# MANCHESTER UNITED

## A COMPLETE RECORD 1878-1992

# MANCHESTER UNITED

## A COMPLETE RECORD 1878-1992

Alan Shury
Ian Morrison

BREEDON
BOOKS
SPORT

First published in Great Britain by
The Breedon Books Publishing Company Limited
44 Friar Gate, Derby DE1 1DA
1992

ISBN 1 873626 22 3

Printed by The Bath Press, Bath and London.
Jacket printed by BDC Printing Services Ltd, Derby.

# Contents

The United Story......................................................9
The Old Trafford Story ........................................53
United Managers....................................................56
A-Z of United Stars...............................................69
Matches to Remember........................................151
Famous Heathens................................................173
United in the Football League
    1892-93 to 1991-92 ..........................................176
United Season-by-Season....................................178
United Against Other League Clubs....................362
United in Wartime...............................................364
United in the FA Cup ..........................................388
United in the Football League Cup.....................406
United in other Cup Competitions ......................413
United in Europe .................................................415
FA Youth Cup Finals ...........................................422
United Internationals...........................................423
Manchester United Career Records.....................436

# Acknowledgements

The authors wish to thank the Football League Ltd for their co-operation in allowing access to the records at Lytham St Anne's. Newspaper libraries across the country were also most helpful and a special word of thanks goes to Richard Wells for his help.

## Photographic Acknowledgements

Photographs have been supplied by Dennis Clareborough, Colorsport, BBC Hulton Picture Library, Illustrated London News Picture Library, Steve Hale, *Manchester Evening News*, Empics of Nottingham, The Photo Source and the Press Association.

## Statistical Note

Information in this book has been diligently researched over a number of years, using both newspaper reports and Football League records at Lytham St Anne's. Inevitably there have been occasional disagreements between those sources, such was the nature of football reporting and record-keeping in the years before World War One. Appearances have been taken from League records except where there has been an obvious error — the transposition of a number to the wrong column for instance — and where there is a difference we have taken the most likely answer and noted the less likely version underneath. Goalscorers, too, can be a minefield of error for the unwary, especially from the days when they were often simply reported as having been 'rushed through in a scrimmage'. Attendances from 1925-6 onwards have been taken from League records; before then they are drawn from newspapers, although it should be stated that even different editions of the same paper sometimes disagreed. Finally, transfer fees (which are not officially divulged by the League or the clubs) have been taken from those reported in the Press. Again, they can vary from paper to paper. All in all, it will be seen that the person who claims to have a wholly accurate record of football since the League was formed is either a fool or a charlatan. We make no such wild claims but present the facts that are available, believing them simply to be a more accurate and comprehensive record of Manchester United's competitive matches than anything else attempted.

# Introduction

MANCHESTER UNITED FOOTBALL CLUB is one of the most famous names in football. Founded as a railway workers' team called Newton Heath, they assumed their present title in 1902 when they were already an established Football League club, albeit a mediocre Second Division one.

Then came their first great manager, Ernest Mangnall, who steered United to two League Championships and an FA Cup Final victory. This was the United of Burgess, Meredith and Sandy Turnbull.

Between the wars, United were once more a mostly average Second Division side. Then came their second great team boss, Matt Busby, who inherited a club whose ground had been severely damaged by German bombs.

But Busby also inherited some fine players and he set forth to build a side which won the FA Cup in 1948 and the League Championship in 1952. More success followed, including successive Championships and the first journey by an English team into the European Cup. By now, the names of Rowley, Carey and Pearson had been replaced by Byrne, Edwards and Taylor.

The Munich air disaster destroyed United's brilliant young team, but Busby survived to rebuild another. In 1968 he had his ultimate reward when Manchester United became the first English club to win the European Cup and Bobby Charlton, a Munich survivor, shed tears of joy with Busby. This was now the United of Best, Law and Crerand.

Since those heady days, Manchester United have experienced the agony of relegation and the joys of FA Cup Final and League Cup Final successes as well as victory in the European Cup-winners' Cup Final. The League title has eluded them, though, and a new generation of United fans have grown up, aching for that triumph. In 1992 they came close before falling away in the last few matches.

Manchester United are easily the best-supported club in Britain and this book has been compiled to give those fans a permanent record of United's long, and mostly illustrious, story.

The first edition sold out quickly when it was published in 1986 and the second edition also quickly disappeared from the bookshops. This third edition updates the United story to include their most recent success, victory in the 1992 Rumbelows Cup Final.

Ian Morrison and Alan Shury
July 1992

*Bobby Charlton and Mario Coluna of Benfica exchange pennants before the 1968 European Cup Final.*

# The United Story

EUROPEAN Cup exploits and full-houses at Old Trafford are a far cry from the humble and poverty-stricken beginnings which Manchester United had to endure in their early days as Newton Heath. It was not uncommon in those times to rely upon a collection from the crowd to pay for transport to the next away fixture.

No records exist to pin-point the exact beginnings but several facts indicate that it all started in 1878. The idea of forming a team came from the railway workers at the carriage and wagon department of the Lancashire & Yorkshire Railway Company's engine shed at Newton Heath. They initially adopted the name Newton Heath (LYR).

Their first ground was on the edge of a clay pit in North Road, Monsall Road, Newton Heath, with the changing rooms some half a mile away in the Three Crowns public house.

After beating all opposition in inter-railway matches Newton Heath looked further afield for fixtures and played against other local teams including a Bolton Wanderers XI, Bootle Reserves and Manchester Arcadians. They turned professional in 1885 and between then and 1891, after impressing against some of the leading sides of the day, Newton Heath were admitted to the Football Alliance after an attempt to join the Football League failed when they received only one vote.

Following the legalization of professionalism in 1885, Newton Heath had started to recruit some useful players. A strong full-back, Jack Powell, joined them in 1886. He was one of many Welsh players to sign for the club around that time and he went on to become captain. Another signing was Tom Hay, the first in a long line of great goalkeepers to play for the club, and he was joined by Pat O'Donnell, a Scot who was so desperate for work that he walked from Glasgow to Manchester to join the railway company and play for Newton Heath. Two other players, brothers Jack and Roger Doughty, came from the top Welsh side Druids, and they were to be an inspirational part of the club's drive towards Football League status, although neither played for Newton Heath in the League. Such was the wealth of talent in the side at the time, that five Newton Heath players (the two Doughtys, Powell, Burke and Davies) appeared for Wales in the 1888 international against Scotland at Edinburgh.

Newton Heath's opening Alliance fixture was a 4-1 win over Sunderland Albion but, despite the new talent in the side, the first two seasons in the Alliance were not successful — they finished eighth and ninth (out of 12).

A second attempt to join the Football League failed in 1891 when Newton Heath did not win a single vote. Ardwick (later to become Manchester City) were also unsuccessful, although they did get four votes. Success, however, did eventually come the Heathens way in 1891-2. Playing in front of their impressive new 1,000-seater stand at North Road, they finished runners-up to Nottingham Forest.

When the Football League enlarged in 1892, the Alliance virtually became, *en bloc*, the new Second Division. As a result of extending the top division to 16 clubs, Newton Heath and Forest (together with Sheffield Wednesday) went straight into the First Division. Promotion to the Football League saw the club remove the letters LYR from their name. That year, they also appointed their first full-time secretary, A.H.Albut, who came from Aston Villa.

Newton Heath started their Football League campaign with a 4-3 defeat at

Blackburn Rovers on 3 September 1892. Seven days later, First Division football came to Manchester when visitors Burnley held the Heathens to a 1-1 draw.

The first season among the élite was a disaster. Newton Heath finished bottom and won only six of their 30 games, although one of them was a 7-1 win over Derby County and another a 10-1 defeat of Wolves. The latter was only Newton Heath's seventh game in the League and today, over 3,000 matches later, it remains the club's biggest League win.

Although they finished bottom, the Heathens stayed in the First Division because of the Test Matches that existed at the time. They drew 1-1 with Second Division champions Small Heath (now Birmingham City), at Stoke, and easily beat the Birmingham side 5-2 at Sheffield. The agony was prolonged for only one season because, twelve months later, Newton Heath lost their Test Match, 2-0 to Liverpool at Blackburn, after again finishing bottom.

The drop to the Second Division brought its financial burdens, and the move to a new ground in September 1893 did little to ease the problem.

Newton Heath's new home was three miles away from North Road, at Bank Lane, Clayton. Set among the smoke-billowing chimneys of the area, like something in a E.S.Lowry painting, the pitch was little better than the clay pitch at Newton Heath. But the increased crowds that were expected, and needed, did not materialize and at the end of their first season at Clayton all the club had to show for the move was relegation.

The drop into the Second Division saw the start of the rivalry with Manchester City and on 3 November 1894, the first League meeting between the two clubs took place at City's old Hyde Road ground. Newton Heath won 5-2 thanks to four goals from Smith and one from Clarkin.

Life was not sweet for the club. The spent 12 years in the Second Division during which time the supporters at Clayton had little to cheer, except perhaps victory over the strong Blackburn Rovers side to win the Lancashire Cup for the first time, in 1898. Newton Heath also temporarily established what would still be a Football League record scoreline when, on 9 March 1895, they beat Walsall 14-0. Walsall subsequently complained about the Bank Lane pitch. The complaint was upheld and when the game was replayed a month later, Newton Heath could manage only nine goals.

A change of colours from green and gold to white shirts and blue shorts brought no change of fortunes. Despite coming close to a First Division return, twice reaching the Test Match stage, Newton Heath remained a struggling Second Division team until one day, in 1902, their saviour came along — thanks to a St Bernard dog.

The financial plight had worsened. Money which Newton Heath could ill-afford was spent on players, but without the desired effect. Ground improvements had been undertaken and in an effort to raise £1,000, a four-day bazaar was held in February and March 1901. A St Bernard dog, belonging to club captain Harry Stafford, was left to wander the bazaar with a collecting box around its neck. The dog strayed from the hall and eventually came into the possession of a wealthy local brewer, John Davies. He traced the owner and was told about the club's difficulties. Davies became interested in the Clayton side and, after creditors foreclosed in 1902, with Newton Heath's debts amounting to over £2,500, he injected £3,000 to pay off those debts and buy players.

A new club was formed on 28 April 1902 and Davies became chairman. The Heathens disappeared and Manchester United was born (despite suggestions that they should be called Manchester Celtic or Central), and changed their colours from white and blue to the now famous red and white.

The first of the new players to join United were Tom Arkesden from Burton United, who had played in the 1899 Cup Final for Derby County; goalscoring forward John Peddie, who had seen service with Third Lanark and Newcastle; and goalkeeper

*United's 1905-06 promotion side. Back row (left to right): Downie, Moger, Bonthron. Middle row: E.Mangnall (manager), Picken, Sagar, Blackstock, Peddie, Bacon (trainer). Front row: Beddow, Roberts, Bell, Arkesden.*

John Sutcliff, a Rugby Union international who was banned from the RU game for alleged professionalism.

United's first game under their new name was at Gainsborough Trinity on 6 September 1902 when, thanks to a goal from inside-right Richards, they won 1-0. Another 1-0 win followed seven days later when they beat Burton United in front of 15,000 fans at Clayton.

In September 1903, James West resigned as secretary and was replaced by Ernest Mangnall who became secretary-manager, a position he had held at Burnley. It was a significant appointment for Mangnall who, like Matt Busby 40 years later, had the dream of turning United into a great club.

Attendances were increasing all the time, and for the opening game of 1903-04, against Bristol City, 40,000 witnessed a 2-2 draw.

Having seen Manchester City win the Second Division title in 1903, United finished fifth that season and in 1903-04 and 1904-05, third. In 1905-06 their efforts began to bear fruit as United finished runners-up to Bristol City and gained promotion. Although four points behind City, United's points tally of 62 was four more than the old Second Division record set by Liverpool the previous season. United lost only four matches all season and wound up the campaign on 28 April 1906 with a 6-0 home win over Burton United. Thus ended a 12-year spell out of the top division and began the start of the most successful period United were to enjoy until after World War Two.

The backbone of their promotion team was the half-back trio of Duckworth, Roberts and Bell, regarded as one of the finest seen in British football until the 1940s and 50s.

11

*Manchester United under pressure during an FA Cup match against Fulham at Craven Cottage in 1905.*

Mangnall was the driving force behind United and he bought shrewdly, signing two unrelated Scots, Alex 'Sandy' Turnbull and James Turnbull, who both proved to be prolific goalscorers, and recruiting Harold Halse and Billy Meredith.

Inside-forward Halse was to play in three FA Cup Finals for three different teams (United, Aston Villa and Chelsea) between 1909 and 1915. Meredith was already one of the game's greatest characters, and one of its finest players. He joined United from Manchester City in 1906 for £500 — with part of an FA ban following alleged illegal payments still to serve — and he was the first in a long line of football legends to wear the Manchester United shirt.

In 1906, Mangnall engineered a shrewd 'bulk buy'. Seventeen Manchester City players were banned by the FA, from May that year until January 1907, for being involved in the same illegal payments scandal. City put all 17 up for sale and Mangnall stepped in to buy Sandy Turnbull, Jimmy Bannister and Herbert Burgess. City's George Livingstone signed later.

The 1907-08 season began with United being floated as a public limited company, while another piece of the team jigsaw was slotted into place when, for the first time, United started a season with Billy Meredith.

It was a season of resounding success. Manchester United won their first League

*April 1906. United and Chelsea battle for promotion at Stamford Bridge. United won back their First Division place but the Londoners finished third.*

Championship and were, by far, the division's outstanding team. They were nine points clear of runners-up Aston Villa, who were only 13 points clear of the bottom club, Birmingham. Meredith, England international winger George Wall, and Sandy Turnbull between them scored over 50 goals. Vittorio Pozzo, the man who was to guide Italy to two World Cup wins in the 1930s, was then a poor student living in England. He watched United during that Championship-winning season and later used some of their techniques in his successful Italian teams.

Twelve months after winning the first League title, United dropped to 13th place. It was a surprising decline, but ample compensation was gained when they won the FA Cup for the first time.

*Action from the 3-2 defeat by Woolwich Arsenal in the fourth-round FA Cup tie at Clayton in March 1906.*

*United's League Championship-winning squad of 1906-07. Back row (left to right): Burgess, Bannister, Berry, Wall. Middle row: Bacon (trainer), Menzies, Meredith, Moger, J.Turnbull, Mills, Stacey, Williams, Broomfield, McGillivray, E.Mangnall (manager). Front row: Duckworth, Dalton, Picken, Whiteside, Holden, Thomson, Bell, A.Turnbull. It was the first time that United had lifted the title.*

United currently possess one of the best post-war FA Cup records, but in the first 16 seasons they entered the competition after joining the League, they reached the quarter-finals only three times. In 1909, however, they were blessed with the good fortune it takes to win the Cup.

With 18 minutes of the quarter-final remaining, they were trailing 1-0 to Burnley when the game was abandoned because of snow. United won the replay 3-2 and in the semi-final met an understrength Newcastle United, who were reduced to ten men in the second half. A solitary goal from Halse gave United victory.

In the Final it was United's turn to be handicapped and they had full-back Hayes limping for most of the match. The issue was settled in the 22nd minute when Sandy Turnbull scored the only goal of the game after a shot from Halse had rebounded off the crossbar.

After the 1909 Cup Final victory, John Davies gave United the then huge sum of £60,000 to purchase a site and build a new stadium, Old Trafford, to where United moved in February 1910. Their last match at Clayton was against Tottenham on 22 January that year and United won 5-0 in front of only 7,000 loyal fans. The official opening of the new ground was on 19 February when 45,000 fans saw United lead 2-0 and then 3-1 against Liverpool, before losing 4-3.

Manchester United, because of the extravagance of their new home, were gaining a reputation for being a rich club which, if Davies' wealth was used as a guideline, was correct. The Old Trafford dream was Mangnall's, but it was to be many years before the club had a team to match the splendour of its stadium.

The first full season saw large crowds regularly pack the new ground and for the visit of Aston Villa, over 65,000 filled Old Trafford. The United team contained new faces: Hofton came from Glossop, brothers James and John Hodge from Scotland. To add power to the forward line there was 'Knocker' West, who signed from Nottingham Forest. Many of the signings were due to the skills of Louis Rocca who served the club as a scout, and in other capacities, for over 40 years until his death in 1950.

United's first full season at Old Trafford brought the reward of a second

*United in 1909 with the FA Cup (note the former trophy). Back row (left to right): J.E.Mangnall (secretary), Bacon, Picken, Edmonds, Mr Murray (director), Moger, Mr Davies (chairman), Homer, Mr Lawson (director), Bell, Mr Deakin (director). Middle row: Meredith, Duckworth, Roberts, Turnbull, West, Stacey. On ground: Whalley, Hofton, Halse, Wall.*

*Manchester United 1909-10. Back row (left to right): Halse, Meredith, Moger, Picken, Wall, Stacey. Middle row: J.Turnbull, Duckworth, Roberts, Bell, Hayes, A.Turnbull. On ground: Livingstone, Downie.*

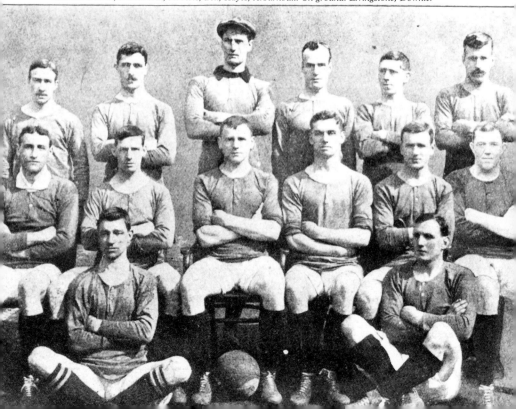

Championship in four seasons, although the battle for the title was a breathtaking affair.

On the penultimate Saturday of 1910-11, United lost 4-2 at Villa Park to their only challengers. Both clubs then had 50 points and Villa had a game in hand. A draw at Blackburn on the following Monday put Villa top, but on the final day of the season Villa lost 3-1 to Liverpool, while United defeated Sunderland 5-1 at Old Trafford to take the Championship by one point.

Meredith, Duckworth, Bell, Sandy Turnbull (who was to lose his life serving with the Manchester Regiment during World War One), Roberts, Wall and goalkeeper Moger each collected their third honour in four seasons. Two world wars would pass by before Manchester United again tasted glory.

Ernest Mangnall left for Manchester City in 1912. Perhaps he realized that this fine United team was on the wane. Certainly, the once great half-back trio of Duckworth, Roberts and Bell was well past its best.

*Manchester United 1913-14. Back row (left to right): James Hodge, Gipps, Knowles, Beale, Stacey, Hamill, Whalley. Front row: Meredith, Woodcock, Anderson, West, Wall.*

*The famous 'Outcasts' team who rebelled on behalf of the Players' Union. Back row (left to right): Picken, Corbett, Holden, Burgess, Clough, Meredith, G.Boswell (PU assistant secretary). Front row: Wall, Sandy Turnbull, Roberts, Coleman, Duckworth. All but Coleman (Everton) were on United's books.*

Mangnall's successor was John Robson, who was appointed in December 1914. He came from the relative seclusion of Brighton and he was soon faced with the unsavoury scandal of 1915 when four United players, together with four Liverpool players, were banned after it was discovered that the match between the two clubs on 2 April, which United won 2-0, had been 'fixed' for betting purposes.

The war years interfered with Robson's plans but when League football resumed in 1919-20, the future looked promising for United. Large crowds flocked to Old Trafford and the current club record, 70,504, witnessed the 3-1 defeat by Aston Villa on Boxing Day 1920.

Despite these large attendances, the first two seasons after the war saw United occupy mid-table positions. Robson resigned at the start of 1921-2, but remained as assistant to the new manager, John Chapman, whose first season in charge saw United drop to the Second Division.

England international Frank Barson was bought from Aston Villa for £5,000. He was seen as the man around whom a promotion-winning side could be built and two seasons were spent moulding that team. The defence had been bolstered with the signing of goalkeeper Alf Steward and full-backs Charlie Moore and Jack Silcock. Others arrived and a new-look team developed. United changed their strip once more when, in 1923, they opted for white shirts with a red 'V' and white shorts.

United finished fourth and 14th before gaining promotion in 1924-5, as runners-up to Leicester City. The building of a solid defence inspired by Barson had worked

*Above: United's Second Division runners-up side of 1924-5. Back row (left to right): Pullen (trainer), Lochhead, Silcock, Steward, Moore, Grimwood, Hilditch. Front row: Mann, Spence, Smith, Barson, Henderson, McPherson.*
*Below: United in action at Upton Park on the first day of the 1925-6 season. They marked their return to Division One with a 1-0 defeat.*

and United conceded only 23 goals, still a Second Division record. They won the one point they needed from their last match of the season in a goalless draw with Barnsley, ironically one of Barson's former clubs.

The return to the First Division brought with it several behind-the-scenes changes. Manager Chapman was dismissed in 1926 after the FA ordered his suspension for alleged improper conduct, the exact details of which were never made public. Clarence Hilditch took over temporarily as player-manager before Herbert Bamlett's appointment in 1927, with Louis Rocca as his assistant. The year started on a sad note with the death of John Davies, the club's saviour in 1902. Perhaps as a token of respect for Davies, United reverted back to their familiar red shirts that year. The following year saw one of their most significant captures when Walter Crickmer, the first link between the United of the pre-war years and that of the successful post-war era, joined the club as secretary in October 1926. He held the post until losing his life at Munich over 30 years later.

United finished a respectable ninth in their first season back in the top flight, but for the next four seasons they were a mediocre bottom-half-of-the-table team. In 1930-31 there was another drop to the Second Division when they went down with Leeds. United finished bottom with 22 points and won only seven matches. By contrast to their near record-breaking start to the 1985-6 season, they lost their first 12 matches, a Football League record. Their first point did not come until 1 November 1930 when they beat Birmingham 2-0 at Old Trafford. That season the Reds conceded 115 goals.

Newcastle beat them 7-4 at Old Trafford and Aston Villa 7-0 at Villa Park, while Huddersfield, Chelsea and Derby each put six goals past them. Towards the end of the season, with the cause a hopeless one, manager Bamlett resigned.

In December 1931, like many businesses, United were feeling the depression and the bank would not extend the club's overdraft when businessman James Gibson (whose son Alan is a United vice-president) appeared as a second saviour. In January 1932, Gibson was co-opted on to the board after he announced he would inject £2,000 immediately to pay wages and meet pressing debts, and a further £20,000 with which to buy players. A new manager was appointed at the start of 1932-3 when former Dumbarton player, Scott Duncan, arrived at a reported salary of £800 per annum.

Although saved from financial disaster, United still failed to prosper on the field. Duncan recruited players, largely from Scotland, yet despite spending over £20,000, United could only finish sixth in the Second Division in 1932-3. In a forlorn effort to find a balanced team, United called upon 60 different players for League duties in three seasons between 1932 and 1934. And in 1933-4, they came within one match of the biggest embarrassment in the club's history.

On 5 May 1934, United travelled to play Millwall in their final Second Division game of the season. United were 21st with 32 points, Millwall 20th with 33 points. The London club had a good home record, despite their position, and had lost only one more game at the Den than Grimsby, recently crowned champions, had done at their home ground. United's future looked bleak, but every player gave his all and United won 2-0 to stay up by one point. Millwall had to wait four years to return to the Second Division, but two seasons later United were Second Division champions for the first time.

Manager Duncan was awarded a new five-year contract during 1936-7, but that season United were relegated once more. They went down with Sheffield Wednesday, while City rubbed salt into the wounds by winning the Championship. There was yet another cliff-hanging finale when United lost their last match to be level on points with Leeds who had one game left. Portsmouth were the visitors to Elland Road and needed to beat Leeds 2-0 for Manchester United to stay safe, but Leeds won 3-1 and the Reds were down again.

Duncan resigned three months into 1937-8 with four years of his contract remaining.

*Above: United's Second Division championship-winning staff of 1935-6. Back row (left to right): J.W.Gibson (chairman), Ferrier, Griffiths, Breedon, Tom Curry (trainer), Hall, Porter, Manley, A.Scott Duncan (manager). Middle row: Cape, Mutch, Bamford, Brown, Rowley, McKay, Vose. On ground: Bryant, Robertson, Owen, Redwood.*

*Below: Another United promotion squad, this time the players who took the club back to Division One as runners-up in Division Two. Back row (left to right): Thompson, Vose, Griffiths, Breen, Tom Curry (trainer), Breedon, Winterbottom, Porter, Manley. Middle row: Mutch, Murray, Roughton, A.Scott Duncan (manager), Baird, Bamford, Bryant. On ground: Whalley, Gladwin, McKay, Brown, Wrigglesworth, Redwood.*

He went to non-League Ipswich Town, who, the following year, were admitted to the League.

Once again United started to build. New players were introduced and three of them, Stan Pearson, Johnny Carey and Jack Rowley, were to be key members of United's successful side of the immediate post-war years.

While Manchester City, League Champions 12 months earlier, were sensationally relegated in 1937-8, United returned immediately to the First Division, although not before giving their fans what had become a traditional end-of-season panic.

Aston Villa had won the title, and Sheffield United had finished their programme on 53 points while Manchester United and Coventry City both had 51. The Reds' goal-average was better than that of their two remaining promotion rivals' and they needed a win. Victory over Bury put United back into the First Division where they were to stay for 40 years.

In 1938 United instituted its now famous youth policy, but the war years intervened and it was 1945 before the next chapter in the story of Manchester United unfolded. Up to then United had been a mostly average side, although they had produced one of the great First Division teams between 1907-11. They had built a fine new stadium, but it waited for a truly great team.

In 1941, the ground was extensively damaged by German bombs and United were the worst hit of all Football League clubs during the hostilities.

By total contrast was the appointment of Matt Busby as manager. Busby rebuilt the shattered club and he was the first man since Ernest Mangnall at the turn of the century, to make United one of the great sides in the Football League. In Busby's case there would later be the added dimension of European football.

Busby had been a fine player with Liverpool and Manchester City, and was Scotland's wartime captain. At a board meeting on 15 February 1945, the directors agreed that he should be offered a five-year contract upon completion of his army duties. The decision of those directors must rank as one of the best ever made by the United board.

Prior to taking up his duties with United, Busby took an army team to Italy and met up with Jimmy Murphy, who he had played against when Murphy was at West Brom. Busby asked Murphy if he would like to join him at Old Trafford, and in 1946 one of soccer's great partnerships was formed. After seven years without a manager, and with a £15,000 overdraft and no ground, Manchester United, led by Busby and Murphy, set off on the trail towards becoming arguably football's most famous club.

When League soccer proper returned in 1946-7, pre-war players Stan Pearson, Charlie Mitten, Jack Rowley, Allenby Chilton and Johnny Carey formed the basis of United's early post-war teams while youngsters like John Aston, Johnny Morris and Joe Walton, who had all progressed with the Manchester United Junior Athletic Club, were given first-team chances.

United finished second in the first post-war season and, perhaps significantly, the reserve side, composed almost entirely of youngsters, won the Central League.

United were runners-up in the First Division four times in the first five seasons after the war, before winning the title for the first time in 40 years. Their first post-war success, however, came in 1948 when they won the FA Cup for the first time since 1909.

On their way to their first Wembley appearance United beat all First Division opposition, including a remarkable 6-4 win at Aston Villa in the third round, in which Villa were one up after 13 seconds, and United 5-1 up at half-time. Stan Pearson scored a hat-trick in the 3-1 semi-final win against Derby County at Hillsborough, and the Final itself, against Blackpool, turned out to be one of Wembley's rare classics.

Both Finalists had scored 18 goals on their way to the Final and a goalscoring

*United in 1946-7, the side that finished runners-up to Liverpool in Division One. Back row (left to right):*
*Warner, Walton, Collinson, Hanlon, McGlen, Cockburn. Front row: Delaney, Morris, Rowley, Pearson,*
*Mitten, Chilton.*

feast was promised. For once, that promise materialized. With only 21 minutes remaining, Blackpool led 2-1 then Rowley equalized, and United scored twice in the last ten minutes, through Pearson and Anderson, to deliver the Cup into the safe hands of skipper Carey.

By now United's financial fortunes had turned around. They had gone from being in the red and in to the black in just two years, and in 1951 all debts were cleared completely. On the playing side the youth framework, started in 1938, was beginning to bear fruit. The Manchester United Junior Athletic Club ran three teams, and United ran official 'A' and reserve teams. This strength in depth was to be United's mainstay in future years.

In 1949, Busby was offered the Spurs' manager's job, and that of coach to the Italian national team. He refused both, such was his commitment to Manchester United, although there were others whose days at Old Trafford were nearing their end.

In 1949, Johnny Morris became Britain's most expensive player when he joined Derby County. The following year, Charlie Mitten set sail for Colombian football to seek his fortune along with England centre-half Neil Franklin. Jimmy Delaney also left United in 1950, a year which saw the death of Louis Rocca. In 1951, a sad period for United continued when James Gibson passed away.

On the positive side, Busby knew that he had many talented youngsters in the

*Roger Byrne carefully carries the League Championship trophy down the steps of Old Trafford's main stand in April 1957.*

junior sides and full-back Roger Byrne, who joined the club in 1949, developed into a regular first-team player. There was also cash to spend and Johnny Berry, a classy winger, was signed from Birmingham City in 1951.

In 1951-2, United won their first Championship for 40 years, lifting the title four points ahead of Spurs and Arsenal. Jack Rowley was the top scorer with 30 goals and Roger Byrne, who started the season at left-back, was switched to outside-left for the last six games and scored seven goals.

Inexplicably United slumped the following season and, in October, along with Manchester City, were bottom of the table. Alarm bells rang, and into the side came youngsters Whitefoot, Pegg, Lewis, Doherty and Blanchflower. Barnsley centre-forward Tommy Taylor signed for United that season and his seven goals in only 11 League games helped to lift United into a respectable eighth position. Johnny Carey retired at the end of the season and Roger Byrne, who was to prove to be a great leader, reverted to his left-back role.

After finishing fourth and fifth in 1953-4 and 1954-5 respectively, United won their second title in four years when in 1956, they finished 11 points clear of Blackpool and Wolves. Their winning margin was a 20th-century First Division record. Only two players, Byrne and Berry, remained from the 1952 Championship winning team. Cockburn, Pearson, Rowley and Chilton had all gone and into their places had stepped members of the Youth Cup winning team — Jones, Edwards, Colman and Greaves. The average age of the side was only 22, one of the youngest ever to win the First Division title. Most of the squad had been developed by the club.

United went to the top of the table following a 2-1 home win over Sunderland on 3 December and on 7 April, they clinched the title with a 2-1 home win over Blackpool. Twelve months later, United retained the title.

Throughout the 20th century teams had dreamed of winning the League Championship and the FA Cup double, a feat last achieved by Aston Villa in 1896-7. United, in 1956-7, had the opportunity of not only emulating Villa and Preston (the only other club to achieve the feat), but also had a chance to go one better with a treble.

The previous season the European Cup had been staged for the first time. Chelsea, the League Champions, were told by the Football League not to enter. After winning the title in 1956, United were similarly discouraged, but Busby convinced the directors otherwise. So began Matt Busby's, and United's, great love affair with Europe.

The first European game was against Anderlecht in Brussels. United created their club record win, 10-0. Viollet (four) and Taylor (three) both scored hat-tricks as United gave, to this day, one of their best European performances.

United fought their way to the semi-final where they lost 5-3 on aggregate to the holders, Real Madrid. Having lost 3-1 in Madrid they drew 2-2, after trailing 2-0, in the first European game under the Old Trafford floodlights. There was still, however, that elusive double.

United went to Wembley as favourites, but the Wembley hoodoo struck once more when United goalkeeper Ray Wood was injured in a collision with Peter McParland — the scorer of both Villa's goals, in their 2-1 win. Although Jackie Blanchflower performed bravely in the United goal, he was powerless, as indeed Wood may well have been, to stop McParland's goals.

Another of United's youngsters to make his debut during that Championship winning season was Bobby Charlton. Coincidentally, his first match was against Charlton at Old Trafford, and he scored twice. For good measure he scored a

*Below: Tommy Taylor (9) scores the goal which gave United a 2-1 victory over Blackpool at Old Trafford in April 1956 and enabled them to lift the League Championship.*
*Opposite, above: Taylor in action again, this time against Cardiff City as the Welshmen's goalkeeper Ron Howells gets ready to block a shot from the United centre-forward.*

*Duncan Edwards and Allenby Chilton go up for the ball during United's FA Cup tie against Reading in January 1955. United won the replay 4-1 after the sides had drawn 1-1 at Elm Park.*

*European Cup action from United's quarter-final tie in Bilbao in February 1956. Despite losing this game 5-3, Busby's team went through 6-5 on aggregate after a magnificent 3-0 win at Maine Road.*

hat-trick in the return match at The Valley, little knowing what a responsibility was going to fall upon his shoulders during the next decade.

On 1 February 1958, United travelled to Highbury for a League game, and came away the winners of an epic match by the odd goal in nine. The previous week they had scored seven goals at home to Bolton and they now lay second in the First Division table, poised for a hat-trick of Championship wins.

Four days after the Highbury thriller, United flew to Belgrade for the second-leg of their European Cup tie against Red Star. A 3-3 draw earned United a 5-4 aggregate victory and their second successive semi-final appearance. The BEA Elizabethan aircraft which carried the United team, officials and journalists stopped to refuel at Munich on the way home. On its third attempt to take off, the 'plane careered off the runway and crashed. In one instant, the greatest team in Britain, and possibly in Europe, was wiped out. Roger Byrne, Geoff Bent, Eddie Colman, Mark Jones, Duncan Edwards, David Pegg, Bill Whelan and Tommy Tayor lost their lives. Secretary Walter Crickmer,

*United's last match before the Munich tragedy, in Belgrade against the Red Star club.*

*The great pre-Munich team. Back row (left to right): Eddie Colman, Billy Foulkes, Ray Wood, Roger Byrne, Mark Jones, Duncan Edwards. Front: Dennis Viollet, Johnny Berry, Tommy Taylor, Bill Whelan, David Pegg.*

trainer Tom Curry, and coach Bert Whalley also perished. Matt Busby came close to death. For a while he was unaware that so many of his stars had been killed. To survive the physical barrier was one thing, but for Busby to overcome the mental pain, and rebuild Manchester United was typical of his courage and determination.

*Wreckage of the BEA Elizabethan aircraft after the crash which killed eight United stars.*

*Billy Foulkes and Sheffield Wednesday's Albert Quixall (later to play for United) before the start of the emotion-charged FA Cup fifth-round game at Old Trafford, just two weeks after the flower of United's team had perished at Munich.*

In Jimmy Murphy, United had the man to carry on while Busby lay in hospital in Munich. Murphy knew how Busby worked, he knew his mind and, despite the tragedy, the Manchester United story rolled on. Murphy was not aboard the 'plane at Munich that day. He was at Cardiff as manager of the Welsh team for a World Cup qualifier against Israel and his place on that fateful trip had been taken by Bert Whalley.

Life had to go on at Old Trafford, and it did. Only Harry Gregg and Bill Foulkes of the survivors, were capable of resuming first-team duties immediately. Ernie Taylor and Stan Crowther were signed and given special permission from the FA to play in the outstanding FA Cup fifth-round tie against Sheffield Wednesday. Crowther had played against United in the previous season's Final, and for Villa in the 1958 competition.

A crowd of almost 59,000 packed Old Trafford on 19 February to watch United miraculously beat Wednesday 3-0, thanks to two goals from Shay Brennan, the reserve full-back who played at outside-left, and one from Alex Dawson. The first League game at Old Trafford after the disaster was a 1-1 draw against Nottingham Forest, and was watched by more than 66,000.

Although United won only one more League game that season, away to Sunderland in April, they were carried along to their second successive FA Cup Final on a wave of national sympathy.

The European dream had already vanished by the time United reached Wembley. AC Milan had ousted them 5-2 on aggregate in the semi-final, despite United's 2-1 win at Old Trafford. And it was not long before their Wembley dream vanished too. After only three minutes Nat Lofthouse put away the first of his two goals and then, in the 55th minute, he scored his second when he bundled Harry Gregg over the goal-line in one of Wembley's most controversial incidents. There is no doubt that the goal would not have been allowed today.

Matt Busby was awarded the CBE in the Birthday Honours List but to make 1958 a completely black year for United, one of its favourite sons, Billy Meridith, died just 10 weeks after the Munich Disaster.

Once Busby returned to his Old Trafford desk, the rebuilding job started in earnest. One man both he and Murphy saw as helping United back to the top was Albert Quixall, for whom they paid Sheffield Wednesday a British transfer record of £45,000. More youngsters were drafted into the side, and players like amateur Warren Bradley of Bishop Auckland, who later played for England at full international level, joined United.

Despite United finishing eighth in the League, UEFA invited them, as a token of respect, to compete in the 1958-9 European Cup along with League Champions Wolves. Both the Football League and Football Association objected to UEFA's compassionate request, although the FA had apparently at first agreed to United taking part.

The first full season after Munich saw the 'Busby Babes' finish second to Wolves in the First Division, but there was disaster in the FA Cup, which had become a United 'speciality', when they were beaten in the third round at Third Division Norwich City — by three goals to nil.

As new blood was introduced, United's League performances slumped and between 1960 and 1963 they finished seventh, seventh, 15th and 19th. One bright spot was the breaking of Jack Rowley's club goalscoring record by Dennis Viollet, with 32 goals in 1959-60. In 1961-2, the average attendance at Old Trafford dropped to 33,491, the third lowest post-war seasonal average, but the following year, with a hint of Wembley in the air, it was above the 40,000 mark again.

Successive FA Cup defeats by Sheffield Wednesday in 1960 and 1961, the latter an embarrassing 7-2 replay defeat at Old Trafford, were followed by a run to the semi-final in 1962, which ended at Hillsborough when Spurs won 3-1. But in 1963, despite finishing 19th, only three points from relegation, United beat the League's fourth-placed club, Leicester City, 3-1 to win the Cup for the third time in five Finals. Noel Cantwell joined Johnny Carey and Charlie Roberts as United captains to proudly hold aloft the trophy.

By now the United team was littered with household names. Denis Law had signed from Torino for £115,000 in 1962 and Pat Crerand came from Celtic in 1963. John Connelly was a £50,000 signing from Burnley, David Herd, Maurice Setters and Johnny Giles were all established First Division players. United were blending together a fine team, although it meant greater use of the cheque book.

Just as the near-drop into the Third Division in 1934 turned the tide for United, so did the scare of relegation to the Second Division in 1963. In 1964 they finished second to Liverpool in the League and reached the FA Cup semi-final for the seventh time since the war, losing 3-1 to West Ham at Hillsborough. United were also back in Europe in 1963-4 and they lost to Sporting Lisbon in the quarter-final of the Cup-winners' Cup. After taking a 4-1 first-leg lead, they inexplicably lost 5-0 in Portugal. One youngster who broke into the United first team in 1963-4, was George Best.

In 1936, two years after nearly going down, United won the Second Division title. In 1965, two years after narrowly missing relegation, they were First Division champions. The third great Busby team was nearly complete, and only two survivors of the Munich disaster, Bill Foulkes and Bobby Charlton, were in the team. United won the title on goal-average ahead of Leeds United as Denis Law, with 28 goals, took his total of League goals in three seasons at Old Trafford to 81.

This latest Championship winning team, like their 1957 predecessors, were also chasing a treble. But this latest assault ended when they were beaten in a play-off in the Inter-Cities Fairs' Cup semi-final by Hungarian side Ferencváros. Leeds United had ended United's FA Cup ambitions by winning a semi-final replay at the City Ground, Nottingham.

*Denis Law celebrates George Best's goal in United's 3-1 win over West Ham before a 45,000 crowd at Old Trafford in September 1964.*

United now had another crack at the European Cup and in 1965-6, their 5-1 defeat of Benfica before 75,000 people in the 'Stadium of Light' is still rated as the Reds' finest all-round team performance. Best (2), Charlton, Connelly and Crerand scored the goals as United powered into the semi-finals.

Alas, a 2-0 away defeat by Partizan Belgrade could not be pulled back in the second leg and Busby may have thought that his one real chance of lifting the European Cup had gone. On the domestic front that season United dropped to fourth in the League, but reached yet another FA Cup semi-final, only to lose 1-0 to Everton at Bolton.

In 1966-7, United regained the League Championship with a four-point margin over Nottingham Forest. They remained undefeated in their last 20 League games, and clinched the title with the division's biggest away win of the season, 6-1 at West Ham. At the end of the season, Busby watched his great friend, and rival, Jock Stein, lead Celtic to victory in the European Cup Final. Busby had been trying for over ten years to win the trophy and now United were back in Europe. In the League, they had to be content with runners-up position, behind Manchester City, as crowds at Old Trafford that season averaged in excess of 57,000 to create a new First Division record, surpassing Newcastle United's 56,283 set in 1947-8.

In the European Cup, relatively easy wins over Hibernian of Malta, Sarajevo, and Gornik Zabrze saw United renew their acquaintance with Real Madrid in the semi-final. A George Best goal gave them a slender 1-0 lead to take to Madrid where the return leg proved one of the greatest nights in United's history to date.

Real were leading 3-1 with 15 minutes to go when Foulkes headed on a Crerand free-kick for Sadler to score. Three minutes later Foulkes, not renowned for his

*United's European Cup-winning squad in 1968. Back row (left to right): Foulkes, Aston, Rimmer, Stepney, Gowling, Herd. Middle row: Sadler, –, Dunn, Brennan, Crerand, Best, Burns, –, Jack Crompton (trainer). Front: Ryan, Stiles, Law, Sir Matt Busby, Charlton, Kidd, Fitzpatrick.*

*Bobby Charlton holds aloft the European Cup after United's great victory over Benfica at Wembley.*

goalscoring, appeared from nowhere to convert a Best centre and United had at last reached the Final of the European Cup.

Some 100,000 mostly United-biased fans packed Wembley on Derby day 1968 and they saw Bobby Charlton give United the lead early in the second half with a rare header. Graca equalized ten minutes from the end and in the closing minutes it was the bravery and instinct of goalkeeper Alex Stepney that kept Benfica, and Eusebio, at bay with two memorable saves. The game went into extra-time and in a magical seven-minute spell, Best, Kidd (celebrating his 19th birthday) and Charlton scored to give United the trophy for which they had waited so long.

For a second time in less than two years Bobby Charlton shed tears of joy at Wembley. First there had been England's World Cup Final triumph over West Germany; now Charlton was at the end of a long, hard and painful road. For Matt Busby, too, a dream had been realized. His 'Babes' had come of age.

It was perhaps inevitable that when Busby made the announcement in January 1969 that he was relinquishing team duties at the end of the season, it heralded a decline in United's fortunes. It was bound to be difficult to follow a man who had done so much for Manchester United over almost a quarter of a century.

Sir Matt — he was knighted in the wake of United's European triumph — remained with the club as General Manager and handed over the day-to-day running of the team to former player Wilf McGuinness. Busby left United in a mid-table position and took them to the European Cup semi-finals where they lost to AC Milan. He also endured two fierce battles with Estudiantes for the World Club championship. On 1 June 1969 the 32-year-old McGuinness took over, not as manager but as chief coach.

McGuinness had worked his way up through the United coaching staff after a bad leg injury ended his playing career in 1959-60. Many big names were tipped

*United's Jimmy Rimmer leaps to push the ball away from Ipswich Town's Trevor Whymark at Portman Road in September 1970. United lost the game 4-0.*

*Spurs' Alan Gilzean gets above United's Denis Law, watched by Martin Chivers (Spurs) and Steve James (United). The sides drew 2-2 at White Hart Lane before 55,693 fans.*

to succeed Busby, but the club thought it better to promote from within. That policy has since worked for Liverpool, but it did not succeed for United. McGuinness spent only 18 months in charge at Old Trafford.

His one full season in charge saw him take United to eighth place in the League and to the semi-finals of both the FA Cup and the League Cup. By Christmas 1970, the club had slumped to a near-relegation position in the First Division, and been knocked out of the League Cup semi-final by Third Division Aston Villa. There were rumours of dressing-room discontent, something Busby had handled when it had rarely arisen. McGuinness, not surprisingly, found difficulty in handling the likes of George Best. It took the might of Busby to do that.

Shortly after Christmas, McGuinness was relieved of his duties, but perhaps realizing their mistake, the board offered him his old job as Reserve-team coach. McGuinness, perhaps realizing *his* mistake in taking over from Busby, accepted.

Sir Matt was beckoned from 'retirement' to take over the reins once more. And as if a magic wand had been waved, United started giving preformances reminiscent of their European Cup winning season. The players responded once more and Busby lifted them away from relegation to finish the season in eighth place. Meanwhile, the search had been on for a new manager, and Frank O'Farrell, the friendly Irishman who had been an inspiration behind the recent transformation of Leicester City into an attractive Second Division championship-winning team, was the man United chose.

35

O'Farrell took over on 1 July 1971, and because of the senseless action of a 'supporter' in the previous season's match with Newcastle United, Old Trafford was closed for United's first two home matches against Arsenal and West Brom. O'Farrell appeared to have motivated the players, however, and victory upon victory followed with nonchalent ease. George Best was playing at his majestic peak. He had scored 17 goals by the end of the year, including hat-tricks against West Ham and Southampton. On 1 January 1972 United were clear leaders with just two defeats, away to Everton and Leeds. But, mysteriously, they started 1972 like a totally different team.

They lost seven matches in succession, and between 11 December and 8 March experienced only one win, in the FA Cup third round against Southampton. In the fourth round, however, United were eliminated by Second Division strugglers, Preston.

After such a promising beginning, United finished eighth for the third successive year. Even the big-money signings of Martin Buchan from Aberdeen, and Ian Storey-Moore from Nottingham Forest could do little to halt the decline.

United started 1972-3 in completely opposite fashion to O'Farrell's first season. They did not register their first win until a 3-0 victory over Derby County at Old Trafford on 23 September, United's tenth League game of the season. They were at the foot of the First Division and once more the chequebook was produced. Ted MacDougall arrived from Bournemouth for £200,000 and Wyn Davies travelled across the city from Maine Road in a £65,000 deal. Neither could help arrest the decline.

Four days after a 5-0 thrashing by Crystal Palace at Selhurst Park, O'Farrell was dismissed. After one man, Busby, had been at the helm for 24 years, now, in just three and a half years, the turnover in managers had doubled.

On 22 December 1972 Tommy Docherty won approval from the Scottish FA to leave his post as national team manager to take up duties at Old Trafford.

'Fantastic!' was how Docherty described the appointment. 'My aim has always been to be the best manager in football. And I know that at Old Trafford I will get the best possible chance of proving that I have what it takes.' But so did McGuinness and O'Farrell.

Docherty's first game in charge was at home to Leeds United who were lying third. MacDougall gave United a dream start and a win was on the cards before Allan Clarke spoilt the celebrations with a last-minute equalizer.

Docherty saw the need to buy players and, for the second time in his career, bought George Graham, this time from Arsenal for £120,000. The following day he invested £100,000 of United's money in Scottish full-back Alex Forsyth from Partick Thistle. In January, another Scot, Lou Macari, signed from Celtic for £200,000 in a deal which turned out to be one of the best of Docherty's managerial career. The buying did not stop there. He bought Jim Holton from Shrewsbury, Stewart Houston from Brentford and the experienced Jim McCalliog from Wolves.

After spending most of the season in the relegation zone United pulled themselves clear, thanks to an unbeaten spell of eight matches which saw them finish 18th, their lowest position since 1962-3 when they won the FA Cup. This time there was no consolation of a Wembley appearance. To add to the club's problems George Best was going through his most troubled period, and he announced, at the same time that O'Farrell was dismissed, that he was quitting the club and the game. Bobby Charlton and Denis Law played their last games for United in the 1972-3 season. Crerand, Foulkes and Stiles had left a couple of years earlier. A new look was beckoning United, but it started with a drop into the Second Division for the first time in 37 years.

United had spent most of the latter half of 1973-4 in the relegation zone and, apart from an unbeaten run of six matches towards the end of the season, never looked like escaping. There was still a mathematical chance which hinged on many imponderables involving United, Birmingham, Southampton, West Ham and Chelsea. The vital factor for United as they went into the last Saturday of the season, was to beat Manchester City at Old Trafford. A draw would probably not be good enough, a defeat would certainly put United down. With eight minutes remaining, there was no score when, with such nonchalance, Denis Law, of all people, back-heeled the ball past Alex Stepney. Old Trafford was invaded by the crowd and the game abandoned, but the scoreline stood. United's former favourite had put his old club into the Second Division with his last goal in League football.

Relegation did United no harm. Their Second Division average attendance in 1974-5 was 48,388 compared with 42,721 the season they came down. Their presence boosted crowds wherever they went, not due simply to the Manchester United name, but because Docherty had blended together a fine team which played attractive, flowing football.

United won their first four matches, the fourth a 1-0 win at Cardiff to put them top of the table. That was on 31 August, and they were never displaced. They won the title by three points from Aston Villa, clinching promotion with a 1-0 win at Southampton, thanks to a Macari goal.

Docherty had developed some fine young players and Brian Greenhoff was proving outstanding in defence. Steve Coppell and Gordon Hill, relative bargain buys from Tranmere and Millwall respectively, were two of the League's best wingers. Sammy McIlroy was the midfield general whilst Martin Buchan was solid in defence.

Even Docherty must have been surprised at how his new team adapted to the pressures in their first season back in the First Division. Never out of the top five,

*United's Stewart Houston gets the better of Arsenal's Liam Brady at Highbury in November 1975. United went down 3-1 but still went on to finish third in Division One.*

*Steve Coppell takes the ball past Derby's Colin Todd in the FA Cup semi-final at Hillsborough in April 1976.*

*Alex Stepney, Tommy Cavanagh and Stewart Houston celebrate the 1977 FA Cup semi-final victory over Leeds United at Hillsborough.*

they chased Liverpool and Queen's Park Rangers for the title until three games from the end when they lost 1-0 at home to Stoke City. Hitherto candidates for the double, United walked out at Wembley alongside Second Division Southampton for the FA Cup Final. The Reds were clear favourites and many thought Wembley's wide open spaces would suit the likes of Coppell and Hill, but the Saints' Bobby Stokes scored the only goal of the game seven minutes from time. Nevertheless, over 59,000 fans turned out at Old Trafford three days after the Wembley appearance to salute their heroes and watch them wind up the season with a 2-0 win over Manchester City, sweet revenge for the last meeting between the two clubs on that ground.

The 1976-7 season saw Gerry Daly depart for Derby County, but Docherty had shrewdly replaced him with Brian Greenhoff's brother, Jimmy, who joined United from Stoke City for £100,000. United were in contention during the second half of the season, before finishing sixth. Back in Europe for the first time in eight years, they lost to Juventus in the second round of the UEFA Cup. They reached the quarter-finals of the League Cup, and Wembley for the second successive year.

United were underdogs when they met champions Liverpool in the 1977 FA Cup Final, and once more the underdogs won as United took the trophy for the fourth time, thanks to 50th and 55th minute goals by Stuart Pearson and Jimmy Greenhoff, which were interrupted by a Jimmy Case equalizer in the 52nd minute. United had spoiled Liverpool's chance of that elusive double, as they themselves have had many such dreams spoiled over the years.

Two months after the Wembley triumph, United had a new manager, when Tommy Docherty's much publicized relationship with Mary Brown, wife of the club's physiotherapist Laurie Brown, led to his departure.

United's players had to re-adjust to the regime of Dave Sexton, who joined the club from QPR. Sexton's approach was totally opposite to Docherty's and all they had in common was that they had formerly managed Chelsea. Sexton, like O'Farrell, was quiet and unassuming and he had a good track record, but whether he would prosper at Old Trafford was a question on supporters' lips. If his first season, 1977-8, was going to be a yardstick, then the answer was 'no'.

Early exits from the FA Cup, League Cup and European Cup-winners' Cup were followed by a final League placing of 10th. Gordon Hill had been allowed to go, and big money had been spent on bringing Joe Jordan and Gordon McQueen from Leeds United. Jordon disappointed, scoring only three goals in his first 14 League games. The following season saw a slight improvement in League form, and although United's final position was ninth when they won only two of their last 13 matches, there was a good FA Cup run.

United met Liverpool at Maine Road in the semi-final, and led 2-1 with six minutes to go, thanks to goals from Jordan and Brian Greenhoff — and a missed penalty from Terry McDermott — but Alan Hansen equalized. Four days later, at Goodison Park, United won thanks to a solitary goal in the 78th minute from Greenhoff. They were back at Wembley for their eighth FA Cup Final appearance, and what a match it turned out to be. After so many dismal Finals, Arsenal and United served up a rare treat.

With four minutes remaining, Arsenal were leading 2-0, but United fought back with goals from McQueen and McIlroy. Fifty-five seconds after the restart, however, Arsenal were back in front through Alan Sunderland after Gary Bailey, who had enjoyed a good first season, appeared to misjudge a cross. It was the most hectic finale of any FA Cup Final.

It was also cruel luck on Dave Sexton, his assistant Tommy Cavanagh, and the entire team. And while the old adage 'one never remembers losers' is generally true, that was not the case at Wembley on 12 May 1979.

Had United not enjoyed that good Cup run, Sexton could well have followed

*Above: Joe Jordan (far right) equalizes for United in the FA Cup semi-final against Liverpool at Maine Road in March 1979.*

*Another equalizing goal for United, this time by Sammy McIlroy against Arsenal in the 1979 FA Cup Final.*

McGuinness and O'Farrell. He took full advantage of his reprieve and paid a club record £825,000 for Chelsea's Ray Wilkins at the start of 1979-80. The rest of the team altered very little from the previous season, but Wilkins was the general and the result was there for all to see as United challenged Liverpool for the title, and were never out of the top two from October to the end of the season when they fell at the very last hurdle. On the final Saturday of the season United were level on points with Liverpool, but had an inferior goal difference. No matter what Liverpool did, United had to get at least one point from their match at Leeds. They failed, losing 2-0, while Liverpool beat Aston Villa 4-1 to confirm themselves as Champions.

Despite coming so close, so often, trophies eluded Sexton and United. The 1980-81 season saw early departures from the League Cup, FA Cup, and UEFA Cup. Only a fine run of seven consecutive wins at the end of the season pulled United into eighth place. The £1,250,000 signing of Garry Birtles had been a disaster. In 25 League games he had failed to score, and overall there was an uneasy atmosphere at the club once more. When the season closed, Dave Sexton was relieved of his duties.

One nice guy, Frank O'Farrell, had failed at Old Trafford, and so had another, Dave Sexton. Tommy Docherty, nothing like O'Farrell and Sexton, had started to get results, so maybe an extrovert character was the answer. In bringing Ron Atkinson away from West Brom, United certainly brought another flamboyant personality to Old Trafford.

Atkinson knew how to communicate with the fans, an area where Sexton had struggled. And he had his own ideas about the kind of players to win success. In his first year, Atkinson spent over £3 million in obtaining those players. Bryan Robson came from Atkinson's old club, West Brom, for a record £1,500,000. Remi Moses was also signed from Albion, while Atkinson paid another large sum for Arsenal striker Frank Stapleton. Full-back John Gidman moved to Old Trafford in a £450,000-rated deal that took Mickey Thomas to Everton. And Dutch international Arnold Muhren signed for United after his contract with Ipswich expired. Also into the side came Ulsterman Norman Whiteside, who was to become the youngest footballer to appear in the World Cup Finals. He joined Dubliner Kevin Moran, a former Gaelic footballer, in United's team.

The new blend was an instant success. United played attractive football, and finished 1981-2 in third place. The following season, Atkinson guided them to their first-ever Milk Cup Final, but injuries robbed United of possible victory over Liverpool, who won 2-1 in extra-time after Whiteside had opened the scoring in the 12th minute.

Less than two months later, United returned to Wembley for the FA Cup Final against Brighton, who had finished bottom of the First Division, while United had finished third. At 2-2, it took a fine save by Gary Bailey from Gordon Smith to keep United in the game, but it was a different story five nights later, again at Wembley, as United rattled in three first-half goals through Robson (two) and Whiteside. An Arnold Muhren penalty in the second half wound up the proceedings as United won the Cup for the fifth time, and with the biggest winning margin since Bury beat Derby County 6-0 in 1903. For the first time since 1977, United had a trophy to show for their efforts and triumph had come on Sir Matt Busby's 74th birthday.

Atkinson made few alterations to his highly-successful side in 1983-4. Arthur Graham was signed from Leeds United for £45,000, and Martin Buchan and Ashley Grimes departed, to Oldham and Coventry City respectively. Alan Davies, who was given his chance, which he took in the two Wembley matches against Brighton, broke an ankle-bone in a pre-season friendly against Stamford, and missed most of the season. But a new starlet appeared during the season when Mark Hughes made his debut as substitute in the 3-2 home win over Southampton.

*Above: United with the FA Cup after the 1983 replay against Brighton. Below: Brighton's Neil Smillie evades Arnold Muhren's tackle in the first game at Wembley.*

United finished fourth in the League, which Liverpool won once more, and were humiliated by Third Division Oxford United in the Milk Cup and by Bournemouth, also from the Third Division, in the FA Cup. United, however, had their eyes on Europe once more but they went into the Cup-winners' Cup semi-finals against Juventus without the suspended Wilkins and the injured Muhren and Robson. Davies was brought into the attack for his first senior game since the previous season's FA Cup Final and celebrated by equalizing Rossi's goal. A 1-1 draw at Old Trafford was never likely to be enough, however, and despite a brave performance in Turin where they held out at 1-1 until the 89th minute, United went out to a Rossi goal.

At the end of the season, Wilkins went to AC Milan, but was immediately replaced by Aberdeen's Gordon Strachan. Atkinson bought Danish international, Jesper Olsen, from Ajax for £350,000, and once more United were in contention for the League title, until they conceded it to Everton. The European Cup-winners' Cup run ended in the quarter-final when United lost 5-4 on penalties to the little-known Hungarian team Videoton, but United gained revenge over Everton at Wembley when they denied the Merseysiders a treble of League Championship, Cup-winners' Cup and FA Cup.

United reached Wembley after two classic semi-final matches against Liverpool. The 100,000 Wembley crowd paid record receipts of £1 million to see two of the most exciting clubs in the country but, as often happens, the contest did not live up to its billing. It came alive only after referee Peter Willis had created Wembley Cup Final history by sending off Kevin Moran. With ten men, United found new motivation and against all the odds they scored the only goal of the match, in extra-time, when a magnificent effort from Whiteside continued his Wembley goal-scoring record.

Three months into the 1985-6 season there was an air of optimism around Old Trafford. United were ten points clear at the top of Division One and unbeaten

*Another victorious United Cup side, this time after beating Everton in the 1985 Final.*

in 15 games. Sheffield Wednesday ended that run when Lee Chapman scored the only goal of the game at Hillsborough on 9 November and set United on a run of six League and Cup games without a win.

The team was hit by a series of injuries, none more cruel than that which sidelined skipper Bryan Robson for three months between October and January. And even when Robson returned, he was soon injured again and spent the frantic last weeks of the season playing in a special harness to protect a dislocated shoulder.

Defeats by Liverpool in the Milk Cup, and at home by West Ham in the FA Cup, left United to concentrate on the League title but with no other distractions they could still not capitalize on their Merseyside neighbours' heavy programme of League and Cup games.

United lost vital points and the crunch came in one April week when they lost successive home matches, to Chelsea and Sheffield Wednesday.

The latter defeat, a match televised live, saw United give one of their worst performances for years and there was the sight — unimagined in the heady opening weeks of the season — of supporters calling for Ron Atkinson's resignation. Two FA Cup Final victories in three years were not enough for United fans who felt that the League Championship, last won 19 years earlier, was long overdue at Old Trafford, especially considering the club's huge spending in the transfer market.

Early-season disasters in 1986-7, including defeats by Charlton and West Ham in the first two home games, made a mockery of United's huge financial investment in top-class players. It was the Reds' worst start to a season since 1972-3 and by the end of September they were languishing near the bottom of the table, after only one win and a draw in their first eight matches.

The poor results of both United and City were refelected in the attendance for the 109th derby — a 'meagre' 32,440. Ten days later, after a 4-1 defeat by Southampton at the Dell in the Littlewoods Cup, the United directors felt it was time to ring the changes. Enough was enough. The spending had brought no positive results and Ron Atkinson was dismissed.

The board wasted no time in seeking out the best man for the hottest job in English football. That man was Alex Ferguson, who had guided unfashionable Aberdeen to glory both in Scottish domestic and in European competition. Only 12 hours after Atkinson's departure, Ferguson agreed to take the United job. "Money did not enter into it. It is just that Manchester United were the only club in the world capable of drawing me away from Aberdeen," he said.

Ferguson had produced success at Pittodrie on a much tighter budget than he would be allocated at Old Trafford and there was optimism that his appointment would bring about the results which the loyal United fans had been seeking for so long.

Midway through November 1986, with United 21st in the League, the club's accounts revealed a loss of £1.5 million on transfer deals — and that was after recouping £2 million from the sale of Mark Hughes to Barcelona in the close season. The announcement could not have come at a worse time.

Nevertheless, despite continued injury problems, notably to skipper Bryan Robson, United had a good run-in to Christmas and on Boxing Day they beat Liverpool 1-0 at Anfield, thanks to a Norman Whiteside goal. It was United's seventh successive visit to Anfield without defeat. But, despite the euphoria of that win, the harsh reality was that United were out of the Littlewoods Cup and were a struggling bottom-half-of-the-table side. To make matters worse, in the New Year they were dumped out of the FA Cup at home by the eventual winners, Coventry City.

Ferguson, however, was taking stock of the talent he had available and was gradually developing a new side which was a blend of enthusiastic youngsters and experience. Young men like Gary Walsh and Liam O'Brien were given their first taste of First Division football. They did not let the manager down and at the end of the season, United were in 11th position. Seven months earlier many United fans would have been grateful for that.

Ferguson had brought a disciplined approach with him and the players responded to the immense talents of the former Scotland team boss. Results in the second half of his first season had been encouraging. Could he now push for the Championship which had eluded Manchester United for so long?

Having spent his first season consolidating, Ferguson knew in which departments he had to find new players and in 1987 he brought the international experience of full-back Viv Anderson from Arsenal, striker Brian McClair from Celtic and midfielder Steve Bruce from Norwich. The trio cost nearly £2 million but all three, notably McClair's goalscoring talents, were to prove invaluable as United pushed for the title in 1987-8.

In contrast to the previous year, the new season started with a run of seven games without defeat and after 15 games, only Everton had beaten United in the League. McClair was finding the net regularly as United challenged at the top of the table. Above them Arsenal were in top spot but Liverpool, with two games in hand, were unbeaten in their first 13 matches. United entertained Liverpool at Old Trafford in November and drew 1-1, thanks to a Norman Whiteside goal.

As the battle at the top of the table intensified, Queen's Park Rangers and Nottingham Forest forced their way into the frame but the real threat, as always, was from Liverpool.

The vital Christmas period came with Liverpool still unbeaten after 20 games and United, Forest and Everton were the most serious challengers to the Anfielders. But, in contrast to 12 months earlier, United's season was far from over. They had a chance of the League and were still in the Littlewoods Cup, having beaten Hull, Crystal Palace and Bury. And the FA Cup was about to start as the season went into 1988.

An excellent 2-1 win in front of the television cameras at Ipswich heralded the start of United's latest FA Cup campaign. Three weeks later, however, it was farewell to the Littlewoods Cup after a 2-0 defeat at Oxford. However, the FA Cup bandwaggon rolled on after United beat Chelsea 2-0 at Old Trafford in the fourth round. And as the fifth-round tie with Arsenal approached United had leap-frogged above the other challengers in the League and were second to Liverpool, who were still unbeaten after 26 matches. After the Cup tie at Highbury, though, United were left with only the League to concentrate on after going down 2-1 to the Gunners.

Liverpool were still in the Cup and also had their minds on an all-time unbeaten First Division record. That could have weighed in United's favour but Liverpool just kept rolling along and by the time they eventually lost their first match, there were only ten League games remaining and United were 14 points adrift. The gap proved too great for the Reds but a good end-of-season run, with only one defeat in their last 16 games, gave renewed hope as they took the runners-up spot by a convincing nine points from third-placed Nottingham Forest.

Having come so close, manager Alex Ferguson sought to strengthen his squad by making more purchases. Shortly after the end of the season, he went back to his old club, Aberdeen, to bring experienced goalkeeper Jim Leighton to Old Trafford for £750,000. A further £1.5 million brought former favourite Mark Hughes back to United and the prospect of a Hughes-McClair strike force was potentially an exciting combination. Alas, it took some time before they struck up a successful goalscoring partnership. Gone from Old Trafford was Kevin Moran, who was seeking to find fame in Spain with Sporting Gijon.

After a promising start to the new season, with three wins and a draw from their first five matches, United then slumped and went nine matches without a win, eight of which were drawn. They were also knocked out of the Littlewoods Cup by Wimbledon during that period and the promise of the previous season was turning into disaster. Jesper Olsen (to Bordeaux) and Peter Davenport (to Middlesbrough) were transferred and the recruitment of Mal Donaghy from Luton Town and Ralph Milne from Bristol City did little to lift United up the table, even though they enjoyed a good spell over Christmas, with wins against Nottingham Forest and Liverpool.

The New Year once again brought a chance of United glory in the shape of the FA Cup and after three tough games against Queen's Park Rangers, they eventually got their chance to avenge the previous season's Littlewoods Cup defeat by Oxford, which they duly did by 4-0. Bournemouth proved to be tough opposition in the fifth round and at the second attempt United scraped through, thanks to a McClair goal.

As the sixth round approached, United had lost only two of the 14 League and Cup games since the beginning of the year but a 1-0 home defeat by Nottingham Forest in the FA Cup heralded the start of a decline which saw United win only three more games before the end of a season in which they finished 11th. It was indeed a disappointment after their impressive runners-up position the previous season.

As Ferguson started his third full season in charge, it was time to make more changes. Gordon Strachan was sold to Leeds United, Paul McGrath joined Aston Villa and Norman Whiteside, after missing most of the 1988-9 season, was transferred to Everton. Into the new-look line-up came Michael Phelan, a £750,000 signing from Norwich City, and Neil Webb, who cost £1.5 million from Nottingham Forest. They teamed up alongside talented youngsters like Clayton Blackmore, Lee Sharpe, Mark Robins and Russell Beardsmore, who cost little or nothing.

But it was not only on the pitch that changes were being made. There was also the much publicized take-over of the club by Michael Knighton. Amidst euphoria of him scoring a 'goal' at the Stretford End and challenging other club chairmen to a penalty shoot-out, Knighton brought a unique, if not unwanted, air to the Old Trafford club, the like of which had not been seen before.

The fans were dubious about the whole affair and were far from happy at the way it had been conducted. The timing of such a transaction was also to be queried because of its unsettling affect on players. Alas, the mockery United received in the Press did nothing to help the image of one of the biggest names in world soccer. After weeks of on-off speculation, it was eventually revealed that Knighton did not have the cash, or guarantees thereof, to go ahead with the deal and it was eventually called off.

United started the season with a great 4-1 win over defending champions Arsenal, but then started a mini-decline. Knighton had promised the manager funds to buy new players and Ferguson got the chequebook out again and delved into the transfer market, although Knighton was obviously not the benefactor.

United acquired Gary Pallister from Middlesbrough for £2.3 million in a club record deal. A further £1.2 million brought the exciting Danny Wallace from Southampton and £800,000, plus a further £5,000 an appearance, brought Paul Ince from West Ham. Ince was valued at some £2 million but doubts over his fitness resulted in the extra-cash-per-game clause which meant that he would have to make 240 appearances before West Ham collected their original asking price.

Wallace made his debut in the derby at Maine Road and, with £11 million worth of talent on display, United were pounded into an embarrassing 5-1 defeat by City.

By the end of October, Spurs had put United out of the Littlewoods Cup and it was apparent that, despite the big spending, United were again not going to be contenders for the League title.

They were unfortunate to lose the services of England midfielder Neil Webb, who was injured after only four League games. He missed a large part of the season and Bryan Robson was also sidelined for nearly four months from Christmas.

By the end of January, United were threatened with relegation, as were City. United were again left with the FA Cup as their only saviour but, this time had the added problem of winning League games to avoid the drop into the Second Division.

A tough away tie at Nottingham Forest in the third round of the FA Cup saw United win, thanks to a Mark Robins goal. Clayton Blackmore scored the only goal of the game as United scraped through against Hereford United at Edgar Street. And in the fourth round it was another away tie, at Newcastle United.

In a five-goal thriller in front of the television cameras, United sealed victory with goals from Robson, Wallace and McClair. But League points were still vital and by the end of February, while they were into the sixth round of the Cup, the Reds had beaten only Millwall in the League since November. Fellow strugglers Sheffield Wednesday were United's next FA Cup opponents and, yet again, the Reds were drawn away from home. This time a McClair goal put them in the semi-final and those two momentous clashes with Oldham Athletic at Maine Road.

Robson, Webb and Wallace scored the goals in the 3-3 draw in the first game as United twice threw away the lead, but the Reds made no mistake in the replay, despite requiring extra-time in which Mark Robins snatched the late winner to put United into their 11th FA Cup Final.

Four successive League wins lifted United clear of the relegation zone and they went into their Cup Final preparations without that additional worry. At Wembley,

*After drawing the first game at Maine Road in the semi-final against Oldham, United were taken to extra-time in the replay. Here Mark Hughes and Holden fight for possession.*

United were pitched against Crystal Palace, who were managed by a former Old Trafford favourite, Steve Coppell.

Having shared six goals with Oldham in their first semi-final United did the same with Palace in the first meeting and were saved from defeat by Mark Hughes, who snatched the equalizer seven minutes from the end of extra-time. At Wembley four days later, and with goalkeeper Jim Leighton dropped in favour of Les Sealey, United won the Cup for a record-equalling seventh time when Lee Martin scored the only goal of the game in the second half. Ironically, amidst the multi-million pound talent around him, Martin was the only home-grown player and cost the club nothing.

United's precarious League position at the end of January gave cause for concern at Old Trafford and the Press, as usual, were predicting Alex Ferguson's imminent departure. But the good Cup run kept him in his job and now that he had brought one piece of silverware to Old Trafford, there was optimism once again that more would follow. United fans, of course, hope it will be that elusive League Championship trophy.

*Above: White-shirted Mark Hughes turns in celebration after giving United the lead at Wembley in the 1990 FA Cup Final but the match ended as a six-goal thriller. It was replayed three days later and United emerged victorious. Below: Lee Martin, who scored the only goal of the replay, keeps possession from Palace's Ian Wright.*

In 1990-91, United never got into the Championship race, which was a two-team contest between Arsenal and Liverpool, the Gunners snatching the prize at the last gasp. United had to be content with sixth place, three points behind their rivals from across the city.

Perhaps the best remembered of all their 38 League games that season — if for the wrong reasons — was the 1-0 home defeat by Arsenal which resulted in a full scale punch-up involving all 22 players on the field with the exception of Arsenal goalkeeper David Seaman. The brawl resulted in the FA taking two points off Arsenal and one off United as well as imposing a £50,000 fine.

Whilst their League hopes were dwindling, United pressed on and enjoyed good runs in the Rumbelows League Cup, FA Cup and European Cup-winners' Cup.

Having overcome Halifax Town, the Football League's bottom club, in the second round of the League Cup, United then played startling football in beating Liverpool 3-1, with goals from Bruce (penalty), Hughes and Sharpe, in front of 42,000 Old Trafford fans. In the next round, United gave what was probably their finest showing of the season to beat Arsenal 6-2 at Highbury. A Lee Sharp hat-trick being the highlight of a great performance.

It was Hughes' turn to claim a hat-trick in the next round as United beat Southampton 3-2 in a controversial replay at Old Trafford which saw referee George Courtney dismiss Jimmy Case for tripping Bryan Robson 40 yards from goal. The referee, though, did not take similar action against Les Sealey, who brought down Rod Wallace.

Only Leeds stood between Manchester United and another Wembley appearance and after the Reds took a 2-1 advantage to Elland Road for the second leg, the tie hung in the balance. But the only goal of the game, from Lee Sharpe, ensured United's passage to the Final.

The League Cup was the only trophy United had been denied and despite starting as clear favourites against Second Division Sheffield Wednesday, it was Ron Atkinson's Yorkshire team who enjoyed victory, thanks to a John Sheridan goal following a shot from the edge of the box in the 37th minute. Victory was a sweet one for the former United boss Atkinson.

The FA Cup did not hold the same success for United. After home wins over Queen's Park Rangers, in a Monday night game, and Bolton, they lost 2-1 at Norwich. After 85 years of trying, United had still not beaten Norwich in the FA Cup, and this latest defeat ended a run of 21 League and Cup games without defeat for United.

However, United saved their best for the European stage. English clubs made a welcome return after the Heysel disaster and it was United and their fans who carried the flag with pride.

Their first game since losing to Videoton of Hungary in the quarter-final of the Cup-winners' Cup in 1985 was in the same competition when they entertained Pécsi Munkás, also of Hungary, and won 2-0 with goals from Blackmore and Webb. They won the return 1-0 and were then drawn against Wrexham. A three-goal advantage from the first leg was a comfortable cushion to take to the Racecourse for a game that was played in a great atmosphere. The home club did their fans proud despite a 2-0 defeat.

United faced a tough draw against the French club, Montpellier, in the quarter-final. The first leg at Old Trafford started with a Brian McClair goal in the first minute, but a Lee Martin own-goal six minutes later cancelled out the advantage and it stayed at 1-1 with United facing an uphill task in the second leg. But they came away with a brilliant 2-0 win, thanks to goals from Blackmore and a Bruce penalty.

McClair, Bruce and Hughes put the outcome of the semi-final beyond doubt when United won 3-1 at Legia Warsaw. A 1-1 home draw was of little significance; United's place in the Final had been won in the away leg.

*Action from the Cup-winners' Cup Final against Barcelona. Left: Mark Hughes in a tussle for the ball; Right: Pallister and Bruce celebrate.*

The Final against the newly-crowned Spanish champions, Barcelona, was played at Rotterdam in front of 44,000 fans. Mark Hughes brought the game to life when he opened the scoring in the 67th minute. He added a second seven minutes later, but within four minutes Ronald Keoman had pulled one back for Barcelona.

The closing 12 minutes were anxious ones as Barcelona looked capable of equalizing with every attack. But the United defence held on and a second European trophy went to Old Trafford and revived memories of that great night at Wembley in 1968.

Optimism was high the following season as Ferguson's team had started to blend together and was now showing the sort of maturity of a team capable of winning the League title.

Indeed, United, along with Leeds, were established as pre-season favourites for the title. And the bookmakers got it right because the two clubs dominated the Championship from start to finish, and to make the season more intriguing, they were drawn together in both the FA Cup and Rumbelows League Cup, with United winning on both occasions.

The FA Cup third-round game saw United win 1-0 at Elland Road with a 44th-minute goal from Mark Hughes. However, Leeds could count themselves unfortunate not to have got at least a draw because they created more chances but could not put the ball in the net.

*Brian McClair seems happy enough with the Rumbelows Cup after United's Wembley victory over Nottingham Forest. Neil Webb looks in more thoughtful mood.*

But when the two teams met in the quarter-finals of the League Cup the previous week, again at Elland Road, the home team were completely swamped by a United side that gave one of its best performances of the season to win 3-1.

Speed put the home team ahead after 16 minutes, but a Blackmore free-kick over the wall levelled the scores on the half-hour. But two quick goals shortly after the kick-off, from Kanchelskis and Giggs, gave United a two-goal lead which they held.

United drew 0-0 at Southampton in the fourth round of the FA Cup and then engaged in a thriller at Old Trafford in the replay. They came back from two goals behind to equalize with a diving Brian McClair header in the 91st minute. The extra-time period failed to produce any further goals, but United lost 4-2 in their first-ever penalty competition in the FA Cup.

United's European challenge did not bear fruit in 1991-2. After drawing 0-0 in Greece against Athinaikos, they only secured victory by scoring two extra-time goals at Old Trafford. But their performance was far from convincing and when the draw paired them with Atlético Madrid in the next round, United knew they would have to raise their game.

The pairing was an interesting one; both clubs were top of their respective leagues at the time, and with unbeaten records. United seemed to have contained the Spaniards in Madrid. With the game entering its last couple of minutes, Atlético held a slim 1-0 lead. But lapses by United resulted in two late goals and the Reds' task in the home leg was turned into a monumental one within the space of those two minutes.

Mark Hughes gave United a brilliant start in the second leg, scoring after four

51

*It's all over. Mark Hughes and Steve Bruce salute United's wonderful supporters after defeat at Anfield in the last match of 1991-2 confirmed the Old Trafford club's failure to clinch the League Championship after such a great season.*

minutes. But the Spaniards contained United and in the 68th minute, Bernd Schuster scored the vital away goal for Atlético and United's dreams of a second successive European trophy disappeared. However, there was another European confrontation a few weeks later when United entertained Red Star Belgrade, in the European Super Cup which United captured, thanks to a 67th-minute goal from Brian McClair. Only 22,110 fans turned up to watch, many of United's fans clearly thinking the match was of little importance.

However, the League Cup show rolled on and after disposing of Leeds in the quarter-final, United had a semi-final meeting with Middlesbrough.

A goalless draw at Ayresome Park was followed by an extra-time victory at Old Trafford as United reached their second successive Final. This time the game against Nottingham Forest at Wembley was decided by an early goal from Brian McClair and the first domestic trophy of the season was United's.

Now United turned their attention to the League Championship but when a disastrous Easter weekend saw them lose successively to Forest at home and then at bottom club West Ham, it was Leeds United who now slipped ahead.

On the penultimate weekend of the season the issue was settled. Leeds won a thriller, 3-2 at Bramall Lane, whilst Manchester United lost 2-0 at Anfield. The title belonged to Leeds. Old Trafford's wait slipped into its 26th year.

# The Old Trafford Story

NEWTON Heath's first ground was at North Road, Monsall, and was set in typical Victorian northern industrial surroundings. When the Heathens joined the Football League in 1892, their playing surface was one of the worst in the competition and could be a mud-bath at one end and rock-hard at the other. The changing-rooms were half a mile away at the Three Crowns public house.

In 1893, the club moved to Bank Street, Clayton. The pitch was little better than the one at North Road and the smoke-billowing chimneys provided a similar backdrop. The only real improvement on the first ground was the subsequent erection of a 1000-seater stand, the result of J.H.Davies, Newton Heath's first major benefactor, investing £500. On 4 April 1904, the Football League beat the Scottish League 2-1 at Clayton.

It was Davies who, in 1909, donated the huge sum of £60,000 for the purchase and development of a site at Trafford Park. The new ground, to be called Old Trafford, was ready for use in 1910 and on 22 January that year, United played their final match at Clayton, beating Spurs 5-0. Their first game at the new stadium nearly a month later, saw 45,000 cram in to witness a seven-goal thriller, won by Liverpool.

The Clayton ground had been sold to Manchester Corporation for £5,000 in January 1909, one week before plans for the new Old Trafford were approved by the Stretford Council.

Old Trafford, with a capacity of 80,000, then had only one stand, situated where the Main Stand is today, but it offered untold luxuries — tea-rooms, tip-up seats and attendants to politely point the way. There were also games rooms, a gymnasium and a plunge bath for the players. The nearest the ground came to being filled to capacity was on 27 December 1920 when Aston Villa were the visitors and 70,504 packed the ground to register what is still United's record home attendance, not withstanding the 80,000-plus crowds who saw them play at Maine Road after World War Two whilst Old Trafford was being rebuilt after war damage. And the actual attendance record for Old Trafford stands at 76,962, for the 1939 FA Cup semi-final between Wolves and Grimsby.

When Old Trafford was built it was one of Britain's great stadiums, but by the outbreak of World War Two, because so little improvement had been made, it no longer stood out as one of the League's outstanding venues. By 1945 it could not be used at all. During a raid on nearby Trafford Park industrial estate, on the night of 11 March 1941, German bombs landed on the ground, virtually destroying the Main Stand, part of the terracing and badly scorching the pitch.

Makeshift offices were erected and United, as determined as ever, set about the long rebuilding job whilst sharing Manchester City's ground for home matches. The worst hit of all League clubs during the war, United were awarded £22,278 by the War Damage Commission to clear the debris and rebuild the ground.

A massive 120,000-capacity ground was planned, but financial restrictions prevented it and instead only the Main Stand was replaced. On 24 August 1949, United played their first Football League game at Old Trafford for ten years when 41,748 saw them beat Bolton.

53

*Scene from the FA Cup semi-final between Wolves and Grimsby Town in 1939. The attendance of 76,962 is still the record 'gate' for the ground.*

United's venture into Europe in 1956 saw them erect floodlights to cater for mid-week matches. The first European Cup match under the Old Trafford lights was the semi-final against Real Madrid on 25 April 1957. For their previous European games that season United had to return to City's Moss Side ground.

The first League game under lights at Old Trafford was on 25 March 1957 when Bolton were the opposition and United's biggest League crowd of the season, 60,826, endured a 2-0 defeat.

One of Old Trafford's most emotional occasions saw nearly 60,000 urge United to FA Cup victory over Sheffield Wednesday in the first post-Munich match. The following Saturday, a crowd of 66,124 saw the visit of Nottingham Forest.

As United moved into the golden era of the 1960s, Old Trafford saw its greatest phase of improvement. The Stretford End was covered in 1959, sheltering 22,000 standing fans from the worst of the Manchester weather.

In readiness for the 1966 World Cup Finals, work started on the magnificent cantilever stand in 1964. Upon its completion, at a cost of £350,000, there remained only one part of the ground still uncovered, the Scoreboard End. In 1973 that was rectified and the next major improvement was the replacement of the Main Stand roof with a cantilever.

Three World Cup matches, in Group Three, were played at Old Trafford in 1966, 40 years after the first full international was staged there — the 1926 England-Scotland match, which the Scots won 1-0.

Bradford City won their one and only FA Cup Final when they beat Newcastle 1-0 in their replayed Final of 1911 at Old Trafford. In 1970, Chelsea beat Leeds to win the Cup at Old Trafford, the first time a Wembley Final had to be replayed. United's ground had been chosen for only one Cup Final, replays excepted, and that was the 1915 game between Sheffield United and Chelsea. It was called the 'Khaki Final' because many of the 49,557 crowd were soldiers either on leave, or about to embark for the trenches. The choice of Old Trafford for that game ended the 19-year dominance of the Crystal Palace as the Cup Final venue.

Old Trafford's 50,000 capacity will shortly be reduced considerably as an 18-month programme of development is undertaken to upgrade the ground.

It was announced that work would start in the summer of 1992 with alterations

*Above and below: Bomb damage at Old Trafford during World War Two. It was to be some time after the war before United could play there again.*

to the Stretford End which would reduce the Old Trafford capacity to 34,000. Naturally, with attendances previously averaging in excess of 40,000 this posed a major problem. Away fans were to be banned, and those United fans fortunate enough to gain admission would have to pay increased charges to compensate for the reduced capacity.

This move brought about much unrest amongst fans and they set up a pressure group called HOSTAGE (Holders of Season Tickets against Gross Exploitation). It is unfortunate that the fans are made to suffer at such a time, but when the redevelopment is complete, Old Trafford will re-state its case as one of the finest soccer grounds in the world and will again be a delight for players and fans to visit.

# United Managers

## Ernest Mangnall
## 1903-1912

TWO men have succeeded in their dream of making Manchester United a great club. Sir Matt Busby achieved it in the post-World War Two era, and the first to that goal was Ernest Mangnall.

Like Busby, Mangnall had the ability to motivate players and the powers to spot and nurture emerging talent. And like Busby, he had a burning, unquenchable thirst for success.

Mangnall joined United from Burnley, succeeding James West as secretary in 1903. Along with the club's first great benefactor, J.H.Davies, he transformed Manchester United into one of the giants of the First Division, a team to be feared and respected.

Mangnall brought players like Roberts, Duckworth and Moger to Clayton and in three years had produced a promotion-winning team. In 1907, when seven Manchester City stars were suspended because of an illegal payments scandal, it was Mangnall who swooped to sign Sandy Turnbull, Herbert Burgess, Jimmy Bannister and the great Billy Meredith. With those stars, United won the League Championship for the first time. They later went on to win the FA Cup for the first time — and another League title.

When that great team began to wane, Mangnall moved across to Manchester City in 1912. Not until Busby's reign, which began over 30 years later, did Manchester United develop anything like the great side which Ernest Mangnall had once assembled.

During his playing career, Mangnall appeared in goal for a Lancashire County team which also included J.J.Bentley, who later succeeded him as secretary at United.

# John Robson
## 1914-1921

JOHN R.Robson was the first official to assume the actual title of manager. Although Ernest Mangnall was the first man to fill the post, his title was that of secretary, as was that of his successors, T.J.Wallworth and J.J.Bentley.

On Bentley's resignation in 1916, Robson took on both roles as United soldiered on through wartime football. He joined United from Brighton, on 28 December 1914 after spells with Middlesbrough and Crystal Palace, and remained in charge until ill health forced his retirement in October 1921. His seven-year reign made him the longest-serving United manager after Sir Matt Busby.

Throughout Robson's managerial career at Old Trafford, United remained a First Division club — albeit with a four-season break because of war — but they were on the decline when he was forced to quit. Upon his resignation, Robson was appointed assistant to his successor, John Chapman.

# John Chapman
## 1921-1926

WHEN John Robson resigned in October 1921, John Chapman was appointed with Robson staying on as his assistant. Chapman came from Airdrieonians and found United to be a struggling First Division team.

His presence made no immediate impact and in his first 15 games in charge, United scored only one victory. The season finished with them bottom of the table and it took Chapman three seasons to haul them back to Division One.

The first season back in the top flight saw United finish ninth and Chapman's side gave Old Trafford fans some hope of success when he took them to their first FA Cup semi-final since they won the trophy in 1909. Manchester City ended United's dreams of their first Wembley Final. Chapman's signings included Frank Barson, Frank Mann, Tom Jones, Jim Hanson and Frank McPherson.

In October 1926, Manchester United received a letter from the Football Association telling them that Chapman was to be suspended forthwith from all involvement with football because of alleged improper conduct whilst acting as the club's secretary-manager.

The full details of the charges were never made public, but United had little option but to dispense with their manager's services.

## Clarence Hilditch
## 1926-1927

CLARRIE Hilditch (see *A-Z of United Stars*) gave Manchester United loyal and devoted service over 16 years. When John Chapman was suspended by the Football Association, and subsequently sacked by United, Hilditch stepped into the breach as player-manager — the only such appointment in the club's history. During his short spell in charge he was reluctant to select himself and United slipped. When Herbert Bamlett was appointed in April 1927, Hilditch made himself available for selection by the new manager and continued to serve the club as a player until his retirement in 1932.

## Herbert Bamlett
## 1927-1931

HERBERT Bamlett took over when United were struggling in Division One and during his four seasons in charge it had to be said that things hardly improved, despite him recruiting the fire-power of strikers Tommy Reid and Henry Rowley. United finished bottom of the table and in 1930-31 after conceding 115 goals and losing their first 12 games, it was inevitable that Bamlett and United would part company at the end of that depressing season.

Before venturing in to the world of management, Bamlett had been one of the country's top referees. Born in Gateshead, he was one of several top-class officials to come from that area and in 1914, aged 32, he became the youngest man to referee an FA Cup Final when he took charge of the game between Burnley and Liverpool at the Crystal Palace.

Bamlett was also the referee for the Burnley-Manchester United FA Cup quarter-final tie in 1909, which he abandoned with 18 minutes to go and United trailing 1-0. United went on to win the re-arranged match and the Cup. Before taking charge at Old Trafford, Bamlett managed Oldham Athletic, Wigan Borough and Middlesbrough.

## Walter Crickmer
## 1931-1932 and 1937-1945

ALTHOUGH Walter Crickmer never assumed the title of manager of Manchester United, he twice dovetailed the duties of team selection with those of his post as club secretary. One of the finest administrators in United's history, Crickmer first took charge of the team, along with Louis Rocca, in 1931-2, between the reigns of Herbert Bamlett and Scott Duncan.

After Duncan resigned in November 1937, United were without a manager until the appointment of Matt Busby in 1945. Once again, Crickmer helped out with the playing affairs and his job took him through the troubled years of 1939-45.

It was Crickmer who, in 1938, was largely responsible for instituting the famous United youth policy that served the club so well in subsequent years. He was appointed secretary in 1926 and lost his life in the Munich air disaster, after 38 years with United.

## A.Scott Duncan
## 1932-1937

FORMER Dumbarton, Glasgow Rangers and Newcastle United player Scott Duncan was offered the post of United manager in August 1932, at a salary reported to be £800 per annum, and after Sir Matt Busby and Robson he is United's longest-serving manager, spending five years at the club.

In his first two seasons he spent a great deal of money, buying several players from his native Scotland, and he came under fire from newspapers and supporters for failing to produce good results, despite his financial outlay.

Duncan had played once for United during World War One. His signings as manager included Scottish internationals Neil Dewar from Third Lanark and Chalmers from Cowdenbeath, together with Shamrock Rovers' Irish international, Byrne, and Welsh international Bamford from Wrexham.

He saw United narrowly escape relegation in 1933-4, but two years later steered them to the Second Division championship. The success was followed by the offer of a five-year contract for the manager, but United were not equipped for life in Division One and a year later they were down again.

After the first 14 games of 1938-9, Duncan resigned and became manager of Ipswich Town who were then in the Southern League. He took them into the Football League whilst United's first game after his departure — a 7-1 win at Chesterfield — began a run which secured them promotion once more, despite having no 'proper' manager for the rest of the season.

Apart from the Second Division championship, Duncan, who also managed Hamilton and Cowdenbeath, made little impact at Old Trafford.

# Sir Matt Busby CBE
# 1945-1969 and 1970-71

WHEN the Manchester United directors appointed Matt Busby manager in 1945 they made probably the most significant decision in the club's history. Like Ernest Mangnall before him, Busby brought glory to the club — and in Busby's case it was to find a stage wider than anyone could have imagined in Mangnall's days before World War One.

Busby, the son of a Scottish miner, was a stylish half-back with Manchester City and Liverpool before World War Two and although he won only one full cap for Scotland, he skippered his country in several wartime internationals.

Busby inherited a club with no home, for Old Trafford had been severely damaged in the war. His team played their home matches at Maine Road as he began to rebuild from the ashes. Busby moulded together his first great team under captain Johnny Carey. They went on to win the FA Cup in 1948, in a Final of breathtaking skill and excitement, and with the addition of talented youth, lifted the Championship in 1952, the club's first League title for 41 years.

In their first six seasons under Busby, United never finished lower than fourth. At his side was Jimmy Murphy and they formed a partnership which could spot raw talent and then nurture it to greatness. Roger Byrne, Tommy Taylor, Duncan Edwards and Bobby Charlton were just some of the players who stand testament to their joint skills.

Busby took United to consecutive League titles, in 1956 and 1957, and in the second of those years he came close to winning for the Reds the first modern 'double' of League and Cup. By then, his quest for the European Cup had started and by now United were one of the best club sides in the world.

The European dream was shattered at Munich where Busby suffered injuries so severe that he was administered the Last Rites. He also had to suffer the cruel knowledge that he had lost many of his young players. Busby was absent from his desk for six months.

With Jimmy Murphy, he began to assemble a new United. Law, Herd, Crerand, Cantwell and others were drafted in and United won the FA Cup again in 1963 — narrowly missing relegation the same season — and the League Championship in 1965.

A Championship two years later set the stage for another attempt at the European Cup and this time Busby's dream was realized. United lifted the trophy with a magnificent win over Benfica at Wembley and he and Bobby Charlton shed tears of joy together. The players had sensed it was Busby's last chance to win the major European club honour.

He made way for Wilf McGuinness, but retained the post of general manager. When McGuinness was relieved of his job in December 1970, Busby took charge once more, steering United away from trouble. He left the manager's chair in 1971, a quarter of a century after he was first appointed.

Sir Matt Busby — he was knighted in the wake of United's European triumph — maintained close links with the club and the city. He was made a Freeman of Manchester in 1967, appointed a United director and then the club's president. He was elected a vice-president of the Football League in 1982 and is now a life member.

In 1945, he was offered jobs as a coach at Liverpool, assistant-manager of Reading, and manager of Ayr United. He turned them all down for a £15-per-week job as manager of Manchester United. Four years later, Spurs offered him £50 a week to become their manager. Every United fan, young or old, can be eternally thankful that he turned them down.

# Jimmy Murphy
## February-August 1958

WELSH international wing-half Jimmy Murphy was with West Brom from 1928 to the outbreak of war. He served in Italy, where he met Matt Busby and when Busby was offered the United manager's job in 1945, Murphy was his first 'signing'. He was initially employed as coach and, always Busby's right-hand man, he was officially appointed assistant manager in 1955.

Shortly afterwards he became the Wales team manager and around this time was offered lucrative jobs in Brazil and with Italian giants, Juventus. A talented coach, Murphy guided the development of many fine players, but he regarded Duncan Edwards as the finest footballer he ever saw.

When the United party flew to Belgrade in 1958, Murphy missed the trip because he was on international duty with the Welsh team for a World Cup qualifier at Cardiff. In the wake of the Munich tragedy, he took charge of United and led them to the 1958 FA Cup Final. In August that year, Murphy made way for the return of Busby. He had been a monumental tower of strength in the months following the disaster.

An avid reader and a pianist in the classical mould, Murphy resigned as assistant manager in 1971, although he continued to scout for the club he had served for over 25 years. He died on 14 November 1989.

# Wilf McGuinness
# 1969-1970

WHEN United appointed Wilf McGuinness as successor to Sir Matt Busby in 1969, no one doubted the enormity of his task. Although he had already served the club for almost 17 years (see *A-Z of United Stars*), he faced a daunting situation as replacement for one of the game's greatest managers, in one of the most prestigious managerial seats in the business.

His playing career ended through injury when he was only 22 and he joined United's training staff. McGuinness was involved in the preparation of several England teams, including the 1966 World Cup squad, and on 9 April 1969 it was announced that he was being appointed United's chief coach in readiness for Busby's retirement at the end of the season.

On 1 June 1969 he was given the manager's job; in December 1970, he lost the position and reverted to trainer-coach of the reserve team. The concept of promoting from within had not worked for United and McGuinness had probably found it difficult to manage players who were established internationals and who had achieved so much more than him as a player.

McGuinness had achieved minor successes as United's manager — two League Cup semi-finals and one FA Cup semi-final — but he could not provide the League and European glory that the club so desperately needed.

He later managed the Greek club, Aris Salonika, and then York City. In 1986, McGuinness was on the coaching staff at Bury and much sought after for his wit as an after-dinner speaker. He spoke at the 1986 PFA Annual Awards dinner.

# Frank O'Farrell
## 1971-1972

WHEN Frank O'Farrell took over as manager of Manchester United in June 1971, he left a Leicester side that he had guided to the Second Division title and which played attractive football.

He was also one of the nicest men in the game but neither that, nor his achievements at Filbert Street, which included taking Leicester to Wembley in 1969, were good enough credentials to help him succeed at Old Trafford.

United finished eighth in O'Farrell's first season in charge, after being five points clear at the top of the table at Christmas. As a decline was evident the following season, O'Farrell and his coach, Malcolm Musgrove, were sacked in December 1972.

He spent a considerable amount of money in his brief spell at Old Trafford. Ian Storey-Moore and Ted MacDougall each cost around £200,000, and Martin Buchan £125,000, but the chequebook failed to halt the slide and O'Farrell, a former West Ham and Preston player, and Torquay manager, paid the price. He was unfortunate to manage United at a time when the wayward genius of George Best was providing a particular headache. O'Farrell later managed Torquay again, for two spells, and coached in the United Arab Emirates.

## Tommy Docherty
## 1972-1977

TOMMY Docherty might be one of the game's most controversial characters, but he certainly assembled an exciting side during his four and a half seasons at Old Trafford. He got a response from his players, the like of which had not been seen since the days of Sir Matt Busby.

Docherty, a former Scottish international wing-half, succeeded Frank O'Farrell in December 1972 and he managed to steer United clear of relegation to finish 18th. The following season, despite the purchase of Jim McCalliog and Stewart Houston, United were relegated.

The drop did the club little harm. Attendances were maintained as they swept to the Second Division title. The addition of Stuart Pearson, and exciting young players like Gerry Daly, Sammy McIlroy and Steve Coppell had made United one of the most attractive teams in the country.

Gordon Hill was added to the line-up and in 1975-6, United finished third in the First Division and reached the FA Cup Final, only to lose to Second Division Southampton.

A year later, Docherty led United out at Wembley again and this time they lifted the FA Cup, beating Liverpool 2-1. It was to be his final achievement at Old Trafford. In the summer of that year it was announced that he was having an affair with the wife of United physiotherapist, Laurie Brown.

Docherty was dismissed and with his United job went his best chance of major managerial success. He had a host of other managerial jobs, both before and after his Old Trafford days, jobs which included being in charge of the Scotland team, but only at Chelsea did he achieve any other honours.

# Dave Sexton
## 1977-1981

AFTER going for nearly 25 years with one man at the helm, Manchester United appointed their fourth manager in eight years when Dave Sexton accepted the job in 1977.

So far, no one had measured up to the massive stature of Busby but United hoped that, in Sexton, they had at last found the man to steady the ship. He had enjoyed a good record as Chelsea manager, guiding them to the 1970 FA Cup Final with victory over Leeds in the Old Trafford replay, as well as to the European Cup-winners' Cup Final the following year.

He took QPR to within a whisker of the League Championship in 1975-6 and just over a year later he was appointed manager at Old Trafford. The directors saw him as the best choice, not just in terms of what he had achieved, but as the most acceptable face in the wake of the scandal which had surrounded Docherty's departure.

The club had nothing to show from Sexton's first year in charge and, despite investing nearly £1 million in Gordon McQueen and Joe Jordan, they finished in a mid-table position.

The following season, although United's League fortunes had changed little, Sexton led them to Wembley for the third time in four seasons. It was to prove a memorable FA Cup Final, if only for the last frantic minutes when United clawed their way back into the game only to see Arsenal grab a dramatic winner.

In 1979-80 Sexton broke the club's outgoing transfer fee record by paying £825,000 to Chelsea for Ray Wilkins. It proved a good move as Wilkins marshalled United's midfield and helped them finish League Championship runners-up to Liverpool.

In 1980-81, despite paying £1 million for Garry Birtles, United found themselves back in mid-table and with no Cup successes either. Sexton lost his job on 30 April 1981, despite the fact that United had won their last seven games.

He was, without doubt, a fine coach but it was said that he was not close enough to his players and lacked the ability to communicate at club level. He went to Coventry as manager and became a member of Bobby Robson's England coaching staff.

It is perhaps ironic that Tommy Docherty offered Sexton his first coaching job, at Chelsea, for Sexton later replaced 'The Doc' as manager at two clubs, Chelsea and United.

# Ron Atkinson
## 1981-86

AS THE 1985-6 season got underway, Ron Atkinson found himself under the same pressure as Scott Duncan when he managed United in the 1930s. Both had spent heavily on buying players, but had little to show for it. Coincidentally, Atkinson was the first non-Roman Catholic to be appointed United manager since Duncan.

United had won the FA Cup twice in Atkinson's first four seasons at Old Trafford, but those successes involved the club in transfer fees grossing several million pounds. And it is League and European honours which most interested United's hungry fans.

Atkinson was born in Liverpool but brought up in the West Midlands. Rejected by Wolves and Aston Villa, he joined Oxford United, along with his brother, Graham. Ron Atkinson was a driving force behind the Oxford team that won a Football League place in 1962 and powered its way to Division Two.

He began his managerial career at Witney Town before moving to Kettering Town, who he took to two Southern League titles. He guided Cambridge United to the Fourth Division title in 1976-7 and the following season helped them towards the Second before West Brom swooped, appointing him successor to Ronnie Allen.

In June 1981 he left The Hawthorns to become United manager and took with him Mick Brown, his assistant at Albion. Atkinson went back to his old club for two players, Bryan Robson and Remi Moses, who cost United a total of £2.4 million. Other Atkinson signings included Frank Stapleton (£1.1 million), Alan Brazil (£700,000), Gordon Strachan (£600,000), Peter Davenport (£575,000), John Gidman (£400,000), Colin Gibson (£275,000), Chris Turner (£275,000), Terry Gibson (£300,000 plus Alan Brazil), Johnny Sivebaek (£250,000) and Jesper Olsen (£350,000).

Atkinson, with his bejewelled image and reputation as a big-spender, found his United team in rampant form at the start of the 1985-6 season when they won ten games on the trot to go clear at the top of the table. Then injuries to key players, notably England skipper Bryan Robson, robbed his side of its greatest influences. United dropped from the top of the First Division and were knocked out of both FA and Milk Cups. Yet again, a season which had promised so much ended with nothing.

Atkinson was replaced by Alex Ferguson in 1986. He returned to West Brom in 1987-8 but quit to take a £250,000-a-year job with Atlético Madrid. He lost that job after only 96 days and returned to Britain, taking over at Sheffield Wednesday in February 1989.

Anderson gained some compensation for his dismissal as United manager by guiding Sheffield Wednesday to victory over the Reds at Wembley in the Rumbelows League Cup Final in 1991. He also guided Wednesday back into the First Division that year. But shortly after gaining promotion he announced he was quitting the club to take charge of Aston Villa, amidst shouts of 'traitor' from the home fans. Ironically the opening day of the 1991-2 season paired Wednesday with Villa.

# Alex Ferguson OBE
# 1986-

WHEN Manchester United appointed Alex Ferguson as their manager, they obtained the services of a man with a proven track record at the highest level, for he had developed one-time unfashionable Aberdeen into three times Scottish League Champions and also European Cup-winners' Cup victors.

Ferguson took over at Aberdeen in 1978, after a playing career spent as a bustling forward with Queen's Park, St Johnstone, Dunfermline, Rangers and Ayr United and managerial spells at East Stirling and St Mirren.

Aberdeen appointed him despite an impending tribunal to settle his differences with St Mirren and although his early days at Pittodrie were difficult ones, he eventually guided Aberdeen to their first League title in 25 years. From 1985 he also stood in as Scotland's team manager, following the death of Jock Stein, until after the 1986 Finals in Mexico.

In earlier years, he had declined offers from Tottenham, Wolves and Rangers but in November 1986 he could not resist the temptation to join Manchester United. At Old Trafford, the man who had wrought such a great influence on Scottish domestic football found life more difficult and as the new decade dawned.

Having spent millions of pounds in the transfer market as a result of signings like Mark Hughes, Neil Webb, Gary Pallister and Danny Wallace, Ferguson was still unable to bring the League Championship to Old Trafford. Midway through the 1989-90 season there was a real threat of relegation and, inevitably, speculation about Ferguson's future. The situation was salvaged when United won the FA Cup in May 1990 and the following year European glory came when United beat Barcelona to win the European Cup-winners' Cup.

Ferguson had moulded together a side that was a mixture of experience with talented youngsters like Lee Sharpe. His team was virtually complete as they went in search of that League title.

Sadly, after engaging in a great season-long battle for the title with Leeds United, the Reds lost out as that first title since 1967 still eluded them.

*Note: Transfer fees quoted above, like all those in this book, are taken from figures widely reported in newspapers at the time.*

# A-Z of United Stars

Edinburgh-born Arthur Albiston holds the distinction of making his FA Cup debut in a Wembley Final. He got his chance as a 19-year-old in 1977, taking over from the injured Stewart Houston, and gave an impressive performance in United's 2-1 win over Liverpool. Having served his apprenticeship at Old Trafford, the Scottish Schoolboy international made his League debut in a 0-0 draw at Portsmouth in October 1974, six days after his senior debut before 55,000 fans at Old Trafford in United's League Cup win over Manchester City. Towards the end of 1976-7 he began to establish himself and, after his surprise Cup Final appearance, became a first-team regular. Subsequent FA Cup Final appearances followed in 1979, 1983 and 1985 and he was also in United's 1983 Milk Cup Final team. Albiston added to his international honours with Under-21 and then full Scotland caps. He made his full international debut in the 1-1 draw with Northern Ireland shortly before the 1982 World Cup Finals but did not make the trip to Spain, although he was in the 1986 squad for Mexico. He joined West Brom in 1988 and after one season moved to Dundee and was later with Chesterfield and Chester.

**ARTHUR ALBISTON**

| | LEAGUE | | FACUP | | FLCUP | | EUROPE | | TOTAL | |
|---|---|---|---|---|---|---|---|---|---|---|
| | App | Gls | App | Gls | App | Gls | App | Gls | App | Gls |
| 1974-75 | 2 | 0 | 0 | 0 | 1 | 0 | 0 | 0 | 3 | 0 |
| 1975-76 | 2/1 | 0 | 0 | 0 | 0 | 0 | 0 | 0 | 2/1 | 0 |
| 1976-77 | 14/3 | 0 | 1 | 0 | 2/2 | 0 | 2/1 | 0 | 19/6 | 0 |
| 1977-78 | 27/1 | 0 | 4 | 0 | 1 | 0 | 4 | 0 | 36/1 | 0 |
| 1978-79 | 32/1 | 0 | 7 | 0 | 2 | 0 | 0 | 0 | 41/1 | 0 |
| 1979-80 | 25 | 0 | 0 | 0 | 3 | 0 | 0 | 0 | 28 | 0 |
| 1980-81 | 42 | 1 | 3 | 0 | 2 | 0 | 2 | 0 | 49 | 1 |
| 1981-82 | 42 | 1 | 1 | 0 | 2 | 0 | 0 | 0 | 45 | 1 |
| 1982-83 | 38 | 1 | 7 | 0 | 9 | 1 | 2 | 0 | 56 | 2 |
| 1983-84 | 40 | 2 | 1 | 0 | 6 | 0 | 8 | 0 | 55 | 2 |
| 1984-85 | 39 | 0 | 7 | 0 | 3 | 0 | 8 | 0 | 57 | 0 |
| 1985-86 | 37 | 1 | 5 | 0 | 3 | 0 | 0 | 0 | 45 | 1 |
| 1986-87 | 19/3 | 0 | 0 | 0 | 4 | 0 | 0 | 0 | 23/3 | 0 |
| 1987-88 | 5/6 | 0 | 0 | 0 | 0 | 0 | 0 | 0 | 5/6 | 0 |
| | 364/15 | 6 | 36 | 0 | 38/2 | 1 | 26/1 | 0 | 464/18 | 7 |

Alex Ferguson's first major signing for Manchester United was the experienced England full-back, Viv Anderson, in the 1987 close season, when United paid Arsenal a tribunal-fixed £250,000. Born in Nottingham, Anderson, a six-footer, served his apprenticeship with Forest before turning professional in 1974 and in September that year he made his League debut against Sheffield Wednesday. Four years later he created history by becoming the first coloured player to win a full England cap, against Czechoslovakia at Wembley. During his spell at Forest he won a League Championship medal, two League Cup winners' medals and was a member of two European Cup winning sides. Anderson moved to Arsenal in a £250,000 deal in July 1984 before joining United at the age of 31. He made his United debut in the 2-2 draw with Southampton at The Dell on the opening day of the 1987-8 season as United pushed for the Championship. Injuries sidelined him the following season and Lee Martin was given the opportunity to take over Anderson's full-back berth. However, Viv is still a valuable member of the first-team squad and has served manager Ferguson well whenever called upon. Anderson came to United as a trialist during the period of upheaval of McGuinness, Busby and O'Farrell and was informed he was not good enough. Anderson moved from Old Trafford on a free transfer in January 1991 and teamed up with former Old Trafford boss Ron Atkinson at Sheffield Wednesday.

**VIV ANDERSON**

|  | LEAGUE | | FA CUP | | FL CUP | | EUROPE | | TOTAL | |
|---|---|---|---|---|---|---|---|---|---|---|
|  | App | Gls | App | Gls | App | Gls | App | Gls | App | Gls |
| 1987-88 | 30/1 | 2 | 3 | 1 | 4 | 0 | - | - | 37/1 | 3 |
| 1988-89 | 5/1 | 0 | 0 | 0 | 0/1 | 0 | - | - | 5/2 | 0 |
| 1989-90 | 14/2 | 0 | 4 | 0 | 1 | 0 | - | - | 19/2 | 0 |
| 1990-91 | 1 | 0 | 0 | 0 | 1 | 1 | 1 | 0 | 3 | 1 |
|  | 50/4 | 2 | 7 | 1 | 6/1 | 1 | 1 | 0 | 64/5 | 4 |

Converted from inside-forward, John Aston joined Johnny Carey as one of the most famous full-back duos of the immediate post-war years. Aston and Carey had a great understanding and it was a treat to see them punting long passes to each other, with deadly accuracy, during the pre-match kick-in. Born locally, Aston signed for United as an amateur in May 1937. He turned professional at the end of the war and made the first of his 250-plus League appearances in the 1-1 draw with Chelsea in September 1946. Aston was a member of United's first 1948 FA Cup winning team, and of the 1952 Championship winning side. Well-built, he used his weight to good advantage but he was also a skilful player. Often called upon to help out in the forward line when injuries took their toll, he scored a number of League goals for United. He won 17 England caps at left-back, partnering several different right-backs including Alf Ramsey. Illness cut short Aston's career and in April 1954 he played his last match, scoring the opening goal in United's 3-1 win over Sheffield United. He took up scouting duties with the club and in 1970 became chief scout. He did not survive the upheaval of Frank O'Farrell's sacking in 1972, when he too left United. His son John was a member of United's 1968 European Cup winning team.

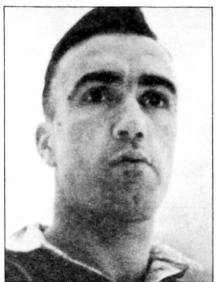

**JOHN ASTON, snr**

|  | LEAGUE | | FA CUP | | TOTAL | |
|---|---|---|---|---|---|---|
|  | App | Gls | App | Gls | App | Gls |
| 1946-47 | 21 | 0 | 2 | 0 | 23 | 0 |
| 1947-48 | 42 | 0 | 6 | 0 | 48 | 0 |
| 1948-49 | 39 | 0 | 8 | 0 | 47 | 0 |
| 1949-50 | 40 | 0 | 5 | 0 | 45 | 0 |
| 1950-51 | 41 | 15 | 4 | 1 | 45 | 16 |
| 1951-52 | 18 | 4 | 1 | 0 | 19 | 4 |
| 1952-53 | 40 | 8 | 3 | 0 | 43 | 8 |
| 1953-54 | 12 | 2 | 0 | 0 | 12 | 2 |
|  | 253 | 29 | 29 | 1 | 282 | 30 |

Like his father before him, John Aston emerged from a Wembley Cup Final with pride and a winners' medal. His father was a member of United's 1948 FA Cup team and John junior had a starring role when the European Cup came to Old Trafford 20 years later. Born in Manchester, John Aston turned professional in 1964 after a two-year apprenticeship with United. A member of that year's FA Youth Cup winning team, Aston made his debut in the home win over Leicester City in April 1965. By the time of United's Wembley triumph over Benfica, he had made the number-11 shirt his own and won a Championship medal. He scored some vital goals for the club but his making of a goal for George Best in the 1-0 European Cup win over Real Madrid,

was perhaps more important than any he netted himself. That goal separated the sides at the end of the two-legged semi-final and sent United on the road to Wembley victory. A broken leg virtually ended his United career and in July 1972 he moved to Luton Town for £30,000. Aston enjoyed a five-year spell at Kenilworth Road and was a member of the Hatters' team which returned to Division One in 1974, after a 14-year absence. He moved to Mansfield Town in 1977 and then to Blackburn Rovers, where he finished his playing career. Aston was a straight-forward winger — there was nothing 'flash' about his style — and perhaps for that reason he did not get the recognition he deserved. His sole representative honour was one Under-23 cap.

**JOHN ASTON, jnr**

|  | LEAGUE | | FACUP | | FLCUP | | EUROPE | | TOTAL | |
|---|---|---|---|---|---|---|---|---|---|---|
|  | App | Gls | App | Gls | App | Gls | App | Gls | App | Gls |
| 1964-65 | 1 | 0 | 0 | 0 | 0 | 0 | 0 | 0 | 1 | 0 |
| 1965-66 | 23 | 4 | 2 | 0 | 0 | 0 | 2 | 0 | 27 | 4 |
| 1966-67 | 26/4 | 5 | 0 | 0 | 1 | 0 | 0 | 0 | 27/4 | 5 |
| 1967-68 | 34/3 | 10 | 2 | 0 | 0 | 0 | 6 | 1 | 42/3 | 11 |
| 1968-69 | 13 | 2 | 0 | 0 | 0 | 0 | 0 | 0 | 13 | 2 |
| 1969-70 | 21/1 | 1 | 1/1 | 0 | 6 | 0 | 0 | 0 | 28/2 | 1 |
| 1970-71 | 19/1 | 3 | 0 | 0 | 3/1 | 0 | 0 | 0 | 22/2 | 3 |
| 1971-72 | 2/7 | 0 | 0/1 | 1 | 2/2 | 0 | 0 | 0 | 4/10 | 1 |
|  | 139/16 | 25 | 5/2 | 1 | 12/3 | 0 | 8 | 1 | 164/21 | 27 |

When Tony Brown of West Brom put two goals past Gary Bailey in December 1978 it created a piece of Football League history as it was the only known instance of the same player scoring past both father and son. Bailey's father, Roy, was Ipswich Town's goalkeeper when they won the Championship in 1961-2, when Brown was starting out on his career. Gary Bailey was born in Ipswich, but was living in South Africa and playing for Witts University when he was sent to Old Trafford for a trial by former United player, Eddie Lewis, in January 1978. He made his debut in November that year, coincidentally against Ipswich Town, and became United's first-choice 'keeper, although in 1985-6, Chris Turner was given an opportunity. Bailey ended his first season with an FA Cup Final appearance and who can forget his despair when he failed to cut out a cross from Graham Rix and allowed Alan Sunderland to score Arsenal's winning goal? More FA Cup Final appearances followed, however, and Bailey now has his winners' medals. After 14 England Under-21 appearances, he was rewarded with his first full cap against the Republic of Ireland in 1985. But he began to suffer from a knee injury and was eventually forced to retire at the age of 29 — returning to South Africa, where he later resumed his playing career with Kaiser Chiefs. In December 1989 he retired from football to take up a job as a television commentator while still coaching soccer.

**GARY BAILEY**

|  | LEAGUE | | FACUP | | FLCUP | | EUROPE | | TOTAL | |
|---|---|---|---|---|---|---|---|---|---|---|
|  | App | Gls | App | Gls | App | Gls | App | Gls | App | Gls |
| 1978-79 | 28 | 0 | 9 | 0 | 0 | 0 | 0 | 0 | 37 | 0 |
| 1979-80 | 42 | 0 | 2 | 0 | 3 | 0 | 0 | 0 | 47 | 0 |
| 1980-81 | 40 | 0 | 3 | 0 | 2 | 0 | 2 | 0 | 47 | 0 |
| 1981-82 | 39 | 0 | 1 | 0 | 2 | 0 | 0 | 0 | 42 | 0 |
| 1982-83 | 37 | 0 | 7 | 0 | 9 | 0 | 2 | 0 | 55 | 0 |
| 1983-84 | 40 | 0 | 1 | 0 | 5 | 0 | 8 | 0 | 54 | 0 |
| 1984-85 | 38 | 0 | 6 | 0 | 3 | 0 | 8 | 0 | 55 | 0 |
| 1985-86 | 25 | 0 | 2 | 0 | 4 | 0 | 0 | 0 | 31 | 0 |
| 1986-87 | 5 | 0 | 0 | 0 | 0 | 0 | 0 | 0 | 5 | 0 |
|  | 294 | 0 | 31 | 0 | 28 | 0 | 20 | 0 | 373 | 0 |

Born in Sheffield, in April 1891, Frank Barson was a blacksmith before becoming a professional footballer. His first club, Barnsley, had a reputation for developing tough players in those days and centre-half Barson was no exception. In 1919 he moved to Aston Villa and was a member of their FA Cup winning side the following year. He won his only England cap in 1920, at Highbury when Wales scored their first victory on English soil since 1881. Often controversial, Barson was once rumoured to have pulled a gun on the Villa manager, but United ignored such tales and paid £5,000 for him at the start of 1922-3. A respected player at Old Trafford, Barson remained there until the end of 1927-8, during which time he helped United into Division One. United gave him a free transfer and he signed for Watford and subsequently played for Hartlepools United, Wigan Borough, was player-manager at Rhyl, manager of Stourbridge and coached Villa and Swansea Town. Ending with Lye Town as trainer in 1954. Barson died in September 1968, aged 77.

| | LEAGUE | | FA CUP | | TOTAL | |
| | App | Gls | App | Gls | App | Gls |
|---|---|---|---|---|---|---|
| 1922-23 | 31 | 0 | 3 | 0 | 34 | 0 |
| 1923-24 | 17 | 0 | 2 | 0 | 19 | 0 |
| 1924-25 | 32 | 0 | 0 | 0 | 32 | 0 |
| 1925-26 | 28 | 2 | 4 | 0 | 32 | 2 |
| 1926-27 | 21 | 2 | 3 | 0 | 24 | 2 |
| 1927-28 | 11 | 0 | 0 | 0 | 11 | 0 |
| | 140 | 4 | 12 | 0 | 152 | 4 |

**FRANK BARSON**

**ROBERT BEALE**

The year after United won the Championship in 1911, they slumped to 13th in the League. Hugh Edmonds had taken over in goal from the veteran Henry Moger, but United conceded 60 goals and it was to Norwich City they turned for a new goalkeeper. United recruited Bobby Beale who hailed from Maidstone and who, whilst he was an experienced Southern League 'keeper, had not played in the Football League. He began his career with Brighton before signing for Norwich in 1908-09. His seven years with the Canaries saw him make over 100 appearances for them. Beale's presence made an immediate difference to United. In 37 League games during his first season, he kept 15 clean sheets as United improved to fourth place. He was over 30 when war broke out and did not play in wartime soccer for United, joining Gillingham for one season of Southern League soccer after the war before retiring at the age of 36. He settled in the south-east again and died at Dymchurch, near Folkestone, in 1950.

| | LEAGUE | | FA CUP | | TOTAL | |
| | App | Gls | App | Gls | App | Gls |
|---|---|---|---|---|---|---|
| 1912-13 | 37 | 0 | 5 | 0 | 42 | 0 |
| 1913-14 | 31 | 0 | 1 | 0 | 32 | 0 |
| 1914-15 | 37 | 0 | 1 | 0 | 38 | 0 |
| | 105 | 0 | 7 | 0 | 112 | 0 |

72

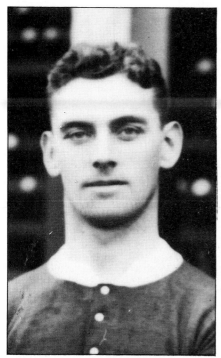

**ALEX BELL**

Alex Bell was born in Cape Town, South Africa, of Scottish parents, and it was from Scottish non-League club Ayr Parkhouse that he signed for United in 1903. United paid £700 for 20-year-old Bell and his 11-year stay saw him play over 300 first-team games. It was as part of the famous half-back line of Duckworth, Roberts and Bell that he achieved greatest recognition. For over a decade it was the backbone of United's team and around those three was built the first great Manchester United side. In 1908, left-half Bell won a League Championship medal, the following year an FA Cup winners' medal, and in 1911 a second Championship medal. Bell was the quiet man of the half-back trio, but no less effective. At the start of 1912-13, the partnership was showing signs of age and by the end of the season it had broken up. Bell moved to Blackburn for £1,000 shortly before World War One. He retired from playing shortly afterwards and after the war, became trainer at Coventry City. In 1925, he took up a similar position with Manchester City, where he stayed until his death in November 1934. He won one Scotland cap, against Ireland in 1912.

|         | LEAGUE | | FA CUP | | TOTAL | |
|---------|-----|-----|-----|-----|-----|-----|
|         | App | Gls | App | Gls | App | Gls |
| 1902-03 | 5   | 1   | 0   | 0   | 5   | 1   |
| 1903-04 | 6   | 1   | 0   | 0   | 6   | 1   |
| 1904-05 | 29  | 1   | 3   | 0   | 32  | 1   |
| 1905-06 | 36  | 2   | 4   | 0   | 40  | 2   |
| 1906-07 | 35  | 2   | 2   | 0   | 37  | 2   |
| 1907-08 | 35  | 1   | 4   | 0   | 39  | 1   |
| 1908-09 | 20  | 2   | 6   | 0   | 26  | 2   |
| 1909-10 | 27  | 0   | 0   | 0   | 27  | 0   |
| 1910-11 | 27  | 0   | 3   | 0   | 30  | 0   |
| 1911-12 | 32  | 0   | 6   | 0   | 38  | 0   |
| 1912-13 | 26  | 0   | 0   | 0   | 26  | 0   |
|         | 278 | 10  | 28  | 0   | 306 | 10  |

In his 13 seasons at Old Trafford, Ray Bennion played more than 300 senior games and won ten full international caps for Wales. A strong right-half, he joined United in April 1920 from Crichton Athletic, but had to wait until the opening day of the 1921-2 season before making his League debut, in the 5-0 drubbing by Everton. Initially understudy to Clarence Hilditch, Bennion was given a regular first-team place when Hilditch moved to the opposite flank. The pair developed a fine partnership. Bennion, born in Wrexham, left United on a free transfer in November 1932 after losing his place to Ernest Vincent. He joined Burnley, who like United were in Division Two, before retiring in 1933-4.

|         | LEAGUE | | FA CUP | | TOTAL | |
|---------|-----|-----|-----|-----|-----|-----|
|         | App | Gls | App | Gls | App | Gls |
| 1921-22 | 15  | 0   | 0   | 0   | 15  | 0   |
| 1922-23 | 14  | 0   | 0   | 0   | 14  | 0   |
| 1923-24 | 34  | 0   | 2   | 0   | 36  | 0   |
| 1924-25 | 17  | 0   | 0   | 0   | 17  | 0   |
| 1925-26 | 7   | 0   | 0   | 0   | 7   | 0   |
| 1926-27 | 37  | 0   | 3   | 1   | 40  | 1   |
| 1927-28 | 36  | 1   | 5   | 0   | 41  | 1   |
| 1928-29 | 34  | 0   | 0   | 0   | 34  | 0   |
| 1929-30 | 28  | 0   | 0   | 0   | 28  | 0   |
| 1930-31 | 36  | 1   | 4   | 0   | 40  | 1   |
| 1931-32 | 28  | 0   | 1   | 0   | 29  | 0   |
|         | 286 | 2   | 15  | 1   | 301 | 3   |

**RAY BENNION**

When Jimmy Delaney left United in November 1950, Matt Busby remembered that when Birmingham City won at Old Trafford towards the end of the previous season, one man virtually beat United on his own. That day, Johnny Berry scored one of the finest goals ever seen at Old Trafford and at the start of 1951-2 Busby signed him for £15,000. Berry made his debut in a 1-0 defeat at Burnden Park but, despite that disappointing start, won a Championship medal at the end of the season. When United next won the title, in 1955-6, Berry and Roger Byrne were the only survivors from the 1952 team and they won a third Championship medal the following year. Born in Aldershot in 1926, Berry joined Birmingham as an 18-year-old and played 103 League games for them before he moved to Old Trafford. Standing only 5ft 5ins tall, he was a speedy, tricky right winger who won four full England caps before the Munich air disaster ended his career. The injuries he received in the crash meant that he never played again. Berry's brother, Peter, also played League soccer.

George Best was hero-worshipped by schoolboys, swooned over by female fans, and many older supporters compared him favourably to Stan Matthews and Tom Finney. Best arrived in Manchester as a 15-year-old, but was homesick enough to return to his native Ulster almost immediately. Matt Busby, who became a father-figure to the teenager, persuaded him to return to Old Trafford and in September 1963 he made his United debut, standing in for Ian Moir against West Brom. Seven months later, Best won his first full Northern Ireland cap, despite having only 15 League games to his name. Outstanding in a team which contained men like Bobby Charlton and Denis Law, Best won Championship medals in 1965 and 1967; and in 1968 when he was Division One's joint top-scorer, he gave a dazzling display in the European Cup Final, setting United on their way to victory with a goal in the opening period of extra-time. That year, Best won the Footballer of the Year award from the Football Writers' Association, and the European Player of the Year trophy. Best had superb balance, close control and acceleration and he was, quite simply, one of the great players of his generation. Occasionally, he retaliated when lesser opponents tried to stop him with unorthodox methods; mostly, he accepted such treatment as the occupational hazard of a world-class footballer. When Sir Matt Busby retired, Best's career began to decline. He walked out on United several times and played his last game for them on New Year's Day 1974, in the defeat at Loftus Road. Four days later, he failed to turn up for training yet again and his United days were over. In November 1975, Best joined Stockport County on loan, playing three games for them. His first appearance saw County's home attendance leap from 2,789 to 9,220, such was his drawing power. After a spell in the United States, Best played a couple of seasons for Fulham. Thereafter it was difficult to keep track of the wayward Irish genius. He turned out for Cork Celtic, in the USA again, Hibernian, Motherwell, Bournemouth and several non-League clubs, all of which delighted at his skills, despite him being past his peak. Skirmishes with the general public and the Press, a succession of glamorous girlfriends, a drink problem and subsequent confrontations with the law, culminated in Best serving a prison sentence in 1985. Perhaps United could have done more to shield him from the bright lights when he was a talented young footballer with a film-star image. Certainly, he seemed unable to handle the pressures and those who saw him play — and those who have enjoyed his skills only on television archives — have reason to feel frustrated that the game was prematurely denied his unique talents. In 1986, he appeared on television as an articulate and knowledgeable pundit. In the USA he played for Los Angeles Aztecs, Fort Lauderdale Strikers and San Jose Earthquakes.

**JOHNNY BERRY**

|  | LEAGUE | | FA CUP | | EUROPE | | TOTAL | |
|  | App | Gls | App | Gls | App | Gls | App | Gls |
|---|---|---|---|---|---|---|---|---|
| 1951-52 | 36 | 6 | 1 | 0 | 0 | 0 | 37 | 6 |
| 1952-53 | 40 | 7 | 4 | 0 | 0 | 0 | 44 | 7 |
| 1953-54 | 37 | 5 | 1 | 0 | 0 | 0 | 38 | 5 |
| 1954-55 | 40 | 3 | 3 | 0 | 0 | 0 | 43 | 3 |
| 1955-56 | 34 | 4 | 1 | 0 | 0 | 0 | 35 | 4 |
| 1956-57 | 40 | 8 | 5 | 4 | 8 | 2 | 53 | 14 |
| 1957-58 | 20 | 4 | 0 | 0 | 3 | 1 | 23 | 5 |
|  | 247 | 37 | 15 | 4 | 11 | 3 | 273 | 44 |

|  | LEAGUE | | FA CUP | | FL CUP | | EUROPE | | TOTAL | |
|  | App | Gls | App | Gls | App | Gls | App | Gls | App | Gls |
|---|---|---|---|---|---|---|---|---|---|---|
| 1963-64 | 17 | 4 | 7 | 2 | 0 | 0 | 2 | 0 | 26 | 6 |
| 1964-65 | 41 | 10 | 7 | 2 | 0 | 0 | 11 | 2 | 59 | 14 |
| 1965-66 | 31 | 9 | 5 | 3 | 0 | 0 | 6 | 4 | 42 | 16 |
| 1966-67 | 42 | 10 | 2 | 0 | 1 | 0 | 0 | 0 | 45 | 10 |
| 1967-68 | 41 | 28 | 2 | 1 | 0 | 0 | 9 | 3 | 52 | 32 |
| 1968-69 | 41 | 19 | 6 | 1 | 0 | 0 | 6 | 2 | 53 | 22 |
| 1969-70 | 37 | 15 | 8 | 6 | 8 | 2 | 0 | 0 | 53 | 23 |
| 1970-71 | 40 | 18 | 2 | 1 | 6 | 2 | 0 | 0 | 48 | 21 |
| 1971-72 | 40 | 18 | 7 | 5 | 6 | 3 | 0 | 0 | 53 | 26 |
| 1972-73 | 19 | 4 | 0 | 0 | 4 | 2 | 0 | 0 | 23 | 6 |
| 1973-74 | 12 | 2 | 0 | 0 | 0 | 0 | 0 | 0 | 12 | 2 |
|  | 361 | 137 | 46 | 21 | 25 | 9 | 34 | 11 | 466 | 178 |

A Welsh international, Clayton Blackmore was born at Neath, a South Wales rugby stronghold, in 1964. He came through the United junior ranks and appeared in both legs of the 1982 FA Youth Cup Final which United lost 7-6 on aggregate to Watford. Blackmore made his first-team debut in the last match of the 1983-4 season, at Nottingham Forest. He scored his first goal in the 5-1 win at West Brom on 21 September 1985, just two days before his 21st birthday. Capped by Wales more than 30 times, he made his international debut when he came on as a substitute against Norway in 1985. It is only in the last couple of seasons that Blackmore has become a regular first-teamer at Old Trafford, but he has been a key member of the first-team squad for the past five seasons or so.

**CLAYTON BLACKMORE**

|  | LEAGUE | | FA CUP | | FL CUP | | EUROPE | | TOTAL | |
|---|---|---|---|---|---|---|---|---|---|---|
|  | App | Gls | App | Gls | App | Gls | App | Gls | App | Gls |
| 1983-84 | 1 | 0 | 0 | 0 | 0 | 0 | 0 | 0 | 1 | 0 |
| 1984-85 | 1 | 0 | 0 | 0 | 1 | 0 | 0 | 0 | 2 | 0 |
| 1985-86 | 12 | 3 | 2/2 | 0 | 2 | 0 | 0 | 0 | 16/2 | 3 |
| 1986-87 | 10/2 | 1 | 1 | 0 | 0 | 0 | 0 | 0 | 11/2 | 1 |
| 1987-88 | 15/7 | 3 | 1/1 | 0 | 3/1 | 0 | 0 | 0 | 19/9 | 3 |
| 1988-89 | 26/2 | 3 | 5/1 | 0 | 3 | 0 | 0 | 0 | 34/3 | 3 |
| 1989-90 | 19/9 | 2 | 2/1 | 1 | 0 | 0 | 0 | 0 | 21/10 | 3 |
| 1990-91 | 35 | 4 | 3 | 0 | 9 | 2 | 9 | 2 | 56 | 8 |
| 1991-92 | 19/14 | 3 | 1 | 0 | 4/1 | 1 | 2 | 0 | 26/15 | 4 |
|  | 138/34 | 19 | 15/5 | 1 | 22/2 | 3 | 11 | 2 | 186/41 | 25 |

**GEORGE BEST**

Jackie Blanchflower is remembered best as a centre-half, yet he played only the last 29 League games of his career in that position. His other appearances were at either wing-half or as goalscoring inside-right, and on one occasion, as a centre-forward. He turned professional in March 1950 after progressing through the junior ranks and made his League debut at right-half against Liverpool in November 1951. Blanchflower's second game was not until April 1953 and he had to wait a further six months before his third appearance. Then he came in as replacement for Stan Pearson and held the number-eight spot for the remainder of 1953-4. He lost his place to John Doherty in 1955-6 and did not regain a regular place until the end of the following season when he took over from Mark Jones at centre-half. His performances earned him a place in the 1957 FA Cup Final and he found himself keeping goal against Aston Villa after Ray Wood was injured. Jones regained the centre-half position in December 1957, but Blanchflower still went on the ill-fated trip to Belgrade in February 1958. The injuries he received at Munich meant he never played again. Born in Belfast in 1933, the younger brother of Danny Blanchflower,

Jackie was also a Northern Ireland international. He later ran a shop close to Old Trafford and became an entertaining after-dinner speaker.

**JACKIE BLANCHFLOWER**

| | LEAGUE | | FA CUP | | EUROPE | | TOTAL | |
|---|---|---|---|---|---|---|---|---|
| | App | Gls | App | Gls | App | Gls | App | Gls |
| 1951-52 | 1 | 0 | 0 | 0 | 0 | 0 | 1 | 0 |
| 1952-53 | 1 | 0 | 0 | 0 | 0 | 0 | 1 | 0 |
| 1953-54 | 27 | 13 | 1 | 1 | 0 | 0 | 28 | 14 |
| 1954-55 | 29 | 10 | 3 | 0 | 0 | 0 | 32 | 10 |
| 1955-56 | 18 | 3 | 0 | 0 | 0 | 0 | 18 | 3 |
| 1956-57 | 11 | 0 | 2 | 0 | 3 | 0 | 16 | 0 |
| 1957-58 | 18 | 0 | 0 | 0 | 2 | 0 | 20 | 0 |
| | 105 | 26 | 6 | 1 | 5 | 0 | 116 | 27 |

*Stand-in goalkeeper Jackie Blanchflower is beaten in the 1957 FA Cup Final against Aston Villa.*

76

Another of the fine Scottish players recruited by Ernest Mangnall at the turn of the century, Robert Bonthron was a solid full-back who joined United from Dundee in 1903. He made his League debut in the opening game of 1903-04 and missed only three games in his first two seasons with the club. He made more than 100 senior appearances for the Clayton outfit, but one he would have wished to forget was against Bradford City on 10 February 1906. United beat City 5-1 at Valley Parade and many of the home fans took exception to Bonthron's uncompromising play, attacking him as he left the ground. Several supporters later faced criminal charges. Bonthron moved to Sunderland in 1907 and spent one season at Roker before signing for Northampton Town, then in the Southern League. After two seasons with the Cobblers, he returned to League action with Birmingham. Bonthron ended his playing career with Leith Athletic.

|         | LEAGUE | | FA CUP | | TOTAL | |
|---------|--------|-----|--------|-----|-------|-----|
|         | App | Gls | App | Gls | App | Gls |
| 1903-04 | 33  | 1   | 7   | 0   | 40  | 1   |
| 1904-05 | 32  | 0   | 3   | 0   | 35  | 0   |
| 1905-06 | 26  | 2   | 4   | 0   | 30  | 2   |
| 1906-07 | 28  | 0   | 1   | 0   | 29  | 0   |
|         | 119 | 3   | 15  | 0   | 134 | 3   |

**ROBERT BONTHRON**

**WARREN BRADLEY**

A small, quick-thinking and speedy winger, who was born at Hyde in June 1933, Warren Bradley joined United after the Munich air disaster. A schoolteacher, he was an amateur player at the time and had two FA Amateur Cup winners' medals gained with northern giants, Bishop Auckland, and 11 England Amateur international caps. Bradley signed professional forms for United in November 1958 and five months later added to his honours with the first of three full England caps. His League career with United was relatively brief, but he had a good striking record and was an important part of the post-Munich rebuilding process at Old Trafford. In March 1962, Bradley moved to Bury for £40,000 and later played non-League football with Northwich Victoria, Macclesfield and Bangor City while he continued as a teacher. After a year out of the game he donned his boots once more and in 1966 turned out for Macclesfield again. In 1970, Bradley became headmaster of a Manchester comprehensive school.

|         | LEAGUE | | FA CUP | | TOTAL | |
|---------|--------|-----|--------|-----|-------|-----|
|         | App | Gls | App | Gls | App | Gls |
| 1958-59 | 24  | 12  | 1   | 0   | 25  | 12  |
| 1959-60 | 29  | 8   | 2   | 1   | 31  | 9   |
| 1960-61 | 4   | 0   | 0   | 0   | 4   | 0   |
| 1961-62 | 6   | 0   | 0   | 0   | 6   | 0   |
|         | 63  | 20  | 3   | 1   | 66  | 21  |

77

Of all the youngsters called upon to help United in the aftermath of the Munich air disaster, Shay Brennan gave the most mature display when he overcame the intensity of the occasion and starred as United beat Sheffield Wednesday in the FA Cup fifth-round match at Old Trafford on 19 February 1958. Brennan joined the club as a 16-year-old in 1953 and two years later was a member of the FA Youth Cup winning team. He was only 20 when Jimmy Murphy threw him into the emotional cauldron of the game against Wednesday and he responded with two goals in United's great victory. What made Brennan's display at outside-left even more remarkable was the fact that, at the time, he was a reserve full-back. Three days after that sensational first-team debut, Brennan made his League bow in the home game against Nottingham Forest. Brennan made over 300 appearances for United — his only League club — and won 19 Republic of Ireland caps. He collected two Championship medals and was a member of the 1968 European Cup winning team — ample compensation for missing the 1963 FA Cup Final. Brennan played his last game for United in January 1970, in the unfamiliar position of left-back in an FA Cup match against Ipswich. Shortly afterwards Brennan, who was Manchester-born of Irish parents, joined League of Ireland club, Waterford as manager. Suffered a heart attack in 1986.

| | LEAGUE | | FACUP | | FLCUP | | EUROPE | | TOTAL | |
|---|---|---|---|---|---|---|---|---|---|---|
| | App | Gls | App | Gls | App | Gls | App | Gls | App | Gls |
| 1957-58 | 5 | 0 | 2 | 3 | 0 | 0 | 0 | 0 | 7 | 3 |
| 1958-59 | 1 | 0 | 0 | 0 | 0 | 0 | 0 | 0 | 1 | 0 |
| 1959-60 | 29 | 0 | 3 | 0 | 0 | 0 | 0 | 0 | 32 | 0 |
| 1960-61 | 41 | 0 | 3 | 0 | 2 | 0 | 0 | 0 | 46 | 0 |
| 1961-62 | 41 | 2 | 6 | 0 | 0 | 0 | 0 | 0 | 47 | 2 |
| 1962-63 | 37 | 0 | 4 | 0 | 0 | 0 | 0 | 0 | 41 | 0 |
| 1963-64 | 17 | 0 | 5 | 0 | 0 | 0 | 2 | 0 | 24 | 0 |
| 1964-65 | 42 | 0 | 7 | 0 | 0 | 0 | 11 | 0 | 60 | 0 |
| 1965-66 | 28 | 0 | 5 | 0 | 0 | 0 | 5 | 0 | 38 | 0 |
| 1966-67 | 16 | 0 | 0 | 0 | 1 | 0 | 0 | 0 | 17 | 0 |
| 1967-68 | 13 | 1 | 0 | 0 | 0 | 0 | 3 | 0 | 16 | 1 |
| 1968-69 | 13 | 0 | 0 | 0 | 0 | 0 | 3 | 0 | 16 | 0 |
| 1969-70 | 8/1 | 0 | 1 | 0 | 1 | 0 | 0 | 0 | 10/1 | 0 |
| | 291/1 | 3 | 36 | 3 | 4 | 0 | 24 | 0 | 355/1 | 6 |

**SEAMUS (SHAY) BRENNAN**

**JAMES BROWN**

After eight seasons without an honour to his name, James Brown moved from Burnley to Manchester United in June 1935 and by the end of the following season had collected a Division Two championship medal. A sound, defensive wing-half, Brown missed only two matches as United lifted the title in 1935-6. He was born in Motherwell and began his career with Wishaw Juniors before joining East Fife — Scottish Cup Finalists in 1927. Brown moved to Turf Moor in 1927 and after 228 League games for Burnley, signed for the Old Trafford club. He left United in February 1939, having taken his overall career total to well over 350 senior appearances, and moved to Park Avenue where he added a further 14 appearances with Bradford.

| | LEAGUE | | FA CUP | | TOTAL | |
|---|---|---|---|---|---|---|
| | App | Gls | App | Gls | App | Gls |
| 1935-36 | 40 | 0 | 3 | 0 | 43 | 0 |
| 1936-37 | 31 | 0 | 2 | 0 | 33 | 0 |
| 1937-38 | 28 | 1 | 3 | 0 | 31 | 1 |
| 1938-39 | 3 | 0 | 0 | 0 | 3 | 0 |
| | 102 | 1 | 8 | 0 | 110 | 1 |

North-Easterner Steve Bruce was born in December 1960. A former England Youth and 'B' international, he started his career at Gillingham, making his debut against Blackpool in August 1979. A midfielder or defender, he was a virtual ever-present in Gillingham's team for five years before Norwich City paid £135,000 for him in July 1984. As Bruce played his part in taking the East Anglian club out of the Second Division in 1986 and then to their highest-ever League position, fifth in 1986-7, his contribution did not go unnoticed and in December 1987, Alex Ferguson bolstered his back line by paying £825,000 for Bruce. He made his United debut in the 2-1 win at Portsmouth but it was not the best of starts, for he conceded a penalty and broke his nose. However United lost only three more League games that season as they finished runners-up to Liverpool. Steve Bruce has since been one of the first names pencilled-in by Ferguson on the team-sheet and in 1990 he added to his 1985 League Cup winners' medal when he played a key role in United's lifting of the FA Cup for a record-equalling seventh time.

|  | LEAGUE | | FA CUP | | FL CUP | | EUROPE | | TOTAL | |
|---|---|---|---|---|---|---|---|---|---|---|
|  | App | Gls | App | Gls | App | Gls | App | Gls | App | Gls |
| 1987-88 | 21 | 2 | 3 | 0 | 0 | 0 | - | - | 24 | 2 |
| 1988-89 | 38 | 2 | 7 | 1 | 3 | 1 | - | - | 48 | 4 |
| 1989-90 | 34 | 3 | 7 | 0 | 2 | 0 | - | - | 43 | 3 |
| 1990-91 | 31 | 13 | 3 | 0 | 7 | 2 | 8 | 4 | 49 | 19 |
| 1991-92 | 38 | 5 | 1 | 0 | 7 | 1 | 4 | 0 | 50 | 6 |
|  | 162 | 25 | 21 | 1 | 19 | 4 | 12 | 4 | 214 | 34 |

**STEVE BRUCE**

**WILLIAM BRYANT**

Although born in the North-East — the great breeding ground for soccer talent, William Bryant's skills were overlooked by local clubs and it was Wolves who gave him his first taste of League soccer. He made his debut for them in the 1932-3 season but after only five League games for them, joined Wrexham the following season. A goalscoring outside-right, Bryant signed for United on 23 October 1934 and scored on his debut, in the 2-1 win at Blackpool on 3 November. Although he missed most of the first half of the following season, he played in United's last 18 games as they swept to the Division Two title. He played for United throughout wartime football, turning out in well over 150 matches. On 26 November 1945, he joined Bradford City for a brief spell before retiring. He died in County Durham in 1975, aged 61

|  | LEAGUE | | FA CUP | | TOTAL | |
|---|---|---|---|---|---|---|
|  | App | Gls | App | Gls | App | Gls |
| 1934-35 | 24 | 6 | 2 | 0 | 26 | 6 |
| 1935-36 | 21 | 8 | 1 | 0 | 22 | 8 |
| 1936-37 | 37 | 10 | 2 | 0 | 39 | 10 |
| 1937-38 | 39 | 12 | 4 | 0 | 43 | 12 |
| 1938-39 | 27 | 6 | 0 | 0 | 27 | 6 |
| 1939-40 | 3 | 2 | 0 | 0 | 3 | 2 |
|  | 151 | 44 | 9 | 0 | 160 | 44 |

79

As well as being a classy defender, Martin Buchan was a great leader and his first club, Aberdeen, soon spotted his qualities and made him their captain when he was only 20. One year later, in 1970, he led the Dons to their first Scottish Cup Final win for 23 years. The following year he was elected Scottish Football Writers'

Player of the Year and in 1977 became the first man since the war to have captained both English and Scottish Cup winning teams when he skippered United to victory over Liverpool. Born in Aberdeen in 1949, Buchan joined his local club in 1965 and after 133 League games for them was snapped up by United manager Frank O'Farrell for a bargain £125,000 in March 1972. Buchan was bought to bolster a team that had gone nine League games without victory. He made his debut at White Hart Lane on 4 March 1972, in United's 2-0 defeat. Apart from his FA Cup winners' medal, Buchan collected a Division Two Championship medal and two FA Cup runners-up medals with United. And all but two of his 34 Scotland caps were earned whilst at Old Trafford. At the start of 1983-4 he joined Oldham Athletic, but the following season retired from playing. He had a brief spell as Burnley manager, taking charge on June 1985 but resigned four months later.

|  | LEAGUE | | FACUP | | FLCUP | | EUROPE | | TOTAL | |
|---|---|---|---|---|---|---|---|---|---|---|
|  | App | Gls | App | Gls | App | Gls | App | Gls | App | Gls |
| 1971-72 | 13 | 1 | 2 | 0 | 0 | 0 | 0 | 0 | 15 | 1 |
| 1972-73 | 42 | 0 | 1 | 0 | 4 | 0 | 0 | 0 | 47 | 0 |
| 1973-74 | 42 | 0 | 2 | 0 | 1 | 0 | 0 | 0 | 45 | 0 |
| 1974-75 | 41 | 0 | 2 | 0 | 7 | 0 | 0 | 0 | 50 | 0 |
| 1975-76 | 42 | 0 | 7 | 0 | 3 | 0 | 0 | 0 | 52 | 0 |
| 1976-77 | 33 | 0 | 7 | 0 | 4 | 0 | 2 | 0 | 46 | 0 |
| 1977-78 | 28 | 1 | 4 | 0 | 1 | 0 | 4 | 0 | 37 | 1 |
| 1978-79 | 37 | 2 | 9 | 0 | 2 | 0 | 0 | 0 | 48 | 2 |
| 1979-80 | 42 | 0 | 2 | 0 | 3 | 0 | 0 | 0 | 47 | 0 |
| 1980-81 | 26 | 0 | 2 | 0 | 2 | 0 | 2 | 0 | 32 | 0 |
| 1981-82 | 27 | 0 | 1 | 0 | 2 | 0 | 0 | 0 | 30 | 0 |
| 1982-83 | 3 | 0 | 0 | 0 | 1 | 0 | 2 | 0 | 6 | 0 |
| | 376 | 4 | 39 | 0 | 30 | 0 | 10 | 0 | 455 | 4 |

**MARTIN BUCHAN**

Francis Burns adopted a simple but effective style from either wing-half or full-back. A Scottish Schoolboy, Youth, Under-23, and full international, Burns, who comes from Glenboig, Lanarkshire, joined United as a 15-year-old in July 1964. He made his debut at West Ham in September 1967 and retained the left-back position for most of the season, playing in all United's European Cup matches until injury ruled him out of the semi-final second-leg match against Real Madrid and the Final. Injuries, particularly cartilage trouble, dogged his career and, after his £60,000 transfer to Southampton in June 1972, he underwent his fourth operation in as many years. After one season at The Dell, Burns joined his former United teammate, Bobby Charlton, then managing Preston. Burns then moved to League of Ireland club, Shamrock Rovers, after a Football League career which spanned 413 matches.

|  | LEAGUE | | FACUP | | FLCUP | | LEAGUE | | TOTAL | |
|---|---|---|---|---|---|---|---|---|---|---|
|  | App | Gls | App | Gls | App | Gls | App | Gls | App | Gls |
| 1967-68 | 36 | 2 | 2 | 0 | 0 | 0 | 7 | 0 | 45 | 2 |
| 1968-69 | 14/2 | 0 | 1 | 0 | 0 | 0 | 3/1 | 1 | 18/3 | 1 |
| 1969-70 | 30/2 | 3 | 3/1 | 0 | 6 | 0 | 0 | 0 | 39/3 | 3 |
| 1970-71 | 16/4 | 0 | 0 | 0 | 1/1 | 0 | 0 | 0 | 17/5 | 0 |
| 1971-72 | 15/2 | 1 | 5 | 0 | 3 | 0 | 0 | 0 | 23/2 | 1 |
| | 111/10 | 6 | 11/1 | 0 | 10/1 | 0 | 10/1 | 1 | 142/13 | 7 |

**FRANCIS BURNS**

Part of Matt Busby's success at Old Trafford was always selecting the right man to lead the team and Roger Byrne was no exception to the tradition of great United captains. He succeeded Johnny Carey as skipper and led the club to successive League Championship wins in the mid-1950s and to the 1957 FA Cup Final. He was also a member of the 1952 Championship winning team. Manchester-born, Byrne joined United, aged 20, in 1949 but had to wait until November 1951 before making his League debut, in the goalless draw at Anfield. He got his chance at left-back in place of Bill Redman but converted successfully to outside-left for the last six games of the season, netting seven goals. Byrne began the following season on the wing but soon reverted to full-back. His experience up front made him one of the great attacking full-backs and he won his 33 consecutive England caps in the number-three shirt. Between his debut and his last League game — the classic encounter with Arsenal in February 1958 — Byrne missed only a handful of matches. He perished at Munich, with seven of his teammates among others, and with them went an era. His remark after the 1957 FA Cup Final defeat was in retrospect, so poignant, when he said: "Never mind, we'll be back next year". United were, Byrne was not.

| | LEAGUE | | FA CUP | | EUROPE | | TOTAL | |
|---|---|---|---|---|---|---|---|---|
| | App | Gls | App | Gls | App | Gls | App | Gls |
| 1951-52 | 24 | 7 | 1 | 0 | 0 | 0 | 25 | 7 |
| 1952-53 | 40 | 2 | 4 | 1 | 0 | 0 | 44 | 3 |
| 1953-54 | 41 | 3 | 1 | 0 | 0 | 0 | 42 | 3 |
| 1954-55 | 39 | 2 | 3 | 0 | 0 | 0 | 42 | 2 |
| 1955-56 | 39 | 3 | 1 | 0 | 0 | 0 | 40 | 3 |
| 1956-57 | 36 | 0 | 6 | 1 | 8 | 0 | 50 | 1 |
| 1957-58 | 26 | 0 | 2 | 0 | 6 | 0 | 34 | 0 |
| | 245 | 17 | 18 | 2 | 14 | 0 | 277 | 19 |

**ROGER BYRNE**

An inspiration to younger players, Noel Cantwell amassed great experience over 15 years with West Ham United and Manchester United. Born in Cork, Cantwell joined West Ham as a 20-year-old in 1952 with Irish Schoolboy international honours before making the first of his 36 appearances for the Republic of Ireland in 1953. A solid, thoughtful full-back, he could also play centre-forward, a position he occasionally filled for both club and country. After 245 League games for the Hammers, Cantwell joined United for just under £30,000 on 21 November 1960 and made his United debut the same day in a friendly against Bayern Munich. He made his League debut at Cardiff five days later. At Old Trafford he followed in a long line of fine captains and led the side to victory in the 1963 FA Cup Final. Towards the end of his career, Cantwell concentrated on the coaching side, gaining his FA badge, and many expected he would succeed Matt Busby as manager. Instead he surprised everyone by replacing Jimmy Hill as Coventry manager in October 1967. Cantwell guided Coventry from the lower reaches

**NOEL CANTWELL**

of Division One to finish sixth in 1969-70, their best-ever position which earned them a place in European football. In 1972, Cantwell took over as manager of Peterborough United. He quit the English game in 1977 and enjoyed brief spells in the NASL (1977-8 as boss of New England Tea Men, 1981-2 as coach with Jacksonville Tea Men) before returning to Peterborough in 1986. He later became general manager but parted company with the club again in April 1989. A former PFA Chairman, Cantwell was Republic of Ireland manager for a while. A double international, he also played cricket for his country.

| | LEAGUE | | FA CUP | | EUROPE | | TOTAL | |
|---|---|---|---|---|---|---|---|---|
| | App | Gls | App | Gls | App | Gls | App | Gls |
| 1960-61 | 24 | 0 | 3 | 2 | 0 | 0 | 27 | 2 |
| 1961-62 | 17 | 2 | 2 | 0 | 0 | 0 | 19 | 2 |
| 1962-63 | 25 | 1 | 5 | 0 | 0 | 0 | 30 | 1 |
| 1963-64 | 28 | 0 | 2 | 0 | 4 | 0 | 34 | 0 |
| 1964-65 | 2 | 1 | 0 | 0 | 0 | 0 | 2 | 1 |
| 1965-66 | 23 | 2 | 2 | 0 | 3 | 0 | 28 | 2 |
| 1966-67 | 4 | 0 | 0 | 0 | 0 | 0 | 4 | 0 |
| | 123 | 6 | 14 | 2 | 7 | 0 | 144 | 8 |

Johnny Carey started his Manchester United career as an inside-left in 1937, was successfully switched to become one of the League's finest right-backs, and ended his career as a polished wing-half. Indeed, the versatile Carey played in every position except on the wing for United in peacetime football, even appearing in goal. He joined United from Dublin side, St James' Gate, in November 1936 for only £250 and made his League debut against Southampton in September the following year. The story goes that United's great talent scout, Louis Rocca, went to Dublin to watch another player but it was Carey, playing only his third game of soccer, who caught the eye and Rocca had his signature on United forms before the youngster could take off his boots. In 17 years at Old Trafford, Carey won almost every honour in the game — FA Cup winners' medal, League Championship medal, international caps for both Northern Ireland and the Republic, the captaincy of the Rest of Europe side against Great Britain in 1947, and Footballer of the Year in 1949. His total of almost 350 League and Cup appearances for United would have been far greater had war not interrupted his career. During the war, Carey served with the Army in Italy and played for several professional, clubs where he earned the nickname 'Cario'. Born in Dublin, he captained the Republic of Ireland side which scored a memorable 2-0 victory over England at Goodison Park in 1949. When he retired in 1953, the United board took the unusual step of inviting him to a meeting to express their personal thanks. He accepted a job as coach, but then became Blackburn manager. He later managed Everton, Leyton Orient, whom he guided to Division One, and Nottingham Forest before returning to Ewood Park as general manager in 1970.

**JOHNNY CAREY**

| | LEAGUE | | FA CUP | | TOTAL | |
|---|---|---|---|---|---|---|
| | App | Gls | App | Gls | App | Gls |
| 1937-38 | 16 | 3 | 3 | 1 | 19 | 4 |
| 1938-39 | 32 | 6 | 2 | 0 | 34 | 6 |
| 1939-40 | 2 | 1 | 0 | 0 | 2 | 1 |
| 1945-46 | 0 | 0 | 4 | 0 | 4 | 0 |
| 1946-47 | 31 | 0 | 2 | 0 | 33 | 0 |
| 1947-48 | 37 | 1 | 6 | 0 | 43 | 1 |
| 1948-49 | 41 | 1 | 7 | 0 | 48 | 1 |
| 1949-50 | 38 | 1 | 5 | 0 | 43 | 1 |
| 1950-51 | 39 | 0 | 4 | 0 | 43 | 0 |
| 1951-52 | 38 | 3 | 1 | 0 | 39 | 3 |
| 1952-53 | 32 | 1 | 4 | 0 | 36 | 1 |
| | 306 | 17 | 38 | 1 | 344 | 18 |

Bobby Charlton offers a host of memories: sweeping crossfield passes of great majesty, deadly shooting from 20 yards and more, and above all, great sportsmanship. A man who gave his all for Manchester United, Charlton climbed dazed from the wreckage of the Munich air disaster to help rebuild the club. The ensuing years saw him become one of the world's best-known footballers. Nephew of the great Newcastle centre-forward, Jackie Milburn, he hails from Ashington, County Durham, and was a product of Manchester United's famous youth team. Charlton was a member of the sides which won the FA Youth Cup in 1954-5 and 1955-6. He made his first-team debut, standing in for Tommy Taylor, on 6 October 1956, scoring two goals against, coincidentally, Charlton Athletic. At the time of Munich, Charlton had established himself as United's regular inside-right, in place of Billy Whelan. After the crash he carried his new-found responsibility well, growing quickly in stature as he helped United through the most difficult period in the club's history. He had played in the Championship side of 1956-7, and in the losing Cup Final side that year and in 1958. In 1963 he won an FA Cup winners' medal and League Championship medals in 1965 and 1967. Two goals — one a rare header — in the 1968 European Cup Final saw him climb the Wembley steps to collect the trophy. Two years earlier, Charlton had collected a World Cup winners' medal when England beat West Germany at Wembley. In the semi-final, against Portugal, he scored two superb goals. Charlton's international career was as outstanding as his club one, with a record 49 goals in his then record 106 full internationals. Charlton was awarded the OBE in 1969, and was elected Footballer of the Year and European Player of the Year in 1966. In 1974, after more than 20 years at Old Trafford, he joined Preston as manager but even his vast experience could not prevent them from slipping into Division Three. His managerial career began and ended at Deepdale (apart from a brief spell in 1983 when he stepped out of the Wigan Athletic boardroom to take charge of team affairs). Like quite a number of fine players his managerial career was nowhere near as successful as his playing days. Today, he runs a school for youngsters learning the games of soccer, whilst United made him a director at Old Trafford. He sold his soccer school business in June 1990 to Conrad Continental.

**BOBBY CHARLTON OBE**

| | LEAGUE | | FACUP | | FLCUP | | EUROPE | | TOTAL | |
|---|---|---|---|---|---|---|---|---|---|---|
| | App | Gls | App | Gls | App | Gls | App | Gls | App | Gls |
| 1956-57 | 14 | 10 | 2 | 1 | 0 | 0 | 1 | 1 | 17 | 12 |
| 1957-58 | 21 | 8 | 7 | 5 | 0 | 0 | 2 | 3 | 30 | 16 |
| 1958-59 | 38 | 29 | 1 | 0 | 0 | 0 | 0 | 0 | 39 | 29 |
| 1959-60 | 37 | 18 | 3 | 3 | 0 | 0 | 0 | 0 | 40 | 21 |
| 1960-61 | 39 | 21 | 3 | 0 | 0 | 0 | 0 | 0 | 42 | 21 |
| 1961-62 | 37 | 8 | 7 | 2 | 0 | 0 | 0 | 0 | 44 | 10 |
| 1962-63 | 28 | 7 | 6 | 2 | 0 | 0 | 0 | 0 | 34 | 9 |
| 1963-64 | 40 | 9 | 7 | 2 | 0 | 0 | 6 | 4 | 53 | 15 |
| 1964-65 | 41 | 10 | 7 | 0 | 0 | 0 | 11 | 8 | 59 | 18 |
| 1965-66 | 38 | 16 | 7 | 0 | 0 | 0 | 8 | 2 | 53 | 18 |
| 1966-67 | 42 | 12 | 2 | 0 | 0 | 0 | 0 | 0 | 44 | 12 |
| 1967-68 | 41 | 15 | 2 | 1 | 0 | 0 | 9 | 2 | 52 | 18 |
| 1968-69 | 32 | 5 | 6 | 0 | 0 | 0 | 8 | 2 | 46 | 7 |
| 1969-70 | 40 | 12 | 9 | 1 | 8 | 1 | 0 | 0 | 57 | 14 |
| 1970-71 | 42 | 5 | 2 | 0 | 6 | 3 | 0 | 0 | 50 | 8 |
| 1971-72 | 40 | 8 | 7 | 2 | 6 | 2 | 0 | 0 | 53 | 12 |
| 1972-73 | 34/2 | 6 | 1 | 0 | 4 | 1 | 0 | 0 | 39/2 | 7 |
| | 604/2 | 199 | 79 | 19 | 24 | 7 | 45 | 22 | 752/2 | 247 |

Allenby Chilton played nearly 400 games for United and, but for World War Two, that total would have been far greater. Signed from north-east club, Seaham Colliery, in November 1938, he made his debut for United on 2 September 1939, against Charlton Athletic. War was declared the following day and coincidentally Chilton guested for Charlton in wartime football, winning a Southern Cup winners' medal with them. By the time the League resumed in 1946, Chilton was two weeks short of his 28th birthday. Despite being in the latter stages of his playing career, and the fact that he had been wounded in Normandy, he stayed with United until 1955, collecting an FA Cup winners' medal and a League Championship medal. A tall and powerful centre-half, Chilton was United's only ever-present when they won the title in 1951-2. The backbone of the defence, he succeeded Johnny Carey as club skipper and when he lost his place to Mark Jones in February 1955, Chilton ended a run of 166 consecutive League appearances, which was a record until broken by Coppell. He moved to Grimsby Town as player-manager and inspired them to the Division Three North title in 1955-6. He ended his playing career shortly afterwards, but continued in management. He left Blundell Park in 1959 and had spells at non-League Wigan Athletic, and at Hartlepools United.

|         | LEAGUE |     | FA CUP |     | TOTAL |     |
|---------|--------|-----|--------|-----|-------|-----|
|         | App    | Gls | App    | Gls | App   | Gls |
| 1939-40 | 1      | 0   | 0      | 0   | 1     | 0   |
| 1945-46 | 0      | 0   | 3      | 0   | 3     | 0   |
| 1946-47 | 41     | 1   | 2      | 0   | 43    | 1   |
| 1947-48 | 41     | 0   | 6      | 0   | 47    | 0   |
| 1948-49 | 42     | 0   | 8      | 0   | 50    | 0   |
| 1949-50 | 35     | 1   | 5      | 0   | 40    | 1   |
| 1950-51 | 38     | 0   | 4      | 0   | 42    | 0   |
| 1951-52 | 42     | 0   | 1      | 0   | 43    | 0   |
| 1952-53 | 42     | 0   | 4      | 0   | 46    | 0   |
| 1953-54 | 42     | 1   | 1      | 0   | 43    | 1   |
| 1954-55 | 29     | 0   | 3      | 0   | 32    | 0   |
|         | 353    | 3   | 37     | 0   | 390   | 3   |

**ALLENBY CHILTON**

|         | LEAGUE |     | FA CUP |     | TOTAL |     |
|---------|--------|-----|--------|-----|-------|-----|
|         | App    | Gls | App    | Gls | App   | Gls |
| 1945-46 | 0      | 0   | 4      | 0   | 4     | 0   |
| 1946-47 | 32     | 0   | 0      | 0   | 32    | 0   |
| 1947-48 | 26     | 1   | 6      | 0   | 32    | 1   |
| 1948-49 | 36     | 0   | 8      | 0   | 44    | 0   |
| 1949-50 | 35     | 1   | 5      | 0   | 40    | 1   |
| 1950-51 | 35     | 0   | 4      | 0   | 39    | 0   |
| 1951-52 | 38     | 2   | 1      | 0   | 39    | 2   |
| 1952-53 | 22     | 0   | 4      | 0   | 26    | 0   |
| 1953-54 | 18     | 0   | 0      | 0   | 18    | 0   |
| 1954-55 | 1      | 0   | 0      | 0   | 1     | 0   |
|         | 243    | 4   | 32     | 0   | 275   | 4   |

Despite standing only 5ft 4ins tall, Henry Cockburn became one of the finest wing-halves in English football in the immediate post-war years. His timing was perfect and he could outjump men much taller than himself. Between 1946 and 1951, Cockburn won 13 full England caps, completing a formidable international half-back line with classy Stoke centre-half, Neil Franklin, and Wolves' Billy Wright. Cockburn's first cap came after he had played only a handful of Football League games, although it should be said that the League proper had only just restarted after the war. Born at Ashton in 1923, Cockburn joined United from local junior club, Goslings, then a Reds' nursery club, and made his first-team debut in wartime football. He made his League debut in the first match of 1946-7, against Grimsby,

**HENRY COCKBURN**

and played in the 1948 FA Cup-winning team and the 1951-2 Championship side. Cockburn left United in October 1954 to join Bury, playing 35 League games at Gigg Lane before signing for Peterborough United, then in the Midland League. Spells with other non-League clubs Corby Town and Sankeys (Wellington) followed before Cockburn returned to the League scene as Oldham's assistant trainer. His final move took him to Huddersfield Town where he was involved in coaching.

84

When Eddie Colman died in the Munich air disaster, he was only 21 years of age but had won two League Championship medals and had appeared in an FA Cup Final. United were thus deprived of one of their brightest prospects, a young player whose career could have reached the greatest heights. A product of United's nursery system, Colman turned professional in November 1953 and played in three FA Youth Cup winning teams before his League debut, at Bolton in November 1955. He was an immediate success and missed only a handful of games throughout the remainder of his all-too-brief career. He was small, yet the 'general' in United's midfield and his deceptive bodyswerve earned him the nickname of 'Snake Hips'. He struck up an uncanny understanding with his colleague at left-half, Duncan Edwards, even though their styles were so different. What they did have in common was a belief that attack was the best form of defence. Despite this Colman never won international honours.

**EDDIE COLMAN**

| | LEAGUE | | FA CUP | | EUROPE | | TOTAL | |
|---|---|---|---|---|---|---|---|---|
| | App | Gls | App | Gls | App | Gls | App | Gls |
| 1955-56 | 25 | 0 | 1 | 0 | 0 | 0 | 26 | 0 |
| 1956-57 | 36 | 1 | 6 | 0 | 8 | 0 | 50 | 1 |
| 1957-58 | 24 | 0 | 2 | 0 | 5 | 1 | 31 | 1 |
| | 85 | 1 | 9 | 0 | 13 | 1 | 107 | 2 |

John Connelly hailed from St Helens, heart of the north-west Rugby League territory, but he preferred soccer and played for St Helens Town before joining Burnley in 1956, remaining an amateur until he had completed his apprenticeship as a joiner at the age of 22. A member of the Turf Moor club's Championship winning side of 1959-60, he also appeared in the 1962 FA Cup Final, when Burnley lost to Spurs. Connelly made 216 League appearances for Burnley, scoring 85 goals, before joining United in 1964 for £56,000. Capable of playing on either wing, Connelly continued to find the net at Old Trafford. He made his United debut in the 2-2 home draw against West Brom at the start of 1964-5 and eight months later added a second Championship medal to his collection when United pipped Leeds on goal-average. Connelly played 20 times for England, the last being their opening match of the 1966 World Cup Finals against Uruguay. Two months later he left United for £40,000, going on to play a further 277 League games for Blackburn and Bury before retiring in 1972.

| | LEAGUE | | FA CUP | | FL CUP | | EUROPE | | TOTAL | |
|---|---|---|---|---|---|---|---|---|---|---|
| | App | Gls | App | Gls | App | Gls | App | Gls | App | Gls |
| 1964-65 | 42 | 15 | 7 | 0 | 0 | 0 | 11 | 5 | 60 | 20 |
| 1965-66 | 31/1 | 5 | 6 | 2 | 0 | 0 | 8 | 6 | 45/1 | 13 |
| 1966-67 | 6 | 2 | 0 | 0 | 1 | 0 | 0 | 0 | 7 | 2 |
| | 79/1 | 22 | 13 | 2 | 1 | 0 | 19 | 11 | 112/1 | 35 |

**JOHN CONNELLY**

Steve Coppell's two-year fight against a serious knee injury ended in October 1983 when he had to retire, aged 28. It was a blow to both United and England, who were to miss his dynamism. Born in Liverpool, Coppell was studying for a university degree when he made his League debut, for Tranmere Rovers against Aldershot, in 1974. Tommy Docherty took him to Old Trafford from under the noses of Liverpool and Everton, for only £60,000, in March 1975. Coppell's great flair on the wing was not supported by his forwards in the 1976 FA Cup Final which United lost, but he returned to Wembley the following year to collect a winners' medal. Losers' medals followed in the 1979 FA Cup Final and the 1983 Milk Cup Final, and injury forced him to miss the 1983 Wembley victory over Brighton. Coppell won 42 full caps, the first in the crucial World Cup qualifying match against Italy at Wembley in November 1977. England missed the 1978 Finals, but Coppell played in the first four games of the 1982 Finals in Spain before injury sidelined him. A former PFA Chairman, he was appointed manager of Second Division Crystal Palace on 3 June 1984, and at 28 was the League's youngest manager. He pulled Palace clear of the relegation zone and turned them into a promotion-winning side in 1989. A year later he proudly led his team out at Wembley in the FA Cup Final . . .against United.

**STEVE COPPELL**

|  | LEAGUE | | FACUP | | FLCUP | | EUROPE | | TOTAL | |
|---|---|---|---|---|---|---|---|---|---|---|
|  | App | Gls | App | Gls | App | Gls | App | Gls | App | Gls |
| 1974-75 | 9/1 | 1 | 0 | 0 | 0 | 0 | 0 | 0 | 9/1 | 1 |
| 1975-76 | 39 | 4 | 7 | 0 | 3 | 1 | 0 | 0 | 49 | 5 |
| 1976-77 | 40 | 6 | 7 | 1 | 5 | 1 | 4 | 0 | 56 | 8 |
| 1977-78 | 42 | 5 | 4 | 1 | 1 | 0 | 4 | 3 | 51 | 9 |
| 1978-79 | 42 | 11 | 9 | 1 | 2 | 0 | 0 | 0 | 53 | 12 |
| 1979-80 | 42 | 8 | 2 | 0 | 2 | 1 | 0 | 0 | 46 | 9 |
| 1980-81 | 42 | 6 | 3 | 0 | 2 | 0 | 2 | 0 | 49 | 6 |
| 1981-82 | 35/1 | 9 | 0 | 0 | 2 | 0 | 1/1 | 0 | 38/2 | 9 |
| 1982-83 | 29 | 4 | 4 | 1 | 8 | 6 | 0 | 0 | 41 | 11 |
|  | 320/2 | 54 | 36 | 4 | 25 | 9 | 11/1 | 3 | 392/3 | 70 |

Born in the Gorbals district of Glasgow, of Irish descent, Paddy Crerand was one of the most constructive — and robust — wing-halves of the 1960s. He was well-built and any lack of pace was more than compensated by magnificent distribution skills. His accurate crossfield passes, perhaps 40 or 50 yards, were a treat to behold and they helped him win 16 Scotland caps. He joined Celtic as a youngster, but won only a Scottish Cup runners-up medal with one of the most successful clubs north of the border. After his £56,000 transfer to United in February 1963, his collection of silverware increased considerably. Three months after his move south he won an FA Cup winners' medal and went on to collect two Championship medals and a European Cup winners' medal. With Stiles and Charlton, he formed one of United's finest-ever midfield trios. After the 4-3 win at Maine Road at the end of 1970-71, Crerand joined United's coaching staff and later became assistant manager before taking over as manager of Northampton Town in 1976. After six months at the County Ground he left the game to run a public house.

**PAT CRERAND**

|  | LEAGUE | | FACUP | | FLCUP | | EUROPE | | TOTAL | |
|---|---|---|---|---|---|---|---|---|---|---|
|  | App | Gls | App | Gls | App | Gls | App | Gls | App | Gls |
| 1962-63 | 19 | 0 | 3 | 0 | 0 | 0 | 0 | 0 | 22 | 0 |
| 1963-64 | 41 | 1 | 7 | 1 | 0 | 0 | 6 | 0 | 54 | 2 |
| 1964-65 | 39 | 3 | 7 | 2 | 0 | 0 | 11 | 0 | 57 | 5 |
| 1965-66 | 41 | 0 | 7 | 0 | 0 | 0 | 7 | 1 | 55 | 1 |
| 1966-67 | 39 | 3 | 2 | 0 | 1 | 0 | 0 | 0 | 42 | 3 |
| 1967-68 | 41 | 1 | 2 | 0 | 0 | 0 | 9 | 0 | 52 | 1 |
| 1968-69 | 35 | 1 | 4 | 1 | 0 | 0 | 8 | 0 | 47 | 2 |
| 1969-70 | 25 | 1 | 9 | 0 | 2 | 0 | 0 | 0 | 36 | 1 |
| 1970-71 | 24 | 0 | 2 | 0 | 1 | 0 | 0 | 0 | 27 | 0 |
|  | 304 | 10 | 43 | 4 | 4 | 0 | 41 | 1 | 392 | 15 |

Goalkeeper Jack Crompton's save from a fierce Stan Mortensen shot 11 minutes from the end of the game was the turning point of the thrilling 1948 FA Cup Final. With the score at 2-2, Crompton cleared the ball quickly, which led to Stan Pearson putting United ahead and, from the jaws of defeat, they went on to grasp victory. It was a closely-guarded secret that 48 hours before the Wembley Final, Crompton had been on an operating table for the removal of an abscess on his spine. Like teammate Henry Cockburn, Crompton joined United from local side, Goslings, in 1944 after a spell as an amateur with Oldham. He was virtually ever-present in United's side from the restart of League soccer in 1946 until losing his place to Reg Allen in 1950-51. Crompton regained a regular place in 1952 but eventually lost it to the younger Ray Wood and, in October 1956, he left United to work as Luton Town coach. A fitness fanatic, both for himself and his players, Crompton was asked to rejoin United to assist Jimmy Murphy in the aftermath of the Munich air disaster. He readily agreed and stayed in the post until Matt Busby took up the reins once more. Crompton returned for his third spell at United, working as part of Tommy Docherty's backroom team. Crompton managed Barrow and had once been offered the manager's job at Luton, but turned it down on doctor's advice. Today he lives in semi-retirement at Amarilla Golf and Country Club in Tenerife.

**JACK CROMPTON**

| | LEAGUE | | FA CUP | | TOTAL | |
|---|---|---|---|---|---|---|
| | App | Gls | App | Gls | App | Gls |
| 1945-46 | 0 | 0 | 4 | 0 | 4 | 0 |
| 1946-47 | 29 | 0 | 1 | 0 | 30 | 0 |
| 1947-48 | 37 | 0 | 6 | 0 | 43 | 0 |
| 1948-49 | 41 | 0 | 8 | 0 | 49 | 0 |
| 1949-50 | 27 | 0 | 1 | 0 | 28 | 0 |
| 1950-51 | 2 | 0 | 0 | 0 | 2 | 0 |
| 1951-52 | 9 | 0 | 0 | 0 | 9 | 0 |
| 1952-53 | 25 | 0 | 0 | 0 | 25 | 0 |
| 1953-54 | 15 | 0 | 0 | 0 | 15 | 0 |
| 1954-55 | 5 | 0 | 0 | 0 | 5 | 0 |
| 1955-56 | 1 | 0 | 0 | 0 | 1 | 0 |
| | 191 | 0 | 20 | 0 | 211 | 0 |

When Stan Crowther played in the victorious Aston Villa side that beat United in the 1957 FA Cup Final, no-one could have imagined that, 12 months later, he would be playing for United at Wembley. Futhermore, the circumstances in which he became a United player were quite unimaginable. Born at Bilston, the tall fair-haired wing-half started his career with Villa and joined United in the wake of the Munich crash, for £35,000. Having played for Villa against Stoke in the third round of the 1957-8 FA Cup competition, he was Cup-tied, but the FA gave him permission to play for the stricken United. Thus Crowther became only the second player since the war (Jimmy Scoular was the other) to play for different clubs in the same season's FA Cup. Crowther was only 22 at the time and had only 50 League games to his name, but in comparison to some of his new colleagues he was a veteran. After helping United to Wembley, Crowther signed for Chelsea the same year for £10,000. He moved to Brighton and retired after only four League games for them, aged 25. An England Under-23 international, Crowther managed non-League club Rugby Town for a short time.

| | LEAGUE | | FA CUP | | EUROPE | | TOTAL | |
|---|---|---|---|---|---|---|---|---|
| | App | Gls | App | Gls | App | Gls | App | Gls |
| 1957-58 | 11 | 0 | 5 | 0 | 2 | 0 | 18 | 0 |
| 1958-59 | 2 | 0 | 0 | 0 | 0 | 0 | 2 | 0 |
| | 13 | 0 | 5 | 0 | 2 | 0 | 20 | 0 |

**STAN CROWTHER**

One of Tommy Docherty's shrewdest buys — as he set about his United reconstruction programme — was Gerry Daly, who joined the club from Irish side, Bohemians, for a fee reported to be in the region of £20,000, just before his 19th birthday in April 1973. Daly proved an effective part of United's midfield which played such attractive football as the team stormed the Second Division title in 1975 and reached the FA Cup Final the following year. Daly eventually found himself in dispute with Docherty and was transferred to Derby County for £175,000 in March 1977, a move that made him Ireland's most expensive footballer. In the summers of 1978 and 1979 he played for New England Tea Men. Enjoying his football at the Baseball Ground, Daly was shattered to learn, six months after his move, that the Derby board had appointed Docherty to succeed manager Colin Murphy. Although he maintained a first-team place, there was an uneasy atmosphere between player and manager and in August 1980 Daly moved to Coventry for £310,000. After four seasons at Highfield Road, including a loan period at Leicester, he was transferred to Birmingham City at the start of 1984-5 and helped them back to Division One. In October 1985, Daly, who has won over 40 Republic of Ireland caps, signed for Shrewsbury Town. He then made 22 League

appearances for Stoke before joining Doncaster Rovers, and then becoming the player-coach at Telford United in 1989. He took over as manager in July 1990.

**GERRY DALY**

| | LEAGUE | | FA CUP | | FL CUP | | EUROPE | | TOTAL | |
|---|---|---|---|---|---|---|---|---|---|---|
| | App | Gls | App | Gls | App | Gls | App | Gls | App | Gls |
| 1973-74 | 14/2 | 1 | 0 | 0 | 1 | 0 | 0 | 0 | 15/2 | 1 |
| 1974-75 | 36/1 | 11 | 2 | 1 | 7 | 1 | 0 | 0 | 45/1 | 13 |
| 1975-76 | 41 | 7 | 7 | 4 | 3 | 0 | 0 | 0 | 51 | 11 |
| 1976-77 | 16/1 | 4 | 0/1 | 0 | 6 | 3 | 4 | 0 | 26/2 | 7 |
| | 107/4 | 23 | 9/1 | 5 | 17 | 4 | 4 | 0 | 137/5 | 32 |

**ALEX DAWSON**

Aberdeen-born Alex Dawson was in fact playing for Hull Schools when United spotted him. He came through the junior ranks and signed professional forms shortly after his 17th birthday, in May 1957. The previous month he had scored on his League debut, against Burnley. After Munich, the bustling centre-forward commanded a regular place and was one of the inspirations behind United's march to the 1958 FA Cup Final. He scored five goals in six matches, including a hat-trick in the 5-3 semi-final replay win over Fulham. After United signed David Herd in the 1961 close season, Dawson found it difficult to get into the side and in October 1961 he moved to Second Division Preston for £18,000. He collected a second FA Cup runners-up medal in 1964, despite scoring in the Final against West Ham. In 1967 Dawson signed for Bury and later played for Brighton and Brentford (on loan). His career spanned 13 years and nearly 400 League games, in which he scored over 200 goals.

| | LEAGUE | | FA CUP | | EUROPE | | TOTAL | |
|---|---|---|---|---|---|---|---|---|
| | App | Gls | App | Gls | App | Gls | App | Gls |
| 1956-57 | 3 | 3 | 0 | 0 | 0 | 0 | 3 | 3 |
| 1957-58 | 12 | 5 | 6 | 5 | 0 | 0 | 18 | 10 |
| 1958-59 | 11 | 4 | 0 | 0 | 0 | 0 | 11 | 4 |
| 1959-60 | 22 | 15 | 1 | 0 | 0 | 0 | 23 | 15 |
| 1960-61 | 28 | 16 | 3 | 3 | 3 | 1 | 34 | 20 |
| 1961-62 | 4 | 2 | 0 | 0 | 0 | 0 | 4 | 2 |
| | 80 | 45 | 10 | 8 | 3 | 1 | 93 | 54 |

When Jimmy Delaney played in the 1954 Irish FA Cup Final, he created football history. It was the first time that a man had won Cup-winners' medals in England, Scotland and Northern Ireland. He won a Scottish medal with his first club, Celtic, in 1937, was a member of the United side which beat Blackpool in the 1948 FA Cup Final and his Irish medal came with Derry City six years later. Two years later he played for Cork Athletic in the FA of Ireland Cup Final but Cork threw away a two-goal lead and lost to Shamrock Rovers, thus denying Delaney, then 32, what would surely have been an unrepeatable feat. Born in 1914, Delaney was bought by United for £4,000 in 1946, which was good business since Sunderland had reportedly bid a staggering £20,000 for him before the war. A speedy winger, he delighted Old Trafford fans with his pace and ability to shoot on the run. By the time he left United, in a £3,500 move to Aberdeen in 1950, he had played over 150 games for the club and, besides his Cup medal, had won a League Championship medal and four Scotland caps to add to the nine gained with Celtic before the war. Delaney joined Celtic from Lanarkshire junior club, Stoneyburn, in 1934. From Aberdeen he moved to Falkirk, then to Derry for a then record Irish fee of £1,500. He became player-manager of Cork in 1955 before returning to Scotland to play for Highland League team, Elgin City. He retired in 1957 after 27 years as a player. Jimmy Delaney died in September 1989 at the age of 74.

| | LEAGUE | | FA CUP | | TOTAL | |
|---|---|---|---|---|---|---|
| | App | Gls | App | Gls | App | Gls |
| 1946-47 | 37 | 8 | 2 | 0 | 39 | 8 |
| 1947-48 | 36 | 8 | 6 | 1 | 42 | 9 |
| 1948-49 | 36 | 4 | 6 | 0 | 42 | 4 |
| 1949-50 | 42 | 4 | 5 | 2 | 47 | 6 |
| 1950-51 | 13 | 1 | 0 | 0 | 13 | 1 |
| | 164 | 25 | 19 | 3 | 183 | 28 |

**JIMMY DELANEY**

It was fitting that Alex Downie should be granted a benefit match during 1907-08, for he had proved a great club man for Manchester United. It was, however, totally incomprehensible that the Manchester public did not respond and the attendance was very disappointing. Totally committed to United, Downie was a wing-half who gave 100 per cent effort in every game he played. Born in Dunoon, he joined Third Lanark as a 20-year-old in 1898. The following year he joined Southern League club Bristol City and, after one season with them, moved to Swindon Town, also in the Southern League. At the start of 1902-03 he joined United, who were beginning their first season under their new name. Downie made his debut against Leicester and scored one of his rare goals. When United won the Championship in 1907-08, he played in only ten games and a year later was left out of the side which won the FA Cup against his former club, Bristol City. After nearly 200 senior games, Downie moved to Oldham Athletic before ending his career with Crewe.

**ALEX DOWNIE**

| | LEAGUE | | FA CUP | | TOTAL | |
|---|---|---|---|---|---|---|
| | App | Gls | App | Gls | App | Gls |
| 1902-03 | 22 | 5 | 5 | 0 | 27 | 5 |
| 1903-04 | 29 | 4 | 6 | 1 | 35 | 5 |
| 1904-05 | 32 | 1 | 3 | 0 | 35 | 1 |
| 1905-06 | 34 | 0 | 4 | 1 | 38 | 1 |
| 1906-07 | 19 | 2 | 1 | 0 | 20 | 2 |
| 1907-08 | 10 | 0 | 0 | 0 | 10 | 0 |
| 1908-09 | 23 | 0 | 0 | 0 | 23 | 0 |
| 1909-10 | 3 | 0 | 0 | 0 | 3 | 0 |
| | 172 | 12 | 19 | 2 | 191 | 14 |

**JOHN DOWNIE**

When Manchester United signed John Downie from Bradford in 1949, they had to pay the Park Avenue club £18,000, which was then a record outgoing transfer fee for United. Downie replaced Johnny Morris, for whom United had collected a British record fee of £24,500 when they sold him to Derby County. Downie justified his own fee by becoming a regular goalscorer during his time at Old Trafford and helped United win the League Championship in 1951-2. Born in Falkirk, he moved to Bradford at the end of World War Two. He made his United debut at Charlton in March 1949 and scored a goal in the Reds' 3-2 win. Midway through the 1952-3 season, he lost his first-team place and in the close season was transferred to Luton Town for £10,000. Subsequent moves took him to Hull City, Mansfield Town and Darlington before he retired in the 1959-60 season, after 284 League games and 92 goals.

|         | LEAGUE | | FA CUP | | TOTAL | |
|---------|-----|-----|-----|-----|-----|-----|
|         | App | Gls | App | Gls | App | Gls |
| 1948-49 | 12  | 5   | 0   | 0   | 12  | 5   |
| 1949-50 | 18  | 6   | 2   | 1   | 20  | 7   |
| 1950-51 | 29  | 10  | 0   | 0   | 29  | 10  |
| 1951-52 | 31  | 11  | 1   | 0   | 32  | 11  |
| 1952-53 | 20  | 3   | 2   | 0   | 22  | 3   |
|         | 110 | 35  | 5   | 1   | 115 | 36  |

Mention of the great Manchester United team of 1907-11 always brings to mind the half-back line of Duckworth, Roberts and Bell. The 'engine-room' of that fine team, they were an outstanding trio and Duckworth was the only one who did not gain full international honours, although he did play in a 'Commonwealth' international against South Africa in 1910 and represented the Football League. He was surely one of the greatest players ever to wear a United shirt. United, whom he joined from non-League Newton Heath, was Duckworth's only club and the locally-born wing-half played well over 200 games before retiring in 1913-14, turning out longer than either of the other members of the 'Triumvirate'. Duckworth had originally decided to retire when Bell and Roberts left United, but he was persuaded to continue for another season. He won two League Championship medals and an FA Cup winners' medal with the club and one outstanding feature of his game was a remarkable understanding with Billy Meredith which led to many United goals.

|         | LEAGUE | | FA CUP | | TOTAL | |
|---------|-----|-----|-----|-----|-----|-----|
|         | App | Gls | App | Gls | App | Gls |
| 1903-04 | 1   | 1   | 0   | 0   | 1   | 1   |
| 1904-05 | 8   | 6   | 0   | 0   | 8   | 6   |
| 1905-06 | 10  | 0   | 0   | 0   | 10  | 0   |
| 1906-07 | 28  | 2   | 2   | 0   | 30  | 2   |
| 1907-08 | 35  | 0   | 3   | 0   | 38  | 0   |
| 1908-09 | 33  | 0   | 6   | 0   | 39  | 0   |
| 1909-10 | 29  | 0   | 1   | 0   | 30  | 0   |
| 1910-11 | 22  | 2   | 3   | 0   | 25  | 2   |
| 1911-12 | 26  | 0   | 6   | 0   | 32  | 0   |
| 1912-13 | 24  | 0   | 5   | 0   | 29  | 0   |
| 1913-14 | 9   | 0   | 0   | 0   | 9   | 0   |
|         | 225 | 11  | 26  | 0   | 251 | 11  |

**DICK DUCKWORTH**

Tony Dunne made his Manchester United debut in the 3-2 defeat at Burnley on 15 October 1960. He appeared in only two more League games that season but midway through the following season established a regular place at full-back. During his 13 years in the first team, Dunne was rarely ousted from the side, playing equally well on either flank. Born in Dublin, he joined United from League of Ireland club Shelbourne United, for £3,500, in August 1960. Dunne made over 500 senior appearances for United, playing in the 1963 FA Cup winning team, the Championship sides of 1965 and 1967, and in the 1968 European Cup Final when he gave one of the finest displays of his career. Capped 32 times by the Republic of Ireland, Dunne made his international debut against Austria in Dublin, a few weeks before his 21st birthday. Small but fast, he was a loyal United servant and gave the same loyalty to Bolton Wanderers, his only other League club, whom he joined in July 1973. Five seasons at Burnden Park took his overall senior appearances tally to 700 games before he went to play in the USA in 1979 for Detroit Express.

**TONY DUNNE**

| | LEAGUE | | FACUP | | FLCUP | | EUROPE | | TOTAL | |
|---|---|---|---|---|---|---|---|---|---|---|
| | App | Gls | App | Gls | App | Gls | App | Gls | App | Gls |
| 1960-61 | 3 | 0 | 0 | 0 | 1 | 0 | 0 | 0 | 4 | 0 |
| 1961-62 | 28 | 0 | 7 | 0 | 0 | 0 | 0 | 0 | 35 | 0 |
| 1962-63 | 25 | 0 | 3 | 0 | 0 | 0 | 0 | 0 | 28 | 0 |
| 1963-64 | 40 | 0 | 7 | 0 | 0 | 0 | 6 | 0 | 53 | 0 |
| 1964-65 | 42 | 0 | 7 | 0 | 0 | 0 | 11 | 0 | 60 | 0 |
| 1965-66 | 40 | 1 | 7 | 0 | 0 | 0 | 8 | 0 | 55 | 1 |
| 1966-67 | 40 | 0 | 2 | 0 | 1 | 0 | 0 | 0 | 43 | 0 |
| 1967-68 | 37 | 1 | 2 | 0 | 0 | 0 | 9 | 0 | 48 | 1 |
| 1968-69 | 33 | 0 | 6 | 0 | 0 | 0 | 6 | 0 | 45 | 0 |
| 1969-70 | 33 | 0 | 7 | 0 | 8 | 0 | 0 | 0 | 48 | 0 |
| 1970-71 | 35 | 0 | 2 | 0 | 5 | 0 | 0 | 0 | 42 | 0 |
| 1971-72 | 34 | 0 | 4 | 0 | 3 | 0 | 0 | 0 | 41 | 0 |
| 1972-73 | 24 | 0 | 0/1 | 0 | 3 | 0 | 0 | 0 | 27/1 | 0 |
| | 414 | 2 | 54/1 | 0 | 21 | 0 | 40 | 0 | 529/1 | 2 |

Mike Duxbury had been at Old Trafford for five years without attracting too much attention, before making his senior debut in the League game against Birmingham City in August 1980. He came on as substitute for Kevin Moran and spent the rest of that season, and the following campaign, filling a variety of positions as a utility player. In 1982, he found himself settled in as United's right-back and it was in that position he won his ten England caps, adding to seven Under-21 appearances. Duxbury's full international appearances came in less than 12 months between November 1983 and October 1984. Although he lost his United right-back spot to John Gidman in 1984-5, Duxbury still maintained a first-team place because of his versatility. Tough and skilful, Duxbury, who was born near Blackburn, served his apprenticeship at Old Trafford before turning professional in 1976. He played in the 1983 and 1985 FA Cup-winning teams and the 1983 Milk Cup Final side. Given a free transfer at the end of the 1989-90 season and he moved to nearby Blackburn Rovers and was later with Bradford City.

**MIKE DUXBURY**

| | LEAGUE | | FACUP | | FLCUP | | EUROPE | | TOTAL | |
|---|---|---|---|---|---|---|---|---|---|---|
| | App | Gls | App | Gls | App | Gls | App | Gls | App | Gls |
| 1980-81 | 27/6 | 2 | 0/2 | 1 | 0 | 0 | 1/1 | 0 | 28/9 | 3 |
| 1981-82 | 19/5 | 0 | 0 | 0 | 0/1 | 0 | 0 | 0 | 19/6 | 0 |
| 1982-83 | 42 | 1 | 7 | 0 | 9 | 0 | 2 | 0 | 60 | 1 |
| 1983-84 | 39 | 0 | 1 | 0 | 6 | 0 | 8 | 0 | 54 | 0 |
| 1984-85 | 27/3 | 1 | 2/1 | 0 | 2 | 0 | 6 | 0 | 37/4 | 1 |
| 1985-86 | 21/2 | 1 | 3 | 0 | 3 | 0 | 0 | 0 | 27/2 | 1 |
| 1986-87 | 32 | 1 | 2 | 0 | 3 | 0 | 0 | 0 | 37 | 1 |
| 1987-88 | 39 | 0 | 3 | 0 | 5 | 0 | 0 | 0 | 47 | 0 |
| 1988-89 | 16/2 | 0 | 0 | 0 | 3 | 0 | 0 | 0 | 19/2 | 0 |
| 1989-90 | 12/7 | 0 | 2/2 | 0 | 1/1 | 0 | 0 | 0 | 15/10 | 0 |
| | 274/25 | 6 | 20/5 | 1 | 32/2 | 0 | 17/1 | 0 | 343/33 | 7 |

There can be few superlatives not used to describe the great Duncan Edwards, and not one of them had ever been used out of context. He was a true football giant and had the Munich air disaster not robbed football of his priceless talent, then he may well have shared in United's European triumph a decade later. Edwards was only 21 when he died and yet he had already achieved so much in the five years since his United debut. His first game was as a 16-year-old amateur in a disastrous 4-1 home defeat by Cardiff, but there were far greater moments in store for the youngster from Dudley, Worcestershire. He went on to win 18 full England caps, the first against Scotland in April 1955 when, aged 18 years and 183 days, he was England's youngest debutant. He won two Championship medals and appeared in the 1957 FA Cup Final. Born in 1936, Edwards was a member of the Dudley Boys team, average age 15, when he was only 11. Two hours into his 16th birthday, he signed for United after Matt Busby had personally made the trip to the West Midlands.

**DUNCAN EDWARDS**

Jimmy Murphy had made an earlier visit to Edwards' home to convince him and his parents that the boys' future lay with United. In Duncan Edwards, the club secured a giant of a wing-half, a hugely talented teenager who had immense natural ability and a fierce shot in either foot. He could play inside-forward as well, once scoring a hat-trick for England Under-23 against Scotland, and his maturity belied his years as he stood out amongst the best in the land. His greatest days were surely yet to come when he boarded the 'plane from Belgrade, but they were denied him. His great physical strength and courage kept him alive for almost two weeks after the crash before he lost his last battle.

| | LEAGUE | | FA CUP | | EUROPE | | TOTAL | |
|---|---|---|---|---|---|---|---|---|
| | App | Gls | App | Gls | App | Gls | App | Gls |
| 1952-53 | 1 | 0 | 0 | 0 | 0 | 0 | 1 | 0 |
| 1953-54 | 24 | 0 | 1 | 0 | 0 | 0 | 25 | 0 |
| 1954-55 | 33 | 6 | 3 | 0 | 0 | 0 | 36 | 6 |
| 1955-56 | 33 | 3 | 0 | 0 | 0 | 0 | 33 | 3 |
| 1956-57 | 34 | 5 | 6 | 1 | 7 | 0 | 47 | 6 |
| 1957-58 | 26 | 6 | 2 | 0 | 5 | 0 | 33 | 6 |
| | 151 | 20 | 12 | 1 | 12 | 0 | 175 | 21 |

When John Fitzpatrick turned out for United at Goodison Park in August 1972, it was his first League appearance for a year and a day and everyone hoped that the injuries which had dogged a promising career were finally over. Sadly they were not and a month later Fitzpatrick made his last appearance in a United shirt. Fitzpatrick was only 26 and had spent nine years at Old Trafford since turning professional in September 1963, after progressing through the junior ranks. Fitzpatrick, who hails from Aberdeen, made his League debut at Sunderland in February 1965, stepping in at left-half for Nobby Stiles. The previous year he had played in the United team which won the FA Youth Cup for the sixth time. A tough-tackling wing-half, with distinctive long, flowing hair, he successfully converted to right-back in the latter stages of his career. Fitzpatrick returned to Scotland on his retirement and set up a wine business, no doubt reflecting on how he spent almost a decade at United, during one of their more successful spells, and never won a major honour himself.

| | LEAGUE | | FA CUP | | FL CUP | | EUROPE | | TOTAL | |
|---|---|---|---|---|---|---|---|---|---|---|
| | App | Gls | App | Gls | App | Gls | App | Gls | App | Gls |
| 1964-65 | 2 | 0 | 0 | 0 | 0 | 0 | 0 | 0 | 2 | 0 |
| 1965-66 | 3/1 | 0 | 0 | 0 | 0 | 0 | 1 | 0 | 4/1 | 0 |
| 1966-67 | 3 | 0 | 0 | 0 | 0 | 0 | 0 | 0 | 3 | 0 |
| 1967-68 | 14/3 | 0 | 2 | 0 | 0 | 0 | 2 | 0 | 18/3 | 0 |
| 1968-69 | 28/2 | 3 | 6 | 1 | 0 | 0 | 4 | 0 | 38/2 | 4 |
| 1969-70 | 20 | 3 | 1 | 0 | 5 | 0 | 0 | 0 | 26 | 3 |
| 1970-71 | 35 | 2 | 2 | 0 | 6 | 1 | 0 | 0 | 43 | 3 |
| 1971-72 | 1 | 0 | 0 | 0 | 0 | 0 | 0 | 0 | 1 | 0 |
| 1972-73 | 5 | 0 | 0 | 0 | 1 | 0 | 0 | 0 | 6 | 0 |
| | 111/6 | 8 | 11 | 1 | 12 | 1 | 7 | 0 | 141/6 | 10 |

**JOHN FITZPATRICK**

When Alex Forsyth stepped out at Highbury to make his United debut in January 1973, just a week after his £100,000 transfer from Partick Thistle, he had a special reason for doing well. Six years earlier, Arsenal released him and he returned home to his native Scotland and signed for Partick Thistle, with whom he won a Scottish League Cup winners' medal in 1972. Forsyth was Tommy Docherty's first signing after taking over at United and he spent nearly six years at Old Trafford, commanding both full-back positions with his hard-tackling and sound all-round defensive work. Forsyth also enjoyed going forward and was regularly seen having a crack at goal. With United, he won a Second Division Championship medal and was a member of the losing 1976 FA Cup Final team. After losing his place to Jimmy Nicholl, Forsyth moved north once more and signed for Rangers after a loan period with them in 1978-9. In 1982 he was transferred from Ibrox to Motherwell.

| | LEAGUE | | FACUP | | FLCUP | | EUROPE | | TOTAL | |
|---|---|---|---|---|---|---|---|---|---|---|
| | App | Gls | App | Gls | App | Gls | App | Gls | App | Gls |
| 1972-73 | 8 | 0 | 1 | 0 | 0 | 0 | 0 | 0 | 9 | 0 |
| 1973-74 | 18/1 | 1 | 2 | 0 | 0 | 0 | 0 | 0 | 20/1 | 1 |
| 1974-75 | 39 | 1 | 0 | 0 | 6 | 0 | 0 | 0 | 45 | 1 |
| 1975-76 | 28 | 2 | 7 | 1 | 0 | 0 | 0 | 0 | 35 | 3 |
| 1976-77 | 3/1 | 0 | 0 | 0 | 1 | 0 | 0 | 0 | 4/1 | 0 |
| 1977-78 | 3 | 0 | 0 | 0 | 0 | 0 | 0/1 | 0 | 3/1 | 0 |
| | 99/2 | 4 | 10 | 1 | 7 | 0 | 0/1 | 0 | 116/3 | 5 |

**ALEX FORSYTH**

It was perhaps fitting that Bill Foulkes should score a goal in the 3-3 draw with Real Madrid which put United into the 1968 European Cup Final. Ten years earlier, Foulkes had been a member of the United squad which was decimated in pursuit of European Cup glory. Foulkes survived Munich to become the backbone of the defence around which rebuilding began. He was one of two Munich survivors — Harry Gregg was the other — to play in the first game after the disaster, the FA Cup match against Sheffield Wednesday. He captained the side to Wembley that year but collected his second successive losers' medal. Compensation was gained in 1963 when United beat Leicester and, in addition to his European Cup winners' medal, Foulkes also won four League Championship medals and one full England cap during his 18-years in United's first team. Born at St Helens, he joined United as an amateur from Whiston Boys Club in 1949 and turned professional in 1951. Strong and resilient, he gave the club sterling service at full-back and centre-half and appeared in over 600 games before retiring to join the coaching staff in 1970. Foulkes subsequently coached in the United States and Norway. In 1989 he managed Japanese side Mazda.

| | LEAGUE | | FACUP | | FLCUP | | EUROPE | | TOTAL | |
|---|---|---|---|---|---|---|---|---|---|---|
| | App | Gls | App | Gls | App | Gls | App | Gls | App | Gls |
| 1952-53 | 2 | 0 | 0 | 0 | 0 | 0 | 0 | 0 | 2 | 0 |
| 1953-54 | 32 | 1 | 1 | 0 | 0 | 0 | 0 | 0 | 33 | 1 |
| 1954-55 | 41 | 0 | 3 | 0 | 0 | 0 | 0 | 0 | 44 | 0 |
| 1955-56 | 26 | 0 | 1 | 0 | 0 | 0 | 0 | 0 | 27 | 0 |
| 1956-57 | 39 | 0 | 6 | 0 | 0 | 0 | 8 | 0 | 53 | 0 |
| 1957-58 | 42 | 0 | 8 | 0 | 0 | 0 | 8 | 0 | 58 | 0 |
| 1958-59 | 32 | 0 | 1 | 0 | 0 | 0 | 0 | 0 | 33 | 0 |
| 1959-60 | 42 | 0 | 3 | 0 | 0 | 0 | 0 | 0 | 45 | 0 |
| 1960-61 | 40 | 0 | 3 | 0 | 2 | 0 | 0 | 0 | 45 | 0 |
| 1961-62 | 40 | 0 | 7 | 0 | 0 | 0 | 0 | 0 | 47 | 0 |
| 1962-63 | 41 | 0 | 6 | 0 | 0 | 0 | 0 | 0 | 47 | 0 |
| 1963-64 | 41 | 1 | 7 | 0 | 0 | 0 | 6 | 0 | 54 | 1 |
| 1964-65 | 42 | 0 | 7 | 0 | 0 | 0 | 11 | 0 | 60 | 0 |
| 1965-66 | 33 | 0 | 7 | 0 | 0 | 0 | 8 | 1 | 48 | 1 |
| 1966-67 | 33 | 4 | 1 | 0 | 1 | 0 | 0 | 0 | 35 | 4 |
| 1967-68 | 24 | 1 | 0 | 0 | 0 | 0 | 6 | 1 | 30 | 2 |
| 1968-69 | 10/3 | 0 | 0 | 0 | 0 | 0 | 5 | 0 | 15/3 | 0 |
| 1969-70 | 3 | 0 | 0 | 0 | 0 | 0 | 0 | 0 | 3 | 0 |
| | 563/3 | 7 | 61 | 0 | 3 | 0 | 52 | 2 | 679/3 | 9 |

**BILL FOULKES**

A former amateur with his home-town club, Liverpool, John Gidman served his apprenticeship with Aston Villa before turning full-time professional in August 1971, making his debut 12 months later against Carlisle United. He won England Youth and Under-23 caps and was a member of Villa's Second Division promotion side in 1974-5, and their League Cup winning team of 1977, the year he made his full England debut. Villa beat Everton to take the League Cup and it was the Goodison club who paid £650,000 for Gidman in October 1979. Two seasons and 64 League games later, he joined United in the deal which took Mickey Thomas to Goodison. A great character, Gidman soon settled into United's defence, enjoying the freedom to display his attacking flair from full-back. Despite suffering more than his share of injuries, including nearly losing an eye in a firework accident, Gidman remained a vital part of the club's thinking and after missing much of the 1982-3 and 1983-4 seasons, he came back in 1984-5 and was a key member of the team which won the FA Cup against his former club, Everton. That victory compensated him for missing the 1983 FA Cup and Milk Cup Finals. In March 1986, United announced that they had given Gidman a free transfer, but then recalled him to the side for vital League games. He eventually moved to rivals Manchester City, then joined Stoke City and Darlington as assistant manager.

|  | LEAGUE | | FA CUP | | FL CUP | | EUROPE | | TOTAL | |
|---|---|---|---|---|---|---|---|---|---|---|
|  | App | Gls | App | Gls | App | Gls | App | Gls | App | Gls |
| 1981-82 | 36/1 | 1 | 1 | 0 | 2 | 0 | 0 | 0 | 39/1 | 1 |
| 1982-83 | 3 | 0 | 0 | 0 | 0 | 0 | 0 | 0 | 3 | 0 |
| 1983-84 | 4 | 0 | 0 | 0 | 1 | 0 | 1/1 | 0 | 6/1 | 0 |
| 1984-85 | 27 | 3 | 6 | 0 | 1 | 0 | 6/1 | 0 | 40/1 | 3 |
| 1985-86 | 24 | 0 | 2 | 0 | 1 | 0 | 0 | 0 | 27 | 0 |
|  | 94/1 | 4 | 9 | 0 | 5 | 0 | 7/2 | 0 | 115/3 | 4 |

**JOHN GIDMAN**

Although Johnny Giles will be best remembered for his days at Leeds United in the 1970s, he began his League career with Manchester United. During his six-year stay at Old Trafford, he won his first club honour, an FA Cup winners' medal in 1963. Born in Dublin in 1940, Giles was signed from Home Farm as a 17-year-old. He made his League debut in the 5-1 home defeat by Spurs in September 1959 when he replaced Albert Quixall. His final competitive game for United was in the 1963 FA Cup Final win over Leicester. Three months later he joined Leeds for £37,500 and began a new career which saw him as part of Leeds' successful midfield. He won a host of honours with the Yorkshire club including League Championship medals in 1969 and 1974, an FA Cup winners' medal in 1972, League Cup winners' medal (1968) and Fairs Cup winners' medals (1968 and 1971). He played in five FA Cup Finals at Wembley (Joe Hulme, Pat Rice and Frank Stapleton are the only other men to do so) and between 1960 and 1979 he won a record 60 Republic of Ireland caps. His last game for Leeds was their 1975 European Cup Final defeat by Bayern Munich. In 1978 he played for Philadelphia Fury. He later guided West Brom into the First Division as player-manager, and managed Shamrock Rovers, Vancouver Whitecaps and the Republic of Ireland national side before a second spell as WBA manager, a job which he later lost to his brother-in-law, Nobby Stiles.

**JOHNNY GILES**

|  | LEAGUE | | FA CUP | | FL CUP | | TOTAL | |
|---|---|---|---|---|---|---|---|---|
|  | App | Gls | App | Gls | App | Gls | App | Gls |
| 1959-60 | 10 | 2 | 0 | 0 | 0 | 0 | 10 | 2 |
| 1960-61 | 23 | 2 | 0 | 0 | 2 | 1 | 25 | 3 |
| 1961-62 | 30 | 2 | 7 | 1 | 0 | 0 | 37 | 3 |
| 1962-63 | 36 | 4 | 6 | 1 | 0 | 0 | 42 | 5 |
|  | 99 | 10 | 13 | 2 | 2 | 1 | 114 | 13 |

Born in Heywood, near Rochdale, Freddie Goodwin was over 20 when he joined United, his first League club, in 1953. He made his League debut against Arsenal in 1954-5, standing in for Duncan Edwards at left-half. Goodwin could play on either flank but he found himself in the shadow of both Edwards and Eddie Colman. After the Munich crash he was a regular at right-half and played there in the 1958 FA Cup Final. After 95 League games for United, Goodwin signed for Leeds United in March 1960, for £10,000. Leeds were relegated that season and Goodwin missed their later successes, moving to Scunthorpe United in December 1964. He later managed the Old Show Ground club and then had a spell in the United States, coaching New York Generals in 1967-8, before returning to Britain in 1968 to manage Brighton. He later managed Birmingham before returning to the States and in 1976 he took over Minnesota Kicks. Goodwin played in 11 first-class cricket matches for Lancashire in 1955 and 1956, scoring 47 runs and taking 27 wickets at 26.48 apiece.

|  | LEAGUE | | FA CUP | | EUROPE | | TOTAL | |
|---|---|---|---|---|---|---|---|---|
|  | App | Gls | App | Gls | App | Gls | App | Gls |
| 1954-55 | 5 | 0 | 0 | 0 | 0 | 0 | 5 | 0 |
| 1955-56 | 8 | 0 | 0 | 0 | 0 | 0 | 8 | 0 |
| 1956-57 | 6 | 0 | 0 | 0 | 0 | 0 | 6 | 0 |
| 1957-58 | 16 | 0 | 6 | 0 | 3 | 0 | 25 | 0 |
| 1958-59 | 42 | 6 | 1 | 0 | 0 | 0 | 43 | 6 |
| 1959-60 | 18 | 1 | 1 | 1 | 0 | 0 | 19 | 2 |
|  | 95 | 7 | 8 | 1 | 3 | 0 | 106 | 8 |

**FREDDIE GOODWIN**

As United endured their worst post-war spell, culminating in relegation in 1974, there was, nevertheless, promise for the future with the emergence of young players like Sammy McIlroy and Brian Greenhoff. Barnsley-born Greenhoff was a United apprentice who turned professional in June 1970, two months after his 17th birthday. He had to wait until September 1973 before making his League debut, at Ipswich. Perhaps his greatest asset was his composure and this was never more evident than in the 1977 FA Cup Final when United held off a magnificent Liverpool team to win the FA Cup for the first time in 14 years. Greenhoff, younger brother of another United star, Jimmy, was also a member of United's team beaten in the 1976 Final, and substitute, although not used, in the 1979 Final. Two years after the Wembley victory, Greenhoff was transferred to Leeds for £350,000. His brother became manager of Rochdale and in November 1983 tempted him to Spotland following a trial period at Hull City. He retired in 1984 with over 300 senior appearances and 18 full England caps to his credit. He then went into pub management in the Rochdale area, but left after disagreement with the Brewery.

|  | LEAGUE | | FA CUP | | FL CUP | | EUROPE | | TOTAL | |
|---|---|---|---|---|---|---|---|---|---|---|
|  | App | Gls | App | Gls | App | Gls | App | Gls | App | Gls |
| 1973-74 | 36 | 3 | 2 | 0 | 1 | 0 | 0 | 0 | 39 | 3 |
| 1974-75 | 39/2 | 4 | 2 | 0 | 6 | 0 | 0 | 0 | 47/2 | 4 |
| 1975-76 | 40 | 0 | 7 | 1 | 3 | 0 | 0 | 0 | 50 | 1 |
| 1976-77 | 40 | 3 | 7 | 0 | 6 | 2 | 4 | 0 | 57 | 5 |
| 1977-78 | 31 | 1 | 1 | 0 | 1 | 0 | 2 | 0 | 35 | 1 |
| 1978-79 | 32/1 | 2 | 5 | 1 | 2 | 0 | 0 | 0 | 39/1 | 3 |
|  | 218/3 | 13 | 24 | 2 | 19 | 2 | 6 | 0 | 267/3 | 17 |

**BRIAN GREENHOFF**

Why Jimmy Greenhoff never won a full England cap is a question that has puzzled many people. He had the ability to turn a match, either with his own scoring ability or with his knack of laying on goals for others. Born in Barnsley, in June 1946, the elder brother of Brian he joined Leeds as a 15-year-old and later played for Birmingham and Stoke where he was a great favourite, inspiring the Potters to victory in the 1972 League Cup Final. It was his second such honour, for he had been in the Leeds team which beat Arsenal in the 1968 Final. Greenhoff became a favourite at Old Trafford after his £100,000 transfer from Stoke in November 1976. He appeared in two FA Cup Finals for United, in 1977 when he scored the winner against Liverpool, and 1979. He moved to Crewe in December 1980, played for Toronto Blizzard and then Port Vale before being appointed Rochdale manager in 1983. When he resigned in March 1984, the League lost one of its characters, although he was not entirely lost to the game and spent part of the following summer coaching youngsters at holiday camps around the country. He gained five England Under-23 caps, played for the Football League and totalled more than 650 appearances for his six clubs. He was coach at Port Vale in 1984 and then worked in insurance in the Stoke area.

**JIMMY GREENHOFF**

| | LEAGUE | | FA CUP | | FL CUP | | EUROPE | | TOTAL | |
|---|---|---|---|---|---|---|---|---|---|---|
| | App | Gls | App | Gls | App | Gls | App | Gls | App | Gls |
| 1976-77 | 27 | 8 | 7 | 4 | 0 | 0 | 0 | 0 | 34 | 12 |
| 1977-78 | 22/1 | 6 | 2/1 | 0 | 0 | 0 | 1 | 0 | 25/2 | 6 |
| 1978-79 | 33 | 11 | 9 | 5 | 2 | 1 | 0 | 0 | 44 | 17 |
| 1979-80 | 4/1 | 1 | 0 | 0 | 0 | 0 | 0 | 0 | 4/1 | 1 |
| 1980-81 | 8/1 | 0 | 0 | 0 | 2 | 0 | 1 | 0 | 11/1 | 0 |
| | 94/3 | 26 | 18/1 | 9 | 4 | 1 | 2 | 0 | 118/4 | 36 |

Four months after surviving the Munich air disaster, Harry Gregg was proving himself one of the outstanding goalkeepers of the 1958 World Cup Finals in Sweden. He gave some tremendous performances in Northern Ireland's goal, notably in the draw with West Germany that ensured the Irish a play-off with Czechoslovakia and ultimately a place in the quarter-finals. Gregg had performed heroically on the Munich runway helping dazed and injured survivors from the crashed 'plane, fighting his way back into the wreckage several times. Born in Magherafelt, County Derry, Gregg was playing in the Irish League when Doncaster Rovers signed him in 1951. He won nine full caps whilst with Second Division Rovers and was noted for his habit of standing well outside his penalty area urging on his team in the days when goalkeepers rarely left their goal area when their team were on the attack. United signed him for £23,500, then a British record for a goalkeeper, in December 1957. Five months later he was being controversially bundled over the line as Nat Lofthouse scored Bolton's second goal in the FA Cup Final. Pat Jennings eventually replaced Gregg in the Northern Ireland goal, and after losing his United place to David Gaskell he signed for Stoke in 1966. A severe shoulder injury restricted Gregg to two League appearances for the Potters before he turned to management with Shrewsbury Town. Subsequently, he managed Swansea City and Crewe Alexandra, coached in Kuwait and was assistant to Lou Macari at Swindon before losing his job in a clash of personalities. He then had 18 months as manager of Carlisle United in May 1986.

**HARRY GREGG**

| | LEAGUE | | FA CUP | | FL CUP | | EUROPE | | TOTAL | |
|---|---|---|---|---|---|---|---|---|---|---|
| | App | Gls | App | Gls | App | Gls | App | Gls | App | Gls |
| 1957-58 | 19 | 0 | 8 | 0 | 0 | 0 | 4 | 0 | 31 | 0 |
| 1958-59 | 41 | 0 | 1 | 0 | 0 | 0 | 0 | 0 | 42 | 0 |
| 1959-60 | 33 | 0 | 3 | 0 | 0 | 0 | 0 | 0 | 36 | 0 |
| 1960-61 | 27 | 0 | 1 | 0 | 2 | 0 | 0 | 0 | 30 | 0 |
| 1961-62 | 13 | 0 | 0 | 0 | 0 | 0 | 0 | 0 | 13 | 0 |
| 1962-63 | 24 | 0 | 4 | 0 | 0 | 0 | 0 | 0 | 28 | 0 |
| 1963-64 | 25 | 0 | 0 | 0 | 0 | 0 | 2 | 0 | 27 | 0 |
| 1965-66 | 26 | 0 | 7 | 0 | 0 | 0 | 5 | 0 | 38 | 0 |
| 1966-67 | 2 | 0 | 0 | 0 | 0 | 0 | 0 | 0 | 2 | 0 |
| | 210 | 0 | 24 | 0 | 2 | 0 | 11 | 0 | 247 | 0 |

**JOHN GRIFFITHS**

After failing to make the grade with Wolverhampton Wanderers, John Griffiths, who was born at Stoke-on-Trent, found a regular League place with Bolton Wanderers, whom he joined in 1932. Towards the end of 1933-4 he left the promotion-chasing Trotters to sign for struggling Manchester United. Griffiths maintained a place at right-back as United fought to stave off relegation and he was a member of the team which beat Millwall in the final game of the season. Two years later he was celebrating United's promotion to Division One. As United returned to the top flight, Griffiths celebrated with his first and only League goal, against Fulham on April Fools' Day. Griffiths also played in an England trial match in 1936. War brought an end to his League career, but he continued to play in regionalized soccer until 1943-4. At the end of the war Griffiths joined nearby non-League Hyde United. He qualified as a masseur.

|  | LEAGUE | | FA CUP | | TOTAL | |
|---|---|---|---|---|---|---|
|  | App | Gls | App | Gls | App | Gls |
| 1933-34 | 10 | 0 | 0 | 0 | 10 | 0 |
| 1934-35 | 40 | 0 | 3 | 0 | 43 | 0 |
| 1935-36 | 41 | 1 | 3 | 0 | 44 | 1 |
| 1936-37 | 21 | 0 | 0 | 0 | 21 | 0 |
| 1937-38 | 18 | 0 | 0 | 0 | 18 | 0 |
| 1938-39 | 35 | 0 | 2 | 0 | 37 | 0 |
| 1939-40 | 3 | 0 | 0 | 0 | 3 | 0 |
|  | 168 | 1 | 8 | 0 | 176 | 1 |

John Grimwood joined United, his first League club, after World War One from South Shields. He made his League debut in the 3-3 draw at Maine Road in October 1919, two weeks before his 21st birthday. He stood in for Clarence Hilditch that day and although he had to wait a couple of months before getting back into the side, he gained a regular place at wing-half before succeeding Hilditch at the centre of the defence. He later switched to left-half where he enjoyed the greater part of his United career. He gave United great service but his only honour came when he was a member of the 1924-5 Second Division promotion side. After over 200 games he left Old Trafford at the end of 1926-7, going temporarily to Aldershot, then a non-League side, before a £2,750 transfer to Blackpool where he ended his career after only eight more League games. Born in South Shields, Grimwood died at Childswickham, Worcestershire, on Boxing Day 1977, aged 79.

**JOHN GRIMWOOD**

|  | LEAGUE | | FA CUP | | TOTAL | |
|---|---|---|---|---|---|---|
|  | App | Gls | App | Gls | App | Gls |
| 1919-20 | 22 | 1 | 2 | 0 | 24 | 1 |
| 1920-21 | 25 | 4 | 2 | 0 | 27 | 4 |
| 1921-22 | 28 | 0 | 0 | 0 | 28 | 0 |
| 1922-23 | 36 | 0 | 3 | 0 | 39 | 0 |
| 1923-24 | 22 | 2 | 0 | 0 | 22 | 2 |
| 1924-25 | 39 | 1 | 1 | 0 | 40 | 1 |
| 1925-26 | 7 | 0 | 1 | 0 | 8 | 0 |
| 1926-27 | 17 | 0 | 0 | 0 | 17 | 0 |
|  | 196 | 8 | 9 | 0 | 205 | 8 |

An inside-right and occasionally a centre-forward, Harold Halse was a great opportunist. Born in Leytonstone, Halse started his career with Barking Town and enjoyed spells with Clapton Orient and Southend United, where he earned a reputation as a prolific goalscorer. United signed him in 1907 and although he was never leading scorer at the club, he complimented Sandy Turnbull well. It was from Halse's shot, which rebounded from the Bristol City crossbar, that Turnbull scored the only goal of the 1909 FA Cup Final. Halse added a Championship medal with United and a second Cup winners' medal in 1913, by which time he was with Aston Villa. Two years later Halse made his third Cup Final appearance, with Chelsea. In 1921, aged 32, he joined Charlton, retiring two years later. Small and slightly built, Halse nevertheless enjoyed a successful 16-year League career. He won one England cap, scoring twice in the 8-1 win over Austria in 1909. He died in April 1951, aged 65.

|         | LEAGUE | | FA CUP | | TOTAL | |
|---------|-----|-----|-----|-----|-----|-----|
|         | App | Gls | App | Gls | App | Gls |
| 1907-08 | 6   | 4   | 0   | 0   | 6   | 4   |
| 1908-09 | 29  | 14  | 6   | 4   | 35  | 18  |
| 1909-10 | 27  | 6   | 1   | 0   | 28  | 6   |
| 1910-11 | 23  | 9   | 2   | 1   | 25  | 10  |
| 1911-12 | 24  | 8   | 6   | 4   | 30  | 12  |
|         | 109 | 41  | 15  | 9   | 124 | 50  |

**HAROLD HALSE**

**JAMES HANSON**

An outstanding schoolboy footballer, Manchester-born James Hanson played three times for England Schools and each time he won a cap in a different county, appearing in Liverpool, Swansea and Glasgow. He played for Bradford Parish, Stalybridge Celtic and Manchester North End before joining United in 1924-5. He made his League debut at home to Hull City on 15 November 1924, nine days after his 20th birthday. Hanson replaced Bill Henderson, the regular centre-forward, and scored a goal. He scored in the next two games but then had to make way for Henderson's return and waited until the following September when, at Villa Park, he scored yet again. Goals came easily to Hanson and he established a regular first-team place. In 1928-9, he was United's only ever-present and the team's leading scorer. He was enjoying a new role as a goalscoring inside-forward when, after 18 matches of the following season, he suffered an injury which ended his career. Hanson's last League game was against Birmingham on Christmas Day, 1929.

|         | LEAGUE | | FA CUP | | TOTAL | |
|---------|-----|-----|-----|-----|-----|-----|
|         | App | Gls | App | Gls | App | Gls |
| 1924-25 | 3   | 3   | 0   | 0   | 3   | 3   |
| 1925-26 | 24  | 5   | 2   | 0   | 26  | 5   |
| 1926-27 | 21  | 5   | 1   | 0   | 22  | 5   |
| 1927-28 | 30  | 10  | 5   | 4   | 35  | 14  |
| 1928-29 | 42  | 19  | 1   | 1   | 43  | 20  |
| 1929-30 | 18  | 5   | 0   | 0   | 18  | 5   |
|         | 138 | 47  | 9   | 5   | 147 | 52  |

Although he played only four League games for United, in 1908-9, Harold Hardman served the club for over half a century as a director, as well as being one of the Edwardian game's best footballers. Born at Kirkmanstwhite, Manchester, in April 1882, Hardman was a small and elusive winger who won an Olympic Games soccer gold medal with the Great Britain team in 1908, the year he left Everton for United. Hardman, who also played for Northern Nomads, Blackpool, Bradford City and Stoke, appeared in consecutive FA Cup Finals for Everton (1906 and 1907), joining Manchester City's S.B.Ashworth and Wolves' Rev K.R.G.Hunt as the only amateurs to win FA Cup winners' medals this century. With Everton, Hardman won four full England caps. After he retired he went on to become one of the game's finest administrators. A solicitor with offices in the centre of Manchester, he was chairman of United from 1951 until his death in June 1965, when he was succeeded by Louis Edwards. Hardman was also an FA councillor, president of the Lancashire FA and associated with the Central League.

| | LEAGUE | | FA CUP | | TOTAL | |
|---|---|---|---|---|---|---|
| | App | Gls | App | Gls | App | Gls |
| 1908-09 | 4 | 0 | 0 | 0 | 4 | 0 |
| | 4 | 0 | 0 | 0 | 4 | 0 |

**HAROLD HARDMAN**

**VINCE HAYES**

Rochdale-born Vince Hayes enjoyed two spells with United. Capable of playing in defence or in the forward line, he made his League debut for Newton Heath at centre-half against Walsall in 1901. The following season he was drafted into the side at inside-left and played in the final 16 games. During the next campaign, the club's first as Manchester United, Hayes played only twice, in his original position of centre-half, and did not regain a regular place until 1903-04, this time at full-back. He then lost his place to Fitchett and in 1905 moved to Brentford. After three years in London, during which time United won their first League title, Hayes returned to the club. He won a place at full-back and played in that season's FA Cup winning team. Despite winning Football League representative honours in 1910, he played only once in United's 1910-11 title-winning side. He moved to Bradford and ended his playing career at Park Avenue in 1912 after nearly 150 League games. Hayes later managed Preston 1919-23.

| | LEAGUE | | FA CUP | | TOTAL | |
|---|---|---|---|---|---|---|
| | App | Gls | App | Gls | App | Gls |
| 1900-01 | 1 | 0 | 0 | 0 | 1 | 0 |
| 1901-02 | 16 | 1 | 0 | 0 | 16 | 1 |
| 1902-03 | 2 | 0 | 0 | 0 | 2 | 0 |
| 1903-04 | 21 | 0 | 3 | 0 | 24 | 0 |
| 1904-05 | 22 | 1 | 3 | 0 | 25 | 1 |
| 1908-09 | 22 | 0 | 6 | 0 | 28 | 0 |
| 1909-10 | 30 | 0 | 1 | 0 | 31 | 0 |
| 1910-11 | 1 | 0 | 0 | 0 | 1 | 0 |
| | 115 | 2 | 13 | 0 | 128 | 2 |

When David Herd turned out at inside-left for Stockport County in the final game of 1950-51 and his father, Alec, played inside-right, it was only the second time that father and son had played in the same League team. Alec Herd won FA Cup and Championship medals with Manchester City and his son was to emulate that feat with Manchester United. After five years at Edgeley Park, David Herd moved to Arsenal in 1954 for £8,000. Well-built, with a powerful shot, he could play inside or centre-forward, although one of his five Scotland caps saw him wear the number-seven shirt. In 1960-61, he finished second to Jimmy Greaves as Division One's leading scorer and that summer United paid £35,000 for his signature. Herd returned to London to make his United debut, against West Ham on the opening day of the season, and he ended the campaign as top scorer for the club. His two goals in the 1963 FA Cup Final repaid a large part of his fee and he was a key member of the 1965 and 1967 Championship teams. He played only a handful of games in United's

**DAVID HERD**

European Cup winning season and in the summer of 1968 moved to Stoke City. He signed for League of Ireland club Waterford in December 1970, but three months later became manager of Lincoln City where he remained for 21 months. In November 1966, Herd scored an unusual hat-trick for United, scoring past three different goalkeepers — Jim Montgomery who went off injured, his replacement Charlie Hurley, and his deputy John Parke. Herd added a fourth in United's 5-0 win over Sunderland. A good cricketer, David is the opening bat for Cheadle Hulme, one of Cheshire's top club sides.

| | LEAGUE | | FA CUP | | FL CUP | | EUROPE | | TOTAL | |
|---|---|---|---|---|---|---|---|---|---|---|
| | App | Gls | App | Gls | App | Gls | App | Gls | App | Gls |
| 1961-62 | 27 | 14 | 5 | 3 | 0 | 0 | 0 | 0 | 32 | 17 |
| 1962-63 | 37 | 19 | 6 | 2 | 0 | 0 | 0 | 0 | 43 | 21 |
| 1963-64 | 30 | 20 | 7 | 4 | 0 | 0 | 6 | 3 | 43 | 27 |
| 1964-65 | 37 | 20 | 7 | 2 | 0 | 0 | 11 | 6 | 55 | 28 |
| 1965-66 | 36/1 | 24 | 7 | 3 | 0 | 0 | 7 | 5 | 50/1 | 32 |
| 1966-67 | 28 | 16 | 2 | 1 | 1 | 1 | 1 | 0 | 32 | 18 |
| 1967-68 | 6 | 1 | 1 | 0 | 0 | 0 | 0 | 0 | 7 | 1 |
| | 201/1 | 114 | 35 | 15 | 1 | 1 | 25 | 14 | 262/1 | 144 |

Clarrie Hilditch had 16 seasons with United, his only club, and there can be few players who spent so long with the Reds without winning a major honour. Born in Hartford, near Northwich, Hilditch began his career as a centre-forward with Witton Albion and joined United from Altrincham in 1916. During the war he served as a London-based clerk in a cavalry regiment. When League soccer resumed, Hilditch went straight into United's first-team as first-choice centre-half and for the next five seasons was a virtual ever-present, equally at home in any of the half-back positions. He played for England against Wales in a 1919 Victory International and against South Africa in the 1920 Commonwealth internationals. When John Chapman was suspended following an FA directive in 1924, Hilditch was appointed player-manager until Herbert Bamlett took over the following April. Hilditch played his last game for United on 30 January 1932, against Nottingham Forest.

| | LEAGUE | | FA CUP | | TOTAL | |
|---|---|---|---|---|---|---|
| | App | Gls | App | Gls | App | Gls |
| 1919-20 | 32 | 2 | 2 | 0 | 34 | 2 |
| 1920-21 | 34 | 1 | 0 | 0 | 34 | 1 |
| 1921-22 | 29 | 0 | 1 | 0 | 30 | 0 |
| 1922-23 | 32 | 1 | 3 | 0 | 35 | 1 |
| 1923-24 | 41 | 0 | 2 | 0 | 43 | 0 |
| 1924-25 | 4 | 0 | 1 | 0 | 5 | 0 |
| 1925-26 | 28 | 1 | 3 | 0 | 31 | 1 |
| 1926-27 | 16 | 0 | 3 | 0 | 19 | 0 |
| 1927-28 | 5 | 0 | 0 | 0 | 5 | 0 |
| 1928-29 | 11 | 1 | 0 | 0 | 11 | 1 |
| 1929-30 | 27 | 1 | 1 | 0 | 28 | 1 |
| 1930-31 | 25 | 0 | 4 | 0 | 29 | 0 |
| 1931-32 | 17 | 0 | 1 | 0 | 18 | 0 |
| | 301 | 7 | 21 | 0 | 322 | 7 |

**CLARRIE HILDITCH**

When Tommy Docherty brought Gordon Hill and Steve Coppell from Division Three football in 1975, he acquired two young wingers with flair who completed his plan for a 4-2-4 formation. United played some of the most attractive football seen for years. Hill cost United £70,000 when he signed from Millwall in November 1975. Within months he was playing for England — which cost United a further £10,000 — and after scoring twice in the FA Cup semi-final against Derby County, stepped out for the 1976 Final against Southampton. United lost but Hill collected a winners' medal the following year against Liverpool. In both games he was replaced by David McCreery, the only instance of a player being substituted in two different Wembley Finals. A disagreement at Old Trafford resulted in Hill joining Derby, when Tommy Docherty signed him for a second time, for £250,000. QPR, who had once released Hill as a junior, bought him for £175,000 in November 1979 and again the buying manager was Docherty. After a career spanning nearly 300 senior games, Hill, who won six full caps, starting with a 3-2 win over Italy in New York, went on to play for Chicago Sting and Montreal Manic in the NASL and later performed in the American indoor soccer league (1982-85). At the beginning of 1985-6, Hill had a trial with Bournemouth. His other clubs included HJK Helsinki and Twente Enschede. He was caretaker manager of Northwich Victoria, played for Stafford Rangers and then returned to Northwich as player-coach in January 1988.

|  | LEAGUE | | FA CUP | | FL CUP | | EUROPE | | TOTAL | |
|---|---|---|---|---|---|---|---|---|---|---|
|  | App | Gls | App | Gls | App | Gls | App | Gls | App | Gls |
| 1975-76 | 26 | 7 | 7 | 3 | 0 | 0 | 0 | 0 | 33 | 10 |
| 1976-77 | 38/1 | 15 | 7 | 2 | 6 | 4 | 4 | 1 | 55/1 | 22 |
| 1977-78 | 36 | 17 | 3 | 1 | 1 | 0 | 4 | 1 | 44 | 19 |
| | 100/1 | 39 | 17 | 6 | 7 | 4 | 8 | 2 | 132/1 | 51 |

**GORDON HILL**

In a career spanning 17 years, Ernest Hine played in 612 League games and scored 287 goals, yet his goalscoring touch deserted him during his spell at Old Trafford. It is fair to say that he played in one of United's poorest sides, the 1933-4 team which narrowly avoided relegation to the Third Division. Hine, a centre-forward or inside-right, signed from Huddersfield Town in February 1933 and left in December 1934 to return to his first-ever League club, Barnsley. Born in Barnsley in April 1900, Hine signed professional for his hometown club in 1922 but it was during his six-year career with Leicester (1926-32) that he enjoyed the best of his career, winning six England caps. From there he went to Huddersfield in May 1932 and less than a year later joined United. After returning to Oakwell, Hine played for another four years before taking up a coaching post with the Colliers. An unassuming character he was a great opportunist and possessed a deadly shot but, sadly, he won no club honours in his lengthy career. Hine died in 1974 at the age of 74.

|  | LEAGUE | | FA CUP | | TOTAL | |
|---|---|---|---|---|---|---|
|  | App | Gls | App | Gls | App | Gls |
| 1932-33 | 14 | 5 | 0 | 0 | 14 | 5 |
| 1933-34 | 33 | 6 | 2 | 0 | 35 | 6 |
| 1934-35 | 4 | 1 | 0 | 0 | 4 | 1 |
| | 51 | 12 | 2 | 0 | 53 | 12 |

**ERNEST HINE**

One of the few local discoveries to break into United's first team in the early part of this century, Dick Holden came from Middleton. He joined the club from Tonge in 1904 and made his debut in the final match of 1904-05, replacing Bonthron at right-back in the home match against Blackpool. He replaced Bonthron again the following season and when the experienced defender returned, Holden switched to left-back to partner him. When Bonthron moved to Sunderland in 1907, Holden returned to right-back and appeared in the first 26 matches of the 1907-08 Championship winning season. He played in an England trial match in 1908. He lost his place to new signing George Stacey and missed an FA Cup winners' medal in 1909, and a second Championship medal in 1911. The knee injury which had dogged his career finally forced his retirement in 1912-13. His loyalty to United was rewarded in 1910 when he shared a benefit match with John Peden, against Newcastle United at Old Trafford.

**DICK HOLDEN**

| | LEAGUE | | FA CUP | | TOTAL | |
|---|---|---|---|---|---|---|
| | App | Gls | App | Gls | App | Gls |
| 1904-05 | 1 | 0 | 0 | 0 | 1 | 0 |
| 1905-06 | 27 | 0 | 4 | 0 | 31 | 0 |
| 1906-07 | 27 | 0 | 2 | 0 | 29 | 0 |
| 1907-08 | 26 | 0 | 3 | 0 | 29 | 0 |
| 1908-09 | 2 | 0 | 0 | 0 | 2 | 0 |
| 1909-10 | 7 | 0 | 0 | 0 | 7 | 0 |
| 1910-11 | 8 | 0 | 0 | 0 | 8 | 0 |
| 1911-12 | 6 | 0 | 2 | 0 | 8 | 0 |
| 1912-13 | 2 | 0 | 0 | 0 | 2 | 0 |
| | 106 | 0 | 11 | 0 | 117 | 0 |

**JIM HOLTON**

Born in the Strathclyde town of Lesmahagow (pop. 3,500), Jim Holton became their favourite 'son' when Tommy Docherty signed him for United in 1973. After failing to make the grade as a West Brom apprentice, Holton played League football for Shrewsbury Town before Docherty signed him for £80,000. Within four months of moving to Old Trafford, the strapping centre-half made the first of his 15 full international appearances for Scotland. He made his United debut along with another newcomer, Lou Macari, against West Ham in January 1973. When United romped away with the Second Division title in 1974-5, the only black mark on the season was when Holton broke a leg. Nine months later he broke it again, in a reserve match and by then Brian Greenhoff had taken over the centre-half spot. Holton signed for Sunderland, for £40,000. He ended his career at Sheffield Wednesday, with nearly 250 League games to his name, he then became a publican. In 1973-4, Holton became the first 'Anglo' to win the Scottish Football Writers' Player of the Year Award. He played in USA for Miami Toros in 1976 and Detroit Express in 1980.

| | LEAGUE | | FA CUP | | FL CUP | | TOTAL | |
|---|---|---|---|---|---|---|---|---|
| | App | Gls | App | Gls | App | Gls | App | Gls |
| 1972-73 | 15 | 3 | 0 | 0 | 0 | 0 | 15 | 3 |
| 1973-74 | 34 | 2 | 2 | 0 | 1 | 0 | 37 | 2 |
| 1974-75 | 14 | 0 | 0 | 0 | 3 | 0 | 17 | 0 |
| | 63 | 5 | 2 | 0 | 4 | 0 | 69 | 5 |

Born in Dunoon, Stewart Houston's first League club was Chelsea who he joined in August 1967 when Tommy Docherty was in charge. Docherty left two months later and Houston never made the grade at Stamford Bridge. He moved to Brentford for a £17,000 fee and it was his performances at left-back for the Bees which persuaded Docherty to buy him for United in December 1973, for £55,000. Houston was one of several Scots recruited by Docherty in his early days at Old Trafford. Houston went straight into United's League side, making his debut against QPR in what was George Best's last game for the Reds. Houston was a member of the side beaten in the 1976 FA Cup Final, and the following year missed the Final, which United won, when he broke an ankle at Ashton Gate only two weeks before the Wembley date. Houston left United in the summer of 1980, joining Sheffield United on a free transfer. In 1983, he moved to Colchester United and scored five goals in over 100 appearances. He gained one full Scotland cap. In 1990 he was a member of the Arsenal coaching staff.

**STEWART HOUSTON**

| | LEAGUE | | FACUP | | FLCUP | | EUROPE | | TOTAL | |
|---|---|---|---|---|---|---|---|---|---|---|
| | App | Gls | App | Gls | App | Gls | App | Gls | App | Gls |
| 1973-74 | 20 | 2 | 0 | 0 | 0 | 0 | 0 | 0 | 20 | 2 |
| 1974-75 | 40 | 6 | 2 | 0 | 6 | 1 | 0 | 0 | 48 | 7 |
| 1975-76 | 42 | 2 | 7 | 0 | 3 | 0 | 0 | 0 | 52 | 2 |
| 1976-77 | 36 | 3 | 6 | 1 | 5 | 1 | 4 | 0 | 51 | 5 |
| 1977-78 | 31 | 0 | 3 | 0 | 0 | 0 | 2/1 | 0 | 36/1 | 0 |
| 1978-79 | 21/1 | 0 | 2 | 0 | 1 | 0 | 0 | 0 | 24/1 | 0 |
| 1979-80 | 14 | 0 | 2 | 0 | 1 | 0 | 0 | 0 | 17 | 0 |
| | 204/1 | 13 | 22 | 1 | 16 | 2 | 6/1 | 0 | 248/2 | 16 |

Mark Hughes' rise established him as one of the hottest properties on the British soccer scene and less than three years after his first-team debut, he was the subject of a £2 million approach by Spanish Champions, Barcelona. A product of United's junior system, Hughes was a midfielder later converted to centre-forward with the Youth and Reserve teams before making his first-team debut. He came on as substitute for Norman Whiteside in the home Milk Cup match against Port Vale in October 1983 and his next game was in the European Cup-winners' Cup tie against Spartak Varna the following month. Hughes had to wait until March 1984 for his first full League match, when he scored against Leicester. Thereafter, he was a regular choice and was top-scorer in his first full season of 1984-5, collecting an FA Cup winners' medal at the end of that campaign. Born in Wrexham, he won his first full cap for Wales on his home-town ground, when he scored the only goal of the game against England in May 1984. He formed a fine dual spearhead in the Welsh side with Ian Rush and although he scored some spectacular goals, few can have bettered his magnificent effort in the World Cup qualifier against Spain at Wrexham in 1985. Hughes was voted PFA Young Player of the Year at the end of that season. In 1985-6, however, Hughes found goals harder to come by and at one point he lost his place. Barcelona were undaunted and at the end of the season, Hughes signed for them for £2,300,000. He had a loan spell at Bayern Munich before returning to United for £1,500,000 in June 1988. He received his second PFA award in 1989 when he was voted Player of the Year by his fellow professionals. The following year his two goals in the 3-3 draw with Crystal Palace at Wembley kept United in the FA Cup. A year later his two goals helped United to win their second European trophy, the Cup-winners' Cup, and Hughes uniquely won the PFA's senior award for the second time.

**MARK HUGHES**

| | LEAGUE | | FACUP | | FLCUP | | EUROPE | | TOTAL | |
|---|---|---|---|---|---|---|---|---|---|---|
| | App | Gls | App | Gls | App | Gls | App | Gls | App | Gls |
| 1983-84 | 7/4 | 4 | 0 | 0 | 1/1 | 1 | 2/2 | 0 | 10/7 | 5 |
| 1984-85 | 38 | 16 | 7 | 3 | 2 | 3 | 8 | 2 | 55 | 24 |
| 1956-86 | 40 | 17 | 3 | 1 | 2 | 0 | - | - | 45 | 18 |
| 1988-89 | 38 | 14 | 7 | 2 | 3 | 0 | - | - | 48 | 16 |
| 1989-90 | 36/1 | 13 | 8 | 2 | 3 | 0 | - | - | 47/1 | 15 |
| 1990-91 | 29/2 | 10 | 3 | 2 | 9 | 6 | 7/1 | 3 | 48/3 | 21 |
| 1991-92 | 39/1 | 11 | 2/1 | 1 | 6 | 0 | 4 | 2 | 51/2 | 14 |
| | 227/8 | 85 | 30/1 | 11 | 26/1 | 10 | 21/3 | 7 | 304/13 | 113 |

Paul Ince moved to Manchester United during the time that Michael Knighton was involved with the club. The West Ham player was all set to follow Gary Pallister and become United's second £2 million player, but a medical examination revealed a pelvic problem. However, a Harley Street specialist eventually gave the all-clear but the fee United agreed with the London club was for a payment of £800,000, followed by instalments of £5,000 per match. Paul made his debut in the 5-1 thrashing of the surprise First Division table-toppers Millwall on 16 September 1989. Two days later, Ince scored two goals in United's 3-2 home win over Portsmouth in the Littlewoods Cup. Those early fitness doubts have subsequently proved unfounded and he has established himself as a regular first-teamer. He won a Rumbelows Cup-winners' medal against Nottingham Forest in 1992, adding this to the European Cup-winners' Cup medal he had gained against Barcelona the previous season. Ince was born in Ilford on 21 October 1967 and joined West Ham as a trainee upon leaving school. He made 72 League appearances for the Hammers, scoring seven goals, before his move to Manchester United. In 1992 he was capped by England 'B' against France.

|  | LEAGUE | | FA CUP | | FLCUP | | EUROPE | | TOTAL | |
|---|---|---|---|---|---|---|---|---|---|---|
|  | App | Gls | App | Gls | App | Gls | App | Gls | App | Gls |
| 1989-90 | 25/1 | 0 | 6/1 | 0 | 3 | 2 | 0 | 0 | 34/2 | 2 |
| 1990-91 | 31 | 3 | 2 | 0 | 6 | 0 | 7 | 0 | 46 | 3 |
| 1991-92 | 31/1 | 3 | 3 | 0 | 6/1 | 0 | 3 | 0 | 43/2 | 3 |
|  | 87/2 | 6 | 11/1 | 0 | 15/1 | 2 | 10 | 0 | 123/4 | 8 |

**PAUL INCE**

*Paul Ince, extreme left, celebrates with his teammates after United's 1990 FA Cup Final replay victory over Crystal Palace.*

Steve James hails from Coseley, near Wolverhampton, and for United he proved an effective defender with a powerful tackle. He joined the club as a 16-year-old and signed professional in December 1966, a few days after his 17th birthday. He made his United debut in front of 53,000 fans at Anfield in October 1968 and won a regular first-team place in the latter half of that season, but was overlooked in 1969-70 after the signing of Ian Ure. James returned to first-team football two years later, but then found himself in and out of the side for three seasons. In January 1976, he joined York City with his final game for United no doubt still fresh in his memory. It was the last match of 1974-5 when United, as Second Division Champions, entertained Blackpool before nearly 59,000 fans. His next League game was for York against West Brom when only 5,628 turned up to watch. After 105 League games for York, James left in May 1980 and returned to his native West Midlands to play for Kidderminster Harriers and later Tipton Town. He became licensee of a pub at Ocker Hill.

| | LEAGUE | | FA CUP | | FL CUP | | EUROPE | | TOTAL | |
|---|---|---|---|---|---|---|---|---|---|---|
| | App | Gls | App | Gls | App | Gls | App | Gls | App | Gls |
| 1968-69 | 21 | 1 | 6 | 0 | 0 | 0 | 2 | 0 | 29 | 1 |
| 1969-70 | 2 | 0 | 0 | 0 | 1 | 0 | 0 | 0 | 3 | 0 |
| 1970-71 | 13 | 0 | 0 | 0 | 3/1 | 0 | 0 | 0 | 16/1 | 0 |
| 1971-72 | 37 | 1 | 5 | 0 | 6 | 0 | 0 | 0 | 48 | 1 |
| 1972-73 | 22 | 0 | 0 | 0 | 4 | 0 | 0 | 0 | 26 | 0 |
| 1973-74 | 21 | 2 | 1 | 0 | 1 | 0 | 0 | 0 | 23 | 2 |
| 1974-75 | 13 | 0 | 0 | 0 | 2 | 0 | 0 | 0 | 15 | 0 |
| | 129 | 4 | 12 | 0 | 17/1 | 0 | 2 | 0 | 160/1 | 4 |

**STEVE JAMES**

In the mid-1950s, the United half-back line of Eddie Colman, Mark Jones and Duncan Edwards was one of the finest in Europe. Colman and Edwards were the footballing wing-halves, whilst Jones was the quite brilliant stopper centre-half. He was born in Barnsley, home of tough footballers, and gained England Schoolboy international honours before going through United's junior ranks then turning professional in July 1950. He made his debut only three months later, in a 3-1 win over Sheffield Wednesday, and eventually won a regular place in 1955 when he took over from Allenby Chilton. Jones was ever-present when United won the Championship in 1955-6 and was a member of the team which retained the title 12 months later, although he lost his place to Jackie Blanchflower towards the end of the season. Jones therefore missed the 1957 FA Cup Final against Aston Villa, but had regained his place by the end of that year and played in the last match before the Munich air disaster in which he was killed.

**MARK JONES**

| | LEAGUE | | FA CUP | | EUROPE | | TOTAL | |
|---|---|---|---|---|---|---|---|---|
| | App | Gls | App | Gls | App | Gls | App | Gls |
| 1950-51 | 4 | 0 | 0 | 0 | 0 | 0 | 4 | 0 |
| 1951-52 | 3 | 0 | 0 | 0 | 0 | 0 | 3 | 0 |
| 1952-53 | 2 | 0 | 0 | 0 | 0 | 0 | 2 | 0 |
| 1953-54 | 0 | 0 | 0 | 0 | 0 | 0 | 0 | 0 |
| 1954-55 | 13 | 0 | 0 | 0 | 0 | 0 | 13 | 0 |
| 1955-56 | 42 | 1 | 1 | 0 | 0 | 0 | 43 | 1 |
| 1956-57 | 29 | 0 | 4 | 0 | 6 | 0 | 39 | 0 |
| 1957-58 | 10 | 0 | 2 | 0 | 4 | 0 | 16 | 0 |
| | 103 | 1 | 7 | 0 | 10 | 0 | 120 | 1 |

Tom Jones was a full-back in the traditional mould, a defender first and foremost. Going forward was not his style and in some 200 games for United he failed to score a goal. Born in Penycae, North Wales, Jones joined United from Oswestry Town in 1924-5 and played right- or left-back depending on whether Charlie Moore or John Silcock was available. In 1927-8, still a deputy, he managed 33 League games, more than either of the men he replaced. He became first choice in 1933-4, playing left-back in the crucial relegation battle against Millwall at the end of that season. By the time United were Second Division champions, two seasons later, Jones had lost his place to Billy Porter. He played only one more League game for the Reds before moving to Scunthorpe & Lindsay United, then a non-League club. Between 1926-30, Jones won four full caps for Wales.

**TOM JONES**

| | LEAGUE | | FA CUP | | TOTAL | |
|---|---|---|---|---|---|---|
| | App | Gls | App | Gls | App | Gls |
| 1924-25 | 15 | 0 | 1 | 0 | 16 | 0 |
| 1925-26 | 10 | 0 | 0 | 0 | 10 | 0 |
| 1926-27 | 21 | 0 | 0 | 0 | 21 | 0 |
| 1927-28 | 33 | 0 | 5 | 0 | 38 | 0 |
| 1928-29 | 0 | 0 | 0 | 0 | 0 | 0 |
| 1929-30 | 16 | 0 | 1 | 0 | 17 | 0 |
| 1930-31 | 5 | 0 | 0 | 0 | 5 | 0 |
| 1931-32 | 12 | 0 | 0 | 0 | 12 | 0 |
| 1932-33 | 10 | 0 | 0 | 0 | 10 | 0 |
| 1933-34 | 39 | 0 | 2 | 0 | 41 | 0 |
| 1934-35 | 27 | 0 | 2 | 0 | 29 | 0 |
| 1935-36 | 0 | 0 | 0 | 0 | 0 | 0 |
| 1936-37 | 1 | 0 | 0 | 0 | 1 | 0 |
| | 189 | 0 | 11 | 0 | 200 | 0 |

Volatile Scotsman, Joe Jordan, certainly gave fine service to all his English clubs and his country, for whom he played 52 times, scoring 11 goals. Born at Carluke, Lanarkshire, in 1951, Jordan signed for Morton who got him from Blantyre Victoria in 1968. After ten Scottish League games, Jordan was snapped up by Leeds United who paid £15,000 for him in October 1970. It proved a bargain fee and when Manchester United signed him from Elland Road in January 1978, they had to pay £350,000. It was former Leeds star, Bobby Collins, then ending his playing days at Morton, who recommended Jordan to his former club. He made his League debut in September 1971 and played in the Yorkshire club's League Championship-winning team of 1974 and in two losing European Cup Final teams, of 1973 and 1975. A great favourite at Old Trafford, Jordan played his first game for United on 28 January 1978, in an FA Cup match against West Brom. After more than 100 League games for the club he joined the exodus of British players to Italy, signing for AC Milan in the summer of 1981, for £175,000. He also played for Verona before Southampton brought him back to England in the 1984 close season, for around £100,000. Jordan soon became a favourite with the crowd at The Dell, scoring 12 goals in 48 League games, before moving to Bristol City for £50,000 in February 1987 where he eventually took over as manager. In October 1990 he became manager of Hearts.

**JOE JORDAN**

| | LEAGUE | | FA CUP | | FL CUP | | EUROPE | | TOTAL | |
|---|---|---|---|---|---|---|---|---|---|---|
| | App | Gls | App | Gls | App | Gls | App | Gls | App | Gls |
| 1977-78 | 14 | 3 | 2 | 0 | 0 | 0 | 0 | 0 | 16 | 3 |
| 1978-79 | 30 | 6 | 4/1 | 2 | 2 | 0 | 0 | 0 | 36/1 | 10 |
| 1979-80 | 32 | 13 | 2 | 0 | 2 | 0 | 0 | 0 | 36 | 13 |
| 1980-81 | 33 | 15 | 3 | 0 | 0 | 0 | 1 | 0 | 37 | 15 |
| | 109 | 37 | 11/1 | 2 | 4 | 2 | 1 | 0 | 125/1 | 41 |

**BRIAN KIDD**

Playing at Wembley is every footballer's dream; to celebrate one's 19th birthday with a goal for a side which is about to win the European Cup is pure *Roy of the Rovers* material. Yet that is exactly what happened to Brian Kidd in May 1968 when his fierce shot hit the roof of the Benfica net during United's European Cup Final triumph. Locally-born, Kidd joined United, his favourite club, as a 15-year-old and began his apprenticeship in 1966. His first-team chance came at the start of 1967-8 when he took over from David Herd, making his senior debut in the FA Charity Shield match against Spurs and he retained his place to win a European Cup-winners' medal. Kidd was involved in the move which brought George Best the only goal of the semi-final first leg against Real Madrid, and then came that Wembley triumph. He was speedy, had great attacking flair, and was capable of scoring with either foot and head. He won two full England caps before moving to Arsenal for £110,000 in 1974. After two years at Highbury, Kidd returned to Manchester in another £100,000 deal, this time to Maine Road. In March 1979, after a successful career with City, he was on the move again, this time to Everton for £150,000. With the Goodison club he had the unwelcome distinction of becoming only the second player since World War Two to be dismissed in an FA Cup semi-final, when he was sent off against West Ham in 1980. Shortly afterwards he signed for Bolton, then went to play in US soccer, with Fort Lauderdale, Atlanta Chiefs and Minnesota Strikers. He returned to play non-League football as player-manager with Barrow in 1985, joining Preston as a non-contract player and assistant manager. When Tommy Booth quit in December 1985, Kidd took over as manager but resigned shortly before Easter 1986. He returned to United on the coaching staff in July 1989 and in August 1991 was appointed assistant manager upon the departure of Archie Knox.

| | LEAGUE | | FA CUP | | FL CUP | | EUROPE | | TOTAL | |
|---|---|---|---|---|---|---|---|---|---|---|
| | App | Gls | App | Gls | App | Gls | App | Gls | App | Gls |
| 1967-68 | 38 | 15 | 2 | 0 | 0 | 0 | 9 | 2 | 49 | 17 |
| 1968-69 | 28/1 | 1 | 5 | 2 | 0 | 0 | 7 | 1 | 40/1 | 4 |
| 1969-70 | 33/1 | 12 | 9 | 6 | 6 | 2 | 0 | 0 | 48/1 | 20 |
| 1970-71 | 24/1 | 8 | 2 | 0 | 6 | 5 | 0 | 0 | 32/1 | 13 |
| 1971-72 | 34 | 10 | 4 | 0 | 5 | 0 | 0 | 0 | 43 | 10 |
| 1972-73 | 17/5 | 4 | 1 | 0 | 2 | 0 | 0 | 0 | 20/5 | 4 |
| 1973-74 | 21 | 2 | 1/1 | 0 | 1 | 0 | 0 | 0 | 23/1 | 2 |
| | 195/8 | 52 | 24/1 | 8 | 20 | 7 | 16 | 3 | 255/9 | 70 |

When Denis Law first arrived at Huddersfield Town from Aberdeen in 1956, he was a thin, bespectacled 16-year-old who looked nothing like a footballer. When Law left the game 18 years later, he looked back on more than 650 senior appearances to his name, over 300 goals, a then record number of Scotland international caps and goals, and virtually every club honour in the game. Law turned professional with Huddersfield in 1957 and the following year became Scotland's youngest player in modern times, at 18 years and 236 days when he made his debut against Wales. Matt Busby was Scotland's manager at the time and he saw Law score a fortunate debut goal when a clearance hit the youngster on the forehead before going into the net via the crossbar. There was nothing lucky about the other 29 goals Law scored for Scotland and he became one of Europe's most feared marksmen. When Manchester City signed him for £55,000 in March 1960, it was a League record fee and when he joined Torino of Italy in July 1961, it was the first time that a British club had been involved in a £100,000 transfer. He broke yet another transfer record 12 months later when United became the first English club to pay a six-figure sum for a player, Law joining them for £115,000. Law enjoyed great days at Old Trafford and thrilled crowds with his style which many older fans likened to the great Peter Doherty, for Law not only scored goals with deadly finishing: he could tackle and hassle like a defender and he covered every inch of the pitch in pursuit of victory. Goalscoring, however, was his first love and he was a great opportunist with lightning reflexes, fast and clever on the ground and quite brilliant in the air. A member of United's 1963 FA Cup winning team, he also won League Championship medals in 1965 and 1967. Honoured with the European Player of the Year award in 1964, he missed United's 1968 European Cup triumph when he was in hospital with a leg injury. Besides his full international honours, Law scored for the FIFA XI which met England in 1963 and played for the Football League and the Italian League. One of the all-time great forwards — he once scored six goals in an FA Cup match for City against Luton only to see the match abandoned and the goals wiped from his record — Law had a tempestuous and often provocative manner. In July 1973, he rejoined City and, ironically, his last League goal was the one which put United into Division Two in April 1974. His 82nd-minute backheeler sealed United's fate and Law confessed later: "I have seldom been so depressed as I was that weekend". He was back in action in 1990 playing exhibition games with George Best in Australia. He is now a commentator for BBC Radio

**DENIS LAW**

| | LEAGUE | | FACUP | | FLCUP | | EUROPE | | TOTAL | |
|---|---|---|---|---|---|---|---|---|---|---|
| | App | Gls | App | Gls | App | Gls | App | Gls | App | Gls |
| 1962-63 | 38 | 23 | 6 | 6 | 0 | 0 | 0 | 0 | 44 | 29 |
| 1963-64 | 30 | 30 | 6 | 10 | 0 | 0 | 5 | 6 | 41 | 46 |
| 1964-65 | 36 | 28 | 6 | 3 | 0 | 0 | 10 | 8 | 52 | 39 |
| 1965-66 | 33 | 15 | 7 | 6 | 0 | 0 | 8 | 3 | 48 | 24 |
| 1966-67 | 36 | 23 | 2 | 2 | 0 | 0 | 0 | 0 | 38 | 25 |
| 1967-68 | 23 | 7 | 1 | 0 | 0 | 0 | 3 | 2 | 27 | 9 |
| 1968-69 | 30 | 14 | 6 | 7 | 0 | 0 | 7 | 9 | 43 | 30 |
| 1969-70 | 10/1 | 2 | 0/2 | 0 | 3 | 1 | 0 | 0 | 13/3 | 3 |
| 1970-71 | 28 | 15 | 2 | 0 | 4 | 1 | 0 | 0 | 34 | 16 |
| 1971-72 | 32/1 | 13 | 7 | 0 | 2 | 0 | 0 | 0 | 41/1 | 13 |
| 1972-73 | 9/2 | 1 | 1 | 0 | 2 | 1 | 0 | 0 | 12/2 | 2 |
| | 305/4 | 171 | 44/2 | 34 | 11 | 3 | 33 | 28 | 393/6 | 236 |

There were many who doubted the shrewdness of Alex Ferguson's decision to bring Jim Leighton from Aberdeen when, in Gary Walsh and Chris Turner, United had two capable contenders for the goalkeeping position.

**JIM LEIGHTON**

But Ferguson knew only too well that Leighton was one of the finest 'keepers produced by Scotland and the two men had shared many moments of triumph at Pittodrie. Born at Johnstone in 1958, Leighton started his career at Deveronvale then Dalry Thistle before making his Aberdeen debut in 1978-9. He played for the Dons more than 250 times and won two League Championship medals and four Scottish FA Cup winners' medals. He also collected a European Cup-winners' Cup medal. After beating off challenges from overseas clubs for his signature, Ferguson paid a British record £750,000 for a goalkeeper in the 1988-9 season. Despite Leighton being 29 at the time, Ferguson knew there was no substitute for experience and Leighton soon gave some classy performances. He has been known to make the occasional mistake but, like all quality goalkeepers, he has the ability to forget about them and get on with the next match. He was an ever-present in his first season at Old Trafford and missed only four games in his second season, but his omission from United's line-up for the FA Cup Final replay against Crystal Palace was seen as the possible end to his United career. Leighton, though, is a great goalkeeper and is professional enough to understand his manager's reasons for leaving him out of the team. However his days at Old Trafford were numbered and after loan spells at Arsenal and Reading he joined Dundee for £200,000 in February 1992.

|  | LEAGUE | | FA CUP | | FL CUP | | TOTAL | |
|---|---|---|---|---|---|---|---|---|
|  | App | Gls | App | Gls | App | Gls | App | Gls |
| 1988-89 | 38 | 0 | 7 | 0 | 3 | 0 | 48 | 0 |
| 1989-90 | 35 | 0 | 7 | 0 | 3 | 0 | 45 | 0 |
| 1990-91 | 0 | 0 | 0 | 0 | 1 | 0 | 1 | 0 |
|  | 73 | 0 | 14 | 0 | 7 | 0 | 94 | 0 |

Born in Busby, Scotland, Arthur Lochhead signed for United in 1921 after only six League appearances for Hearts. An inside-forward who averaged a goal every three games for United, he made his debut at centre-forward in the opening game of 1921-2. It was a 5-0 defeat by Everton and set the pattern for the rest of that season as United were eventually relegated. The following season, Lochhead was joint top scorer with Ernest Goldthorpe. Outright top scorer the following season, Lochhead scored 13 times when United won promotion in 1924-5. After only five First Division appearances, he found his place under threat from Chat Rennox and in October 1926 he moved to Leicester City where he enjoyed ten seasons at Filbert Street in one of that club's most successful periods. He was a member of their side which finished League Championship runners-up in 1928-9. He scored 105 goals in 303 League games for Leicester to take his career tally to 155 goals in 450 League games. He retired during 1934-5, as Leicester dropped to Division Two. He was player-manager of City at the time.

|  | LEAGUE | | FA CUP | | TOTAL | |
|---|---|---|---|---|---|---|
|  | App | Gls | App | Gls | App | Gls |
| 1921-22 | 31 | 8 | 1 | 0 | 32 | 8 |
| 1922-23 | 34 | 13 | 3 | 0 | 37 | 13 |
| 1923-24 | 40 | 14 | 2 | 0 | 42 | 14 |
| 1924-25 | 37 | 13 | 0 | 0 | 37 | 13 |
| 1925-26 | 5 | 2 | 0 | 0 | 5 | 2 |
|  | 147 | 50 | 6 | 0 | 153 | 50 |

**ARTHUR LOCHHEAD**

Luigi Macari was born in Edinburgh, of Italian parents, in June 1949. One of the many Scottish players recruited by Tommy Docherty, Macari repaid every penny of the £200,000 United paid Celtic for him in January 1973. He spent seven years at Parkhead before moving south, and in 11 years with United he made over 400 senior appearances. A player of great flair, Macari was part of United's attractive side of the mid-1970s. He had already won two League Championship and two Scottish Cup-winners' and losers' medals with Celtic. He scored on his debut, against West Ham, but the following season saw United relegated for the first time in 37 years. Macari scored the only goal of the victory over Southampton which secured his club's promotion at the first attempt and after playing in the losing 1976 FA Cup Final team, he had a major hand in victory over Liverpool in the 1977 Final, when his shot was deflected over the line by Jimmy Greenhoff for the winning goal. Two years later he was back at Wembley again when United lost to Arsenal, but by the 1980s, although still an important member of the squad, he had made way for younger men. In July 1984, Macari took over as player-manager of Swindon Town and survived the 'sack' following a row with his assistant, former United goalkeeper Harry Gregg, to steer the Wiltshire club to promotion from Division Four in 1986. He took over from John Lyall at West Ham in 1989, but he was dogged by problems including allegations about a betting scandal and irregularities while he was at Swindon, he left West Ham in 1990 to join Stoke City who he guided back towards the Second Division.

**LOU MACARI**

| | LEAGUE | | FA CUP | | FL CUP | | EUROPE | | TOTAL | |
|---|---|---|---|---|---|---|---|---|---|---|
| | App | Gls | App | Gls | App | Gls | App | Gls | App | Gls |
| 1972-73 | 16 | 5 | 0 | 0 | 0 | 0 | 0 | 0 | 16 | 5 |
| 1973-74 | 34/1 | 5 | 2 | 1 | 1 | 0 | 0 | 0 | 37/1 | 6 |
| 1974-75 | 36/2 | 11 | 2 | 0 | 6/1 | 7 | 0 | 0 | 44/3 | 18 |
| 1975-76 | 36 | 12 | 6 | 1 | 3 | 2 | 0 | 0 | 45 | 15 |
| 1976-77 | 38 | 9 | 7 | 3 | 4 | 1 | 4 | 1 | 53 | 14 |
| 1977-78 | 32 | 8 | 4 | 3 | 1 | 0 | 2 | 0 | 39 | 11 |
| 1978-79 | 31/1 | 6 | 5 | 0 | 1 | 0 | 0 | 0 | 37/1 | 6 |
| 1979-80 | 39 | 9 | 2 | 0 | 3 | 0 | 0 | 0 | 44 | 9 |
| 1980-81 | 37/1 | 9 | 3 | 0 | 2 | 0 | 1 | 0 | 43/1 | 9 |
| 1981-82 | 10/1 | 2 | 0/1 | 0 | 0 | 0 | 0 | 0 | 10/2 | 2 |
| 1982-83 | 2/7 | 2 | 0/1 | 0 | 1/2 | 0 | 0/1 | 0 | 3/11 | 2 |
| 1983-84 | 0/5 | 0 | 0/1 | 0 | 0/2 | 0 | 2 | 0 | 2/8 | 0 |
| | 311/18 | 78 | 31/3 | 8 | 22/5 | 10 | 9/1 | 1 | 373/27 | 97 |

**NEIL McBAIN**

Neil McBain's senior playing career spanned a record 32 years. He joined his first major club, Ayr United, from his home-town team, Campbeltown Academicals, just before World War One. He played his final League game on 15 March 1947 when, as manager of New Brighton, he kept goal against Hartlepools United during an injury crisis — at the age of 51 years four months — to become the Football League's oldest player. During his long career, however, it was as a stylish wing-half or centre-half that McBain excelled. He guided the ball so delicately and delighted crowds with his artistry, as well as being a dominant figure in the air. United paid £4,600 for him in November 1921 and in his short stay at Old Trafford he won the first of three Scotland caps. In January 1923, he signed for Everton for £4,000, and later played for St Johnstone, Liverpool and Watford where he eventually became manager, the first of several such posts. He later managed Ayr United (twice), Luton Town, Leyton Orient and Watford again, and coached the Argentinian club, Estudiantes de la Plata. McBain died, aged 78, in May 1974.

| | LEAGUE | | FA CUP | | TOTAL | |
|---|---|---|---|---|---|---|
| | App | Gls | App | Gls | App | Gls |
| 1921-22 | 21 | 0 | 1 | 0 | 22 | 0 |
| 1922-23 | 21 | 2 | 0 | 0 | 21 | 2 |
| | 42 | 2 | 1 | 0 | 43 | 2 |

Alex Ferguson is a manager who has that knack of spotting talented players as well as developing his own home-bred players. And one player that Ferguson saw as a vital part of the Old Trafford machinery was Celtic striker, Brian McClair. A great opportunist in front of the goal, McClair took over the goalscoring role from Charlie Nicholas at Parkhead. Born at Belshill, he joined Celtic from Motherwell for £100,000 in 1983, having previously been on Aston Villa's books. A former university student, he did not finish his studies because of the pull of his first love, soccer. If honours degrees were awarded for goalscoring, then McClair would have passed with flying colours, for in 143 League games for Celtic he found the net 99 times. He was Scotland's Player of the Year in 1987. Celtic asked £2 million for the striker but United got him for £850,000 in 1987. In his first season he became the first United player since George Best in 1967-8 to score 20 League goals in a season. McClair's total played a large part in United's push for the League title. However, after Mark Hughes returned to United the following season, McClair found goalscoring difficult as the Welshman took control of that department. They eventually built up a relationship but towards the end of the season, McClair was played more in a midfield role. In 1989-90, his total in all three major domestic tournaments was a mere eight goals and, whilst he collected an FA Cup winners' medal, he was left out of Scotland's World Cup squad.

**BRIAN McCLAIR**

|  | LEAGUE | | FACUP | | FLCUP | | EUROPE | | TOTAL | |
|---|---|---|---|---|---|---|---|---|---|---|
|  | App | Gls | App | Gls | App | Gls | App | Gls | App | Gls |
| 1987-88 | 40 | 24 | 3 | 2 | 5 | 5 | - | - | 48 | 31 |
| 1988-89 | 38 | 10 | 7 | 3 | 3 | 3 | - | - | 48 | 16 |
| 1989-90 | 37 | 5 | 8 | 3 | 3 | 0 | - | - | 48 | 8 |
| 1990-91 | 34/2 | 13 | 3 | 2 | 9 | 2 | 9 | 4 | 55/2 | 21 |
| 1991-92 | 41/1 | 18 | 3 | 1 | 8 | 4 | 4 | 1 | 56/1 | 24 |
|  | 190/3 | 70 | 24 | 11 | 28 | 14 | 13 | 5 | 255/3 | 100 |

United's own 'super-sub', midfielder David McCreery, came on as a substitute in nearly half the League games in which he appeared for the club. He also wore the number-12 shirt in the 1976 and 1977 FA Cup Finals, replacing Gordon Hill in both games. McCreery developed through the junior ranks at Old Trafford during Tommy Docherty's spell as manager. McCreery turned professional in October 1974 and made his League debut almost immediately when he came on as substitute for Willie Morgan at Portsmouth. Docherty left United for Derby County, but when the former United boss began a second spell as QPR manager, he took McCreery to Loftus Road for £200,000 in August 1979. In the summer months, he played NASL soccer with Tulsa Roughnecks. In October 1982, he joined Newcastle United teaming up with former Liverpool stars Keegan and McDermott, and helped the Magpies win promotion to Division One at the end of 1983-4. McCreery made his full international debut for Northern Ireland in 1976 and has won over 60 caps, playing in all five of his country's matches in the 1982 World Cup Finals in Spain. He left Newcastle in the summer of 1989 and had a couple of months in Sweden and with Sundsvaal before joining Hearts in September 1989. In 1992 he signed for Hartlepool United.

**DAVID McCREERY**

|  | LEAGUE | | FACUP | | FLCUP | | EUROPE | | TOTAL | |
|---|---|---|---|---|---|---|---|---|---|---|
|  | App | Gls | App | Gls | App | Gls | App | Gls | App | Gls |
| 1974-75 | 0/2 | 0 | 0 | 0 | 0 | 0 | 0 | 0 | 0/2 | 0 |
| 1975-76 | 12/16 | 4 | 1/2 | 0 | 0/1 | 0 | 0 | 0 | 13/19 | 4 |
| 1976-77 | 9/16 | 2 | 0/3 | 0 | 3/2 | 0 | 1/3 | 0 | 13/24 | 2 |
| 1977-78 | 13/4 | 1 | 0/1 | 0 | 1 | 1 | 3 | 0 | 17/5 | 2 |
| 1978-79 | 14/1 | 0 | 0 | 0 | 0/1 | 0 | 0 | 0 | 14/2 | 0 |
|  | 48/39 | 7 | 1/6 | 0 | 4/4 | 1 | 4/3 | 0 | 57/52 | 8 |

**BILL McGLEN**

Born in Bedlington, Bill McGlen left his native North-East in 1946 when he joined United from Blyth Spartans as a 25-year-old. He was left-back in the United team which met Grimsby Town in the opening League game after the war but, towards the end of that season, moved to left-half to make way for John Aston. McGlen spent most of his days at Old Trafford as a wing-half, except for a spell at the start of 1950-51 when he was tried on the left wing. Unspectacular but steady, McGlen played only twice in 1951-2 when United won the Championship and in the close season he signed for Lincoln. He moved to Oldham Athletic in February 1953 and the Latics went on to win the season's Third Division North championship. On his retirement in May 1956, McGlen was over 35 and had totalled more than 200 appearances in senior soccer.

|  | LEAGUE | | FA CUP | | TOTAL | |
|---|---|---|---|---|---|---|
|  | App | Gls | App | Gls | App | Gls |
| 1946-47 | 33 | 1 | 2 | 0 | 35 | 1 |
| 1947-48 | 13 | 0 | 0 | 0 | 13 | 0 |
| 1948-49 | 23 | 1 | 8 | 0 | 31 | 1 |
| 1949-50 | 13 | 0 | 1 | 0 | 14 | 0 |
| 1950-51 | 26 | 0 | 1 | 0 | 27 | 0 |
| 1951-52 | 2 | 0 | 0 | 0 | 2 | 0 |
|  | 110 | 2 | 12 | 0 | 122 | 2 |

Although born in Ealing, Paul McGrath is qualified to play for the Republic of Ireland and he arrived at Old Trafford from Dublin club St Patrick's Athletic, for £30,000 in March 1982. He made his first appearance in the first team before the start of 1982-3, in the South Atlantic Fund match at Aldershot, but had to wait until that November for his League debut. McGrath took over from Kevin Moran, having been given his first competitive run-out three days earlier in the Milk Cup match against Bradford City. Tall and powerful, and cool under pressure, McGrath has been held back by a series of injuries, but since regaining his place midway through 1984-5 he held on to appear in the FA Cup Final win over Everton. He has also become an established member of the Republic of Ireland squad. McGrath was runner-up to Gary Lineker in the 1985-6 PFA Player of the Year poll. Further injuries threatened his career at Old Trafford and in 1989 he moved to Aston Villa in a £450,000 deal. He played for the Republic of Ireland in the 1990 World Cup Finals.

|  | LEAGUE | | FACUP | | FLCUP | | EUROPE | | TOTAL | |
|---|---|---|---|---|---|---|---|---|---|---|
|  | App | Gls | App | Gls | App | Gls | App | Gls | App | Gls |
| 1982-83 | 14 | 3 | 0/1 | 0 | 1 | 0 | 0 | 0 | 15/1 | 3 |
| 1983-84 | 9 | 1 | 0 | 0 | 1 | 0 | 2 | 0 | 12 | 1 |
| 1984-85 | 23 | 0 | 7 | 2 | 0 | 0 | 2 | 0 | 32 | 2 |
| 1985-86 | 40 | 3 | 4 | 0 | 4 | 1 | 0 | 0 | 48 | 4 |
| 1986-87 | 34/1 | 2 | 0/1 | 0 | 4 | 0 | 0 | 0 | 38/2 | 2 |
| 1987-88 | 21/1 | 2 | 0 | 0 | 2 | 1 | 0 | 0 | 23/1 | 3 |
| 1988-89 | 18/2 | 1 | 4/1 | 0 | 1 | 0 | 0 | 0 | 23/3 | 1 |
|  | 159/4 | 12 | 15/3 | 2 | 13 | 2 | 4 | 0 | 191/7 | 16 |

**PAUL McGRATH**

Along with Duncan Edwards, Jackie Blanchflower and Eddie Colman, Wilf McGuinness was one of the players to emerge from United's youth policy of the early 1950s. The first three gave United great service before the Munich air disaster, but McGuinness did not make the trip and his career with his home-town club spanned 18 years and ended in the managerial chair. (See *United Managers*). Born on 25 October 1937, McGuinness joined United's groundstaff as a 16-year-old, turning professional on his 17th birthday. One of the stars of the highly successful Youth team of the 1950s, he appeared in three FA Youth Cup winning teams and captained the England Youth side. He made his League debut against Wolves in October 1955, but did not make the left-half position his own until after the Munich tragedy. Even then he could not retain the position for the 1958 FA Cup Final against Bolton and was replaced by the more experienced Stan Crowther. McGuinness's career ended after he broke a leg in a Central League game against Stoke in December 1959. Forced to retire at the age of 22, he joined United's backroom staff, succeeding Sir Matt Busby at the helm in June 1969.

**WILF McGUINNESS**

|         | LEAGUE | | FA CUP | | EUROPE | | TOTAL | |
|---------|--------|-----|--------|-----|--------|-----|-------|-----|
|         | App    | Gls | App    | Gls | App    | Gls | App   | Gls |
| 1955-56 | 3      | 1   | 0      | 0   | 0      | 0   | 3     | 1   |
| 1956-57 | 13     | 0   | 1      | 0   | 1      | 0   | 15    | 0   |
| 1957-58 | 7      | 0   | 0      | 0   | 1      | 0   | 8     | 0   |
| 1958-59 | 39     | 1   | 1      | 0   | 0      | 0   | 40    | 1   |
| 1959-60 | 19     | 0   | 0      | 0   | 0      | 0   | 19    | 0   |
|         | 81     | 2   | 2      | 0   | 2      | 0   | 85    | 2   |

Even as a 15-year-old schoolboy player in 1969, Sammy McIlroy impressed Sir Matt Busby who foresaw a long and successful career for the Irish youngster. He signed for United in September 1969, turning professional two years later. On his debut, in front of 63,000 fans at Maine Road in November 1971, McIlroy scored and although he spent much of that season in a sort of 'supersub' role, he found a regular place in 1973-4 — United's relegation season — after missing half the previous season following a motor accident. McIlroy was ever-present in the Second Division Championship side of 1974-5 and by then he was an established Northern Ireland international, having won his first cap against Spain in 1972. Today, McIlroy has over 80 caps to his name. A clever midfielder also capable of scoring goals, his glancing header in the 1976 FA Cup Final defeat by Southampton might have swung the game United's way had it not hit the crossbar. McIlroy collected a winners' medal the following year when United defeated Liverpool. In 1979, he made his third FA Cup Final appearance in four years when United were beaten by Arsenal. McIlroy moved to Stoke for £350,000 in February 1982, but found himself in a struggling team. In 1984-5, as Stoke set the worst First Division record of all-time and were relegated, McIlroy battled alone and at the end of the season moved to Manchester City on a free transfer. But he played only 13 League games before joining Bury in 1986-7, after short spells in Sweden and Austria. He then became player-coach at Preston North End. Injury ended his playing career and he was appointed manager of Northwich Victoria.

**SAMMY McILROY MBE**

|         | LEAGUE | | FA CUP | | FL CUP | | EUROPE | | TOTAL | |
|---------|--------|-----|--------|-----|--------|-----|--------|-----|-------|-----|
|         | App    | Gls | App    | Gls | App    | Gls | App    | Gls | App   | Gls |
| 1971-72 | 8/8    | 4   | 1/2    | 0   | 2      | 0   | 0      | 0   | 11/10 | 4   |
| 1972-73 | 4/6    | 0   | 0      | 0   | 0/3    | 1   | 0      | 0   | 4/9   | 1   |
| 1973-74 | 24/5   | 6   | 1/1    | 0   | 0      | 0   | 0      | 0   | 25/6  | 6   |
| 1974-75 | 41/1   | 7   | 2      | 0   | 7      | 2   | 0      | 0   | 50/1  | 9   |
| 1975-76 | 41     | 10  | 7      | 3   | 3      | 1   | 0      | 0   | 51    | 14  |
| 1976-77 | 39/1   | 2   | 7      | 0   | 6      | 0   | 4      | 1   | 56/1  | 3   |
| 1977-78 | 39     | 9   | 4      | 0   | 0      | 0   | 4      | 0   | 47    | 9   |
| 1978-79 | 40     | 5   | 9      | 2   | 2      | 1   | 0      | 0   | 51    | 8   |
| 1979-80 | 41     | 6   | 2      | 1   | 2      | 1   | 0      | 0   | 45    | 8   |
| 1980-81 | 31/1   | 5   | 1      | 0   | 2      | 0   | 2      | 1   | 36/1  | 6   |
| 1981-82 | 12     | 3   | 1      | 0   | 1      | 0   | 0      | 0   | 14    | 3   |
|         | 320/22 | 57  | 35/3   | 6   | 25/3   | 6   | 10     | 2   | 390/28| 71  |

Two months after joining United, Bill McKay was involved in one of the most crucial games in the club's history. A member of the Bolton side relegated to Division Two in 1932-3, he looked certain to drop into the Third Division with United. However, McKay helped United through their vital end-of-the-season game at Millwall and two years later was collecting his first honour in the game, a Second Division championship medal. An outstanding left-half who was particularly reliable in defence, McKay was born at Harthill, Lanarkshire, and his first senior club was East Stirlingshire followed by Hamilton Academicals. After 78 Scottish League games he joined Bolton in 1929-30, the season they won the FA Cup. He was one of four newcomers recruited by United in March 1934 as they struggled to avoid relegation. All four — McKay, Griffiths (Bolton), Robertson (Stoke), and Hacking (Oldham) — made their debuts against Fulham that month and were ever-present for the rest of the season. McKay played for United right into wartime football but when League soccer resumed in 1946, he had signed for Stalybridge Celtic.

|  | LEAGUE | | FA CUP | | TOTAL | |
|---|---|---|---|---|---|---|
|  | App | Gls | App | Gls | App | Gls |
| 1933-34 | 10 | 0 | 0 | 0 | 10 | 0 |
| 1934-35 | 38 | 3 | 3 | 0 | 41 | 3 |
| 1935-36 | 35 | 0 | 3 | 0 | 38 | 0 |
| 1936-37 | 29 | 4 | 2 | 0 | 31 | 4 |
| 1937-38 | 37 | 7 | 3 | 0 | 40 | 7 |
| 1938-39 | 20 | 1 | 2 | 0 | 22 | 1 |
| 1939-40 | 2 | 0 | 0 | 0 | 2 | 0 |
|  | 171 | 15 | 13 | 0 | 184 | 15 |

**BILL McKAY**

Born in Glasgow, George McLachlan was one of a small number of footballers to have enjoyed League soccer with English, Scottish and Welsh clubs. He joined Clyde from Rutherglen in 1922-3, previously having played for Queens Park Reserves, moving to Cardiff City three years later. McLachlan's finest hour came when he played in Cardiff's 1927 FA Cup winning team, the first and only time the trophy has been won by a non-English club. A fine ball-playing outside-left, McLachlan was not noted for his goalscoring but as Cardiff dropped towards the Second Division in 1929-30, United showed no reservations in continuing the player's Division One career. They signed him on 18 December 1929 and he made his debut three days later in the 3-1 home win over Leeds United. McLachlan had four seasons at Old Trafford, making more than 100 appearances before his move to Third Division North club Chester. After one season at Sealand Road, he retired from playing and returned to Scotland to seek a new career in management.

|  | LEAGUE | | FA CUP | | TOTAL | |
|---|---|---|---|---|---|---|
|  | App | Gls | App | Gls | App | Gls |
| 1929-30 | 23 | 2 | 1 | 0 | 24 | 2 |
| 1930-31 | 42 | 2 | 4 | 0 | 46 | 2 |
| 1931-32 | 28 | 0 | 1 | 0 | 29 | 0 |
| 1932-33 | 17 | 0 | 0 | 0 | 17 | 0 |
|  | 110 | 4 | 6 | 0 | 116 | 4 |

**GEORGE McLACHLAN**

Yet another result of Louis Rocca's shrewd eye, Hugh McLenahan's transfer to United from Stockport County must rank as one of the strangest in League history — he cost United three freezers full of ice-cream. Born in Manchester, he attended St Francis' School, Gorton, and established himself as a model wing-half with Manchester, Lancashire and England Schoolboys. He joined Stockport as an amateur, after playing for Ambrose, Stalybridge Celtic and Ashton Brothers. It was not long before United spotted the youngster and signed him in 1927. Although he never held down a regular first-team place at Old Trafford, due to injuries which included a broken leg, his versatility was vital to United and he performed well in any of the half-back positions and also proved a goalscoring inside-forward when, in 1929-30, he scored six goals in five consecutive matches — and he scored only 12 in his entire career. He signed for Notts County in December 1936 and they narrowly missed promotion from Division Three South. When League soccer resumed in 1946, McLenahan was 37 and well past his best. He later became an electrician.

| | LEAGUE | | FA CUP | | TOTAL | |
|---|---|---|---|---|---|---|
| | App | Gls | App | Gls | App | Gls |
| 1927-28 | 10 | 1 | 0 | 0 | 10 | 1 |
| 1928-29 | 1 | 0 | 0 | 0 | 1 | 0 |
| 1929-30 | 10 | 6 | 0 | 0 | 10 | 6 |
| 1930-31 | 21 | 1 | 0 | 0 | 21 | 1 |
| 1931-32 | 11 | 0 | 1 | 0 | 12 | 0 |
| 1932-33 | 24 | 2 | 1 | 0 | 25 | 2 |
| 1933-34 | 22 | 0 | 2 | 1 | 24 | 1 |
| 1934-35 | 10 | 1 | 0 | 0 | 10 | 1 |
| 1936-37 | 3 | 0 | 0 | 0 | 3 | 0 |
| | 112 | 11 | 4 | 1 | 116 | 12 |

**HUGH McLENAHAN**

**FRANK McPHERSON**

Between 1923 and 1928 Frank McPherson played in all four divisions of the Football League. Born in Barrow-in-Furness, he made his debut for his home-town club in Division Three North in 1921-2. At the end of the following season, United offered him Second Division football. He slotted straight in at outside-left and, at the end of his second season at Old Trafford, he was a member of the side which won promotion from the Second Division. Second top-scorer in United's first season back in Division One, his scoring touch then largely deserted him and in September 1928 he moved to Manchester Central. Watford signed him and in his first season of Third Division South football, he netted 33 goals (six penalties) in 33 League games. The following season he scored 22 goals in 28 games before Second Division Reading signed him just before the transfer deadline. He helped them stave off relegation with eight goals in 11 games. The following season, however, Reading went down and McPherson never played outside the Third Division again. He returned to Watford in 1933, then rejoined Barrow in 1936. He was only 51 when he died in Daveyhulme in 1953.

| | LEAGUE | | FA CUP | | TOTAL | |
|---|---|---|---|---|---|---|
| | App | Gls | App | Gls | App | Gls |
| 1923-24 | 34 | 1 | 2 | 1 | 36 | 2 |
| 1924-25 | 38 | 7 | 1 | 0 | 39 | 7 |
| 1925-26 | 29 | 16 | 7 | 4 | 36 | 20 |
| 1926-27 | 32 | 15 | 3 | 1 | 35 | 16 |
| 1927-28 | 26 | 6 | 3 | 1 | 29 | 7 |
| | 159 | 45 | 16 | 7 | 175 | 52 |

Shortly after his move to Leeds United in 1972, Gordon McQueen could be found most Sunday mornings watching local amateur teams in Roundhay Park, such was his love for the game. One of the game's best 'attacking defenders', McQueen was difficult to beat and was always looking to add his name to the scorers. Born in Kilbirnie, Ayrshire, in June 1952, the 6ft 3ins centre-half joined Leeds from St Mirren for £40,000. Leeds saw him as Jackie Charlton's replacement and in over 150 games for them he won a Championship medal before his £495,000 move to Old Trafford in February 1978. A month earlier, United manager Dave Sexton had bought McQueen's great friend and Elland Road teammate, Joe Jordan. Eleven days after his move McQueen made his United debut in the toughest circumstances, defeat at Anfield. It was at Anfield in January 1984 that McQueen received the injury which kept him out of the team for the rest of the season. After a handful of appearances the following season, McQueen joined Seiko of Hong Kong. He appeared in three Wembley Finals for United: the 1979 FA Cup defeat by Arsenal, the 1983 Milk Cup defeat by Liverpool, and United's two matches against Brighton which brought them the FA Cup in 1983. Capped 30 times by Scotland, McQueen, who made his international debut against Belgium in 1974, nevertheless missed his country's appearances in the World Cup Finals, due to injury. He took over as manager of Airdrie in June 1987 but quit in May 1989 and ran a greetings card shop in Paisley. He is now coach at St Mirren. His father played League soccer for Accrington Stanley.

|  | LEAGUE | | FA CUP | | FL CUP | | EUROPE | | TOTAL | |
|---|---|---|---|---|---|---|---|---|---|---|
|  | App | Gls | App | Gls | App | Gls | App | Gls | App | Gls |
| 1977-78 | 14 | 1 | 0 | 0 | 0 | 0 | 0 | 0 | 14 | 1 |
| 1978-79 | 36 | 6 | 9 | 1 | 2 | 0 | 0 | 0 | 47 | 7 |
| 1979-80 | 33 | 9 | 2 | 0 | 2 | 0 | 0 | 0 | 37 | 9 |
| 1980-81 | 11 | 2 | 2 | 0 | 0 | 0 | 0 | 0 | 13 | 2 |
| 1981-82 | 21 | 0 | 0 | 0 | 0 | 0 | 0 | 0 | 21 | 0 |
| 1982-83 | 37 | 0 | 7 | 0 | 8 | 3 | 1 | 0 | 53 | 3 |
| 1983-84 | 20 | 1 | 0 | 0 | 4 | 1 | 4 | 0 | 28 | 2 |
| 1984-85 | 12 | 1 | 1 | 1 | 0 | 0 | 2 | 0 | 15 | 2 |
|  | 184 | 20 | 21 | 2 | 16 | 4 | 7 | 0 | 228 | 26 |

**GORDON McQUEEN**

**TOM MANLEY**

When Tom Manley hung up his boots during 1950-51, he was in his 39th year and had enjoyed a career that spanned 20 years. Born in Northwich, Cheshire, he played for the local Victoria side before signing for United in 1931-2. He was an effective outside-left, capable of scoring goals in dramatic fashion. The most important goal he ever scored — or made — came on 5 May 1934, at The Den, when his 80th-minute effort set United on the way to victory and thus, safety from the drop to Division Three. Two seasons later, United were Second Division champions. Manley scored 14 goals to supplement the goalscoring feats of the three main forwards, Bamford, Mutch and Rowley. After eight seasons at Old Trafford, he joined Brentford for the start of 1939-40 and played in their three League games before the season was abandoned because of war. Manley returned to United to play in wartime soccer, but resumed his career at Griffin Park after the war.

|  | LEAGUE | | FA CUP | | TOTAL | |
|---|---|---|---|---|---|---|
|  | App | Gls | App | Gls | App | Gls |
| 1931-32 | 3 | 0 | 0 | 0 | 3 | 0 |
| 1932-33 | 19 | 0 | 0 | 0 | 19 | 0 |
| 1933-34 | 30 | 2 | 2 | 0 | 32 | 2 |
| 1934-35 | 30 | 9 | 1 | 0 | 31 | 9 |
| 1935-36 | 31 | 14 | 3 | 1 | 34 | 15 |
| 1936-37 | 31 | 5 | 0 | 0 | 31 | 5 |
| 1937-38 | 21 | 7 | 1 | 0 | 22 | 7 |
| 1938-39 | 23 | 3 | 0 | 0 | 23 | 3 |
|  | 188 | 40 | 7 | 1 | 195 | 41 |

116

Although he won an FA Cup winners' medal with Huddersfield Town in 1922, Frank Mann missed most of the glory years at Leeds Road. An important factor in the Yorkshire club's rise to the top in the 1920s, he was the link between attack and defence, playing at inside-right or right-half. He could also score goals and netted 18 in 1919-20. Many thought he was nearing the end of his playing career when he signed for United in 1923, at the age of 32. Mann's early days at Old Trafford were spent in the Second Division, while his former Huddersfield colleagues were winning the first of three consecutive First Division titles — the first team ever to achieve that feat. Mann did, however, enjoy his moment of glory as he helped United to promotion in 1924-5 and thereafter spent the rest of his League career in the top flight. He continued to be used in the role of linkman at Old Trafford, by now using his quick-thinking brain to compensate for ageing legs. He bowed out of League soccer following United's 7-2 defeat by Sheffield Wednesday at Hillsborough in November 1929, then joined non-League Mossley.

| | LEAGUE | | FA CUP | | TOTAL | |
|---|---|---|---|---|---|---|
| | App | Gls | App | Gls | App | Gls |
| 1922-23 | 10 | 0 | 0 | 0 | 10 | 0 |
| 1923-24 | 25 | 3 | 2 | 0 | 27 | 3 |
| 1924-25 | 32 | 0 | 1 | 0 | 33 | 0 |
| 1925-26 | 34 | 0 | 7 | 0 | 41 | 0 |
| 1926-27 | 14 | 0 | 0 | 0 | 14 | 0 |
| 1927-28 | 26 | 0 | 5 | 0 | 31 | 0 |
| 1928-29 | 25 | 1 | 2 | 0 | 27 | 1 |
| 1929-30 | 14 | 1 | 0 | 0 | 14 | 1 |
| | 180 | 5 | 17 | 0 | 197 | 5 |

**FRANK MANN**

When Charlie Moore retired in 1930, United struggled to find a replacement. Tom Jones, who could play on either flank, was the immediate deputy before John Mellor was recruited from non-League Witton Albion. Mellor made his League debut in the 3-0 defeat at Huddersfield in September 1930 as United continued what was to prove the worst-ever start to a season by a League club — 12 consecutive defeats. Playing in one of United's poorest teams, Mellor missed only two League games in season 1932-3. The drop into Division Two meant that the Oldham-born defender spent most of his career in that division. When United regained their First Division place in 1936, Mellor had lost his place to John Griffiths. He played only two more matches in Division One, the last a 6-2 defeat at Grimsby, before transferring to Cardiff City who were then in Division Three South. After two seasons at Ninian Park, Mellor ended his League career.

| | LEAGUE | | FA CUP | | TOTAL | |
|---|---|---|---|---|---|---|
| | App | Gls | App | Gls | App | Gls |
| 1930-31 | 35 | 0 | 4 | 0 | 39 | 0 |
| 1931-32 | 33 | 0 | 1 | 0 | 34 | 0 |
| 1932-33 | 40 | 0 | 1 | 0 | 41 | 0 |
| 1933-34 | 5 | 0 | 0 | 0 | 5 | 0 |
| 1934-35 | 1 | 0 | 0 | 0 | 1 | 0 |
| 1935-36 | 0 | 0 | 0 | 0 | 0 | 0 |
| 1936-37 | 2 | 0 | 0 | 0 | 2 | 0 |
| | 116 | 0 | 6 | 0 | 122 | 0 |

**JOHN MELLOR**

117

Billy Meredith ranks alongside Stanley Matthews as one of the greatest outside-rights of all time. He was certainly the most celebrated Welsh international, winning 48 full caps when Welsh international soccer was restricted to the Home International Championship, and his last cap came when he was 43. His international career spanned 25 years and his League career 29 years and nearly 700 games. Born in Chirk, North Wales, the boney, bandy-legged youngster whose trade-mark became the toothpick he chewed, played with the Chirk team which was then one of Wales' finest and Northwich Victoria before joining Manchester City as an amateur in 1894. Meredith was soon thrilling Hyde Road crowds with his darting runs to the corner-flag, and his pin-point centres. He was also a deadly finisher, cutting in from the wing, and one of his 300-plus goals

won the 1904 FA Cup Final for City. Meredith moved to United in May 1906, in the wake of the bribes and illegal payments scandal which saw him and others receive lengthy suspensions. He made his United debut when the ban was lifted, on 1 January 1907 against Aston Villa, along with former City colleagues, Burgess, Bannister and Sandy Turnbull, all of whom ended their suspensions too. Meredith collected a second FA Cup winners' medal with United and was a vital member of their 1908 and 1911 Championship sides. He returned to City as a wartime guest player, and permanently in July 1921 after a row with United concerning wages.

**BILLY MEREDITH**

|  | LEAGUE | | FA CUP | | TOTAL | |
|--|--|--|--|--|--|--|
|  | App | Gls | App | Gls | App | Gls |
| 1906-07 | 16 | 5 | 2 | 0 | 18 | 5 |
| 1907-08 | 37 | 10 | 4 | 0 | 41 | 10 |
| 1908-09 | 34 | 0 | 4 | 0 | 38 | 0 |
| 1909-10 | 31 | 5 | 1 | 0 | 32 | 5 |
| 1910-11 | 35 | 5 | 3 | 0 | 38 | 5 |
| 1911-12 | 35 | 3 | 6 | 0 | 41 | 3 |
| 1912-13 | 22 | 2 | 5 | 0 | 27 | 2 |
| 1913-14 | 34 | 2 | 1 | 0 | 35 | 2 |
| 1914-15 | 26 | 0 | 1 | 0 | 27 | 0 |
| 1919-20 | 19 | 2 | 2 | 0 | 21 | 2 |
| 1920-21 | 14 | 1 | 0 | 0 | 14 | 1 |
|  | 303 | 35 | 29 | 0 | 332 | 35 |

Although small, John Mew was a safe goalkeeper who served United well between 1912 and 1926. Born in Sunderland, he joined United from Marley Hill Colliery in September 1912. After the four-week trial, United signed him and he made his League debut the following March, in a 3-2 home defeat at the hands of Middlesbrough. Edmonds, who had succeeded Moger, was the regular United goalkeeper at the time and it was during the war that Mew finally won a regular first-team place. He had exceptionally strong wrists and his excellent handling and ability to narrow the angle made him first choice. He won one England cap, in the 2-0 win over Ireland in 1920, at Sunderland. Mew was one of several goalkeepers tried by England as a possible replacement for the great Sam Hardy. In September 1926, Mew joined Barrow and a year later left to coach in Belgium and South America before returning to Manchester.

|  | LEAGUE | | FA CUP | | TOTAL | |
|--|--|--|--|--|--|--|
|  | App | Gls | App | Gls | App | Gls |
| 1912-13 | 1 | 0 | 0 | 0 | 1 | 0 |
| 1913-14 | 2 | 0 | 0 | 0 | 2 | 0 |
| 1914-15 | 1 | 0 | 0 | 0 | 1 | 0 |
| 1919-20 | 42 | 0 | 2 | 0 | 44 | 0 |
| 1920-21 | 40 | 0 | 2 | 0 | 42 | 0 |
| 1921-22 | 41 | 0 | 1 | 0 | 42 | 0 |
| 1922-23 | 41 | 0 | 3 | 0 | 44 | 0 |
| 1923-24 | 12 | 0 | 0 | 0 | 12 | 0 |
| 1925-26 | 6 | 0 | 5 | 0 | 11 | 0 |
|  | 186 | 0 | 13 | 0 | 199 | 0 |

**JOHN MEW**

118

Of the great United forward line of 1948, only Charlie Mitten never won a full international cap, although he played in a Victory international. Born at Rangoon, Burma, in January 1921, Mitten was a speedy, clever goalscoring outside-left and one of the stars of United's epic FA Cup Final win over Blackpool. He joined the club straight from school in 1936 and made wartime appearances for United and as a guest for Tranmere Rovers and Aston Villa. In 1945, he signed professional forms for United and made his debut in the first post-war League game, at home to Grimsby Town. Against Aston Villa on 8 March 1950, he became only the second man, after Villa's own Billy Walker in 1921, to score a hat-trick of penalties in a First Division game. In 1950, Mitten became one of the several players tempted to Colombian football where, it was alleged, huge rewards awaited them in the days of maximum wages for footballers in England. He left at the end of the 1949-50 season, ending a run of 113 consecutive League and Cup games for United. But the Colombian adventure failed and a year later he was back in England. United immediately transfer-listed him and in January 1952 he moved to Fulham. Four years later he signed for Mansfield Town, where he ended his League career after 395 games. He later managed Newcastle and his two sons, John and Charles, followed him into League football and were both on United's books for a while.

|         | LEAGUE |     | FA CUP |     | TOTAL |     |
|---------|--------|-----|--------|-----|-------|-----|
|         | App    | Gls | App    | Gls | App   | Gls |
| 1946-47 | 20     | 8   | 0      | 0   | 20    | 8   |
| 1947-48 | 38     | 8   | 6      | 3   | 44    | 11  |
| 1948-49 | 42     | 18  | 8      | 5   | 50    | 23  |
| 1949-50 | 42     | 16  | 5      | 3   | 47    | 19  |
|         | 142    | 50  | 19     | 11  | 161   | 61  |

**CHARLIE MITTEN**

Harry Moger was United's regular goalkeeper during their first really successful period between 1908 and 1911 when they won the League Championship twice and the FA Cup. Between 1904-05 and 1910-11 he was rarely absent from the United team. Very tall, he was safe in the air and inspired confidence in his defenders. He joined United from Southampton, then in the Southern League, in 1903 and made his United debut in the 4-0 home win over Barnsley in October that year. He bowed out in 1912, aged 33. When he joined United, Moger was regarded as the best goalkeeper in the south of England and he soon gained similar recognition in the north but surprisingly never gained international selection, despite winning three major honours with United.

**HARRY MOGER**

|         | LEAGUE |     | FA CUP |     | TOTAL |     |
|---------|--------|-----|--------|-----|-------|-----|
|         | App    | Gls | App    | Gls | App   | Gls |
| 1903-04 | 13     | 0   | 0      | 0   | 13    | 0   |
| 1904-05 | 32     | 0   | 3      | 0   | 35    | 0   |
| 1905-06 | 27     | 0   | 4      | 0   | 31    | 0   |
| 1906-07 | 38     | 0   | 2      | 0   | 40    | 0   |
| 1907-08 | 29     | 0   | 4      | 0   | 33    | 0   |
| 1908-09 | 36     | 0   | 6      | 0   | 42    | 0   |
| 1909-10 | 36     | 0   | 1      | 0   | 37    | 0   |
| 1910-11 | 25     | 0   | 2      | 0   | 27    | 0   |
| 1911-12 | 6      | 0   | 0      | 0   | 6     | 0   |
|         | 242    | 0   | 22     | 0   | 264   | 0   |

**CHARLIE MOORE**

Born in Cheslyn Hay, near Cannock, Staffordshire, Charlie Moore was 21 when he joined United from non-League Hednesford Town in May 1919. He immediately went into the League side, making his bow at Derby's Baseball Ground in the opening game of 1919-20. Totally dependable, Moore was one of the safest full-backs in the Football League. His 11-year spell at Old Trafford saw him develop a fine partnership with John Silcock, who played on the left flank. It was perhaps significant that when Moore was absent in the 1921-2 season, United finished bottom of Division One. To underline the point, he was near ever-present when they won promotion in 1925. During the 1920s, England had difficulty in finding a regular right-back and it was surprising that Moore was overlooked, even though he was playing in a struggling team. He played over 300 senior games for United, his only League club, and never got his name of the score-sheet.

| | LEAGUE | | FA CUP | | TOTAL | |
|---|---|---|---|---|---|---|
| | App | Gls | App | Gls | App | Gls |
| 1919-20 | 36 | 0 | 2 | 0 | 38 | 0 |
| 1920-21 | 26 | 0 | 0 | 0 | 26 | 0 |
| 1921-22 | 0 | 0 | 0 | 0 | 0 | 0 |
| 1922-23 | 12 | 0 | 0 | 0 | 12 | 0 |
| 1923-24 | 42 | 0 | 2 | 0 | 44 | 0 |
| 1924-25 | 40 | 0 | 1 | 0 | 41 | 0 |
| 1925-26 | 33 | 0 | 7 | 0 | 40 | 0 |
| 1926-27 | 30 | 0 | 3 | 0 | 33 | 0 |
| 1927-28 | 25 | 0 | 1 | 0 | 26 | 0 |
| 1928-29 | 37 | 0 | 2 | 0 | 39 | 0 |
| 1929-30 | 28 | 0 | 1 | 0 | 29 | 0 |
| | 309 | 0 | 19 | 0 | 328 | 0 |

The name of Kevin Moran will be in football's record books for ever, but the Manchester United central defender would gladly opt out of his place in the game's history as the first man to be sent off in an FA Cup Final. Durham referee, Peter Willis, was the man who ensured Moran's infamy when he controversially dismissed the Dublin-born footballer in the 1985 Final against Everton. Many felt that Moran's challenge on Peter Reid hardly deserved a booking, but the Irishman had to go and was also denied his medal until a few weeks later. In happier circumstances, Moran had collected a winners' medal two years earlier, when United beat Brighton in a Wembley replay. In his native Dublin, Moran was a noted Gaelic footballer but it was his ability as a soccer player which induced Dave Sexton to pay a nominal fee to the Pegasus (Eire Gaelic) club for his transfer in February 1978. Moran, a tough-tackling defender, made his United debut at Southampton in April 1979 and since the 1980-81 season was a virtual ever-present. His international career has been similarly consistent since he won his first cap for the Republic of Ireland against Switzerland in 1980. He left Old Trafford at the end of 1987-8 to join Sporting Gijon, but returned to team-up with Frank Stapleton at Blackburn in January 1990. Played for Republic of Ireland in the 1990 World Cup Finals.

| | LEAGUE | | FACUP | | FLCUP | | EUROPE | | TOTAL | |
|---|---|---|---|---|---|---|---|---|---|---|
| | App | Gls | App | Gls | App | Gls | App | Gls | App | Gls |
| 1978-79 | 1 | 0 | 0 | 0 | 0 | 0 | 0 | 0 | 1 | 0 |
| 1979-80 | 9 | 1 | 0 | 0 | 0 | 0 | 0 | 0 | 9 | 1 |
| 1980-81 | 32 | 0 | 1 | 0 | 0 | 0 | 0/1 | 0 | 33/1 | 0 |
| 1981-82 | 30 | 7 | 1 | 0 | 2 | 0 | 0 | 0 | 33 | 7 |
| 1982-83 | 29 | 2 | 7 | 1 | 7 | 2 | 1 | 0 | 44 | 5 |
| 1983-84 | 38 | 7 | 0 | 0 | 5 | 0 | 8 | 0 | 51 | 7 |
| 1984-85 | 19 | 4 | 3 | 0 | 2 | 0 | 4 | 0 | 28 | 4 |
| 1985-86 | 18/1 | 0 | 3 | 0 | 4 | 0 | 0 | 0 | 25/1 | 0 |
| 1986-87 | 32/1 | 0 | 2 | 0 | 2/1 | 0 | 0 | 0 | 36/2 | 0 |
| 1987-88 | 20/1 | 0 | 1 | 0 | 2 | 0 | 0 | 0 | 23/1 | 0 |
| | 228/3 | 21 | 18 | 1 | 24/1 | 2 | 13/1 | 0 | 283/5 | 24 |

**KEVIN MORAN**

Willie Morgan's arrival at Old Trafford, in August 1968, continued the tradition of ball-playing wing play to which United's fans had been treated over the years. Born at Sauchie, near Alloa, in October 1944, Morgan joined Burnley in 1960 as an amateur before turning professional the following year. He made his League debut in 1963 and played over 200 games before his £110,000 transfer to United. Not renowned for scoring goals, Morgan nevertheless created many for Law, Charlton, Best, Pearson and Macari. When Frank O'Farrell converted Morgan to a midfield role, he was equally effective and helped United to the Second Division title in 1974-5. He returned to Burnley in the 1975 close season and then signed for Bolton Wanderers in March 1976. In four and a half years at Burnden Park he collected another Second Division championship medal, in 1977-8. In their first season back in the top flight, Bolton completed the double over United and Morgan played in both games. In November 1978, Morgan was at the centre of a court sensation when his former United boss, Tommy Docherty, brought a libel action against him and Granada TV. The action collapsed when Docherty admitted lying under oath. In September 1980, after a spell in America with Chicago Sting and Minnesota Kicks, Morgan signed for Blackpool. He retired at the end of 1981-2 with well over 600 senior games and 21 full Scotland caps to his credit.

**WILLIE MORGAN**

| | LEAGUE | | FA CUP | | FL CUP | | EUROPE | | TOTAL | |
|---|---|---|---|---|---|---|---|---|---|---|
| | App | Gls | App | Gls | App | Gls | App | Gls | App | Gls |
| 1968-69 | 29 | 6 | 5 | 1 | 0 | 0 | 4 | 1 | 38 | 8 |
| 1969-70 | 35 | 7 | 9 | 2 | 5 | 0 | 0 | 0 | 49 | 9 |
| 1970-71 | 25 | 3 | 2 | 0 | 2 | 0 | 0 | 0 | 29 | 3 |
| 1971-72 | 35 | 1 | 7 | 1 | 6 | 1 | 0 | 0 | 48 | 3 |
| 1972-73 | 39 | 3 | 1 | 0 | 4 | 1 | 0 | 0 | 44 | 4 |
| 1973-74 | 41 | 2 | 2 | 0 | 1 | 0 | 0 | 0 | 44 | 2 |
| 1974-75 | 32/2 | 3 | 1 | 0 | 6/1 | 1 | 0 | 0 | 39/3 | 4 |
| | 236/2 | 25 | 27 | 4 | 24/1 | 3 | 4 | 1 | 291/3 | 33 |

**JOHNNY MORRIS**

It was quick-thinking inside-forward Johnny Morris, with his hurriedly-taken free-kick, who helped turn the tide for United in the 1948 FA Cup Final. Jack Rowley collected Morris' free-kick to level the scores and two late goals took the Cup to Old Trafford. Morris hailed from Radcliffe — he was born in September 1924 — and was spotted by Louis Rocca as a 15-year-old. United paid him a £10 signing-on fee and later collected a British record fee of £24,500 when Derby bought him in March 1949. Curly-haired Morris had great dribbling skills and was difficult to dispossess. He starred in United's early post-war forward line, having few peers on the field. Off it he had the audacity to query some of manager Busby's theories, which led to United transferring him. Liverpool were keenly interested in Morris, but Derby beat them for his signature and at the Baseball Ground he won three England caps. He went to Leicester City — where he was once sent-off in a pre-season public practice match — and moved to wing-half. At Filbert Street, Morris won a Division Two championship medal in 1954. In 1958 he took over as player-manager of Corby Town, then had spells with Kettering Town, Great Harwood and Oswestry Town. His brother, William, played for Rochdale.

| | LEAGUE | | FA CUP | | TOTAL | |
|---|---|---|---|---|---|---|
| | App | Gls | App | Gls | App | Gls |
| 1946-47 | 24 | 8 | 2 | 0 | 26 | 8 |
| 1947-48 | 38 | 18 | 6 | 3 | 44 | 21 |
| 1948-49 | 21 | 6 | 1 | 0 | 22 | 6 |
| | 83 | 32 | 9 | 3 | 92 | 35 |

When Ron Atkinson returned to his former club, West Brom, to buy Remi Moses in September 1981, it was a dream come true for Moses who returned home to the club he had supported since boyhood. Moses signed for Albion after leaving school in Manchester, where he was born in November 1960. He turned professional in November 1978 and made his League debut at Crystal Palace in January 1980. After three seasons at The Hawthorns, Moses signed for United in a dual-transaction which also took Bryan Robson to Old Trafford. The double-deal involved a staggering £2 million, of which Moses was rated at around £650,000. He made his United debut when he came on as substitute against Swansea City on 12 September 1981, having signed before the Robson part of the deal was finalized. Things rarely went right for this aggressive England Under-21 midfielder after he joined the Old Trafford staff. He missed the 1983 FA Cup Final through suspension and the 1985 Final through the injury which sidelined him for much of the following season. He did play in United's 1983 losing Milk Cup Final team, but struggled with injuries after that, and finally retired in 1988.

| | LEAGUE | | FA CUP | | FL CUP | | EUROPE | | TOTAL | |
|---|---|---|---|---|---|---|---|---|---|---|
| | App | Gls | App | Gls | App | Gls | App | Gls | App | Gls |
| 1981-82 | 20/1 | 2 | 1 | 0 | 1 | 0 | 0 | 0 | 22/1 | 2 |
| 1982-83 | 29 | 0 | 5 | 1 | 8 | 1 | 1 | 0 | 43 | 2 |
| 1983-84 | 31/4 | 2 | 1 | 0 | 5/1 | 1 | 5/1 | 0 | 42/6 | 3 |
| 1984-85 | 26 | 3 | 3 | 0 | 3 | 0 | 6 | 0 | 38 | 3 |
| 1985-86 | 4 | 0 | 0 | 0 | 0 | 0 | 0 | 0 | 4 | 0 |
| 1986-87 | 17/1 | 0 | 0 | 0 | 4 | 2 | 0 | 0 | 21/1 | 2 |
| 1987-88 | 16/1 | 0 | 1 | 0 | 1/1 | 0 | 0 | 0 | 18/2 | 0 |
| | 143/7 | 7 | 11 | 1 | 22/2 | 4 | 12/1 | 0 | 188/1012 | |

**REMI MOSES**

**ARNOLDUS MUHREN**

A classy midfielder, Dutch international Arnoldus Muhren started his career with the great Ajax team of the 1970s and was substitute for them in the 1972 and 1973 European Cup finals, although he never came on in either game. He moved to Twente Enschede before joining Ipswich Town for £165,000 in 1978. Muhren returned to Holland in 1981, to collect a UEFA Cup-winners' medal with Ipswich. After his contract at Portman Road expired in the summer of 1982, United acquired his services. At the end of his first season at Old Trafford, Muhren helped United to victory in the FA Cup Final replay against Brighton, scoring a second-half penalty. Earlier that season, he had to be content with a Milk Cup runners-up medal when United lost to Liverpool. He was hit by injuries towards the end of 1983-4 and his demise coincided with United dropping out of the Championship race. Thereafter, however, the Dutchman struggled to find a regular first-team place and in June 1985 he returned to Ajax and appeared in the 1987 Cup-winners' Cup Final. He was in the Dutch side that captured the 1988 European Championship. He retired from international football after the final. He was capped before and after his United days, but never when a United player.

| | LEAGUE | | FA CUP | | FL CUP | | EUROPE | | TOTAL | |
|---|---|---|---|---|---|---|---|---|---|---|
| | App | Gls | App | Gls | App | Gls | App | Gls | App | Gls |
| 1982-83 | 32 | 5 | 6 | 1 | 8 | 1 | 0 | 0 | 46 | 7 |
| 1983-84 | 26 | 8 | 1 | 0 | 2 | 0 | 5 | 0 | 34 | 8 |
| 1984-85 | 7/5 | 0 | 1 | 0 | 1 | 0 | 3 | 3 | 12/5 | 3 |
| | 65/5 | 13 | 8 | 1 | 11 | 1 | 8 | 3 | 92/5 | 18 |

Aberdeen-born George Mutch joined United from Arbroath, for £800 in May 1934. He soon adapted to English football and was an instant success at Old Trafford. He was bought as a goalscoring forward who could perhaps revive United's flagging fortunes. The previous season they had narrowly avoided relegation to the Third Division. Mutch was leading scorer in his first season, and again a year later when United won the Second Division title. High-flying Preston secured his goalscoring prowess with a £5,000 bid in September 1937 and in his first season at Deepdale, he helped North End to third place in Division One and into the FA Cup Final. At Wembley, Mutch was involved in a fairy-tale ending to the Final. With only 30 seconds to play, he was upended by Huddersfield skipper Alf Young. Mutch took the penalty himself and his shot rebounded off the bar and over the line for the only goal of the game. After the war, Mutch joined Bury before ending his playing career at Southport. Later he managed the Scottish junior club he played for as a youngster, Banks o'Dee. A schoolboy international, Mutch gained one full Scotland cap.

|  | LEAGUE | | FA CUP | | TOTAL | |
|---|---|---|---|---|---|---|
|  | App | Gls | App | Gls | App | Gls |
| 1934-35 | 40 | 18 | 3 | 1 | 43 | 19 |
| 1935-36 | 42 | 21 | 3 | 2 | 45 | 23 |
| 1936-37 | 28 | 7 | 2 | 0 | 30 | 7 |
| 1937-38 | 2 | 0 | 0 | 0 | 2 | 0 |
| | 112 | 46 | 8 | 3 | 120 | 49 |

**GEORGE MUTCH**

Born in Canada in February 1956, Jimmy Nicholl served his apprenticeship at Old Trafford before becoming a full-time professional in 1974. A fine defender, he was one of a new breed of young footballers developed by the club who blossomed in the mid-1970s. He made his League debut by coming on as substitute for Martin Buchan at Southampton in April 1975 and took over the right-back position from Alex Forsyth in 1975-6 before staking a regular place the following season. He lost his place when United signed John Gidman. After a loan spell at Sunderland, Nicholl joined Toronto Blizzard before returning to Roker Park in September 1982. He had a brief spell with Glasgow Rangers in 1983-4 before signing for West Brom. He returned to Rangers in 1986-7 for £50,000 after making 56 League appearances for West Brom. He joined Dunfermline in 1989 and a year later was appointed manager of Raith Rovers. Nicholl has an impressive international record, with Northern Ireland caps at Youth and Under-21 levels, and more than 70 full international appearances. One of the Northern Ireland stars of the 1982 World Cup Finals, Nicholl went with his country to the 1986 Finals in Mexico. In January 1992 he was appointed part-time assistant manager of Northern Ireland.

|  | LEAGUE | | FA CUP | | FL CUP | | EUROPE | | TOTAL | |
|---|---|---|---|---|---|---|---|---|---|---|
|  | App | Gls | App | Gls | App | Gls | App | Gls | App | Gls |
| 1974-75 | 0/1 | 0 | 0 | 0 | 0 | 0 | 0 | 0 | 0/1 | 0 |
| 1975-76 | 15/5 | 0 | 0/2 | 0 | 3 | 0 | 0 | 0 | 18/7 | 0 |
| 1976-77 | 39 | 0 | 7 | 0 | 5 | 1 | 4 | 0 | 55 | 1 |
| 1977-78 | 37 | 2 | 4 | 0 | 1 | 0 | 4 | 1 | 46 | 3 |
| 1978-79 | 19/2 | 0 | 6/2 | 0 | 0 | 0 | 0 | 0 | 25/4 | 0 |
| 1979-80 | 42 | 0 | 2 | 0 | 3 | 0 | 0 | 0 | 47 | 0 |
| 1980-81 | 36 | 1 | 3 | 1 | 2 | 0 | 2 | 0 | 43 | 2 |
| 1981-82 | 0/1 | 0 | 0 | 0 | 0 | 0 | 0 | 0 | 0/1 | 0 |
| | 188/9 | 3 | 22/4 | 1 | 14 | 1 | 10 | 1 | 234/13 | 6 |

**JIMMY NICHOLL**

123

Although Les Olive played only two League games for United, his outstanding devotion to the club means that he is included alongside the great players who have worn the Manchester United shirt. Olive joined the United groundstaff as a 14-year-old in 1942. He worked in the club office and played for the Junior and Reserve teams as an amateur, normally in an outfield position. In April 1953, when goalkeepers Ray Wood, Jack Crompton and Reg Allen were all injured, Olive, who had regarded himself as a full-back when he first joined the club, turned out in goal. He played in a 2-1 win at Newcastle and a 2-2 draw at home to West Brom — so he can look back on an unbeaten League career. At the time of the Munich crash, he was combining playing with the duties of assistant secretary to Walter Crickmer. Crickmer perished in the disaster and Olive took over. At the age of 30 he was one of the youngest secretaries in the League and became regarded as one of the game's most able administrators. He took his administrative skills to nearby Oldham Athletic in 1990.

|  | LEAGUE | | FA CUP | | TOTAL | |
|---|---|---|---|---|---|---|
|  | *App* | *Gls* | *App* | *Gls* | *App* | *Gls* |
| 1952-53 | 2 | 0 | 0 | 0 | 2 | 0 |
|  | 2 | 0 | 0 | 0 | 2 | 0 |

**LES OLIVE**

A Danish international, Jesper Olsen was one of a long list of world-class players to have donned a Manchester United shirt. He began his career with Danish club Naestved before joining the top Dutch side, Ajax, in 1981-2. British fans were given a taste of his skills when he scored a memorable goal for Denmark against England in a European Championship match in 1982. A self-confessed United fan since boyhood, Olsen's dreams were fulfilled when he signed for the Old Trafford club in July 1984 for a fee believed to be in the region of £350,000. He stands only 5ft 4ins tall and weighs less than 10st, but his speed and artistry make up for that. In his first season with United, Olsen won an FA Cup-winners' medal although in 1985-6, some commentators were questioning his contribution to United's cause when things were not going well. He made only ten League appearances in 1988-9 before leaving for Bordeaux in a £400,000 deal. He then joined Caen in June 1990. In March 1992 he had a trial with Stoke City.

|  | LEAGUE | | FACUP | | FLCUP | | EUROPE | | TOTAL | |
|---|---|---|---|---|---|---|---|---|---|---|
|  | *App* | *Gls* | *App* | *Gls* | *App* | *Gls* | *App* | *Gls* | *App* | *Gls* |
| 1984-85 | 36 | 5 | 6 | 0 | 2 | 1 | 6/1 | 0 | 50/1 | 6 |
| 1985-86 | 25/3 | 11 | 3/2 | 2 | 3 | 0 | 0 | 0 | 31/5 | 13 |
| 1986-87 | 22/6 | 3 | 2 | 0 | 1/1 | 0 | 0 | 0 | 25/7 | 3 |
| 1987-88 | 30/7 | 2 | 2/1 | 0 | 3/1 | 0 | 0 | 0 | 35/9 | 2 |
| 1988-89 | 6/4 | 0 | 0 | 0 | 1/1 | 0 | 0 | 0 | 7/5 | 0 |
|  | 119/20 | 21 | 13/3 | 2 | 10/3 | 1 | 6/1 | 0 | 148/27 | 24 |

**JESPER OLSEN**

124

There were many who thought Gary Pallister was overpriced when Alex Ferguson made him United's costliest signing after paying Middlesbrough £2.3 million for his services in 1989. But the England defender is a quality player and appears to be an excellent investment for United's future. Born at Ramsgate in 1965, he joined Middlesbrough from non-League Billingham Town in November 1984. He made his Middlesbrough debut against Wimbledon in 1985 and then spent a period on loan at nearby Darlington. He nearly signed permanently for the Feethams club but they could not afford the £4,000 fee. Pallister became a 'Boro regular in 1986-7 and when he signed for United in August 1989 he had 160 League games and two full caps to his credit. At 6ft 4ins, he is reminiscent of Liverpool's Alan Hansen and rarely lets anything fluster him. He made his United debut in the disappointing 2-0 home defeat by Norwich City on 30 August 1989, but the season ended on a happy note as he collected his first major domestic honour when United won the FA Cup. Pallister was the PFA Player of the Year in 1991-2.

**GARY PALLISTER**

| | LEAGUE | | FA CUP | | FL CUP | | EUROPE | | TOTAL | |
|---|---|---|---|---|---|---|---|---|---|---|
| | App | Gls | App | Gls | App | Gls | App | Gls | App | Gls |
| 1989-90 | 35 | 3 | 8 | 0 | 3 | 0 | - | - | 46 | 3 |
| 1990-91 | 36 | 0 | 3 | 0 | 9 | 0 | 9 | 1 | 57 | 1 |
| 1991-92 | 37/3 | 1 | 3 | 0 | 8 | 0 | 3/1 | 0 | 51/4 | 1 |
| | 108/3 | 4 | 14 | 0 | 20 | 0 | 12/1 | 1 | 154/4 | 5 |

**ALBERT PAPE**

Albert Pape's career with United was short — only 18 League games — but he has a special place in the club's history because he was involved in one of football's most curious transfers. Pape was a member of the Clapton Orient team selected for their game at Old Trafford on 7 February 1925, and the United match programme showed him as the London club's centre-forward. Shortly before kick-off, officials of both clubs met to discuss Pape's possible transfer to United and a deal was struck. The Football League cleared the transfer by telephone and one can imagine the fans' surprise when they were told that Pape, who was Orient's leading scorer, would be playing for United, not against them. Pape, a former Notts County and Rotherham County player, stayed at Old Trafford for eight months before signing for Fulham on 10 November 1925 staying two seasons. He then dropped out of League football returning in 1930 with Halifax Town. He died November 1955, aged 58, at Doncaster.

| | LEAGUE | | FA CUP | | TOTAL | |
|---|---|---|---|---|---|
| | App | Gls | App | Gls | App | Gls |
| 1924-25 | 16 | 5 | 0 | 0 | 16 | 5 |
| 1925-26 | 2 | 0 | 0 | 0 | 2 | 0 |
| | 18 | 5 | 0 | 0 | 18 | 5 |

125

Ted Partridge was born in the West Midlands town of Lye, but found his way to Old Trafford via Welsh club, Ebbw Vale, in 1920. A left winger or inside-left, he had great individual flair and talent. Unselfish, he was happier making goals for his fellow forwards than scoring himself. Indeed, he averaged only one League goal every 11 games throughout his career. He went into the United team shortly after signing, against Oldham in a League game, and held his place for three seasons before making way for new signing, Frank McPherson, and in United's promotion-winning season of 1924-5, he played only once. By the time he won back his place, he was approaching the age of 30 and in 1929-30, he signed for Halifax Town, playing for them for one more season of League football. He died in November 1966 aged 65.

|  | LEAGUE | | FA CUP | | TOTAL | |
|---|---|---|---|---|---|---|
|  | App | Gls | App | Gls | App | Gls |
| 1920-21 | 28 | 7 | 2 | 1 | 30 | 8 |
| 1921-22 | 37 | 4 | 1 | 0 | 38 | 4 |
| 1922-23 | 30 | 0 | 3 | 1 | 33 | 1 |
| 1923-24 | 5 | 0 | 0 | 0 | 5 | 0 |
| 1924-25 | 1 | 0 | 0 | 0 | 1 | 0 |
| 1925-26 | 3 | 0 | 0 | 0 | 3 | 0 |
| 1926-27 | 16 | 0 | 3 | 0 | 19 | 0 |
| 1927-28 | 23 | 5 | 3 | 0 | 26 | 5 |
| 1928-29 | 5 | 0 | 0 | 0 | 5 | 0 |
|  | 148 | 16 | 12 | 2 | 160 | 18 |

**TED PARTRIDGE**

United's forward line of the immediate post-war era was one of the finest ever produced by the club and Stan Pearson was its inside-left, a player of immense power who was always scheming to outwit opposing defenders. Stylish, he had the ability to score goals as well as create them for others and none can have been more important than the one he netted in the 1948 FA Cup Final which gave United a lead they were not to relinquish against Blackpool. Pearson's hat-trick in the semi-final against Derby had assured United of a Wembley place and he enjoyed a highly-successful partnership with Jack Rowley. Between them they totalled 52 of United's 95 goals on their way to the League Championship in 1951-2. Salford-born Pearson joined United from local soccer and made his League debut in a 7-1 win at Chesterfield in November 1937, aged 18. He went on to play nearly 350 first-team games for United and served them with distinction until, with Busby's youth policy bearing fruit, he ended his 17-year career with the club and signed for Bury in 1954, later playing for Chester where he eventually became manager. He found the managerial side of football much harder than playing and exchanged the pressures of League club management for the less demanding task of running a newsagent's shop.

**STAN PEARSON**

|  | LEAGUE | | FA CUP | | TOTAL | |
|---|---|---|---|---|---|---|
|  | App | Gls | App | Gls | App | Gls |
| 1937-38 | 11 | 2 | 1 | 1 | 12 | 3 |
| 1938-39 | 9 | 1 | 0 | 0 | 9 | 1 |
| 1939-40 | 3 | 1 | 0 | 0 | 3 | 1 |
| 1946-47 | 42 | 19 | 2 | 0 | 44 | 19 |
| 1947-48 | 40 | 18 | 6 | 8 | 46 | 26 |
| 1948-49 | 39 | 14 | 8 | 3 | 47 | 17 |
| 1949-50 | 41 | 15 | 4 | 2 | 45 | 17 |
| 1950-51 | 39 | 18 | 4 | 5 | 43 | 23 |
| 1951-52 | 41 | 22 | 1 | 0 | 42 | 22 |
| 1952-53 | 39 | 16 | 4 | 2 | 43 | 18 |
| 1953-54 | 11 | 2 | 0 | 0 | 11 | 2 |
|  | 315 | 128 | 30 | 21 | 345 | 149 |

When Tommy Docherty paid Hull City £200,000 for Stuart Pearson at the end of United's relegation season, 1973-4, he saw the powerful goalscorer as the man to help his side back to the top flight. Pearson responded with 17 goals as United won the Second Division championship the following season, and many of his goals were provided by Lou Macari, enjoying his new midfield role. Hull-born Pearson was an apprentice with the Tigers before signing full-time professional forms in 1968. He made his League debut at Boothferry Park, against Portsmouth on 15 April 1970. Pearson played 129 League games for Hull before his move to Old Trafford and during five years with United he won 15 full England caps. A great favourite with United's fans, he enjoyed the Wembley stage in the 1976 and 1977 FA Cup Finals, scoring in the latter game when United beat Liverpool. He was back at Wembley in 1980 as a member of West Ham's FA Cup-winning team. Pearson had signed for the Hammers for £220,000 in September 1979. The London club released him at the end of 1981-2 and he went on Jimmy Hill's 'rebel' soccer tour to South Africa and played in the NASL before a knee injury, which had frequently threatened his career, forced his retirement from the professional game. He turned to Rugby Union, occasionally playing on the wing for Sale. But he returned to soccer, as manager of Northwich Victoria in 1986 then as a coach at West Brom in 1988. He left Albion in March 1992.

**STUART PEARSON**

| | LEAGUE | | FA CUP | | FL CUP | | EUROPE | | TOTAL | |
|---|---|---|---|---|---|---|---|---|---|---|
| | App | Gls | App | Gls | App | Gls | App | Gls | App | Gls |
| 1974-75 | 30/1 | 17 | 2 | 0 | 4 | 1 | 0 | 0 | 36/1 | 18 |
| 1975-76 | 39 | 13 | 7 | 1 | 3 | 0 | 0 | 0 | 49 | 14 |
| 1976-77 | 39 | 15 | 7 | 1 | 4 | 3 | 3 | 0 | 53 | 19 |
| 1977-78 | 30 | 10 | 4 | 3 | 1 | 1 | 3 | 1 | 38 | 15 |
| 1978-79 | 0 | 0 | 2 | 0 | 0 | 0 | 0 | 0 | 2 | 0 |
| | 138/1 | 55 | 22 | 5 | 12 | 5 | 6 | 1 | 178/1 | 66 |

Born in Glasgow in 1877, John Peddie joined Third Lanark from local side, Bentinck, in 1895. Newcastle saw the 20-year-old's potential and signed him in 1897, bringing out his instinctive goalscoring ability. In his first 20 League games for Newcastle, he scored 17 goals. He totalled 62 goals in 125 League games for the Magpies, but failed to get amongst the scorers in 1901-02 and was transferred to Manchester United. He figured in United's first game under their new name, missing only four games that season and scoring 11 goals. The following season, Peddie was playing Southern League football for Plymouth Argyle, but after one season returned to Old Trafford and was once again top scorer. He stayed until 1907-08 when he returned to Scotland, joining Hearts in a deal which also took United colleagues Wombwell and Yates to Tynecastle. In 236 League games, he scored 113 goals. Peddie later emigrated to Canada where he died.

| | LEAGUE | | FA CUP | | TOTAL | |
|---|---|---|---|---|---|---|
| | App | Gls | App | Gls | App | Gls |
| 1902-03 | 30 | 11 | 6 | 4 | 36 | 15 |
| 1904-05 | 32 | 17 | 0 | 0 | 32 | 17 |
| 1905-06 | 34 | 18 | 3 | 2 | 37 | 20 |
| 1906-07 | 16 | 6 | 0 | 0 | 16 | 6 |
| | 112 | 52 | 9 | 6 | 121 | 58 |

**JOHN PEDDIE**

David Pegg was a member of United's splendid left-wing trio — Duncan Edwards and Albert Scanlon were the others — who destroyed Wolves in the first-leg of the first FA Youth Cup Final in 1953 before 21,000 spectators. Pegg played inside-left that evening as United built up a 7-1 lead. It was, however, as an outside-left that Pegg played all his senior games for United, starting with a League match at Middlesbrough in December 1952, less than three months after his 17th birthday. Born near Doncaster, Pegg joined United in September 1950, from Doncaster schools football. He won two League Championship medals, in 1956 and 1957, and played in the 1957 FA Cup Final against Aston Villa. His short career was tragically ended at Munich. He had lost his first-team place to Scanlon shortly before the Belgrade European Cup match but still made the fateful trip. An England Schoolboy, 'B' and Under-23 international, Pegg played once for the full international team, against the Republic of Ireland in 1957 when he joined United colleagues Roger Byrne, Duncan Edwards and Tommy Taylor in the England team.

|         | LEAGUE | | FA CUP | | EUROPE | | TOTAL | |
|---------|-----|-----|-----|-----|-----|-----|-----|-----|
|         | App | Gls | App | Gls | App | Gls | App | Gls |
| 1952-53 | 19  | 4   | 2   | 0   | 0   | 0   | 21  | 4   |
| 1953-54 | 9   | 0   | 0   | 0   | 0   | 0   | 9   | 0   |
| 1954-55 | 6   | 1   | 0   | 0   | 0   | 0   | 6   | 1   |
| 1955-56 | 35  | 9   | 1   | 0   | 0   | 0   | 36  | 9   |
| 1956-57 | 37  | 6   | 6   | 0   | 8   | 1   | 51  | 7   |
| 1957-58 | 21  | 4   | 0   | 0   | 4   | 3   | 25  | 7   |
|         | 127 | 24  | 9   | 0   | 12  | 4   | 148 | 28  |

**DAVID PEGG**

**JOHN PICKEN**

Inside-forward John Picken, or Jack as he liked to be called, was one of several Scots in United's team in the early part of the century. Born at Hurlford, near Kilmarnock, he played local amateur football with Hurlford before being snapped up by Bolton Wanderers in 1899. He was a member of the Bolton side which won promotion to Division One that season. After four seasons at Burnden Park, in which he scored 22 goals in 101 League games, Picken moved to Plymouth Argyle, then a Southern League team. He scored regularly for them for two seasons before United signed him in 1905. He scored on his United debut, against Bristol City, and was top-scorer in his first season. He helped United to promotion, just as he had done in his first season with Bolton, but lost his place to Sandy Turnbull at the start of 1907-08 and consequently did not win a League Championship medal, nor an FA Cup winners' medal the following season. He was rewarded with a benefit match in 1910 (along with Dick Holden) and in 1911 he collected a League Championship medal when United took the title for a second time. By the start of the following season, Picken was playing for Burnley and he later moved to Bristol City. He died at his Plymouth home in 1952.

|         | LEAGUE | | FA CUP | | TOTAL | |
|---------|-----|-----|-----|-----|-----|-----|
|         | App | Gls | App | Gls | App | Gls |
| 1905-06 | 33  | 20  | 4   | 5   | 37  | 25  |
| 1906-07 | 26  | 4   | 2   | 1   | 28  | 5   |
| 1907-08 | 8   | 1   | 0   | 0   | 8   | 1   |
| 1908-09 | 13  | 3   | 0   | 0   | 13  | 3   |
| 1909-10 | 19  | 7   | 1   | 0   | 20  | 7   |
| 1910-11 | 14  | 4   | 1   | 1   | 15  | 5   |
|         | 113 | 39  | 8   | 7   | 121 | 46  |

Despite his youthful looks, Albert Quixall brought immense experience to a team being carried along by a new generation of younger players in the aftermath of the Munich tragedy. Quixall cost United a British record £45,000 — almost £10,000 more than the previous record — when he signed from Sheffield Wednesday in September 1958. United bought a man who had scored 63 goals in 243 League games for the Owls and one, ironically, who had skippered Wednesday against United in the Reds' first game after Munich. His goalscoring touch deserted him in his first season at Old Trafford, but he rediscovered it the following year and became a regular scorer. A product of Wednesday's junior scheme, Quixall, who was born in Sheffield in August 1933, turned professional in 1950 and won two Second Division championship medals with his home town club. He also collected five full England caps to add to those won at Schoolboy, Under-23 and 'B' levels. He had to wait five years before collecting his only trophy with United, an FA Cup winners' medal in 1963. The following season he played only a handful of games and in September 1964 signed for Oldham Athletic for £7,000. In July 1966, he moved to Stockport County but retired after one season at Edgeley Park, after a career spanning more than 500 senior games. He had a short spell with non-League Altrincham before concentrating on his scrap metal business.

| | LEAGUE | | FA CUP | | FL CUP | | EUROPE | | TOTAL | |
|---|---|---|---|---|---|---|---|---|---|---|
| | App | Gls | App | Gls | App | Gls | App | Gls | App | Gls |
| 1958-59 | 33 | 4 | 1 | 0 | 0 | 0 | 0 | 0 | 34 | 4 |
| 1959-60 | 33 | 13 | 3 | 0 | 0 | 0 | 0 | 0 | 36 | 13 |
| 1960-61 | 38 | 13 | 2 | 0 | 1 | 2 | 0 | 0 | 41 | 15 |
| 1961-62 | 21 | 10 | 3 | 0 | 0 | 0 | 0 | 0 | 24 | 10 |
| 1962-63 | 31 | 7 | 5 | 4 | 0 | 0 | 0 | 0 | 36 | 11 |
| 1963-64 | 9 | 3 | 0 | 0 | 0 | 0 | 3 | 0 | 12 | 3 |
| | 165 | 50 | 14 | 4 | 1 | 2 | 3 | 0 | 183 | 56 |

**ALBERT QUIXALL**

Another of the fine soccer players to hail from the Rugby League stronghold of St Helens, Hubert Redwood was nearly 22 years of age when he joined Manchester United from Sherdley Albion in 1934-5. A right-back, Redwood made his debut in the Reds' goalless draw with Tottenham Hotspur in 1935-6. United won the Second Division title that season but Redwood's contribution was minimal and he did not play again. The following season, however, he shared the right-back berth with the established John Griffiths before his performances meant that Griffiths was switched to the left flank. Redwood played for United in wartime football, but in October 1943, after being invalided out of the army because of tuberculosis, he died at the age of 30.

| | LEAGUE | | FA CUP | | TOTAL | |
|---|---|---|---|---|---|
| | App | Gls | App | Gls | App | Gls |
| 1935-36 | 1 | 0 | 0 | 0 | 1 | 0 |
| 1936-37 | 21 | 0 | 1 | 0 | 22 | 0 |
| 1937-38 | 29 | 2 | 4 | 0 | 33 | 2 |
| 1938-39 | 35 | 1 | 2 | 1 | 37 | 2 |
| 1939-40 | 3 | 0 | 0 | 0 | 3 | 0 |
| | 89 | 3 | 7 | 1 | 96 | 4 |

**HUBERT REDWOOD**

129

Tom Reid, born in Motherwell, was discovered by Clydebank where he soon developed his goalscoring talents. The robust centre-forward moved to England in 1925-6 to join Liverpool. Reid scored 31 goals in only 51 League games for the Anfield club and that scoring form tempted United to sign him in 1929. He was soon in the scoring groove at Old Trafford but, despite his efforts, the club was relegated in 1931 when he finished top-scorer with little support. After a season and a half in Division Two, United released Reid to Oldham in March 1933 and in the final 13 League games of that season he continued his scoring touch with ten goals for his new club.

|  | LEAGUE | | FA CUP | | TOTAL | |
|---|---|---|---|---|---|---|
|  | App | Gls | App | Gls | App | Gls |
| 1928-29 | 17 | 14 | 0 | 0 | 17 | 14 |
| 1929-30 | 13 | 5 | 0 | 0 | 13 | 5 |
| 1930-31 | 30 | 17 | 3 | 3 | 33 | 20 |
| 1931-32 | 25 | 17 | 1 | 1 | 26 | 18 |
| 1932-33 | 11 | 10 | 1 | 0 | 12 | 10 |
|  | 96 | 63 | 5 | 4 | 101 | 67 |

**TOM REID**

Charlie Roberts, who led United to glory in the early years of the 20th century, was one of the club's greatest captains, taking them to their first League Championship and their first FA Cup Final win. Born in Darlington, Roberts was 20 when United signed him from Grimsby Town for £400 in April 1904, beating off several other clubs for his signature. He had been at Grimsby, whom he joined from Bishop Auckland, for only a season when United bought him. They saw his natural ability as an attacking centre-half, despite his pale

appearance which earned him the nickname of 'The Ghost in Boots'. He went straight into United's League side and the stamina he showed no doubt stemmed from his summers spent working on East Coast trawlers. Skilled and quick-thinking, Roberts could run 100 yards in 11 seconds at a time when the world record stood at 9.6 seconds. One of the poineers of the Players' Union, he became its chairman. Because of his sympathies for the players' cause, and partly because Bristol City's Billy Wedlock was firmly established as England's centre-half, Roberts gained only three England caps. He rarely endeared himself to the game's rulers and insisted on wearing short shorts when the FA ordered that 'players should cover their knees'. In August 1913, Roberts signed for Oldham. He retired during the war and in July 1921 became Oldham manager. He held the job for 18 months before resigning, confessing that he could not stand the strain of watching. Roberts, whose sons still run the wholesale tobacconists' business he started, died just before World War Two, aged 56.

**CHARLIE ROBERTS**

|  | LEAGUE | | FA CUP | | TOTAL | |
|---|---|---|---|---|---|---|
|  | App | Gls | App | Gls | App | Gls |
| 1903-04 | 2 | 0 | 0 | 0 | 2 | 0 |
| 1904-05 | 28 | 5 | 0 | 0 | 28 | 5 |
| 1905-06 | 34 | 4 | 4 | 0 | 38 | 4 |
| 1906-07 | 31 | 2 | 1 | 0 | 32 | 2 |
| 1907-08 | 32 | 2 | 3 | 0 | 35 | 2 |
| 1908-09 | 27 | 1 | 6 | 0 | 33 | 1 |
| 1909-10 | 28 | 4 | 1 | 0 | 29 | 4 |
| 1910-11 | 33 | 1 | 3 | 0 | 36 | 1 |
| 1911-12 | 32 | 2 | 5 | 0 | 37 | 2 |
| 1912-13 | 24 | 1 | 5 | 1 | 29 | 2 |
|  | 271 | 22 | 28 | 1 | 299 | 23 |

When Bryan Robson moved from his native North-East to join West Brom, as a 15-year-old, he was only 5ft 2ins tall and weighed around 7st. Albion built him up with raw eggs in Guinness and he made his League debut against York City in April 1975. Breaking a leg three times in 1976-7, Robson emerged an even more determined individual and when Albion manager Ron Atkinson moved to Old Trafford he wasted little time in signing Robson for United, for a British record fee of around £1.5 million in October 1981, in the deal which also took Remi Moses to Old Trafford. Robson's League debut came in a derby match against Manchester City and he soon showed his creative skills. He established a notable partnership with Ray Wilkins, displaying his own versatility in defence, attack and as a creative midfielder. It is perhaps as a captain that Robson made his deepest impression, both for his club and country. He has led United to FA Cup Final victories and was the two-goal hero of their 4-0 replay win over Brighton in 1983. The 1985-6 season saw him once more seriously affected by injuries and there was talk that he was being pushed too hard and was physically not up to the strains of First Division and international football. No sooner had he returned to the United side than he was injured again. Yet he has played more than 500 games at senior level

**BRYAN ROBSON OBE**

and proved himself arguably the best all-round footballer in Britain and possibly Europe. He was born in Chester-le-Street in January 1957 and it now seems remarkable that at one time, England's captain could not get into the Durham School's team. In 1990 Robson created history by becoming the first captain to hold aloft the FA Cup three times as United won the coveted trophy for a record-equalling seventh time. Played for England in the 1990 World Cup Finals before injury forced an early return home.

| | LEAGUE | | FA CUP | | FL CUP | | EUROPE | | TOTAL | |
|---|---|---|---|---|---|---|---|---|---|---|
| | App | Gls | App | Gls | App | Gls | App | Gls | App | Gls |
| 1981-82 | 32 | 5 | 1 | 0 | 2 | 0 | 0 | 0 | 35 | 5 |
| 1982-83 | 33 | 10 | 6 | 3 | 8 | 1 | 2 | 1 | 49 | 15 |
| 1983-84 | 33 | 12 | 1 | 0 | 6 | 0 | 6 | 4 | 46 | 16 |
| 1984-85 | 32/1 | 9 | 4 | 2 | 2 | 1 | 7 | 2 | 45/1 | 14 |
| 1985-86 | 21 | 7 | 3 | 0 | 2 | 0 | 0 | 0 | 26 | 7 |
| 1986-87 | 29/1 | 7 | 0 | 0 | 3 | 0 | 0 | 0 | 32/1 | 7 |
| 1987-88 | 36 | 11 | 2 | 0 | 5 | 0 | 0 | 0 | 43 | 11 |
| 1988-89 | 34 | 4 | 6 | 2 | 3 | 2 | 0 | 0 | 43 | 8 |
| 1989-90 | 20 | 2 | 4 | 2 | 3 | 0 | 0 | 0 | 27 | 4 |
| 1990-91 | 15/2 | 1 | 3 | 0 | 5 | 0 | 4 | 0 | 27/2 | 1 |
| 1991-92 | 25/1 | 4 | 2 | 0 | 5/1 | 1 | 3 | 0 | 35/2 | 5 |
| | 310/5 | 72 | 32 | 9 | 44/1 | 5 | 22 | 7 | 408/6 | 93 |

Bilston-born Harry Rowley spent two spells with United, each time suffering relegation with them. He first joined the club from non-League Shrewsbury Town in 1928 and made his League debut in the 2-1 win at Huddersfield in October that year. A powerful inside-left, Rowley complemented the goalscoring talents of centre-forward Reid. He was joint top-scorer in 1929-30 but the following year found goals hard to come by as United were relegated. After one game in Division Two, Rowley returned to the top flight with Manchester City but struggled to find his form at Maine Road and two seasons later returned to Division Two with Oldham. In 1934 he rejoined United and in 1935-6, despite being in his 31st year, enjoyed his best spell with the club, finding the net regularly as United won the Second Division title. As the club made an immediate return to Division Two, Rowley played less than half the games in what turned out to be his last season. His last game was the goalless draw with Leeds United at Old Trafford on 3 April 1937. Altogether, Rowley scored 74 goals in 261 League games. Rowley died in December 1985 aged 81.

**HENRY ROWLEY**

| | LEAGUE | | FA CUP | | TOTAL | |
|---|---|---|---|---|---|---|
| | App | Gls | App | Gls | App | Gls |
| 1928-29 | 25 | 5 | 0 | 0 | 25 | 5 |
| 1929-30 | 40 | 12 | 1 | 0 | 41 | 12 |
| 1930-31 | 29 | 7 | 0 | 0 | 29 | 7 |
| 1931-32 | 1 | 0 | 0 | 0 | 1 | 0 |
| 1934-35 | 24 | 8 | 3 | 0 | 27 | 8 |
| 1935-36 | 37 | 19 | 3 | 0 | 40 | 19 |
| 1936-37 | 17 | 4 | 0 | 0 | 17 | 4 |
| | 173 | 55 | 7 | 0 | 180 | 55 |

Jack Rowley was one of the finest goalscoring centre-forwards of the immediate post-war era. Many of his goals came from his head, but most were the result of his deadly left-footed shooting. Born in Wolverhampton, he was signed for Wolves by Major Frank Buckley, a former United player, but was transferred to Bournemouth before he had played a League game for the Molineux club. Rowley returned to the Black Country to make his League debut against Walsall in February 1937. After 23 League games for Bournemouth, he signed for United for £3,000 in October 1937. Rowley, made his debut the same week, against Sheffield Wednesday, but feeling that he was not ready for Second Division football, asked to play in the Reserves. Six weeks later he was back in the first team, scoring four of United's five goals against Swansea Town and thereafter goals were his business. United were promoted that season and Rowley played his part, but soon he found himself playing wartime football. He guested for Spurs, Wolves (winning a War Cup winners' medal) and Irish club, Distillery. His goalscoring exploits — eight in one game for Wolves and seven in a match for Spurs —

won him a wartime cap, against Wales in 1944, but he had to wait four years before the first of six full caps. Two goals in the 1948 FA Cup Final made him a United hero, and when the club won the League Championship in 1951-2, his 30 goals (including hat-tricks in the first two games of the season) were a United record which stood until Viollet beat it eight years later. Released on a free transfer in 1955, he joined Plymouth Argyle as player-manager and hung up his boots in 1957. He later managed Oldham (twice), Wrexham, Bradford and Ajax of Amsterdam.

**JACK ROWLEY**

|  | LEAGUE | | FA CUP | | TOTAL | |
|---|---|---|---|---|---|---|
|  | App | Gls | App | Gls | App | Gls |
| 1937-38 | 25 | 9 | 4 | 0 | 29 | 9 |
| 1938-39 | 38 | 10 | 1 | 0 | 39 | 10 |
| 1945-46 | 0 | 0 | 4 | 2 | 4 | 2 |
| 1946-47 | 37 | 26 | 2 | 2 | 39 | 28 |
| 1947-48 | 39 | 23 | 6 | 5 | 45 | 28 |
| 1948-49 | 39 | 20 | 8 | 9 | 47 | 29 |
| 1949-50 | 39 | 20 | 5 | 3 | 44 | 23 |
| 1950-51 | 39 | 14 | 3 | 1 | 42 | 15 |
| 1951-52 | 40 | 30 | 1 | 0 | 41 | 30 |
| 1952-53 | 26 | 11 | 4 | 3 | 30 | 14 |
| 1953-54 | 36 | 12 | 1 | 0 | 37 | 12 |
| 1954-55 | 22 | 7 | 3 | 1 | 25 | 8 |
|  | 380 | 182 | 42 | 26 | 422 | 208 |

United beat several League clubs to the signature of Maidstone United's England Amateur international inside-forward, David Sadler, in November 1962. They converted him to a centre-half, signed him on professional forms in February 1963, and gave him his League debut in place of David Herd later that year. Sadler converted to his defensive role and it was as a solid centre-half that he is best remembered at Old Trafford. He scored a hat-trick in the second-leg of the 1964 FA Youth Cup Final against Swindon, and added a League Championship medal, in 1967, and a European Cup winners' medal to his honours. Born at Yalding in February 1946, Sadler was also capped at Youth, Under-23 and full levels. Tall and well-built, his style was unspectacular but effective. In 1973 he played for Miami Toros in the USA. In November 1973, he signed for Preston for £25,000 and stayed at Deepdale until injury forced his retirement in May 1977. His career had spanned 14 years and 375 League games. He returned to Preston, managing them in 1981.

|  | LEAGUE | | FACUP | | FLCUP | | EUROPE | | TOTAL | |
|---|---|---|---|---|---|---|---|---|---|---|
|  | App | Gls | App | Gls | App | Gls | App | Gls | App | Gls |
| 1963-64 | 19 | 5 | 0 | 0 | 0 | 0 | 2 | 0 | 21 | 5 |
| 1964-65 | 6 | 1 | 0 | 0 | 0 | 0 | 0 | 0 | 6 | 1 |
| 1965-66 | 10 | 4 | 0 | 0 | 0 | 0 | 0 | 0 | 10 | 4 |
| 1966-67 | 35/1 | 5 | 2 | 0 | 1 | 0 | 0 | 0 | 38/1 | 5 |
| 1967-68 | 40/1 | 3 | 2 | 0 | 0 | 0 | 9 | 3 | 51/1 | 6 |
| 1968-69 | 26/3 | 0 | 0/1 | 0 | 0 | 0 | 5 | 0 | 31/4 | 0 |
| 1969-70 | 40 | 2 | 9 | 0 | 8 | 1 | 0 | 0 | 57 | 3 |
| 1970-71 | 32 | 1 | 2 | 0 | 5 | 0 | 0 | 0 | 39 | 1 |
| 1971-72 | 37 | 1 | 6 | 1 | 6 | 0 | 0 | 0 | 49 | 2 |
| 1972-73 | 19 | 0 | 1 | 0 | 2 | 0 | 0 | 0 | 22 | 0 |
| 1973-74 | 2/1 | 0 | 0 | 0 | 0 | 0 | 0 | 0 | 2/1 | 0 |
|  | 266/6 | 22 | 22/1 | 1 | 22 | 1 | 16 | 3 | 326/7 | 27 |

**DAVID SADLER**

132

Charles Sagar was one of the first great players developed by Bury. He was capped twice for England. A native of Turton, he joined the Gigg Lane club in 1898 as a 20-year-old. Two years later, he was a member of the Shakers' FA Cup winning team which beat Southampton 4-0. In 1903, he was in the side which beat Derby County by a record FA Cup Final score of 6-0, scoring Bury's second goal just after half-time. A tricky player, he could play at either centre-forward or inside-left. United signed him in 1905 and he scored regularly in his first season, including a hat-trick in the 5-1 home win over Bristol City. Sagar lost his place to Wombwell and then Scottish international Menzies the following season and made his last appearance for the club, against Everton, in April 1907. Shortly afterwards he moved back to the Bury area and played for Haslingden. Sagar died in December 1919, aged 41.

|  | LEAGUE | | FA CUP | | TOTAL | |
|---|---|---|---|---|---|---|
|  | App | Gls | App | Gls | App | Gls |
| 1905-06 | 20 | 16 | 3 | 4 | 23 | 20 |
| 1906-07 | 10 | 4 | 0 | 0 | 10 | 4 |
|  | 30 | 20 | 3 | 4 | 33 | 24 |

**CHARLES SAGAR**

Albert Scanlon followed his uncle, Charlie Mitten, into United's first team after coming through the Old Trafford youth scheme. Manchester-born, in October 1935, he played in the 1953 and 1954 FA Youth Cup winning teams. He turned professional in 1952, but had to wait until November 1954 before making his League debut against Arsenal. Six weeks before the Munich air disaster, Scanlon established a regular place and came to be regarded as one of the best outside-lefts in the League, although he was not honoured beyond Under-23 level or Football League XI level. He survived the Munich crash, but the injuries he sustained meant that he missed the remainder of the season. As United rebuilt in 1958-9, Scanlon was ever-present. In November 1960, after being a key member of the recovery programme, he went to Newcastle United for £18,000 and later played for Lincoln City and Mansfield Town, where he made the last of his 292 League appearances.

| | LEAGUE | | FACUP | | FLCUP | | EUROPE | | TOTAL | |
|---|---|---|---|---|---|---|---|---|---|---|
| | App | Gls | App | Gls | App | Gls | App | Gls | App | Gls |
| 1954-55 | 14 | 4 | 0 | 0 | 0 | 0 | 0 | 0 | 14 | 4 |
| 1955-56 | 6 | 1 | 0 | 0 | 0 | 0 | 0 | 0 | 6 | 1 |
| 1956-57 | 5 | 2 | 0 | 0 | 0 | 0 | 0 | 0 | 5 | 2 |
| 1957-58 | 9 | 3 | 2 | 0 | 0 | 0 | 3 | 0 | 14 | 3 |
| 1958-59 | 42 | 16 | 1 | 0 | 0 | 0 | 0 | 0 | 43 | 16 |
| 1959-60 | 31 | 7 | 3 | 1 | 0 | 0 | 0 | 0 | 34 | 8 |
| 1960-61 | 8 | 1 | 0 | 0 | 3 | 0 | 0 | 0 | 11 | 1 |
| | 115 | 34 | 6 | 1 | 3 | 0 | 3 | 0 | 127 | 35 |

**ALBERT SCANLON**

After five seasons with Everton, during which time he made only 13 League appearances, Liverpool-born Alf Schofield signed for Newton Heath as a replacement for outside-right William Bryant. Schofield's career at Clayton was in direct contrast to his Goodison days and in seven seasons he played over 150 League games. He made his Newton Heath debut on 1 September 1900, at Glossop, and was a member of the team which won promotion from Division Two in 1906. But, just as the first great United team was taking shape, he retired, having played ten First Division matches the following season. His last game was against Liverpool on Christmas Day 1906 and a week later he was succeeded in the United team by the great Billy Meredith.

**ALF SCHOFIELD**

| | LEAGUE | | FA CUP | | TOTAL | |
|---|---|---|---|---|---|---|
| | App | Gls | App | Gls | App | Gls |
| 1900-01 | 29 | 7 | 3 | 1 | 32 | 8 |
| 1901-02 | 29 | 4 | 1 | 0 | 30 | 4 |
| 1902-03 | 16 | 3 | 4 | 1 | 20 | 4 |
| 1903-04 | 26 | 6 | 7 | 3 | 33 | 9 |
| 1904-05 | 24 | 4 | 3 | 0 | 27 | 4 |
| 1905-06 | 23 | 4 | 4 | 0 | 27 | 4 |
| 1906-07 | 10 | 2 | 0 | 0 | 10 | 2 |
| | 157 | 30 | 22 | 5 | 179 | 35 |

Crew-cut Devonian Maurice Setters looked like a hard player and his appearance did not deceive. A member of the old school of tough-tackling wing-halves, he was born at Honiton in December 1936 and his first club was Exeter City. After only ten League games he was signed by West Brom in January 1955 and after five years at The Hawthorns he moved to United in January 1960. They wanted the bandy-legged terrier to strengthen a defence which had conceded 54 goals in 25 League games, including seven at Newcastle only days earlier. Setters, an England Schoolboy and Youth international, settled into the side and went on to win a further five Under-23 caps, adding to the 11 he won at West Brom, although he was never honoured at full level. His one club honour came in the 1964 FA Cup Final win over Leicester City and his last game for United was the 7-0 thrashing of Aston Villa in October 1964. The following month he joined Stoke City for £30,000 and built up a partnership with Calvin Palmer. He moved to Coventry in 1967 and Charlton in 1970, where he finished his playing career which took in over 500 senior appearances. He became Doncaster manager and later teamed up with Jack Charlton at Sheffield Wednesday before becoming Rotherham assistant manager. He then followed Charlton to Newcastle where he was appointed chief scout. And the two men teamed up again when Jack was appointed manager of the Republic of Ireland international team.

| | LEAGUE | | FACUP | | FLCUP | | EUROPE | | TOTAL | |
|---|---|---|---|---|---|---|---|---|---|---|
| | App | Gls | App | Gls | App | Gls | App | Gls | App | Gls |
| 1959-60 | 17 | 0 | 2 | 0 | 0 | 0 | 0 | 0 | 19 | 0 |
| 1960-61 | 40 | 4 | 3 | 0 | 2 | 0 | 0 | 0 | 45 | 4 |
| 1961-62 | 38 | 3 | 7 | 1 | 0 | 0 | 0 | 0 | 45 | 4 |
| 1962-63 | 27 | 1 | 6 | 0 | 0 | 0 | 0 | 0 | 33 | 1 |
| 1963-64 | 32 | 4 | 7 | 0 | 0 | 0 | 6 | 1 | 45 | 5 |
| 1964-65 | 5 | 0 | 0 | 0 | 0 | 0 | 1 | 0 | 6 | 0 |
| | 159 | 12 | 25 | 1 | 2 | 0 | 7 | 1 | 193 | 14 |

**MAURICE SETTERS**

One of the classic full-backs to have played for United, Wigan-born John Silcock gave his only League club loyal and dedicated service in a career spanning 15 seasons and nearly 450 senior games. He signed for United as an amateur in April 1916, from Wigan junior club Atherton, and turned professional the following year. Silcock made his Football League debut at Derby in August 1919, after more than 100 wartime games. He struck up a fine partnership with right-back Charlie Moore and they were to prove the backbone of United's defence in the early post-war years. Silcock's ability to clear the ball with pinpoint accuracy, particularly on the volley, was almost uncanny and apparently a treat to watch. His talents earned him three full England caps and Football League honours. Retiring at the end of 1933-4, Silcock was persuaded to have a trial with Oldham at the age of 37, but did not pursue it. He ran a pub in the Manchester area until his death in 1966.

**JOHN SILCOCK**

| | LEAGUE | | FA CUP | | TOTAL | |
|---|---|---|---|---|---|---|
| | App | Gls | App | Gls | App | Gls |
| 1919-20 | 40 | 0 | 1 | 0 | 41 | 0 |
| 1920-21 | 37 | 1 | 2 | 0 | 39 | 1 |
| 1921-22 | 36 | 0 | 0 | 0 | 36 | 0 |
| 1922-23 | 37 | 0 | 3 | 0 | 40 | 0 |
| 1923-24 | 8 | 0 | 1 | 0 | 9 | 0 |
| 1924-25 | 29 | 0 | 0 | 0 | 29 | 0 |
| 1925-26 | 33 | 0 | 7 | 0 | 40 | 0 |
| 1926-27 | 26 | 0 | 3 | 0 | 29 | 0 |
| 1927-28 | 26 | 0 | 4 | 0 | 30 | 0 |
| 1928-29 | 27 | 1 | 2 | 0 | 29 | 1 |
| 1929-30 | 21 | 0 | 0 | 0 | 21 | 0 |
| 1930-31 | 25 | 0 | 0 | 0 | 25 | 0 |
| 1931-32 | 35 | 0 | 1 | 0 | 36 | 0 |
| 1932-33 | 27 | 0 | 1 | 0 | 28 | 0 |
| 1933-34 | 16 | 0 | 1 | 0 | 17 | 0 |
| | 423 | 2 | 26 | 0 | 449 | 2 |

In 14 years at Old Trafford, Joe Spence created a club record of 481 appearances which was to remain unbeaten until Bill Foulkes passed the total 40 years later. An outside-right or centre-forward, Spence was a great favourite with United's fans and from his wing position he went on many famous runs that ended in some memorable goals. Born in Throckley, Northumberland, Spence joined United from north-east amateur side, Scotswood, in March 1919. When League soccer resumed in August that year, he made his debut in the opening match, against Derby County. He was United's top scorer that season and during his stay at Old Trafford was top or joint-top scorer on seven occasions. In June 1933, he moved to Bradford City, signing for Chesterfield two years later. He retired in 1938, aged 40, and remained in the Chesterfield area, working and scouting for the Saltergate club. He died on the last day of 1966.

**JOE SPENCE**

| | LEAGUE | | FA CUP | | TOTAL | |
|---|---|---|---|---|---|---|
| | App | Gls | App | Gls | App | Gls |
| 1919-20 | 32 | 14 | 1 | 0 | 33 | 14 |
| 1920-21 | 15 | 7 | 0 | 0 | 15 | 7 |
| 1921-22 | 35 | 15 | 1 | 0 | 36 | 15 |
| 1922-23 | 35 | 11 | 2 | 0 | 37 | 11 |
| 1923-24 | 36 | 10 | 2 | 0 | 38 | 10 |
| 1924-25 | 42 | 5 | 1 | 0 | 43 | 5 |
| 1925-26 | 39 | 7 | 7 | 4 | 46 | 11 |
| 1926-27 | 40 | 18 | 3 | 1 | 43 | 19 |
| 1927-28 | 38 | 22 | 5 | 2 | 43 | 24 |
| 1928-29 | 36 | 5 | 2 | 1 | 38 | 6 |
| 1929-30 | 42 | 12 | 1 | 0 | 43 | 12 |
| 1930-31 | 35 | 6 | 2 | 1 | 37 | 7 |
| 1931-32 | 37 | 19 | 1 | 0 | 38 | 19 |
| 1932-33 | 19 | 7 | 1 | 1 | 20 | 8 |
| | 481 | 158 | 29 | 10 | 510 | 168 |

135

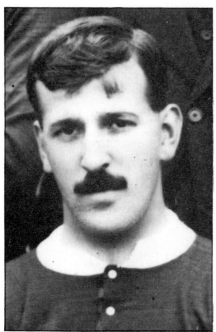

South Yorkshire had a tradition for breeding tough footballers before World War One, and George Stacey was a typical example. Born at Thorpe Hesley, near Rotherham, he joined Sheffield Wednesday as a youngster but never made the grade and moved to Barnsley where he soon established himself as a solid right-back in the true Oakwell mould. United, meanwhile, were building a side ready to take the League Championship and they bought Stacey for £400 to provide them with cover. He soon forced his way into the first team and towards the end of the 1907-08 Championship winning season, had established himself as the first-choice full-back. Originally a right-back, Stacey switched to the left flank and over the years enjoyed a successful partnership with several right-backs. He was in the United side that won the 1909 FA Cup Final and he won a second Championship medal in 1911. He played in an England trial match in 1912. He stayed with United until the outbreak of war and after the conflict returned to his old job as a coalminer.

| | LEAGUE | | FA CUP | | TOTAL | |
|---|---|---|---|---|---|---|
| | App | Gls | App | Gls | App | Gls |
| 1907-08 | 18 | 1 | 3 | 0 | 21 | 1 |
| 1908-09 | 32 | 0 | 6 | 0 | 38 | 0 |
| 1909-10 | 32 | 0 | 1 | 0 | 33 | 0 |
| 1910-11 | 36 | 0 | 3 | 0 | 39 | 0 |
| 1911-12 | 29 | 2 | 6 | 0 | 35 | 2 |
| 1912-13 | 36 | 1 | 5 | 0 | 41 | 1 |
| 1913-14 | 34 | 1 | 1 | 0 | 35 | 1 |
| 1914-15 | 24 | 4 | 1 | 0 | 25 | 4 |
| | 241 | 9 | 26 | 0 | 267 | 9 |

**GEORGE STACEY**

Manchester United probably owe their continued existence to Harry Stafford — or rather his dog. It was during a bazaar in 1901, when Newton Heath were desperately trying to raise money, that Stafford's St Bernard dog, a collecting tin around its neck, wandered off. It came into the possession of John Davies and when he reunited Stafford with the dog, Davies learned of the Heathens' financial plight. Davies stepped in and his cash saved the club from possible closure. Stafford gave United much more than this chance encounter with their saviour, however. A full-back from Crewe who appeared for Southport Central and Crewe Alexandra, he was the first of many great United captains, skippering the side in their first game under their present title. He ended his seven-year career after the 2-1 home defeat by Lincoln in March 1903. Granted a benefit towards the end of his playing career, Stafford regained his amateur status after retiring from League football and later served United as a director. When he emigrated because of ill health in 1911, United's board gave him £50.

| | LEAGUE | | FA CUP | | TOTAL | |
|---|---|---|---|---|---|---|
| | App | Gls | App | Gls | App | Gls |
| 1895-96 | 4 | 0 | 0 | 0 | 4 | 0 |
| 1896-97 | 24 | 0 | 8 | 0 | 32 | 0 |
| 1897-98 | 25 | 0 | 0 | 0 | 25 | 0 |
| 1898-99 | 33 | 0 | 2 | 0 | 35 | 0 |
| 1899-1900 | 31 | 0 | 1 | 0 | 32 | 0 |
| 1900-01 | 30 | 0 | 3 | 1 | 33 | 1 |
| 1901-02 | 26 | 0 | 1 | 0 | 27 | 0 |
| 1902-03 | 10 | 0 | 2 | 0 | 12 | 0 |
| | 183 | 0 | 17 | 1 | 200 | 1 |

**HARRY STAFFORD**

When Frank Stapleton scored United's first goal in the 1983 FA Cup Final against Brighton he made history by becoming the first man to score for different clubs in two Wembley FA Cup Finals. His first Final goal had come in 1979 when he scored for Arsenal — against United. Stapleton has now appeared in a host of major Finals — FA Cup, Milk Cup — and in a European Cup-winners' Cup Final (for Arsenal). Born in Dublin, he was on United's books as a schoolboy but they allowed him to leave and he joined the Gunners, turning professional in 1973 shortly after his 17th birthday. He played over 200 games for the London club and in August 1981 it cost United in the region of £1 million to sign the player they could have had for nothing. An experienced Republic of Ireland international who has captained his country, Stapleton has proved himself a brave, artistic and creative striker. He left United in 1987-8 to join Ajax but made only four appearances before joining Derby County, then French club Le Havre and Blackburn Rovers. He was in the Republic's squad for the World Cup in Italy 1990. In May 1991 he was released by Blackburn and became player-manager of Huddersfield.

**FRANK STAPLETON**

|  | LEAGUE | | FACUP | | FLCUP | | EUROPE | | TOTAL | |
|---|---|---|---|---|---|---|---|---|---|---|
|  | App | Gls | App | Gls | App | Gls | App | Gls | App | Gls |
| 1981-82 | 41 | 13 | 1 | 0 | 2 | 0 | 0 | 0 | 44 | 13 |
| 1982-83 | 41 | 14 | 7 | 3 | 9 | 2 | 2 | 0 | 59 | 19 |
| 1983-84 | 42 | 13 | 1 | 0 | 6 | 2 | 8 | 4 | 57 | 19 |
| 1984-85 | 21/3 | 6 | 5 | 2 | 1/1 | 0 | 4/1 | 1 | 31/5 | 9 |
| 1985-86 | 34/7 | 7 | 5 | 2 | 4 | 0 | 0 | 0 | 43/7 | 9 |
| 1986-87 | 25/9 | 7 | 2 | 0 | 4 | 2 | 0 | 0 | 31/9 | 9 |
|  | 204/19 | 60 | 21 | 7 | 26/1 | 6 | 14/1 | 5 | 265/21 | 78 |

It was the heroics of Alex Stepney, with two instinctive saves from Eusebio in the closing minutes of normal time, which kept United alive in the 1968 European Cup Final. The extra-time goals will always be the highlight of the famous victory, but Stepney's part should never be forgotten. A solid, secure and unspectacular goalkeeper, he began his career with non-League Tooting and Mitcham before turning professional with Millwall in 1963, making nearly 150 appearances for the Lions. Tommy Docherty signed him for Chelsea in May 1966, for £50,000, but he made only one League appearance for them before joining United for £55,000, only four months after his move to Stamford Bridge. He immediately replaced David Gaskell, making his debut in front of 62,000 fans in a Manchester 'derby' match. Over the next 12 seasons his name was one of the first to be written on the team-sheet. After 21 games of United's relegation season of 1973-4, Stepney was joint leading scorer after converting two penalties. He won a Second Division championship medal the following season to add to his League Championship medal won in 1966-7. Later he won an FA Cup winners' medal when United beat Liverpool at Wembley in 1977. At the end of 1977-8 he left United and went to play in the USA with Dallas Tornadoes and with non-League Altrincham. Stepney won one England cap and was a member of the 1970 World Cup Finals squad, although he did not play in Mexico.

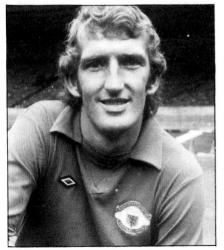

**ALEX STEPNEY**

|  | LEAGUE | | FACUP | | FLCUP | | EUROPE | | TOTAL | |
|---|---|---|---|---|---|---|---|---|---|---|
|  | App | Gls | App | Gls | App | Gls | App | Gls | App | Gls |
| 1966-67 | 35 | 0 | 2 | 0 | 0 | 0 | 0 | 0 | 37 | 0 |
| 1967-68 | 41 | 0 | 2 | 0 | 0 | 0 | 9 | 0 | 52 | 0 |
| 1968-69 | 38 | 0 | 5 | 0 | 0 | 0 | 6 | 0 | 49 | 0 |
| 1969-70 | 37 | 0 | 9 | 0 | 8 | 0 | 0 | 0 | 54 | 0 |
| 1970-71 | 22 | 0 | 0 | 0 | 0 | 0 | 0 | 0 | 22 | 0 |
| 1971-72 | 39 | 0 | 7 | 0 | 6 | 0 | 0 | 0 | 52 | 0 |
| 1972-73 | 38 | 0 | 1 | 0 | 4 | 0 | 0 | 0 | 43 | 0 |
| 1973-74 | 42 | 2 | 2 | 0 | 1 | 0 | 0 | 0 | 45 | 2 |
| 1974-75 | 40 | 0 | 2 | 0 | 7 | 0 | 0 | 0 | 49 | 0 |
| 1975-76 | 38 | 0 | 7 | 0 | 2 | 0 | 0 | 0 | 47 | 0 |
| 1976-77 | 40 | 0 | 7 | 0 | 6 | 0 | 4 | 0 | 57 | 0 |
| 1977-78 | 23 | 0 | 0 | 0 | 1 | 0 | 4 | 0 | 28 | 0 |
|  | 433 | 2 | 44 | 0 | 35 | 0 | 23 | 0 | 535 | 2 |

Just after World War One, United found themselves without adequate cover for long-serving goalkeeper John Mew, who was approaching the end of his career. They recruited Manchester-born Alf Steward from Stalybridge Celtic. Steward himself was no youngster, being in his early 20s, and he got his first chance to impress when he replaced Mew in United's 1-0 home win against Preston in October 1920. He did, however, wait three seasons before being handed the goalkeeper's jersey permanently. That was in 1923-4 and between then and 1932, when he lost his place to Moody, Steward was a difficult man to displace from the team. An all-round sportsman, he was a fine cricketer and was on Lancashire's books for a time. It was his misfortune to play through one of United's bad patches and after 13 seasons he left Old Trafford without a single honour to his name. In 1932, Steward joined Manchester North End and, for a short time immediately before World War Two, he managed Torquay United from 1938 to 1940.

| | LEAGUE | | FA CUP | | TOTAL | |
|---|---|---|---|---|---|---|
| | App | Gls | App | Gls | App | Gls |
| 1920-21 | 2 | 0 | 0 | 0 | 2 | 0 |
| 1921-22 | 1 | 0 | 0 | 0 | 1 | 0 |
| 1922-23 | 1 | 0 | 0 | 0 | 1 | 0 |
| 1923-24 | 30 | 0 | 2 | 0 | 32 | 0 |
| 1924-25 | 42 | 0 | 1 | 0 | 43 | 0 |
| 1925-26 | 35 | 0 | 2 | 0 | 37 | 0 |
| 1926-27 | 42 | 0 | 3 | 0 | 45 | 0 |
| 1927-28 | 10 | 0 | 1 | 0 | 11 | 0 |
| 1928-29 | 37 | 0 | 2 | 0 | 39 | 0 |
| 1929-30 | 39 | 0 | 1 | 0 | 40 | 0 |
| 1930-31 | 38 | 0 | 4 | 0 | 42 | 0 |
| 1931-32 | 32 | 0 | 1 | 0 | 33 | 0 |
| | 309 | 0 | 17 | 0 | 326 | 0 |

**ALF STEWARD**

The sight of toothless Nobby Stiles dancing around the Wembley pitch after England's 1966 World Cup Final win is an indelible soccer memory. Stiles, who played a great part in England's 4-2 win over West Germany, was a tough, aggressive little Mancunian with a burning desire to win. He joined United as a schoolboy in 1957, turning professional in 1959. He made his debut as an 18-year-old, at Bolton in 1960, and in his 14 years at Old Trafford won two League Championship medals and a European Cup winners' medal. His international career spanned 28 full caps as well as Schoolboy, Youth and Under-23 appearances. In 1971 he moved to Middlesbrough for £20,000, where he was later joined by former England teammate, Jackie Charlton. Released in August 1973, Stiles joined Bobby Charlton at Preston, eventually taking over as manager. Like his predecessor, he could not bring back the glory days to Deeepdale and after spells in the USA joined his brother-in-law, Johnny Giles, at West Brom. In 1985, he succeeded Giles as Albion manager but reverted to assistant when Ron Saunders took over in February 1986. He left the Albion staff at the end of 1988-9, and returned to United as coach to the youth team in July 1989.

**NOBBY STILES**

| | LEAGUE | | FA CUP | | FL CUP | | EUROPE | | TOTAL | |
|---|---|---|---|---|---|---|---|---|---|---|
| | App | Gls | App | Gls | App | Gls | App | Gls | App | Gls |
| 1960-61 | 26 | 2 | 3 | 0 | 2 | 0 | 0 | 0 | 31 | 2 |
| 1961-62 | 34 | 7 | 4 | 0 | 0 | 0 | 0 | 0 | 38 | 7 |
| 1962-63 | 31 | 2 | 4 | 0 | 0 | 0 | 0 | 0 | 35 | 2 |
| 1963-64 | 17 | 0 | 2 | 0 | 0 | 0 | 2 | 0 | 21 | 0 |
| 1964-65 | 41 | 0 | 7 | 0 | 0 | 0 | 11 | 0 | 59 | 0 |
| 1965-66 | 39 | 2 | 7 | 0 | 0 | 0 | 8 | 1 | 54 | 3 |
| 1966-67 | 37 | 3 | 2 | 0 | 1 | 0 | 0 | 0 | 40 | 3 |
| 1967-68 | 20 | 0 | 0 | 0 | 0 | 0 | 7 | 0 | 27 | 0 |
| 1968-69 | 41 | 1 | 6 | 0 | 0 | 0 | 8 | 1 | 55 | 2 |
| 1969-70 | 8 | 0 | 3 | 0 | 2 | 0 | 0 | 0 | 13 | 0 |
| 1970-71 | 17 | 0 | 0 | 0 | 2 | 0 | 0 | 0 | 19 | 0 |
| | 311 | 17 | 38 | 0 | 7 | 0 | 36 | 2 | 392 | 19 |

**GORDON STRACHAN**

When Ray Wilkins left United at the end of 1983-4, the club invested the incoming cash in three class players, Jesper Olsen, Alan Brazil and Gordon Strachan. Olsen and Strachan soon proved successful at Old Trafford and in his first full season, Strachan missed only one League game and was the second-highest scorer. He played in every game — and scored two goals — in United's victorious FA Cup run. The fiery, red-haired Scot began his career with Dundee before moving to Aberdeen in November 1977. He was one of the reasons for the Dons' rise which broke the domination of Celtic and Rangers and he won Premier League Championship medals in 1980 and 1984, Scottish FA Cup-winners' medals in 1982-3-4, and a European Cup-winners' Cup medal in 1983. He won his first full Scotland cap in 1980 and now has over 40 to his name. United signed him for £600,000 in May 1984 and the tireless midfielder repaid them with some sparkling performances. In 1988-9 he left to join ambitious Leeds United in a £300,000 deal. Strachan, who has now played over 500 senior games, was Scottish Football Writers' Player of the Year in 1980. In 1991 he was the English FWA Player of the Year having been the inspiration behind a revived Leeds United team who, the following year, pushed United all the way in the First Division title race.

| | LEAGUE | | FA CUP | | FL CUP | | EUROPE | | TOTAL | |
|---|---|---|---|---|---|---|---|---|---|---|
| | App | Gls | App | Gls | App | Gls | App | Gls | App | Gls |
| 1984-85 | 41 | 15 | 7 | 2 | 2 | 0 | 6 | 2 | 56 | 19 |
| 1985-86 | 27/1 | 5 | 5 | 0 | 1 | 0 | 0 | 0 | 33/1 | 5 |
| 1986-87 | 33/1 | 4 | 2 | 0 | 2 | 0 | 0 | 0 | 37/1 | 4 |
| 1987-88 | 33/3 | 8 | 3 | 0 | 5 | 1 | 0 | 0 | 41/3 | 9 |
| 1988-89 | 21 | 1 | 5 | 0 | 2/1 | 0 | 0 | 0 | 28/1 | 1 |
| | 155/5 | 33 | 22 | 2 | 12/1 | 1 | 6 | 2 | 195/6 | 38 |

John Sutcliffe holds the distinction of being the last Englishman to play international soccer and Rugby Union. He was also the first man to keep goal for Bolton Wanderers in an FA Cup Final, in 1894. By an odd coincidence, the next man to keep goal for the Trotters in a Cup Final was Dai Davies, the last man to play soccer and Rugby League at full international level. Sutcliffe, a Yorkshireman who was born in Shibden, near Halifax, in April 1868, played RU for Heckmondwike before being expelled for alleged professionalism. He turned to soccer, starting his new career as a centre-forward before Bolton converted him to goalkeeper. He won the first of five England caps in 1893 and left the Football League to join Millwall in April 1902. Twelve months later he joined United. He was 35 and well past his best, keeping goal for United for one season, when they missed promotion to the First Division by one point. In 1904, he joined Plymouth Argyle, taking over as Southend United coach in 1911-12. During World War One, he coached abroad for a spell, returning to become Bradford City trainer in 1919. Sutcliffe died in 1947, aged 79.

| | LEAGUE | | FA CUP | | TOTAL | |
|---|---|---|---|---|---|---|
| | App | Gls | App | Gls | App | Gls |
| 1903-04 | 21 | 0 | 7 | 0 | 28 | 0 |
| | 21 | 0 | 7 | 0 | 28 | 0 |

**JOHN SUTCLIFFE**

139

Although Ernie Taylor played only a handful of League games for United, his contribution in the aftermath of Munich was enormous. Recruited to guide United's youngsters through a tremendously difficult period, his vast experience did just that. Taylor stood only 5ft 4in tall, but his defence-splitting passing caused panic amongst the opposition and he could score goals too. When he joined United in 1958 he was in his 33rd year and already had over 300 League games to his name. A naval submariner, he joined Newcastle United in 1942 and won two FA Cup winners' medals, with the Magpies in 1951, and Blackpool in 1953 when he played in the famous 'Matthews Final'. It was said that when Taylor played well, Blackpool played well. After signing from Blackpool for £8,000, he made his United debut in the emotional FA Cup match against Sheffield Wednesday and played at Wembley that season, but Bolton ended his dreams of a third winners' medal. Before the end of 1958, Sunderland, his home-town club, paid £6,000 for him and after 68 games with the Roker club he went into non-League football with Altrincham and then Irish club, Derry. He emigrated to New Zealand where he did some coaching before returning to England and a job at the Vauxhall car plant in Cheshire. Taylor, who died at Birkenhead in April 1985, won one full England cap as well as 'B' international honours.

|  | LEAGUE | | FA CUP | | EUROPE | | TOTAL | |
|  | App | Gls | App | Gls | App | Gls | App | Gls |
|---|---|---|---|---|---|---|---|---|
| 1957-58 | 11 | 2 | 6 | 1 | 2 | 1 | 19 | 4 |
| 1958-59 | 11 | 0 | 0 | 0 | 0 | 0 | 11 | 0 |
|  | 22 | 2 | 6 | 1 | 2 | 1 | 30 | 4 |

**ERNIE TAYLOR**

Tommy Taylor was a superb leader of the United attack in the years leading to the Munich crash. A powerful header of the ball, he also possessed great positional sense and could scheme as well as score. Born in Barnsley, Taylor joined the Yorkshire club as a junior before turning professional in 1949. United paid £29,999 — Busby did not want to burden him with a £30,000 tag — in March 1953. Originally an inside-forward at Barnsley, United converted him to one of the most successful centre-forwards in the country. Two months after his transfer, Taylor won the first of his 19 England caps, in the abandoned game against Argentina in May 1953; a week later he scored the first of his 16 English goals. Although he played twice in the 1954 World Cup Finals, he did not establish himself as an England regular until he replaced Nat Lofthouse in 1956. He helped his country qualify for the 1958 World Cup Finals but by the time England took their place in Sweden, Taylor had tragically lost his life at Munich. In five years at Old Trafford, he won two Championship medals and scored United's only goal of the 1957 FA Cup Final. Europe provided his greatest stage and he scored 11 goals in 14 European

Cup matches. One of his finest performances was in the 3-0 win over Atletico Bilbao in the 1956-7 quarter-finals.

|  | LEAGUE | | FA CUP | | EUROPE | | TOTAL | |
|  | App | Gls | App | Gls | App | Gls | App | Gls |
|---|---|---|---|---|---|---|---|---|
| 1952-53 | 11 | 7 | 0 | 0 | 0 | 0 | 11 | 7 |
| 1953-54 | 35 | 22 | 1 | 1 | 0 | 0 | 36 | 23 |
| 1954-55 | 30 | 20 | 1 | 0 | 0 | 0 | 31 | 20 |
| 1955-56 | 33 | 25 | 1 | 0 | 0 | 0 | 34 | 25 |
| 1956-57 | 32 | 22 | 4 | 4 | 8 | 8 | 44 | 34 |
| 1957-58 | 25 | 16 | 2 | 0 | 6 | 3 | 33 | 19 |
|  | 166 | 112 | 9 | 5 | 14 | 11 | 189 | 128 |

**TOMMY TAYLOR**

Swansea-born Henry Thomas signed for United on 7 April 1922, from Welsh non-League side Porth. Two weeks after his transfer, Thomas was given his first taste of League football in a side already doomed to relegation to the Second Division. He played in the 1-1 draw at Oldham and held his place for the opening ten games of the following season. Thereafter, he did not regain a regular first-team place until 1925-6. An outside-left who was not renowned for scoring goals, Thomas nevertheless created plenty for Frank McPherson. He played his last game for United in the home match against Huddersfield Town in April 1930, although he remained on United's books for another season. Thomas was capped once by Wales, playing in the 3-3 draw with England at Wrexham in 1927.

| | LEAGUE | | FA CUP | | TOTAL | |
|---|---|---|---|---|---|---|
| | App | Gls | App | Gls | App | Gls |
| 1921-22 | 3 | 0 | 0 | 0 | 3 | 0 |
| 1922-23 | 18 | 0 | 0 | 0 | 18 | 0 |
| 1923-24 | 6 | 0 | 0 | 0 | 6 | 0 |
| 1924-25 | 3 | 0 | 0 | 0 | 3 | 0 |
| 1925-26 | 29 | 5 | 6 | 1 | 35 | 6 |
| 1926-27 | 16 | 0 | 0 | 0 | 16 | 0 |
| 1927-28 | 13 | 2 | 0 | 0 | 13 | 2 |
| 1928-29 | 19 | 4 | 1 | 0 | 20 | 4 |
| 1929-30 | 21 | 1 | 0 | 0 | 21 | 1 |
| | 128 | 12 | 7 | 1 | 135 | 13 |

**HENRY THOMAS**

When United paid Wrexham £300,000 for Mickey Thomas in November 1978, they bought a hard-working and energetic forward who had made 230 League appearances for his local team. He made his United debut in a 1-0 win at Chelsea who, in 1983-4, were to become his sixth club. A professional since 1972, Thomas played 110 League and Cup games for United in his familiar number-11 shirt, including the 1979 FA Cup Final defeat by Arsenal. In July 1981 he signed for Everton in a deal which took John Gidman to Old Trafford. Thomas could not settle at Goodison and after only ten League games joined Brighton for £400,000. His wife found it difficult to settle so far from her North Wales home and in August 1982, Thomas moved to Stoke City for £200,000. Beleaguered Stoke were forced to sell Thomas to Chelsea in 1984, for only £75,000. The small, tempestuous but clever footballer was still playing First Division football in 1985-6, with struggling West Brom, and won his 50th cap for Wales. But when Ron Saunders took over at The Hawthorns he decreed that Thomas must move his home nearer to the West Midlands or leave. Thomas joined Third Division promotion-chasing Derby on loan. He made nine League appearances before trying his luck with Wichita Wings USA for £35,000 and then Shrewsbury before a shock move to Leeds United in the summer of 1989 for £10,000. But he was soon on his way again — back to Stoke. Another move took him back to where it all started, at Wrexham, and during the 1992 FA Cup competition Thomas enjoyed the thrill of the Cup once more as the Welsh side dumped mighty Arsenal in the third round.

**MICKEY THOMAS**

| | LEAGUE | | FA CUP | | FL CUP | | EUROPE | | TOTAL | |
|---|---|---|---|---|---|---|---|---|---|---|
| | App | Gls | App | Gls | App | Gls | App | Gls | App | Gls |
| 1978-79 | 25 | 1 | 8 | 1 | 0 | 0 | 0 | 0 | 33 | 2 |
| 1979-80 | 35 | 8 | 2 | 0 | 3 | 2 | 0 | 0 | 40 | 10 |
| 1980-81 | 30 | 2 | 3 | 1 | 2 | 0 | 2 | 0 | 37 | 3 |
| | 90 | 11 | 13 | 2 | 5 | 2 | 2 | 0 | 110 | 15 |

141

Alex 'Sandy' Turnbull was one of the several Manchester City players, banned by the FA in 1906 over an illegal payments scandal, who played for United once their suspensions were lifted. Alongside former City colleagues Meredith, Bannister and Burgess, Turnbull made his debut in the 1-0 home win over Aston Villa in January 1907. It was Turnbull who scored the winning goal that day, the first of many such efforts for United. The following season he was the club's leading scorer as they surged to their first League Championship, and he scored the only goal of the 1909 FA Cup Final when United lifted the trophy for the first time. Nicknamed 'Turnbull the Terrible' in his City days, he continued his understanding with Meredith at United. With his namesake Jimmy Turnbull, who joined United from Clapton Orient in May 1907, Sandy formed a lethal striking force. He won a second Championship medal in 1911 and continued playing until World War One. Born in Hurlford, Scotland, he joined City in 1902. He was killed in action in France on 3 May 1917.

| | LEAGUE | | FA CUP | | TOTAL | |
|---|---|---|---|---|---|---|
| | App | Gls | App | Gls | App | Gls |
| 1906-07 | 15 | 6 | 0 | 0 | 15 | 6 |
| 1907-08 | 30 | 25 | 4 | 2 | 34 | 27 |
| 1908-09 | 19 | 5 | 6 | 4 | 25 | 9 |
| 1909-10 | 26 | 13 | 1 | 0 | 27 | 13 |
| 1910-11 | 35 | 18 | 3 | 1 | 38 | 19 |
| 1911-12 | 30 | 7 | 6 | 3 | 36 | 10 |
| 1912-13 | 35 | 10 | 4 | 0 | 39 | 10 |
| 1913-14 | 17 | 4 | 1 | 0 | 18 | 4 |
| 1914-15 | 13 | 2 | 0 | 0 | 13 | 2 |
| | 220 | 90 | 25 | 10 | 245 | 100 |

**SANDY TURNBULL**

Manchester-born Dennis Viollet joined United as a 16-year-old and gave them 13 years loyal service. He made his League debut at Newcastle in April 1953. Viollet went on to play in nearly 300 first-team games. Of frail appearance, his skills and stamina belied his frame and he was an accurate passer of the ball and possessed a delicate body-swerve. He made goals and scored them and his 32 League goals in 1959-60 is still a United record. After winning two Championship medals and an FA Cup runners-up medal, Viollet moved to Stoke City in a £25,000-deal in January 1962. He scored 59 League goals in 182 games for the Potters and helped them to the Second Division championship in 1962-3. He spent 18 months in the United States with Baltimore Bays before returning to play for non-League Witton Albion. He won an Irish FA Cup winners' medal with Linfield and joined the coaching staff at Preston, then Crewe where he had a brief period as manager. Viollet later coached NASL team Washington Diplomats. He won two full England caps, plus Schoolboy and football League honours.

| | LEAGUE | | FA CUP | | FL CUP | | EUROPE | | TOTAL | |
|---|---|---|---|---|---|---|---|---|---|---|
| | App | Gls | App | Gls | App | Gls | App | Gls | App | Gls |
| 1952-53 | 3 | 1 | 0 | 0 | 0 | 0 | 0 | 0 | 3 | 1 |
| 1953-54 | 29 | 11 | 1 | 1 | 0 | 0 | 0 | 0 | 30 | 12 |
| 1954-55 | 34 | 20 | 3 | 1 | 0 | 0 | 0 | 0 | 37 | 21 |
| 1955-56 | 34 | 20 | 1 | 0 | 0 | 0 | 0 | 0 | 35 | 20 |
| 1956-57 | 27 | 16 | 5 | 0 | 0 | 0 | 6 | 9 | 38 | 25 |
| 1957-58 | 22 | 16 | 3 | 3 | 0 | 0 | 6 | 4 | 31 | 23 |
| 1958-59 | 37 | 21 | 1 | 0 | 0 | 0 | 0 | 0 | 38 | 21 |
| 1959-60 | 36 | 32 | 3 | 0 | 0 | 0 | 0 | 0 | 39 | 32 |
| 1960-61 | 24 | 15 | 1 | 0 | 2 | 1 | 0 | 0 | 27 | 16 |
| 1961-62 | 13 | 7 | 0 | 0 | 0 | 0 | 0 | 0 | 13 | 7 |
| | 259 | 159 | 18 | 5 | 2 | 1 | 12 | 13 | 291 | 178 |

**DENNIS VIOLLET**

The Rugby League stronghold of St Helens has produced some fine soccer players over the years and United have been fortunate to have fielded some of them. George Vose was one such player. He joined United in September 1932, after being spotted playing for his local team, Peasley Cross. He made his debut the following season when he started as first-choice centre-half. Most of his League appearances were made in that position. After World War Two he joined Cheshire League side Runcorn. Vose was a member of the United team which went up and down between the First and Second Divisions in the 1930s. His only honour from the game was a Second Division championship medal in 1936, but his skills should have earned him many more. He was a natural ball-player, always quick to see and exploit an opening. He played in an England trial match in 1936.

|         | LEAGUE | | FA CUP | | TOTAL | |
|---------|--------|-----|--------|-----|--------|-----|
|         | App | Gls | App | Gls | App | Gls |
| 1933-34 | 17 | 1 | 2 | 0 | 19 | 1 |
| 1934-35 | 39 | 0 | 3 | 0 | 42 | 0 |
| 1935-36 | 41 | 0 | 3 | 0 | 44 | 0 |
| 1936-37 | 26 | 0 | 1 | 0 | 27 | 0 |
| 1937-38 | 33 | 0 | 4 | 0 | 37 | 0 |
| 1938-39 | 39 | 0 | 1 | 0 | 40 | 0 |
| 1939-40 | 2 | 0 | 0 | 0 | 2 | 0 |
|         | 197 | 1 | 14 | 0 | 211 | 1 |

**GEORGE VOSE**

**GEORGE WALL**

One of the many players bred in the tough Barnsley 'school' before World War One, George Wall was a goalscoring outside-left. Born in Boldon, County Durham, in February 1885, Wall joined Barnsley in 1902. Louis Rocca took him to United in 1906 and he scored the only goal on his League debut, against Clapton Orient in April that year. He was a member of the United team which won the club's first League Championship, and their first FA Cup. He won seven England caps and helped United to a second League title. Wall played his last game for United just after the outbreak of war. After hostilities ceased he signed for Oldham and in 1922 transferred to Hamilton Academicals before returning to Lancashire and a brief stay with Rochdale. He retired in 1923 and worked on Manchester docks. A fast winger, Wall could cross the ball accurately and was capable of producing a fierce shot on the run. His 20-year playing career saw him play 503 League games in England and Scotland.

|         | LEAGUE | | FA CUP | | TOTAL | |
|---------|--------|-----|--------|-----|--------|-----|
|         | App | Gls | App | Gls | App | Gls |
| 1905-06 | 6 | 3 | 0 | 0 | 6 | 3 |
| 1906-07 | 38 | 11 | 2 | 2 | 40 | 13 |
| 1907-08 | 36 | 19 | 4 | 3 | 40 | 22 |
| 1908-09 | 34 | 11 | 6 | 0 | 40 | 11 |
| 1909-10 | 32 | 14 | 1 | 0 | 33 | 14 |
| 1910-11 | 26 | 5 | 3 | 1 | 29 | 6 |
| 1911-12 | 33 | 3 | 6 | 1 | 39 | 4 |
| 1912-13 | 36 | 10 | 5 | 2 | 41 | 12 |
| 1913-14 | 29 | 11 | 1 | 0 | 30 | 11 |
| 1914-15 | 17 | 2 | 1 | 0 | 18 | 2 |
|         | 287 | 89 | 29 | 9 | 316 | 98 |

The war years deprived John Warner of what would have been a distinguished career with United. He was in his 27th year when he joined them from Swansea Town in June 1938, and that made him nearly 35 when League soccer resumed after the war. Warner, a strong wing-half, appeared in over 100 peacetime games for the club but made more than 150 appearances in wartime football. He commanded a regular place immediately after the war but his appearances were limited from 1948 until the 1951 close season when he moved to Oldham Athletic. After 12 months at Boundary Park he moved to Rochdale for what proved to be his final season of League football, retiring at the age of 42. His career spanned 20 years and more than 400 senior games, excluding his wartime appearances. He won two Wales caps before the war, one with Swansea and one with United.

|  | LEAGUE | | FA CUP | | TOTAL | |
|---|---|---|---|---|---|---|
|  | App | Gls | App | Gls | App | Gls |
| 1938-39 | 29 | 0 | 2 | 0 | 31 | 0 |
| 1939-40 | 3 | 0 | 0 | 0 | 3 | 0 |
| 1945-46 | 0 | 0 | 4 | 0 | 4 | 0 |
| 1946-47 | 34 | 1 | 2 | 0 | 36 | 1 |
| 1947-48 | 15 | 0 | 1 | 1 | 16 | 1 |
| 1948-49 | 3 | 0 | 0 | 0 | 3 | 0 |
| 1949-50 | 21 | 0 | 4 | 0 | 25 | 0 |
|  | 105 | 1 | 13 | 1 | 118 | 2 |

**JOHN WARNER**

**NEIL WEBB**

Neil Webb joined United in the 1989 close season from Nottingham Forest for £1.5 million. He started his career at Reading before a move to Portsmouth and then joined Brian Clough at Forest. By the time Webb arrived at Old Trafford, he had a wealth of experience behind him and had appeared in nearly 250 League games and scored over 100 goals. He had also gained full England international honours, winning 11 caps at the time of his move to United. He has since gone on to win 20 full caps and was a member of the 1990 World Cup squad, playing in one game, as a substitute in the third-place play-off against Italy. It was something of a comeback, though, for he had been out with injury for some time. Webb scored on his United debut, in the 3-1 win over Arsenal on the opening day of the 1989 season, but after only four games he damaged an Achilles tendon playing for England in a World Cup qualifier against Sweden and was out of action for six months, returning as sub at Southampton the following March. He ended what seemed like being a miserable debut season at Old Trafford by collecting an FA Cup winners' medal.

|  | LEAGUE | | FACUP | | FLCUP | | EUROPE | | TOTAL | |
|---|---|---|---|---|---|---|---|---|---|---|
|  | App | Gls | App | Gls | App | Gls | App | Gls | App | Gls |
| 1989-90 | 10/1 | 2 | 4 | 1 | 0 | 0 | 0 | 0 | 14/1 | 3 |
| 1990-91 | 31/1 | 3 | 2 | 0 | 7 | 1 | 6 | 1 | 46/1 | 5 |
| 1991-92 | 29/2 | 3 | 3 | 0 | 6 | 0 | 3 | 0 | 41/2 | 3 |
|  | 70/4 | 8 | 9 | 1 | 13 | 1 | 9 | 1 | 101/4 | 11 |

Cardiff-born Welsh international Colin Webster was on the books of three of Wales' four Football League clubs. He joined Cardiff as a 17-year-old in 1949 but failed to make the grade with them. Jimmy Murphy's contacts put United in touch with the youngster and in May 1952 Webster signed for the Old Trafford club. He was too old to take part in the club's FA Youth Cup successes and had to serve his apprenticeship in the Central League. He was given one League game in 1953-4 when he replaced Johnny Berry at Portsmouth. Thereafter his first-team appearances were spasmodic, but he always gave maximum effort whenever and wherever he was called upon. Although a natural centre-forward, he could also play on either wing and at inside-forward or wing-half. He played enough games to qualify for a League Championship medal in 1956 and after Munich established himself as a regular, playing outside-left in the 1958 FA Cup Final. The following October he signed for Swansea Town and in March 1963 made his final move, to Newport County. Webster played 255 League games and scored 95 goals. He won four full Welsh caps, three of them in the 1958 World Cup Finals in Sweden.

|         | LEAGUE | | FA CUP | | EUROPE | | TOTAL | |
|---------|-----|-----|-----|-----|-----|-----|-----|-----|
|         | App | Gls | App | Gls | App | Gls | App | Gls |
| 1953-54 | 1   | 0   | 0   | 0   | 0   | 0   | 1   | 0   |
| 1954-55 | 17  | 8   | 2   | 3   | 0   | 0   | 19  | 11  |
| 1955-56 | 15  | 4   | 0   | 0   | 0   | 0   | 15  | 4   |
| 1956-57 | 5   | 3   | 1   | 0   | 0   | 0   | 6   | 3   |
| 1957-58 | 20  | 6   | 6   | 1   | 5   | 1   | 31  | 8   |
| 1958-59 | 7   | 5   | 0   | 0   | 0   | 0   | 7   | 5   |
|         | 65  | 26  | 9   | 4   | 5   | 1   | 79  | 31  |

**COLIN WEBSTER**

Enoch 'Knocker' West joined Manchester United before the start of 1910-11 and scored a goal on the opening day of the season, in a 2-1 win at Woolwich Arsenal. It was the first of many goals that helped United to their second League title in four seasons and West played his full part. Only Sandy Turnbull scored more goals for United that season, but in the next two, West finished top scorer. Born at Hucknall, Nottinghamshire, West started his career with Nottingham Forest and scored almost 100 goals in five seasons with them, being the First Division's leading scorer in 1907-08. His powerful shooting from centre-forward brought him many goals for United and he played his final game for them in April 1915. Earlier that month he had been involved in a plot to 'fix' the result of United's game against Liverpool. He was suspended for life along with other players, and his ban, the longest in Football League history was eventually lifted in November 1945, after 30 years. West won representative honours with the Football League.

|         | LEAGUE | | FA CUP | | TOTAL | |
|---------|-----|-----|-----|-----|-----|-----|
|         | App | Gls | App | Gls | App | Gls |
| 1910-11 | 35  | 19  | 3   | 1   | 38  | 20  |
| 1911-12 | 32  | 17  | 6   | 6   | 38  | 23  |
| 1912-13 | 36  | 21  | 4   | 1   | 40  | 22  |
| 1913-14 | 30  | 6   | 1   | 0   | 31  | 6   |
| 1914-15 | 33  | 9   | 1   | 0   | 34  | 9   |
|         | 166 | 72  | 15  | 8   | 181 | 80  |

**ENOCH WEST**

**ARTHUR WHALLEY**

Born in Openshaw, Arthur Whalley was a powerfully-built centre-half who joined United from Blackpool in May 1909 after six League games for the Seasiders. He could also perform well at wing-half, although he was bought as cover for centre-half Charlie Roberts. He made over 100 first-team appearances for United and won a League Championship medal in 1910-11. When Roberts signed for Oldham Athletic in 1913, Whalley became United's regular pivot until he lost his place to Pat O'Connell the following season. He played in the football League in 1913 and in an England trial match in 1914. Whalley did not appear for United in the wartime Lancashire Section, but he returned after the conflict to take up the left-half position alongside Clarrie Hilditch. In the 1920 close season he was transferred to Southend United and after one season there, moved to Charlton. He stayed at The Valley for three years moving to Millwall in 1924. In 1926 he became trainer at Barrow and made his final League appearance in 1927. He returned to Manchester where he became a bookmaker. He died in 1952 aged 66.

|         | LEAGUE | | FA CUP | | TOTAL | |
|---------|-----|-----|-----|-----|-----|-----|
|         | App | Gls | App | Gls | App | Gls |
| 1909-10 | 9   | 0   | 0   | 0   | 9   | 0   |
| 1910-11 | 15  | 0   | 0   | 0   | 15  | 0   |
| 1911-12 | 5   | 0   | 1   | 0   | 6   | 0   |
| 1912-13 | 26  | 4   | 5   | 0   | 31  | 4   |
| 1913-14 | 18  | 2   | 1   | 0   | 19  | 2   |
| 1914-15 | 1   | 0   | 0   | 0   | 1   | 0   |
| 1919-20 | 23  | 0   | 2   | 0   | 25  | 0   |
|         | 97  | 6   | 9   | 0   | 106 | 6   |

Bert Whalley's record of only 33 League games for Manchester United does not begin to tell the full story of his contribution to the club. His career with United lasted from May 1934, when he joined them from Stalybridge Celtic, until February 1958 when he lost his life in the Munich air disaster. A strong wing-half, Whalley made his United debut against Doncaster Rovers in November 1935, but it was during the war that he gave the club his best years as a player. A virtual ever-present, Whalley played around 190 games for the Reds in wartime soccer. After the war he appeared in three more League games before taking up a coaching position. Well-loved and respected, he played a significant part in the development of many youngsters who went on to give United inestimable value. Ironically, Bert Whalley was not scheduled to make the fateful European Cup trip to Belgrade. His seat should have been filled by Jimmy Murphy, but he was on international duty as manager of the Wales team at Cardiff. Whalley was killed instantly in the crash and his death was mourned in particular by the many young players whose formative years he had overseen.

|         | LEAGUE | | FA CUP | | TOTAL | |
|---------|-----|-----|-----|-----|-----|-----|
|         | App | Gls | App | Gls | App | Gls |
| 1935-36 | 2   | 0   | 0   | 0   | 2   | 0   |
| 1936-37 | 19  | 0   | 2   | 0   | 21  | 0   |
| 1937-38 | 6   | 0   | 0   | 0   | 6   | 0   |
| 1938-39 | 2   | 0   | 0   | 0   | 2   | 0   |
| 1939-40 | 1   | 0   | 0   | 0   | 1   | 0   |
| 1945-46 | 0   | 0   | 4   | 0   | 4   | 0   |
| 1946-47 | 3   | 0   | 0   | 0   | 3   | 0   |
|         | 33  | 0   | 6   | 0   | 39  | 0   |

**BERT WHALLEY**

Known as Billy, or Liam, Whelan was the artist of the 'pre-Munich' United team. His ball control was a delight to witness and his overall command of the game's skills was a model for any young footballer to study. He was born in Dublin and joined United from Home Farm FC in 1953. He went on to play almost 100 games for United, scoring over 50 goals and collecting Championship medals in 1956 and 1957 and an FA Cup losers' medal in 1957. Capped four times by the Republic of Ireland, Whelan was vying with Bobby Charlton for the number-eight shirt at the time of the Munich air disaster. Charlton played in the last seven League games before the crash and although Whelan did not play in the game against Red Star Belgrade, he was a member of the squad that made that trip and was one of those who lost their lives.

|  | LEAGUE | | FA CUP | | EUROPE | | TOTAL | |
|  | App | Gls | App | Gls | App | Gls | App | Gls |
|---|---|---|---|---|---|---|---|---|
| 1954-55 | 7 | 1 | 0 | 0 | 0 | 0 | 7 | 1 |
| 1955-56 | 13 | 4 | 0 | 0 | 0 | 0 | 13 | 4 |
| 1956-57 | 39 | 26 | 6 | 4 | 8 | 3 | 53 | 33 |
| 1957-58 | 20 | 12 | 0 | 0 | 3 | 2 | 23 | 14 |
|  | 79 | 43 | 6 | 4 | 11 | 5 | 96 | 52 |

**BILLY WHELAN**

**JEFF WHITEFOOT**

Although Jeff Whitefoot's career stretched to nearly 400 League games, only 93 of them were with his first club, Manchester United. He spent eight seasons with United after joining them in 1949. He made his League debut, against Portsmouth in April 1950, at the age of 16 years and 105 days, which makes him the youngest player ever to appear in a League game for the club. He gained a regular first-team place during the 1953-4 season. Whitefoot was a powerful wing-half but despite winning a Championship medal in 1955-6, he lost his right-half place to another youngster, Eddie Colman. An England Schoolboy international, Whitefoot won one Under-23 cap before his transfer to Grimsby Town in 1957. The following close season he signed for Nottingham Forest, for whom he played almost 300 games in ten seasons. In 1959, he won an FA Cup winners' medal with Forest and played his final League game in 1967-8, 18 years after his debut.

|  | LEAGUE | | FA CUP | | TOTAL | |
|  | App | Gls | App | Gls | App | Gls |
|---|---|---|---|---|---|---|
| 1949-50 | 1 | 0 | 0 | 0 | 1 | 0 |
| 1950-51 | 2 | 0 | 0 | 0 | 2 | 0 |
| 1951-52 | 3 | 0 | 0 | 0 | 3 | 0 |
| 1952-53 | 10 | 0 | 0 | 0 | 10 | 0 |
| 1953-54 | 38 | 0 | 1 | 0 | 39 | 0 |
| 1954-55 | 24 | 0 | 0 | 0 | 24 | 0 |
| 1955-56 | 15 | 0 | 1 | 0 | 16 | 0 |
|  | 93 | 0 | 2 | 0 | 95 | 0 |

Norman Whiteside capped his first full season in United's first team with a goal in the 4-0 FA Cup Final replay over Brighton in 1983. It made him the youngest-ever FA Cup Final scorer and came a few weeks after he had become the youngest-ever scorer of a League (Milk) Cup Final goal. In the 1982 World Cup Finals, Whiteside, then 17, was the youngest player ever to appear in the final stages of the competition. Born in Belfast in 1965, he was still an apprentice when he made his United debut against Brighton in 1982. After only two appearances in the League he was chosen for the full Northern Ireland squad and played in all five games in Spain. A footballer with great talent, and his effort which won the 1985 FA Cup Final — a wickedly swerving shot which completely defeated Neville Southall — was a typical effort. Still only 21, and already a Wembley veteran for club and country, Whiteside proved his worth as a striker and a midfielder and skippered United when Robson was injured. But he struggled with injuries in 1988-9, making only six League appearances, and he signed for Everton for £750,000 in 1989. However, after only 29 League games for Everton he was forced to quit through injury and became phsyiotherapist with Northwich Victoria.

**NORMAN WHITESIDE**

|  | LEAGUE | | FACUP | | FLCUP | | EUROPE | | TOTAL | |
|---|---|---|---|---|---|---|---|---|---|---|
|  | App | Gls | App | Gls | App | Gls | App | Gls | App | Gls |
| 1981-82 | 1/1 | 1 | 0 | 0 | 0 | 0 | 0 | 0 | 1/1 | 1 |
| 1982-83 | 39 | 8 | 7 | 3 | 7/2 | 3 | 2 | 0 | 55/2 | 14 |
| 1983-84 | 30/7 | 10 | 1 | 0 | 6 | 1 | 5/1 | 1 | 42/8 | 12 |
| 1984-85 | 23/4 | 9 | 6 | 4 | 1 | 0 | 4/1 | 0 | 34/5 | 13 |
| 1985-86 | 37 | 4 | 5 | 1 | 4 | 2 | 0 | 0 | 46 | 7 |
| 1986-87 | 31 | 8 | 2 | 1 | 3/1 | 1 | 0 | 0 | 36/1 | 10 |
| 1987-88 | 26/1 | 7 | 3 | 1 | 5 | 2 | 0 | 0 | 34/1 | 10 |
| 1988-89 | 6 | 0 | 0 | 0 | 0 | 0 | 0 | 0 | 6 | 0 |
|  | 193/13 | 47 | 24 | 10 | 26/3 | 9 | 11/2 | 1 | 254/18 | 67 |

Nicknamed 'Butch' by his father, a former Brentford professional, Ray Wilkins joined Chelsea as a 15-year-old when Dave Sexton signed him. He obtained Schoolboy international honours. Captain of the England Youth team, he became Chelsea's youngest-ever skipper when he was 18. He led them to promotion from the Second Division in 1976-7. Wilkins' great features were the coolness of his play and his passing and shooting skills. After going through a phase when he ceased to enjoy his football at Stamford Bridge, Wilkins joined United when Sexton, then manager at Old Trafford, signed him for £825,000 in August 1979. He took a while to settle but eventually succeeded Martin Buchan as club captain. He later captained England but then lost both jobs to Bryan Robson. Wilkins with over 80 England caps to his name, perhaps plays best when he is captain. He appeared in the 1983 FA Cup and Milk Cup Finals and scored a memorable goal in the first Wembley game against Brighton. In May 1984, he left United to play for AC Milan, who paid £1.5 million for him. He joined Rangers, via Paris St Germain, and then returned to the top flight in England with QPR.

**RAY WILKINS**

|  | LEAGUE | | FACUP | | FLCUP | | EUROPE | | TOTAL | |
|---|---|---|---|---|---|---|---|---|---|---|
|  | App | Gls | App | Gls | App | Gls | App | Gls | App | Gls |
| 1979-80 | 37 | 2 | 2 | 0 | 3 | 0 | 0 | 0 | 42 | 2 |
| 1980-81 | 11/2 | 0 | 2 | 0 | 0 | 0 | 0 | 0 | 13/2 | 0 |
| 1981-82 | 42 | 1 | 1 | 0 | 2 | 0 | 0 | 0 | 45 | 1 |
| 1982-83 | 26 | 1 | 4 | 1 | 3/1 | 0 | 2 | 0 | 35/1 | 2 |
| 1983-84 | 42 | 3 | 1 | 0 | 6 | 1 | 6 | 1 | 55 | 5 |
|  | 158/2 | 7 | 10 | 1 | 14/1 | 1 | 8 | 1 | 190/3 | 10 |

148

John Wilson started his Football League career in the
First Division with Newcastle United in 1919-20, but
it was not until he joined Manchester United, seven
years and 139 League games later, that he played in
the First Division again. He left the League to play
for Leadgate Park, one of the clubs from his home
town of Leadgate. Durham City, who were then a Third
Division North club, tempted him back to League
football and after one season with Durham, Wilson
moved to Stockport County. The solidly-built wing-
half had four seasons at Edgeley Park, until they were
relegated at the end of 1925-6. United signed him before
the start of the following season and Wilson found
himself back in the First Division. After five seasons
at the top, he suffered relegation once more and after
nine games of the 1931-2 season, signed for Bristol
City where he finished his career.

|  | LEAGUE | | FA CUP | | TOTAL | |
|  | App | Gls | App | Gls | App | Gls |
|---|---|---|---|---|---|---|
| 1926-27 | 21 | 0 | 0 | 0 | 21 | 0 |
| 1927-28 | 33 | 0 | 5 | 0 | 38 | 0 |
| 1928-29 | 19 | 1 | 2 | 0 | 21 | 1 |
| 1929-30 | 28 | 1 | 1 | 0 | 29 | 1 |
| 1930-31 | 20 | 1 | 2 | 0 | 22 | 1 |
| 1931-32 | 9 | 0 | 0 | 0 | 9 | 0 |
|  | 130 | 3 | 10 | 0 | 140 | 3 |

**JOHN WILSON**

**WALTER WINTERBOTTOM OBE**

Although Walter Winterbottom's Football League
career was undistinguished, he served as FA Director
of Coaching and as the first England team manager
between 1946 and 1963. Born in Lancashire,
Winterbottom went to Oldham Grammar School and
spent three years as a schoolteacher before Louis Rocca
saw him playing for Cheshire League side, Mossley.
Winterbottom made his League debut at wing-half at
Elland Road in November 1936. One of his best games
for the club was against Manchester City in January
1937 when he shut out Freddie Tilson, even though
City won 1-0. A spinal injury ended Winterbottom's
League career but during the war he led several
representative sides. He enjoyed the theory of the game
and after the war was offered the FA's top coaching
job, as well as being appointed England team manager.
Although he never had the complete control enjoyed
by his successor, Sir Alf Ramsey, Winterbottom guided
England to four successive World Cup Finals and
worked for the Central Council of Physical Education.
A member of the Sports Council, in 1985 Winterbottom
was appointed chairman of a committee to review the
development of Karate in Great Britain.

|  | LEAGUE | | FA CUP | | TOTAL | |
|  | App | Gls | App | Gls | App | Gls |
|---|---|---|---|---|---|---|
| 1936-37 | 21 | 0 | 2 | 0 | 23 | 0 |
| 1937-38 | 4 | 0 | 0 | 0 | 4 | 0 |
|  | 25 | 0 | 2 | 0 | 27 | 0 |

**RICHARD WOMBWELL**

Dicky Wombwell was a clever outside-left who was more adept at creating goals for his fellow forwards than he was at scoring them himself. His Football League career covered nearly 250 games, he started with Derby County whom he joined in May 1899 from Ilkeston Town. After three seasons and 95 League and Cup games for the Rams he dropped to the Second Division with Bristol City. Towards the end of 1904-05, Wombwell moved to Manchester United, who were Bristol's close promotion rivals. That season United finished third in the Second Division. City were fourth. A year later, the West Country side were champions with United second. After only half a season back in Division One, Wombwell, together with Peddie and Yates, signed for Hearts. Wombwell returned to England the following season to play Southern League football for Brighton, then joined Blackburn Rovers for two seasons before returning to his first club, Ilkeston.

|  | LEAGUE | | FA CUP | | TOTAL | |
|---|---|---|---|---|---|---|
|  | App | Gls | App | Gls | App | Gls |
| 1904-05 | 8 | 1 | 0 | 0 | 8 | 1 |
| 1905-06 | 25 | 2 | 2 | 0 | 27 | 2 |
| 1906-07 | 14 | 0 | 2 | 0 | 16 | 0 |
|  | 47 | 3 | 4 | 0 | 51 | 3 |

Born at Hebburn-on-Tyne, goalkeeper Ray Wood was another of the fine players from the North-East who joined United in the 1940s. He had been a professional with Darlington for only six months when United signed him as an 18-year-old in December 1949. He made his debut, against Newcastle United for whom he had played as an amateur, the day after he signed, but he was basically a cover for Jack Crompton. The following summer, United signed Reg Allen and Wood had to be content with a further spell in the Central League. When Allen retired through illness, Wood shared the first-team spot with Crompton. He started 1954-5 as first-choice goalkeeper and was a member of the 1956 and 1957 Championship sides, also appearing in the 1957 FA Cup Final when he was injured in a collision with Peter McParland and had to leave the field. He returned for a brief spell on the wing, and then went off again and went back in goal for the final few minutes. Wood survived the Munich crash, but by the time he was fit again, he had lost his place to Harry Gregg. He played only one more game before moving to Huddersfield Town in 1958, later playing for Bradford City and Barnsley and in the USA for Los Angeles Wolves, and coaching in Cyprus and the United Arab Emirates. Wood won three full England caps.

**RAY WOOD**

|  | LEAGUE | | FA CUP | | EUROPE | | TOTAL | |
|---|---|---|---|---|---|---|---|---|
|  | App | Gls | App | Gls | App | Gls | App | Gls |
| 1949-50 | 1 | 0 | 0 | 0 | 0 | 0 | 1 | 0 |
| 1950-51 | 0 | 0 | 0 | 0 | 0 | 0 | 0 | 0 |
| 1951-52 | 0 | 0 | 0 | 0 | 0 | 0 | 0 | 0 |
| 1952-53 | 12 | 0 | 4 | 0 | 0 | 0 | 16 | 0 |
| 1953-54 | 27 | 0 | 1 | 0 | 0 | 0 | 28 | 0 |
| 1954-55 | 37 | 0 | 3 | 0 | 0 | 0 | 40 | 0 |
| 1955-56 | 41 | 0 | 1 | 0 | 0 | 0 | 42 | 0 |
| 1956-57 | 39 | 0 | 6 | 0 | 8 | 0 | 53 | 0 |
| 1957-58 | 20 | 0 | 0 | 0 | 4 | 0 | 24 | 0 |
| 1958-59 | 1 | 0 | 0 | 0 | 0 | 0 | 1 | 0 |
|  | 178 | 0 | 15 | 2 | 12 | 0 | 205 | 0 |

*Newton Heath 1901-02, the last season under this name. Back row (left to right): James West (secretary), Stafford, Whitehouse, F.Erentz. Middle row: Schofield, Williams, Morgan, Griffiths, Banks. On ground: Preston, Lapping, Fisher. Fred Erentz was the only survivor from Newton Heath's first League game.*

## Match to Remember 1        3 September 1892

# Blackburn Rovers 4    Newton Heath 3

AFTER three years in the Alliance, Newton Heath were admitted to the Football League and their first taste of action in the competition they had been trying to join for some time came at Ewood Park, home of one of the leading sides of the day, Blackburn Rovers.

Rovers, five times winners of the FA Cup and with four years of League experience behind them, were expected to score an easy victory over the newcomers. But when the game kicked-off at four o'clock, they were surprised by the attacking play of the Heathens, who forced their way forward, despite kicking into the wind.

It took only five minutes, however, for Blackburn to take the lead, thanks to an individual effort by Jack Southworth. Two minutes later, Hall scored a second for the home team, although the Heathens hotly disputed the legitimacy of the goal.

Blackburn now dominated the proceedings and came close on several occasions before Chippendale pulled the ball back for Hall to score their third in the 15th minute.

Eventually, Newton Heath scored their first goal in the Football League when Donaldson broke away. And just before half-time, Coupar caused a stir among home fans when he reduced Rovers' lead to a single goal.

There was to be no great fight-back, however, and Rovers had the better of a fast-moving second half. Chippendale restored their two-goal average but in the closing minutes a Farman goal closed the gap again and left Newton Heath's first League scoreline looking slightly more respectable.

**Blackburn Rovers:** Pennington; Murray, Forbes, Almond, Dewar, Forrest, Chippendale, Walton, Southworth, Hall, Bowdler.
**Newton Heath:** Warner; Clements, Brown, Perrins, Stewart, F.C.Erentz, Farman, Coupar, Donaldson, Carson, Mathieson.

*Attendance: 8,000*            *Referee: T.Helme (Farnworth)*

151

# Manchester City 2  Newton Heath 5

THE first Football League encounter between Manchester's two giants took place at City's Hyde Road ground over 90 years ago. City had recently changed their name from Ardwick, but United were to be known as Newton Heath for another eight years.

The Heathens had just been relegated and Manchester fans eagerly awaited the first clash between the two clubs since they had joined the League two years earlier. Billy Meredith, who joined City two weeks earlier, was making his home debut and although they did not know it, supporters were witnessing the start of a career which would serve both clubs with distinction.

A 14,000 crowd braved a dull, miserable day and they saw Meredith mount the first attack, although his solo effort came to nothing. It was Newton Heath who opened the scoring through inside-left Smith and they added a second in the 13th minute when the same player gave Hutchinson no chance with a powerful, low shot.

City mounted several attacks late in the first half and only a series of fine saves by Douglas prevented them from getting back into the game.

City full-back Smith limped off shortly after the restart and soon afterwards Clarkin scored the Heathens' third. Two quick goals from Newton Heath's Smith brought his personal tally to four and made the score 5-0.

For City it was another big disappointment following defeat in their previous home match, 4-2 at the hands of Darwen, and on Meredith's debut, at Newcastle where they went down 5-4. They salvaged a little pride with two goals, one each from Meredith and Sharples.

**Manchester City:** Hutchinson; H.Smith, Walker, Mann, Nash, Dyer, Meredith, Finnerhan, Rowan, Sharples, Milarvie.
**Newton Heath:** Douglas; McCartney, F.Erentz, Perrins, McNaught, Davidson, Clarkin, Donaldson, Dow, R.Smith, Peters.

*Attendance 14,000*                            *Referee: Lewis (Blackburn)*

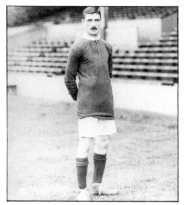

*Billy Meredith made his home debut for Manchester City in the first Mancunian derby game. He was later to serve United with distinction before rejoining City after World War One.*

152

*Sandy Turnbull's shot beats Bristol City goalkeeper Harry Clay at the Crystal Palace.*

# Manchester United 1   Bristol City 0

ALTHOUGH the 1909 FA Cup Final at the Crystal Palace was a disappointing affair, with both sides occasionally indulging in rough play, it will stand out in the story of Manchester United as the first time United won the trophy.

United were favourites, despite being below City in Division One. They were the previous season's Champions and many felt that their greater experience would give them the edge.

Skipper Charlie Roberts won the toss and the United forwards mounted several early attacks, but they missed their chances and that was to be the pattern of the game for both sides.

The difference between the teams was Billy Meredith. He was United's great motivator, adding to the winners' medal he had won with Manchester City five years earlier.

The only goal of the game came in the 22nd minute when Sandy Turnbull turned home a Harold Halse shot that had rebounded off the crossbar. There were few other notable incidents. Harry Moger made a fine save from Hardy, and at the other end Wall brought Clay to an equally good save.

Sandy Turnbull had decided to play only at the last minute when Charlie Roberts persuaded him that, even with an injured knee, he would be capable of winning the match on his own. He certainly did not disappoint his skipper.

Another United casualty was full-back Hayes, who played for part of the game with a broken rib. In the closing stages, tempers began to fray as City pressed for an equalizer and United were cautioned for time-wasting.

Nothing, however, could cloud the moment when Charlie Roberts became the first United captain to proudly hold aloft the FA Cup.

**Manchester United:** Moger; Stacey, Hayes, Duckworth, Roberts, Bell, Meredith, Halse, J.Turnbull, A.Turnbull, Wall.
**Bristol City:** Clay; Annan, Cottle, Hanlin, Wedlock, Spear, Staniforth, Hardy, Gilligan, Burton, Hilton.

*Attendance: 71,401*                    *Referee: J.Mason (Burslem)*

# Millwall 0   Manchester United 2

UNITED travelled to Millwall on the last Saturday of the 1933-4 season for the most crucial match in their history. Defeat, or even a draw, would see them relegated to the Third Division for the first time — and one London newspaper that week had even reviewed United's prospects in the lowest division.

To compound the difficulty of United's task, Millwall were also fighting to stave off relegation, yet their home record was impressive for a club so low in the table. Nevertheless, United had a good record in London that season, having won at Brentford and Fulham.

Lincoln were already down and the other relegation place lay between United (32 points from 41 games), Millwall (33 from 41) and Swansea (33 from 41). The Old Trafford club, who had not lost in their previous four games, brought back Vose at the heart of their defence, and introduced Hugh McLenahan and Manley to the forward line.

While United's defence withstood some frenzied Millwall attacks, it was the wing pairing of Manley and Cape that did the damage. After eight minutes, Manley started and finished the move which brought United's first goal when he sent Cape away and then netted from the centre.

Injury left Hine a virtual passenger with only a quarter of the game played but United hung on to their slender lead and then, two minutes after the interval, Cape scored his most important goal of the season with a powerful shot.

United's cool heads and stout hearts held on and it was Millwall who were relegated. On the corresponding Saturday two years later, United drew 1-1 with Hull to assure themselves of the Second Division championship.

**Manchester United:** Hacking; Griffiths, Jones, Robertson, Vose, McKay, Cape, McLenahan, Ball, Hine, Manley.
**Millwall:** Yuill; Walsh, Pipe, Newcomb, Turnbull, Forsyth, McCartney, Alexander, Yardley, Roberts, Fishlock.

*Attendance: 24,003*                                      *Referee: J.H.Whittle (Worcester)*

*George Vose returned to the heart of United's defence and gave a sterling display as Millwall mounted a series of frenzied attacks.*

# Manchester United 4   Blackpool 2

IT WAS 39 years to the day since Manchester United had last appeared in an FA Cup Final. On that occasion they beat Bristol City in a dull affair, but the 1948 Final was so different, hailed as one of the finest ever seen.

A capacity crowd filled Wembley Stadium and they were treated to a display of attacking football as both sides signalled an early push forward in search of goals. They were privileged to witness not only classic skills, but also fine sportsmanship. Even when Blackpool took a 12th minute lead through Shimwell's penalty, United accepted it with grace although many felt that Allenby Chilton's foul on Mortensen was outside the penalty area.

A mix-up between Hayward and Robinson allowed Jack Rowley to level the scores in the 28th minute, but Blackpool regained the lead seven minutes later when Kelly headed on a Matthews free-kick and Mortensen scored.

In the second half, United managed to shut out Matthews and in a 14-minute spell they scored three times to climax a magnificent Final.

Rowley got between two defenders to head home a Johnny Morris free-kick — a superb goal — in the 69th minute, and United took the lead for the first time when Stan Pearson took Anderson's pass and placed the ball wide of the onrushing goalkeeper. Seconds earlier, Jack Crompton had brought off a tremendous save from Mortensen and it was the 'keeper's quick clearance to Anderson that set up the third goal.

Seven minutes from time Anderson's centre found the back of the net via Kelly and soon Johnny Carey was accepting the Cup from King George VI. Both sets of fans were left with memories of a truly great match.

**Manchester United:** Crompton; Carey, Aston, Anderson, Chilton, Cockburn, Delaney, Morris, Rowley, Pearson, Mitten.
**Blackpool:** Robinson; Shimwell, Crosland, Johnston, Hayward, Kelly, Matthews, Munro, Mortensen, Dick, Rickett.

*Attendance: 99,000*                          *Referee: C.J.Barrick (Northampton)*

*Blackpool's Eddie Shimwell puts the Seasiders ahead with a 12th-minute penalty.*

155

*The United team that hammered Anderlecht. Back row (left to right): Edwards, Foulkes, Jones, Wood, Colman, Pegg. Front: Berry, Whelan, Byrne, Taylor, Viollet.*

## Match to Remember 6      26 September 1956

# Manchester United 10    RSC Anderlecht 0

UNITED had opened their European Cup campaign two weeks earlier with a 2-0 win in Brussels. The return leg, played on a wet night at Manchester City's Maine Road because United did not have floodlights at the time, gave England its first taste of European Cup Football.

Anderlecht's trainer-coach was 46-year-old Blackpool-born Bill Gormlie, a former Blackburn Rovers goalkeeper and old schoolmate of Frank Swift. In an effort to resist the formidable United team, Gormlie made several changes from the home leg. United made only one alteration, Duncan Edwards coming in for Jackie Blanchflower.

Anderlecht mounted the first attack, but it was United who mastered the muddy conditions to take the lead with a classic goal after only nine minutes. Roger Byrne's clearance found David Pegg who beat several defenders before finding Taylor with a perfect cross. Taylor headed home and then scored a second, toe-poking the ball home.

Dennis Viollet scored United's third and fourth goals, both from defensive errors, and then completed his hat-trick with a fierce shot from the edge of the penalty area.

In the second half, Taylor completed his own hat-trick with United's sixth goal following a goalmouth scramble. Billy Whelan added number seven and Viollet scored his fourth from Byrne's pass. Johnny Berry made it 9-0 before Whelan took the score into double-figures.

Only Pegg, of the forwards, did not score but he played as well as anyone in this magnificent United performance. Welsh referee Mervyn Griffiths summed up: "They couldn't pick an England side to beat this United team."

**Manchester United:** Wood; Foulkes, Byrne, Colman, Jones, Edwards, Berry, Whelan, Taylor, Viollet, Pegg.
**RSC Anderlecht:** Week; Gettemans, Culot, Hanon, De Koster, Vanderwilt, DeDryver, Vandenbosche, Mermans, Dewael, Jurion.

*Attendance: 40,000*              *Referee: B.M.Griffiths (Newport)*

*Tommy Taylor (falling, far right of picture) heads a fine goal for United. Injured goalkeeper Ray Wood is facing the goal.*

## Match to Remember 7                     4 May 1957

# Aston Villa 2    Manchester United 1

TWO weeks before the 1957 FA Cup Final, Manchester United had hopes of becoming the first club to win the treble of League Championship, FA Cup and European Cup. United took the Championship, but Real Madrid ended their European hopes in the semi-final and now Villa stood in the way of United becoming the first club this century to complete the double.

Villa had an extra reason for denying United that glory, for the Black Country club had been the last side to win the double, in the gaslit days of Victorian soccer.

After only six minutes United goalkeeper, Ray Wood, was stretchered off after a collision with Villa's Peter McParland.

Jackie Blanchflower took over in goal and Duncan Edwards moved to the centre-half position, with Billy Whelan dropping back to wing-half.

Despite their handicap, United were the better side in a dull first half. In the 15th minute, they might have had a penalty when Bobby Charlton was toppled. Wood returned for the last ten minutes of the first-half, a right-wing passenger, but did not emege after the interval.

The second period saw United produce some of their best football but Villa, with Stan Crowther outstanding, defended well. Then McParland headed a fine goal past Blanchflower. Five minutes later, he scored a second.

Apparently well offside when Johnny Dixon thundered a shot against the crossbar, McParland scored from the rebound. Referee Frank Coultas ruled that, at the time of Dixon's shot, McParland was not interfering with play.

Tommy Taylor pulled a goal back, whereupon Wood reappeared in goal, but it was too late and Villa, with seven victories, became the most prolific FA Cup-winners of all time.

**Aston Villa:** Sims; Lynn, Aldis, Crowther, Dugdale, Saward, Smith, Sewell, Myerscough, Dixon, McParland.
**Manchester United:** Wood; Foulkes, Byrne, Colman, Blanchflower, Edwards, Berry, Whelan, Taylor, Charlton, Pegg.

*Attendance: 100,000*                     *Referee: F.Coultas (Hull)*

157

# Arsenal 4   Manchester United 5

THE names Manchester United and Arsenal have a special ring to them and the game played at Highbury in the winter of 1958 gave a near-capacity crowd nine goals and, although they did not know it at the time, the last opportunity to see this great United team perform on English soil.

United were chasing the First Division title once again and at half-time they led the Gunners 3-0. The hugely-talented Duncan Edwards opened the scoring with a low shot into the corner of Jack Kelsey's net and Tommy Taylor and Bobby Charlton added the others as United stormed ahead.

Gunners fans were resigned to a big defeat, for United looked unstoppable. Instead they saw their own side contribute to a memorable second half.

The first 15 minutes after the restart were goalless, then Arsenal scored three times in less than three minutes and suddenly the scores were level. Harry Gregg was powerless to stop Herd's shot, then Bloomfield scored two in quick succession. Arsenal fans could hardly believe it.

Lesser sides might have crumbled after losing a seemingly invincible lead, but United's answer was to fight back in turn and Dennis Viollet headed them back into the lead. Tommy Taylor made it 5-3 from a near-impossible angle, but even then Arsenal were not outdone and Tapscott reduced United's lead to a single goal.

The fans who poured out of Highbury reflected on the great match. They could also say that they had seen Duncan Edwards, Roger Byrne, Tommy Taylor, Mark Jones and Eddie Colman. Five days later those great players lay dead or dying in the ashes of the Munich air disaster.

**Arsenal:** Kelsey; S.Charlton, Evans, Ward, Fotheringham, Bowen, Groves, Tapscott, Herd, Bloomfield, Nutt.
**Manchester United:** Gregg; Foulkes, Byrne, Colman, Jones, Edwards, Morgans, R.Charlton, Taylor, Viollet, Scanlon.

*Attendance: 63,578*                    *Referee: G.W.Pullin (Bristol)*

*Bobby Charlton watches the ball narrowly miss the Arsenal post.*

158

# Manchester United 3    Sheffield Wednesday 0

ALL BRITAIN was anxious to see how Manchester United would fare in their first match since the Munich air disaster had cut the very heart from the club. And if there was ever proof that the United system of nurturing young talent worked, then it was on this February night of a thousand emotions.

Into the side were drafted youngsters Ian Greaves, Freddie Goodwin, Ron Cope, Colin Webster, Alex Dawson, Mark Pearson and Shay Brennan. Their sum total of Football League experience totalled only 75 games yet, aided by the experience of players like Harry Gregg, Bill Foulkes, and new signings Ernie Taylor and Stan Crowther, both of whom were given FA permission to play, although they were ineligible, the United youngsters secured a famous victory.

The reception which greeted the team when they ran out before a near-60,000 crowd was deafening, but there was soon a hush around the ground as everyone stood in one minute's silent remembrance of the fallen United heroes.

For Wednesday, who seemed to have the whole country against them, it was an impossible task and only Albert Quixall, later to join United, showed any attacking flair as the Owls were dumped out of the FA Cup fifth-round match.

United opened the scoring in the 27th minute when Wednesday goalkeeper Ryalls made two mistakes. First he punched a Foulkes free-kick out for a corner when the ball looked to be sailing harmlessly wide; then he helped Brennan's corner into the net. For Brennan, a reserve full-back who had been called up at outside-left, it was a moment to treasure.

And for Brennan there was more to remember when he scored United's second goal after Pearson's shot had rebounded off Ryalls' knees. Pearson was involved in the third goal five minutes from time when he pulled the ball back for Dawson to score.

United's win earned them a quarter-final tie at West Brom on the next step of an amazing journey that ended at Wembley.

**Manchester United:** Gregg; Foulkes, Greaves, Goodwin, Cope, Crowther, Webster, E.Taylor, Dawson, Pearson, Brennan.
**Sheffield Wednesday:** Ryalls; Martin, Baker, Kay, Swan, O'Donnell, Wilkinson, Quixall, Johnson, Froggatt, Cargill.

*Attendance: 59,848*                    *Referee: A.Bond (Middlesex)*

*Billy Foulkes leads a makeshift United team to meet Sheffield Wednesday in the first match after Munich.*

159

# Bolton Wanderers 2   Manchester United 0

IF FAIRY stories come true, then the Empire Stadium, Wembley, on 3 May 1958 should have been one of those occasions.

Manchester United, their side rebuilt from the ruins of the Munich air disaster and carried along on a wave of national sympathy, defied all the odds to reach the FA Cup Final. But the dream was ruined by Nat Lofthouse and his Bolton teammates.

United became the first 20th-century team to lose consecutive FA Cup Finals and for the second year running they had their goalkeeper injured. This latest occasion proved to be one of Wembley's most controversial incidents.

Lofthouse put Wanderers into a third-minute lead, so he was hardly popular with the United fans, and when he scored the second in the 55th-minute, he incurred their wrath — and the doubts of probably every soccer fan outside Bolton.

Gregg appeared to have the ball in his hands when Lofthouse charged him heavily and forced both goalkeeper and ball over the line. Almost 30 years later, television archive film of the goal makes astonishing viewing, but in those days the goalkeeper was not afforded protection and was fair game for marauding forwards.

In reality, United were outplayed by a fine Bolton side and the controversial second goal perhaps clouds the issue. Lofthouse was a superb leader and in defence Bolton were efficient, with Tommy Banks particularly effective.

United had only two real chances, both from Bobby Charlton. The first effort was brilliantly saved by Eddie Hopkinson; the second struck a post before rebounding into the grateful goalkeeper's arms.

**Bolton Wanderers:** Hopkinson; Hartle, Banks, Hennin, Higgins, Edwards, Birch, Stevens, Lofthouse, Parry, Holden.

**Manchester United:** Gregg; Foulkes, Greaves, Goodwin, Cope, Crowther, Dawson, E.Taylor, Charlton, Viollet, Webster.

*Attendance: 100,000*                    *Referee: J.U.Sherlock (Sheffield)*

*Eddie Hopkinson is beaten but a Bolton defender clears Dennis Viollet's shot off the line.*

*Denis Law (10, partly hidden) in a heading duel with Leicester City's Richie Norman.*

Match to Remember 11                                25 May 1963

# Manchester United 3   Leicester City 1

AFTER spending most of the season battling against relegation, United went into the 1963 FA Cup Final against a Leicester side which had finished fourth in Division One by playing some of the most attractive football in the country.

For once United were the underdogs but at Wembley in late May — the Final was staged three weeks later than normal because of that winter's terrible weather — it was the Midlanders who froze. Even Gordon Banks made some uncharacteristic mistakes.

In contrast, Pat Crerand and Denis Law were outstanding in midfield and attack respectively and they helped United to an emphatic victory in the FA's Centenary Year.

It was United's Scots who made the first goal after 29 minutes. Law took a pass from Crerand, feinted and then shot hard on the turn beyond Banks.

Fifteen minutes earlier it might have been a different tale when United skipper Noel Cantwell almost headed Stringfellow's shot into his own net. The luck of the Irish was with United and thereafter they dominated Leicester.

After 57 minutes, David Herd, whose father had played for Manchester City in the 1933 and 1934 Finals, rammed home a Bobby Charlton shot which Banks had only half saved.

Ten minutes from the end Keyworth dived to head home a twice-taken free-kick, but five minutes from time Herd put the issue beyond doubt when Banks dropped a Johnny Giles cross and the United centre-forward crashed it over the line.

Leicester's defeat was their third in three post-war FA Cup Finals, but few would have denied Bill Foulkes and Bobby Charlton their medals. They were the Munich survivors who collected losers' medals in 1957 and 1958.

**Manchester United:** Gaskell; Dunne, Cantwell, Crerand, Foulkes, Setters, Giles, Quixall, Herd, Law, Charlton.
**Leicester City:** Banks; Sjoberg, Norman, McLintock, King, Appleton, Riley, Cross, Keyworth, Gibson, Stringfellow.

*Attendance: 100,000*                          *Referee: K.Aston (Essex)*

161

# Benfica 1   Manchester United 5

WHEN Manchester United travelled to Lisbon for their European Cup quarter-final second-leg match against Benfica, they took with them the most slender of leads after a 3-2 victory at Old Trafford.

United fans need not have worried. Led by the dazzling skills of George Best, the Reds gave one of the finest displays of attacking football ever mounted by an away side in European competition. United left Benfica, the previous season's losing finalists, beaten and bemused.

Three goals in the first 16 minutes settled the issue. After six minutes Best rose above a packed defence to head past Costa Pereira. Six minutes later, the United star collected a ball from David Herd and raced through to hit a low shot under the goalkeeper.

Best was also involved in the third goal when his pass was hammered home by John Connelly. Eusebio, who had been presented with the European Footballer of the Year trophy before the kick-off, hit a post with a free-kick but in comparison to Best he looked an ordinary player on the night.

Even when Benfica did score, it was through an own-goal by Shay Brennan, but United were so composed and ten minutes from time, Pat Crerand pounced on a defence-splitting pass from Denis Law to make it 4-1. In the dying seconds, Bobby Charlton strode almost casually through a tired defence to pause before netting United's fifth.

Destruction of their side complete, Benfica fans hurled cushions on the pitch. The much-vaunted 'Eagles of Lisbon' had been outfought and outplayed as United reached their third semi-final. Final European glory, however, was still a little way off.

**Benfica:** Costa Pereira; Carem, Germano, Cruz, Pinto, Coluna, Augusto Silva, Eusebio, Torres, Jose Augusto, Simoes.
**Manchester United:** Gregg; Brennan, A.Dunne, Crerand, Foulkes, Stiles, Best, Law, Charlton, Herd, Connelly.

*Attendance: 75,000*                    *Referee: C.Lo Bello (Italy)*

*George Best wheels away after giving United a sixth-minute lead.*

# Manchester United 4    Benfica 1

(after extra-time)

MATT Busby realized a dream in 1968. After 12 years of trying, he saw his team step out for a European Cup Final at the end of a trail which had started in Anderlecht in September 1956.

After three unsuccessful semi-final appearances, and a tragedy that had wiped out one of the finest teams ever produced by an English club, United walked out at Wembley led by Bobby Charlton.

The first half was an uninspiring affair. The second half, however, whilst no classic, certainly lived up to the occasion in terms of excitement. United took the lead when Dave Sadler and Tony Dunne combined on the left. Sadler crossed and Charlton glanced a rare header past Henrique. The goal gave United confidence. John Aston was the star and they might have gone further ahead, but Sadler wasted the chance.

Ten minutes from the end Benfica equalized through Graca and four minutes from the final whistle United's dream was almost shattered. Eusebio broke free of Nobby Stiles and sent in a stinging shot which Alex Stepney blocked. It was Eusebio's desire to score a dramatic winner, rather than the simple goal which presented itself, that kept United alive.

Two minutes into extra-time, George Best emerged to score a goal of rare brilliance, leaving the defence trailing before rounding Henrique. One minute later, Brian Kidd — celebrating his 19th birthday — settled the issue with a header; a third goal in the space of eight minutes came from Charlton.

Most British fans savoured one of football's most emotional nights whilst United, particularly Munich survivors Busby, Charlton and Foulkes, thought back to the men who were denied their chance of glory.

**Manchester United:** Stepney; Brennan, Dunne, Crerand, Foulkes, Stiles, Best, Kidd, Charlton, Sadler, Aston.
**Benfica:** Henrique; Adolfo, Humberto, Jacinto, Cruz, Graca, Coluna, Augusto, Eusebio, Torres, Simoes.

*Attendance: 100,000*                                    *Referee: C.Lo Bello (Italy)*

*David Sadler tries a spectacular effort but Henrique saved the situation for Benfica.*

# Manchester United 0    Manchester City 1

UNITED went into their final home match of 1973-4 facing the irony of a situation which left Manchester City holding the key to the Old Trafford club's immediate fate.

Defeat would almost certainly put United into the Second Division for the first time in 36 years, a draw could possibly have ensured their safety but there were so many imponderables on this, the last Saturday of the League season.

Almost 57,000 fans packed Old Trafford and they gave Denis Law, a favourite 'son' of both clubs, a warm reception on his last Football League appearance. He was made City's captain for the day, but little did United's fans know that, before the day was out, he would be the villain who sent their team down.

Apart from the final few minutes, the game had little to offer in entertainment. Gerry Daly, Lou Macari and Stewart Houston played well for United, and Doyle, Barrett and Oakes were City's best performers. Little else can be said to describe the greater part of a match full of tension.

United did most of the attacking and were unlucky when Donachie and then Barrett cleared shots off the City line.

With eight minutes remaining, Bell and Lee combined before finding Law. The City man casually back-heeled the ball — straight past Alex Stepney and into the United net. It was to be Law's last touch in League football. United fans invaded the pitch and when the game restarted three minutes later, Law had been replaced by Hanson.

A second pitch invasion, and a fire on the Stretford End, caused Gloucestershire referee David Smith, who was refereeing his last match, to abandon the game. The League ordered the result to stand and United were down.

**Manchester United:** Stepney; Forsyth, Houston, B.Greenhoff, Holton, M.Buchan, Morgan, Macari, McIlroy, McCalliog, Daly.
**Manchester City:** Corrigan; Barrett, Donachie, Doyle, Booth, Oakes, Summerbee, Bell, Lee, Law(Hanson), Tueart.

*Attendance: 56,996*                    *Referee: D.W.Smith (Stonehouse)*

*United fans force an abandonment but the result stood and their club were relegated after all.*

*Lou Macari (second left) watches his shot fly into the net for the winning goal.*

# Manchester United 2    Liverpool 1

AFTER losing the previous year's FA Cup Final to Second Division Southampton, United had an even tougher-looking assignment when they met League Champions Liverpool in the 1977 Final.

But the Cup had no regard for favourites or predictability, and United went on to prevent the Merseysiders from completing a League and Cup double, just as United had been denied 20 years earlier.

The game was not a memorable affair for the uncommitted, apart from a five-minute spell at the beginning of the second half. Liverpool were the better team until that point, and they were the better side after it. In between, United scored two goals to Liverpool's one.

In the 50th minute Stuart Pearson showed why he was considered one of the game's great opportunists when he took a pass from Jimmy Greenhoff and shot low under Clemence's body.

Two minutes later it was Liverpool's turn to celebrate and Reds' fans drowned the United cheering when Jimmy Case put the Merseysiders level. Case, along with Keegan, had been Liverpool's inspiration and his goal was the best of the game. Turning on the edge of the penalty area, he hit a Joey Jones cross into the left-hand corner of the net.

Three minutes later United were back in the lead with a fortunate goal. Jimmy Greenhoff seized upon Tommy Smith's error and his shot rebounded to Lou Macari. Macari's snap shot could have gone almost anywhere but struck Jimmy Greenhoff and flew past Clemence.

Ray Kennedy, who nearly opened the scoring in the first half when his header hit a post, crashed a thunderous shot against the stanchion as Liverpool pressed for another equalizer, but the Cup was on its way to Manchester.

**Manchester United:** Stepney; Nicholl, Albiston, McIlroy, B.Greenhoff, Buchan, Coppell, J.Greenhoff, Pearson, Macari, Hill(McCreery).
**Liverpool:** Clemence; Neal, Jones, Smith, Kennedy, Hughes, Keegan, Case, Heighway, Johnson(Callaghan), McDermott.

*Attendance: 100,000*                          *Referee: R.Matthewson (Bolton)*

*Brian Talbot (third right) gets the final touch and United are behind at Wembley.*

## Match to Remember 16        12 May 1979

# Arsenal 3    Manchester United 2

TWO goals ahead with four minutes to play in a Wembley Final — it was hardly surprising that Arsenal fans were ecstatic. United supporters were still roaring on their team, but they knew deep down that the cause was lost. Then came a sensational fightback by the Red Devils — and ultimate agony as Arsenal came back again in one of the most rousing finales ever seen at Wembley.

United's previous Cup Final appearance in 1977 was brought to life with a three-goal burst in the second half. This latest excursion to Wembley saw another three-goal flourish in less than three minutes.

Arsenal took the lead in the 12th minute when Sunderland and Talbot, who had played for Ipswich in the previous year's Final, both claimed they had touched David Price's cross before it entered the net. Talbot was officially credited with the goal. Liam Brady had been the architect behind that effort and the same player set up a goal for Frank Stapleton, later to play for United, just before half-time.

Joe Jordan had won the aerial battle with Willie Young, but with four minutes left Arsenal still had their 2-0 lead. Then Gordon McQueen turned the ball past Jennings with an outstretched left leg and less than two minutes later, McIlroy danced through before stroking home the equalizer with one minute and 45 seconds remaining.

United had clawed back from the jaws of defeat, or so they thought. Brady had no intention of letting the game slip now and he started the move which saw Rix take the ball down the left before crossing to where Sunderland was racing in to snatch a dramatic winner.

**Arsenal:** Jennings; Rice, Nelson, Talbot, O'Leary, Young, Brady, Sunderland, Stapleton, Price (Walford), Rix.
**Manchester United:** Bailey; Nicholl, Albiston, McIlroy, McQueen, Buchan, Coppell, J.Greenhoff, Jordan, Macari, Thomas.

*Attendance: 100,000*        *Referee: R.Challis (Tonbridge)*

*Bryan Robson stabs home the ball to take United towards Cup glory.*

26 May 1983

# Manchester United 4   Brighton & Hove Albion 0

MANCHESTER United won the FA Cup on a Thursday evening and finished the job they should have completed the previous Saturday. In the first Wembley game they came back from a goal down to lead Brighton 2-1, but then allowed the Seagulls to draw level. A relatively easy chance was missed by Brighton's Smith in extra-time and it was back to Wembley five days later.

Brighton skipper Foster, suspended for the first match, returned to the heart of his side's defence and yet the south coast club were not the same 'nothing-to-lose' side that had come so close to winning the Cup for the first time in their history.

United were by far the better team in the replay and two goals in a four-minute spell midway through the first half put the issue beyond Brighton's reach. Arthur Albiston and Alan Davies set up Bryan Robson's opener, and Davies was involved in the second when he touched on Arnold Muhren's corner for Norman Whiteside to score. Whiteside thus became the first man to score in both the FA Cup and Milk Cup Finals in the same season.

Robson scored his second just before the interval and United's 3-0 lead was the biggest in an FA Cup Final since 1900 when Bury led Southampton 3-0. Bury went on to win 4-0 and so did United when Muhren scored from the penalty-spot after Robson had been held by Stevens.

It was the biggest margin in a Wembley FA Cup Final and it came on Sir Matt Busby's 74th birthday.

**Manchester United:** Bailey; Duxbury, Albiston, Wilkins, Moran, McQueen, Robson, Muhren, Stapleton, Whiteside, Davies.
**Brighton & Hove Albion:** Moseley; Gatting, Pearce, Grealish, Foster, Stevens, Case, Howlett, Robinson, Smith, Smillie.

*Attendance: 92,000*                *Referee: A.W.Grey (Great Yarmouth)*

# Manchester United 1  Everton 0

IN 1977 United ended Liverpool's hopes of a League, FA Cup and European treble by winning at Wembley. In 1985 United did the same to the other Merseyside giants, Everton.

With the Canon League trophy and European Cup-winners' Cup already gracing the magnificent Goodison Park trophy room, Everton were set to achieve what no other club had done — win the League and Cup double and a European prize in the same season.

As so often happens in the electric atmosphere of Wembley, the expected classic between two of the country's finest football teams did not materialize.

The first 78 minutes of the game produced nothing special. Only when retired police inspector Peter Willis of County Durham sent off United's Kevin Moran did the game burst into live. Willis felt that Moran's challenge on Peter Reid deserved the sending-off. Many observers felt that Moran's tackle was the kind seen every Saturday of a League season. Whatever the views, Moran became the first man to be sent off in an FA Cup Final.

The loss of Moran, far from hindering United, spurred them on and even when extra-time began, United's ten lion-hearts were far from finished. Olsen and Strachan, in particular, menaced with long runs deep into Everton's defence.

Ten minutes from the end of 120 minutes play, United achieved a breakthrough. Norman Whiteside produced a curling shot which totally deceived Southall.

Moran had to wait several weeks before collecting his medal and Ron Atkinson called the victory 'arguably the best Cup win any side will have at Wembley'. It was certainly one of the most courageous.

**Manchester United:** Bailey; Gidman, Albiston(Duxbury), Whiteside, McGrath, Moran, Robson, Strachan, Hughes, Stapleton, Olsen.
**Everton:** Southall; Stevens, Van den Hauwe, Ratcliffe, Mountfield, Reid, Steven, Sharp, Gray, Bracewell, Sheedy.

*Attendance: 100,000*                    *Referee: R.Willis (Meadowfield)*

*Bailey, Moran and Whiteside celebrate Cup Final victory over Everton.*

# Liverpool 3   Manchester United 3

A VISIT to Anfield is always a daunting task but Manchester United are one of the few clubs in recent years to have had more than their fair share of success against their old rivals. And on Easter Monday 1988, United came away with a 3-3 draw after staging a remarkable recovery.

Although United opened the scoring with a Bryan Robson goal in the second minute, the Merseysiders soon fought back. With Beardsley and Houghton back in the Liverpool team, their attack moved with more fluency and in the 37th minute the combination worked well for Beardsley to score his 14th goal of the season. Three minutes later, Beardsley had a hand in Liverpool's second goal when Gillespie headed home with the United defence in disarray.

A minute after the interval, the Liverpool celebrations resumed as McMahon scored with a 25-yard shot. All seemed lost for United supporters, but then came that thrilling recovery.

In the 54th minute, Alex Ferguson gambled with his two substitutes, Whiteside and Olsen who, he knew, would add attacking flair. Six minutes later, however, Colin Gibson was given his marching orders after a second bookable offence. United were now trailing 3-1, were down to ten men and had 30 minutes left. Then in the 65th minute, Robson scored his second goal, aided by a Hansen deflection.

United now felt that, despite their numerical disadvantage, they could snatch a draw and in the 77th minute Davenport put Strachan through to level the scores.

After the match, Ferguson, bitter at Gibson's sending-off, commented about Anfield's intimidating atmosphere upon referees. His remarks did not go without comment from Kenny Dalglish and led to further ill-feeling between the two clubs.

**Liverpool:** Grobbelaar; Gillespie, Ablett, Nicol, Spackman, Hansen, Beardsley, Aldridge(Johnston), Houghton, Barnes, McMahon.

**Manchester United:** Turner; Anderson, Blackmore(Olsen), Bruce, McGrath, Duxbury(Whiteside), Robson, Strachan, McClair, Davenport, Gibson.

*Attendance: 43,497*                                    *Referee: J.Key (Rotherham)*

# Manchester United 3   Oldham Athletic 3

ON their way to winning a record-equalling seventh FA Cup Final, United had been drawn away from home in every round. The nearest they got to a 'home' match was in the semi-final when they played Oldham Athletic at Maine Road. But, of their five opponents thus far, the Latics provided the sternest test.

Joe Royle's side were the 'team of the season' in many respects, having already reached the Littlewoods Cup Final and still being involved, albeit tenuously, in the Second Division promotion race. United, on the other hand, had been battling against relegation. A good Cup run was to be their salvation.

The semi-final clash was the second part of a live television 'double header'. In the first game, Crystal Palace had beaten Liverpool in a seven-goal extra-time thriller. The pundits commented that the second match surely could not live up to that. Well, it may have produced 'only' six goals, but for sheer excitement the United-Oldham clash certainly matched the excitement of Villa Park.

Oldham's Barrett took advantage of a Jim Leighton error to open the scoring

*Neil Webb scores Manchester United's second in the six-goal thriller against Oldham Athletic.*

in the fifth minute but then United responded with two goals. The first, after half an hour, was scored by skipper Bryan Robson, playing his first senior game since Christmas. He took an excellent pass from Neil Webb and netted past the despairing Hallworth.

An exhausted Robson was taken off in the 71st minute and a minute later Webb headed United in front. But Oldham refused to give up and in the 76th minute their stand-in centre-forward, Marshall, blasted a shot into the roof of the net from the edge of the penalty area. Hughes and Webb both had chances to win the match in the dying seconds of normal time.

A minute into the extra period, United were back in front when Wallace scored after receiving a great ball from McClair. And a couple of minutes into the second half of extra-time, Oldham pulled themselves back into the game for a second time when Palmer ran on to a Marshall cross to level the scores at 3-3.

The result was a fair one, for neither side deserved to lose. Three days later they resumed the battle and after another 120 minutes' football, United eventually reached their 11th Final.

**Manchester United:** Leighton; Martin(Robins), Gibson, Bruce, Phelan, Pallister, Robson(Wallace), Ince, McClair, Hughes, Webb.
**Oldham Athletic:** Hallworth; Irwin, Barlow, Henry(Warhurst), Barrett, A.Holden, Redfearn, Ritchie(Palmer), Marshall, Milligan, R.Holden.
*Attendance: 44,026*                                    *Referee: J.Worrall (Warrington)*

# Arsenal 2    Manchester United 6

UNITED faced a daunting task when they went to Highbury for this fourth-round clash in the Rumbelows League Cup. Arsenal were second in the First Division, had gone 16 League and Cup games without defeat and had conceded only one goal at home.

United's confidence, however, was sky-high after their 3-1 win over Liverpool in the previous round. But even they could not have imagined they would have come away from the capital with six goals to their credit.

The avalanche started in the very first minute when Clayton Blackmore latched on to a Paul Ince free-kick after Wallace had been fouled by Davis. United should have added further goals before Mark Hughes eventually made it 2-0, after a move involving Sharpe and Wallace.

A minute later, Sharpe got his own name on the score-sheet when his 25-yard shot curled over the top of the stranded Arsenal goalkeeper, David Seaman.

Arsenal came out for the second half in a determined mood and the second period was barely three minutes old when Smith scored after Sealey had initially made a good save from a Thomas volley. And when Smith scored a second in the 68th minute, it looked as though an Arsenal recovery was on its way.

But Lee Sharpe had other ideas and he scored his second goal 15 minutes from time to restore United's two-goal advantage. Three minutes later, the 19-year-old made it a memorable night when he completed his hat-trick.

Eight minutes from time Wallace rounded off the evening as Arsenal slumped to their biggest defeat for 69 years. But for United, and Lee Sharpe in particular, it was a night to remember as they gave a wonderful display of attacking football.

**Arsenal:** Seaman; Dixon, Winterburn, Thomas, Bould, Admas, Groves, Davis, Smith, Merson, Limpar(Campbell).
**Manchester United:** Sealey; Irwin, Blackmore, Bruce(Donaghy), Phelan, Pallister, Sharpe, Ince, McClair, Hughes, Wallace.

*Referee: J.Martin (Alton)*                          *Attendance: 40,884*

# Manchester United 2    Barcelona 1

UNITED arrived in Rotterdam for the European Cup-winners' Cup Final, hoping to end a 23-year drought at Old Trafford without a European trophy. They did it with two goals from Mark Hughes, the man who was rejected by the Spaniards nearly four years earlier.

Driving rain came down from the start and Barcelona's goalkeeper, Busquets, making his first-team debut, was surprisingly calm and confident in the conditions.

Much pressure was on Lee Sharpe to fare well on such an important stage, but he failed to impress on a night that saw him marked closely by two Barcelona defenders. But the danger man for United was Mark Hughes, who was keen to

*Goalscorer Mark Hughes with the Cup-winners' Cup after United's victory against Barcelona.*

show the Spaniards they had made a mistake in letting him go. Such were his darting attacks into the Barcelona danger zone, that Ronald Koeman was penned into his own half in an unusually defensive role.

United deserved a goal in the first half but it was not forthcoming. However, after 68 minutes, Hughes was fouled on the edge of the box. Robson took the kick and Bruce rose to beat Busquets in the air. Hughes was on hand to make sure the ball went over the line and, whilst the Welshman got credit for the goal, the real work was done by Bruce.

Seven minutes later, Hughes took a through pass from Robson and the Welsh international rounded the 'keeper and blasted the ball into the net to make it 2-0.

Ronald Koeman pulled one back in the 79th minute when his free-kick deceived Sealey. For the next ten minutes it was an anxious time for the United defence, but they held on and in the dying seconds, Hughes looked destined to get his hat-trick but was pulled down on the edge of the box by Nando, who was duly sent off.

United emulated thir 1968 counterparts and brought European glory back to Old Trafford. All the credit does not go solely to Alex Ferguson and his players, but also to the United fans who were true ambassadors for the English game as they vindicated UEFA's decision to allow English clubs back into Europe. It was truly a welcome and successful return for Manchester United and English football.

**Manchester United:** Sealey; Irwin, Blackmore, Bruce, Phelan, Pallister, Robson, Ince, McClair, Hughes, Sharpe.
**Barcelona:** Busquets; Nando, Alexanco, Koemen, Ferrer, Bakero, Goicoechea, Eusebio, Salinas, Laudrup, Beguiristan.

*Referee: Bo Karlsson (Sweden)*                    *Attendance 44,000*

# Famous Heathens

WHEN Newton Heath was formed in 1878, one man who was a tower of strength behind the new club was **Sam Black**. Black was a tower in more ways than one. He was a solidly-built player with enormous thighs, and both on and off the field, he made a huge contribution to the task of getting Newton Heath off the ground.

He joined the Heathens from Burton and spent six years in Manchester. A great defensive player, he was one of the first Newton Heath players to gain representative honours when he played for Manchester & District against Liverpool & District at Bootle Cricket Ground in 1884. Having completed his task at Newton Heath, Black returned to Burton and later became secretary of Derby Town. An all-round sportsman, he remained an amateur throughout his career.

Black was not around to see Newton Heath join the Combination in 1888, but a new mentor arrived in the shape of **Jack Powell**. Powell, a full-back who weighed over 14st and was over six feet tall, was born near Wrexham and joined the famous Welsh club, Druids, in 1878. He had never played soccer before but after only three games made his international debut, against Scotland in Glasgow. He went on to win 15 caps.

He joined Bolton Wanderers in 1883 and three years later, joined Newton Heath. He was a member of the first Heathens team to appear in the FA Cup, against Fleetwood Rangers in October 1886. Powell captained Newton Heath's Combination side and, on 21 September 1889, skippered the Heathens' first Alliance team, against Sunderland Albion.

In those Alliance days, Newton Heath's strike force revolved around the brothers **Jack** and **Roger Doughty**. Both were prolific scorers and appeared in Welsh Cup Finals with Druids before turning out in Manchester Cup Finals for Newton Heath. Jack led the attack in three such Manchester Finals, scoring a hat-trick against Denton in the 1888 Final which Newton Heath won 7-1.

Jack usually played centre-forward whilst Roger was his inside-right, and together they scored many goals. Against Ireland at Wrexham in 1888, Jack scored four and Roger two in Wales' 11-0 win. They won 11 Welsh caps between them and although neither played for Newton Heath in the Football League, Roger did appear in three Test Matches, and Jack Doughty continued to work for the Newton Heath Railway Company until the 1920s.

When Newton Heath turned their attentions to the League, it was obvious that they would have to sign new players. Down from Scotland came **Joe Cassidy** and **Robert Donaldson**.

Cassidy came from Celtic and whilst he made four appearances in Newton Heath's first League season, he had to wait until 9 March 1895 for his fifth game. On that occasion, he scored four goals in the 14-0 win over Walsall that was subsequently deleted from the records. He continued to prove his worth as a lethal goalscorer and was Newton Heath's top-scorer four times before moving to Manchester City in 1899.

Robert Donaldson had the distinction of scoring Newton Heath's first League goal, against Blackburn on 3 September 1892. Against Wolves the same season, he scored the first League hat-trick for the club. Mainly an inside-right, Donaldson left Newton Heath in 1897-8, after his scoring touch deserted him, and signed for Luton Town before ending his career with Glossop North End.

Backbone of Newton Heath's defence in those early days was **Fred Erentz**, another

*Cartoonist's impression of the Heathens' first season in Division One, after they beat Derby County 7-1 at North Road on 31 December 1892. Robert Donaldson scored a hat-trick for the Manchester club.*

Scot who played for Dundee Old Boys before joining the Heathens in 1892. A wing-half or full-back, Fred Erentz played over 300 games for the club. His career neatly spanned Newton Heath's League days. He played in their first League game in 1892, and his last appearance was against Chesterfield in April 1902, just before the Heathens changed their name to Manchester United. Fred's brother, Harry, also played for the Heathens before moving to Spurs where he won an FA Cup winners' medal in 1901.

One of the finest ball-players seen at Clayton in those days was centre-half **James McNaught**. He could play wing-half or inside-forward but preferred the centre of the defence. His skills earned him the nickname, 'The Little Wonder'.

McNaught moved to Manchester from Linfield in 1893 and played over 150 games for the Heathens before joining Southern League Tottenham in 1898. Despite four seasons at the London club, he never matched his performances in a Newton Heath shirt. A gentlemanly character, both on and off the field, McNaught was heavily involved in the players' union movement at the turn of the century.

McNaught was succeeded at the heart of the defence by local lad **William Griffiths**, who gave nine years service to the club as both Newton Heath and Manchester United. A member of the first team to play under the United banner, he established a regular first-team role in 1898-9 after McNaught's departure to Spurs. He played over 150 League games for the club and scored 27 goals, including 11 in the 1903-04 season when he was joint top scorer.

**Walter Cartwright** played for the Heathens during one of the club's most difficult times, often unsure whether he would have his rail fare reimbursed. He was loyal and dedicated, though, and gave the club nine years' service, making over 250 appearances. He signed for Newton Heath from Crewe in 1895, soon developing into one of the best left-halves in Division Two. He could also play left-back, and towards the end of his career, turned out at outside-left and even kept goal in two games. Cartwright played his last League game for United in April 1904, at Chesterfield.

Newton Heath had a glimpse of the man who could be called the 'first George Best' when **John Peden** had a brief flirtation with the club. Like Best, Peden was a brilliant match-winner — and like Best he could be difficult, temperamental and unreliable.

An Irish international, he joined the Heathens from Linfield before the start of their second League campaign and missed only two games in his first season, scoring seven goals from his favourite position on the left wing. He joined Sheffield United the following season and then, feeling homesick, returned to Ireland and signed for Distillery.

One of the club's first great goalkeepers was **Frank Barrett**, who signed from Dundee in 1896 with two full Scotland caps to his name. Born in Dundee, Barrett made the jersey his own property from the moment he made his debut, in a 4-0 home win over Newcastle in September 1896. At the end of 1899-1900, Barrett signed for New Brighton Tower.

Along with Griffiths and Cartwright, **William Morgan** was a member of the solid Newton Heath defence at the turn of the century. They were not a spectacular trio, but they proved immensely difficult to beat and frustrated many attackers. In the three years of their prime, between 1899 and 1902, the Heathens conceded only 32 League goals at Clayton. Normally, Morgan was the team's right-half but he made his debut as stand-in centre-half for Welsh international Caesar Jenkyns, against Darwen in March 1897.

Morgan played in the first game under the Manchester United banner, at Gainsborough Trinity in September 1902, but the following March was transferred to Bolton Wanderers. He played only three more League games for the Trotters that season before ending his career.

All the above players — and many more not mentioned — played important parts in the birth and early years of Manchester United. Their contributions should never be forgotten.

# United in the Football League 1892-93 to 1991-92

| | | | HOME | | | | | AWAY | | | | |
|---|---|---|---|---|---|---|---|---|---|---|---|---|
| | P | W | D | L | F | A | W | D | L | F | A | Pts | Pos |

| | P | W | D | L | F | A | W | D | L | F | A | Pts | Pos |
|---|---|---|---|---|---|---|---|---|---|---|---|---|---|
| **FIRST DIVISION** | | | | | | | | | | | | | |
| 1892-93 | 30 | 6 | 3 | 6 | 39 | 35 | 0 | 3 | 12 | 11 | 50 | 18 | 16th |
| 1893-94 | 30 | 5 | 2 | 8 | 29 | 33 | 1 | 0 | 14 | 7 | 39 | 14 | 16th |
| **SECOND DIVISION** | | | | | | | | | | | | | |
| 1894-95 | 30 | 9 | 6 | 0 | 52 | 18 | 6 | 2 | 7 | 26 | 26 | 38 | 3rd |
| 1895-96 | 30 | 12 | 2 | 1 | 48 | 15 | 3 | 1 | 11 | 18 | 42 | 33 | 6th |
| 1896-97 | 30 | 11 | 4 | 0 | 37 | 10 | 6 | 1 | 8 | 19 | 24 | 39 | 2nd |
| 1897-98 | 30 | 11 | 2 | 2 | 42 | 10 | 5 | 4 | 6 | 22 | 25 | 38 | 4th |
| 1898-99 | 34 | 12 | 4 | 1 | 51 | 14 | 7 | 1 | 9 | 16 | 29 | 43 | 4th |
| 1899-1900 | 34 | 15 | 1 | 1 | 44 | 11 | 5 | 3 | 9 | 19 | 16 | 44 | 4th |
| 1900-01 | 34 | 11 | 3 | 3 | 31 | 9 | 3 | 1 | 13 | 11 | 29 | 32 | 10th |
| 1901-02 | 34 | 10 | 2 | 5 | 27 | 12 | 1 | 4 | 12 | 11 | 41 | 28 | 15th |
| 1902-03 | 34 | 9 | 4 | 4 | 32 | 15 | 6 | 4 | 7 | 21 | 23 | 38 | 5th |
| 1903-04 | 34 | 14 | 2 | 1 | 42 | 14 | 6 | 6 | 5 | 23 | 19 | 48 | 3rd |
| 1904-05 | 34 | 16 | 0 | 1 | 60 | 10 | 8 | 5 | 4 | 21 | 20 | 53 | 3rd |
| 1905-06 | 38 | 15 | 3 | 1 | 55 | 13 | 13 | 3 | 3 | 35 | 15 | 62 | 2nd |
| **FIRST DIVISION** | | | | | | | | | | | | | |
| 1906-07 | 38 | 10 | 6 | 3 | 33 | 15 | 7 | 2 | 10 | 20 | 41 | 42 | 8th |
| 1907-08 | 38 | 15 | 1 | 3 | 43 | 19 | 8 | 5 | 6 | 38 | 29 | 52 | 1st |
| 1908-09 | 38 | 10 | 3 | 6 | 37 | 33 | 5 | 4 | 10 | 21 | 35 | 37 | 13th |
| 1909-10 | 38 | 14 | 2 | 3 | 41 | 20 | 5 | 5 | 9 | 28 | 41 | 45 | 5th |
| 1910-11 | 38 | 14 | 4 | 1 | 47 | 18 | 8 | 4 | 7 | 25 | 22 | 52 | 1st |
| 1911-12 | 38 | 9 | 5 | 5 | 29 | 19 | 4 | 6 | 9 | 16 | 41 | 37 | 13th |
| 1912-13 | 38 | 13 | 3 | 3 | 41 | 14 | 6 | 5 | 8 | 28 | 29 | 46 | 4th |
| 1913-14 | 38 | 8 | 4 | 7 | 27 | 23 | 7 | 2 | 10 | 25 | 39 | 36 | 14th |
| 1914-15 | 38 | 8 | 6 | 5 | 27 | 19 | 1 | 6 | 12 | 19 | 43 | 30 | 18th |
| 1919-20 | 42 | 6 | 8 | 7 | 20 | 17 | 7 | 6 | 8 | 34 | 33 | 40 | 12th |
| 1920-21 | 42 | 9 | 4 | 8 | 34 | 26 | 6 | 6 | 9 | 30 | 42 | 40 | 13th |
| 1921-22 | 42 | 7 | 7 | 7 | 25 | 26 | 1 | 5 | 15 | 16 | 47 | 28 | 22nd |
| **SECOND DIVISION** | | | | | | | | | | | | | |
| 1922-23 | 42 | 10 | 6 | 5 | 25 | 17 | 7 | 8 | 6 | 26 | 19 | 48 | 4th |
| 1923-24 | 42 | 10 | 7 | 4 | 37 | 15 | 3 | 7 | 11 | 15 | 29 | 40 | 14th |
| 1924-25 | 42 | 17 | 3 | 1 | 40 | 6 | 6 | 8 | 7 | 17 | 17 | 57 | 2nd |
| **FIRST DIVISION** | | | | | | | | | | | | | |
| 1925-26 | 42 | 12 | 4 | 5 | 40 | 26 | 7 | 2 | 12 | 26 | 47 | 44 | 9th |
| 1926-27 | 42 | 9 | 8 | 4 | 29 | 19 | 4 | 6 | 11 | 23 | 45 | 40 | 15th |
| 1927-28 | 42 | 12 | 6 | 3 | 51 | 27 | 4 | 1 | 16 | 21 | 53 | 39 | 18th |
| 1928-29 | 42 | 8 | 8 | 5 | 32 | 23 | 6 | 5 | 10 | 34 | 53 | 41 | 12th |
| 1929-30 | 42 | 11 | 4 | 6 | 39 | 34 | 4 | 4 | 13 | 28 | 54 | 38 | 17th |
| 1930-31 | 42 | 6 | 6 | 9 | 30 | 37 | 1 | 2 | 18 | 23 | 78 | 22 | 22nd |
| **SECOND DIVISION** | | | | | | | | | | | | | |
| 1931-32 | 42 | 12 | 3 | 6 | 44 | 31 | 5 | 5 | 11 | 27 | 41 | 42 | 12th |
| 1932-33 | 42 | 11 | 5 | 5 | 40 | 24 | 4 | 8 | 9 | 31 | 44 | 43 | 6th |
| 1933-34 | 42 | 9 | 3 | 9 | 29 | 33 | 5 | 3 | 13 | 30 | 52 | 34 | 20th |
| 1934-35 | 42 | 16 | 2 | 3 | 50 | 21 | 7 | 2 | 12 | 26 | 34 | 50 | 5th |
| 1935-36 | 42 | 16 | 3 | 2 | 55 | 16 | 6 | 9 | 6 | 30 | 27 | 56 | 1st |
| **FIRST DIVISION** | | | | | | | | | | | | | |
| 1936-37 | 42 | 8 | 9 | 4 | 29 | 26 | 2 | 3 | 16 | 26 | 52 | 32 | 21st |

|  | P | W | D | L | F | A | W | D | L | F | A | Pts | Pos |
|---|---|---|---|---|---|---|---|---|---|---|---|---|---|
|  |  | *HOME* |  |  |  |  | *AWAY* |  |  |  |  |  |  |
|  | **SECOND DIVISION** |  |  |  |  |  |  |  |  |  |  |  |  |
| 1937-38 | 42 | 15 | 3 | 3 | 50 | 18 | 7 | 6 | 8 | 32 | 32 | 53 | 2nd |
|  | **FIRST DIVISION** |  |  |  |  |  |  |  |  |  |  |  |  |
| 1938-39 | 42 | 7 | 9 | 5 | 30 | 20 | 4 | 7 | 10 | 27 | 45 | 38 | 14th |
| 1946-47 | 42 | 17 | 3 | 1 | 61 | 19 | 5 | 9 | 7 | 34 | 35 | 56 | 2nd |
| 1947-48 | 42 | 11 | 7 | 3 | 50 | 27 | 8 | 7 | 6 | 31 | 21 | 52 | 2nd |
| 1948-49 | 42 | 11 | 7 | 3 | 40 | 20 | 10 | 4 | 7 | 37 | 24 | 53 | 2nd |
| 1949-50 | 42 | 11 | 5 | 5 | 42 | 20 | 7 | 9 | 5 | 27 | 24 | 50 | 4th |
| 1950-51 | 42 | 14 | 4 | 3 | 42 | 16 | 10 | 4 | 7 | 32 | 24 | 56 | 2nd |
| 1951-52 | 42 | 15 | 3 | 3 | 55 | 21 | 8 | 8 | 5 | 40 | 31 | 57 | 1st |
| 1952-53 | 42 | 11 | 5 | 5 | 35 | 30 | 7 | 5 | 9 | 34 | 42 | 46 | 8th |
| 1953-54 | 42 | 11 | 6 | 4 | 41 | 27 | 7 | 6 | 8 | 32 | 31 | 48 | 4th |
| 1954-55 | 42 | 12 | 4 | 5 | 44 | 30 | 8 | 3 | 10 | 40 | 44 | 47 | 5th |
| 1955-56 | 42 | 18 | 3 | 0 | 51 | 20 | 7 | 7 | 7 | 32 | 31 | 60 | 1st |
| 1956-57 | 42 | 14 | 4 | 3 | 55 | 25 | 14 | 4 | 3 | 48 | 29 | 64 | 1st |
| 1957-58 | 42 | 10 | 4 | 7 | 45 | 31 | 6 | 7 | 8 | 40 | 44 | 43 | 9th |
| 1958-59 | 42 | 14 | 4 | 3 | 58 | 27 | 10 | 3 | 8 | 45 | 39 | 55 | 2nd |
| 1959-60 | 42 | 13 | 3 | 5 | 53 | 30 | 6 | 4 | 11 | 49 | 50 | 45 | 7th |
| 1960-61 | 42 | 14 | 5 | 2 | 58 | 20 | 4 | 4 | 13 | 30 | 56 | 45 | 7th |
| 1961-62 | 42 | 10 | 3 | 8 | 44 | 31 | 5 | 6 | 10 | 28 | 44 | 39 | 15th |
| 1962-63 | 42 | 6 | 6 | 9 | 36 | 38 | 6 | 4 | 11 | 31 | 43 | 34 | 19th |
| 1963-64 | 42 | 15 | 3 | 3 | 54 | 19 | 8 | 4 | 9 | 36 | 43 | 53 | 2nd |
| 1964-65 | 42 | 16 | 4 | 1 | 52 | 13 | 10 | 5 | 6 | 37 | 26 | 61 | 1st |
| 1965-66 | 42 | 12 | 8 | 1 | 50 | 20 | 6 | 7 | 8 | 34 | 39 | 51 | 4th |
| 1966-67 | 42 | 17 | 4 | 0 | 51 | 13 | 7 | 8 | 6 | 33 | 32 | 60 | 1st |
| 1967-68 | 42 | 15 | 2 | 4 | 49 | 21 | 9 | 6 | 6 | 40 | 34 | 56 | 2nd |
| 1968-69 | 42 | 13 | 5 | 3 | 38 | 18 | 2 | 7 | 12 | 19 | 35 | 42 | 11th |
| 1969-70 | 42 | 8 | 9 | 4 | 37 | 27 | 6 | 8 | 7 | 29 | 34 | 45 | 8th |
| 1970-71 | 42 | 9 | 6 | 6 | 29 | 24 | 7 | 5 | 9 | 36 | 42 | 43 | 8th |
| 1971-72 | 42 | 13 | 2 | 6 | 39 | 26 | 6 | 8 | 7 | 30 | 35 | 48 | 8th |
| 1972-73 | 42 | 9 | 7 | 5 | 24 | 19 | 3 | 6 | 12 | 20 | 41 | 37 | 18th |
| 1973-74 | 42 | 7 | 7 | 7 | 23 | 20 | 3 | 5 | 13 | 15 | 28 | 32 | 21st |
|  | **SECOND DIVISION** |  |  |  |  |  |  |  |  |  |  |  |  |
| 1974-75 | 42 | 17 | 3 | 1 | 45 | 12 | 9 | 6 | 6 | 21 | 18 | 61 | 1st |
|  | **FIRST DIVISION** |  |  |  |  |  |  |  |  |  |  |  |  |
| 1975-76 | 42 | 16 | 4 | 1 | 40 | 13 | 7 | 6 | 8 | 28 | 29 | 56 | 3rd |
| 1976-77 | 42 | 12 | 6 | 3 | 41 | 22 | 6 | 5 | 10 | 30 | 40 | 47 | 6th |
| 1977-78 | 42 | 9 | 6 | 6 | 32 | 23 | 7 | 4 | 10 | 35 | 40 | 42 | 10th |
| 1978-79 | 42 | 9 | 7 | 5 | 29 | 25 | 6 | 8 | 7 | 31 | 38 | 45 | 9th |
| 1979-80 | 42 | 17 | 3 | 1 | 43 | 8 | 7 | 7 | 7 | 22 | 27 | 58 | 2nd |
| 1980-81 | 42 | 9 | 11 | 1 | 30 | 14 | 6 | 7 | 8 | 21 | 22 | 48 | 8th |
| 1981-82 | 42 | 12 | 6 | 3 | 27 | 9 | 10 | 6 | 5 | 32 | 20 | 78 | 3rd |
| 1982-83 | 42 | 14 | 7 | 0 | 39 | 10 | 5 | 6 | 10 | 17 | 28 | 70 | 3rd |
| 1983-84 | 42 | 14 | 3 | 4 | 43 | 18 | 6 | 11 | 4 | 28 | 23 | 74 | 4th |
| 1984-85 | 42 | 13 | 6 | 2 | 47 | 13 | 9 | 4 | 8 | 30 | 34 | 76 | 4th |
| 1985-86 | 42 | 12 | 5 | 4 | 35 | 12 | 10 | 5 | 6 | 35 | 24 | 76 | 4th |
| 1986-87 | 42 | 13 | 3 | 5 | 38 | 18 | 1 | 11 | 9 | 14 | 27 | 56 | 11th |
| 1987-88 | 40 | 14 | 5 | 1 | 41 | 17 | 9 | 7 | 4 | 30 | 21 | 81 | 2nd |
| 1988-89 | 38 | 10 | 5 | 4 | 27 | 13 | 3 | 7 | 9 | 18 | 22 | 51 | 11th |
| 1989-90 | 38 | 8 | 6 | 5 | 26 | 14 | 5 | 3 | 11 | 20 | 33 | 48 | 13th |
| 1990-91 | 38 | 11 | 4 | 4 | 34 | 17 | 5 | 8 | 6 | 24 | 28 | 59 | 6th |
| 1991-92 | 42 | 12 | 7 | 2 | 34 | 13 | 9 | 8 | 4 | 29 | 20 | 78 | 2nd |

In seasons 1946-7, 1947-8 and 1948-9, United played all their home games at Maine Road. Since 1981-2, three points have been awarded for a win.

# Football Alliance 1889-90

Secretary: A.H.Albut

| 1 | Sep | 21 | (h) | Sunderland A | W | 4-1 | Wilson 2, J.Doughty, Stewart | 3,000 |
|---|---|---|---|---|---|---|---|---|
| 2 | | 23 | (a) | Bootle | L | 1-4 | Tait | 3,000 |
| 3 | | 28 | (a) | Crewe A | D | 2-2 | Stewart, Opp own-goal | 2,000 |
| 4 | Oct | 19 | (a) | Walsall TS | L | 0-4 | | 2,000 |
| 5 | | 26 | (a) | Birmingham St G | L | 1-5 | J.Doughty | 3,000 |
| 6 | Nov | 9 | (h) | Long Eaton R | W | 3-0 | J.Doughty 2, Farman | 3,000 |
| 7 | | 30 | (a) | Sheffield W | L | 1-3 | J.Doughty | 5,000 |
| 8 | Dec | 7 | (h) | Bootle | W | 3-0 | J.Doughty, Farman, Stewart | 5,000 |
| 9 | | 28 | (a) | Darwen | L | 1-4 | G.Owen | 5,000 |
| 10 | Jan | 25 | (a) | Sunderland A | L | 0-2 | | 3,000 |
| 11 | Feb | 8 | (a) | Grimsby T | L | 0-7 | | 3,000 |
| 12 | | 15 | (a) | Nottingham F | W | 3-1 | Stewart 2, Wilson | 800 |
| 13 | Mar | 1 | (h) | Crewe A | L | 1-2 | G.Owen | 2,000 |
| 14 | | 15 | (a) | Small Heath | D | 1-1 | Farman | 2,000 |
| 15 | | 22 | (a) | Long Eaton R | W | 3-1 | Wilson 2, Farman | 2,000 |
| 16 | | 29 | (h) | Darwen | W | 2-1 | Davies, Stewart | 5,000 |
| 17 | Apr | 5 | (h) | Nottingham F | L | 0-1 | | 4,000 |
| 18 | | 7 | (h) | Small Heath | W | 9-1 | Stewart 3, J.Doughty 2, Craig, R.Doughty, Farman, Wilson | 4,000 |
| 19 | | 14 | (h) | Grimsby T | L | 0-1 | | 3,000 |
| 20 | | 19 | (h) | Birmingham St G | W | 2-1 | Craig, J.Doughty | 3,000 |
| 21 | | 21 | (h) | Walsall | W | 2-1 | Davies, Stewart | 1,000 |
| 22 | | 26 | (h) | Sheffield W | L | 1-2 | Craig | 8,000 |

FINAL LEAGUE POSITION: 8th in Football Alliance

Appearances
Goals

FA Cup

| 1 | Jan | 18 | (a) | Preston NE | L | 1-6 | |
|---|---|---|---|---|---|---|---|

178

| Hay | Mitchell | Powell | Doughty R | Davies, Joe E | Owen J | Tait | Stewart | Doughty J | Wilson | Gotheridge | Burke | Pedley | Felton | Owen G | Farman | Craig | Harrison | No. |
|---|---|---|---|---|---|---|---|---|---|---|---|---|---|---|---|---|---|---|
| 1 | 2 | 3 | 4 | 5 | 6 | 7 | 8 | 9 | 10 | 11 | | | | | | | | 1 |
| 1 | 2 | | 4 | 5 | 3 | 7 | 8 | 9 | 10 | 11 | 6 | | | | | | | 2 |
| | 2 | 3 | 4 | 5 | 6 | 7 | 8 | 9 | 10 | 11 | | 1 | | | | | | 3 |
| 1 | 2 | 3 | 4 | 5 | 6 | 7 | 8 | 9 | 10 | 11 | | | | | | | | 4 |
| 1 | 2 | | 4 | 5 | 6 | 7 | 8 | 9 | | 11 | | | 3 | 10 | | | | 5 |
| 1 | 2 | 3 | 4 | 5 | 6 | | 8 | 9 | 11 | | | | | 10 | 7 | | | 6 |
| 1 | 2 | 3 | 4 | 5 | 6 | | 8 | 9 | 11 | | | | 10 | | 7 | | | 7 |
| 1 | 2 | 3 | 4 | 5 | 6 | | 8 | 9 | 11 | | | | | 10 | 7 | | | 8 |
| 1 | | 3 | 4 | 5 | 6 | | | 9 | 11 | | | | 2 | 10 | 7 | 8 | | 9 |
| 1 | | | 4 | 5 | | | | 9 | 11 | | 6 | | 2 | 10 | 7 | 8 | 3 | 10 |
| | 2 | 3 | | 5 | | | | 9 | 11 | | 6 | | 4 | 10 | 7 | 8 | 1 | 11 |
| 1 | 2 | 3 | 4 | 5 | 6 | | 8 | 9 | 11 | | | | | 10 | 7 | | | 12 |
| | 2 | 3 | 4 | 5 | 6 | | 8 | 9 | 11 | | | | | 10 | 7 | | 1 | 13 |
| 1 | 2 | 3 | | | 6 | | 8 | 9 | 11 | | | | | 10 | 7 | 4 | 5 | 14 |
| 1 | 2 | 3 | 4 | 5 | 6 | | 8 | 9 | 11 | | | | | | 7 | 10 | | 15 |
| 1 | 2 | 3 | 4 | 5 | 6 | | 8 | 9 | 11 | | | | | | 7 | 10 | | 16 |
| 1 | 2 | 3 | 4 | 5 | 6 | 10 | 8 | 9 | 11 | | | | | | 7 | | | 17 |
| 1 | | 3 | 4 | 5 | 6 | | 8 | 9 | 11 | | | | | | 7 | 10 | 2 | 18 |
| | 2 | 3 | 4 | 5 | | | 8 | 9 | 11 | | | | | 10 | 7 | 6 | 1 | 19 |
| | 2 | | 4 | 5 | | 11 | 8 | 9 | | | 3 | | | 10 | 7 | 6 | 1 | 20 |
| | 2 | 3 | 4 | 5 | 6 | | 8 | 9 | 11 | | | | | | 7 | 10 | 1 | 21 |
| | 2 | | 4 | 5 | 6 | | 8 | 9 | | | 3 | | | 10 | 7 | 11 | 1 | 22 |
| 15 | 19 | 17 | 20 | 21 | 18 | 7 | 19 | 22 | 19 | 5 | 5 | 1 | 5 | 12 | 17 | 11 | 9 | |
| | | 1 | 2 | | 1 | | 10 | 9 | 6 | | | | | 2 | 5 | 3 | | |

1 own-goal

# Football Alliance 1890-91

Secretary: A.H.Albut

| 1 | Sep | 6 | (h) | Darwen | W 4-2 | J.Doughty, Evans, Farman, Owen | 6,000 |
|---|---|---|---|---|---|---|---|
| 2 | | 13 | (a) | Grimsby T | L 1-3 | Stewart | 3,000 |
| 3 | | 20 | (h) | Nottingham F | D 1-1 | J.Doughty | 5,000 |
| 4 | | 27 | (a) | Stoke | L 1-2 | Milarvie | 2,000 |
| 5 | Oct | 11 | (a) | Bootle | L 0-5 | | 4,000 |
| 6 | | 18 | (h) | Grimsby T | W 3-1 | Evans, Ramsey, Sharpe | 3,000 |
| 7 | Nov | 1 | (h) | Crewe A | W 6-3 | Stewart 2, Craig, Farman, Ramsey, Evans | 4,000 |
| 8 | | 8 | (a) | Walsall TS | L 1-2 | Evans | 3,000 |
| 9 | | 22 | (a) | Nottingham F | L 2-8 | Evans, Sharpe | 2,000 |
| 10 | | 29 | (h) | Sunderland A | L 1-5 | Unknown | 2,000 |
| 11 | Dec | 13 | (h) | Small Heath | W 3-1 | Milarvie, Sharpe, Speller (og) | 1,000 |
| 12 | | 27 | (h) | Bootle | W 2-1 | Milarvie, Stewart | 5,000 |
| 13 | Jan | 5 | (h) | Stoke | L 0-1 | | 3,000 |
| 14 | | 10 | (a) | Birmingham St G | L 1-6 | Farman | 1,000 |
| 15 | | 17 | (h) | Walsall TS | D 3-3 | Milarvie, Owen, Ramsey | 1,500 |
| 16 | | 24 | (a) | Sheffield W | W 2-1 | Sharpe, Stewart | 3,000 |
| 17 | Feb | 14 | (a) | Crewe A | W 1-0 | Farman | 3,000 |
| 18 | | 21 | (h) | Sheffield W | D 1-1 | Craig | 4,000 |
| 19 | Mar | 7 | (a) | Small Heath | L 1-2 | Sharpe | 2,000 |
| 20 | | 14 | (h) | Birmingham St G | L 1-3 | Sharpe | 2,000 |
| 21 | | 28 | (a) | Darwen | L 1-2 | Ramsey | 2,000 |
| 22 | Apr | 11 | (a) | Sunderland A | L 1-2 | Ramsey | 3,500 |

FINAL LEAGUE POSITION: 9th in Football Alliance

Appearances
Goals

FA Cup

| Q1 | Oct | 4 | (h*) | Higher Walton | W 2-0 | (*Higher Walton drawn at home but switched venue to obtain greater receipts) |
|---|---|---|---|---|---|---|
| Q2 | | 25 | (a) | Bootle Res | L 0-1 | (Fixture fulfilled by Newton Heath Reserves) |

| Slater | Mitchell | McMillan | Doughty R | Ramsey | Owen J | Farman | Doughty J | Evans | Milarvie | Sharpe | Stewart | Powell | Sadler | Clements | Craig | Felton | Phasey | Denman | |
|---|---|---|---|---|---|---|---|---|---|---|---|---|---|---|---|---|---|---|---|
| 1 | 2 | 3 | 4 | 5 | 6 | 7 | 8 | 9 | 10 | 11 | | | | | | | | | 1 |
| 1 | 2 | 3 | 4 | 5 | 6 | 7 | | 9 | 10 | 11 | 8 | | | | | | | | 2 |
| 1 | | | 4 | 5 | 6 | 7 | 8 | 9 | 10 | 11 | 3 | 2 | | | | | | | 3 |
| 1 | 2 | | 4 | 5 | | 7 | 8 | 9 | 10 | 11 | 6 | 3 | | | | | | | 4 |
| 1 | | | 4 | 5 | 6 | 7 | | 9 | 10 | 11 | 8 | 3 | 2 | | | | | | 5 |
| 1 | 2 | | 4 | 5 | 6 | 7 | | 9 | 10 | 11 | 8 | 3 | | | | | | | 6 |
| 1 | 2 | | 4 | 5 | | 7 | | 9 | 10 | 11 | 8 | | | 3 | 6 | | | | 7 |
| 1 | 2 | | 4 | 5 | | 7 | | 9 | 10 | 6 | 8 | | | 3 | 11 | | | | 8 |
| 1 | 2 | | 4 | 5 | 6 | 7 | | 9 | 10 | 11 | 8 | | | 3 | | | | | 9 |
| 1 | 2 | | 4 | 5 | 6 | 7 | | 9 | 10 | 11 | 8 | | | 3 | | | | | 10 |
| 1 | 2 | | 4 | 5 | | 7 | | 9 | 10 | 11 | 8 | | | 3 | 6 | | | | 11 |
| 1 | 2 | | 4 | 5 | 6 | 7 | | | 10 | 11 | 8 | | | 3 | 9 | | | | 12 |
| 1 | 2 | | 4 | 5 | 6 | 7 | | | 10 | 11 | 9 | | | 3 | 8 | | | | 13 |
| 1 | | | 4 | 5 | 6 | 7 | | | 10 | | 8 | | | 3 | 9 | 2 | 11 | | 14 |
| 1 | 2 | | 4 | 5 | 6 | 7 | | | 10 | 11 | 8 | | | 3 | 9 | | | | 15 |
| 1 | 2 | | 4 | 5 | 6 | 7 | | | 10 | 11 | 8 | | | 3 | 9 | | | | 16 |
| 1 | 2 | | | 5 | 6 | 7 | | 4 | 10 | 11 | 8 | | | 3 | 9 | | | | 17 |
| 1 | 2 | | 4 | 5 | 6 | 7 | | | 10 | 11 | 8 | | | 3 | 9 | | | | 18 |
| 1 | 2 | | 4 | 5 | 6 | 7 | | | 10 | 11 | 8 | | | 3 | 9 | | | | 19 |
| 1 | 2 | | 4 | 5 | 6 | 7 | | | 10 | 11 | 8 | | | 3 | 9 | | | | 20 |
| 1 | | | 4 | 5 | 6 | 7 | 11 | | 10 | | 8 | | | | 9 | 2 | | 3 | 21 |
| 1 | | | 4 | 5 | 6 | 7 | | | 10 | 11 | 8 | | | 3 | 9 | | | 2 | 22 |
| 22 | 17 | 2 | 21 | 22 | 18 | 22 | 4 | 12 | 22 | 20 | 21 | 4 | 1 | 15 | 14 | 2 | 1 | 2 | |
| | | | | 5 | 2 | 4 | 2 | 5 | 4 | 6 | 5 | | | 2 | | | | | |

1 Unknown scorer, 1 own-goal

# Football Alliance 1891-92

Secretary: A.H.Albut

| | | | | | | | |
|---|---|---|---|---|---|---|---|
| 1 | Sep | 12 | (a) | Burton S | L | 2-3 | Donaldson, Farman | 2,000 |
| 2 | | 19 | (h) | Bootle | W | 4-0 | Edge 3, Farman | 5,000 |
| 3 | | 26 | (a) | Birmingham St G | W | 3-1 | Donaldson 2, Stewart | 300 |
| 4 | Oct | 10 | (h) | Ardwick | W | 3-1 | Farman 2, Donaldson | 4,000 |
| 5 | | 17 | (a) | Grimsby T | D | 2-2 | Donaldson 2 | 3,000 |
| 6 | | 31 | (h) | Burton S | W | 3-1 | R.Doughty, Farman, Edge | 4,000 |
| 7 | Nov | 7 | (a) | Crewe A | W | 2-0 | Donaldson, Stafford (og) | 3,000 |
| 8 | | 21 | (h) | Lincoln C | W | 10-1 | Donaldson 3, Hood 2, Stewart 2, Farman, Sneddon, Bates (og) | 6,000 |
| 9 | | 28 | (a) | Walsall TS | W | 4-1 | Donaldson 3, Farman | 1,000 |
| 10 | Dec | 12 | (a) | Sheffield W | W | 4-2 | Farman 2, Sneddon, Owen | 3,000 |
| 11 | | 19 | (a) | Ardwick | D | 2-2 | Farman 2 | 10,000 |
| 12 | | 26 | (h) | Small Heath | D | 3-3 | Edge, Farman, Unknown | 7,000 |
| 13 | Jan | 1 | (h) | Nottingham F | D | 1-1 | Edge | 16,000 |
| 14 | | 9 | (a) | Bootle | D | 1-1 | Hood | 2,000 |
| 15 | | 30 | (h) | Crewe A | W | 5-3 | Donaldson 3, Sneddon, R.Doughty | 3,000 |
| 16 | Feb | 20 | (h) | Sheffield W | D | 1-1 | Hood | 6,000 |
| 17 | | 27 | (a) | Small Heath | L | 2-3 | Farman, Unknown | 3,000 |
| 18 | Mar | 5 | (h) | Walsall TS | W | 5-0 | Farman 2, Sneddon 2, McFarlane | 4,000 |
| 19 | | 19 | (a) | Nottingham F | L | 0-3 | | 8,000 |
| 20 | | 26 | (h) | Grimsby T | D | 3-3 | Donaldson 2, Farman | 6,000 |
| 21 | Apr | 2 | (a) | Lincoln C | W | 6-1 | Mathieson, Sneddon, Unknown 4 | 2,000 |
| 22 | | 9 | (h) | Birmingham St G | W | 3-0 | Donaldson 2, Hood | 6,000 |

FINAL LEAGUE POSITION: 2nd in Football Alliance

Appearances  
Goals

## FA Cup

| | | | | | | |
|---|---|---|---|---|---|---|
| Q1 | Oct | 3 | (h) | Ardwick | W | 5-1 | |
| Q2 | | 24 | (h) | Heywood | W | * | (*Walked-over after Heywood scratched) |
| Q3 | Nov | 14 | (a) | South Shore | W | 2-0 | |
| Q4 | Dec | 5 | (h) | Blackpool | L | 3-4 | |

| Slater | McFarlane | Clements | Doughty R | Stewart | Sharpe | Farman | Edge | Donaldson | Sneddon | Henrys | Owen J | Denman | Hood | Davies J | Mathieson | |
|---|---|---|---|---|---|---|---|---|---|---|---|---|---|---|---|---|
| 1 | 2 | 3 | 4 | 5 | 6 | 7 | 8 | 9 | 10 | 11 | | | | | | 1 |
| 1 | 2 | 3 | 4 | 5 | | 7 | 8 | 9 | 10 | 11 | 6 | | | | | 2 |
| 1 | 2 | 3 | 4 | 5 | | 7 | 8 | 9 | 10 | 11 | 6 | | | | | 3 |
| 1 | 2 | 3 | | 5 | 4 | 7 | 8 | 9 | 10 | 11 | 6 | | | | | 4 |
| 1 | 2 | 3 | | 5 | 4 | 7 | 8 | 9 | 10 | 11 | 6 | | | | | 5 |
| 1 | 2 | 3 | 4 | 5 | | 7 | 8 | 9 | 10 | 11 | 6 | | | | | 6 |
| 1 | 2 | 3 | 4 | 5 | | 7 | 8 | 9 | 10 | 11 | | 6 | | | | 7 |
| 1 | 2 | 3 | 4 | 5 | | 7 | 8 | 9 | 10 | 11 | | | 6 | | | 8 |
| 1 | 2 | 3 | | 5 | | 7 | 8 | 9 | 10 | 11 | 6 | | 4 | | | 9 |
| 1 | 2 | 3 | | 5 | | 7 | 8 | 9 | 10 | 11 | 4 | | 6 | | | 10 |
| 1 | | 3 | | 5 | | 7 | 8 | 9 | 10 | 11 | 4 | 2 | 6 | | | 11 |
| 1 | | 3 | | 5 | | 7 | 8 | 9 | 10 | 11 | 4 | 2 | 6 | | | 12 |
| 1 | | 3 | 4 | 5 | | 7 | 8 | 9 | 10 | 2 | 6 | | 11 | | | 13 |
| 1 | | 3 | 4 | 5 | | 7 | 8 | 9 | 10 | | 6 | 2 | 11 | | | 14 |
| 1 | 2 | 3 | 4 | 5 | | | 8 | 9 | 10 | 11 | 6 | | 7 | | | 15 |
| 1 | 2 | 3 | | 5 | | 7 | 8 | 9 | 10 | 11 | 6 | | 4 | | | 16 |
| 1 | 2 | 3 | 4 | 5 | | 7 | 8 | 9 | 10 | 11 | | | 6 | | | 17 |
| 1 | 2 | 3 | 4 | 5 | | 7 | 8 | 9 | 10 | 11 | | | 6 | | | 18 |
| 1 | 2 | 3 | 4 | 5 | | 7 | 8 | 9 | 10 | 11 | | | 6 | | | 19 |
| | 2 | 3 | 4 | 5 | | 7 | | 9 | 10 | | 6 | | 8 | 1 | 11 | 20 |
| | 2 | | 4 | 5 | | 7 | | 9 | 10 | 3 | 6 | | 8 | 1 | 11 | 21 |
| | 2 | 3 | 4 | 5 | | 7 | | 9 | | 10 | 4 | | 8 | 1 | 11 | 22 |
| 19 | 18 | 21 | 15 | 22 | 3 | 21 | 19 | 22 | 21 | 20 | 16 | 4 | 15 | 3 | 3 | |
| 1 | | | 2 | 3 | | 16 | 6 | 20 | 6 | | 1 | | 5 | | 1 | |

6 Unknown scorers, 2 own-goals

# 1892-93

| 1 | Sep | 3 | (a) | Blackburn R | L 3-4 | Coupar, Donaldson, Farman | 8,000 |
|---|---|---|---|---|---|---|---|
| 2 | | 10 | (h) | Burnley | D 1-1 | Donaldson | 10,000 |
| 3 | | 17 | (a) | Burnley | L 1-4 | Donaldson | 7,000 |
| 4 | | 24 | (a) | Everton | L 0-6 | | 10,000 |
| 5 | Oct | 1 | (a) | West Brom A | D 0-0 | | 4,000 |
| 6 | | 8 | (h) | West Brom A | L 2-4 | Donaldson, Hood | 9,000 |
| 7 | | 15 | (h) | Wolves | W 10-1 | Donaldson 3, Stewart 3, Carson, Farman, Hendry, Hood | 4,000 |
| 8 | | 19 | (h) | Everton | L 3-4 | Donaldson, Farman, Hood | 4,000 |
| 9 | | 22 | (a) | Sheffield W | L 0-1 | | 6,000 |
| 10 | | 29 | (a) | Nottingham F | D 1-1 | Farman | 6,000 |
| 11 | Nov | 5 | (h) | Blackburn R | D 4-4 | Farman 2, Carson, Hood | 12,000 |
| 12 | | 12 | (h) | Notts C | L 1-3 | Carson | 8,000 |
| 13 | | 19 | (h) | Aston Villa | W 2-0 | Coupar, Fitzsimmons | 7,000 |
| 14 | | 26 | (a) | Accrington | D 1-1 | Colville, Fitzsimmons | 3,000 |
| 15 | Dec | 3 | (a) | Bolton W | L 1-4 | Coupar | 3,000 |
| 16 | | 10 | (h) | Bolton W | W 1-0 | Donaldson | 4,000 |
| 17 | | 17 | (a) | Wolves | L 0-2 | | 5,000 |
| 18 | | 24 | (h) | Sheffield W | L 1-5 | Hood | 4,000 |
| 19 | | 26 | (a) | Preston NE | L 1-2 | Coupar | 4,000 |
| 20 | | 31 | (h) | Derby C | W 7-1 | Donaldson 3, Farman 3, Fitzsimmons | 3,000 |
| 21 | Jan | 7 | (a) | Stoke | L 1-7 | Coupar | 1,000 |
| 22 | | 14 | (h) | Nottingham F | L 1-3 | Donaldson | 8,000 |
| 23 | | 26 | (a) | Notts C | L 0-4 | | 1,000 |
| 24 | Feb | 11 | (a) | Derby C | L 1-5 | Fitzsimmons | 5,000 |
| 25 | Mar | 4 | (h) | Sunderland | L 0-5 | | 15,000 |
| 26 | | 6 | (a) | Aston Villa | L 0-2 | | 4,000 |
| 27 | | 31 | (h) | Stoke | W 1-0 | Farman | 10,000 |
| 28 | Apr | 1 | (h) | Preston NE | W 2-1 | Donaldson 2 | 9,000 |
| 29 | | 4 | (a) | Sunderland | L 0-6 | | 3,500 |
| 30 | | 8 | (h) | Accrington | D 3-3 | Donaldson, Fitzsimmons, Stewart | 3,000 |

FINAL LEAGUE POSITION: 16th in Division One

Appearances
Goals

## Test Matches

Apr 22 v Small Heath (Stoke) 1-1 Scorer: Farman
Team: Davies; Mitchell, Clements, Perrins, Stewart, Erentz, Farman, Coupar, Donaldson, Fitzsimmons, Cassidy. Att: 4,000
Apr 27 v Small Heath (Bramall Lane, Sheffield) 5-2 Scorers: Farman 3, Cassidy, Coupar
Team: Davies; Mitchell, Clements, Hood, Perrins, Erentz, Farman, Coupar, Donaldson, Fitzsimmons, Cassidy. Att: 6,000

## FA Cup

| 1 | Jan | 21 | (a) | Blackburn R | L 0-4 |
|---|---|---|---|---|---|

| Warner | Clements | Brown | Perrins | Stewart | Erentz | Farman | Coupar | Donaldson | Carson | Mathieson | Mitchell | Hood | Hendry | Kinloch | Colville | Fitzsimmons | Henrys | Davies | Cassidy | |
|---|---|---|---|---|---|---|---|---|---|---|---|---|---|---|---|---|---|---|---|---|
| 1 | 2 | 3 | 4 | 5 | 6 | 7 | 8 | 9 | 10 | 11 | | | | | | | | | | 1 |
| 1 | | 3 | 4 | 5 | 6 | 7 | 8 | 9 | 10 | 11 | 2 | | | | | | | | | 2 |
| 1 | | 3 | 4 | 5 | 6 | 7 | 8 | 9 | 10 | 11 | 2 | | | | | | | | | 3 |
| 1 | | 3 | 4 | 5 | 6 | 7 | 8 | 9 | 10 | 11 | 2 | | | | | | | | | 4 |
| 1 | | 3 | 4 | 5 | 6 | | 8 | 9 | 10 | 11 | 2 | 7 | | | | | | | | 5 |
| 1 | | 3 | 4 | 5 | 6 | | 8 | 9 | 10 | 11 | 2 | 7 | | | | | | | | 6 |
| 1 | 3 | | 4 | 5 | 6 | 7 | | 9 | 10 | | 2 | 8 | 11 | | | | | | | 7 |
| 1 | 3 | | 4 | 5 | 6 | 7 | | 9 | 10 | 11 | 2 | 8 | | | | | | | | 8 |
| 1 | 3 | | 4 | 5 | 6 | 7 | | 9 | 10 | | 2 | 8 | 11 | | | | | | | 9 |
| 1 | 3 | | 4 | 5 | 6 | 7 | 11 | | 10 | | 2 | 8 | | 9 | | | | | | 10 |
| 1 | 3 | | 4 | 5 | 6 | 7 | | 9 | 10 | 11 | 2 | 8 | | | | | | | | 11 |
| 1 | 3 | | 4 | 5 | 6 | 7 | | 9 | 10 | | 2 | 8 | | | 11 | | | | | 12 |
| 1 | 3 | | 4 | 5 | 6 | 7 | 9 | | | | 2 | 8 | | | 11 | 10 | | | | 13 |
| 1 | 3 | | 4 | | 6 | 7 | 9 | | | | 2 | 8 | | | 11 | 10 | 5 | | | 14 |
| 1 | 3 | | 4 | 5 | 6 | 7 | 8 | 9 | | | 2 | | | | 11 | 10 | | | | 15 |
| 1 | 3 | | 4 | 5 | 6 | 7 | 9 | | | | 2 | 8 | | | 11 | 10 | | | | 16 |
| 1 | 3 | | 4 | 5 | 6 | 7 | 9 | 11 | | | 2 | 8 | | | | 10 | | | | 17 |
| 1 | 3 | | 4 | 5 | 6 | 7 | 11 | 9 | | | 2 | 8 | | | | 10 | | | | 18 |
| 1 | 3 | | 4 | 5 | 6 | 7 | 11 | 9 | | | 2 | 8 | | | | 10 | | | | 19 |
| 1 | 3 | | 4 | 5 | 6 | 7 | 11 | 9 | | | 2 | 8 | | | | 10 | | | | 20 |
| | 3 | | 4 | 1 | 6 | 7 | 11 | 9 | | | 2 | 8 | | | | 10 | | | | *21 |
| | 3 | | | 5 | 6 | 7 | | 9 | | | 2 | 8 | | | 11 | 10 | 4 | 1 | | 22 |
| | 3 | 4 | 5 | | 6 | 7 | | 9 | | | 2 | 8 | | | 11 | 10 | | 1 | | 23 |
| 1 | 3 | | 4 | 5 | | 7 | | 9 | | | 2 | 8 | | | 11 | 10 | | 6 | | 24 |
| 1 | 3 | | 4 | 5 | 6 | 7 | | 9 | | | 2 | 8 | | | 11 | 10 | | 1 | | 25 |
| | 3 | | 4 | 5 | 6 | 7 | 8 | 9 | | | 2 | | | | 11 | 10 | | 1 | | 26 |
| | 3 | | 4 | 5 | 6 | 7 | 8 | 9 | | | 2 | | | | | 10 | | 1 | 11 | 27 |
| | 3 | | 4 | 5 | 6 | 7 | 8 | 9 | | | 2 | | | | | 10 | | 1 | 11 | 28 |
| | 3 | | 4 | 5 | 6 | 7 | 8 | 9 | | | 2 | | | | | 10 | | 1 | 11 | 29 |
| | 3 | | | 5 | 6 | 7 | 8 | 9 | | | 2 | 4 | | | | 10 | | 1 | 11 | 30 |
| 22 | 24 | 7 | 28 | 29 | 29 | 28 | 21 | 26 | 13 | 8 | 29 | 21 | 2 | 1 | 9 | 18 | 3 | 7 | 4 | |
| | | | | | | | 4 | 10 | 5 | 16 | 3 | | | | 5 | 1 | 1 | 5 | | |

*Match 21: United played with only 10 men.

Match 5: Clements listed as playing number 3 by the Football League.
Match 10: Coupar listed as playing number 10 by the Football League.
Match 21: Colville listed as playing number 11 by the Football League.
Match 24: Colville listed as playing number 9 by the Football League.
　　　　　Davies listed as playing number 1 by the Football League.
　　　　　Erentz listed as playing number 6 by the Football League.
Match 27: Colville listed as playing number 11 by the Football League.
Match 28: Colville listed as playing number 11 by the Football League.
Match 29: Colville listed as playing number 11 by the Football League.

# 1893-94

Secretary: A.H.Albut

| 1 | Sep | 2 | (h) | Burnley | W | 3-2 | Farman 3 | 10,000 |
|---|---|---|---|---|---|---|---|---|
| 2 | | 9 | (a) | West Brom A | L | 1-3 | Donaldson | 4,500 |
| 3 | | 16 | (a) | Sheffield W | W | 1-0 | Farman | 7,000 |
| 4 | | 23 | (h) | Nottingham F | D | 1-1 | Donaldson | 10,000 |
| 5 | | 30 | (a) | Darwen | L | 0-1 | | 4,000 |
| 6 | Oct | 7 | (a) | Derby C | L | 0-2 | | 7,000 |
| 7 | | 14 | (h) | West Brom A | W | 4-1 | Peden 2, Donaldson, Erentz | 8,000 |
| 8 | | 21 | (a) | Burnley | L | 1-4 | Hood | 7,000 |
| 9 | | 28 | (a) | Wolves | L | 0-2 | | 4,000 |
| 10 | Nov | 4 | (h) | Darwen | L | 0-1 | | 8,000 |
| 11 | | 11 | (h) | Wolves | W | 1-0 | Davidson | 5,000 |
| 12 | | 25 | (a) | Sheffield U | L | 1-3 | Fitzsimmons | 2,000 |
| 13 | Dec | 2 | (h) | Everton | L | 0-3 | | 6,000 |
| 14 | | 6 | (a) | Sunderland | L | 1-4 | Campbell | 5,000 |
| 15 | | 9 | (a) | Bolton W | L | 0-2 | | 5,000 |
| 16 | | 16 | (h) | Aston Villa | L | 1-3 | Peden | 8,000 |
| 17 | | 23 | (a) | Preston NE | L | 0-2 | | 5,000 |
| 18 | Jan | 6 | (a) | Everton | L | 0-2 | | 8,000 |
| 19 | | 13 | (h) | Sheffield W | L | 1-2 | Peden | 9,000 |
| 20 | Feb | 3 | (a) | Aston Villa | L | 1-5 | Mathieson | 5,000 |
| 21 | Mar | 3 | (h) | Sunderland | L | 2-4 | McNaught, Peden | 10,000 |
| 22 | | 10 | (h) | Sheffield U | L | 0-2 | | 5,000 |
| 23 | | 12 | (h) | Blackburn R | W | 5-1 | Donaldson 3, Clarkin, Farman | 5,000 |
| 24 | | 17 | (h) | Derby C | L | 2-6 | Clarkin 2 | 7,000 |
| 25 | | 23 | (h) | Stoke | W | 6-2 | Farman 2, Peden 2, Clarkin, Erentz | 8,000 |
| 26 | | 24 | (h) | Bolton W | D | 2-2 | Donaldson, Farman | 10,000 |
| 27 | | 26 | (a) | Blackburn R | L | 0-4 | | 5,000 |
| 28 | | 31 | (a) | Stoke | L | 1-3 | Clarkin | 4,000 |
| 29 | Apr | 7 | (a) | Nottingham F | L | 0-2 | | 4,000 |
| 30 | | 14 | (h) | Preston NE | L | 1-3 | Mathieson | 4,000 |

FINAL LEAGUE POSITION: 16th in Division One

Appearances
Goals

Test Match

Apr 28 v Liverpool (Ewood Park) 0-2
Team: Fall; Mitchell, Erentz, Perrins, McNaught, Davidson, Clarkin, Farman, Donaldson, Hood, Peden. Att: 3,000

FA Cup

| 1 | Jan | 27 | (h) | Middlesbrough | W | 4-0 | |
|---|---|---|---|---|---|---|---|
| 2 | Feb | 10 | (h) | Blackburn R | D | 0-0 | (After extra-time) |
| R | | 17 | (a) | Blackburn R | L | 1-5 | |

186

| Fall | Mitchell | Clements | Perrins | Stewart | Davidson | Farman | McNaught | Fitzsimmons | Peden | Donaldson | Erentz | Hood | Thompson | Prince | Graham | Campbell | Rothwell | Clarkin | Parker | Douglas | Mathieson | Dow | Stone | |
|---|---|---|---|---|---|---|---|---|---|---|---|---|---|---|---|---|---|---|---|---|---|---|---|---|
| 1 | 2 | 3 | 4 | 5 | 6 | 7 | 8 | 9 | 10 | 11 | | | | | | | | | | | | | | 1 |
| 1 | 2 | 3 | 4 | 5 | 6 | 7 | 8 | 9 | 10 | 11 | | | | | | | | | | | | | | 2 |
| 1 | 2 | 3 | | 5 | 6 | 7 | 10 | | 11 | 9 | 4 | 8 | | | | | | | | | | | | 3 |
| 1 | 2 | 3 | 4 | 5 | 6 | 7 | 10 | | 11 | 9 | 8 | | | | | | | | | | | | | 4 |
| 1 | 2 | 3 | 4 | 5 | 6 | 7 | 8 | 10 | 11 | 9 | | | | | | | | | | | | | | 5 |
| 1 | 2 | 3 | 4 | 5 | 6 | | 8 | 10 | 11 | 9 | 7 | | | | | | | | | | | | | 6 |
| 1 | 2 | 3 | 4 | 5 | 6 | | 7 | 10 | 11 | 9 | 8 | | | | | | | | | | | | | 7 |
| 1 | 2 | 3 | 4 | 5 | 6 | | 7 | | 11 | 9 | | 10 | 8 | | | | | | | | | | | 8 |
| 1 | 2 | 3 | 4 | 5 | 6 | | 7 | 10 | 11 | 9 | 8 | | | | | | | | | | | | | 9 |
| 1 | 2 | | | 5 | 6 | | 7 | 10 | 9 | | 3 | 4 | 8 | 11 | | | | | | | | | | 10 |
| 1 | 2 | | | 5 | 6 | 7 | 8 | 10 | 11 | | 3 | 4 | | | 9 | | | | | | | | | 11 |
| 1 | 2 | 3 | 4 | 5 | 6 | 7 | 10 | | 11 | 9 | | | | | | 8 | | | | | | | | 12 |
| 1 | 2 | 3 | 4 | 5 | 6 | | 10 | | 11 | 9 | | | | | | 8 | 7 | | | | | | | 13 |
| 1 | 2 | | 4 | 5 | 6 | 7 | 10 | | 11 | | 3 | | | | 9 | 8 | | | | | | | | 14 |
| 1 | 2 | | | 5 | 6 | 7 | 10 | | 11 | 9 | 3 | 4 | | | | 8 | | | | | | | | 15 |
| 1 | 2 | | 4 | 5 | 6 | 7 | 10 | | 11 | 9 | 3 | | | | | 8 | | | | | | | | 16 |
| 1 | 2 | | 4 | 5 | 6 | 7 | 10 | | 11 | 9 | 3 | 8 | | | | | | | | | | | | 17 |
| | 2 | | 4 | 5 | 6 | 7 | 10 | | 11 | | 3 | 8 | | | 9 | | | | | | | | | 18 |
| 1 | 2 | | 4 | 5 | 6 | | | | 10 | 11 | 3 | | | | 9 | | | 7 | 8 | | | | | 19 |
| | 2 | | 4 | 5 | 6 | | | | 10 | 9 | 3 | | | | | | | 7 | 8 | 1 | 11 | | | 20 |
| 1 | 2 | | 4 | 5 | 6 | | 10 | | 11 | 9 | 3 | | | | | | | 7 | 8 | | | | | 21 |
| | 2 | | | 5 | 6 | | 10 | | 11 | 9 | 3 | 4 | | | | | | 7 | 8 | 1 | | | | 22 |
| 1 | 2 | | 4 | 5 | 6 | | 8 | | 11 | 9 | 3 | | | | | | | 7 | 10 | | | | | 23 |
| 1 | 2 | | 4 | 5 | 6 | | 8 | | 11 | 9 | 3 | | | | | | | 7 | 10 | | | | | 24 |
| | | | 4 | | 6 | | 8 | 5 | 11 | 9 | 3 | 2 | | | | | | 7 | 10 | 1 | | | | 25 |
| | | | 4 | 5 | 6 | | 8 | | 11 | 9 | 3 | | | | | | | 7 | 10 | 1 | | 2 | | 26 |
| | | | 4 | | 6 | | 8 | | 11 | | 3 | 10 | | | | | | 7 | 9 | 1 | | 2 | 5 | 27 |
| | | | 4 | | 6 | | 8 | 5 | 11 | 9 | 3 | 2 | | | | | | 7 | 10 | 1 | | | | 28 |
| | 2 | | 4 | 5 | 6 | | 8 | | | 9 | 3 | | | 11 | | | | 7 | 10 | 1 | | | | 29 |
| 1 | 2 | | 4 | 5 | 3 | | | | 11 | 9 | | 8 | | | | | | 7 | | | 10 | | 6 | 30 |
| 23 | 25 | 12 | 27 | 25 | 28 | 18 | 26 | 9 | 28 | 24 | 22 | 12 | 3 | 2 | 4 | 5 | 1 | 12 | 11 | 7 | 2 | 2 | 2 | |
| | | | | | 1 | 8 | 1 | 1 | 7 | 7 | 2 | 1 | | | 1 | | | | 5 | | | 2 | | |

Match 27: Donaldson listed as playing number 1 by the Football League.
Match 29: Hood listed as playing number 1 by the Football League.
Matches 26 & 27: M.J.Woods was listed as playing number 2 in newspapers; the Football League have J.M.Dow as number 2 in both games and this is accepted here as there was no player M.J.Woods registered for Newton Heath. The name may have been a pseudonym.

187

# 1894-95

Secretary: A.H.Albut

| 1 | Sep | 8 | (a) | Burton W | L 0-1 | | 3,000 |
|---|---|---|---|---|---|---|---|
| 2 | | 15 | (h) | Crewe A | W 6-1 | Dow 2, Smith 2, Clarkin, McCartney | 6,000 |
| 3 | | 22 | (a) | Leicester F | W 3-2 | Dow 2, Smith | 6,000 |
| 4 | Oct | 6 | (a) | Darwen | D 1-1 | Donaldson | 6,000 |
| 5 | | 13 | (h) | W Arsenal | D 3-3 | Donaldson 2, Clarkin | 4,000 |
| 6 | | 20 | (a) | Burton S | W 2-1 | Donaldson 2 | 5,000 |
| 7 | | 27 | (h) | Leicester F | D 2-2 | McNaught, Smith | 3,000 |
| 8 | Nov | 3 | (a) | Manchester C | W 5-2 | Smith 4, Clarkin | 14,000 |
| 9 | | 10 | (h) | Rotherham T | W 3-2 | Davidson, Donaldson, Peters | 4,000 |
| 10 | | 17 | (a) | Grimsby T | L 1-2 | Clarkin | 3,000 |
| 11 | | 24 | (h) | Darwen | D 1-1 | Donaldson | 5,000 |
| 12 | Dec | 1 | (a) | Crewe A | W 2-0 | Clarkin, Smith | 600 |
| 13 | | 8 | (h) | Burton S | W 5-1 | Peters 2, Smith 2, Dow | 4,000 |
| 14 | | 15 | (a) | Notts C | D 1-1 | Donaldson | 3,000 |
| 15 | | 22 | (h) | Lincoln C | W 3-0 | Donaldson, Millar, Smith | 2,000 |
| 16 | | 24 | (a) | Burslem PVale | W 5-2 | Clarkin, Donaldson, McNaught, Millar, Smith | 1,000 |
| 17 | | 26 | (a) | Walsall TS | W 2-1 | Millar, Stewart | 1,000 |
| 18 | | 29 | (a) | Lincoln C | L 0-3 | | 3,000 |
| 19 | Jan | 1 | (h) | Burslem PVale | W 3-0 | Millar 2, Rothwell | 5,000 |
| 20 | | 5 | (h) | Manchester C | W 4-1 | Clarkin 2, Donaldson, Smith | 12,000 |
| 21 | | 12 | (a) | Rotherham T | L 1-2 | Erentz | 2,000 |
| 22 | Mar | 2 | (h) | Burton W | D 1-1 | Peters | 6,000 |
| 23 | | 23 | (h) | Grimsby T | W 2-0 | Cassidy 2 | 9,000 |
| 24 | | 30 | (a) | W Arsenal | L 2-3 | Clarkin, Donaldson | 6,000 |
| 25 | Apr | 3 | (h) | Walsall TS | W 9-0 | Cassidy 2, Donaldson 2, Peters 2, Smith 2, Clarkin | 6,000 |
| 26 | | 6 | (h) | Newcastle U | W 5-1 | Cassidy 2, Smith 2, McDermidd (og) | 5,000 |
| 27 | | 12 | (h) | Bury | D 2-2 | Cassidy, Donaldson | 15,000 |
| 28 | | 13 | (a) | Newcastle U | L 0-3 | | 4,000 |
| 29 | | 15 | (a) | Bury | L 1-2 | Peters | 10,000 |
| 30 | | 20 | (h) | Notts C | D 3-3 | Cassidy, Clarkin, Smith | 12,000 |

FINAL LEAGUE POSITION: 3rd in Division Two

Appearances

Goals

Test Match

Apr 27 v Stoke (Burslem) 0-3
Team: Douglas; Dow, McCartney, Perrins, Stone, Stewart, Clarkin, Donaldson, Cassidy, Smith, Peters. Att: 10,000

FA Cup

| 1 | Feb | 2 | (h) | Stoke | | L 2-3 |
|---|---|---|---|---|---|---|

| Douglas | McCartney | Erentz | Stewart | McNaught | Davidson | Clarkin | Farman | Dow | Smith | Peters | Perrins | Donaldson | Millar | Stone | Rothwell | Cassidy | McFetteridge | Cairns | Longair | |
|---|---|---|---|---|---|---|---|---|---|---|---|---|---|---|---|---|---|---|---|---|
| 1 | 2 | 3 | 4 | 5 | 6 | 7 | 8 | 9 | 10 | 11 | | | | | | | | | | 1 |
| 1 | 2 | 3 | | 5 | 6 | 7 | 8 | 9 | 10 | 11 | 4 | | | | | | | | | 2 |
| 1 | 2 | 3 | | 5 | 6 | 7 | | 9 | 10 | 11 | 4 | 8 | | | | | | | | 3 |
| 1 | 2 | 3 | | 5 | 6 | 7 | | 9 | 10 | 11 | 4 | 8 | | | | | | | | 4 |
| 1 | 2 | 3 | | 5 | 6 | 7 | | 9 | 10 | 11 | 4 | 8 | | | | | | | | 5 |
| 1 | | 3 | 9 | 5 | 6 | 7 | | 2 | 10 | 11 | 4 | 8 | | | | | | | | 6 |
| 1 | 2 | 3 | 9 | 5 | 6 | 7 | | | 10 | 11 | 4 | 8 | | | | | | | | 7 |
| 1 | 2 | 3 | | 5 | 6 | 7 | | 9 | 10 | 11 | 4 | 8 | | | | | | | | 8 |
| 1 | 2 | 3 | | 5 | 6 | 7 | | 9 | 10 | 11 | 4 | 8 | | | | | | | | 9 |
| 1 | | 3 | 4 | 5 | 6 | 7 | 8 | 9 | 10 | 11 | | 2 | | | | | | | | 10 |
| 1 | 2 | 3 | | 5 | 6 | 7 | | 9 | 10 | 11 | 4 | 8 | | | | | | | | 11 |
| 1 | 2 | 3 | 4 | 5 | 6 | 7 | | 9 | 10 | 11 | | 8 | | | | | | | | 12 |
| 1 | 2 | 3 | 5 | 6 | | 7 | | 9 | 10 | 11 | 4 | 8 | | | | | | | | 13 |
| 1 | 2 | 3 | 5 | 6 | | 7 | | 9 | 10 | 11 | 4 | 8 | | | | | | | | 14 |
| 1 | 2 | 6 | 5 | | | 7 | | 3 | 10 | 11 | 4 | 8 | 9 | | | | | | | 15 |
| 1 | 2 | 3 | 6 | 5 | | 7 | | | 10 | 11 | 4 | 8 | 9 | | | | | | | 16 |
| 1 | | 3 | 6 | 5 | | 7 | 10 | 2 | | 11 | 4 | 8 | 9 | | | | | | | 17 |
| 1 | | 3 | 6 | 5 | | 7 | | 2 | 10 | 11 | 4 | 8 | 9 | | | | | | | 18 |
| 1 | 2 | 3 | | 6 | | 7 | | | 10 | 11 | | 4 | 9 | 5 | 8 | | | | | 19 |
| 1 | 2 | 3 | 6 | 5 | | 7 | | 9 | 10 | 11 | | 8 | | 4 | | | | | | 20 |
| 1 | 2 | 3 | 6 | 5 | | | 7 | 9 | 10 | 11 | 4 | 8 | | | | | | | | 21 |
| 1 | 2 | 3 | 6 | 5 | | 7 | | 9 | 10 | 11 | 4 | 8 | | | | | | | | 22 |
| 1 | | 3 | 6 | 5 | | 7 | | 2 | 10 | 11 | 4 | 8 | | | | 9 | | | | 23 |
| 1 | | 3 | 6 | 5 | | 7 | | 2 | 10 | 11 | 4 | 8 | | | | 9 | | | | 24 |
| 1 | | 3 | 6 | 5 | | 7 | | 2 | 10 | 11 | 4 | 8 | | | | 9 | | | | 25 |
| 1 | | 3 | 6 | 5 | | 7 | | 2 | 10 | 11 | 4 | 8 | | | | 9 | | | | 26 |
| 1 | | 3 | 6 | 5 | | 7 | | 2 | 10 | 11 | 4 | 8 | | | | 9 | | | | 27 |
| 1 | | 6 | | | | 7 | | 3 | 10 | 11 | 4 | 2 | | 5 | | 9 | 8 | | | 28 |
| 1 | | 6 | | | | 7 | | 2 | 10 | 11 | 4 | | 8 | 5 | | 9 | | 3 | | 29 |
| 1 | | 3 | 6 | | | 7 | | 2 | 10 | 11 | 4 | 8 | | | | 9 | | | 5 | 30 |
| 30 | 18 | 28 | 22 | 26 | 12 | 29 | 5 | 27 | 29 | 30 | 25 | 27 | 6 | 4 | 1 | 8 | 1 | 1 | 1 | |
| | 1 | 1 | 1 | 2 | 1 | 11 | | 5 | 19 | 7 | | 15 | 5 | | 1 | 8 | | | | |

1 own-goal

Match 23: McCartney listed as playing number 5 by the Football League.
Match 25: McCartney listed as playing number 2 by the Football League.

189

# 1895-96

Secretary: A.H.Albut

| | | | | | | | | |
|---|---|---|---|---|---|---|---|---|
| 1 | Sep | 7 | (h) | Crewe A | W | 5-0 | Cassidy 2, Aitken, Kennedy, Smith | 6,000 |
| 2 | | 14 | (a) | Loughborough T | D | 3-3 | Cassidy 2, McNaught | 3,000 |
| 3 | | 21 | (h) | Burton S | W | 5-0 | Donaldson 2, Cassidy 2, Kennedy | 9,000 |
| 4 | | 28 | (a) | Crewe A | W | 2-0 | Smith 2 | 2,000 |
| 5 | Oct | 5 | (h) | Manchester C | D | 1-1 | Clarkin | 12,000 |
| 6 | | 12 | (a) | Liverpool | L | 1-7 | Cassidy | 7,000 |
| 7 | | 19 | (h) | Newcastle U | W | 2-1 | Cassidy, Peters | 8,000 |
| 8 | | 26 | (a) | Newcastle U | L | 1-2 | Kennedy | 8,000 |
| 9 | Nov | 2 | (h) | Liverpool | W | 5-2 | Peters 3, Clarkin, Smith | 10,000 |
| 10 | | 9 | (a) | W Arsenal | L | 1-2 | Cassidy | 9,000 |
| 11 | | 16 | (h) | Lincoln C | D | 5-5 | Clarkin 2, Cassidy, Collinson, Peters | 8,000 |
| 12 | | 23 | (a) | Notts C | W | 2-0 | Cassidy, Kennedy | 3,000 |
| 13 | | 30 | (h) | W Arsenal | W | 5-1 | Cartwright 2, Clarkin, Kennedy, Peters | 6,000 |
| 14 | Dec | 7 | (a) | Manchester C | L | 1-2 | Cassidy | 18,000 |
| 15 | | 14 | (h) | Notts C | W | 3-0 | Cassidy, Clarkin, Donaldson | 3,000 |
| 16 | | 21 | (a) | Darwen | L | 0-3 | | 3,000 |
| 17 | Jan | 1 | (h) | Grimsby T | W | 3-2 | Cassidy 3 | 8,000 |
| 18 | | 4 | (a) | Leicester F | L | 0-3 | | 7,000 |
| 19 | | 11 | (h) | Rotherham T | W | 3-0 | Donaldson 2, Stephenson | 3,000 |
| 20 | Feb | 3 | (h) | Leicester F | W | 2-0 | Kennedy, Smith | 1,000 |
| 21 | | 8 | (a) | Burton S | L | 1-4 | Vance | 2,000 |
| 22 | | 29 | (h) | Burton W | L | 1-2 | McNaught | 1,000 |
| 23 | Mar | 7 | (a) | Rotherham T | W | 3-2 | Donaldson, Kennedy, Smith | 1,500 |
| 24 | | 14 | (a) | Grimsby T | L | 2-4 | Kennedy, Smith | 2,000 |
| 25 | | 18 | (a) | Burton W | L | 1-5 | Dow | 2,000 |
| 26 | | 23 | (a) | Burslem PVale | L | 0-3 | | 3,000 |
| 27 | Apr | 3 | (h) | Darwen | W | 4-0 | Kennedy 3, McNaught | 1,000 |
| 28 | | 4 | (h) | Loughborough T | W | 2-0 | Donaldson, Smith | 4,000 |
| 29 | | 6 | (h) | Burslem PVale | W | 2-1 | Clarkin, Smith | 5,000 |
| 30 | | 11 | (a) | Lincoln C | L | 0-2 | | 2,000 |

FINAL LEAGUE POSITION: 6th in Division Two

Appearances
Goals

FA Cup

| | | | | | | | |
|---|---|---|---|---|---|---|---|
| 1 | Feb | 1 | (h) | Kettering T | W | 2-1 | |
| 2 | | 15 | (h) | Derby C | D | 1-1 | |
| R | | 19 | (a) | Derby C | L | 1-5 | |

190

| Douglas | Dow | Erentz | Fitzsimmons | McNaught | Cartwright | Clarkin | Kennedy | Cassidy | Smith R | Aitken | Peters | Perrins | Donaldson | Collinson | Ridgway | Stephenson | Vance | Whitney | Whittaker | Stafford | # |
|---|---|---|---|---|---|---|---|---|---|---|---|---|---|---|---|---|---|---|---|---|---|
| 1 | 2 | 3 | 4 | 5 | 6 | 7 | 8 | 9 | 10 | 11 |  |  |  |  |  |  |  |  |  |  | 1 |
| 1 | 2 | 3 | 4 | 5 | 6 | 7 | 8 | 9 | 10 |  | 11 |  |  |  |  |  |  |  |  |  | 2 |
| 1 | 2 | 3 | 4 | 5 |  | 7 | 8 | 11 | 10 |  |  | 6 | 9 |  |  |  |  |  |  |  | 3 |
| 1 | 2 | 3 | 6 | 5 |  | 7 | 8 | 9 | 10 | 11 |  | 4 |  |  |  |  |  |  |  |  | 4 |
| 1 | 2 | 3 |  | 5 | 6 | 7 | 8 | 9 | 10 |  | 11 | 4 |  |  |  |  |  |  |  |  | 5 |
| 1 | 2 | 3 |  | 5 | 6 | 7 | 8 | 9 | 10 |  | 11 | 4 |  |  |  |  |  |  |  |  | 6 |
| 1 | 2 | 3 |  | 5 | 6 | 7 | 8 | 9 | 10 |  | 11 | 4 |  |  |  |  |  |  |  |  | 7 |
| 1 | 2 |  | 4 | 3 | 6 | 7 | 8 | 9 | 10 |  | 11 | 5 |  |  |  |  |  |  |  |  | 8 |
| 1 | 2 | 3 | 4 | 5 | 6 | 7 | 8 | 9 | 10 |  | 11 |  |  |  |  |  |  |  |  |  | 9 |
| 1 | 2 | 3 | 4 | 5 | 6 | 7 | 8 | 9 | 10 |  | 11 |  |  |  |  |  |  |  |  |  | 10 |
| 1 | 2 |  | 4 | 5 | 6 | 7 | 8 | 9 | 10 |  | 11 |  |  | 3 |  |  |  |  |  |  | 11 |
| 1 |  | 3 | 4 | 5 | 6 | 7 | 8 | 9 | 10 |  | 11 |  |  | 2 |  |  |  |  |  |  | 12 |
| 1 | 2 | 3 | 4 | 5 | 6 | 7 | 8 | 9 | 10 |  | 11 |  |  |  |  |  |  |  |  |  | 13 |
| 1 | 2 | 3 | 4 | 5 | 6 | 7 | 8 | 9 | 10 |  | 11 |  |  |  |  |  |  |  |  |  | 14 |
| 1 |  | 3 | 4 | 5 | 6 | 7 | 8 | 11 | 10 |  |  |  | 9 | 2 |  |  |  |  |  |  | 15 |
| 1 |  | 3 | 4 | 5 | 6 | 7 | 8 |  | 10 |  | 11 |  | 9 | 2 |  |  |  |  |  |  | 16 |
| 1 | 2 |  |  | 6 | 5 | 3 | 7 | 8 | 11 |  | 10 | 4 | 9 |  |  |  |  |  |  |  | 17 |
| 1 | 2 |  |  | 4 | 5 | 6 | 7 | 8 | 11 |  | 10 |  | 9 | 3 |  |  |  |  |  |  | 18 |
|  | 2 |  | 4 | 5 | 6 |  | 7 | 11 |  |  | 8 |  | 9 | 3 | 1 | 10 |  |  |  |  | 19 |
| 9 |  | 4 |  | 3 |  | 7 |  |  | 6 |  | 11 | 5 | 8 | 2 | 1 |  | 10 |  |  |  | 20 |
| 9 | 3 | 4 | 5 | 6 |  | 7 |  |  | 11 |  |  |  | 8 | 2 | 1 |  | 10 |  |  |  | 21 |
|  | 3 | 4 | 5 |  |  | 7 | 8 |  | 10 |  | 11 | 1 | 9 | 2 |  |  |  | 6 |  |  | 22 |
|  | 3 |  | 1 |  |  | 7 | 8 |  | 11 |  | 4 | 5 | 9 | 2 |  |  | 10 | 6 |  |  | 23 |
|  | 3 | 4 | 5 | 6 | 7 | 8 |  |  | 11 |  |  |  | 9 | 2 |  |  | 10 |  | 1 |  | 24 |
| 7 | 3 | 4 | 5 | 6 |  | 8 |  |  | 11 |  |  | 1 | 9 | 2 |  |  | 10 |  |  |  | 25 |
|  | 3 | 4 | 5 | 6 | 7 | 8 |  |  | 11 |  |  |  | 9 | 2 |  |  | 10 |  | 1 |  | 26 |
|  | 3 | 4 | 5 | 6 | 7 | 8 |  |  | 11 |  |  |  | 9 |  | 1 |  | 10 |  |  | 2 | 27 |
|  | 3 | 4 | 5 | 6 | 7 | 8 |  |  | 11 |  |  |  | 9 |  | 1 |  | 10 |  |  | 2 | 28 |
|  | 3 | 4 | 5 | 6 | 7 | 8 |  |  | 11 |  |  |  | 9 |  | 1 |  | 10 |  |  | 2 | 29 |
|  | 3 | 4 | 8 | 6 | 7 |  |  |  | 11 |  |  | 5 | 9 |  |  |  | 10 |  | 1 | 2 | 30 |
| 18 | 19 | 24 | 26 | 28 | 27 | 26 | 29 | 19 | 28 | 2 | 16 | 12 | 17 | 13 | 6 | 1 | 10 | 2 | 3 | 4 |  |
| 1 |  |  | 3 | 2 | 7 | 11 | 16 | 9 | 1 |  | 6 |  | 7 | 1 |  | 1 | 1 |  |  |  |  |

Match 16: Perrins listed as playing number 6 by the Football League.
Match 19: Alec Smith listed as playing number 10 by the Football League. *Manchester Evening Mail* and *Manchester Courier* state B.Stephenson although the League had no player by that name registered for Newton Heath.
Match 25: Clarkin listed as playing number 2 by the Football League.

# 1896-97

Secretary: A.H.Albut

| 1 | Sep | 1 | (h) | Gainsborough T | W | 2-0 | McNaught 2 | 4,000 |
| 2 | | 5 | (a) | Burton S | W | 5-3 | Brown, Bryant, Cassidy, Draycott, McNaught | 3,000 |
| 3 | | 7 | (h) | Walsall | W | 2-0 | Cassidy, Donaldson | 7,000 |
| 4 | | 12 | (h) | Lincoln C | W | 3-1 | Cassidy 2, Donaldson | 7,000 |
| 5 | | 19 | (a) | Grimsby T | L | 0-2 | | 3,000 |
| 6 | | 21 | (a) | Walsall | W | 3-2 | Brown, Draycott, McNaught | 7,000 |
| 7 | | 26 | (h) | Newcastle U | W | 4-0 | Cassidy 3, Donaldson | 7,000 |
| 8 | Oct | 3 | (a) | Manchester C | D | 0-0 | | 20,000 |
| 9 | | 10 | (h) | Small Heath | D | 1-1 | Draycott | 7,000 |
| 10 | | 17 | (a) | Blackpool | L | 2-4 | Bryant, Draycott | 5,000 |
| 11 | | 21 | (a) | Gainsborough T | L | 0-2 | | 4,000 |
| 12 | | 24 | (h) | Burton W | W | 3-0 | Cassidy 3 | 4,000 |
| 13 | Nov | 7 | (h) | Grimsby T | W | 4-2 | Cassidy 2, Donaldson, Jenkyns | 5,000 |
| 14 | | 28 | (a) | Small Heath | L | 0-1 | | 4,000 |
| 15 | Dec | 19 | (a) | Notts C | L | 0-3 | | 5,000 |
| 16 | | 25 | (h) | Manchester C | W | 2-1 | Donaldson, Smith | 18,000 |
| 17 | | 26 | (h) | Blackpool | W | 2-0 | Cassidy 2 | 9,000 |
| 18 | | 28 | (a) | Leicester F | L | 0-1 | | 8,000 |
| 19 | Jan | 1 | (a) | Newcastle U | L | 0-2 | | 17,000 |
| 20 | | 9 | (h) | Burton S | D | 1-1 | Donaldson | 3,000 |
| 21 | Feb | 6 | (h) | Loughborough T | W | 6-0 | Smith 2, Boyd, Donaldson, Draycott, Jenkyns | 5,000 |
| 22 | | 20 | (h) | Leicester F | W | 2-1 | Boyd, Donaldson | 8,000 |
| 23 | Mar | 2 | (h) | Darwen | W | 3-1 | Cassidy 2, Boyd | 3,000 |
| 24 | | 13 | (a) | Darwen | W | 2-0 | Cassidy, Gillespie | 2,000 |
| 25 | | 20 | (a) | Burton W | W | 2-1 | Gillespie, Opp own-goal | 3,000 |
| 26 | | 22 | (h) | W Arsenal | D | 1-1 | Boyd | 3,000 |
| 27 | | 27 | (h) | Notts C | D | 1-1 | Bryant | 10,000 |
| 28 | Apr | 1 | (a) | Lincoln C | W | 3-1 | Jenkyns 3 | 1,000 |
| 29 | | 3 | (a) | W Arsenal | W | 2-0 | Boyd, Donaldson | 6,000 |
| 30 | | 10 | (a) | Loughborough T | L | 0-2 | | 3,000 |

FINAL LEAGUE POSITION: 2nd in Division Two

Appearances
Goals

## Test Matches

Apr 19 v Burnley (a) 0-2
Team: Barrett; Cartwright, Erentz, Draycott, Jenkyns, McNaught, Bryant, Doughty, Donaldson, Gillespie, Cassidy. Att: 10,000
Apr 21 v Burnley (h) 2-0 Scorers: Boyd, Jenkyns
Team: Barrett; Cartwright, Erentz, Draycott, Jenkyns, McNaught, Bryant, Boyd, Donaldson, Gillespie, Cassidy. Att: 7,000
Apr 24 v Sunderland (h) 1-1 Scorer: Boyd
Team: Barrett; Doughty, Erentz, Draycott, Jenkyns, McNaught, Bryant, Boyd, Donaldson, Gillespie, Cassidy. Att: 18,000
Apr 26 v Sunderland (a) 0-2
Team: Barrett; Doughty, Erentz, Draycott, Jenkyns, McNaught, Bryant, Boyd, Donaldson, Gillespie, Cassidy. Att: 6,000

## FA Cup

| Q1 | Dec | 12 | (h) | West Manchester | W | 7-0 |
| Q2 | Jan | 2 | (h) | Nelson | W | 3-0 |
| Q3 | | 16 | (h) | Blackpool | D | 2-2 |
| R | | 20 | (a) | Blackpool | W | 2-1 |
| 1 | | 30 | (h) | Kettering T | W | 5-1 |
| 2 | Feb | 13 | (a) | Southampton | D | 1-1 |
| R | | 17 | (h) | Southampton | W | 3-1 |
| 3 | | 27 | (a) | Derby C | L | 0-2 |

| Ridgway | Stafford | Erentz | Draycott | Jenkyns | Cartwright | Bryant | Donaldson | Brown | McNaught | Cassidy | Smith | Wetherell | Barrett | Kennedy | Vance | Gillespie | Boyd | Morgan | |
|---|---|---|---|---|---|---|---|---|---|---|---|---|---|---|---|---|---|---|---|
| 1 | 2 | 3 | 4 | 5 | 6 | 7 | 8 | 9 | 10 | 11 |  |  |  |  |  |  |  |  | 1 |
| 1 | 2 | 3 | 4 | 5 | 6 | 7 | 8 | 9 | 10 | 11 |  |  |  |  |  |  |  |  | 2 |
| 1 | 2 | 3 | 4 | 5 | 6 | 7 | 8 | 9 | 10 | 11 |  |  |  |  |  |  |  |  | 3 |
| 1 | 2 | 3 |  | 5 | 6 | 7 | 8 | 9 | 10 | 11 | 4 |  |  |  |  |  |  |  | 4 |
| 1 | 2 | 3 | 4 | 5 |  | 7 | 8 | 9 | 10 | 11 | 6 |  |  |  |  |  |  |  | 5 |
|  | 2 | 3 | 4 | 5 |  | 7 | 8 | 9 | 10 | 11 | 6 | 1 |  |  |  |  |  |  | 6 |
|  | 2 | 3 | 4 | 5 | 6 | 7 | 8 |  | 10 | 11 | 9 |  | 1 |  |  |  |  |  | 7 |
|  | 2 | 3 | 4 | 5 | 6 | 7 | 8 |  | 10 | 9 | 11 |  | 1 |  |  |  |  |  | 8 |
|  | 2 | 3 | 4 | 5 | 6 | 7 | 8 |  | 10 | 9 | 11 | 1 |  |  |  |  |  |  | 9 |
|  | 2 | 3 | 4 | 5 | 6 | 7 | 8 | 9 | 10 |  | 11 |  | 1 |  |  |  |  |  | 10 |
|  | 2 | 3 | 4 | 5 | 6 | 7 | 9 |  | 10 | 11 |  |  | 1 | 8 |  |  |  |  | 11 |
|  | 2 | 3 | 4 | 5 | 6 | 7 |  |  | 8 | 9 | 11 |  | 1 |  | 10 |  |  |  | 12 |
|  | 2 | 3 | 4 | 5 | 6 | 7 | 11 |  | 8 | 9 | 10 |  | 1 |  |  |  |  |  | 13 |
|  | 2 | 3 | 4 | 5 | 6 | 7 | 11 |  | 8 | 9 |  |  | 1 |  |  | 10 |  |  | 14 |
|  | 2 | 3 | 4 | 5 | 6 | 7 | 11 |  | 8 | 9 |  |  | 1 |  |  | 10 |  |  | 15 |
|  | 2 | 3 | 4 | 5 |  | 7 | 11 |  | 6 | 9 | 8 |  | 1 |  |  | 10 |  |  | 16 |
|  | 2 | 3 | 4 | 5 |  | 7 | 11 |  | 6 | 9 | 8 |  | 1 |  |  | 10 |  |  | 17 |
|  | 2 |  | 4 | 5 | 3 | 7 | 11 |  | 6 | 9 | 8 |  | 1 |  |  | 10 |  |  | 18 |
|  | 2 | 3 | 4 | 5 | 6 | 7 | 11 |  | 8 | 9 |  |  | 1 |  |  | 10 |  |  | 19 |
|  | 2 | 3 | 4 | 5 | 6 | 7 | 11 |  | 8 | 9 |  |  | 1 |  |  | 10 |  |  | 20 |
|  | 2 | 3 | 4 | 5 |  |  | 8 |  | 6 | 11 | 7 |  | 1 |  |  | 10 | 9 |  | 21 |
|  | 2 |  | 4 | 5 | 3 | 7 | 8 |  | 6 | 11 |  |  | 1 |  |  | 10 | 9 |  | 22 |
|  | 2 |  | 4 |  | 3 | 7 | 8 |  | 6 | 11 |  |  | 1 |  |  | 10 | 9 | 5 | 23 |
|  |  | 3 | 4 | 5 | 2 | 7 | 8 |  | 6 | 11 |  |  | 1 |  |  | 10 | 9 |  | 24 |
|  |  | 3 | 4 |  | 2 | 7 | 8 |  | 6 | 11 |  |  | 1 |  |  | 10 | 9 | 5 | 25 |
|  |  | 3 | 4 | 5 | 2 | 7 | 8 |  | 6 |  | 11 |  | 1 |  |  | 10 | 9 |  | 26 |
|  |  | 3 | 4 | 5 | 2 | 7 | 8 |  | 6 | 11 |  |  | 1 |  |  | 10 | 9 |  | 27 |
|  |  | 3 | 4 | 5 | 2 | 7 | 8 |  | 6 | 11 |  |  | 1 |  |  | 10 | 9 |  | 28 |
|  |  | 3 | 4 | 5 | 2 | 7 | 8 |  | 6 | 11 |  |  | 1 |  |  | 10 | 9 |  | 29 |
|  | 2 | 3 | 4 |  | 6 | 7 | 8 |  | 5 | 11 |  |  | 1 |  |  | 10 | 9 |  | 30 |
| 5 | 24 | 27 | 29 | 27 | 25 | 29 | 29 | 7 | 30 | 28 | 14 | 2 | 23 | 1 | 1 | 17 | 10 | 2 | |
|  |  |  | 5 | 5 |  | 3 | 9 | 2 | 4 | 17 | 3 |  |  |  |  | 2 | 5 |  | |

1 own-goal

193

# 1897-98

Secretary: A.H.Albut

| 1 | Sep | 4 | (h) | Lincoln C | W | 5-0 | Boyd 3, Cassidy, Bryant | 5,000 |
|---|---|---|---|---|---|---|---|---|
| 2 | | 11 | (a) | Burton S | W | 4-0 | Boyd 3, Cassidy | 2,000 |
| 3 | | 18 | (h) | Luton T | L | 1-2 | Cassidy | 8,000 |
| 4 | | 25 | (a) | Blackpool | W | 1-0 | Smith | 2,000 |
| 5 | Oct | 2 | (h) | Leicester F | W | 2-0 | Boyd 2 | 6,000 |
| 6 | | 9 | (a) | Newcastle U | L | 0-2 | | 12,000 |
| 7 | | 16 | (h) | Manchester C | D | 1-1 | Gillespie | 20,000 |
| 8 | | 23 | (a) | Small Heath | L | 1-2 | Bryant | 6,000 |
| 9 | | 30 | (h) | Walsall | W | 6-0 | Cassidy 2, Donaldson 2, Bryant, Gillespie | 6,000 |
| 10 | Nov | 6 | (a) | Lincoln C | L | 0-1 | | 2,000 |
| 11 | | 13 | (h) | Newcastle U | L | 0-1 | | 7,000 |
| 12 | | 20 | (a) | Leicester F | D | 1-1 | Wedge | 6,000 |
| 13 | | 27 | (h) | Grimsby T | W | 2-1 | Bryant, Wedge | 5,000 |
| 14 | Dec | 11 | (a) | Walsall | D | 1-1 | Boyd | 2,000 |
| 15 | | 25 | (h) | Manchester C | W | 1-0 | Cassidy | 16,000 |
| 16 | | 27 | (a) | Gainsborough T | L | 1-2 | Boyd | 3,000 |
| 17 | Jan | 1 | (h) | Burton S | W | 4-0 | Boyd, Bryant, Carman, McNaught | 6,000 |
| 18 | | 8 | (a) | W Arsenal | L | 1-5 | F.C.Erentz | 8,000 |
| 19 | | 12 | (h) | Burnley | D | 0-0 | | 7,000 |
| 20 | | 15 | (h) | Blackpool | W | 4-0 | Boyd 2, Cartwright, Cassidy | 4,000 |
| 21 | Feb | 26 | (h) | W Arsenal | W | 5-1 | Bryant 2, Boyd, Cassidy, Collinson | 6,000 |
| 22 | Mar | 7 | (a) | Burnley | L | 3-6 | Bryant 2, Collinson | 3,000 |
| 23 | | 19 | (a) | Darwen | W | 3-2 | Boyd 2, McNaught | 2,000 |
| 24 | | 21 | (a) | Luton T | D | 2-2 | Boyd, Cassidy | 2,000 |
| 25 | | 29 | (h) | Loughborough T | W | 5-1 | Boyd 3, Cassidy 2 | 2,000 |
| 26 | Apr | 2 | (a) | Grimsby T | W | 3-1 | Cassidy 2, Boyd | 2,000 |
| 27 | | 8 | (h) | Gainsborough T | W | 1-0 | Cassidy | 5,000 |
| 28 | | 9 | (h) | Small Heath | W | 3-1 | Boyd, Gillespie, Morgan | 4,000 |
| 29 | | 16 | (a) | Loughborough T | D | 0-0 | | 1,200 |
| 30 | | 23 | (h) | Darwen | W | 3-2 | Collinson 2, Bryant | 4,000 |

FINAL LEAGUE POSITION: 4th in Division Two

Appearances
Goals

FA Cup

| 1 | Jan | 29 | (h) | Walsall | W | 1-0 |
|---|---|---|---|---|---|---|
| 2 | Feb | 12 | (h) | Liverpool | D | 0-0 |
| R | | 16 | (a) | Liverpool | L | 1-2 |

| Barrett | Stafford | Erentz FC | Morgan | McNaught | Cartwright | Bryant | Dunn | Boyd | Gillespie | Cassidy | Jenkyns | Donaldson | Smith | Ridgway | Draycott | Wedge | Carman | Erentz H | Collinson | |
|---|---|---|---|---|---|---|---|---|---|---|---|---|---|---|---|---|---|---|---|---|
| 1 | 2 | 3 | 4 | 5 | 6 | 7 | 8 | 9 | 10 | 11 | | | | | | | | | | 1 |
| 1 | 2 | 3 | 4 | 5 | 6 | 7 | 8 | 9 | 10 | 11 | | | | | | | | | | 2 |
| 1 | 2 | 3 | 4 | 5 | 6 | 7 | 8 | 9 | 10 | 11 | | | | | | | | | | 3 |
| 1 | 2 | 3 | | 4 | 6 | 7 | | 9 | | 11 | 5 | 8 | 10 | | | | | | | 4 |
| 1 | 2 | 3 | | 4 | 6 | 7 | | 9 | | 11 | 5 | 8 | 10 | | | | | | | 5 |
| 1 | 2 | 3 | | 4 | 6 | 7 | | 9 | | 11 | 5 | 8 | 10 | | | | | | | 6 |
| 1 | 2 | 3 | | 4 | 6 | 7 | | 9 | 10 | 11 | 5 | 8 | | | | | | | | 7 |
| | 2 | 3 | | 4 | 6 | 7 | | 9 | 10 | 11 | 5 | 8 | | 1 | | | | | | 8 |
| 1 | 2 | 3 | | 4 | | 7 | | 9 | 10 | 11 | 5 | 8 | | | 6 | | | | | 9 |
| 1 | 2 | 3 | | 4 | 6 | 7 | | 9 | 10 | 11 | 5 | 8 | | | | | | | | 10 |
| 1 | | 3 | 6 | 2 | | 7 | | 9 | 10 | 11 | 5 | 8 | | | 4 | | | | | 11 |
| 1 | 2 | 3 | | 5 | 6 | 7 | 11 | 9 | | 10 | | | | | 4 | | | | 8 | 12 |
| 1 | 2 | 3 | | 5 | 6 | 7 | 11 | 9 | | 10 | | | | | 4 | | | | 8 | 13 |
| 1 | 2 | 3 | 8 | 5 | 6 | 7 | 11 | 9 | | 10 | | | | | 4 | | | | | 14 |
| 1 | 2 | 3 | | 5 | 6 | 7 | 11 | 9 | | 10 | | | | | 4 | 8 | | | | 15 |
| 1 | 2 | 3 | | 5 | 6 | 7 | 11 | 9 | | 10 | | | | | 4 | 8 | | | | 16 |
| 1 | 2 | 3 | | 5 | 6 | 7 | 11 | 9 | | 10 | | | | | 4 | 8 | | | | 17 |
| 1 | | 3 | 8 | 5 | 6 | 7 | | 9 | 11 | 10 | | | | | 4 | | 2 | | | 18 |
| 1 | 2 | 3 | | 5 | 6 | 7 | | 9 | 11 | 10 | | | | | 4 | | | | 8 | 19 |
| 1 | | 3 | | 5 | 6 | 7 | | 9 | 11 | 10 | | | | | 4 | | 2 | | 8 | 20 |
| 1 | 2 | 3 | | 5 | 6 | 7 | | 9 | 11 | 10 | | | | | 4 | | | | 8 | 21 |
| 1 | 2 | 3 | | 5 | 6 | 7 | | 9 | 11 | 10 | | | | | 4 | | | | 8 | 22 |
| | 2 | 3 | | 5 | 6 | 7 | | 9 | 11 | 10 | | | | 1 | 4 | | | | 8 | 23 |
| | 2 | 3 | | 5 | 6 | 7 | | 9 | 11 | 10 | | | | 1 | 4 | | | | 8 | 24 |
| 1 | | | 4 | 5 | 3 | 7 | | 9 | 11 | 10 | | | | | 6 | | 2 | | 8 | 25 |
| 1 | 2 | | 6 | 5 | | 7 | | 9 | 11 | 10 | | | | | 4 | | | 3 | 8 | 26 |
| 1 | | 3 | | 5 | 6 | 7 | | 9 | 11 | 10 | | | | | 4 | | 2 | | 8 | 27 |
| 1 | 2 | 3 | 8 | 5 | 6 | 7 | | 9 | 11 | 10 | | | | | 4 | | | | | 28 |
| 1 | 2 | 3 | 8 | 5 | | 7 | | 9 | 11 | 10 | | | | | 4 | | | 6 | | 29 |
| 1 | 2 | 3 | | 5 | 6 | 7 | | 9 | 11 | 10 | | | | | 4 | | | | 8 | 30 |
| 27 | 25 | 28 | 9 | 30 | 27 | 29 | 10 | 30 | 19 | 30 | 8 | 8 | 5 | 3 | 21 | 2 | 3 | 6 | 10 | |
| | 1 | 1 | 2 | 1 | 10 | | | 22 | 3 | 14 | | 2 | 1 | | | 2 | 1 | | 4 | |

Match 14: Carman listed as playing number 7 by the Football League.

195

# 1898-99

Secretary: A.H.Albut

| 1 | Sep | 3 | (a) | Gainsborough T | W | 2-0 | Bryant, Cassidy | 2,000 |
|---|---|---|---|---|---|---|---|---|
| 2 | | 10 | (h) | Manchester C | W | 3-0 | Boyd, Cassidy, Collinson | 20,000 |
| 3 | | 17 | (a) | Glossop NE | W | 2-1 | Bryant, Cassidy | 6,000 |
| 4 | | 24 | (h) | Walsall | W | 1-0 | Gillespie | 8,000 |
| 5 | Oct | 1 | (a) | Burton S | L | 1-5 | Boyd | 2,000 |
| 6 | | 8 | (h) | Burslem PVale | W | 2-1 | Bryant, Cassidy | 10,000 |
| 7 | | 15 | (a) | Small Heath | L | 1-4 | Cassidy | 5,000 |
| 8 | | 22 | (h) | Loughborough T | W | 6-1 | Brooks 2, Cassidy 2, Collinson 2 | 2,000 |
| 9 | Nov | 5 | (h) | Grimsby T | W | 3-2 | Brooks, Cassidy, Gillespie | 5,000 |
| 10 | | 12 | (h) | Barnsley | D | 0-0 | | 5,000 |
| 11 | | 19 | (a) | New Brighton T | W | 3-0 | Collinson 2, Cassidy | 5,000 |
| 12 | | 26 | (h) | Lincoln C | W | 1-0 | Bryant | 4,000 |
| 13 | Dec | 3 | (a) | W Arsenal | L | 1-5 | Collinson | 7,000 |
| 14 | | 10 | (h) | Blackpool | W | 3-1 | Cassidy, Collinson, Cunningham | 5,000 |
| 15 | | 17 | (a) | Leicester F | L | 0-1 | | 8,000 |
| 16 | | 24 | (h) | Darwen | W | 9-0 | Bryant 3, Cassidy 3, Gillespie 2, Opp own-goal | 2,000 |
| 17 | | 26 | (a) | Manchester C | L | 0-4 | | 25,000 |
| 18 | | 31 | (h) | Gainsborough T | W | 6-1 | Collinson 2, Bryant, Boyd, Cartwright, Draycott | 2,000 |
| 19 | Jan | 2 | (h) | Burton S | D | 2-2 | Boyd, Cassidy | 6,000 |
| 20 | | 14 | (h) | Glossop NE | W | 3-0 | Cunningham, Erentz, Gillespie | 12,000 |
| 21 | | 21 | (a) | Walsall | L | 0-2 | | 3,000 |
| 22 | Feb | 4 | (a) | Burslem PVale | L | 0-1 | | 6,000 |
| 23 | | 18 | (a) | Loughborough T | W | 1-0 | Bryant | 1,500 |
| 24 | | 25 | (h) | Small Heath | W | 2-0 | Boyd, Roberts | 12,000 |
| 25 | Mar | 4 | (a) | Grimsby T | L | 0-3 | | 4,000 |
| 26 | | 18 | (h) | New Brighton T | L | 1-2 | Cassidy | 20,000 |
| 27 | | 25 | (a) | Lincoln C | L | 0-2 | | 3,000 |
| 28 | Apr | 1 | (h) | W Arsenal | D | 2-2 | Bryant, Cassidy | 5,000 |
| 29 | | 3 | (a) | Blackpool | W | 1-0 | Cassidy | 3,000 |
| 30 | | 4 | (a) | Barnsley | W | 2-0 | Lee 2 | 4,000 |
| 31 | | 8 | (a) | Luton T | W | 1-0 | Lee | 1,500 |
| 32 | | 12 | (h) | Luton T | W | 5-0 | Cartwright, Cassidy, Gillespie, Lee, Morgan | 3,000 |
| 33 | | 15 | (h) | Leicester F | D | 2-2 | Cassidy, Gillespie | 6,000 |
| 34 | | 22 | (a) | Darwen | D | 1-1 | Morgan | 1,000 |

FINAL LEAGUE POSITION: 4th in Division Two

Appearances

Goals

FA Cup

| 1 | Jan | 28 | (a) | Tottenham H | D | 1-1 | |
|---|---|---|---|---|---|---|---|
| R | Feb | 1 | (h) | Tottenham H | L | 3-5 | |

Appearance and goalscoring grid (numbers indicate shirt number worn by each player in each match):

| Barrett | Stafford | Erentz | Draycott | Morgan | Cartwright | Bryant | Collinson | Jones | Cassidy | Gillespie | Boyd | Turner R | Cairns | Owen | Turner J | Brooks | Connachan | Cunningham | Pepper | Walker | Roberts | Gourlay | Hopkins | Lee | Griffiths | Radcliffe | Match |
|---|---|---|---|---|---|---|---|---|---|---|---|---|---|---|---|---|---|---|---|---|---|---|---|---|---|---|---|
| 1 | 2 | 3 | 4 | 5 | 6 | 7 | 8 | 9 | 10 | 11 |  |  |  |  |  |  |  |  |  |  |  |  |  |  |  |  | 1 |
| 1 | 2 | 3 | 4 | 5 | 6 | 7 | 8 |  | 10 | 11 | 9 |  |  |  |  |  |  |  |  |  |  |  |  |  |  |  | 2 |
| 1 | 2 | 3 | 4 | 5 | 6 | 7 | 8 |  | 10 | 11 | 9 |  |  |  |  |  |  |  |  |  |  |  |  |  |  |  | 3 |
| 1 | 2 | 3 | 4 | 5 | 6 | 7 | 8 |  | 10 | 11 | 9 |  |  |  |  |  |  |  |  |  |  |  |  |  |  |  | 4 |
| 1 | 2 | 3 | 4 | 5 | 6 | 7 |  | 8 | 10 | 11 | 9 |  |  |  |  |  |  |  |  |  |  |  |  |  |  |  | 5 |
| 1 | 2 | 3 |  | 5 | 6 | 7 |  |  | 10 | 11 | 9 | 4 | 8 |  |  |  |  |  |  |  |  |  |  |  |  |  | 6 |
| 1 | 2 | 3 | 4 | 5 | 6 | 9 | 8 |  | 10 | 11 |  |  |  | 7 |  |  |  |  |  |  |  |  |  |  |  |  | 7 |
| 1 | 2 | 3 |  | 4 | 6 | 7 | 8 |  | 10 | 11 |  |  |  |  | 5 | 9 |  |  |  |  |  |  |  |  |  |  | 8 |
| 1 | 2 | 3 |  |  | 6 | 7 |  |  | 10 | 11 |  |  |  |  | 5 | 9 | 4 | 8 |  |  |  |  |  |  |  |  | 9 |
| 1 | 2 | 3 | 4 |  | 6 | 7 | 5 |  | 10 | 11 |  |  |  |  |  | 9 | 8 |  |  |  |  |  |  |  |  |  | 10 |
| 1 | 2 | 3 | 4 | 5 | 6 | 7 | 8 |  | 10 | 11 |  |  |  |  |  |  | 9 |  |  |  |  |  |  |  |  |  | 11 |
| 1 | 2 | 3 | 4 | 5 | 6 | 7 | 8 |  | 9 | 11 |  |  |  |  |  |  | 10 |  |  |  |  |  |  |  |  |  | 12 |
| 1 | 2 | 3 | 4 | 5 | 6 | 7 | 8 |  | 9 | 11 |  |  |  |  |  |  | 10 |  |  |  |  |  |  |  |  |  | 13 |
| 1 |  | 3 | 4 |  | 2 |  | 8 | 9 | 11 |  |  |  |  |  | 6 | 7 | 10 | 5 |  |  |  |  |  |  |  |  | 14 |
| 1 | 2 | 3 | 4 |  | 6 | 7 |  | 9 | 11 |  |  |  |  |  |  | 8 | 10 | 5 |  |  |  |  |  |  |  |  | 15 |
| 1 | 2 | 3 | 4 |  | 6 | 7 | 8 |  | 10 | 11 | 9 |  |  |  |  |  |  | 5 |  |  |  |  |  |  |  |  | 16 |
| 1 | 2 | 3 | 4 |  | 6 | 7 | 8 |  | 9 | 11 |  |  |  |  |  | 10 |  | 5 |  |  |  |  |  |  |  |  | 17 |
| 1 | 2 | 3 | 4 |  | 6 | 7 | 8 |  | 9 | 10 |  |  |  |  |  |  |  | 11 | 5 |  |  |  |  |  |  |  | 18 |
| 1 | 2 | 3 | 4 |  | 6 | 7 | 8 |  | 9 | 10 |  |  |  |  |  |  |  | 11 | 5 |  |  |  |  |  |  |  | 19 |
| 1 | 2 | 3 | 4 |  | 6 | 7 | 8 |  | 9 | 11 |  |  |  |  |  |  |  | 10 | 5 |  |  |  |  |  |  |  | 20 |
| 1 | 2 | 3 | 4 |  | 6 | 7 | 8 |  | 9 | 11 |  |  |  |  |  |  |  | 10 | 5 |  |  |  |  |  |  |  | 21 |
| 1 | 2 |  | 4 | 6 | 3 | 7 | 8 |  | 10 |  | 9 |  |  |  |  |  |  | 11 | 5 |  |  |  |  |  |  |  | 22 |
| 1 | 2 |  | 4 | 6 | 3 | 7 |  |  | 10 |  | 9 |  |  |  |  |  |  | 5 | 8 |  | 11 |  |  |  |  |  | 23 |
| 1 | 2 | 3 | 4 |  | 6 | 5 | 7 |  | 10 |  | 9 |  |  |  |  |  |  | 8 |  |  | 11 |  |  |  |  |  | 24 |
| 1 | 2 | 3 | 4 |  | 6 | 5 | 7 | 8 | 10 |  | 9 |  |  |  |  |  |  |  |  |  | 11 |  |  |  |  |  | 25 |
| 1 | 2 | 3 | 4 |  | 6 | 5 | 7 |  | 9 | 10 |  |  |  |  |  |  |  | 11 | 8 |  |  |  |  |  |  |  | 26 |
| 1 | 2 | 3 | 4 |  | 6 | 5 | 7 | 8 | 10 | 11 |  |  |  |  |  |  |  |  |  |  |  |  |  | 9 |  |  | 27 |
| 1 | 2 | 3 | 4 | 6 | 10 | 7 | 8 |  | 9 | 11 |  |  |  |  |  |  |  |  |  |  |  |  |  |  | 5 |  | 28 |
| 1 | 2 | 3 | 4 | 8 | 6 | 7 |  |  | 11 | 10 |  |  |  |  |  |  |  |  |  |  |  |  |  | 9 | 5 |  | 29 |
| 1 | 2 | 3 | 4 | 8 | 6 | 7 |  |  | 11 | 10 |  |  |  |  |  |  |  |  |  |  |  |  |  | 9 | 5 |  | 30 |
| 1 | 2 | 3 | 4 | 8 | 6 | 7 |  |  | 11 | 10 |  |  |  |  |  |  |  |  |  |  |  |  |  | 9 | 5 |  | 31 |
| 1 | 2 | 3 | 4 | 8 | 6 |  |  |  | 11 | 10 |  |  |  |  |  |  |  |  |  |  |  |  |  | 9 | 5 | 7 | 32 |
| 1 | 2 | 3 | 4 | 8 | 6 | 7 |  |  | 11 | 10 |  |  |  |  |  |  |  |  |  |  |  |  |  | 9 | 5 |  | 33 |
| 1 | 2 | 3 | 4 | 8 | 6 | 7 |  |  | 11 | 10 |  |  |  |  |  |  |  |  |  |  |  |  |  | 9 | 5 |  | 34 |
| 34 | 33 | 32 | 31 | 24 | 33 | 32 | 21 | 2 | 34 | 28 | 12 | 2 | 1 | 1 | 3 | 3 | 4 | 15 | 7 | 2 | 3 | 1 | 1 | 7 | 7 | 1 |  |
|  | 1 | 1 | 2 | 2 | 10 | 9 |  |  | 19 | 7 | 5 |  |  |  |  | 3 | 2 | 1 | 4 |  |  |  |  |  |  |  |  |

1 own-goal

Match 7: Although Owen is reported in newspapers as having played number 7, Football League records show George Pare as playing in that position. League records do not list Owen as being registererd.

197

# 1899-1900

| | | | | | | | |
|---|---|---|---|---|---|---|---|
| 1 | Sep | 2 | (h) | Gainsborough T | D | 2-2 | Cassidy, Lee | 8,000 |
| 2 | | 9 | (a) | Bolton W | L | 1-2 | Ambler | 5,000 |
| 3 | | 16 | (h) | Loughborough T | W | 4-0 | Bain, Cassidy, Griffiths, Opp own-goal | 6,000 |
| 4 | | 23 | (a) | Burton S | D | 0-0 | | 2,000 |
| 5 | | 30 | (a) | Sheffield W | L | 1-2 | Bryant | 8,000 |
| 6 | Oct | 7 | (h) | Lincoln C | W | 1-0 | Cassidy | 5,000 |
| 7 | | 14 | (a) | Small Heath | L | 0-1 | | 10,000 |
| 8 | | 21 | (h) | New Brighton T | W | 2-1 | Cassidy 2 | 5,000 |
| 9 | Nov | 4 | (h) | W Arsenal | W | 2-0 | Jackson, Roberts | 5,000 |
| 10 | | 11 | (a) | Barnsley | D | 0-0 | | 3,000 |
| 11 | | 25 | (a) | Luton T | W | 1-0 | Jackson | 3,000 |
| 12 | Dec | 2 | (h) | Burslem PVale | W | 3-0 | Cassidy 2, Jackson | 5,000 |
| 13 | | 16 | (h) | Middlesbrough | W | 2-1 | Erentz, Parkinson | 4,000 |
| 14 | | 23 | (a) | Chesterfield | L | 1-2 | Griffiths | 2,000 |
| 15 | | 26 | (a) | Grimsby T | W | 7-0 | Bryant 2, Cassidy 2, Jackson, Parkinson, Opp own-goal | 2,000 |
| 16 | | 30 | (a) | Gainsborough T | W | 1-0 | Parkinson | 2,000 |
| 17 | Jan | 6 | (h) | Bolton W | L | 1-2 | Parkinson | 5,000 |
| 18 | | 13 | (a) | Loughborough T | W | 2-0 | Jackson, Parkinson | 1,000 |
| 19 | | 20 | (h) | Burton S | W | 4-0 | Gillespie 3, Parkinson | 4,000 |
| 20 | Feb | 3 | (h) | Sheffield W | W | 1-0 | Bryant | 10,000 |
| 21 | | 10 | (a) | Lincoln C | L | 0-1 | | 2,000 |
| 22 | | 17 | (h) | Small Heath | W | 3-2 | Cassidy, Godsmark, Parkinson | 10,000 |
| 23 | | 24 | (a) | New Brighton T | W | 4-1 | Collinson 2, Godsmark, Smith | 8,000 |
| 24 | Mar | 3 | (h) | Grimsby T | W | 1-0 | Smith | 4,000 |
| 25 | | 10 | (a) | W Arsenal | L | 1-2 | Cassidy | 3,000 |
| 26 | | 17 | (h) | Barnsley | W | 3-0 | Cassidy 2, Leigh | 6,000 |
| 27 | | 24 | (a) | Leicester F | L | 0-2 | | 8,000 |
| 28 | | 31 | (h) | Luton T | W | 5-0 | Cassidy 3, Godsmark 2 | 6,000 |
| 29 | Apr | 7 | (a) | Burslem PVale | L | 0-1 | | 3,000 |
| 30 | | 13 | (h) | Leicester F | W | 3-2 | Gillespie, Griffiths, Unknown | 10,000 |
| 31 | | 14 | (h) | Walsall | W | 5-0 | Jackson 2, Erentz, Foley, Gillespie | 4,000 |
| 32 | | 17 | (a) | Walsall | D | 0-0 | | 3,000 |
| 33 | | 21 | (a) | Middlesbrough | L | 0-2 | | 8,000 |
| 34 | | 28 | (h) | Chesterfield | W | 2-1 | Holt, Grundy | 6,000 |

FINAL LEAGUE POSITION: 4th in Division Two

Appearances
Goals

FA Cup

| | | | | | | | |
|---|---|---|---|---|---|---|---|
| Q1 | Oct | 28 | (a) | South Shore | L | 1-3 | |

| Barrett | Stafford | Erentz | Morgan | Fitzsimmons | Cartwright | Bryant | Jackson | Lee | Cassidy | Ambler | Griffiths | Bain | Roberts | Clark | Collinson | Gillespie | Sawyer | Blackmore | Parkinson | Heathcote | Godsmark | Smith | Foley | Leigh | Holt | Grundy | |
|---|---|---|---|---|---|---|---|---|---|---|---|---|---|---|---|---|---|---|---|---|---|---|---|---|---|---|---|
| 1 | 2 | 3 | 4 | 5 | 6 | 7 | 8 | 9 | 10 | 11 | | | | | | | | | | | | | | | | | 1 |
| 1 | 2 | 3 | 4 | | 6 | 7 | 8 | 9 | 10 | 11 | 5 | | | | | | | | | | | | | | | | 2 |
| 1 | 2 | 3 | 4 | | 6 | 7 | 8 | 11 | 10 | | 5 | 9 | | | | | | | | | | | | | | | 3 |
| 1 | 2 | 3 | 4 | | 6 | 7 | 8 | | 10 | | 5 | 9 | 11 | | | | | | | | | | | | | | 4 |
| 1 | 2 | 3 | 4 | | 6 | 7 | 8 | | 10 | | 5 | | 11 | 9 | | | | | | | | | | | | | 5 |
| 1 | 2 | 3 | 4 | | 6 | | 8 | | 10 | | 5 | | | 7 | 9 | 11 | | | | | | | | | | | 6 |
| 1 | 2 | 3 | 4 | | 6 | | 8 | | 10 | | 5 | | | | 9 | 11 | 7 | | | | | | | | | | 7 |
| 1 | 2 | 3 | 4 | 6 | | 7 | 8 | | 10 | | 5 | | | 11 | | | | 9 | | | | | | | | | 8 |
| 1 | 2 | 3 | 4 | | 6 | 7 | 8 | | 10 | | 5 | | 11 | 9 | | | | | | | | | | | | | 9 |
| 1 | 2 | 3 | 4 | | 6 | 7 | 10 | | | 11 | 5 | | | | | | | | 9 | | 8 | | | | | | 10 |
| 1 | 2 | 3 | 4 | | 6 | 7 | 10 | | | 11 | 5 | | | | | | | | 9 | | 8 | | | | | | 11 |
| 1 | 2 | 3 | 4 | | 6 | 7 | 10 | | | 11 | 5 | | | | | | | | 9 | | 8 | | | | | | 12 |
| 1 | 2 | 3 | 4 | | 6 | 7 | 10 | | | 11 | 5 | | | | | | | | 9 | | 8 | | | | | | 13 |
| 1 | 2 | 3 | 4 | | 6 | 7 | 8 | | 10 | 11 | 5 | | | | | | | | 9 | | | | | | | | 14 |
| 1 | 2 | 3 | 4 | | 6 | 7 | 10 | | | 11 | 5 | | | | | | | | 9 | | 8 | | | | | | 15 |
| 1 | 2 | 3 | 4 | | 6 | 7 | 10 | | | 11 | 5 | | | | | | | | 9 | | 8 | | | | | | 16 |
| 1 | 2 | 3 | 4 | | 6 | 7 | 10 | | | 11 | 5 | | | | | | | | 9 | | 8 | | | | | | 17 |
| 1 | 2 | 3 | 4 | | 6 | | 8 | | 10 | 11 | 5 | | | | | | 7 | | 9 | | | | | | | | 18 |
| 1 | 2 | 3 | 4 | | 6 | 7 | 8 | | 10 | | 5 | | | | | 11 | | | 9 | | | | | | | | 19 |
| 1 | 2 | 3 | 4 | | 6 | 7 | 8 | | 10 | | 5 | | | | | 11 | | | 9 | | | | | | | | 20 |
| 1 | 2 | 3 | 4 | | 6 | 7 | 8 | | 10 | | 5 | | | | | 11 | | | 9 | | | | | | | | 21 |
| 1 | | 3 | 4 | | 6 | 7 | 8 | | 10 | | 5 | | | 2 | | 11 | | | 9 | | | | | | | | 22 |
| 1 | 2 | 3 | 4 | | 6 | | | | 10 | | 5 | | 11 | | 7 | | | | 9 | | 8 | | | | | | 23 |
| 1 | 2 | 3 | 4 | | 6 | | | | 10 | | 5 | | 11 | | 7 | | | | 9 | | 8 | | | | | | 24 |
| 1 | 2 | 3 | 4 | | 6 | 7 | | | 10 | | 5 | | | | 9 | | | | | | | 8 | 11 | | | | 25 |
| 1 | 2 | 3 | 4 | | 6 | | | | 10 | 11 | 5 | | | | | | | | | | | 8 | 7 | 9 | | | 26 |
| 1 | | 3 | 4 | | | | | | 10 | 11 | 5 | | | 2 | | | | | | | | 8 | 7 | 9 | 6 | | 27 |
| 1 | 2 | 3 | 4 | | 6 | | | | 10 | 11 | 5 | | | | | | | | | | | 8 | 7 | 9 | | | 28 |
| 1 | 2 | 3 | 4 | | 6 | | | | 10 | 11 | 5 | | | | | | | | | | | 8 | 7 | 9 | | | 29 |
| 1 | 2 | 3 | 4 | | 6 | | | | 10 | 11 | 5 | | | | | | | | | | | 8 | 7 | 9 | | | 30 |
| 1 | 2 | 3 | 4 | | 6 | | | | 10 | 11 | 5 | | | | | | | | | | | 8 | 7 | 9 | | | 31 |
| 1 | | 3 | 4 | | 6 | | | | 10 | | 5 | | | 2 | | 11 | | | | | | 8 | 7 | 9 | | | 32 |
| 1 | 2 | 3 | 4 | | 6 | | | | 10 | 11 | 5 | | | | | | | | | | | 8 | 7 | 9 | | | 33 |
| 1 | 2 | 3 | 4 | | 6 | | | | 10 | | 5 | | | | | | | | | | | 8 | 7 | 9 | | 11 | 34 |
| 34 | 31 | 34 | 30 | 2 | 25 | 19 | 32 | 4 | 29 | 9 | 33 | 2 | 6 | 9 | 7 | 10 | 2 | 1 | 15 | 1 | 9 | 12 | 7 | 9 | 1 | 1 | |
| | 2 | | | | 4 | 7 | 1 | | 16 | 1 | 3 | 1 | 1 | | 2 | 5 | | | 7 | | 4 | 2 | 1 | 1 | 1 | 1 | |

1 Unknown scorer, 2 own-goals

Match  6: Clark listed as playing number 9 by the Football League.
Match  8: Bain listed as playing number 9 by the Football League.
Match 10: Roberts listed as playing number 9 by the Football League.
Match 23: Sharp listed as playing number 11 by the Football League.
Match 24: Sharp listed as playing number 11 by the Football League.

# 1900-01

Secretary: James West

| 1 | Sep | 1 | (a) | Glossop | L | 0-1 | | 8,000 |
|---|---|---|---|---|---|---|---|---|
| 2 | | 8 | (h) | Middlesbrough | W | 4-0 | Griffiths, Grundy, Jackson, Leigh | 5,500 |
| 3 | | 15 | (a) | Burnley | L | 0-1 | | 4,000 |
| 4 | | 22 | (h) | Burslem PVale | W | 4-0 | Grundy, Leigh, Schofield, Smith | 6,000 |
| 5 | | 29 | (a) | Leicester F | L | 0-1 | | 6,000 |
| 6 | Oct | 6 | (h) | New Brighton T | W | 1-0 | Jackson | 5,000 |
| 7 | | 13 | (a) | Gainsborough T | W | 1-0 | Leigh | 2,000 |
| 8 | | 20 | (h) | Walsall | D | 1-1 | Schofield | 8,000 |
| 9 | | 27 | (a) | Burton S | L | 1-3 | Leigh | 2,000 |
| 10 | Nov | 10 | (a) | W Arsenal | L | 1-2 | Jackson | 8,000 |
| 11 | | 24 | (a) | Stockport C | L | 0-1 | | 5,000 |
| 12 | Dec | 1 | (h) | Small Heath | L | 0-1 | | 5,000 |
| 13 | | 8 | (a) | Grimsby T | L | 0-2 | | 4,000 |
| 14 | | 15 | (h) | Lincoln C | W | 4-1 | Leigh 2, H.Morgan, Schofield | 4,000 |
| 15 | | 22 | (a) | Chesterfield | L | 1-2 | Hancock (og) | 4,000 |
| 16 | | 26 | (h) | Blackpool | W | 4-0 | Griffiths, Leigh, W.Morgan, Schofield | 10,000 |
| 17 | | 29 | (h) | Glossop | W | 3-0 | Leigh 2, H.Morgan | 8,000 |
| 18 | Jan | 1 | (a) | Middlesbrough | W | 2-1 | Schofield 2 | 12,000 |
| 19 | | 12 | (h) | Burnley | L | 0-1 | | 10,000 |
| 20 | | 19 | (a) | Burslem PVale | L | 0-2 | | 1,000 |
| 21 | Feb | 16 | (h) | Gainsborough T | D | 0-0 | | 7,000 |
| 22 | | 19 | (a) | New Brighton T | L | 0-2 | | 2,000 |
| 23 | | 25 | (a) | Walsall | D | 1-1 | W.Morgan | 2,000 |
| 24 | Mar | 2 | (h) | Burton S | D | 1-1 | Leigh | 5,000 |
| 25 | | 13 | (h) | Barnsley | W | 1-0 | Leigh | 6,000 |
| 26 | | 16 | (h) | W Arsenal | W | 1-0 | Leigh | 5,000 |
| 27 | | 20 | (h) | Leicester F | L | 2-3 | Fisher, Jackson | 2,000 |
| 28 | | 23 | (a) | Blackpool | W | 2-1 | Griffiths 2 | 2,000 |
| 29 | | 30 | (h) | Stockport C | W | 3-1 | Leigh, H.Morgan, Schofield | 4,000 |
| 30 | Apr | 5 | (a) | Lincoln C | L | 0-2 | | 5,000 |
| 31 | | 6 | (a) | Small Heath | L | 0-1 | | 6,000 |
| 32 | | 9 | (a) | Barnsley | L | 2-6 | Jackson, W.Morgan | 3,000 |
| 33 | | 13 | (h) | Grimsby T | W | 1-0 | H.Morgan | 3,000 |
| 34 | | 27 | (h) | Chesterfield | W | 1-0 | Leigh | 1,000 |

FINAL LEAGUE POSITION: 10th in Division Two

Appearances
Goals

## FA Cup

| S1 | Jan | 5 | (h) | Portsmouth | W | 3-0 | |
|---|---|---|---|---|---|---|---|
| 1 | Feb | 9 | (h) | Burnley | D | 0-0 | |
| R | | 13 | (a) | Burnley | L | 1-7 | |

| Garvey | Stafford | Erentz | Morgan W | Griffiths | Cartwright | Schofield | Lawson | Leigh | Jackson | Grundy | Whitehouse | Smith | Ambler | Fisher | Greenwood | Collinson | Morgan H | Booth | Heathcote | Hayes | Whitney | Johnson | Sawyer | Lappin | Match |
|---|---|---|---|---|---|---|---|---|---|---|---|---|---|---|---|---|---|---|---|---|---|---|---|---|---|
| 1 | 2 | 3 | 4 | 5 | 6 | 7 | 8 | 9 | 10 | 11 | | | | | | | | | | | | | | | 1 |
| 1 | 2 | 3 | 4 | 5 | 6 | 7 | 8 | 9 | 10 | 11 | | | | | | | | | | | | | | | 2 |
| | 2 | 3 | 4 | 5 | 6 | 7 | 8 | 9 | 10 | 11 | 1 | | | | | | | | | | | | | | 3 |
| | 2 | 3 | 4 | 5 | 6 | 7 | | 9 | 10 | 11 | 1 | 8 | | | | | | | | | | | | | 4 |
| | 2 | 3 | 4 | 5 | 6 | 7 | | 9 | 10 | 11 | 1 | 8 | | | | | | | | | | | | | 5 |
| | 2 | 3 | 4 | 5 | 6 | 7 | | 9 | 10 | 11 | 1 | 8 | | | | | | | | | | | | | 6 |
| | 2 | 3 | 4 | 5 | | 7 | | 9 | 10 | 11 | 1 | 8 | | | 6 | | | | | | | | | | 7 |
| | 2 | 3 | 4 | 5 | 6 | 7 | | 9 | 10 | | 1 | 8 | | | | 11 | | | | | | | | | 8 |
| | 2 | 3 | | 5 | | | | 9 | 6 | 11 | 1 | | 4 | 10 | 7 | 8 | | | | | | | | | 9 |
| | 2 | 3 | 4 | 5 | 6 | 11 | | 9 | 8 | | 1 | | | 7 | 10 | | | | | | | | | | 10 |
| | 2 | 3 | 4 | 5 | 6 | 7 | | 9 | 10 | 11 | 1 | | | 8 | | | | | | | | | | | 11 |
| | 2 | 3 | 4 | 5 | 6 | 7 | | 9 | 10 | | 1 | | | 8 | | 11 | | | | | | | | | 12 |
| | 2 | 3 | 4 | 5 | 6 | 7 | | 9 | 10 | 11 | 1 | | | 8 | | | | | | | | | | | 13 |
| 1 | 2 | 3 | 4 | 5 | 6 | 7 | | 9 | 10 | | | | | 8 | | 11 | | | | | | | | | 14 |
| | 2 | 3 | 4 | 5 | 6 | 7 | | 9 | 10 | | 1 | | | 8 | | 11 | | | | | | | | | 15 |
| | 2 | 3 | 4 | 5 | 6 | 7 | | 9 | 10 | | 1 | | | 8 | | | | 11 | | | | | | | 16 |
| | 2 | 3 | 4 | 5 | 6 | 7 | | 9 | 10 | | 1 | | | 8 | | | | 11 | | | | | | | 17 |
| | 2 | 3 | 4 | 5 | 6 | 7 | | 9 | 10 | | 1 | | | 8 | | | 11 | | | | | | | | 18 |
| | 2 | 3 | 4 | 5 | 6 | 7 | | 9 | 10 | | 1 | | | 8 | | | 11 | | | | | | | | 19 |
| | 2 | 3 | 4 | 5 | | 7 | | 9 | 10 | | 1 | | | 8 | | 11 | 6 | | | | | | | | 20 |
| | 2 | 3 | 4 | | 6 | 7 | | 9 | | | 1 | | | 8 | | 11 | 5 | | 10 | | | | | | 21 |
| | 2 | 3 | 4 | | 6 | 7 | | 9 | | | 1 | | | 8 | | 11 | 5 | | 10 | | | | | | 22 |
| 1 | | 3 | 4 | 2 | | 7 | | 9 | 10 | | | | | 8 | | 11 | | | | 5 | 6 | | | | 23 |
| | 2 | 3 | 4 | 5 | 6 | 7 | | 9 | | | 1 | | | 8 | | 11 | | | 10 | | | | | | 24 |
| 1 | 2 | 3 | 4 | 5 | 6 | 7 | | 9 | 10 | | | | | 8 | | 11 | | | | | | | | | 25 |
| | 2 | 3 | 4 | 5 | 6 | 7 | | 9 | 10 | | 1 | | | 8 | | 11 | | | | | | | | | 26 |
| 1 | 2 | | 4 | 5 | 6 | | | 9 | 10 | | | | | | | 11 | 3 | | | | | 8 | 7 | | 27 |
| | 2 | | 4 | 5 | 6 | 7 | | 9 | 10 | | 1 | | | 8 | | 11 | 3 | | | | | | | | 28 |
| | 2 | | 4 | 5 | 6 | 7 | | 9 | 10 | | 1 | | | 8 | | 11 | 3 | | | | | | | | 29 |
| | 2 | 3 | 4 | 5 | 6 | 7 | | 9 | 10 | | 1 | | | 8 | | 11 | | | | | | | | | 30 |
| | | 3 | 4 | 5 | 6 | | | 9 | 10 | | 1 | | | 8 | | 11 | 2 | | | | | | 7 | | 31 |
| | | 3 | 4 | 5 | 6 | | | 9 | 10 | | 1 | | | 8 | | 11 | 2 | | | | | | 7 | | 32 |
| | | 3 | 4 | 5 | 6 | | | 9 | 10 | | 1 | | | 8 | | 11 | 2 | | | | | | 7 | | 33 |
| | 2 | 3 | 4 | 5 | 6 | 7 | | 9 | | | 1 | | | | | 11 | 8 | | | | | | | 10 | 34 |
| 6 | 30 | 31 | 33 | 31 | 31 | 29 | 3 | 34 | 29 | 10 | 29 | 5 | 1 | 25 | 3 | 11 | 20 | 2 | 3 | 1 | 1 | 1 | 4 | 1 | |
| | | 3 | 4 | | | 7 | | 14 | 5 | 2 | | | 1 | 1 | | | 4 | | | | | | | | |

1 own-goal

Match 25: Whitehouse listed as playing number 1 by the Football League.
Heathcote listed as playing number 10 by the Football League.
Match 26: Heathcote listed as playing number 10 by the Football League.
Match 30: Collinson listed as playing number 2 by the Football League.
Match 34: H.Morgan listed as playing number 8 by the Football League.

# 1901-02

| 1 | Sep | 7 | (h) | Gainsborough T | W 3-0 | Preston 2, Lappin | 3,000 |
|---|---|---|---|---|---|---|---|
| 2 | | 14 | (a) | Middlesbrough | L 0-5 | | 12,000 |
| 3 | | 21 | (h) | Bristol C | W 1-0 | Griffiths | 5,000 |
| 4 | | 28 | (a) | Blackpool | W 4-2 | Preston 2, Schofield, Opp own-goal | 3,000 |
| 5 | Oct | 5 | (h) | Stockport C | D 3-3 | Schofield 2, Preston | 5,000 |
| 6 | | 12 | (a) | Burton U | D 0-0 | | 3,000 |
| 7 | | 19 | (a) | Glossop | D 0-0 | | 7,000 |
| 8 | | 26 | (h) | Doncaster R | W 6-0 | Coupar 3, Griffiths, Preston, Opp own-goal | 7,000 |
| 9 | Nov | 9 | (h) | West Brom A | L 1-2 | Fisher | 13,000 |
| 10 | | 16 | (a) | W Arsenal | L 0-2 | | 3,000 |
| 11 | | 23 | (h) | Barnsley | W 1-0 | Griffiths | 4,000 |
| 12 | | 30 | (a) | Leicester F | L 2-3 | Cartwright, Preston | 4,000 |
| 13 | Dec | 7 | (a) | Preston NE | L 1-5 | Preston | 2,000 |
| 14 | | 21 | (h) | Burslem PVale | W 1-0 | Richards | 3,000 |
| 15 | | 26 | (a) | Lincoln C | L 0-2 | | 4,000 |
| 16 | Jan | 1 | (h) | Preston NE | L 0-2 | | 10,000 |
| 17 | | 4 | (a) | Gainsborough T | D 1-1 | Lappin | 2,000 |
| 18 | | 18 | (a) | Bristol C | L 0-4 | | 6,000 |
| 19 | | 25 | (h) | Blackpool | L 0-1 | | 2,500 |
| 20 | Feb | 1 | (a) | Stockport C | L 0-1 | | 2,000 |
| 21 | | 11 | (h) | Burnley | W 2-0 | Lappin, Preston | 1,000 |
| 22 | | 15 | (h) | Glossop | W 1-0 | Erentz | 5,000 |
| 23 | | 22 | (a) | Doncaster R | L 0-4 | | 3,000 |
| 24 | Mar | 1 | (h) | Lincoln C | D 0-0 | | 6,000 |
| 25 | | 8 | (a) | West Brom A | L 0-4 | | 10,000 |
| 26 | | 15 | (h) | W Arsenal | L 0-1 | | 4,000 |
| 27 | | 17 | (a) | Chesterfield | L 0-3 | | 2,000 |
| 28 | | 22 | (a) | Barnsley | L 2-3 | Cartwright, Higson | 2,500 |
| 29 | | 28 | (a) | Burnley | L 0-1 | | 3,000 |
| 30 | | 29 | (h) | Leicester F | W 2-0 | Griffiths, Hayes | 2,000 |
| 31 | Apr | 7 | (h) | Middlesbrough | L 1-2 | Erentz | 2,000 |
| 32 | | 19 | (a) | Burslem PVale | D 1-1 | Schofield | 2,000 |
| 33 | | 21 | (h) | Burton U | W 3-1 | Cartwright, Griffiths, Preston | 500 |
| 34 | | 23 | (h) | Chesterfield | W 2-0 | Coupar, Preston | 2,000 |

FINAL LEAGUE POSITION: 15th in Division Two

Appearances
Goals

FA Cup

| I | Dec | 14 | (h) | Lincoln C | L 1-2 | | |
|---|---|---|---|---|---|---|---|

202

| Whitehouse | Stafford | Erentz | Morgan | Banks | Cartwright | Schofield | Williams | Preston | Lappin | Fisher | Smith | Griffiths | Higgins | Coupar | Heathcote | Richards | Saunders | Hayes | Higson | O'Brien | Match |
|---|---|---|---|---|---|---|---|---|---|---|---|---|---|---|---|---|---|---|---|---|---|
| 1 | 2 | 3 | 4 | 5 | 6 | 7 | 8 | 9 | 10 | 11 |  |  |  |  |  |  |  |  |  |  | 1 |
| 1 | 2 | 3 | 4 | 5 | 6 |  | 8 | 9 | 10 | 11 | 7 |  |  |  |  |  |  |  |  |  | 2 |
| 1 | 2 | 3 | 4 |  | 6 | 7 | 8 | 9 | 10 | 11 |  | 5 |  |  |  |  |  |  |  |  | 3 |
| 1 | 2 | 3 | 4 |  | 6 |  | 7 | 9 | 10 | 11 | 8 | 5 |  |  |  |  |  |  |  |  | 4 |
| 1 | 2 |  | 4 | 6 | 3 | 7 |  | 9 | 10 | 11 | 8 | 5 |  |  |  |  |  |  |  |  | 5 |
| 1 | 2 |  | 4 | 6 | 3 | 7 |  |  | 10 | 11 | 8 | 5 | 9 |  |  |  |  |  |  |  | 6 |
| 1 |  | 2 | 6 | 3 |  | 7 |  | 9 |  | 11 | 8 | 5 | 4 | 10 |  |  |  |  |  |  | 7 |
| 1 |  | 2 | 6 | 3 | 7 |  |  | 9 |  | 11 | 8 | 5 | 4 | 10 |  |  |  |  |  |  | 8 |
| 1 |  | 2 | 6 | 3 | 7 |  |  | 9 |  | 11 | 8 | 5 | 4 | 10 |  |  |  |  |  |  | 9 |
| 1 |  | 2 | 6 | 3 | 7 |  |  | 9 | 10 | 11 | 8 | 5 | 4 |  |  |  |  |  |  |  | 10 |
| 1 | 2 |  | 5 | 6 | 3 | 7 |  |  |  | 11 | 8 | 9 | 4 | 10 |  |  |  |  |  |  | 11 |
| 1 | 2 | 3 |  | 6 | 8 | 7 |  | 9 | 10 | 11 |  | 5 | 4 |  |  |  |  |  |  |  | 12 |
| 1 | 2 | 3 | 4 | 6 |  | 7 |  | 10 | 11 | 9 | 5 | 8 |  |  |  |  |  |  |  |  | 13 |
| 1 |  | 3 | 4 | 6 | 2 | 7 |  | 10 |  | 11 |  | 5 | 8 | 9 |  |  |  |  |  |  | 14 |
|  |  | 3 | 4 | 6 | 2 | 7 |  | 10 |  | 11 |  | 5 | 8 | 9 |  |  | 1 |  |  |  | 15 |
|  |  | 2 | 4 | 6 | 3 | 7 |  | 10 |  | 11 |  | 5 | 8 | 9 |  |  | 1 |  |  |  | 16 |
|  |  | 2 | 4 | 6 | 3 | 7 |  | 10 |  | 11 | 8 | 5 |  | 9 |  |  | 1 |  |  |  | 17 |
| 1 | 2 | 3 | 4 |  | 6 | 7 |  | 10 |  | 11 | 8 | 5 |  | 9 |  |  |  |  |  |  | 18 |
| 1 | 2 | 3 | 4 |  | 6 | 7 |  |  |  | 11 | 8 | 5 |  | 9 |  |  |  | 10 |  |  | 19 |
|  |  | 3 | 4 | 6 | 2 | 7 |  | 9 |  | 11 | 8 | 5 |  |  |  |  | 1 | 10 |  |  | 20 |
|  | 2 | 3 | 7 | 6 | 4 |  |  | 9 |  | 11 | 8 | 5 |  |  |  |  | 1 | 10 |  |  | 21 |
|  | 2 | 3 | 7 | 6 | 4 |  |  | 9 |  | 11 | 8 | 5 |  |  |  |  | 1 | 10 |  |  | 22 |
|  | 2 | 3 | 4 | 6 | 9 | 7 |  |  |  | 11 | 8 | 5 |  |  |  |  | 1 | 10 |  |  | 23 |
|  | 2 | 3 | 4 | 6 | 11 | 7 |  | 9 |  |  |  | 5 |  |  |  |  | 1 | 10 | 8 |  | 24 |
| 1 | 2 | 3 | 4 | 6 | 11 | 7 |  | 9 |  |  |  | 5 |  |  |  |  |  | 10 | 8 |  | 25 |
| 1 | 2 | 3 | 4 | 6 |  | 7 |  | 9 |  | 11 |  | 5 |  |  |  |  |  | 10 | 8 |  | 26 |
| 1 |  | 3 | 2 | 6 | 4 | 7 |  | 9 |  | 11 | 8 | 5 |  |  |  |  |  | 10 |  |  | 27 |
|  | 2 | 3 | 4 | 6 | 11 | 7 |  | 9 |  |  |  | 5 |  |  |  |  | 1 | 10 | 8 |  | 28 |
| 1 | 2 | 3 | 4 | 6 | 11 | 7 |  | 9 |  |  | 8 | 5 |  |  |  |  |  | 10 |  |  | 29 |
|  | 2 | 3 | 4 | 6 | 11 | 7 |  | 9 |  |  | 8 | 5 |  |  |  |  | 1 | 10 |  |  | 30 |
| 1 | 2 | 3 | 4 | 6 |  | 7 |  | 9 |  |  |  | 5 |  |  |  |  |  | 10 | 8 | 11 | 31 |
| 1 | 2 | 3 | 4 | 6 |  | 7 |  | 9 |  | 11 | 8 | 5 |  |  |  |  |  | 10 |  |  | 32 |
| 1 | 2 | 3 | 4 | 6 |  | 7 |  | 9 |  | 11 | 8 | 5 |  |  |  |  |  | 10 |  |  | 33 |
|  | 2 | 3 | 4 | 6 |  | 7 |  | 9 |  | 11 | 8 | 5 |  |  |  |  | 1 | 10 |  |  | 34 |
| 23 | 26 | 25 | 33 | 27 | 29 | 29 | 4 | 29 | 21 | 17 | 16 | 29 | 10 | 11 | 3 | 9 | 11 | 16 | 5 | 1 |  |
|  | 2 |  |  | 3 | 4 |  |  | 11 | 3 | 1 |  | 5 |  | 4 |  | 1 |  | 1 | 1 |  |  |

2 own-goals

Match 2: Schofield listed as playing number 7 by the Football League.
Match 5: Erentz listed as playing number 3 by the Football League.
Match 12: Morgan listed as playing number 10 by the Football League.
Match 34: Whitehouse listed as playing number 1 by the Football League.

# 1902-03

Secretary: James West

| 1 | Sep | 6 | (a) | Gainsborough T | W | 1-0 | Richards | 4,000 |
|---|---|---|---|---|---|---|---|---|
| 2 | | 13 | (h) | Burton U | W | 1-0 | Hurst | 15,000 |
| 3 | | 20 | (a) | Bristol C | L | 1-3 | Hurst | 6,000 |
| 4 | | 27 | (h) | Glossop | D | 1-1 | Hurst | 12,000 |
| 5 | Oct | 4 | (h) | Chesterfield | W | 2-1 | Preston 2 | 12,000 |
| 6 | | 11 | (a) | Stockport C | L | 1-2 | Pegg | 6,000 |
| 7 | | 25 | (a) | W Arsenal | W | 1-0 | Beadsworth | 12,000 |
| 8 | Nov | 8 | (a) | Lincoln C | W | 3-1 | Peddie 2, Hurst | 3,000 |
| 9 | | 15 | (h) | Small Heath | L | 0-1 | | 25,000 |
| 10 | | 22 | (a) | Leicester F | D | 1-1 | Downie | 5,000 |
| 11 | Dec | 6 | (a) | Burnley | W | 2-0 | Pegg, Lockhart (og) | 4,000 |
| 12 | | 20 | (a) | Burslem PVale | D | 1-1 | Peddie | 1,000 |
| 13 | | 25 | (h) | Manchester C | D | 1-1 | Pegg | 40,000 |
| 14 | | 26 | (h) | Blackpool | D | 2-2 | Downie, Morrison | 10,000 |
| 15 | | 27 | (h) | Barnsley | W | 2-1 | Peddie, Lappin | 9,000 |
| 16 | Jan | 3 | (h) | Gainsborough T | W | 3-1 | Downie, Peddie, Pegg | 8,000 |
| 17 | | 10 | (a) | Burton U | L | 1-3 | Peddie | 3,000 |
| 18 | | 17 | (h) | Bristol C | L | 1-2 | Preston | 12,000 |
| 19 | | 24 | (a) | Glossop | W | 3-1 | Downie, Griffiths, Morrison | 5,000 |
| 20 | | 31 | (a) | Chesterfield | L | 0-2 | | 6,000 |
| 21 | Feb | 14 | (a) | Blackpool | L | 0-2 | | 3,000 |
| 22 | | 28 | (a) | Doncaster R | D | 2-2 | Morrison 2 | 4,000 |
| 23 | Mar | 7 | (h) | Lincoln C | L | 1-2 | Downie | 4,000 |
| 24 | | 9 | (h) | W Arsenal | W | 3-0 | Arkesden, Peddie, Pegg | 5,000 |
| 25 | | 21 | (h) | Leicester F | W | 5-1 | Fitchett, Griffiths, Morrison, Pegg, Smith | 8,000 |
| 26 | | 23 | (h) | Stockport C | D | 0-0 | | 2,000 |
| 27 | | 30 | (h) | Preston NE | L | 0-1 | | 3,000 |
| 28 | Apr | 4 | (h) | Burnley | W | 4-0 | Peddie 2, Griffiths, Morrison | 5,000 |
| 29 | | 10 | (a) | Manchester C | W | 2-0 | Peddie, Schofield | 30,000 |
| 30 | | 11 | (a) | Preston NE | L | 1-3 | Pegg | 7,000 |
| 31 | | 13 | (h) | Doncaster R | W | 4-0 | Arkesden, Bell, Griffiths, Morrison | 6,000 |
| 32 | | 18 | (a) | Burslem PVale | W | 2-1 | Schofield 2 | 8,000 |
| 33 | | 20 | (a) | Small Heath | L | 1-2 | Peddie | 6,000 |
| 34 | | 25 | (a) | Barnsley | D | 0-0 | | 2,000 |

FINAL LEAGUE POSITION: 5th in Division Two

Appearances
Goals

FA Cup

| Q1 | Nov | 1 | (h) | Accrington S | W | 7-0 | |
|---|---|---|---|---|---|---|---|
| Q2 | | 13 | (h) | Oswaldtwistle R | W | 3-2 | |
| Q3 | | 29 | (h) | Southport Cen | W | 4-1 | |
| I | Dec | 13 | (h) | Burton U | D | 1-1 | |
| R | | 17 | (h) | Burton U | W | 3-1 | |
| 1 | Feb | 7 | (h) | Liverpool | W | 2-1 | |
| 2 | | 21 | (a) | Everton | L | 1-3 | |

Appearance grid (numbers indicate the shirt/position number each player wore in that match; the right-hand column is the match number).

| Whitehouse | Stafford | Read | Morgan | Griffiths | Cartwright | Richards | Pegg | Peddie | Williams | Hurst | Schofield | Bunce | Hayes | Banks | Preston | Birchenough | Rothwell | Beadsworth | Ball | Downie | Smith | Lappin | Morrison | Saunders | Bell | Arkesden | Christie | Street | Marshall | Fitchett | Cleaver | # |
|---|---|---|---|---|---|---|---|---|---|---|---|---|---|---|---|---|---|---|---|---|---|---|---|---|---|---|---|---|---|---|---|---|
| 1 | 2 | 3 | 4 | 5 | 6 | 7 | 8 | 9 | 10 | 11 | | | | | | | | | | | | | | | | | | | | | | 1 |
| 1 | 2 | 3 | 4 | 5 | 6 | | 8 | 9 | 10 | 11 | 7 | | | | | | | | | | | | | | | | | | | | | 2 |
| 1 | 2 | 3 | 4 | 5 | 6 | | 8 | 9 | 10 | 11 | 7 | | | | | | | | | | | | | | | | | | | | | 3 |
| 1 | 2 | 3 | 4 | 5 | 6 | | 8 | 9 | 10 | 11 | 7 | | | | | | | | | | | | | | | | | | | | | 4 |
| 1 | | 3 | | | | 4 | 8 | 7 | 9 | | 11 | 2 | 5 | 6 | 10 | | | | | | | | | | | | | | | | | 5 |
| 1 | | 3 | | | | 4 | 8 | 7 | 9 | | 11 | 2 | 5 | 6 | 10 | | | | | | | | | | | | | | | | | 6 |
| | | 3 | 4 | 5 | | | 8 | 7 | | 10 | 11 | | | 6 | | 1 | 2 | 9 | | | | | | | | | | | | | | 7 |
| | | 3 | 4 | | | | | 7 | 9 | 10 | 11 | | | 6 | | 1 | 2 | 8 | 5 | | | | | | | | | | | | | 8 |
| | 2 | | 4 | | | | | 7 | 9 | 10 | 11 | | | 6 | | 1 | 3 | 8 | 5 | | | | | | | | | | | | | 9 |
| | 2 | | 4 | | | | | 7 | 9 | | 11 | | | 6 | | 1 | 3 | 8 | | 5 | 10 | | | | | | | | | | | 10 |
| | | 2 | | 5 | | | 10 | 9 | 8 | 11 | 7 | | | 6 | | 1 | 3 | | 4 | | | | | | | | | | | | | 11 |
| | | 3 | | 5 | 6 | 8 | | 9 | 10 | | 7 | | | | | 1 | 2 | | 4 | | 11 | | | | | | | | | | | 12 |
| | | 3 | | 5 | 6 | | | 9 | 10 | | 7 | | | | | 1 | 2 | 11 | | 4 | | 8 | | | | | | | | | | 13 |
| 1 | | 3 | | 5 | 6 | | | 9 | 10 | | | | | | | 2 | 8 | 4 | | 11 | 7 | | | | | | | | | | | 14 |
| | 2 | 3 | 6 | 5 | | | 8 | 9 | 10 | | | | | | | | | 4 | | 11 | 7 | 1 | | | | | | | | | | 15 |
| | | 3 | 4 | | | | | 9 | 10 | | | | | 8 | | 1 | 2 | | 6 | 5 | 11 | 7 | | | | | | | | | | 16 |
| | | 3 | 4 | | 6 | | | | 10 | | 7 | | | | | 1 | 2 | 5 | | 9 | 11 | 8 | | | | | | | | | | 17 |
| | | 3 | 4 | | 6 | 8 | | | 10 | | 11 | | | 9 | | 1 | 2 | | 5 | | 7 | | | | | | | | | | | 18 |
| | | 3 | | 5 | | | 9 | 8 | | | 11 | | | 6 | | 1 | 2 | 4 | | 7 | | | 10 | | | | | | | | | 19 |
| | 2 | | | 5 | | | 8 | 10 | | | 11 | | | 6 | | 1 | 3 | 4 | | 7 | | | 9 | | | | | | | | | 20 |
| | 2 | | 4 | | | | | 10 | | | 11 | | | 6 | | 1 | 3 | 5 | | 8 | 7 | | 9 | | | | | | | | | 21 |
| | | 3 | | 5 | | | 8 | 9 | | | 6 | | | | | 1 | | | | 4 | 11 | | 7 | | 10 | 2 | | | | | | 22 |
| | 2 | | | 5 | 6 | | | 9 | | | 11 | | | | | 1 | 3 | | | 4 | | | 7 | | 10 | | 8 | | | | | 23 |
| | | 3 | | 5 | 6 | | | 9 | 10 | | 7 | | | | | 1 | | | | 4 | | | 8 | | 11 | | | | 2 | | | 24 |
| | | | | 5 | 6 | | | 9 | 10 | | 7 | | | | | 1 | 3 | | | | 11 | | 8 | | | | | | 2 | 4 | | 25 |
| | | | | 5 | 6 | | | 9 | 10 | | 7 | | | | | 1 | 3 | | | | 11 | | 8 | | | | | | 2 | 4 | | 26 |
| | | 3 | | 5 | 6 | | | | 10 | 11 | 7 | | | | | 1 | | | | 4 | | | 8 | | | | | | 2 | 9 | | 27 |
| | | 3 | | 5 | 6 | | | | 10 | | 7 | | | | | 1 | 2 | | | 4 | 11 | | 8 | | | | | | | 9 | | 28 |
| | | 3 | | 5 | 6 | | | 9 | 10 | | 7 | | | | | 1 | 2 | | | 4 | | | 8 | | | 11 | | | | | | 29 |
| | | 3 | | 5 | | | 8 | | 10 | | | | | | | 1 | 11 | | | 4 | | | 7 | | | 9 | | | 2 | 6 | | 30 |
| | | 3 | | 5 | 6 | | | 7 | | | | | | | | 1 | | | | 4 | 11 | | 8 | | | 9 | 10 | | 2 | | | 31 |
| | | 3 | | 5 | 10 | | 8 | | | | | | | 11 | | 1 | 2 | | | 4 | 6 | | 7 | | | 9 | | | | | | 32 |
| | | 3 | | | | | | 9 | 8 | | 7 | | | | 6 | 1 | 2 | 10 | | 4 | 11 | | | | 5 | | | | | | | 33 |
| | | 3 | | 5 | 10 | | 8 | | | | 7 | | | | 6 | 1 | | | | | 11 | 4 | | | | 9 | | | 2 | | | 34 |
| 7 | 10 | 27 | 12 | 25 | 22 | 8 | 28 | 30 | 8 | 16 | 16 | 2 | 2 | 13 | 4 | 25 | 22 | 9 | 4 | 22 | 8 | 5 | 20 | 1 | 5 | 9 | 1 | 1 | 6 | 5 | 1 | |
| | | | | 4 | | 1 | 7 | 11 | | | | | 4 | 3 | | 3 | | | 1 | 5 | 1 | 1 | 7 | | | 1 | 2 | | 1 | | | |

1 own-goal

Match 12: Ball listed as playing number 6 by the Football League.
Match 16: Banks listed as playing number 6 by the Football League.
Match 27: Banks listed as playing number 6 by the Football League.

# 1903-04

Secretary-Manager: Ernest Mangnall

| 1 | Sep | 5 | (h) | Bristol C | D | 2-2 | Griffiths 2 | 40,000 |
|---|---|---|---|---|---|---|---|---|
| 2 | | 7 | (a) | Burnley | L | 0-2 | | 5,000 |
| 3 | | 12 | (a) | Burslem PVale | L | 0-1 | | 3,000 |
| 4 | | 19 | (a) | Glossop | W | 5-0 | Griffiths 2, A.Robertson, Downie, Arkesden | 3,000 |
| 5 | | 26 | (h) | Bradford C | W | 3-1 | Pegg 3 | 30,000 |
| 6 | Oct | 3 | (a) | W Arsenal | L | 0-4 | | 20,000 |
| 7 | | 10 | (h) | Barnsley | W | 4-0 | Pegg 2, Griffiths, A.Robertson | 20,000 |
| 8 | | 17 | (a) | Lincoln C | D | 0-0 | | 5,000 |
| 9 | | 24 | (h) | Stockport C | W | 3-1 | Arkesden, Grassam, A.J.Schofield | 15,000 |
| 10 | Nov | 7 | (h) | Bolton W | D | 0-0 | | 30,000 |
| 11 | | 21 | (h) | Preston NE | L | 0-2 | | 15,000 |
| 12 | Dec | 19 | (h) | Gainsborough T | W | 4-2 | Arkesden, Duckworth, Grassam, A.Robertson | 6,000 |
| 13 | | 25 | (h) | Chesterfield | W | 3-1 | Arkesden 2, A.Robertson | 15,000 |
| 14 | | 26 | (a) | Burton U | D | 2-2 | Arkesden 2 | 4,000 |
| 15 | Jan | 2 | (a) | Bristol C | D | 1-1 | Griffiths | 8,000 |
| 16 | | 9 | (h) | Burslem PVale | W | 2-0 | Arkesden, Grassam | 10,000 |
| 17 | | 16 | (h) | Glossop | W | 3-1 | Arkesden 2, Downie | 10,000 |
| 18 | | 23 | (a) | Bradford C | D | 3-3 | Griffiths 2, Downie | 12,000 |
| 19 | | 30 | (h) | W Arsenal | W | 1-0 | A.Robertson | 40,000 |
| 20 | Feb | 13 | (h) | Lincoln C | W | 2-0 | Downie, Griffiths | 8,000 |
| 21 | Mar | 9 | (a) | Blackpool | L | 1-2 | Grassam | 3,000 |
| 22 | | 12 | (h) | Burnley | W | 3-1 | Grassam 2, Griffiths | 14,000 |
| 23 | | 19 | (a) | Preston NE | D | 1-1 | Arkesden | 7,000 |
| 24 | | 26 | (h) | Grimsby T | W | 2-0 | A.Robertson 2 | 12,000 |
| 25 | | 28 | (a) | Stockport C | W | 3-0 | Hall, Pegg, A.J.Schofield | 2,500 |
| 26 | Apr | 1 | (a) | Chesterfield | W | 2-0 | Bell, Hall | 5,000 |
| 27 | | 2 | (a) | Leicester F | W | 1-0 | McCartney | 4,000 |
| 28 | | 5 | (a) | Barnsley | W | 2-0 | Grassam, A.J.Schofield | 5,000 |
| 29 | | 9 | (h) | Blackpool | W | 3-1 | Grassam 2, A.J.Schofield | 10,000 |
| 30 | | 12 | (a) | Grimsby T | L | 1-3 | Grassam | 8,000 |
| 31 | | 16 | (a) | Gainsborough T | W | 1-0 | A.Robertson | 4,000 |
| 32 | | 23 | (h) | Burton U | W | 2-0 | Grassam, A.Robertson | 8,000 |
| 33 | | 25 | (a) | Bolton W | D | 0-0 | | 10,000 |
| 34 | | 30 | (h) | Leicester F | W | 5-2 | A.J.Schofield 2, Bonthron, Griffiths, A.Robertson | 7,000 |

FINAL LEAGUE POSITION: 3rd in Division Two

Appearances
Goals

## FA Cup

| 1 | Dec | 12 | (h) | Small Heath | D | 1-1 | |
|---|---|---|---|---|---|---|---|
| R | | 16 | (a) | Small Heath | D | 1-1 | (After extra-time) |
| 2R | | 21 | (n*) | Small Heath | D | 1-1 | (After extra-time. *Played at Bramall Lane, Sheffield.) |
| 3R | Jan | 11 | (n†) | Small Heath | W | 3-1 | (†Played at Hyde Road, Manchester.) |
| 1 | Feb | 6 | (a) | Notts C | D | 3-3 | |
| R | | 10 | (h) | Notts C | W | 2-1 | |
| 2 | | 20 | (a) | Sheffield W | L | 0-6 | |

| Sutcliffe | Bonthron | Read | Downie | Griffiths | Robertson A* | Gaudie | Robertson T | Arkesden | Robertson A | McCartney | Cartwright | Schofield AJ | Hayes | Bell | Pegg | Blackstock | Grassam | Morrison | Moger | Duckworth | Wilkinson | Kerr | Hall | Schofield J | Roberts | Lyons | Hartwell | Match |
|---|---|---|---|---|---|---|---|---|---|---|---|---|---|---|---|---|---|---|---|---|---|---|---|---|---|---|---|---|
| 1 | 2 | 3 | 4 | 5 | 6 | 7 | 8 | 9 | 10 | 11 |  |  |  |  |  |  |  |  |  |  |  |  |  |  |  |  |  | 1 |
| 1 | 2 | 3 | 4 | 5 |  | 7 | 11 | 10 | 9 | 8 | 6 |  |  |  |  |  |  |  |  |  |  |  |  |  |  |  |  | 2 |
| 1 | 2 | 3 | 4 | 5 |  | 7 | 11 | 10 | 9 |  | 6 | 8 |  |  |  |  |  |  |  |  |  |  |  |  |  |  |  | 3 |
| 1 | 2 | 3 | 4 | 5 |  | 8 |  | 9 | 11 |  |  | 7 |  | 6 | 10 |  |  |  |  |  |  |  |  |  |  |  |  | 4 |
| 1 | 2 | 3 | 4 | 5 |  | 7 |  | 10 | 11 |  | 6 | 8 |  | 9 |  |  |  |  |  |  |  |  |  |  |  |  |  | 5 |
| 1 | 2 |  | 4 | 5 |  |  | 10 | 11 |  | 6 |  | 7 |  |  | 8 |  | 9 | 3 |  |  |  |  |  |  |  |  |  | 6 |
|  | 2 |  | 4 | 5 |  |  | 10 | 11 |  | 6 |  | 7 |  |  | 8 |  | 9 | 3 | 1 |  |  |  |  |  |  |  |  | 7 |
| 1 | 2 |  | 4 | 5 |  |  | 10 | 11 |  | 6 |  | 7 |  |  | 8 |  | 9 | 3 |  |  |  |  |  |  |  |  |  | 8 |
| 1 | 2 |  | 4 | 5 | 6 |  | 10 | 11 |  |  |  | 7 |  |  | 8 |  | 9 | 3 |  |  |  |  |  |  |  |  |  | 9 |
| 1 | 3 |  | 4 | 5 |  |  | 10 | 11 |  | 6 |  | 7 |  |  | 8 |  | 9 | 2 |  |  |  |  |  |  |  |  |  | 10 |
| 1 | 2 |  | 4 | 5 | 6 |  | 10 | 11 |  |  |  | 7 |  |  | 8 |  | 9 | 3 |  |  |  |  |  |  |  |  |  | 11 |
| 1 |  |  |  | 5 | 3 |  | 10 | 11 |  | 6 |  | 7 |  |  | 8 |  | 9 | 2 |  | 4 |  |  |  |  |  |  |  | 12 |
| 1 | 2 | 3 |  | 5 | 6 | 4 |  | 10 | 11 | 8 |  | 7 |  |  |  |  | 9 |  |  |  |  |  |  |  |  |  |  | 13 |
|  | 2 |  |  | 5 | 6 | 4 |  | 10 |  | 8 |  | 7 |  |  |  |  | 9 | 3 | 1 |  | 11 |  |  |  |  |  |  | 14 |
| 1 | 2 |  |  | 6 | 10 |  |  | 7 | 8 | 5 |  | 3 | 4 |  | 9 |  |  |  |  |  | 11 |  |  |  |  |  |  | 15 |
| 1 | 2 | 3 |  | 5 | 6 |  |  | 10 | 9 | 7 |  |  | 4 |  | 8 |  |  |  |  |  | 11 |  |  |  |  |  |  | 16 |
| 1 | 2 | 3 | 6 | 5 | 4 |  |  | 10 |  | 7 |  |  |  |  | 8 |  | 9 |  |  |  | 11 |  |  |  |  |  |  | 17 |
|  | 2 |  | 6 | 5 | 4 |  |  | 10 |  |  |  | 7 | 3 |  | 8 |  | 9 |  | 1 |  | 11 |  |  |  |  |  |  | 18 |
| 1 | 2 |  | 4 | 5 | 6 |  |  | 10 | 11 |  |  | 7 | 3 |  | 8 |  | 9 |  |  |  |  |  |  |  |  |  |  | 19 |
| 1 | 2 |  | 4 | 5 |  |  |  | 10 | 11 |  |  | 7 | 3 |  | 9 |  | 8 | 6 |  |  |  |  |  |  |  |  |  | 20 |
| 1 | 2 |  | 4 | 5 | 6 |  |  | 10 |  |  |  | 7 | 3 |  | 8 |  |  |  |  |  | 11 | 9 |  |  |  |  |  | 21 |
| 1 | 2 |  | 4 | 5 | 6 |  |  | 10 |  |  |  | 7 | 3 |  | 8 |  | 9 |  |  |  | 11 |  |  |  |  |  |  | 22 |
| 1 | 2 |  | 4 | 5 | 6 |  |  | 10 |  |  |  | 7 | 3 |  | 8 |  | 9 |  |  |  | 11 |  |  |  |  |  |  | 23 |
| 1 | 2 |  | 4 | 5 | 6 |  |  |  | 10 |  |  | 7 | 3 |  |  |  |  |  |  |  |  | 9 | 8 | 11 |  |  |  | 24 |
|  | 2 |  | 4 | 5 | 6 |  |  | 11 |  |  |  | 7 | 3 |  |  |  | 9 |  | 1 |  |  |  | 8 | 10 |  |  |  | 25 |
|  | 2 |  | 4 |  |  |  |  | 11 |  | 5 |  | 7 | 3 |  |  |  | 9 |  | 1 |  |  |  | 8 |  | 6 | 10 |  | 26 |
|  | 2 |  | 4 |  | 6 |  |  | 11 | 10 | 5 |  | 7 | 3 |  |  |  | 9 |  | 1 |  |  |  | 8 |  |  |  |  | 27 |
|  | 2 |  | 4 | 5 | 6 |  |  | 11 | 8 |  |  | 7 | 3 |  |  |  | 9 |  | 1 |  |  |  | 10 |  |  |  |  | 28 |
|  | 2 |  | 4 | 5 | 6 |  |  | 11 | 10 |  |  | 7 | 3 |  |  |  | 9 |  | 1 |  |  |  | 8 |  |  |  |  | 29 |
|  | 2 |  | 4 | 5 | 6 |  |  | 11 | 10 |  |  | 7 | 3 |  |  |  | 9 |  | 1 |  |  |  | 8 |  |  |  |  | 30 |
|  | 2 |  | 4 | 5 | 6 |  |  | 11 | 10 |  |  | 7 | 3 |  |  |  | 9 |  | 1 |  |  |  | 8 |  |  |  |  | 31 |
|  | 2 |  | 4 |  | 6 |  |  | 10 | 11 |  |  | 7 | 3 |  |  |  | 9 |  | 1 |  |  |  |  |  | 5 | 8 |  | 32 |
|  | 2 |  | 4 |  | 6 |  |  | 11 | 10 |  |  | 7 | 3 |  |  |  | 9 |  | 1 |  |  |  |  |  | 5 | 8 |  | 33 |
|  | 2 |  | 4 | 5 | 6 |  |  | 10 | 9 |  |  | 7 | 3 |  |  |  | 8 |  | 1 |  |  |  |  |  |  |  | 11 | 34 |
| 21 | 33 | 8 | 29 | 30 | 24 | 7 | 3 | 26 | 27 | 13 | 9 | 26 | 21 | 6 | 13 | 7 | 23 | 9 | 13 | 1 | 8 | 2 | 8 | 2 | 2 | 2 | 1 |  |
| 1 |  | 4 | 11 |  |  |  |  | 11 | 10 | 1 |  | 6 |  | 1 | 6 |  | 11 |  |  | 1 |  |  | 2 |  |  |  |  |  |

Match 9: T.Robertson listed as playing number 6 by the Football League.
Match 26: Roberts listed as playing number 6 by the Football League.
Lyons listed as playing number 10 by the Football League.
Match 32: McCartney listed as playing number 1 by the Football League.

# 1904-05

Secretary-Manager: Ernest Mangnall

| 1 | Sep | 3 | (a) | Burslem PVale | D | 2-2 | Allan 2 | 4,000 |
|---|---|---|---|---|---|---|---|---|
| 2 | | 10 | (h) | Bristol C | W | 4-1 | Peddie, Robertson, Schofield, Williams | 20,000 |
| 3 | | 17 | (h) | Bolton W | L | 1-2 | Mackie | 25,000 |
| 4 | | 24 | (a) | Glossop | W | 2-1 | Allan, Roberts | 6,000 |
| 5 | Oct | 8 | (a) | Bradford C | D | 1-1 | Arkesden | 12,000 |
| 6 | | 15 | (h) | Lincoln C | W | 2-0 | Arkesden, Schofield | 15,000 |
| 7 | | 22 | (a) | Leicester F | W | 3-0 | Arkesden, Peddie, Schofield | 7,000 |
| 8 | | 29 | (h) | Barnsley | W | 4-0 | Allan, Downie, Peddie, Schofield | 15,000 |
| 9 | Nov | 5 | (a) | West Brom A | W | 2-0 | Arkesden, Williams | 5,000 |
| 10 | | 12 | (h) | Burnley | W | 1-0 | Arkesden | 15,000 |
| 11 | | 19 | (a) | Grimsby T | W | 1-0 | Bell | 4,000 |
| 12 | Dec | 3 | (a) | Doncaster R | W | 1-0 | Peddie | 10,000 |
| 13 | | 10 | (h) | Gainsborough T | W | 3-1 | Arkesden 2, Allan | 12,000 |
| 14 | | 17 | (a) | Burton U | W | 3-2 | Peddie 3 | 3,000 |
| 15 | | 24 | (h) | Liverpool | W | 3-1 | Arkesden, Roberts, Williams | 40,000 |
| 16 | | 26 | (h) | Chesterfield | W | 3-0 | Allan 2, Williams | 20,000 |
| 17 | | 31 | (h) | Burslem PVale | W | 6-1 | Allan 3, Arkesden, Hayes, Roberts | 8,000 |
| 18 | Jan | 2 | (h) | Bradford C | W | 7-0 | Arkesden 2, Roberts 2, Allan, Peddie, Robinson (og) | 10,000 |
| 19 | | 3 | (a) | Bolton W | W | 4-2 | Allan 2, Peddie, Williams | 35,000 |
| 20 | | 7 | (a) | Bristol C | D | 1-1 | Arkesden | 12,000 |
| 21 | | 21 | (h) | Glossop | W | 4-1 | Mackie 2, Arkesden, Grassam | 20,000 |
| 22 | Feb | 11 | (a) | Lincoln C | L | 0-3 | | 2,000 |
| 23 | | 18 | (h) | Leicester F | W | 4-1 | Peddie 3, Allan | 7,000 |
| 24 | | 25 | (a) | Barnsley | D | 0-0 | | 5,000 |
| 25 | Mar | 4 | (h) | West Brom A | W | 2-0 | Peddie, Williams | 8,000 |
| 26 | | 11 | (a) | Burnley | L | 0-2 | | 7,000 |
| 27 | | 18 | (h) | Grimsby T | W | 2-1 | Allan, Duckworth | 12,000 |
| 28 | | 25 | (a) | Blackpool | W | 1-0 | Grassam | 6,000 |
| 29 | Apr | 1 | (h) | Doncaster R | W | 6-0 | Duckworth 3, Beddow, Peddie, Wombwell | 6,000 |
| 30 | | 8 | (a) | Gainsborough T | D | 0-0 | | 6,000 |
| 31 | | 15 | (h) | Burton U | W | 5-0 | Duckworth 2, Peddie 2, Arkesden | 16,000 |
| 32 | | 21 | (a) | Chesterfield | L | 0-2 | | 10,000 |
| 33 | | 22 | (a) | Liverpool | L | 0-4 | | 28,000 |
| 34 | | 24 | (h) | Blackpool | W | 3-1 | Allan, Arkesden, Peddie | 4,000 |

FINAL LEAGUE POSITION: 3rd in Division Two

Appearances

Goals

FA Cup

| 1 | Jan | 14 | (h) | Fulham | D | 2-2 | |
| R | | 18 | (a) | Fulham | D | 0-0 | |
| 2R | | 23 | (n*) | Fulham | L | 0-1 | (*Played at Villa Park, Birmingham.) |

| Moger | Bonthron | Hayes | Downie | Roberts | Robertson A* | Schofield | Allan | Mackie | Peddie | Arkesden | Williams | Bell | Robertson A | Duckworth | Hartwell | Grassam | Blackstock | Fitchett | Beddow | Griffiths | Wombwell | Valentine | Holden | Match |
|---|---|---|---|---|---|---|---|---|---|---|---|---|---|---|---|---|---|---|---|---|---|---|---|---|
| 1 | 2 | 3 | 4 | 5 | 6 | 7 | 8 | 9 | 10 | 11 |  |  |  |  |  |  |  |  |  |  |  |  |  | 1 |
| 1 | 2 | 3 | 4 | 5 | 6 | 7 | 8 | 9 | 10 |  | 11 |  |  |  |  |  |  |  |  |  |  |  |  | 2 |
| 1 | 2 | 3 | 4 | 5 | 6 | 7 | 8 | 9 | 10 |  | 11 |  |  |  |  |  |  |  |  |  |  |  |  | 3 |
| 1 | 2 | 3 | 4 | 5 |  | 7 | 8 | 9 | 10 |  | 11 | 6 |  |  |  |  |  |  |  |  |  |  |  | 4 |
| 1 | 2 | 3 | 4 |  | 6 | 7 | 8 |  | 9 | 10 |  | 5 | 11 |  |  |  |  |  |  |  |  |  |  | 5 |
| 1 | 2 | 3 | 4 | 5 |  | 7 | 8 |  | 9 | 10 | 11 | 6 |  |  |  |  |  |  |  |  |  |  |  | 6 |
| 1 | 2 | 3 |  | 5 |  | 7 | 8 |  | 9 | 10 | 11 | 6 |  | 4 |  |  |  |  |  |  |  |  |  | 7 |
| 1 | 2 | 3 | 4 |  | 6 | 7 | 8 |  | 9 | 10 | 11 | 5 |  |  |  |  |  |  |  |  |  |  |  | 8 |
| 1 | 2 | 3 | 4 | 5 | 6 | 7 | 8 |  | 9 | 10 | 11 |  |  |  |  |  |  |  |  |  |  |  |  | 9 |
| 1 | 2 | 3 | 4 | 5 | 6 | 7 | 8 |  | 9 | 10 | 11 |  |  |  |  |  |  |  |  |  |  |  |  | 10 |
| 1 | 2 | 3 | 4 | 5 |  | 7 | 8 |  | 9 | 10 | 11 | 6 |  |  |  |  |  |  |  |  |  |  |  | 11 |
| 1 | 2 | 3 | 4 | 5 |  | 7 | 8 |  | 9 | 10 | 11 | 6 |  |  |  |  |  |  |  |  |  |  |  | 12 |
| 1 | 2 | 3 | 4 | 5 |  | 7 | 8 |  | 9 | 10 | 11 | 6 |  |  |  |  |  |  |  |  |  |  |  | 13 |
| 1 | 2 | 3 | 4 | 5 |  | 7 | 8 |  | 9 | 10 |  | 6 |  |  | 11 |  |  |  |  |  |  |  |  | 14 |
| 1 | 2 | 3 | 4 | 5 |  | 7 | 8 |  | 9 | 10 | 11 | 6 |  |  |  |  |  |  |  |  |  |  |  | 15 |
| 1 | 2 | 3 | 4 | 5 |  |  | 8 |  | 9 | 10 | 11 | 6 |  |  | 7 |  |  |  |  |  |  |  |  | 16 |
| 1 | 2 | 3 | 4 | 5 |  | 7 | 8 |  | 9 | 10 | 11 | 6 |  |  |  |  |  |  |  |  |  |  |  | 17 |
| 1 | 2 | 3 | 4 | 5 |  | 7 | 8 |  | 9 | 10 |  | 6 |  |  |  | 11 |  |  |  |  |  |  |  | 18 |
| 1 | 2 | 3 | 4 | 5 |  | 7 | 8 |  | 9 | 10 | 11 | 6 |  |  |  |  |  |  |  |  |  |  |  | 19 |
| 1 | 2 |  | 4 | 5 |  | 7 |  | 9 | 10 | 11 |  | 6 |  |  |  | 8 | 3 |  |  |  |  |  |  | 20 |
| 1 | 2 | 3 | 4 |  |  | 7 |  | 9 | 10 |  | 11 | 6 |  |  |  | 8 | 5 |  |  |  |  |  |  | 21 |
| 1 | 2 | 3 | 4 | 5 |  | 7 | 8 |  | 9 | 10 | 11 | 6 |  |  |  |  |  |  |  |  |  |  |  | 22 |
| 1 | 2 | 3 | 4 | 5 |  | 7 | 8 |  | 9 | 10 | 11 | 6 |  |  |  |  |  |  |  |  |  |  |  | 23 |
| 1 |  |  | 4 |  |  |  | 8 | 9 | 10 | 11 |  | 6 |  |  |  | 3 | 2 | 7 | 5 |  |  |  |  | 24 |
| 1 | 2 |  | 4 | 5 |  |  | 8 | 9 | 10 | 11 |  | 6 |  |  |  | 3 |  | 7 |  |  |  |  |  | 25 |
| 1 | 2 |  | 4 |  |  |  | 8 | 9 | 10 | 11 |  | 6 |  |  |  | 3 |  | 7 | 5 |  |  |  |  | 26 |
| 1 | 2 |  | 4 | 5 |  |  | 8 |  | 10 |  |  | 6 |  | 9 |  |  |  | 3 | 7 |  | 11 |  |  | 27 |
|  | 2 |  | 4 | 5 |  |  |  |  | 10 |  |  | 6 |  | 9 |  | 8 |  | 3 | 7 |  | 11 |  | 1 | 28 |
| 1 | 2 |  | 4 |  | 6 |  |  |  | 10 |  |  | 5 |  | 9 |  | 8 |  | 3 | 7 |  | 11 |  |  | 29 |
| 1 | 2 |  | 4 | 5 |  |  |  |  | 10 |  |  | 6 |  | 9 |  | 8 |  | 3 | 7 |  | 11 |  |  | 30 |
| 1 | 2 |  | 4 | 5 |  |  |  | 9 | 10 |  |  | 6 |  |  |  | 8 |  | 3 | 7 |  | 11 |  |  | 31 |
| 1 | 2 |  | 4 | 5 |  |  | 8 | 9 | 10 |  |  | 6 |  |  |  |  |  | 3 | 7 |  | 11 |  |  | 32 |
| 1 | 2 |  | 4 | 5 |  | 7 |  | 9 | 10 |  |  | 6 |  |  |  | 8 |  | 3 |  |  | 11 |  |  | 33 |
|  |  |  |  | 5 |  | 7 | 8 | 9 | 10 |  |  | 6 |  | 4 |  |  |  | 3 |  | 11 | 1 | 2 |  | 34 |
| 32 | 32 | 22 | 32 | 28 | 8 | 24 | 27 | 5 | 32 | 28 | 22 | 29 | 1 | 8 | 2 | 6 | 3 | 11 | 9 | 2 | 8 | 2 | 1 |  |
|  | 1 | 1 | 5 | 1 | 4 | 16 | 3 | 17 | 15 | 6 | 1 |  |  | 6 |  | 2 |  | 1 |  |  | 1 |  |  |  |

1 own-goal

Match 28: Moger listed as playing number 1 by the Football League.

# 1905-06

Secretary-Manager: Ernest Mangnall

| 1 | Sep | 2 | (h) | Bristol C | W | 5-1 | Sagar 3, Beddow, Picken | 25,000 |
|---|---|---|---|---|---|---|---|---|
| 2 | | 4 | (h) | Blackpool | W | 2-1 | Peddie 2 | 7,000 |
| 3 | | 9 | (a) | Grimsby T | W | 1-0 | Sagar | 6,000 |
| 4 | | 16 | (a) | Glossop | W | 2-1 | Bell, Beddow | 7,000 |
| 5 | | 23 | (h) | Stockport C | W | 3-1 | Peddie 2, Sagar | 15,000 |
| 6 | | 30 | (a) | Blackpool | W | 1-0 | Roberts | 7,000 |
| 7 | Oct | 7 | (h) | Bradford C | D | 0-0 | | 17,000 |
| 8 | | 14 | (a) | West Brom A | L | 0-1 | | 15,000 |
| 9 | | 21 | (h) | Leicester F | W | 3-2 | Peddie 2, Sagar | 12,000 |
| 10 | | 25 | (a) | Gainsborough T | D | 2-2 | Bonthron 2 | 4,000 |
| 11 | | 28 | (h) | Hull C | W | 1-0 | Picken | 14,000 |
| 12 | Nov | 4 | (h) | Lincoln C | W | 2-1 | Picken, Roberts | 15,000 |
| 13 | | 11 | (a) | Chesterfield | L | 0-1 | | 3,000 |
| 14 | | 18 | (h) | Burslem PVale | W | 3-0 | Beddow, Peddie, Hamilton (og) | 8,000 |
| 15 | | 25 | (a) | Barnsley | W | 3-0 | Beddow, Picken, Silto (og) | 3,000 |
| 16 | Dec | 2 | (h) | Clapton O | W | 4-0 | Peddie 2, Picken 2 | 12,000 |
| 17 | | 9 | (a) | Burnley | W | 3-1 | Beddow, Peddie, Picken | 8,000 |
| 18 | | 23 | (a) | Burton U | W | 2-0 | Schofield 2 | 5,000 |
| 19 | | 25 | (h) | Chelsea | D | 0-0 | | 35,000 |
| 20 | | 30 | (a) | Bristol C | D | 1-1 | Roberts | 18,000 |
| 21 | Jan | 6 | (h) | Grimsby T | W | 5-0 | Beddow 3, Picken 2 | 10,000 |
| 22 | | 15 | (h) | Leeds C | L | 0-3 | | 6,000 |
| 23 | | 20 | (h) | Glossop | W | 5-2 | Picken 2, Beddow, Peddie, Williams | 7,000 |
| 24 | | 27 | (a) | Stockport C | W | 1-0 | Peddie | 15,000 |
| 25 | Feb | 10 | (a) | Bradford C | W | 5-1 | Beddow 2, Roberts, Schofield, Wombwell | 8,000 |
| 26 | | 17 | (h) | West Brom A | D | 0-0 | | 30,000 |
| 27 | Mar | 3 | (h) | Hull C | W | 5-0 | Picken 2, Peddie, Sagar, Schofield | 16,000 |
| 28 | | 17 | (h) | Chesterfield | W | 4-1 | Picken 3, Sagar | 16,000 |
| 29 | | 24 | (a) | Burslem PVale | L | 0-1 | | 3,000 |
| 30 | | 29 | (a) | Leicester F | W | 5-2 | Peddie 3, Picken, Sagar | 5,000 |
| 31 | | 31 | (h) | Barnsley | W | 5-1 | Sagar 3, Bell, Picken | 15,000 |
| 32 | Apr | 7 | (a) | Clapton O | W | 1-0 | Wall | 8,000 |
| 33 | | 13 | (a) | Chelsea | D | 1-1 | Sagar | 60,000 |
| 34 | | 14 | (h) | Burnley | W | 1-0 | Sagar | 12,000 |
| 35 | | 16 | (h) | Gainsborough T | W | 2-0 | Allan 2 | 20,000 |
| 36 | | 21 | (a) | Leeds C | W | 3-1 | Allan, Peddie, Wombwell | 15,000 |
| 37 | | 25 | (a) | Lincoln C | W | 3-2 | Allan 2, Wall | 1,500 |
| 38 | | 28 | (h) | Burton U | W | 6-0 | Sagar 2, Picken 2, Peddie, Wall | 16,000 |

FINAL LEAGUE POSITION: 2nd in Division Two

Appearances

Goals

FA Cup

| 1 | Jan | 13 | (h) | Staple Hill | W | 7-2 |
|---|---|---|---|---|---|---|
| 2 | Feb | 3 | (h) | Norwich C | W | 3-0 |
| 3 | | 24 | (h) | Aston Villa | W | 5-1 |
| 4 | Mar | 10 | (h) | W Arsenal | L | 2-3 |

210

| Moger | Bonthron | Blackstock | Downie | Roberts | Bell | Beddow | Picken | Sagar | Peddie | Arkesden | Wombwell | Montgomery | Valentine | Lyons | Dyer | Schofield | Holden | Donaghey | Duckworth | Williams | Allan | Robertson | Wall | Blew | |
|---|---|---|---|---|---|---|---|---|---|---|---|---|---|---|---|---|---|---|---|---|---|---|---|---|---|
| 1 | 2 | 3 | 4 | 5 | 6 | 7 | 8 | 9 | 10 | 11 | | | | | | | | | | | | | | | 1 |
| 1 | 2 | 3 | 4 | 5 | 6 | 7 | 8 | 9 | 10 | 11 | | | | | | | | | | | | | | | 2 |
| 1 | 2 | 3 | 4 | 5 | 6 | 7 | 8 | 9 | 10 | | 11 | | | | | | | | | | | | | | 3 |
| | 2 | 3 | 4 | 5 | 6 | 7 | 8 | | 9 | 10 | 11 | 1 | | | | | | | | | | | | | 4 |
| | 2 | 3 | 4 | 5 | 6 | 7 | 8 | 9 | 10 | | 11 | 1 | | | | | | | | | | | | | 5 |
| | 2 | 3 | 4 | 5 | 6 | 7 | 8 | | 9 | 10 | 11 | 1 | | | | | | | | | | | | | 6 |
| | 2 | 3 | 4 | 5 | 6 | 7 | 8 | 9 | 10 | | 11 | | 1 | | | | | | | | | | | | 7 |
| | 2 | 3 | 4 | 5 | 6 | 7 | | | 10 | | 11 | | 1 | 8 | 9 | | | | | | | | | | 8 |
| | 2 | 3 | 4 | 5 | 6 | | 8 | 9 | 10 | | 11 | | 1 | | | 7 | | | | | | | | | 9 |
| | 2 | 3 | 4 | 5 | 6 | | 8 | 9 | 10 | | 11 | | 1 | | | 7 | | | | | | | | | 10 |
| | | 3 | 4 | 5 | 6 | | 8 | 9 | 10 | | 11 | | 1 | | | 7 | 2 | | | | | | | | 11 |
| | | 3 | 4 | 5 | 6 | | 10 | 9 | | | 11 | | 1 | | | 7 | 2 | 8 | | | | | | | 12 |
| | 2 | 3 | 4 | 5 | 6 | | 10 | | 9 | | 11 | | 1 | | | 7 | | 8 | | | | | | | 13 |
| 1 | | 3 | | 5 | 6 | | 9 | | 10 | | 8 | | | | | 7 | 2 | | 4 | 11 | | | | | 14 |
| 1 | | 3 | | 5 | 6 | | 9 | | 10 | | 8 | | | | | 7 | 2 | | 4 | 11 | | | | | 15 |
| 1 | | 3 | | 5 | 6 | | 9 | | 10 | | 8 | | | | | 7 | 2 | | 4 | 11 | | | | | 16 |
| 1 | 2 | | | 5 | 6 | | 9 | | 10 | | 8 | | | | | 7 | 3 | | 4 | 11 | | | | | 17 |
| 1 | 2 | | 4 | 5 | 6 | | 9 | | 10 | | 8 | | | | | 7 | 3 | | | 11 | | | | | 18 |
| 1 | 2 | | 4 | 5 | 6 | | 9 | | 10 | 8 | 11 | | | | | 7 | 3 | | | | | | | | 19 |
| 1 | 2 | | 4 | 5 | 6 | | 9 | | 10 | | 8 | | | | | 7 | 3 | | | 11 | | | | | 20 |
| 1 | 2 | | 4 | 5 | 6 | | 9 | | 10 | | | | | | | 7 | 3 | | 11 | 8 | | | | | 21 |
| 1 | | 3 | 4 | 5 | 6 | | 9 | | 10 | | | | | | | 7 | 2 | | 11 | 8 | | | | | 22 |
| 1 | | | 4 | 5 | | | 9 | | 10 | | 8 | | | | | 7 | 3 | 2 | 11 | 6 | | | | | 23 |
| 1 | 2 | | 4 | 5 | 6 | | 9 | | 10 | | 8 | | | | | 7 | 3 | | | 11 | | | | | 24 |
| 1 | 2 | | 4 | 5 | 6 | | 9 | | 10 | 8 | 11 | | | | | 7 | 3 | | | | | | | | 25 |
| 1 | 2 | | 4 | 5 | 6 | | 9 | | 10 | 8 | 11 | | | | | 7 | 3 | | | | | | | | 26 |
| 1 | 2 | | 4 | 5 | 6 | | 10 | 9 | 8 | | 11 | | | | | 7 | 3 | | | | | | | | 27 |
| 1 | 2 | | 4 | 5 | 6 | | 10 | 9 | 8 | | 11 | | | | | 7 | 3 | | | | | | | | 28 |
| 1 | 2 | | 4 | 5 | 6 | | 10 | 9 | 8 | | 11 | | | | | 7 | 3 | | | | | | | | 29 |
| 1 | 2 | | 4 | 5 | 6 | | 10 | 9 | 8 | | 11 | | | | | 7 | 3 | | | | | | | | 30 |
| 1 | 2 | | 4 | 5 | 6 | | 10 | 9 | 8 | | 11 | | | | | 7 | 3 | | | | | | | | 31 |
| 1 | 2 | | 4 | 5 | 6 | | 10 | 9 | 8 | | | | | | | 7 | 3 | | | | | 11 | | | 32 |
| 1 | | | 4 | 5 | | | 10 | 9 | 8 | | | | | | | 7 | 3 | | 6 | | | | 11 | 2 | 33 |
| 1 | 2 | | 4 | 5 | 6 | | 10 | 9 | 8 | | | | | | | 7 | 3 | | | | | | 11 | | 34 |
| | | 3 | 4 | 5 | 6 | | 10 | | 8 | | 11 | | 1 | | | 7 | 2 | | | | | | 9 | | 35 |
| 1 | | 3 | 4 | 5 | 6 | | 10 | | 8 | | | | | | | 7 | 2 | | | | 9 | | 11 | | 36 |
| 1 | | 3 | 4 | 5 | | | 10 | | 8 | | | | | | | 7 | 2 | | 6 | | 9 | | 11 | | 37 |
| 1 | | 3 | 4 | 5 | | | 10 | 9 | 8 | | | | | | | 7 | 2 | | 6 | | | | 11 | | 38 |
| 27 | 26 | 21 | 34 | 34 | 36 | 21 | 33 | 20 | 34 | 7 | 25 | 3 | 8 | 2 | 1 | 23 | 27 | 3 | 10 | 10 | 5 | 1 | 6 | 1 | |
| | 2 | | 4 | 2 | 11 | 20 | 16 | 18 | | | 2 | | | | | 4 | | | 1 | 5 | | | 3 | | |

2 own-goals

# 1906-07

Secretary-Manager: Ernest Mangnall

| | | | | | | | | |
|---|---|---|---|---|---|---|---|---|
| 1 | Sep | 1 | (a) | Bristol C | W | 2-1 | Picken, Roberts | 5,000 |
| 2 | | 3 | (a) | Derby C | D | 2-2 | Schofield 2 | 5,000 |
| 3 | | 8 | (h) | Notts C | D | 0-0 | | 30,000 |
| 4 | | 15 | (a) | Sheffield U | W | 2-0 | Bell, Downie | 12,000 |
| 5 | | 22 | (h) | Bolton W | L | 1-2 | Peddie | 45,000 |
| 6 | | 29 | (h) | Derby C | D | 1-1 | Bell | 25,000 |
| 7 | Oct | 6 | (a) | Stoke | W | 2-1 | Duckworth 2 | 7,000 |
| 8 | | 13 | (h) | Blackburn R | D | 1-1 | Wall | 20,000 |
| 9 | | 20 | (a) | Sunderland | L | 1-4 | Peddie | 18,000 |
| 10 | | 27 | (h) | Birmingham | W | 2-1 | Peddie 2 | 14,000 |
| 11 | Nov | 3 | (a) | Everton | L | 0-3 | | 20,000 |
| 12 | | 10 | (h) | W Arsenal | W | 1-0 | Downie | 20,000 |
| 13 | | 17 | (a) | Sheffield W | L | 2-5 | Menzies, Peddie | 7,000 |
| 14 | | 24 | (h) | Bury | L | 2-4 | Peddie, Wall | 30,000 |
| 15 | Dec | 1 | (a) | Manchester C | L | 0-3 | | 40,000 |
| 16 | | 8 | (h) | Middlesbrough | W | 3-1 | Wall 2, Sagar | 12,000 |
| 17 | | 15 | (a) | Preston NE | L | 0-2 | | 9,000 |
| 18 | | 22 | (h) | Newcastle U | L | 1-3 | Menzies | 18,000 |
| 19 | | 25 | (h) | Liverpool | D | 0-0 | | 20,000 |
| 20 | | 26 | (a) | Aston Villa | L | 0-2 | | 20,000 |
| 21 | | 29 | (h) | Bristol C | D | 0-0 | | 10,000 |
| 22 | Jan | 1 | (h) | Aston Villa | W | 1-0 | Turnbull | 40,000 |
| 23 | | 5 | (a) | Notts C | L | 0-3 | | 10,000 |
| 24 | | 19 | (h) | Sheffield U | W | 2-0 | Turnbull, Wall | 15,000 |
| 25 | | 26 | (a) | Bolton W | W | 1-0 | Turnbull | 25,000 |
| 26 | Feb | 2 | (a) | Newcastle U | L | 0-5 | | 30,000 |
| 27 | | 9 | (h) | Stoke | W | 4-1 | Picken 2, Meredith, Holford (og) | 15,000 |
| 28 | | 16 | (a) | Blackburn R | W | 4-2 | Meredith 2, Sagar, Wall | 5,000 |
| 29 | | 23 | (h) | Preston NE | W | 3-0 | Wall 2, Sagar | 16,000 |
| 30 | Mar | 2 | (a) | Birmingham | D | 1-1 | Menzies | 20,000 |
| 31 | | 16 | (a) | W Arsenal | L | 0-4 | | 6,000 |
| 32 | | 25 | (h) | Sunderland | W | 2-0 | Turnbull, Williams | 12,000 |
| 33 | | 30 | (a) | Bury | W | 2-1 | Menzies, Meredith | 25,000 |
| 34 | Apr | 1 | (a) | Liverpool | W | 1-0 | Turnbull | 20,000 |
| 35 | | 6 | (h) | Manchester C | D | 1-1 | Roberts | 40,000 |
| 36 | | 10 | (h) | Sheffield W | W | 5-0 | Wall 3, Picken, Sagar | 10,000 |
| 37 | | 13 | (a) | Middlesbrough | L | 0-2 | | 15,000 |
| 38 | | 22 | (h) | Everton | W | 3-0 | Bannister, Meredith, Turnbull | 10,000 |

FINAL LEAGUE POSITION: 8th in Division One

Appearances
Goals

FA Cup

| | | | | | | | |
|---|---|---|---|---|---|---|---|
| 1 | Jan | 12 | (a) | Portsmouth | D | 2-2 | |
| R | | 16 | (h) | Portsmouth | L | 1-2 | |

212

Appearance and goalscoring grid (player shirt numbers by match):

| Moger | Bonthron | Holden | Downie | Roberts | Bell | Schofield | Peddie | Sagar | Picken | Wall | Beddow | Yates | Wombwell | Buckley | Allan | Blackstock | Duckworth | Young | Berry | Menzies | Burgess | Meredith | Turnbull | Bannister | Williams | # |
|---|---|---|---|---|---|---|---|---|---|---|---|---|---|---|---|---|---|---|---|---|---|---|---|---|---|---|
| 1 | 2 | 3 | 4 | 5 | 6 | 7 | 8 | 9 | 10 | 11 |  |  |  |  |  |  |  |  |  |  |  |  |  |  |  | 1 |
| 1 | 2 | 3 | 4 | 5 | 6 | 7 | 8 | 9 | 10 | 11 |  |  |  |  |  |  |  |  |  |  |  |  |  |  |  | 2 |
| 1 | 2 | 3 | 4 | 5 | 6 | 7 | 8 | 9 | 10 | 11 |  |  |  |  |  |  |  |  |  |  |  |  |  |  |  | 3 |
| 1 | 2 | 3 | 4 | 5 | 6 |  |  |  | 10 | 11 |  | 7 | 8 | 9 |  |  |  |  |  |  |  |  |  |  |  | 4 |
| 1 | 2 | 3 | 4 | 5 | 6 |  |  | 9 | 10 | 11 |  |  | 8 | 7 |  |  |  |  |  |  |  |  |  |  |  | 5 |
| 1 | 2 |  | 4 | 5 | 6 | 7 | 8 |  | 10 | 11 |  |  |  |  | 3 | 9 |  |  |  |  |  |  |  |  |  | 6 |
| 1 | 2 |  | 4 | 5 | 6 |  | 8 |  | 10 | 11 |  |  |  |  | 9 | 3 | 7 |  |  |  |  |  |  |  |  | 7 |
| 1 | 2 | 3 | 4 |  | 5 | 7 | 8 |  |  | 11 |  | 10 |  | 9 | 6 |  |  |  |  |  |  |  |  |  |  | 8 |
| 1 | 2 | 3 | 4 | 5 | 6 |  | 8 |  | 9 | 11 |  | 10 |  | 7 |  |  |  |  |  |  |  |  |  |  |  | 9 |
| 1 | 2 | 3 | 4 | 5 | 6 |  | 9 |  | 10 | 11 |  |  | 8 | 7 |  |  |  |  |  |  |  |  |  |  |  | 10 |
| 1 | 2 | 3 | 4 | 5 | 6 |  | 9 |  |  | 11 |  | 10 | 8 | 7 |  |  |  |  |  |  |  |  |  |  |  | 11 |
| 1 | 2 | 3 | 4 |  | 6 | 7 | 9 |  | 10 | 11 |  |  | 8 |  | 5 |  |  |  |  |  |  |  |  |  |  | 12 |
| 1 | 2 | 3 | 4 |  | 6 |  | 10 |  |  | 11 |  |  | 8 |  | 5 |  | 7 | 9 |  |  |  |  |  |  |  | 13 |
| 1 | 2 |  | 4 | 5 | 6 |  | 10 |  |  | 11 |  |  | 8 |  | 3 |  | 7 | 9 |  |  |  |  |  |  |  | 14 |
| 1 | 2 |  | 4 | 5 | 6 |  |  |  | 10 | 11 |  | 7 | 8 |  | 3 |  | 9 |  |  |  |  |  |  |  |  | 15 |
| 1 | 2 | 3 |  | 5 | 6 | 7 |  | 9 | 10 | 11 |  |  | 8 | 4 |  |  |  |  |  |  |  |  |  |  |  | 16 |
| 1 | 2 | 3 |  | 5 | 6 | 7 |  | 9 | 10 | 11 |  |  | 8 | 4 |  |  |  |  |  |  |  |  |  |  |  | 17 |
| 1 | 2 | 3 |  | 5 | 6 | 7 | 8 |  | 10 | 11 |  |  |  | 4 |  | 9 |  |  |  |  |  |  |  |  |  | 18 |
| 1 |  | 2 |  | 5 | 6 | 7 |  |  | 10 | 11 |  |  | 3 | 4 |  | 8 | 9 |  |  |  |  |  |  |  |  | 19 |
| 1 |  | 3 | 4 | 5 |  |  | 8 |  | 10 | 11 |  | 6 |  |  | 2 |  | 7 | 9 |  |  |  |  |  |  |  | 20 |
| 1 | 2 | 3 | 4 | 5 |  |  |  |  | 10 | 11 |  | 7 |  | 6 |  |  | 8 | 9 |  |  |  |  |  |  |  | 21 |
| 1 | 2 |  |  | 5 | 6 |  |  |  |  | 11 |  |  |  |  |  |  | 4 |  |  | 9 | 3 | 7 | 10 | 8 |  | 22 |
| 1 | 2 |  |  |  | 6 |  |  |  |  | 11 |  |  |  | 5 |  |  | 4 |  |  | 9 | 3 | 7 | 10 | 8 |  | 23 |
| 1 | 2 | 5 |  |  | 6 |  | 8 | 9 |  | 11 |  |  |  |  |  |  | 4 |  |  |  | 3 | 7 | 10 |  |  | 24 |
| 1 | 2 |  |  | 5 | 6 |  |  | 8 |  | 11 |  |  |  |  |  |  | 4 | 9 |  |  | 3 | 7 | 10 |  |  | 25 |
| 1 |  | 2 |  | 5 | 6 |  |  |  | 10 | 11 |  |  |  |  |  |  | 4 | 9 | 8 |  | 3 | 7 |  |  |  | 26 |
| 1 |  | 2 |  | 5 | 6 |  | 8 |  |  | 11 |  |  |  |  |  |  | 4 | 9 | 10 |  | 3 | 7 |  |  |  | 27 |
| 1 |  | 2 |  | 5 | 6 |  | 9 | 8 |  | 11 |  |  |  |  |  |  | 4 |  |  |  | 3 | 7 | 10 |  |  | 28 |
| 1 |  | 2 |  | 5 | 6 |  | 9 | 8 |  | 11 |  |  |  |  |  |  | 4 | 7 |  |  | 3 |  | 10 |  |  | 29 |
| 1 |  | 2 |  |  | 6 |  |  | 8 |  | 11 | 5 |  |  |  |  |  | 4 |  |  | 9 | 3 | 7 | 10 |  |  | 30 |
| 1 | 2 | 5 |  |  | 6 |  |  |  |  | 11 |  |  |  |  |  |  | 4 |  |  | 9 | 3 | 7 | 10 | 8 |  | 31 |
| 1 |  | 2 |  | 5 | 6 |  |  |  |  | 11 |  |  |  |  |  |  | 4 |  |  | 9 | 3 | 7 | 10 |  | 8 | 32 |
| 1 |  | 2 |  | 5 | 6 |  |  |  |  | 11 |  |  |  |  |  |  | 4 |  |  | 9 | 3 | 7 | 10 |  | 8 | 33 |
| 1 | 2 |  |  | 5 | 6 |  |  |  |  | 11 |  |  |  |  |  |  | 4 |  |  | 9 | 3 | 7 | 10 |  | 8 | 34 |
| 1 | 2 |  | 4 | 5 | 6 |  | 8 |  |  | 11 |  |  |  |  |  |  |  | 9 |  |  | 3 | 7 | 10 |  |  | 35 |
| 1 | 2 |  | 6 | 5 |  |  |  | 9 | 8 | 11 |  |  |  |  |  |  | 4 |  |  |  | 3 | 7 | 10 |  |  | 36 |
| 1 | 2 |  |  | 5 | 6 |  |  | 9 | 8 | 11 |  |  |  |  |  |  | 4 |  |  |  | 3 | 7 | 10 |  |  | 37 |
| 1 |  | 8 |  | 5 | 6 |  |  | 9 |  | 11 |  |  |  |  |  |  | 4 |  |  |  | 3 | 7 | 10 |  | 2 | 38 |
| 38 | 28 | 27 | 19 | 31 | 35 | 10 | 16 | 10 | 26 | 38 | 3 | 3 | 14 | 3 | 3 |  | 28 | 2 | 9 | 17 | 17 | 16 | 15 | 4 | 3 |  |
|  |  | 2 | 2 | 2 | 2 | 6 | 4 | 4 | 11 |  |  |  |  |  |  |  | 2 |  |  | 4 |  | 5 | 6 | 1 | 1 |  |

1 own-goal

# 1907-08

Secretary-Manager: Ernest Mangnall

| | | | | | | | | |
|---|---|---|---|---|---|---|---|---|
| 1 | Sep | 2 | (a) | Aston Villa | W | 4-1 | Meredith 2, Bannister, Wall | 20,000 |
| 2 | | 7 | (h) | Liverpool | W | 4-0 | A.Turnbull 3, Wall | 24,000 |
| 3 | | 9 | (h) | Middlesbrough | W | 2-1 | A.Turnbull 2 | 20,000 |
| 4 | | 14 | (a) | Middlesbrough | L | 1-2 | Bannister | 18,000 |
| 5 | | 21 | (h) | Sheffield U | W | 2-1 | A.Turnbull 2 | 25,000 |
| 6 | | 28 | (a) | Chelsea | W | 4-1 | Meredith 2, Bannister, A.Turnbull | 40,000 |
| 7 | Oct | 5 | (h) | Nottingham F | W | 4-0 | Bannister, J.Turnbull, Wall, Maltby (og) | 20,000 |
| 8 | | 12 | (a) | Newcastle U | W | 6-1 | Wall 2, Meredith, Roberts, A.Turnbull, J.Turnbull | 25,000 |
| 9 | | 19 | (a) | Blackburn R | W | 5-1 | A.Turnbull 3, J.Turnbull 2 | 30,000 |
| 10 | | 26 | (h) | Bolton W | W | 2-1 | A.Turnbull, J.Turnbull | 35,000 |
| 11 | Nov | 2 | (a) | Birmingham | W | 4-3 | Meredith 2, J.Turnbull, Wall | 20,000 |
| 12 | | 9 | (h) | Everton | W | 4-3 | Wall 2, Meredith, Roberts | 30,000 |
| 13 | | 16 | (a) | Sunderland | W | 2-1 | A.Turnbull 2 | 30,000 |
| 14 | | 23 | (h) | W Arsenal | W | 4-2 | A.Turnbull 4 | 10,000 |
| 15 | | 30 | (a) | Sheffield W | L | 0-2 | | 40,000 |
| 16 | Dec | 7 | (h) | Bristol C | W | 2-1 | Wall 2 | 20,000 |
| 17 | | 14 | (a) | Notts C | D | 1-1 | Meredith | 11,000 |
| 18 | | 21 | (h) | Manchester C | W | 3-1 | A.Turnbull 2, Wall | 35,000 |
| 19 | | 25 | (h) | Bury | W | 2-1 | Meredith, J.Turnbull | 45,000 |
| 20 | | 28 | (a) | Preston NE | D | 0-0 | | 12,000 |
| 21 | Jan | 1 | (a) | Bury | W | 1-0 | Wall | 29,500 |
| 22 | | 18 | (a) | Sheffield U | L | 0-2 | | 17,000 |
| 23 | | 25 | (h) | Chelsea | W | 1-0 | J.Turnbull | 20,000 |
| 24 | Feb | 8 | (h) | Newcastle U | D | 1-1 | J.Turnbull | 50,000 |
| 25 | | 15 | (h) | Blackburn R | L | 1-2 | A.Turnbull | 15,000 |
| 26 | | 29 | (h) | Birmingham | W | 1-0 | A.Turnbull | 12,000 |
| 27 | Mar | 14 | (h) | Sunderland | W | 3-0 | Bell, Berry, Wall | 15,000 |
| 28 | | 21 | (a) | W Arsenal | L | 0-1 | | 20,000 |
| 29 | | 25 | (a) | Liverpool | L | 4-7 | Wall 2, Bannister, J.Turnbull | 10,000 |
| 30 | | 28 | (h) | Sheffield W | W | 4-1 | Wall 2, Halse, A.Turnbull | 30,000 |
| 31 | Apr | 4 | (a) | Bristol C | D | 1-1 | Wall | 12,000 |
| 32 | | 8 | (a) | Everton | W | 3-1 | Halse, A.Turnbull, Wall | 17,000 |
| 33 | | 11 | (h) | Notts C | L | 0-1 | | 20,000 |
| 34 | | 17 | (a) | Nottingham F | L | 0-2 | | 22,000 |
| 35 | | 18 | (a) | Manchester C | D | 0-0 | | 40,000 |
| 36 | | 20 | (h) | Aston Villa | L | 1-2 | Picken | 10,000 |
| 37 | | 22 | (a) | Bolton W | D | 2-2 | Halse, Stacey | 18,000 |
| 38 | | 25 | (h) | Preston NE | W | 2-1 | Halse, Rodway (og) | 8,000 |

FINAL LEAGUE POSITION: 1st in Division One

Appearances

Goals

FA Cup

| | | | | | | | |
|---|---|---|---|---|---|---|---|
| 1 | Jan | 11 | (h) | Blackpool | W | 3-1 | |
| 2 | Feb | 1 | (h) | Chelsea | W | 1-0 | |
| 3 | | 22 | (a) | Aston Villa | W | 2-0 | |
| 4 | Mar | 7 | (a) | Fulham | L | 1-2 | |

214

| Moger | Holden | Burgess | Duckworth | Roberts | Bell | Meredith | Bannister | Menzies | Turnbull A | Wall | Thomson | Turnbull J | Stacey | Picken | Williams | Whiteside | McGillivray | Downie | Wilson | Berry | Broomfield | Dalton | Halse | Hulme | |
|---|---|---|---|---|---|---|---|---|---|---|---|---|---|---|---|---|---|---|---|---|---|---|---|---|---|
| 1 | 2 | 3 | 4 | 5 | 6 | 7 | 8 | 9 | 10 | 11 | | | | | | | | | | | | | | | 1 |
| 1 | 2 | 3 | 4 | 5 | 6 | 7 | 8 | 9 | 10 | 11 | | | | | | | | | | | | | | | 2 |
| 1 | 2 | 3 | 4 | 5 | 6 | 7 | 8 | 9 | 10 | 11 | | | | | | | | | | | | | | | 3 |
| 1 | 2 | 3 | 4 | 5 | | 7 | 8 | 9 | 10 | 11 | 6 | | | | | | | | | | | | | | 4 |
| 1 | 2 | 3 | 4 | 5 | 6 | 7 | 8 | 9 | 10 | 11 | | | | | | | | | | | | | | | 5 |
| 1 | 2 | 3 | 4 | 5 | 6 | 7 | 8 | | 10 | 11 | | 9 | | | | | | | | | | | | | 6 |
| 1 | 2 | 3 | 4 | 5 | 6 | 7 | 8 | | 10 | 11 | | 9 | | | | | | | | | | | | | 7 |
| 1 | 2 | | 4 | 5 | 6 | 7 | 8 | | 10 | 11 | | 9 | 3 | | | | | | | | | | | | 8 |
| 1 | 2 | 3 | 4 | 5 | 6 | 7 | 8 | | 10 | 11 | | 9 | | | | | | | | | | | | | 9 |
| 1 | 2 | 3 | 4 | 5 | 6 | 7 | 8 | | 10 | 11 | | 9 | | | | | | | | | | | | | 10 |
| 1 | 2 | 3 | 4 | 5 | 6 | 7 | 8 | | | 11 | | 9 | | 10 | | | | | | | | | | | 11 |
| 1 | 2 | 3 | 4 | 5 | 6 | 7 | 8 | | 10 | 11 | | 9 | | | | | | | | | | | | | 12 |
| 1 | 2 | 3 | 4 | 5 | 6 | 7 | 8 | | 10 | 11 | | 9 | | | | | | | | | | | | | 13 |
| 1 | 2 | 3 | 4 | 5 | 6 | 7 | 8 | | 10 | | | 9 | | | 11 | | | | | | | | | | 14 |
| 1 | 2 | 3 | 4 | 5 | 6 | 7 | 8 | | 10 | 11 | | 9 | | | | | | | | | | | | | 15 |
| 1 | 2 | | 4 | 5 | 6 | 7 | 8 | | 10 | 11 | | 9 | 3 | | | | | | | | | | | | 16 |
| 1 | 2 | 3 | 4 | 5 | 6 | 7 | 8 | | 10 | 11 | | 9 | | | | | | | | | | | | | 17 |
| 1 | 2 | 3 | 4 | 5 | 6 | 7 | 8 | | 10 | 11 | | 9 | | | | | | | | | | | | | 18 |
| 1 | 2 | | 4 | 5 | 6 | 7 | 8 | | 10 | 11 | | 9 | 3 | | | | | | | | | | | | 19 |
| 1 | 2 | | 4 | 5 | 6 | 7 | 8 | | 10 | 11 | | 9 | 3 | | | | | | | | | | | | 20 |
| 1 | 2 | | 4 | 5 | 6 | 7 | 8 | | 10 | 11 | | 9 | 3 | | | | | | | | | | | | 21 |
| 1 | 2 | 3 | | | 6 | 7 | 8 | | | 11 | | | 9 | 10 | | 4 | 5 | | | | | | | | 22 |
| 1 | 2 | 3 | | 5 | 6 | 7 | | | 10 | 11 | | | 9 | | | | | 8 | | 4 | | | | | 23 |
| 1 | 2 | 3 | 4 | | 6 | 7 | 8 | | 10 | 11 | | | 9 | | | | 5 | | | | | | | | 24 |
| 1 | 2 | 3 | 4 | 5 | 6 | 7 | 8 | | 10 | | | 9 | | | | | | 11 | | | | | | | 25 |
| 1 | 2 | | 4 | 5 | 6 | 7 | 8 | | 10 | 11 | | 9 | 3 | | | | | | | | | | | | 26 |
| 1 | | 3 | 4 | 5 | 6 | 7 | 8 | | 10 | 11 | | | | 2 | | | | 9 | | | | | | | 27 |
| | | 3 | 4 | 5 | 6 | 7 | 8 | | | 11 | | | | 2 | | | | 9 | | 10 | 1 | | | | 28 |
| 1 | | | 4 | 5 | | 7 | 8 | | | 11 | | | 9 | 2 | | | | 10 | | | | 3 | 6 | | 29 |
| | | 3 | 4 | | 6 | 7 | 8 | | 10 | 11 | | | | 2 | | | | 5 | | | 1 | | 9 | | 30 |
| | | 3 | 4 | 5 | 6 | 7 | 8 | | 10 | 11 | | | | 2 | | | | | | | 1 | | 9 | | 31 |
| | | 3 | 4 | 5 | | 7 | 8 | | 10 | 11 | | | | 2 | | | | 6 | | | 1 | | 9 | | 32 |
| | | 3 | 4 | | 6 | | 8 | | 10 | 11 | | | 9 | 2 | | | | 5 | | 7 | 1 | | | | 33 |
| | | 3 | 4 | 5 | 6 | 7 | | | 10 | 11 | | | 9 | 2 | | | | | | | 1 | | 8 | | 34 |
| | | 2 | | 5 | 6 | 7 | 8 | | 10 | 11 | | 9 | 3 | | | | | 4 | | | 1 | | | | 35 |
| | | 2 | | 5 | 6 | 7 | 8 | | | 11 | 10 | 3 | 9 | | | | | 4 | | | 1 | | | | 36 |
| | | 2 | | | 6 | 7 | 8 | | | 11 | 5 | | 3 | 10 | | | | 4 | | | 1 | | 9 | | 37 |
| 1 | | | | | 6 | 7 | 8 | | | 11 | | | 5 | 2 | 10 | | | 4 | | | | 3 | 9 | | 38 |
| 29 | 26 | 27 | 35 | 32 | 35 | 37 | 36 | 6 | 30 | 36 | 3 | 26 | 18 | 8 | 1 | 1 | 1 | 10 | 1 | 3 | 9 | 1 | 6 | 1 | |
| | | | | 2 | 1 | 10 | 5 | | 25 | 19 | | 10 | 1 | 1 | | | | 4 | | 1 | | | 4 | | |

2 own-goals

215

# 1908-09

Secretary-Manager: Ernest Mangnall

| | | | | | | | |
|---|---|---|---|---|---|---|---|
| 1 | Sep | 5 | (a) | Preston NE | W 3-0 | J.Turnbull 2, Halse | 18,000 |
| 2 | | 7 | (h) | Bury | W 2-1 | J.Turnbull 2 | 16,000 |
| 3 | | 12 | (h) | Middlesbrough | W 6-3 | J.Turnbull 4, Halse, Wall | 25,000 |
| 4 | | 19 | (a) | Manchester C | W 2-1 | Halse, J.Turnbull | 40,000 |
| 5 | | 26 | (h) | Liverpool | W 3-2 | Halse 2, J.Turnbull | 25,000 |
| 6 | Oct | 3 | (a) | Bury | D 2-2 | Halse, Wall | 25,000 |
| 7 | | 10 | (h) | Sheffield U | W 2-1 | Bell 2 | 14,000 |
| 8 | | 17 | (a) | Aston Villa | L 1-3 | Halse | 40,000 |
| 9 | | 24 | (h) | Nottingham F | D 2-2 | A.Turnbull 2 | 20,000 |
| 10 | | 31 | (a) | Sunderland | L 1-6 | A.Turnbull | 30,000 |
| 11 | Nov | 7 | (h) | Chelsea | L 0-1 | | 15,000 |
| 12 | | 14 | (a) | Blackburn R | W 3-1 | Halse, J.Turnbull, Wall | 25,000 |
| 13 | | 21 | (h) | Bradford C | W 2-0 | Picken, Wall | 15,000 |
| 14 | | 28 | (h) | Sheffield W | W 3-1 | Halse, Picken, J.Turnbull | 20,000 |
| 15 | Dec | 5 | (a) | Everton | L 2-3 | Bannister, Halse | 35,000 |
| 16 | | 12 | (h) | Leicester F | W 4-2 | Wall 3, Picken | 10,000 |
| 17 | | 19 | (a) | W Arsenal | W 1-0 | Halse | 10,000 |
| 18 | | 25 | (a) | Newcastle U | L 1-2 | Wall | 35,000 |
| 19 | | 26 | (h) | Newcastle U | W 1-0 | Halse | 40,000 |
| 20 | Jan | 1 | (h) | Notts C | W 4-3 | Halse 2, Roberts, A.Turnbull | 15,000 |
| 21 | | 2 | (h) | Preston NE | L 0-2 | | 18,000 |
| 22 | | 9 | (a) | Middlesbrough | L 0-5 | | 15,000 |
| 23 | | 23 | (h) | Manchester C | W 3-1 | Livingstone 2, Wall | 40,000 |
| 24 | | 30 | (a) | Liverpool | L 1-3 | A.Turnbull | 30,000 |
| 25 | Feb | 13 | (a) | Sheffield U | D 0-0 | | 12,000 |
| 26 | | 27 | (a) | Nottingham F | L 0-2 | | 7,000 |
| 27 | Mar | 13 | (a) | Chelsea | D 1-1 | Wall | 30,000 |
| 28 | | 15 | (h) | Sunderland | D 2-2 | Payne, J.Turnbull | 10,000 |
| 29 | | 20 | (h) | Blackburn R | L 0-3 | | 11,000 |
| 30 | | 31 | (h) | Aston Villa | L 0-2 | | 10,000 |
| 31 | Apr | 3 | (a) | Sheffield W | L 0-2 | | 15,000 |
| 32 | | 9 | (h) | Bristol C | L 0-1 | | 18,000 |
| 33 | | 10 | (h) | Everton | D 2-2 | J.Turnbull 2 | 8,000 |
| 34 | | 12 | (a) | Bristol C | D 0-0 | | 18,000 |
| 35 | | 13 | (a) | Notts C | W 1-0 | Livingstone | 7,000 |
| 36 | | 17 | (a) | Leicester F | L 2-3 | J.Turnbull, Wall | 8,000 |
| 37 | | 27 | (h) | W Arsenal | L 1-4 | J.Turnbull | 10,000 |
| 38 | | 29 | (a) | Bradford C | L 0-1 | | 30,000 |

FINAL LEAGUE POSITION: 13th in Division One

Appearances
Goals

FA Cup

| | | | | | | |
|---|---|---|---|---|---|---|
| 1 | Jan | 16 | (h) | Brighton & HA | W 1-0 | |
| 2 | Feb | 6 | (h) | Everton | W 1-0 | |
| 3 | | 20 | (h) | Blackburn R | W 6-1 | |
| 4 | Mar | 10 | (a) | Burnley | W 3-2 | (Original match played on 6 March but abandoned after 72 minutes with Burnley leading 1-0) |
| SF | | 27 | (n*) | Newcastle U | W 1-0 | (*Played at Bramall Lane, Sheffield.) |
| F | Apr | 24 | (n†) | Bristol C | W 1-0 | (†Played at the Crystal Palace) |

216

| Moger | Stacey | Burgess | Duckworth | Roberts | Bell | Meredith | Halse | Turnbull J | Picken | Wall | Christie D | Bannister | Downie | Hardman | Turnbull A | Hulme | Wilcox | Linkson | Thomson | Hayes | Curry | Berry | Livingstone | Payne | Donnelly | Holden | McGillivray | Ford | Quinn | Match |
|---|---|---|---|---|---|---|---|---|---|---|---|---|---|---|---|---|---|---|---|---|---|---|---|---|---|---|---|---|---|---|
| 1 | 2 | 3 | 4 | 5 | 6 | 7 | 8 | 9 | 10 | 11 |  |  |  |  |  |  |  |  |  |  |  |  |  |  |  |  |  |  |  | 1 |
| 1 | 2 | 3 | 4 | 5 | 6 | 7 | 8 | 9 |  | 11 | 10 |  |  |  |  |  |  |  |  |  |  |  |  |  |  |  |  |  |  | 2 |
| 1 | 2 | 3 | 4 | 5 | 6 | 7 | 10 | 9 |  | 11 |  | 8 |  |  |  |  |  |  |  |  |  |  |  |  |  |  |  |  |  | 3 |
| 1 | 3 |  | 2 | 5 |  | 7 | 10 | 9 |  | 11 |  |  | 4 | 6 | 8 |  |  |  |  |  |  |  |  |  |  |  |  |  |  | 4 |
| 1 | 3 |  | 2 | 5 | 6 | 7 | 8 | 9 |  | 11 |  |  | 4 |  | 10 |  |  |  |  |  |  |  |  |  |  |  |  |  |  | 5 |
| 1 | 3 |  | 4 | 5 |  | 7 | 8 | 9 |  | 11 |  |  | 6 |  | 10 | 2 |  |  |  |  |  |  |  |  |  |  |  |  |  | 6 |
| 1 | 3 |  | 4 | 5 | 6 | 7 |  | 9 |  | 11 |  | 8 |  |  | 10 | 2 |  |  |  |  |  |  |  |  |  |  |  |  |  | 7 |
| 1 | 3 |  | 4 | 5 | 6 | 7 |  | 9 |  | 11 |  | 8 |  |  | 10 | 2 |  |  |  |  |  |  |  |  |  |  |  |  |  | 8 |
|  | 3 |  | 4 | 5 |  | 7 | 8 | 9 |  | 11 |  |  | 6 |  | 10 | 1 | 2 |  |  |  |  |  |  |  |  |  |  |  |  | 9 |
| 1 | 2 | 3 | 4 |  |  | 7 | 8 | 9 |  | 11 |  |  | 5 |  | 10 |  |  |  | 6 |  |  |  |  |  |  |  |  |  |  | 10 |
| 1 | 2 |  | 4 |  | 6 | 7 |  | 9 | 5 | 11 |  | 8 |  |  | 10 |  |  |  |  | 3 |  |  |  |  |  |  |  |  |  | 11 |
| 1 | 2 |  | 4 | 5 |  | 7 | 8 | 9 |  | 10 |  |  | 6 | 11 |  |  |  |  |  | 3 |  |  |  |  |  |  |  |  |  | 12 |
| 1 | 2 |  | 4 |  |  | 7 | 8 | 9 | 10 | 11 |  |  | 6 |  |  |  |  |  |  | 3 | 5 |  |  |  |  |  |  |  |  | 13 |
| 1 | 2 |  | 4 | 5 |  | 7 | 8 | 9 | 10 | 11 |  |  | 6 |  |  |  |  |  |  | 3 |  |  |  |  |  |  |  |  |  | 14 |
| 1 | 2 |  | 4 | 5 | 6 | 7 |  | 9 | 10 | 11 |  | 8 |  |  |  |  |  |  |  | 3 |  |  |  |  |  |  |  |  |  | 15 |
| 1 |  |  | 4 |  |  | 7 | 8 | 9 | 10 |  |  |  | 6 | 11 |  |  |  | 2 |  | 3 | 5 |  |  |  |  |  |  |  |  | 16 |
| 1 |  |  | 4 | 5 |  | 7 |  | 9 | 10 | 11 |  | 8 | 6 |  |  |  |  | 2 |  | 3 |  |  |  |  |  |  |  |  |  | 17 |
| 1 | 2 |  | 4 | 5 | 6 | 7 |  | 9 |  | 11 |  | 8 |  |  | 10 |  |  |  |  | 3 |  |  |  |  |  |  |  |  |  | 18 |
| 1 | 2 |  | 4 | 5 | 6 | 7 |  | 9 |  | 11 |  | 8 |  |  | 10 |  |  |  |  | 3 |  |  |  |  |  |  |  |  |  | 19 |
| 1 | 2 |  | 4 | 5 | 6 | 7 |  | 9 |  | 11 |  | 8 |  |  | 10 |  |  |  |  | 3 |  |  |  |  |  |  |  |  |  | 20 |
| 1 | 2 |  | 4 | 5 | 6 | 7 |  | 9 |  | 11 |  | 8 |  |  | 10 |  |  |  |  | 3 |  |  |  |  |  |  |  |  |  | 21 |
| 1 | 2 |  | 4 | 5 | 6 | 7 |  |  |  | 11 |  | 8 |  |  | 10 |  |  |  |  | 3 | 9 |  |  |  |  |  |  |  |  | 22 |
| 1 | 2 |  | 4 | 5 |  | 7 |  | 9 |  | 11 |  |  | 6 |  | 10 |  |  |  |  | 3 |  |  | 8 |  |  |  |  |  |  | 23 |
| 1 | 2 |  | 4 | 5 |  | 7 |  | 9 |  | 11 |  |  | 6 |  | 10 |  |  |  |  | 3 |  |  | 8 |  |  |  |  |  |  | 24 |
| 1 | 2 |  |  |  | 6 | 7 |  | 9 |  | 11 |  |  | 4 |  | 10 |  |  |  |  | 3 | 5 |  | 8 |  |  |  |  |  |  | 25 |
| 1 | 2 |  |  |  | 6 |  |  | 9 | 10 | 11 |  | 8 | 4 |  |  |  |  |  |  | 3 | 5 |  |  |  | 7 |  |  |  |  | 26 |
| 1 | 2 |  | 4 | 5 |  | 7 | 8 | 9 |  | 11 |  |  | 6 |  | 10 |  |  |  |  | 3 |  |  |  |  |  |  |  |  |  | 27 |
| 1 |  |  |  | 5 | 6 |  |  | 9 |  | 11 |  |  | 4 |  | 10 |  |  |  |  | 3 |  |  | 8 | 7 | 2 |  |  |  |  | 28 |
| 1 |  |  | 4 |  |  | 7 |  | 9 | 10 | 11 |  |  | 6 |  |  |  |  |  |  | 3 | 5 |  | 8 | 2 |  |  |  |  |  | 29 |
| 1 |  |  | 4 |  |  | 7 |  |  | 10 |  |  | 8 | 6 |  |  |  |  |  |  | 3 |  | 9 | 2 | 5 | 11 |  |  |  |  | 30 |
|  | 3 |  |  | 5 |  | 7 |  |  |  |  |  | 8 |  |  |  | 1 | 2 | 4 |  | 10 |  |  |  |  |  | 6 | 11 | 9 |  | 31 |
| 1 | 3 |  | 4 | 5 |  | 7 |  | 9 |  | 11 |  | 8 | 6 |  |  |  | 2 |  |  | 10 |  |  |  |  |  |  |  |  |  | 32 |
| 1 | 2 |  | 4 |  |  | 7 | 8 | 9 | 10 |  |  |  | 6 |  |  |  |  |  |  | 3 | 5 |  |  |  |  |  | 11 |  |  | 33 |
| 1 | 2 |  | 4 | 5 |  | 7 |  | 9 | 10 | 11 |  |  | 6 |  |  |  |  |  |  | 3 |  |  | 8 |  |  |  |  |  |  | 34 |
| 1 | 2 |  | 4 | 5 |  | 7 |  | 9 | 10 |  |  |  | 6 |  |  |  |  |  |  | 3 |  |  | 8 |  |  |  | 11 |  |  | 35 |
| 1 |  |  |  |  | 6 | 7 |  | 9 | 10 | 11 |  |  | 4 |  |  |  | 2 |  |  | 3 | 5 |  | 8 |  |  |  |  |  |  | 36 |
| 1 | 2 |  | 4 | 5 | 6 | 7 | 8 | 9 |  | 11 |  |  |  |  | 10 |  |  |  |  | 3 |  |  |  |  |  |  |  |  |  | 37 |
| 1 | 2 |  | 4 | 5 | 6 | 7 | 8 | 9 |  | 11 |  |  |  |  | 10 |  |  |  |  | 3 |  |  |  |  |  |  |  |  |  | 38 |
| 36 | 32 | 4 | 33 | 27 | 20 | 34 | 29 | 22 | 13 | 34 | 2 | 16 | 23 | 4 | 19 | 3 | 2 | 10 | 1 | 22 | 8 | 1 | 11 | 2 | 1 | 2 | 2 | 4 | 1 |  |
|  |  |  | 1 | 2 |  |  | 14 | 17 | 3 | 11 |  |  | 1 |  | 5 |  |  |  |  |  |  |  | 3 | 1 |  |  |  |  |  |  |

Match 6: Bell listed as playing number 6 by the Football League.

# 1909-10

Secretary-Manager: Ernest Mangnall

| 1 | Sep | 1 | (h) | Bradford C | W | 1-0 | Wall | 12,000 |
|---|---|---|---|---|---|---|---|---|
| 2 | | 4 | (h) | Bury | W | 2-0 | J.Turnbull 2 | 12,000 |
| 3 | | 6 | (h) | Notts C | W | 2-1 | J.Turnbull, Wall | 6,000 |
| 4 | | 11 | (a) | Tottenham H | D | 2-2 | J.Turnbull, Wall | 40,000 |
| 5 | | 18 | (h) | Preston NE | D | 1-1 | Roberts | 13,000 |
| 6 | | 25 | (a) | Notts C | L | 2-3 | A.Turnbull 2 | 11,000 |
| 7 | Oct | 2 | (h) | Newcastle U | D | 1-1 | Wall | 30,000 |
| 8 | | 9 | (a) | Liverpool | L | 2-3 | A.Turnbull 2 | 30,000 |
| 9 | | 16 | (h) | Aston Villa | W | 2-0 | Halse, A.Turnbull | 20,000 |
| 10 | | 23 | (a) | Sheffield U | W | 1-0 | Wall | 30,000 |
| 11 | | 30 | (h) | W Arsenal | W | 1-0 | Wall | 20,000 |
| 12 | Nov | 6 | (a) | Bolton W | W | 3-2 | Homer 2, Halse | 20,000 |
| 13 | | 13 | (h) | Chelsea | W | 2-0 | A.Turnbull, Wall | 10,000 |
| 14 | | 20 | (a) | Blackburn R | L | 2-3 | Homer 2 | 40,000 |
| 15 | | 27 | (h) | Nottingham F | L | 2-6 | Halse, Wall | 12,000 |
| 16 | Dec | 4 | (a) | Sunderland | L | 0-3 | | 12,000 |
| 17 | | 18 | (a) | Middlesbrough | W | 2-1 | Homer, A.Turnbull | 10,000 |
| 18 | | 25 | (h) | Sheffield W | L | 0-3 | | 25,000 |
| 19 | | 27 | (a) | Sheffield W | L | 1-4 | Wall | 37,000 |
| 20 | Jan | 1 | (a) | Bradford C | W | 2-0 | A.Turnbull, Wall | 25,000 |
| 21 | | 8 | (a) | Bury | D | 1-1 | Homer | 10,000 |
| 22 | | 22 | (h) | Tottenham H | W | 5-0 | Roberts 2, Connor, Hooper, Meredith | 7,000 |
| 23 | Feb | 5 | (a) | Preston NE | L | 0-1 | | 4,000 |
| 24 | | 12 | (a) | Newcastle U | W | 4-3 | A.Turnbull 2, Blott, Roberts | 20,000 |
| 25 | | 19 | (h) | Liverpool | L | 3-4 | Homer, A.Turnbull, Wall | 45,000 |
| 26 | | 26 | (a) | Aston Villa | L | 1-7 | Meredith | 20,000 |
| 27 | Mar | 5 | (h) | Sheffield U | W | 1-0 | Picken | 40,000 |
| 28 | | 12 | (a) | W Arsenal | D | 0-0 | | 4,000 |
| 29 | | 19 | (h) | Bolton W | W | 5-0 | Halse, Meredith, Picken, J.Turnbull, Wall | 20,000 |
| 30 | | 25 | (h) | Bristol C | W | 2-1 | Picken, J.Turnbull | 50,000 |
| 31 | | 26 | (a) | Chelsea | D | 1-1 | J.Turnbull | 25,000 |
| 32 | | 28 | (a) | Bristol C | L | 1-2 | Meredith | 18,000 |
| 33 | Apr | 2 | (h) | Blackburn R | W | 2-0 | Halse 2 | 20,000 |
| 34 | | 6 | (h) | Everton | W | 3-2 | J.Turnbull 2, Meredith | 5,500 |
| 35 | | 9 | (a) | Nottingham F | L | 0-2 | | 7,000 |
| 36 | | 16 | (h) | Sunderland | W | 2-0 | A.Turnbull, Wall | 12,000 |
| 37 | | 23 | (a) | Everton | D | 3-3 | Homer, A.Turnbull, Wall | 10,000 |
| 38 | | 30 | (h) | Middlesbrough | W | 4-1 | Picken 4 | 10,000 |

FINAL LEAGUE POSITION: 5th in Division One

Appearances

Goals

FA Cup

| 1 | Jan | 15 | (a) | Burnley | L | 0-2 | |
|---|---|---|---|---|---|---|---|

218

| Moger | Stacey | Hayes | Duckworth | Roberts | Bell | Halse | Blott | Bannister | Turnbull A | Wall | Livingstone | Turnbull J | Picken | Downie | Meredith | Rounds | Ford | Homer | Holden | Burgess | Donnelly | Whalley | Connor | Quinn | Hooper | |
|---|---|---|---|---|---|---|---|---|---|---|---|---|---|---|---|---|---|---|---|---|---|---|---|---|---|---|
| 1 | 2 | 3 | 4 | 5 | 6 | 7 | 8 | 9 | 10 | 11 |  |  |  |  |  |  |  |  |  |  |  |  |  |  |  | 1 |
| 1 | 2 | 3 | 4 | 5 | 6 | 7 |  |  | 10 | 11 | 8 | 9 |  |  |  |  |  |  |  |  |  |  |  |  |  | 2 |
| 1 | 2 | 3 | 4 | 5 | 6 | 7 |  |  |  | 11 | 8 | 9 | 10 |  |  |  |  |  |  |  |  |  |  |  |  | 3 |
| 1 | 2 | 3 | 4 | 5 |  | 8 | 7 |  | 10 | 11 |  |  | 9 | 6 |  |  |  |  |  |  |  |  |  |  |  | 4 |
| 1 | 2 | 3 | 4 | 5 |  |  | 8 |  | 10 | 11 |  |  | 9 | 6 | 7 |  |  |  |  |  |  |  |  |  |  | 5 |
| 1 | 2 | 3 |  | 5 |  |  | 8 | 6 | 10 | 11 |  |  | 9 | 4 | 7 |  |  |  |  |  |  |  |  |  |  | 6 |
| 1 | 2 | 3 | 4 | 5 | 6 |  | 8 |  | 10 | 11 |  |  | 9 |  | 7 |  |  |  |  |  |  |  |  |  |  | 7 |
|  | 2 | 3 | 4 | 5 | 6 |  | 8 |  | 10 |  |  |  | 9 |  | 7 | 1 | 11 |  |  |  |  |  |  |  |  | 8 |
| 1 | 2 | 3 | 4 | 5 | 6 |  | 8 |  | 10 | 11 |  |  | 9 |  | 7 |  |  |  |  |  |  |  |  |  |  | 9 |
| 1 | 2 | 3 | 4 | 5 | 6 |  | 8 |  | 10 | 11 |  |  | 9 |  | 7 |  |  |  |  |  |  |  |  |  |  | 10 |
| 1 | 2 | 3 | 4 | 5 |  |  |  | 6 | 10 | 11 | 8 |  |  |  | 7 |  |  | 9 |  |  |  |  |  |  |  | 11 |
| 1 | 2 | 3 | 4 | 5 | 6 |  | 8 |  | 10 | 11 |  |  |  |  | 7 |  |  | 9 |  |  |  |  |  |  |  | 12 |
| 1 | 2 | 3 | 4 | 5 | 6 |  | 8 |  | 10 | 11 |  |  |  |  | 7 |  |  | 9 |  |  |  |  |  |  |  | 13 |
| 1 |  | 3 | 4 | 5 | 6 |  |  |  | 10 | 11 | 8 |  |  |  | 7 |  |  | 9 | 2 |  |  |  |  |  |  | 14 |
| 1 | 2 | 3 | 4 | 5 | 6 |  | 8 |  |  | 11 |  | 10 |  |  | 7 |  |  | 9 |  |  |  |  |  |  |  | 15 |
| 1 |  | 3 | 4 | 5 | 6 |  |  |  | 10 | 11 | 8 |  |  |  | 7 |  |  | 9 | 2 |  |  |  |  |  |  | 16 |
| 1 |  | 3 | 4 | 5 | 6 |  |  |  | 10 | 11 | 9 |  |  |  | 7 |  |  | 8 | 2 |  |  |  |  |  |  | 17 |
| 1 |  |  | 4 | 5 | 6 |  |  |  | 10 | 11 | 9 |  |  |  | 7 |  |  | 8 | 2 | 3 |  |  |  |  |  | 18 |
| 1 | 2 |  | 6 |  |  |  |  |  |  | 4 |  | 8 | 10 |  | 7 |  |  | 9 |  |  | 3 | 5 | 11 |  |  | 19 |
| 1 | 2 | 3 |  |  | 6 |  |  |  | 10 | 11 | 4 | 8 |  |  |  |  |  | 9 |  |  |  | 5 | 7 |  |  | 20 |
| 1 | 2 | 3 |  |  | 6 |  |  |  | 10 |  | 4 | 8 |  |  | 7 |  |  | 9 |  |  |  | 5 | 11 |  |  | 21 |
| 1 | 2 | 3 |  | 5 | 8 | 6 |  |  |  |  | 4 |  |  |  | 7 |  |  | 9 |  |  |  |  | 11 |  | 10 | 22 |
| 1 | 2 | 3 |  | 5 | 9 | 6 |  |  |  | 11 | 4 | 8 |  |  | 7 |  |  |  |  |  |  |  |  |  | 10 | 23 |
| 1 | 2 | 3 |  | 5 | 9 | 6 |  |  | 10 | 11 | 4 | 8 |  |  | 7 |  |  |  |  |  |  |  |  |  |  | 24 |
| 1 | 2 | 3 | 4 | 5 | 8 | 6 |  |  | 10 | 11 |  |  |  |  | 7 |  |  | 9 |  |  |  |  |  |  |  | 25 |
|  | 2 |  | 4 | 5 | 6 | 8 |  |  | 10 |  |  |  |  |  | 7 | 1 |  | 9 | 3 |  |  |  | 11 |  |  | 26 |
| 1 | 2 | 3 | 4 |  | 6 | 8 |  |  |  | 11 | 5 | 9 | 10 |  | 7 |  |  |  |  |  |  |  |  |  |  | 27 |
| 1 | 2 | 3 | 4 |  | 6 | 8 |  |  |  | 11 |  | 9 | 10 |  | 7 |  |  |  |  |  |  | 5 |  |  |  | 28 |
| 1 |  | 3 | 2 | 5 | 6 | 8 |  |  |  | 11 | 4 | 9 | 10 |  | 7 |  |  |  |  |  |  |  |  |  |  | 29 |
| 1 |  | 3 | 2 | 4 | 6 | 8 |  |  |  | 11 |  | 9 | 10 |  | 7 |  |  |  |  |  |  | 5 |  |  |  | 30 |
| 1 | 2 | 3 | 4 |  | 6 | 8 |  |  | 10 | 11 |  | 9 |  |  | 7 |  |  |  |  |  |  | 5 |  |  |  | 31 |
| 1 |  | 3 | 2 |  | 6 | 8 |  |  | 4 | 11 |  | 9 | 10 |  | 7 |  |  |  |  |  |  | 5 |  |  |  | 32 |
| 1 | 2 | 3 | 4 |  |  | 8 |  |  |  |  | 6 | 9 | 10 |  | 7 |  |  |  |  |  |  | 5 | 11 |  |  | 33 |
| 1 | 2 | 3 | 4 |  |  | 8 |  |  |  | 11 | 6 | 9 | 10 |  | 7 |  |  |  |  |  |  | 5 |  |  |  | 34 |
| 1 | 2 | 3 |  | 5 | 6 | 9 |  |  | 10 | 11 | 4 | 8 |  |  | 7 |  |  |  |  |  |  |  |  |  |  | 35 |
| 1 | 2 |  |  | 5 | 6 |  |  |  | 10 | 11 | 4 | 8 |  |  | 7 |  |  | 9 |  |  | 3 |  |  |  |  | 36 |
| 1 |  |  | 4 | 5 | 6 |  |  |  | 10 | 11 | 8 |  |  |  |  |  |  | 9 | 2 |  | 3 |  | 7 |  |  | 37 |
| 1 |  |  | 4 | 5 |  |  |  |  | 10 |  | 6 | 8 |  |  | 7 |  |  | 9 | 2 |  | 3 |  | 11 |  |  | 38 |
| 36 | 32 | 30 | 29 | 28 | 27 | 27 | 10 | 1 | 26 | 32 | 16 | 19 | 19 | 3 | 31 | 2 | 1 | 17 | 7 | 1 | 4 | 9 | 8 | 1 | 2 |  |
|  |  |  |  |  | 4 |  | 6 | 1 |  | 13 | 14 |  | 9 | 7 |  |  | 5 | 8 |  |  |  |  |  | 1 | 1 |  |

Match 11: Bell listed as playing number 6 by the Football League.
Match 19: Duckworth listed as playing number 3 by the Football League.
Match 26: Moger listed as playing number 1 by the Football League.

219

# 1910-11

Secretary-Manager: Ernest Mangnall

| | | | | | | | |
|---|---|---|---|---|---|---|---|
| 1 | Sep | 1 | (a) | W Arsenal | W | 2-1 | Halse, West | 15,000 |
| 2 | | 3 | (h) | Blackburn R | W | 3-2 | Meredith, Turnbull, West | 40,000 |
| 3 | | 10 | (a) | Nottingham F | L | 1-2 | Turnbull | 20,000 |
| 4 | | 17 | (h) | Manchester C | W | 2-1 | Turnbull, West | 60,000 |
| 5 | | 24 | (a) | Everton | W | 1-0 | Turnbull | 25,000 |
| 6 | Oct | 1 | (h) | Sheffield W | W | 3-2 | Wall 2, West | 20,000 |
| 7 | | 8 | (a) | Bristol C | W | 1-0 | Halse | 20,000 |
| 8 | | 15 | (h) | Newcastle U | W | 2-0 | Halse, Turnbull | 50,000 |
| 9 | | 22 | (a) | Tottenham H | D | 2-2 | West 2 | 30,000 |
| 10 | | 29 | (h) | Middlesbrough | L | 1-2 | Turnbull | 35,000 |
| 11 | Nov | 5 | (a) | Preston NE | W | 2-0 | Turnbull, West | 13,000 |
| 12 | | 12 | (h) | Notts C | D | 0-0 | | 13,000 |
| 13 | | 19 | (a) | Oldham A | W | 3-1 | Turnbull 2, Wall | 25,000 |
| 14 | | 26 | (a) | Liverpool | L | 2-3 | Roberts, Turnbull | 8,000 |
| 15 | Dec | 3 | (h) | Bury | W | 3-2 | Homer 2, Turnbull | 7,000 |
| 16 | | 10 | (a) | Sheffield U | L | 0-2 | | 8,000 |
| 17 | | 17 | (h) | Aston Villa | W | 2-0 | Turnbull, West | 20,000 |
| 18 | | 24 | (a) | Sunderland | W | 2-1 | Meredith, Turnbull | 30,000 |
| 19 | | 26 | (h) | W Arsenal | W | 5-0 | Picken 2, West 2, Meredith | 40,000 |
| 20 | | 27 | (a) | Bradford C | L | 0-1 | | 35,000 |
| 21 | | 31 | (a) | Blackburn R | L | 0-1 | | 20,000 |
| 22 | Jan | 2 | (h) | Bradford C | W | 1-0 | Meredith | 40,000 |
| 23 | | 7 | (h) | Nottingham F | W | 4-2 | Homer, Picken, Wall, Needham (og) | 10,000 |
| 24 | | 21 | (a) | Manchester C | D | 1-1 | Turnbull | 40,000 |
| 25 | | 28 | (h) | Everton | D | 2-2 | Duckworth, Wall | 45,000 |
| 26 | Feb | 11 | (h) | Bristol C | W | 3-1 | Homer, Picken, West | 14,000 |
| 27 | | 18 | (a) | Newcastle U | W | 1-0 | Halse | 45,000 |
| 28 | Mar | 4 | (a) | Middlesbrough | D | 2-2 | Turnbull, West | 8,000 |
| 29 | | 11 | (h) | Preston NE | W | 5-0 | WEst 2, Connor, Duckworth, Turnbull | 25,000 |
| 30 | | 15 | (h) | Tottenham H | W | 3-2 | Meredith, Turnbull, West | 10,000 |
| 31 | | 18 | (a) | Notts C | L | 0-1 | | 12,000 |
| 32 | | 25 | (h) | Oldham A | D | 0-0 | | 35,000 |
| 33 | Apr | 1 | (h) | Liverpool | W | 2-0 | West 2 | 20,000 |
| 34 | | 8 | (a) | Bury | W | 3-0 | Homer 2, Halse | 20,000 |
| 35 | | 15 | (h) | Sheffield U | D | 1-1 | West | 22,000 |
| 36 | | 17 | (a) | Sheffield W | D | 0-0 | | 25,000 |
| 37 | | 22 | (a) | Aston Villa | L | 2-4 | Halse 2 | 50,000 |
| 38 | | 29 | (h) | Sunderland | W | 5-1 | Halse 2, Turnbull, West, Milton (og) | 10,000 |

FINAL LEAGUE POSITION: 1st in Division One

Appearances
Goals

FA Cup

| | | | | | | | |
|---|---|---|---|---|---|---|---|
| 1 | Jan | 14 | (a) | Blackpool | W | 2-1 |
| 2 | Feb | 4 | (h) | Aston Villa | W | 2-1 |
| 3 | | 25 | (a) | West Ham U | L | 1-2 |

This page presents a player appearances-and-goals grid (one row per match, numbers are shirt numbers 1–11). Column headers (left to right): Moger, Holden, Stacey, Duckworth, Roberts, Bell, Meredith, Halse, West, Turnbull, Wall, Hayes, Linkson, Livingstone, Picken, Connor, Curry, Hooper, Homer, Whalley, Donnelly, Sheldon, Edmonds, Hofton, Hodge James, Blott.

| Moger | Holden | Stacey | Duckworth | Roberts | Bell | Meredith | Halse | West | Turnbull | Wall | Hayes | Linkson | Livingstone | Picken | Connor | Curry | Hooper | Homer | Whalley | Donnelly | Sheldon | Edmonds | Hofton | Hodge James | Blott | Match |
|---|---|---|---|---|---|---|---|---|---|---|---|---|---|---|---|---|---|---|---|---|---|---|---|---|---|---|
| 1 | 2 | 3 | 4 | 5 | 6 | 7 | 8 | 9 | 10 | 11 | | | | | | | | | | | | | | | | 1 |
| 1 | 2 | 3 | 4 | 5 | 6 | 7 | 8 | 9 | 10 | 11 | | | | | | | | | | | | | | | | 2 |
| 1 | | 2 | 4 | 5 | 6 | 7 | 8 | 9 | 10 | 11 | 3 | | | | | | | | | | | | | | | 3 |
| 1 | | 3 | 4 | 5 | 6 | 7 | 8 | 9 | 10 | 11 | | 2 | | | | | | | | | | | | | | 4 |
| 1 | 2 | 3 | 4 | 5 | 6 | 7 | 8 | 9 | 10 | 11 | | | | | | | | | | | | | | | | 5 |
| 1 | 2 | 3 | 4 | 5 | 6 | 7 | 8 | 9 | 10 | 11 | | | | | | | | | | | | | | | | 6 |
| 1 | 2 | 3 | | 5 | 6 | 7 | 8 | 9 | | 11 | | | 4 | 10 | | | | | | | | | | | | 7 |
| 1 | 2 | 3 | 4 | 5 | | 7 | 8 | 9 | 10 | 11 | | | | 6 | | | | | | | | | | | | 8 |
| 1 | 2 | 3 | 4 | 5 | | 7 | 8 | 9 | 10 | | | | | 6 | 11 | | | | | | | | | | | 9 |
| 1 | | 3 | 4 | 5 | | 7 | 8 | 9 | 10 | | | 2 | | 6 | 11 | | | | | | | | | | | 10 |
| 1 | | 3 | 4 | 5 | | 7 | 8 | 9 | 10 | | | 2 | | | 11 | 6 | | | | | | | | | | 11 |
| 1 | | 3 | 4 | 5 | | 7 | 8 | 9 | 10 | 11 | | 2 | | | | 6 | | | | | | | | | | 12 |
| 1 | | 3 | | 5 | | 7 | 8 | 9 | 10 | 11 | | 2 | 4 | | | 6 | | | | | | | | | | 13 |
| 1 | | 3 | | 5 | | 7 | 8 | | 10 | 11 | | 2 | 4 | | | 6 | 9 | | | | | | | | | 14 |
| 1 | | 3 | | 5 | | 7 | | | 10 | 11 | | 2 | 4 | 8 | | 6 | 9 | | | | | | | | | 15 |
| 1 | 2 | 3 | | 5 | | 7 | | | 10 | 11 | | | 4 | 8 | | | | 9 | 6 | | | | | | | 16 |
| 1 | | 3 | | 5 | 6 | 7 | | 9 | 10 | 11 | | | | 8 | | | | | 4 | 2 | | | | | | 17 |
| 1 | | 3 | | 5 | 6 | 7 | | 9 | 10 | 11 | | | | 8 | | | | | 4 | 2 | | | | | | 18 |
| 1 | | 3 | | 5 | 6 | 7 | | 9 | 10 | 11 | | | | 8 | | | | | 4 | 2 | | | | | | 19 |
| 1 | | 3 | | 5 | | | | 9 | 10 | 11 | | | 6 | 8 | | | | | 4 | 2 | 7 | | | | | 20 |
| 1 | | 3 | | 5 | 6 | | | 9 | 10 | 11 | | | | 8 | | | | | 4 | 2 | 7 | | | | | 21 |
| 1 | | 3 | | | 6 | 7 | | 9 | 10 | 11 | | | 4 | 8 | | | | | 5 | 2 | | | | | | 22 |
| 1 | | 3 | | 5 | 6 | 7 | | | 10 | 11 | | | | 8 | | | | 9 | 4 | 2 | | | | | | 23 |
| 1 | | 3 | 4 | 5 | 6 | 7 | 8 | 9 | 10 | 11 | | | | | | | | | | 2 | | | | | | 24 |
| 1 | | 3 | 4 | 5 | 6 | | 8 | 9 | 10 | 11 | | | | | | | | | | 2 | 7 | | | | | 25 |
| | | 3 | 4 | 5 | 6 | 7 | | 9 | | 11 | | | 10 | | | | | 8 | | 2 | | 1 | | | | 26 |
| | | | 4 | 5 | 6 | 7 | 8 | 9 | 10 | 11 | | | | | | | | | | 3 | | 1 | 2 | | | 27 |
| | | 3 | 4 | | 6 | 7 | | 9 | 10 | 11 | | | | | | | | 8 | 5 | 2 | | 1 | | | | 28 |
| | | 3 | 4 | 5 | 6 | 7 | | 9 | 10 | | | | | 8 | 11 | | | | | | | 1 | 2 | | | 29 |
| | | 3 | 4 | 5 | 6 | 7 | | 9 | 10 | | | | | | 11 | | | 8 | | | | 1 | 2 | | | 30 |
| | | 3 | 4 | 5 | 6 | 7 | | 9 | 10 | | | | | | 11 | | | | | 2 | 8 | 1 | | | | 31 |
| | | 3 | 4 | 5 | 6 | 7 | | 9 | 10 | 11 | | | | | | | | | | | 8 | 1 | 2 | | | 32 |
| | | 3 | | 5 | 6 | 7 | 8 | 9 | 10 | | | | 4 | | 11 | | | | | | | 1 | 2 | | | 33 |
| | | 3 | | 5 | 6 | 7 | 8 | | 11 | 10 | | | | | | | | 9 | 4 | | | 1 | 2 | | | 34 |
| | | 3 | | 5 | 6 | 7 | 8 | | 11 | 10 | | | | | | | | 9 | 4 | | | 1 | 2 | | | 35 |
| | | | | 5 | | 7 | 8 | | 11 | 10 | | | | | | | | 9 | 6 | 3 | | 1 | 2 | 4 | | 36 |
| | | 3 | 4 | | | 7 | 8 | 9 | 10 | | | | | | | | | | 5 | | | 1 | 2 | 6 | 11 | 37 |
| | | 3 | 4 | | | 7 | 8 | 9 | 10 | 11 | | | | | | | | | 5 | 2 | | 1 | 6 | | | 38 |
| **25** | **8** | **36** | **22** | **33** | **27** | **35** | **23** | **35** | **35** | **26** | **1** | **7** | **10** | **14** | **7** | **5** | **2** | **7** | **15** | **15** | **5** | **13** | **9** | **2** | **1** | |
| | | | 2 | 1 | | 5 | 9 | 19 | 18 | 5 | | | 4 | 1 | 6 | | | | | | | | | | | |

2 own-goals

Match 27: Moger listed as playing number 1 by the Football League.
Match 34: Wall listed as playing number 11 by the Football League.
Match 38: Hofton listed as playing number 6 by the Football League.

221

# 1911-12

Secretary-Manager: Ernest Mangnall

| | | | | | | | |
|---|---|---|---|---|---|---|---|
| 1 | Sep | 2 | (a) | Manchester C | D | 0-0 | 35,000 |
| 2 | | 9 | (h) | Everton | W | 2-1 Halse, Turnbull | 20,000 |
| 3 | | 16 | (a) | West Brom A | L | 0-1 | 35,000 |
| 4 | | 23 | (h) | Sunderland | D | 2-2 Stacey 2 | 20,000 |
| 5 | | 30 | (a) | Blackburn R | D | 2-2 West 2 | 30,000 |
| 6 | Oct | 7 | (h) | Sheffield W | W | 3-1 Halse 2, West | 30,000 |
| 7 | | 14 | (a) | Bury | W | 1-0 Turnbull | 18,000 |
| 8 | | 21 | (h) | Middlesbrough | L | 3-4 Halse, Turnbull, West | 20,000 |
| 9 | | 28 | (a) | Notts C | W | 1-0 Turnbull | 15,000 |
| 10 | Nov | 4 | (h) | Tottenham H | L | 1-2 Halse | 20,000 |
| 11 | | 11 | (h) | Preston NE | D | 0-0 | 10,000 |
| 12 | | 18 | (a) | Liverpool | L | 2-3 Roberts, West | 15,000 |
| 13 | | 25 | (h) | Aston Villa | W | 3-1 West 2, Roberts | 20,000 |
| 14 | Dec | 2 | (a) | Newcastle U | W | 3-2 West 2, Halse | 40,000 |
| 15 | | 9 | (h) | Sheffield U | W | 1-0 Halse | 12,000 |
| 16 | | 16 | (a) | Oldham A | D | 2-2 Turnbull, West | 20,000 |
| 17 | | 23 | (h) | Bolton W | W | 2-0 Halse, Turnbull | 20,000 |
| 18 | | 25 | (h) | Bradford C | L | 0-1 | 50,000 |
| 19 | | 26 | (a) | Bradford C | W | 1-0 West | 40,000 |
| 20 | | 30 | (h) | Manchester C | D | 0-0 | 50,000 |
| 21 | Jan | 1 | (h) | W Arsenal | W | 2-0 Meredith, West | 20,000 |
| 22 | | 6 | (a) | Everton | L | 0-4 | 12,000 |
| 23 | | 20 | (h) | West Brom A | L | 1-2 Wall | 8,000 |
| 24 | | 27 | (a) | Sunderland | L | 0-5 | 12,000 |
| 25 | Feb | 10 | (a) | Sheffield W | L | 0-3 | 25,000 |
| 26 | | 17 | (h) | Bury | D | 0-0 | 6,000 |
| 27 | Mar | 2 | (h) | Notts C | W | 2-0 West 2 | 10,000 |
| 28 | | 16 | (a) | Preston NE | D | 0-0 | 7,000 |
| 29 | | 23 | (h) | Liverpool | D | 1-1 Nuttall | 10,000 |
| 30 | | 30 | (a) | Aston Villa | L | 0-6 | 15,000 |
| 31 | Apr | 5 | (a) | W Arsenal | L | 1-2 Turnbull | 14,000 |
| 32 | | 6 | (h) | Newcastle U | L | 0-2 | 14,000 |
| 33 | | 9 | (a) | Tottenham H | D | 1-1 Wall | 20,000 |
| 34 | | 13 | (a) | Sheffield U | L | 1-6 Nuttall | 7,000 |
| 35 | | 17 | (a) | Middlesbrough | L | 0-3 | 5,000 |
| 36 | | 20 | (h) | Oldham A | W | 3-1 West 2, Wall | 15,000 |
| 37 | | 27 | (a) | Bolton W | D | 1-1 Meredith | 20,000 |
| 38 | | 29 | (h) | Blackburn R | W | 3-1 Hamill, Meredith, West | 20,000 |

FINAL LEAGUE POSITION: 13th in Division One

Appearances

Goals

FA Cup

| | | | | | | |
|---|---|---|---|---|---|---|
| 1 | Jan | 13 | (h) | Huddersfield T | W | 3-1 |
| 2 | Feb | 3 | (a) | Coventry C | W | 5-1 |
| 3 | | 24 | (a) | Reading | D | 1-1 |
| R | | 29 | (h) | Reading | W | 3-0 |
| 4 | Mar | 9 | (h) | Blackburn R | D | 1-1 |
| R | | 14 | (a) | Blackburn R | L | 2-4 (After extra-time) |

| Edmonds | Hofton | Stacey | Duckworth | Roberts | Bell | Meredith | Halse | Homer | Turnbull | Wall | Anderson | Hamill | Sheldon | West | Holden | Donnelly | Whalley | Blott | Moger | Linkson | McCarthy | Livingstone | Hodge, James | Royals | Nuttall | Capper | Knowles | Match |
|---|---|---|---|---|---|---|---|---|---|---|---|---|---|---|---|---|---|---|---|---|---|---|---|---|---|---|---|---|
| 1 | 2 | 3 | 4 | 5 | 6 | 7 | 8 | 9 | 10 | 11 |  |  |  |  |  |  |  |  |  |  |  |  |  |  |  |  |  | 1 |
| 1 | 2 | 3 | 4 | 5 | 6 | 7 | 8 |  | 10 | 11 | 9 |  |  |  |  |  |  |  |  |  |  |  |  |  |  |  |  | 2 |
| 1 | 2 | 3 | 4 | 5 | 6 | 7 |  | 9 | 10 | 11 |  | 8 |  |  |  |  |  |  |  |  |  |  |  |  |  |  |  | 3 |
| 1 | 2 | 3 | 4 | 5 | 6 | 7 |  | 9 | 10 | 11 |  | 8 |  |  |  |  |  |  |  |  |  |  |  |  |  |  |  | 4 |
| 1 | 2 | 3 | 4 | 5 | 6 |  | 8 |  | 10 | 11 |  |  | 7 | 9 |  |  |  |  |  |  |  |  |  |  |  |  |  | 5 |
| 1 | 2 | 3 | 4 | 5 | 6 | 7 | 8 |  | 10 | 11 |  |  |  | 9 |  |  |  |  |  |  |  |  |  |  |  |  |  | 6 |
| 1 | 2 | 3 | 4 | 5 | 6 | 7 | 8 |  | 10 | 11 |  |  |  | 9 |  |  |  |  |  |  |  |  |  |  |  |  |  | 7 |
| 1 |  | 3 | 4 | 5 | 6 | 7 | 8 |  | 10 | 11 |  |  |  | 9 | 2 |  |  |  |  |  |  |  |  |  |  |  |  | 8 |
| 1 |  | 3 |  | 5 | 6 | 7 | 8 |  | 10 |  |  |  |  | 9 |  | 2 | 4 | 11 |  |  |  |  |  |  |  |  |  | 9 |
| 1 |  | 3 |  | 5 | 6 | 7 | 8 |  | 10 | 11 |  |  |  | 9 |  | 2 | 4 |  |  |  |  |  |  |  |  |  |  | 10 |
| 1 |  | 3 | 4 | 5 | 6 | 7 | 8 |  | 10 |  |  |  |  | 9 |  | 2 |  | 11 |  |  |  |  |  |  |  |  |  | 11 |
| 1 |  | 3 | 4 | 5 | 6 | 7 | 8 |  | 10 |  |  |  |  | 9 |  | 2 |  | 11 |  |  |  |  |  |  |  |  |  | 12 |
|  |  | 3 | 4 | 5 | 6 | 7 | 8 |  | 10 | 11 |  |  |  | 9 |  |  |  |  | 1 | 2 |  |  |  |  |  |  |  | 13 |
| 1 |  | 3 | 4 | 5 | 6 | 7 | 8 |  | 10 | 11 |  |  |  | 9 |  |  |  |  |  | 2 |  |  |  |  |  |  |  | 14 |
| 1 |  | 3 | 4 | 5 | 6 | 7 | 8 |  | 10 | 11 |  |  |  | 9 |  |  |  |  |  | 2 |  |  |  |  |  |  |  | 15 |
| 1 |  | 3 | 4 | 5 | 6 | 7 | 8 |  | 10 | 11 |  |  |  | 9 |  |  |  |  |  | 2 |  |  |  |  |  |  |  | 16 |
| 1 |  | 3 | 4 | 5 | 6 | 7 | 8 |  | 10 | 11 |  |  |  | 9 |  |  |  |  |  | 2 |  |  |  |  |  |  |  | 17 |
| 1 |  | 3 | 4 | 5 | 6 | 7 | 8 |  | 10 | 11 |  |  |  | 9 |  |  |  |  |  | 2 |  |  |  |  |  |  |  | 18 |
| 1 |  | 3 | 4 | 5 |  | 7 |  |  | 10 | 11 |  | 8 |  | 9 |  |  | 6 |  |  | 2 |  |  |  |  |  |  |  | 19 |
| 1 |  | 3 | 4 | 5 | 6 | 7 |  |  | 10 | 11 |  | 8 |  | 9 |  |  |  |  |  | 2 |  |  |  |  |  |  |  | 20 |
| 1 |  | 3 | 4 | 5 | 6 | 7 |  |  | 10 | 11 |  | 8 |  | 9 |  |  |  |  |  | 2 |  |  |  |  |  |  |  | 21 |
| 1 |  |  | 4 | 5 | 6 | 7 |  |  |  | 11 |  | 8 |  | 9 |  | 2 | 3 | 10 |  |  |  |  |  |  |  |  |  | 22 |
| 1 |  | 3 | 4 | 5 | 6 | 7 | 8 |  | 10 | 11 |  |  |  |  | 2 |  |  |  |  |  | 9 |  |  |  |  |  |  | 23 |
| 1 |  | 3 | 4 | 5 | 6 | 7 |  |  | 10 | 11 |  | 8 |  |  | 2 | 9 |  |  |  |  |  |  |  |  |  |  |  | 24 |
| 1 |  | 3 |  |  | 6 |  | 8 |  | 10 | 11 |  |  | 7 | 9 | 2 |  |  | 5 | 4 |  |  |  |  |  |  |  |  | 25 |
| 1 |  | 3 |  | 5 |  | 7 | 8 |  | 10 | 11 |  |  |  | 9 | 2 |  |  |  |  |  |  | 4 | 6 |  |  |  |  | 26 |
| 1 |  | 3 | 4 | 5 |  |  | 8 |  | 10 | 11 |  |  | 7 | 9 | 2 |  |  |  |  |  |  |  | 6 |  |  |  |  | 27 |
| 1 |  |  | 4 | 5 |  | 7 | 8 |  | 10 | 11 |  |  |  | 9 |  | 3 |  |  |  | 2 |  |  | 6 |  |  |  |  | 28 |
|  |  |  | 4 | 5 |  | 7 | 8 |  |  |  |  |  |  | 9 |  | 3 |  |  |  | 2 |  |  | 6 | 1 | 10 |  | 11 | 29 |
|  |  |  | 4 |  |  | 7 | 8 |  | 10 |  |  |  |  | 9 |  | 3 |  | 11 |  | 2 |  |  | 6 | 1 |  |  | 5 | 30 |
| 1 |  |  | 4 |  | 6 | 7 |  |  | 10 | 11 |  | 8 |  | 9 |  | 3 |  |  |  | 2 |  |  |  |  |  |  | 5 | 31 |
|  |  |  |  |  | 6 | 7 |  |  | 10 | 11 |  | 8 |  | 9 |  | 3 |  |  | 1 | 2 |  |  |  |  |  | 4 | 5 | 32 |
| 1 |  |  |  |  | 6 | 7 |  |  | 10 | 11 |  | 8 |  | 9 |  | 3 |  |  |  | 2 |  |  |  |  | 4 |  | 5 | 33 |
| 1 |  |  |  | 5 | 6 | 7 |  |  |  | 11 |  | 8 |  | 9 |  | 3 |  |  |  | 2 |  |  | 4 |  | 10 |  |  | 34 |
|  |  |  |  | 5 | 6 | 7 |  |  |  | 11 |  | 8 |  | 9 |  | 3 |  |  | 1 | 2 |  |  | 4 |  | 10 |  |  | 35 |
|  |  | 3 |  | 5 | 6 | 7 |  |  |  | 11 |  | 8 |  | 9 |  |  |  |  | 1 | 2 |  |  | 10 |  | 4 |  |  | 36 |
|  |  | 3 |  | 5 | 6 | 7 |  |  |  | 11 |  | 8 |  | 9 |  |  |  |  | 1 | 2 |  |  | 10 |  | 4 |  |  | 37 |
|  |  | 3 |  | 5 | 6 | 7 |  |  |  | 11 |  | 8 |  | 9 |  |  |  |  | 1 | 2 |  |  | 10 |  | 4 |  |  | 38 |
| 30 | 7 | 29 | 26 | 32 | 32 | 35 | 24 | 1 | 30 | 33 | 1 | 16 | 5 | 32 | 6 | 13 | 5 | 6 | 6 | 21 | 1 | 1 | 10 | 2 | 6 | 1 | 7 |  |
|  | 2 |  | 2 |  |  | 3 | 8 |  | 7 | 3 |  | 1 |  | 17 |  |  |  | 2 |  |  |  |  |  |  |  |  |  |  |

Match 18: Moger listed as playing number 1 by the Football League.
Whalley listed as playing number 6 by the Football League.

# 1912-13

Secretary: J.J.Bentley

| 1 | Sep | 2 | (a) | W Arsenal | D | 0-0 | | 11,000 |
|---|---|---|---|---|---|---|---|---|
| 2 | | 7 | (h) | Manchester C | L | 0-1 | | 40,000 |
| 3 | | 14 | (a) | West Brom A | W | 2-1 | Livingstone, Turnbull | 25,000 |
| 4 | | 21 | (h) | Everton | W | 2-0 | West 2 | 40,000 |
| 5 | | 28 | (a) | Sheffield W | D | 3-3 | West 2, Turnbull | 30,000 |
| 6 | Oct | 5 | (h) | Blackburn R | D | 1-1 | Wall | 45,000 |
| 7 | | 12 | (a) | Derby C | L | 1-2 | Turnbull | 15,000 |
| 8 | | 19 | (h) | Tottenham H | W | 2-0 | Turnbull, West | 12,000 |
| 9 | | 26 | (a) | Middlesbrough | L | 2-3 | Nuttall 2 | 10,000 |
| 10 | Nov | 2 | (h) | Notts C | W | 2-1 | Anderson, Meredith | 12,000 |
| 11 | | 9 | (a) | Sunderland | L | 1-3 | West | 20,000 |
| 12 | | 16 | (a) | Aston Villa | L | 2-4 | Wall, West | 20,000 |
| 13 | | 23 | (h) | Liverpool | W | 3-1 | Anderson 2, Wall | 8,000 |
| 14 | | 30 | (a) | Bolton W | L | 1-2 | Wall | 25,000 |
| 15 | Dec | 7 | (h) | Sheffield U | W | 4-0 | Anderson, Turnbull, Wall, West | 12,000 |
| 16 | | 14 | (a) | Newcastle U | W | 3-1 | West 3 | 20,000 |
| 17 | | 21 | (h) | Oldham A | D | 0-0 | | 30,000 |
| 18 | | 25 | (a) | Chelsea | W | 4-1 | West 2, Anderson, Whalley | 33,000 |
| 19 | | 26 | (h) | Chelsea | W | 4-2 | Turnbull 2, Anderson, Wall | 20,000 |
| 20 | | 28 | (a) | Manchester C | W | 2-0 | West 2 | 38,000 |
| 21 | Jan | 1 | (h) | Bradford C | W | 2-0 | Anderson 2 | 30,000 |
| 22 | | 4 | (h) | West Brom A | D | 1-1 | Roberts | 25,000 |
| 23 | | 18 | (a) | Everton | L | 1-4 | Hamill | 20,000 |
| 24 | | 25 | (h) | Sheffield W | W | 2-0 | West, Whalley | 45,000 |
| 25 | Feb | 8 | (a) | Blackburn R | D | 0-0 | | 38,000 |
| 26 | | 15 | (h) | Derby C | W | 4-0 | West 2, Anderson, Turnbull | 30,000 |
| 27 | Mar | 1 | (h) | Middlesbrough | L | 2-3 | Meredith, Whalley | 15,000 |
| 28 | | 8 | (a) | Notts C | W | 2-1 | Anderson, Turnbull | 10,000 |
| 29 | | 15 | (h) | Sunderland | L | 1-3 | Sheldon | 15,000 |
| 30 | | 21 | (h) | W Arsenal | W | 2-0 | Anderson, Whalley | 20,000 |
| 31 | | 22 | (h) | Aston Villa | W | 4-0 | Turnbull, Stacey, Wall, West | 30,000 |
| 32 | | 25 | (a) | Bradford C | L | 0-1 | | 25,000 |
| 33 | | 29 | (a) | Liverpool | W | 2-0 | Wall, West | 12,000 |
| 34 | | 31 | (a) | Tottenham H | D | 1-1 | Blott | 12,000 |
| 35 | Apr | 5 | (h) | Bolton W | W | 2-1 | Anderson, Wall | 30,000 |
| 36 | | 12 | (a) | Sheffield U | L | 1-2 | Wall | 12,000 |
| 37 | | 19 | (h) | Newcastle U | W | 3-0 | Hunter 2, West | 10,000 |
| 38 | | 26 | (a) | Oldham A | D | 0-0 | | 3,000 |

FINAL LEAGUE POSITION: 4th in Division One

Appearances
Goals

FA Cup

| 1 | Jan | 11 | (h) | Coventry C | D | 1-1 | |
|---|---|---|---|---|---|---|---|
| R | | 16 | (a) | Coventry C | W | 2-1 | |
| 2 | Feb | 1 | (a) | Plymouth A | W | 2-0 | |
| 3 | | 22 | (a) | Oldham A | D | 0-0 | |
| R | | 26 | (h) | Oldham A | L | 1-2 | |

| Beale | Linkson | Stacey | Duckworth | Roberts | Bell | Meredith | Hamill | West | Turnbull | Wall | Holden | Whalley | Livingstone | Nuttall | Donnelly | Hodge, James | Anderson | Sheldon | Knowles | Gipps | Blott | Mew | Hunter | |
|---|---|---|---|---|---|---|---|---|---|---|---|---|---|---|---|---|---|---|---|---|---|---|---|---|
| 1 | 2 | 3 | 4 | 5 | 6 | 7 | 8 | 9 | 10 | 11 | | | | | | | | | | | | | | 1 |
| 1 | 2 | 3 | 4 | 5 | 6 | 7 | 8 | 9 | 10 | 11 | | | | | | | | | | | | | | 2 |
| 1 | | 3 | | 5 | 6 | 7 | | 9 | 10 | 11 | 2 | 4 | 8 | | | | | | | | | | | 3 |
| 1 | | 3 | 2 | 5 | 6 | 7 | | 9 | 10 | 11 | | 4 | | 8 | | | | | | | | | | 4 |
| 1 | 2 | 3 | 4 | | 6 | 7 | | 9 | 10 | 11 | | 5 | | 8 | | | | | | | | | | 5 |
| 1 | 2 | 3 | | 5 | 6 | 7 | | 9 | 10 | 11 | | 4 | | 8 | | | | | | | | | | 6 |
| 1 | 2 | | 4 | 5 | 6 | 7 | | 9 | 10 | 11 | | | | 8 | 3 | | | | | | | | | 7 |
| 1 | 2 | 3 | | 5 | | 7 | | 9 | 10 | 11 | | 4 | | 8 | | 6 | | | | | | | | 8 |
| 1 | 2 | 3 | 4 | 5 | | 7 | | 9 | 10 | 11 | | | | 8 | | 6 | | | | | | | | 9 |
| 1 | 2 | 3 | 4 | 5 | 6 | 7 | | | 10 | 11 | | | | 8 | | | 9 | | | | | | | 10 |
| 1 | | 3 | | 5 | | 7 | | 9 | 10 | 11 | 2 | 4 | | | | 6 | 8 | | | | | | | 11 |
| 1 | 2 | 3 | 4 | 5 | 6 | | | 9 | 10 | 11 | | | | 8 | | 7 | | | | | | | | 12 |
| 1 | | 3 | 2 | 5 | 6 | 7 | | | 10 | 11 | | | | 8 | | 9 | | 4 | | | | | | 13 |
| 1 | | 3 | 2 | | 6 | 7 | | | 10 | 11 | | 5 | | 8 | | 9 | | 4 | | | | | | 14 |
| 1 | 2 | 3 | 4 | 5 | 6 | 7 | | 10 | 8 | 11 | | | | | | 9 | | | | | | | | 15 |
| 1 | 2 | 3 | | 5 | 6 | | | 10 | 8 | 11 | | 4 | | | | 9 | | 7 | | | | | | 16 |
| 1 | 2 | 3 | 4 | 5 | 6 | | | 10 | 8 | 11 | | | | | | 9 | | 7 | | | | | | 17 |
| 1 | 2 | 3 | 4 | | | | | 10 | 8 | 11 | | 6 | | | | 9 | | 7 | | 5 | | | | 18 |
| 1 | 2 | 3 | 4 | | | | | 10 | 8 | 11 | | 5 | | | | 9 | | 7 | | 6 | | | | 19 |
| 1 | | 3 | 4 | 5 | | 7 | | 10 | 8 | 11 | | 6 | | | | 2 | 9 | | | | | | | 20 |
| 1 | | 3 | 4 | 5 | | | | 10 | 8 | 11 | | 6 | | | | 2 | 9 | 7 | | | | | | 21 |
| 1 | | 3 | 4 | 5 | | 7 | | 10 | 8 | 11 | | 6 | | | | 2 | 9 | | | | | | | 22 |
| 1 | | 3 | 4 | | 6 | | | 10 | 8 | 11 | | 5 | | | | 9 | 2 | 7 | | | | | | 23 |
| 1 | | 3 | 4 | 5 | | 7 | 8 | 10 | | 11 | | 6 | | | | 2 | 9 | | | | | | | 24 |
| 1 | | 3 | 4 | 5 | | 7 | | 10 | 8 | 11 | | 6 | | | | 2 | 9 | | | | | | | 25 |
| 1 | | 3 | 4 | 5 | | 7 | | 10 | 8 | | | 6 | | | | 2 | 9 | | 11 | | | | | 26 |
| | | 3 | 4 | | 6 | 7 | 8 | 10 | 9 | 11 | | 5 | | | | 2 | | | | | | 1 | | 27 |
| 1 | | 3 | 4 | | 6 | | | 10 | 8 | 11 | | 5 | | | | 2 | 9 | 7 | | | | | | 28 |
| 1 | 2 | 3 | | | 6 | | | 10 | 8 | 11 | | 5 | 4 | | | | 9 | 7 | | | | | | 29 |
| 1 | 2 | 3 | 4 | | 6 | | | 10 | 8 | 11 | | 5 | | | | | 9 | 7 | | | | | | 30 |
| 1 | 2 | 3 | 4 | | 6 | | | 10 | 8 | 11 | | 5 | | | | | 9 | 7 | | | | | | 31 |
| 1 | | 3 | | | 6 | | 4 | 10 | 8 | 11 | | 5 | | | | 2 | 9 | 7 | | | | | | 32 |
| 1 | | 3 | | | 6 | | 4 | 10 | 8 | 11 | | 5 | | | | 2 | | 7 | | | 9 | | | 33 |
| 1 | | 3 | | | 6 | | 4 | 10 | 8 | | | 5 | | | | 2 | 9 | 7 | 11 | | | | | 34 |
| 1 | | 3 | | | 6 | | 4 | 10 | 8 | 11 | | 5 | | | | 2 | 9 | 7 | | | | | | 35 |
| 1 | | 3 | | 5 | 6 | | 4 | 10 | 8 | 11 | | | | | | 2 | 9 | 7 | | | | | | 36 |
| 1 | | 3 | | 5 | 6 | 7 | 4 | 10 | 8 | 11 | | | | | | 2 | | | | | | | 9 | 37 |
| 1 | | 3 | | 5 | 6 | 7 | 4 | 10 | 8 | 11 | | | | | | 2 | | | | | | | 9 | 38 |
| 37 | 17 | 36 | 24 | 24 | 26 | 22 | 15 | 36 | 35 | 36 | 2 | 26 | 2 | 10 | 1 | 19 | 24 | 16 | 2 | 2 | 2 | 1 | 3 | |
| | 1 | | 1 | | 2 | 1 | 21 | 10 | 10 | | 4 | 1 | 2 | | | | 12 | 1 | | | 1 | | 2 | |

225

# 1913-14

Secretary: J.J.Bentley

| | | | | | | | |
|---|---|---|---|---|---|---|---|
| 1 | Sep | 6 | (a) | Sheffield W | W | 3-1 | Turnbull, West, Spoors (og) | 32,000 |
| 2 | | 8 | (h) | Sunderland | W | 3-1 | Anderson, Turnbull, Whalley | 25,000 |
| 3 | | 13 | (h) | Bolton W | L | 0-1 | | 45,000 |
| 4 | | 20 | (a) | Chelsea | W | 2-0 | Anderson, Wall | 40,000 |
| 5 | | 27 | (h) | Oldham A | W | 4-1 | West 2, Anderson, Wall | 55,000 |
| 6 | Oct | 4 | (h) | Tottenham H | W | 3-1 | Stacey, Wall, Whalley | 25,000 |
| 7 | | 11 | (a) | Burnley | W | 2-1 | Anderson 2 | 30,000 |
| 8 | | 18 | (h) | Preston NE | W | 3-0 | Anderson 3 | 30,000 |
| 9 | | 25 | (a) | Newcastle U | W | 1-0 | West | 35,000 |
| 10 | Nov | 1 | (h) | Liverpool | W | 3-0 | Wall 2, West | 30,000 |
| 11 | | 8 | (a) | Aston Villa | L | 1-3 | Woodcock | 20,000 |
| 12 | | 15 | (h) | Middlesbrough | L | 0-1 | | 15,000 |
| 13 | | 22 | (a) | Sheffield U | L | 0-2 | | 30,000 |
| 14 | | 29 | (h) | Derby C | D | 3-3 | Turnbull 2, Meredith | 20,000 |
| 15 | Dec | 6 | (a) | Manchester C | W | 2-0 | Anderson 2 | 40,000 |
| 16 | | 13 | (h) | Bradford C | D | 1-1 | Knowles | 18,000 |
| 17 | | 20 | (a) | Blackburn R | W | 1-0 | Crompton (og) | 35,000 |
| 18 | | 25 | (h) | Everton | L | 0-1 | | 25,000 |
| 19 | | 26 | (a) | Everton | L | 0-5 | | 40,000 |
| 20 | | 27 | (h) | Sheffield W | W | 2-1 | Meredith, Wall | 10,000 |
| 21 | Jan | 1 | (h) | West Brom A | W | 1-0 | Wall | 35,000 |
| 22 | | 3 | (a) | Bolton W | L | 1-6 | West | 35,000 |
| 23 | | 17 | (h) | Chelsea | L | 0-1 | | 20,000 |
| 24 | | 24 | (a) | Oldham A | D | 2-2 | Wall, Woodcock | 10,000 |
| 25 | Feb | 7 | (a) | Tottenham H | L | 1-2 | Wall | 22,000 |
| 26 | | 14 | (h) | Burnley | L | 0-1 | | 35,000 |
| 27 | | 21 | (a) | Middlesbrough | L | 1-3 | Anderson | 12,000 |
| 28 | | 28 | (h) | Newcastle U | D | 2-2 | Anderson, Potts | 30,000 |
| 29 | Mar | 5 | (a) | Preston NE | L | 2-4 | Travers, Wall | 12,000 |
| 30 | | 14 | (h) | Aston Villa | L | 0-6 | | 30,000 |
| 31 | Apr | 4 | (a) | Derby C | L | 2-4 | Anderson, Travers | 7,000 |
| 32 | | 10 | (a) | Sunderland | L | 0-2 | | 20,000 |
| 33 | | 11 | (h) | Manchester C | L | 0-1 | | 36,000 |
| 34 | | 13 | (a) | West Brom A | L | 1-2 | Travers | 20,000 |
| 35 | | 15 | (a) | Liverpool | W | 2-1 | Travers, Wall | 28,000 |
| 36 | | 18 | (a) | Bradford C | D | 1-1 | Thomson | 10,000 |
| 37 | | 22 | (h) | Sheffield U | W | 2-1 | Anderson 2 | 4,500 |
| 38 | | 25 | (h) | Blackburn R | D | 0-0 | | 20,000 |

FINAL LEAGUE POSITION: 14th in Division One

Appearances
Goals

FA Cup

| | | | | | | |
|---|---|---|---|---|---|---|
| 1 | Jan | 10 | (a) | Swindon T | L | 0-1 |

226

Appearances and goals grid (players across the top, match numbers 1–38 down the right):

| Beale | Hodge, James | Stacey | Duckworth | Whalley | Hamill | Meredith | Turnbull | Anderson | West | Wall | Knowles | Cashmore | Hooper | Chorlton | Gipps | Woodcock | Mew | Haywood | Thomson | Potts | Roberts | Hodge, John | Livingstone | Hudson | Norton | Travers | Rowe | Hunter | Royals | Match |
|---|---|---|---|---|---|---|---|---|---|---|---|---|---|---|---|---|---|---|---|---|---|---|---|---|---|---|---|---|---|---|
| 1 | 2 | 3 | 4 | 5 | 6 | 7 | 8 | 9 | 10 | 11 |  |  |  |  |  |  |  |  |  |  |  |  |  |  |  |  |  |  |  | 1 |
| 1 | 2 | 3 | 4 | 5 | 6 | 7 | 8 | 9 | 10 | 11 |  |  |  |  |  |  |  |  |  |  |  |  |  |  |  |  |  |  |  | 2 |
| 1 | 2 | 3 | 4 | 5 |  | 7 |  | 9 | 10 | 11 | 6 | 8 |  |  |  |  |  |  |  |  |  |  |  |  |  |  |  |  |  | 3 |
| 1 | 2 | 3 | 4 | 5 | 6 | 7 | 8 | 9 | 10 | 11 |  |  |  |  |  |  |  |  |  |  |  |  |  |  |  |  |  |  |  | 4 |
| 1 | 2 | 3 | 4 | 5 | 6 | 7 | 8 | 9 | 10 | 11 |  |  |  |  |  |  |  |  |  |  |  |  |  |  |  |  |  |  |  | 5 |
| 1 | 2 | 3 | 4 | 5 | 6 | 7 |  | 9 | 10 | 11 |  |  | 8 |  |  |  |  |  |  |  |  |  |  |  |  |  |  |  |  | 6 |
| 1 |  | 3 | 4 | 5 | 6 | 7 | 8 | 9 | 10 | 11 |  |  |  | 2 |  |  |  |  |  |  |  |  |  |  |  |  |  |  |  | 7 |
| 1 | 2 | 3 | 4 | 5 | 6 | 7 | 8 | 9 | 10 | 11 |  |  |  |  |  |  |  |  |  |  |  |  |  |  |  |  |  |  |  | 8 |
| 1 | 2 | 3 |  | 5 |  | 7 | 8 | 9 | 10 | 11 | 6 |  |  |  | 4 |  |  |  |  |  |  |  |  |  |  |  |  |  |  | 9 |
| 1 | 2 | 3 |  | 5 | 6 | 7 |  | 9 | 10 | 11 |  |  |  |  | 4 | 8 |  |  |  |  |  |  |  |  |  |  |  |  |  | 10 |
| 1 | 2 | 3 |  | 5 | 6 | 7 |  | 9 | 10 | 11 |  |  |  |  | 4 | 8 |  |  |  |  |  |  |  |  |  |  |  |  |  | 11 |
| 1 | 2 | 3 | 4 | 5 | 6 | 7 | 8 | 9 |  | 11 |  |  | 10 |  |  |  |  |  |  |  |  |  |  |  |  |  |  |  |  | 12 |
|  | 2 | 3 |  | 5 |  | 7 | 8 | 9 | 10 | 11 |  |  |  |  | 4 |  | 1 | 6 |  |  |  |  |  |  |  |  |  |  |  | 13 |
|  | 2 | 3 |  | 5 |  | 7 | 8 | 9 |  | 11 | 10 |  |  |  | 4 |  | 1 | 6 |  |  |  |  |  |  |  |  |  |  |  | 14 |
| 1 | 2 | 3 |  | 5 | 6 | 7 | 8 | 9 | 10 | 11 | 4 |  |  |  |  |  |  |  |  |  |  |  |  |  |  |  |  |  |  | 15 |
| 1 | 2 | 3 |  |  | 6 | 7 | 8 | 9 | 10 |  | 5 |  |  |  |  |  |  | 4 | 11 |  |  |  |  |  |  |  |  |  |  | 16 |
| 1 | 2 | 3 |  |  | 6 | 7 | 8 | 9 | 10 | 11 | 5 |  |  |  |  |  |  | 4 |  |  |  |  |  |  |  |  |  |  |  | 17 |
| 1 | 2 | 3 |  | 5 | 6 | 7 | 8 | 9 | 10 | 11 | 4 |  |  |  |  |  |  |  |  |  |  |  |  |  |  |  |  |  |  | 18 |
| 1 | 2 | 3 |  | 5 | 6 | 7 | 10 |  | 9 | 11 | 4 |  |  |  |  |  |  |  | 8 |  |  |  |  |  |  |  |  |  |  | 19 |
| 1 |  | 3 |  |  | 6 | 7 |  |  |  | 11 | 4 |  | 10 |  | 9 |  |  |  | 8 | 2 | 5 |  |  |  |  |  |  |  |  | 20 |
| 1 | 2 | 3 |  |  | 5 | 7 |  | 9 |  | 11 |  |  |  | 4 | 10 |  |  | 6 | 8 |  |  |  |  |  |  |  |  |  |  | 21 |
| 1 |  | 3 |  |  |  | 7 | 8 | 9 | 10 | 11 | 5 |  |  |  | 4 |  |  | 6 |  | 2 |  |  |  |  |  |  |  |  |  | 22 |
| 1 | 2 | 3 |  | 5 | 6 | 7 |  |  | 10 | 11 | 4 |  |  |  | 9 |  |  |  | 8 |  |  |  |  |  |  |  |  |  |  | 23 |
| 1 | 2 | 3 |  |  |  | 7 |  | 9 | 10 |  | 4 |  |  |  | 8 |  |  |  |  |  |  |  |  | 5 | 6 | 11 |  |  |  | 24 |
| 1 | 2 | 3 |  |  | 6 | 7 | 10 | 9 |  | 11 |  |  |  |  |  |  |  |  |  |  |  |  |  | 5 | 4 |  | 8 |  |  | 25 |
| 1 | 2 | 3 |  |  |  | 7 |  | 9 | 5 | 6 |  |  |  |  | 8 |  |  | 4 |  |  |  |  |  |  |  | 11 | 10 |  |  | 26 |
| 1 |  | 3 |  |  | 6 | 7 |  | 9 | 10 | 11 | 5 |  | 2 |  | 8 |  |  | 4 |  |  |  |  |  |  |  |  |  |  |  | 27 |
| 1 |  | 3 |  |  | 6 |  |  | 9 |  | 11 |  |  | 2 |  |  |  |  | 4 |  | 8 | 5 |  |  |  |  | 7 | 10 |  |  | 28 |
| 1 |  | 3 |  |  | 6 |  |  | 9 |  | 11 |  |  |  |  |  |  |  | 4 |  | 8 | 5 |  |  |  |  | 7 | 10 | 2 |  | 29 |
| 1 |  | 3 |  |  |  | 7 |  | 9 |  | 11 |  |  | 2 |  | 8 |  |  | 6 |  |  |  |  | 4 |  |  | 10 |  | 5 |  | 30 |
| 1 |  | 3 |  |  | 6 | 7 |  | 9 | 10 |  |  |  |  |  |  |  |  | 4 |  |  | 2 |  |  |  |  | 11 | 8 | 5 |  | 31 |
|  | 2 |  |  |  |  |  |  | 9 | 10 |  |  |  |  |  | 4 | 6 |  |  | 11 |  |  |  |  | 3 | 7 | 8 |  | 5 | 1 | 32 |
|  | 3 |  |  |  |  | 7 |  | 9 | 10 |  |  |  |  | 4 | 6 |  |  |  | 11 |  |  |  |  | 2 |  | 8 |  | 5 | 1 | 33 |
|  | 3 |  |  |  |  | 7 |  | 9 |  |  |  |  |  | 4 | 6 | 10 |  |  | 11 |  |  |  |  | 2 |  | 8 |  | 5 | 1 | 34 |
|  | 3 |  |  |  | 6 | 7 |  | 9 |  | 11 | 4 |  |  |  |  | 10 |  |  |  |  |  |  |  | 2 |  | 8 |  | 5 | 1 | 35 |
|  | 3 |  |  |  | 6 | 7 |  |  | 10 |  | 4 | 9 |  |  |  |  |  |  | 11 |  |  |  |  | 2 |  | 8 |  | 5 | 1 | 36 |
| 1 | 4 | 3 |  |  |  | 7 |  | 9 | 10 |  | 5 |  |  | 6 |  |  |  |  |  |  |  |  |  |  | 2 | 11 | 8 |  |  | 37 |
| 1 |  | 3 |  |  | 6 |  |  | 9 | 10 |  | 5 |  |  |  | 4 |  |  |  | 11 |  |  |  |  | 2 | 7 | 8 |  |  |  | 38 |
| 31 | 28 | 34 | 9 | 18 | 26 | 34 | 17 | 32 | 30 | 29 | 18 | 3 | 3 | 4 | 11 | 11 | 2 | 14 | 6 | 6 | 2 | 4 | 3 | 9 | 8 | 13 | 1 | 7 | 5 |  |
|  | 1 |  | 2 |  | 2 | 4 | 15 | 6 | 11 | 1 |  |  |  |  | 2 |  |  | 1 | 1 |  |  |  |  |  |  | 4 |  |  |  |  |

2 own-goals

# 1914-15

Manager: John Robson

| | | | | | | | |
|---|---|---|---|---|---|---|---|
| 1 | Sep | 2 | (h) | Oldham A | L | 1-3 | O'Connell | 13,000 |
| 2 | | 5 | (h) | Manchester C | D | 0-0 | | 20,000 |
| 3 | | 12 | (a) | Bolton W | L | 0-3 | | 10,000 |
| 4 | | 19 | (h) | Blackburn R | W | 2-0 | West 2 | 15,000 |
| 5 | | 26 | (a) | Notts C | L | 2-4 | Turnbull, Wall | 12,000 |
| 6 | Oct | 3 | (h) | Sunderland | W | 3-0 | Anderson, Stacey, West | 16,000 |
| 7 | | 10 | (a) | Sheffield W | L | 0-1 | | 19,000 |
| 8 | | 17 | (h) | West Brom A | D | 0-0 | | 18,000 |
| 9 | | 24 | (a) | Everton | L | 2-4 | Anderson, Wall | 15,000 |
| 10 | | 31 | (h) | Chelsea | D | 2-2 | Anderson, Hunter | 15,000 |
| 11 | Nov | 7 | (a) | Bradford C | L | 2-4 | Hunter, West | 12,000 |
| 12 | | 14 | (h) | Burnley | L | 0-2 | | 12,000 |
| 13 | | 21 | (a) | Tottenham H | L | 0-2 | | 12,000 |
| 14 | | 28 | (h) | Newcastle U | W | 1-0 | West | 5,000 |
| 15 | Dec | 5 | (a) | Middlesbrough | D | 1-1 | Anderson | 7,000 |
| 16 | | 12 | (h) | Sheffield U | L | 1-2 | Anderson | 8,000 |
| 17 | | 19 | (a) | Aston Villa | D | 3-3 | Norton 2, Anderson | 10,000 |
| 18 | | 26 | (a) | Liverpool | D | 1-1 | Stacey | 25,000 |
| 19 | Jan | 1 | (h) | Bradford | L | 1-2 | Anderson | 8,000 |
| 20 | | 2 | (a) | Manchester C | D | 1-1 | West | 30,000 |
| 21 | | 16 | (h) | Bolton W | W | 4-1 | Potts 2, Stacey, Woodcock | 8,000 |
| 22 | | 23 | (a) | Blackburn R | D | 3-3 | Woodcock 2, Robinson (og) | 7,000 |
| 23 | | 30 | (h) | Notts C | D | 2-2 | Potts, Stacey | 7,000 |
| 24 | Feb | 6 | (a) | Sunderland | L | 0-1 | | 5,000 |
| 25 | | 13 | (h) | Sheffield W | W | 2-0 | West, Woodcock | 7,000 |
| 26 | | 20 | (a) | West Brom A | D | 0-0 | | 10,000 |
| 27 | | 27 | (h) | Everton | L | 1-2 | Woodcock | 10,000 |
| 28 | Mar | 13 | (h) | Bradford C | W | 1-0 | Potts | 14,000 |
| 29 | | 20 | (a) | Burnley | L | 0-3 | | 12,000 |
| 30 | | 27 | (h) | Tottenham H | D | 1-1 | Woodcock | 15,000 |
| 31 | Apr | 2 | (h) | Liverpool | W | 2-0 | Anderson 2 | 18,000 |
| 32 | | 3 | (a) | Newcastle U | L | 0-2 | | 12,000 |
| 33 | | 5 | (a) | Bradford | L | 0-5 | | 15,000 |
| 34 | | 6 | (a) | Oldham A | L | 0-1 | | 2,000 |
| 35 | | 10 | (h) | Middlesbrough | D | 2-2 | O'Connell, Turnbull | 15,000 |
| 36 | | 17 | (a) | Sheffield U | L | 1-3 | West | 14,000 |
| 37 | | 19 | (a) | Chelsea | W | 3-1 | Norton, West, Woodcock | 13,000 |
| 38 | | 26 | (h) | Aston Villa | W | 1-0 | Anderson | 8,000 |

FINAL LEAGUE POSITION: 18th in Division One

Appearances
Goals

FA Cup

| | | | | | | | |
|---|---|---|---|---|---|---|---|
| 1 | Jan | 9 | (a) | Sheffield W | L | 0-1 | |

228

| Beale | Hodge, John | Stacey | Hunter | O'Connell | Knowles | Meredith | Anderson | Travers | West | Wall | Woodcock | Norton | Gipps | Turnbull | Potts | Hudson | Whalley | Mew | Hodge, James | Cookson | Spratt | Haywood | Allman | Prince | Montgomery | |
|---|---|---|---|---|---|---|---|---|---|---|---|---|---|---|---|---|---|---|---|---|---|---|---|---|---|---|
| 1 | 2 | 3 | 4 | 5 | 6 | 7 | 8 | 9 | 10 | 11 | | | | | | | | | | | | | | | | 1 |
| 1 | 2 | 3 | 4 | 5 | 6 | 7 | | 8 | 9 | 11 | 10 | | | | | | | | | | | | | | | 2 |
| 1 | 2 | 3 | 4 | 5 | 6 | | | 8 | 9 | 11 | 10 | 7 | | | | | | | | | | | | | | 3 |
| 1 | 2 | 3 | 5 | | 6 | 7 | | 9 | 10 | 11 | | | 4 | | 8 | | | | | | | | | | | 4 |
| 1 | 2 | 3 | 5 | | 6 | 7 | | 9 | 10 | 11 | | | 4 | | 8 | | | | | | | | | | | 5 |
| 1 | 2 | 3 | 5 | 4 | 6 | 7 | | 9 | 10 | | | 11 | | | 8 | | | | | | | | | | | 6 |
| 1 | 2 | 3 | 4 | 5 | 6 | 7 | 9 | 8 | 10 | | | 11 | | | | | | | | | | | | | | 7 |
| 1 | 2 | 3 | | | 5 | 6 | | 9 | | 10 | | 7 | 11 | 4 | | 8 | | | | | | | | | | 8 |
| 1 | 2 | | | 4 | 6 | | | 9 | 8 | 10 | 7 | 11 | 3 | | | 5 | | | | | | | | | | 9 |
| 1 | 2 | 3 | 5 | | 6 | | | 9 | 8 | | 7 | 11 | 4 | 10 | | | | | | | | | | | | 10 |
| 1 | 2 | 3 | 5 | | 6 | | | 9 | 10 | | 7 | 11 | 4 | | 8 | | | | | | | | | | | 11 |
| | 2 | 3 | 5 | 4 | 6 | 7 | | 9 | | 11 | 10 | | | | 8 | | | 1 | | | | | | | | 12 |
| 1 | | 2 | 6 | 4 | | | | 9 | | 10 | 7 | | 11 | 5 | 8 | | | | 3 | | | | | | | 13 |
| 1 | 2 | 3 | 5 | 4 | 6 | | | 9 | | 10 | 7 | | 11 | | 8 | | | | | | | | | | | 14 |
| 1 | 2 | 3 | 5 | 4 | 6 | | | 9 | | 10 | 7 | | 11 | | 8 | | | | | | | | | | | 15 |
| 1 | 2 | 3 | 5 | 4 | 6 | | | 9 | | 10 | 7 | | 11 | | 8 | | | | | | | | | | | 16 |
| 1 | 2 | 3 | 5 | 4 | | 7 | 9 | | 10 | | | 11 | 6 | | 8 | | | | | | | | | | | 17 |
| 1 | 2 | 3 | | 5 | | 7 | 9 | | 10 | | | 11 | 6 | | 8 | | | | | 4 | | | | | | 18 |
| 1 | 2 | 3 | | 5 | | 7 | 9 | | 10 | | | 11 | 4 | | 8 | | | | | 6 | | | | | | 19 |
| 1 | 2 | 3 | | 5 | | 7 | 9 | | 10 | | | 11 | 4 | | 8 | | | | | 6 | | | | | | 20 |
| 1 | 2 | 3 | | 5 | 4 | 7 | | | 10 | | 6 | 11 | | | 8 | | | | | 9 | | | | | | 21 |
| 1 | 2 | 3 | | 5 | 4 | 7 | | | 10 | | 9 | 11 | | | 8 | | | | | 6 | | | | | | 22 |
| 1 | 2 | 3 | | 5 | 4 | 7 | | | 10 | | 9 | 11 | | | 8 | | | | | 6 | | | | | | 23 |
| 1 | | 3 | | 5 | | 7 | | | 10 | | 9 | 11 | | | 8 | | | | | 6 | 2 | 4 | | | | 24 |
| 1 | | | | 5 | | 7 | | | 10 | | 9 | 11 | | | 8 | | | | | 6 | 3 | 4 | 2 | | | 25 |
| 1 | | | | 5 | | | | | 10 | | 7 | 9 | 11 | | 8 | | | | | 6 | 3 | 4 | 2 | | | 26 |
| 1 | | | | 5 | | 7 | | | 9 | | | 11 | 6 | | 8 | | | | | | 3 | 4 | 2 | | 10 | 27 |
| 1 | | | | 5 | | | 10 | | 9 | 11 | 7 | | | | 8 | | | | | 6 | 3 | | 2 | | 4 | 28 |
| 1 | | | | 5 | | | 10 | | 9 | 11 | 7 | | | | 8 | | | | | 6 | 3 | | 2 | | 4 | 29 |
| 1 | | | | 5 | | 7 | | | 10 | 11 | 9 | | | | 8 | | | | 3 | 6 | | | 2 | | 4 | 30 |
| 1 | 2 | | | 5 | | 7 | 9 | | 10 | | 11 | | | | 8 | | | | 3 | 6 | | | | | 4 | 31 |
| 1 | 2 | | | 5 | | 7 | 9 | | 10 | | 11 | | | | 8 | | | | 3 | 6 | | | | | 4 | 32 |
| 1 | | | | 5 | | 7 | | | 10 | | 9 | 11 | | | 8 | | | | 3 | 6 | | | 2 | | 4 | 33 |
| 1 | | 3 | | 5 | 6 | 7 | 9 | | 10 | | | | | | 8 | | 11 | | | | | | 2 | | 4 | 34 |
| 1 | | | | 5 | | 7 | 9 | | 8 | | | 10 | | | 11 | | | | 3 | 6 | 2 | | | | 4 | 35 |
| 1 | | | | 5 | | 7 | | 8 | 9 | | 10 | | | | 11 | | | | 3 | 6 | 2 | | | | 4 | 36 |
| 1 | 3 | | | 5 | | 7 | 9 | | 10 | 8 | 11 | | | | | | | | | 6 | 2 | | | | 4 | 37 |
| 1 | 3 | | | 5 | | 7 | 9 | | 10 | 8 | 11 | | | | | | | | | 6 | 2 | | | | 4 | 38 |
| 37 | 26 | 24 | 15 | 34 | 19 | 26 | 23 | 8 | 33 | 17 | 19 | 29 | 10 | 13 | 17 | 2 | 1 | 1 | 4 | 12 | 12 | 12 | 12 | 1 | 11 | |
| | | | 4 | 2 | 2 | | | | 10 | | | 9 | 2 | 7 | 3 | | | | | | | | 2 | | 4 | |

1 own-goal

# 1919-20

Manager: John Robson

| 1 | Aug | 30 | (a) | Derby C | D | 1-1 | Woodcock | 12,000 |
|---|---|---|---|---|---|---|---|---|
| 2 | Sep | 1 | (h) | Sheffield W | D | 0-0 | | 13,000 |
| 3 | | 6 | (h) | Derby C | L | 0-2 | | 15,000 |
| 4 | | 8 | (a) | Sheffield W | W | 3-1 | Meehan, Spence, Woodcock | 10,000 |
| 5 | | 13 | (a) | Preston NE | W | 3-2 | Spence 2, Meehan | 15,000 |
| 6 | | 20 | (h) | Preston NE | W | 5-1 | Spence 2, Woodcock 2, Montgomery | 18,000 |
| 7 | | 27 | (a) | Middlesbrough | D | 1-1 | Woodcock | 20,000 |
| 8 | Oct | 4 | (h) | Middlesbrough | D | 1-1 | Woodcock | 28,000 |
| 9 | | 11 | (a) | Manchester C | D | 3-3 | Hodge, Hopkin, Spence | 30,000 |
| 10 | | 18 | (h) | Manchester C | W | 1-0 | Spence | 40,000 |
| 11 | | 25 | (a) | Sheffield U | D | 2-2 | Hopkin, Woodcock | 18,000 |
| 12 | Nov | 1 | (h) | Sheffield U | W | 3-0 | Hodges, Spence, Woodcock | 24,500 |
| 13 | | 8 | (a) | Burnley | L | 1-2 | Hodge | 15,000 |
| 14 | | 15 | (h) | Burnley | L | 0-1 | | 25,000 |
| 15 | | 22 | (a) | Oldham A | W | 3-0 | Hodges, Hopkin, Spence | 15,000 |
| 16 | Dec | 6 | (a) | Aston Villa | L | 0-2 | | 40,000 |
| 17 | | 13 | (h) | Aston Villa | L | 1-2 | Hilditch | 30,000 |
| 18 | | 20 | (h) | Newcastle U | W | 2-1 | Hodges, Spence | 20,000 |
| 19 | | 26 | (h) | Liverpool | D | 0-0 | | 45,000 |
| 20 | | 27 | (a) | Newcastle U | L | 1-2 | Hilditch | 45,000 |
| 21 | Jan | 1 | (a) | Liverpool | D | 0-0 | | 30,000 |
| 22 | | 3 | (h) | Chelsea | L | 0-2 | | 25,000 |
| 23 | | 17 | (a) | Chelsea | L | 0-1 | | 40,000 |
| 24 | | 24 | (a) | West Brom A | L | 1-2 | Woodcock | 20,000 |
| 25 | Feb | 7 | (a) | Sunderland | L | 0-3 | | 25,000 |
| 26 | | 11 | (h) | Oldham A | D | 1-1 | Bissett | 15,000 |
| 27 | | 14 | (h) | Sunderland | W | 2-0 | Harris, Hodges | 35,000 |
| 28 | | 21 | (a) | Arsenal | W | 3-0 | Spence 2, Hopkin | 25,000 |
| 29 | | 25 | (h) | West Brom A | L | 1-2 | Spence | 20,000 |
| 30 | | 28 | (h) | Arsenal | L | 0-1 | | 20,000 |
| 31 | Mar | 6 | (h) | Everton | W | 1-0 | Bissett | 25,000 |
| 32 | | 13 | (a) | Everton | D | 0-0 | | 30,000 |
| 33 | | 20 | (h) | Bradford C | D | 0-0 | | 25,000 |
| 34 | | 27 | (a) | Bradford C | L | 1-2 | Bissett | 18,000 |
| 35 | Apr | 2 | (h) | Bradford | L | 0-1 | | 30,000 |
| 36 | | 3 | (h) | Bolton W | D | 1-1 | Toms | 39,000 |
| 37 | | 6 | (a) | Bradford | W | 4-1 | Bissett, Grimwood, Toms, Woodcock | 14,000 |
| 38 | | 10 | (a) | Bolton W | W | 5-3 | Bissett 2, Meredith, Toms, Woodcock | 25,000 |
| 39 | | 17 | (h) | Blackburn R | D | 1-1 | Hopkin | 40,000 |
| 40 | | 24 | (a) | Blackburn R | L | 0-5 | | 30,000 |
| 41 | | 26 | (h) | Notts C | D | 0-0 | | 30,000 |
| 42 | May | 1 | (a) | Notts C | W | 2-0 | Meredith, Spence | 20,000 |

FINAL LEAGUE POSITION: 12th in Division One

Appearances

Goals

FA Cup

| 1 | Jan | 10 | (a) | Port Vale | W | 1-0 | |
|---|---|---|---|---|---|---|---|
| 2 | | 31 | (h) | Aston Villa | L | 1-2 | |

| Mew | Moore | Silcock | Montgomery | Hilditch | Whalley | Hodge JA | Woodcock | Spence | Potts | Hopkin | Meehan | Toms | Grimwood | Hodges | Forster | Bissett | Meredith | Robinson | Barlow | Harris | Spratt | Williamson | Prentice | Sapsford | # |
|---|---|---|---|---|---|---|---|---|---|---|---|---|---|---|---|---|---|---|---|---|---|---|---|---|---|
| 1 | 2 | 3 | 4 | 5 | 6 | 7 | 8 | 9 | 10 | 11 |  |  |  |  |  |  |  |  |  |  |  |  |  |  | 1 |
| 1 | 2 | 3 | 4 | 5 | 6 | 7 | 10 | 9 |  | 11 | 8 |  |  |  |  |  |  |  |  |  |  |  |  |  | 2 |
| 1 | 2 | 3 | 4 | 5 | 6 | 7 | 8 | 9 |  | 11 | 10 |  |  |  |  |  |  |  |  |  |  |  |  |  | 3 |
| 1 | 2 | 3 | 4 | 5 | 6 | 7 | 8 | 9 |  | 11 | 10 |  |  |  |  |  |  |  |  |  |  |  |  |  | 4 |
| 1 | 2 | 3 | 4 | 5 | 6 | 7 | 8 | 9 |  | 11 | 10 |  |  |  |  |  |  |  |  |  |  |  |  |  | 5 |
| 1 | 2 | 3 | 4 | 5 | 6 | 7 | 8 | 9 |  | 11 | 10 |  |  |  |  |  |  |  |  |  |  |  |  |  | 6 |
| 1 | 2 | 3 | 4 | 5 | 6 | 7 | 8 | 9 |  | 11 | 10 |  |  |  |  |  |  |  |  |  |  |  |  |  | 7 |
| 1 | 2 | 3 |  | 5 | 6 | 7 | 8 | 9 |  | 11 | 4 | 10 |  |  |  |  |  |  |  |  |  |  |  |  | 8 |
| 1 | 2 | 3 |  |  | 4 | 7 | 8 | 9 |  | 11 | 6 | 10 | 5 |  |  |  |  |  |  |  |  |  |  |  | 9 |
| 1 | 2 | 3 |  | 5 | 6 | 7 | 10 | 9 |  | 11 | 4 |  |  | 8 |  |  |  |  |  |  |  |  |  |  | 10 |
| 1 | 2 | 3 |  | 5 | 6 | 7 | 10 | 9 |  | 11 | 4 |  |  | 8 |  |  |  |  |  |  |  |  |  |  | 11 |
| 1 | 2 | 3 |  | 5 | 6 |  | 10 | 9 | 8 | 11 | 4 |  |  |  |  | 7 |  |  |  |  |  |  |  |  | 12 |
| 1 | 2 | 3 |  | 5 |  | 7 | 10 | 9 |  | 11 | 4 |  |  | 8 | 6 |  |  |  |  |  |  |  |  |  | 13 |
| 1 | 2 | 3 |  | 5 |  |  | 10 | 9 |  | 11 | 4 |  |  | 8 | 6 | 7 |  |  |  |  |  |  |  |  | 14 |
| 1 | 2 | 3 |  | 5 | 6 |  | 10 | 9 |  | 11 | 4 |  |  | 8 |  | 7 |  |  |  |  |  |  |  |  | 15 |
| 1 | 2 | 3 |  | 5 | 6 |  | 8 | 9 |  | 11 | 4 | 10 |  |  |  | 7 |  |  |  |  |  |  |  |  | 16 |
| 1 | 2 | 3 | 6 | 5 |  | 7 |  | 9 |  | 11 | 4 | 10 |  | 8 |  |  |  |  |  |  |  |  |  |  | 17 |
| 1 | 2 | 3 |  | 5 | 6 |  | 8 | 9 |  | 11 | 10 |  | 4 |  |  | 7 |  |  |  |  |  |  |  |  | 18 |
| 1 | 2 | 3 |  | 5 | 6 |  |  | 9 |  | 11 | 10 |  | 4 | 8 |  | 7 |  |  |  |  |  |  |  |  | 19 |
| 1 | 2 | 3 |  | 5 | 6 |  |  | 9 |  | 11 | 10 |  | 4 | 8 |  | 7 |  |  |  |  |  |  |  |  | 20 |
| 1 | 2 | 3 |  | 5 | 6 |  | 10 | 9 |  | 11 |  |  | 4 | 8 |  | 7 |  |  |  |  |  |  |  |  | 21 |
| 1 | 2 | 3 |  | 5 | 6 |  | 10 | 9 |  |  |  |  | 4 | 8 |  | 7 | 11 |  |  |  |  |  |  |  | 22 |
| 1 | 2 | 3 |  | 5 | 6 |  | 10 | 9 |  | 11 | 8 |  | 4 |  |  | 7 |  |  |  |  |  |  |  |  | 23 |
| 1 | 2 | 3 |  | 5 | 6 |  |  | 9 | 8 | 11 |  | 10 | 4 |  |  | 7 |  |  |  |  |  |  |  |  | 24 |
| 1 | 2 | 3 |  | 5 |  |  | 10 | 9 |  | 11 | 6 |  | 4 | 8 |  | 7 |  |  |  |  |  |  |  |  | 25 |
| 1 | 2 | 3 |  | 5 |  |  | 10 | 9 |  | 11 | 6 |  | 4 | 8 |  | 7 |  |  |  |  |  |  |  |  | 26 |
| 1 |  | 3 | 6 |  |  |  |  | 9 |  | 11 | 10 |  | 4 | 8 |  | 7 |  |  | 2 | 5 |  |  |  |  | 27 |
| 1 |  | 3 | 6 |  |  |  |  | 9 |  | 11 | 10 |  | 4 | 8 |  | 7 |  |  | 2 | 5 |  |  |  |  | 28 |
| 1 |  | 3 | 6 |  |  |  |  | 9 |  | 11 | 10 |  | 4 | 8 |  | 7 |  |  | 2 | 5 |  |  |  |  | 29 |
| 1 | 2 |  | 6 |  |  |  |  | 9 |  | 11 | 10 |  | 4 | 8 |  | 7 |  |  |  | 5 |  | 3 |  |  | 30 |
| 1 | 2 | 3 |  | 5 |  |  | 10 |  |  | 11 | 6 |  | 4 | 8 |  | 7 |  |  |  | 9 |  |  |  |  | 31 |
| 1 | 2 | 3 |  | 5 |  |  | 10 | 9 |  | 11 | 6 |  | 4 | 8 |  | 7 |  |  |  |  |  |  |  |  | 32 |
| 1 | 2 |  |  | 5 |  |  | 10 | 9 |  | 11 | 6 |  | 4 | 8 |  | 7 |  | 3 |  |  |  |  |  |  | 33 |
| 1 | 2 | 3 | 6 |  |  |  |  | 9 | 10 | 11 |  |  | 4 | 8 |  | 7 |  |  |  | 5 |  |  |  |  | 34 |
| 1 | 2 | 3 | 6 |  |  |  |  | 9 |  |  |  | 10 | 4 | 8 |  | 7 |  |  |  | 5 | 11 |  |  |  | 35 |
| 1 |  | 3 |  | 5 |  |  | 8 | 9 |  | 11 | 6 |  | 4 |  | 10 | 7 |  |  | 2 |  |  |  |  |  | 36 |
| 1 |  | 3 |  | 5 |  |  | 8 | 9 |  | 11 | 6 |  | 4 |  | 10 | 7 |  |  | 2 |  |  |  |  |  | 37 |
| 1 | 2 | 3 |  | 5 |  |  | 8 | 9 |  | 11 | 6 |  | 4 |  | 10 | 7 |  |  |  |  |  |  |  |  | 38 |
| 1 | 2 | 3 |  | 5 |  |  | 8 | 9 |  | 11 | 6 |  |  |  | 10 | 7 |  |  |  |  |  | 4 |  |  | 39 |
| 1 | 2 | 3 |  | 5 |  |  |  | 9 | 8 | 11 | 6 | 10 |  |  |  | 7 |  |  |  |  |  |  | 4 |  | 40 |
| 1 |  | 3 |  | 5 | 6 |  |  | 9 |  |  |  |  | 4 | 8 |  | 7 | 11 | 2 |  |  |  |  |  | 10 | 41 |
| 1 | 2 | 3 |  | 5 |  |  |  | 9 |  | 11 | 6 |  | 4 | 8 |  | 7 |  |  |  |  |  |  |  | 10 | 42 |
| 42 | 36 | 40 | 14 | 32 | 23 | 16 | 28 | 32 | 4 | 39 | 36 | 12 | 22 | 18 | 5 | 22 | 19 | 2 | 7 | 7 | 1 | 2 | 1 | 2 |  |
|  |  | 1 | 2 |  | 2 | 11 | 14 |  |  | 5 | 2 | 3 | 1 | 4 |  | 6 | 2 |  |  | 1 |  |  |  |  |  |

# 1920-21

Manager: John Robson

| 1 | Aug | 28 | (h) | Bolton W | L | 2-3 | Hopkin, Meehan | 50,000 |
|---|-----|----|-----|----------|---|-----|----------------|--------|
| 2 | | 30 | (a) | Arsenal | L | 0-2 | | 40,000 |
| 3 | Sep | 4 | (a) | Bolton W | D | 1-1 | Sapsford | 35,000 |
| 4 | | 6 | (h) | Arsenal | D | 1-1 | Spence | 45,000 |
| 5 | | 11 | (h) | Chelsea | W | 3-1 | Meehan 2, Leonard | 40,000 |
| 6 | | 18 | (a) | Chelsea | W | 2-1 | Leonard 2 | 35,000 |
| 7 | | 25 | (h) | Tottenham H | L | 0-1 | | 50,000 |
| 8 | Oct | 2 | (a) | Tottenham H | L | 1-4 | Spence | 45,000 |
| 9 | | 9 | (h) | Oldham A | W | 4-1 | Sapsford 2, Meehan, Miller | 50,000 |
| 10 | | 16 | (a) | Oldham A | D | 2-2 | Spence, Hemsley (og) | 20,000 |
| 11 | | 23 | (h) | Preston NE | W | 1-0 | Miller | 42,000 |
| 12 | | 30 | (a) | Preston NE | D | 0-0 | | 25,000 |
| 13 | Nov | 6 | (h) | Sheffield U | W | 2-1 | Leonard 2 | 30,000 |
| 14 | | 13 | (a) | Sheffield U | D | 0-0 | | 18,000 |
| 15 | | 20 | (h) | Manchester C | D | 1-1 | Miller | 63,000 |
| 16 | | 27 | (a) | Manchester C | L | 0-3 | | 35,000 |
| 17 | Dec | 4 | (h) | Bradford | W | 5-1 | Miller 2, Myerscough 2, Partridge | 25,000 |
| 18 | | 11 | (a) | Bradford | W | 4-2 | Myerscough 2, Miller, Partridge | 10,000 |
| 19 | | 18 | (h) | Newcastle U | W | 2-0 | Hopkin, Miller | 40,000 |
| 20 | | 25 | (a) | Aston Villa | W | 4-3 | Grimwood 2, Harrison, Partridge | 38,000 |
| 21 | | 27 | (h) | Aston Villa | L | 1-3 | Harrison | 45,000 |
| 22 | Jan | 1 | (a) | Newcastle U | L | 3-6 | Hopkin, Partridge, Silcock | 40,000 |
| 23 | | 15 | (h) | West Brom A | L | 1-4 | Partridge | 30,000 |
| 24 | | 22 | (a) | West Brom A | W | 2-0 | Myerscough, Partridge | 30,000 |
| 25 | Feb | 5 | (h) | Liverpool | D | 1-1 | Grimwood | 30,000 |
| 26 | | 9 | (a) | Liverpool | L | 0-2 | | 35,000 |
| 27 | | 12 | (h) | Everton | L | 1-2 | Meredith | 30,000 |
| 28 | | 20 | (h) | Sunderland | W | 3-0 | Harrison, Hilditch, Robinson | 40,000 |
| 29 | Mar | 5 | (a) | Sunderland | W | 3-2 | Sapsford 2, Goodwin | 25,000 |
| 30 | | 9 | (a) | Everton | L | 0-2 | | 38,000 |
| 31 | | 12 | (h) | Bradford C | D | 1-1 | Robinson | 30,000 |
| 32 | | 19 | (a) | Bradford C | D | 1-1 | Sapsford | 25,000 |
| 33 | | 25 | (a) | Burnley | L | 0-1 | | 20,000 |
| 34 | | 26 | (a) | Huddersfield T | L | 2-5 | Harris, Partridge | 17,000 |
| 35 | | 28 | (h) | Burnley | L | 0-3 | | 28,000 |
| 36 | Apr | 2 | (h) | Huddersfield T | W | 2-0 | Bissett 2 | 30,000 |
| 37 | | 9 | (a) | Middlesbrough | W | 4-2 | Spence 2, Bissett, Grimwood | 15,000 |
| 38 | | 16 | (a) | Middlesbrough | L | 0-1 | | 25,000 |
| 39 | | 23 | (a) | Blackburn R | L | 0-2 | | 18,000 |
| 40 | | 30 | (h) | Blackburn R | L | 0-1 | | 20,000 |
| 41 | May | 2 | (a) | Derby C | D | 1-1 | Bissett | 8,000 |
| 42 | | 7 | (h) | Derby C | W | 3-0 | Spence 2, Sapsford | 10,000 |

FINAL LEAGUE POSITION: 13th in Division One

Appearances
Goals

FA Cup

| 1 | Jan | 8 | (a) | Liverpool | D | 1-1 |
|---|-----|---|-----|-----------|---|-----|
| R | | 12 | (h) | Liverpool | L | 1-2 |

232

Appearances and goals grid (shirt numbers by match). Columns are players; the rightmost column is the match number.

| Mew | Moore | Silcock | Meehan | Grimwood | Hilditch | Meredith | Bissett | Goodwin | Sapsford | Hopkin | Hofton | Harris | Spence | Toms | Barlow | Schofield | Myerscough | Hodges | Leonard | Miller | Montgomery | Forster | Partridge | Steward | Harrison | Robinson | Radford | # |
|---|---|---|---|---|---|---|---|---|---|---|---|---|---|---|---|---|---|---|---|---|---|---|---|---|---|---|---|---|
| 1 | 2 | 3 | 4 | 5 | 6 | 7 | 8 | 9 | 10 | 11 |  |  |  |  |  |  |  |  |  |  |  |  |  |  |  |  |  | 1 |
| 1 |  | 3 |  | 6 | 5 | 7 |  |  | 10 | 11 |  | 2 | 4 | 8 | 9 |  |  |  |  |  |  |  |  |  |  |  |  | 2 |
| 1 |  | 3 | 6 | 4 | 5 |  |  |  | 10 | 11 |  | 9 | 2 | 7 | 8 |  |  |  |  |  |  |  |  |  |  |  |  | 3 |
| 1 |  | 3 | 6 | 4 | 5 |  |  | 8 | 10 | 11 |  | 7 | 2 |  | 9 |  |  |  |  |  |  |  |  |  |  |  |  | 4 |
| 1 |  | 3 |  | 6 | 5 | 7 |  |  | 10 | 11 |  | 4 | 2 |  |  |  |  | 8 | 9 |  |  |  |  |  |  |  |  |  | 5 |
| 1 |  | 3 |  | 6 | 5 | 7 |  |  | 10 | 11 |  | 4 | 8 |  | 2 |  |  | 9 |  |  |  |  |  |  |  |  |  |  | 6 |
| 1 | 2 |  |  | 6 | 5 | 7 |  |  | 10 | 11 |  | 4 |  |  | 3 |  |  | 9 | 8 |  |  |  |  |  |  |  |  |  | 7 |
| 1 | 2 |  |  | 6 |  | 7 |  |  |  | 11 |  | 4 | 10 |  | 3 |  | 9 |  | 8 | 5 |  |  |  |  |  |  |  |  | 8 |
| 1 |  | 3 | 7 |  | 5 |  |  |  | 10 |  |  | 4 | 9 |  | 2 |  | 8 |  |  | 6 |  | 11 |  |  |  |  |  |  | 9 |
| 1 |  | 3 | 7 |  | 5 |  |  |  | 10 |  |  | 4 | 9 |  | 2 |  | 8 |  |  | 6 |  | 11 |  |  |  |  |  |  | 10 |
|  |  | 3 |  | 6 | 5 |  |  |  | 10 |  |  | 4 | 2 |  | 8 |  | 9 |  | 11 |  | 1 |  | 7 |  |  |  |  | 11 |
| 1 |  | 3 |  | 6 | 5 |  |  |  | 10 | 11 |  | 4 | 2 |  | 9 |  | 8 |  |  |  |  | 7 |  |  |  |  |  | 12 |
| 1 |  | 3 |  | 5 |  |  |  |  |  | 11 |  | 4 | 2 |  | 9 |  | 8 |  | 6 | 10 |  | 7 |  |  |  |  |  | 13 |
| 1 | 2 | 3 |  | 6 | 5 |  |  |  |  | 11 |  | 4 | 9 |  | 8 |  |  |  | 10 |  |  | 7 |  |  |  |  |  | 14 |
| 1 | 2 | 3 |  | 6 |  |  |  |  | 10 | 11 |  | 5 | 9 |  | 8 |  |  |  | 4 |  |  | 7 |  |  |  |  |  | 15 |
| 1 | 2 | 3 |  | 6 | 5 |  |  |  |  | 11 |  | 4 | 10 |  | 9 |  |  |  | 8 |  |  | 7 |  |  |  |  |  | 16 |
| 1 | 2 | 3 |  | 5 |  |  |  |  |  | 11 |  | 4 |  |  | 8 |  | 9 |  |  | 6 |  | 10 | 7 |  |  |  |  | 17 |
| 1 | 2 | 3 |  | 5 |  |  |  |  |  | 11 |  | 4 |  |  | 8 |  | 9 |  |  | 6 |  | 10 | 7 |  |  |  |  | 18 |
| 1 | 2 | 3 |  | 5 |  |  |  |  |  | 11 |  | 4 |  |  | 8 |  | 9 |  |  | 6 |  | 10 | 7 |  |  |  |  | 19 |
| 1 | 2 | 3 |  | 5 |  |  |  |  |  | 11 |  | 4 |  |  | 8 |  | 9 |  |  | 6 |  | 10 | 7 |  |  |  |  | 20 |
| 1 | 2 | 3 |  | 5 |  |  |  |  |  | 11 |  | 4 |  |  | 8 |  | 9 |  |  | 6 |  | 10 | 7 |  |  |  |  | 21 |
| 1 | 2 | 3 |  | 5 | 6 |  |  |  |  | 11 |  | 4 |  |  | 9 |  |  |  | 8 |  |  | 10 | 7 |  |  |  |  | 22 |
| 1 |  | 3 |  | 5 | 8 |  |  |  |  | 11 |  | 4 | 2 |  | 9 |  |  |  |  | 6 |  | 10 | 7 |  |  |  |  | 23 |
| 1 | 2 |  | 5 | 4 |  |  |  |  |  | 11 |  | 3 |  |  | 8 |  | 9 |  |  | 6 |  | 10 | 7 |  |  |  |  | 24 |
| 1 |  | 3 | 5 | 4 |  |  |  |  |  | 11 |  | 2 |  |  | 8 |  | 9 |  |  | 6 |  | 10 | 7 |  |  |  |  | 25 |
| 1 |  | 3 | 5 | 4 | 7 |  |  |  |  | 11 |  | 9 | 2 |  | 8 |  |  |  |  | 6 |  | 10 |  |  |  |  |  | 26 |
| 1 |  | 3 | 5 | 4 | 7 |  |  |  |  | 11 |  | 2 | 8 |  | 9 |  |  |  |  | 6 |  | 10 |  |  |  |  |  | 27 |
| 1 | 2 | 3 |  | 5 | 4 |  |  | 9 | 10 |  |  |  |  |  |  |  |  |  |  |  |  | 6 | 8 |  | 7 | 11 |  | 28 |
| 1 | 2 | 3 |  | 5 | 4 |  |  | 9 | 10 |  |  |  |  |  |  |  |  |  |  |  |  | 6 | 8 |  | 7 | 11 |  | 29 |
| 1 | 2 |  | 5 | 4 |  |  |  | 9 | 10 |  |  | 6 |  |  | 3 |  |  |  |  |  |  |  | 8 |  | 7 | 11 |  | 30 |
|  | 2 |  | 5 | 4 |  |  |  | 9 | 10 |  |  | 3 |  |  |  |  |  |  |  |  |  | 8 | 6 | 1 | 7 | 11 |  | 31 |
| 1 | 2 | 3 |  | 4 |  |  |  | 9 |  |  |  |  |  |  | 8 |  |  |  | 5 | 6 |  | 10 |  |  | 7 | 11 |  | 32 |
| 1 | 2 | 3 |  | 5 |  |  |  |  |  | 11 |  | 4 | 8 |  |  |  | 9 |  |  | 6 |  | 10 | 7 |  |  |  |  | 33 |
| 1 | 2 | 3 |  | 5 | 7 |  |  |  |  | 11 |  | 4 | 8 |  |  |  | 9 |  |  | 6 |  | 10 |  |  |  |  |  | 34 |
| 1 | 2 | 3 |  | 4 |  |  | 8 |  | 10 |  |  | 5 |  |  |  |  | 9 |  |  | 6 |  | 11 | 7 |  |  |  |  | 35 |
| 1 | 2 | 3 |  | 5 | 4 | 7 | 8 |  |  |  |  |  |  |  |  |  | 9 |  |  | 6 |  | 10 | 11 |  |  |  |  | 36 |
| 1 | 2 |  | 5 | 4 | 7 | 8 |  |  |  | 11 |  |  | 9 |  | 3 |  |  |  |  | 6 |  | 10 |  |  |  |  |  | 37 |
| 1 | 2 | 3 |  | 5 | 4 | 7 | 8 |  |  | 11 |  |  | 9 |  |  |  |  |  |  | 6 |  | 10 |  |  |  |  |  | 38 |
| 1 | 2 | 3 |  | 5 | 4 |  | 8 |  |  | 11 |  | 6 |  |  |  |  | 9 |  |  |  |  | 10 | 7 |  |  |  |  | 39 |
| 1 | 2 | 3 |  | 5 | 4 | 7 | 8 |  |  | 11 |  | 6 |  |  |  |  | 9 |  |  |  |  | 10 |  |  |  |  |  | 40 |
| 1 | 2 | 3 |  | 5 | 4 | 7 | 8 |  | 10 |  |  | 9 |  |  |  |  |  |  |  | 6 |  |  |  |  | 11 |  |  | 41 |
| 1 |  | 3 |  | 5 | 4 | 7 | 8 |  | 10 | 11 |  | 9 |  |  |  |  |  |  |  | 6 |  |  |  |  | 2 |  |  | 42 |
| 40 | 26 | 37 | 15 | 25 | 34 | 14 | 12 | 5 | 21 | 31 | 1 | 26 | 15 | 1 | 19 | 1 | 13 | 2 | 10 | 25 | 2 | 26 | 28 | 2 | 23 | 7 | 1 | |
|  | 1 | 4 | 4 | 1 | 1 | 4 | 1 | 7 | 3 |  | 1 | 7 |  | 5 |  | 5 | 7 |  | 7 |  | 3 | 2 |  | 7 |  | 3 | 2 | |

1 own-goal

Match 8: Silcock listed as playing number 3 by the Football League.

# 1921-22

Manager: John Robson until October 1921, then John Chapman.

| 1 | Aug | 27 | (a) | Everton | L 0-5 | | 30,000 |
|---|---|---|---|---|---|---|---|
| 2 | | 29 | (h) | West Brom A | L 2-3 | Partridge, Robinson | 20,000 |
| 3 | Sep | 3 | (h) | Everton | W 2-1 | Harrison, Spence | 25,000 |
| 4 | | 7 | (a) | West Brom A | D 0-0 | | 15,000 |
| 5 | | 10 | (a) | Chelsea | D 0-0 | | 35,000 |
| 6 | | 17 | (h) | Chelsea | D 0-0 | | 28,000 |
| 7 | | 24 | (a) | Preston NE | L 2-3 | Lochhead, Partridge | 25,000 |
| 8 | Oct | 1 | (h) | Preston NE | D 1-1 | Spence | 30,000 |
| 9 | | 8 | (a) | Tottenham H | D 2-2 | Sapsford, Spence | 35,000 |
| 10 | | 15 | (h) | Tottenham H | W 2-1 | Sapsford, Spence | 30,000 |
| 11 | | 22 | (a) | Manchester C | L 1-4 | Spence | 24,000 |
| 12 | | 29 | (h) | Manchester C | W 3-1 | Spence 3 | 56,000 |
| 13 | Nov | 5 | (h) | Middlesbrough | L 3-5 | Lochhead, Sapsford, Spence | 30,000 |
| 14 | | 12 | (a) | Middlesbrough | L 0-2 | | 18,000 |
| 15 | | 19 | (a) | Aston Villa | L 1-3 | Spence | 30,000 |
| 16 | | 26 | (h) | Aston Villa | W 1-0 | Henderson | 33,000 |
| 17 | Dec | 3 | (a) | Bradford C | L 1-2 | Spence | 15,000 |
| 18 | | 10 | (h) | Bradford C | D 1-1 | Henderson | 9,000 |
| 19 | | 17 | (a) | Liverpool | L 1-2 | Sapsford | 40,000 |
| 20 | | 24 | (h) | Liverpool | D 0-0 | | 30,000 |
| 21 | | 26 | (h) | Burnley | L 0-1 | | 15,000 |
| 22 | | 27 | (a) | Burnley | L 2-4 | Lochhead, Sapsford | 10,000 |
| 23 | | 31 | (a) | Newcastle U | L 0-3 | | 20,000 |
| 24 | Jan | 2 | (a) | Sheffield U | L 0-3 | | 18,000 |
| 25 | | 14 | (h) | Newcastle U | L 0-1 | | 20,000 |
| 26 | | 21 | (a) | Sunderland | L 1-2 | Sapsford | 10,000 |
| 27 | | 28 | (h) | Sunderland | W 3-1 | Lochhead, Sapsford, Spence | 18,000 |
| 28 | Feb | 11 | (h) | Huddersfield T | D 1-1 | Spence | 30,000 |
| 29 | | 18 | (a) | Birmingham | W 1-0 | Spence | 20,000 |
| 30 | | 25 | (h) | Birmingham | D 1-1 | Sapsford | 35,000 |
| 31 | | 27 | (a) | Huddersfield T | D 1-1 | Sapsford | 30,000 |
| 32 | Mar | 11 | (h) | Arsenal | W 1-0 | Spence | 30,000 |
| 33 | | 18 | (h) | Blackburn R | L 0-1 | | 30,000 |
| 34 | | 25 | (a) | Blackburn R | L 0-3 | | 15,000 |
| 35 | Apr | 1 | (h) | Bolton W | L 0-1 | | 28,000 |
| 36 | | 5 | (a) | Arsenal | L 1-3 | Lochhead | 25,000 |
| 37 | | 8 | (a) | Bolton W | L 0-1 | | 28,000 |
| 38 | | 15 | (h) | Oldham A | L 0-3 | | 30,000 |
| 39 | | 17 | (h) | Sheffield U | W 3-2 | Harrison, Lochhead, Partridge | 28,000 |
| 40 | | 22 | (a) | Oldham A | D 1-1 | Lochhead | 30,000 |
| 41 | | 29 | (h) | Cardiff C | D 1-1 | Partridge | 18,000 |
| 42 | May | 6 | (a) | Cardiff C | L 1-3 | Lochhead | 16,000 |

FINAL LEAGUE POSITION: 22nd in Division One

Appearances

Goals

FA Cup

| 1 | Jan | 7 | (h) | Cardiff C | L 1-4 | |
|---|---|---|---|---|---|---|

234

| Mew | Brett | Silcock | Bennion | Grimwood | Scott | Gibson | Myerscough | Lochhead | Sapsford | Partridge | Harris | Harrison | Spence | Goodwin | Robinson | Bissett | Hilditch | Radford | Schofield P | Forster | Barlow | McBain | Henderson | Steward | Howarth | Taylor W | Haslam | Thomas | Pugh | |
|---|---|---|---|---|---|---|---|---|---|---|---|---|---|---|---|---|---|---|---|---|---|---|---|---|---|---|---|---|---|---|
| 1 | 2 | 3 | 4 | 5 | 6 | 7 | 8 | 9 | 10 | 11 | | | | | | | | | | | | | | | | | | | | 1 |
| 1 | 2 | 3 | | 5 | 6 | | | | 10 | | 4 | 7 | 8 | 9 | 11 | | | | | | | | | | | | | | | 2 |
| 1 | 2 | 3 | | 5 | 6 | | | | 10 | | 4 | 7 | 8 | 9 | 11 | | | | | | | | | | | | | | | 3 |
| 1 | 2 | 3 | | 5 | 6 | | | | 10 | | 4 | 7 | 9 | | | 11 | 8 | | | | | | | | | | | | | 4 |
| 1 | 2 | 3 | | 5 | 6 | | | | 10 | | 4 | 7 | 9 | | | 11 | 8 | | | | | | | | | | | | | 5 |
| 1 | 2 | 3 | | 5 | 6 | | | 9 | 10 | | | 7 | 8 | | | 11 | 4 | | | | | | | | | | | | | 6 |
| 1 | | 3 | | 5 | 6 | | | 9 | 10 | | | 7 | 8 | | | 11 | 4 | 2 | | | | | | | | | | | | 7 |
| 1 | | 3 | 4 | | 6 | | | 9 | 10 | 11 | | 7 | 8 | | | | 5 | 2 | | | | | | | | | | | | 8 |
| 1 | | 3 | 4 | | 6 | | 8 | | 10 | 11 | | 7 | 9 | | | | 5 | 2 | | | | | | | | | | | | 9 |
| 1 | | 3 | 4 | | 6 | | 8 | | 10 | 11 | | 7 | 9 | | | | 5 | 2 | | | | | | | | | | | | 10 |
| 1 | | 3 | 4 | | 6 | | 8 | | 10 | 11 | | 7 | 9 | | | | 5 | 2 | | | | | | | | | | | | 11 |
| 1 | | 3 | | | 6 | | 8 | | 10 | 11 | | 7 | 9 | | | | 5 | 2 | | | 4 | | | | | | | | | 12 |
| 1 | | 3 | | | 6 | | 8 | | 10 | 11 | | 7 | 9 | | | | 5 | 2 | | | 4 | | | | | | | | | 13 |
| 1 | | 3 | | | 6 | 7 | 8 | | 10 | 11 | | | 9 | | | | 5 | 2 | | | 4 | | | | | | | | | 14 |
| 1 | | | 4 | | 6 | | 8 | | 10 | 11 | | 7 | 9 | | | | 5 | 2 | | | | 3 | | | | | | | | 15 |
| 1 | | 3 | | | 6 | | | | 10 | 11 | 4 | 7 | 8 | | | | | 2 | | | | 5 | 9 | | | | | | | 16 |
| 1 | 2 | 3 | | | 6 | | | | 10 | 11 | 4 | 7 | 8 | | | | | | | | | 5 | 9 | | | | | | | 17 |
| 1 | | 3 | | | 6 | 7 | | | 10 | 11 | | | 8 | | | | 4 | 2 | | | | 5 | 9 | | | | | | | 18 |
| 1 | | 3 | | | 6 | 7 | 8 | | 10 | 11 | | | 9 | | | | 4 | 2 | | | | 5 | | | | | | | | 19 |
| 1 | | 3 | | | 6 | 7 | 8 | | 10 | | | | 9 | | 11 | | 4 | 2 | | | | 5 | | | | | | | | 20 |
| 1 | | 3 | | | 6 | 7 | 8 | | 10 | 11 | | | | | | | 4 | 2 | | | | 5 | 9 | | | | | | | 21 |
| 1 | | 3 | | | 6 | 7 | 8 | | 10 | 11 | | | | | | | 4 | 2 | | | | 5 | 9 | | | | | | | 22 |
| 1 | | 3 | | 5 | 6 | 7 | 8 | | 10 | 11 | | | | | | | 4 | 2 | | | | | 9 | | | | | | | 23 |
| | | | | 5 | 6 | | 8 | | 10 | 11 | | | | | | | 4 | | 3 | | | | 9 | 1 | 2 | 7 | | | | 24 |
| 1 | | 3 | | | 6 | 7 | 8 | | 10 | 11 | | | 9 | | | | 4 | 2 | | | | 5 | | | | | | | | 25 |
| 1 | | 3 | | | 6 | | 8 | | 10 | 11 | | 7 | | | | | 4 | 2 | | | | 5 | 9 | | | | | | | 26 |
| 1 | | 3 | | | 6 | | 8 | | 10 | 11 | | 7 | | | | | 4 | 2 | | | | 5 | 9 | | | | | | | 27 |
| 1 | | 3 | | | 6 | | 8 | | 10 | 11 | | 7 | | | | | 4 | 2 | | | | 5 | 9 | | | | | | | 28 |
| 1 | | 3 | 4 | | 6 | | 8 | | 10 | 11 | | 7 | 9 | | | | | 2 | | | | 5 | | | | | | | | 29 |
| 1 | | 3 | 4 | | | | 8 | | 10 | 11 | | 7 | 9 | | | | | 2 | | | | 6 | | | | 5 | | | | 30 |
| 1 | | 3 | 4 | 5 | | | 8 | | 10 | 11 | | 7 | 9 | | | | | 2 | | | | 6 | | | | | | | | 31 |
| 1 | | 3 | 4 | 5 | | | 8 | | 10 | 11 | | 7 | 9 | | | | | 2 | | | | 6 | | | | | | | | 32 |
| 1 | | 3 | 4 | 5 | | | 8 | | 10 | 11 | | 7 | 9 | | | | | 2 | | | | 6 | | | | | | | | 33 |
| 1 | | 3 | 4 | | | | | | 10 | 11 | | 7 | 9 | | | | 8 | 2 | | | | 6 | 5 | | | | | | | 34 |
| 1 | | 3 | 4 | | | | | 9 | 10 | 11 | | 7 | 8 | | | | | 2 | | | | 5 | 6 | | | | | | | 35 |
| 1 | 2 | 3 | 4 | | 6 | | 8 | | 10 | 11 | | 7 | 9 | | | | | | | | | 5 | | | | | | | | 36 |
| 1 | | 3 | 4 | | 6 | | 8 | | 10 | 11 | | 7 | 9 | | | | | | | | | 5 | | | 2 | | | | | 37 |
| 1 | | 3 | 4 | | 6 | | | | 10 | 11 | | 7 | 9 | | | | 8 | | | | | 5 | | | 2 | | | | | 38 |
| 1 | | 3 | | | 6 | | 8 | | 10 | 11 | | 7 | 9 | | | | 4 | | | | | 5 | | | 2 | | | | | 39 |
| 1 | | 3 | | | 6 | | 8 | 9 | 10 | | | 7 | | | | | 4 | 2 | | | | 5 | | | | | 11 | | | 40 |
| 1 | | | | | 6 | | 8 | 9 | 10 | | | 7 | | | | | 4 | 2 | | | | 5 | | | | | | 11 | 3 | 41 |
| 1 | | 3 | | | 6 | | 8 | 9 | 10 | | | 7 | | | | | 4 | 2 | | | | 5 | | | | | | 11 | | 42 |
| 41 | 10 | 36 | 15 | 28 | 23 | 11 | 7 | 31 | 29 | 37 | 13 | 21 | 35 | 2 | 12 | 6 | 29 | 26 | 1 | 4 | 3 | 21 | 10 | 1 | 4 | 1 | 1 | 3 | 1 | |
| | | | | | | | | 8 | 9 | 4 | | 2 | 15 | | | | | 1 | | | | 2 | | | | | | | | |

235

# 1922-23

Manager: John Chapman

| | | | | | | | |
|---|---|---|---|---|---|---|---:|
| 1 | Aug | 26 | (h) | Crystal P | W | 2-1 | Spence, Wood | 30,000 |
| 2 | | 28 | (a) | Sheffield W | L | 0-1 | | 12,500 |
| 3 | Sep | 2 | (a) | Crystal P | W | 3-2 | Spence 2, Williams | 8,500 |
| 4 | | 4 | (h) | Sheffield W | W | 1-0 | Spence | 22,000 |
| 5 | | 9 | (a) | Wolves | W | 1-0 | Williams | 18,000 |
| 6 | | 16 | (h) | Wolves | W | 1-0 | Spence | 28,000 |
| 7 | | 23 | (a) | Coventry C | L | 0-2 | | 19,000 |
| 8 | | 30 | (h) | Coventry C | W | 2-1 | Henderson, Spence | 25,000 |
| 9 | Oct | 7 | (h) | Port Vale | L | 1-2 | Spence | 25,000 |
| 10 | | 14 | (a) | Port Vale | L | 0-1 | | 16,000 |
| 11 | | 21 | (h) | Fulham | D | 1-1 | Myerscough | 18,000 |
| 12 | | 28 | (a) | Fulham | D | 0-0 | | 20,000 |
| 13 | Nov | 4 | (h) | Clapton O | D | 0-0 | | 16,500 |
| 14 | | 11 | (a) | Clapton O | D | 1-1 | Goldthorpe | 11,000 |
| 15 | | 18 | (a) | Bury | D | 2-2 | Goldthorpe 2 | 21,000 |
| 16 | | 25 | (h) | Bury | L | 0-1 | | 28,000 |
| 17 | Dec | 2 | (h) | Rotherham C | W | 3-0 | Lochhead, McBain, Spence | 13,500 |
| 18 | | 9 | (a) | Rotherham C | D | 1-1 | Goldthorpe | 7,500 |
| 19 | | 16 | (h) | Stockport C | W | 1-0 | McBain | 24,000 |
| 20 | | 23 | (a) | Stockport C | L | 0-1 | | 15,500 |
| 21 | | 25 | (h) | West Ham U | L | 1-2 | Lochhead | 17,500 |
| 22 | | 26 | (a) | West Ham U | W | 2-0 | Lochhead 2 | 25,000 |
| 23 | | 30 | (a) | Hull C | L | 1-2 | Lochhead | 6,750 |
| 24 | Jan | 1 | (h) | Barnsley | W | 1-0 | Lochhead | 29,000 |
| 25 | | 6 | (h) | Hull C | W | 3-2 | Goldthorpe, Lochhead, Bell (og) | 15,000 |
| 26 | | 20 | (h) | Leeds U | D | 0-0 | | 25,000 |
| 27 | | 27 | (a) | Leeds U | W | 1-0 | Lochhead | 24,500 |
| 28 | Feb | 10 | (a) | Notts C | W | 6-1 | Goldthorpe 4, Myerscough 2 | 10,000 |
| 29 | | 17 | (h) | Derby C | D | 0-0 | | 27,500 |
| 30 | | 21 | (h) | Notts C | D | 1-1 | Lochhead | 12,100 |
| 31 | Mar | 3 | (h) | Southampton | L | 1-2 | Lochhead | 30,000 |
| 32 | | 14 | (a) | Derby C | D | 1-1 | MacDonald | 12,000 |
| 33 | | 17 | (a) | Bradford C | D | 1-1 | Goldthorpe | 10,000 |
| 34 | | 21 | (h) | Bradford C | D | 1-1 | Spence | 15,000 |
| 35 | | 30 | (h) | South Shields | W | 3-0 | Goldthorpe 2, Lochhead | 26,000 |
| 36 | | 31 | (a) | Blackpool | L | 0-1 | | 21,000 |
| 37 | Apr | 2 | (a) | South Shields | W | 3-0 | Goldthorpe, Hilditch, Spence | 6,500 |
| 38 | | 7 | (h) | Blackpool | W | 2-1 | Lochhead, Radford | 20,000 |
| 39 | | 11 | (a) | Southampton | D | 0-0 | | 5,500 |
| 40 | | 14 | (a) | Leicester C | W | 1-0 | Bain | 25,000 |
| 41 | | 21 | (h) | Leicester C | L | 0-2 | | 30,000 |
| 42 | | 28 | (a) | Barnsley | D | 2-2 | Lochhead, Spence | 8,000 |

FINAL LEAGUE POSITION: 4th in Division Two

Appearances
Goals

FA Cup

| | | | | | | |
|---|---|---|---|---|---|---|
| 1 | Jan | 13 | (a) | Bradford C | D | 1-1 |
| R | | 17 | (h) | Bradford C | W | 2-0 |
| 2 | Feb | 3 | (a) | Tottenham H | L | 0-4 |

| Mew | Radford | Silcock | Hilditch | McBain | Grimwood | Wood | Lochhead | Spence | Partridge | Thomas | Williams | Moore | Barson | Lyner | Sarvis | Henderson | Bain | Pugh | Myerscough | Goldthorpe | Cartman | Bennion | Barber | Lievesley | MacDonald | Mann | Steward | Broome | # |
|---|---|---|---|---|---|---|---|---|---|---|---|---|---|---|---|---|---|---|---|---|---|---|---|---|---|---|---|---|---|
| 1 | 2 | 3 | 4 | 5 | 6 | 7 | 8 | 9 | 10 | 11 |  |  |  |  |  |  |  |  |  |  |  |  |  |  |  |  |  |  | 1 |
| 1 | 2 | 3 | 4 | 5 | 6 | 7 | 8 | 9 |  | 11 | 10 |  |  |  |  |  |  |  |  |  |  |  |  |  |  |  |  |  | 2 |
| 1 |  | 3 | 4 | 5 | 6 | 7 | 8 | 9 |  | 11 | 10 | 2 |  |  |  |  |  |  |  |  |  |  |  |  |  |  |  |  | 3 |
| 1 |  | 3 | 4 | 5 | 6 | 7 | 8 | 9 |  | 11 | 10 | 2 |  |  |  |  |  |  |  |  |  |  |  |  |  |  |  |  | 4 |
| 1 |  | 3 | 4 |  | 6 | 7 | 8 | 9 |  | 11 | 10 | 2 | 5 |  |  |  |  |  |  |  |  |  |  |  |  |  |  |  | 5 |
| 1 |  | 3 | 4 |  | 6 | 7 | 8 | 9 | 10 | 11 |  | 2 | 5 |  |  |  |  |  |  |  |  |  |  |  |  |  |  |  | 6 |
| 1 |  | 3 | 4 |  | 6 |  |  | 9 | 10 | 11 |  | 2 | 5 | 7 | 8 |  |  |  |  |  |  |  |  |  |  |  |  |  | 7 |
| 1 |  | 3 | 4 |  | 6 |  | 8 | 9 |  | 11 |  | 2 | 5 | 7 |  | 10 |  |  |  |  |  |  |  |  |  |  |  |  | 8 |
| 1 |  | 3 | 4 |  | 6 |  | 8 | 9 |  | 11 |  | 2 | 5 | 7 |  | 10 |  |  |  |  |  |  |  |  |  |  |  |  | 9 |
| 1 | 2 | 3 | 4 |  | 6 | 7 |  | 9 | 10 | 11 |  |  | 5 |  |  |  | 8 |  |  |  |  |  |  |  |  |  |  |  | 10 |
| 1 | 2 |  | 4 |  | 6 | 7 |  | 9 |  | 11 | 10 |  | 5 |  |  |  |  | 3 | 8 |  |  |  |  |  |  |  |  |  | 11 |
| 1 | 2 | 3 | 4 | 10 | 6 | 7 |  | 9 |  | 11 |  |  | 5 |  |  |  |  |  | 8 |  |  |  |  |  |  |  |  |  | 12 |
| 1 | 2 | 3 | 4 | 10 | 6 | 7 |  | 9 |  | 11 |  |  | 5 |  |  |  |  |  | 8 |  |  |  |  |  |  |  |  |  | 13 |
| 1 | 2 | 3 | 4 | 10 | 6 | 7 |  |  |  | 11 |  |  | 5 |  |  |  |  |  | 8 | 9 |  |  |  |  |  |  |  |  | 14 |
| 1 | 2 | 3 | 4 | 10 | 6 | 7 |  |  |  | 11 |  |  | 5 |  |  |  |  |  | 8 | 9 |  |  |  |  |  |  |  |  | 15 |
| 1 | 2 | 3 | 4 | 10 | 6 | 7 |  |  |  | 11 |  |  | 5 |  |  |  |  |  | 8 | 9 |  |  |  |  |  |  |  |  | 16 |
| 1 | 2 | 3 | 4 | 10 | 6 | 7 |  | 9 | 8 | 11 |  |  | 5 |  |  |  |  |  |  |  |  |  |  |  |  |  |  |  | 17 |
| 1 | 2 |  | 4 |  | 6 | 7 | 8 | 10 |  | 11 |  | 3 | 5 |  |  |  |  |  |  | 9 |  |  |  |  |  |  |  |  | 18 |
| 1 | 2 | 3 | 4 | 10 | 6 |  | 8 |  |  | 11 |  |  | 5 |  |  |  |  |  |  | 9 | 7 |  |  |  |  |  |  |  | 19 |
| 1 | 2 | 3 | 4 | 10 | 6 |  | 8 |  |  | 11 |  |  | 5 |  |  |  |  |  |  | 9 | 7 |  |  |  |  |  |  |  | 20 |
| 1 | 2 | 3 | 4 |  | 6 |  | 8 | 10 |  | 11 |  |  | 5 |  |  |  |  |  |  | 9 | 7 |  |  |  |  |  |  |  | 21 |
| 1 | 2 | 3 |  | 5 | 6 | 7 | 8 | 10 |  | 11 |  |  |  |  |  |  |  |  |  | 9 |  | 4 |  |  |  |  |  |  | 22 |
| 1 | 2 | 3 |  | 5 | 6 | 7 | 8 | 10 |  | 11 |  |  |  |  |  |  |  |  |  | 9 |  | 4 |  |  |  |  |  |  | 23 |
| 1 | 2 |  | 4 |  | 6 |  |  | 10 | 7 | 11 |  | 3 | 5 |  |  |  |  |  | 8 | 9 |  |  |  |  |  |  |  |  | 24 |
| 1 | 2 |  | 4 |  | 6 | 7 |  | 10 |  | 11 |  | 3 | 5 |  |  |  |  |  |  | 9 |  |  | 8 |  |  |  |  |  | 25 |
| 1 |  | 3 | 4 |  | 6 |  |  | 10 |  | 11 |  | 2 | 5 |  |  |  |  |  |  | 9 |  |  | 8 | 7 |  |  |  |  | 26 |
| 1 | 2 | 3 | 4 |  | 6 |  |  | 10 |  | 11 |  |  | 5 |  |  |  |  |  | 8 | 9 |  |  |  | 7 |  |  |  |  | 27 |
| 1 | 2 | 3 |  |  | 6 |  |  | 10 |  | 11 |  | 7 | 5 |  |  |  |  |  | 8 | 9 |  | 4 |  |  |  |  |  |  | 28 |
| 1 | 2 | 3 |  |  | 6 |  |  | 10 |  | 11 |  | 7 | 5 |  |  |  |  |  | 8 | 9 |  | 4 |  |  |  |  |  |  | 29 |
| 1 | 2 | 3 |  |  | 6 |  |  | 10 | 7 | 11 |  |  | 5 |  |  |  |  |  | 8 | 9 |  | 4 |  |  |  |  |  |  | 30 |
| 1 | 2 | 3 | 4 |  | 6 |  |  | 10 | 7 | 11 |  |  | 5 |  |  |  |  |  | 8 |  |  |  |  |  | 9 |  |  |  | 31 |
| 1 | 2 | 3 |  |  | 6 |  |  | 10 | 7 | 11 |  |  | 5 |  |  |  |  |  | 8 |  |  |  |  |  | 9 |  |  |  | 32 |
| 1 | 2 | 3 |  |  | 6 |  |  | 10 | 7 | 11 |  |  | 5 |  |  |  |  |  |  | 9 |  | 4 |  |  |  | 8 |  |  | 33 |
| 1 | 2 |  |  |  | 6 |  |  | 10 | 7 | 11 |  | 3 | 5 |  |  |  |  |  |  | 9 |  | 4 |  |  |  | 8 |  |  | 34 |
| 1 | 2 | 3 | 4 |  | 6 |  |  | 10 | 7 | 11 |  |  | 5 |  |  |  |  |  |  | 9 |  |  |  |  |  | 8 |  |  | 35 |
| 1 | 2 | 3 | 4 |  | 6 |  |  | 10 | 7 | 11 |  |  | 5 |  |  |  |  |  |  | 9 |  |  |  |  |  | 8 |  |  | 36 |
| 1 | 2 | 3 |  | 5 | 6 |  |  | 10 | 7 | 11 |  |  |  |  |  |  |  |  |  | 9 |  | 4 |  |  |  | 8 |  |  | 37 |
| 1 | 2 | 3 |  | 5 | 6 |  |  | 10 | 7 | 11 |  |  |  |  |  |  |  |  |  | 9 |  | 4 |  |  |  | 8 |  |  | 38 |
| 1 | 2 | 3 |  | 5 | 6 |  |  | 10 | 7 | 11 |  |  |  |  |  |  |  |  |  | 9 |  | 4 |  |  |  | 8 |  |  | 39 |
|  | 2 | 3 |  | 5 | 6 |  |  | 10 | 7 | 11 |  |  |  |  |  |  |  |  |  | 9 |  | 4 |  |  |  | 8 | 1 |  | 40 |
| 1 | 2 | 3 |  | 5 | 6 |  |  | 10 | 7 | 11 |  |  |  |  |  |  |  |  |  | 9 |  | 4 |  |  |  | 8 |  |  | 41 |
| 1 | 2 | 3 |  |  | 6 |  |  | 10 | 9 | 11 |  |  | 5 |  |  |  |  |  |  |  |  | 4 |  |  |  | 7 |  | 8 | 42 |
| 41 | 34 | 37 | 32 | 21 | 36 | 15 | 34 | 35 | 30 | 18 | 5 | 12 | 31 | 3 | 1 | 2 | 4 | 1 | 13 | 22 | 3 | 14 | 2 | 2 | 2 | 10 | 1 | 1 |  |
|  | 1 |  | 1 | 2 | 1 |  | 13 | 11 |  | 2 |  |  | 1 | 1 |  |  |  |  | 3 | 13 |  | 1 |  |  |  |  |  |  |  |

1 own-goal

# 1923-24

Manager: John Chapman

| 1 | Aug | 25 | (a) | Bristol C | W | 2-1 | Lochhead, MacDonald | 20,500 |
|---|---|---|---|---|---|---|---|---|
| 2 | | 27 | (h) | Southampton | W | 1-0 | Goldthorpe | 21,750 |
| 3 | Sep | 1 | (h) | Bristol C | W | 2-1 | Lochhead, Spence | 21,000 |
| 4 | | 3 | (a) | Southampton | D | 0-0 | | 11,500 |
| 5 | | 8 | (a) | Bury | L | 0-2 | | 19,000 |
| 6 | | 15 | (h) | Bury | L | 0-1 | | 43,000 |
| 7 | | 22 | (a) | South Shields | L | 0-1 | | 9,750 |
| 8 | | 29 | (h) | South Shields | D | 1-1 | Lochhead | 22,250 |
| 9 | Oct | 6 | (a) | Oldham A | L | 2-3 | Wynne 2 (2 og's) | 12,250 |
| 10 | | 13 | (h) | Oldham A | W | 2-0 | Bain 2 | 26,000 |
| 11 | | 20 | (h) | Stockport C | W | 3-0 | Mann 2, Bain | 31,500 |
| 12 | | 27 | (a) | Stockport C | L | 2-3 | Barber, Lochhead | 16,500 |
| 13 | Nov | 3 | (a) | Leicester C | D | 2-2 | Lochhead 2 | 17,000 |
| 14 | | 10 | (h) | Leicester C | W | 3-0 | Lochhead, Mann, Spence | 20,000 |
| 15 | | 17 | (h) | Coventry C | D | 1-1 | Randle (og) | 13,580 |
| 16 | Dec | 1 | (a) | Leeds U | D | 0-0 | | 20,000 |
| 17 | | 8 | (h) | Leeds U | W | 3-1 | Lochhead 2, Spence | 22,250 |
| 18 | | 15 | (a) | Port Vale | W | 1-0 | Grimwood | 7,500 |
| 19 | | 22 | (h) | Port Vale | W | 5-0 | Bain 3, Lochhead, Spence | 11,750 |
| 20 | | 25 | (h) | Barnsley | L | 1-2 | Grimwood | 34,000 |
| 21 | | 26 | (a) | Barnsley | L | 0-1 | | 12,000 |
| 22 | | 29 | (a) | Bradford C | D | 0-0 | | 11,500 |
| 23 | Jan | 2 | (h) | Coventry C | L | 1-2 | Bain | 7,000 |
| 24 | | 5 | (h) | Bradford C | W | 3-0 | Bain, Lochhead, McPherson | 18,000 |
| 25 | | 19 | (a) | Fulham | L | 1-3 | Lochhead | 15,500 |
| 26 | | 26 | (h) | Fulham | D | 0-0 | | 25,000 |
| 27 | Feb | 6 | (a) | Blackpool | L | 0-1 | | 6,000 |
| 28 | | 9 | (h) | Blackpool | D | 0-0 | | 13,000 |
| 29 | | 16 | (a) | Derby C | L | 0-3 | | 12,000 |
| 30 | | 23 | (h) | Derby C | D | 0-0 | | 25,000 |
| 31 | Mar | 1 | (a) | Nelson | W | 2-0 | Kennedy, Spence | 2,750 |
| 32 | | 8 | (h) | Nelson | L | 0-1 | | 8,500 |
| 33 | | 15 | (h) | Hull C | D | 1-1 | Lochhead | 13,000 |
| 34 | | 22 | (a) | Hull C | D | 1-1 | Miller | 6,250 |
| 35 | | 29 | (h) | Stoke | D | 2-2 | Smith 2 | 13,000 |
| 36 | Apr | 5 | (a) | Stoke | L | 0-3 | | 11,000 |
| 37 | | 12 | (h) | Crystal P | W | 5-1 | Spence 4, Smith | 8,000 |
| 38 | | 18 | (a) | Clapton O | L | 0-1 | | 18,000 |
| 39 | | 19 | (a) | Crystal P | D | 1-1 | Spence | 7,000 |
| 40 | | 21 | (h) | Clapton O | D | 2-2 | Evans 2 | 11,000 |
| 41 | | 26 | (h) | Sheffield W | W | 2-0 | Lochhead, Smith | 7,500 |
| 42 | May | 3 | (a) | Sheffield W | L | 0-2 | | 7,250 |

FINAL LEAGUE POSITION: 14th in Division Two

Appearances
Goals

FA Cup

| 1 | Jan | 12 | (h) | Plymouth A | W | 1-0 |
|---|---|---|---|---|---|---|
| 2 | Feb | 2 | (h) | Huddersfield T | L | 0-3 |

Appearances and goals grid (shirt numbers by player and match):

| Mew | Radford | Moore | Bennion | Barson | Hilditch | Ellis | Goldthorpe | MacDonald | Lochhead | McPherson | Spence | Steward | Grimwood | Mann | Kennedy | Dennis | Haslam | Bain | Barber | Tyler | Thomas | Smith | Partridge | Miller | Silcock | Evans | No. |
|---|---|---|---|---|---|---|---|---|---|---|---|---|---|---|---|---|---|---|---|---|---|---|---|---|---|---|---|
| 1 | 2 | 3 | 4 | 5 | 6 | 7 | 8 | 9 | 10 | 11 | | | | | | | | | | | | | | | | | 1 |
| 1 | 2 | 3 | 4 | 5 | 6 | 7 | 8 | 9 | 10 | 11 | | | | | | | | | | | | | | | | | 2 |
| 1 | 2 | 3 | 4 | 5 | 6 | 7 | | 9 | 10 | 11 | 8 | | | | | | | | | | | | | | | | 3 |
| 1 | 2 | 3 | 4 | 5 | 6 | 7 | | 9 | 10 | 11 | 8 | | | | | | | | | | | | | | | | 4 |
| 1 | 2 | 3 | 4 | 5 | 6 | 7 | | 9 | 10 | 11 | 8 | | | | | | | | | | | | | | | | 5 |
| | 2 | 3 | | 5 | 4 | 7 | | 9 | 10 | 11 | | 1 | 6 | 8 | | | | | | | | | | | | | 6 |
| 1 | 2 | 3 | | 5 | 4 | 7 | | | 10 | 11 | 9 | | 6 | 8 | | | | | | | | | | | | | 7 |
| 1 | 2 | 3 | | 5 | 4 | 7 | 8 | 9 | 10 | 11 | | | 6 | | | | | | | | | | | | | | 8 |
| 1 | 2 | 3 | 4 | 5 | | | 8 | | 10 | 11 | 7 | | 9 | 6 | | | | | | | | | | | | | 9 |
| | | 2 | 4 | | 6 | | | | 10 | 11 | 7 | 1 | 8 | | | 3 | 5 | 9 | | | | | | | | | 10 |
| | | 2 | 4 | | 6 | | | | 10 | 11 | 7 | 1 | 8 | | | 3 | 5 | 9 | | | | | | | | | 11 |
| | | 2 | 4 | | 6 | | | | 10 | 11 | 7 | 1 | | | | 3 | 5 | 9 | 8 | | | | | | | | 12 |
| | 3 | 2 | 4 | | 6 | | | | 10 | 11 | 7 | 1 | 8 | | | | 5 | 9 | | | | | | | | | 13 |
| | | 3 | 4 | | 6 | | | | 10 | 11 | 7 | 1 | 5 | 8 | | | | 9 | | | 2 | | | | | | 14 |
| | 2 | 3 | 4 | | 6 | | | | 10 | 11 | 7 | 1 | 5 | 8 | | | | 9 | | | | | | | | | 15 |
| | 2 | 3 | 4 | 5 | 6 | | | | 10 | 11 | 7 | 1 | | 8 | | | | 9 | | | | | | | | | 16 |
| | 2 | 3 | 4 | | 6 | | | | 10 | 11 | 7 | 1 | 5 | 8 | | | | 9 | | | | | | | | | 17 |
| | 2 | 3 | 4 | | 6 | | | | 10 | | 7 | 1 | 5 | 8 | | | | 9 | | | 11 | | | | | | 18 |
| | 2 | 3 | 4 | | 6 | | | | 10 | 11 | 7 | 1 | 5 | 8 | | | | 9 | | | | | | | | | 19 |
| | 2 | 3 | 6 | | 4 | | | | 10 | 11 | 7 | 1 | 5 | 8 | | | | 9 | | | | | | | | | 20 |
| | 2 | 3 | 6 | | 4 | | | | 10 | 11 | 7 | 1 | 5 | 8 | | | | 9 | | | | | | | | | 21 |
| | 2 | 3 | 4 | 5 | 6 | | | | 10 | 11 | 7 | 1 | | 8 | | | | 9 | | | | | | | | | 22 |
| | 2 | 3 | 4 | 5 | 6 | | | | 10 | 11 | 7 | 1 | | 8 | | | | 9 | | | | | | | | | 23 |
| | 2 | 3 | 4 | 5 | 6 | | | | 10 | 11 | 7 | 1 | | 8 | | | | 9 | | | | | | | | | 24 |
| | 2 | 3 | 4 | 5 | 6 | | | | 10 | 11 | 7 | 1 | | 9 | | | | | | | | 8 | | | | | 25 |
| | 2 | 3 | 4 | 5 | 6 | | | | 10 | 11 | 7 | 1 | | 8 | | | | | | | | 9 | | | | | 26 |
| | 2 | 3 | 4 | 5 | 6 | | | | | | 7 | 1 | | 8 | | | | 9 | | | | 11 | 10 | | | | 27 |
| | 2 | 3 | 4 | 5 | 6 | | | | 10 | 11 | 7 | 1 | | 8 | | | | 9 | | | | | | | | | 28 |
| | 2 | 3 | 4 | 5 | | 7 | | | 10 | 11 | 9 | 1 | 6 | 8 | | | | | | | | | | | | | 29 |
| | 2 | 3 | 4 | | 6 | 7 | | | 9 | 11 | 8 | 1 | 5 | 10 | | | | | | | | | | | | | 30 |
| | 2 | 3 | 4 | | 6 | 7 | | | 9 | 11 | 8 | 1 | 5 | 10 | | | | | | | | | | | | | 31 |
| | 2 | 3 | 4 | | 6 | | | | 9 | 11 | 7 | 1 | 5 | 8 | | | | | | | | 10 | | | | | 32 |
| 1 | 2 | 3 | 4 | | 6 | | | | 9 | | 7 | | 5 | | | | | | | | 11 | 8 | 10 | | | | 33 |
| 1 | 2 | 3 | 4 | | 6 | | | | 9 | | 7 | | 5 | | | | | | | | 11 | 8 | 10 | | | | 34 |
| 1 | | 2 | 4 | | 6 | | | | 9 | 11 | 7 | | 5 | | | | | | | | | 8 | 10 | | 3 | | 35 |
| 1 | | 2 | 4 | | 6 | | | | 9 | 11 | 7 | | 5 | | | | | | | | | 8 | 10 | | 3 | | 36 |
| | | 2 | | | 6 | | | | 10 | | 9 | 1 | | | 5 | | | | | 4 | | 8 | 11 | | 3 | 7 | 37 |
| | | 2 | | | 6 | | | | 10 | | 9 | 1 | | | 5 | | | | | | 11 | 8 | | 4 | 3 | 7 | 38 |
| | | 2 | | | 6 | | | | 10 | | 9 | 1 | | | 5 | | | | | | 11 | 8 | | 4 | 3 | 7 | 39 |
| | | 2 | 4 | | 6 | | | | 10 | 11 | | 1 | 9 | | 5 | | | | | | | 8 | | | 3 | 7 | 40 |
| | | 2 | | | 6 | | | | 10 | | | 1 | 9 | | 5 | | | | | | 11 | 8 | | 4 | 3 | 7 | 41 |
| | | 2 | | | 6 | | | | 10 | | | 1 | 9 | | 5 | | | | | | 11 | 8 | | 4 | 3 | 7 | 42 |
| 12 | 30 | 42 | 34 | 17 | 41 | 11 | 4 | 7 | 40 | 34 | 36 | 30 | 22 | 25 | 6 | 3 | 7 | 18 | 1 | 1 | 6 | 12 | 5 | 4 | 8 | 6 | |
| | | | | | | | 1 | 1 | 14 | 1 | 10 | | 2 | 3 | 1 | | | 8 | 1 | | | 4 | | 1 | | 2 | |

3 own-goals

# 1924-25

Manager: John Chapman

| | | | | | | | |
|---|---|---|---|---|---|---|---|
| 1 | Aug | 30 | (h) | Leicester C | W 1-0 | Goldthorpe | 21,250 |
| 2 | Sep | 1 | (a) | Stockport C | L 1-2 | Lochhead | 12,500 |
| 3 | | 6 | (a) | Stoke | D 0-0 | | 15,250 |
| 4 | | 8 | (h) | Barnsley | W 1-0 | Henderson | 9,500 |
| 5 | | 13 | (h) | Coventry C | W 5-1 | Henderson 2, Lochhead, McPherson, Spence | 12,000 |
| 6 | | 20 | (a) | Oldham A | W 3-0 | Henderson 3 | 14,500 |
| 7 | | 27 | (h) | Sheffield W | W 2-0 | McPherson, Smith | 29,500 |
| 8 | Oct | 4 | (a) | Clapton O | W 1-0 | Lochhead | 15,000 |
| 9 | | 11 | (h) | Crystal P | W 1-0 | Lochhead | 27,750 |
| 10 | | 18 | (a) | Southampton | W 2-0 | Lochhead 2 | 10,000 |
| 11 | | 25 | (a) | Wolves | D 0-0 | | 17,500 |
| 12 | Nov | 1 | (h) | Fulham | W 2-0 | Henderson, Lochhead | 24,000 |
| 13 | | 8 | (a) | Portsmouth | D 1-1 | Smith | 19,500 |
| 14 | | 15 | (h) | Hull C | W 2-0 | Hanson, McPherson | 29,750 |
| 15 | | 22 | (a) | Blackpool | D 1-1 | Hanson | 9,500 |
| 16 | | 29 | (h) | Derby C | D 1-1 | Hanson | 59,500 |
| 17 | Dec | 6 | (a) | South Shields | W 2-1 | Henderson, McPherson | 6,500 |
| 18 | | 13 | (h) | Bradford C | W 3-0 | Henderson 2, McPherson | 18,250 |
| 19 | | 20 | (a) | Port Vale | L 1-2 | Lochhead | 11,000 |
| 20 | | 25 | (a) | Middlesbrough | D 1-1 | Henderson | 18,500 |
| 21 | | 26 | (h) | Middlesbrough | W 2-0 | Henderson, Smith | 44,000 |
| 22 | | 27 | (a) | Leicester C | L 0-3 | | 18,250 |
| 23 | Jan | 1 | (h) | Chelsea | W 1-0 | Grimwood | 30,500 |
| 24 | | 3 | (h) | Stoke | W 2-0 | Henderson 2 | 24,500 |
| 25 | | 17 | (a) | Coventry C | L 0-1 | | 9,000 |
| 26 | | 24 | (h) | Oldham A | L 0-1 | | 20,000 |
| 27 | Feb | 7 | (h) | Clapton O | W 4-2 | Kennedy 2, McPherson, Pape | 18,250 |
| 28 | | 14 | (a) | Crystal P | L 1-2 | Lochhead | 11,250 |
| 29 | | 23 | (a) | Sheffield W | D 1-1 | Pape | 3,000 |
| 30 | | 28 | (h) | Wolves | W 3-0 | Spence 2, Kennedy | 21,250 |
| 31 | Mar | 7 | (a) | Fulham | L 0-1 | | 16,000 |
| 32 | | 14 | (h) | Portsmouth | W 2-0 | Lochhead, Spence | 22,000 |
| 33 | | 21 | (a) | Hull C | W 1-0 | Lochhead | 6,250 |
| 34 | | 28 | (h) | Blackpool | D 0-0 | | 26,250 |
| 35 | Apr | 4 | (a) | Derby C | L 0-1 | | 24,000 |
| 36 | | 10 | (h) | Stockport C | W 2-0 | Pape 2 | 43,500 |
| 37 | | 11 | (h) | South Shields | W 1-0 | Lochhead | 24,000 |
| 38 | | 13 | (a) | Chelsea | D 0-0 | | 16,500 |
| 39 | | 18 | (a) | Bradford C | W 1-0 | Smith | 13,250 |
| 40 | | 22 | (h) | Southampton | D 1-1 | Pape | 26,500 |
| 41 | | 25 | (h) | Port Vale | W 4-0 | Lochhead, McPherson, Smith, Spence | 33,500 |
| 42 | May | 2 | (a) | Barnsley | D 0-0 | | 11,250 |

FINAL LEAGUE POSITION: 2nd in Division Two

Appearances
Goals

FA Cup

| | | | | | | |
|---|---|---|---|---|---|---|
| 1 | Jan | 10 | (a) | Sheffield W | L 0-2 | |

240

| Steward | Moore | Silcock | Bennion | Barson | Hilditch | Spence | Smith | Goldthorpe | Lochhead | McPherson | Henderson | Mann | Grimwood | Jones | Thomas | Hanson | Kennedy | Haslam | Taylor C | Bain | Pape | Partridge | Rennox | |
|---|---|---|---|---|---|---|---|---|---|---|---|---|---|---|---|---|---|---|---|---|---|---|---|---|
| 1 | 2 | 3 | 4 | 5 | 6 | 7 | 8 | 9 | 10 | 11 | | | | | | | | | | | | | | 1 |
| 1 | 2 | 3 | 4 | 5 | 6 | 7 | 8 | | 10 | 11 | 9 | | | | | | | | | | | | | 2 |
| 1 | 2 | 3 | | 5 | 6 | 7 | 8 | | 10 | 11 | 9 | 4 | | | | | | | | | | | | 3 |
| 1 | 2 | 3 | | | 6 | 7 | 8 | | 10 | 11 | 9 | 4 | 5 | | | | | | | | | | | 4 |
| 1 | 2 | 3 | | 5 | | 7 | 8 | | 10 | 11 | 9 | 4 | 6 | | | | | | | | | | | 5 |
| 1 | 2 | 3 | | 5 | | 7 | 8 | | 10 | 11 | 9 | 4 | 6 | | | | | | | | | | | 6 |
| 1 | 2 | 3 | | 5 | | 7 | 8 | | 10 | 11 | 9 | 4 | 6 | | | | | | | | | | | 7 |
| 1 | 2 | 3 | | 5 | | 7 | 8 | | 10 | 11 | 9 | 4 | 6 | | | | | | | | | | | 8 |
| 1 | 2 | 3 | | 5 | | 7 | 8 | | 10 | 11 | 9 | 4 | 6 | | | | | | | | | | | 9 |
| 1 | 2 | 3 | | 5 | | 7 | 8 | | 10 | 11 | 9 | 4 | 6 | | | | | | | | | | | 10 |
| 1 | 2 | 3 | | 5 | | 7 | 8 | | 10 | 11 | 9 | 4 | 6 | | | | | | | | | | | 11 |
| 1 | 2 | 3 | | 5 | | 7 | 8 | | 10 | 11 | 9 | 4 | 6 | | | | | | | | | | | 12 |
| 1 | 2 | | | 5 | | 7 | 8 | | 10 | | 9 | 4 | 6 | 3 | 11 | | | | | | | | | 13 |
| 1 | 2 | 3 | | 5 | | 7 | 8 | | 10 | 11 | | 4 | 6 | | | 9 | | | | | | | | 14 |
| 1 | 2 | 3 | | 5 | | 7 | 8 | | 10 | 11 | | 4 | 6 | | | 9 | | | | | | | | 15 |
| 1 | 2 | 3 | | 5 | | 7 | 8 | | 10 | 11 | | 4 | 6 | | | 9 | | | | | | | | 16 |
| 1 | 2 | 3 | | 5 | | 7 | 8 | | 10 | 11 | 9 | 4 | 6 | | | | | | | | | | | 17 |
| 1 | | 3 | | 5 | | 7 | 8 | | 10 | 11 | 9 | 4 | 6 | | | | 2 | | | | | | | 18 |
| 1 | | 3 | | 5 | | 7 | 8 | | 10 | 11 | 9 | 4 | 6 | | | | 2 | | | | | | | 19 |
| 1 | 2 | 3 | | 5 | | 7 | 8 | | | 11 | 9 | 4 | 6 | | | | 10 | | | | | | | 20 |
| 1 | 2 | 3 | | 5 | | 7 | 8 | | | 11 | 9 | 4 | 6 | | | | 10 | | | | | | | 21 |
| 1 | 2 | 3 | | 5 | | 7 | 8 | | | 11 | 9 | 4 | 6 | | | | 10 | | | | | | | 22 |
| 1 | 2 | 3 | | 5 | | 7 | 8 | | | 11 | 9 | 4 | 6 | | | | 10 | | | | | | | 23 |
| 1 | 2 | 3 | | 5 | | 7 | | | | 11 | 9 | 4 | 6 | 8 | | | 10 | | | | | | | 24 |
| 1 | 2 | 3 | | | | 7 | | | 10 | 11 | 9 | 4 | 6 | | | | | 5 | 8 | | | | | 25 |
| 1 | 2 | 3 | | 5 | | 7 | 8 | | | 11 | 9 | 4 | 6 | | | | 10 | | | | | | | 26 |
| 1 | 2 | 3 | 4 | | | 7 | 8 | | | 11 | | 5 | 6 | | | | 10 | | | 9 | | | | 27 |
| 1 | 2 | 3 | 4 | | | 7 | 8 | | | 11 | | 5 | 6 | | | | 10 | | | 9 | | | | 28 |
| 1 | 2 | 3 | 4 | | | 7 | 8 | | | 11 | | 5 | 6 | | | | 10 | | | 9 | | | | 29 |
| 1 | 2 | | 4 | | | 7 | 8 | | | | | 5 | 6 | 3 | | | 10 | | | 9 | 11 | | | 30 |
| 1 | 2 | | 4 | | | 7 | 8 | | | 11 | | 5 | 6 | 3 | | | 10 | | | 9 | | | | 31 |
| 1 | 2 | | 4 | | | 7 | | | 10 | 11 | | 5 | 6 | 3 | | | | | | 9 | | 8 | | 32 |
| 1 | 2 | | 4 | | | 7 | | | 10 | 11 | | 5 | 6 | 3 | | | | | | 9 | | 8 | | 33 |
| 1 | 2 | | 4 | | | 7 | | | 10 | 11 | | 5 | 6 | 3 | | | | | | 9 | | 8 | | 34 |
| 1 | 2 | | | 5 | | 7 | | | 10 | | | 4 | 6 | 3 | 11 | | | | | 9 | | 8 | | 35 |
| 1 | 2 | | 4 | 5 | | 7 | 8 | | 10 | | | | 6 | 3 | 11 | | | | | 9 | | | | 36 |
| 1 | 2 | 3 | 4 | 5 | | 7 | 8 | | 10 | 11 | | | 6 | | | | | | | 9 | | | | 37 |
| 1 | 2 | | 4 | 5 | | 7 | 8 | | 10 | 11 | | | 6 | 3 | | | | | | 9 | | | | 38 |
| 1 | 2 | | 4 | 5 | | 7 | 8 | | 10 | 11 | | | 6 | 3 | | | | | | 9 | | | | 39 |
| 1 | 2 | | 4 | 5 | | 7 | 8 | | 10 | 11 | | | 6 | 3 | | | | | | 9 | | | | 40 |
| 1 | 2 | | 4 | 5 | | 7 | 8 | | 10 | 11 | | | 6 | 3 | | | | | | 9 | | | | 41 |
| 1 | 2 | | 4 | 5 | | 7 | 8 | | 10 | 11 | | | 6 | 3 | | | | | | 9 | | | | 42 |
| 42 | 40 | 29 | 17 | 32 | 4 | 42 | 31 | 1 | 37 | 38 | 22 | 32 | 39 | 15 | 3 | 3 | 11 | 1 | 1 | 16 | 1 | 4 | | |
| | | | | | | 5 | 5 | 1 | 13 | 7 | 14 | | 1 | | | 3 | 3 | | | 5 | | | | |

# 1925-26

Manager: John Chapman

| 1 | Aug | 29 | (a) | West Ham U | L | 0-1 | | 25,630 |
|---|---|---|---|---|---|---|---|---|
| 2 | Sep | 2 | (h) | Aston Villa | W | 3-0 | Barson, Lochhead, Spence | 41,717 |
| 3 | | 5 | (h) | Arsenal | L | 0-1 | | 32,288 |
| 4 | | 7 | (a) | Aston Villa | D | 2-2 | Hanson, Rennox | 27,701 |
| 5 | | 12 | (a) | Manchester C | D | 1-1 | Rennox | 62,994 |
| 6 | | 16 | (h) | Leicester C | W | 3-2 | Rennox 2, Lochhead | 21,275 |
| 7 | | 19 | (a) | Liverpool | L | 0-5 | | 18,824 |
| 8 | | 26 | (h) | Burnley | W | 6-1 | Rennox 3, Hanson, Hilditch, Smith | 17,259 |
| 9 | Oct | 3 | (a) | Leeds U | L | 0-2 | | 26,265 |
| 10 | | 10 | (h) | Newcastle U | W | 2-1 | Rennox, Thomas | 39,651 |
| 11 | | 17 | (h) | Tottenham H | D | 0-0 | | 26,496 |
| 12 | | 24 | (a) | Cardiff C | W | 2-0 | McPherson 2 | 15,846 |
| 13 | | 31 | (h) | Huddersfield T | D | 1-1 | Thomas | 37,213 |
| 14 | Nov | 7 | (a) | Everton | W | 3-1 | McPherson, Rennox, Spence | 12,387 |
| 15 | | 14 | (h) | Birmingham | W | 3-1 | Barson, Spence, Thomas | 23,559 |
| 16 | | 21 | (a) | Bury | W | 3-1 | McPherson 2, Spence | 16,591 |
| 17 | | 28 | (h) | Blackburn R | W | 2-0 | McPherson, Thomas | 33,660 |
| 18 | Dec | 5 | (a) | Sunderland | L | 1-2 | Rennox | 25,507 |
| 19 | | 12 | (h) | Sheffield U | L | 1-2 | McPherson | 31,132 |
| 20 | | 19 | (a) | West Brom A | L | 1-5 | McPherson | 17,651 |
| 21 | | 25 | (h) | Bolton W | W | 2-1 | Hanson, Spence | 38,503 |
| 22 | | 28 | (a) | Leicester C | W | 3-1 | McPherson 3 | 28,367 |
| 23 | Jan | 2 | (h) | West Ham U | W | 2-1 | Rennox 2 | 29,612 |
| 24 | | 16 | (a) | Arsenal | L | 2-3 | McPherson, Spence | 25,252 |
| 25 | | 23 | (h) | Manchester C | L | 1-6 | Rennox | 48,657 |
| 26 | Feb | 6 | (a) | Burnley | W | 1-0 | McPherson | 17,141 |
| 27 | | 13 | (h) | Leeds U | W | 2-1 | McPherson, Sweeney | 29,584 |
| 28 | | 27 | (a) | Tottenham H | W | 1-0 | Smith | 25,466 |
| 29 | Mar | 10 | (h) | Liverpool | D | 3-3 | Hanson, Rennox, Spence | 9,214 |
| 30 | | 13 | (a) | Huddersfield T | L | 0-5 | | 27,842 |
| 31 | | 17 | (a) | Bolton W | L | 1-3 | McPherson | 10,794 |
| 32 | | 20 | (h) | Everton | D | 0-0 | | 30,058 |
| 33 | Apr | 2 | (a) | Notts C | W | 3-0 | Rennox 2, McPherson | 18,453 |
| 34 | | 3 | (h) | Bury | L | 0-1 | | 41,085 |
| 35 | | 5 | (h) | Notts C | L | 0-1 | | 19,606 |
| 36 | | 10 | (a) | Blackburn R | L | 0-7 | | 15,870 |
| 37 | | 14 | (a) | Newcastle U | L | 1-4 | Hanson | 9,829 |
| 38 | | 19 | (a) | Birmingham | L | 1-2 | Rennox | 8,948 |
| 39 | | 21 | (h) | Sunderland | W | 5-1 | Taylor 3, Smith, Thomas | 10,918 |
| 40 | | 24 | (a) | Sheffield U | L | 0-2 | | 15,571 |
| 41 | | 28 | (h) | Cardiff C | W | 1-0 | Inglis | 9,116 |
| 42 | May | 1 | (h) | West Brom A | W | 3-2 | Taylor 3 | 9,974 |

FINAL LEAGUE POSITION: 9th in Division One

Appearances
Goals

## FA Cup

| 3 | Jan | 9 | (a) | Port Vale | W | 3-2 |
|---|---|---|---|---|---|---|
| 4 | | 30 | (a) | Tottenham H | D | 2-2 |
| R | Feb | 3 | (h) | Tottenham H | W | 2-0 |
| 5 | | 20 | (a) | Sunderland | D | 3-3 |
| R | | 24 | (h) | Sunderland | W | 2-1 |
| 6 | Mar | 6 | (a) | Fulham | W | 2-1 |
| SF | | 27 | (n*) | Manchester C | L | 0-3 | (*Played at Bramall Lane, Sheffield.) |

242

Player appearance/shirt-number grid (numbers indicate the shirt number each player wore in that match; blank = did not play).

| Steward | Moore | Silcock | Bennion | Barson | Bain | Spence | Smith | Iddon | Lochhead | McPherson | Mann | Hilditch | Pape | Hanson | Rennox | Grimwood | Thomas | Haslam | Taylor | Hannaford | McCrae | Jones T | Mew | Hall | Sweeney | Partridge | Astley | Inglis | Richardson | |
|---|---|---|---|---|---|---|---|---|---|---|---|---|---|---|---|---|---|---|---|---|---|---|---|---|---|---|---|---|---|---|
| 1 | 2 | 3 | 4 | 5 | 6 | 7 | 8 | 9 | 10 | 11 |  |  |  |  |  |  |  |  |  |  |  |  |  |  |  |  |  |  |  | 1 |
| 1 | 2 | 3 |  | 5 |  | 7 | 8 |  | 10 | 11 | 4 | 6 | 9 |  |  |  |  |  |  |  |  |  |  |  |  |  |  |  |  | 2 |
| 1 | 2 | 3 |  | 5 |  | 7 | 8 |  | 10 | 11 | 4 | 6 | 9 |  |  |  |  |  |  |  |  |  |  |  |  |  |  |  |  | 3 |
| 1 | 2 | 3 | 4 | 5 |  | 7 | 8 |  |  | 11 |  | 6 |  |  | 9 | 10 |  |  |  |  |  |  |  |  |  |  |  |  |  | 4 |
| 1 | 2 | 3 | 4 | 5 |  | 7 | 8 |  |  | 11 |  | 6 |  |  | 9 | 10 |  |  |  |  |  |  |  |  |  |  |  |  |  | 5 |
| 1 | 2 | 3 | 4 | 5 |  | 7 | 8 |  | 9 | 11 |  | 6 |  |  |  | 10 |  |  |  |  |  |  |  |  |  |  |  |  |  | 6 |
| 1 | 2 | 3 |  | 5 |  | 7 | 8 |  | 9 | 11 |  | 6 |  | 4 |  | 10 |  |  |  |  |  |  |  |  |  |  |  |  |  | 7 |
| 1 | 2 | 3 |  | 5 |  | 7 | 8 |  |  |  |  |  |  | 4 | 9 | 10 | 6 | 11 |  |  |  |  |  |  |  |  |  |  |  | 8 |
| 1 | 2 | 3 |  | 5 |  | 7 | 8 |  |  |  |  |  |  | 4 | 9 | 10 | 6 | 11 |  |  |  |  |  |  |  |  |  |  |  | 9 |
| 1 | 2 | 3 |  | 5 |  | 7 | 8 |  |  |  |  |  |  | 4 | 9 | 10 | 6 | 11 |  |  |  |  |  |  |  |  |  |  |  | 10 |
| 1 | 2 | 3 |  | 5 |  | 7 | 8 |  |  |  |  |  |  | 4 | 9 | 10 | 6 | 11 |  |  |  |  |  |  |  |  |  |  |  | 11 |
| 1 | 2 | 3 |  | 5 |  | 7 |  |  |  |  | 4 |  |  | 9 | 8 | 10 | 6 | 11 |  |  |  |  |  |  |  |  |  |  |  | 12 |
| 1 | 2 | 3 |  | 5 |  | 7 |  |  |  |  | 4 |  |  | 9 | 8 | 10 | 6 | 11 |  |  |  |  |  |  |  |  |  |  |  | 13 |
| 1 | 2 | 3 |  |  |  | 7 | 8 |  |  | 9 |  | 6 |  | 4 |  | 10 |  | 11 | 5 |  |  |  |  |  |  |  |  |  |  | 14 |
| 1 | 2 | 3 |  | 5 |  | 7 | 8 |  |  | 9 |  | 6 |  | 4 |  | 10 |  | 11 |  |  |  |  |  |  |  |  |  |  |  | 15 |
| 1 | 2 | 3 |  | 5 |  | 7 | 8 |  |  | 9 |  | 6 |  | 4 |  | 10 |  | 11 |  |  |  |  |  |  |  |  |  |  |  | 16 |
| 1 | 2 | 3 |  | 5 |  | 7 | 8 |  |  | 9 |  | 6 |  | 4 |  | 10 |  | 11 |  |  |  |  |  |  |  |  |  |  |  | 17 |
| 1 | 2 | 3 |  |  |  | 7 | 8 |  |  |  |  | 6 |  | 4 | 9 | 10 |  | 11 | 5 |  |  |  |  |  |  |  |  |  |  | 18 |
| 1 | 2 | 3 |  | 5 |  | 7 | 8 |  |  | 9 |  | 6 |  | 4 |  | 10 |  | 11 |  |  |  |  |  |  |  |  |  |  |  | 19 |
| 1 | 2 | 3 | 4 |  |  | 7 |  |  |  | 9 |  | 6 |  |  |  | 10 |  | 11 | 5 | 8 |  |  |  |  |  |  |  |  |  | 20 |
| 1 | 2 | 3 |  | 5 |  | 7 |  |  |  | 9 |  | 6 |  | 4 | 8 | 10 |  | 11 |  |  |  |  |  |  |  |  |  |  |  | 21 |
| 1 | 2 | 3 |  |  |  | 7 |  |  |  | 9 |  | 6 |  | 4 | 5 | 8 | 10 |  |  |  | 11 |  |  |  |  |  |  |  |  | 22 |
| 1 | 2 | 3 |  |  |  | 7 |  |  |  | 9 |  | 6 |  | 4 | 8 | 10 | 5 | 11 |  |  |  |  |  |  |  |  |  |  |  | 23 |
| 1 |  | 3 |  |  |  | 7 |  |  |  | 9 |  | 4 |  | 5 | 8 | 10 |  | 11 |  |  | 6 | 2 |  |  |  |  |  |  |  | 24 |
| 1 |  | 3 | 4 |  |  | 7 |  |  |  | 9 |  | 6 | 5 |  |  | 10 |  | 11 |  | 8 |  | 2 |  |  |  |  |  |  |  | 25 |
|  | 2 | 3 |  |  |  |  | 8 |  |  | 9 |  | 6 |  |  |  | 10 |  |  | 5 |  | 11 | 4 |  | 1 | 7 |  |  |  |  | 26 |
|  | 2 | 3 |  |  |  |  |  |  |  | 9 |  | 6 |  | 8 |  |  |  |  | 5 |  | 11 | 4 |  | 1 | 7 | 10 |  |  |  | 27 |
|  | 2 |  |  |  |  |  | 8 |  |  | 9 |  | 6 |  |  |  | 10 |  | 11 | 5 |  | 4 | 3 | 1 | 7 |  |  |  |  |  | 28 |
|  | 2 | 3 |  | 5 | 4 | 7 | 8 |  |  |  |  | 6 |  |  | 9 | 10 |  |  |  |  |  | 1 |  |  | 11 |  |  |  |  | 29 |
|  | 2 |  | 4 | 5 |  | 7 | 8 |  |  |  |  | 6 |  |  | 9 | 10 |  |  |  |  | 3 | 1 |  |  | 11 |  |  |  |  | 30 |
|  | 2 |  |  | 5 |  | 7 | 8 |  |  | 9 |  | 6 |  |  |  | 10 | 11 | 4 |  |  |  | 1 |  |  |  | 3 |  |  |  | 31 |
| 1 |  |  |  | 5 |  | 7 | 8 |  |  | 9 |  | 6 |  | 10 |  |  | 11 |  |  |  | 4 | 3 |  |  |  | 2 |  |  |  | 32 |
| 1 | 2 | 3 |  | 5 |  | 7 | 8 |  |  | 9 | 4 |  |  |  | 10 |  | 11 |  |  |  | 6 |  |  |  |  |  |  |  |  | 33 |
| 1 | 2 | 3 |  | 5 |  | 7 |  |  |  | 9 | 4 |  |  | 8 | 10 |  | 11 |  |  |  | 6 |  |  |  |  |  |  |  |  | 34 |
| 1 | 2 |  |  |  |  | 7 | 8 |  |  | 9 | 6 |  |  | 4 | 10 |  | 11 |  |  |  | 5 | 3 |  |  |  |  |  |  |  | 35 |
| 1 | 2 | 3 |  | 5 |  | 7 |  |  |  | 9 | 6 | 4 |  | 10 |  |  |  |  | 8 | 11 |  |  |  |  |  |  |  |  |  | 36 |
| 1 |  |  |  |  |  | 7 | 8 |  |  | 6 | 4 |  |  | 10 | 9 |  | 11 |  |  |  | 6 | 3 |  |  |  | 2 |  |  |  | 37 |
| 1 |  |  |  |  |  | 7 | 8 |  |  | 6 | 4 |  |  | 9 | 10 |  | 11 | 5 |  |  |  | 3 |  |  |  | 2 |  |  |  | 38 |
| 1 |  |  |  | 5 |  | 7 | 8 |  |  | 6 | 4 |  |  | 10 |  |  | 11 |  | 9 |  |  | 3 |  |  |  | 2 |  |  |  | 39 |
| 1 |  |  |  |  |  | 7 | 8 |  |  | 6 | 4 |  |  | 10 |  |  | 11 | 5 | 9 |  |  | 3 |  |  |  | 2 |  |  |  | 40 |
| 1 |  | 3 | 5 |  |  | 7 | 8 |  |  | 6 | 4 |  |  | 9 |  |  | 11 |  |  |  |  |  |  | 10 |  |  | 2 |  |  | 41 |
|  |  | 3 | 5 |  |  | 7 |  |  |  | 6 | 4 |  |  | 8 |  |  |  | 9 |  |  |  |  | 10 | 11 |  |  | 2 | 1 |  | 42 |
| 35 | 33 | 33 | 7 | 28 | 2 | 39 | 30 | 1 | 5 | 29 | 34 | 28 | 2 | 24 | 34 | 7 | 29 | 9 | 6 | 4 | 9 | 10 | 6 | 3 | 3 | 3 | 1 | 7 | 1 | |
|  |  | 2 |  |  |  | 7 | 3 |  |  |  |  | 2 | 16 |  |  |  | 1 |  | 5 | 17 |  | 5 |  | 6 |  |  | 1 |  | 1 | |

243

# 1926-27

Manager: John Chapman until October 1926, then Clarrie Hilditch to April 1927, then Herbert Bamlett.

| 1 | Aug | 28 | (a) | Liverpool | L | 2-4 | McPherson 2 | 34,795 |
|---|---|---|---|---|---|---|---|---|
| 2 | | 30 | (a) | Sheffield U | D | 2-2 | McPherson 2 | 14,844 |
| 3 | Sep | 4 | (h) | Leeds U | D | 2-2 | McPherson 2 | 26,338 |
| 4 | | 11 | (a) | Newcastle U | L | 2-4 | McPherson, Spence | 28,050 |
| 5 | | 15 | (h) | Arsenal | D | 2-2 | Hanson, Spence | 15,259 |
| 6 | | 18 | (h) | Burnley | W | 2-1 | Spence 2 | 32,593 |
| 7 | | 25 | (a) | Cardiff C | W | 2-0 | Rennox, Spence | 17,267 |
| 8 | Oct | 2 | (h) | Aston Villa | W | 2-1 | Barson, Rennox | 31,234 |
| 9 | | 9 | (a) | Bolton W | L | 0-4 | | 17,869 |
| 10 | | 16 | (a) | Bury | W | 3-0 | Spence 2, McPherson | 22,728 |
| 11 | | 23 | (h) | Birmingham | L | 0-1 | | 32,010 |
| 12 | | 30 | (a) | West Ham U | L | 0-4 | | 19,733 |
| 13 | Nov | 6 | (h) | Sheffield W | D | 0-0 | | 16,166 |
| 14 | | 13 | (a) | Leicester C | W | 3-2 | McPherson 2, Rennox | 18,521 |
| 15 | | 20 | (h) | Everton | W | 2-1 | Rennox 2 | 24,361 |
| 16 | | 27 | (a) | Blackburn R | L | 1-2 | Spence | 17,280 |
| 17 | Dec | 4 | (h) | Huddersfield T | D | 0-0 | | 33,135 |
| 18 | | 11 | (a) | Sunderland | L | 0-6 | | 15,385 |
| 19 | | 18 | (h) | West Brom A | W | 2-0 | Sweeney 2 | 18,585 |
| 20 | | 25 | (a) | Tottenham H | D | 1-1 | Spence | 37,287 |
| 21 | | 27 | (h) | Tottenham H | W | 2-1 | McPherson 2 | 50,665 |
| 22 | | 28 | (a) | Arsenal | L | 0-1 | | 30,111 |
| 23 | Jan | 1 | (h) | Sheffield U | W | 5-0 | McPherson 2, Barson, Rennox, Sweeney | 33,593 |
| 24 | | 15 | (h) | Liverpool | L | 0-1 | | 30,304 |
| 25 | | 22 | (a) | Leeds U | W | 3-2 | McPherson, Rennox, Spence | 16,816 |
| 26 | Feb | 5 | (a) | Burnley | L | 0-1 | | 22,010 |
| 27 | | 9 | (h) | Newcastle U | W | 3-1 | Hanson, Harris, Spence | 25,402 |
| 28 | | 12 | (h) | Cardiff C | D | 1-1 | Hanson | 26,213 |
| 29 | | 19 | (a) | Aston Villa | L | 0-2 | | 32,467 |
| 30 | | 26 | (h) | Bolton W | D | 0-0 | | 29,618 |
| 31 | Mar | 5 | (h) | Bury | L | 1-2 | A.Smith | 14,709 |
| 32 | | 12 | (a) | Birmingham | L | 0-4 | | 14,392 |
| 33 | | 19 | (h) | West Ham U | L | 0-3 | | 18,347 |
| 34 | | 26 | (a) | Sheffield W | L | 0-2 | | 11,997 |
| 35 | Apr | 2 | (h) | Leicester C | W | 1-0 | Spence | 17,119 |
| 36 | | 9 | (a) | Everton | D | 0-0 | | 22,564 |
| 37 | | 15 | (h) | Derby C | D | 2-2 | Spence 2 | 31,110 |
| 38 | | 16 | (h) | Blackburn R | W | 2-0 | Hanson, Spence | 24,845 |
| 39 | | 18 | (a) | Derby C | D | 2-2 | Spence 2 | 17,306 |
| 40 | | 23 | (a) | Huddersfield T | D | 0-0 | | 13,870 |
| 41 | | 30 | (h) | Sunderland | D | 0-0 | | 17,300 |
| 42 | May | 7 | (a) | West Brom A | D | 2-2 | Hanson, Spence | 6,668 |

FINAL LEAGUE POSITION: 15th in Division One

Appearances
Goals

FA Cup

| 3 | Jan | 8 | (a) | Reading | D | 1-1 | |
|---|---|---|---|---|---|---|---|
| R | | 12 | (h) | Reading | D | 2-2 | (After extra-time) |
| 2R | | 17 | (n*) | Reading | L | 1-2 | (*Played at Villa Park, Birmingham.) |

244

| Steward | Inglis | Silcock | Hilditch | Barson | Mann | Spence | Smith T | McPherson | Haworth | Thomas | Bennion | Haslam | Hanson | Wilson | Partridge | Rennox | Jones | Grimwood | Chapman | Hamaford | Sweeney | Moore | Harris | Smith A | Iddon | Astley | No |
|---|---|---|---|---|---|---|---|---|---|---|---|---|---|---|---|---|---|---|---|---|---|---|---|---|---|---|---|
| 1 | 2 | 3 | 4 | 5 | 6 | 7 | 8 | 9 | 10 | 11 | | | | | | | | | | | | | | | | | 1 |
| 1 | 2 | 3 | | | 6 | 7 | | 9 | 10 | 11 | 4 | 5 | 8 | | | | | | | | | | | | | | 2 |
| 1 | 2 | 3 | | 5 | 6 | 7 | | 9 | | | 4 | | 8 | 10 | 11 | | | | | | | | | | | | 3 |
| 1 | 2 | 3 | | 5 | 6 | 7 | | 9 | | | 4 | | 8 | 11 | 10 | | | | | | | | | | | | 4 |
| 1 | 2 | | | 5 | 6 | 7 | | 9 | | | 4 | | 8 | 11 | 10 | 3 | | | | | | | | | | | 5 |
| 1 | 2 | | | | 6 | | | 9 | | 11 | 4 | | 8 | | 10 | 3 | 5 | 7 | | | | | | | | | 6 |
| 1 | | 3 | | 5 | | | | 9 | | | 4 | | 8 | 6 | 10 | 2 | | 7 | 11 | | | | | | | | 7 |
| 1 | | 3 | | 5 | | | | 9 | | | 4 | 5 | 8 | | 10 | 2 | | 7 | 11 | | | | | | | | 8 |
| 1 | | 3 | | | | | | 9 | | | 4 | 5 | 8 | 6 | 10 | 2 | | 7 | 11 | | | | | | | | 9 |
| 1 | | 3 | | | | | | 9 | | 11 | 4 | | | 6 | 10 | 2 | 5 | 7 | | | 8 | | | | | | 10 |
| 1 | | 3 | | 5 | | | | 9 | | 11 | 4 | | | 6 | 10 | 2 | | 7 | | | 8 | | | | | | 11 |
| 1 | | | 4 | 5 | 6 | 7 | | 9 | | 11 | | | | | 10 | 3 | | | | | 8 | 2 | | | | | 12 |
| 1 | | | | 5 | | | 8 | 9 | | 11 | 4 | | | 6 | 10 | 3 | | 7 | | | | 2 | | | | | 13 |
| 1 | | | | | | 7 | 8 | 9 | | 11 | 4 | | | 6 | 10 | 3 | 5 | | | | | 2 | | | | | 14 |
| 1 | | | | | | 7 | 8 | 9 | | 11 | 4 | | | 6 | 10 | 3 | 5 | | | | | 2 | | | | | 15 |
| 1 | | | | | | 7 | 8 | 9 | | 11 | 4 | | | 6 | 10 | 3 | 5 | | | | | 2 | | | | | 16 |
| 1 | | | | | | 7 | 8 | 9 | | 11 | 4 | | | 6 | 10 | 3 | 5 | | | | | 2 | | | | | 17 |
| 1 | | | | | | 7 | 8 | 9 | | 11 | 4 | | | 6 | 10 | 3 | 5 | | | | | 2 | | | | | 18 |
| 1 | | 3 | | | | 7 | 8 | 9 | | 11 | 4 | | | 6 | | 5 | | | | | 10 | 2 | | | | | 19 |
| 1 | | 3 | | 5 | 8 | 7 | | 9 | | | 4 | | | 6 | 11 | | | | | | 10 | 2 | | | | | 20 |
| 1 | | 3 | | 5 | | 7 | | 9 | | | 4 | | | 6 | 11 | | | 8 | | | 10 | 2 | | | | | 21 |
| 1 | | 3 | 10 | | | 7 | | 9 | | | 4 | | | 6 | 11 | | | 8 | | | | 2 | | 5 | | | 22 |
| 1 | | 3 | 6 | 5 | | 7 | | 9 | | | 4 | | | | 11 | | | 8 | | | 10 | 2 | | | | | 23 |
| 1 | | | | | 6 | 7 | | 9 | | | 4 | | 8 | | 11 | 3 | 5 | | | | 10 | 2 | | | | | 24 |
| 1 | | 6 | | | | 7 | | | | 11 | 4 | | | | 8 | 3 | 5 | | | | 10 | 2 | | 9 | | | 25 |
| 1 | | 6 | | 5 | | 7 | | | | 11 | 4 | | | | | 3 | | | | | 10 | 2 | 9 | 8 | | | 26 |
| 1 | | 3 | 6 | 4 | | 7 | | 9 | | | | | | | 11 | | 5 | | | | 10 | 2 | 8 | | | | 27 |
| 1 | | 3 | 6 | 4 | | 7 | | 9 | | | | | | | 11 | | 5 | | | | 10 | 2 | 8 | | | | 28 |
| 1 | | 3 | | 5 | 6 | 7 | | | | 11 | 4 | | | 9 | 10 | | | | | | | 2 | 8 | | | | 29 |
| 1 | | 3 | 6 | | | | 8 | 9 | | | 4 | | | | 10 | | 5 | 7 | 11 | | | 2 | | | | | 30 |
| 1 | | 6 | | 8 | | 10 | | | | | 4 | 5 | | | 11 | 3 | | 7 | | | | 2 | | 9 | | | 31 |
| 1 | | 6 | | 8 | | 10 | | | | | 4 | 5 | | | | 3 | | 7 | 11 | | | 2 | | 9 | | | 32 |
| 1 | | 3 | | 5 | | 7 | | 9 | | | 4 | | 8 | 6 | | | | | | 11 | 10 | 2 | | | | | 33 |
| 1 | | 3 | | | | 7 | 8 | | | | 4 | | 9 | 6 | 10 | | 5 | | | 11 | | 2 | | | | | 34 |
| 1 | | 3 | 6 | 5 | | | | 9 | | 11 | 4 | | 8 | | 10 | | | 7 | | | | 2 | | | | | 35 |
| 1 | | 3 | 6 | 5 | | | | 9 | | | 4 | | 8 | 11 | 10 | | | 7 | | | | 2 | | | | | 36 |
| 1 | | 3 | 6 | 5 | | | | 9 | | 11 | 4 | | 8 | | | | | 7 | | | 10 | 2 | | | | | 37 |
| 1 | | 3 | 6 | 5 | | | | 9 | | | 4 | | 8 | 11 | 10 | | | 7 | | | | 2 | | | | | 38 |
| 1 | | 3 | 6 | | | | | 9 | | | 4 | | 8 | 11 | 10 | | 5 | 7 | | | | 2 | | | | | 39 |
| 1 | | 3 | 6 | 5 | | | | 9 | | | 4 | | | | 11 | | | 7 | | | 10 | 2 | 8 | | | | 40 |
| 1 | | | | 5 | | | | 9 | | 11 | 4 | | 8 | 6 | 10 | | | | | | | 2 | 7 | 3 | | | 41 |
| 1 | | | | | | | | 9 | | 11 | 4 | | 8 | 6 | 10 | 3 | 5 | 7 | | | | 2 | | | | | 42 |
| 42 | 6 | 26 | 16 | 21 | 14 | 40 | 10 | 32 | 2 | 16 | 37 | 4 | 21 | 21 | 16 | 22 | 21 | 17 | 17 | 7 | 13 | 30 | 4 | 5 | 1 | 1 | |
| | | | | 2 | | 18 | | 15 | | 5 | | | 7 | | | | | 3 | | | | | 1 | 1 | | | |

# 1927-28

Manager: Herbert Bamlett

| 1 | Aug | 27 | (h) | Middlesbrough | W | 3-0 | Spence 2, Hanson | 44,957 |
|---|---|---|---|---|---|---|---|---|
| 2 | | 29 | (a) | Sheffield W | W | 2-0 | Hanson, Partridge | 17,944 |
| 3 | Sep | 3 | (a) | Birmingham | D | 0-0 | | 25,863 |
| 4 | | 7 | (h) | Sheffield W | D | 1-1 | McPherson | 18,759 |
| 5 | | 10 | (h) | Newcastle U | L | 1-7 | Spence | 50,217 |
| 6 | | 17 | (a) | Huddersfield T | L | 2-4 | Spence 2 | 17,307 |
| 7 | | 19 | (a) | Blackburn R | L | 0-3 | | 18,243 |
| 8 | | 24 | (h) | Tottenham H | W | 3-0 | Hanson 2, Spence | 13,952 |
| 9 | Oct | 1 | (a) | Leicester C | L | 0-1 | | 22,385 |
| 10 | | 8 | (a) | Everton | L | 2-5 | Bennion, Spence | 40,080 |
| 11 | | 15 | (h) | Cardiff C | D | 2-2 | Spence, Sweeney | 31,090 |
| 12 | | 22 | (h) | Derby C | W | 5-0 | Spence 3, Johnston, McPherson | 18,304 |
| 13 | | 29 | (a) | West Ham U | W | 2-1 | McPherson, Barrett (og) | 21,972 |
| 14 | Nov | 5 | (h) | Portsmouth | W | 2-0 | McPherson, Clifford (og) | 13,119 |
| 15 | | 12 | (a) | Sunderland | L | 1-4 | Spence | 13,319 |
| 16 | | 19 | (h) | Aston Villa | W | 5-1 | Partridge 2, Johnston, McPherson, Spence | 25,991 |
| 17 | | 26 | (a) | Burnley | L | 0-4 | | 18,509 |
| 18 | Dec | 3 | (h) | Bury | L | 0-1 | | 23,581 |
| 19 | | 10 | (a) | Sheffield U | L | 1-2 | Spence | 11,984 |
| 20 | | 17 | (h) | Arsenal | W | 4-1 | Hanson, McPherson, Partridge, Spence | 18,120 |
| 21 | | 24 | (a) | Liverpool | L | 0-2 | | 14,971 |
| 22 | | 26 | (h) | Blackburn R | D | 1-1 | Spence | 31,131 |
| 23 | | 31 | (a) | Middlesbrough | W | 2-1 | Hanson, Johnston | 19,652 |
| 24 | Jan | 7 | (h) | Birmingham | D | 1-1 | Hanson | 16,853 |
| 25 | | 21 | (a) | Newcastle U | L | 1-4 | Partridge | 25,912 |
| 26 | Feb | 4 | (a) | Tottenham H | L | 1-4 | Johnston | 23,545 |
| 27 | | 11 | (h) | Leicester C | W | 5-2 | Nicol 2, Spence 2, Hanson | 16,640 |
| 28 | | 25 | (a) | Cardiff C | L | 0-2 | | 15,579 |
| 29 | Mar | 7 | (h) | Huddersfield T | D | 0-0 | | 35,413 |
| 30 | | 10 | (h) | West Ham U | D | 1-1 | Johnston | 21,577 |
| 31 | | 14 | (h) | Everton | W | 1-0 | Rawlings | 25,667 |
| 32 | | 17 | (a) | Portsmouth | L | 0-1 | | 25,400 |
| 33 | | 28 | (a) | Derby C | L | 0-5 | | 8,323 |
| 34 | | 31 | (a) | Aston Villa | L | 1-3 | Rawlings | 24,691 |
| 35 | Apr | 6 | (a) | Bolton W | L | 2-3 | Spence, Thomas | 23,795 |
| 36 | | 7 | (h) | Burnley | W | 4-3 | Rawlings 3, Williams | 28,311 |
| 37 | | 9 | (h) | Bolton W | W | 2-1 | Johnston, Rawlings | 28,590 |
| 38 | | 14 | (a) | Bury | L | 3-4 | Johnston, McLenahan, Williams | 17,440 |
| 39 | | 21 | (h) | Sheffield U | L | 2-3 | Rawlings, Thomas | 27,137 |
| 40 | | 25 | (h) | Sunderland | W | 2-1 | Hanson, Johnston | 9,545 |
| 41 | | 28 | (a) | Arsenal | W | 1-0 | Rawlings | 22,452 |
| 42 | May | 5 | (h) | Liverpool | W | 6-1 | Spence 3, Rawlings 2, Hanson | 30,625 |

FINAL LEAGUE POSITION: 18th in Division One

Appearances
Goals

## FA Cup

| 3 | Jan | 14 | (h) | Brentford | W | 7-1 |
|---|---|---|---|---|---|---|
| 4 | | 28 | (a) | Bury | D | 1-1 |
| R | Feb | 1 | (h) | Bury | W | 1-0 |
| 5 | | 18 | (h) | Birmingham | W | 1-0 |
| 6 | Mar | 3 | (a) | Blackburn R | L | 0-2 |

| Steward | Moore | Silcock | Bennion | Barson | Wilson | Chapman | Hanson | Spence | Partridge | McPherson | Hilditch | Jones | Thomas | Haslam | Bain | Richardson | Mann | Ramsden | Sweeney | Williams | Johnston | Taylor | McLenahan | Nicol | Rawlings | Ferguson | |
|---|---|---|---|---|---|---|---|---|---|---|---|---|---|---|---|---|---|---|---|---|---|---|---|---|---|---|---|
| 1 | 2 | 3 | 4 | 5 | 6 | 7 | 8 | 9 | 10 | 11 | | | | | | | | | | | | | | | | | 1 |
| 1 | 2 | 3 | 4 | | | 6 | 7 | 8 | 9 | 10 | 11 | 5 | | | | | | | | | | | | | | | 2 |
| 1 | | 3 | 4 | 5 | 6 | 7 | 8 | 9 | 10 | 11 | | 2 | | | | | | | | | | | | | | | 3 |
| 1 | | 3 | 4 | 5 | 6 | 7 | 8 | 9 | 10 | 11 | | 2 | | | | | | | | | | | | | | | 4 |
| 1 | 2 | 3 | 4 | | | 6 | 7 | 8 | 9 | 10 | | 5 | 11 | | | | | | | | | | | | | | 5 |
| 1 | 2 | 3 | 4 | | | | 7 | 8 | 9 | 10 | | 6 | 11 | 5 | | | | | | | | | | | | | 6 |
| 1 | 2 | 3 | 4 | | | | 7 | 8 | 9 | 10 | | | 11 | 5 | 6 | | | | | | | | | | | | 7 |
| | 2 | 3 | 4 | | | | 8 | 9 | 10 | 11 | | | | 5 | | 1 | 6 | 7 | | | | | | | | | 8 |
| | 2 | 3 | 4 | | 6 | | | 9 | 10 | 11 | | | | | | 1 | 5 | 7 | 8 | | | | | | | | 9 |
| | 2 | 3 | 4 | | 6 | | 8 | 9 | 10 | 11 | 5 | | | | | 1 | | | | 7 | | | | | | | 10 |
| | 2 | 3 | 4 | 5 | 6 | | | 9 | | 11 | | | | | | 1 | | 8 | | 7 | 10 | | | | | | 11 |
| | | 3 | 4 | 5 | 6 | | | 9 | | 11 | | 2 | | | | 1 | | 8 | | 7 | 10 | | | | | | 12 |
| | | 3 | | 5 | 6 | | 8 | 9 | | 11 | | 2 | | | | 1 | 4 | | | 7 | 10 | | | | | | 13 |
| | | 3 | 4 | 5 | 6 | | 8 | 9 | | 11 | | 2 | | | | 1 | | | | 7 | 10 | | | | | | 14 |
| | | 3 | 4 | 5 | 6 | | 8 | 9 | | 11 | | 2 | | | | 1 | | | | 7 | 10 | | | | | | 15 |
| | 2 | | 4 | 5 | 6 | | | 9 | 8 | 11 | | | 3 | | | 1 | | | | 7 | 10 | | | | | | 16 |
| | 2 | | 4 | 5 | 6 | | | 9 | 8 | 11 | | 3 | | | | 1 | | | | 7 | 10 | | | | | | 17 |
| | | 3 | 4 | | 6 | | | 9 | 8 | 11 | 5 | 2 | | | | 1 | | | | 7 | 10 | | | | | | 18 |
| | 2 | | 4 | | 6 | | | 9 | 8 | | | 3 | 11 | | | 1 | 5 | | | 7 | 10 | | | | | | 19 |
| | 2 | | 4 | | 6 | | | 9 | 7 | 8 | 11 | 3 | | | | 1 | 5 | | | | 10 | | | | | | 20 |
| | 2 | | 4 | | 6 | | | 9 | 7 | 8 | 11 | 3 | | | | 1 | 5 | | | | 10 | | | | | | 21 |
| | 2 | | 4 | | 6 | | | 9 | 7 | 8 | 11 | 3 | | | | 1 | 5 | | | | 10 | | | | | | 22 |
| | 2 | | 4 | | 6 | | | 9 | 7 | | 11 | 3 | | | | 1 | 5 | | | | 10 | 8 | | | | | 23 |
| | 2 | | 4 | | 6 | | | 9 | 7 | | 11 | 3 | | | | 1 | 5 | | | | 10 | 8 | | | | | 24 |
| | | 3 | 4 | | 6 | | | 9 | 7 | 8 | 11 | 2 | | | | 1 | 5 | | | | 10 | | | | | | 25 |
| | | 3 | | | 6 | 7 | 8 | 9 | | 11 | | 2 | | | | 1 | 5 | | | | 10 | | 4 | | | | 26 |
| | 2 | | 4 | | 6 | | 8 | 7 | | 11 | | 3 | | | | 1 | 5 | | | | 10 | | | 9 | | | 27 |
| | | 3 | 4 | | 6 | | 8 | 7 | | 11 | | 2 | | | | 1 | 5 | | | | 10 | | | 9 | | | 28 |
| | | 3 | 4 | | 6 | | | 9 | 7 | 8 | 11 | 2 | | | | 1 | 5 | | | | 10 | | | | | | 29 |
| | 2 | | 4 | | 6 | 7 | | 9 | 8 | 11 | | 3 | | | | 1 | 5 | | | | 10 | | | | | | 30 |
| | 2 | | 4 | | 6 | | 8 | 7 | | 11 | | 3 | | | | 1 | 5 | | | | 10 | | | 9 | | | 31 |
| | 2 | | 4 | 5 | 6 | | 8 | 7 | | | | 3 | 11 | | | 1 | | | | | 10 | | | 9 | | | 32 |
| | | 3 | 4 | | 6 | | 8 | 7 | | | | 2 | 11 | | | 1 | 5 | | | | 10 | | | | | | 33 |
| | 2 | | 4 | | | | | 7 | | | 11 | 3 | | | | 1 | 5 | | | | 10 | | 6 | 9 | 8 | | 34 |
| | 2 | | 4 | | | | | 7 | | | | 3 | 11 | | | 1 | 5 | | | | 10 | | 6 | 9 | 8 | | 35 |
| | | 3 | 4 | | | | | | | | | 2 | 11 | | | 1 | 5 | | | 7 | 10 | | 6 | | 9 | 8 | 36 |
| | | 3 | | | | | 4 | | | | | 2 | 11 | | | 1 | 5 | | | 7 | 10 | | 6 | | 9 | 8 | 37 |
| | | 3 | 4 | | | | | | | | 11 | 2 | | | | 1 | 5 | | | 7 | 10 | | 6 | | 9 | 8 | 38 |
| | | 3 | 4 | | | | | 7 | | | | 2 | 11 | | | 1 | 5 | | | | 10 | | 6 | | 9 | 8 | 39 |
| 1 | | 3 | | | 6 | | 8 | 7 | | | | 2 | 11 | | | | 5 | | | | 10 | | 4 | | 9 | | 40 |
| 1 | 2 | | | | 6 | | 8 | 7 | | | | 3 | 11 | | | | 5 | | | | 10 | | 4 | | 9 | | 41 |
| 1 | 2 | | | | 6 | | 8 | 7 | | | | 3 | 11 | | | | 5 | | | | 10 | | 4 | | 9 | | 42 |
| 10 | 25 | 26 | 36 | 11 | 33 | 9 | 30 | 38 | 23 | 26 | 5 | 33 | 13 | 3 | 1 | 32 | 26 | 2 | 4 | 13 | 31 | 2 | 10 | 4 | 12 | 4 | |
| | | 1 | | | | | 10 | 22 | 5 | 6 | | | 2 | | | | 1 | | | 2 | 8 | | 1 | 2 | 10 | | |

2 own-goals

# 1928-29

Manager: Herbert Bamlett

| | | | | | | | |
|---|---|---|---|---|---|---|---|
| 1 | Aug | 25 | (h) | Leicester C | D 1-1 | Rawlings | 20,129 |
| 2 | | 27 | (a) | Aston Villa | D 0-0 | | 30,356 |
| 3 | Sep | 1 | (a) | Manchester C | D 2-2 | Johnston, Wilson | 61,007 |
| 4 | | 8 | (a) | Leeds U | L 2-3 | Johnston, Spence | 28,723 |
| 5 | | 15 | (h) | Liverpool | D 2-2 | Hanson, Silcock | 24,077 |
| 6 | | 22 | (a) | West Ham U | L 1-3 | Rawlings | 20,788 |
| 7 | | 29 | (h) | Newcastle U | W 5-0 | Rawlings 2, Hanson, Johnston, Spence | 25,243 |
| 8 | Oct | 6 | (a) | Burnley | W 4-3 | Hanson 2, Spence 2 | 17,493 |
| 9 | | 13 | (h) | Cardiff C | D 1-1 | Johnston | 26,010 |
| 10 | | 20 | (h) | Birmingham | W 1-0 | Johnston | 17,522 |
| 11 | | 27 | (a) | Huddersfield T | W 2-1 | Hanson, Spence | 13,648 |
| 12 | Nov | 3 | (h) | Bolton W | D 1-1 | Hanson | 31,185 |
| 13 | | 10 | (a) | Sheffield W | L 1-2 | Hanson | 18,113 |
| 14 | | 17 | (h) | Derby C | L 0-1 | | 26,122 |
| 15 | | 24 | (a) | Sunderland | L 1-5 | Rowley | 15,932 |
| 16 | Dec | 1 | (h) | Blackburn R | L 1-4 | Ramsden | 19,589 |
| 17 | | 8 | (a) | Arsenal | L 1-3 | Hanson | 18,923 |
| 18 | | 15 | (h) | Everton | D 1-1 | Hanson | 17,080 |
| 19 | | 22 | (a) | Portsmouth | L 0-3 | | 12,836 |
| 20 | | 25 | (h) | Sheffield U | D 1-1 | Ramsden | 22,202 |
| 21 | | 26 | (a) | Sheffield U | L 1-6 | Rawlings | 34,696 |
| 22 | | 29 | (a) | Leicester C | L 1-2 | Hanson | 21,535 |
| 23 | Jan | 1 | (h) | Aston Villa | D 2-2 | Hilditch, Rowley | 25,935 |
| 24 | | 5 | (h) | Manchester C | L 1-2 | Rawlings | 42,555 |
| 25 | | 19 | (h) | Leeds U | L 1-2 | Sweeney | 21,995 |
| 26 | Feb | 2 | (h) | West Ham U | L 2-3 | Reid, Rowley | 12,020 |
| 27 | | 9 | (a) | Newcastle U | L 0-5 | | 34,134 |
| 28 | | 13 | (a) | Liverpool | W 3-2 | Reid 2, Thomas | 8,852 |
| 29 | | 16 | (h) | Burnley | W 1-0 | Rowley | 12,516 |
| 30 | | 23 | (a) | Cardiff C | D 2-2 | Hanson, Reid | 13,070 |
| 31 | Mar | 2 | (a) | Birmingham | D 1-1 | Hanson | 16,738 |
| 32 | | 9 | (h) | Huddersfield T | W 1-0 | Hanson | 28,183 |
| 33 | | 16 | (a) | Bolton W | D 1-1 | Hanson | 17,354 |
| 34 | | 23 | (h) | Sheffield W | W 2-1 | Reid, Rowley | 27,095 |
| 35 | | 29 | (a) | Bury | W 3-1 | Reid 2, Thomas | 27,167 |
| 36 | | 30 | (a) | Derby C | L 1-6 | Hanson | 14,319 |
| 37 | Apr | 1 | (h) | Bury | W 1-0 | Thomas | 29,742 |
| 38 | | 6 | (h) | Sunderland | W 3-0 | Hanson, Mann, Reid | 27,772 |
| 39 | | 13 | (a) | Blackburn R | W 3-0 | Reid 2, Ramsden | 8,193 |
| 40 | | 20 | (h) | Arsenal | W 4-1 | Reid 2, Hanson, Thomas | 22,858 |
| 41 | | 27 | (a) | Everton | W 4-2 | Hanson 2, Reid 2 | 19,442 |
| 42 | May | 4 | (h) | Portsmouth | D 0-0 | | 17,728 |

FINAL LEAGUE POSITION: 12th in Division One

Appearances
Goals

FA Cup

| | | | | | | | |
|---|---|---|---|---|---|---|---|
| 3 | Jan | 12 | (a) | Port Vale | W 3-0 | |
| 4 | | 26 | (h) | Bury | L 0-1 | |

248

| Steward | Dale | Silcock | Bennion | Mann | Wilson | Spence | Hanson | Rawlings | Johnston | Williams | Moore | McLenahan | Spencer | Taylor | Rowley | Thomas | Hilditch | Ramsden | Richardson | Nicol | Sweeney | Partridge | Inglis | Reid | Boyle | |
|---|---|---|---|---|---|---|---|---|---|---|---|---|---|---|---|---|---|---|---|---|---|---|---|---|---|---|
| 1 | 2 | 3 | 4 | 5 | 6 | 7 | 8 | 9 | 10 | 11 | | | | | | | | | | | | | | | | 1 |
| 1 | | 3 | | 5 | 6 | 7 | 8 | 9 | 10 | 11 | 2 | 4 | | | | | | | | | | | | | | 2 |
| 1 | | 3 | 4 | 5 | 6 | 7 | 8 | 9 | 10 | 11 | 2 | | | | | | | | | | | | | | | 3 |
| 1 | | 3 | 4 | 5 | 6 | 7 | 8 | 9 | 10 | 11 | 2 | | | | | | | | | | | | | | | 4 |
| 1 | | 3 | 4 | | 6 | 7 | 8 | 9 | 10 | 11 | 2 | | 5 | | | | | | | | | | | | | 5 |
| 1 | | 3 | 4 | | 6 | 7 | | 9 | 10 | 11 | 2 | | 5 | 8 | | | | | | | | | | | | 6 |
| 1 | | 3 | 4 | | 6 | 7 | 8 | 9 | 10 | 11 | 2 | | 5 | | | | | | | | | | | | | 7 |
| 1 | | 3 | 4 | | 6 | 7 | 8 | 9 | 10 | 11 | 2 | | 5 | | | | | | | | | | | | | 8 |
| 1 | | 3 | 4 | | 6 | 7 | 8 | 9 | 10 | 11 | 2 | | 5 | | | | | | | | | | | | | 9 |
| 1 | | 3 | 4 | | 6 | 7 | 8 | 9 | 10 | 11 | 2 | | 5 | | | | | | | | | | | | | 10 |
| 1 | | 3 | 4 | | 6 | 7 | 8 | 9 | | | 2 | | 5 | | 10 | 11 | | | | | | | | | | 11 |
| 1 | | 3 | 4 | | 6 | 7 | 8 | 9 | | 11 | 2 | | 5 | | 10 | | | | | | | | | | | 12 |
| 1 | | 3 | 4 | | 6 | 7 | 8 | 9 | | 11 | 2 | | 5 | | 10 | | | | | | | | | | | 13 |
| 1 | | 3 | | | 6 | 7 | 8 | 9 | | | 2 | | 5 | | 10 | 11 | 4 | | | | | | | | | 14 |
| 1 | | 3 | 4 | 5 | | 7 | 8 | 9 | | 11 | 2 | | | | 10 | | 6 | | | | | | | | | 15 |
| 1 | | 3 | 4 | 5 | | | 8 | 9 | | 11 | 2 | | | | 10 | | 6 | 7 | | | | | | | | 16 |
| 1 | 3 | 4 | | | | 7 | | 9 | | 11 | 2 | | 5 | 8 | 10 | | 6 | | | | | | | | | 17 |
| | 3 | | | | 6 | 7 | 8 | | | | 2 | | 5 | | | | 4 | 1 | 9 | 10 | 11 | | | | | 18 |
| | 3 | | | | 6 | 7 | 8 | | | | 2 | | 5 | | | 11 | 4 | 1 | 9 | 10 | | | | | | 19 |
| | 2 | 3 | 4 | | 6 | | 8 | 9 | 10 | | | | 5 | | | | 7 | 1 | | 11 | | | | | | 20 |
| | 3 | | 4 | | | | 8 | 9 | | | | | 5 | | | | 6 | 7 | 1 | 10 | 11 | 2 | | | | 21 |
| | 2 | 3 | 4 | | | | | 9 | 10 | | | | 5 | | | | 6 | 7 | 1 | | 8 | 11 | | | | 22 |
| 1 | | 3 | 4 | | | 7 | | 9 | | | 2 | | 5 | | 10 | | 6 | | | | 8 | 11 | | | | 23 |
| 1 | | 3 | 4 | | | 7 | 8 | 9 | | 11 | 2 | | 5 | | 10 | | 6 | | | | | | | | | 24 |
| 1 | | 3 | 4 | | 6 | 7 | | 9 | | 11 | 2 | | 5 | 8 | | | | | 10 | | | | | | | 25 |
| 1 | 2 | 3 | | | 6 | 7 | 8 | | | | | | 5 | | 10 | 11 | 4 | | | | | | | 9 | | 26 |
| 1 | | 3 | 4 | | 6 | 7 | 8 | | | | 2 | | 5 | | 10 | 11 | | | | | | | | 9 | | 27 |
| 1 | | 3 | 4 | | 6 | 7 | 8 | | | | 2 | | 5 | | 10 | 11 | | | | | | | | 9 | | 28 |
| 1 | 3 | | 4 | | 6 | 7 | 8 | | | | 2 | | 5 | | 10 | 11 | | | | | | | | 9 | | 29 |
| 1 | 3 | | 4 | | 6 | 7 | 8 | | | | 2 | | 5 | | 10 | 11 | | | | | | | | 9 | | 30 |
| 1 | 3 | | 4 | | 6 | 7 | 8 | | | | 2 | | 5 | | 10 | 11 | | | | | | | | 9 | | 31 |
| 1 | 3 | | 4 | | 6 | 7 | 8 | | | | 2 | | 5 | | 10 | 11 | | | | | | | | 9 | | 32 |
| 1 | 3 | | 4 | | 6 | 7 | 8 | | | | 2 | | 5 | | 10 | 11 | | | | | | | | 9 | | 33 |
| 1 | | 3 | 4 | | 6 | 7 | 8 | | | | 2 | | 5 | | 10 | 11 | | | | | | | | 9 | | 34 |
| 1 | | 3 | 4 | | 6 | 7 | 8 | | | | 2 | | 5 | | 10 | 11 | | | | | | | | 9 | | 35 |
| 1 | | 3 | 4 | | 6 | 7 | 8 | | | 11 | 2 | | 5 | | | | | | | | | | | 9 | 10 | 36 |
| 1 | 3 | | 4 | | 6 | 7 | 8 | | | | 2 | | 5 | | 10 | 11 | | | | | | | | 9 | | 37 |
| 1 | 3 | | 4 | | 6 | 7 | 8 | | | | 2 | | 5 | | 10 | 11 | | | | | | | | 9 | | 38 |
| 1 | 3 | | 4 | | 6 | | 8 | | | | 2 | | 5 | | 10 | 11 | | 7 | | | | | | 9 | | 39 |
| 1 | 3 | | 4 | | 6 | 7 | 8 | | | | 2 | | 5 | | 10 | 11 | | | | | | | | 9 | | 40 |
| 1 | 3 | | 4 | | 6 | 7 | 8 | | | | 2 | | 5 | | 10 | 11 | | | | | | | | 9 | | 41 |
| 1 | 3 | | 4 | | 6 | 7 | 8 | | | | 2 | | 5 | | 10 | 11 | | | | | | | | 9 | | 42 |
| 37 | 19 | 27 | 34 | 25 | 19 | 36 | 42 | 19 | 12 | 18 | 37 | 1 | 36 | 3 | 25 | 19 | 11 | 5 | 5 | 2 | 6 | 5 | 1 | 17 | 1 | |
| | | 1 | | 1 | 1 | 5 | 19 | 6 | 5 | | | | | | 5 | 4 | 1 | 3 | | | 1 | | | 14 | | |

249

# 1929-30

Manager: Herbert Bamlett

| 1 | Aug | 31 | (a) | Newcastle U | L | 1-4 | Spence | 43,489 |
|---|---|---|---|---|---|---|---|---|
| 2 | Sep | 2 | (a) | Leicester C | L | 1-4 | Rowley | 20,490 |
| 3 | | 7 | (h) | Blackburn R | W | 1-0 | Mann | 22,362 |
| 4 | | 11 | (h) | Leicester C | W | 2-1 | Ball, Spence | 16,445 |
| 5 | | 14 | (a) | Middlesbrough | W | 3-2 | Rawlings 3 | 26,428 |
| 6 | | 21 | (h) | Liverpool | L | 1-2 | Spence | 20,788 |
| 7 | | 28 | (a) | West Ham U | L | 1-2 | Hanson | 20,695 |
| 8 | Oct | 5 | (h) | Manchester C | L | 1-3 | Thomas | 57,201 |
| 9 | | 7 | (a) | Sheffield U | L | 1-3 | Boyle | 7,987 |
| 10 | | 12 | (h) | Grimsby T | L | 2-5 | Ball, Rowley | 21,494 |
| 11 | | 19 | (a) | Portsmouth | L | 0-3 | | 18,070 |
| 12 | | 26 | (h) | Arsenal | W | 1-0 | Ball | 12,662 |
| 13 | Nov | 2 | (a) | Aston Villa | L | 0-1 | | 24,292 |
| 14 | | 9 | (h) | Derby C | W | 3-2 | Ball, Hanson, Rowley | 15,174 |
| 15 | | 16 | (a) | Sheffield W | L | 2-7 | Ball, Hanson | 14,264 |
| 16 | | 23 | (h) | Burnley | W | 1-0 | Rowley | 9,060 |
| 17 | | 30 | (a) | Sunderland | W | 4-2 | Spence 2, Ball, Hanson | 11,508 |
| 18 | Dec | 7 | (h) | Bolton W | D | 1-1 | Ball | 5,656 |
| 19 | | 14 | (a) | Everton | D | 0-0 | | 18,182 |
| 20 | | 21 | (h) | Leeds U | W | 3-1 | Ball 2, Hanson | 15,054 |
| 21 | | 25 | (h) | Birmingham | D | 0-0 | | 18,626 |
| 22 | | 26 | (a) | Birmingham | W | 1-0 | Rowley | 35,682 |
| 23 | | 28 | (h) | Newcastle U | W | 5-0 | Boyle 2, McLachlan, Rowley, Spence | 14,862 |
| 24 | Jan | 4 | (a) | Blackburn R | L | 4-5 | Boyle 2, Ball, Rowley | 23,923 |
| 25 | | 18 | (h) | Middlesbrough | L | 0-3 | | 21,028 |
| 26 | | 25 | (a) | Liverpool | L | 0-1 | | 28,592 |
| 27 | Feb | 1 | (h) | West Ham U | W | 4-2 | Spence 4 | 15,424 |
| 28 | | 8 | (a) | Manchester C | W | 1-0 | Reid | 64,472 |
| 29 | | 15 | (a) | Grimsby T | D | 2-2 | Reid, Rowley | 9,337 |
| 30 | | 22 | (h) | Portsmouth | W | 3-0 | Reid 2, Boyle | 17,317 |
| 31 | Mar | 1 | (a) | Bolton W | L | 1-4 | Reid | 17,714 |
| 32 | | 8 | (h) | Aston Villa | L | 2-3 | McLachlan, Warburton | 25,407 |
| 33 | | 12 | (a) | Arsenal | L | 2-4 | Ball, Wilson | 18,082 |
| 34 | | 15 | (a) | Derby C | D | 1-1 | Rowley | 9,102 |
| 35 | | 29 | (a) | Burnley | L | 0-4 | | 11,659 |
| 36 | Apr | 5 | (h) | Sunderland | W | 2-1 | McLenahan 2 | 13,230 |
| 37 | | 14 | (h) | Sheffield W | D | 2-2 | McLenahan, Rowley | 12,806 |
| 38 | | 18 | (h) | Huddersfield T | W | 1-0 | McLenahan | 26,496 |
| 39 | | 19 | (h) | Everton | D | 3-3 | McLenahan, Rowley, Spence | 13,320 |
| 40 | | 22 | (a) | Huddersfield T | D | 2-2 | Hilditch, McLenahan | 20,716 |
| 41 | | 26 | (a) | Leeds U | L | 1-3 | Spence | 10,596 |
| 42 | May | 3 | (h) | Sheffield U | L | 1-5 | Rowley | 15,268 |

FINAL LEAGUE POSITION: 17th in Division One

Appearances

Goals

FA Cup

| 3 | Jan | 11 | (h) | Swindon T | L | 0-2 | |
|---|---|---|---|---|---|---|---|

250

| Steward | Moore | Dale | Bennion | Spencer | Mann | Spence | Hanson | Reid | Rowley | Thomas | Silcock | Ball | Rawlings | Wilson | Boyle | Sweeney | Hilditch | Taylor | McLenahan | Jones | McLachlan | Chesters | Warburton | Thomson | # |
|---|---|---|---|---|---|---|---|---|---|---|---|---|---|---|---|---|---|---|---|---|---|---|---|---|---|
| 1 | 2 | 3 | 4 | 5 | 6 | 7 | 8 | 9 | 10 | 11 |  |  |  |  |  |  |  |  |  |  |  |  |  |  | 1 |
| 1 | 2 | 3 | 4 | 5 | 6 | 7 | 8 | 9 | 10 | 11 |  |  |  |  |  |  |  |  |  |  |  |  |  |  | 2 |
| 1 | 2 |  | 4 | 5 | 6 | 7 | 8 | 9 | 10 | 11 | 3 |  |  |  |  |  |  |  |  |  |  |  |  |  | 3 |
| 1 | 2 |  | 4 | 5 | 6 | 7 | 8 |  | 10 | 11 | 3 | 9 |  |  |  |  |  |  |  |  |  |  |  |  | 4 |
| 1 | 2 | 3 | 4 | 5 | 6 | 7 | 8 |  | 10 | 11 |  |  | 9 |  |  |  |  |  |  |  |  |  |  |  | 5 |
| 1 | 2 | 3 | 4 | 5 | 6 | 7 | 8 |  | 10 | 11 |  |  | 9 |  |  |  |  |  |  |  |  |  |  |  | 6 |
| 1 | 2 | 3 | 4 |  | 5 | 7 | 8 |  | 10 | 11 |  |  | 9 | 6 |  |  |  |  |  |  |  |  |  |  | 7 |
| 1 | 2 |  | 4 | 5 | 6 | 7 | 8 | 9 | 10 | 11 | 3 |  |  |  |  |  |  |  |  |  |  |  |  |  | 8 |
| 1 | 2 |  | 4 | 5 | 6 | 7 |  |  |  | 11 | 3 |  | 9 |  | 8 | 10 |  |  |  |  |  |  |  |  | 9 |
| 1 | 2 | 3 |  |  |  | 7 |  |  | 10 | 11 |  | 9 |  |  | 8 |  | 4 | 5 | 6 |  |  |  |  |  | 10 |
| 1 | 2 | 3 | 4 |  | 6 | 7 |  | 9 | 10 | 11 |  |  |  |  | 8 |  | 5 |  |  |  |  |  |  |  | 11 |
| 1 | 2 | 3 |  | 5 | 6 | 7 | 8 |  | 10 | 11 |  | 9 |  |  |  |  | 4 |  |  |  |  |  |  |  | 12 |
| 1 | 2 | 3 |  | 5 | 6 | 7 | 8 |  | 10 | 11 |  | 9 |  |  |  |  | 4 |  |  |  |  |  |  |  | 13 |
| 1 | 2 | 3 | 4 |  | 6 | 7 | 8 |  | 10 | 11 |  | 9 |  |  |  |  | 5 |  |  |  |  |  |  |  | 14 |
| 1 | 2 | 3 | 4 |  | 6 | 7 | 8 |  | 10 | 11 |  | 9 |  |  |  |  | 5 |  |  |  |  |  |  |  | 15 |
| 1 | 2 | 3 | 4 |  |  | 7 | 8 |  | 10 | 11 |  | 9 |  | 6 |  |  | 5 |  |  |  |  |  |  |  | 16 |
| 1 | 2 | 3 |  |  |  | 7 | 8 |  | 10 | 11 |  | 9 |  | 6 |  |  | 4 | 5 |  |  |  |  |  |  | 17 |
| 1 | 2 | 3 |  |  |  | 7 | 8 |  | 10 | 11 |  | 9 |  | 6 |  |  | 4 | 5 |  |  |  |  |  |  | 18 |
| 1 | 2 | 3 |  |  |  | 7 | 8 |  | 10 | 11 |  | 9 |  | 6 |  |  | 4 | 5 |  |  |  |  |  |  | 19 |
| 1 | 2 |  |  |  |  | 7 | 8 |  | 10 |  |  | 9 |  | 6 |  |  | 4 | 5 |  | 3 | 11 |  |  |  | 20 |
| 1 | 2 |  |  |  |  | 7 | 8 |  | 10 |  |  | 9 |  | 6 |  |  | 4 | 5 |  | 3 | 11 |  |  |  | 21 |
| 1 | 2 |  |  |  |  | 7 |  |  | 10 |  |  | 9 |  | 6 | 8 |  | 4 | 5 |  | 3 | 11 |  |  |  | 22 |
|  | 2 |  |  |  |  | 7 |  |  | 10 |  |  | 9 |  | 6 | 8 |  | 4 | 5 |  | 3 | 11 | 1 |  |  | 23 |
| 1 | 2 |  |  |  |  | 7 |  |  | 10 |  |  | 9 |  | 6 | 8 |  | 4 | 5 |  | 3 | 11 |  |  |  | 24 |
| 1 | 2 |  |  |  |  | 7 |  |  | 10 |  |  | 9 |  | 6 | 8 |  | 4 | 5 |  | 3 | 11 |  |  |  | 25 |
| 1 | 2 |  | 4 |  |  | 7 |  | 9 | 10 |  | 3 |  |  | 6 | 8 |  | 5 |  |  |  | 11 |  |  |  | 26 |
| 1 | 2 |  | 4 |  |  | 7 |  | 9 | 10 |  | 3 |  |  | 6 | 8 |  | 5 |  |  |  | 11 |  |  |  | 27 |
| 1 |  |  | 4 |  |  | 7 |  | 9 | 10 |  | 3 |  |  | 6 | 8 |  | 5 |  |  | 2 | 11 |  |  |  | 28 |
| 1 | 2 |  | 4 |  |  | 7 |  | 9 | 10 |  | 3 |  |  | 6 | 8 |  | 5 |  |  |  | 11 |  |  |  | 29 |
| 1 | 2 |  | 4 |  |  | 7 |  | 9 | 10 |  | 3 |  |  | 6 | 8 |  | 5 |  |  |  | 11 |  |  |  | 30 |
| 1 | 2 |  | 4 |  |  | 7 |  | 9 | 10 |  | 3 |  |  | 6 | 8 |  | 5 |  |  |  | 11 |  |  |  | 31 |
| 1 | 2 |  | 4 |  |  | 7 |  | 9 | 10 |  | 3 |  |  | 6 |  |  | 5 |  |  |  | 11 |  | 8 |  | 32 |
| 1 | 2 |  | 4 |  |  | 7 |  |  |  | 11 | 3 | 9 |  | 6 |  |  | 5 |  |  |  | 10 |  | 8 |  | 33 |
|  |  |  |  |  |  | 7 |  |  | 10 |  | 3 | 9 |  | 6 | 8 |  | 5 |  | 4 | 2 | 11 | 1 |  |  | 34 |
|  |  |  |  |  |  | 7 |  |  | 10 |  | 3 | 9 |  | 6 | 8 |  | 5 |  | 4 | 2 | 11 | 1 |  |  | 35 |
| 1 |  |  | 4 |  |  | 7 |  |  | 10 |  | 3 | 9 |  | 6 |  |  |  | 5 | 8 | 2 | 11 |  |  |  | 36 |
| 1 |  |  | 4 |  |  | 7 |  | 9 | 10 |  | 3 |  |  | 6 |  |  |  | 5 | 8 | 2 | 11 |  |  |  | 37 |
| 1 |  |  | 4 |  |  | 7 |  |  | 10 | 11 | 3 |  |  | 6 |  |  |  | 5 | 8 | 2 | 9 |  |  |  | 38 |
| 1 |  |  | 4 |  |  | 7 |  |  | 10 |  | 3 |  |  | 6 |  |  |  | 5 | 8 | 2 | 11 |  |  | 9 | 39 |
| 1 |  |  | 4 |  |  | 7 |  |  | 10 |  | 3 | 9 |  | 6 |  |  |  | 5 | 8 | 2 | 11 |  |  |  | 40 |
| 1 |  |  | 4 |  |  | 7 |  |  | 10 |  | 3 | 9 |  | 6 |  |  |  | 5 | 8 | 2 | 11 |  |  |  | 41 |
| 1 |  |  | 4 |  |  | 7 |  |  | 10 |  | 3 | 9 |  | 6 |  |  |  | 5 | 8 | 2 | 11 |  |  |  | 42 |
| **39** | **28** | **19** | **28** | **10** | **14** | **42** | **18** | **13** | **40** | **21** | **21** | **23** | **4** | **28** | **15** | **1** | **27** | **16** | **10** | **16** | **23** | **3** | **2** | **1** |  |
|  |  | 1 |  |  | 12 | 5 | 5 | 12 | 1 |  |  | 11 | 3 | 1 | 6 |  | 1 |  | 6 |  | 2 |  | 1 |  |  |

# 1930-31

Manager: Herbert Bamlett

| 1 | Aug | 30 | (h) | Aston Villa | L | 3-4 | Reid, Rowley, Warburton | 18,004 |
|---|---|---|---|---|---|---|---|---|
| 2 | Sep | 3 | (a) | Middlesbrough | L | 1-3 | Rowley | 15,712 |
| 3 | | 6 | (a) | Chelsea | L | 2-6 | Reid, Spence | 48,648 |
| 4 | | 10 | (h) | Huddersfield T | L | 0-6 | | 11,836 |
| 5 | | 13 | (h) | Newcastle U | L | 4-7 | Reid 3, Rowley | 10,907 |
| 6 | | 15 | (a) | Huddersfield T | L | 0-3 | | 14,028 |
| 7 | | 20 | (a) | Sheffield W | L | 0-3 | | 18,705 |
| 8 | | 27 | (h) | Grimsby T | L | 0-2 | | 14,695 |
| 9 | Oct | 4 | (a) | Manchester C | L | 1-4 | Spence | 41,757 |
| 10 | | 11 | (a) | West Ham U | L | 1-5 | Reid | 20,003 |
| 11 | | 18 | (h) | Arsenal | L | 1-2 | McLachlan | 23,406 |
| 12 | | 25 | (a) | Portsmouth | L | 1-4 | Rowley | 19,262 |
| 13 | Nov | 1 | (h) | Birmingham | W | 2-0 | Gallimore, Rowley | 11,479 |
| 14 | | 8 | (a) | Leicester C | L | 4-5 | Bullock 3, McLachlan | 17,466 |
| 15 | | 15 | (h) | Blackpool | D | 0-0 | | 14,765 |
| 16 | | 22 | (a) | Sheffield U | L | 1-3 | Gallimore | 12,698 |
| 17 | | 29 | (h) | Sunderland | D | 1-1 | Gallimore | 10,971 |
| 18 | Dec | 6 | (a) | Blackburn R | L | 1-4 | Rowley | 10,802 |
| 19 | | 13 | (h) | Derby C | W | 2-1 | Reid, Spence | 9,701 |
| 20 | | 20 | (a) | Leeds U | L | 0-5 | | 11,282 |
| 21 | | 25 | (a) | Bolton W | L | 1-3 | Reid | 22,662 |
| 22 | | 26 | (h) | Bolton W | D | 1-1 | Reid | 12,741 |
| 23 | | 27 | (a) | Aston Villa | L | 0-7 | | 32,505 |
| 24 | Jan | 1 | (h) | Leeds U | D | 0-0 | | 9,875 |
| 25 | | 3 | (h) | Chelsea | W | 1-0 | Warburton | 8,966 |
| 26 | | 17 | (a) | Newcastle U | L | 3-4 | Warburton 2, Reid | 24,835 |
| 27 | | 28 | (h) | Sheffield W | W | 4-1 | Hopkinson, Reid, Spence, Warburton | 6,077 |
| 28 | | 31 | (a) | Grimsby T | L | 1-2 | Reid | 9,305 |
| 29 | Feb | 7 | (h) | Manchester C | L | 1-3 | Spence | 39,876 |
| 30 | | 14 | (h) | West Ham U | W | 1-0 | Gallimore | 9,745 |
| 31 | | 21 | (a) | Arsenal | L | 1-4 | Thomson | 41,510 |
| 32 | Mar | 7 | (a) | Birmingham | D | 0-0 | | 17,678 |
| 33 | | 16 | (h) | Portsmouth | L | 0-1 | | 4,808 |
| 34 | | 21 | (a) | Blackpool | L | 1-5 | Hopkinson | 13,612 |
| 35 | | 25 | (h) | Leicester C | D | 0-0 | | 3,679 |
| 36 | | 28 | (h) | Sheffield U | L | 1-2 | Hopkinson | 5,420 |
| 37 | Apr | 3 | (a) | Liverpool | D | 1-1 | Wilson | 27,782 |
| 38 | | 4 | (a) | Sunderland | W | 2-1 | Hopkinson, Reid | 13,590 |
| 39 | | 6 | (h) | Liverpool | W | 4-1 | Reid 2, McLenahan, Rowley | 8,058 |
| 40 | | 11 | (h) | Blackburn R | L | 0-1 | | 6,414 |
| 41 | | 18 | (a) | Derby C | L | 1-6 | Spence | 6,610 |
| 42 | May | 2 | (h) | Middlesbrough | D | 4-4 | Reid 2, Bennion, Gallimore | 3,969 |

FINAL LEAGUE POSITION: 22nd in Division One

Appearances
Goals

FA Cup

| 3 | Jan | 10 | (a) | Stoke C | D | 3-3 | |
|---|---|---|---|---|---|---|---|
| R | | 14 | (h) | Stoke C | D | 0-0 | (After extra-time) |
| 2R | | 19 | (n*) | Stoke C | W | 4-2 | (*Played at Anfield, Liverpool.) |
| 4 | | 24 | (a) | Grimsby T | L | 0-1 | |

| Steward | Jones | Silcock | Bennion | McLenahan | Wilson | Spence | Warburton | Reid | Rowley | McLachlan | Chesters | Dale | Ramsden | Hilditch | Williams | Mellor | Bullock | Parker | Gallimore | Lydon | Hopkinson | Thomson | # |
|---|---|---|---|---|---|---|---|---|---|---|---|---|---|---|---|---|---|---|---|---|---|---|---|
| 1 | 2 | 3 | 4 | 5 | 6 | 7 | 8 | 9 | 10 | 11 |  |  |  |  |  |  |  |  |  |  |  |  | 1 |
|  |  | 3 | 4 | 5 | 6 |  | 8 | 9 | 10 | 11 | 1 | 2 | 7 |  |  |  |  |  |  |  |  |  | 2 |
|  |  | 3 | 4 | 5 |  | 7 | 8 | 9 | 10 | 11 | 1 | 2 |  | 6 |  |  |  |  |  |  |  |  | 3 |
|  |  | 3 | 4 |  | 6 | 7 | 8 | 9 | 10 | 11 | 1 | 2 |  | 5 |  |  |  |  |  |  |  |  | 4 |
|  |  | 3 |  |  | 6 | 7 | 8 | 9 | 10 | 11 | 1 | 2 | 5 | 4 |  |  |  |  |  |  |  |  | 5 |
| 1 |  | 3 |  | 6 |  | 7 | 8 | 9 | 10 | 11 | 5 |  |  | 4 | 2 |  |  |  |  |  |  |  | 6 |
| 1 |  | 3 |  | 6 |  | 7 | 8 |  | 10 | 11 | 5 |  |  | 4 | 2 | 9 |  |  |  |  |  |  | 7 |
| 1 | 2 | 3 | 4 | 6 |  | 7 | 8 |  | 10 | 11 | 5 |  |  |  |  | 9 |  |  |  |  |  |  | 8 |
| 1 | 2 | 3 |  | 5 | 6 | 7 | 8 | 9 | 10 | 11 |  |  | 4 |  |  |  |  |  |  |  |  |  | 9 |
| 1 |  |  | 4 |  | 6 | 7 |  | 9 | 10 | 11 |  |  | 3 |  |  | 2 |  | 5 | 8 |  |  |  | 10 |
| 1 |  | 3 | 4 |  | 6 | 7 |  | 9 | 10 | 11 |  |  |  |  |  | 2 |  | 5 | 8 |  |  |  | 11 |
| 1 |  | 3 | 4 |  | 6 | 7 |  | 9 | 10 | 11 |  |  |  |  |  | 2 |  | 5 | 8 |  |  |  | 12 |
| 1 |  | 3 | 4 |  | 6 | 7 |  |  | 10 | 11 |  |  |  |  |  | 2 | 9 | 5 | 8 |  |  |  | 13 |
| 1 |  | 3 | 4 |  | 6 | 7 |  |  | 10 | 11 |  |  |  |  |  | 2 | 9 | 5 | 8 |  |  |  | 14 |
| 1 |  |  | 4 |  | 6 | 7 |  |  | 10 | 11 |  |  | 3 |  |  | 2 | 9 | 5 | 8 |  |  |  | 15 |
| 1 |  |  | 4 |  | 6 | 7 |  |  | 10 | 11 |  |  | 3 |  |  | 2 | 9 | 5 | 8 |  |  |  | 16 |
| 1 |  | 3 | 4 |  | 6 |  |  |  | 10 | 11 |  |  | 7 |  |  | 2 | 9 | 5 | 8 |  |  |  | 17 |
| 1 |  | 3 | 4 |  | 6 |  |  |  | 10 | 11 |  |  | 7 |  |  | 2 | 9 | 5 | 8 |  |  |  | 18 |
| 1 |  | 3 | 4 | 5 | 6 | 7 |  | 9 | 10 | 11 |  |  |  |  |  | 2 |  |  | 8 |  |  |  | 19 |
| 1 |  | 3 | 4 | 5 | 6 | 7 |  | 9 | 10 | 11 |  |  |  |  |  | 2 |  |  | 8 |  |  |  | 20 |
| 1 |  | 3 | 4 | 5 | 10 | 7 |  | 9 |  | 11 |  |  |  |  |  | 2 |  |  | 8 | 6 |  |  | 21 |
| 1 |  | 3 | 4 |  | 6 |  |  | 9 | 10 | 11 |  |  | 7 | 5 |  | 2 |  |  | 8 |  |  |  | 22 |
| 1 |  |  | 4 |  | 6 |  |  | 9 | 10 | 11 |  | 3 | 7 | 5 |  | 2 |  |  | 8 |  |  |  | 23 |
| 1 |  |  | 4 |  | 6 |  |  | 9 | 10 | 11 |  | 3 | 7 | 5 |  | 2 |  |  | 8 |  |  |  | 24 |
| 1 |  |  | 4 |  | 6 |  | 8 | 9 |  | 11 |  | 3 | 7 | 5 |  | 2 |  | 10 |  |  |  |  | 25 |
| 1 |  | 3 | 4 |  |  | 7 | 8 | 9 |  | 6 |  |  |  | 5 |  | 2 |  | 10 |  |  | 11 |  | 26 |
| 1 |  |  | 4 |  |  | 7 | 8 | 9 | 10 | 6 |  | 3 |  | 5 |  | 2 |  |  |  |  | 11 |  | 27 |
| 1 |  |  | 4 |  |  | 7 | 8 | 9 | 10 | 6 |  | 3 |  | 5 |  | 2 |  |  |  |  | 11 |  | 28 |
| 1 |  |  | 4 |  |  | 7 | 8 | 9 |  | 6 |  | 3 |  | 5 |  | 2 |  | 10 |  |  | 11 |  | 29 |
| 1 |  |  | 4 |  |  | 7 |  | 9 |  | 6 |  | 3 |  | 5 |  | 2 |  | 10 |  |  | 11 | 8 | 30 |
| 1 |  |  | 4 |  |  | 7 |  |  |  | 6 |  | 3 |  | 5 |  | 2 | 9 | 10 |  |  | 11 | 8 | 31 |
| 1 |  |  | 4 |  |  | 7 | 8 |  |  | 6 |  | 3 |  | 5 |  | 2 | 9 | 10 |  |  | 11 |  | 32 |
| 1 |  |  | 4 |  |  | 7 | 8 | 9 |  | 6 |  | 3 |  | 5 |  | 2 |  | 10 |  |  | 11 |  | 33 |
| 1 |  | 3 | 4 |  |  | 7 | 8 | 9 |  | 6 |  |  |  | 5 |  | 2 |  | 10 |  |  | 11 |  | 34 |
| 1 |  |  | 4 | 8 |  | 7 |  |  | 10 | 6 |  | 3 |  | 5 |  | 2 |  | 9 |  |  | 11 |  | 35 |
| 1 |  |  | 4 | 9 |  | 7 | 8 |  |  | 6 |  | 3 |  | 5 |  | 2 |  | 10 |  |  | 11 |  | 36 |
| 1 |  | 3 | 4 | 8 | 9 | 7 |  |  | 10 | 6 |  |  |  | 5 |  | 2 |  |  |  |  | 11 |  | 37 |
| 1 |  | 3 | 4 | 8 |  | 7 |  | 9 |  | 6 |  |  |  | 5 |  | 2 |  | 10 |  |  | 11 |  | 38 |
| 1 |  | 3 | 4 | 8 |  | 7 |  | 9 | 10 | 6 |  |  |  | 5 |  | 2 |  |  |  |  | 11 |  | 39 |
| 1 |  | 3 | 4 | 8 |  | 7 |  | 9 | 10 | 6 |  |  |  | 5 |  | 2 |  |  |  |  | 11 |  | 40 |
| 1 |  | 3 | 4 | 8 |  | 7 |  | 9 |  | 6 |  |  |  | 5 |  | 2 |  | 10 |  |  | 11 |  | 41 |
| 1 |  | 3 | 4 | 8 |  | 7 |  | 9 |  | 6 |  |  |  | 5 |  | 2 |  | 10 |  |  | 11 |  | 42 |
| 38 | 5 | 25 | 36 | 21 | 20 | 35 | 18 | 30 | 29 | 42 | 4 | 22 | 7 | 25 | 3 | 35 | 10 | 9 | 28 | 1 | 17 | 2 |  |
|  |  |  | 1 | 1 | 1 | 6 | 5 | 17 | 7 | 2 |  |  |  | 3 |  |  | 5 |  | 4 | 1 |  |  |  |

253

# 1931-32

| 1 | Aug | 29 | (a) | Bradford | L | 1-3 | Reid | 16,239 |
|---|---|---|---|---|---|---|---|---|
| 2 | Sep | 2 | (h) | Southampton | L | 2-3 | Ferguson, Johnston | 3,507 |
| 3 | | 5 | (h) | Swansea T | W | 2-1 | Hopkinson, Reid | 6,763 |
| 4 | | 7 | (a) | Stoke C | L | 0-3 | | 10,518 |
| 5 | | 12 | (h) | Tottenham H | D | 1-1 | Johnston | 9,557 |
| 6 | | 16 | (h) | Stoke C | D | 1-1 | Spence | 5,025 |
| 7 | | 19 | (a) | Nottingham F | L | 1-2 | Gallimore | 10,166 |
| 8 | | 26 | (h) | Chesterfield | W | 3-1 | Warburton 2, Johnston | 10,834 |
| 9 | Oct | 3 | (a) | Burnley | L | 0-2 | | 9,719 |
| 10 | | 10 | (h) | Preston NE | W | 3-2 | Gallimore, Johnston, Spence | 8,496 |
| 11 | | 17 | (a) | Barnsley | D | 0-0 | | 4,052 |
| 12 | | 24 | (h) | Notts C | D | 3-3 | Gallimore, Mann, Spence | 6,694 |
| 13 | | 31 | (a) | Plymouth A | L | 1-3 | Johnston | 22,555 |
| 14 | Nov | 7 | (h) | Leeds U | L | 2-5 | Spence 2 | 9,512 |
| 15 | | 14 | (a) | Oldham A | W | 5-1 | Johnston 2, Spence 2, Mann | 10,922 |
| 16 | | 21 | (h) | Bury | L | 1-2 | Spence | 11,745 |
| 17 | | 28 | (a) | Port Vale | W | 2-1 | Spence 2 | 6,955 |
| 18 | Dec | 5 | (h) | Millwall | W | 2-0 | Gallimore, Spence | 6,396 |
| 19 | | 12 | (a) | Bradford C | L | 3-4 | Spence 2, Johnston | 13,215 |
| 20 | | 19 | (h) | Bristol C | L | 0-1 | | 4,697 |
| 21 | | 25 | (h) | Wolves | W | 3-2 | Hopkinson, Reid, Spence | 33,123 |
| 22 | | 26 | (a) | Wolves | L | 0-7 | | 37,207 |
| 23 | Jan | 2 | (h) | Bradford | L | 0-2 | | 6,056 |
| 24 | | 16 | (a) | Swansea T | L | 1-3 | Warburton | 5,888 |
| 25 | | 23 | (a) | Tottenham H | L | 1-4 | Reid | 19,139 |
| 26 | | 30 | (h) | Nottingham F | W | 3-2 | Reid 3 | 11,152 |
| 27 | Feb | 6 | (a) | Chesterfield | W | 3-1 | Reid 2, Spence | 9,457 |
| 28 | | 17 | (h) | Burnley | W | 5-1 | Johnston 2, Ridding 2, Gallimore | 11,036 |
| 29 | | 20 | (a) | Preston NE | D | 0-0 | | 13,353 |
| 30 | | 27 | (h) | Barnsley | W | 3-0 | Hopkinson 2, Gallimore | 18,223 |
| 31 | Mar | 5 | (a) | Notts C | W | 2-1 | Hopkinson, Reid | 10,817 |
| 32 | | 12 | (h) | Plymouth A | W | 2-1 | Spence 2 | 24,827 |
| 33 | | 19 | (a) | Leeds U | W | 4-1 | Reid 2, Johnston, Ridding | 13,644 |
| 34 | | 25 | (h) | Charlton A | L | 0-2 | | 37,012 |
| 35 | | 26 | (h) | Oldham A | W | 5-1 | Reid 3, Fitton, Spence | 17,886 |
| 36 | | 28 | (a) | Charlton A | L | 0-1 | | 16,256 |
| 37 | Apr | 2 | (a) | Bury | D | 0-0 | | 12,592 |
| 38 | | 9 | (h) | Port Vale | W | 2-0 | Reid, Spence | 10,916 |
| 39 | | 16 | (a) | Millwall | D | 1-1 | Reid | 9,087 |
| 40 | | 23 | (h) | Bradford C | W | 1-0 | Fitton | 17,765 |
| 41 | | 30 | (a) | Bristol C | L | 1-2 | Black | 5,874 |
| 42 | May | 7 | (a) | Southampton | D | 1-1 | Black | 6,128 |

FINAL LEAGUE POSITION: 12th in Division Two

Appearances
Goals

FA Cup

| 3 | Jan | 9 | (a) | Plymouth A | L | 1-4 | | |
|---|---|---|---|---|---|---|---|---|

| Steward | Mellor | Silcock | Bennion | Parker | McLachlan | Ferguson | Warburton | Reid | Johnston | Mann | McLenahan | Spence | Hopkinson | Rowley | Hilditch | Wilson | Gallimore | Jones | Dean | Robinson | Dale | Lydon | Manley | Chesters | Ridding | Whittle | Vincent | Lievesley | Page | Moody | Fitton | McDonald | Black | |
|---|---|---|---|---|---|---|---|---|---|---|---|---|---|---|---|---|---|---|---|---|---|---|---|---|---|---|---|---|---|---|---|---|---|---|
| 1 | 2 | 3 | 4 | 5 | 6 | 7 | 8 | 9 | 10 | 11 | | | | | | | | | | | | | | | | | | | | | | | | 1 |
| 1 | 2 | 3 | 4 | 5 | 11 | 7 | 8 | 9 | 10 | | | 6 | | | | | | | | | | | | | | | | | | | | | | 2 |
| 1 | 2 | 3 | | 5 | 6 | 7 | | 9 | 10 | | | 4 | 8 | | 11 | | | | | | | | | | | | | | | | | | | 3 |
| 1 | 2 | 3 | | 5 | 6 | | | 9 | 8 | | | 4 | 7 | | 11 | 10 | | | | | | | | | | | | | | | | | | 4 |
| 1 | 2 | 3 | 4 | | | 7 | | | 10 | | | 9 | | | 11 | 5 | 6 | 8 | | | | | | | | | | | | | | | | 5 |
| 1 | 2 | 3 | 4 | | | 7 | | | 10 | 11 | | 9 | | | | 5 | 6 | 8 | | | | | | | | | | | | | | | | 6 |
| 1 | | 3 | 4 | 5 | | 7 | | 9 | 10 | | | 11 | | | | 6 | 8 | 2 | | | | | | | | | | | | | | | | 7 |
| 1 | | 3 | 4 | | | 7 | 8 | | 10 | | | 9 | | | | 5 | 6 | | 2 | 11 | | | | | | | | | | | | | | 8 |
| 1 | | 3 | 4 | | | 7 | 8 | | 10 | | | 9 | | | | 5 | 6 | | 2 | 11 | | | | | | | | | | | | | | 9 |
| 1 | 2 | 3 | 4 | | | | | 10 | 7 | 6 | | 9 | 5 | | | | 8 | | | 11 | | | | | | | | | | | | | | 10 |
| 1 | 2 | 3 | 4 | | | | | 10 | 7 | 6 | | 9 | 5 | | | | 8 | | | 11 | | | | | | | | | | | | | | 11 |
| 1 | 2 | 3 | 4 | | | | | 10 | 7 | | | 9 | 5 | | | 6 | 8 | | | 11 | | | | | | | | | | | | | | 12 |
| 1 | 2 | 3 | 4 | | 6 | | | 10 | 7 | | | 9 | 5 | | | | 8 | | | 11 | | | | | | | | | | | | | | 13 |
| 1 | 2 | 3 | 4 | | 6 | | | 10 | 7 | | | 9 | 5 | | | | 8 | | | 11 | | | | | | | | | | | | | | 14 |
| 1 | 2 | | 4 | 5 | | | | 10 | 7 | 6 | | 9 | | | | | 8 | | | 11 | | | 3 | | | | | | | | | | | 15 |
| 1 | 2 | | 4 | | | | | 10 | 7 | 6 | | 9 | 5 | | | | 8 | | | 11 | | | 3 | | | | | | | | | | | 16 |
| 1 | 2 | | 4 | | | | 8 | | 7 | 6 | | 9 | 5 | | | | | | | 11 | 10 | | 3 | | | | | | | | | | | 17 |
| 1 | 2 | | | | | | | | 10 | 8 | 7 | 9 | 5 | | | | | | | 11 | | | 3 | 4 | 6 | | | | | | | | | 18 |
| 1 | 2 | 3 | | | | | | | 10 | 8 | 7 | 9 | 5 | | | | | | | 11 | | | | 4 | 6 | | | | | | | | | 19 |
| | 2 | 3 | 4 | | | | | | 10 | 8 | 7 | 9 | 5 | | | | | | | 11 | | | | | 6 | 1 | | | | | | | | 20 |
| | 2 | 3 | 4 | | 6 | | | | 10 | | | 9 | 7 | | 5 | | | | | 11 | | | | | | 1 | 8 | | | | | | | 21 |
| 1 | 2 | 3 | 4 | | 6 | | | | 10 | | | 9 | 7 | | 5 | | | | | 11 | | | | | | | 8 | | | | | | | 22 |
| 1 | 2 | 3 | 4 | | 6 | | | | 10 | | | 9 | 7 | | 5 | | | | | 11 | | | | | | | 8 | | | | | | | 23 |
| 1 | 2 | 3 | 4 | 5 | 6 | | 8 | 9 | 10 | | | 7 | | | | | | | | | | | | | | | 11 | | | | | | | 24 |
| 1 | 2 | 3 | 4 | 5 | 6 | | | | 9 | | | 7 | | | 11 | | | | | | 10 | | | | | | 8 | | | | | | | 25 |
| 1 | 2 | 3 | 4 | | 6 | | 8 | | 9 | | | 7 | | | 11 | 5 | | | | | 10 | | | | | | | | | | | | | 26 |
| 1 | 2 | | 4 | | 6 | | | 9 | | | | 7 | | | 11 | | | | | | 10 | | 3 | | 8 | | 5 | | | | | | | 27 |
| 1 | | 3 | 4 | | 6 | | | | 10 | | | 7 | | | 11 | | 8 | | | | 2 | | | | 9 | | 5 | | | | | | | 28 |
| 1 | | 3 | | | 6 | | 8 | | | | | 4 | 7 | | 11 | | | | | 10 | 2 | | | | 9 | | 5 | | | | | | | 29 |
| 1 | | 3 | | | 6 | | | 9 | 10 | | | 4 | 7 | | 11 | | 8 | | | | 2 | | | | | | 5 | | | | | | | 30 |
| 1 | 2 | | | | 6 | | | 9 | 10 | | | 4 | 7 | | 11 | | 8 | | | | 3 | | | | | | 5 | | | | | | | 31 |
| 1 | 2 | | | | 6 | | | 9 | 10 | | | 7 | | | 11 | 4 | 3 | | | | | | | | 8 | | 5 | | | | | | | 32 |
| 1 | | 3 | | | 6 | | | 9 | 10 | | | 7 | | | 11 | 4 | | | | | 2 | | | | 8 | | 5 | | | | | | | 33 |
| 1 | | 3 | | | 6 | | | 9 | | | | 7 | | | | | | | | 10 | 2 | | | | 8 | | 5 | 4 | 11 | | | | | 34 |
| | | 3 | | | 6 | | | 9 | | | | 7 | | | | | | | | | 2 | | | | 8 | | 5 | 4 | | 10 | 1 | | 11 | 35 |
| | 2 | 3 | 4 | | 6 | | | 9 | | | | 7 | | | | | | | | | | | | | 8 | | 5 | | | 10 | 1 | | 11 | 36 |
| | 2 | 3 | 4 | | 6 | | | 9 | | | | 7 | | | | | | | | | | | | | 8 | | 5 | | | 10 | 1 | | 11 | 37 |
| | 2 | 3 | 4 | | 6 | | | 9 | 10 | | | 7 | | | | | | | | | | | | | 8 | | 5 | | | | 1 | | 11 | 38 |
| | 2 | 3 | | | 6 | | | 9 | | | | 7 | | | | | | | | | | | | | 8 | | 5 | 4 | | 10 | 1 | | 11 | 39 |
| | 2 | 3 | | | 6 | | | | | | | 7 | | | | 4 | | | | | | | | | | | 5 | | 11 | 10 | 1 | 8 | 9 | 40 |
| | 2 | 3 | 4 | | 6 | | | | 10 | | | 7 | | | | | | | | | | | | | 8 | | 5 | | | | 1 | 9 | 11 | 41 |
| | 2 | 3 | | | 6 | | | | | | | 7 | | | | 4 | | | | | | | | | | | 5 | | 11 | 10 | 1 | 8 | 9 | 42 |
| 32 | 33 | 35 | 28 | 8 | 28 | 8 | 7 | 25 | 28 | 13 | 11 | 37 | 19 | 1 | 17 | 9 | 25 | 12 | 2 | 10 | 4 | 2 | 3 | 2 | 14 | 1 | 16 | 2 | 9 | 8 | 8 | 2 | 3 | |
| | | | | | | | 1 | 3 | 17 | 11 | 2 | 19 | 5 | | | | 6 | | | | | | | | 3 | | | | | | 2 | 2 | | |

255

# 1932-33

Manager: A.Scott Duncan

| | | | | | | | |
|---|---|---|---|---|---|---|---|
| 1 | Aug | 27 | (h) | Stoke C | L 0-2 | | 24,996 |
| 2 | | 29 | (a) | Charlton A | W 1-0 | Spence | 12,946 |
| 3 | Sep | 3 | (a) | Southampton | L 2-4 | Reid, Campbell (og) | 7,978 |
| 4 | | 7 | (h) | Charlton A | D 1-1 | McLenahan | 9,480 |
| 5 | | 10 | (a) | Tottenham H | L 1-6 | Ridding | 23,333 |
| 6 | | 17 | (h) | Grimsby T | D 1-1 | Brown | 17,662 |
| 7 | | 24 | (a) | Oldham A | D 1-1 | Spence | 14,403 |
| 8 | Oct | 1 | (h) | Preston NE | D 0-0 | | 20,800 |
| 9 | | 8 | (a) | Burnley | W 3-2 | Brown, Gallimore, Spence | 5,314 |
| 10 | | 15 | (h) | Bradford | W 2-1 | Reid 2 | 18,918 |
| 11 | | 22 | (h) | Millwall | W 7-1 | Reid 3, Brown 2, Gallimore, Spence | 15,860 |
| 12 | | 29 | (a) | Port Vale | D 3-3 | Ridding 2, Brown | 7,138 |
| 13 | Nov | 5 | (h) | Notts C | W 2-0 | Gallimore, Ridding | 24,178 |
| 14 | | 12 | (a) | Bury | D 2-2 | Brown, Ridding | 21,663 |
| 15 | | 19 | (h) | Fulham | W 4-3 | Gallimore 2, Brown, Ridding | 28,803 |
| 16 | | 26 | (a) | Chesterfield | D 1-1 | Ridding | 10,277 |
| 17 | Dec | 3 | (h) | Bradford C | L 0-1 | | 28,513 |
| 18 | | 10 | (a) | West Ham U | L 1-3 | Ridding | 13,435 |
| 19 | | 17 | (h) | Lincoln C | W 4-1 | Reid 3, Worthy (og) | 18,021 |
| 20 | | 24 | (a) | Swansea T | L 1-2 | Brown | 10,727 |
| 21 | | 26 | (a) | Plymouth A | W 3-2 | Spence 2, Reid | 33,776 |
| 22 | | 31 | (a) | Stoke C | D 0-0 | | 14,115 |
| 23 | Jan | 2 | (h) | Plymouth A | W 4-0 | Ridding 2, Chalmers, Spence | 30,257 |
| 24 | | 7 | (h) | Southampton | L 1-2 | McDonald | 21,364 |
| 25 | | 21 | (h) | Tottenham H | W 2-1 | Frame, McDonald | 20,661 |
| 26 | | 31 | (a) | Grimsby T | D 1-1 | Stewart | 4,020 |
| 27 | Feb | 4 | (h) | Oldham A | W 2-0 | Ridding, Stewart | 15,275 |
| 28 | | 11 | (a) | Preston NE | D 3-3 | Dewar, Hopkinson, Stewart | 15,662 |
| 29 | | 22 | (h) | Burnley | W 2-1 | McDonald, Warburton | 18,533 |
| 30 | Mar | 4 | (a) | Millwall | L 0-2 | | 22,578 |
| 31 | | 11 | (h) | Port Vale | D 1-1 | Hine | 24,690 |
| 32 | | 18 | (a) | Notts C | L 0-1 | | 13,018 |
| 33 | | 25 | (h) | Bury | L 1-3 | McLenahan | 27,687 |
| 34 | Apr | 1 | (a) | Fulham | L 1-3 | Dewar | 21,477 |
| 35 | | 5 | (a) | Bradford | D 1-1 | Vincent | 6,314 |
| 36 | | 8 | (h) | Chesterfield | W 2-1 | Dewar, Frame | 16,031 |
| 37 | | 14 | (a) | Nottingham F | L 2-3 | Brown, Dewar | 12,963 |
| 38 | | 15 | (a) | Bradford C | W 2-1 | Brown, Hine | 11,195 |
| 39 | | 17 | (h) | Nottingham F | W 2-1 | Hine, McDonald | 16,849 |
| 40 | | 22 | (h) | West Ham U | L 1-2 | Dewar | 14,958 |
| 41 | | 29 | (a) | Lincoln C | L 2-3 | Dewar, Hine | 8,507 |
| 42 | May | 6 | (h) | Swansea C | D 1-1 | Hine | 9,588 |

FINAL LEAGUE POSITION: 6th in Division Two

Appearances

Goals

FA Cup

3 Jan 14 (h) Middlesbrough L 1-4

256

Football appearances and goals grid (shirt numbers by match, 1–42).

| Moody | Mellor | Silcock | McLenahan | Vincent | McLachlan | Spence | Ridding | Black | McDonald | Page | Warburton | Reid | Fitton | Hopkinson | Gallimore | Manley | Brown | Frame | Chalmers | Jones T | Stewart | Hine | Dewar | Mitchell | Topping | Heywood | # |
|---|---|---|---|---|---|---|---|---|---|---|---|---|---|---|---|---|---|---|---|---|---|---|---|---|---|---|---|
| 1 | 2 | 3 | 4 | 5 | 6 | 7 | 8 | 9 | 10 | 11 | | | | | | | | | | | | | | | | | 1 |
| 1 | 2 | 3 | 4 | 5 | 6 | 7 | | | 10 | | 8 | 9 | 11 | | | | | | | | | | | | | | 2 |
| 1 | 2 | 3 | 4 | 5 | 6 | 7 | | | 10 | | 8 | 9 | | 11 | | | | | | | | | | | | | 3 |
| 1 | 2 | 3 | 4 | 5 | 6 | 7 | 8 | | 10 | | | 9 | | 11 | | | | | | | | | | | | | 4 |
| 1 | 2 | 3 | | 5 | 6 | 7 | 9 | 8 | | | | | 11 | 4 | 10 | | | | | | | | | | | | 5 |
| 1 | 2 | 3 | | 5 | 6 | | 9 | 8 | 10 | | | | 11 | | | 4 | 7 | | | | | | | | | | 6 |
| 1 | 2 | 3 | 8 | 5 | 6 | | 9 | | | | | | 11 | | 10 | 4 | 7 | | | | | | | | | | 7 |
| 1 | 2 | 3 | 6 | 4 | | 7 | | | | | | 9 | | | 10 | 11 | 5 | 8 | | | | | | | | | 8 |
| 1 | 2 | 3 | 6 | 4 | | 7 | | | | | | 9 | | | 10 | 11 | 5 | 8 | | | | | | | | | 9 |
| 1 | 2 | 3 | 6 | 4 | | 7 | | | | | | 9 | | | 10 | 11 | 5 | 8 | | | | | | | | | 10 |
| 1 | 2 | 3 | 6 | 4 | | 7 | | | | | | 9 | | | 10 | 11 | 5 | 8 | | | | | | | | | 11 |
| 1 | 2 | | 6 | 4 | | 7 | | | | | | 9 | | | 10 | 3 | 11 | 5 | 8 | | | | | | | | 12 |
| 1 | 2 | | 6 | 4 | | 7 | | | | | | 9 | | | 10 | 3 | 11 | 5 | 8 | | | | | | | | 13 |
| 1 | 2 | 3 | 6 | 4 | | | 9 | | 10 | | 8 | | 11 | | | | 7 | 5 | | | | | | | | | 14 |
| 1 | 2 | | 6 | 4 | | | 9 | | 10 | | | | | | | | 7 | 5 | 8 | 3 | 11 | | | | | | 15 |
| 1 | 2 | | 6 | 4 | | | 9 | | 10 | | | | | | | | 7 | 5 | 8 | 3 | 11 | | | | | | 16 |
| 1 | 2 | | 6 | 4 | | | 9 | | 10 | | | | | | | | 7 | 5 | 8 | 3 | 11 | | | | | | 17 |
| 1 | 2 | 3 | 6 | 4 | | | 9 | | 10 | | | | | | | | 7 | 5 | 8 | | 11 | | | | | | 18 |
| 1 | 2 | 3 | 6 | 4 | | | 8 | | | | | 9 | | | | | 7 | 5 | 10 | | 11 | | | | | | 19 |
| 1 | 2 | 3 | 6 | 4 | | | 8 | | | | | 9 | | | | | 7 | 5 | 10 | | 11 | | | | | | 20 |
| 1 | | 3 | | 4 | | 7 | 8 | | | | | 9 | | | | 6 | | 5 | 10 | 2 | 11 | | | | | | 21 |
| 1 | 2 | 3 | | 4 | | 7 | 8 | | | | | 9 | | | | 6 | | 5 | 10 | | 11 | | | | | | 22 |
| 1 | | 3 | 6 | 4 | 11 | 7 | 9 | | | | 8 | | | | | | | 5 | 10 | 2 | | | | | | | 23 |
| 1 | 2 | 3 | 6 | 5 | | 7 | 9 | | | | 8 | | | | | 4 | | | 10 | | 11 | | | | | | 24 |
| 1 | 2 | 3 | | 4 | | | 9 | | 10 | | | | | | | 6 | 7 | 5 | 8 | | 11 | | | | | | 25 |
| 1 | 2 | | | 4 | | | 9 | | 10 | | | | | | | 6 | 7 | 5 | 8 | 3 | 11 | | | | | | 26 |
| 1 | 2 | | | 4 | | 7 | 9 | | 10 | | | | | | | 6 | | 5 | 8 | 3 | 11 | | | | | | 27 |
| 1 | 2 | | | 4 | | | | | | 10 | | 7 | | | | 6 | | 5 | | 3 | 11 | 8 | 9 | | | | 28 |
| 1 | 2 | 3 | | 4 | | | | | | 10 | 7 | | | | | 6 | | 5 | | | 11 | 8 | 9 | | | | 29 |
| 1 | 2 | | | 4 | 6 | | | | | 10 | 7 | | | | | | | 5 | | 3 | 11 | 8 | 9 | | | | 30 |
| 1 | 2 | | | 4 | | | 8 | | | | | 7 | | | | 6 | | 5 | | 3 | 11 | 10 | 9 | | | | 31 |
| 1 | 2 | 3 | 6 | 4 | | | 8 | | | | | | | | | | | 5 | | | 11 | 10 | 9 | 7 | | | 32 |
| 1 | 2 | 3 | 4 | 5 | 6 | 7 | | | | 10 | | | | | | | | | | | 11 | 8 | 9 | | | | 33 |
| 1 | 2 | 3 | 4 | | 6 | 7 | 8 | | | | | | | | | | | 5 | | | 11 | 10 | 9 | | | | 34 |
| 1 | 2 | | 4 | | 6 | | 8 | | | | | | | | | | 7 | 5 | | | 11 | 10 | 9 | 3 | | | 35 |
| 1 | 2 | | 4 | | 6 | | | | | | | | | | 10 | | 7 | 5 | 8 | | 11 | | 9 | 3 | | | 36 |
| 1 | 2 | | 4 | | 11 | | | | | | | | | | | 6 | 7 | 5 | 8 | | | 10 | 9 | 3 | | | 37 |
| 1 | 2 | 3 | 4 | | 11 | | | | | 10 | | | | | | 6 | 7 | 5 | | | | 8 | 9 | | | | 38 |
| 1 | 2 | 3 | 4 | | 11 | | | | | 10 | | | | | | 6 | 7 | 5 | | | | 8 | 9 | | | | 39 |
| 1 | 2 | | 4 | | 11 | | | | | 10 | | | | | | 6 | 7 | 5 | | | | 8 | 9 | 3 | | | 40 |
| 1 | 2 | 3 | 4 | | | | | | | 10 | | 11 | | | | 6 | 7 | 5 | | | | 8 | 9 | | | | 41 |
| 1 | 2 | | 4 | | | | | | | | | | | | | 6 | 11 | 5 | 10 | | | 8 | 9 | 3 | 7 | | 42 |
| 42 | 40 | 27 | 24 | 40 | 17 | 19 | 23 | 1 | 21 | 3 | 6 | 11 | 4 | 6 | 12 | 19 | 25 | 33 | 22 | 10 | 21 | 14 | 15 | 1 | 5 | 1 | |
| | | 2 | 1 | | | 7 | 11 | | 4 | | | 1 | | | 10 | 1 | 5 | 10 | 2 | | 1 | | 3 | 5 | 6 | | |

2 own-goals

# 1933-34

Manager: A.Scott Duncan

| | | | | | | |
|---|---|---|---|---|---|---|
| 1 | Aug | 26 | (a) | Plymouth A · | L 0-4 | 25,700 |
| 2 | | 30 | (h) | Nottingham F | L 0-1 | 16,934 |
| 3 | Sep | 2 | (h) | Lincoln C | D 1-1 Green | 16,987 |
| 4 | | 7 | (a) | Nottingham F | D 1-1 Stewart | 10,650 |
| 5 | | 9 | (h) | Bolton W | L 1-5 Stewart | 21,779 |
| 6 | | 16 | (a) | Brentford | W 4-3 Brown 2, Frame, Hine | 17,180 |
| 7 | | 23 | (h) | Burnley | W 5-2 Dewar 4, Brown | 18,411 |
| 8 | | 30 | (a) | Oldham A | L 0-2 | 22,736 |
| 9 | Oct | 7 | (h) | Preston NE | W 1-0 Hine | 22,303 |
| 10 | | 14 | (a) | Bradford | L 1-6 Hine | 11,033 |
| 11 | | 21 | (a) | Bury | L 1-2 Byrne | 15,008 |
| 12 | | 28 | (h) | Hull C | W 4-1 Heywood 2, Green, Hine | 16,269 |
| 13 | Nov | 4 | (a) | Fulham | W 2-0 Stewart, Keeping (og) | 17,049 |
| 14 | | 11 | (h) | Southampton | W 1-0 Manley | 18,149 |
| 15 | | 18 | (a) | Blackpool | L 1-3 Brown | 14,384 |
| 16 | | 25 | (h) | Bradford C | W 2-1 Dewar, Barkas (og) | 20,902 |
| 17 | Dec | 2 | (a) | Port Vale | W 3-2 Black, Brown, Dewar | 10,316 |
| 18 | | 9 | (h) | Notts C | L 1-2 Dewar | 15,564 |
| 19 | | 16 | (a) | Swansea T | L 1-2 Hine | 6,591 |
| 20 | | 23 | (h) | Millwall | D 1-1 Dewar | 12,043 |
| 21 | | 25 | (h) | Grimsby T | L 1-3 Vose | 29,443 |
| 22 | | 26 | (a) | Grimsby T | L 3-7 Byrne 2, Frame | 15,801 |
| 23 | | 30 | (h) | Plymouth A | L 0-3 | 12,206 |
| 24 | Jan | 6 | (a) | Lincoln C | L 1-5 Brown | 6,075 |
| 25 | | 20 | (a) | Bolton W | L 1-3 Ball | 11,887 |
| 26 | | 27 | (h) | Brentford | L 1-3 Ball | 16,891 |
| 27 | Feb | 3 | (a) | Burnley | W 4-1 Cape 2, Green, Stewart | 9,906 |
| 28 | | 10 | (h) | Oldham A | L 2-3 Cape, Green | 24,480 |
| 29 | | 21 | (a) | Preston NE | L 2-3 Gallimore 2 | 9,173 |
| 30 | | 24 | (h) | Bradford | L 0-4 | 13,389 |
| 31 | Mar | 3 | (h) | Bury | W 2-1 Ball, Gallimore | 11,176 |
| 32 | | 10 | (a) | Hull C | L 1-4 Ball | 5,771 |
| 33 | | 17 | (h) | Fulham | W 1-0 Ball | 17,565 |
| 34 | | 24 | (a) | Southampton | L 0-1 | 4,840 |
| 35 | | 30 | (h) | West Ham U | L 0-1 | 29,114 |
| 36 | | 31 | (h) | Blackpool | W 2-0 Cape, Hine | 20,038 |
| 37 | Apr | 2 | (a) | West Ham U | L 1-2 Cape | 20,085 |
| 38 | | 7 | (a) | Bradford C | D 1-1 Cape | 9,258 |
| 39 | | 14 | (h) | Port Vale | W 2-0 Brown, McMillen | 14,777 |
| 40 | | 21 | (a) | Notts C | D 0-0 | 9,645 |
| 41 | | 28 | (h) | Swansea T | D 1-1 Topping | 16,678 |
| 42 | May | 5 | (a) | Millwall | W 2-0 Cape, Manley | 24,003 |

FINAL LEAGUE POSITION: 20th in Division Two

Appearances
Goals

FA Cup

| | | | | | | |
|---|---|---|---|---|---|---|
| 3 | Jan | 13 | (h) | Portsmouth | D 1-1 | |
| R | | 17 | (a) | Portsmouth | L 1-4 | |

258

| Hillam | Mellor | Jones | McLenahan | Vose | Manley | McGillivray | Hine | Dewar | Green | Stewart | Vincent | Frame | Chalmers | Silcock | McMillen | Brown | Warburton | Hall | Hopkinson | Ridding | Byrne | Heywood | Black | Topping | McDonald | Ball | Nevin | Cape | Manns | Newton | Gallimore | Behan | Ainsworth | Hacking | Griffiths | Robertson | McKay | | |
|---|---|---|---|---|---|---|---|---|---|---|---|---|---|---|---|---|---|---|---|---|---|---|---|---|---|---|---|---|---|---|---|---|---|---|---|---|---|---|---|
| 1 | 2 | 3 | 4 | 5 | 6 | 7 | 8 | 9 | 10 | 11 | | | | | | | | | | | | | | | | | | | | | | | | | | | | | 1 |
| 1 | 2 | 3 | 4 | 5 | 6 | 7 | 8 | 9 | 10 | 11 | | | | | | | | | | | | | | | | | | | | | | | | | | | | | 2 |
| 1 | 2 | 3 | 6 | | | 7 | 8 | 9 | 10 | 11 | 4 | 5 | | | | | | | | | | | | | | | | | | | | | | | | | | | 3 |
| 1 | 2 | 3 | 6 | 4 | | 7 | 8 | 9 | | 11 | | 5 | 10 | | | | | | | | | | | | | | | | | | | | | | | | | | 4 |
| 1 | 2 | 3 | 6 | | | 7 | 8 | 9 | | 11 | 4 | 5 | 10 | | | | | | | | | | | | | | | | | | | | | | | | | | 5 |
| 1 | | 2 | | | 6 | | 10 | 9 | | 11 | | 4 | | 3 | 5 | 7 | 8 | | | | | | | | | | | | | | | | | | | | | | 6 |
| 1 | | 2 | | 4 | 6 | | 10 | 9 | | 11 | | 8 | | 3 | 5 | 7 | | | | | | | | | | | | | | | | | | | | | | | 7 |
| | | 2 | | 4 | 6 | | 10 | 9 | | 11 | | 8 | | 3 | 5 | 7 | | 1 | | | | | | | | | | | | | | | | | | | | | 8 |
| | | 2 | | 4 | 6 | | 10 | 9 | | | | | 8 | 3 | 5 | 7 | | 1 | 11 | | | | | | | | | | | | | | | | | | | | 9 |
| | | 2 | 3 | 4 | 6 | | 10 | 9 | | | 5 | | | | | 7 | | 1 | 11 | 8 | | | | | | | | | | | | | | | | | | | 10 |
| | | 2 | 4 | | 6 | | 10 | 8 | | 11 | | | | 3 | 5 | | 7 | 1 | | | 9 | | | | | | | | | | | | | | | | | | 11 |
| | | 2 | 4 | | 6 | | 8 | 9 | 10 | 11 | | | | 3 | 5 | | | 1 | | | | 7 | | | | | | | | | | | | | | | | | 12 |
| | | 2 | 4 | | 6 | | 8 | 9 | 10 | 11 | | | | 3 | 5 | | | 1 | | | | 7 | | | | | | | | | | | | | | | | | 13 |
| | | 2 | 4 | | 6 | | 8 | 9 | 10 | 11 | | | | 3 | 5 | | | 1 | | | | 7 | | | | | | | | | | | | | | | | | 14 |
| | | 2 | 4 | | 6 | | 8 | 9 | 10 | 11 | | | | 3 | 5 | 7 | | 1 | | | | | | | | | | | | | | | | | | | | | 15 |
| | | 2 | | 5 | 6 | | 10 | 9 | | | 4 | | | 3 | | 7 | | 1 | | 8 | | | 11 | | | | | | | | | | | | | | | | 16 |
| | | 2 | | 5 | 6 | | 10 | 9 | | | 4 | | | | | 7 | | 1 | | 8 | | | 11 | 3 | | | | | | | | | | | | | | | 17 |
| | | 2 | 6 | 5 | | | 10 | 9 | | | 4 | | | 3 | | 7 | | 1 | | 8 | | | 11 | | | | | | | | | | | | | | | | 18 |
| | | 2 | 4 | 5 | 6 | | 10 | 9 | | | | | 8 | 3 | | 7 | | 1 | | | | | 11 | | | | | | | | | | | | | | | | 19 |
| | | 2 | 4 | | 6 | | 10 | 9 | | | | 3 | 8 | | 5 | 7 | | 1 | 11 | | | | | | | | | | | | | | | | | | | | 20 |
| | | 2 | | 4 | 6 | | 8 | 9 | | 11 | | 3 | 10 | | 5 | | | 1 | | | 7 | | | | | | | | | | | | | | | | | | 21 |
| | | | | 4 | 6 | 7 | | | | 11 | | 2 | 10 | | 5 | | | 1 | | | 9 | | | 3 | 8 | | | | | | | | | | | | | | 22 |
| | | 3 | | 4 | 6 | | 8 | | | 11 | | 2 | 10 | | 5 | | | 1 | | | 7 | | | | | 9 | | | | | | | | | | | | | 23 |
| | | | 10 | | 6 | 8 | | | | 11 | | 4 | | | 5 | 7 | | 1 | | | | | | 3 | | 9 | 2 | | | | | | | | | | | | 24 |
| | | | | | 6 | 7 | 8 | | | 11 | | 4 | | 3 | 5 | | | 1 | | | | | | | 10 | 9 | 2 | | | | | | | | | | | | 25 |
| | | 2 | 4 | | 6 | | 8 | | | 11 | | | | 3 | 5 | | | 1 | | | | | | | 10 | 9 | | 7 | | | | | | | | | | | 26 |
| | | 2 | 8 | | 6 | | | | 10 | 11 | | | | | | | | 1 | | | | | | | | 9 | 3 | 7 | 4 | 5 | | | | | | | | | 27 |
| | | 2 | 8 | | 6 | | | | 10 | 11 | | | | | | | | 1 | | | | | | | | 9 | 3 | 7 | 4 | 5 | | | | | | | | | 28 |
| | | 2 | 4 | | 6 | | | | | 11 | | 5 | 8 | | | | | 1 | | | | | | 3 | | 9 | | 7 | | | 10 | | | | | | | | 29 |
| | | 2 | 4 | | 6 | | 8 | | | 11 | | 5 | | | | | | 1 | | | | | | 3 | | 9 | | 7 | | | 10 | | | | | | | | 30 |
| | | 2 | 4 | 5 | | | | | | 11 | | | | 3 | | | | | 6 | | | | | | | 9 | | 7 | | | 10 | 1 | 8 | | | | | | 31 |
| 1 | | 2 | | 5 | | | | | | 11 | | | | 3 | 4 | | | | 6 | | | | | | 8 | 9 | | 7 | | | 10 | | | | | | | | 32 |
| | | 3 | | | | | | | | | | 5 | | | | | | | 11 | | | | | | | 9 | | 7 | | | 10 | | 8 | 1 | 2 | 4 | 6 | | 33 |
| | | 3 | | | 11 | | | | | | | 5 | | | | | | | | 8 | | | | | | 9 | | 7 | | | 10 | | | 1 | 2 | 4 | 6 | | 34 |
| | | 3 | | | | | 10 | | | | | 5 | | | 8 | | | | | | | | | | | 9 | | 7 | | | 11 | | | 1 | 2 | 4 | 6 | | 35 |
| | | 3 | | | 11 | | 10 | | | | | 5 | 8 | | | | | | | | | | | | | 9 | | 7 | | | | | | 1 | 2 | 4 | 6 | | 36 |
| | | 3 | | | 11 | | 10 | | | | | | 8 | | 5 | | | | | | | | | | | 9 | | 7 | | | | | | 1 | 2 | 4 | 6 | | 37 |
| | | 3 | | | | | 10 | | | | | | 8 | | 5 | 11 | | | | | | | | | | 9 | | 7 | | | | | | 1 | 2 | 4 | 6 | | 38 |
| | | 3 | | | | | 10 | | | | 5 | | | | 8 | 9 | | | 11 | | | | | | | | | 7 | | | | | | 1 | 2 | 4 | 6 | | 39 |
| | | 3 | | | | | 10 | | | | 5 | | | | 8 | 9 | | | 11 | | | | | | | | | 7 | | | | | | 1 | 2 | 4 | 6 | | 40 |
| | | 3 | | | | | 10 | | | | | | | | 5 | | | | 6 | | | | | 11 | | 9 | | 7 | | | | | | 1 | 2 | 4 | 8 | | 41 |
| | | 3 | 8 | 5 | 11 | | 10 | | | | | | | | | | | | | | | | | | | 9 | | 7 | | | | | | 1 | 2 | 4 | 6 | | 42 |
| 8 | 5 | 39 | 22 | 17 | 30 | 8 | 33 | 21 | 9 | 25 | 8 | 18 | 12 | 16 | 23 | 15 | 2 | 23 | 9 | 5 | 4 | 3 | 4 | 6 | 4 | 18 | 4 | 17 | 2 | 2 | 7 | 1 | 2 | 10 | 10 | 10 | 10 | | |
| | | | | 1 | 2 | | 6 | 8 | 4 | 4 | | 2 | | | 1 | 7 | | | | | 3 | 2 | 1 | 1 | | 5 | | 7 | | | 3 | | | | | | | | |

2 own-goals

# 1934-35

Manager: A.Scott Duncan

| 1 | Aug | 25 | (h) | Bradford C | W | 2-0 | Manley 2 | 27,573 |
|---|-----|----|-----|------------|---|-----|----------|--------|
| 2 | Sep | 1 | (a) | Sheffield U | L | 2-3 | Ball, Manley | 18,468 |
| 3 | | 3 | (a) | Bolton W | L | 1-3 | Finney (og) | 16,238 |
| 4 | | 8 | (h) | Barnsley | W | 4-1 | Mutch 3, Manley | 22,315 |
| 5 | | 12 | (h) | Bolton W | L | 0-3 | | 24,760 |
| 6 | | 15 | (a) | Port Vale | L | 2-3 | T.J.Jones, Mutch | 9,307 |
| 7 | | 22 | (h) | Norwich C | W | 5-0 | Cape, T.J.Jones, McLenahan, Mutch, Owen | 13,052 |
| 8 | | 29 | (h) | Swansea T | W | 3-1 | Cape 2, Mutch | 14,865 |
| 9 | Oct | 6 | (a) | Burnley | W | 2-1 | Cape, Manley | 16,757 |
| 10 | | 13 | (h) | Oldham A | W | 4-0 | Manley 2, McKay, Mutch | 29,143 |
| 11 | | 20 | (a) | Newcastle U | W | 1-0 | Bamford | 24,752 |
| 12 | | 27 | (h) | West Ham U | W | 3-1 | Mutch 2, McKay | 31,950 |
| 13 | Nov | 3 | (a) | Blackpool | W | 2-1 | Bryant, McKay | 15,663 |
| 14 | | 10 | (h) | Bury | W | 1-0 | Mutch | 41,415 |
| 15 | | 17 | (a) | Hull C | L | 2-3 | Bamford 2 | 6,494 |
| 16 | | 24 | (h) | Nottingham F | W | 3-2 | Mutch 2, Hine | 27,192 |
| 17 | Dec | 1 | (a) | Brentford | L | 1-3 | Bamford | 21,744 |
| 18 | | 8 | (h) | Fulham | W | 1-0 | Mutch | 25,706 |
| 19 | | 15 | (a) | Bradford | W | 2-1 | Manley, Mutch | 8,405 |
| 20 | | 22 | (h) | Plymouth A | W | 3-1 | Bamford, Bryant, Rowley | 24,896 |
| 21 | | 25 | (h) | Notts C | W | 2-1 | Mutch, Rowley | 32,965 |
| 22 | | 26 | (a) | Notts C | L | 0-1 | | 24,599 |
| 23 | | 29 | (a) | Bradford C | L | 0-2 | | 11,908 |
| 24 | Jan | 1 | (h) | Southampton | W | 3-0 | Cape 2, Rowley | 15,174 |
| 25 | | 5 | (a) | Sheffield U | D | 3-3 | Bryant, Mutch, Rowley | 28,300 |
| 26 | | 19 | (a) | Barnsley | W | 2-0 | Bryant, T.J.Jones | 10,177 |
| 27 | Feb | 2 | (a) | Norwich C | L | 2-3 | Manley, Rowley | 14,260 |
| 28 | | 6 | (h) | Port Vale | W | 2-1 | T.J.Jones, Rowley | 7,372 |
| 29 | | 9 | (a) | Swansea T | L | 0-1 | | 8,876 |
| 30 | | 23 | (a) | Oldham A | L | 1-3 | Mutch | 14,432 |
| 31 | Mar | 2 | (h) | Newcastle U | L | 0-1 | | 20,728 |
| 32 | | 9 | (a) | West Ham U | D | 0-0 | | 19,718 |
| 33 | | 16 | (h) | Blackpool | W | 3-2 | Bamford, Mutch, Rowley | 25,704 |
| 34 | | 23 | (a) | Bury | W | 1-0 | Cape | 7,229 |
| 35 | | 27 | (h) | Burnley | L | 3-4 | Boyd, Cape, McMillen | 10,247 |
| 36 | | 30 | (h) | Hull C | W | 3-0 | Boyd 3 | 15,358 |
| 37 | Apr | 6 | (a) | Nottingham F | D | 2-2 | Bryant 2 | 8,618 |
| 38 | | 13 | (h) | Brentford | D | 0-0 | | 32,969 |
| 39 | | 20 | (a) | Fulham | L | 1-3 | Bamford | 11,059 |
| 40 | | 22 | (a) | Southampton | L | 0-1 | | 12,458 |
| 41 | | 27 | (h) | Bradford | W | 2-0 | Bamford, Robertson | 8,606 |
| 42 | May | 4 | (a) | Plymouth A | W | 2-0 | Bamford, Rowley | 10,767 |

FINAL LEAGUE POSITION: 5th in Division Two

Appearances
Goals

FA Cup

| 3 | Jan | 12 | (a) | Bristol R | W | 3-1 |
|---|-----|----|-----|-----------|---|-----|
| 4 | | 26 | (a) | Nottingham F | D | 0-0 |
| R | | 30 | (h) | Nottingham F | L | 0-3 |

| Hacking | Griffiths | Jones T | Robertson | Vose | McKay | Cape | Mutch | Ball | Jones T J | Manley | McLenahan | Topping | Hine | Langford | Mellor | Owen | Bamford | Bryant | Rowley | McMillen | Hall | Porter | Boyd | |
|---|---|---|---|---|---|---|---|---|---|---|---|---|---|---|---|---|---|---|---|---|---|---|---|---|
| 1 | 2 | 3 | 4 | 5 | 6 | 7 | 8 | 9 | 10 | 11 |  |  |  |  |  |  |  |  |  |  |  |  |  | 1 |
| 1 | 2 | 3 | 4 | 5 | 6 | 7 | 8 | 9 | 10 | 11 |  |  |  |  |  |  |  |  |  |  |  |  |  | 2 |
| 1 | 2 | 3 | 4 | 5 | 6 | 7 | 8 | 9 | 10 | 11 |  |  |  |  |  |  |  |  |  |  |  |  |  | 3 |
| 1 | 2 | 3 |  | 5 | 6 | 7 | 8 | 9 | 10 | 11 | 4 |  |  |  |  |  |  |  |  |  |  |  |  | 4 |
| 1 | 2 | 3 |  | 5 | 6 | 7 | 8 | 9 | 10 | 11 | 4 |  |  |  |  |  |  |  |  |  |  |  |  | 5 |
| 1 |  | 2 |  | 5 | 6 | 7 | 8 | 9 |  | 11 |  | 4 | 3 | 10 |  |  |  |  |  |  |  |  |  | 6 |
|  | 3 | 4 | 5 | 6 | 9 | 8 |  | 7 |  | 10 |  |  | 1 | 2 | 11 |  |  |  |  |  |  |  |  | 7 |
|  | 2 | 3 | 4 | 5 | 10 | 9 | 8 |  | 7 | 6 |  |  | 1 | 11 |  |  |  |  |  |  |  |  |  | 8 |
| 1 | 2 | 3 | 4 | 5 | 10 | 9 | 8 |  | 7 | 6 |  |  |  | 11 |  |  |  |  |  |  |  |  |  | 9 |
| 1 | 2 | 3 | 4 | 5 | 10 |  | 8 |  | 7 | 6 |  |  | 9 | 11 |  |  |  |  |  |  |  |  |  | 10 |
| 1 | 2 | 3 | 4 | 5 | 10 |  | 8 |  | 7 | 6 |  |  |  |  |  | 11 | 9 |  |  |  |  |  |  | 11 |
| 1 | 2 | 3 | 4 | 5 | 10 |  | 8 |  | 7 | 6 |  |  |  |  |  | 11 | 9 |  |  |  |  |  |  | 12 |
| 1 | 2 | 3 | 4 | 5 | 10 |  | 8 |  | 11 | 6 |  |  |  |  |  |  | 9 | 7 |  |  |  |  |  | 13 |
| 1 | 2 | 3 | 4 | 5 | 10 |  | 8 |  | 11 | 6 |  |  |  |  |  |  | 9 | 7 |  |  |  |  |  | 14 |
| 1 | 2 | 3 | 4 | 5 | 10 |  | 8 |  |  | 6 |  |  |  |  |  | 11 | 9 | 7 |  |  |  |  |  | 15 |
| 1 | 2 | 3 | 4 | 5 |  |  | 8 |  | 6 | 11 |  |  |  |  |  | 10 | 9 | 7 |  |  |  |  |  | 16 |
| 1 | 2 | 3 | 4 | 5 |  |  | 8 |  | 6 | 11 |  |  |  |  |  | 10 | 9 | 7 |  |  |  |  |  | 17 |
| 1 | 2 | 3 |  | 5 | 6 |  | 8 |  | 11 |  | 4 |  |  |  |  |  | 9 | 7 | 10 |  |  |  |  | 18 |
| 1 | 2 | 3 | 4 | 5 | 6 |  | 8 |  | 11 |  |  |  |  |  |  |  | 9 | 7 | 10 |  |  |  |  | 19 |
| 1 | 2 | 3 | 4 | 5 | 6 |  | 8 |  | 11 |  |  |  |  |  |  |  | 9 | 7 | 10 |  |  |  |  | 20 |
| 1 | 2 | 3 | 4 | 5 | 6 |  | 8 |  |  |  |  |  |  |  |  | 11 | 9 | 7 | 10 |  |  |  |  | 21 |
| 1 | 2 | 3 | 4 |  | 6 |  | 8 |  |  |  |  |  |  |  |  | 11 | 9 | 7 | 10 | 5 |  |  |  | 22 |
|  | 2 | 3 | 4 | 5 | 6 | 9 | 8 |  |  |  |  |  |  |  |  | 11 |  | 7 | 10 |  | 1 |  |  | 23 |
|  | 2 | 3 | 4 | 5 | 6 | 9 | 8 |  | 11 |  |  |  |  |  |  |  |  | 7 | 10 |  | 1 |  |  | 24 |
|  | 2 | 3 | 4 | 5 | 6 | 9 | 8 |  | 11 |  |  |  |  |  |  |  |  | 7 | 10 |  | 1 |  |  | 25 |
| 1 | 2 |  | 4 | 5 | 6 |  | 8 |  | 11 |  |  |  |  |  |  |  | 9 | 7 | 10 |  |  | 3 |  | 26 |
| 1 | 2 | 3 | 4 | 5 | 6 | 9 | 8 |  | 7 |  |  |  |  |  |  | 11 |  |  | 10 |  |  |  |  | 27 |
|  | 2 | 3 | 5 | 4 | 9 |  | 8 |  | 11 | 6 |  |  |  |  |  |  |  | 7 | 10 |  | 1 |  |  | 28 |
|  | 2 |  | 4 |  | 6 |  | 8 |  | 11 |  |  |  |  |  |  |  |  | 7 | 10 | 5 | 1 | 3 | 9 | 29 |
|  | 2 |  | 5 | 4 |  |  | 8 |  | 11 | 6 |  |  |  |  |  |  |  | 7 | 10 |  | 1 | 3 | 9 | 30 |
|  | 2 |  | 4 | 5 | 6 | 7 | 8 |  | 11 |  |  |  |  |  |  |  |  |  | 10 |  | 1 | 3 | 9 | 31 |
|  | 2 |  | 4 | 5 | 6 | 7 | 8 |  | 11 |  |  |  |  |  |  |  |  |  | 10 |  | 1 | 3 | 9 | 32 |
|  | 2 |  | 4 | 5 |  |  | 8 |  |  | 6 |  |  |  |  |  | 11 | 9 | 7 | 10 |  | 1 | 3 |  | 33 |
|  | 2 |  | 4 | 5 |  | 7 | 8 |  |  | 6 |  |  |  |  |  | 11 | 9 |  | 10 |  | 1 | 3 |  | 34 |
|  | 2 |  | 5 | 4 |  | 7 | 8 |  |  | 6 |  |  |  |  |  | 11 |  |  | 10 |  | 1 | 3 | 9 | 35 |
|  | 2 |  | 4 | 5 | 10 | 7 | 8 |  |  | 6 |  |  |  |  |  | 11 |  |  |  |  | 1 | 3 | 9 | 36 |
|  | 2 |  | 4 | 5 | 10 | 9 | 8 |  |  | 6 |  |  |  |  |  | 11 |  | 7 |  |  | 1 | 3 |  | 37 |
|  | 2 |  | 4 | 5 | 6 | 9 | 8 |  |  |  |  |  |  |  |  | 11 |  | 7 | 10 |  | 1 | 3 |  | 38 |
|  | 2 |  | 4 | 5 | 10 |  | 8 |  | 11 | 6 |  |  |  |  |  |  | 9 | 7 |  |  | 1 | 3 |  | 39 |
|  | 2 |  | 4 | 5 | 10 |  | 8 |  |  | 6 |  |  |  |  |  | 11 | 9 | 7 |  |  | 1 | 3 |  | 40 |
|  | 2 |  | 4 | 5 |  |  | 8 |  | 11 | 6 |  |  |  |  |  |  | 9 | 7 | 10 |  | 1 | 3 |  | 41 |
|  | 2 |  | 4 | 5 |  |  | 8 |  | 11 | 6 |  |  |  |  |  |  | 9 | 7 | 10 |  | 1 | 3 |  | 42 |
| 22 | 40 | 27 | 36 | 39 | 38 | 21 | 40 | 6 | 20 | 30 | 10 | 1 | 4 | 12 | 1 | 15 | 19 | 24 | 24 | 4 | 8 | 15 | 6 | |
|  |  | 1 |  | 3 | 8 | 18 | 1 | 4 | 9 | 1 |  |  | 1 |  |  | 1 | 9 | 6 | 8 | 1 |  |  | 4 | |

1 own-goal

261

# 1935-36

Manager: A.Scott Duncan

| 1 | Aug | 31 | (a) | Plymouth A | L | 1-3 | Bamford | 22,366 |
|---|---|---|---|---|---|---|---|---|
| 2 | Sep | 4 | (h) | Charlton A | W | 3-0 | Bamford, Cape, Chester | 21,211 |
| 3 | | 7 | (h) | Bradford C | W | 3-1 | Bamford 2, Mutch | 30,754 |
| 4 | | 9 | (a) | Charlton A | D | 0-0 | | 13,178 |
| 5 | | 14 | (a) | Newcastle U | W | 2-0 | Bamford, Rowley | 28,520 |
| 6 | | 18 | (h) | Hull C | W | 2-0 | Bamford 2 | 15,739 |
| 7 | | 21 | (h) | Tottenham H | D | 0-0 | | 34,718 |
| 8 | | 28 | (a) | Southampton | L | 1-2 | Rowley | 17,678 |
| 9 | Oct | 5 | (a) | Port Vale | W | 3-0 | Mutch 2, Bamford | 9,703 |
| 10 | | 12 | (h) | Fulham | W | 1-0 | Rowley | 22,723 |
| 11 | | 19 | (h) | Sheffield U | W | 3-1 | Cape, Mutch, Rowley | 18,636 |
| 12 | | 26 | (a) | Bradford | L | 0-1 | | 12,216 |
| 13 | Nov | 2 | (h) | Leicester C | L | 0-1 | | 39,074 |
| 14 | | 9 | (a) | Swansea T | L | 1-2 | Bamford | 9,731 |
| 15 | | 16 | (h) | West Ham U | L | 2-3 | Rowley 2 | 24,440 |
| 16 | | 23 | (a) | Norwich C | W | 5-3 | Rowley 3, Manley 2 | 17,266 |
| 17 | | 30 | (h) | Doncaster R | D | 0-0 | | 23,569 |
| 18 | Dec | 7 | (a) | Blackpool | L | 1-4 | Mutch | 13,218 |
| 19 | | 14 | (h) | Nottingham F | W | 5-0 | Bamford 2, Manley, Mutch, Rowley | 15,284 |
| 20 | | 26 | (h) | Barnsley | D | 1-1 | Mutch | 20,993 |
| 21 | | 28 | (h) | Plymouth A | W | 3-2 | Mutch 2, Manley | 20,894 |
| 22 | Jan | 1 | (a) | Barnsley | W | 3-0 | Gardner, Manley, Mutch | 20,957 |
| 23 | | 4 | (a) | Bradford C | L | 0-1 | | 11,286 |
| 24 | | 18 | (h) | Newcastle U | W | 3-1 | Mutch 2, Rowley | 22,968 |
| 25 | Feb | 1 | (h) | Southampton | W | 4-0 | Mutch 2, Bryant, Curry (og) | 23,205 |
| 26 | | 5 | (a) | Tottenham H | D | 0-0 | | 20,085 |
| 27 | | 8 | (h) | Port Vale | W | 7-2 | Manley 4, Rowley 2, Mutch | 22,265 |
| 28 | | 22 | (a) | Sheffield U | D | 1-1 | Manley | 25,852 |
| 29 | | 29 | (h) | Blackpool | W | 3-2 | Bryant, Manley, Mutch | 18,423 |
| 30 | Mar | 7 | (a) | West Ham U | W | 2-1 | Bryant, Mutch | 29,684 |
| 31 | | 14 | (h) | Swansea T | W | 3-0 | Manley, Mutch, Rowley | 27,580 |
| 32 | | 21 | (a) | Leicester C | D | 1-1 | Bryant | 18,200 |
| 33 | | 28 | (h) | Norwich C | W | 2-1 | Rowley 2 | 31,596 |
| 34 | Apr | 1 | (a) | Fulham | D | 2-2 | Bryant, Griffiths | 11,137 |
| 35 | | 4 | (a) | Doncaster R | D | 0-0 | | 13,474 |
| 36 | | 10 | (a) | Burnley | D | 2-2 | Bamford 2 | 27,245 |
| 37 | | 11 | (h) | Bradford | W | 4-0 | Mutch 2, Bamford, Bryant | 33,517 |
| 38 | | 13 | (h) | Burnley | W | 4-0 | Bryant 2, Rowley 2 | 39,855 |
| 39 | | 18 | (a) | Nottingham F | D | 1-1 | Bamford | 12,156 |
| 40 | | 25 | (h) | Bury | W | 2-1 | Lang, Rowley | 35,027 |
| 41 | | 29 | (a) | Bury | W | 3-2 | Manley 2, Mutch | 31,562 |
| 42 | May | 2 | (a) | Hull C | D | 1-1 | Bamford | 4,540 |

FINAL LEAGUE POSITION: 1st in Division Two

Appearances

Goals

FA Cup

| 3 | Jan | 11 | (a) | Reading | W | 3-1 | |
|---|---|---|---|---|---|---|---|
| 4 | | 25 | (a) | Stoke C | D | 0-0 | |
| R | | 29 | (h) | Stoke C | L | 0-2 | |

| Match | Breedon | Griffiths | Porter | Brown | Vose | McKay | Bryant | Mutch | Bamford | Rowley | Chester | Hall | Cape | Ferrier | Manley | Redwood | Robbie | Owen | Wassall | Morton | Langford | Whalley | Robertson | Gardner | Lang |
|---|---|---|---|---|---|---|---|---|---|---|---|---|---|---|---|---|---|---|---|---|---|---|---|---|---|
| 1 | 1 | 2 | 3 | 4 | 5 | 6 | 7 | 8 | 9 | 10 | 11 | | | | | | | | | | | | | | |
| 2 | | 2 | 3 | 4 | 5 | 6 | | 8 | 9 | | 11 | 1 | 7 | 10 | | | | | | | | | | | |
| 3 | | 2 | 3 | 4 | 5 | 6 | | 8 | 9 | | 11 | 1 | 7 | 10 | | | | | | | | | | | |
| 4 | | 2 | 3 | 4 | 5 | 6 | | 8 | 9 | | 11 | 1 | 7 | 10 | | | | | | | | | | | |
| 5 | | 2 | 3 | 4 | 5 | | | 8 | 9 | 10 | 11 | 1 | 7 | | 6 | | | | | | | | | | |
| 6 | | 2 | 3 | 4 | 5 | | 7 | 8 | 9 | 10 | 11 | 1 | | | 6 | | | | | | | | | | |
| 7 | 1 | | 3 | 4 | 5 | 6 | 7 | 8 | 9 | | 11 | | | | 10 | 2 | | | | | | | | | |
| 8 | | 2 | 3 | 4 | 5 | 6 | | 8 | 9 | 10 | 11 | 1 | 7 | | | | | | | | | | | | |
| 9 | | 2 | 3 | 4 | 5 | 6 | | 8 | 9 | 10 | 11 | 1 | 7 | | | | | | | | | | | | |
| 10 | | 2 | 3 | 4 | 5 | 6 | | 8 | 9 | 10 | 11 | 1 | 7 | | | | | | | | | | | | |
| 11 | | 2 | 3 | 4 | 5 | 6 | | 8 | 9 | 10 | 11 | 1 | 7 | | | | | | | | | | | | |
| 12 | | 2 | 3 | 4 | 5 | 6 | | 8 | 9 | 10 | 11 | 1 | 7 | | | | | | | | | | | | |
| 13 | | 2 | 3 | 4 | 5 | 6 | | 8 | 9 | 10 | | 1 | 7 | | 11 | | | | | | | | | | |
| 14 | | 2 | 3 | 4 | 5 | | | 8 | 9 | 10 | | 1 | | | 6 | | 7 | | | 11 | | | | | |
| 15 | | 2 | 3 | 4 | 5 | 6 | | 8 | | 10 | 11 | 1 | 7 | | | | | | 9 | | | | | | |
| 16 | | 2 | 3 | 4 | 5 | 6 | | 8 | 9 | 10 | | | 7 | | 11 | | | | | | 1 | | | | |
| 17 | | 2 | 3 | | 5 | 6 | | 8 | 9 | 10 | | | 7 | | 11 | | | | | | 1 | 4 | | | |
| 18 | | 2 | 3 | | 5 | 6 | | 8 | 9 | 10 | | | 7 | | 11 | | | | | | 1 | 4 | | | |
| 19 | | 2 | 3 | 4 | 5 | 6 | | 8 | 9 | 10 | | 1 | 7 | | 11 | | | | | | | | | | |
| 20 | | 2 | 3 | 4 | 5 | 6 | | 8 | 9 | 10 | | 1 | 7 | | 11 | | | | | | | | | | |
| 21 | | 2 | 3 | 4 | 5 | 6 | | 9 | | 10 | | 1 | 7 | | 11 | | | | | | | | | 8 | |
| 22 | | 2 | 3 | 4 | 5 | 6 | | 9 | | 10 | | 1 | 7 | | 11 | | | | | | | | | 8 | |
| 23 | | 2 | 3 | 4 | 5 | 6 | | 9 | | 10 | | 1 | 7 | | 11 | | | | | | | | | 8 | |
| 24 | | 2 | 3 | 4 | 5 | 6 | | 9 | | | 10 | 1 | 7 | | 11 | | | | | | | | | 8 | |
| 25 | | 2 | 3 | 4 | 5 | 6 | 7 | 9 | | | | 1 | | 10 | 11 | | | | | | | | | 8 | |
| 26 | | 2 | 3 | 4 | 5 | 6 | 7 | 9 | | 10 | | 1 | | | 11 | | | | 8 | | | | | | |
| 27 | | 2 | 3 | 4 | 5 | 6 | 7 | 9 | | 10 | | 1 | | | 11 | | | | | | | | | 8 | |
| 28 | | 2 | 3 | 4 | 5 | 6 | 7 | 9 | | 10 | | 1 | | | 11 | | | | | | | | | 8 | |
| 29 | | 2 | 3 | 4 | 5 | 6 | 7 | 9 | | 10 | | 1 | | | 11 | | | | | | | | | 8 | |
| 30 | | 2 | 3 | 4 | 5 | 6 | 7 | 9 | | 10 | | 1 | | | 11 | | | | | | | | | 8 | |
| 31 | | 2 | 3 | 4 | 5 | 6 | 7 | 9 | | 10 | | 1 | | | 11 | | | | | | | | | 8 | |
| 32 | | 2 | 3 | 4 | 5 | 6 | 7 | 9 | | 10 | | 1 | | | 11 | | | | | | | | | 8 | |
| 33 | | 2 | 3 | 4 | 5 | 6 | 7 | 9 | | 10 | | 1 | | | 11 | | | 8 | | | | | | | |
| 34 | | 2 | 3 | 4 | 5 | 6 | 7 | 9 | | 10 | | 1 | | | 11 | | | 8 | | | | | | | |
| 35 | | 2 | 3 | 4 | 5 | 6 | 7 | 9 | | 10 | | 1 | | | 11 | | | | | | | | | 8 | |
| 36 | | 2 | 3 | 4 | 5 | 6 | 7 | 8 | 9 | 10 | | 1 | | | 11 | | | | | | | | | | |
| 37 | 1 | 2 | 3 | 4 | 5 | | 7 | 8 | 9 | 10 | | | | | 6 | | | | | | | | | | 11 |
| 38 | | 2 | 3 | | 5 | | 7 | 8 | 9 | 10 | | 1 | | | 6 | | | | | | | | 4 | | 11 |
| 39 | | 2 | 3 | 4 | 5 | | 7 | 8 | 9 | 10 | | 1 | | | 6 | | | | | | | | | | 11 |
| 40 | | 2 | 3 | 4 | 5 | | 7 | 8 | 9 | 10 | | 1 | | | 6 | | | | | | | | | | 11 |
| 41 | | 2 | 3 | 4 | 5 | 6 | 7 | 8 | 9 | 10 | | 1 | | | 11 | | | | | | | | | | |
| 42 | | 2 | 3 | 4 | 5 | 6 | 7 | 8 | 9 | 10 | | 1 | | | 11 | | | | | | | | | | |
| **Apps** | 3 | 41 | 42 | 40 | 41 | 35 | 21 | 42 | 27 | 37 | 13 | 36 | 17 | 7 | 31 | 1 | 1 | 2 | 2 | 1 | 3 | 2 | 1 | 12 | 4 |
| **Goals** | | 1 | | | | | 8 | 21 | 16 | 19 | 1 | | 2 | | 14 | | | | | | | | | 1 | 1 |

1 own-goal

# 1936-37

Manager: A.Scott Duncan until 9 November 1937, then Walter Crickmer.

| 1 | Aug | 29 | (h) | Wolves | D | 1-1 | Bamford | 42,731 |
|---|---|---|---|---|---|---|---|---|
| 2 | Sep | 2 | (a) | Huddersfield T | L | 1-3 | Manley | 12,616 |
| 3 | | 5 | (a) | Derby C | L | 4-5 | Bamford 3, Wassall | 21,194 |
| 4 | | 9 | (h) | Huddersfield T | W | 3-1 | Bamford, Bryant, Mutch | 26,839 |
| 5 | | 12 | (h) | Manchester C | W | 3-2 | Bamford, Bryant, Manley | 68,796 |
| 6 | | 19 | (h) | Sheffield W | D | 1-1 | Bamford | 40,933 |
| 7 | | 26 | (a) | Preston NE | L | 1-3 | Bamford | 24,149 |
| 8 | Oct | 3 | (h) | Arsenal | W | 2-0 | Bryant, Rowley | 55,884 |
| 9 | | 10 | (a) | Brentford | L | 0-4 | | 28,019 |
| 10 | | 17 | (a) | Portsmouth | L | 1-2 | Manley | 19,845 |
| 11 | | 24 | (h) | Chelsea | D | 0-0 | | 29,859 |
| 12 | | 31 | (a) | Stoke C | L | 0-3 | | 22,464 |
| 13 | Nov | 7 | (h) | Charlton A | D | 0-0 | | 26,084 |
| 14 | | 14 | (a) | Grimsby T | L | 2-6 | Bryant, Mutch | 9,844 |
| 15 | | 21 | (h) | Liverpool | L | 2-5 | Manley, Thompson | 26,419 |
| 16 | | 28 | (a) | Leeds U | L | 1-2 | Bryant | 17,610 |
| 17 | Dec | 5 | (h) | Birmingham | L | 1-2 | Mutch | 16,544 |
| 18 | | 12 | (a) | Middlesbrough | L | 2-3 | Halton, Manley | 11,790 |
| 19 | | 19 | (h) | West Brom A | D | 2-2 | McKay, Mutch | 21,051 |
| 20 | | 25 | (h) | Bolton W | W | 1-0 | Bamford | 47,658 |
| 21 | | 26 | (a) | Wolves | L | 1-3 | McKay | 41,525 |
| 22 | | 28 | (a) | Bolton W | W | 4-0 | Bryant 2, McKay 2 | 11,801 |
| 23 | Jan | 1 | (h) | Sunderland | W | 2-1 | Bryant, Mutch | 46,257 |
| 24 | | 2 | (h) | Derby C | D | 2-2 | Rowley 2 | 31,883 |
| 25 | | 9 | (a) | Manchester C | L | 0-1 | | 64,862 |
| 26 | | 23 | (a) | Sheffield W | L | 0-1 | | 8,658 |
| 27 | Feb | 3 | (h) | Preston NE | D | 1-1 | Wrigglesworth | 13,225 |
| 28 | | 6 | (a) | Arsenal | D | 1-1 | Rowley | 37,236 |
| 29 | | 13 | (h) | Brentford | L | 1-3 | Baird | 31,942 |
| 30 | | 20 | (h) | Portsmouth | L | 0-1 | | 19,416 |
| 31 | | 27 | (a) | Chelsea | L | 2-4 | Bamford, Gladwin | 16,382 |
| 32 | Mar | 6 | (h) | Stoke C | W | 2-1 | Baird, McClelland | 24,660 |
| 33 | | 13 | (a) | Charlton A | L | 0-3 | | 25,943 |
| 34 | | 20 | (h) | Grimsby T | D | 1-1 | Cape | 26,636 |
| 35 | | 26 | (h) | Everton | W | 2-1 | Baird, Mutch | 30,071 |
| 36 | | 27 | (a) | Liverpool | L | 0-2 | | 25,319 |
| 37 | | 29 | (a) | Everton | W | 3-2 | Bryant, Ferrier, Mutch | 28,395 |
| 38 | Apr | 3 | (h) | Leeds U | D | 0-0 | | 34,429 |
| 39 | | 10 | (a) | Birmingham | D | 2-2 | Bamford 2 | 19,130 |
| 40 | | 17 | (h) | Middlesbrough | W | 2-1 | Bamford, Bryant | 17,656 |
| 41 | | 21 | (a) | Sunderland | D | 1-1 | Bamford | 12,876 |
| 42 | | 24 | (a) | West Brom A | L | 0-1 | | 16,234 |

FINAL LEAGUE POSITION: 21st in Division One

Appearances

Goals

FA Cup

| 3 | Jan | 16 | (h) | Reading | W | 1-0 | |
|---|---|---|---|---|---|---|---|
| 4 | | 30 | (a) | Arsenal | L | 0-5 | |

264

| John | Redwood | Porter | Brown | Vose | McKay | Bryant | Mutch | Bamford | Rowley | Manley | McLenahan | McClelland | Wassall | Ferrier | Mellor | Roughton | Griffiths | Whalley | Thompson | Breen | Winterbottom | Halton | Lang | Breedon | Cape | Baird | Wrigglesworth | Gladwin | Jones | Gardner | |
|---|---|---|---|---|---|---|---|---|---|---|---|---|---|---|---|---|---|---|---|---|---|---|---|---|---|---|---|---|---|---|---|
| 1 | 2 | 3 | 4 | 5 | 6 | 7 | 8 | 9 | 10 | 11 | | | | | | | | | | | | | | | | | | | | | 1 |
| 1 | 2 | | 4 | 5 | 6 | 7 | | 9 | 10 | 11 | 3 | 8 | | | | | | | | | | | | | | | | | | | 2 |
| 1 | 2 | | 4 | 5 | 6 | 7 | | 9 | | 11 | 3 | | 8 | 10 | | | | | | | | | | | | | | | | | 3 |
| 1 | 2 | | 4 | 5 | 6 | 7 | 10 | 9 | | 11 | | | 8 | 3 | | | | | | | | | | | | | | | | | 4 |
| 1 | 2 | | 4 | 5 | 6 | 7 | 10 | 9 | | 11 | | | 8 | | | 3 | | | | | | | | | | | | | | | 5 |
| 1 | 2 | | 4 | 5 | 6 | 7 | 10 | 9 | | 11 | | | 8 | | | 3 | | | | | | | | | | | | | | | 6 |
| 1 | 2 | | 4 | 5 | 6 | 7 | | 9 | | 11 | | | 8 | 10 | | 3 | | | | | | | | | | | | | | | 7 |
| 1 | 2 | | 4 | 5 | 6 | 7 | 8 | 9 | 10 | 11 | | | | | | 3 | | | | | | | | | | | | | | | 8 |
| 1 | 2 | | 4 | 5 | 6 | 7 | 8 | 9 | 10 | 11 | | | | | | 3 | | | | | | | | | | | | | | | 9 |
| 1 | | | 4 | 5 | 6 | 7 | | 9 | 10 | 11 | | | 8 | | | 3 | 2 | | | | | | | | | | | | | | 10 |
| 1 | | | 4 | 5 | | 7 | 8 | 9 | 10 | 11 | | | | | | 3 | 2 | 6 | | | | | | | | | | | | | 11 |
| 1 | | | 4 | 5 | | 7 | 8 | 9 | 10 | 11 | | | | | | 3 | 2 | 6 | | | | | | | | | | | | | 12 |
| 1 | | | 4 | 5 | 6 | 7 | 8 | 9 | | 11 | | | | 10 | | 3 | 2 | | | | | | | | | | | | | | 13 |
| 1 | | | 4 | 5 | 6 | 7 | 8 | 9 | | 11 | | | | 10 | 3 | 2 | | | | | | | | | | | | | | | 14 |
| 1 | | | 4 | | 6 | 7 | 8 | | | 11 | | | 5 | | 10 | 3 | 2 | | 9 | | | | | | | | | | | | 15 |
| | | 3 | | 5 | 6 | 7 | 8 | 9 | | 11 | | | | | | 2 | | | 10 | 1 | | 4 | | | | | | | | | 16 |
| | 2 | | | 5 | 6 | 7 | 8 | 9 | 10 | 11 | | | | | | 3 | | | | 1 | | 4 | | | | | | | | | 17 |
| | 2 | | | 5 | | 7 | | 9 | 10 | | 6 | | 8 | | | 3 | | | | 1 | | 4 | 11 | | | | | | | | 18 |
| | 2 | | | 5 | 10 | 7 | 8 | 9 | | | 6 | | | | | 3 | | | | 1 | | 4 | 11 | | | | | | | | 19 |
| | 2 | | 4 | | 10 | 7 | 8 | 9 | | | 6 | | | | | 3 | | | | 1 | 5 | | 11 | | | | | | | | 20 |
| | 2 | | 4 | | 10 | 7 | 8 | 9 | | | 6 | | | | | 3 | | | | 1 | 5 | | 11 | | | | | | | | 21 |
| | 2 | | 4 | | 10 | 7 | 8 | 9 | | | | | | | | 3 | 6 | | | 1 | 5 | | 11 | | | | | | | | 22 |
| | 2 | | 4 | | 10 | 7 | 8 | 9 | | | | | | | | 3 | 6 | | | 1 | 5 | | 11 | | | | | | | | 23 |
| | 2 | | 4 | | 10 | | 8 | 9 | | | | | | | | 3 | 6 | | | | 5 | | 11 | 1 | 7 | | | | | | 24 |
| | 2 | | 4 | 8 | 10 | 7 | | 9 | | | | | | | | 3 | 6 | | | 1 | 5 | | 11 | | | | | | | | 25 |
| | 2 | | 4 | | | 7 | 8 | 9 | | | | | | | | 3 | 6 | | | 1 | 5 | | | | | 10 | 11 | | | | 26 |
| | 2 | | 4 | | 10 | 7 | | 9 | | | | | | | | 3 | 6 | | | 1 | 5 | | | | | 8 | 11 | | | | 27 |
| | | | | 5 | 10 | 7 | | 9 | | | | 6 | | | | | 2 | 4 | | 1 | 3 | | | | | 11 | 8 | | | | 28 |
| | | | | 5 | 10 | 7 | | 9 | | | | 6 | | | | | 2 | 4 | | 1 | 3 | | | | | 11 | 8 | | | | 29 |
| | | | | 5 | | 7 | 8 | 9 | | | 11 | | | | | 3 | 2 | 6 | | 1 | 4 | | | | | 10 | | | | | 30 |
| | | | | 5 | | 7 | | 9 | | | | | | | | 3 | 2 | 6 | | 1 | 4 | | | | | 10 | 11 | 8 | | | 31 |
| | | | | | 6 | 7 | | 9 | | | | 8 | | | | 3 | 2 | 4 | | 1 | 5 | | | | | 10 | 11 | | | | 32 |
| | | | | | 6 | 7 | 8 | 9 | | | | | | | | 3 | 2 | 4 | | 1 | 5 | | | | | 10 | 11 | | | | 33 |
| | | | 4 | | | | 11 | 9 | | | | | | | | 3 | 2 | 6 | | 1 | 5 | | | | 7 | 10 | | 8 | | | 34 |
| | | | 4 | | | | | 9 | | 11 | | | | | | 3 | 2 | 6 | | 1 | 5 | | | | 7 | 10 | | 8 | | | 35 |
| | | | 4 | | | | | 9 | | 11 | | | | | | 3 | 2 | 6 | | 1 | 5 | | | | 7 | 10 | | 8 | | | 36 |
| | | | 4 | 5 | | 7 | | 9 | | | | 6 | | | 10 | 3 | 2 | | | 1 | | | | | | | 11 | 8 | | | 37 |
| | | | 4 | 5 | | 7 | | 9 | | | | 6 | | | 10 | 3 | 2 | | | 1 | | | | | | | 11 | 8 | | | 38 |
| | | | | 5 | | | | 9 | | 11 | | | | | 10 | | 2 | 6 | | 1 | | | | | | | 7 | 4 | 3 | 8 | 39 |
| | | 3 | | 5 | | 7 | | 9 | | | | | | | 10 | | 2 | 6 | | 1 | | | | | | | 11 | 4 | | 8 | 40 |
| | | | | 5 | 6 | 7 | | 9 | | 11 | | | | 10 | | 3 | 2 | | | 1 | | | | | | | | 4 | | 8 | 41 |
| | | | | 5 | 6 | 7 | | 9 | | 11 | | | | | | 3 | 2 | | | 1 | | | | | | 10 | | 4 | | 8 | 42 |
| 15 | 21 | 2 | 31 | 26 | 29 | 37 | 28 | 29 | 17 | 31 | 3 | 5 | 7 | 6 | 2 | 33 | 21 | 19 | 2 | 26 | 21 | 4 | 8 | 1 | 4 | 14 | 7 | 8 | 1 | 4 | |
| | | | | | 4 | 10 | 7 | 14 | 4 | 5 | | | | 1 | 1 | 1 | 1 | 1 | | | 1 | | | | | 3 | 1 | 1 | | | |

# 1937-38

Secretary: Walter Crickmer

| | | | | | | | |
|---|---|---|---|---|---|---|---|
| 1 | Aug | 28 | (h) | Newcastle U | W 3-0 | Manley 2, Bryant | 29,446 |
| 2 | | 30 | (a) | Coventry C | L 0-1 | | 30,575 |
| 3 | Sep | 4 | (a) | Luton T | L 0-1 | | 20,610 |
| 4 | | 8 | (h) | Coventry C | D 2-2 | Bamford, Bryant | 17,455 |
| 5 | | 11 | (h) | Barnsley | W 4-1 | Bamford 3, Manley | 22,394 |
| 6 | | 13 | (a) | Bury | W 2-1 | Ferrier 2 | 9,954 |
| 7 | | 18 | (a) | Stockport C | L 0-1 | | 24,386 |
| 8 | | 25 | (h) | Southampton | L 1-2 | Manley | 22,729 |
| 9 | Oct | 2 | (h) | Sheffield U | L 0-1 | | 20,105 |
| 10 | | 9 | (a) | Tottenham H | W 1-0 | Manley | 31,189 |
| 11 | | 16 | (a) | Blackburn R | D 1-1 | Bamford | 19,580 |
| 12 | | 23 | (h) | Sheffield W | W 1-0 | Ferrier | 16,379 |
| 13 | | 30 | (a) | Fulham | L 0-1 | | 17,350 |
| 14 | Nov | 6 | (h) | Plymouth A | D 0-0 | | 18,359 |
| 15 | | 13 | (a) | Chesterfield | W 7-1 | Bamford 4, Baird, Bryant, Manley | 17,407 |
| 16 | | 20 | (h) | Aston Villa | W 3-1 | Bamford, Manley, Pearson | 33,193 |
| 17 | | 27 | (a) | Norwich C | W 3-2 | Baird, Bryant, Pearson | 17,397 |
| 18 | Dec | 4 | (h) | Swansea T | W 5-1 | Rowley 4, Bryant | 17,782 |
| 19 | | 11 | (a) | Bradford | L 0-4 | | 12,004 |
| 20 | | 27 | (h) | Nottingham F | W 4-3 | Baird 2, McKay, Wrigglesworth | 30,778 |
| 21 | | 28 | (a) | Nottingham F | W 3-2 | Bamford, Bryant, Carey | 19,283 |
| 22 | Jan | 1 | (a) | Newcastle U | D 2-2 | Bamford, Rowley | 40,088 |
| 23 | | 15 | (h) | Luton T | W 4-2 | Bamford, Bryant, Carey, McKay | 16,845 |
| 24 | | 29 | (h) | Stockport C | W 3-1 | Bamford, Bryant, McKay | 31,852 |
| 25 | Feb | 2 | (a) | Barnsley | D 2-2 | Rowley, Smith | 7,859 |
| 26 | | 5 | (a) | Southampton | D 3-3 | Redwood 2, Baird | 20,354 |
| 27 | | 17 | (a) | Sheffield U | W 2-1 | Bryant, Smith | 17,754 |
| 28 | | 19 | (h) | Tottenham H | L 0-1 | | 34,631 |
| 29 | | 23 | (h) | West Ham U | W 4-0 | Baird 2, Smith, Wassell | 14,572 |
| 30 | | 26 | (h) | Blackburn R | W 2-1 | Baird, Bryant | 30,892 |
| 31 | Mar | 5 | (a) | Sheffield W | W 3-1 | Baird, Brown, Rowley | 37,156 |
| 32 | | 12 | (h) | Fulham | W 1-0 | Barid | 30,363 |
| 33 | | 19 | (a) | Plymouth A | D 1-1 | Rowley | 20,311 |
| 34 | | 26 | (h) | Chesterfield | W 4-1 | Smith 2, Bryant, Carey | 27,311 |
| 35 | Apr | 2 | (a) | Aston Villa | L 0-3 | | 54,654 |
| 36 | | 9 | (h) | Norwich C | D 0-0 | | 25,879 |
| 37 | | 15 | (a) | Burnley | L 0-1 | | 28,459 |
| 38 | | 16 | (a) | Swansea T | D 2-2 | Rowley, Smith | 13,811 |
| 39 | | 18 | (h) | Burnley | W 4-0 | McKay 2, Baird, Bryant | 35,808 |
| 40 | | 23 | (h) | Bradford | W 3-1 | Baird, McKay, Smith | 28,919 |
| 41 | | 30 | (a) | West Ham U | L 0-1 | | 14,816 |
| 42 | May | 7 | (h) | Bury | W 2-0 | McKay, Smith | 53,604 |

FINAL LEAGUE POSITION: 2nd in Division Two 

Appearances
Goals


FA Cup

| | | | | | | |
|---|---|---|---|---|---|---|
| 3 | Jan | 8 | (h) | Yeovil T | W 3-0 | |
| 4 | | 22 | (a) | Barnsley | D 2-2 | |
| R | | 26 | (h) | Barnsley | W 1-0 | |
| 5 | Feb | 12 | (a) | Brentford | L 0-2 | |

| Breen | Griffiths | Roughton | Gladwin | Vose | McKay | Bryant | Murray | Bamford | Baird | Manley | Mutch | Wassall | Brown | Winterbottom | Ferrier | Thompson | Carey | Wrigglesworth | Breedon | Rowley | Whalley | Redwood | Pearson | Jones | Savage | Porter | Smith | No. |
|---|---|---|---|---|---|---|---|---|---|---|---|---|---|---|---|---|---|---|---|---|---|---|---|---|---|---|---|---|
| 1 | 2 | 3 | 4 | 5 | 6 | 7 | 8 | 9 | 10 | 11 |  |  |  |  |  |  |  |  |  |  |  |  |  |  |  |  |  | 1 |
| 1 | 2 | 3 | 4 | 5 | 6 | 7 | 8 | 9 | 10 | 11 |  |  |  |  |  |  |  |  |  |  |  |  |  |  |  |  |  | 2 |
| 1 | 2 | 3 | 4 | 5 | 6 | 7 | 8 |  | 10 | 11 | 9 |  |  |  |  |  |  |  |  |  |  |  |  |  |  |  |  | 3 |
| 1 | 2 | 3 | 4 | 5 | 6 | 7 |  | 9 | 10 | 11 | 8 |  |  |  |  |  |  |  |  |  |  |  |  |  |  |  |  | 4 |
| 1 | 2 | 3 |  |  | 6 | 7 |  | 9 |  | 11 |  |  | 8 | 4 | 5 |  | 10 |  |  |  |  |  |  |  |  |  |  | 5 |
| 1 | 2 | 3 |  |  | 6 | 7 |  | 9 |  | 11 |  |  | 8 | 4 | 5 |  | 10 |  |  |  |  |  |  |  |  |  |  | 6 |
| 1 | 2 | 3 |  |  | 6 | 7 |  | 9 |  | 11 |  |  | 8 | 4 | 5 |  | 10 |  |  |  |  |  |  |  |  |  |  | 7 |
| 1 | 2 | 3 | 8 |  | 6 | 7 |  |  |  | 11 |  |  |  | 4 | 5 |  | 9 | 10 |  |  |  |  |  |  |  |  |  | 8 |
| 1 | 2 | 3 |  | 5 | 6 | 7 |  | 9 | 10 | 11 |  |  | 8 |  | 4 |  |  |  |  |  |  |  |  |  |  |  |  | 9 |
| 1 | 2 | 3 |  | 5 | 6 | 7 |  |  | 10 | 11 |  | 4 | 8 |  |  |  | 9 |  |  |  |  |  |  |  |  |  |  | 10 |
| 1 | 2 | 3 |  | 5 | 6 | 7 |  | 9 | 10 | 11 |  | 4 | 8 |  |  |  |  |  |  |  |  |  |  |  |  |  |  | 11 |
|  | 2 | 3 |  | 5 | 6 | 7 |  | 9 | 10 | 11 |  | 4 | 8 |  |  |  |  |  | 1 |  |  |  |  |  |  |  |  | 12 |
| 1 | 2 | 3 |  | 5 | 6 |  |  | 9 | 10 | 11 |  | 4 | 8 |  |  |  | 7 |  |  |  |  |  |  |  |  |  |  | 13 |
| 1 |  | 3 |  | 5 |  |  |  | 9 | 10 | 11 |  | 4 | 8 |  |  |  | 7 |  |  |  | 6 | 2 |  |  |  |  |  | 14 |
|  |  | 3 |  | 5 |  | 7 |  | 9 |  | 11 |  | 4 | 8 |  |  |  |  |  | 1 |  | 6 | 2 | 10 |  |  |  |  | 15 |
|  |  | 3 |  | 5 | 6 | 7 |  | 9 |  | 11 |  | 4 | 8 |  |  |  |  |  | 1 |  |  | 2 | 10 |  |  |  |  | 16 |
|  |  | 3 |  | 5 | 6 | 7 |  | 9 |  | 11 |  | 4 | 8 |  |  |  |  |  | 1 |  |  | 2 | 10 |  |  |  |  | 17 |
|  |  | 3 |  | 5 | 6 | 7 |  | 9 |  |  |  |  | 8 |  |  |  | 4 |  | 1 | 11 |  | 2 | 10 |  |  |  |  | 18 |
|  |  | 3 |  |  | 6 | 7 |  | 9 |  |  |  |  | 8 |  |  |  | 4 |  | 1 | 11 |  | 2 | 10 | 5 |  |  |  | 19 |
|  |  | 3 |  | 5 | 6 |  |  | 9 |  |  |  |  | 8 |  |  |  | 7 |  | 1 | 11 | 4 | 2 | 10 |  |  |  |  | 20 |
|  | 4 | 3 |  | 5 | 6 | 7 |  | 9 |  |  |  |  | 8 |  |  |  | 10 |  | 1 | 11 |  | 2 |  |  |  |  |  | 21 |
|  | 5 | 3 |  |  | 6 | 7 |  | 9 |  |  |  |  | 8 |  |  |  | 10 |  | 1 | 11 |  | 2 |  |  | 4 |  |  | 22 |
| 1 |  | 3 |  | 5 | 6 | 7 |  | 9 |  |  |  |  | 8 |  |  |  | 10 |  |  | 11 |  | 2 |  |  | 4 |  |  | 23 |
| 1 | 2 |  |  | 5 | 6 | 7 |  | 9 |  |  |  |  | 8 |  |  |  | 10 |  |  | 11 |  | 3 |  |  | 4 |  |  | 24 |
| 1 | 2 |  |  | 5 |  | 7 |  |  |  |  |  |  | 8 |  |  |  | 10 |  |  | 11 |  | 3 |  |  | 4 | 6 | 9 | 25 |
| 1 | 2 |  |  | 5 |  | 7 |  |  |  |  |  |  | 8 |  |  |  | 10 |  |  | 11 |  | 3 | 4 |  |  | 6 | 9 | 26 |
| 1 |  | 3 |  | 5 | 6 | 7 |  |  |  |  |  |  | 8 |  |  |  | 10 |  |  | 11 |  | 2 | 4 |  |  |  | 9 | 27 |
| 1 |  | 3 |  | 5 | 6 | 7 |  |  |  |  |  |  | 8 |  |  |  | 10 |  |  | 11 |  | 2 | 4 |  |  |  | 9 | 28 |
| 1 |  | 3 |  | 5 | 6 | 7 |  |  | 10 |  |  |  | 8 |  |  |  | 4 |  |  | 11 |  | 2 |  |  |  |  | 9 | 29 |
| 1 |  | 3 |  | 5 | 6 | 7 |  |  | 10 |  |  |  | 8 |  |  |  | 4 |  |  | 11 |  | 2 |  |  |  |  | 9 | 30 |
| 1 |  | 3 |  | 5 | 6 | 7 |  |  |  |  |  |  | 8 |  |  |  | 4 |  |  | 11 |  | 2 | 10 |  |  |  | 9 | 31 |
| 1 |  | 3 |  | 5 | 6 | 7 |  |  |  |  |  |  | 8 |  |  |  | 4 |  |  | 11 |  | 2 | 10 |  |  |  | 9 | 32 |
| 1 |  | 3 |  | 5 | 6 | 7 |  | 9 |  |  |  |  | 8 |  |  |  | 4 |  |  | 11 |  | 2 | 10 |  |  |  |  | 33 |
| 1 |  | 3 |  | 5 | 6 | 7 |  |  |  |  |  |  | 8 |  |  |  | 4 |  |  | 11 |  | 2 | 10 |  |  |  | 9 | 34 |
| 1 |  | 3 |  | 5 | 6 | 7 |  |  |  |  |  |  | 8 |  |  |  | 4 |  |  | 11 |  | 2 | 10 |  |  |  | 9 | 35 |
| 1 |  | 3 |  | 5 | 6 | 7 |  |  |  |  |  |  | 8 |  |  |  | 4 |  |  | 11 |  | 2 | 10 |  |  |  | 9 | 36 |
| 1 |  | 3 |  | 5 | 6 | 7 |  |  |  |  |  |  | 8 |  |  |  | 4 |  |  | 11 |  | 2 | 10 |  |  |  | 9 | 37 |
| 1 |  | 3 | 4 | 5 | 6 | 7 |  | 9 |  |  |  |  | 8 |  |  |  |  |  |  | 11 |  | 2 | 10 |  |  |  |  | 38 |
| 1 |  | 3 |  | 5 | 6 | 7 |  |  |  |  |  |  | 8 |  |  |  | 4 |  |  | 11 |  | 2 | 10 |  |  |  | 9 | 39 |
| 1 |  | 3 |  | 5 | 6 | 7 |  |  |  |  |  |  | 8 |  |  |  | 4 |  |  | 11 |  | 2 | 10 |  |  |  | 9 | 40 |
| 1 |  | 3 | 4 | 5 | 6 | 7 |  |  |  |  |  |  | 8 |  |  |  |  |  |  | 11 |  | 2 | 10 |  |  |  | 9 | 41 |
| 1 |  | 3 |  |  | 6 | 7 |  |  |  |  |  | 5 | 8 |  |  |  | 4 |  |  | 11 |  | 2 | 10 |  |  |  | 9 | 42 |
| 33 | 18 | 39 | 7 | 33 | 37 | 39 | 4 | 23 | 35 | 21 | 2 | 9 | 28 | 4 | 5 | 1 | 16 | 4 | 9 | 25 | 6 | 29 | 11 | 1 | 4 | 2 | 17 |  |
|  |  |  |  |  | 7 | 12 |  | 14 | 12 | 7 |  |  | 1 | 1 |  |  | 3 |  |  | 3 | 1 | 9 | 2 | 2 |  |  | 8 |  |

# 1938-39

Secretary: Walter Crickmer

| | | | | | | | |
|---|---|---|---|---|---|---|---|
| 1 | Aug | 27 | (a) | Middlesbrough | L 1-3 | Smith | 25,539 |
| 2 | | 31 | (h) | Bolton W | D 2-2 | Craven, Hubbick (og) | 37,950 |
| 3 | Sep | 3 | (h) | Birmingham | W 4-1 | Smith 2, Bryant, Craven | 22,228 |
| 4 | | 7 | (a) | Liverpool | L 0-1 | | 25,070 |
| 5 | | 10 | (a) | Grimsby T | L 0-1 | | 14,077 |
| 6 | | 17 | (a) | Stoke C | D 1-1 | Smith | 21,526 |
| 7 | | 24 | (h) | Chelsea | W 5-1 | Carey, Manley, Redwood, Rowley, Smith | 34,557 |
| 8 | Oct | 1 | (a) | Preston NE | D 1-1 | Bryant | 25,964 |
| 9 | | 8 | (h) | Charlton A | L 0-2 | | 35,730 |
| 10 | | 15 | (h) | Blackpool | D 0-0 | | 39,723 |
| 11 | | 22 | (a) | Derby C | L 1-5 | Smith | 26,612 |
| 12 | | 29 | (h) | Sunderland | L 0-1 | | 33,565 |
| 13 | Nov | 5 | (a) | Aston Villa | W 2-0 | Rowley, Wrigglesworth | 38,357 |
| 14 | | 12 | (h) | Wolves | L 1-3 | Rowley | 32,821 |
| 15 | | 19 | (a) | Everton | L 0-3 | | 31,809 |
| 16 | | 26 | (h) | Huddersfield T | D 1-1 | Hanlon | 23,164 |
| 17 | Dec | 3 | (a) | Portsmouth | D 0-0 | | 18,692 |
| 18 | | 10 | (h) | Arsenal | W 1-0 | Bryant | 42,008 |
| 19 | | 17 | (a) | Brentford | W 5-2 | Hanlon 2, Bryant, Manley, Rowley | 14,919 |
| 20 | | 24 | (h) | Middlesbrough | D 1-1 | Wassall | 33,235 |
| 21 | | 26 | (h) | Leicester C | W 3-0 | Wrigglesworth 2, Carey | 26,332 |
| 22 | | 27 | (a) | Leicester C | D 1-1 | Hanlon | 21,434 |
| 23 | | 31 | (a) | Birmingham | D 3-3 | Hanlon, McKay, Pearson | 20,787 |
| 24 | Jan | 14 | (h) | Grimsby T | W 3-1 | Rowley 2, Wassall | 25,654 |
| 25 | | 21 | (h) | Stoke C | L 0-1 | | 37,384 |
| 26 | | 28 | (a) | Chelsea | W 1-0 | Bradbury | 31,265 |
| 27 | Feb | 4 | (h) | Preston NE | D 1-1 | Rowley | 41,061 |
| 28 | | 11 | (a) | Charlton A | L 1-7 | Hanlon | 23,721 |
| 29 | | 18 | (a) | Blackpool | W 5-3 | Hanlon 3, Bryant, Carey | 15,253 |
| 30 | | 25 | (h) | Derby C | D 1-1 | Carey | 37,166 |
| 31 | Mar | 4 | (a) | Sunderland | L 2-5 | Manley, Rowley | 11,078 |
| 32 | | 11 | (h) | Aston Villa | D 1-1 | Wassall | 28,292 |
| 33 | | 18 | (a) | Wolves | L 0-3 | | 31,498 |
| 34 | | 29 | (h) | Everton | L 0-2 | | 18,348 |
| 35 | Apr | 1 | (a) | Huddersfield T | D 1-1 | Rowley | 14,007 |
| 36 | | 7 | (h) | Leeds U | D 0-0 | | 35,564 |
| 37 | | 8 | (h) | Portsmouth | D 1-1 | Rowley | 25,457 |
| 38 | | 10 | (a) | Leeds U | L 1-3 | Carey | 13,771 |
| 39 | | 15 | (a) | Arsenal | L 1-2 | Hanlon | 25,741 |
| 40 | | 22 | (h) | Brentford | W 3-0 | Bryant, Carey, Wassall | 15,353 |
| 41 | | 29 | (a) | Bolton W | D 0-0 | | 10,314 |
| 42 | May | 6 | (h) | Liverpool | W 2-0 | Hanlon 2 | 12,073 |

FINAL LEAGUE POSITION: 14th in Division One

Appearances
Goals

FA Cup

| | | | | | | |
|---|---|---|---|---|---|---|
| 3 | Jan | 7 | (a) | West Brom A | D 0-0 | |
| R | | 11 | (h) | West Brom A | L 1-5 | |

| Breen | Redwood | Roughton | Gladwin | Vose | McKay | Bryant | Wassall | Smith | Craven | Rowley | Breedon | Pearson | Griffiths | Manley | Carey | Wrigglesworth | Brown | Warner | Whalley | Hanlon | Tapken | Bradbury | Dougan | |
|---|---|---|---|---|---|---|---|---|---|---|---|---|---|---|---|---|---|---|---|---|---|---|---|---|
| 1 | 2 | 3 | 4 | 5 | 6 | 7 | 8 | 9 | 10 | 11 | | | | | | | | | | | | | | 1 |
| | 2 | 3 | 4 | 5 | 6 | 7 | | 9 | 8 | 11 | 1 | 10 | | | | | | | | | | | | 2 |
| | 3 | | 4 | 5 | | 7 | | 9 | 8 | 11 | 1 | 10 | 2 | 6 | | | | | | | | | | 3 |
| | 3 | | 4 | 5 | | 7 | | 9 | 8 | 11 | 1 | 10 | 2 | 6 | | | | | | | | | | 4 |
| | 3 | | 4 | 5 | | 7 | | 9 | 8 | 11 | 1 | | 2 | 6 | 10 | | | | | | | | | 5 |
| | 2 | 3 | 4 | 5 | | 7 | | 9 | 8 | 11 | 1 | | | 6 | 10 | | | | | | | | | 6 |
| | 2 | | 4 | 5 | | 7 | | 9 | 8 | 11 | 1 | | 3 | 6 | 10 | | | | | | | | | 7 |
| | 2 | | 4 | 5 | | 7 | | 9 | 8 | 11 | 1 | | 3 | 6 | 10 | | | | | | | | | 8 |
| | 2 | | 4 | 5 | | 7 | | 9 | 8 | 11 | 1 | | 3 | 6 | 10 | | | | | | | | | 9 |
| | 2 | | 4 | 5 | | | 8 | 9 | | 11 | 1 | | 3 | 6 | 10 | 7 | | | | | | | | 10 |
| | | 3 | 4 | 5 | | | 8 | 9 | | 11 | 1 | | 2 | 6 | 10 | 7 | | | | | | | | 11 |
| | 2 | 3 | | | 6 | 7 | | 9 | | | 1 | 10 | | 5 | 8 | 11 | 4 | | | | | | | 12 |
| 1 | 2 | | | 5 | 6 | | | 9 | | 7 | | 10 | 3 | | 8 | 11 | | 4 | | | | | | 13 |
| | 2 | | | 5 | 6 | | | 9 | | 7 | 1 | 10 | 3 | | 8 | 11 | | 4 | | | | | | 14 |
| | 2 | 3 | 8 | | | | | 9 | | 7 | 1 | | | 5 | 10 | 11 | | 4 | 6 | | | | | 15 |
| | 2 | | | 5 | | 7 | 8 | | 10 | 11 | 1 | | 3 | 6 | | | | 4 | | 9 | | | | 16 |
| | 2 | | | 5 | | | 8 | | 10 | 11 | 1 | | 3 | 6 | | 7 | | 4 | | 9 | | | | 17 |
| | 2 | | | 5 | | 7 | 8 | | | 11 | 1 | | 3 | 6 | 10 | | | 4 | | 9 | | | | 18 |
| | 2 | | | 5 | | 7 | 8 | | | 11 | 1 | | 3 | 6 | 10 | | | 4 | | 9 | | | | 19 |
| | 2 | | | 5 | 6 | 7 | 8 | | | 11 | 1 | | 3 | | 10 | | | 4 | | 9 | | | | 20 |
| | 2 | | | 5 | | | 8 | | | 11 | | | 3 | | 10 | 7 | 6 | 4 | | 9 | 1 | | | 21 |
| | 2 | | | 5 | | | 8 | | | 11 | | | 3 | | 10 | 7 | 6 | 4 | | 9 | 1 | | | 22 |
| | 2 | | | 5 | 6 | | 7 | | | | | 10 | 3 | | 8 | 11 | | 4 | | 9 | 1 | | | 23 |
| | 2 | | | 5 | 6 | 7 | 8 | | | 11 | | | 3 | | 10 | | | 4 | | 9 | 1 | | | 24 |
| | 2 | | | 5 | 6 | 7 | 8 | | | 11 | | | 3 | | 10 | | | 4 | | 9 | 1 | | | 25 |
| | 2 | | | 5 | 6 | 7 | 8 | | | 11 | | | 3 | | | | | 4 | | 9 | 1 | 10 | | 26 |
| | 2 | | | 5 | 6 | 7 | 8 | | | 11 | | | 3 | | 10 | | | 4 | | 9 | 1 | | | 27 |
| | 2 | | | 5 | 6 | 7 | 8 | | | 11 | | | 3 | | | | | 4 | | 9 | 1 | 10 | | 28 |
| | 2 | | | 5 | 6 | 7 | 8 | | | 11 | | | 3 | | 10 | | | 4 | | 9 | 1 | | | 29 |
| | 2 | | | 5 | 6 | 7 | 8 | | | 11 | | | 3 | | 10 | | | 4 | | 9 | 1 | | | 30 |
| | 2 | | | 5 | 6 | | 8 | | | 7 | | | 3 | 11 | 10 | | | 4 | | 9 | 1 | | | 31 |
| 1 | 2 | | | 5 | | | 8 | 7 | | 11 | | | 3 | 6 | 10 | | | 4 | | 9 | | | | 32 |
| 1 | 2 | | | 5 | | 7 | 8 | | | 11 | | 10 | 3 | 6 | | | | 4 | | 9 | | | | 33 |
| 1 | 2 | | | 5 | | | 8 | | | 11 | | 10 | 3 | 6 | | | | 4 | | 9 | | | 7 | 34 |
| 1 | | 3 | | 5 | | | | 8 | | 11 | | | 2 | 6 | 10 | | | 4 | | 9 | | | 7 | 35 |
| | | 3 | | 5 | | | | 8 | | 11 | | | 2 | 6 | 10 | | | 4 | | 9 | 1 | | 7 | 36 |
| | | 3 | | 5 | | | 8 | | | 11 | | | 2 | 6 | 10 | | | 4 | | 9 | 1 | | 7 | 37 |
| | | 3 | | | 6 | 7 | | 8 | | 11 | | | 2 | 5 | 10 | | | | 4 | 9 | 1 | | | 38 |
| | | 3 | | 5 | 6 | 7 | 8 | | | 11 | 1 | | 2 | | 10 | | | 4 | | 9 | | | | 39 |
| | | 3 | | 5 | 6 | 7 | 8 | | | | 1 | | 2 | | 10 | 11 | | 4 | | 9 | | | | 40 |
| | 2 | 3 | | 5 | 6 | 7 | 8 | | | | 1 | | | | 10 | 11 | | 4 | | 9 | | | | 41 |
| | 2 | 3 | | 5 | 6 | 7 | 8 | | | 11 | 1 | | | | 10 | | | 4 | | 9 | | | | 42 |
| 6 | 35 | 14 | 12 | 39 | 20 | 27 | 27 | 19 | 11 | 38 | 22 | 9 | 35 | 23 | 32 | 12 | 3 | 29 | 2 | 27 | 14 | 2 | 4 | |
| | 1 | | | | 1 | 6 | 4 | 6 | 2 | 10 | | 1 | | 3 | 6 | 3 | | | | 12 | | 1 | | |

1 own-goal

# 1946-47

Manager: Matt Busby

| 1 | Aug | 31 | (h) | Grimsby T | W | 2-1 | Mitten, Rowley | 41,025 |
|---|---|---|---|---|---|---|---|---|
| 2 | Sep | 4 | (a) | Chelsea | W | 3-0 | Mitten, Pearson, Rowley | 27,750 |
| 3 | | 7 | (a) | Charlton A | W | 3-1 | Hanlon, Rowley, Johnson (og) | 44,088 |
| 4 | | 11 | (h) | Liverpool | W | 5-0 | Pearson 3, Mitten, Rowley | 41,657 |
| 5 | | 14 | (h) | Middlesbrough | W | 1-0 | Rowley | 65,112 |
| 6 | | 18 | (h) | Chelsea | D | 1-1 | Chilton | 30,275 |
| 7 | | 21 | (a) | Stoke C | L | 2-3 | Delaney, Hanlon | 41,699 |
| 8 | | 28 | (h) | Arsenal | W | 5-2 | Hanlon 2, Rowley 2, Wrigglesworth | 62,718 |
| 9 | Oct | 5 | (h) | Preston NE | D | 1-1 | Wrigglesworth | 55,395 |
| 10 | | 12 | (a) | Sheffield U | D | 2-2 | Rowley 2 | 35,543 |
| 11 | | 19 | (a) | Blackpool | L | 1-3 | Delaney | 26,307 |
| 12 | | 26 | (h) | Sunderland | L | 0-3 | | 48,385 |
| 13 | Nov | 2 | (a) | Aston Villa | D | 0-0 | | 53,668 |
| 14 | | 9 | (h) | Derby C | W | 4-1 | Pearson 2, Mitten, Rowley | 57,340 |
| 15 | | 16 | (a) | Everton | D | 2-2 | Pearson, Rowley | 45,832 |
| 16 | | 23 | (h) | Huddersfield T | W | 5-2 | Mitten 2, Morris 2, Rowley | 39,216 |
| 17 | | 30 | (a) | Wolves | L | 2-3 | Hanlon, Delaney | 46,704 |
| 18 | Dec | 7 | (h) | Brentford | W | 4-1 | Rowley 3, Mitten | 31,962 |
| 19 | | 14 | (a) | Blackburn R | L | 1-2 | Morris | 21,455 |
| 20 | | 25 | (a) | Bolton W | D | 2-2 | Rowley 2 | 28,505 |
| 21 | | 26 | (h) | Bolton W | W | 1-0 | Pearson | 57,186 |
| 22 | | 28 | (a) | Grimsby T | D | 0-0 | | 17,183 |
| 23 | Jan | 4 | (h) | Charlton A | W | 4-1 | Burke 2, Buckle, Pearson | 43,406 |
| 24 | | 18 | (a) | Middlesbrough | W | 4-2 | Pearson 2, Buckle, Morris | 37,435 |
| 25 | Feb | 1 | (a) | Arsenal | L | 2-6 | Morris, Pearson | 29,415 |
| 26 | | 5 | (h) | Stoke C | D | 1-1 | Buckle | 8,456 |
| 27 | | 22 | (h) | Blackpool | W | 3-0 | Rowley 2, Hanlon | 29,993 |
| 28 | Mar | 1 | (a) | Sunderland | D | 1-1 | Delaney | 25,038 |
| 29 | | 8 | (h) | Aston Villa | W | 2-1 | Burke, Pearson | 36,965 |
| 30 | | 15 | (a) | Derby C | L | 3-4 | Burke 2, Pearson | 19,579 |
| 31 | | 22 | (h) | Everton | W | 3-0 | Burke, Delaney, Warner | 43,441 |
| 32 | | 29 | (a) | Huddersfield T | D | 2-2 | Delaney, Pearson | 18,509 |
| 33 | Apr | 5 | (h) | Wolves | W | 3-1 | Rowley 2, Hanlon | 66,967 |
| 34 | | 7 | (h) | Leeds U | W | 3-1 | Burke 2, Delaney | 41,772 |
| 35 | | 8 | (a) | Leeds U | W | 2-0 | Burke, McGlen | 15,528 |
| 36 | | 12 | (a) | Brentford | D | 0-0 | | 21,714 |
| 37 | | 19 | (h) | Blackburn R | W | 4-0 | Pearson 2, Rowley, Higgins (og) | 46,196 |
| 38 | | 26 | (a) | Portsmouth | W | 1-0 | Delaney | 30,623 |
| 39 | May | 3 | (a) | Liverpool | L | 0-1 | | 48,800 |
| 40 | | 10 | (a) | Preston NE | D | 1-1 | Pearson | 23,278 |
| 41 | | 17 | (h) | Portsmouth | W | 3-0 | Mitten, Morris, Rowley | 37,614 |
| 42 | | 26 | (h) | Sheffield U | W | 6-2 | Rowley 3, Morris 2, Pearson | 34,059 |

FINAL LEAGUE POSITION: 2nd in Division One

Appearances
Goals

FA Cup

| 3 | Jan | 11 | (a) | Bradford | W | 3-0 |
|---|---|---|---|---|---|---|
| 4 | | 25 | (h) | Nottingham F | L | 0-2 |

| Crompton | Carey | McGlen | Warner | Chilton | Cockburn | Delaney | Pearson | Hanlon | Rowley | Mitten | Whalley | Aston | Walton | Wrigglesworth | Morris | Burke | Collinson | Worrall | Buckle | Fielding | No. |
|---|---|---|---|---|---|---|---|---|---|---|---|---|---|---|---|---|---|---|---|---|---|
| 1 | 2 | 3 | 4 | 5 | 6 | 7 | 8 | 9 | 10 | 11 | | | | | | | | | | | 1 |
| 1 | 2 | 3 | 4 | 5 | 6 | 7 | 8 | 9 | 10 | 11 | | | | | | | | | | | 2 |
| 1 | 2 | 3 | 4 | 5 | 6 | 7 | 8 | 9 | 10 | 11 | | | | | | | | | | | 3 |
| 1 | 2 | 3 | 4 | 5 | 6 | 7 | 8 | 9 | 10 | 11 | | | | | | | | | | | 4 |
| 1 | 2 | 3 | 4 | 5 | 6 | 7 | 8 | 9 | 10 | 11 | | | | | | | | | | | 5 |
| 1 | 2 | | 4 | 3 | 6 | 7 | 8 | 9 | | 11 | 5 | 8 | | | | | | | | | 6 |
| 1 | 2 | 3 | 4 | 5 | 6 | 7 | 8 | 9 | 10 | 11 | | | | | | | | | | | 7 |
| 1 | | 3 | 4 | 5 | | 7 | 8 | 9 | 10 | | | 6 | 2 | 11 | | | | | | | 8 |
| 1 | 2 | 3 | 4 | 5 | 6 | 7 | 8 | 9 | 10 | | | | | 11 | | | | | | | 9 |
| 1 | 6 | 3 | 4 | 5 | | 7 | 8 | 9 | 10 | | | | 2 | 11 | | | | | | | 10 |
| 1 | 4 | 3 | | | 5 | 6 | 7 | 8 | 9 | 10 | | | 2 | 11 | | | | | | | 11 |
| 1 | | 3 | 4 | 5 | 6 | 7 | 10 | | | 11 | | | 2 | | 8 | 9 | | | | | 12 |
| | | 3 | 4 | 5 | 6 | 7 | 10 | | 9 | 11 | | | 2 | | 8 | | 1 | | | | 13 |
| | | 3 | 4 | 5 | 6 | 7 | 10 | | 9 | 11 | | | 2 | | 8 | | 1 | | | | 14 |
| | | 3 | 4 | 5 | 6 | 7 | 10 | | 9 | 11 | | | 2 | | 8 | | 1 | | | | 15 |
| | 4 | 3 | | 5 | 6 | 7 | 10 | | 9 | 11 | | | 2 | | 8 | | 1 | | | | 16 |
| | 4 | 3 | | 5 | 6 | 7 | 10 | | 9 | 11 | | | | | 8 | | 1 | 2 | | | 17 |
| | 2 | 3 | 4 | 5 | 6 | | 10 | 7 | 9 | 11 | | | | | 8 | | 1 | | | | 18 |
| | 2 | 3 | 4 | 5 | 6 | | 10 | 7 | 9 | 11 | | | | | 8 | | 1 | | | | 19 |
| 1 | 2 | 3 | 4 | 5 | 6 | 7 | 10 | | 9 | 11 | | | | | 8 | | | | | | 20 |
| 1 | 2 | 3 | 4 | 5 | 6 | 7 | 10 | | 9 | 11 | | | | | 8 | | | | | | 21 |
| 1 | | | 4 | 5 | 6 | 7 | 10 | | 9 | 11 | 2 | 3 | | | 8 | | | | | | 22 |
| 1 | | 3 | 4 | 5 | 6 | 7 | 10 | | | | | | 2 | | 8 | 9 | | | 11 | | 23 |
| 1 | 6 | 3 | 4 | 5 | | 7 | 10 | | 9 | | | | 2 | | 8 | | | | 11 | | 24 |
| | | 3 | 4 | 5 | 6 | 7 | 10 | | 9 | | | | 2 | | 8 | | | | 11 | 1 | 25 |
| | | | 4 | 5 | 6 | 7 | 10 | | 9 | | | 2 | 3 | | 8 | | | | 11 | 1 | 26 |
| | 6 | | 4 | 5 | | 7 | 10 | | 9 | 11 | | 2 | 3 | | 8 | | | | | 1 | 27 |
| | | | 4 | 5 | 6 | 7 | 10 | | 9 | 11 | | 2 | 3 | | 8 | | | | | 1 | 28 |
| | 6 | | 4 | 5 | | 7 | 10 | | | 11 | | 2 | 3 | | 8 | 9 | | | | 1 | 29 |
| | 6 | 3 | 4 | 5 | | 7 | 10 | | | 11 | | | 2 | | 8 | 9 | | | | 1 | 30 |
| 1 | 2 | 3 | 4 | 5 | 6 | 7 | 10 | | | 11 | | | | | 8 | 9 | | | | | 31 |
| 1 | 2 | 6 | | 5 | 4 | 7 | 10 | 8 | 11 | | | 3 | | | 9 | | | | | | 32 |
| 1 | 2 | 6 | | 5 | 4 | 7 | 10 | 8 | 11 | | | 3 | | | 9 | | | | | | 33 |
| 1 | 2 | 6 | | 5 | 4 | 7 | 10 | 8 | 11 | | | 3 | | | 9 | | | | | | 34 |
| 1 | 2 | 6 | | 5 | 4 | 7 | 10 | 8 | 11 | | | 3 | | | 9 | | | | | | 35 |
| 1 | 2 | | 4 | 5 | 6 | | 10 | 8 | 7 | 11 | | 3 | | | 9 | | | | | | 36 |
| 1 | 2 | | 4 | | 6 | 7 | 10 | | 9 | 11 | 5 | 3 | | | 8 | | | | | | 37 |
| 1 | 2 | 6 | | 5 | 4 | 7 | 10 | 8 | 11 | | | 3 | | | 9 | | | | | | 38 |
| 1 | 2 | 6 | 4 | 5 | | 7 | 10 | 8 | 11 | | | 3 | | | 9 | | | | | | 39 |
| 1 | | 6 | 4 | 5 | | 7 | 10 | | | 11 | | 3 | 2 | | 8 | 9 | | | | | 40 |
| 1 | 6 | | 4 | 5 | | | 10 | | 9 | 11 | | 3 | 2 | | 8 | | | | 7 | | 41 |
| 1 | 2 | 6 | 4 | 5 | | | 10 | 7 | 9 | 11 | | 3 | | | 8 | | | | | | 42 |
| 29 | 31 | 33 | 34 | 41 | 32 | 37 | 42 | 27 | 37 | 20 | 3 | 21 | 15 | 4 | 24 | 13 | 7 | 1 | 5 | 6 | |
| | 1 | 1 | 1 | | | 8 | 19 | 7 | 26 | 8 | | | 2 | | 8 | 9 | | | 3 | | |

2 own-goals

# 1947-48

Manager: Matt Busby

| | | | | | | | |
|---|---|---|---|---|---|---|---|
| 1 | Aug | 23 | (a) | Middlesbrough | D | 2-2 | Rowley 2 | 39,554 |
| 2 | | 27 | (h) | Liverpool | W | 2-0 | Morris, Pearson | 52,385 |
| 3 | | 30 | (h) | Charlton A | W | 6-2 | Rowley 4, Morris, Pearson | 52,659 |
| 4 | Sep | 3 | (a) | Liverpool | D | 2-2 | Mitten, Pearson | 48,081 |
| 5 | | 6 | (a) | Arsenal | L | 1-2 | Morris | 64,905 |
| 6 | | 8 | (a) | Burnley | D | 0-0 | | 37,517 |
| 7 | | 13 | (h) | Sheffield U | L | 0-1 | | 49,808 |
| 8 | | 20 | (a) | Manchester C | D | 0-0 | | 71,364 |
| 9 | | 27 | (a) | Preston NE | L | 1-2 | Morris | 34,372 |
| 10 | Oct | 4 | (h) | Stoke C | D | 1-1 | Hanlon | 45,745 |
| 11 | | 11 | (h) | Grimsby T | L | 3-4 | Mitten, Morris, Rowley | 40,035 |
| 12 | | 18 | (a) | Sunderland | L | 0-1 | | 37,148 |
| 13 | | 25 | (h) | Aston Villa | W | 2-0 | Delaney, Rowley | 47,078 |
| 14 | Nov | 1 | (a) | Wolves | W | 6-2 | Morris 2, Pearson 2, Delaney, Mitten | 44,309 |
| 15 | | 8 | (h) | Huddersfield T | W | 4-4 | Rowley 4 | 59,772 |
| 16 | | 15 | (a) | Derby C | D | 1-1 | Carey | 32,990 |
| 17 | | 22 | (h) | Everton | D | 2-2 | Cockburn, Morris | 35,509 |
| 18 | | 29 | (a) | Chelsea | W | 4-0 | Morris 3, Rowley | 43,617 |
| 19 | Dec | 6 | (h) | Blackpool | D | 1-1 | Pearson | 63,683 |
| 20 | | 13 | (a) | Blackburn R | D | 1-1 | Morris | 22,784 |
| 21 | | 20 | (h) | Middlesbrough | W | 2-1 | Pearson 2 | 46,666 |
| 22 | | 25 | (h) | Portsmouth | W | 3-2 | Morris 2, Rowley | 42,776 |
| 23 | | 27 | (a) | Portsmouth | W | 3-1 | Morris 2, Delaney | 27,674 |
| 24 | Jan | 1 | (h) | Burnley | W | 5-0 | Rowley 3, Mitten 2 | 59,838 |
| 25 | | 3 | (a) | Charlton A | W | 2-1 | Morris, Pearson | 40,484 |
| 26 | | 17 | (h) | Arsenal | D | 1-1 | Rowley | 81,962 |
| 27 | | 31 | (a) | Sheffield U | L | 1-2 | Rowley | 45,189 |
| 28 | Feb | 14 | (h) | Preston NE | D | 1-1 | Delaney | 61,765 |
| 29 | | 21 | (a) | Stoke C | W | 2-0 | Buckle, Pearson | 36,794 |
| 30 | Mar | 6 | (h) | Sunderland | W | 3-1 | Delaney, Mitten, Rowley | 55,160 |
| 31 | | 17 | (a) | Grimsby T | D | 1-1 | Rowley | 12,284 |
| 32 | | 20 | (h) | Wolves | W | 3-2 | Delaney, Mitten, Morris | 50,667 |
| 33 | | 22 | (a) | Aston Villa | W | 1-0 | Pearson | 52,366 |
| 34 | | 26 | (h) | Bolton W | L | 0-2 | | 71,623 |
| 35 | | 27 | (a) | Huddersfield T | W | 2-0 | Burke, Pearson | 38,266 |
| 36 | | 29 | (a) | Bolton W | W | 1-0 | Anderson | 44,225 |
| 37 | Apr | 3 | (h) | Derby C | W | 1-0 | Pearson | 49,609 |
| 38 | | 7 | (h) | Manchester C | D | 1-1 | Rowley | 71,690 |
| 39 | | 10 | (a) | Everton | L | 0-2 | | 44,198 |
| 40 | | 17 | (h) | Chelsea | W | 5-0 | Pearson 2, Delaney, Mitten, Rowley | 43,225 |
| 41 | | 28 | (a) | Blackpool | L | 0-1 | | 32,236 |
| 42 | May | 1 | (h) | Blackburn R | W | 4-1 | Pearson 3, Delaney | 44,439 |

FINAL LEAGUE POSITION: 2nd in Division One

Appearances
Goals

FA Cup

| | | | | | | |
|---|---|---|---|---|---|---|
| 3 | Jan | 10 | (a) | Aston Villa | W | 6-4 | |
| 4 | | 24 | (h*) | Liverpool | W | 3-0 | (*Played at Goodison Park, Liverpool.) |
| 5 | Feb | 7 | (h†) | Charlton A | W | 2-0 | (†Played at Leeds Road, Huddersfield.) |
| 6 | | 28 | (h‡) | Preston NE | W | 4-1 | (‡Played at Maine Road, Manchester.) |
| SF | Mar 13 | | (n§) | Derby C | W | 3-1 | (§Played at Hillsborough, Sheffield) |
| F | Apr 24 | | (n¹) | Blackpool | W | 4-2 | (¹Played at Wembley Stadium) |

272

| Crompton | Carey | Aston | Warner | Chilton | McGlen | Delaney | Morris | Rowley | Pearson | Mitten | Burke | Lowrie | Ball | Cockburn | Dale | Hanlon | Walton | Worrall | Pegg | Anderson | Lynn | Brown | Buckle | Cassidy | |
|---|---|---|---|---|---|---|---|---|---|---|---|---|---|---|---|---|---|---|---|---|---|---|---|---|---|
| 1 | 2 | 3 | 4 | 5 | 6 | 7 | 8 | 9 | 10 | 11 | | | | | | | | | | | | | | | 1 |
| 1 | 2 | 3 | 4 | 5 | 6 | 7 | 8 | 9 | 10 | 11 | | | | | | | | | | | | | | | 2 |
| 1 | 2 | 3 | 4 | 5 | 6 | 7 | 8 | 9 | 10 | 11 | | | | | | | | | | | | | | | 3 |
| 1 | 2 | 3 | 4 | 5 | 6 | 7 | 8 | 9 | 10 | 11 | | | | | | | | | | | | | | | 4 |
| 1 | 2 | 3 | 4 | 5 | 6 | 7 | 8 | 9 | 10 | 11 | | | | | | | | | | | | | | | 5 |
| 1 | 2 | 3 | 4 | 5 | 6 | 7 | 8 | 9 | 10 | 11 | | | | | | | | | | | | | | | 6 |
| 1 | 2 | 3 | 4 | 5 | 6 | 7 | 8 | 11 | 10 | | 9 | | | | | | | | | | | | | | 7 |
| 1 | 2 | 3 | 4 | 5 | 6 | 7 | 8 | 9 | 10 | 11 | | | | | | | | | | | | | | | 8 |
| 1 | | 2 | 4 | 5 | 3 | | 8 | 11 | 10 | | | | | 6 | 7 | 9 | | | | | | | | | 9 |
| 1 | | 2 | 4 | 5 | 3 | | 8 | 11 | 10 | | | | | 6 | 7 | 9 | | | | | | | | | 10 |
| 1 | | 2 | 4 | 5 | 3 | 7 | 8 | 10 | 6 | 11 | | | | | | 9 | | | | | | | | | 11 |
| 1 | 4 | 3 | | 5 | 6 | 7 | | 10 | 8 | 11 | | | | | | 9 | 2 | | | | | | | | 12 |
| 1 | 4 | 2 | | 5 | | 7 | 8 | 9 | 10 | 11 | | | | 6 | | | 3 | | | | | | | | 13 |
| 1 | 4 | 2 | | 5 | | 7 | 8 | 9 | 10 | 11 | | | | 6 | | | 3 | | | | | | | | 14 |
| 1 | 4 | 2 | | 5 | | 7 | 8 | 9 | 10 | 11 | | | | 6 | | | 3 | | | | | | | | 15 |
| | 4 | 2 | | 5 | | 7 | 8 | 9 | 10 | 11 | | | | 6 | | | 3 | 1 | | | | | | | 16 |
| | 4 | 2 | | 5 | | 7 | 8 | 9 | 10 | 11 | | | | 6 | | | 3 | 1 | | | | | | | 17 |
| 1 | 4 | 2 | | 5 | | 7 | 8 | 9 | 10 | 11 | | | | 6 | | | 3 | | | | | | | | 18 |
| 1 | 4 | 3 | | 5 | | 7 | 8 | 9 | 10 | 11 | | | | 6 | | 2 | | | | | | | | | 19 |
| 1 | 4 | 3 | | 5 | | 7 | 8 | 9 | 10 | 11 | | | | 6 | | 2 | | | | | | | | | 20 |
| 1 | | 3 | | | | 7 | 8 | 9 | 10 | 11 | | | | 6 | | 2 | | | | 4 | | | | | 21 |
| 1 | 4 | 3 | | 5 | | 7 | 8 | 9 | 10 | 11 | | | | 6 | | 2 | | | | | | | | | 22 |
| 1 | 2 | 3 | | 5 | | 7 | 8 | 9 | 10 | 11 | | | | 6 | | | | | | 4 | | | | | 23 |
| 1 | 2 | 3 | | 5 | | 7 | 8 | 9 | 10 | 11 | | | | 6 | | | | | | 4 | | | | | 24 |
| 1 | 2 | 3 | 4 | 5 | | 7 | 8 | 9 | 10 | 11 | | | | | | | | | | | 6 | | | | 25 |
| 1 | 2 | 3 | | 5 | | 7 | 8 | 9 | 10 | 11 | | | | 6 | | | | | | 4 | | | | | 26 |
| | 2 | 3 | | 5 | | 7 | 8 | 9 | 10 | 11 | | | | 6 | | | | | | 4 | | 1 | | | 27 |
| 1 | 2 | 3 | 4 | 5 | | 7 | 8 | 9 | 10 | 11 | | | | 6 | | | | | | | | | | | 28 |
| 1 | 2 | 3 | | 5 | | 7 | 8 | 9 | 10 | | | | | 6 | | | | | | 4 | | 11 | | | 29 |
| 1 | 2 | 3 | | 5 | | 7 | 8 | 9 | 10 | 11 | | | | 6 | | | | | | 4 | | | | | 30 |
| 1 | 2 | 3 | | 5 | | 7 | | 9 | 10 | 11 | | | | 6 | 8 | | | | | 4 | | | | | 31 |
| 1 | 2 | 3 | 4 | 5 | | 7 | 8 | 9 | 10 | 11 | | | | 6 | | | | | | | | | | | 32 |
| 1 | 2 | 3 | | 5 | | 7 | 8 | 9 | 10 | 11 | | | | | | | | 6 | | 4 | | | | | 33 |
| 1 | 2 | 3 | | 5 | | 7 | 8 | 9 | 10 | 11 | | | | | | | | 6 | | 4 | | | | | 34 |
| | 2 | 3 | 4 | 5 | | 7 | 8 | | 10 | 11 | 9 | | | 6 | | | | | | | 1 | | | | 35 |
| | 2 | 3 | | 5 | | | 8 | | 10 | 11 | 9 | | | 6 | | | | | 7 | 4 | 1 | | | | 36 |
| 1 | 2 | 3 | | 5 | | 7 | 8 | 9 | 10 | 11 | | | | 6 | | | | | | 4 | | | | | 37 |
| 1 | 2 | 3 | | 5 | | | 8 | 10 | | 11 | 9 | 6 | | | | | | | 7 | 4 | | | | | 38 |
| 1 | | 3 | | 5 | | | 8 | | | 11 | 9 | 6 | 2 | | | | | | | 4 | | 7 | 10 | | 39 |
| 1 | 2 | 3 | | 5 | | 7 | 8 | 9 | 10 | 11 | | | | 6 | | | | | | 4 | | | | | 40 |
| 1 | 2 | 3 | | 5 | | | 9 | 10 | 11 | 8 | | | | 6 | 8 | | | | | 4 | | 7 | | | 41 |
| 1 | 2 | 3 | | 5 | | 7 | | 9 | 10 | 11 | 8 | | | 6 | | | | | | 4 | | | | | 42 |
| 37 | 37 | 42 | 15 | 41 | 13 | 36 | 38 | 39 | 40 | 38 | 6 | 2 | 1 | 26 | 2 | 8 | 6 | 5 | 2 | 18 | 3 | 3 | 3 | 1 | |
| 1 | | | | | | | 8 | 18 | 23 | 18 | 8 | 1 | | 1 | | 1 | | | | 1 | | 1 | | | |

# 1948-49

Manager: Matt Busby

| | | | | | | | |
|---|---|---|---|---|---|---|---|
| 1 | Aug | 21 | (h) | Derby C | L 1-2 | Pearson | 52,620 |
| 2 | | 23 | (a) | Blackpool | W 3-0 | Rowley 2, Mitten | 36,880 |
| 3 | | 28 | (a) | Arsenal | W 1-0 | Mitten | 64,150 |
| 4 | Sep | 1 | (h) | Blackpool | L 3-4 | Delaney, Mitten, Morris | 51,187 |
| 5 | | 4 | (h) | Huddersfield T | W 4-1 | Pearson 2, Delaney, Mitten | 57,714 |
| 6 | | 8 | (a) | Wolves | L 2-3 | Morris, Rowley | 42,617 |
| 7 | | 11 | (a) | Manchester C | D 0-0 | | 64,502 |
| 8 | | 15 | (h) | Wolves | W 2-0 | Buckle, Pearson | 33,871 |
| 9 | | 18 | (a) | Sheffield U | D 2-2 | Buckle, Pearson | 36,880 |
| 10 | | 25 | (h) | Aston Villa | W 3-1 | Mitten 2, Pearson | 53,820 |
| 11 | Oct | 2 | (a) | Sunderland | L 1-2 | Rowley | 54,419 |
| 12 | | 9 | (h) | Charlton A | D 1-1 | Burke | 46,964 |
| 13 | | 16 | (a) | Stoke C | L 1-2 | Morris | 45,830 |
| 14 | | 23 | (h) | Burnley | D 1-1 | Mitten | 47,093 |
| 15 | | 30 | (a) | Preston NE | W 6-1 | Mitten 2, Pearson 2, Morris, Rowley | 37,372 |
| 16 | Nov | 6 | (h) | Everton | W 2-0 | Delaney, Morris | 42,789 |
| 17 | | 13 | (a) | Chelsea | D 1-1 | Rowley | 62,542 |
| 18 | | 20 | (h) | Birmingham C | W 3-0 | Morris, Pearson, Rowley | 45,482 |
| 19 | | 27 | (a) | Middlesbrough | W 4-1 | Rowley 3, Delaney | 31,331 |
| 20 | Dec | 4 | (h) | Newcastle U | D 1-1 | Mitten | 70,787 |
| 21 | | 11 | (a) | Portsmouth | D 2-2 | McGlen, Mitten | 29,966 |
| 22 | | 18 | (a) | Derby C | W 3-1 | Burke 2, Pearson | 31,498 |
| 23 | | 25 | (h) | Liverpool | D 0-0 | | 47,788 |
| 24 | | 26 | (a) | Liverpool | W 2-0 | Burke, Pearson | 53,325 |
| 25 | Jan | 1 | (h) | Arsenal | W 2-0 | Burke, Mitten | 58,688 |
| 26 | | 22 | (h) | Manchester C | D 0-0 | | 66,485 |
| 27 | Feb | 19 | (a) | Aston Villa | L 1-2 | Rowley | 68,354 |
| 28 | Mar | 5 | (a) | Charlton A | W 3-2 | Pearson 2, Downie | 55,291 |
| 29 | | 12 | (h) | Stoke C | W 3-0 | Downie, Mitten, Rowley | 55,949 |
| 30 | | 19 | (a) | Birmingham C | L 0-1 | | 46,819 |
| 31 | Apr | 6 | (a) | Huddersfield T | L 1-2 | Rowley | 17,256 |
| 32 | | 9 | (h) | Chelsea | D 1-1 | Mitten | 27,304 |
| 33 | | 15 | (a) | Bolton W | W 1-0 | Carey | 44,999 |
| 34 | | 16 | (a) | Burnley | W 2-0 | Rowley 2 | 37,722 |
| 35 | | 18 | (h) | Bolton W | W 3-0 | Rowley 2, Mitten | 47,653 |
| 36 | | 21 | (h) | Sunderland | L 1-2 | Mitten | 30,640 |
| 37 | | 23 | (h) | Preston NE | D 2-2 | Downie 2 | 43,214 |
| 38 | | 27 | (a) | Everton | L 0-2 | | 39,106 |
| 39 | | 30 | (a) | Newcastle U | W 1-0 | Burke | 38,266 |
| 40 | May | 2 | (h) | Middlesbrough | W 1-0 | Rowley | 20,158 |
| 41 | | 4 | (h) | Sheffield U | W 3-2 | Downie, Mitten, Pearson | 20,880 |
| 42 | | 7 | (h) | Portsmouth | W 3-2 | Rowley 2, Mitten | 49,808 |

FINAL LEAGUE POSITION: 2nd in Division One

Appearances

Goals

FA Cup

| | | | | | | |
|---|---|---|---|---|---|---|
| 3 | Jan | 8 | (h) | Bournemouth | W 6-0 | |
| 4 | | 29 | (h) | Bradford | D 1-1 | (After extra-time) |
| R | Feb | 5 | (a) | Bradford | D 1-1 | (After extra-time) |
| 2R | | 7 | (h) | Bradford | W 5-0 | |
| 5 | | 12 | (h) | Yeovil T | W 8-0 | |
| 6 | | 26 | (a) | Hull C | W 1-0 | |
| SF | Mar | 26 | (n*) | Wolves | D 1-1 | (After extra-time. *Played at Hillsborough, Sheffield.) |
| R | Apr | 2 | (n†) | Wolves | L 0-1 | (†Played at Goodison Park, Liverpool.) |

| No. | Crompton | Carey | Aston | Anderson | Chilton | Cockburn | Delaney | Morris | Rowley | Pearson | Mitten | Ball | McGlen | Brown | Buckle | Hanlon | Warner | Burke | Downie | Lowrie | Cassidy |
|---|---|---|---|---|---|---|---|---|---|---|---|---|---|---|---|---|---|---|---|---|---|
| 1 | 1 | 2 | 3 | 4 | 5 | 6 | 7 | 8 | 9 | 10 | 11 |  |  |  |  |  |  |  |  |  |  |
| 2 | 1 | 3 |  | 4 | 5 |  | 7 | 8 | 9 | 10 | 11 | 2 | 6 |  |  |  |  |  |  |  |  |
| 3 | 1 | 2 | 3 | 4 | 5 | 6 | 7 | 8 | 9 | 10 | 11 |  |  |  |  |  |  |  |  |  |  |
| 4 |  | 2 | 3 | 4 | 5 | 6 | 7 | 8 | 9 | 10 | 11 |  | 1 |  |  |  |  |  |  |  |  |
| 5 | 1 | 2 | 3 | 4 | 5 |  | 7 | 8 | 9 | 10 | 11 |  | 6 |  |  |  |  |  |  |  |  |
| 6 | 1 | 2 | 3 | 4 | 5 |  | 7 | 8 | 9 | 10 | 11 |  | 6 |  |  |  |  |  |  |  |  |
| 7 | 1 | 2 | 3 |  | 5 | 4 | 7 | 8 | 9 | 10 | 11 |  | 6 |  |  |  |  |  |  |  |  |
| 8 | 1 | 2 | 3 | 4 | 5 | 6 |  | 8 | 9 | 10 | 11 |  |  | 7 |  |  |  |  |  |  |  |
| 9 | 1 | 2 | 3 |  | 5 | 4 |  | 8 | 9 | 10 | 11 |  | 6 |  | 7 |  |  |  |  |  |  |
| 10 | 1 | 2 | 3 |  | 5 | 4 | 7 |  | 9 | 10 | 11 |  | 6 |  | 8 |  |  |  |  |  |  |
| 11 | 1 | 2 | 3 |  | 5 | 4 | 7 |  | 9 | 10 | 11 |  | 6 |  | 8 |  |  |  |  |  |  |
| 12 | 1 |  | 3 | 4 | 5 |  | 7 | 8 | 10 |  | 11 | 2 |  |  |  | 6 | 9 |  |  |  |  |
| 13 | 1 | 2 | 3 | 4 | 5 | 6 | 7 | 8 | 9 | 10 | 11 |  |  |  |  |  |  |  |  |  |  |
| 14 | 1 | 2 | 3 | 4 | 5 | 6 | 7 | 8 | 9 | 10 | 11 |  |  |  |  |  |  |  |  |  |  |
| 15 | 1 | 2 | 3 |  | 5 | 6 | 7 | 8 | 9 | 10 | 11 |  |  |  |  |  | 4 |  |  |  |  |
| 16 | 1 | 2 | 3 |  | 5 | 6 | 7 | 8 | 9 | 10 | 11 |  |  |  |  |  | 4 |  |  |  |  |
| 17 | 1 | 2 | 3 | 4 | 5 | 6 | 7 | 8 | 9 | 10 | 11 |  |  |  |  |  |  |  |  |  |  |
| 18 | 1 | 2 | 3 |  | 5 | 4 | 7 | 8 | 9 | 10 | 11 |  | 6 |  |  |  |  |  |  |  |  |
| 19 | 1 | 2 | 3 |  | 5 | 4 | 7 | 8 | 9 | 10 | 11 |  | 6 |  |  |  |  |  |  |  |  |
| 20 | 1 | 2 | 3 |  | 5 | 4 | 7 | 8 | 9 | 10 | 11 |  | 6 |  |  |  |  |  |  |  |  |
| 21 | 1 | 2 | 3 |  | 5 | 4 | 7 | 8 | 9 | 10 | 11 |  | 6 |  |  |  |  |  |  |  |  |
| 22 | 1 | 2 | 3 |  | 5 | 4 | 7 |  | 10 | 8 | 11 |  | 6 |  |  |  |  | 9 |  |  |  |
| 23 | 1 | 2 | 3 |  | 5 | 4 | 7 |  | 10 | 8 | 11 |  | 6 |  |  |  |  | 9 |  |  |  |
| 24 | 1 | 2 | 3 |  | 5 | 4 |  |  | 10 | 8 | 11 |  | 6 |  | 7 |  |  | 9 |  |  |  |
| 25 | 1 | 2 | 3 |  | 5 | 4 | 7 | 8 |  | 10 | 11 |  | 6 |  |  |  |  | 9 |  |  |  |
| 26 | 1 | 2 | 3 |  | 5 | 4 | 7 | 8 | 9 | 10 | 11 |  | 6 |  |  |  |  |  |  |  |  |
| 27 | 1 | 2 | 3 |  | 5 | 4 | 7 |  | 10 | 8 | 11 |  | 6 |  |  |  |  | 9 |  |  |  |
| 28 | 1 | 2 | 3 |  | 5 | 4 | 7 |  | 9 | 10 | 11 |  | 6 |  |  |  |  |  | 8 |  |  |
| 29 | 1 | 2 | 3 |  | 5 | 4 | 7 |  | 9 | 10 | 11 |  | 6 |  |  |  |  |  | 8 |  |  |
| 30 | 1 | 2 | 3 |  | 5 | 4 | 7 |  | 9 | 10 | 11 |  | 6 |  |  |  |  |  | 8 |  |  |
| 31 | 1 | 2 |  | 4 | 5 |  | 7 |  | 10 |  | 11 | 3 | 6 |  |  |  |  | 9 | 8 |  |  |
| 32 | 1 | 2 |  | 4 | 5 |  |  |  | 10 |  | 11 | 3 | 6 |  | 7 |  |  | 9 | 8 |  |  |
| 33 | 1 | 7 | 3 |  | 5 | 6 |  |  | 9 | 10 | 11 | 2 |  |  |  |  |  | 8 |  | 4 |  |
| 34 | 1 | 7 | 3 |  | 5 | 6 |  |  | 9 | 10 | 11 | 2 |  |  |  |  |  | 8 |  | 4 |  |
| 35 | 1 | 8 | 3 |  | 5 | 6 | 7 |  | 9 | 10 | 11 | 2 |  |  |  |  |  |  |  | 4 |  |
| 36 | 1 | 8 | 3 |  | 5 | 6 | 7 |  | 9 | 10 | 11 | 2 |  |  |  |  |  |  |  | 4 |  |
| 37 | 1 | 2 | 3 |  | 5 | 6 | 7 |  | 9 | 10 | 11 |  |  |  |  |  |  | 8 |  | 4 |  |
| 38 | 1 | 2 | 3 |  | 5 | 6 | 7 |  |  | 10 | 11 |  |  |  |  |  |  | 8 |  | 4 | 9 |
| 39 | 1 | 2 | 3 |  | 5 | 6 | 7 |  |  | 10 | 11 |  |  |  |  |  |  | 9 | 8 | 4 |  |
| 40 | 1 | 2 | 3 |  | 5 | 6 | 7 |  | 9 | 10 | 11 |  |  |  |  |  |  | 8 |  | 4 |  |
| 41 | 1 | 2 | 3 |  | 5 | 4 | 7 |  | 9 | 10 | 11 |  | 6 |  |  |  |  |  | 8 |  |  |
| 42 | 1 | 2 | 3 | 4 | 5 | 6 | 7 |  | 9 | 10 | 11 |  |  |  |  |  |  |  | 8 |  |  |
| Apps | 41 | 41 | 39 | 15 | 42 | 36 | 36 | 21 | 39 | 39 | 42 | 8 | 23 | 1 | 5 | 1 | 3 | 9 | 12 | 8 | 1 |
| Goals |  | 1 |  |  |  |  | 4 | 6 | 20 | 14 | 18 |  | 1 |  | 2 |  |  | 6 | 5 |  |  |

# 1949-50

Manager: Matt Busby

| | | | | | | | | |
|---|---|---|---|---|---|---|---|---|
| 1 | Aug | 20 | (a) | Derby C | W | 1-0 | Rowley | 35,687 |
| 2 | | 24 | (h) | Bolton W | W | 3-0 | Mitten, Rowley, Gillies (og) | 41,748 |
| 3 | | 27 | (h) | West Brom A | D | 1-1 | Pearson | 44,655 |
| 4 | | 31 | (a) | Bolton W | W | 2-1 | Mitten, Pearson | 36,277 |
| 5 | Sep | 3 | (h) | Manchester C | W | 2-1 | Pearson 2 | 47,760 |
| 6 | | 7 | (a) | Liverpool | D | 1-1 | Mitten | 51,587 |
| 7 | | 10 | (a) | Chelsea | D | 1-1 | Rowley | 61,357 |
| 8 | | 17 | (h) | Stoke C | D | 2-2 | Rowley 2 | 43,522 |
| 9 | | 24 | (a) | Burnley | L | 0-1 | | 41,072 |
| 10 | Oct | 1 | (h) | Sunderland | L | 1-3 | Pearson | 49,260 |
| 11 | | 8 | (h) | Charlton A | W | 3-2 | Mitten 2, Rowley | 43,809 |
| 12 | | 15 | (a) | Aston Villa | W | 4-0 | Mitten 2, Bogan, Rowley | 47,483 |
| 13 | | 22 | (h) | Wolves | W | 3-0 | Pearson 2, Bogan | 51,427 |
| 14 | | 29 | (a) | Portsmouth | D | 0-0 | | 41,098 |
| 15 | Nov | 5 | (h) | Huddersfield T | W | 6-0 | Pearson 2, Rowley 2, Delaney, Mitten | 40,295 |
| 16 | | 12 | (a) | Everton | D | 0-0 | | 46,672 |
| 17 | | 19 | (h) | Middlesbrough | W | 2-0 | Pearson, Rowley | 42,626 |
| 18 | | 26 | (a) | Blackpool | D | 3-3 | Pearson 2, Bogan | 27,742 |
| 19 | Dec | 3 | (h) | Newcastle U | D | 1-1 | Mitten | 30,343 |
| 20 | | 10 | (a) | Fulham | L | 0-1 | | 35,362 |
| 21 | | 17 | (h) | Derby C | L | 0-1 | | 33,753 |
| 22 | | 24 | (a) | West Brom A | W | 2-1 | Bogan, Rowley | 46,973 |
| 23 | | 26 | (h) | Arsenal | W | 2-0 | Pearson 2 | 53,928 |
| 24 | | 27 | (a) | Arsenal | D | 0-0 | | 65,133 |
| 25 | | 31 | (a) | Manchester C | W | 2-1 | Delaney, Pearson | 63,704 |
| 26 | Jan | 14 | (h) | Chelsea | W | 1-0 | Mitten | 46,954 |
| 27 | | 21 | (a) | Stoke C | L | 1-3 | Mitten | 38,877 |
| 28 | Feb | 4 | (h) | Burnley | W | 3-2 | Rowley 2, Mitten | 46,702 |
| 29 | | 18 | (a) | Sunderland | D | 2-2 | Chilton, Rowley | 63,251 |
| 30 | | 25 | (a) | Charlton A | W | 2-1 | Carey, Rowley | 44,920 |
| 31 | Mar | 8 | (h) | Aston Villa | W | 7-0 | Mitten 4, Downie 2, Rowley | 22,149 |
| 32 | | 11 | (a) | Middlesbrough | W | 3-2 | Downie 2, Rowley | 46,702 |
| 33 | | 15 | (h) | Liverpool | D | 0-0 | | 43,456 |
| 34 | | 18 | (h) | Blackpool | L | 1-2 | Delaney | 53,688 |
| 35 | | 25 | (a) | Huddersfield T | L | 1-3 | Downie | 34,348 |
| 36 | Apr | 1 | (h) | Everton | D | 1-1 | Delaney | 35,381 |
| 37 | | 7 | (h) | Birmingham C | L | 0-2 | | 47,170 |
| 38 | | 8 | (a) | Wolves | D | 1-1 | Rowley | 54,296 |
| 39 | | 10 | (a) | Birmingham C | D | 0-0 | | 35,863 |
| 40 | | 15 | (h) | Portsmouth | L | 0-2 | | 44,908 |
| 41 | | 22 | (a) | Newcastle U | L | 1-2 | Downie | 52,203 |
| 42 | | 29 | (h) | Fulham | W | 3-0 | Rowley 2, Cockburn | 11,968 |

FINAL LEAGUE POSITION: 4th in Division One

Appearances
Goals

FA Cup

| | | | | | | |
|---|---|---|---|---|---|---|
| 3 | Jan | 7 | (h) | Weymouth | W | 4-0 |
| 4 | | 28 | (a) | Watford | W | 1-0 |
| 5 | Feb | 11 | (h) | Portsmouth | D | 3-3 |
| R | | 15 | (a) | Portsmouth | W | 3-1 |
| 6 | Mar | 4 | (a) | Chelsea | L | 0-2 |

| Crompton | Carey | Aston | Warner | Lynn | Cockburn | Delaney | Downie | Rowley | Pearson | Mitten | Birch | Buckle | Lowrie | Chilton | Ball | McGlen | Bogan | Feehan | Wood | Lancaster | Clempson | McNulty | Whitefoot | No. |
|---|---|---|---|---|---|---|---|---|---|---|---|---|---|---|---|---|---|---|---|---|---|---|---|---|
| 1 | 2 | 3 | 4 | 5 | 6 | 7 | 8 | 9 | 10 | 11 | | | | | | | | | | | | | | 1 |
| 1 | 2 | 3 | 4 | 5 | 6 | 7 | 8 | 9 | 10 | 11 | | | | | | | | | | | | | | 2 |
| 1 | 2 | 3 | 4 | 5 | 6 | 7 | | 9 | 8 | 11 | 10 | | | | | | | | | | | | | 3 |
| 1 | 2 | 3 | 4 | 5 | 6 | 7 | | 9 | 8 | 11 | | 10 | | | | | | | | | | | | 4 |
| 1 | 2 | 3 | 4 | 5 | 6 | 7 | | 9 | 8 | 11 | | 10 | | | | | | | | | | | | 5 |
| 1 | 2 | 3 | | 5 | | 7 | | 9 | 8 | 11 | | 10 | 4 | 6 | | | | | | | | | | 6 |
| 1 | 2 | 3 | | 5 | | 7 | | 9 | 8 | 11 | | 10 | 4 | 6 | | | | | | | | | | 7 |
| 1 | 2 | 3 | | 5 | 6 | 7 | | 9 | 8 | 11 | | 10 | | 4 | | | | | | | | | | 8 |
| 1 | 2 | 3 | | 5 | 6 | 7 | | 9 | 8 | 11 | | 10 | | 4 | | | | | | | | | | 9 |
| 1 | 2 | 3 | | | 6 | 7 | | 9 | 8 | 11 | | 10 | 4 | 5 | | | | | | | | | | 10 |
| 1 | | 3 | 4 | | | 7 | | 9 | 10 | 11 | | | | 5 | 2 | 6 | 8 | | | | | | | 11 |
| 1 | | 3 | 4 | 5 | 6 | 7 | | 9 | 10 | 11 | | | | | 2 | | 8 | | | | | | | 12 |
| 1 | 2 | 3 | 4 | | 6 | 7 | | 9 | 10 | 11 | | | | 5 | | | 8 | | | | | | | 13 |
| 1 | 2 | 3 | 4 | | 6 | 7 | | 9 | 10 | 11 | | | | 5 | | | 8 | | | | | | | 14 |
| | 2 | 3 | 4 | | | 7 | | 9 | 10 | 11 | | | | 5 | | 6 | 8 | 1 | | | | | | 15 |
| 1 | 2 | 3 | 4 | | 6 | 7 | | 9 | 10 | 11 | | | | 5 | | | 8 | | | | | | | 16 |
| 1 | 2 | 3 | | | 4 | 7 | | 9 | 10 | 11 | | | | 5 | | 6 | 8 | | | | | | | 17 |
| | 2 | 3 | | | 4 | 7 | 8 | | 10 | 11 | | | | 5 | | 6 | 9 | 1 | | | | | | 18 |
| | 2 | 3 | | | 4 | 7 | 8 | | 10 | 11 | | | | 5 | | 6 | 9 | | 1 | | | | | 19 |
| | 2 | 3 | | | 4 | 7 | | 9 | 10 | 11 | | | | 5 | | 6 | 8 | 1 | | | | | | 20 |
| | 2 | 3 | | | 4 | 7 | | 9 | 10 | 11 | | | | 5 | | 6 | 8 | 1 | | | | | | 21 |
| | 2 | 3 | | | 4 | 7 | | 9 | 10 | 11 | | | | 5 | | 6 | 8 | 1 | | | | | | 22 |
| | 2 | 3 | 4 | | | 7 | | 9 | 10 | 11 | | | | 5 | | 6 | 8 | 1 | | | | | | 23 |
| | 2 | 3 | 4 | | | 7 | | 9 | 10 | 11 | | | | 5 | | 6 | 8 | 1 | | | | | | 24 |
| | 2 | 3 | 4 | | | 7 | | 9 | 10 | 11 | | | | 5 | | 6 | 8 | 1 | | | | | | 25 |
| | 2 | 3 | | | 4 | 7 | 8 | 9 | 10 | 11 | | | | 5 | | 6 | | 1 | | | | | | 26 |
| | 2 | 3 | | | 4 | 7 | | 9 | 10 | 11 | | | | 5 | | 6 | 8 | 1 | | | | | | 27 |
| | 2 | 3 | 4 | | 6 | 7 | | 9 | 10 | 11 | | | | 5 | | | 8 | 1 | | | | | | 28 |
| | 2 | 3 | 4 | | 6 | 7 | 10 | 9 | | 11 | | | | 5 | | | 8 | 1 | | | | | | 29 |
| 1 | 4 | 3 | | | 6 | 7 | 8 | 9 | 10 | 11 | | | | 5 | 2 | | | | | | | | | 30 |
| 1 | 5 | 3 | 4 | | 6 | 7 | 8 | 9 | 10 | 11 | | | | | 2 | | | | | | | | | 31 |
| 1 | 6 | 3 | 4 | | | 7 | 8 | 9 | 10 | 11 | | | | 5 | 2 | | | | | | | | | 32 |
| 1 | 2 | 3 | 4 | | 6 | 7 | 8 | 9 | 10 | 11 | | | | 5 | | | | | | | | | | 33 |
| 1 | 2 | 3 | 4 | | 6 | 9 | 8 | | 10 | 11 | | | | 5 | | | | | | | 7 | | | 34 |
| 1 | 9 | 3 | 4 | | 6 | 7 | 8 | | 10 | 11 | | | | 5 | 2 | | | | | | | | | 35 |
| | 4 | 3 | | | 6 | 7 | 8 | 9 | 10 | 11 | | | | 5 | 2 | | | | | 1 | | | | 36 |
| | 4 | 3 | | | 6 | 7 | 10 | 9 | 8 | 11 | | | | 5 | 2 | | | | | 1 | | | | 37 |
| 1 | 4 | 3 | | | 6 | 7 | 10 | 9 | 8 | 11 | | | | 5 | 2 | | | | | | | | | 38 |
| 1 | 4 | 3 | | | 6 | 7 | 10 | 9 | 8 | 11 | | | | 5 | 2 | | | | | | | | | 39 |
| 1 | | | | | 6 | 7 | 10 | 9 | 8 | 11 | | | | 5 | 3 | | | | | | | 2 | 4 | 40 |
| 1 | | 3 | 4 | | 6 | 7 | 10 | 9 | 8 | 11 | | | | 5 | 2 | | | | | | | | | 41 |
| 1 | | 4 | | | 6 | 7 | 10 | 9 | 8 | 11 | | | | 5 | 3 | | | | | | | 2 | | 42 |
| 27 | 38 | 40 | 21 | 10 | 35 | 42 | 18 | 39 | 41 | 42 | 1 | 7 | 3 | 35 | 13 | 13 | 18 | 12 | 1 | 2 | 1 | 2 | 1 | |
| | 1 | | | | 1 | 4 | 6 | 20 | 15 | 16 | | | | 1 | | | 4 | | | | | | | |

1 own-goal

# 1950-51

Manager: Matt Busby

| | | | | | | | Attendance |
|---|---|---|---|---|---|---|---|
| 1 | Aug | 19 | (h) | Fulham | W | 1-0 Pearson | 44,042 |
| 2 | | 23 | (a) | Liverpool | L | 1-2 Rowley | 30,211 |
| 3 | | 26 | (a) | Bolton W | L | 0-1 | 40,431 |
| 4 | | 30 | (h) | Liverpool | W | 1-0 Downie | 34,835 |
| 5 | Sep | 2 | (h) | Blackpool | W | 1-0 Bogan | 53,260 |
| 6 | | 4 | (a) | Aston Villa | W | 3-1 Rowley 2, Pearson | 42,724 |
| 7 | | 9 | (a) | Tottenham H | L | 0-1 | 60,621 |
| 8 | | 13 | (h) | Aston Villa | D | 0-0 | 33,021 |
| 9 | | 16 | (h) | Charlton A | W | 3-0 Delaney, Pearson, Rowley | 36,619 |
| 10 | | 23 | (a) | Middlesbrough | W | 2-1 Pearson 2 | 48,051 |
| 11 | | 30 | (a) | Wolves | D | 0-0 | 45,898 |
| 12 | Oct | 7 | (h) | Sheffield W | W | 3-1 Downie, McShane, Rowley | 40,651 |
| 13 | | 14 | (a) | Arsenal | L | 0-3 | 66,150 |
| 14 | | 21 | (h) | Portsmouth | D | 0-0 | 41,842 |
| 15 | | 28 | (a) | Everton | W | 4-1 Rowley 2, Aston, Pearson | 51,142 |
| 16 | Nov | 4 | (h) | Burnley | D | 1-1 McShane | 39,454 |
| 17 | | 11 | (a) | Chelsea | L | 0-1 | 51,882 |
| 18 | | 18 | (h) | Stoke C | D | 0-0 | 30,031 |
| 19 | | 25 | (a) | West Brom A | W | 1-0 Birch | 28,146 |
| 20 | Dec | 2 | (h) | Newcastle U | L | 1-2 Birch | 34,502 |
| 21 | | 9 | (a) | Huddersfield T | W | 3-2 Aston 2, Birkett | 26,713 |
| 22 | | 16 | (a) | Fulham | D | 2-2 Pearson 2 | 19,649 |
| 23 | | 23 | (h) | Bolton W | L | 2-3 Aston, Pearson | 35,382 |
| 24 | | 25 | (a) | Sunderland | L | 1-2 Aston | 41,215 |
| 25 | | 26 | (h) | Sunderland | L | 3-5 Bogan 2, Aston | 35,176 |
| 26 | Jan | 13 | (h) | Tottenham H | W | 2-1 Birch, Rowley | 43,283 |
| 27 | | 20 | (a) | Charlton A | W | 2-1 Aston, Birkett | 31,978 |
| 28 | Feb | 3 | (h) | Middlesbrough | W | 1-0 Pearson | 44,633 |
| 29 | | 17 | (h) | Wolves | W | 2-1 Birch, Rowley | 42,022 |
| 30 | | 26 | (a) | Sheffield W | W | 4-0 McShane, Downie, Pearson, Rowley | 25,693 |
| 31 | Mar | 3 | (h) | Arsenal | W | 3-1 Aston 2, Downie | 46,202 |
| 32 | | 10 | (a) | Portsmouth | D | 0-0 | 33,148 |
| 33 | | 17 | (a) | Everton | W | 3-0 Aston, Downie, Pearson | 29,317 |
| 34 | | 23 | (h) | Derby C | W | 2-0 Aston, Downie | 42,009 |
| 35 | | 24 | (a) | Burnley | W | 2-1 Aston, McShane | 36,656 |
| 36 | | 26 | (a) | Derby C | W | 4-2 Aston, Downie, Pearson, Rowley | 25,860 |
| 37 | | 31 | (h) | Chelsea | W | 4-1 Pearson 3, McShane | 25,779 |
| 38 | Apr | 7 | (a) | Stoke C | L | 0-2 | 25,690 |
| 39 | | 14 | (h) | West Brom A | W | 3-0 Downie, Pearson, Rowley | 24,764 |
| 40 | | 21 | (a) | Newcastle U | W | 2-0 Rowley, Pearson | 45,209 |
| 41 | | 28 | (h) | Huddersfield T | W | 6-0 Aston 2, McShane 2, Downie, Rowley | 25,560 |
| 42 | May | 5 | (a) | Blackpool | D | 1-1 Downie | 22,864 |

FINAL LEAGUE POSITION: 2nd in Division One

Appearances
Goals

FA Cup

| 3 | Jan | 6 | (h) | Oldham A | W | 4-1 |
|---|---|---|---|---|---|---|
| 4 | | 27 | (h) | Leeds U | W | 4-0 |
| 5 | Feb | 10 | (h) | Arsenal | W | 1-0 |
| 6 | | 24 | (a) | Birmingham C | L | 0-1 |

Appearance / shirt-number grid:

| Allen | Carey | Aston | McIlvenney | Chilton | Cockburn | Delaney | Downie | Rowley | Pearson | McGlen | Gibson | Bogan | Cassidy | McShane | Redman | Jones | Crompton | Birch | McNulty | Birkett | Whitefoot | Clempson | # |
|---|---|---|---|---|---|---|---|---|---|---|---|---|---|---|---|---|---|---|---|---|---|---|---|
| 1 | 2 | 3 | 4 | 5 | 6 | 7 | 8 | 9 | 10 | 11 | | | | | | | | | | | | | 1 |
| 1 | 2 | 3 | 4 | 5 | 6 | 7 | 8 | 9 | 10 | 11 | | | | | | | | | | | | | 2 |
| 1 | 2 | 3 | | 5 | 6 | 7 | 8 | 9 | 10 | 11 | 4 | | | | | | | | | | | | 3 |
| 1 | 2 | 3 | | 5 | 6 | | 8 | 9 | 10 | 11 | 4 | 7 | | | | | | | | | | | 4 |
| 1 | 2 | 3 | | 5 | 6 | | 8 | 9 | 10 | 11 | 4 | 7 | | | | | | | | | | | 5 |
| 1 | 2 | 3 | | 5 | 6 | | 8 | 9 | 10 | 11 | 4 | 7 | | | | | | | | | | | 6 |
| 1 | 2 | 3 | | 5 | 6 | | 8 | 9 | 10 | 11 | 4 | 7 | | | | | | | | | | | 7 |
| 1 | 2 | 3 | | 5 | 6 | 7 | | 9 | | | 4 | 8 | 10 | 11 | | | | | | | | | 8 |
| 1 | 2 | 3 | | 5 | 6 | 7 | 8 | 9 | 10 | | 4 | | | 11 | | | | | | | | | 9 |
| 1 | 2 | 3 | | 5 | 6 | 7 | 8 | 9 | 10 | | 4 | | | 11 | | | | | | | | | 10 |
| 1 | 2 | 3 | | 5 | 6 | 7 | 8 | 9 | 10 | | 4 | | | 11 | | | | | | | | | 11 |
| 1 | 2 | | | | | 7 | 8 | 9 | 10 | 6 | 4 | | | 11 | 3 | 5 | | | | | | | 12 |
| 1 | 2 | 3 | | 5 | 6 | 7 | 8 | 9 | 10 | | 4 | | | 11 | | | | | | | | | 13 |
| 1 | 2 | 3 | | 5 | | 7 | 8 | 9 | 10 | 6 | 4 | | | 11 | | | | | | | | | 14 |
| | 2 | 3 | | | 6 | 7 | | 9 | 10 | | 4 | 8 | | 11 | 5 | 1 | | | | | | | 15 |
| 1 | 2 | 3 | | 5 | 6 | 7 | | 9 | 10 | | 4 | 8 | | 11 | | | | | | | | | 16 |
| 1 | 2 | 3 | | 5 | 6 | 7 | 10 | 9 | 8 | | 4 | | | 11 | | | | | | | | | 17 |
| 1 | 2 | 3 | | 5 | 6 | | | 9 | 8 | | 4 | 7 | | 11 | | | 10 | | | | | | 18 |
| 1 | | 3 | | 5 | 6 | | | 9 | 8 | | 4 | 7 | | 11 | | | 10 | 2 | | | | | 19 |
| 1 | 2 | 3 | | 5 | 6 | | | 9 | 8 | | 4 | | | 11 | | | | 10 | | 7 | | | 20 |
| 1 | | 9 | | 5 | 6 | | | 8 | 3 | | 4 | | | 11 | | | | 10 | 2 | 7 | | | 21 |
| 1 | | 9 | | 5 | 6 | | 10 | 8 | 3 | | 4 | | | 11 | | | | | 2 | 7 | | | 22 |
| 1 | 2 | 9 | | 5 | 6 | | 10 | 8 | 3 | | 4 | | | 11 | | | | | | 7 | | | 23 |
| 1 | 2 | 9 | | 5 | 6 | | | 11 | 8 | 3 | 4 | | | | | | | 10 | | 7 | | | 24 |
| 1 | 2 | 9 | | 5 | 6 | | | 11 | 8 | 3 | 4 | | | | | | | 10 | | 7 | | | 25 |
| 1 | 2 | 9 | | 5 | 6 | | | 11 | 10 | | 4 | 3 | | | | | | 8 | | 7 | | | 26 |
| | 2 | 9 | | 5 | 6 | | | 11 | 10 | | 4 | | | | 3 | | 1 | 8 | | 7 | | | 27 |
| 1 | 2 | 9 | | 5 | 6 | | | 11 | 10 | | 4 | | | 8 | 3 | | | | | 7 | | | 28 |
| 1 | 3 | 9 | | 5 | 6 | | | 11 | 8 | | 4 | | | | | | | 10 | 2 | 7 | | | 29 |
| 1 | 2 | 9 | | | 6 | | 10 | 11 | 8 | 3 | 4 | | | 7 | | 5 | | | | | | | 30 |
| 1 | 2 | 9 | | | 6 | | 10 | 11 | 8 | | | | | 7 | 3 | 5 | | | | | 4 | | 31 |
| 1 | 2 | 9 | | 5 | | | 10 | 11 | 8 | 6 | | | | 7 | 3 | 4 | | | | | | | 32 |
| 1 | 2 | 9 | | 5 | | | 10 | 11 | 8 | 6 | 4 | | | 7 | 3 | | | | | | | | 33 |
| 1 | 2 | 9 | | 5 | | | 10 | 11 | | 6 | 4 | | | 7 | 3 | | | | | | | 8 | 34 |
| 1 | 2 | 9 | | 5 | | | 10 | 11 | | 6 | 4 | | | 7 | 3 | | | | | | | 8 | 35 |
| 1 | 2 | 9 | | 5 | 4 | | 10 | 11 | 8 | 6 | | | | 7 | 3 | | | | | | | | 36 |
| 1 | 2 | 9 | | 5 | 4 | | 10 | 11 | 8 | 6 | | | | 7 | 3 | | | | | | | | 37 |
| 1 | 2 | 9 | | 5 | 4 | | 10 | 11 | 8 | 6 | | | | 7 | 3 | | | | | | | | 38 |
| 1 | 2 | 9 | | 5 | | | 10 | 11 | 8 | 6 | 4 | | | 7 | 3 | | | | | | | | 39 |
| 1 | 2 | 9 | | 5 | 4 | | 10 | 11 | 8 | 6 | | | | 7 | 3 | | | | | | | | 40 |
| 1 | 2 | 9 | | 5 | 4 | | 10 | 11 | 8 | 6 | | | | 7 | 3 | | | | | | | | 41 |
| 1 | 2 | 9 | | 5 | 4 | | 10 | 11 | 8 | 6 | | | | 7 | 3 | | | | | | | | 42 |
| 40 | 39 | 41 | 2 | 38 | 35 | 13 | 29 | 39 | 39 | 26 | 32 | 11 | 1 | 30 | 16 | 4 | 2 | 8 | 4 | 9 | 2 | 2 | |
| | | 15 | | | 1 | | 10 | 14 | 18 | | | 3 | | 7 | | | | 4 | 2 | | | | |

# 1951-52

Manager: Matt Busby

| 1 | Aug | 18 | (a) | West Brom A | D | 3-3 | Rowley 3 | 27,486 |
|---|---|---|---|---|---|---|---|---|
| 2 | | 22 | (h) | Middlesbrough | W | 4-2 | Rowley 3, Pearson | 37,339 |
| 3 | | 25 | (h) | Newcastle U | W | 2-1 | Downie, Rowley | 51,850 |
| 4 | | 29 | (a) | Middlesbrough | W | 4-1 | Pearson 2, Rowley 2 | 44,212 |
| 5 | Sep | 1 | (a) | Bolton W | L | 0-1 | | 52,239 |
| 6 | . | 5 | (h) | Charlton A | W | 3-2 | Rowley 2, Downie | 26,773 |
| 7 | | 8 | (h) | Stoke C | W | 4-0 | Rowley 3, Pearson | 43,660 |
| 8 | | 12 | (a) | Charlton A | D | 2-2 | Downie 2 | 28,806 |
| 9 | | 15 | (a) | Manchester C | W | 2-1 | Berry, McShane | 52,571 |
| 10 | | 22 | (a) | Tottenham H | L | 0-2 | | 70,882 |
| 11 | | 29 | (h) | Preston NE | L | 1-2 | Aston | 53,454 |
| 12 | Oct | 6 | (h) | Derby C | W | 2-1 | Berry, Pearson | 39,767 |
| 13 | | 13 | (a) | Aston Villa | W | 5-2 | Pearson 2, Rowley 2, Bond | 47,795 |
| 14 | | 20 | (h) | Sunderland | L | 0-1 | | 40,915 |
| 15 | | 27 | (a) | Wolves | W | 2-0 | Pearson, Rowley | 46,167 |
| 16 | Nov | 3 | (h) | Huddersfield T | D | 1-1 | Pearson | 25,616 |
| 17 | | 10 | (a) | Chelsea | L | 2-4 | Pearson, Rowley | 48,960 |
| 18 | | 17 | (h) | Portsmouth | L | 1-3 | Downie | 35,914 |
| 19 | | 24 | (a) | Liverpool | D | 0-0 | | 42,378 |
| 20 | Dec | 1 | (h) | Blackpool | W | 3-1 | Downie 3, Rowley | 34,154 |
| 21 | | 8 | (a) | Arsenal | W | 3-1 | Pearson, Rowley, Daniels (og) | 55,451 |
| 22 | | 15 | (h) | West Brom A | W | 5-1 | Downie 2, Pearson 2, Berry | 27,584 |
| 23 | | 22 | (a) | Newcastle U | D | 2-2 | Bond, Cockburn | 45,414 |
| 24 | | 25 | (h) | Fulham | W | 3-2 | Berry, Bond, Rowley | 33,802 |
| 25 | | 26 | (a) | Fulham | D | 3-3 | Bond, Pearson, Rowley | 32,671 |
| 26 | | 29 | (h) | Bolton W | W | 1-0 | Pearson | 53,205 |
| 27 | Jan | 5 | (a) | Stoke C | D | 0-0 | | 36,389 |
| 28 | | 19 | (h) | Manchester C | D | 1-1 | Carey | 54,245 |
| 29 | | 26 | (h) | Tottenham H | W | 2-0 | Pearson, Ramsey (og) | 40,845 |
| 30 | Feb | 9 | (a) | Preston NE | W | 2-1 | Aston, Berry | 38,792 |
| 31 | | 16 | (a) | Derby C | W | 3-0 | Aston, Pearson, Rowley | 27,693 |
| 32 | Mar | 1 | (h) | Aston Villa | D | 1-1 | Berry | 39,910 |
| 33 | | 8 | (a) | Sunderland | W | 2-1 | Cockburn, Rowley | 48,078 |
| 34 | | 15 | (h) | Wolves | W | 2-0 | Aston, Clempson | 45,109 |
| 35 | | 22 | (a) | Huddersfield T | L | 2-3 | Clempson, Pearson | 30,316 |
| 36 | Apr | 5 | (a) | Portsmouth | L | 0-1 | | 25,522 |
| 37 | | 11 | (a) | Burnley | D | 1-1 | Byrne | 38,907 |
| 38 | | 12 | (h) | Liverpool | W | 4-0 | Byrne 2, Downie, Rowley | 42,970 |
| 39 | | 14 | (h) | Burnley | W | 6-1 | Byrne 2, Carey, Downie, Pearson, Rowley | 44,508 |
| 40 | | 19 | (a) | Blackpool | D | 2-2 | Byrne, Rowley | 29,118 |
| 41 | | 21 | (h) | Chelsea | W | 3-0 | Carey, Pearson, McKnight (og) | 37,436 |
| 42 | | 26 | (h) | Arsenal | W | 6-1 | Rowley 3, Pearson 2, Byrne | 53,651 |

FINAL LEAGUE POSITION: 1st in Division One — Appearances / Goals

FA Cup

| 3 | Jan | 12 | (h) | Hull C | | L | 0-2 | |
|---|---|---|---|---|---|---|---|---|

280

| Allen | Carey | Redman | Cockburn | Chilton | McGlen | McShane | Pearson | Rowley | Downie | Bond | Gibson | Berry | Cassidy | Walton | Aston | McNulty | Birch | Crompton | Byrne | Blanchflower | Jones | Clempson | Whitefoot | No. |
|---|---|---|---|---|---|---|---|---|---|---|---|---|---|---|---|---|---|---|---|---|---|---|---|---|
| 1 | 2 | 3 | 4 | 5 | 6 | 7 | 8 | 9 | 10 | 11 |  |  |  |  |  |  |  |  |  |  |  |  |  | 1 |
| 1 | 2 | 3 | 6 | 5 |  | 7 | 8 | 9 | 10 | 11 | 4 |  |  |  |  |  |  |  |  |  |  |  |  | 2 |
| 1 | 2 | 3 | 6 | 5 |  | 7 | 8 | 9 | 10 | 11 | 4 |  |  |  |  |  |  |  |  |  |  |  |  | 3 |
| 1 | 2 | 3 | 6 | 5 |  | 7 | 8 | 9 | 10 | 11 | 4 |  |  |  |  |  |  |  |  |  |  |  |  | 4 |
| 1 | 2 | 3 | 6 | 5 |  |  | 8 | 9 | 10 | 11 | 4 | 7 |  |  |  |  |  |  |  |  |  |  |  | 5 |
| 1 | 2 | 3 | 6 | 5 |  |  | 8 | 9 | 10 | 11 | 4 | 7 |  |  |  |  |  |  |  |  |  |  |  | 6 |
| 1 | 2 | 3 | 6 | 5 |  | 11 | 8 | 9 | 10 |  | 4 | 7 |  |  |  |  |  |  |  |  |  |  |  | 7 |
| 1 | 2 | 3 | 6 | 5 |  | 11 | 8 | 9 | 10 |  | 4 | 7 |  |  |  |  |  |  |  |  |  |  |  | 8 |
| 1 | 2 | 3 | 6 | 5 |  | 11 | 8 |  | 10 |  | 4 | 7 | 9 |  |  |  |  |  |  |  |  |  |  | 9 |
| 1 | 2 | 3 | 6 | 5 |  | 11 | 8 | 9 | 10 |  | 4 | 7 |  |  |  |  |  |  |  |  |  |  |  | 10 |
| 1 | 2 | 3 | 6 | 5 |  |  |  | 10 | 11 |  | 4 | 7 |  | 8 | 9 |  |  |  |  |  |  |  |  | 11 |
| 1 | 2 | 3 | 6 | 5 |  | 11 |  | 10 | 9 |  | 4 | 7 |  | 8 |  |  |  |  |  |  |  |  |  | 12 |
| 1 |  | 3 | 6 | 5 |  |  | 8 | 9 | 10 | 11 | 4 | 7 |  |  |  | 2 |  |  |  |  |  |  |  | 13 |
| 1 | 2 | 3 |  | 5 | 6 | 11 | 10 | 9 | 8 |  | 4 | 7 |  |  |  |  |  |  |  |  |  |  |  | 14 |
| 1 | 2 | 3 | 6 | 5 |  | 7 | 8 | 9 |  | 11 | 4 |  |  |  |  |  | 10 |  |  |  |  |  |  | 15 |
| 1 | 2 | 3 | 6 | 5 |  | 7 | 8 | 9 |  | 11 | 4 |  |  |  |  |  | 10 |  |  |  |  |  |  | 16 |
| 1 | 2 | 3 | 6 | 5 |  |  | 8 | 11 | 10 |  | 4 | 7 |  |  | 9 |  |  |  |  |  |  |  |  | 17 |
| 1 | 2 | 3 | 6 | 5 |  |  | 8 | 11 | 10 |  | 4 | 7 |  |  | 9 |  |  |  |  |  |  |  |  | 18 |
|  | 2 |  | 6 | 5 |  |  | 8 | 9 | 10 | 11 |  | 7 |  |  |  |  |  | 1 | 3 | 4 |  |  |  | 19 |
|  | 4 |  | 6 | 5 |  |  | 8 | 9 | 10 | 11 |  | 7 |  |  |  | 2 |  | 1 | 3 |  |  |  |  | 20 |
|  | 4 |  | 6 | 5 |  |  | 8 | 9 | 10 | 11 |  | 7 |  |  |  | 2 |  | 1 | 3 |  |  |  |  | 21 |
| 1 | 4 |  | 6 | 5 |  |  | 8 | 9 | 10 | 11 |  | 7 |  |  |  | 2 |  |  | 3 |  |  |  |  | 22 |
| 1 | 4 |  | 6 | 5 |  |  | 8 | 9 | 10 | 11 |  | 7 |  |  |  | 2 |  |  | 3 |  |  |  |  | 23 |
| 1 |  |  | 6 | 4 |  |  | 8 | 9 | 10 | 11 |  | 7 |  |  |  | 2 |  |  | 3 |  | 5 |  |  | 24 |
| 1 |  |  | 6 | 4 |  |  | 8 | 9 | 10 | 11 |  | 7 |  |  |  | 2 |  |  | 3 |  | 5 |  |  | 25 |
| 1 |  |  | 6 | 4 |  |  | 8 | 9 | 10 | 11 |  | 7 |  |  |  | 2 |  |  | 3 |  | 5 |  |  | 26 |
| 1 | 4 |  | 6 | 5 |  |  | 8 | 9 | 10 | 11 |  | 7 |  |  |  | 2 |  |  | 3 |  |  |  |  | 27 |
| 1 | 4 |  | 6 | 5 |  |  | 8 | 11 | 10 |  |  | 7 |  |  | 9 | 2 |  |  | 3 |  |  |  |  | 28 |
| 1 | 4 |  | 6 | 5 |  |  | 10 | 11 |  |  |  | 7 |  |  | 9 | 2 |  |  | 3 |  |  | 8 |  | 29 |
| 1 | 4 |  | 6 | 5 |  |  | 10 | 11 |  |  |  | 7 |  |  | 9 | 2 |  |  | 3 |  |  | 8 |  | 30 |
|  | 4 |  | 6 | 5 |  |  | 10 | 11 |  |  |  | 7 |  |  | 9 | 2 |  | 1 | 3 |  |  | 8 |  | 31 |
|  | 4 |  | 6 | 5 |  |  | 10 | 11 |  |  |  | 7 |  |  | 9 | 2 |  | 1 | 3 |  |  | 8 |  | 32 |
|  | 4 |  | 6 | 5 |  |  | 10 | 11 |  |  |  | 7 |  |  | 9 | 2 |  | 1 | 3 |  |  | 8 |  | 33 |
|  | 4 |  | 6 | 5 |  |  | 10 | 11 |  |  |  | 7 |  |  | 9 | 2 |  | 1 | 3 |  |  | 8 |  | 34 |
|  | 4 |  | 6 | 5 |  |  | 10 | 11 |  |  |  | 7 |  |  | 9 | 2 |  | 1 | 3 |  |  | 8 |  | 35 |
|  | 4 |  |  | 5 |  |  | 10 | 11 |  |  |  | 7 |  |  | 9 | 2 |  | 1 | 3 |  |  | 8 | 6 | 36 |
| 1 | 4 |  | 6 | 5 |  |  | 10 | 9 | 8 |  |  | 7 |  |  | 3 | 2 |  |  | 11 |  |  |  |  | 37 |
| 1 | 4 |  |  | 5 |  |  | 10 | 9 | 8 |  |  | 7 |  |  | 3 | 2 |  |  | 11 |  |  |  | 6 | 38 |
| 1 | 4 |  |  | 5 |  |  | 10 | 9 | 8 |  |  | 7 |  |  | 3 | 2 |  |  | 11 |  |  |  | 6 | 39 |
| 1 | 4 |  | 6 | 5 |  |  | 10 | 9 | 8 |  |  | 7 |  |  | 3 | 2 |  |  | 11 |  |  |  |  | 40 |
| 1 | 4 |  | 6 | 5 |  |  | 10 | 9 | 8 |  |  | 7 |  |  | 3 | 2 |  |  | 11 |  |  |  |  | 41 |
| 1 | 4 |  | 6 | 5 |  |  | 10 | 9 | 8 |  |  | 7 |  |  | 3 | 2 |  |  | 11 |  |  |  |  | 42 |
| 33 | 38 | 18 | 38 | 42 | 2 | 12 | 41 | 40 | 31 | 19 | 17 | 36 | 1 | 2 | 18 | 24 | 2 | 9 | 24 | 1 | 3 | 8 | 3 |  |
|  | 3 |  |  | 2 |  | 1 | 22 | 30 | 11 | 4 |  | 6 |  |  | 4 |  |  |  | 7 |  |  | 2 |  |  |

3 own-goals

# 1952-53

Manager: Matt Busby

| 1 | Aug | 23 | (h) | Chelsea | W | 2-0 | Berry, Downie | 43,629 |
|---|---|---|---|---|---|---|---|---|
| 2 | | 27 | (a) | Arsenal | L | 1-2 | Rowley | 58,831 |
| 3 | | 30 | (a) | Manchester C | L | 1-2 | Downie | 56,140 |
| 4 | Sep | 3 | (h) | Arsenal | D | 0-0 | | 39,193 |
| 5 | | 6 | (a) | Portsmouth | L | 0-2 | | 37,278 |
| 6 | | 10 | (a) | Derby C | W | 3-2 | Pearson 3 | 20,226 |
| 7 | | 13 | (h) | Bolton W | W | 1-0 | Berry | 40,531 |
| 8 | | 20 | (a) | Aston Villa | D | 3-3 | Rowley 2, Downie | 43,490 |
| 9 | | 27 | (h) | Sunderland | L | 0-1 | | 28,967 |
| 10 | Oct | 4 | (a) | Wolves | L | 2-6 | Rowley 2 | 40,132 |
| 11 | | 11 | (h) | Stoke C | L | 0-2 | | 28,968 |
| 12 | | 18 | (a) | Preston NE | W | 5-0 | Aston 2, Pearson 2, Rowley | 33,502 |
| 13 | | 25 | (h) | Burnley | L | 1-3 | Aston | 36,913 |
| 14 | Nov | 1 | (a) | Tottenham H | W | 2-1 | Berry 2 | 44,300 |
| 15 | | 8 | (h) | Sheffield W | D | 1-1 | Pearson | 48,571 |
| 16 | | 15 | (a) | Cardiff C | W | 2-1 | Aston, Pearson | 40,096 |
| 17 | | 22 | (h) | Newcastle U | D | 2-2 | Aston, Pearson | 33,528 |
| 18 | | 29 | (a) | West Brom A | L | 1-3 | Lewis | 23,499 |
| 19 | Dec | 6 | (h) | Middlesbrough | W | 3-2 | Pearson 2, Aston | 27,617 |
| 20 | | 13 | (a) | Liverpool | W | 2-1 | Aston, Pearson | 34,450 |
| 21 | | 20 | (a) | Chelsea | W | 3-2 | Doherty 2, Aston | 23,261 |
| 22 | | 25 | (a) | Blackpool | D | 0-0 | | 27,778 |
| 23 | | 26 | (h) | Blackpool | W | 2-1 | Carey, Lewis | 48,077 |
| 24 | Jan | 1 | (h) | Derby C | W | 1-0 | Lewis | 34,813 |
| 25 | | 3 | (h) | Manchester C | D | 1-1 | Pearson | 47,883 |
| 26 | | 17 | (h) | Portsmouth | W | 1-0 | Lewis | 32,341 |
| 27 | | 24 | (a) | Bolton W | L | 1-2 | Lewis | 43,638 |
| 28 | Feb | 7 | (h) | Aston Villa | W | 3-1 | Rowley 2, Lewis | 34,339 |
| 29 | | 18 | (a) | Sunderland | D | 2-2 | Lewis, Pegg | 24,263 |
| 30 | | 21 | (h) | Wolves | L | 0-3 | | 38,269 |
| 31 | | 28 | (a) | Stoke C | L | 1-3 | Berry | 30,219 |
| 32 | Mar | 7 | (h) | Preston NE | W | 5-2 | Pegg 2, Taylor 2, Rowley | 52,590 |
| 33 | | 14 | (a) | Burnley | L | 1-2 | Byrne | 45,682 |
| 34 | | 25 | (h) | Tottenham H | W | 3-2 | Pearson 2, Pegg | 18,384 |
| 35 | | 28 | (a) | Sheffield W | D | 0-0 | | 36,509 |
| 36 | Apr | 3 | (a) | Charlton A | D | 2-2 | Berry, Taylor | 41,814 |
| 37 | | 4 | (h) | Cardiff C | L | 1-4 | Byrne | 37,163 |
| 38 | | 6 | (h) | Charlton A | W | 3-2 | Taylor 2, Rowley | 30,105 |
| 39 | | 11 | (a) | Newcastle U | W | 2-1 | Taylor 2 | 38,970 |
| 40 | | 18 | (h) | West Brom A | D | 2-2 | Pearson, Viollet | 31,380 |
| 41 | | 20 | (h) | Liverpool | W | 3-1 | Berry, Pearson, Rowley | 20,869 |
| 42 | | 25 | (a) | Middlesbrough | L | 0-5 | | 34,344 |

FINAL LEAGUE POSITION: 8th in Division One

Appearances
Goals

FA Cup

| 3 | Jan | 10 | (a) | Millwall | W | 1-0 | |
|---|---|---|---|---|---|---|---|
| 4 | | 31 | (h) | Walthamstow A | D | 1-1 | |
| R | Feb | 5 | (a*) | Walthamstow A | W | 5-2 | (*Played at Arsenal Stadium, Highbury, London.) |
| 5 | | 14 | (a) | Everton | L | 1-2 | |

282

| Wood | McNulty | Aston | Carey | Chilton | Gibson | Berry | Downie | Rowley | pearson | Byrne | Crompton | Cockburn | Clempson | Bond | Allen | Jones | Scott | Whitefoot | McShane | Lewis | Doherty | Pegg | Foulkes | Redman | Taylor | Blanchflower | Edwards | Olive | Viollet | No. |
|---|---|---|---|---|---|---|---|---|---|---|---|---|---|---|---|---|---|---|---|---|---|---|---|---|---|---|---|---|---|---|
| 1 | 2 | 3 | 4 | 5 | 6 | 7 | 8 | 9 | 10 | 11 |  |  |  |  |  |  |  |  |  |  |  |  |  |  |  |  |  |  |  | 1 |
|  | 2 | 3 | 4 | 5 |  | 7 | 8 | 9 | 10 | 11 | 1 | 6 |  |  |  |  |  |  |  |  |  |  |  |  |  |  |  |  |  | 2 |
|  | 2 | 3 | 4 | 5 |  | 7 | 8 | 9 | 10 | 11 | 1 | 6 |  |  |  |  |  |  |  |  |  |  |  |  |  |  |  |  |  | 3 |
|  |  | 9 | 2 | 5 | 4 | 7 |  |  | 10 | 3 | 1 | 6 | 8 | 11 |  |  |  |  |  |  |  |  |  |  |  |  |  |  |  | 4 |
|  | 2 | 9 |  | 5 | 4 | 7 |  | 11 | 10 | 3 | 1 | 6 | 8 |  |  |  |  |  |  |  |  |  |  |  |  |  |  |  |  | 5 |
|  | 2 | 3 | 4 | 5 | 6 | 7 | 8 | 9 | 10 | 11 | 1 |  |  |  |  |  |  |  |  |  |  |  |  |  |  |  |  |  |  | 6 |
|  | 2 | 3 | 4 | 5 | 6 | 7 | 8 | 9 | 10 | 11 |  |  |  |  | 1 |  |  |  |  |  |  |  |  |  |  |  |  |  |  | 7 |
| 1 | 2 | 3 | 4 | 5 | 6 | 7 | 8 | 9 | 10 | 11 |  |  |  |  |  |  |  |  |  |  |  |  |  |  |  |  |  |  |  | 8 |
| 1 | 2 | 3 |  | 5 | 6 | 7 | 8 |  | 10 | 11 |  |  | 9 |  |  | 4 |  |  |  |  |  |  |  |  |  |  |  |  |  | 9 |
|  | 2 | 3 | 4 | 5 | 6 | 7 | 8 | 9 | 10 |  |  |  |  | 1 |  | 11 |  |  |  |  |  |  |  |  |  |  |  |  |  | 10 |
| 1 | 2 | 3 | 4 | 5 | 6 | 7 | 10 | 9 |  |  |  |  |  | 8 |  | 11 |  |  |  |  |  |  |  |  |  |  |  |  |  | 11 |
|  |  | 9 | 2 | 5 | 6 | 7 | 8 | 11 | 10 | 3 | 1 |  |  |  |  |  | 4 |  |  |  |  |  |  |  |  |  |  |  |  | 12 |
|  |  | 9 | 2 | 5 | 6 | 7 | 8 | 11 | 10 | 3 | 1 |  |  |  |  |  | 4 |  |  |  |  |  |  |  |  |  |  |  |  | 13 |
|  | 2 | 9 |  | 5 | 6 | 7 | 8 |  | 10 | 3 | 1 |  |  |  |  |  |  | 4 | 11 |  |  |  |  |  |  |  |  |  |  | 14 |
|  | 2 | 9 |  | 5 | 6 | 7 | 8 |  | 10 | 3 | 1 |  |  |  |  |  |  | 4 | 11 |  |  |  |  |  |  |  |  |  |  | 15 |
|  | 2 | 9 |  | 5 | 6 | 7 | 8 |  | 10 | 3 | 1 |  |  |  |  |  |  | 4 | 11 |  |  |  |  |  |  |  |  |  |  | 16 |
|  | 2 | 9 |  | 5 | 6 | 7 | 8 |  | 10 | 3 | 1 |  |  |  |  |  |  | 4 | 11 |  |  |  |  |  |  |  |  |  |  | 17 |
|  | 2 |  |  | 5 | 6 | 7 | 8 |  | 10 | 3 | 1 |  |  |  |  |  |  | 4 | 11 | 9 |  |  |  |  |  |  |  |  |  | 18 |
|  | 2 | 9 | 4 | 5 |  | 7 |  |  | 10 | 3 | 1 | 6 |  |  |  |  |  |  |  |  | 8 | 11 |  |  |  |  |  |  |  | 19 |
|  |  | 9 | 4 | 5 |  | 7 |  |  | 10 | 3 | 1 | 6 |  |  |  |  |  |  |  |  | 8 | 11 | 2 |  |  |  |  |  |  | 20 |
|  |  | 9 | 4 | 5 |  | 7 |  |  | 10 | 3 | 1 | 6 |  |  |  |  |  |  |  |  | 8 | 11 | 2 |  |  |  |  |  |  | 21 |
| 1 | 2 | 9 | 4 | 5 |  | 7 |  |  | 10 | 3 |  | 6 |  |  |  |  |  |  |  |  | 8 | 11 |  |  |  |  |  |  |  | 22 |
| 1 | 2 | 9 | 4 | 5 |  | 7 |  |  | 10 | 3 |  | 6 |  |  |  |  |  |  |  |  | 8 | 11 |  |  |  |  |  |  |  | 23 |
| 1 |  | 8 | 4 | 5 |  | 7 |  |  | 10 | 3 |  | 6 |  |  |  |  |  |  |  | 9 |  | 11 | 2 |  |  |  |  |  |  | 24 |
| 1 | 2 |  | 4 | 5 |  | 7 |  |  | 10 | 3 |  | 6 |  |  |  |  |  |  |  | 9 | 8 | 11 |  |  |  |  |  |  |  | 25 |
| 1 | 2 |  | 4 | 5 |  | 7 | 8 |  | 10 | 3 |  | 6 |  |  |  |  |  |  |  | 9 |  | 11 |  |  |  |  |  |  |  | 26 |
| 1 | 2 |  | 4 | 5 |  | 7 | 8 |  | 10 | 3 |  | 6 |  |  |  |  |  |  |  | 9 |  | 11 |  |  |  |  |  |  |  | 27 |
| 1 | 2 |  | 4 | 5 |  | 7 |  | 9 | 10 | 3 |  | 6 |  |  |  |  |  |  |  |  | 8 | 11 |  |  |  |  |  |  |  | 28 |
| 1 | 2 |  | 5 | 4 |  | 7 |  | 9 | 10 | 3 |  | 6 |  |  |  |  |  |  |  |  | 8 | 11 |  |  |  |  |  |  |  | 29 |
| 1 | 2 |  | 4 | 5 |  | 7 |  | 9 | 10 | 3 |  | 6 |  |  |  |  |  |  |  |  | 8 | 11 |  |  |  |  |  |  |  | 30 |
|  | 2 | 8 | 4 | 6 |  | 7 |  | 9 | 10 | 3 | 1 |  |  |  | 5 |  |  |  |  |  |  | 11 |  |  |  |  |  |  |  | 31 |
|  | 2 |  | 4 | 5 |  | 7 | 8 |  | 10 | 3 | 1 | 6 |  |  |  |  |  |  |  |  |  | 11 |  |  | 9 |  |  |  |  | 32 |
|  | 2 |  | 4 | 5 |  | 7 | 8 |  | 10 | 3 | 1 | 6 |  |  |  |  |  |  |  |  |  | 11 |  |  | 9 |  |  |  |  | 33 |
|  | 2 |  | 5 | 4 |  | 7 | 8 |  | 10 | 3 | 1 | 6 |  |  |  |  |  |  |  |  |  | 11 |  |  | 9 |  |  |  |  | 34 |
|  | 2 |  | 4 | 5 |  | 7 | 8 |  | 10 | 3 | 1 | 6 |  |  |  |  |  |  |  |  |  | 11 |  |  | 9 |  |  |  |  | 35 |
|  | 2 |  | 4 | 5 |  | 7 | 8 |  | 10 | 3 | 1 |  |  |  |  |  |  |  |  |  |  | 11 |  |  | 9 | 6 |  |  |  | 36 |
|  | 2 |  | 5 | 4 |  | 7 | 8 |  | 10 | 3 | 1 |  |  |  |  |  |  |  |  |  |  | 11 |  |  | 9 |  | 6 |  |  | 37 |
|  | 2 |  | 4 | 5 |  | 7 |  | 11 | 10 | 3 | 1 | 6 |  |  |  |  |  |  |  |  | 8 |  |  |  |  |  |  |  |  | 38 |
|  | 2 | 9 | 4 | 5 |  |  | 8 | 11 | 10 | 3 |  | 6 |  |  |  |  |  |  |  |  |  |  |  |  |  |  |  | 1 | 7 | 39 |
|  | 2 | 9 | 4 | 5 |  |  | 8 | 11 | 10 | 3 |  | 6 |  |  |  |  |  |  |  |  |  |  |  |  |  |  |  | 1 | 7 | 40 |
|  | 2 |  | 4 | 5 |  | 7 | 8 | 11 | 10 | 3 | 1 | 6 |  |  |  |  |  |  |  |  |  |  |  |  | 9 |  |  |  |  | 41 |
|  | 2 | 9 | 4 | 5 |  | 7 |  | 11 | 10 | 3 | 1 | 6 |  |  |  |  |  |  |  |  |  |  |  |  |  |  |  |  | 8 | 42 |
| 12 | 23 | 40 | 32 | 42 | 20 | 40 | 20 | 26 | 39 | 40 | 25 | 22 | 4 | 1 | 2 | 2 | 2 | 10 | 5 | 10 | 5 | 19 | 2 | 1 | 11 | 1 | 1 | 2 | 3 |  |
|  |  | 8 | 1 |  |  | 7 | 3 | 11 | 16 | 2 |  |  |  |  |  |  |  |  |  | 7 | 2 | 4 |  |  | 7 |  |  |  | 1 |  |

283

# 1953-54

Manager: Matt Busby

| | | | | | | | |
|---|---|---|---|---|---|---|---|
| 1 | Aug | 19 | (h) | Chelsea | D 1-1 | Pearson | 28,936 |
| 2 | | 22 | (a) | Liverpool | D 4-4 | Byrne, Lewis, Rowley, Taylor | 48,422 |
| 3 | | 26 | (h) | West Brom A | L 1-3 | Taylor | 31,806 |
| 4 | | 29 | (h) | Newcastle U | D 1-1 | Chilton | 27,837 |
| 5 | Sep | 2 | (a) | West Brom A | L 0-2 | | 28,892 |
| 6 | | 5 | (a) | Manchester C | L 0-2 | | 53,097 |
| 7 | | 9 | (h) | Middlesbrough | D 2-2 | Rowley 2 | 18,161 |
| 8 | | 12 | (a) | Bolton W | D 0-0 | | 43,544 |
| 9 | | 16 | (a) | Middlesbrough | W 4-1 | Taylor 2, Byrne, Rowley | 23,607 |
| 10 | | 19 | (h) | Preston NE | W 1-0 | Byrne | 41,171 |
| 11 | | 26 | (a) | Tottenham H | D 1-1 | Rowley | 52,837 |
| 12 | Oct | 3 | (h) | Burnley | L 1-2 | Pearson | 37,696 |
| 13 | | 10 | (h) | Sunderland | W 1-0 | Rowley | 34,617 |
| 14 | | 17 | (a) | Wolves | L 1-3 | Taylor | 40,084 |
| 15 | | 24 | (h) | Aston Villa | W 1-0 | Berry | 30,266 |
| 16 | | 31 | (a) | Huddersfield T | D 0-0 | | 34,175 |
| 17 | Nov | 7 | (h) | Arsenal | D 2-2 | Blanchflower, Rowley | 28,141 |
| 18 | | 14 | (a) | Cardiff C | W 6-1 | Viollet 2, Berry, Blanchflower, Rowley, Taylor | 26,844 |
| 19 | | 21 | (h) | Blackpool | W 4-1 | Taylor 3, Viollet | 49,853 |
| 20 | | 28 | (a) | Portsmouth | D 1-1 | Taylor | 29,233 |
| 21 | Dec | 5 | (h) | Sheffield U | D 2-2 | Blanchflower 2 | 31,693 |
| 22 | | 12 | (a) | Chelsea | L 1-3 | Berry | 37,153 |
| 23 | | 19 | (h) | Liverpool | W 5-1 | Blanchflower 2, Taylor 2, Viollet | 26,074 |
| 24 | | 25 | (h) | Sheffield W | W 5-2 | Taylor 3, Blanchflower, Viollet | 27,123 |
| 25 | | 26 | (a) | Sheffield W | W 1-0 | Viollet | 44,196 |
| 26 | Jan | 2 | (a) | Newcastle U | W 2-1 | Blanchflower, Foulkes | 55,780 |
| 27 | | 16 | (h) | Manchester C | D 1-1 | Berry | 46,379 |
| 28 | | 23 | (h) | Bolton W | L 1-5 | Taylor | 46,663 |
| 29 | Feb | 6 | (a) | Preston NE | W 3-1 | Blanchflower, Rowley, Taylor | 30,064 |
| 30 | | 13 | (h) | Tottenham H | W 2-0 | Rowley, Taylor | 35,485 |
| 31 | | 20 | (a) | Burnley | L 0-2 | | 29,576 |
| 32 | | 27 | (a) | Sunderland | W 2-0 | Blanchflower, Taylor | 58,440 |
| 33 | Mar | 6 | (h) | Wolves | W 1-0 | Berry | 38,939 |
| 34 | | 13 | (a) | Aston Villa | D 2-2 | Taylor 2 | 26,023 |
| 35 | | 20 | (h) | Huddersfield T | W 3-1 | Blanchflower, Rowley, Viollet | 40,181 |
| 36 | | 27 | (a) | Arsenal | L 1-3 | Taylor | 42,753 |
| 37 | Apr | 3 | (h) | Cardiff C | L 2-3 | Rowley, Viollet | 22,832 |
| 38 | | 10 | (a) | Blackpool | L 0-2 | | 25,996 |
| 39 | | 16 | (h) | Charlton A | W 2-0 | Aston, Viollet | 31,876 |
| 40 | | 17 | (h) | Portsmouth | W 2-0 | Blanchflower, Viollet | 29,663 |
| 41 | | 19 | (a) | Charlton A | L 0-1 | | 19,111 |
| 42 | | 24 | (a) | Sheffield U | W 3-1 | Aston, Blanchflower, Viollet | 29,189 |

FINAL LEAGUE POSITION: 4th in Division One

Appearances
Goals

FA Cup

| 3 | Jan | 9 | (a) | Burnley | L 3-5 | |

| Crompton | Aston | Byrne | Gibson | Chilton | Cockburn | Berry | Rowley | Taylor | Pearson | Pegg | Lewis | Wood | McNulty | Whitefoot | Viollet | McShane | Foulkes | Edwards | Blanchflower | Webster | McFarlane | Redman | |
|---|---|---|---|---|---|---|---|---|---|---|---|---|---|---|---|---|---|---|---|---|---|---|---|
| 1 | 2 | 3 | 4 | 5 | 6 | 7 | 8 | 9 | 10 | 11 |  |  |  |  |  |  |  |  |  |  |  |  | 1 |
| 1 | 2 | 3 | 4 | 5 | 6 | 7 | 8 | 9 |  | 11 | 10 |  |  |  |  |  |  |  |  |  |  |  | 2 |
| 1 | 2 | 3 | 4 | 5 | 6 | 7 | 8 | 9 |  | 11 | 10 |  |  |  |  |  |  |  |  |  |  |  | 3 |
|  | 3 | 8 |  | 5 | 6 | 7 | 11 | 9 |  |  | 10 | 1 | 2 | 4 |  |  |  |  |  |  |  |  | 4 |
|  | 2 | 3 |  | 5 | 6 | 7 | 11 | 9 |  |  | 8 | 1 |  | 4 | 10 |  |  |  |  |  |  |  | 5 |
|  | 2 | 3 |  | 5 | 6 | 7 | 11 | 9 | 10 |  |  | 1 |  | 4 | 8 |  |  |  |  |  |  |  | 6 |
|  |  | 3 |  | 5 | 6 | 7 |  | 9 | 10 |  | 8 | 1 | 2 | 4 |  | 11 |  |  |  |  |  |  | 7 |
|  |  | 3 |  | 5 | 6 | 7 | 9 | 8 | 10 |  |  | 1 | 2 | 4 |  | 11 |  |  |  |  |  |  | 8 |
|  |  | 3 |  | 5 | 6 | 7 | 9 | 8 | 10 |  |  | 1 | 2 | 4 |  | 11 |  |  |  |  |  |  | 9 |
|  |  | 3 |  | 5 | 6 | 7 | 9 | 8 | 10 |  |  | 1 |  | 4 |  | 11 | 2 |  |  |  |  |  | 10 |
|  |  | 3 |  | 5 | 6 | 7 | 9 | 8 | 10 |  |  | 1 |  | 4 |  | 11 | 2 |  |  |  |  |  | 11 |
|  |  | 3 |  | 5 | 6 | 7 | 9 | 8 | 10 |  |  | 1 |  | 4 |  | 11 | 2 |  |  |  |  |  | 12 |
|  | 2 | 3 |  | 5 | 6 | 7 | 9 | 8 | 10 |  |  | 1 |  | 4 |  | 11 |  |  |  |  |  |  | 13 |
|  |  | 3 |  | 5 | 6 | 7 | 10 | 9 | 8 |  |  | 1 |  | 4 |  | 11 | 2 |  |  |  |  |  | 14 |
|  |  | 3 |  | 5 | 6 | 7 | 10 | 9 | 8 |  |  | 1 |  | 4 |  | 11 | 2 |  |  |  |  |  | 15 |
|  |  | 3 |  | 5 |  | 7 | 11 | 9 |  |  |  | 1 |  | 4 | 10 |  | 2 | 6 | 8 |  |  |  | 16 |
|  |  | 3 |  | 5 |  | 7 | 11 | 9 |  |  |  | 1 |  | 4 | 10 |  | 2 | 6 | 8 |  |  |  | 17 |
|  |  | 3 |  | 5 |  | 7 | 11 | 9 |  |  |  | 1 |  | 4 | 10 |  | 2 | 6 | 8 |  |  |  | 18 |
|  |  | 3 |  | 5 |  | 7 | 11 | 9 |  |  |  | 1 |  | 4 | 10 |  | 2 | 6 | 8 |  |  |  | 19 |
|  |  | 3 |  | 5 |  |  | 11 | 9 |  |  |  | 1 |  | 4 | 10 |  | 2 | 6 | 8 | 7 |  |  | 20 |
|  |  | 3 |  | 5 |  | 7 | 11 | 9 |  |  |  | 1 |  | 4 | 10 |  | 2 | 6 | 8 |  |  |  | 21 |
|  |  | 3 |  | 5 |  | 7 | 11 | 9 |  |  |  | 1 |  | 4 | 10 |  | 2 | 6 | 8 |  |  |  | 22 |
|  |  | 3 |  | 5 |  | 7 | 11 | 9 |  |  |  | 1 |  | 4 | 10 |  | 2 | 6 | 8 |  |  |  | 23 |
|  |  | 3 |  | 5 |  | 7 | 11 | 9 |  |  |  | 1 |  | 4 | 10 |  | 2 | 6 | 8 |  |  |  | 24 |
|  |  | 3 |  | 5 |  | 7 | 11 | 9 |  |  |  | 1 |  | 4 | 10 |  | 2 | 6 | 8 |  |  |  | 25 |
|  |  | 3 |  | 5 |  | 7 | 11 | 9 |  |  |  | 1 |  | 4 | 10 |  | 2 | 6 | 8 |  |  |  | 26 |
|  |  | 3 |  | 5 |  | 7 |  | 9 |  | 11 |  | 1 |  | 4 | 10 |  | 2 | 6 | 8 |  |  |  | 27 |
|  |  | 3 |  | 5 |  | 7 |  | 9 |  | 11 |  | 1 |  | 4 | 10 |  | 2 | 6 | 8 |  |  |  | 28 |
| 1 |  | 3 |  | 5 |  | 7 | 11 | 9 |  |  |  |  |  | 4 | 10 |  | 2 | 6 | 8 |  |  |  | 29 |
| 1 |  | 3 |  | 5 |  |  | 11 | 9 |  |  |  |  |  | 4 | 10 |  | 2 | 6 | 8 |  | 7 |  | 30 |
| 1 |  | 3 |  | 5 |  | 7 |  | 9 |  | 11 |  |  |  | 4 | 10 |  | 2 | 6 | 8 |  |  |  | 31 |
|  |  | 3 |  | 5 |  | 7 | 11 | 9 |  |  |  | 1 |  | 4 | 10 |  | 2 | 6 | 8 |  |  |  | 32 |
|  |  | 3 |  | 5 |  | 7 | 11 | 9 |  |  |  | 1 |  | 4 | 10 |  | 2 | 6 | 8 |  |  |  | 33 |
| 1 |  | 3 |  | 5 | 6 | 7 | 11 | 9 |  |  |  |  |  | 4 | 10 |  | 2 |  | 8 |  |  |  | 34 |
| 1 |  | 3 |  | 5 |  | 7 | 11 | 9 |  |  |  |  |  | 4 | 10 |  | 2 | 6 | 8 |  |  |  | 35 |
| 1 |  | 3 | 4 | 5 |  | 7 | 11 | 9 |  |  |  |  |  |  | 10 |  | 2 | 6 | 8 |  |  |  | 36 |
| 1 |  | 3 |  | 5 |  | 7 |  |  |  |  | 9 |  |  | 4 | 10 |  | 2 | 6 | 8 |  |  | 3 | 37 |
| 1 | 9 | 3 |  | 5 |  | 7 | 11 |  |  |  |  |  |  | 4 | 10 |  | 2 | 6 | 8 |  |  |  | 38 |
| 1 | 9 | 3 | 7 | 5 |  |  |  |  |  | 11 |  |  |  | 4 | 10 |  | 2 | 6 | 8 |  |  |  | 39 |
| 1 | 9 | 3 | 7 | 5 |  |  |  |  |  | 11 |  |  |  | 4 | 10 |  | 2 | 6 | 8 |  |  |  | 40 |
| 1 | 9 | 3 | 7 | 5 | 6 |  |  |  |  | 11 |  |  |  | 4 | 10 |  | 2 |  | 8 |  |  |  | 41 |
| 1 | 9 | 3 |  | 5 | 6 | 7 | 11 |  |  |  |  |  |  | 4 | 10 |  | 2 |  | 8 |  |  |  | 42 |
| 15 | 12 | 41 | 7 | 42 | 18 | 37 | 36 | 35 | 11 | 9 | 6 | 27 | 4 | 38 | 29 | 9 | 32 | 24 | 27 | 1 | 1 | 1 | |
|  | 2 | 3 |  | 1 |  | 5 | 12 | 22 | 2 |  | 1 |  |  |  | 11 |  | 1 |  | 13 |  |  |  | |

285

# 1954-55

Manager: Matt Busby

| | | | | | | | |
|---|---|---|---|---|---|---|---|
| 1 | Aug | 21 | (h) | Portsmouth | L 1-3 | Rowley | 38,203 |
| 2 | | 23 | (a) | Sheffield W | W 4-2 | Blanchflower 2, Viollet 2 | 38,118 |
| 3 | | 28 | (a) | Blackpool | W 4-2 | Webster 2, Blanchflower, Viollet | 31,855 |
| 4 | Sep | 1 | (h) | Sheffield W | W 2-0 | Viollet 2 | 31,371 |
| 5 | | 4 | (h) | Charlton A | W 3-1 | Rowley 2, Taylor | 38,105 |
| 6 | | 8 | (a) | Tottenham H | W 2-0 | Berry, Webster | 35,162 |
| 7 | | 11 | (a) | Bolton W | D 1-1 | Webster | 44,661 |
| 8 | | 15 | (h) | Tottenham H | W 2-1 | Rowley, Viollet | 29,212 |
| 9 | | 18 | (h) | Huddersfield T | D 1-1 | Viollet | 45,648 |
| 10 | | 25 | (a) | Manchester C | L 2-3 | Blanchflower, Taylor | 54,105 |
| 11 | Oct | 2 | (a) | Wolves | L 2-4 | Rowley, Viollet | 39,617 |
| 12 | | 9 | (h) | Cardiff C | W 5-2 | Taylor 4, Viollet | 39,378 |
| 13 | | 16 | (a) | Chelsea | W 6-5 | Viollet 3, Taylor 2, Blanchflower | 55,966 |
| 14 | | 23 | (h) | Newcastle U | D 2-2 | Taylor, Scoular (og)* | 29,217 |
| 15 | | 30 | (a) | Everton | L 2-4 | Taylor, Rowley | 63,021 |
| 16 | Nov | 6 | (h) | Preston NE | W 2-1 | Viollet 2 | 30,063 |
| 17 | | 13 | (a) | Sheffield U | L 0-3 | | 26,257 |
| 18 | | 20 | (h) | Arsenal | W 2-1 | Blanchflower, Taylor | 33,373 |
| 19 | | 27 | (a) | West Brom A | L 0-2 | | 33,931 |
| 20 | Dec | 4 | (h) | Leicester C | W 3-1 | Webster, Rowley, Viollet | 19,369 |
| 21 | | 11 | (a) | Burnley | W 4-2 | Webster 3, Viollet | 24,977 |
| 22 | | 18 | (a) | Portsmouth | D 0-0 | | 26,019 |
| 23 | | 27 | (h) | Aston Villa | L 0-1 | | 49,136 |
| 24 | | 28 | (a) | Aston Villa | L 1-2 | Taylor | 48,718 |
| 25 | Jan | 1 | (h) | Blackpool | W 4-1 | Blanchflower 2, Edwards, Viollet | 51,918 |
| 26 | | 22 | (h) | Bolton W | D 1-1 | Taylor | 39,873 |
| 27 | Feb | 5 | (a) | Huddersfield T | W 3-1 | Berry, Edwards, Pegg | 31,408 |
| 28 | | 12 | (h) | Manchester C | L 0-5 | | 47,914 |
| 29 | | 23 | (h) | Wolves | L 2-4 | Edwards, Taylor | 15,679 |
| 30 | | 26 | (a) | Cardiff C | L 0-3 | | 16,329 |
| 31 | Mar | 5 | (h) | Burnley | W 1-0 | Edwards | 31,729 |
| 32 | | 19 | (a) | Everton | L 1-2 | Scanlon | 32,295 |
| 33 | | 26 | (a) | Preston NE | W 2-0 | Byrne, Scanlon | 13,327 |
| 34 | Apr | 2 | (h) | Sheffield U | W 5-0 | Taylor 2, Berry, Viollet, Whelan | 21,158 |
| 35 | | 8 | (a) | Sunderland | L 3-4 | Edwards 2, Scanlon | 43,882 |
| 36 | | 9 | (a) | Leicester C | L 0-1 | | 34,362 |
| 37 | | 11 | (h) | Sunderland | D 2-2 | Byrne, Taylor | 36,013 |
| 38 | | 16 | (h) | West Brom A | W 3-0 | Taylor 2, Viollet | 24,765 |
| 39 | | 18 | (a) | Newcastle U | L 0-2 | | 35,540 |
| 40 | | 23 | (a) | Arsenal | W 3-2 | Blanchflower 2, Goring (og) | 42,754 |
| 41 | | 26 | (a) | Charlton A | D 1-1 | Viollet | 13,149 |
| 42 | | 30 | (h) | Chelsea | W 2-1 | Scanlon, Taylor | 34,933 |

FINAL LEAGUE POSITION: 5th in Division One

*Some sources credit Taylor with this goal

Appearances
Goals

FA Cup

| | | | | | | |
|---|---|---|---|---|---|---|
| 3 | Jan | 8 | (a) | Reading | D 1-1 | |
| R | | 12 | (h) | Reading | W 4-1 | |
| 4 | | 29 | (a) | Manchester C | L 0-2 | |

| Wood | Foulkes | Byrne | Whitefoot | Chilton | Edwards | Berry | Blanchflower | Webster | Viollet | Rowley | Taylor | Gibson | Crompton | Greaves | Kennedy | Cockburn | Goodwin | Scanlon | Bent | Pegg | Jones | Whelan | |
|---|---|---|---|---|---|---|---|---|---|---|---|---|---|---|---|---|---|---|---|---|---|---|---|
| 1 | 2 | 3 | 4 | 5 | 6 | 7 | 8 | 9 | 10 | 11 | | | | | | | | | | | | | 1 |
| 1 | 2 | 3 | 4 | 5 | 6 | 7 | 8 | 9 | 10 | 11 | | | | | | | | | | | | | 2 |
| 1 | 2 | 3 | 4 | 5 | 6 | 7 | 8 | 9 | 10 | 11 | | | | | | | | | | | | | 3 |
| 1 | 2 | 3 | 4 | 5 | 6 | 7 | 8 | 9 | 10 | 11 | | | | | | | | | | | | | 4 |
| 1 | 2 | 3 | 4 | 5 | 6 | 7 | 8 | | 10 | 11 | 9 | | | | | | | | | | | | 5 |
| 1 | 2 | 3 | 4 | 5 | 6 | 7 | 8 | 9 | 10 | 11 | | | | | | | | | | | | | 6 |
| 1 | 2 | 3 | 4 | 5 | 6 | 7 | 8 | 9 | 10 | 11 | | | | | | | | | | | | | 7 |
| 1 | 2 | 3 | 4 | 5 | 6 | 7 | 8 | | 10 | 11 | 9 | | | | | | | | | | | | 8 |
| 1 | 2 | 3 | 4 | 5 | 6 | 7 | 8 | | 10 | 11 | 9 | | | | | | | | | | | | 9 |
| 1 | 2 | 3 | | 5 | 6 | 7 | 8 | | 10 | 11 | 9 | 4 | | | | | | | | | | | 10 |
| | | | | 5 | 8 | 7 | | | 10 | 11 | 9 | 4 | 1 | 2 | 3 | 6 | | | | | | | 11 |
| 1 | 2 | 3 | | 5 | 6 | 7 | 8 | | 10 | 11 | 9 | 4 | | | | | | | | | | | 12 |
| 1 | 2 | 3 | | 5 | 6 | 7 | 8 | | 10 | 11 | 9 | 4 | | | | | | | | | | | 13 |
| 1 | 2 | 3 | | 5 | 6 | 7 | 8 | | 10 | 11 | 9 | 4 | | | | | | | | | | | 14 |
| 1 | 2 | 3 | | 5 | 6 | 7 | 8 | | 10 | 11 | 9 | 4 | | | | | | | | | | | 15 |
| 1 | 2 | 3 | | 5 | 6 | 7 | 8 | | 10 | 11 | 9 | 4 | | | | | | | | | | | 16 |
| 1 | 2 | 3 | | 5 | 6 | 7 | 8 | | 10 | 11 | 9 | 4 | | | | | | | | | | | 17 |
| 1 | 2 | 3 | | 5 | | 7 | 8 | | 10 | | 9 | 4 | | | | | 6 | 11 | | | | | 18 |
| 1 | 2 | 3 | | 5 | 6 | 7 | 8 | | 10 | | 9 | 4 | | | | | | 11 | | | | | 19 |
| 1 | 2 | 3 | 6 | 5 | | 7 | 8 | 9 | 10 | 11 | | 4 | | | | | | | | | | | 20 |
| 1 | 2 | | 6 | 5 | | 7 | 8 | 9 | 10 | 11 | | 4 | | | 3 | | | | | | | | 21 |
| 1 | 2 | 3 | | 5 | 6 | 7 | 8 | 9 | 10 | 11 | | 4 | | | | | | | | | | | 22 |
| 1 | 2 | 3 | | 5 | 6 | 7 | 8 | 9 | 10 | 11 | | 4 | | | | | | | | | | | 23 |
| 1 | 2 | 3 | | 5 | 6 | 7 | | 8 | 10 | | 9 | 4 | | | | | | | | 11 | | | 24 |
| 1 | 2 | 3 | | 5 | 6 | 7 | 8 | | 10 | | 9 | 4 | | | | | | | | 11 | | | 25 |
| 1 | 2 | 3 | | 5 | 6 | 7 | 8 | | 10 | 11 | 9 | 4 | | | | | | | | | | | 26 |
| 1 | 2 | 3 | 6 | 5 | 10 | 7 | 8 | 9 | | | | 4 | | | | | | | | 11 | | | 27 |
| 1 | 2 | 3 | 6 | 5 | 10 | 7 | 8 | 9 | | | | 4 | | | | | | | | 11 | | | 28 |
| 1 | 2 | 3 | 6 | 5 | 10 | 7 | 8 | 9 | | | | 4 | | | | | | | | 11 | | | 29 |
| 1 | 2 | 3 | 6 | | 10 | 7 | 8 | 9 | | | | 4 | | | | | | | | 11 | 5 | | 30 |
| 1 | 2 | 3 | 6 | | 10 | 7 | 8 | 9 | | | | 4 | | | | | | 11 | | | 5 | | 31 |
| 1 | 2 | 3 | 6 | | 10 | 7 | 8 | 9 | | | | 4 | | | | | | 11 | | | 5 | | 32 |
| 1 | 2 | 3 | 6 | | 10 | 7 | | | | | 9 | 4 | | | | | | 11 | | | 5 | 8 | 33 |
| 1 | 2 | | 6 | | | 7 | | | 10 | | 9 | 4 | | | | | | 11 | 3 | | 5 | 8 | 34 |
| 1 | 2 | 3 | 6 | | 10 | 7 | | | | | 9 | 4 | | | | | | 11 | | | 5 | 8 | 35 |
| | 2 | 3 | 6 | | 10 | 7 | | | | | 9 | 4 | 1 | | | | | 11 | | | 5 | 8 | 36 |
| | 2 | 3 | 6 | | 10 | 7 | | | | | 9 | 4 | 1 | | | | | 11 | | | 5 | 8 | 37 |
| | 2 | 3 | 6 | | | 7 | | | 10 | | 9 | | 1 | | | | 4 | 11 | | | 5 | 8 | 38 |
| | 2 | 3 | 6 | | | 7 | | | 10 | | 9 | 4 | 1 | | | | | 11 | | | 5 | 8 | 39 |
| 1 | 2 | 3 | | | | 7 | 8 | | 10 | | 9 | 4 | | | | | 6 | 11 | | | 5 | | 40 |
| 1 | 2 | 3 | | | | 7 | 8 | | 10 | | 9 | 4 | | | | | 6 | 11 | | | 5 | | 41 |
| 1 | 2 | 3 | | | | 7 | 8 | | 10 | | 9 | 4 | | | | | 6 | 11 | | | 5 | | 42 |
| 37 | 41 | 39 | 24 | 29 | 33 | 40 | 29 | 17 | 34 | 22 | 30 | 32 | 5 | 1 | 1 | 1 | 5 | 14 | 2 | 6 | 13 | 7 | |
| | | 2 | | | 6 | 3 | 10 | 8 | 20 | 7 | 20 | | | | | | | 4 | | 1 | | 1 | |

2 own-goals

# 1955-56

Manager: Matt Busby

| | | | | | | | |
|---|---|---|---|---|---|---|---|
| 1 | Aug | 20 | (a) | Birmingham C | D | 2-2 | Viollet 2 | 37,994 |
| 2 | | 24 | (h) | Tottenham H | D | 2-2 | Berry, Webster | 25,406 |
| 3 | | 27 | (h) | West Brom A | W | 3-1 | Lewis, Scanlon, Viollet | 31,996 |
| 4 | | 31 | (a) | Tottenham H | W | 2-1 | Edwards 2 | 27,453 |
| 5 | Sep | 3 | (a) | Manchester C | L | 0-1 | | 59,162 |
| 6 | | 7 | (h) | Everton | W | 2-1 | Blanchflower, Edwards | 27,843 |
| 7 | | 10 | (a) | Sheffield U | L | 0-1 | | 28,241 |
| 8 | | 14 | (a) | Everton | L | 2-4 | Blanchflower, Webster | 34,897 |
| 9 | | 17 | (h) | Preston NE | W | 3-2 | Pegg, Taylor, Viollet | 33,078 |
| 10 | | 24 | (a) | Burnley | D | 0-0 | | 26,873 |
| 11 | Oct | 1 | (h) | Luton T | W | 3-1 | Taylor 2, Webster | 34,409 |
| 12 | | 8 | (h) | Wolves | W | 3-2 | Taylor 2, Doherty, Pegg | 48,638 |
| 13 | | 15 | (a) | Aston Villa | D | 4-4 | Pegg 2, Blanchflower, Webster | 29,478 |
| 14 | | 22 | (h) | Huddersfield T | W | 3-0 | Berry, Pegg, Taylor | 34,150 |
| 15 | | 29 | (a) | Cardiff C | W | 1-0 | Taylor | 27,795 |
| 16 | Nov | 5 | (h) | Arsenal | D | 1-1 | Taylor | 41,586 |
| 17 | | 12 | (a) | Bolton W | L | 1-3 | Taylor | 38,109 |
| 18 | | 19 | (h) | Chelsea | W | 3-0 | Taylor 2, Byrne | 22,192 |
| 19 | | 26 | (a) | Blackpool | D | 0-0 | | 26,240 |
| 20 | Dec | 3 | (h) | Sunderland | W | 2-1 | Doherty, Viollet | 39,901 |
| 21 | | 10 | (a) | Portsmouth | L | 2-3 | Pegg, Taylor | 24,594 |
| 22 | | 17 | (h) | Birmingham C | W | 2-1 | Jones, Viollet | 27,704 |
| 23 | | 24 | (a) | West Brom A | W | 4-1 | Viollet 3, Taylor | 25,168 |
| 24 | | 26 | (h) | Charlton A | W | 5-1 | Viollet 2, Byrne, Doherty, Taylor | 44,611 |
| 25 | | 27 | (a) | Charlton A | L | 0-3 | | 42,040 |
| 26 | | 31 | (h) | Manchester C | W | 2-1 | Taylor, Viollet | 60,956 |
| 27 | Jan | 14 | (h) | Sheffield U | W | 3-1 | Berry, Pegg, Taylor | 30,162 |
| 28 | | 21 | (a) | Preston NE | L | 1-3 | Whelan | 28,047 |
| 29 | Feb | 4 | (h) | Burnley | W | 2-0 | Taylor, Viollet | 27,342 |
| 30 | | 11 | (a) | Luton T | W | 2-0 | Viollet, Whelan | 16,354 |
| 31 | | 18 | (a) | Wolves | W | 2-0 | Taylor 2 | 40,014 |
| 32 | | 25 | (h) | Aston Villa | W | 1-0 | Whelan | 36,277 |
| 33 | Mar | 3 | (a) | Chelsea | W | 4-2 | Viollet 2, Pegg, Taylor | 32,050 |
| 34 | | 10 | (h) | Cardiff C | D | 1-1 | Byrne | 44,693 |
| 35 | | 17 | (a) | Arsenal | D | 1-1 | Taylor | 50,758 |
| 36 | | 24 | (h) | Bolton W | W | 1-0 | Taylor | 46,114 |
| 37 | | 30 | (h) | Newcastle U | W | 5-2 | Viollet 2, Doherty, Pegg, Taylor | 58,994 |
| 38 | | 31 | (a) | Huddersfield T | W | 2-0 | Taylor 2 | 37,780 |
| 39 | Apr | 2 | (a) | Newcastle U | D | 0-0 | | 37,395 |
| 40 | | 7 | (h) | Blackpool | W | 2-1 | Berry, Taylor | 62,277 |
| 41 | | 14 | (a) | Sunderland | D | 2-2 | McGuinness, Whelan | 19,865 |
| 42 | | 21 | (h) | Portsmouth | W | 1-0 | Viollet | 38,417 |

FINAL LEAGUE POSITION: 1st in Division One

Appearances
Goals

FA Cup

| | | | | | | |
|---|---|---|---|---|---|---|
| 3 | Jan | 7 | (a) | Bristol R | L | 0-4 |

| Wood | Foulkes | Byrne | Whitefoot | Jones | Edwards | Webster | Blanchflower | Taylor | Viollet | Scanlon | Berry | Lewis | Goodwin | Whelan | Pegg | Whitehurst | Doherty | Bent | McGuinness | Crompton | Colman | Greaves | Scott | |
|---|---|---|---|---|---|---|---|---|---|---|---|---|---|---|---|---|---|---|---|---|---|---|---|---|
| 1 | 2 | 3 | 4 | 5 | 6 | 7 | 8 | 9 | 10 | 11 | | | | | | | | | | | | | | 1 |
| 1 | 2 | 3 | 4 | 5 | 6 | 9 | 8 | | 10 | 11 | 7 | | | | | | | | | | | | | 2 |
| 1 | 2 | 3 | 4 | 5 | 6 | 7 | 8 | | 10 | 11 | | 9 | | | | | | | | | | | | 3 |
| 1 | 2 | 3 | 4 | 5 | 6 | 7 | 8 | | 10 | 11 | | 9 | | | | | | | | | | | | 4 |
| 1 | 2 | 3 | 4 | 5 | 10 | 7 | 8 | | | 11 | | 9 | 6 | | | | | | | | | | | 5 |
| 1 | 2 | 3 | 4 | 5 | 10 | 7 | 8 | | | 11 | | 9 | 6 | | | | | | | | | | | 6 |
| 1 | 2 | 3 | 4 | 5 | | 9 | 10 | | | | 7 | | 6 | 8 | 11 | | | | | | | | | 7 |
| 1 | 2 | 3 | | 5 | | 7 | 9 | | | | | | 6 | 8 | 11 | 4 | 10 | | | | | | | 8 |
| 1 | 2 | 3 | 4 | 5 | | 7 | 8 | 9 | 10 | | | | 6 | | 11 | | | | | | | | | 9 |
| 1 | 2 | 3 | 4 | 5 | | 7 | 8 | 9 | 10 | | | | 6 | | 11 | | | | | | | | | 10 |
| 1 | 2 | | 4 | 5 | | 10 | 8 | 9 | | | 7 | | 6 | | 11 | | | 3 | | | | | | 11 |
| 1 | | 2 | 4 | 5 | | 10 | | 9 | | | 7 | | | | 11 | | 8 | 3 | 6 | | | | | 12 |
| 1 | 2 | 3 | 4 | 5 | | 10 | 8 | 9 | | | 7 | | | | 11 | | | | 6 | | | | | 13 |
| | 2 | | 4 | 5 | 6 | | 8 | 9 | 10 | | 7 | | | | 11 | | | 3 | | 1 | | | | 14 |
| 1 | 2 | 3 | 4 | 5 | 6 | | 8 | 9 | 10 | | 7 | | | | 11 | | | | | | | | | 15 |
| 1 | 2 | 3 | 4 | 5 | 6 | | 8 | 9 | 10 | | 7 | | | | 11 | | | | | | | | | 16 |
| 1 | 2 | 3 | | 5 | 6 | 10 | 8 | 9 | | | 7 | | | | 11 | | | | | | 4 | | | 17 |
| 1 | 2 | 3 | | 5 | 6 | | | 9 | 10 | | 7 | | | | 11 | | 8 | | | | 4 | | | 18 |
| 1 | | 3 | | 5 | 6 | | | 9 | 10 | | 7 | | | | 11 | | 8 | | | | 4 | 2 | | 19 |
| 1 | 2 | 3 | | 5 | 6 | | | 9 | 10 | | 7 | | | | 11 | | 8 | | | | 4 | | | 20 |
| 1 | 2 | 3 | | 5 | 6 | | | 9 | 10 | | 7 | | | | 11 | | 8 | | | | 4 | | | 21 |
| 1 | 2 | 3 | | 5 | 6 | | | 9 | 10 | | 7 | | | | 11 | | 8 | | | | 4 | | | 22 |
| 1 | 2 | 3 | | 5 | 6 | | | 9 | 10 | | 7 | | | | 11 | | 8 | | | | 4 | | | 23 |
| 1 | 2 | 3 | | 5 | 6 | | | 9 | 10 | | 7 | | | | 11 | | 8 | | | | 4 | | | 24 |
| 1 | 2 | 3 | | 5 | 6 | | | 9 | 10 | | 7 | | | | 11 | | 8 | | | | 4 | | | 25 |
| 1 | 2 | 3 | | 5 | 6 | | | 9 | 10 | | 7 | | | | 11 | | 8 | | | | 4 | | | 26 |
| 1 | 2 | 3 | | 5 | 6 | | | 9 | 10 | | 7 | | | 8 | 11 | | | | | | 4 | | | 27 |
| 1 | 2 | 3 | | 5 | 6 | 9 | | | 10 | | | | | 8 | 11 | | | | | | 4 | | 7 | 28 |
| 1 | | 3 | | 5 | 6 | | | 9 | 10 | | 7 | | | 8 | 11 | | | | | | 4 | 2 | | 29 |
| 1 | | 3 | | 5 | 6 | | | 9 | 10 | | 7 | | 4 | 8 | 11 | | | | | | | 2 | | 30 |
| 1 | | 3 | | 5 | 6 | | | 9 | 10 | | 7 | | | | 11 | | 8 | | | | 4 | 2 | | 31 |
| 1 | | 3 | | 5 | 6 | | | 9 | 10 | | 7 | | | | 11 | | 8 | | | | 4 | 2 | | 32 |
| 1 | | 3 | | 5 | 6 | | | 9 | 10 | | 7 | | | | 11 | | 8 | | | | 4 | 2 | | 33 |
| 1 | | 3 | | 5 | 6 | | | 9 | 10 | | 7 | | | | 11 | | 8 | | | | 4 | 2 | | 34 |
| 1 | | 3 | | 5 | 6 | | | 9 | 10 | | 7 | | | | 11 | | 8 | | | | 4 | 2 | | 35 |
| 1 | | 3 | | 5 | 6 | | | 9 | 10 | | 7 | | | 8 | 11 | | | | | | 4 | 2 | | 36 |
| 1 | | 3 | | 5 | 6 | | | 9 | 10 | | 7 | | | | 11 | | 8 | | | | 4 | 2 | | 37 |
| 1 | | 3 | | 5 | 6 | | | 9 | 10 | | 7 | | | | 11 | | 8 | | | | 4 | 2 | | 38 |
| 1 | | 3 | | 5 | 6 | | | 9 | 10 | | 7 | | | | 11 | | 8 | | | | 4 | 2 | | 39 |
| 1 | | 3 | | 5 | 6 | | | 9 | 10 | | 7 | | | | 11 | | 8 | | | | 4 | 2 | | 40 |
| 1 | | | | 5 | | 9 | | | 10 | | 7 | | | 8 | 11 | | | 3 | 6 | | 4 | 2 | | 41 |
| 1 | | 3 | | 5 | 6 | | | 9 | 10 | | 7 | | | | 11 | | 8 | | | | 4 | 2 | | 42 |
| 41 | 26 | 39 | 15 | 42 | 33 | 15 | 18 | 33 | 34 | 6 | 34 | 4 | 8 | 13 | 35 | 1 | 16 | 4 | 3 | 1 | 25 | 15 | 1 | |
| | | | 3 | 1 | 3 | 4 | 3 | 25 | 20 | 1 | 4 | 1 | | 4 | 9 | | 4 | | 1 | | | | | |

# 1956-57

Manager: Matt Busby

| | | | | | | | | |
|---|---|---|---|---|---|---|---|---|
| 1 | Aug | 18 | (h) | Birmingham C | D | 2-2 | Viollet 2 | 32,752 |
| 2 | | 20 | (a) | Preston NE | W | 3-1 | Taylor 2, Whelan | 32,569 |
| 3 | | 25 | (a) | West Brom A | W | 3-2 | Taylor, Viollet, Whelan | 26,387 |
| 4 | | 29 | (h) | Preston NE | W | 3-2 | Viollet 3 | 32,515 |
| 5 | Sep | 1 | (h) | Portsmouth | W | 3-0 | Berry, Pegg, Viollet | 40,369 |
| 6 | | 5 | (a) | Chelsea | W | 2-1 | Taylor, Whelan | 29,082 |
| 7 | | 8 | (a) | Newcastle U | D | 1-1 | Whelan | 50,130 |
| 8 | | 15 | (h) | Sheffield W | W | 4-1 | Berry, Taylor, Viollet, Whelan | 48,078 |
| 9 | | 22 | (h) | Manchester C | W | 2-0 | Whelan, Viollet | 53,525 |
| 10 | | 29 | (a) | Arsenal | W | 2-1 | Berry, Whelan | 62,479 |
| 11 | Oct | 6 | (h) | Charlton A | W | 4-2 | Charlton 2, Berry, Whelan | 41,439 |
| 12 | | 13 | (a) | Sunderland | W | 3-1 | Whelan, Viollet, Opp own-goal | 49,487 |
| 13 | | 20 | (h) | Everton | L | 2-5 | Charlton, Whelan | 43,451 |
| 14 | | 27 | (a) | Blackpool | D | 2-2 | Taylor 2 | 32,632 |
| 15 | Nov | 3 | (h) | Wolves | W | 3-0 | Pegg, Taylor, Whelan | 59,835 |
| 16 | | 10 | (a) | Bolton W | L | 0-2 | | 39,922 |
| 17 | | 17 | (h) | Leeds U | W | 3-2 | Whelan 2, Charlton | 51,131 |
| 18 | | 24 | (a) | Tottenham H | D | 2-2 | Berry, Colman | 57,724 |
| 19 | Dec | 1 | (h) | Luton T | W | 3-1 | Edwards, Pegg, Taylor | 34,736 |
| 20 | | 8 | (a) | Aston Villa | W | 3-1 | Taylor 2, Viollet | 42,530 |
| 21 | | 15 | (a) | Birmingham C | L | 1-3 | Whelan | 36,146 |
| 22 | | 26 | (h) | Cardiff C | W | 3-1 | Taylor, Whelan, Viollet | 28,607 |
| 23 | | 29 | (a) | Portsmouth | W | 3-1 | Edwards, Pegg, Viollet | 32,147 |
| 24 | Jan | 1 | (h) | Chelsea | W | 3-0 | Taylor 2, Whelan | 42,116 |
| 25 | | 12 | (h) | Newcastle U | W | 6-1 | Pegg 2, Whelan 2, Viollet 2 | 44,911 |
| 26 | | 19 | (a) | Sheffield W | L | 1-2 | Taylor | 51,068 |
| 27 | Feb | 2 | (a) | Manchester C | W | 4-2 | Edwards, Taylor, Whelan, Viollet | 63,872 |
| 28 | | 9 | (h) | Arsenal | W | 6-2 | Berry 2, Whelan 2, Edwards, Taylor | 60,384 |
| 29 | | 18 | (a) | Charlton A | W | 5-1 | Charlton 3, Taylor 2 | 16,308 |
| 30 | | 23 | (h) | Blackpool | L | 0-2 | | 42,602 |
| 31 | Mar | 6 | (a) | Everton | W | 2-1 | Webster 2 | 34,029 |
| 32 | | 9 | (h) | Aston Villa | D | 1-1 | Charlton | 55,484 |
| 33 | | 16 | (a) | Wolves | D | 1-1 | Charlton | 53,228 |
| 34 | | 25 | (h) | Bolton W | L | 0-2 | | 60,862 |
| 35 | | 30 | (a) | Leeds U | W | 2-1 | Berry, Charlton | 47,216 |
| 36 | Apr | 6 | (h) | Tottenham H | D | 0-0 | | 60,349 |
| 37 | | 13 | (a) | Luton T | W | 2-0 | Taylor 2 | 21,227 |
| 38 | | 19 | (a) | Burnley | W | 3-1 | Whelan 3 | 41,321 |
| 39 | | 20 | (h) | Sunderland | W | 4-0 | Whelan 2, Edwards, Taylor | 58,725 |
| 40 | | 22 | (h) | Burnley | W | 2-0 | Dawson, Webster | 41,321 |
| 41 | | 27 | (a) | Cardiff C | W | 3-2 | Scanlon 2, Dawson* | 17,708 |
| 42 | | 29 | (h) | West Brom A | D | 1-1 | Dawson | 20,357 |

FINAL LEAGUE POSITION: 1st in Division One

Appearances

*Some sources credit McSeveney(og)

Goals

FA Cup

| | | | | | | | |
|---|---|---|---|---|---|---|---|
| 3 | Jan | 5 | (a) | Hartlepools U | W | 4-3 | |
| 4 | | 26 | (a) | Wrexham | W | 5-0 | |
| 5 | Feb | 16 | (h) | Everton | W | 1-0 | |
| 6 | Mar | 2 | (a) | Bournemouth | W | 2-1 | |
| SF | | 23 | (n‡) | Birmingham C | W | 2-0 | (‡Played at Hillsborough, Sheffield) |
| F | May | 4 | (n†) | Aston Villa | L | 1-2 | (†Played at Wembley Stadium) |

Manchester United also reached the semi-final of the European Cup (see *United in Europe*).

| Wood | Foulkes | Byrne | Colman | Jones | Edwards | Berry | Whelan | Taylor | Viollet | Pegg | Cope | Bent | McGuinness | Charlton | Hawksworth | Blanchflower | Goodwin | Webster | Doherty | Clayton | Scanlon | Greaves | Dawson | |
|---|---|---|---|---|---|---|---|---|---|---|---|---|---|---|---|---|---|---|---|---|---|---|---|---|
| 1 | 2 | 3 | 4 | 5 | 6 | 7 | 8 | 9 | 10 | 11 | | | | | | | | | | | | | | 1 |
| 1 | 2 | 3 | 4 | 5 | 6 | 7 | 8 | 9 | 10 | 11 | | | | | | | | | | | | | | 2 |
| 1 | 2 | 3 | 4 | 5 | 6 | 7 | 8 | 9 | 10 | 11 | | | | | | | | | | | | | | 3 |
| 1 | 2 | 3 | 4 | 5 | 6 | 7 | 8 | 9 | 10 | 11 | | | | | | | | | | | | | | 4 |
| 1 | 2 | 3 | 4 | 5 | 6 | 7 | 8 | 9 | 10 | 11 | | | | | | | | | | | | | | 5 |
| 1 | 2 | 3 | 4 | 5 | 6 | 7 | 8 | 9 | 10 | 11 | | | | | | | | | | | | | | 6 |
| 1 | 2 | 3 | 4 | 5 | 6 | 7 | 8 | 9 | 10 | 11 | | | | | | | | | | | | | | 7 |
| 1 | 2 | 3 | 4 | 5 | 6 | 7 | 8 | 9 | 10 | 11 | | | | | | | | | | | | | | 8 |
| 1 | 2 | 3 | 4 | 5 | 6 | 7 | 8 | 9 | 10 | 11 | | | | | | | | | | | | | | 9 |
| 1 | 2 | 3 | 4 | | 6 | 7 | 8 | 9 | 10 | 11 | 5 | | | | | | | | | | | | | 10 |
| 1 | 2 | | 4 | 5 | | 7 | 8 | | 10 | 11 | | 3 | 6 | 9 | | | | | | | | | | 11 |
| 1 | 2 | 3 | 4 | 5 | 6 | 7 | 8 | 9 | 10 | 11 | | | | | | | | | | | | | | 12 |
| 1 | 2 | 3 | 4 | 5 | 6 | 7 | 8 | 9 | | 11 | | | | 10 | | | | | | | | | | 13 |
| | 2 | 3 | 4 | 5 | 6 | 7 | 8 | 9 | 10 | 11 | | | | | 1 | | | | | | | | | 14 |
| 1 | 2 | 3 | 4 | 5 | 6 | 7 | 8 | 9 | | 11 | | | | 10 | | | | | | | | | | 15 |
| 1 | 2 | 3 | 4 | 5 | 6 | 7 | 8 | 9 | | 11 | | | | 10 | | | | | | | | | | 16 |
| 1 | 2 | 3 | 4 | 5 | | 7 | 8 | 9 | | 11 | | | 6 | 10 | | | | | | | | | | 17 |
| 1 | 2 | 3 | 4 | | 10 | 7 | 8 | 9 | | 11 | | | 6 | | | 5 | | | | | | | | 18 |
| 1 | 2 | 3 | 4 | 5 | 10 | 7 | 8 | 9 | | 11 | | | 6 | | | | | | | | | | | 19 |
| 1 | 2 | | 4 | 5 | 6 | 7 | 8 | 9 | 10 | 11 | | 3 | | | | | | | | | | | | 20 |
| 1 | 2 | | 4 | 5 | 6 | 7 | 8 | 9 | 10 | 11 | | 3 | | | | | | | | | | | | 21 |
| 1 | 2 | 3 | 4 | 5 | 6 | 7 | 8 | 9 | 10 | 11 | | | | | | | | | | | | | | 22 |
| 1 | 2 | 3 | 4 | 5 | 9 | 7 | 8 | | 10 | 11 | | | 6 | | | | | | | | | | | 23 |
| 1 | 2 | 3 | 4 | 5 | 6 | 7 | 8 | 9 | 10 | 11 | | | | | | | | | | | | | | 24 |
| 1 | 2 | 3 | 4 | 5 | 6 | 7 | 8 | 9 | 10 | 11 | | | | | | | | | | | | | | 25 |
| 1 | 2 | 3 | 4 | 5 | 6 | 7 | 8 | 9 | 10 | 11 | | | | | | | | | | | | | | 26 |
| 1 | 2 | 3 | 4 | 5 | 6 | 7 | 8 | 9 | 10 | 11 | | | | | | | | | | | | | | 27 |
| 1 | 2 | 3 | 4 | 5 | 6 | 7 | 8 | 9 | 10 | 11 | | | | | | | | | | | | | | 28 |
| 1 | | 2 | 4 | 5 | | 7 | 8 | 9 | | 11 | | 3 | 6 | 10 | | | | | | | | | | 29 |
| 1 | 2 | 3 | 4 | 5 | 6 | 7 | 8 | 9 | | 11 | | | | 10 | | | | | | | | | | 30 |
| 1 | | 2 | | | | 7 | 8 | | | 11 | | 3 | 6 | | | 5 | 4 | 9 | 10 | | | | | 31 |
| 1 | 2 | 3 | | | 9 | 7 | 8 | | | 11 | | | 6 | 10 | | 5 | 4 | | | | | | | 32 |
| | 2 | 3 | 4 | | 6 | 7 | 8 | | | 11 | | | | 10 | | 5 | | 9 | | 1 | | | | 33 |
| 1 | 2 | 3 | 4 | | 9 | 7 | 8 | | | 11 | | | 6 | 10 | | 5 | | | | | | | | 34 |
| 1 | 2 | 3 | 4 | | 6 | 7 | 8 | | | 11 | | | | 10 | | 5 | | 9 | | | | | | 35 |
| 1 | 2 | | 4 | | | 7 | 8 | 9 | 10 | | | 3 | 6 | | | 5 | | | | | 11 | | | 36 |
| 1 | 2 | 3 | | | 6 | 7 | | 9 | 8 | | | | | 10 | | 5 | 4 | | | | 11 | | | 37 |
| 1 | 2 | 3 | | | 6 | 7 | 8 | 9 | | 11 | | | | 10 | | 5 | 4 | | | | | | | 38 |
| 1 | 2 | 3 | 4 | | 6 | 7 | 8 | 9 | | 11 | | | | 10 | | 5 | | | | | | | | 39 |
| 1 | 2 | | | | | | | | 10 | | 5 | | 6 | | | | 4 | 7 | 8 | | 11 | 3 | 9 | 40 |
| 1 | 2 | | 4 | | | | 8 | | 10 | | | | 6 | | | 5 | | 7 | | | 11 | 3 | 9 | 41 |
| | | 3 | | 5 | | 7 | | | 10 | | | | 6 | | | | 4 | 8 | | 1 | 11 | 2 | 9 | 42 |
| 39 | 39 | 36 | 36 | 29 | 34 | 40 | 39 | 32 | 27 | 37 | 2 | 6 | 13 | 14 | 1 | 11 | 6 | 5 | 3 | 2 | 5 | 3 | 3 | |
| | | | 1 | | 5 | 8 | 26 | 22 | 16 | 6 | | | | 10 | | | | | 3 | | 2 | | 3 | |

1 own-goal

# 1957-58

Manager: Matt Busby (Jimmy Murphy took temporary control from February 1958)

| 1 | Aug | 24 | (a) | Leicester C | W 3-0 | Whelan 3 | 40,214 |
|---|---|---|---|---|---|---|---|
| 2 | | 28 | (h) | Everton | W 3-0 | T.Taylor, Viollet, Opp own-goal | 59,103 |
| 3 | | 31 | (h) | Manchester C | W 4-1 | Berry, Edwards, T.Taylor, Viollet | 63,347 |
| 4 | Sep | 4 | (a) | Everton | D 3-3 | Berry, Viollet, Whelan | 72,077 |
| 5 | | 7 | (h) | Leeds U | W 5-0 | Berry 2, T.Taylor 2, Viollet | 50,842 |
| 6 | | 9 | (a) | Blackpool | W 4-1 | Viollet 2, Whelan 2 | 34,181 |
| 7 | | 14 | (a) | Bolton W | L 0-4 | | 48,003 |
| 8 | | 18 | (h) | Blackpool | L 1-2 | Edwards | 40,763 |
| 9 | | 21 | (h) | Arsenal | W 4-2 | Whelan 2, Pegg, T.Taylor | 47,142 |
| 10 | | 28 | (a) | Wolves | L 1-3 | Doherty | 48,825 |
| 11 | Oct | 5 | (h) | Aston Villa | W 4-1 | T.Taylor 2, Pegg, Opp own-goal | 43,102 |
| 12 | | 12 | (a) | Nottingham F | W 2-1 | Viollet, Whelan | 47,654 |
| 13 | | 19 | (h) | Portsmouth | L 0-3 | | 38,253 |
| 14 | | 26 | (a) | West Brom A | L 3-4 | T.Taylor 2, Whelan | 52,160 |
| 15 | Nov | 2 | (h) | Burnley | W 1-0 | T.Taylor | 49,449 |
| 16 | | 9 | (a) | Preston NE | D 1-1 | Whelan | 39,063 |
| 17 | | 16 | (h) | Sheffield W | W 2-1 | Webster 2 | 40,366 |
| 18 | | 23 | (a) | Newcastle U | W 2-1 | Edwards, T.Taylor | 53,890 |
| 19 | | 30 | (h) | Tottenham H | L 3-4 | Pegg 2, Whelan | 43,077 |
| 20 | Dec | 7 | (a) | Birmingham C | D 3-3 | Viollet 2, T.Taylor | 35,791 |
| 21 | | 14 | (h) | Chelsea | L 0-1 | | 36,853 |
| 22 | | 21 | (h) | Leicester C | W 4-0 | Viollet 2, Charlton, Scanlon | 41,631 |
| 23 | | 25 | (h) | Luton T | W 3-0 | Charlton, Edwards, T.Taylor | 39,444 |
| 24 | | 26 | (a) | Luton T | D 2-2 | Scanlon, T.Taylor | 26,458 |
| 25 | | 28 | (a) | Manchester C | D 2-2 | Charlton, Viollet | 70,483 |
| 26 | Jan | 11 | (a) | Leeds U | D 1-1 | Viollet | 39,401 |
| 27 | | 18 | (h) | Bolton W | W 7-2 | Charlton 3, Viollet 2, Edwards, Scanlon | 41,141 |
| 28 | Feb | 1 | (a) | Arsenal | W 5-4 | T.Taylor 2, Charlton, Edwards, Viollet | 63,578 |
| 29 | | 22 | (h) | Nottingham F | D 1-1 | Dawson | 66,124 |
| 30 | Mar | 8 | (h) | West Brom A | L 0-4 | | 63,278 |
| 31 | | 15 | (a) | Burnley | L 0-3 | | 37,247 |
| 32 | | 29 | (a) | Sheffield W | L 0-1 | | 35,608 |
| 33 | | 31 | (a) | Aston Villa | L 2-3 | Dawson, Webster | 16,631 |
| 34 | Apr | 4 | (h) | Sunderland | D 2-2 | Charlton, Dawson | 47,421 |
| 35 | | 5 | (h) | Preston NE | D 0-0 | | 47,816 |
| 36 | | 7 | (a) | Sunderland | W 2-1 | Webster 2 | 51,302 |
| 37 | | 12 | (a) | Tottenham H | L 0-1 | | 59,836 |
| 38 | | 16 | (a) | Portsmouth | D 3-3 | Dawson, E.Taylor, Webster | 39,975 |
| 39 | | 19 | (h) | Birmingham C | L 0-2 | | 38,991 |
| 40 | | 21 | (h) | Wolves | L 0-4 | | 33,267 |
| 41 | | 23 | (h) | Newcastle U | D 1-1 | Dawson | 28,393 |
| 42 | | 26 | (a) | Chelsea | L 1-2 | E.Taylor | 45,011 |

FINAL LEAGUE POSITION: 9th in Division One

Appearances
Goals

FA Cup

| 3 | Jan | 4 | (a) | Workington | W 3-1 | |
|---|---|---|---|---|---|---|
| 4 | | 25 | (h) | Ipswich T | W 2-0 | |
| 5 | Feb | 19 | (h) | Sheffield W | W 3-0 | |
| 6 | Mar | 1 | (a) | West Brom A | D 2-2 | |
| R | | 5 | (h) | West Brom A | W 1-0 | |
| SF | | 22 | (n*) | Fulham | D 2-2 | (*Played at Villa Park, Birmingham.) |
| R | | 26 | (n†) | Fulham | W 5-3 | (†Played at Arsenal Stadium, Highbury, London.) |
| F | May | 3 | (n‡) | Bolton W | L 0-2 | (‡Played at Wembley Stadium) |

Manchester United also reached the semi-final of the European Cup (see *United in Europe*).

292

| Wood | Foulkes | Byrne | Colman | Blanchflower | Edwards | Berry | Whelan | Taylor T | Viollet | Pegg | McGuinness | Goodwin | Doherty | Charlton | Jones M | Jones P | Dawson | Webster | Scanlon | Gaskell | Gregg | Morgans | Greaves | Cope | Crowther | Taylor E | Pearson | Brennan | Harrop | Heron | No. |
|---|---|---|---|---|---|---|---|---|---|---|---|---|---|---|---|---|---|---|---|---|---|---|---|---|---|---|---|---|---|---|---|
| 1 | 2 | 3 | 4 | 5 | 6 | 7 | 8 | 9 | 10 | 11 | | | | | | | | | | | | | | | | | | | | | 1 |
| 1 | 2 | 3 | 4 | 5 | 6 | 7 | 8 | 9 | 10 | 11 | | | | | | | | | | | | | | | | | | | | | 2 |
| 1 | 2 | 3 | 4 | 5 | 6 | 7 | 8 | 9 | 10 | 11 | | | | | | | | | | | | | | | | | | | | | 3 |
| 1 | 2 | 3 | 4 | 5 | 6 | 7 | 8 | 9 | 10 | 11 | | | | | | | | | | | | | | | | | | | | | 4 |
| 1 | 2 | 3 | 4 | 5 | 6 | 7 | 8 | 9 | 10 | 11 | | | | | | | | | | | | | | | | | | | | | 5 |
| 1 | 2 | 3 | 4 | 5 | 6 | 7 | 8 | 9 | 10 | 11 | | | | | | | | | | | | | | | | | | | | | 6 |
| 1 | 2 | 3 | 4 | 5 | 6 | 7 | 8 | 9 | 10 | 11 | | | | | | | | | | | | | | | | | | | | | 7 |
| 1 | 2 | 3 | 4 | 5 | 6 | 7 | 8 | 9 | 10 | 11 | | | | | | | | | | | | | | | | | | | | | 8 |
| 1 | 2 | 3 | 4 | 5 | 6 | 7 | 8 | 9 | 10 | 11 | | | | | | | | | | | | | | | | | | | | | 9 |
| 1 | 2 | | | 5 | 6 | 7 | | 9 | | 11 | 3 | 4 | 8 | 10 | | | | | | | | | | | | | | | | | 10 |
| 1 | 2 | 3 | 4 | | | 7 | 8 | 9 | | 11 | 6 | | | 10 | 5 | | | | | | | | | | | | | | | | 11 |
| 1 | 2 | 3 | 4 | 5 | 6 | 7 | 8 | 9 | 10 | 11 | | | | | | | | | | | | | | | | | | | | | 12 |
| 1 | 2 | | 4 | 5 | | 7 | 8 | | 10 | 11 | 6 | | | | | 3 | 9 | | | | | | | | | | | | | | 13 |
| 1 | 2 | 3 | | 5 | 6 | 7 | 8 | 9 | | 11 | | 4 | | 10 | | | | | | | | | | | | | | | | | 14 |
| 1 | 2 | 3 | | 5 | 6 | 7 | 8 | 9 | | 11 | | 4 | | | | | | 10 | | | | | | | | | | | | | 15 |
| 1 | 2 | 3 | | 5 | 6 | 7 | 8 | 9 | | 11 | | 4 | | | | | | 10 | | | | | | | | | | | | | 16 |
| 1 | 2 | 3 | 4 | 5 | 6 | 7 | 8 | 9 | | 11 | | | | | | | | 10 | | | | | | | | | | | | | 17 |
| 1 | 2 | 3 | 4 | 5 | 6 | | 8 | 9 | | 11 | | | | | | | | 10 | 7 | | | | | | | | | | | | 18 |
| | 2 | 3 | 4 | 5 | 6 | | 8 | | | 11 | | | | 10 | | | 9 | 7 | | 1 | | | | | | | | | | | 19 |
| 1 | 2 | 3 | 4 | | 6 | 7 | 8 | 9 | 10 | 11 | | | | | 5 | | | | | | | | | | | | | | | | 20 |
| 1 | 2 | 3 | 4 | | 6 | 7 | 8 | 9 | 10 | 11 | | | | | 5 | | | | | | | | | | | | | | | | 21 |
| | 2 | 3 | 4 | | 6 | | | 9 | 10 | | | | | 8 | 5 | | | | 11 | | 1 | 7 | | | | | | | | | 22 |
| | 2 | 3 | 4 | | 6 | | | 9 | 10 | | | | | 8 | 5 | | | | 11 | | 1 | 7 | | | | | | | | | 23 |
| | 2 | 3 | 4 | | 6 | 7 | | 9 | 10 | | | | | 8 | 5 | | | | 11 | | 1 | | | | | | | | | | 24 |
| | 2 | 3 | 4 | | 6 | | | | 10 | | | | | 8 | 5 | | 9 | | 11 | | 1 | 7 | | | | | | | | | 25 |
| | 2 | 3 | 4 | | 6 | | | 9 | 10 | | | | | 8 | 5 | | | | 11 | | 1 | 7 | | | | | | | | | 26 |
| | 2 | 3 | 4 | | 6 | | | 9 | 10 | | | | | 8 | 5 | | | | 11 | | 1 | 7 | | | | | | | | | 27 |
| | 2 | 3 | 4 | | 6 | | | 9 | 10 | | | | | 8 | 5 | | | | 11 | | 1 | 7 | | | | | | | | | 28 |
| | 2 | | | | | | | | | | | 4 | | | | | 9 | 7 | | | 1 | 3 | 5 | 6 | 8 | 10 | 11 | | | | 29 |
| | 2 | | | | | | | | | | | 4 | | 11 | | | 9 | 7 | | | 1 | 3 | 5 | | 8 | 10 | | 6 | | | 30 |
| | 2 | | | | | | | | | | | 4 | | 11 | | | 9 | 7 | | | 1 | 3 | 5 | 6 | | 10 | | 8 | | | 31 |
| | 2 | | | | | | | | | | | 4 | | 10 | | | 9 | 7 | | | 1 | 3 | | 6 | 8 | | 11 | | 5 | | 32 |
| | 2 | | | | | | | | | | | 4 | | 10 | | | 9 | 7 | | | 1 | 3 | | 6 | 8 | | 11 | | 5 | | 33 |
| | 2 | | | | | | | | | | | 4 | | 10 | | | 9 | 7 | | | 1 | 3 | 5 | 6 | 8 | | 11 | | | | 34 |
| | 2 | | | | | | | | | | | 4 | | 10 | | | 9 | | | | 1 | 7 | 3 | 5 | 6 | 8 | 11 | | | | 35 |
| | 2 | | | | | | | | | | 6 | 4 | | 10 | | | 9 | | | | 1 | 7 | 3 | | 8 | | 11 | | 5 | | 36 |
| | 2 | | | | | | | | | | | 4 | | 10 | | | 9 | | | | 1 | 7 | 3 | 5 | 6 | 8 | 11 | | | | 37 |
| | 2 | | | | | | | | | | 6 | | | | | | 7 | 9 | | 1 | | 11 | 3 | 5 | 4 | 8 | 10 | | | | 38 |
| | 2 | | | | | | | | | | | 4 | | | | | 7 | 9 | | | 1 | 11 | 3 | 5 | 6 | 8 | 10 | | | | 39 |
| | 2 | | | | | | | | 10 | | 6 | 4 | | | | | 7 | 9 | | 1 | | 11 | 3 | 5 | 8 | | | | | | 40 |
| | 2 | | | | | | | | | | 6 | | | 10 | | | 7 | 9 | | | 1 | 11 | 3 | 5 | 4 | 8 | | | | | 41 |
| | 2 | | | | | | | | 10 | | | 4 | | | | | 9 | 7 | 11 | | 1 | 3 | 5 | 6 | 8 | | | | | | 42 |
| 20 | 42 | 26 | 24 | 18 | 26 | 20 | 20 | 25 | 22 | 21 | 7 | 16 | 1 | 21 | 10 | 1 | 12 | 20 | 9 | 3 | 19 | 13 | 12 | 13 | 11 | 11 | 8 | 5 | 5 | 1 | |
| | | | | | 6 | 4 | 12 | 16 | 16 | 4 | | | 1 | 8 | | | 5 | 6 | 3 | | | | | | | 2 | | | | | |

2 own-goals

# 1958-59

Manager: Matt Busby

| 1 | Aug | 23 | (h) | Chelsea | W | 5-2 | Charlton 3, Dawson 2 | 52,382 |
|---|---|---|---|---|---|---|---|---|
| 2 | | 27 | (a) | Nottingham F | W | 3-0 | Charlton 2, Scanlon | 44,971 |
| 3 | | 30 | (a) | Blackpool | L | 1-2 | Viollet | 36,719 |
| 4 | Sep | 3 | (h) | Nottingham F | D | 1-1 | Charlton | 51,880 |
| 5 | | 6 | (h) | Blackburn R | W | 6-1 | Charlton 2, Viollet 2, Scanlon, Webster | 65,187 |
| 6 | | 8 | (a) | West Ham U | L | 2-3 | McGuinness, Webster | 35,672 |
| 7 | | 13 | (a) | Newcastle U | D | 1-1 | Charlton | 60,670 |
| 8 | | 17 | (h) | West Ham U | W | 4-1 | Scanlon 3, Webster | 53,276 |
| 9 | | 20 | (h) | Tottenham H | D | 2-2 | Webster 2 | 62,277 |
| 10 | | 27 | (a) | Manchester C | D | 1-1 | Charlton | 62,912 |
| 11 | Oct | 4 | (a) | Wolves | L | 0-4 | | 36,840 |
| 12 | | 8 | (h) | Preston NE | L | 0-2 | | 46,163 |
| 13 | | 11 | (h) | Arsenal | D | 1-1 | Viollet | 56,148 |
| 14 | | 18 | (a) | Everton | L | 2-3 | Cope 2 | 64,079 |
| 15 | | 25 | (h) | West Brom A | L | 1-2 | Goodwin | 51,721 |
| 16 | Nov | 1 | (a) | Leeds U | W | 2-1 | Goodwin, Scanlon | 48,574 |
| 17 | | 8 | (h) | Burnley | L | 1-3 | Quixall | 48,509 |
| 18 | | 15 | (a) | Bolton W | L | 3-6 | Dawson 2, Charlton | 33,358 |
| 19 | | 22 | (h) | Luton T | W | 2-1 | Charlton, Viollet | 42,428 |
| 20 | | 29 | (a) | Birmingham C | W | 4-0 | Charlton 2, Bradley, Scanlon | 28,658 |
| 21 | Dec | 6 | (h) | Leicester C | W | 4-1 | Bradley, Charlton, Scanlon, Viollet | 38,482 |
| 22 | | 13 | (a) | Preston NE | W | 4-3 | Bradley, Charlton, Scanlon, Viollet | 26,290 |
| 23 | | 20 | (a) | Chelsea | W | 3-2 | Charlton, Goodwin, Scott (og) | 48,550 |
| 24 | | 26 | (h) | Aston Villa | W | 2-1 | Quixall, Viollet | 63,098 |
| 25 | | 27 | (a) | Aston Villa | W | 2-0 | Pearson, Viollet | 56,450 |
| 26 | Jan | 3 | (h) | Blackpool | W | 3-1 | Charlton 2, Viollet | 61,961 |
| 27 | | 31 | (h) | Newcastle U | D | 4-4 | Charlton, Scanlon, Quixall, Viollet | 49,008 |
| 28 | Feb | 7 | (a) | Tottenham H | W | 3-1 | Charlton 2, Scanlon | 48,401 |
| 29 | | 16 | (h) | Manchester C | W | 4-1 | Bradley 2, Goodwin, Scanlon | 59,846 |
| 30 | | 21 | (h) | Wolves | W | 2-1 | Charlton, Viollet | 62,794 |
| 31 | | 28 | (a) | Arsenal | L | 2-3 | Bradley, Viollet | 67,162 |
| 32 | Mar | 2 | (a) | Blackburn R | W | 3-1 | Bradley 2, Scanlon | 40,401 |
| 33 | | 7 | (h) | Everton | W | 2-1 | Goodwin, Scanlon | 51,254 |
| 34 | | 14 | (a) | West Brom A | W | 3-1 | Bradley, Scanlon, Viollet | 35,463 |
| 35 | | 21 | (h) | Leeds U | W | 4-0 | Viollet 3, Charlton | 45,473 |
| 36 | | 27 | (h) | Portsmouth | W | 6-1 | Charlton 2, Viollet 2, Bradley, Hayward (og) | 52,004 |
| 37 | | 28 | (a) | Burnley | L | 2-4 | Goodwin, Viollet | 44,577 |
| 38 | | 30 | (a) | Portsmouth | W | 3-1 | Charlton 2, Bradley | 29,359 |
| 39 | Apr | 4 | (h) | Bolton W | W | 3-0 | Charlton, Scanlon, Viollet | 61,528 |
| 40 | | 11 | (a) | Luton T | D | 0-0 | | 27,025 |
| 41 | | 18 | (h) | Birmingham C | W | 1-0 | Quixall | 43,006 |
| 42 | | 25 | (a) | Leicester C | L | 1-2 | Bradley | 38,466 |

FINAL LEAGUE POSITION: 2nd in Division One    Appearances

Goals

FA Cup

3  Jan   10  (a)  Norwich C        L  0-3

294

| Gregg | Foulkes | Greaves | Goodwin | Cope | McGuinness | Dawson | Taylor E | Viollet | Charlton | Scanlon | Webster | Crowther | Quixall | Wood | Harrop | Pearson | Morgans | Bradley | Carolan | Hunter | Brennan | |
|---|---|---|---|---|---|---|---|---|---|---|---|---|---|---|---|---|---|---|---|---|---|---|
| 1 | 2 | 3 | 4 | 5 | 6 | 7 | 8 | 9 | 10 | 11 | | | | | | | | | | | | 1 |
| 1 | 2 | 3 | 4 | 5 | 6 | 7 | 8 | 9 | 10 | 11 | | | | | | | | | | | | 2 |
| 1 | 2 | 3 | 4 | 5 | 6 | 7 | 8 | 9 | 10 | 11 | | | | | | | | | | | | 3 |
| 1 | 2 | 3 | 4 | 5 | 6 | 7 | 8 | 9 | 10 | 11 | | | | | | | | | | | | 4 |
| 1 | 2 | 3 | 4 | 5 | 6 | | 8 | 9 | 10 | 11 | 7 | | | | | | | | | | | 5 |
| 1 | 2 | 3 | 4 | 5 | 6 | | 8 | 9 | 10 | 11 | 7 | | | | | | | | | | | 6 |
| 1 | 2 | 3 | 4 | 5 | | 9 | 8 | | 10 | 11 | 7 | 6 | | | | | | | | | | 7 |
| 1 | 2 | 3 | 4 | 5 | 6 | | 8 | 9 | 10 | 11 | 7 | | | | | | | | | | | 8 |
| 1 | 2 | 3 | 4 | 5 | 6 | 9 | | | 10 | 11 | 7 | | 8 | | | | | | | | | 9 |
| 1 | 2 | 3 | 4 | 5 | 6 | 7 | | | 10 | 11 | 9 | | 8 | | | | | | | | | 10 |
| | 2 | 3 | 4 | | | | | 7 | | 11 | 9 | 6 | 8 | 1 | 5 | 10 | | | | | | 11 |
| 1 | 2 | 3 | 4 | 5 | 6 | 7 | 8 | 9 | 10 | 11 | | | | | | | | | | | | 12 |
| 1 | 2 | 3 | 4 | 5 | 6 | | 10 | 7 | 9 | 11 | | | 8 | | | | | | | | | 13 |
| 1 | 2 | 3 | 4 | 5 | 6 | | 10 | 7 | 9 | 11 | | | 8 | | | | | | | | | 14 |
| 1 | 2 | 3 | 4 | | 6 | 9 | | 7 | 10 | 11 | | | 8 | | 5 | | | | | | | 15 |
| 1 | 2 | 3 | 4 | | 6 | 9 | | | 10 | 11 | | | 8 | | 5 | | 7 | | | | | 16 |
| 1 | 2 | 3 | 4 | | 6 | 9 | | | 10 | 11 | | | 8 | | 5 | | 7 | | | | | 17 |
| 1 | 2 | 3 | 4 | 5 | 6 | 9 | | | 10 | 11 | | | 8 | | | | | 7 | | | | 18 |
| 1 | 2 | | 4 | 5 | 6 | | | 9 | 10 | 11 | | | 8 | | | | | 7 | 3 | | | 19 |
| 1 | 2 | | 4 | 5 | 6 | | | 9 | 10 | 11 | | | 8 | | | | | 7 | 3 | | | 20 |
| 1 | 2 | | 4 | 5 | 6 | | | 9 | 10 | 11 | | | 8 | | | | | 7 | 3 | | | 21 |
| 1 | 2 | | 4 | 5 | 6 | | | 9 | 10 | 11 | | | 8 | | | | | 7 | 3 | | | 22 |
| 1 | 2 | | 4 | 5 | 6 | | | 9 | 10 | 11 | | | 8 | | | | | 7 | 3 | | | 23 |
| 1 | 2 | | 4 | 5 | 6 | | | 9 | | 11 | | | 8 | | | 10 | | 7 | 3 | | | 24 |
| 1 | 2 | 3 | 4 | 5 | 6 | | | 9 | | 11 | | | 8 | | | 10 | | | 7 | | | 25 |
| 1 | 2 | | 4 | 5 | 6 | | | 9 | 10 | 11 | | | 8 | | | | | 7 | 3 | | | 26 |
| 1 | 2 | | 5 | | 6 | | | 9 | 10 | 11 | | | 8 | | 4 | | | 7 | 3 | | | 27 |
| 1 | | 2 | 4 | 5 | 6 | | | 9 | 10 | 11 | | | 8 | | | | | 7 | 3 | | | 28 |
| 1 | | 2 | 4 | 5 | 6 | | | 9 | 10 | 11 | | | 8 | | | | | 7 | 3 | | | 29 |
| 1 | | 2 | 4 | 5 | 6 | | | 9 | 10 | 11 | | | 8 | | | | | 7 | 3 | | | 30 |
| 1 | | 2 | 4 | 5 | 6 | | | 9 | 10 | 11 | | | 8 | | | | | 7 | 3 | | | 31 |
| 1 | | 2 | 4 | 5 | 6 | | | 9 | 10 | 11 | | | 8 | | | | | 7 | 3 | | | 32 |
| 1 | | 2 | 4 | 5 | 6 | | | 9 | 10 | 11 | | | 8 | | | | | 7 | 3 | | | 33 |
| 1 | | 2 | 4 | 5 | 6 | | | 9 | 10 | 11 | | | 8 | | | | | 7 | 3 | | | 34 |
| 1 | | 2 | 4 | 5 | 6 | | | 9 | 10 | 11 | | | 8 | | | | | 7 | 3 | | | 35 |
| 1 | | 2 | 4 | 5 | 6 | | | 9 | 10 | 11 | | | 8 | | | | | 7 | 3 | | | 36 |
| 1 | | 2 | 4 | 5 | 6 | | | 9 | 10 | 11 | | | 8 | | | | | 7 | 3 | | | 37 |
| 1 | 5 | 2 | 4 | | 6 | | | 9 | 10 | 11 | | | 8 | | | | | 7 | 3 | | | 38 |
| 1 | 5 | 2 | 4 | | 6 | | | 9 | 10 | 11 | | | 8 | | | | | 7 | 3 | | | 39 |
| 1 | 5 | 2 | 4 | | 6 | | | 9 | | 11 | | | 8 | | | 10 | | 7 | 3 | | | 40 |
| 1 | 5 | 2 | 4 | | 6 | | | 9 | 10 | 11 | | | 8 | | | | | 7 | 3 | | | 41 |
| 1 | 5 | 2 | 4 | | | | | 9 | 10 | 11 | | | 8 | | | | | 7 | 3 | 6 | | 42 |
| 41 | 32 | 34 | 42 | 32 | 39 | 11 | 11 | 37 | 38 | 42 | 7 | 2 | 33 | 1 | 5 | 4 | 2 | 24 | 23 | 1 | 1 | |
| | | 6 | 2 | 1 | 4 | | 21 | 29 | 16 | 5 | | 4 | | | 1 | | | 12 | | | | |

2 own-goals

# 1959-60

Manager: Matt Busby

| | | | | | | | |
|---|---|---|---|---|---|---|---|
| 1 | Aug | 22 | (a) | West Brom A | L | 2-3 | Viollet 2 | 40,076 |
| 2 | | 26 | (h) | Chelsea | L | 0-1 | | 57,674 |
| 3 | | 29 | (h) | Newcastle U | W | 3-2 | Viollet 2, Charlton | 53,257 |
| 4 | Sep | 2 | (a) | Chelsea | W | 6-3 | Bradley 2, Viollet 2, Charlton, Quixall | 66,579 |
| 5 | | 5 | (a) | Birmingham C | D | 1-1 | Quixall | 38,220 |
| 6 | | 9 | (h) | Leeds U | W | 6-0 | Bradley 2, Charlton 2, Scanlon, Viollet | 48,407 |
| 7 | | 12 | (h) | Tottenham H | L | 1-5 | Viollet | 55,402 |
| 8 | | 16 | (a) | Leeds U | D | 2-2 | Charlton Opp own-goal | 34,048 |
| 9 | | 19 | (a) | Manchester C | L | 0-3 | | 58,300 |
| 10 | | 26 | (a) | Preston NE | L | 0-4 | | 35,016 |
| 11 | Oct | 3 | (h) | Leicester C | W | 4-1 | Viollet 2, Charlton, Quixall | 41,637 |
| 12 | | 10 | (h) | Arsenal | W | 4-2 | Charlton, Quixall, Viollet, Opp own-goal | 51,626 |
| 13 | | 17 | (a) | Wolves | L | 2-3 | Viollet, Opp own-goal | 45,451 |
| 14 | | 24 | (h) | Sheffield W | W | 3-1 | Viollet 2, Bradley | 39,259 |
| 15 | | 31 | (a) | Blackburn R | D | 1-1 | Quixall | 39,621 |
| 16 | Nov | 7 | (h) | Fulham | D | 3-3 | Charlton, Scanlon, Viollet | 44,063 |
| 17 | | 14 | (a) | Bolton W | D | 1-1 | Dawson | 37,892 |
| 18 | | 21 | (h) | Luton T | W | 4-1 | Viollet 2, Goodwin, Quixall | 40,572 |
| 19 | | 28 | (a) | Everton | L | 1-2 | Viollet | 46,095 |
| 20 | Dec | 5 | (h) | Blackpool | W | 3-1 | Viollet 2, Pearson | 45,558 |
| 21 | | 12 | (a) | Nottingham F | W | 5-1 | Viollet 3, Dawson, Scanlon | 31,666 |
| 22 | | 19 | (a) | West Brom A | L | 2-3 | Dawson, Quixall | 33,677 |
| 23 | | 26 | (h) | Burnley | L | 1-2 | Quixall | 62,376 |
| 24 | | 28 | (a) | Burnley | W | 4-1 | Scanlon 2, Viollet 2 | 47,253 |
| 25 | Jan | 2 | (a) | Newcastle U | L | 3-7 | Quixall 2, Dawson | 57,200 |
| 26 | | 16 | (h) | Birmingham C | W | 2-1 | Quixall, Viollet | 47,361 |
| 27 | | 23 | (a) | Tottenham H | L | 1-2 | Bradley | 62,602 |
| 28 | Feb | 6 | (h) | Manchester C | D | 0-0 | | 59,450 |
| 29 | | 13 | (h) | Preston NE | D | 1-1 | Viollet | 44,014 |
| 30 | | 24 | (a) | Leicester C | L | 1-3 | Scanlon | 33,191 |
| 31 | | 27 | (a) | Blackpool | W | 6-0 | Charlton 3, Viollet 2, Scanlon | 23,996 |
| 32 | Mar | 5 | (h) | Wolves | L | 0-2 | | 60,560 |
| 33 | | 19 | (h) | Nottingham F | W | 3-1 | Charlton 2, Dawson | 35,269 |
| 34 | | 26 | (a) | Fulham | W | 5-0 | Viollet 2, Dawson, Giles, Pearson | 38,250 |
| 35 | | 30 | (a) | Sheffield W | L | 2-4 | Charlton, Viollet | 26,821 |
| 36 | Apr | 2 | (h) | Bolton W | W | 2-0 | Charlton 2 | 45,298 |
| 37 | | 9 | (a) | Luton T | W | 3-2 | Dawson 2, Bradley | 21,242 |
| 38 | | 15 | (a) | West Ham U | L | 1-2 | Dawson | 34,969 |
| 39 | | 16 | (h) | Blackburn R | W | 1-0 | Dawson | 45,945 |
| 40 | | 18 | (h) | West Ham U | W | 5-3 | Charlton 2, Dawson 2, Quixall | 34,676 |
| 41 | | 23 | (a) | Arsenal | L | 2-5 | Giles, Pearson | 41,057 |
| 42 | | 30 | (h) | Everton | W | 5-0 | Dawson 3, Bradley, Quixall | 43,823 |

FINAL LEAGUE POSITION: 7th in Division One

Appearances
Goals

FA Cup

| | | | | | | |
|---|---|---|---|---|---|---|
| 3 | Jan | 9 | (a) | Derby C | W | 4-2 |
| 4 | | 30 | (a) | Liverpool | W | 3-1 |
| 5 | Feb | 20 | (h) | Sheffield W | L | 0-1 |

| Gregg | Greaves | Carolan | Goodwin | Foulkes | McGuinness | Bradley | Quixall | Viollet | Charlton | Scanlon | Dawson | Cope | Brennan | Giles | Gaskell | Pearson | Setters | Heron | Lawton | |
|---|---|---|---|---|---|---|---|---|---|---|---|---|---|---|---|---|---|---|---|---|
| 1 | 2 | 3 | 4 | 5 | 6 | 7 | 8 | 9 | 10 | 11 |  |  |  |  |  |  |  |  |  | 1 |
| 1 | 2 | 3 | 4 | 5 | 6 | 7 | 8 | 10 | 11 |  | 9 |  |  |  |  |  |  |  |  | 2 |
| 1 |  | 3 |  | 5 | 6 | 7 | 8 | 9 | 10 | 11 |  | 2 | 4 |  |  |  |  |  |  | 3 |
| 1 |  | 3 |  | 5 | 6 | 7 | 8 | 9 | 10 | 11 |  | 2 | 4 |  |  |  |  |  |  | 4 |
| 1 |  | 3 |  | 5 | 6 | 7 | 8 | 9 | 10 | 11 |  | 2 | 4 |  |  |  |  |  |  | 5 |
| 1 |  | 3 |  | 5 | 6 | 7 | 8 | 9 | 10 | 11 |  | 2 | 4 |  |  |  |  |  |  | 6 |
| 1 |  | 3 | 4 | 5 | 6 | 7 |  | 9 | 10 | 11 |  | 2 |  | 8 |  |  |  |  |  | 7 |
| 1 |  | 3 |  | 5 | 6 | 7 | 8 | 9 | 10 | 11 |  | 2 | 4 |  |  |  |  |  |  | 8 |
| 1 |  | 3 |  | 2 | 6 | 7 | 8 | 9 | 10 | 11 |  | 5 | 4 |  |  |  |  |  |  | 9 |
| 1 |  | 3 |  | 2 | 6 | 7 | 8 | 4 | 10 | 11 | 9 | 5 |  |  |  |  |  |  |  | 10 |
|  |  | 3 | 4 | 2 | 6 | 7 | 8 | 9 | 10 | 11 |  | 5 |  |  | 1 |  |  |  |  | 11 |
| 1 |  | 3 | 4 | 2 | 6 | 7 | 8 | 9 | 10 | 11 |  | 5 |  |  |  |  |  |  |  | 12 |
| 1 |  | 3 | 4 | 2 | 6 | 7 |  | 9 |  | 11 |  | 5 |  | 8 |  | 10 |  |  |  | 13 |
| 1 |  | 3 | 4 | 2 | 6 | 7 | 8 | 9 | 10 | 11 |  | 5 |  |  |  |  |  |  |  | 14 |
| 1 |  | 3 | 4 | 2 | 6 | 7 | 8 | 9 | 10 | 11 |  | 5 |  |  |  |  |  |  |  | 15 |
| 1 |  | 3 | 4 | 2 | 6 | 7 | 8 | 9 | 10 | 11 |  | 5 |  |  |  |  |  |  |  | 16 |
| 1 |  | 3 | 4 | 2 | 6 | 7 | 8 | 9 | 10 |  | 11 | 5 |  |  |  |  |  |  |  | 17 |
| 1 |  | 3 | 4 | 2 | 6 | 7 | 8 | 9 | 10 | 11 |  | 5 |  |  |  |  |  |  |  | 18 |
| 1 |  | 3 | 4 | 2 | 6 | 7 | 8 | 9 | 10 | 11 |  | 5 |  |  |  |  |  |  |  | 19 |
|  |  | 3 | 4 | 2 |  |  | 8 | 9 |  | 11 | 7 | 5 | 6 |  | 1 | 10 |  |  |  | 20 |
|  |  | 3 | 4 | 2 |  |  | 8 | 9 |  | 11 | 7 | 5 | 6 |  | 1 | 10 |  |  |  | 21 |
|  |  | 3 | 4 | 2 |  |  | 8 | 9 |  | 11 | 7 | 5 | 6 |  | 1 | 10 |  |  |  | 22 |
|  |  | 3 | 4 | 2 |  |  | 8 | 9 | 10 | 11 | 7 | 5 | 6 |  | 1 |  |  |  |  | 23 |
|  |  | 3 | 4 | 2 |  |  | 8 | 9 | 10 | 11 | 7 | 5 | 6 |  | 1 |  |  |  |  | 24 |
|  |  | 3 | 4 | 2 |  |  | 8 | 9 | 10 | 11 | 7 | 5 | 6 |  | 1 |  |  |  |  | 25 |
| 1 |  | 3 |  | 2 |  | 7 | 8 | 9 | 10 | 11 |  | 5 | 6 |  |  |  | 4 |  |  | 26 |
| 1 |  | 3 |  | 2 |  | 7 | 8 | 9 | 10 | 11 |  | 5 | 6 |  |  |  | 4 |  |  | 27 |
| 1 |  | 3 |  | 2 |  | 7 | 8 | 9 | 10 | 11 |  | 5 | 6 |  |  |  | 4 |  |  | 28 |
| 1 |  | 3 |  | 2 |  | 7 | 8 | 9 | 10 | 11 |  | 5 | 6 |  |  |  | 4 |  |  | 29 |
| 1 |  | 3 |  | 2 |  |  | 8 | 7 | 10 | 11 | 9 | 5 | 6 |  |  |  | 4 |  |  | 30 |
| 1 |  | 3 |  | 2 |  |  | 8 | 7 | 10 | 11 | 9 | 5 | 6 |  |  |  | 4 |  |  | 31 |
| 1 |  | 3 |  | 2 |  |  | 8 | 7 | 10 | 11 | 9 | 5 | 6 |  |  |  | 4 |  |  | 32 |
| 1 |  | 3 |  | 2 |  |  | 8 |  |  | 11 | 9 | 5 | 6 | 7 |  | 10 | 4 |  |  | 33 |
| 1 |  | 3 |  | 2 |  |  | 8 |  |  | 11 | 9 | 5 | 6 | 7 |  | 10 | 4 |  |  | 34 |
|  |  |  |  | 2 |  | 7 |  | 9 |  | 11 |  | 5 | 6 | 8 | 1 | 10 | 4 | 3 |  | 35 |
|  |  | 3 |  | 2 |  | 7 |  | 9 |  | 11 |  | 5 | 6 | 8 | 1 | 10 | 4 |  |  | 36 |
| 1 |  | 3 |  | 2 |  | 7 |  |  |  | 11 | 9 | 5 | 6 | 8 |  | 10 | 4 |  |  | 37 |
| 1 |  | 3 |  | 2 |  | 7 |  |  |  | 11 | 9 | 5 | 6 | 8 |  | 10 | 4 |  |  | 38 |
| 1 |  | 3 |  | 2 |  | 7 |  |  |  | 11 | 9 | 5 | 6 | 8 |  | 10 | 4 |  |  | 39 |
| 1 |  | 3 |  | 2 |  |  | 8 |  | 10 | 11 | 9 | 5 | 6 | 7 |  |  | 4 |  |  | 40 |
| 1 |  | 3 |  | 2 |  |  | 8 |  |  | 11 | 9 | 5 | 6 |  |  | 10 | 4 |  |  | 41 |
| 1 |  | 3 |  | 2 |  | 7 | 8 |  |  | 11 | 9 | 5 | 6 |  |  | 10 | 4 |  |  | 42 |
| 33 | 2 | 41 | 18 | 42 | 19 | 29 | 33 | 36 | 37 | 31 | 22 | 40 | 29 | 10 | 9 | 10 | 17 | 1 | 3 | |
|  |  |  | 1 |  |  | 8 | 13 | 32 | 18 | 7 | 15 |  | 2 |  |  | 3 |  |  |  | |

3 own-goals

# 1960-61

Manager: Matt Busby

| | | | | | | | | | |
|---|---|---|---|---|---|---|---|---|---|
| 1 | Aug | 20 | (h) | Blackburn R | L | 1-3 | Charlton | | 47,778 |
| 2 | | 24 | (a) | Everton | L | 0-4 | | | 51,602 |
| 3 | | 31 | (h) | Everton | W | 4-0 | Dawson 2, Charlton, Nicholson | | 51,818 |
| 4 | Sep | 3 | (a) | Tottenham H | L | 1-4 | Viollet | | 55,445 |
| 5 | | 5 | (a) | West Ham U | L | 1-2 | Quixall | | 30,506 |
| 6 | | 10 | (h) | Leicester C | D | 1-1 | Giles | | 35,493 |
| 7 | | 14 | (h) | West Ham U | W | 6-1 | Charlton 2, Viollet 2, Quixall, Scanlon | | 33,695 |
| 8 | | 17 | (a) | Aston Villa | L | 1-3 | Viollet | | 43,593 |
| 9 | | 24 | (h) | Wolves | L | 1-3 | Charlton | | 44,458 |
| 10 | Oct | 1 | (a) | Bolton W | D | 1-1 | Giles | | 39,197 |
| 11 | | 15 | (a) | Burnley | L | 3-5 | Viollet 3 | | 32,011 |
| 12 | | 22 | (h) | Newcastle U | W | 3-2 | Dawson, Setters, Stiles | | 37,516 |
| 13 | | 24 | (h) | Nottingham F | W | 2-1 | Viollet 2 | | 23,628 |
| 14 | | 29 | (a) | Arsenal | L | 1-2 | Quixall | | 45,715 |
| 15 | Nov | 5 | (h) | Sheffield W | D | 0-0 | | | 36,855 |
| 16 | | 12 | (a) | Birmingham C | L | 1-3 | Charlton | | 31,549 |
| 17 | | 19 | (h) | West Brom A | W | 3-0 | Dawson, Quixall, Viollet | | 32,756 |
| 18 | | 26 | (a) | Cardiff C | L | 0-3 | | | 21,122 |
| 19 | Dec | 3 | (h) | Preston NE | W | 1-0 | Dawson | | 24,904 |
| 20 | | 10 | (a) | Fulham | D | 4-4 | Quixall 2, Charlton, Dawson | | 23,625 |
| 21 | | 17 | (a) | Blackburn R | W | 2-1 | Pearson 2 | | 17,285 |
| 22 | | 24 | (a) | Chelsea | W | 2-1 | Dawson, Charlton | | 37,601 |
| 23 | | 26 | (h) | Chelsea | W | 6-0 | Dawson 3, Nicholson 2, Charlton | | 50,164 |
| 24 | | 31 | (h) | Manchester C | W | 5-1 | Dawson 3, Charlton 2 | | 61,213 |
| 25 | Jan | 14 | (h) | Tottenham H | W | 2-0 | Pearson, Stiles | | 65,295 |
| 26 | | 21 | (a) | Leicester C | L | 0-6 | | | 31,308 |
| 27 | Feb | 4 | (h) | Aston Villa | D | 1-1 | Charlton | | 33,525 |
| 28 | | 11 | (a) | Wolves | L | 1-2 | Nicholson | | 38,526 |
| 29 | | 18 | (h) | Bolton W | W | 3-1 | Dawson 2, Quixall | | 37,558 |
| 30 | | 25 | (a) | Nottingham F | L | 2-3 | Charlton, Quixall | | 26,850 |
| 31 | Mar | 4 | (a) | Manchester C | W | 3-1 | Charlton, Dawson, Pearson | | 50,479 |
| 32 | | 11 | (a) | Newcastle U | D | 1-1 | Charlton | | 28,870 |
| 33 | | 18 | (h) | Arsenal | D | 1-1 | Moir | | 29,732 |
| 34 | | 25 | (a) | Sheffield W | L | 1-5 | Charlton | | 35,901 |
| 35 | | 31 | (h) | Blackpool | L | 0-2 | | | 30,835 |
| 36 | Apr | 1 | (h) | Fulham | W | 3-1 | Charlton, Quixall, Viollet | | 24,654 |
| 37 | | 3 | (h) | Blackpool | W | 2-0 | Nicholson, Opp own-goal | | 39,169 |
| 38 | | 8 | (a) | West Brom A | D | 1-1 | Pearson | | 27,750 |
| 39 | | 12 | (h) | Burnley | W | 6-0 | Quixall 3, Viollet 3 | | 25,019 |
| 40 | | 15 | (h) | Birmingham C | W | 4-1 | Pearson 2, Quixall, Viollet | | 28,376 |
| 41 | | 22 | (a) | Preston NE | W | 4-2 | Charlton 2, Setters 2 | | 21,252 |
| 42 | | 29 | (h) | Cardiff C | D | 3-3 | Charlton 2, Setters | | 30,320 |

FINAL LEAGUE POSITION: 7th in Division One

Appearances
Goals

## FA Cup

| | | | | | | |
|---|---|---|---|---|---|---|
| 3 | Jan | 7 | (h) | Middlesbrough | W | 3-0 |
| 4 | | 28 | (a) | Sheffield W | D | 1-1 |
| R | Feb | 1 | (h) | Sheffield W | L | 2-7 |

## League Cup

| | | | | | | |
|---|---|---|---|---|---|---|
| 1 | Oct | 19 | (a) | Exeter C | D | 1-1 |
| R | | 26 | (h) | Exeter C | W | 4-1 |
| 2 | Nov | 2 | (a) | Bradford C | L | 1-2 |

| Gregg | Cope | Carolan | Setters | Haydock | Brennan | Giles | Quixall | Viollet | Charlton | Scanlon | Nicholson | Foulkes | Dawson | Stiles | Moir | Dunne | Pearson | Heron | Bradley | Cantwell | Briggs | Pinner | Morgans | Lawton | Gaskell | |
|---|---|---|---|---|---|---|---|---|---|---|---|---|---|---|---|---|---|---|---|---|---|---|---|---|---|---|
| 1 | 2 | 3 | 4 | 5 | 6 | 7 | 8 | 9 | 10 | 11 | | | | | | | | | | | | | | | | 1 |
| 1 | | 3 | 4 | 5 | 2 | 7 | 8 | 9 | 10 | 11 | 6 | | | | | | | | | | | | | | | 2 |
| 1 | | | 4 | 5 | 3 | 8 | 7 | 10 | 11 | | 6 | 2 | 9 | | | | | | | | | | | | | 3 |
| 1 | | | 4 | 5 | 3 | 8 | 7 | 10 | 11 | | 6 | 2 | 9 | | | | | | | | | | | | | 4 |
| 1 | 5 | | 4 | | 3 | 8 | 7 | 10 | 11 | | 6 | 2 | 9 | | | | | | | | | | | | | 5 |
| 1 | 5 | | 4 | | 3 | 8 | 7 | 10 | 11 | | 6 | 2 | 9 | | | | | | | | | | | | | 6 |
| 1 | 5 | | 4 | | 3 | 8 | 7 | 9 | 10 | 11 | 6 | 2 | | | | | | | | | | | | | | 7 |
| 1 | 5 | | 4 | | 3 | 7 | 8 | 9 | 10 | 11 | 6 | 2 | | | | | | | | | | | | | | 8 |
| 1 | 5 | | 4 | | 3 | 7 | 8 | 9 | 10 | 11 | 6 | 2 | | | | | | | | | | | | | | 9 |
| 1 | 2 | | | | 3 | | 8 | 10 | 11 | | 6 | 5 | 9 | 4 | 7 | | | | | | | | | | | 10 |
| 1 | 2 | | | | | 8 | 7 | 9 | 11 | | 6 | 5 | | 4 | | 3 | 10 | | | | | | | | | 11 |
| 1 | 2 | | | | 3 | 8 | | 9 | 11 | | 6 | 5 | | 4 | 7 | | 10 | | | | | | | | | 12 |
| 1 | | | | | 3 | 8 | | 9 | 11 | | 6 | 5 | | 4 | 7 | 2 | 10 | | | | | | | | | 13 |
| 1 | 2 | | | | | 8 | 10 | 9 | 11 | | 6 | 5 | | 4 | 7 | 3 | | | | | | | | | | 14 |
| 1 | 2 | | | | 3 | 8 | 10 | 9 | 11 | | 6 | 5 | | 4 | 7 | | | | | | | | | | | 15 |
| 1 | 2 | | | | 3 | 8 | | 9 | 11 | | 6 | 5 | | 4 | 7 | | 10 | | | | | | | | | 16 |
| 1 | 2 | | | | 3 | | 8 | 10 | 11 | | 6 | 5 | 9 | 4 | 7 | | | | | | | | | | | 17 |
| 1 | | | 4 | | 2 | | 8 | 10 | 11 | | 6 | 5 | 9 | | 7 | | | | | 3 | | | | | | 18 |
| 1 | | | 4 | | 2 | | 8 | | 11 | | 6 | 5 | 9 | | | | 10 | | 7 | 3 | | | | | | 19 |
| 1 | | | 4 | | 2 | | 8 | | 11 | | 6 | 5 | 9 | | | | 10 | | 7 | 3 | | | | | | 20 |
| 1 | | | 4 | | 2 | | 7 | | 11 | | 6 | 5 | 9 | 8 | | | 10 | | | 3 | | | | | | 21 |
| 1 | | | 4 | | 2 | | 7 | | 11 | | 6 | 5 | 9 | 8 | | | 10 | | | 3 | | | | | | 22 |
| 1 | | | 4 | | 2 | | 7 | | 11 | | 6 | 5 | 9 | 8 | | | 10 | | | 3 | | | | | | 23 |
| 1 | | | 4 | | 2 | | 7 | | 11 | | 6 | 5 | 9 | 8 | | | 10 | | | 3 | | | | | | 24 |
| 1 | | | 4 | | 2 | | 7 | | 11 | | 6 | 5 | 9 | 8 | | | 10 | | | 3 | | | | | | 25 |
| | | | 4 | | 2 | | 7 | | 11 | | 6 | 5 | 9 | 8 | | | 10 | | | 3 | | 1 | | | | 26 |
| | | | 4 | | 2 | | 7 | | 11 | | 6 | 5 | 9 | 8 | | | 10 | | | 3 | 1 | | | | | 27 |
| | | | 4 | | 2 | | 7 | | 11 | | 6 | 5 | 9 | 8 | | | 10 | | | 3 | 1 | | | | | 28 |
| | | | 6 | | 2 | | 8 | | 11 | | | 5 | 9 | 4 | | | 10 | | | 3 | 1 | 7 | | | | 29 |
| 1 | | | 4 | | 2 | | 8 | | 11 | | 6 | 5 | 9 | | | | 10 | | | 3 | | | 7 | | | 30 |
| 1 | | | 4 | | 2 | | 8 | | 11 | | 6 | 5 | 9 | | 7 | | 10 | | | 3 | | | | | | 31 |
| | | | 4 | | 2 | | 8 | | 11 | | 6 | 5 | | | 7 | | 10 | | | 3 | 1 | | | 9 | | 32 |
| | | | 4 | | 2 | | 8 | | 11 | | 6 | 5 | 9 | | 7 | | 10 | | | 3 | | | | | 1 | 33 |
| | | | 4 | | 2 | | 8 | | 11 | | 6 | 5 | 9 | | 7 | | 10 | | | 3 | | | | | 1 | 34 |
| | | | 4 | | 2 | | 8 | | 11 | | 6 | 5 | 9 | | 7 | | 10 | | | 3 | | | | | 1 | 35 |
| | | | 4 | | 2 | 7 | 8 | | 11 | | 6 | 5 | 9 | | | | 10 | | | 3 | | | | | 1 | 36 |
| | | | 4 | | 2 | 7 | 8 | | 11 | | 6 | 5 | 9 | | | | 10 | | | 3 | | | | | 1 | 37 |
| | | | 4 | | 2 | 7 | 8 | | 11 | | 6 | 5 | 9 | | | | 10 | | | 3 | | | | | 1 | 38 |
| | | | 4 | | 2 | 7 | 8 | | 11 | | 6 | 5 | 9 | | | | 10 | | | 3 | | | | | 1 | 39 |
| | | | 4 | | 2 | 7 | 8 | | 11 | | 6 | 5 | 9 | | | | 10 | | | 3 | | | | | 1 | 40 |
| | | | 4 | | 3 | 7 | 8 | | 11 | | 6 | 5 | 9 | | | | 10 | | | 2 | | | | | 1 | 41 |
| | | | 4 | | 2 | 7 | 8 | | 11 | | 6 | 5 | 9 | | | | 10 | | | 3 | | | | | 1 | 42 |
| 27 | 6 | 2 | 40 | 4 | 41 | 23 | 38 | 24 | 39 | 8 | 31 | 40 | 28 | 26 | 8 | 3 | 27 | 1 | 4 | 24 | 1 | 4 | 2 | 1 | 10 | |
| | | | 4 | | | 2 | 13 | 15 | 21 | 1 | 5 | | 16 | 2 | 1 | | 7 | | | | | | | | | |

1 own-goal

# 1961-62

Manager: Matt Busby

| | | | | | | | | |
|---|---|---|---|---|---|---|---|---|
| 1 | Aug | 19 | (a) | West Ham U | D | 1-1 | Stiles | 32,628 |
| 2 | | 23 | (h) | Chelsea | W | 3-2 | Herd, Pearson, Viollet | 45,847 |
| 3 | | 26 | (h) | Blackburn R | W | 6-1 | Herd 2, Quixall 2, Charlton, Setters | 45,302 |
| 4 | | 30 | (a) | Chelsea | L | 0-2 | | 42,248 |
| 5 | Sep | 2 | (a) | Blackpool | W | 3-2 | Viollet 2, Charlton | 28,156 |
| 6 | | 9 | (h) | Tottenham H | W | 1-0 | Quixall | 57,135 |
| 7 | | 16 | (a) | Cardiff C | W | 2-1 | Dawson, Quixall | 29,251 |
| 8 | | 18 | (a) | Aston Villa | D | 1-1 | Stiles | 38,837 |
| 9 | | 23 | (h) | Manchester C | W | 3-2 | Stiles, Viollet, Ewing (og) | 56,345 |
| 10 | | 30 | (h) | Wolves | L | 0-2 | | 39,457 |
| 11 | Oct | 7 | (a) | West Brom A | D | 1-1 | Dawson | 25,645 |
| 12 | | 14 | (h) | Birmingham C | L | 0-2 | | 30,674 |
| 13 | | 21 | (a) | Arsenal | L | 1-5 | Viollet | 54,245 |
| 14 | | 28 | (h) | Bolton W | L | 0-3 | | 31,442 |
| 15 | Nov | 4 | (a) | Sheffield W | L | 1-3 | Viollet | 35,998 |
| 16 | | 11 | (h) | Leicester C | D | 2-2 | Giles, Viollet | 21,567 |
| 17 | | 18 | (a) | Ipswich T | L | 1-4 | McMillan | 25,755 |
| 18 | | 25 | (h) | Burnley | L | 1-4 | Herd | 41,029 |
| 19 | Dec | 2 | (a) | Everton | L | 1-5 | Herd | 48,099 |
| 20 | | 9 | (h) | Fulham | W | 3-0 | Herd 2, Lawton | 22,193 |
| 21 | | 16 | (h) | West Ham U | L | 1-2 | Herd | 29,472 |
| 22 | | 26 | (h) | Nottingham F | W | 6-3 | Lawton 3, Brennan, Charlton, Herd | 30,822 |
| 23 | Jan | 13 | (h) | Blackpool | L | 0-1 | | 26,999 |
| 24 | | 15 | (h) | Aston Villa | W | 2-0 | Charlton, Quixall | 20,807 |
| 25 | | 20 | (a) | Tottenham H | D | 2-2 | Charlton, Stiles | 55,225 |
| 26 | Feb | 3 | (a) | Cardiff C | W | 3-0 | Giles, Lawton, Stiles | 29,200 |
| 27 | | 10 | (a) | Manchester C | W | 2-0 | Chisnall, Herd | 49,959 |
| 28 | | 24 | (h) | West Brom A | W | 4-1 | Charlton 2, Setters, Quixall | 32,456 |
| 29 | | 28 | (a) | Wolves | D | 2-2 | Herd, Lawton | 27,565 |
| 30 | Mar | 3 | (a) | Birmingham C | D | 1-1 | Herd | 25,817 |
| 31 | | 17 | (a) | Bolton W | L | 0-1 | | 34,366 |
| 32 | | 20 | (a) | Nottingham F | L | 0-1 | | 27,833 |
| 33 | | 24 | (h) | Sheffield W | D | 1-1 | Charlton | 31,322 |
| 34 | Apr | 4 | (a) | Leicester C | L | 3-4 | McMillan 2, Quixall | 15,318 |
| 35 | | 7 | (h) | Ipswich T | W | 5-0 | Quixall 3, Setters, Stiles | 24,976 |
| 36 | | 10 | (a) | Blackburn R | L | 0-3 | | 14,623 |
| 37 | | 14 | (a) | Burnley | W | 3-1 | Brennan, Cantwell, Herd | 36,240 |
| 38 | | 16 | (h) | Arsenal | L | 2-3 | Cantwell, McMillan | 24,258 |
| 39 | | 21 | (h) | Everton | D | 1-1 | Herd | 31,926 |
| 40 | | 23 | (h) | Sheffield U | L | 0-1 | | 30,073 |
| 41 | | 24 | (a) | Sheffield U | W | 3-2 | McMillan 2, Stiles | 25,324 |
| 42 | | 28 | (a) | Fulham | L | 0-2 | | 40,113 |

FINAL LEAGUE POSITION: 15th in Division One

Appearances
Goals

## FA Cup

| | | | | | | | |
|---|---|---|---|---|---|---|---|
| 3 | Jan | 6 | (h) | Bolton W | W | 2-1 | |
| 4 | | 31 | (h) | Arsenal | W | 1-0 | |
| 5 | Feb | 17 | (h) | Sheffield W | D | 0-0 | |
| R | | 21 | (a) | Sheffield W | W | 2-0 | |
| 6 | Mar | 10 | (a) | Preston NE | D | 0-0 | |
| R | | 14 | (h) | Preston NE | W | 2-1 | |
| SF | | 31 | (n*) | Tottenham H | L | 1-3 | (*Played at Hillsborough, Sheffield.) |

Appearances and goals grid (shirt numbers worn per match):

| Gregg | Brennan | Cantwell | Stiles | Foulkes | Setters | Quixall | Viollet | Herd | Pearson | Charlton | Bradley | Dawson | Gaskell | Dunne | Lawton | Giles | Moir | Haydock | Nicholson | McMillan | Chisnall | Briggs | Match |
|---|---|---|---|---|---|---|---|---|---|---|---|---|---|---|---|---|---|---|---|---|---|---|---|
| 1 | 2 | 3 | 4 | 5 | 6 | 7 | 8 | 9 | 10 | 11 | | | | | | | | | | | | | 1 |
| 1 | 2 | 3 | 4 | 5 | 6 | 7 | 8 | 9 | 10 | 11 | | | | | | | | | | | | | 2 |
| 1 | 2 | 3 | 4 | 5 | 6 | 7 | 8 | 9 | 10 | 11 | | | | | | | | | | | | | 3 |
| 1 | 2 | 3 | 4 | 5 | 6 | 7 | 8 | 9 | 10 | 11 | | | | | | | | | | | | | 4 |
| 1 | 2 | 3 | 4 | 5 | 6 | | 8 | 9 | 10 | 11 | 7 | | | | | | | | | | | | 5 |
| 1 | 2 | 3 | 4 | 5 | 6 | 7 | 8 | 9 | 10 | 11 | | | | | | | | | | | | | 6 |
| 1 | 2 | 3 | 4 | 5 | 6 | 7 | 8 | | 10 | 11 | 9 | | | | | | | | | | | | 7 |
| | 2 | | 4 | 5 | 6 | 7 | 8 | 9 | 10 | 11 | | | 1 | 3 | | | | | | | | | 8 |
| 1 | 2 | | 4 | 5 | 6 | 7 | 8 | 9 | 10 | 11 | | | | 3 | | | | | | | | | 9 |
| 1 | 2 | 3 | 4 | 5 | | 7 | | | 10 | 11 | 9 | | | | 6 | 8 | | | | | | | 10 |
| | 2 | 3 | 4 | 5 | | | 8 | | | 11 | 9 | 1 | | | 6 | 10 | 7 | | | | | | 11 |
| 1 | 2 | 3 | 4 | | | | | 10 | | | 7 | 9 | | 6 | 8 | 11 | 5 | | | | | | 12 |
| 1 | 2 | 3 | | 5 | | | 10 | 9 | | 11 | | | | 6 | 8 | 7 | | | 4 | | | | 13 |
| 1 | 2 | | | 5 | 6 | 8 | 10 | 9 | | 11 | | | 3 | | | 7 | | | 4 | | | | 14 |
| 1 | 2 | 3 | 4 | 5 | 6 | | | 9 | | 10 | 7 | | | | 8 | | | | 11 | | | | 15 |
| | 2 | 3 | 4 | 5 | 6 | | | 9 | | 10 | 7 | 1 | | | 8 | | | | 11 | | | | 16 |
| | 2 | | 4 | 5 | 6 | | | 9 | | 10 | 7 | | 1 | 3 | 8 | | | | 11 | | | | 17 |
| | 2 | | 4 | 5 | 6 | 10 | | 9 | | 11 | 7 | | 1 | 3 | 8 | | | | | | | | 18 |
| | 2 | | | 5 | 6 | | | 9 | | 11 | | | 1 | 3 | 10 | 8 | | | 4 | | 7 | | 19 |
| | 2 | | | 5 | 6 | | | 9 | | 11 | | | 1 | 3 | 10 | 8 | | | 4 | | 7 | | 20 |
| | 2 | | | 5 | 6 | | | 9 | | 11 | | | 1 | 3 | 10 | 8 | | | 4 | | 7 | | 21 |
| | 2 | | | 5 | 6 | | | 9 | | 11 | | | 1 | 3 | 10 | 8 | | | 4 | | 7 | | 22 |
| | 2 | | | 5 | 6 | | | 9 | | 11 | | | 1 | 3 | 10 | 8 | | | 4 | | 7 | | 23 |
| | 2 | | | 5 | 6 | 9 | | | | 11 | | | 1 | 3 | 10 | 8 | | | 4 | | 7 | | 24 |
| | 2 | 8 | | 5 | 6 | | | | | 11 | | | 1 | 3 | 9 | 10 | | | 4 | | 7 | | 25 |
| | 2 | 8 | | 5 | 6 | | | | | 11 | | | 1 | 3 | 9 | 10 | | | 4 | | 7 | | 26 |
| | 2 | | 4 | | 5 | | | 9 | | 11 | | | 1 | 3 | 10 | 8 | | | 6 | | 7 | | 27 |
| | 2 | | 4 | 5 | 6 | 7 | | 9 | | 11 | | | | 3 | 10 | 8 | | | | 1 | | | 28 |
| | 2 | 8 | 5 | 4 | 7 | | | 9 | | 11 | | | | 3 | 10 | | | | 6 | 1 | | | 29 |
| | 2 | 8 | 5 | 6 | 7 | | | 9 | | 11 | | | | 3 | 10 | 8 | | | | 1 | | | 30 |
| | 2 | 10 | 5 | 6 | 7 | | | | | 11 | | | | 3 | 9 | 8 | | | 4 | 1 | | | 31 |
| | 2 | 10 | 5 | 6 | 7 | | | | | | | | | 3 | 9 | 8 | 11 | | 4 | 1 | | | 32 |
| | 2 | | 4 | 5 | 6 | 9 | | | | 11 | | | 1 | 3 | 10 | 8 | 7 | | | | | | 33 |
| | | 4 | 5 | 2 | 8 | | 9 | | | | | | 1 | 3 | 10 | | 7 | | 6 | 11 | | | 34 |
| | 2 | | 4 | 5 | 6 | 9 | | | | 11 | | | | 3 | 8 | 7 | | | 10 | 1 | | | 35 |
| | 2 | 9 | 4 | 5 | 6 | | | 10 | | | | | 1 | 3 | 8 | 7 | | | 11 | | | | 36 |
| | 2 | 9 | 4 | 5 | 6 | | 10 | 8 | | | | | | 3 | | 7 | | | 11 | 1 | | | 37 |
| | 2 | 3 | 4 | 5 | 6 | | 9 | 8 | 11 | | | | | | | 7 | | | 10 | 1 | | | 38 |
| | 2 | 9 | 4 | 5 | 6 | | 10 | 8 | 11 | | | 1 | 3 | | 7 | | | | | | | | 39 |
| | 2 | | 4 | 5 | 6 | | 9 | 8 | 11 | | | 1 | 3 | | 7 | | | | 10 | | | | 40 |
| | 2 | 10 | 5 | 6 | | | 8 | | 11 | | | 1 | 3 | | 7 | | | | 4 | 9 | | | 41 |
| | 2 | 10 | 5 | 4 | | | 8 | | 11 | | | 1 | 3 | | 7 | | | | 6 | 9 | | | 42 |
| 13 | 41 | 17 | 34 | 40 | 38 | 21 | 13 | 27 | 17 | 37 | 6 | 4 | 21 | 28 | 20 | 30 | 9 | 1 | 17 | 11 | 9 | 8 | |
| | 2 | 2 | 7 | | 3 | 10 | 7 | 14 | 1 | 8 | | | | 2 | | 6 | 2 | | | 6 | 1 | | |

1 own-goal

301

# 1962-63

Manager: Matt Busby

| | | | | | | | |
|---|---|---|---|---|---|---|---|
| 1 | Aug | 18 | (h) | West Brom A | D | 2-2 Herd, Law | 51,685 |
| 2 | | 22 | (a) | Everton | L | 1-3 Moir | 69,501 |
| 3 | | 25 | (a) | Arsenal | W | 3-1 Herd 2, Chisnall | 62,308 |
| 4 | | 29 | (h) | Everton | L | 0-1 | 63,437 |
| 5 | Sep | 1 | (h) | Birmingham C | W | 2-0 Giles, Herd | 39,847 |
| 6 | | 5 | (a) | Bolton W | L | 0-3 | 44,859 |
| 7 | | 8 | (a) | Leyton O | L | 0-1 | 24,901 |
| 8 | | 12 | (h) | Bolton W | W | 3-0 Herd 2, Cantwell | 37,721 |
| 9 | | 15 | (h) | Manchester C | L | 2-3 Law 2 | 49,193 |
| 10 | | 22 | (h) | Burnley | L | 2-5 Law, Stiles | 45,954 |
| 11 | | 29 | (a) | Sheffield W | L | 0-1 | 40,520 |
| 12 | Oct | 6 | (a) | Blackpool | D | 2-2 Herd 2 | 33,242 |
| 13 | | 13 | (h) | Blackburn R | L | 0-3 | 42,252 |
| 14 | | 20 | (a) | Tottenham H | L | 2-6 Herd, Quixall | 51,314 |
| 15 | | 27 | (h) | West Ham U | W | 3-1 Quixall 2, Law | 29,204 |
| 16 | Nov | 3 | (a) | Ipswich T | W | 5-3 Law 4, Herd | 18,483 |
| 17 | | 10 | (h) | Liverpool | D | 3-3 Giles, Herd, Quixall | 43,810 |
| 18 | | 17 | (a) | Wolves | W | 3-2 Law 2, Herd | 27,305 |
| 19 | | 24 | (h) | Aston Villa | D | 2-2 Quixall 2 | 36,852 |
| 20 | Dec | 1 | (a) | Sheffield U | D | 1-1 Charlton | 25,173 |
| 21 | | 8 | (h) | Nottingham F | W | 5-1 Herd 2, Charlton, Giles, Law | 27,946 |
| 22 | | 15 | (a) | West Brom A | L | 0-3 | 18,113 |
| 23 | | 26 | (a) | Fulham | W | 1-0 Charlton | 23,928 |
| 24 | Feb | 23 | (h) | Blackpool | D | 1-1 Herd | 43,121 |
| 25 | Mar | 2 | (a) | Blackburn R | D | 2-2 Charlton, Law | 27,924 |
| 26 | | 9 | (h) | Tottenham H | L | 0-2 | 53,416 |
| 27 | | 18 | (a) | West Ham U | L | 1-3 Herd | 28,950 |
| 28 | | 23 | (h) | Ipswich T | L | 0-1 | 32,792 |
| 29 | Apr | 1 | (h) | Fulham | L | 0-2 | 28,124 |
| 30 | | 9 | (a) | Aston Villa | W | 2-1 Charlton, Stiles | 26,867 |
| 31 | | 13 | (a) | Liverpool | L | 0-1 | 51,529 |
| 32 | | 15 | (h) | Leicester C | D | 2-2 Charlton, Herd | 50,005 |
| 33 | | 16 | (a) | Leicester C | L | 3-4 Law 3 | 37,002 |
| 34 | | 20 | (h) | Sheffield U | D | 1-1 Law | 31,179 |
| 35 | | 22 | (h) | Wolves | W | 2-1 Herd, Law | 36,147 |
| 36 | May | 1 | (h) | Sheffield W | L | 1-3 Setters | 31,878 |
| 37 | | 4 | (a) | Burnley | W | 1-0 Law | 30,266 |
| 38 | | 6 | (h) | Arsenal | L | 2-3 Law 2 | 35,999 |
| 39 | | 10 | (a) | Birmingham C | L | 1-2 Law | 21,814 |
| 40 | | 15 | (a) | Manchester C | D | 1-1 Quixall | 52,424 |
| 41 | | 18 | (h) | Leyton O | W | 3-1 Charlton, Law, Opp own-goal | 32,759 |
| 42 | | 20 | (a) | Nottingham F | L | 2-3 Giles, Herd | 16,130 |

FINAL LEAGUE POSITION: 19th in Division One

Appearances
Goals

FA Cup

| | | | | | | |
|---|---|---|---|---|---|---|
| 3 | Mar | 4 | (h) | Huddersfield T | W | 5-0 |
| 4 | | 11 | (h) | Aston Villa | W | 1-0 |
| 5 | | 16 | (h) | Chelsea | W | 2-1 |
| 6 | | 30 | (a) | Coventry C | W | 3-1 |
| SF | Apr | 27 | (n*) | Southampton | W | 1-0 (*Played at Villa Park, Birmingham.) |
| F | May | 25 | (n†) | Leicester C | W | 3-1 (†Played at Wembley Stadium) |

302

| Gaskell | Brennan | Dunne | Stiles | Foulkes | Setters | Giles | Quixall | Herd | Law | Moir | Pearson | Nicholson | Lawton | Chisnall | McMillan | Cantwell | Gregg | Charlton | Crerand | Haydock | Walker | |
|---|---|---|---|---|---|---|---|---|---|---|---|---|---|---|---|---|---|---|---|---|---|---|
| 1 | 2 | 3 | 4 | 5 | 6 | 7 | 8 | 9 | 10 | 11 | | | | | | | | | | | | 1 |
| 1 | 2 | 3 | 4 | 5 | 6 | 7 | | 9 | 10 | 11 | 8 | | | | | | | | | | | 2 |
| 1 | 2 | 3 | | 5 | | 7 | | 9 | 10 | 11 | | 4 | 6 | 8 | | | | | | | | 3 |
| 1 | 2 | 3 | | 5 | | 7 | | 9 | 10 | 11 | | 4 | 6 | 8 | | | | | | | | 4 |
| 1 | 2 | 3 | | 5 | | 7 | | 9 | 10 | 11 | | 4 | 6 | 8 | | | | | | | | 5 |
| 1 | 2 | 3 | | 5 | | 7 | 8 | 9 | 10 | 11 | | 4 | 6 | | | | | | | | | 6 |
| 1 | 2 | 3 | | 5 | 8 | | | 9 | 10 | 7 | | 4 | 6 | | | 11 | | | | | | 7 |
| 1 | 2 | 3 | 4 | 5 | 6 | 7 | | 9 | 10 | | | | 8 | | | 11 | | | | | | 8 |
| 1 | 2 | 3 | 4 | 5 | | 7 | | 9 | 10 | | | 6 | 8 | | | 11 | | | | | | 9 |
| 1 | 2 | 3 | 4 | 5 | | 7 | | 9 | 8 | 11 | 10 | | 6 | | | | | | | | | 10 |
| | 2 | 3 | 4 | 5 | | 7 | | 9 | 8 | | | 6 | 10 | 11 | | | 1 | | | | | 11 |
| | 2 | 3 | 4 | 5 | | 7 | | 9 | 8 | | | 6 | 10 | 11 | | | 1 | | | | | 12 |
| | 2 | 3 | 4 | 5 | | 7 | | 9 | 8 | | | 6 | | 11 | | | 1 | 10 | | | | 13 |
| | 2 | | 4 | 5 | 6 | 7 | 8 | 9 | 10 | | | | | | | 3 | 1 | 11 | | | | 14 |
| | 2 | | 4 | 5 | 6 | 7 | 8 | 9 | 10 | | | | | | | 3 | 1 | 11 | | | | 15 |
| | 2 | | 4 | 5 | 6 | 7 | 8 | 9 | 10 | | | | | | | 3 | 1 | 11 | | | | 16 |
| | 2 | | 4 | 5 | 6 | 7 | 8 | 9 | 10 | | | | | | | 3 | 1 | 11 | | | | 17 |
| | 2 | | 4 | 5 | 6 | 7 | 8 | 9 | 10 | | | | | | | 3 | 1 | 11 | | | | 18 |
| | 2 | | 4 | 5 | 6 | 7 | 8 | 9 | 10 | | | | | | | 3 | 1 | 11 | | | | 19 |
| | 2 | | 4 | 5 | 6 | 7 | 8 | 9 | | | | 10 | | | | 3 | 1 | 11 | | | | 20 |
| | 2 | | | 5 | | 7 | 8 | 9 | 10 | 11 | | 4 | 6 | | | 3 | 1 | | | | | 21 |
| | 2 | | 4 | 5 | | 7 | 8 | 9 | 10 | 11 | | 6 | | | | 3 | 1 | | | | | 22 |
| | 2 | | 4 | 5 | 6 | 7 | 8 | 9 | 10 | | | | | | | 3 | 1 | 11 | | | | 23 |
| | 2 | | | 5 | 6 | 7 | 8 | 9 | | | | 10 | | | | 3 | 1 | 11 | 4 | | | 24 |
| | 2 | | | 5 | 6 | 7 | 8 | 9 | 10 | | | | | | | 3 | 1 | 11 | 4 | | | 25 |
| | 2 | 6 | | 5 | | 7 | 8 | 9 | 10 | | | | | | | 3 | 1 | 11 | 4 | | | 26 |
| | 2 | 8 | | 5 | 6 | 7 | | 9 | 10 | | | | | | | 3 | 1 | 11 | 4 | | | 27 |
| | 2 | | | 5 | 6 | 7 | 8 | 9 | 10 | | | | | | | 3 | 1 | 11 | 4 | | | 28 |
| | 2 | 3 | | 5 | 6 | 7 | | 9 | 10 | | | | 8 | | | | 1 | 11 | 4 | | | 29 |
| | 2 | 8 | | 5 | 6 | 7 | 10 | 9 | | | | | | | | 3 | 1 | 11 | 4 | | | 30 |
| | 2 | 3 | 8 | 5 | 6 | 7 | | 9 | 10 | | | | | | | | 1 | 11 | 4 | | | 31 |
| | 2 | 3 | 8 | 5 | 6 | 7 | | 9 | 10 | | | | | | | | 1 | 11 | 4 | | | 32 |
| | 2 | 3 | 8 | 5 | 6 | 7 | | 9 | 10 | | | | | | | | 1 | 11 | 4 | | | 33 |
| | 2 | 3 | 8 | 5 | 6 | 7 | | 9 | 10 | | | | | | | | 1 | 11 | 4 | | | 34 |
| 1 | 2 | 3 | 8 | 5 | 6 | 7 | | 9 | 10 | | | | | | | | | 11 | 4 | | | 35 |
| 1 | 2 | | 8 | 5 | 6 | 7 | | 9 | 10 | | | | | | | 3 | | 11 | 4 | | | 36 |
| 1 | 2 | | 8 | 5 | 6 | 7 | | 9 | 10 | | | | | | | 3 | | 11 | 4 | | | 37 |
| 1 | 2 | | 8 | 5 | 6 | 7 | | 9 | 10 | | | | | | | 3 | | 11 | 4 | | | 38 |
| 1 | 2 | 6 | | 5 | 8 | 7 | | 9 | 10 | | | | | | | 3 | | 11 | 4 | | | 39 |
| 1 | 2 | 6 | | 5 | 8 | 7 | | 9 | 10 | | | | | | | 3 | | 11 | 4 | | | 40 |
| 1 | 2 | | | 5 | 6 | 8 | 7 | 9 | 10 | | | | | | | 3 | | 11 | 4 | | | 41 |
| 1 | 6 | 2 | 8 | | | 10 | 7 | 9 | | | | | | | | 3 | | | 4 | 5 | 11 | 42 |
| 18 | 37 | 25 | 31 | 41 | 27 | 36 | 31 | 37 | 38 | 9 | 2 | 10 | 12 | 6 | 4 | 25 | 24 | 28 | 19 | 1 | 1 | |
| | | | | 2 | 1 | 4 | 7 | 19 | 23 | 1 | | | 1 | | | 1 | | 7 | | | | |

1 own-goal

# 1963-64

Manager: Matt Busby

| | | | | | | | |
|---|---|---|---|---|---|---|---|
| 1 | Aug | 24 | (a) | Sheffield W | D 3-3 | Charlton 2, Moir | 32,177 |
| 2 | | 28 | (h) | Ipswich T | W 2-0 | Law 2 | 39,921 |
| 3 | | 31 | (h) | Everton | W 5-1 | Chisnall 2, Law 2, Sadler | 62,965 |
| 4 | Sep | 3 | (a) | Ipswich T | W 7-2 | Law 3, Chisnall, Moir, Sadler, Setters | 28,113 |
| 5 | | 7 | (a) | Birmingham C | D 1-1 | Chisnall | 36,874 |
| 6 | | 11 | (h) | Blackpool | W 3-0 | Charlton 2, Law | 47,400 |
| 7 | | 14 | (h) | West Brom A | W 1-0 | Sadler | 50,453 |
| 8 | | 16 | (a) | Blackpool | L 0-1 | | 29,806 |
| 9 | | 21 | (a) | Arsenal | L 1-2 | Herd | 56,776 |
| 10 | | 28 | (h) | Leicester C | W 3-1 | Herd 2, Setters | 41,374 |
| 11 | Oct | 2 | (a) | Chelsea | D 1-1 | Setters | 45,351 |
| 12 | | 5 | (a) | Bolton W | W 1-0 | Herd | 35,872 |
| 13 | | 19 | (a) | Nottingham F | W 2-1 | Chisnall, Quixall | 41,426 |
| 14 | | 26 | (h) | West Ham U | L 0-1 | | 45,120 |
| 15 | | 28 | (h) | Blackburn R | D 2-2 | Quixall 2 | 41,169 |
| 16 | Nov | 2 | (a) | Wolves | L 0-2 | | 34,159 |
| 17 | | 9 | (h) | Tottenham H | W 4-1 | Law 3, Herd | 57,413 |
| 18 | | 16 | (a) | Aston Villa | L 0-4 | | 36,276 |
| 19 | | 23 | (h) | Liverpool | L 0-1 | | 54,654 |
| 20 | | 30 | (a) | Sheffield U | W 2-1 | Law 2 | 30,615 |
| 21 | Dec | 7 | (h) | Stoke C | W 5-2 | Law 4, Herd | 52,232 |
| 22 | | 14 | (h) | Sheffield W | W 3-1 | Herd 3 | 35,139 |
| 23 | | 21 | (a) | Everton | L 0-4 | | 48,027 |
| 24 | | 26 | (a) | Burnley | L 1-6 | Herd | 35,764 |
| 25 | | 28 | (h) | Burnley | W 5-1 | Herd 2, Moore 2, Best | 47,834 |
| 26 | Jan | 11 | (h) | Birmingham C | L 1-2 | Sadler | 44,695 |
| 27 | | 18 | (a) | West Brom A | W 4-1 | Law 2, Best, Charlton | 25,624 |
| 28 | Feb | 1 | (h) | Arsenal | W 3-1 | Herd, Law, Setters | 48,340 |
| 29 | | 8 | (a) | Leicester C | L 2-3 | Herd, Law | 35,538 |
| 30 | | 19 | (h) | Bolton W | W 5-0 | Best 2, Herd 2, Charlton | 33,926 |
| 31 | | 22 | (a) | Blackburn R | W 3-1 | Law 2, Chisnall | 36,726 |
| 32 | Mar | 7 | (a) | West Ham U | W 2-0 | Herd, Sadler | 27,027 |
| 33 | | 21 | (a) | Tottenham H | W 3-2 | Charlton, Law, Moore | 56,392 |
| 34 | | 23 | (h) | Chelsea | D 1-1 | Law | 42,931 |
| 35 | | 27 | (a) | Fulham | D 2-2 | Herd, Law | 41,769 |
| 36 | | 28 | (h) | Wolves | D 2-2 | Charlton, Herd | 44,470 |
| 37 | | 30 | (h) | Fulham | W 3-0 | Crerand, Foulkes, Herd | 42,279 |
| 38 | Apr | 4 | (a) | Liverpool | L 0-3 | | 52,559 |
| 39 | | 6 | (h) | Aston Villa | W 1-0 | Law | 25,848 |
| 40 | | 13 | (h) | Sheffield U | W 2-1 | Law, Moir | 27,587 |
| 41 | | 18 | (a) | Stoke C | L 1-3 | Charlton | 45,670 |
| 42 | | 25 | (h) | Nottingham F | W 3-1 | Law 2, Moore | 31,671 |

FINAL LEAGUE POSITION: 2nd in Division One

Appearances
Goals

FA Cup

| | | | | | | |
|---|---|---|---|---|---|---|
| 3 | Jan | 4 | (a) | Southampton | W 3-2 | |
| 4 | | 25 | (h) | Bristol R | W 4-1 | |
| 5 | Feb | 15 | (a) | Barnsley | W 4-0 | |
| 6 | | 29 | (h) | Sunderland | D 3-3 | |
| R | Mar | 4 | (a) | Sunderland | D 2-2 | (After extra-time) |
| 2R | | 9 | (n*) | Sunderland | W 5-1 | (*Played at Leeds Road, Huddersfield.) |
| SF | | 14 | (n†) | West Ham U | L 1-3 | (†Played at Hillsborough, Sheffield.) |

Manchester United also reached the third round of the European Cup-winners' Cup (see *United in Europe*).

304

| Gregg | Dunne | Cantwell | Crerand | Foulkes | Setters | Moir | Chisnall | Sadler | Law | Charlton | Stiles | Best | Herd | Quixall | Moore | Gaskell | Brennan | Anderson | Tranter | |
|---|---|---|---|---|---|---|---|---|---|---|---|---|---|---|---|---|---|---|---|---|
| 1 | 2 | 3 | 4 | 5 | 6 | 7 | 8 | 9 | 10 | 11 | | | | | | | | | | 1 |
| 1 | 2 | 3 | 4 | 5 | 6 | 7 | 8 | 9 | 10 | 11 | | | | | | | | | | 2 |
| 1 | 2 | 3 | 4 | 5 | | 7 | 8 | 9 | 10 | 11 | 6 | | | | | | | | | 3 |
| 1 | 2 | 3 | 4 | 5 | 6 | 7 | 8 | 9 | 10 | 11 | | | | | | | | | | 4 |
| 1 | 2 | 3 | 4 | 5 | 6 | 7 | 8 | 9 | 10 | 11 | | | | | | | | | | 5 |
| 1 | 2 | 3 | 4 | 5 | 6 | 7 | 8 | 9 | 10 | 11 | | | | | | | | | | 6 |
| 1 | 2 | 3 | 4 | 5 | 6 | | | 10 | 9 | 11 | | 8 | 7 | | | | | | | 7 |
| 1 | 2 | 3 | 4 | 5 | 6 | 7 | | 10 | 9 | 11 | | 8 | | | | | | | | 8 |
| 1 | 2 | 3 | 4 | 5 | 6 | | 8 | 9 | 10 | 11 | | | 7 | | | | | | | 9 |
| 1 | 2 | 3 | 4 | 5 | 6 | 7 | 8 | 9 | | 11 | | | 10 | | | | | | | 10 |
| 1 | 2 | 3 | 4 | 5 | 6 | 7 | 8 | 9 | | 11 | | | 10 | | | | | | | 11 |
| 1 | 2 | 3 | 4 | 5 | 6 | | 8 | 9 | | 11 | 10 | | 7 | | | | | | | 12 |
| 1 | 2 | 3 | 4 | 5 | 6 | | 8 | | 10 | 11 | | | 9 | 7 | | | | | | 13 |
| 1 | 2 | 3 | 4 | 5 | 6 | 7 | 8 | | 10 | 11 | | | 9 | | | | | | | 14 |
| 1 | 2 | 3 | 4 | 5 | | 7 | 8 | | 10 | 11 | 6 | | 9 | | | | | | | 15 |
| 1 | 2 | 3 | 4 | 5 | 6 | 7 | 8 | | 10 | 11 | | | 9 | | | | | | | 16 |
| 1 | 2 | 3 | 4 | 5 | 6 | | | | 10 | 11 | | | 9 | 7 | 8 | | | | | 17 |
| 1 | 2 | 3 | 4 | 5 | 6 | | | | 10 | 11 | | | 9 | 7 | 8 | | | | | 18 |
| 1 | 2 | 3 | 4 | 5 | 6 | | | | 10 | 11 | | | 9 | 7 | 8 | | | | | 19 |
| | 2 | 3 | 4 | 5 | 6 | | | | 10 | 11 | | | 9 | 7 | 8 | 1 | | | | 20 |
| | 2 | 3 | 4 | 5 | 6 | | | | 10 | 11 | | | 9 | 7 | 8 | 1 | | | | 21 |
| | | 3 | 4 | 5 | 6 | 7 | | 9 | | 11 | | | 10 | | 8 | 1 | 2 | | | 22 |
| | 2 | 3 | 4 | 5 | 6 | 7 | | 9 | | 11 | | | 10 | | 8 | 1 | | | | 23 |
| | 2 | 3 | 4 | 5 | 6 | | | 9 | 10 | 11 | | | | 7 | 8 | 1 | | | | 24 |
| | 2 | 3 | 4 | 5 | 6 | | | 9 | | 11 | | | 10 | 7 | 8 | 1 | | | | 25 |
| | 2 | 3 | 4 | 5 | 6 | | | 9 | 10 | 11 | | | | 7 | 8 | 1 | | | | 26 |
| | 2 | 3 | 4 | 5 | 6 | | | 9 | 10 | 11 | | | | 7 | 8 | 1 | | | | 27 |
| | 3 | | 4 | 5 | 6 | | | | 10 | 11 | | | 9 | 7 | 8 | 1 | 2 | | | 28 |
| | 3 | | 4 | 5 | 6 | | | | 10 | 11 | | | 9 | 7 | 8 | 1 | 2 | | | 29 |
| | 3 | | 4 | 5 | 6 | | | | 10 | 11 | | 8 | 9 | 7 | | 1 | 2 | | | 30 |
| | 3 | | 4 | 5 | 6 | | 8 | | 10 | 11 | | | 9 | 7 | | 1 | 2 | | | 31 |
| | 3 | | 4 | | 6 | | 8 | | 10 | 11 | | | 9 | | | 1 | 2 | 7 | 5 | 32 |
| | 3 | | 4 | 5 | | | | 9 | 10 | 11 | 6 | | | 7 | 8 | 1 | 2 | | | 33 |
| | 3 | | 4 | 5 | | | | 9 | 10 | 11 | 6 | | | 7 | 8 | 1 | 2 | | | 34 |
| | 3 | | 4 | 5 | | | | | 10 | 11 | 6 | | 9 | 7 | 8 | 1 | 2 | | | 35 |
| 1 | 3 | | 4 | 5 | | | 8 | | 10 | 11 | 6 | | 9 | 7 | | | 2 | | | 36 |
| 1 | 3 | | 4 | 5 | | | | | 10 | 11 | 6 | | 9 | 7 | 8 | | 2 | | | 37 |
| 1 | 3 | | 4 | 5 | 6 | | 8 | | 10 | 11 | | | 9 | 7 | | | 2 | | | 38 |
| 1 | 3 | | 4 | 5 | | | 8 | | 10 | 11 | 6 | | 9 | 7 | | | 2 | | | 39 |
| 1 | 3 | | 4 | 5 | | | 8 | | 10 | 11 | 6 | | 9 | 7 | | | 2 | | | 40 |
| 1 | 3 | | 4 | 5 | | | 8 | | 10 | 11 | 6 | | 9 | 7 | | | 2 | | | 41 |
| | 3 | | 4 | 5 | 6 | | | | 10 | 11 | | | 9 | 7 | 8 | 1 | 2 | | | 42 |
| 25 | 40 | 28 | 41 | 41 | 32 | 18 | 20 | 19 | 30 | 40 | 17 | 17 | 30 | 9 | 18 | 17 | 17 | 2 | 1 | |
| | | | 1 | 1 | 4 | 3 | 6 | 5 | 30 | 9 | | 4 | 20 | 3 | 4 | | | | | |

# 1964-65

Manager: Matt Busby

| 1 | Aug | 22 | (h) | West Brom A | D | 2-2 | Charlton, Law | 52,007 |
|---|---|---|---|---|---|---|---|---|
| 2 | | 24 | (a) | West Ham U | L | 1-3 | Law | 37,070 |
| 3 | | 29 | (a) | Leicester C | D | 2-2 | Law, Sadler | 32,373 |
| 4 | Sep | 2 | (h) | West Ham U | W | 3-1 | Best, Connelly, Law | 45,123 |
| 5 | | 5 | (a) | Fulham | L | 1-2 | Connelly | 36,291 |
| 6 | | 8 | (a) | Everton | D | 3-3 | Connelly, Herd, Law | 63,024 |
| 7 | | 12 | (h) | Nottingham F | W | 3-0 | Herd 2, Connelly | 45,012 |
| 8 | | 16 | (h) | Everton | W | 2-1 | Best, Law | 49,968 |
| 9 | | 19 | (a) | Stoke C | W | 2-1 | Connelly, Herd | 40,031 |
| 10 | | 26 | (h) | Tottenham H | W | 4-1 | Crerand 2, Law 2 | 53,058 |
| 11 | | 30 | (a) | Chelsea | W | 2-0 | Best, Law | 60,769 |
| 12 | Oct | 6 | (a) | Burnley | D | 0-0 | | 30,761 |
| 13 | | 10 | (h) | Sunderland | W | 1-0 | Herd | 48,577 |
| 14 | | 17 | (a) | Wolves | W | 4-2 | Law 2, Herd, Opp own-goal | 26,763 |
| 15 | | 24 | (h) | Aston Villa | W | 7-0 | Law 4, Herd 2, Connelly | 35,807 |
| 16 | | 31 | (a) | Liverpool | W | 2-0 | Crerand, Herd | 52,402 |
| 17 | Nov | 7 | (h) | Sheffield W | W | 1-0 | Herd | 50,178 |
| 18 | | 14 | (a) | Blackpool | W | 2-1 | Connelly, Herd | 31,129 |
| 19 | | 21 | (h) | Blackburn R | W | 3-0 | Best, Connelly, Herd | 49,633 |
| 20 | | 28 | (a) | Arsenal | W | 3-2 | Law 2, Connelly | 59,627 |
| 21 | Dec | 5 | (h) | Leeds U | L | 0-1 | | 53,374 |
| 22 | | 12 | (a) | West Brom A | D | 1-1 | Law | 28,126 |
| 23 | | 16 | (h) | Birmingham C | D | 1-1 | Charlton | 25,721 |
| 24 | | 26 | (a) | Sheffield U | W | 1-0 | Best | 37,295 |
| 25 | | 28 | (h) | Sheffield U | D | 1-1 | Herd | 42,219 |
| 26 | Jan | 16 | (a) | Nottingham F | D | 2-2 | Law 2 | 43,009 |
| 27 | | 23 | (h) | Stoke C | D | 1-1 | Law | 50,392 |
| 28 | Feb | 6 | (a) | Tottenham H | L | 0-1 | | 58,639 |
| 29 | | 13 | (h) | Burnley | W | 3-2 | Best, Charlton, Herd | 38,865 |
| 30 | | 24 | (a) | Sunderland | L | 0-1 | | 51,336 |
| 31 | | 27 | (h) | Wolves | W | 3-0 | Charlton 2, Connelly | 37,018 |
| 32 | Mar | 13 | (h) | Chelsea | W | 4-0 | Herd 2, Best, Law | 56,261 |
| 33 | | 15 | (h) | Fulham | W | 4-1 | Connelly 2, Herd 2 | 45,402 |
| 34 | | 20 | (a) | Sheffield W | L | 0-1 | | 33,549 |
| 35 | | 22 | (h) | Blackpool | W | 2-0 | Law 2 | 42,318 |
| 36 | Apr | 3 | (a) | Blackburn R | W | 5-0 | Law 3, Connelly, Herd | 29,363 |
| 37 | | 12 | (h) | Leicester C | W | 1-0 | Herd | 34,114 |
| 38 | | 17 | (a) | Leeds U | W | 1-0 | Connelly | 52,368 |
| 39 | | 19 | (a) | Birmingham C | W | 4-2 | Best 2, Cantwell, Charlton | 28,907 |
| 40 | | 24 | (h) | Liverpool | W | 3-0 | Law 2, Connelly | 55,772 |
| 41 | | 26 | (h) | Arsenal | W | 3-1 | Law 2, Best | 51,625 |
| 42 | | 28 | (a) | Aston Villa | L | 1-2 | Charlton | 36,081 |

FINAL LEAGUE POSITION: 1st in Division One

Appearances
Goals

FA Cup

| 3 | Jan | 9 | (h) | Chester | W | 2-1 | |
|---|---|---|---|---|---|---|---|
| 4 | | 30 | (a) | Stoke C | D | 0-0 | |
| R | Feb | 3 | (h) | Stoke C | W | 1-0 | |
| 5 | | 20 | (h) | Burnley | W | 2-1 | |
| 6 | Mar | 10 | (a) | Wolves | W | 5-3 | |
| SF | | 27 | (n*) | Leeds U | D | 0-0 | (*Played at Hillsborough, Sheffield.) |
| R | | 31 | (n†) | Leeds U | L | 0-1 | (†Played at the City Ground, Nottingham.) |

Manchester United also reached the semi-final of the Inter-Cities Fairs' Cup (see *United in Europe*).

| Gaskell | Brennan | Dunne | Setters | Foulkes | Stiles | Connelly | Charlton | Herd | Law | Best | Crerand | Sadler | Dunne | Moir | Fitzpatrick | Aston | Cantwell | # |
|---|---|---|---|---|---|---|---|---|---|---|---|---|---|---|---|---|---|---|
| 1 | 2 | 3 | 4 | 5 | 6 | 7 | 8 | 9 | 10 | 11 | | | | | | | | 1 |
| 1 | 2 | 3 | 4 | 5 | 6 | 7 | 8 | 9 | 10 | 11 | | | | | | | | 2 |
| 1 | 2 | 3 | | 5 | 6 | 7 | 8 | | 10 | 11 | 4 | 9 | | | | | | 3 |
| 1 | 2 | 3 | | 5 | 6 | 7 | 8 | | 10 | 11 | 4 | 9 | | | | | | 4 |
| 1 | 2 | 3 | | 5 | 6 | 7 | 8 | | 10 | 11 | 4 | 9 | | | | | | 5 |
| | 2 | 3 | | 5 | 6 | 7 | 8 | 9 | 10 | 11 | 4 | | 1 | | | | | 6 |
| | 2 | 3 | 6 | 5 | 10 | 7 | 8 | 9 | | 11 | 4 | | 1 | | | | | 7 |
| | 2 | 3 | | 5 | 6 | 7 | 8 | 9 | 10 | 11 | 4 | | 1 | | | | | 8 |
| | 2 | 3 | 6 | 5 | 10 | 7 | 8 | 9 | | 11 | 4 | | 1 | | | | | 9 |
| | 2 | 3 | | 5 | 6 | 7 | 8 | 9 | 10 | 11 | 4 | | 1 | | | | | 10 |
| | 2 | 3 | | 5 | 6 | 7 | 8 | 9 | 10 | 11 | 4 | | 1 | | | | | 11 |
| | 2 | 3 | | 5 | 6 | 7 | 8 | 9 | 10 | 11 | 4 | | 1 | | | | | 12 |
| | 2 | 3 | | 5 | 6 | 7 | 8 | 9 | 10 | 11 | 4 | | 1 | | | | | 13 |
| | 2 | 3 | | 5 | 6 | 7 | 8 | 9 | 10 | 11 | 4 | | 1 | | | | | 14 |
| | 2 | 3 | 6 | 5 | 8 | 7 | | 9 | 10 | 11 | 4 | | 1 | | | | | 15 |
| | 2 | 3 | | 5 | 6 | 7 | 8 | 9 | 10 | 11 | 4 | | 1 | | | | | 16 |
| | 2 | 3 | | 5 | 6 | 7 | 8 | 9 | 10 | 11 | 4 | | 1 | | | | | 17 |
| | 2 | 3 | | 5 | 6 | 7 | 8 | 9 | 10 | | 4 | | 1 | 11 | | | | 18 |
| | 2 | 3 | | 5 | 6 | 7 | 8 | 9 | 10 | 11 | 4 | | 1 | | | | | 19 |
| | 2 | 3 | | 5 | 6 | 7 | 8 | 9 | 10 | 11 | 4 | | 1 | | | | | 20 |
| | 2 | 3 | | 5 | 6 | 7 | 8 | 9 | 10 | 11 | 4 | | 1 | | | | | 21 |
| | 2 | 3 | | 5 | 6 | 7 | 8 | 9 | 10 | 11 | 4 | | 1 | | | | | 22 |
| | 2 | 3 | | 5 | 6 | 7 | 8 | 10 | | 11 | 4 | 9 | 1 | | | | | 23 |
| | 2 | 3 | | 5 | 6 | 7 | 8 | 10 | | 11 | 4 | 9 | 1 | | | | | 24 |
| | 2 | 3 | | 5 | 6 | 7 | 8 | 10 | | 11 | 4 | 9 | 1 | | | | | 25 |
| | 2 | 3 | | 5 | 6 | 7 | 8 | 9 | 10 | 11 | 4 | | 1 | | | | | 26 |
| | 2 | 3 | | 5 | 6 | 7 | 8 | 9 | 10 | 11 | 4 | | 1 | | | | | 27 |
| | 2 | 3 | | 5 | 6 | 7 | 8 | 9 | 10 | 11 | 4 | | 1 | | | | | 28 |
| | 2 | 3 | | 5 | 6 | 7 | 8 | 9 | 10 | 11 | 4 | | 1 | | | | | 29 |
| | 2 | 3 | | 5 | | 7 | 8 | 9 | 10 | 11 | 4 | | 1 | | | | 6 | 30 |
| | 2 | 3 | | 5 | 6 | 7 | 8 | 9 | 10 | 11 | 4 | | 1 | | | | | 31 |
| | 2 | 3 | | 5 | 6 | 7 | 8 | 9 | 10 | 11 | 4 | | 1 | | | | | 32 |
| | 2 | 3 | | 5 | 6 | 7 | 8 | 9 | 10 | 11 | 4 | | 1 | | | | | 33 |
| | 2 | 3 | | 5 | 6 | 7 | 8 | 9 | 10 | 11 | 4 | | 1 | | | | | 34 |
| | 2 | 3 | | 5 | 6 | 7 | 8 | 9 | 10 | 11 | 4 | | 1 | | | | | 35 |
| | 2 | 3 | | 5 | 6 | 7 | 8 | 9 | 10 | 11 | 4 | | 1 | | | | | 36 |
| | 2 | 3 | | 5 | 6 | 7 | 8 | 9 | | 10 | 4 | | 1 | | | 11 | | 37 |
| | 2 | 3 | | 5 | 6 | 7 | 8 | 9 | 10 | 11 | 4 | | 1 | | | | | 38 |
| | 2 | 3 | | 5 | 6 | 7 | 8 | | 10 | 11 | 4 | | 1 | | 9 | | | 39 |
| | 2 | 3 | | 5 | 6 | 7 | 8 | | 10 | 11 | 4 | | 1 | | 9 | | | 40 |
| | 2 | 3 | | 5 | 6 | 7 | 8 | 9 | 10 | 11 | 4 | | 1 | | | | | 41 |
| | 2 | 3 | | 5 | 6 | 7 | 8 | 9 | 10 | 11 | | | 1 | | | | 4 | 42 |
| 5 | 42 | 42 | 5 | 42 | 41 | 42 | 41 | 37 | 36 | 41 | 39 | 6 | 37 | 1 | 2 | 1 | 2 | |
| | | | | | | 15 | 10 | 20 | 28 | 10 | 3 | 1 | | 1 | | | | |

1 own-goal

# 1965-66

Manager: Matt Busby

| | | | | | | | |
|---|---|---|---|---|---|---|---|
| 1 | Aug | 21 | (h) | Sheffield W | W 1-0 | Herd | 37,524 |
| 2 | | 24 | (a) | Nottingham F | L 2-4 | Aston, Best | 33,744 |
| 3 | | 28 | (a) | Northampton T | D 1-1 | Connelly | 21,140 |
| 4 | Sep | 1 | (h) | Nottingham F | D 0-0 | | 38,777 |
| 5 | | 4 | (h) | Stoke C | D 1-1 | Herd | 37,603 |
| 6 | | 8 | (a) | Newcastle U | W 2-1 | Herd, Law | 57,380 |
| 7 | | 11 | (a) | Burnley | L 0-3 | | 30,235 |
| 8 | | 15 | (h) | Newcastle U | D 1-1 | Stiles | 30,401 |
| 9 | | 18 | (h) | Chelsea | W 4-1 | Law 3, Charlton | 37,917 |
| 10 | | 25 | (a) | Arsenal | L 2-4 | Aston, Charlton | 56,757 |
| 11 | Oct | 9 | (h) | Liverpool | W 2-0 | Best, Law | 58,161 |
| 12 | | 16 | (a) | Tottenham H | L 1-5 | Charlton | 58,051 |
| 13 | | 23 | (h) | Fulham | W 4-1 | Herd 3, Charlton | 32,716 |
| 14 | | 30 | (a) | Blackpool | W 2-1 | Herd 2 | 24,703 |
| 15 | Nov | 6 | (h) | Blackburn R | D 2-2 | Charlton, Law | 38,823 |
| 16 | | 13 | (a) | Leicester C | W 5-0 | Herd 2, Best, Charlton, Connelly | 34,551 |
| 17 | | 20 | (h) | Sheffield U | W 3-1 | Best 2, Law | 37,922 |
| 18 | Dec | 4 | (h) | West Ham U | D 0-0 | | 32,924 |
| 19 | | 11 | (a) | Sunderland | W 3-2 | Best 2, Herd | 37,417 |
| 20 | | 15 | (h) | Everton | W 3-0 | Best, Charlton, Herd | 32,624 |
| 21 | | 18 | (h) | Tottenham H | W 5-1 | Law 2, Charlton, Herd, Beal (og) | 39,270 |
| 22 | | 27 | (h) | West Brom A | D 1-1 | Law | 54,102 |
| 23 | Jan | 1 | (a) | Liverpool | L 1-2 | Law | 53,790 |
| 24 | | 8 | (h) | Sunderland | D 1-1 | Best | 39,162 |
| 25 | | 12 | (a) | Leeds U | D 1-1 | Herd | 49,672 |
| 26 | | 15 | (a) | Fulham | W 1-0 | Charlton | 33,018 |
| 27 | | 29 | (a) | Sheffield W | D 0-0 | | 39,281 |
| 28 | Feb | 5 | (h) | Northampton T | W 6-2 | Charlton 3, Law 2, Connelly | 34,986 |
| 29 | | 19 | (a) | Stoke C | D 2-2 | Connelly, Herd | 36,667 |
| 30 | | 26 | (h) | Burnley | W 4-2 | Herd 3, Charlton | 49,892 |
| 31 | Mar | 12 | (a) | Chelsea | L 0-2 | | 60,269 |
| 32 | | 19 | (h) | Arsenal | W 2-1 | Law, Stiles | 47,246 |
| 33 | Apr | 6 | (a) | Aston Villa | D 1-1 | Cantwell | 28,211 |
| 34 | | 9 | (h) | Leicester C | L 1-2 | Connelly | 42,593 |
| 35 | | 16 | (a) | Sheffield U | L 1-3 | Sadler | 22,330 |
| 36 | | 25 | (a) | Everton | D 0-0 | | 50,843 |
| 37 | | 27 | (h) | Blackpool | W 2-1 | Charlton, Law | 26,953 |
| 38 | | 30 | (a) | West Ham U | L 2-3 | Aston, Cantwell | 36,416 |
| 39 | May | 4 | (a) | West Brom A | D 3-3 | Aston, A.Dunne, Herd | 22,609 |
| 40 | | 7 | (a) | Blackburn R | W 4-1 | Herd 2, Charlton, Sadler | 14,513 |
| 41 | | 9 | (h) | Aston Villa | W 6-1 | Herd 2, Sadler 2, Charlton, Ryan | 23,039 |
| 42 | | 19 | (h) | Leeds U | D 1-1 | Herd | 35,008 |

FINAL LEAGUE POSITION: 4th in Division One

Appearances
Sub Appearances
Goals

## FA Cup

| | | | | | | | |
|---|---|---|---|---|---|---|---|
| 3 | Jan | 22 | (a) | Derby C | W 5-2 | | |
| 4 | Feb | 12 | (h) | Rotherham U | D 0-0 | | |
| R | | 15 | (a) | Rotherham U | W 1-0 | (After extra-time) | |
| 5 | Mar | 5 | (a) | Wolves | W 4-2 | | |
| 6 | | 26 | (a) | Preston NE | D 1-1 | | |
| R | | 30 | (h) | Preston NE | W 3-1 | | |
| SF | Apr | 23 | (n*) | Everton | L 0-1 | (*Played at Burnden Park, Bolton.) | |

Manchester United also reached the semi-final of the European Cup (see *United in Europe*).

| Dunne P | Brennan | Dunne A | Crerand | Foulkes | Stiles | Anderson | Charlton | Herd | Best | Aston | Connelly | Gaskell | Cantwell | Law | Fitzpatrick | Gregg | Sadler | Noble | Ryan | |
|---|---|---|---|---|---|---|---|---|---|---|---|---|---|---|---|---|---|---|---|---|
| 1 | 2 | 3 | 4 | 5 | 6 | 7 | 8 | 9 | 10 | 11 |  |  |  |  |  |  |  |  |  | 1 |
| 1 | 2 | 3 | 4 | 5 | 6 |  | 8 | 9 | 10 | 11 | 7 |  |  |  |  |  |  |  |  | 2 |
|  | 2 |  | 4 | 5 | 6 |  | 8 | 9 |  | 11 | 7 | 1 | 3 | 10 |  |  |  |  |  | 3 |
|  | 2 | 3 | 4 | 5 | 6 |  | 8 | 9 |  | 11 | 7 | 1 |  | 10 |  |  |  |  |  | 4 |
|  | 2 | 3 | 4 | 5 | 6 |  | 8 | 9 |  | 11 | 7 | 1 |  | 10 |  |  |  |  |  | 5 |
|  | 2 | 3 | 4 | 5 | 6 |  | 8 | 9 |  | 11 | 7 | 1 |  | 10 |  |  |  |  |  | 6 |
|  | 2 | 3 | 4 | 5 | 6 |  | 8 | 9 |  | 11 | 7 | 1 |  | 10 |  |  |  |  |  | 7 |
|  | 2 | 3 | 4 | 5 | 6 |  | 8 | 9 |  | 11 | 7 | 1 |  | 10 |  |  |  |  |  | 8 |
|  | 2 | 3 | 4 | 5 | 6 |  | 8 | 9 |  | 11 | 7 | 1 |  | 10 |  |  |  |  |  | 9 |
| 1 | 2 | 3 | 4 | 5 | 6 |  | 8 | 9 |  | 11 | 7 |  |  | 10 |  |  |  |  |  | 10 |
| 1 | 2 | 3 | 4 | 5 | 6 |  | 9 |  | 8 | 11 | 7 |  |  | 10 |  |  |  |  |  | 11 |
| 1 | 2 | 3 | 4 | 5 | 6 |  | 9 |  | 8 | 11 | 7 |  |  | 10* | 12 |  |  |  |  | 12 |
| 1 | 2 | 3 | 4 | 5 | 6 |  | 9 | 10 | 8 | 11 | 7 |  |  |  |  |  |  |  |  | 13 |
|  | 2 | 3 | 4 | 5 | 6 |  | 9 | 10 | 8 | 11 | 7 |  |  |  |  | 1 |  |  |  | 14 |
|  | 2 | 3 | 4 | 5 | 6 |  | 9 | 10 | 7 | 11* | 12 |  |  | 8 |  | 1 |  |  |  | 15 |
|  | 2 |  | 4 | 5 | 6 |  | 9 | 10 | 7 | 11 |  |  | 3 | 8 |  | 1 |  |  |  | 16 |
|  | 2 |  | 4 |  | 6 |  | 9 | 10 | 7 | 11 |  |  | 3 | 8 |  | 1 | 5 |  |  | 17 |
| 1 | 2 |  | 4 | 5 | 6 |  | 9 | 10 | 7 | 11 |  |  | 3 | 8 |  |  |  |  |  | 18 |
| 1 | 2 |  | 4 | 5 | 6 |  | 9 | 10 | 7 | 11 |  |  | 3 | 8 |  |  |  |  |  | 19 |
|  | 2 |  | 4 | 5 | 6 |  | 9 | 10 | 7 | 11 |  |  | 3 | 8 |  | 1 |  |  |  | 20 |
|  | 2 |  | 4 | 5 | 6 |  | 9 | 10 | 7 | 11 |  |  | 3 | 8 |  | 1 |  |  |  | 21 |
|  | 2 |  | 4 | 5 | 6 |  | 9 | 10 | 7 | 11 |  |  | 3 | 8 |  | 1 |  |  |  | 22 |
|  | 2 |  | 4 | 5 | 6 |  | 9 | 10 | 7 | 11 |  |  | 3 | 8 |  | 1 |  |  |  | 23 |
|  | 2 |  | 4 | 5 | 6 |  | 9 | 10 | 7 | 11 |  |  | 3 | 8 |  | 1 |  |  |  | 24 |
|  | 2 |  | 4 | 5 | 6 |  | 9 | 10 | 7 | 11 |  |  | 3 | 8 |  | 1 |  |  |  | 25 |
|  | 2 |  | 4 | 5 | 6 |  | 9 | 10 | 7 | 11 |  |  | 3 | 8 |  | 1 |  |  |  | 26 |
|  | 2 |  | 4 | 5 | 6 |  | 9 | 10 | 7 | 11 |  |  | 3 | 8 |  | 1 |  |  |  | 27 |
|  | 2 |  | 4 | 5 | 6 |  | 9 | 10 | 7 | 11 |  |  | 3 | 8 |  | 1 |  |  |  | 28 |
|  | 2 | 3 | 4 | 5 | 6 |  | 9 | 10 | 8 | 11 | 7 |  |  |  |  | 1 |  |  |  | 29 |
|  | 2 | 3 | 4 | 5 | 6 |  | 9 | 10 | 7 | 11 |  |  |  | 8 |  | 1 |  |  |  | 30 |
|  | 2 | 3 | 4 | 5 | 6 |  | 9 | 10 | 7 | 11 |  |  |  | 8 |  | 1 |  |  |  | 31 |
|  | 2 | 3 | 4 | 5 | 6 |  | 9 | 10 | 7 | 11 |  |  |  | 8 |  | 1 |  |  |  | 32 |
|  | 2 | 3 | 4 | 5 |  |  | 9 |  | 11 | 7 |  | 1 | 10 | 8 | 6 |  |  |  |  | 33 |
|  | 2 |  | 4 |  | 6 | 8 | 9 | 10 | 7 | 11 |  |  |  |  |  | 1 | 5 | 3 |  | 34 |
|  | 2 |  |  | 5 | 6 | 8 |  | 10 |  | 11 | 7 |  | 3 |  | 4 | 1 | 9 |  |  | 35 |
|  | 2 | 3 | 4 |  | 6 | 7 | 10 | 11 |  |  |  |  | 5 | 8 |  | 1 | 9 |  |  | 36 |
|  | 2 | 3 | 4 |  | 6 |  | 10 | 11 | 7 |  |  |  | 5 | 8 |  | 1 | 9 |  |  | 37 |
|  | 2 | 3* | 4 |  | 6 |  | 10 | 12 | 7 | 11 |  |  | 5 | 8 | 6* | 1 | 9 |  |  | 38 |
|  | 2 | 3 | 4 | 12 |  |  | 10 | 11 |  |  |  |  | 5 | 8 | 6* | 1 | 9 |  | 7 | 39 |
|  | 2 | 3 | 4 |  | 6 | 8 | 8 | 10 |  | 11 |  |  | 5 |  |  | 1 | 9 |  | 7 | 40 |
|  | 2 | 3 | 4 |  | 6 |  | 10 | 8 |  | 11 |  |  | 5 |  |  | 1 | 9 |  | 7 | 41 |
|  | 2 | 6 | 4 |  |  |  | 8 | 11 |  |  |  |  | 5 | 10 |  | 1 | 9 | 3 | 7 | 42 |
| 8 | 28 | 40 | 41 | 33 | 39 | 5 | 38 | 36 | 31 | 23 | 31 | 8 | 23 | 33 | 3 | 26 | 10 | 2 | 4 |  |
|  |  |  |  | 1 |  |  |  |  | 1 |  |  |  | 1 |  | 1 |  |  |  |  |  |
|  | 1 |  |  | 2 |  |  | 16 | 24 | 9 | 4 | 5 |  | 2 | 15 |  |  | 4 |  | 1 |  |

1 own-goal

# 1966-67

Manager: Matt Busby

| | | | | | | | | |
|---|---|---|---|---|---|---|---|---|
| 1 | Aug | 20 | (h) | West Brom A | W | 5-3 | Law 2, Best, Herd, Stiles | 41,343 |
| 2 | | 23 | (a) | Everton | W | 2-1 | Law 2 | 60,657 |
| 3 | | 27 | (a) | Leeds U | L | 1-3 | Best | 45,092 |
| 4 | | 31 | (h) | Everton | W | 3-0 | Connelly, Foulkes, Law | 61,114 |
| 5 | Sep | 3 | (h) | Newcastle U | W | 3-2 | Connelly, Herd, Law | 44,448 |
| 6 | | 7 | (a) | Stoke C | L | 0-3 | | 44,337 |
| 7 | | 10 | (a) | Tottenham H | L | 1-2 | Law | 56,295 |
| 8 | | 17 | (h) | Manchester C | W | 1-0 | Law | 62,085 |
| 9 | | 24 | (h) | Burnley | W | 4-1 | Crerand, Herd, Law, Sadler | 52,697 |
| 10 | Oct | 1 | (a) | Nottingham F | L | 1-4 | Charlton | 41,854 |
| 11 | | 8 | (a) | Blackpool | W | 2-1 | Law 2 | 33,555 |
| 12 | | 15 | (h) | Chelsea | D | 1-1 | Law | 56,789 |
| 13 | | 29 | (h) | Arsenal | W | 1-0 | Sadler | 45,387 |
| 14 | Nov | 5 | (a) | Chelsea | W | 3-1 | Aston 2, Best | 55,958 |
| 15 | | 12 | (h) | Sheffield W | W | 2-0 | Charlton, Herd | 46,942 |
| 16 | | 19 | (a) | Southampton | W | 2-1 | Charlton 2 | 29,458 |
| 17 | | 26 | (h) | Sunderland | W | 5-0 | Herd 4, Law | 44,687 |
| 18 | | 30 | (a) | Leicester C | W | 2-1 | Best, Law | 39,014 |
| 19 | Dec | 3 | (a) | Aston Villa | L | 1-2 | Herd | 39,937 |
| 20 | | 10 | (h) | Liverpool | D | 2-2 | Best 2 | 61,768 |
| 21 | | 17 | (a) | West Brom A | W | 4-3 | Herd 3, Law | 32,080 |
| 22 | | 26 | (a) | Sheffield U | L | 1-2 | Herd | 42,752 |
| 23 | | 27 | (h) | Sheffield U | W | 2-0 | Crerand, Herd | 59,392 |
| 24 | | 31 | (h) | Leeds U | D | 0-0 | | 53,486 |
| 25 | Jan | 14 | (h) | Tottenham H | W | 1-0 | Herd | 57,366 |
| 26 | | 21 | (a) | Manchester C | D | 1-1 | Foulkes | 62,983 |
| 27 | Feb | 4 | (a) | Burnley | D | 1-1 | Sadler | 40,165 |
| 28 | | 11 | (h) | Nottingham F | W | 1-0 | Law | 62,727 |
| 29 | | 25 | (h) | Blackpool | W | 4-0 | Charlton 2, Law, Hughes (og) | 47,158 |
| 30 | Mar | 3 | (a) | Arsenal | D | 1-1 | Aston | 63,363 |
| 31 | | 11 | (a) | Newcastle U | D | 0-0 | | 37,430 |
| 32 | | 18 | (h) | Leicester C | W | 5-2 | Aston, Charlton, Herd, Law, Sadler | 50,281 |
| 33 | | 25 | (a) | Liverpool | D | 0-0 | | 53,813 |
| 34 | | 27 | (a) | Fulham | D | 2-2 | Best, Stiles | 47,290 |
| 35 | | 28 | (h) | Fulham | W | 2-1 | Foulkes, Stiles | 51,673 |
| 36 | Apr | 1 | (h) | West Ham U | W | 3-0 | Best, Charlton, Law | 61,308 |
| 37 | | 10 | (a) | Sheffield W | D | 2-2 | Charlton 2 | 51,101 |
| 38 | | 18 | (h) | Southampton | W | 3-0 | Charlton, Law, Sadler | 54,291 |
| 39 | | 22 | (a) | Sunderland | D | 0-0 | | 43,570 |
| 40 | | 29 | (h) | Aston Villa | W | 3-1 | Aston, Best, Law | 55,782 |
| 41 | May | 6 | (a) | West Ham U | W | 6-1 | Law 2, Best, Charlton, Crerand, Foulkes | 38,424 |
| 42 | | 13 | (h) | Stoke C | D | 0-0 | | 61,071 |

FINAL LEAGUE POSITION: 1st in Division One

Appearances
Sub Appearances
Goals

FA Cup

| | | | | | | | |
|---|---|---|---|---|---|---|---|
| 3 | Jan | 28 | (h) | Stoke C | W | 2-0 | |
| 4 | Feb | 18 | (h) | Norwich C | L | 1-2 | |

League Cup

| | | | | | | | |
|---|---|---|---|---|---|---|---|
| 2 | Sep | 14 | (a) | Blackpool | L | 1-5 | |

310

| Gaskell | Brennan | Dunne | Fitzpatrick | Foulkes | Stiles | Best | Law | Charlton | Herd | Connelly | Crerand | Gregg | Sadler | Aston | Stepney | Noble | Cantwell | Ryan | Anderson | # |
|---|---|---|---|---|---|---|---|---|---|---|---|---|---|---|---|---|---|---|---|---|
| 1 | 2 | 3 | 4 | 5 | 6 | 7 | 8 | 9 | 10 | 11 | | | | | | | | | | 1 |
| 1 | 2 | 3 | 4 | 5 | 6 | 7 | 8 | 9 | 10 | 11 | | | | | | | | | | 2 |
| 1 | 2 | 3 | 4 | 5 | 6 | 7 | 8 | 9 | 10 | 11 | | | | | | | | | | 3 |
| 1 | 2 | 3 | | 5 | 6 | 11 | 8 | 9 | 10 | 7 | 4 | | | | | | | | | 4 |
| | 2 | 3 | | 5 | 6 | 11 | 8 | 9 | 10 | 7 | 4 | 1 | | | | | | | | 5 |
| | 2 | 3 | | 5 | 6 | 11 | 8 | 9 | 10 | 7 | 4 | 1 | | | | | | | | 6 |
| 1 | 2 | 3 | | 5 | 6 | 7 | 8 | 11 | 10 | | 4 | | 9* | 12 | | | | | | 7 |
| | 2 | 3 | | 5 | 6 | 7 | 8 | 10 | | | 4 | | 9 | 11 | 1 | | | | | 8 |
| | 2 | 3 | | 5 | 6 | 11 | 8* | 10 | 7 | | 4 | | 9 | 12 | 1 | | | | | 9 |
| | 2 | 3 | | 5 | 6 | 7 | | 8 | 10 | | 4 | | 9 | 11 | 1 | | | | | 10 |
| | | 2 | | | 6 | 11 | 8 | 10 | 7 | | 4 | | 9 | | 1 | 3 | 5 | | | 11 |
| | | 2 | | | 6 | 11 | 8 | 10 | 7 | | 4 | | 9 | | 1 | 3 | 5 | | | 12 |
| | | 2 | | | 6 | 11 | 8 | 10 | 7 | | 4 | | 9 | | 1 | 3 | 5 | | | 13 |
| | | 2 | | 5 | 6 | 11 | | 10 | 7 | | 4 | | 9 | 8 | 1 | 3 | | | | 14 |
| | | 2 | | 5* | 6 | 11 | 8 | 10 | 7 | | 4 | | 9 | 12 | 1 | 3 | | | | 15 |
| | | 2 | | | 6 | 11 | 8 | 10 | 7 | | 4 | | 9 | 12 | 1 | 3 | 5* | | | 16 |
| | | 2 | | | 6 | 7 | 8 | 9 | 10 | | 4 | | 5 | 11 | 1 | 3 | | | | 17 |
| | | 2 | | | 6 | 7 | 8 | 9 | 10 | | 4 | | 5 | 11 | 1 | 3 | | | | 18 |
| | | 2 | | | 6 | 7 | 8 | 9 | 10 | | 4 | | 5 | 11 | 1 | 3 | | | | 19 |
| | | 2 | | | 6* | 7 | | 9 | 10 | | 4 | | 5 | 11 | 1 | 3 | 8 | 12 | | 20 |
| | | 2 | | | 6 | 7 | 8 | 9 | 10 | | 4 | | 5 | 11 | 1 | 3 | | | | 21 |
| | | 2 | | 5 | | 7 | 8 | 9 | 10 | | 4 | | 6 | 11 | 1 | 3 | | | | 22 |
| | | 2 | | 5 | | 7 | 8 | 9 | 10 | | 4 | | 6 | 11 | 1 | 3 | | | | 23 |
| | | 2 | | 5 | | 7 | 8 | 9 | 10 | | 4 | | 6 | 11 | 1 | 3 | | | | 24 |
| | | 2 | | 5 | | 7 | | 9 | 10 | | 4 | | 6 | 11 | 1 | 3 | | 8 | | 25 |
| | | 2 | | 5 | 6 | 11 | 8 | 10 | | | 4 | | 9 | | 1 | 3 | | 7 | | 26 |
| | | 2 | | 5 | 6 | 7 | 8 | 11 | 10 | | 4 | | 9 | | 1 | 3 | | | | 27 |
| | | 2 | | 5* | 6 | 7 | 8 | 11 | 10 | | 4 | | 9 | | 1 | 3 | | 12 | | 28 |
| | | 2 | | 5 | 6 | 7 | 8 | 10 | | | 4 | | 9 | 11 | 1 | 3 | | | | 29 |
| | | 2 | | 5 | 6 | 7 | 8 | 10 | | | 4 | | 9 | 11 | 1 | 3 | | | | 30 |
| | | 2 | | 5 | 6 | 7 | 8 | 10 | | | 4 | | 9 | 11 | 1 | 3 | | | | 31 |
| | | 2 | | 5 | 6 | 7 | 8 | 9 | 10* | | 4 | | 12 | 11 | 1 | 3 | | | | 32 |
| | | 2 | | 5 | 6 | 7 | 8 | 10 | | | 4 | | 9 | 11 | 1 | 3 | | | | 33 |
| | | 2 | | 5 | 6 | 7 | 8 | 10 | | | 4 | | 9 | 11 | 1 | 3 | | | | 34 |
| | | 2 | | 5 | 6 | 7 | 8 | 10 | | | 4 | | 9 | 11 | 1 | 3 | | | | 35 |
| | | 2 | | 5 | 6 | 7 | 8 | 10 | | | 4 | | 9 | 11 | 1 | 3 | | | | 36 |
| | | 2 | | 5 | 6 | 7 | 8 | 10 | | | 4 | | 9 | 11 | 1 | 3 | | | | 37 |
| | | 2 | | 5 | 6 | 7 | 8 | 10 | | | 4 | | 9 | 11 | 1 | 3 | | | | 38 |
| | | 2 | | 5 | 6 | 7 | 8 | 10 | | | 4 | | 9 | 11 | 1 | 3 | | | | 39 |
| | 2 | 3 | | 5 | 6 | 7 | 8 | 10 | | | 4 | | 9 | 11 | 1 | | | | | 40 |
| | 2 | 3 | | 5 | 6 | 7 | 8 | 10 | | | 4 | | 9 | 11 | 1 | | | | | 41 |
| | 2 | 3 | | 5 | 6 | 7 | | 10 | | | 4 | | 9 | 11 | 1 | | 8 | | | 42 |
| 5 | 16 | 40 | 3 | 33 | 37 | 42 | 36 | 42 | 28 | 6 | 39 | 2 | 35 | 26 | 35 | 29 | 4 | 4 | | |
| | | | | | | | | | | | | | 1 | 4 | | | 1 | 1 | | |
| | | | | 4 | 3 | 10 | 23 | 12 | 16 | 2 | 3 | | 5 | 5 | | | | | | |

1 own-goal

# 1967-68

Manager: Matt Busby

| # | | | | | | Result | Scorers | Attendance |
|---|---|---|---|---|---|---|---|---|
| 1 | Aug | 19 | (a) | Everton | L | 1-3 | Charlton | 61,452 |
| 2 | | 23 | (h) | Leeds U | W | 1-0 | Charlton | 53,016 |
| 3 | | 26 | (h) | Leicester C | D | 1-1 | Foulkes | 51,256 |
| 4 | Sep | 2 | (a) | West Ham U | W | 3-1 | Kidd, Ryan, Sadler | 36,562 |
| 5 | | 6 | (a) | Sunderland | D | 1-1 | Kidd | 51,527 |
| 6 | | 9 | (h) | Burnley | D | 2-2 | Burns, Crerand | 55,809 |
| 7 | | 16 | (a) | Sheffield W | D | 1-1 | Best | 47,274 |
| 8 | | 23 | (h) | Tottenham H | W | 3-1 | Best 2, Law | 58,779 |
| 9 | | 30 | (a) | Manchester C | W | 2-1 | Charlton 2 | 62,942 |
| 10 | Oct | 7 | (h) | Arsenal | W | 1-0 | Aston | 60,197 |
| 11 | | 14 | (a) | Sheffield U | W | 3-0 | Aston, Kidd, Law | 29,170 |
| 12 | | 25 | (h) | Coventry C | W | 4-0 | Aston 2, Best, Charlton | 54,253 |
| 13 | | 28 | (a) | Nottingham F | L | 1-3 | Best | 49,946 |
| 14 | Nov | 4 | (h) | Stoke C | W | 1-0 | Charlton | 51,041 |
| 15 | | 8 | | Leeds U | L | 0-1 | | 43,999 |
| 16 | | 11 | (a) | Liverpool | W | 2-1 | Best 2 | 54,515 |
| 17 | | 18 | (h) | Southampton | W | 3-2 | Aston, Charlton, Kidd | 48,732 |
| 18 | | 25 | (a) | Chelsea | D | 1-1 | Kidd | 54,712 |
| 19 | Dec | 2 | (h) | West Brom A | W | 2-1 | Best 2 | 52,568 |
| 20 | | 9 | (a) | Newcastle U | D | 2-2 | Dunne, Kidd | 48,639 |
| 21 | | 16 | (h) | Everton | W | 3-1 | Aston, Law, Sadler | 60,736 |
| 22 | | 23 | (a) | Leicester C | D | 2-2 | Charlton, Law | 40,104 |
| 23 | | 26 | (h) | Wolves | W | 4-0 | Best 2, Charlton, Kidd | 63,450 |
| 24 | | 30 | (a) | Wolves | W | 3-2 | Aston, Charlton, Kidd | 53,940 |
| 25 | Jan | 6 | (a) | West Ham U | W | 3-1 | Aston, Best, Charlton | 54,498 |
| 26 | | 20 | (h) | Sheffield W | W | 4-2 | Best 2, Charlton, Kidd | 55,254 |
| 27 | Feb | 3 | (a) | Tottenham H | W | 2-1 | Best, Charlton | 57,790 |
| 28 | | 17 | (a) | Burnley | L | 1-2 | Best | 31,965 |
| 29 | | 24 | (a) | Arsenal | W | 2-0 | Best, Storey (og) | 46,417 |
| 30 | Mar | 2 | (h) | Chelsea | L | 1-3 | Kidd | 62,978 |
| 31 | | 16 | (a) | Coventry C | L | 0-2 | | 47,110 |
| 32 | | 23 | (h) | Nottingham F | W | 3-0 | Herd, Brennan, Burns | 61,978 |
| 33 | | 27 | (h) | Manchester C | L | 1-3 | Best | 63,004 |
| 34 | | 30 | (a) | Stoke C | W | 4-2 | Aston, Best, Gowling, Ryan | 30,141 |
| 35 | Apr | 6 | (h) | Liverpool | L | 1-2 | Best | 63,059 |
| 36 | | 12 | (h) | Fulham | W | 4-0 | Best 2, Kidd, Law | 40,152 |
| 37 | | 13 | (a) | Southampton | D | 2-2 | Best, Charlton | 30,079 |
| 38 | | 15 | (h) | Fulham | W | 3-0 | Aston, Best, Charlton | 60,465 |
| 39 | | 20 | (h) | Sheffield U | W | 1-0 | Law | 55,033 |
| 40 | | 27 | (a) | West Brom A | L | 3-6 | Kidd 2, Law | 43,412 |
| 41 | May | 4 | (h) | Newcastle U | W | 6-0 | Best 3, Kidd 2, Sadler | 59,976 |
| 42 | | 11 | (h) | Sunderland | L | 1-2 | Best | 62,963 |

FINAL LEAGUE POSITION: 2nd in Division One

Appearances
Sub Appearances
Goals

FA Cup

| 3 | Jan | 27 | (h) | Tottenham H | D | 2-2 | |
| R | | 31 | (a) | Tottenham H | L | 0-1 | (After extra-time) |

Manchester United also won the European Cup (see *United in Europe*).

| Stepney | Brennan | Dunne | Crerand | Foulkes | Stiles | Best | Law | Charlton | Kidd | Aston | Sadler | Ryan | Burns | Fitzpatrick | Kopel | Herd | Gowling | Rimmer | No. |
|---|---|---|---|---|---|---|---|---|---|---|---|---|---|---|---|---|---|---|---|
| 1 | 2 | 3 | 4* | 5 | 6 | 7 | 8 | 9 | 10 | 11 | 12 |  |  |  |  |  |  |  | 1 |
| 1 | 2 | 3 | 4 | 5 | 6 |  | 8 | 9 | 10 | 11 |  | 7 |  |  |  |  |  |  | 2 |
| 1 | 2 | 3 |  | 5 | 6 | 7 | 8 | 9 | 10 | 11 | 4 |  |  |  |  |  |  |  | 3 |
| 1 |  | 2 | 4 | 5 | 6 | 11 |  | 9 | 10 |  | 8 | 7 | 3 |  |  |  |  |  | 4 |
| 1 |  | 2 | 4 | 5 | 6* | 11 |  | 9 | 10 |  | 8 | 7 | 3 | 12 |  |  |  |  | 5 |
| 1 |  | 2 | 4 | 5 |  | 11 |  | 9 | 10 |  | 8 | 7 | 3 | 6* | 12 |  |  |  | 6 |
| 1 |  | 2 | 4 | 5 | 6 | 7 | 10 | 9 | 11 |  | 8 |  | 3 |  |  |  |  |  | 7 |
| 1 |  | 2 | 4 | 5 | 6 | 7 | 10 | 9 | 11 |  | 8 |  | 3 |  |  |  |  |  | 8 |
| 1 |  | 2 | 4 | 5* | 6 | 7 | 10 | 9 | 11 | 12 | 8 |  | 3 |  |  |  |  |  | 9 |
| 1 |  | 2 | 4 |  | 6 | 7 | 10 | 9 | 8 | 11 | 5 |  | 3 |  |  |  |  |  | 10 |
| 1 |  | 2 | 4 |  | 6* | 7 | 10 | 9 | 8 | 11 | 5 |  | 3 | 12 |  |  |  |  | 11 |
| 1 |  | 2 | 4 |  |  | 7 | 10 | 9 | 8 | 11 | 5 |  | 3 | 6 |  |  |  |  | 12 |
| 1 |  |  | 4 |  |  | 7 | 10 | 9 | 8 | 11 | 5 |  | 3 | 6 | 2 |  |  |  | 13 |
| 1 |  | 2 | 4 | 5 |  | 10 |  | 9 | 8 | 11 | 6 | 7 | 3 |  |  |  |  |  | 14 |
| 1 |  | 2 | 4 | 5 |  | 10 |  | 9 | 8 | 11 | 6 | 7* | 3 | 12 |  |  |  |  | 15 |
| 1 |  | 2 | 4 | 5 |  | 10 |  | 9 | 8 | 11 | 6 |  | 3 | 7 |  |  |  |  | 16 |
| 1 |  | 2 | 4 | 5 |  | 10 |  | 9 | 8 | 11 | 6 |  | 3 | 7 |  |  |  |  | 17 |
| 1 | 2 | 3 | 4 | 5 |  | 10 |  | 9 | 8 | 11 | 6 |  |  | 7 |  |  |  |  | 18 |
| 1 | 2 | 3 | 4 | 5 |  | 10 |  | 9 | 8 | 11 | 6 |  |  | 7 |  |  |  |  | 19 |
| 1 | 2 | 3 | 4 | 5 |  | 10 |  | 9 | 8 | 11 | 6 |  |  | 7 |  |  |  |  | 20 |
| 1 |  | 2 | 4 | 5 |  | 7 | 10 | 9 | 8 | 11 | 6 |  | 3 |  |  |  |  |  | 21 |
| 1 |  | 2 | 4 | 5 |  | 7 | 10 | 9 | 8 | 11 | 6 |  | 3 |  |  |  |  |  | 22 |
| 1 |  | 2 | 4 | 5 |  | 7 | 10 | 9 | 8 | 11 | 6 |  | 3 |  |  |  |  |  | 23 |
| 1 |  | 2 | 4 | 5 |  | 7 | 10 | 9 | 8 | 11 | 6 |  | 3 |  |  |  |  |  | 24 |
| 1 |  | 2 | 4 |  |  | 7 | 10 | 9 | 8 | 11 | 5 |  | 3 | 6 |  |  |  |  | 25 |
| 1 |  | 2 | 4 |  |  | 7 | 10 | 9 | 8 | 11 | 5 |  | 3 | 6 |  |  |  |  | 26 |
| 1 |  | 2 | 4 |  |  | 7 |  | 9 | 8 | 11 | 5 |  | 3 | 6 |  | 10 |  |  | 27 |
| 1 |  | 2 | 4 |  | 6 | 7 | 10 | 9 | 8 | 11 | 5 |  | 3 |  |  |  |  |  | 28 |
| 1 |  | 2 | 4 |  | 6 | 7 | 10 |  | 8 | 11 | 5 |  | 3 | 9 |  |  |  |  | 29 |
| 1 |  | 2 | 4 |  | 6 | 7 |  | 9 | 8 | 11 | 5 | 10 | 3 |  |  |  |  |  | 30 |
| 1 | 2 |  | 4 |  | 6 | 7 |  | 9 | 8* | 12 | 5 |  | 3 | 10 |  | 11 |  |  | 31 |
| 1 | 2 |  | 4 |  | 6 | 10 |  | 9 |  | 11 | 5 |  | 3 | 7 |  | 8 |  |  | 32 |
| 1 | 2 |  | 4 |  | 6 | 10 | 8 | 9 |  | 12 | 5 |  | 3 | 7 |  | 11* |  |  | 33 |
| 1 | 2 |  | 4 |  |  | 7 |  | 9 |  | 11 | 5 | 12 | 3 | 6 |  | 10* | 8 |  | 34 |
| 1 |  | 2 | 4 |  |  | 7 |  | 9 |  | 11 | 5 |  | 3 | 6 |  | 10 | 8 |  | 35 |
| 1 |  | 2 | 4 |  | 6 | 7 | 10 | 9 | 8 | 11 | 5 |  | 3 |  |  |  |  |  | 36 |
| 1 |  | 2 | 4 | 5 |  | 7 |  | 9 | 8 | 11 | 6 |  | 3 |  |  |  | 10 |  | 37 |
|  |  | 2 | 4 | 5 |  | 7 | 10 | 9 | 8 | 11 | 6 |  | 3 |  |  |  |  | 1 | 38 |
| 1 | 2 | 3 | 4 |  | 6 | 7 | 10 | 9 | 8 | 11 | 5 |  |  |  |  |  |  |  | 39 |
| 1 |  | 2 | 4 |  | 6 | 7 | 10 | 9 | 8 | 11 | 5 |  | 3 |  |  |  |  |  | 40 |
| 1 | 2 | 3 | 4 | 5 |  | 7 |  | 9 | 8 | 11 | 6 |  |  |  |  |  | 10 |  | 41 |
| 1 | 2 | 3 | 4 | 5* | 6 | 7 |  | 9 | 8 | 11 | 10 |  |  |  |  |  |  |  | 42 |
| 41 | 13 | 37 | 41 | 24 | 20 | 41 | 23 | 41 | 38 | 34 | 40 | 7 | 36 | 14 | 1 | 6 | 4 | 1 |  |
|  |  |  |  |  |  |  |  |  |  | 3 | 1 | 1 |  | 3 | 1 | 1 |  |  |  |
|  |  | 1 | 1 | 1 | 1 | 28 | 7 | 15 | 15 | 10 | 3 | 2 | 2 |  |  | 1 | 1 |  |  |

1 own-goal

# 1968-69

Manager: Sir Matt Busby

| 1 | Aug | 10 | (h) | Everton | W | 2-1 | Best, Charlton | 61,311 |
|---|---|---|---|---|---|---|---|---|
| 2 | | 14 | (a) | West Brom A | L | 1-3 | Charlton | 38,299 |
| 3 | | 17 | (a) | Manchester C | D | 0-0 | | 63,052 |
| 4 | | 21 | (h) | Coventry C | W | 1-0 | Ryan | 51,201 |
| 5 | | 24 | (h) | Chelsea | L | 0-4 | | 55,114 |
| 6 | | 28 | (h) | Tottenham H | W | 3-1 | Fitzpatrick 2, Beal (og) | 62,649 |
| 7 | | 31 | (a) | Sheffield W | L | 4-5 | Law 2, Best, Charlton | 50,490 |
| 8 | Sep | 7 | (h) | West Ham U | D | 1-1 | Law | 63,274 |
| 9 | | 14 | (a) | Burnley | L | 0-1 | | 32,935 |
| 10 | | 21 | (h) | Newcastle U | W | 3-1 | Best 2, Law | 47,262 |
| 11 | Oct | 5 | (h) | Arsenal | D | 0-0 | | 61,843 |
| 12 | | 9 | (a) | Tottenham H | D | 2-2 | Crerand, Law | 56,205 |
| 13 | | 12 | (a) | Liverpool | L | 0-2 | | 53,392 |
| 14 | | 19 | (h) | Southampton | L | 1-2 | Best | 46,526 |
| 15 | | 26 | (a) | Queen's Park R | W | 3-2 | Best 2, Law | 31,138 |
| 16 | Nov | 2 | (h) | Leeds U | D | 0-0 | | 53,839 |
| 17 | | 9 | (a) | Sunderland | D | 1-1 | Hurley (og) | 33,151 |
| 18 | | 16 | (h) | Ipswich T | D | 0-0 | | 45,796 |
| 19 | | 23 | (a) | Stoke C | D | 0-0 | | 30,562 |
| 20 | | 30 | (h) | Wolves | W | 2-0 | Best, Law | 50,165 |
| 21 | Dec | 7 | (a) | Leicester C | L | 1-2 | Law | 36,303 |
| 22 | | 14 | (h) | Liverpool | W | 1-0 | Law | 55,354 |
| 23 | | 21 | (a) | Southampton | L | 0-2 | | 26,194 |
| 24 | | 26 | (a) | Arsenal | L | 0-3 | | 62,300 |
| 25 | Jan | 11 | (a) | Leeds U | L | 1-2 | Charlton | 48,145 |
| 26 | | 18 | (h) | Sunderland | W | 4-1 | Law 3, Best | 45,670 |
| 27 | Feb | 1 | (a) | Ipswich T | L | 0-1 | | 30,837 |
| 28 | | 15 | (a) | Wolves | D | 2-2 | Best, Charlton | 44,023 |
| 29 | Mar | 8 | (h) | Manchester C | L | 0-1 | | 63,264 |
| 30 | | 10 | (a) | Everton | D | 0-0 | | 57,514 |
| 31 | | 15 | (a) | Chelsea | L | 2-3 | James, Law | 60,436 |
| 32 | | 19 | (h) | Queen's Park R | W | 8-1 | Morgan 3, Best 2, Aston, Kidd, Stiles | 36,638 |
| 33 | | 22 | (h) | Sheffield W | W | 1-0 | Best | 45,527 |
| 34 | | 24 | (h) | Stoke C | D | 1-1 | Aston | 39,931 |
| 35 | | 29 | (a) | West Ham U | D | 0-0 | | 41,546 |
| 36 | | 31 | (a) | Nottingham F | W | 1-0 | Best | 41,892 |
| 37 | Apr | 2 | (h) | West Brom A | W | 2-1 | Best 2 | 38,846 |
| 38 | | 5 | (h) | Nottingham F | W | 3-1 | Morgan 2, Best | 51,952 |
| 39 | | 8 | (a) | Coventry C | L | 1-2 | Fitzpatrick | 45,402 |
| 40 | | 12 | (a) | Newcastle U | L | 0-2 | | 46,379 |
| 41 | | 19 | (h) | Burnley | W | 2-0 | Best, Waldron (og) | 52,626 |
| 42 | May | 17 | (h) | Leicester C | W | 3-2 | Best, Law, Morgan | 45,860 |

FINAL LEAGUE POSITION: 11th in Division One

Appearances
Sub Appearances
Goals

FA Cup

| 3 | Jan | 4 | (a) | Exeter C | W | 3-1 |
|---|---|---|---|---|---|---|
| 4 | | 25 | (h) | Watford | D | 1-1 |
| R | Feb | 3 | (a) | Watford | W | 2-0 |
| 5 | | 8 | (a) | Birmingham C | D | 2-2 |
| R | | 24 | (h) | Birmingham C | W | 6-2 |
| 6 | Mar | 1 | (h) | Everton | L | 0-1 |

Manchester United also reached the semi-final of the European Cup (see *United in Europe*).

| Stepney | Brennan | Dunne | Crerand | Foulkes | Stiles | Best | Kidd | Charlton | Law | Aston | Sadler | Kopel | Fitzpatrick | Gowling | Burns | Ryan | Morgan | Sartori | James | Rimmer | |
|---|---|---|---|---|---|---|---|---|---|---|---|---|---|---|---|---|---|---|---|---|---|
| 1 | 2 | 3 | 4 | 5 | 6 | 7 | 8 | 9 | 10 | 11 | | | | | | | | | | | 1 |
| 1 | 2 | 3 | 4 | 5* | 6 | 7 | 8 | 9 | 10 | 11 | 12 | | | | | | | | | | 2 |
| 1 | | 3 | | | 6 | 7 | 10 | 9 | | 11* | 5 | 2 | 4 | 8 | 12 | | | | | | 3 |
| 1 | | 3 | | | 6 | 11 | 8 | 9 | | | 5 | 2 | 4 | | 10 | 7 | | | | | 4 |
| 1 | | 3 | 4 | | 6 | 11 | 8 | 9 | | | 5 | 2 | | | 10 | 7 | | | | | 5 |
| 1 | 2 | 3 | | | 6 | 11 | 8 | 9 | 10 | | 5 | | 4 | | | | 7 | | | | 6 |
| 1 | 2 | 3* | | | 6 | 11 | 8 | 9 | 10 | | 5 | | 4 | | 12 | | 7 | | | | 7 |
| 1 | | 2 | | 5 | 6 | 11 | | 9 | 10 | | 8 | | 4 | | 3 | | 7 | | | | 8 |
| 1 | | 2 | | 5 | 6 | 11 | | 9 | 10 | | 8 | | 4 | | 3 | | 7 | | | | 9 |
| 1 | | 2 | 4* | | 6 | 11 | 12 | 9 | 10 | | 5 | | 8 | | 3 | | 7 | | | | 10 |
| 1 | | 2 | 4 | 5 | 6 | 11 | | 9 | 10 | | | | 8 | | 3 | | 7 | | | | 11 |
| 1 | | 2 | 4 | 5 | 6 | 11 | | 9 | 10 | | | | 8 | | 3* | | 7 | 12 | | | 12 |
| 1 | 2 | | 4 | | 6 | | | 9 | | | | 3 | 8 | 10 | | 7 | | 11 | 5 | | 13 |
| 1 | | 3 | 4 | 5* | 6 | 11 | | 9 | | | 8 | 2 | 12 | | | | 7 | 10 | | | 14 |
| 1 | 2 | 3 | 4 | | 6 | 11 | 8 | 9 | 10 | | 5 | | | | | | 7 | | | | 15 |
| 1 | 2 | 3 | 4 | | 6 | 11 | 8 | 9 | 10 | | 5 | | | | | | 7 | | | | 16 |
| 1 | 2 | 3 | 4 | | 6 | 11 | 8 | 9 | | | 5 | | | | | | 7 | 10 | | | 17 |
| 1 | 2 | 3 | 4 | | 6 | 11 | 8* | 9 | 10 | | | 12 | | | | | 7 | | 5 | | 18 |
| 1 | | 3 | 4 | | 6 | 8 | | 9 | | | | 2 | 10 | | | | 7 | 11 | 5 | | 19 |
| 1 | | 3 | 4 | | 6* | 11 | | 9 | 10 | | 5 | 2 | 12 | | | | 7 | 8 | | | 20 |
| 1 | | 2 | 4 | | 6 | 11 | | 9 | 10 | | 5 | | | | 3 | | 7 | 8 | | | 21 |
| 1 | | 2 | 4 | | 6 | 7 | | 9 | 10 | | 8 | | | | 3 | | | 11 | 5 | | 22 |
| 1 | | 2 | 4 | | 6 | 7 | | 9 | 10 | | 8 | | | | 3 | | | 11 | 5 | | 23 |
| 1 | | 2 | 4* | | 6 | 7 | 11 | 9 | 10 | | 8 | | | | 3 | | | 12 | 5 | | 24 |
| 1 | | 2 | 4 | | 6 | 7 | | 9 | 10 | | | | 8 | | 3 | | | 11 | 5 | | 25 |
| | | 2 | | | 6 | 11 | | 9 | 10 | | | | 4 | | 3 | | 7 | 8 | 5 | 1 | 26 |
| 1 | | 3 | 4 | | 6 | 11 | 8 | 9 | 10 | | | | 2 | | | | 7 | | 5 | | 27 |
| 1 | | 3 | 4 | 12 | | 11 | 8 | 9 | | | 6 | | 2 | | | | 7 | 10* | 5 | | 28 |
| 1 | 2 | | 4 | 5 | 6 | 11 | 8 | 9 | | | 10 | | 3 | | | | 7 | | | | 29 |
| 1 | 2* | 3 | 4 | 12 | 6 | 7 | 8 | | | 11 | 10 | | 9 | | | | | | 5 | | 30 |
| 1 | | 3 | 4 | | 6 | 11 | 8 | | 10 | | 9 | | 2 | | | | 7 | | 5 | | 31 |
| 1 | | 3 | 4 | | 6 | 11 | 8 | | 10 | 9 | | | 2 | | | | 7 | | 5 | | 32 |
| 1 | | 3 | 4 | | 6 | 9 | 8 | | 10 | 11 | | | 2 | | | | 7 | | 5 | | 33 |
| 1 | | 3 | 4 | | 6 | 11 | 8 | | 10 | 9 | 12 | | 2 | | | | 7* | | 5 | | 34 |
| 1 | | 3* | 4 | | 6 | 11 | 8 | | 10 | 9 | 12 | | 2 | | | 7 | | | 5 | | 35 |
| 1 | | | 4 | | 3 | 11 | 8 | | 10 | 9 | 6 | | 2 | | | 7 | | | 5 | | 36 |
| 1 | | | 4 | 12 | 3 | 11 | 10 | | | 9 | 6 | | 2 | | | 8* | 7 | | 5 | | 37 |
| 1 | | | 4 | | 3 | 11 | 8 | | 10 | 9 | 6 | | 2 | | | | 7 | | 5 | | 38 |
| 1 | | | 4 | | 3 | 11 | 8 | 10 | | 9 | 6 | | 2 | | | | 7 | | 5 | | 39 |
| | | | 4 | | 3 | 11 | 8 | 9 | 10 | | 6 | | 2 | | | | 7 | | 5 | 1 | 40 |
| | 2 | | 4 | 5 | 6 | 11 | 8 | | 10 | 9 | | | 3 | | | | 7 | | | 1 | 41 |
| | 2 | | 4 | 5 | 6 | 11 | 8 | 9 | 10 | | | | | | 3 | | 7 | | | 1 | 42 |
| 38 | 13 | 33 | 35 | 10 | 41 | 41 | 28 | 32 | 30 | 13 | 26 | 7 | 28 | 2 | 14 | 6 | 29 | 11 | 21 | 4 | |
| | | | | 3 | | | 1 | | | | 3 | 1 | 2 | | 2 | | | 2 | | | |
| | | | 1 | | 1 | 19 | 1 | 5 | 14 | 2 | | | 3 | | | 1 | 6 | | 1 | | |

3 own-goals

# 1969-70

Manager: Wilf McGuinness

| | | | | | | | |
|---|---|---|---|---|---|---|---|
| 1 | Aug | 9 | (a) | Crystal P | D 2-2 | Charlton, Morgan | 48,610 |
| 2 | | 13 | (h) | Everton | L 0-2 | | 57,752 |
| 3 | | 16 | (h) | Southampton | L 1-4 | Morgan | 46,328 |
| 4 | | 19 | (a) | Everton | L 0-3 | | 53,185 |
| 5 | | 23 | (a) | Wolves | D 0-0 | | 50,783 |
| 6 | | 27 | (h) | Newcastle U | D 0-0 | | 52,774 |
| 7 | | 30 | (h) | Sunderland | W 3-1 | Best, Givens, Kidd | 50,570 |
| 8 | Sep | 6 | (a) | Leeds U | D 2-2 | Best 2 | 44,271 |
| 9 | | 13 | (h) | Liverpool | W 1-0 | Morgan | 56,509 |
| 10 | | 17 | (a) | Sheffield W | W 3-1 | Best 2, Kidd | 39,298 |
| 11 | | 20 | (a) | Arsenal | D 2-2 | Best, Sadler | 59,498 |
| 12 | | 27 | (h) | West Ham U | W 5-2 | Best 2, Burns, Charlton, Kidd | 58,579 |
| 13 | Oct | 4 | (a) | Derby C | L 0-2 | | 40,724 |
| 14 | | 8 | (a) | Southampton | W 3-0 | Best, Burns, Kidd | 31,044 |
| 15 | | 11 | (h) | Ipswich T | W 2-1 | Best, Kidd | 52,281 |
| 16 | | 18 | (h) | Nottingham F | D 1-1 | Best | 53,702 |
| 17 | | 25 | (a) | West Brom A | L 1-2 | Kidd | 45,120 |
| 18 | Nov | 1 | (h) | Stoke C | D 1-1 | Charlton | 53,406 |
| 19 | | 8 | (a) | Coventry C | W 2-1 | Aston, Law | 43,446 |
| 20 | | 15 | (a) | Manchester C | L 0-4 | | 63,013 |
| 21 | | 22 | (h) | Tottenham H | W 3-1 | Charlton 2, Burns | 50,003 |
| 22 | | 29 | (a) | Burnley | D 1-1 | Best | 23,770 |
| 23 | Dec | 6 | (h) | Chelsea | L 0-2 | | 49,344 |
| 24 | | 13 | (a) | Liverpool | W 4-1 | Charlton, Morgan, Ure, Yeats (og) | 47,682 |
| 25 | | 26 | (h) | Wolves | D 0-0 | | 50,806 |
| 26 | | 27 | (a) | Sunderland | D 1-1 | Kidd | 36,504 |
| 27 | Jan | 10 | (h) | Arsenal | W 2-1 | Morgan, Sartori | 41,055 |
| 28 | | 17 | (a) | West Ham U | D 0-0 | | 41,643 |
| 29 | | 26 | (h) | Leeds U | D 2-2 | Kidd, Sadler | 59,879 |
| 30 | | 31 | (h) | Derby C | W 1-0 | Charlton | 59,315 |
| 31 | Feb | 10 | (a) | Ipswich T | W 1-0 | Kidd | 29,755 |
| 32 | | 14 | (h) | Crystal P | D 1-1 | Kidd | 54,711 |
| 33 | | 28 | (a) | Stoke C | D 2-2 | Morgan, Sartori | 38,917 |
| 34 | Mar | 17 | (h) | Burnley | D 3-3 | Best, Crerand, Law | 38,377 |
| 35 | | 21 | (a) | Chelsea | L 1-2 | Morgan | 61,479 |
| 36 | | 28 | (h) | Manchester C | L 1-2 | Kidd | 59,777 |
| 37 | | 30 | (h) | Coventry C | D 1-1 | Kidd | 38,647 |
| 38 | | 31 | (a) | Nottingham F | W 2-1 | Charlton, Gowling | 39,228 |
| 39 | Apr | 4 | (a) | Newcastle U | L 1-5 | Charlton | 43,094 |
| 40 | | 8 | (h) | West Brom A | W 7-0 | Charlton 2, Fitzpatrick 2, Gowling 2, Best | 26,582 |
| 41 | | 13 | (a) | Tottenham H | L 1-2 | Fitzpatrick | 41,808 |
| 42 | | 15 | (h) | Sheffield W | D 2-2 | Best, Charlton | 36,649 |

FINAL LEAGUE POSITION: 8th in Division One

Appearances
Sub Appearances
Goals

## FA Cup

| | | | | | | |
|---|---|---|---|---|---|---|
| 3 | Jan | 3 | (a) | Ipswich T | W 1-0 | |
| 4 | | 24 | (h) | Manchester C | W 3-0 | |
| 5 | Feb | 7 | (a) | Northampton T | W 8-2 | |
| 6 | | 21 | (a) | Middlesbrough | D 1-1 | |
| R | | 25 | (h) | Middlesbrough | W 2-1 | |
| SF | Mar | 14 | (n*) | Leeds U | D 0-0 | (*Played at Hillsborough, Sheffield.) |
| R | | 23 | (n†) | Leeds U | D 0-0 | (After extra-time. †Played at Villa Park, Birmingham.) |
| 2R | | 26 | (n‡) | Leeds U | L 0-1 | (‡Played at Burnden Park, Bolton.) |
| PO | Apr | 10 | (n§) | Watford | W 2-0 | (§Played at Arsenal Stadium, Highbury, London.) |

316

| Rimmer | Dunne | Burns | Crerand | Foulkes | Sadler | Morgan | Kidd | Charlton | Law | Best | Givens | Brennan | Stepney | Fitzpatrick | Edwards | Aston | Ure | Gowling | Sartori | Stiles | Ryan | James | |
|---|---|---|---|---|---|---|---|---|---|---|---|---|---|---|---|---|---|---|---|---|---|---|---|
| 1 | 2* | 3 | 4 | 5 | 6 | 7 | 8 | 9 | 10 | 11 | 12 | | | | | | | | | | | | 1 |
| | | 3 | 4 | 5* | 6 | 7 | 8 | 9 | 10 | 11 | 12 | 2 | | | | | | | | | | | 2 |
| 1 | | 3 | 4 | 5 | 6 | 7 | 8 | 9 | 10 | 11 | | 2 | | | | | | | | | | | 3 |
| | | 3 | 4 | | 6 | 7 | 8 | 10 | 9 | | | | 1 | 2 | 5 | 11 | | | | | | | 4 |
| | | 3 | 4 | | 6 | 7 | 8 | 9 | 10* | 11 | 12 | | 1 | 2 | 5 | | | | | | | | 5 |
| | 3 | | 4 | | 6 | 7 | 8 | 9 | 10 | 11 | | | 1 | 2 | 5 | | | | | | | | 6 |
| | 3 | | 4 | | 6 | 7 | 8 | 9 | 10 | 11 | | | 1 | 2 | 5 | | | | | | | | 7 |
| | | 3 | 4 | | 6 | 7 | 8 | 9 | | 11 | | | 1 | 2 | 5 | 10 | | | | | | | 8 |
| | | 3 | 4 | | 6 | 7 | 8 | 9 | | 11 | | | 1 | 2 | 5 | 10 | | | | | | | 9 |
| | | 3 | 4 | | 6 | 7 | 8 | 9 | | 11 | | | 1 | 2 | 12 | 5 | 10* | | | | | | 10 |
| | | 3 | 4 | | 6 | 7 | 8 | 9 | | 11 | | | 1 | 2 | | 10 | 5 | | | | | | 11 |
| | | 3 | 4 | | 6 | 7 | 8 | 9 | | 11 | | | 1 | 2 | | 10 | 5 | | | | | | 12 |
| | | 3 | 4 | | 6 | 7 | 8 | 9 | | 11 | | | 1 | 2 | | 10* | 5 | | 12 | | | | 13 |
| | | 3 | 4 | | 6 | 7 | 8 | 9 | | 11 | | | 1 | 2 | | 10 | 5 | | | | | | 14 |
| | | 3 | 4 | | 6 | 7 | 8 | 9 | | 11* | 12 | | 1 | 2 | | 10 | 5 | | | | | | 15 |
| | | 3 | 4 | | 6 | 7 | 8 | 9 | | 11 | | | 1 | 2 | | 10 | 5 | | | | | | 16 |
| | | 3 | 4 | | 6 | | 8 | 9 | | 11 | 12 | 2 | 1 | | | 10* | 5 | | 7 | | | | 17 |
| | | 3 | 4 | | 6 | | 8 | 9 | 7 | 11 | | 2 | 1 | | | 10 | 5 | | | | | | 18 |
| | | 3 | 4 | | 6 | | | 9 | 10 | 8 | | 2 | 1 | | | 11 | 5 | | 7 | | | | 19 |
| | | 3 | 4 | | 6 | | 12 | 9 | 10 | 8 | | 2 | 1 | | | 11 | 5 | | 7* | | | | 20 |
| | | 3 | 4 | | 6 | | 8 | 9 | | 10 | | 1 | 2* | 12 | | 11 | 5 | | 7 | | | | 21 |
| | | 3 | 4 | | 6 | | 8 | 9 | | 7 | | | 1 | | 2 | 11 | 5 | | | | | | 22 |
| | | 3 | 4 | | 6 | | 8* | 9 | | 7 | | | 1 | | 2 | 11 | 5 | | 10 | 12 | | | 23 |
| | | 3 | 4 | 10 | 6 | 7 | | 9 | | 8 | | 2 | 1 | | | 11* | 5 | | 12 | | | | 24 |
| | | 3 | 4 | 8 | 6 | 7 | 10 | 9 | | 11 | | | 1 | 2 | | | 5 | | | | | | 25 |
| | | | 4 | 8 | 6 | 7 | 10 | 9 | | 11 | | 3 | 1 | 2 | | | 5 | | | | | | 26 |
| | 3* | | 4 | 8 | 6 | 7 | 10 | 9 | | | | | 1 | 2 | | 11 | 5 | | 12 | | | | 27 |
| 1 | | 3 | 4 | | 6 | 7 | 10 | 9 | | | | | | 2 | | 11 | 5 | | 8 | | | | 28 |
| | | 3 | 4 | | 6 | 7 | 10 | 9 | | | | 1 | | 2 | | 11 | 5 | | 8 | | | | 29 |
| | | 3 | 4 | | 6 | 7 | 10 | 9 | | | | 1 | | 2 | | 11 | 5 | | 8 | | | | 30 |
| | 3 | | 4 | | 6 | 7 | 10 | 9 | | 11 | | 1 | | 2 | | | 5 | | 8 | | | | 31 |
| | 3 | | 4 | | 6 | 7 | 10 | 9 | | 11 | | 1 | | 2 | | | 5 | | 8 | | | | 32 |
| | 3 | 12 | 4 | | 6* | 7 | 10 | 9 | | 11 | | 1 | | 2 | | | 5 | | 8 | | | | 33 |
| 1 | 3 | | 4 | | 6 | 7 | | 9 | 10 | 11 | | | | 2 | | | 5 | | 8 | | | | 34 |
| | | 3 | 4 | | | 7 | | 9 | 10 | 11 | | 1 | | 2 | | | 5 | | 8 | 6 | | | 35 |
| | 3 | 6 | 4 | | 5 | 7 | 10 | 9 | 12 | 11 | | 1 | | 2 | | | | | 8* | | | | 36 |
| | 3 | 12 | | | 6 | 7 | 10* | 9 | 8 | | | | 1 | 4 | 2 | 11 | 5 | | | | | | 37 |
| | 3 | | 4 | | 6 | 7 | | 9 | | 11 | | | 1 | 8 | | | | 10 | 2 | 5 | | | 38 |
| | 3 | | 4 | | 6 | 7 | | 9 | | | | | 1 | 2 | 11* | | 8 | 12 | 10 | 5 | | | 39 |
| | 3 | | 4 | | 6 | 7 | | 9 | | 11 | | | 1 | 8 | | | 5 | 10 | 2 | | | | 40 |
| | 3 | | 4 | | | 7* | 10 | 9 | | 11 | | | 1 | 8 | 2 | | 5 | 12 | 6 | | | | 41 |
| | 3 | | 4 | | 5 | 7 | 10 | 9 | | 11 | | | 1 | 8 | 2 | | | | 6 | | | | 42 |
| 5 | 33 | 30 | 25 | 3 | 40 | 35 | 33 | 40 | 10 | 37 | 4 | 8 | 37 | 20 | 18 | 21 | 34 | 6 | 13 | 8 | | 2 | |
| | 2 | | | | 1 | | 1 | | 4 | 1 | | | | 1 | 1 | | | 1 | 4 | | 1 | | |
| | | 3 | 1 | | 2 | 7 | 12 | 12 | 2 | 15 | 1 | | | | 3 | | 1 | 1 | 1 | 3 | | 2 | |

1 own-goal

League Cup

| | | | | | | |
|---|---|---|---|---|---|---|
| 2 | Sep | 3 | (h) | Middlesbrough | W | 1-0 |
| 3 | | 23 | (h) | Wrexham | W | 2-0 |
| 4 | Oct | 14 | (a) | Burnley | D | 0-0 |
| R | | 20 | (h) | Burnley | W | 1-0 |
| 5 | Nov | 12 | (a) | Derby C | D | 0-0 |
| R | | 19 | (h) | Derby C | W | 1-0 |
| SF | Dec | 3 | (a) | Manchester C | L | 1-2 |
| | | 17 | (h) | Manchester C | D | 2-2 |

# 1970-71

Manager: Wilf McGuinnes to December 1970, then Sir Matt Busby.

| 1 | Aug | 15 | (h) | Leeds U | L | 0-1 | | 59,365 |
|---|---|---|---|---|---|---|---|---|
| 2 | | 19 | (h) | Chelsea | D | 0-0 | | 50,979 |
| 3 | | 22 | (a) | Arsenal | L | 0-4 | | 54,117 |
| 4 | | 25 | (a) | Burnley | W | 2-0 | Law 2 | 29,385 |
| 5 | | 29 | (h) | West Ham U | D | 1-1 | Fitzpatrick | 50,643 |
| 6 | Sep | 2 | (h) | Everton | W | 2-0 | Best, Charlton | 51,346 |
| 7 | | 5 | (a) | Liverpool | D | 1-1 | Kidd | 52,542 |
| 8 | | 12 | (h) | Coventry C | W | 2-0 | Best, Charlton | 48,939 |
| 9 | | 19 | (a) | Ipswich T | L | 0-4 | | 27,776 |
| 10 | | 26 | (h) | Blackpool | D | 1-1 | Best | 46,647 |
| 11 | Oct | 3 | (a) | Wolves | L | 2-3 | Gowling, Kidd | 38,629 |
| 12 | | 10 | (h) | Crystal P | L | 0-1 | | 42,979 |
| 13 | | 17 | (a) | Leeds U | D | 2-2 | Charlton, Fitzpatrick | 50,190 |
| 14 | | 24 | (h) | West Brom A | W | 2-1 | Kidd, Law | 43,278 |
| 15 | | 31 | (a) | Newcastle U | L | 0-1 | | 45,140 |
| 16 | Nov | 7 | (h) | Stoke C | D | 2-2 | Law, Sadler | 47,451 |
| 17 | | 14 | (a) | Nottingham F | W | 2-1 | Gowling, Sartori | 36,364 |
| 18 | | 21 | (a) | Southampton | L | 0-1 | | 30,202 |
| 19 | | 28 | (h) | Huddersfield T | D | 1-1 | Best | 45,306 |
| 20 | Dec | 5 | (a) | Tottenham H | D | 2-2 | Best, Law | 55,693 |
| 21 | | 12 | (h) | Manchester C | L | 1-4 | Kidd | 52,636 |
| 22 | | 19 | (h) | Arsenal | L | 1-3 | Sartori | 33,182 |
| 23 | | 26 | (a) | Derby C | D | 4-4 | Law 2, Best, Kidd | 34,068 |
| 24 | Jan | 9 | (a) | Chelsea | W | 2-1 | Gowling, Morgan | 53,482 |
| 25 | | 16 | (h) | Burnley | D | 1-1 | Aston | 40,135 |
| 26 | | 30 | (a) | Huddersfield T | W | 2-1 | Aston, Law | 41,464 |
| 27 | Feb | 6 | (h) | Tottenham H | W | 2-1 | Best, Morgan | 48,965 |
| 28 | | 20 | (h) | Southampton | W | 5-1 | Gowling 4, Morgan | 36,060 |
| 29 | | 23 | (a) | Everton | L | 0-1 | | 52,544 |
| 30 | | 27 | (h) | Newcastle U | W | 1-0 | Kidd | 41,902 |
| 31 | Mar | 6 | (a) | West Brom A | L | 3-4 | Aston, Best, Kidd | 41,112 |
| 32 | | 13 | (h) | Nottingham F | W | 2-0 | Best, Law | 40,473 |
| 33 | | 20 | (a) | Stoke C | W | 2-1 | Best 2 | 40,005 |
| 34 | Apr | 3 | (a) | West Ham U | L | 1-2 | Best | 38,507 |
| 35 | | 10 | (h) | Derby C | L | 1-2 | Law | 45,691 |
| 36 | | 12 | (h) | Wolves | W | 1-0 | Gowling | 41,886 |
| 37 | | 13 | (a) | Coventry C | L | 1-2 | Best | 33,818 |
| 38 | | 17 | (a) | Crystal P | W | 5-3 | Law 3, Best 2 | 39,145 |
| 39 | | 19 | (h) | Liverpool | L | 0-2 | | 44,004 |
| 40 | | 24 | (h) | Ipswich T | W | 3-2 | Charlton, Best, Kidd | 33,566 |
| 41 | May | 1 | (a) | Blackpool | D | 1-1 | Law | 29,857 |
| 42 | | 5 | (a) | Manchester C | W | 4-3 | Best 2, Charlton, Law | 43,626 |

FINAL LEAGUE POSITION: 8th in Division One

Appearances
Sub Appearances
Goals

## FA Cup

| 3 | Jan | 2 | (h) | Middlesbrough | D | 0-0 |
|---|---|---|---|---|---|---|
| R | | 5 | (a) | Middlesbrough | L | 1-2 |

## League Cup

| 2 | Sep | 9 | (a) | Aldershot | W | 3-1 |
|---|---|---|---|---|---|---|
| 3 | Oct | 7 | (h) | Portsmouth | W | 1-0 |
| 4 | | 28 | (h) | Chelsea | W | 2-1 |
| 5 | Nov | 18 | (h) | Crystal P | W | 4-2 |
| SF | Dec | 16 | (h) | Aston Villa | D | 1-1 |
| | | 23 | (a) | Aston Villa | L | 1-2 |

318

Appearance grid (shirt numbers worn by each player per match). Columns left-to-right: Stepney, Edwards, Dunne, Crerand, Ure, Sadler, Fitzpatrick, Stiles, Charlton, Kidd, Best, Gowling, Morgan, Law, Rimmer, Young, James, Watson, Burns, Sartori, Aston, O'Neil.

| Stepney | Edwards | Dunne | Crerand | Ure | Sadler | Fitzpatrick | Stiles | Charlton | Kidd | Best | Gowling | Morgan | Law | Rimmer | Young | James | Watson | Burns | Sartori | Aston | O'Neil | No. |
|---|---|---|---|---|---|---|---|---|---|---|---|---|---|---|---|---|---|---|---|---|---|---|
| 1 | 2 | 3 | 4 | 5 | 6 | 7 | 8* | 9 | 10 | 11 | 12 | | | | | | | | | | | 1 |
| 1 | 2 | 3 | 4 | 5 | 6 | | 8 | 10 | 9 | 11 | | 7 | | | | | | | | | | 2 |
| 1* | 12 | 3 | 4 | 5 | 6† | 8 | 2 | 9 | | 11 | | 7 | 10 | | | | | | | | | 3 |
| | 2 | 3 | | 5 | 6 | 4 | | 10 | 9 | 11 | | | 7 | 8 | 1 | | | | | | | 4 |
| | 2 | 3 | | 5 | 6 | 4 | | 10* | 9 | 11 | 12 | | 7 | 8 | 1 | | | | | | | 5 |
| | 2 | 3 | | 5 | 6 | 4 | 7 | 9 | 10 | 11 | | | | 8 | 1 | | | | | | | 6 |
| | 2 | 3 | | 5 | 6 | 4 | 7 | 9 | 10 | 11 | | | | 8 | 1 | | | | | | | 7 |
| | 2 | 3 | | 5 | 6 | 4 | 7 | 9 | 10 | 11 | | | | 8 | 1 | | | | | | | 8 |
| | 2 | 3* | | 5 | 6 | 4 | 7 | 9 | | 11 | | | 10 | 8 | 1 | 12 | | | | | | 9 |
| | | | | | 6 | 4 | | 9 | 10 | 11 | | | 8 | 7 | 1 | 5 | 2 | 3 | | | | 10 |
| | | | | | 6 | 4 | | 9 | 10 | 11 | | | 8 | 7 | 1 | 5* | 2 | 3 | 12 | | | 11 |
| | 2 | 3 | | 5 | 6 | 4 | | 9 | 10 | | | | 8 | 7 | 1 | | | | 11 | | | 12 |
| | 2 | 3 | | 5 | 6* | 4 | | 9 | 10 | | | | 8 | 7 | 1 | 12 | | | 11 | | | 13 |
| | 2 | 3 | | 5 | | 4 | | 9 | 10 | | | | 8 | 7 | 1 | 6 | | | 11 | | | 14 |
| | 2 | 3 | | | 6 | 4 | | 9 | 10 | | | | 8 | 7 | 1 | 5 | | | 11 | | | 15 |
| | 2 | | | | 6 | 4 | | 9 | 10 | | | | 8 | 7 | 1 | 5 | | 3 | 11 | | | 16 |
| | | 3 | | | 6 | 4 | | 9 | 10 | | | | 8 | 7 | 1 | 5 | 2 | | 11 | | | 17 |
| | | 3 | | | 6 | 4* | | 9 | 10 | | | | 8 | 7 | 1 | 5 | 2 | | 12 | 11 | | 18 |
| | | 3 | | | 6 | 4 | | 9 | 10 | | | | 8 | 7 | 1 | 5 | 2 | | 11 | | | 19 |
| | | 3 | | | 6 | 4 | | 9 | 10 | | | | 8 | 7 | 1 | 5 | 2 | | 11 | | | 20 |
| | | 3 | 4 | | 6 | | | 9 | 10 | | | | 8 | 7* | 1 | 5 | 2 | | 12 | 11 | | 21 |
| | | 3 | 4 | | 6 | | | 9 | 10 | | | | 8 | 7 | 1 | 5 | 2 | | 11 | | | 22 |
| | | 3 | 4 | 5 | 6 | 2 | | 9 | 10 | | | | 8 | 7 | 11 | 1 | | | | | | 23 |
| 1 | 5 | 3 | 4 | | | 2 | | 6 | 9 | | | | 10 | 7 | 8 | | | | 11 | | | 24 |
| 1 | 5 | 3 | 4 | | | 2 | | 6 | 9 | | | | 10 | 7 | 8 | | | | 11 | | | 25 |
| 1 | 5 | | 4 | | 6 | 2 | | 9 | 11 | 10 | | | 7 | 8* | | | | 3 | 12 | | | 26 |
| 1 | 5 | | 4 | | 6 | 2 | | 9 | 8 | 11 | 10 | | 7 | | | | | 3 | | | | 27 |
| 1 | 5 | | 4 | | 6 | 2 | | 9 | 8 | | 10 | | 7 | | | | | 3 | 11 | | | 28 |
| 1 | 5 | 3 | 4 | | 6 | 2 | | 9 | 8 | 10* | | | 7 | | | | | | 12 | 11 | | 29 |
| 1 | 5 | 3 | 4 | | 6 | 2 | | 9 | 10 | 8 | | | 7 | | | | | | 11 | | | 30 |
| 1 | 5 | 3 | 4 | | 6 | 2 | | 9 | 10 | 8 | | | 7 | | | | | | 11 | | | 31 |
| 1 | 5 | 3 | 4 | | 6 | 2 | | 9 | 8 | | | | 7 | 10 | | | | | 12 | 11* | | 32 |
| 1 | 5 | 3 | 4 | | 6 | 2 | | 9 | 8 | | | | 7 | 10 | | | | | 11 | | | 33 |
| 1 | 5 | 3 | 4 | | 6* | 2 | | 9 | 8 | | | | 7 | 10 | | | | | 12 | 11 | | 34 |
| 1 | 5 | 2 | 4 | | | 6 | | 9 | 8 | 12 | | | 7 | 10 | | | | 3 | | 11* | | 35 |
| 1 | 5 | 2 | 4 | | | 6 | | 9 | 12 | 7 | | | 8 | 11 | 10* | | | 3 | | | | 36 |
| 1 | 5 | 2 | 4 | | | 6 | | 9 | 10 | 7 | | | 8 | 11 | | | | 3 | | | | 37 |
| 1 | 5 | 3 | 4* | | 6 | 2 | | 9 | | 7 | | | 8 | 11 | 10 | | | | 12 | | | 38 |
| 1 | 5 | 2 | 4 | | 6 | | | 9 | | 7 | | | 8 | 11 | 10 | | | 3 | | | | 39 |
| 1 | | 2 | 4 | | 6* | | | 9 | 10 | 11 | 8 | | 7 | | | 5 | | | 3 | 12 | | 40 |
| 1 | | 2 | 4 | | 6 | | | 9 | 10 | 11 | 8 | | 7 | | | 5 | | | 3 | | | 41 |
| 1 | | | 4 | | 6 | | | 9 | 10 | 11 | 8 | | 7 | | | 5 | | 3 | 2 | | | 42 |
| 22 | 29 | 35 | 24 | 13 | 32 | 35 | 17 | 42 | 24 | 40 | 17 | 25 | 28 | 20 | 13 | 8 | 16 | 2 | 19 | 1 | | |
| | 1 | | | | | | | 1 | 3 | | | | 1 | | | 4 | 5 | 1 | | | | |
| | | | 1 | 2 | | 5 | 8 | 18 | 8 | 3 | 15 | | | | | | | | 2 | 3 | | |

†Sadler acted as substitute goalkeeper

319

# 1971-72

Manager: Frank O'Farrell

| 1 | Aug | 14 | (a) | Derby C | D | 2-2 | Gowling, Law | 35,886 |
|---|-----|----|-----|---------|---|-----|--------------|--------|
| 2 |  | 18 | (a) | Chelsea | W | 3-2 | Charlton, Kidd, Morgan | 54,763 |
| 3 |  | 20 | (h) | Arsenal | W | 3-1 | Charlton, Gowling, Kidd | 27,649 |
| 4 |  | 23 | (h) | West Brom A | W | 3-1 | Best 2, Gowling | 23,146 |
| 5 |  | 28 | (a) | Wolves | D | 1-1 | Best | 46,471 |
| 6 |  | 31 | (a) | Everton | L | 0-1 |  | 52,151 |
| 7 | Sep | 4 | (h) | Ipswich T | W | 1-0 | Best | 45,656 |
| 8 |  | 11 | (a) | Crystal P | W | 3-1 | Law 2, Kidd | 44,020 |
| 9 |  | 18 | (h) | West Ham U | W | 4-2 | Best 3, Charlton | 53,339 |
| 10 |  | 25 | (a) | Liverpool | D | 2-2 | Charlton, Law | 55,634 |
| 11 | Oct | 2 | (h) | Sheffield U | W | 2-0 | Best, Gowling | 51,735 |
| 12 |  | 9 | (a) | Huddersfield T | W | 3-0 | Best, Charlton, Law | 33,458 |
| 13 |  | 16 | (h) | Derby C | W | 1-0 | Best | 53,247 |
| 14 |  | 23 | (a) | Newcastle U | W | 1-0 | Best | 52,411 |
| 15 |  | 30 | (h) | Leeds U | L | 0-1 |  | 53,960 |
| 16 | Nov | 6 | (a) | Manchester C | D | 3-3 | Gowling, Kidd, McIlroy | 63,326 |
| 17 |  | 13 | (h) | Tottenham H | W | 3-1 | Law 2, McIlroy | 54,058 |
| 18 |  | 20 | (h) | Leicester C | W | 3-2 | Law 2, Kidd | 48,757 |
| 19 |  | 27 | (a) | Southampton | W | 5-2 | Best 3, Kidd, McIlroy | 30,323 |
| 20 | Dec | 4 | (h) | Nottingham F | W | 3-2 | Kidd 2, Law | 45,411 |
| 21 |  | 11 | (a) | Stoke C | D | 1-1 | Law | 33,857 |
| 22 |  | 18 | (a) | Ipswich T | D | 0-0 |  | 29,229 |
| 23 |  | 27 | (h) | Coventry C | D | 2-2 | James, Law | 52,117 |
| 24 | Jan | 1 | (a) | West Ham U | L | 0-3 |  | 41,892 |
| 25 |  | 8 | (h) | Wolves | L | 1-3 | McIlroy | 46,781 |
| 26 |  | 22 | (h) | Chelsea | L | 0-1 |  | 55,927 |
| 27 |  | 29 | (a) | West Brom A | L | 1-2 | Kidd | 47,012 |
| 28 | Feb | 12 | (h) | Newcastle U | L | 0-2 |  | 44,983 |
| 29 |  | 19 | (a) | Leeds U | L | 1-5 | Burns | 45,399 |
| 30 | Mar | 4 | (a) | Tottenham H | L | 0-2 |  | 54,814 |
| 31 |  | 8 | (h) | Everton | D | 0-0 |  | 38,415 |
| 32 |  | 11 | (h) | Huddersfield T | W | 2-0 | Best, Storey-Moore | 53,581 |
| 33 |  | 25 | (h) | Crystal P | W | 4-0 | Charlton, Gowling, Law, Storey-Moore | 41,550 |
| 34 | Apr | 1 | (a) | Coventry C | W | 3-2 | Best, Charlton, Storey-Moore | 37,901 |
| 35 |  | 3 | (h) | Liverpool | L | 0-3 |  | 53,826 |
| 36 |  | 4 | (a) | Sheffield U | D | 1-1 | Sadler | 45,045 |
| 37 |  | 8 | (a) | Leicester C | L | 0-2 |  | 35,970 |
| 38 |  | 12 | (h) | Manchester C | L | 1-3 | Buchan | 56,362 |
| 39 |  | 15 | (h) | Southampton | W | 3-2 | Best, Kidd, Storey-Moore | 38,437 |
| 40 |  | 22 | (a) | Nottingham F | D | 0-0 |  | 35,063 |
| 41 |  | 25 | (a) | Arsenal | L | 0-3 |  | 49,125 |
| 42 |  | 29 | (h) | Stoke C | W | 3-0 | Best, Charlton, Storey-Moore | 34,959 |

FINAL LEAGUE POSITION: 8th in Division One

Appearances
Sub Appearances
Goals

FA Cup

| 3 | Jan | 15 | (a) | Southampton | D | 1-1 | |
|---|-----|----|-----|-------------|---|-----|---|
| R |  | 19 | (h) | Southampton | W | 4-1 | (After extra-time) |
| 4 | Feb | 5 | (a) | Preston NE | W | 2-0 | |
| 5 |  | 26 | (h) | Middlesbrough | D | 0-0 | |
| R |  | 29 | (a) | Middlesbrough | W | 3-0 | |
| 6 | Mar | 18 | (h) | Stoke C | D | 1-1 | |
| R |  | 22 | (a) | Stoke C | L | 1-2 | (After extra-time) |

In the League, Manchester United's first two home games (Matches 3 & 4) were played at Anfield, Liverpool and the Victoria Ground, Stoke, respectively due to Old Trafford being closed by the FA following crowd disturbances.

320

| Stepney | O'Neil | Dunne | Gowling | James | Sadler | Morgan | Kidd | Charlton | Law | Best | Fitzpatrick | Aston | Burns | Sartori | McIlroy | Edwards | Buchan | Storey-Moore | Young | Connaughton | # |
|---|---|---|---|---|---|---|---|---|---|---|---|---|---|---|---|---|---|---|---|---|---|
| 1 | 2 | 3 | 4 | 5 | 6 | 7 | 8 | 9 | 10 | 11 |  |  |  |  |  |  |  |  |  |  | 1 |
| 1 |  | 3 | 4 | 5 | 6 | 7 | 8 | 9 | 10 | 11 | 2 |  |  |  |  |  |  |  |  |  | 2 |
| 1 | 2 | 3 | 4 | 5 | 6 | 7 | 8 | 9 | 10 | 11* |  | 12 |  |  |  |  |  |  |  |  | 3 |
| 1 | 2 | 3 | 4 | 5 | 6 | 7 | 8 | 9* |  | 10 |  | 11 | 12 |  |  |  |  |  |  |  | 4 |
| 1 | 2 | 3 | 4 | 5 | 6 | 7 | 8 | 9 | 10 | 11 |  |  |  |  |  |  |  |  |  |  | 5 |
| 1 | 2 | 3 | 4 | 5 | 6 | 7 | 8 | 9 | 10 | 11 |  |  |  |  |  |  |  |  |  |  | 6 |
| 1 | 2 | 3 | 4 | 5 | 6 | 7 | 8 | 9 | 10* | 11 |  | 12 |  |  |  |  |  |  |  |  | 7 |
| 1 | 2 | 3 | 4* | 5 | 6 | 7 | 8 | 9 | 10 | 11 |  | 12 |  |  |  |  |  |  |  |  | 8 |
| 1 | 2 | 3 | 4 | 5 | 6 | 7 | 8 | 9 | 10 | 11 |  |  |  |  |  |  |  |  |  |  | 9 |
| 1 | 2 |  | 4 | 5 | 6 | 7 | 8 | 9 | 10 | 11 |  |  | 3 |  |  |  |  |  |  |  | 10 |
| 1 | 2 | 3* | 4 | 5 | 6 | 7 | 8 | 9 |  | 10 |  | 11 | 12 |  |  |  |  |  |  |  | 11 |
| 1 | 2 | 3 | 4 | 5 | 6 | 7 | 8 | 9 | 10 | 11 |  |  |  |  |  |  |  |  |  |  | 12 |
| 1 | 2 | 3 | 4 | 5 | 6 | 7 | 8 | 9 | 10 | 11 |  |  |  |  |  |  |  |  |  |  | 13 |
| 1 | 2 | 3* | 4 | 5 | 6 | 7 | 8 | 9 | 10 | 11 |  | 12 |  |  |  |  |  |  |  |  | 14 |
| 1 | 2 | 3 | 4 | 5 | 6 | 7 | 8* | 9 | 10 | 11 |  |  | 12 |  |  |  |  |  |  |  | 15 |
| 1 | 2 | 3* | 4 | 5 | 6 | 7 | 8 | 9 |  | 11 |  | 12 |  | 10 |  |  |  |  |  |  | 16 |
| 1 | 2 |  | 4 | 5 | 6 | 7 |  | 9 | 10 | 11 |  |  | 3 | 8 |  |  |  |  |  |  | 17 |
| 1 | 2 |  | 4 | 5 |  | 7 | 8 | 9 | 10* | 11 |  |  | 3 | 12 | 6 |  |  |  |  |  | 18 |
| 1 | 2 |  | 4 | 5 | 6 | 7 | 8 | 9 |  | 11* | 12 |  | 3 | 10 |  |  |  |  |  |  | 19 |
| 1 | 2 |  | 4 | 5 | 6 | 7 | 8 | 9 | 10 | 11 |  |  | 3 |  |  |  |  |  |  |  | 20 |
| 1 | 2 |  | 4 | 5 | 6 | 7 | 8* | 9 | 10 | 11 |  |  | 3 | 12 |  |  |  |  |  |  | 21 |
| 1 |  | 2 | 4 | 5 | 6 | 7 | 8 | 9 | 10 | 11 |  |  | 3 |  |  |  |  |  |  |  | 22 |
| 1 |  | 2 | 4 | 5* | 6 | 7 | 8 | 9 | 10 | 11 |  |  | 3 | 12 |  |  |  |  |  |  | 23 |
| 1 |  | 2 | 4 |  | 6 | 7 | 8 | 9 | 10 | 11 |  |  | 3 |  | 5 |  |  |  |  |  | 24 |
| 1 |  | 2 | 4* |  | 6 | 7 | 8 | 9 | 10 |  |  |  | 3 | 12 | 11 | 5 |  |  |  |  | 25 |
| 1 | 2 |  | 4 |  | 6 | 7 |  | 9 | 10 | 11 | 12 |  | 3 | 8* | 5 |  |  |  |  |  | 26 |
| 1 | 2 | 3 |  | 5 | 6 | 7 | 8 | 9 | 10 | 11 |  |  | 4 |  |  |  |  |  |  |  | 27 |
| 1 | 2 |  | 4 | 5 | 6 | 7 | 8 | 9 | 10 | 11 |  |  | 3 |  |  |  |  |  |  |  | 28 |
| 1 | 2 | 3 | 10 | 5 | 6 | 7 | 8* | 9 |  | 11 |  |  | 4 | 12 |  |  |  |  |  |  | 29 |
| 1 | 2 | 3 | 8 | 5 | 6 | 7 |  | 9 | 10 | 11 |  |  |  |  |  |  | 4 |  |  |  | 30 |
| 1 | 2 | 3 | 8* | 5 | 6 |  |  | 9 | 10 | 11 |  |  | 7 | 12 |  |  | 4 |  |  |  | 31 |
| 1 | 2 | 3 |  | 5 | 6 |  | 8* | 9 | 10 |  |  |  | 7 | 12 |  |  | 4 | 11 |  |  | 32 |
| 1 | 2 | 3 | 6 | 5 |  |  | 8* | 9 | 10 |  |  |  | 7 | 12 |  |  | 4 | 11 |  |  | 33 |
| 1 | 2 | 3 | 6 | 5 |  | 7 |  | 9 | 10 |  |  |  |  | 8 |  |  | 4 | 11 |  |  | 34 |
| 1 | 2 | 3 | 6 | 5 |  | 7 |  | 9 | 10* |  |  |  |  | 8 |  |  | 4 | 11 | 12 |  | 35 |
|  | 2 | 3 |  | 5 | 6 |  |  | 9 |  |  |  |  | 7 | 8 |  |  | 4 | 11 | 10 | 1 | 36 |
|  | 2 | 3 | 12 | 5 | 6 |  |  | 9 |  |  |  |  | 7 | 8* |  |  | 4 | 11 | 10 | 1 | 37 |
|  | 2 | 3 | 8* | 5 | 6 |  | 10 | 9 | 12 |  |  |  | 7 |  |  |  | 4 | 11 |  | 1 | 38 |
| 1 | 2 | 3 |  | 5 | 6 |  | 9* |  | 10 |  |  |  | 7 | 12 |  |  | 4 | 11 | 8 |  | 39 |
| 1 | 2 | 3 | 5* | 6 | 7 | 8 | 9 | 10 |  |  |  |  |  |  |  |  | 4 | 11 | 12 |  | 40 |
| 1 | 2 | 3 | 6 |  | 5 |  | 10 | 9 | 7 |  |  |  | 12 |  |  |  | 4 | 11 | 8* |  | 41 |
| 1 | 2 | 3 | 12 | 5 |  | 9* | 10 | 7 |  |  |  |  | 8 |  |  |  | 4 | 11 | 6 |  | 42 |
| 39 | 37 | 34 | 35 | 37 | 37 | 35 | 34 | 40 | 32 | 40 | 1 | 2 | 15 |  | 8 | 4 | 13 | 11 | 5 | 3 | |
|  |  | 2 |  |  |  |  |  | 1 |  | 7 | 2 | 2 | 8 |  |  | 2 |  |  |  |  | |
|  |  | 6 | 1 | 1 | 1 | 10 | 8 | 13 | 18 |  |  |  | 1 |  | 4 |  | 1 | 5 |  |  | |

### League Cup

| | | | | | | |
|---|---|---|---|---|---|---|
| 2 | Sep | 7 | (a) | Ipswich T | W | 3-1 |
| 3 | Oct | 6 | (h) | Burnley | D | 1-1 |
| R | | 18 | (a) | Burnley | W | 1-0 |
| 4 | | 27 | (h) | Stoke C | D | 1-1 |
| R | Nov | 8 | (a) | Stoke C | D | 0-0 (After extra-time) |
| 2R | | 15 | (a) | Stoke C | L | 1-2 |

# 1972-73

Manager: Frank O'Farrell to December 1972, then Tommy Docherty.

| 1 | Aug | 12 | (h) | Ipswich T | L | 1-2 | Law | 51,459 |
|---|---|---|---|---|---|---|---|---|
| 2 | | 15 | (a) | Liverpool | L | 0-2 | | 54,799 |
| 3 | | 19 | (a) | Everton | L | 0-2 | | 52,348 |
| 4 | | 23 | (h) | Leicester C | D | 1-1 | Best | 40,067 |
| 5 | | 26 | (h) | Arsenal | D | 0-0 | | 48,108 |
| 6 | | 30 | (h) | Chelsea | D | 0-0 | | 44,482 |
| 7 | Sep | 2 | (a) | West Ham U | D | 2-2 | Best, Storey-Moore | 31,939 |
| 8 | | 9 | (h) | Coventry C | L | 0-1 | | 37,073 |
| 9 | | 16 | (a) | Wolves | L | 0-2 | | 34,049 |
| 10 | | 23 | (h) | Derby C | W | 3-0 | Davies, Morgan, Storey-Moore | 48,255 |
| 11 | | 30 | (a) | Sheffield U | L | 0-1 | | 37,347 |
| 12 | Oct | 7 | (a) | West Brom A | D | 2-2 | Best, Storey-Moore | 39,209 |
| 13 | | 14 | (h) | Birmingham C | W | 1-0 | MacDougall | 52,104 |
| 14 | | 21 | (a) | Newcastle U | L | 1-2 | Charlton | 38,170 |
| 15 | | 28 | (h) | Tottenham H | L | 1-4 | Charlton | 52,497 |
| 16 | Nov | 4 | (a) | Leicester C | D | 2-2 | Best, Davies | 32,575 |
| 17 | | 11 | (h) | Liverpool | W | 2-0 | Davies, MacDougall | 53,944 |
| 18 | | 18 | (a) | Manchester C | L | 0-3 | | 52,050 |
| 19 | | 25 | (h) | Southampton | W | 2-1 | Davies, MacDougall | 36,073 |
| 20 | Dec | 2 | (a) | Norwich C | W | 2-0 | MacDougall, Storey-Moore | 35,910 |
| 21 | | 9 | (h) | Stoke C | L | 0-2 | | 41,347 |
| 22 | | 16 | (a) | Crystal P | L | 0-5 | | 39,484 |
| 23 | | 23 | (h) | Leeds U | D | 1-1 | MacDougall | 46,382 |
| 24 | | 26 | (a) | Derby C | L | 1-3 | Storey-Moore | 35,098 |
| 25 | Jan | 6 | (a) | Arsenal | L | 1-3 | Kidd | 51,194 |
| 26 | | 20 | (h) | West Ham U | D | 2-2 | Charlton, Macari | 50,878 |
| 27 | | 24 | (h) | Everton | D | 0-0 | | 58,970 |
| 28 | | 27 | (a) | Coventry C | D | 1-1 | Holton | 42,767 |
| 29 | Feb | 10 | (h) | Wolves | W | 2-1 | Charlton 2 | 52,089 |
| 30 | | 17 | (a) | Ipswich T | L | 1-4 | Macari | 31,918 |
| 31 | Mar | 3 | (h) | West Brom A | W | 2-1 | Kidd, Macari | 46,735 |
| 32 | | 10 | (a) | Birmingham C | L | 1-3 | Macari | 51,278 |
| 33 | | 17 | (h) | Newcastle U | W | 2-1 | Holton, Martin | 48,426 |
| 34 | | 24 | (a) | Tottenham H | D | 1-1 | Graham | 49,751 |
| 35 | | 31 | (a) | Southampton | W | 2-0 | Charlton, Holton | 23,161 |
| 36 | Apr | 7 | (h) | Norwich C | W | 1-0 | Martin | 48,593 |
| 37 | | 11 | (h) | Crystal P | W | 2-0 | Kidd, Morgan | 46,891 |
| 38 | | 14 | (a) | Stoke C | D | 2-2 | Macari, Morgan | 37,051 |
| 39 | | 18 | (a) | Leeds U | W | 1-0 | Anderson | 45,450 |
| 40 | | 21 | (h) | Manchester C | D | 0-0 | | 61,676 |
| 41 | | 23 | (h) | Sheffield U | L | 1-2 | Kidd | 57,280 |
| 42 | | 28 | (a) | Chelsea | L | 0-1 | | 44,184 |

FINAL LEAGUE POSITION: 18th in Division One

Appearances
Sub Appearances
Goals

FA Cup

| 3 | Jan | 13 | (a) | Wolves | L | 0-1 | |
|---|---|---|---|---|---|---|---|

League Cup

| 2 | Sep | 6 | (a) | Oxford U | D | 2-2 | |
|---|---|---|---|---|---|---|---|
| R | | 12 | (h) | Oxford U | W | 3-1 | |
| 3 | Oct | 3 | (a) | Bristol R | D | 1-1 | |
| R | | 11 | (h) | Bristol R | L | 1-2 | |

| Stepney | O'Neil | Dunne | Morgan | James | Buchan | Best | Kidd | Charlton | Law | Storey-Moore | McIlroy | Young | Sadler | Fitzpatrick | Donald | Davies W | MacDougall | Watson | Edwards | Graham | Forsyth | Holton | Macari | Martin | Rimmer | Anderson | Fletcher | Sidebottom | # |
|---|---|---|---|---|---|---|---|---|---|---|---|---|---|---|---|---|---|---|---|---|---|---|---|---|---|---|---|---|---|
| 1 | 2 | 3 | 4 | 5 | 6 | 7 | 8 | 9* | 10 | 11 | 12 | | | | | | | | | | | | | | | | | | 1 |
| 1 | 2 | 3 | 7 | 5 | 6 | 10 | 8* | 9 | | 11 | 12 | 4 | | | | | | | | | | | | | | | | | 2 |
| 1 | 2 | 3 | 7 | 5* | 4 | 10 | | 9 | | 11 | 12 | | | 6 | 8 | | | | | | | | | | | | | | 3 |
| 1 | 2 | 3 | 7 | 5 | 4 | 10 | 12 | | | 11 | 9* | | | 6 | 8 | | | | | | | | | | | | | | 4 |
| 1 | 2 | 3 | 7 | 5 | 4 | 10 | | | | 11 | 9 | 8 | 6 | | | | | | | | | | | | | | | | 5 |
| 1 | 2 | 3 | 7 | 5 | 4 | 10 | 12 | 9 | | 11* | | | 6 | 8 | | | | | | | | | | | | | | | 6 |
| 1 | 2 | 3 | 7 | 5 | 4 | 10 | | 9 | 8* | 11 | 12 | | 6 | | | | | | | | | | | | | | | | 7 |
| 1 | 2 | | 5 | 3 | 10 | | 9 | 8* | 11 | 7 | 12 | 6 | 4 | | | | | | | | | | | | | | | | 8 |
| 1 | | 3 | | 5 | 2 | 10 | 12 | 9 | | 11 | 8 | 7 | 6* | 4 | | | | | | | | | | | | | | | 9 |
| 1 | | 3 | 7 | 5 | 6 | 10 | | 9 | | 11 | | 4 | | | | 2 | 8 | | | | | | | | | | | | 10 |
| 1 | | 3 | 7 | 5 | 6 | 10 | | 9 | | 11* | 12 | 4 | | | | 2 | 8 | | | | | | | | | | | | 11 |
| 1 | | 3 | 7 | 5 | 6 | 10 | | | | 11 | | 4 | | | | 2 | 9 | 8 | | | | | | | | | | | 12 |
| 1 | | 3 | 7 | | 6 | 10 | | | | 11 | | 4 | 5 | | | 9 | 8 | 2 | | | | | | | | | | | 13 |
| 1 | | 3 | 7 | | 6 | 10 | | 12 | | 11* | | 4 | 5 | | | 9 | 8 | 2 | | | | | | | | | | | 14 |
| 1 | | 3 | 7 | | 6 | 10 | | 11 | 4 | | | 5 | | | | 9 | 8 | 2 | | | | | | | | | | | 15 |
| 1 | | 3 | 4 | | 6 | 7 | | 10 | | 11 | | 5 | | | | 2 | 9 | 8 | | | | | | | | | | | 16 |
| 1 | 2 | 3* | 4 | | 6 | 7 | | 9 | | 11 | 12 | 5 | | | | 10 | 8 | | | | | | | | | | | | 17 |
| 1 | 2 | 3 | 4* | | 6 | 7 | 12 | 9 | | 11 | | 5 | | | | 10 | 8 | | | | | | | | | | | | 18 |
| 1 | 2 | 3 | 4 | | 6 | 7 | | 9 | | 11 | | | | | | 10 | 8 | 5 | | | | | | | | | | | 19 |
| 1 | 2 | 3 | 4 | | 6 | | | 9 | | 11 | 7 | 5 | | | | 10 | 8 | | | | | | | | | | | | 20 |
| 1 | 2 | 3 | 7 | | 6 | | | 9 | 12 | 11 | 4* | 5 | | | | 10 | 8 | | | | | | | | | | | | 21 |
| 1 | 2 | 3* | 7 | | 6 | | 9 | | 12 | 11 | 4 | 5 | | | | 10 | 8 | | | | | | | | | | | | 22 |
| 1 | 2 | 3 | 7 | | 6 | | 12 | 9 | 4* | 11 | | 5 | | | | 10 | 8 | | | | | | | | | | | | 23 |
| 1 | 2 | 3* | 7 | | 6 | | 4 | 9 | | 11 | | 12 | 5 | | | 10 | 8 | | | | | | | | | | | | 24 |
| 1 | | | 7 | | 6 | | 8 | 9 | 10 | 11 | | 2 | 5 | | | | | | | 4 | 3 | | | | | | | | 25 |
| 1 | | 7 | | 6 | | | 9 | 4* | | | | 2 | | | | 12 | 8 | | | 11 | 3 | 5 | 10 | | | | | | 26 |
| 1 | | 7 | | 6 | 12 | | 9 | | | | | 2 | | | | | 8* | | | 11 | 3 | 5 | 10 | 4 | | | | | 27 |
| 1 | | 7 | | 6 | | | 9 | | | | | 2 | | | | | 8 | | | 4 | 3 | 5 | 10 | 11 | | | | | 28 |
| 1 | | 7 | | 6 | | | 9 | | | | | 2 | | | | | 8 | | | 4 | 3 | 5 | 10 | 11 | | | | | 29 |
| 1 | 3 | | 6 | | 11 | 9 | | | | | | | | | | | 8 | | | 4 | 2 | 5 | 10 | 7 | | | | | 30 |
| 1 | | 7 | 5 | 6 | | 8 | 9 | | | 11* | | 2 | | | | | | | | 4 | 3 | | 10 | 12 | | | | | 31 |
| | | 7 | 5 | 6 | | 8 | 9 | | | 11* | | 2 | | | | | | | | 4 | 3 | | 10 | 12 | 1 | | | | 32 |
| | | 7 | 3 | 6 | | 8 | 9 | | | | | 2 | | | | | | | | 4 | | 5 | 10 | 11 | 1 | | | | 33 |
| | | 7 | 3 | 6 | | 8 | 9 | | | | | 2 | | | | | | | | 4 | | 5 | 10 | 11 | 1 | | | | 34 |
| | | 7 | 3 | 6 | | 8* | 9 | | | | | 2 | | | | | | | | 4 | | 5 | 10 | 11 | 1 | 12 | | | 35 |
| 1 | | 7 | 3 | 6 | | 8* | 9 | 10 | | 12 | | 2 | | | | | | | | 4 | | 5 | 10 | 11 | | 12 | | | 36 |
| 1 | | 7 | 3 | 6 | | 8* | 9 | | | | | 2 | | | | | | | | 4 | | 5 | 10 | 11 | | 12 | | | 37 |
| 1 | | 7 | 3 | 6 | | | 9 | | | | | 2 | | | | | | | | 4 | | 5 | 10 | 11 | | 8* | 12 | | 38 |
| 1 | | 7 | 3 | 6 | | | 9 | | | | | 2 | | | | | | | | 4 | | 5 | 10 | 11 | | 8* | 12 | | 39 |
| 1 | | 7 | 3* | 6 | | 8 | 9 | | | | | 2 | | | | | | | | 4 | | 5 | 10 | 11 | | | 12 | | 40 |
| 1 | | 7 | | 6 | | 8 | 9 | | | | | 2 | | | | | | | | 4 | | 5 | 10 | 11 | | | | 3 | 41 |
| 1 | | 7 | | 6 | | 8* | 9 | | | | | 2 | | | | | | | | 4 | | 5 | 10 | 11 | | 12 | | 3 | 42 |
| 38 | 16 | 24 | 39 | 22 | 42 | 19 | 17 | 34 | 9 | 26 | 4 | 28 | 19 | 5 | 4 | 15 | 18 | 3 | 1 | 18 | 8 | 15 | 16 | 14 | 4 | 2 | | 2 | |
| | | | | | 5 | 2 | 2 | | | 6 | 2 | | | | | 1 | | | | | | 2 | | 5 | 2 | | | | |
| | | 3 | | | 4 | 4 | 6 | 1 | 5 | | | 4 | 5 | | | 1 | | | | 3 | 5 | 2 | 1 | | | | | | |

# 1973-74

Manager: Tommy Docherty

| | | | | | | | | |
|---|---|---|---|---|---|---|---|---|
| 1 | Aug | 25 | (a) | Arsenal | L | 0-3 | | 51,501 |
| 2 | | 29 | (h) | Stoke C | W | 1-0 | James | 43,614 |
| 3 | Sep | 1 | (h) | Queen's Park R | W | 2-1 | Holton, McIlroy | 44,156 |
| 4 | | 5 | (a) | Leicester C | L | 0-1 | | 29,152 |
| 5 | | 8 | (a) | Ipswich T | L | 1-2 | Anderson | 22,023 |
| 6 | | 12 | (h) | Leicester C | L | 1-2 | Stepney | 40,793 |
| 7 | | 15 | (h) | West Ham U | W | 3-1 | Kidd 2, Storey-Moore | 44,757 |
| 8 | | 22 | (a) | Leeds U | D | 0-0 | | 47,058 |
| 9 | | 29 | (h) | Liverpool | D | 0-0 | | 53,882 |
| 10 | Oct | 6 | (a) | Wolves | L | 1-2 | McIlroy | 32,962 |
| 11 | | 13 | (h) | Derby C | L | 0-1 | | 43,724 |
| 12 | | 20 | (h) | Birmingham C | W | 1-0 | Stepney | 48,937 |
| 13 | | 27 | (a) | Burnley | D | 0-0 | | 31,976 |
| 14 | Nov | 3 | (h) | Chelsea | D | 2-2 | Greenhoff, Young | 48,036 |
| 15 | | 10 | (a) | Tottenham H | L | 1-2 | Best | 42,756 |
| 16 | | 17 | (a) | Newcastle U | L | 2-3 | Graham, Macari | 41,768 |
| 17 | | 24 | (h) | Norwich C | D | 0-0 | | 36,338 |
| 18 | Dec | 8 | (h) | Southampton | D | 0-0 | | 31,648 |
| 19 | | 15 | (h) | Coventry C | L | 2-3 | Best, Morgan | 28,589 |
| 20 | | 22 | (a) | Liverpool | L | 0-2 | | 40,420 |
| 21 | | 26 | (h) | Sheffield U | L | 1-2 | Macari | 38,653 |
| 22 | | 29 | (h) | Ipswich T | W | 2-0 | Macari, McIlroy | 36,365 |
| 23 | Jan | 1 | (a) | Queen's Park R | L | 0-3 | | 32,339 |
| 24 | | 12 | (a) | West Ham U | L | 1-2 | McIlroy | 34,147 |
| 25 | | 19 | (h) | Arsenal | D | 1-1 | James | 38,589 |
| 26 | Feb | 2 | (a) | Coventry C | L | 0-1 | | 25,313 |
| 27 | | 9 | (h) | Leeds U | L | 0-2 | | 60,025 |
| 28 | | 16 | (a) | Derby C | D | 2-2 | Greenhoff, Houston | 29,987 |
| 29 | | 23 | (h) | Wolves | D | 0-0 | | 39,260 |
| 30 | Mar | 2 | (a) | Sheffield U | W | 1-0 | Macari | 29,203 |
| 31 | | 13 | (a) | Manchester C | D | 0-0 | | 51,331 |
| 32 | | 16 | (a) | Birmingham C | L | 0-1 | | 37,768 |
| 33 | | 23 | (h) | Tottenham H | L | 0-1 | | 36,278 |
| 34 | | 30 | (a) | Chelsea | W | 3-1 | Daly, McIlroy, Morgan | 29,602 |
| 35 | Apr | 3 | (h) | Burnley | D | 3-3 | Forsyth, Holton, McIlroy | 33,336 |
| 36 | | 6 | (a) | Norwich C | W | 2-0 | Greenhoff, Macari | 28,223 |
| 37 | | 13 | (h) | Newcastle U | W | 1-0 | McCalliog | 44,751 |
| 38 | | 15 | (h) | Everton | W | 3-0 | McCalliog 2, Houston | 48,424 |
| 39 | | 20 | (a) | Southampton | D | 1-1 | McCalliog | 30,789 |
| 40 | | 23 | (a) | Everton | L | 0-1 | | 46,093 |
| 41 | | 27 | (h) | Manchester C | L | 0-1 | | 56,996 |
| 42 | | 29 | (a) | Stoke C | L | 0-1 | | 27,392 |

FINAL LEAGUE POSITION: 21st in Division One

Appearances
Sub Appearances
Goals

FA Cup

| | | | | | | |
|---|---|---|---|---|---|---|
| 3 | Jan | 5 | (h) | Plymouth A | W | 1-0 |
| 4 | | 26 | (h) | Ipswich T | L | 0-1 |

League Cup

| | | | | | | |
|---|---|---|---|---|---|---|
| 2 | Oct | 8 | (h) | Middlebrough | L | 0-1 |

| Stepney | Young | Buchan M | Daly | Holton | James | Morgan | Anderson | Macari | Graham | Martin | McIlroy | Fletcher | Sidebottom | Sadler | Kidd | Greenhoff | Storey-Moore | Buchan G | Forsyth | Best | Griffiths | Houston | Bielby | McCalliog | |
|---|---|---|---|---|---|---|---|---|---|---|---|---|---|---|---|---|---|---|---|---|---|---|---|---|---|
| 1 | 2 | 3 | 4* | 5 | 6 | 7 | 8 | 9 | 10 | 11 | 12 |  |  |  |  |  |  |  |  |  |  |  |  |  | 1 |
| 1 | 2 | 3 |  | 5 | 6* | 7 | 8 | 9 | 10 | 4 | 11 | 12 |  |  |  |  |  |  |  |  |  |  |  |  | 2 |
| 1 | 2 | 3 |  | 5 |  | 7 | 8 | 9 | 10 | 4* | 11 | 12 |  |  | 6 |  |  |  |  |  |  |  |  |  | 3 |
| 1 | 2 | 3 | 4* | 5 |  | 7 | 8 |  | 10 | 12 | 11 |  |  | 6 | 9 |  |  |  |  |  |  |  |  |  | 4 |
| 1 | 2 | 3 | 4 |  |  | 7 | 8 | 12 | 10 |  | 11 |  |  | 5 | 9* | 6 |  |  |  |  |  |  |  |  | 5 |
| 1 | 3 | 2 |  | 5 | 6 | 7 | 8 | 9 | 10 | 4 |  |  |  |  |  | 11 |  |  |  |  |  |  |  |  | 6 |
| 1 | 3 | 2 | 5* | 6 | 7 | 9 |  |  | 10 | 4 |  |  |  |  | 8 | 11 | 12 |  |  |  |  |  |  |  | 7 |
| 1 | 3 | 2 |  | 5 | 6 | 7 | 8 | 9* | 11 |  |  |  |  |  | 10 | 4 | 12 |  |  |  |  |  |  |  | 8 |
| 1 | 3 | 2 |  | 5 | 6 | 7 | 8 | 9 | 11* |  |  |  |  |  | 10 | 4 | 12 |  |  |  |  |  |  |  | 9 |
| 1 | 3 | 2 |  | 5 | 6 | 7 | 8* | 9 | 11 |  | 12 |  |  |  | 10 | 4 |  |  |  |  |  |  |  |  | 10 |
| 1 | 8 | 2 |  | 5 | 6 | 7 | 10 |  | 11 |  |  |  |  |  | 9 | 4 |  |  |  |  |  | 3 |  |  | 11 |
| 1 | 3 | 2 |  | 5 | 6 | 7 |  | 9 | 10 | 12 |  |  |  |  | 8 | 4 |  |  | 11* |  |  |  |  |  | 12 |
| 1 | 3 | 2 |  |  | 5 | 7 |  | 9 | 10 |  |  |  |  | 12 | 8* | 4 |  |  | 11 |  | 6 |  |  |  | 13 |
| 1 | 3 | 2 |  |  | 5 | 7 |  | 8 | 10 |  |  |  |  |  | 9 | 4 |  |  | 11 |  | 6 |  |  |  | 14 |
| 1 | 3 | 2 |  | 5 | 6 | 7 |  | 8 | 10 |  |  |  |  |  | 9 | 4 |  |  | 11 |  |  |  |  |  | 15 |
| 1 | 3 | 2 |  | 5 | 6 | 7 |  | 8 | 10 |  |  |  |  |  | 9 | 4 |  |  | 11 |  |  |  |  |  | 16 |
| 1 | 3 | 2 |  | 5 | 6 | 7* |  | 8 | 10 |  | 12 |  |  |  | 9 | 4 |  |  | 11 |  |  |  |  |  | 17 |
| 1 | 8 | 2 |  |  | 5 | 7 | 12 |  |  |  | 10 |  |  |  | 9* | 4 |  |  | 11 |  | 6 | 3 |  |  | 18 |
| 1 | 10 | 2 | 5* |  |  | 7 | 8 |  | 12 | 9 |  |  |  |  |  | 4 |  |  | 11 |  | 6 | 3 |  |  | 19 |
| 1 | 3 | 2 |  |  |  | 7 | 8 |  | 10 |  | 12 |  |  | 5 | 9* | 4 |  |  | 11 |  | 6 |  |  |  | 20 |
| 1 | 2 | 6 | 5 |  |  | 7 | 8 |  | 10 |  |  |  |  |  | 9 | 4 |  |  | 11 |  |  | 3 |  |  | 21 |
| 1 | 2 | 6 | 5 |  |  | 7 | 8 |  | 10 |  |  |  |  |  | 9 | 4 |  |  | 11 |  |  | 3 |  |  | 22 |
| 1 | 2 | 6 | 5 |  |  | 7 | 8 |  | 10 |  |  |  |  |  | 9 | 4 |  |  | 11 |  |  | 3 |  |  | 23 |
| 1 | 10 | 6 | 5 |  |  | 7 | 8 |  | 11 |  | 12 |  |  |  | 9* | 4 |  |  | 2 |  |  | 3 |  |  | 24 |
| 1 | 10 | 2 | 5 | 6 |  | 7 | 8 |  | 11 |  |  |  |  |  | 9 | 4 |  |  |  |  |  | 3 |  |  | 25 |
| 1 | 11 | 2 | 5 | 6 |  | 7 | 8 | 9* | 10 |  |  |  |  |  |  | 4 |  |  | 12 |  |  | 3 |  |  | 26 |
| 1 | 10 | 2 | 5 | 6 |  | 7 | 8 |  | 12 |  |  |  |  |  | 9 | 4 |  |  | 11* |  |  | 3 |  |  | 27 |
| 1 | 6 | 12 | 5 | 7* |  | 10 | 11 | 8 | 9 |  |  |  |  |  |  | 4 |  |  | 2 |  |  | 3 |  |  | 28 |
| 1 | 6 | 12 | 5 | 7 |  | 10 | 11* | 8 | 9 |  |  |  |  |  |  | 4 |  |  | 2 |  |  | 3 |  |  | 29 |
| 1 | 6 | 10 | 5 |  |  | 7 |  | 8 | 11 |  |  |  |  |  | 9 | 4 |  |  | 2 |  |  | 3 |  |  | 30 |
| 1 | 6 | 10 | 5 |  |  | 7 |  | 8 | 12 |  |  |  |  |  | 4* | 9 |  |  | 2 |  |  | 3 | 11 |  | 31 |
| 1 | 6 |  | 5 |  |  |  |  | 8 | 10 |  |  |  |  |  | 9 | 4 |  |  | 2 |  |  | 3 | 11 | 7 | 32 |
| 1 | 6 | 11 | 5 |  |  | 7 |  | 8 |  |  |  |  |  |  | 9* | 4 |  |  | 2 |  |  | 3 | 12 | 10 | 33 |
| 1 | 6 | 4 | 5* |  |  | 7 | 11 | 8 | 9 |  |  |  |  |  |  |  |  |  | 2 |  |  | 3 | 12 | 10 | 34 |
| 1 | 6 | 4 | 5 |  |  | 7 | 11 | 8 | 9 |  |  |  |  |  |  |  |  |  | 2 |  |  | 3 |  | 10 | 35 |
| 1 | 6 | 11 | 5 |  |  | 7 |  | 8 | 9 |  |  |  |  |  |  | 4 |  |  | 2 |  |  | 3 |  | 10 | 36 |
| 1 | 6 | 8 | 5 |  |  | 7 |  | 10 | 11 |  |  |  |  |  |  | 4 |  |  | 2 |  |  | 3 |  | 9 | 37 |
| 1 | 2 | 6 | 11 | 5 |  | 7 |  | 8 | 12 |  |  |  |  |  | 9* | 4 |  |  |  |  |  | 3 |  | 10 | 38 |
| 1 | 2 | 6 | 11 | 5 |  | 7 |  | 8 | 9 |  |  |  |  |  |  | 4 |  |  |  |  |  | 3 |  | 10 | 39 |
| 1 | 6 | 11 | 5 |  |  | 7 |  | 8 | 9 |  |  |  |  |  |  | 4 |  |  | 2 |  |  | 3 |  | 10 | 40 |
| 1 | 6 | 11 | 5 |  |  | 7 |  | 8 | 9 |  |  |  |  |  |  | 4 |  |  | 2 |  |  | 3 |  | 10 | 41 |
| 1 | 6 | 11 | 5 |  |  | 7 |  | 8 | 9 |  | 11 |  |  |  |  | 4 |  |  | 2 |  |  | 3 |  | 10 | 42 |
| 42 | 29 | 42 | 14 | 34 | 21 | 41 | 11 | 34 | 23 | 12 | 24 | 2 | 2 | 2 | 21 | 36 | 2 |  | 18 | 12 | 7 | 20 | 2 | 11 | |
|  |  |  | 2 |  |  | 1 | 1 | 1 |  |  | 4 | 5 | 3 |  | 1 |  | 3 | 1 |  |  |  | 2 |  |  | |
|  | 2 | 1 |  | 1 | 2 | 2 | 2 | 1 | 5 | 1 | 6 |  |  |  | 2 | 3 | 1 |  | 1 | 2 |  | 2 |  | 4 | |

# 1974-75

Manager: Tommy Docherty

| | | | | | | | |
|---|---|---|---|---|---|---|---|
| 1 | Aug | 17 | (a) | Orient | W 2-0 | Houston, Morgan | 17,772 |
| 2 | | 24 | (h) | Millwall | W 4-0 | Daly 3, Pearson | 44,756 |
| 3 | | 28 | (h) | Portsmouth | W 2-1 | Daly, McIlroy | 42,547 |
| 4 | | 31 | (a) | Cardiff C | W 1-0 | Daly | 22,344 |
| 5 | Sep | 7 | (h) | Nottingham F | D 2-2 | Greenhoff, McIlroy | 40,671 |
| 6 | | 14 | (a) | West Brom A | D 1-1 | Pearson | 23,721 |
| 7 | | 16 | (a) | Millwall | W 1-0 | Daly | 16,988 |
| 8 | | 21 | (h) | Bristol R | W 2-0 | Greenhoff, Prince (og) | 42,948 |
| 9 | | 25 | (h) | Bolton W | W 3-0 | Houston, Macari, McAllister (og) | 47,084 |
| 10 | | 28 | (a) | Norwich C | L 0-2 | | 24,586 |
| 11 | Oct | 5 | (a) | Fulham | W 2-1 | Pearson 2 | 26,513 |
| 12 | | 12 | (h) | Notts C | W 1-0 | McIlroy | 46,565 |
| 13 | | 15 | (a) | Portsmouth | D 0-0 | | 25,608 |
| 14 | | 19 | (a) | Blackpool | W 3-0 | Forsyth, Macari, McCalliog | 25,370 |
| 15 | | 26 | (h) | Southampton | W 1-0 | Pearson | 48,724 |
| 16 | Nov | 2 | (h) | Oxford U | W 4-0 | Pearson 3, Macari | 41,909 |
| 17 | | 9 | (a) | Bristol C | L 0-1 | | 28,104 |
| 18 | | 16 | (h) | Aston Villa | W 2-1 | Daly 2 | 55,615 |
| 19 | | 23 | (a) | Hull C | L 0-2 | | 23,287 |
| 20 | | 30 | (h) | Sunderland | W 3-2 | McIlroy, Morgan, Pearson | 60,585 |
| 21 | Dec | 7 | (a) | Sheffield W | D 4-4 | Macari 2, Houston, Pearson | 35,230 |
| 22 | | 14 | (h) | Orient | D 0-0 | | 41,200 |
| 23 | | 21 | (a) | York C | W 1-0 | Pearson | 15,567 |
| 24 | | 26 | (h) | West Brom A | W 2-1 | Daly, McIlroy | 51,104 |
| 25 | | 28 | (a) | Oldham A | L 0-1 | | 26,384 |
| 26 | Jan | 11 | (h) | Sheffield W | W 2-0 | McCalliog 2 | 45,662 |
| 27 | | 18 | (a) | Sunderland | D 0-0 | | 45,976 |
| 28 | Feb | 1 | (h) | Bristol C | L 0-1 | | 47,118 |
| 29 | | 8 | (a) | Oxford U | L 0-1 | | 15,959 |
| 30 | | 15 | (h) | Hull C | W 2-0 | Houston, Pearson | 44,712 |
| 31 | | 22 | (a) | Aston Villa | L 0-2 | | 39,156 |
| 32 | Mar | 1 | (h) | Cardiff C | W 4-0 | Houston, McIlroy, Macari, Pearson | 43,601 |
| 33 | | 8 | (a) | Bolton W | W 1-0 | Pearson | 38,152 |
| 34 | | 15 | (h) | Norwich C | D 1-1 | Pearson | 56,202 |
| 35 | | 22 | (a) | Nottingham F | W 1-0 | Daly | 21,893 |
| 36 | | 28 | (a) | Bristol R | D 1-1 | Macari | 19,337 |
| 37 | | 29 | (h) | York C | W 2-1 | Macari, Morgan | 46,802 |
| 38 | | 31 | (h) | Oldham A | W 3-2 | Coppell, Macari, McIlroy | 56,618 |
| 39 | Apr | 5 | (a) | Southampton | W 1-0 | Macari | 21,866 |
| 40 | | 12 | (h) | Fulham | W 1-0 | Daly | 52,971 |
| 41 | | 19 | (a) | Notts C | D 2-2 | Greenhoff, Houston | 17,320 |
| 42 | | 26 | (h) | Blackpool | W 4-0 | Pearson 2, Greenhoff, Macari | 58,769 |

FINAL LEAGUE POSITION: 1st in Division Two

Appearances
Sub Appearances
Goals

FA Cup

| | | | | | | |
|---|---|---|---|---|---|---|
| 3 | Jan | 4 | (h) | Walsall | D 0-0 | |
| R | | 7 | (a) | Walsall | L 2-3 | (After extra-time) |

League Cup

| | | | | | | |
|---|---|---|---|---|---|---|
| 2 | Sep | 11 | (h) | Charlton A | W 5-1 | |
| 3 | Oct | 9 | (h) | Manchester C | W 1-0 | |
| 4 | Nov | 13 | (h) | Burnley | W 3-2 | |
| 5 | Dec | 4 | (a) | Middlesbrough | D 0-0 | |
| R | | 18 | (h) | Middlesbrough | W 3-0 | |
| SF | Jan | 15 | (h) | Norwich C | D 2-2 | |
| | | 22 | (a) | Norwich C | L 0-1 | |

| Stepney | Forsyth | Houston | Greenhoff | Holton | Buchan M | Morgan | Macari | Pearson | McCalliog | Daly | McIlroy | Martin | Young | Sidebottom | Albiston | McCreery | Graham | Davies R | James | Baldwin | Roche | Coppell | Nicholl | |
|---|---|---|---|---|---|---|---|---|---|---|---|---|---|---|---|---|---|---|---|---|---|---|---|---|
| 1 | 2 | 3 | 4 | 5 | 6 | 7 | 8* | 9 | 10 | 11 | 12 |  |  |  |  |  |  |  |  |  |  |  |  | 1 |
| 1 | 2 | 3 | 4 | 5 | 6 | 7 |  | 9 |  | 11 | 8 | 10 |  |  |  |  |  |  |  |  |  |  |  | 2 |
| 1 | 2 | 3 | 4 | 5 | 6 | 7 |  | 9 |  | 11 | 8 | 10 |  |  |  |  |  |  |  |  |  |  |  | 3 |
| 1 | 2 | 3 | 4 | 5 | 6 | 7 |  | 9* |  | 11 | 8 | 10 | 12 |  |  |  |  |  |  |  |  |  |  | 4 |
| 1 | 2 | 3 | 4* | 5 | 6 | 7 | 12 |  | 10 | 11 | 8 | 9 |  |  |  |  |  |  |  |  |  |  |  | 5 |
| 1 | 2 | 3 | 12 | 5 | 6 | 7 |  | 9 | 10 | 11 | 8 | 4* |  |  |  |  |  |  |  |  |  |  |  | 6 |
| 1 | 2 | 3 | 4 |  | 6 | 7 |  | 9 | 10 | 11* | 8 |  | 12 | 5 |  |  |  |  |  |  |  |  |  | 7 |
| 1 | 2 | 3 | 4 | 5 | 6 | 7 |  | 9 | 10* | 11 | 8 |  | 12 |  |  |  |  |  |  |  |  |  |  | 8 |
| 1 | 2 | 3 | 4 |  | 6 | 7 |  | 9 | 10 | 11 | 8 |  |  | 5 |  |  |  |  |  |  |  |  |  | 9 |
| 1 | 2 | 3 | 4 |  | 6 | 7* |  | 9 | 10 | 11 | 8 |  | 12 | 5 |  |  |  |  |  |  |  |  |  | 10 |
| 1 | 2 | 3 | 4 | 5 | 6 | 7 | 12 | 9 | 10 | 11* | 8 |  |  |  |  |  |  |  |  |  |  |  |  | 11 |
| 1 | 2 | 3 | 4 | 5 | 6 | 7 |  | 9 | 10* | 11 | 8 |  |  |  |  |  |  | 12 |  |  |  |  |  | 12 |
| 1 | 2 |  | 4 | 5 | 6 | 7* |  | 9 | 10 | 11 | 8 |  |  |  | 3 |  |  | 12 |  |  |  |  |  | 13 |
| 1 | 2 | 3 | 4 | 5 | 6 | 7 |  | 9 | 10 | 11* | 8 |  |  |  |  |  |  | 12 |  |  |  |  |  | 14 |
| 1 | 2 | 3 | 4 | 5 | 6 | 7* | 12 | 9 | 10 | 11 | 8 |  |  |  |  |  |  |  |  |  |  |  |  | 15 |
| 1 | 2 | 3 | 4* |  | 6 | 12 | 7 | 9 | 10 | 11 | 8 |  |  | 5 |  |  |  |  |  |  |  |  |  | 16 |
| 1 | 2 | 3 | 4 |  | 6 | 7 |  | 9 | 10 | 11* | 8 |  |  | 5 |  |  |  | 12 |  |  |  |  |  | 17 |
| 1 | 2 | 3 | 12 |  | 6 | 7 | 4 | 9* | 10 | 11 | 8 |  |  | 5 |  |  |  |  |  |  |  |  |  | 18 |
| 1 | 2 | 3 | 9 |  | 6 | 7 | 4 |  | 10 | 11 | 8 |  |  | 5 |  |  |  |  |  |  |  |  |  | 19 |
| 1 | 2 | 3 | 4* | 5 | 6 | 7 | 10 | 9 |  | 11 | 8 |  |  |  |  |  |  | 12 |  |  |  |  |  | 20 |
| 1 | 2 | 3 | 4 | 5* | 6 | 7 | 10 | 9 |  | 11 | 8 |  |  |  |  |  |  | 12 |  |  |  |  |  | 21 |
| 1 | 2 | 3 | 4* |  | 6 | 7 | 10 | 9 |  | 11 | 8 |  |  | 5 |  |  |  | 12 |  |  |  |  |  | 22 |
| 1 |  | 3 | 4 |  | 6 | 7 | 10 | 9 |  | 11 | 8 |  | 2 | 5* |  |  |  | 12 |  |  |  |  |  | 23 |
| 1 |  | 3 | 4 |  | 6 | 7 | 10 | 9 |  | 11 | 8 |  | 2 | 5 |  |  |  | 12 |  |  |  |  |  | 24 |
| 1 |  |  | 4* |  | 6 | 7 | 10 | 9 |  | 11 | 8 |  | 2 | 5 | 3 |  |  | 12 |  |  |  |  |  | 25 |
| 1 | 2 | 3 | 4 |  | 6 | 7* | 10 | 9 |  | 11 | 8 |  |  | 5 |  |  |  | 12 |  |  |  |  |  | 26 |
| 1 | 2 | 3 | 4 |  | 6 | 7 | 10 |  |  | 11 | 8 |  |  |  |  |  |  |  | 5 | 9 |  |  |  | 27 |
| 1 | 2 | 3 | 4* |  | 6 | 7 | 10 |  |  | 11 | 8 |  |  |  |  | 12 |  |  | 5 | 9 |  |  |  | 28 |
|  | 2 | 3 | 4 |  | 6 | 7* | 10 | 9 |  | 11 | 8 |  |  |  |  | 12 |  |  | 5 |  | 1 |  |  | 29 |
|  | 2 | 3 | 4 |  | 6 |  | 10 | 9 |  | 11 | 8 |  |  |  |  | 12 |  |  | 5* |  | 1 | 7 |  | 30 |
| 1 | 2 | 3 | 4 |  | 6 |  | 10 | 9 |  | 11* | 8 |  |  |  |  | 12 |  |  | 5 |  |  | 7 |  | 31 |
| 1 | 2 | 3 | 4 |  | 6 | 7* | 10 | 9 |  | 11 | 8 |  |  |  |  | 12 |  |  | 5 |  |  |  |  | 32 |
| 1 | 2 | 3* | 4 |  | 6 |  | 10 | 9 |  | 11 | 8 |  |  |  |  | 12 |  |  | 5 |  |  | 7 |  | 33 |
| 1 | 2 | 3 | 4 |  | 6 |  | 10 | 9 |  | 11 | 8 |  |  |  |  | 12 |  |  | 5 |  |  | 7* |  | 34 |
| 1 | 2 | 3 | 4 |  | 6 |  | 10 | 9 |  | 11 | 8 |  |  |  |  |  |  |  | 5 |  |  | 7 |  | 35 |
| 1 | 2 | 3 | 4 |  | 6 | 12 | 10 | 9 |  | 11 | 8 |  |  |  |  |  |  |  | 5* |  |  | 7 |  | 36 |
| 1 | 2 | 3 | 4 | 5 | 6 |  | 10 | 9 |  | 11 | 8 |  |  |  |  |  |  |  |  |  |  | 7 |  | 37 |
| 1 | 2 | 3 | 4 | 5 | 6 |  | 10 | 9 |  | 11* | 8 |  |  |  |  | 12 |  |  |  |  |  | 7 |  | 38 |
| 1 | 2 | 3 | 4 | 5 | 6* | 7 | 10 | 9 |  | 11 | 8 |  |  |  |  |  | 12 |  |  |  |  |  |  | 39 |
| 1 | 2 | 3 | 4 |  | 6 |  | 10 | 9 |  | 11 | 8 |  |  |  |  |  |  |  | 5 |  |  | 7 |  | 40 |
| 1 | 2 | 3 | 4 |  | 6 |  | 10 | 9 |  | 11 | 8 |  |  |  |  |  |  |  | 5 |  |  | 7 |  | 41 |
| 1 | 2 | 3 | 4 |  | 6 |  | 10 | 9 |  | 11 | 8 |  |  |  |  |  |  |  | 5 |  |  | 7 |  | 42 |
| 40 | 39 | 40 | 39 | 14 | 41 | 32 | 36 | 30 | 20 | 36 | 41 | 7 | 7 | 12 | 2 |  |  |  | 13 | 2 | 2 | 9 |  |  |
|  |  |  | 2 |  |  | 2 | 2 | 1 | 1 | 1 |  |  | 1 |  |  | 8 | 2 | 1 | 8 |  |  | 1 | 1 |  |
|  |  | 1 | 6 | 4 |  | 3 | 11 | 17 | 3 | 11 | 7 |  |  |  |  |  |  |  |  |  |  | 1 |  |  |

2 own-goals

# 1975-76

Manager: Tommy Docherty

| | | | | | | | |
|---|---|---|---|---|---|---|---|
| 1 | Aug | 16 | (a) | Wolves | W | 2-0 | Macari 2 | 32,348 |
| 2 | | 19 | (a) | Birmingham C | W | 2-0 | McIlroy 2 | 33,177 |
| 3 | | 23 | (h) | Sheffield U | W | 5-1 | Pearson 2, Daly, McIlroy, Badger (og) | 55,949 |
| 4 | | 27 | (h) | Coventry C | D | 1-1 | Pearson | 52,169 |
| 5 | | 30 | (a) | Stoke C | W | 1-0 | Dodd (og) | 33,092 |
| 6 | Sep | 6 | (h) | Tottenham H | W | 3-2 | Daly 2, Pratt (og) | 51,641 |
| 7 | | 13 | (a) | Queen's Park R | L | 0-1 | | 29,237 |
| 8 | | 20 | (h) | Ipswich T | W | 1-0 | Houston | 50,513 |
| 9 | | 24 | (a) | Derby C | L | 1-2 | Daly | 33,187 |
| 10 | | 27 | (a) | Manchester C | D | 2-2 | Macari, McCreery | 46,931 |
| 11 | Oct | 4 | (h) | Leicester C | D | 0-0 | | 47,878 |
| 12 | | 11 | (a) | Leeds U | W | 2-1 | McIlroy 2 | 40,264 |
| 13 | | 18 | (h) | Arsenal | W | 3-1 | Coppell 2, Pearson | 53,885 |
| 14 | | 25 | (a) | West Ham U | L | 1-2 | Macari | 38,528 |
| 15 | Nov | 1 | (h) | Norwich C | W | 1-0 | Pearson | 50,587 |
| 16 | | 8 | (a) | Liverpool | L | 1-3 | Coppell | 49,136 |
| 17 | | 15 | (h) | Aston Villa | W | 2-0 | Coppell, McIlroy | 51,682 |
| 18 | | 22 | (a) | Arsenal | L | 1-3 | Pearson | 40,102 |
| 19 | | 29 | (h) | Newcastle U | W | 1-0 | Daly | 52,624 |
| 20 | Dec | 6 | (a) | Middlesbrough | D | 0-0 | | 32,454 |
| 21 | | 13 | (a) | Sheffield U | W | 4-1 | Pearson 2, Hill, Macari | 31,741 |
| 22 | | 20 | (h) | Wolves | W | 1-0 | Hill | 44,269 |
| 23 | | 23 | (a) | Everton | D | 1-1 | Macari | 41,732 |
| 24 | | 27 | (h) | Burnley | W | 2-1 | Macari, McIlroy | 59,726 |
| 25 | Jan | 10 | (h) | Queen's Park R | W | 2-1 | Hill, McIlroy | 58,312 |
| 26 | | 17 | (a) | Tottenham H | D | 1-1 | Hill | 49,189 |
| 27 | | 31 | (h) | Birmingham C | W | 3-1 | Forsyth, Macari, McIlroy | 50,724 |
| 28 | Feb | 7 | (a) | Coventry C | D | 1-1 | Macari | 33,922 |
| 29 | | 18 | (h) | Liverpool | D | 0-0 | | 59,709 |
| 30 | | 21 | (a) | Aston Villa | L | 1-2 | Macari | 50,094 |
| 31 | | 25 | (h) | Derby C | D | 1-1 | Pearson | 59,632 |
| 32 | | 28 | (h) | West Ham U | W | 4-0 | Forsyth, Macari, McCreery, Pearson | 57,220 |
| 33 | Mar | 13 | (h) | Leeds U | W | 3-2 | Daly, Houston, Pearson | 59,429 |
| 34 | | 17 | (a) | Norwich C | D | 1-1 | Hill | 27,787 |
| 35 | | 20 | (a) | Newcastle U | W | 4-3 | Pearson 2, Bird (og), Howard (og) | 45,043 |
| 36 | | 27 | (h) | Middlesbrough | W | 3-0 | Daly, Hill, McCreery | 58,527 |
| 37 | Apr | 10 | (a) | Ipswich T | L | 0-3 | | 34,886 |
| 38 | | 17 | (h) | Everton | W | 2-1 | McCreery, Kenyon (og) | 61,879 |
| 39 | | 19 | (a) | Burnley | W | 1-0 | Macari | 27,418 |
| 40 | | 21 | (h) | Stoke C | L | 0-1 | | 53,879 |
| 41 | | 24 | (a) | Leicester C | L | 1-2 | Coyne | 31,053 |
| 42 | May | 4 | (h) | Manchester C | W | 2-0 | Hill, McIlroy | 59,517 |

FINAL LEAGUE POSITION: 3rd in Division One

Appearances
Sub Appearances
Goals

FA Cup

| | | | | | | |
|---|---|---|---|---|---|---|
| 3 | Jan | 3 | (h) | Oxford U | W | 2-1 |
| 4 | | 24 | (h) | Peterborough U | W | 3-1 |
| 5 | Feb | 14 | (a) | Leicester C | W | 2-1 |
| 6 | Mar | 6 | (h) | Wolves | D | 1-1 |
| R | | 9 | (a) | Wolves | W | 3-2 (After extra-time) |
| SF | Apr | 3 | (n*) | Derby C | W | 2-0 (*Played at Hillsborough, Sheffield.) |
| F | May | 1 | (n†) | Southampton | L | 0-1 (†Played at Wembley Stadium) |

League Cup

| | | | | | | |
|---|---|---|---|---|---|---|
| 2 | Sep | 10 | (h) | Brentford | W | 2-1 |
| 3 | Oct | 8 | (a) | Aston Villa | W | 2-1 |
| 4 | Nov | 12 | (a) | Manchester C | L | 0-4 |

| Stepney | Forsyth | Houston | Jackson | Greenhoff | Buchan | Coppell | McIlroy | Pearson | Macari | Daly | Nicholl | McCreery | Young | Albiston | Grimshaw | Roche | Hill | Kelly | Coyne | No. |
|---|---|---|---|---|---|---|---|---|---|---|---|---|---|---|---|---|---|---|---|---|
| 1 | 2 | 3 | 4 | 5 | 6 | 7 | 8 | 9* | 10 | 11 | 12 | | | | | | | | | 1 |
| 1* | 2 | 3 | 4 | 5† | 6 | 7 | 8 | | 10 | 11 | 12 | 9 | | | | | | | | 2 |
| 1 | 2* | 3 | 4 | 5 | 6 | 7 | 8 | 9 | 10 | 11 | 12 | | | | | | | | | 3 |
| 1 | 2 | 3 | 4 | 5 | 6 | 7 | 8 | 9 | 10 | 11 | | | | | | | | | | 4 |
| 1 | 2 | 3 | 4 | 5 | 6 | 7 | 8 | 9 | 10 | 11 | | | | | | | | | | 5 |
| 1 | | 3 | 4 | 5 | 6 | 7 | 8 | 9 | 10 | 11 | 2 | | | | | | | | | 6 |
| 1 | | 3 | 4* | | 6 | 7 | 8 | 9 | 10 | 11 | 2 | 12 | 5 | | | | | | | 7 |
| 1 | | 3 | | 5 | 6 | 7 | 8 | 9 | 10 | 11 | 2 | 4 | | | | | | | | 8 |
| 1 | | 3 | | 5 | 6 | 7 | 8 | 9 | 10 | 11 | 2 | 4 | | | | | | | | 9 |
| 1 | | 3 | | 5 | 6 | 7 | 8 | 9 | 10 | 11 | 2 | 4 | | | | | | | | 10 |
| 1 | | 3 | 4* | 5 | 6 | 7 | 8 | 9 | 10 | 11 | 2 | 12 | | | | | | | | 11 |
| 1 | | 3* | 4 | 5 | 6 | 7 | 8 | 9 | 10 | 11 | 2 | | 12 | | | | | | | 12 |
| 1 | | 3 | 4 | 5 | 6 | 7 | 8 | 9 | 10 | 11 | 2 | | | | | | | | | 13 |
| 1 | | 3 | 4 | 5 | 6 | 7 | 8 | 9 | 10 | 11* | 2 | 12 | | | | | | | | 14 |
| | | 3 | 4 | 5 | 6 | 7 | 8 | 9 | 10 | 11 | 2 | | | | | 1 | | | | 15 |
| | | 3 | 4* | 5 | 6 | 7 | 8 | 9 | 10 | 11 | 2 | 12 | | | | 1 | | | | 16 |
| | | 3 | | 5 | 6 | 7 | 8* | 9 | 10 | 4 | 2 | 12 | | | | 1 | 11 | | | 17 |
| | | 3 | | 5 | 6 | 7 | 8* | 9 | 10 | 4 | 2 | 12 | | | | 1 | 11 | | | 18 |
| 1 | | 3 | | 5 | 6 | 7 | 8 | 9* | 10 | 4 | 2 | 12 | | | | | 11 | | | 19 |
| 1 | 2* | 3 | | 5 | 6 | 7 | 8 | 9 | 10 | 4 | | 12 | | | | | 11 | | | 20 |
| 1 | 2 | 3 | | 5 | 6 | 7 | 8* | 9 | 10 | 4 | | 12 | | | | | 11 | | | 21 |
| 1 | 2 | 3 | 5* | | 6 | 7 | 8 | 9 | 10 | 4 | | | | | | | 11 | 12 | | 22 |
| 1 | 2 | 3 | | 5 | 6 | 7 | 8 | 9 | 10 | 4 | | | | | | | 11 | | | 23 |
| 1 | 2 | 3 | | 5 | 6 | 7 | 8 | 9* | 10 | 4 | | 12 | | | | | 11 | | | 24 |
| 1 | 2 | 3 | | 5 | 6 | 7 | 8 | 9 | 10 | 4 | | | | | | | 11 | | | 25 |
| 1 | 2 | 3 | | 5 | 6 | 7 | 8* | 9 | 10 | 4 | | 12 | | | | | 11 | | | 26 |
| 1 | 2 | 3 | | 5 | 6 | 7 | 8 | 9* | 10 | 4 | | 12 | | | | | 11 | | | 27 |
| 1 | 2 | 3 | | 5 | 6 | 7 | 8 | 9* | 10 | 4 | | 12 | | | | | 11 | | | 28 |
| 1 | 2 | 3 | | 5 | 6 | 7 | 8* | 9 | 10 | 4 | | 12 | | | | | 11 | | | 29 |
| 1 | 2 | 3 | | 5 | 6 | 7 | 8 | 9* | 10 | 4 | | | | | | | 11 | 12 | | 30 |
| 1 | 2 | 3 | | 5 | 6 | 7 | 8 | 9 | 10 | 4 | | 12 | | | | | 11* | | | 31 |
| 1 | 2 | 3 | | 5 | 6 | 7 | 8* | 9 | 10 | 4 | | 12 | | | | | 11 | | | 32 |
| 1 | 2 | 3 | | 5 | 6 | 7 | 8 | 9 | | 4 | | 10 | | | | | 11 | | | 33 |
| 1 | 2 | 3 | | 5 | 6 | 7 | 8 | 9 | | 4 | | 10 | | | | | 11 | | | 34 |
| 1 | 2 | 3 | | 5 | 6 | 7 | 8 | 9 | | 4 | | 10 | | | | | 11 | | | 35 |
| 1 | 2 | 3 | | 5 | 6 | 7 | 8 | 9 | | 4 | | 10 | | | | | 11 | | | 36 |
| 1 | 2 | 3 | | 5 | 6 | 7 | 8 | 9 | | 4 | | 10 | | | | | 11 | | | 37 |
| 1 | 2 | 3 | | 5 | 6 | 7* | 8 | 9 | 10 | 4 | | 12 | | | | | 11 | | | 38 |
| 1 | 2 | 3 | 12 | 5 | 6 | | 8 | 9* | 10 | 4 | | 7 | | | | | 11 | | | 39 |
| 1 | 2 | 3 | 7* | 5 | 6 | | 8 | | 10 | 4 | | 12 | 9 | | | | 11 | | | 40 |
| 1 | 2 | 3* | 7 | 5 | 6 | | | 10 | | 4 | | 8 | 12 | 5 | | | 11 | 9 | | 41 |
| 1 | 2 | 3 | 10 | | 6 | 7 | 8 | 9* | | 4 | | 12 | 5 | | | | 11 | | | 42 |
| 38 | 28 | 42 | 16 | 40 | 42 | 39 | 41 | 39 | 36 | 41 | 15 | 12 | 2 | | | 4 | 26 | 1 | | |
| | | | | 1 | | | | | | | 5 | 16 | 1 | 1 | 1 | | 1 | 1 | | |
| | 2 | 2 | | | | 4 | 10 | 13 | 12 | 7 | | 4 | | | | | 7 | | 1 | |

†Greenhoff acted as substitute goalkeeper

6 own-goals

# 1976-77

Manager: Tommy Docherty

| 1 | Aug | 21 | (h) | Birmingham C | D | 2-2 | Coppell, Pearson | 58,898 |
|---|---|---|---|---|---|---|---|---|
| 2 | | 24 | (a) | Coventry C | W | 2-0 | Hill, Macari | 26,775 |
| 3 | | 28 | (a) | Derby C | D | 0-0 | | 30,054 |
| 4 | Sep | 4 | (h) | Tottenham H | L | 2-3 | Coppell, Pearson | 60,723 |
| 5 | | 11 | (a) | Newcastle U | D | 2-2 | B.Greenhoff, Pearson | 39,037 |
| 6 | | 18 | (h) | Middlesbrough | W | 2-0 | Pearson, McAndrew (og) | 56,712 |
| 7 | | 25 | (a) | Manchester C | W | 3-1 | Coppell, Daly, McCreery | 48,861 |
| 8 | Oct | 2 | (a) | Leeds U | W | 2-0 | Coppell, Daly | 44,512 |
| 9 | | 16 | (a) | West Brom A | L | 0-4 | | 36,615 |
| 10 | | 23 | (h) | Norwich C | D | 2-2 | Daly, Hill | 54,356 |
| 11 | | 30 | (h) | Ipswich T | L | 0-1 | | 57,416 |
| 12 | Nov | 6 | (a) | Aston Villa | L | 2-3 | Hill, Pearson | 44,789 |
| 13 | | 10 | (h) | Sunderland | D | 3-3 | B.Greenhoff, Hill, Pearson | 42,685 |
| 14 | | 20 | (a) | Leicester C | D | 1-1 | Daly | 26,421 |
| 15 | | 27 | (h) | West Ham U | L | 0-2 | | 55,366 |
| 16 | Dec | 18 | (a) | Arsenal | L | 1-3 | McIlroy | 39,572 |
| 17 | | 27 | (h) | Everton | W | 4-0 | J.Greenhoff, Hill, Macari, Pearson | 56,786 |
| 18 | Jan | 1 | (h) | Aston Villa | W | 2-0 | Pearson 2 | 55,446 |
| 19 | | 3 | (a) | Ipswich T | L | 1-2 | Pearson | 30,105 |
| 20 | | 15 | (h) | Coventry C | W | 2-0 | Macari 2 | 46,567 |
| 21 | | 19 | (h) | Bristol C | W | 2-1 | B.Greenhoff, Pearson | 43,051 |
| 22 | | 22 | (a) | Birmingham C | W | 3-2 | J.Greenhoff, Houston, Pearson | 35,316 |
| 23 | Feb | 5 | (h) | Derby C | W | 3-1 | Houston, Macari, Powell (og) | 54,044 |
| 24 | | 12 | (a) | Tottenham H | W | 3-1 | Hill, Macari, McIlroy | 46,946 |
| 25 | | 16 | (h) | Liverpool | D | 0-0 | | 57,487 |
| 26 | | 19 | (h) | Newcastle U | W | 3-1 | J.Greenhoff 3 | 51,828 |
| 27 | Mar | 5 | (h) | Manchester C | W | 3-1 | Coppell, Hill, Pearson | 58,595 |
| 28 | | 12 | (h) | Leeds U | W | 1-0 | Cherry (og) | 60,612 |
| 29 | | 23 | (h) | West Brom A | D | 2-2 | Coppell, Hill | 51,053 |
| 30 | Apr | 2 | (a) | Norwich C | L | 1-2 | Powell (og) | 24,161 |
| 31 | | 5 | (a) | Everton | W | 2-1 | Hill 2 | 38,216 |
| 32 | | 9 | (h) | Stoke C | W | 3-0 | Houston, Macari, Pearson | 53,102 |
| 33 | | 11 | (a) | Sunderland | L | 1-2 | Hill | 38,785 |
| 34 | | 16 | (h) | Leicester C | D | 1-1 | J.Greenhoff | 49,161 |
| 35 | | 19 | (a) | Queen's Park R | L | 0-4 | | 28,848 |
| 36 | | 26 | (a) | Middlesbrough | L | 0-3 | | 21,744 |
| 37 | | 30 | (h) | Queen's Park R | W | 1-0 | Macari | 50,788 |
| 38 | May | 3 | (a) | Liverpool | L | 0-1 | | 53,046 |
| 39 | | 7 | (a) | Bristol C | D | 1-1 | J.Greenhoff | 28,864 |
| 40 | | 10 | (a) | Stoke C | D | 3-3 | Hill 2, McCreery | 24,204 |
| 41 | | 14 | (h) | Arsenal | W | 3-2 | J.Greenhoff, Hill, Macari | 53,232 |
| 42 | | 16 | (a) | West Ham U | L | 2-4 | Hill, Pearson | 29,904 |

FINAL LEAGUE POSITION: 6th in Division One

Appearances
Sub Appearances
Goals

FA Cup

| 3 | Jan | 8 | (h) | Walsall | W | 1-0 | |
|---|---|---|---|---|---|---|---|
| 4 | | 29 | (h) | Queen's Park R | W | 1-0 | |
| 5 | Feb | 26 | (a) | Southampton | D | 2-2 | |
| R | Mar | 8 | (h) | Southampton | W | 2-1 | |
| 6 | | 19 | (h) | Aston Villa | W | 2-1 | |
| SF | Apr | 23 | (n*) | Leeds U | W | 2-1 | (*Played at Hillsborough, Sheffield.) |
| F | May | 21 | (n†) | Liverpool | W | 2-1 | (†Played at Wembley Stadium) |

Manchester United also reached the second round of the UEFA Cup (see *United in Europe*).

| Stepney | Nicholl | Houston | Daly | Greenhoff B | Buchan | Coppell | McIlroy | Pearson | Macari | Hill | Foggon | McCreery | Waldron | McGrath | Albiston | Roche | Paterson | Clark | Greenhoff J | Forsyth | Jackson | № |
|---|---|---|---|---|---|---|---|---|---|---|---|---|---|---|---|---|---|---|---|---|---|---|
| 1 | 2 | 3 | 4* | 5 | 6 | 7 | 8 | 9 | 10 | 11 | 12 |  |  |  |  |  |  |  |  |  |  | 1 |
| 1 | 2 | 3 | 4 | 5 | 6 | 7 | 8 | 9 | 10 | 11 |  |  |  |  |  |  |  |  |  |  |  | 2 |
| 1 | 2 | 3 | 4 | 5 | 6 | 7 | 8 | 9 | 10 | 11 |  |  |  |  |  |  |  |  |  |  |  | 3 |
| 1 | 2 | 3 | 4 | 5 | 6 | 7 | 8* | 9 | 10 | 11 |  | 12 |  |  |  |  |  |  |  |  |  | 4 |
| 1 | 2 | 3 | 4 | 5 | 6 | 7 | 8 | 9 | 10 | 11* | 12 |  |  |  |  |  |  |  |  |  |  | 5 |
| 1 | 2 | 3 | 4* | 5 | 6 | 7 | 8 | 9 | 10 | 11 | 12 |  |  |  |  |  |  |  |  |  |  | 6 |
| 1 | 2 | 3 | 4 | 5 | 6 | 7 | 8 | 9* | 10 | 11 |  | 12 |  |  |  |  |  |  |  |  |  | 7 |
| 1 | 2 | 3 | 4 | 5 | 6 | 7 | 8 | 9* | 10 | 11 |  | 12 |  |  |  |  |  |  |  |  |  | 8 |
| 1 | 2 | 3 | 4 | 5 |  | 7 | 8 | 9 | 10* | 11 | 12 | 6 |  |  |  |  |  |  |  |  |  | 9 |
| 1 | 2 | 3 | 4 | 5 |  | 7 | 8* | 9 | 10 | 11 |  | 6 | 12 |  |  |  |  |  |  |  |  | 10 |
| 1 | 2 | 6 | 4 | 5 |  | 7 | 8 | 9 | 10* | 11 | 12 |  |  | 3 |  |  |  |  |  |  |  | 11 |
| 1 | 2 | 6 | 4 | 5 |  | 10 | 8 | 9 |  | 11 |  |  | 7 | 3 |  |  |  |  |  |  |  | 12 |
|  |  | 3 | 4 | 8 |  | 7 |  | 9 | 10 | 11 |  | 6* |  |  | 2 | 1 | 5 | 12 |  |  |  | 13 |
| 1 | 2 |  | 4 | 5 |  | 7 | 8 | 9 |  | 11 |  |  |  | 3 | 6 |  |  | 10 |  |  |  | 14 |
| 1 |  | 6 | 4 | 5 |  | 7 | 8 | 9 |  | 11 |  |  |  | 3 |  |  |  | 10 | 2 |  |  | 15 |
| 1 |  | 3 |  | 5* | 6 | 4 |  | 9 | 10 | 11 | 7 |  |  | 12 |  |  |  | 8 |  | 2 |  | 16 |
| 1 | 2 | 3 |  | 5 | 6 | 7* | 4 | 9 | 10 | 11 |  |  |  | 12 |  |  |  | 8 |  |  |  | 17 |
| 1 | 2 | 3 |  | 5 | 6 | 7 | 4 | 9* | 10 | 11 |  |  |  | 12 |  |  |  | 8 |  |  |  | 18 |
| 1 | 2 |  |  | 5 | 6 |  | 4 | 9* | 10 | 11 | 7 |  | 12 | 3 |  |  |  | 8 |  |  |  | 19 |
| 1 | 2 | 3 |  | 5 | 6 | 7 | 4 | 9 | 10 | 11* |  |  |  | 12 |  |  |  | 8 |  |  |  | 20 |
| 1 | 2 | 3 |  | 5 | 6 | 7 | 4 | 9 | 10 | 11 |  |  |  |  |  |  |  | 8 |  |  |  | 21 |
| 1 | 2 | 3 | 12 | 5 | 6 | 7 | 4 | 9 | 10 | 11* |  |  |  |  |  |  |  | 8 |  |  |  | 22 |
| 1 | 2 | 3 | 11 | 5 | 6 | 7 | 4 | 9 | 10 |  |  |  |  |  |  |  |  | 8 |  |  |  | 23 |
| 1 | 2 | 3 |  | 5 | 6 | 7 | 4 | 9 | 10 | 11 |  |  |  |  |  |  |  | 8 |  |  |  | 24 |
| 1 | 2 | 3 |  | 5 | 6 | 7 | 4 | 9 | 10 | 11 |  |  |  |  |  |  |  | 8 |  |  |  | 25 |
| 1 | 2 | 3 |  | 5 | 6 | 7 | 4 | 9 | 10 | 11* |  |  |  | 12 |  |  |  | 8 |  |  |  | 26 |
| 1 | 2 | 3 |  | 5 | 6 | 7 | 4 | 9 | 10 | 11* | 12 |  |  |  |  |  |  | 8 |  |  |  | 27 |
| 1 | 2 | 3 |  | 5 | 6 | 7 | 4 | 9 | 10 | 11* |  |  |  | 12 |  |  |  | 8 |  |  |  | 28 |
| 1 | 2 |  |  | 5 | 6 | 7 | 4* | 9 | 10 | 11 | 12 |  |  | 3 |  |  |  | 8 |  |  |  | 29 |
| 1 | 2 | 3 |  | 5 | 6 | 7 | 4 |  | 10 | 11* | 9 |  | 12 |  |  |  |  | 8 |  |  |  | 30 |
| 1 | 2 | 3 |  | 5 | 6 | 7 | 4 | 9 |  | 11* | 10 |  | 12 |  |  |  |  | 8 |  |  |  | 31 |
| 1 | 2 | 3 |  | 5 | 6 | 7 | 4 | 9 | 10* | 11 |  |  |  | 12 |  |  |  | 8* |  |  |  | 32 |
| 1 | 2 | 3 |  | 5 | 6 | 7 | 4 | 9 | 10* | 11 | 8 |  |  | 12 |  |  |  | 8 |  |  |  | 33 |
| 1 | 2 |  |  | 5 | 6 | 7 | 4 | 9 | 10 | 11* | 12 |  |  | 3 |  |  |  | 8 |  |  |  | 34 |
| 1 | 2 | 6 |  | 5* |  | 7 | 4 | 9 | 10 | 11 |  |  |  | 3 |  |  |  | 8 | 12 |  |  | 35 |
| 1 | 2 | 3 |  | 5 | 6 | 7 | 4 | 9 | 10 | 11 |  |  |  |  |  |  |  | 8 |  |  |  | 36 |
| 1 | 2 | 3 |  | 5 | 6 | 7 | 4 | 9 | 10 | 11* | 12 |  |  |  |  |  |  | 8 |  |  |  | 37 |
| 1 | 2 | 3 |  |  |  | 7 | 4 | 9 | 10 | 11 | 12 |  |  |  | 6 |  |  | 8* | 5 |  |  | 38 |
| 1 | 2 | 3* |  | 5 | 6 | 7 | 12 |  | 10 |  | 9 |  |  | 11 |  |  |  | 8 | 4 |  |  | 39 |
| 1 | 2 |  |  | 5 | 6 | 7 |  |  | 10 | 11 | 8 | 9 |  | 3 |  |  |  |  | 4 |  |  | 40 |
| 1 | 2 |  |  | 5 | 6 | 7 | 4 | 9* | 10 | 11 | 12 |  |  | 3 |  |  |  | 8 |  |  |  | 41 |
|  | 2 |  |  | 5 | 6 | 7 | 4 | 9 | 10 | 11 | 12 |  |  | 3 |  | 1 |  | 8* |  |  |  | 42 |
| 40 | 39 | 36 | 16 | 40 | 33 | 40 | 39 | 39 | 38 | 38 | 9 | 3 | 2 | 14 | 2 | 2 |  | 27 | 3 | 2 |  |  |
|  | 1 |  |  |  |  |  |  |  |  | 1 | 1 | 3 | 16 | 4 | 3 |  |  | 1 | 1 |  |  |  |
|  |  | 3 | 4 | 3 |  | 6 | 2 | 15 | 9 | 15 | 2 |  |  |  |  |  |  | 8 |  |  |  |  |

4 own-goals

League Cup

| 2 | Sep | 1 | (h) | Tranmere R | W 5-0 |
| 3 |  | 22 | (h) | Sunderland | D 2-2 |
| R | Oct | 4 | (a) | Sunderland | D 2-2 (After extra-time) |
| 2R |  | 6 | (h) | Sunderland | W 1-0 |
| 4 |  | 27 | (h) | Newcastle U | W 7-2 |
| 5 | Dec | 1 | (h) | Everton | L 0-3 |

# 1977-78

Manager: Dave Sexton

| | | | | | | | | |
|---|---|---|---|---|---|---|---|---|
| 1 | Aug | 20 | (a) | Birmingham C | W | 4-1 | Macari 3, Hill | 28,005 |
| 2 | | 24 | (h) | Coventry C | W | 2-1 | Hill, McCreery | 55,726 |
| 3 | | 27 | (h) | Ipswich T | D | 0-0 | | 57,904 |
| 4 | Sep | 3 | (a) | Derby C | W | 1-0 | Macari | 21,279 |
| 5 | | 10 | (a) | Manchester C | L | 1-3 | Nicholl | 50,856 |
| 6 | | 17 | (h) | Chelsea | L | 0-1 | | 54,951 |
| 7 | | 24 | (a) | Leeds U | D | 1-1 | Hill | 33,517 |
| 8 | Oct | 1 | (h) | Liverpool | W | 2-0 | Macari, McIlroy | 55,089 |
| 9 | | 8 | (a) | Middlesbrough | L | 1-2 | Coppell | 26,822 |
| 10 | | 15 | (h) | Newcastle U | W | 3-2 | Coppell, J.Greenhoff, Macari | 55,056 |
| 11 | | 22 | (a) | West Brom A | L | 0-4 | | 27,526 |
| 12 | | 29 | (a) | Aston Villa | L | 1-2 | Nicholl | 39,144 |
| 13 | Nov | 5 | (h) | Arsenal | L | 1-2 | Hill | 53,055 |
| 14 | | 12 | (a) | Nottingham F | L | 1-2 | Pearson | 30,183 |
| 15 | | 19 | (h) | Norwich C | W | 1-0 | Pearson | 48,729 |
| 16 | | 26 | (a) | Queen's Park R | D | 2-2 | Hill 2 | 25,367 |
| 17 | Dec | 3 | (h) | Wolves | W | 3-1 | J.Greenhoff, McIlroy, Pearson | 48,874 |
| 18 | | 10 | (a) | West Ham U | L | 1-2 | McGrath | 20,242 |
| 19 | | 17 | (h) | Nottingham F | L | 0-4 | | 54,374 |
| 20 | | 26 | (a) | Everton | W | 6-2 | Macari 2, Coppell, J.Greenhoff, Hill, McIlroy | 48,335 |
| 21 | | 27 | (h) | Leicester C | W | 3-1 | Coppell, J.Greenhoff, Hill | 57,396 |
| 22 | | 31 | (a) | Coventry C | L | 0-3 | | 24,706 |
| 23 | Jan | 2 | (h) | Birmingham C | L | 1-2 | J.Greenhoff | 53,501 |
| 24 | | 14 | (a) | Ipswich T | W | 2-1 | McIlroy, Pearson | 23,321 |
| 25 | | 21 | (h) | Derby C | W | 4-0 | Hill 2, Buchan, Pearson | 57,115 |
| 26 | Feb | 8 | (a) | Bristol C | D | 1-1 | Hill | 43,457 |
| 27 | | 11 | (a) | Chelsea | D | 2-2 | Hill, McIlroy | 32,849 |
| 28 | | 25 | (a) | Liverpool | L | 1-3 | McIlroy | 49,094 |
| 29 | Mar | 1 | (h) | Leeds U | L | 0-1 | | 49,101 |
| 30 | | 4 | (h) | Middlesbrough | D | 0-0 | | 46,332 |
| 31 | | 11 | (a) | Newcastle U | D | 2-2 | Hill, Jordan | 25,825 |
| 32 | | 15 | (h) | Manchester C | D | 2-2 | Hill 2 | 58,398 |
| 33 | | 18 | (h) | West Brom A | D | 1-1 | McQueen | 46,329 |
| 34 | | 25 | (a) | Leicester C | W | 3-2 | J.Greenhoff, Hill, Pearson | 20,299 |
| 35 | | 27 | (h) | Everton | L | 1-2 | Hill | 55,277 |
| 36 | | 29 | (h) | Aston Villa | D | 1-1 | McIlroy | 41,625 |
| 37 | Apr | 1 | (a) | Arsenal | L | 1-3 | Jordan | 40,829 |
| 38 | | 8 | (h) | Queen's Park R | W | 3-1 | Pearson 2, Grimes | 42,677 |
| 39 | | 15 | (a) | Norwich C | W | 3-1 | Coppell, Jordan, McIlroy | 19,778 |
| 40 | | 22 | (h) | West Ham U | W | 3-0 | Grimes, McIlroy, Pearson | 54,089 |
| 41 | | 25 | (a) | Bristol C | W | 1-0 | Pearson | 26,035 |
| 42 | | 29 | (a) | Wolves | L | 1-2 | B.Greenhoff | 24,774 |

FINAL LEAGUE POSITION: 10th in Division One

Appearances
Sub Appearances
Goals

---

FA Cup

| | | | | | | | |
|---|---|---|---|---|---|---|---|
| 3 | Jan | 7 | (a) | Carlisle U | D | 1-1 | |
| R | | 11 | (h) | Carlsile U | W | 4-2 | |
| 4 | | 28 | (h) | West Brom A | D | 1-1 | |
| R | Feb | 1 | (a) | West Brom A | L | 2-3 | (After extra-time) |

League Cup

| | | | | | | |
|---|---|---|---|---|---|---|
| 2 | Aug | 30 | (a) | Arsenal | L | 2-3 |

Manchester United also reached the second round of the European Cup-winners' Cup (see *United in Europe*).

| Stepney | Nicholl | Albiston | McIlroy | Greenhoff B | Buchan | Coppell | McCreery | Pearson | Macari | Hill | Grimes | McGrath | Forsyth | Houston | Greenhoff J | Rogers | Roche | Ritchie | Jordan | McQueen | |
|---|---|---|---|---|---|---|---|---|---|---|---|---|---|---|---|---|---|---|---|---|---|
| 1 | 2 | 3 | 4 | 5 | 6 | 7 | 8 | 9* | 10 | 11 | 12 | | | | | | | | | | 1 |
| 1 | 2 | 3 | 4 | 5 | 6 | 7 | 8 | 9 | 10 | 11 | | | | | | | | | | | 2 |
| 1 | 2 | 3 | 4* | 5 | 6 | 9 | 8 | | 10 | 11 | 12 | 7 | | | | | | | | | 3 |
| 1 | 5 | 3 | 4 | | 6 | 7 | 8 | 9 | 10 | 11 | | | 2 | | | | | | | | 4 |
| 1 | 5 | 3 | 4 | | 6 | 7 | 8 | 9 | 10* | 11 | | 12 | 2 | | | | | | | | 5 |
| 1 | 2 | 3 | 4 | 5 | 6* | 7 | 8 | 9 | 10 | 11 | 12 | | | | | | | | | | 6 |
| 1 | 2 | 3 | 4 | 5 | | 7 | 8 | 9 | 10 | 11 | | | | | 6 | | | | | | 7 |
| 1 | 2 | 3 | 4 | 5 | 6 | 7 | 8 | | 10 | 11 | | | | | 9 | | | | | | 8 |
| 1 | 2 | 3 | | 5 | 6 | 9 | 4 | | 10 | 11 | | 7 | | | 8 | | | | | | 9 |
| 1 | 2 | 3 | 4 | | 6 | 9 | | | 10 | 11 | | 7 | | 5 | 8 | | | | | | 10 |
| 1 | 5 | | 4 | | 6 | 7 | 8* | 9 | 10 | 11 | | 12 | 2 | | 3 | | | | | | 11 |
| 1 | 2 | 3 | 4 | | 6 | 8 | 10 | 9 | 11* | 12 | | 7 | | 5 | | | | | | | 12 |
| 1 | 2 | 3 | 4 | | 6 | 8 | 10 | 9 | 11 | 12 | | 7* | | 5 | | | | | | | 13 |
| | 2 | | 4 | 5 | 6 | 7 | | 9 | 10 | 11 | | | | 3 | 8 | | 1 | | | | 14 |
| | 2 | | 4* | 5 | 6 | 7 | 12 | 9 | 10 | 11 | | | | 3 | 8 | | 1 | | | | 15 |
| | 2 | | 4 | 5 | 6 | 7 | | 9 | 10* | 11 | 12 | | | 3 | 8 | | 1 | | | | 16 |
| | 2 | 3 | 4 | 5 | | 7 | | 9 | 10* | 11 | 12 | | | 6 | 8 | | 1 | | | | 17 |
| | 2 | 3 | 4 | 5 | | 7 | | 9 | 10 | 11 | | | | 6 | 8 | | 1 | | | | 18 |
| | 2 | | 4 | 5 | 6 | 7 | | 9* | 10 | 11 | 12 | | | 3 | 8 | | 1 | | | | 19 |
| | 2 | | 4 | 5* | 6 | 7 | | | 10 | 11 | 12 | | | 3 | 8 | | 1 | 9 | | | 20 |
| | 2 | 3 | 4 | | 6 | 7 | | | 10 | 11 | | | | 5 | 8 | | 1 | 9 | | | 21 |
| | 2 | | 4 | 5 | 6 | 7 | | | 10 | 11 | 12 | | | 3* | 8 | | 1 | 9 | | | 22 |
| | 2 | 3 | 4 | 5 | 6 | 7 | | | 10 | 11 | | | | | 8 | | 1 | 9 | | | 23 |
| | 2 | 3 | 4 | | 6 | 7 | | 9 | 10 | 11 | | | | 5 | 8 | | 1 | | | | 24 |
| | 2 | 3 | 4 | | 6 | 7 | | 9 | 10 | 11 | | | | 5 | 8 | | 1 | | | | 25 |
| | 2 | 3 | 4 | | 6* | 7 | | 9 | 10 | 11 | 12 | | | 5 | 8 | | 1 | | | | 26 |
| | 2 | 3 | 4 | | 6 | 7 | | 9 | 10 | 11 | | | | 5 | 8 | | 1 | | | | 27 |
| | 2 | 3 | 4 | | | 7 | | 9 | 10 | 11 | | | | 6 | 8 | | 1 | | | 5 | 28 |
| | 2 | 3 | 4 | 5 | | 7 | | | 10 | 11* | 12 | | | 6 | 8 | | 1 | | 9 | | 29 |
| | 2 | | 4 | | 6 | 7 | | | 10 | 11 | | | | 3 | 8 | | 1 | | 9 | 5 | 30 |
| | 2 | | 4 | | 6 | 7 | | | 10 | 11 | | | | 3 | 8 | | 1 | | 9 | 5 | 31 |
| 1 | 2 | 12 | 4 | | 6 | 7 | | | 10 | 11 | | | | 3 | 8 | 9* | | | | 5 | 32 |
| 1 | 2 | | 4 | | 6 | 7 | | 9 | 10 | 11* | | | | 3 | 8 | | | | 12 | 5 | 33 |
| 1 | 2 | | 4 | | 6 | 7 | | 9 | 10 | 11 | | | | 3 | 8 | | | | | 5 | 34 |
| 1 | 2 | 3 | 4 | | 6 | 7 | | 9 | 10 | 11 | | | | | 8 | | | | | 5 | 35 |
| 1 | | 2 | 4 | | 6 | 7 | 12 | 9 | 10 | | | | | 3 | 8* | | | | 11 | 5 | 36 |
| 1 | | 2 | 4 | | 6 | 7 | 12 | 9 | | 11* | | | | 3 | 8 | | | | | 5 | 37 |
| 1 | | 2 | 4 | | 6 | 7 | | 9 | | 11 | | 10 | | 3 | 8 | | | | | 5 | 38 |
| 1 | 2 | | 4 | | 6 | 7 | | 9 | 10 | 11* | 12 | | | 3 | 8 | | | | | 5 | 39 |
| 1 | 2 | | 4 | | 6 | 7 | | 9 | 10 | 11 | | | | 3 | 8 | | | | | 5 | 40 |
| | 2 | | 4 | 6 | | 7 | | 9 | 10 | 11 | | | | 3 | 8 | | 1 | | | 5 | 41 |
| 1 | | 2 | 4 | | 6 | 7 | 12 | 9 | 10* | 11 | | | | 3 | 8 | | | | | 5 | 42 |
| 23 | 37 | 27 | 39 | 31 | 28 | 42 | 13 | 30 | 32 | 36 | 7 | 9 | 3 | 31 | 22 | 1 | 19 | 4 | 14 | 14 | |
| | 1 | | | | | | | | 4 | | 6 | 9 | | 1 | | | | | | | |
| | 2 | | 9 | 1 | 1 | 5 | 1 | 10 | 8 | 17 | 2 | 1 | | 6 | | | | 3 | 1 | | |

# 1978-79

Manager: Dave Sexton

| 1 | Aug | 19 | (h) | Birmingham C | W | 1-0 | Jordan | 56,139 |
|---|---|---|---|---|---|---|---|---|
| 2 | | 23 | (a) | Leeds U | W | 3-2 | Macari, McIlroy, McQueen | 36,845 |
| 3 | | 26 | (a) | Ipswich T | L | 0-3 | | 21,802 |
| 4 | Sep | 2 | (h) | Everton | D | 1-1 | Buchan | 53,982 |
| 5 | | 9 | (a) | Queen's Park R | D | 1-1 | J.Greenhoff | 23,477 |
| 6 | | 16 | (h) | Nottingham F | D | 1-1 | J.Greenhoff | 53,039 |
| 7 | | 23 | (a) | Arsenal | D | 1-1 | Coppell | 45,393 |
| 8 | | 30 | (h) | Manchester C | W | 1-0 | Jordan | 55,301 |
| 9 | Oct | 7 | (h) | Middlesbrough | W | 3-2 | Macari 2, Jordan | 45,402 |
| 10 | | 14 | (a) | Aston Villa | D | 2-2 | Macari, McIlroy | 36,204 |
| 11 | | 21 | (h) | Bristol C | L | 1-3 | J.Greenhoff | 47,211 |
| 12 | | 28 | (a) | Wolves | W | 4-2 | J.Greenhoff 2, B.Greenhoff, Jordan | 23,141 |
| 13 | Nov | 4 | (h) | Southampton | D | 1-1 | J.Greenhoff | 46,259 |
| 14 | | 11 | (a) | Birmingham C | L | 1-5 | Jordan | 23,550 |
| 15 | | 18 | (h) | Ipswich T | W | 2-0 | Coppell, J.Greenhoff | 42,109 |
| 16 | | 21 | (a) | Everton | L | 0-3 | | 42,126 |
| 17 | | 25 | (a) | Chelsea | W | 1-0 | J.Greenhoff | 28,162 |
| 18 | Dec | 9 | (a) | Derby C | W | 3-1 | Ritchie 2, J.Greenhoff | 23,180 |
| 19 | | 16 | (h) | Tottenham H | W | 2-0 | McIlroy, Ritchie | 52,026 |
| 20 | | 22 | (a) | Bolton W | L | 0-3 | | 32,390 |
| 21 | | 26 | (h) | Liverpool | L | 0-3 | | 54,910 |
| 22 | | 30 | (h) | West Brom A | L | 3-5 | B.Greenhoff, McIlroy, McQueen | 45,091 |
| 23 | Feb | 3 | (h) | Arsenal | L | 0-2 | | 45,460 |
| 24 | | 10 | (a) | Manchester C | W | 3-0 | Coppell 2, Ritchie | 46,151 |
| 25 | | 24 | (h) | Aston Villa | D | 1-1 | J.Greenhoff | 44,437 |
| 26 | | 28 | (h) | Queen's Park R | W | 2-0 | Coppell, J.Greenhoff | 36,085 |
| 27 | Mar | 3 | (a) | Bristol C | W | 2-1 | McQueen, Ritchie | 24,583 |
| 28 | | 20 | (a) | Coventry C | L | 3-4 | Coppell 2, McIlroy | 25,382 |
| 29 | | 24 | (h) | Leeds U | W | 4-1 | Ritchie 3, Thomas | 51,191 |
| 30 | | 27 | (a) | Middlesbrough | D | 2-2 | Coppell, McQueen | 20,138 |
| 31 | Apr | 7 | (a) | Norwich C | D | 2-2 | Macari, McQueen | 19,382 |
| 32 | | 11 | (h) | Bolton W | L | 1-2 | Buchan | 49,617 |
| 33 | | 14 | (a) | Liverpool | L | 0-2 | | 46,608 |
| 34 | | 16 | (h) | Coventry C | D | 0-0 | | 43,035 |
| 35 | | 18 | (a) | Nottingham F | D | 1-1 | Jordan | 33,074 |
| 36 | | 21 | (a) | Tottenham H | D | 1-1 | McQueen | 36,665 |
| 37 | | 25 | (h) | Norwich C | W | 1-0 | Macari | 33,678 |
| 38 | | 28 | (h) | Derby C | D | 0-0 | | 42,546 |
| 39 | | 30 | (a) | Southampton | D | 1-1 | Ritchie | 21,616 |
| 40 | May | 5 | (a) | West Brom A | L | 0-1 | | 27,960 |
| 41 | | 7 | (h) | Wolves | W | 3-2 | Coppell 2, Ritchie | 39,402 |
| 42 | | 16 | (h) | Chelsea | D | 1-1 | Coppell | 38,109 |

FINAL LEAGUE POSITION: 9th in Division One

Appearances
Sub Appearances
Goals

## FA Cup

| 3 | Jan | 15 | (h) | Chelsea | W | 3-0 | |
|---|---|---|---|---|---|---|---|
| 4 | | 31 | (a) | Fulham | D | 1-1 | |
| R | Feb | 12 | (h) | Fulham | W | 1-0 | |
| 5 | | 20 | (a) | Colchester U | W | 1-0 | |
| 6 | Mar | 10 | (a) | Tottenham H | D | 1-1 | |
| R | | 14 | (h) | Tottenham H | W | 2-0 | |
| SF | | 31 | (n*) | Liverpool | D | 2-2 | (*Played at Maine Road, Manchester.) |
| R | Apr | 4 | (n†) | Liverpool | W | 1-0 | (†Played at Goodison Park, Liverpool.) |
| F | May | 12 | (n‡) | Arsenal | L | 2-3 | (‡Played at Wembley Stadium) |

## League Cup

| 2 | Aug | 30 | (a§) | Stockport C | W | 3-2 | (§Played at Old Trafford, Manchester.) |
|---|---|---|---|---|---|---|---|
| 3 | Oct | 4 | (h) | Watford | L | 1-2 | |

334

| Roche | Greenhoff B | Albiston | McIlroy | McQueen | Buchan | Coppell | Greenhoff J | Jordan | Macari | McCreery | McGrath | Nicholl | Grimes | Houston | Bailey | Sloan | Thomas | Ritchie | Paterson | Connell | Moran | # |
|---|---|---|---|---|---|---|---|---|---|---|---|---|---|---|---|---|---|---|---|---|---|---|
| 1 | 2 | 3 | 4 | 5 | 6 | 7 | 8 | 9 | 10 | 11 | | | | | | | | | | | | 1 |
| 1 | 2 | 3 | 4 | 5 | 6 | 7 | 8 | 9 | 10 | 11 | | | | | | | | | | | | 2 |
| 1 | 2 | 3 | 4 | 5 | 6 | 7 | 8 | 9 | 10 | 11* | 12 | | | | | | | | | | | 3 |
| 1 | 5 | 3 | 4 | | 6 | 7 | 8 | 9 | 10 | 11* | | 2 | 12 | | | | | | | | | 4 |
| 1 | 2 | 3 | 4 | 5 | 6 | 7 | 8 | 9 | 10 | 11 | | | | | | | | | | | | 5 |
| 1 | 2 | 3 | 4 | 5 | 6 | 7 | 8 | 9 | 10 | 11* | | | 12 | | | | | | | | | 6 |
| 1 | 4 | 2 | 11 | 5 | 6 | 7 | 8 | 9 | 10 | | | | | 3 | | | | | | | | 7 |
| 1 | 4 | 2 | 11 | 5 | 6 | 7 | 8 | 9 | 10 | | | | | 3 | | | | | | | | 8 |
| 1 | | 2 | 4 | 5 | 6 | 7 | 8* | 9 | 10 | 11 | | | 12 | 3 | | | | | | | | 9 |
| 1 | | 2 | 4 | 5 | 6 | 7 | 8 | 9 | 10 | | | | 11 | 3 | | | | | | | | 10 |
| 1 | 12 | 2 | 4* | 5 | 6 | 7 | 8 | 9 | 10 | | | | 11 | 3 | | | | | | | | 11 |
| 1 | | 4 | 11 | 5* | 6 | 7 | 8 | 9 | 10 | | | 2 | 12 | 3 | | | | | | | | 12 |
| 1 | 5 | | 4 | | 6 | 7 | 8 | 9 | 10 | | | 2 | 11 | 3 | | | | | | | | 13 |
| 1 | 5 | 12 | 11 | | 6 | 7 | 8 | 9 | 10 | 4 | | 2* | | 3 | | | | | | | | 14 |
| | 4 | 2 | 11 | 5 | 6 | 7 | 8 | 9 | | 12 | | | | 3 | 1 | 10* | | | | | | 15 |
| | 4 | 2 | 11 | 5 | 6 | 7 | 8 | 9 | 12 | | | | | 3 | 1 | 10* | | | | | | 16 |
| | | 2 | 4 | 5 | 6 | 7 | 8 | 9 | 10 | | | | | 3 | 1 | | 11 | | | | | 17 |
| | | 2 | 4 | 5 | 6 | 7 | 8 | | | | | | | 3* | 1 | | 11 | 9 | 12 | | | 18 |
| | | 2 | 4 | 5 | 6 | 7 | 8 | | | | | | | 3 | 1 | | 11 | 9 | | | | 19 |
| | | 2 | 4 | 5 | 6 | 7 | 8* | | 10 | | | 12 | | | 1 | | 11 | 9 | | 3 | | 20 |
| | | 2 | 4 | 5 | 6 | 7 | 8 | | 10 | | | | | | 1 | | 11 | 9 | | 3 | | 21 |
| | | 2 | 4 | 5 | 6 | 7 | 8* | | 10 | | | | | 3 | 1 | 12 | 11 | 9 | | | | 22 |
| | | 2 | 10 | 5 | 6 | 7 | 8* | 9 | | 4 | | | | 3 | 1 | | 11 | 12 | | | | 23 |
| | 2 | 3 | 4 | 5 | 6 | 7 | 8 | | 10 | | | | | | 1 | | 11 | 9 | | | | 24 |
| | 2 | 3 | 4 | 5 | 6 | 7 | 8 | | 10* | | | 12 | | | 1 | | 11 | 9 | | | | 25 |
| | 2 | 3 | 4 | 5 | 6 | 7 | 8 | | 10 | | | | | | 1 | | 11 | 9 | | | | 26 |
| | | 3 | 4 | 5 | 6 | 7 | 8 | | 10 | | | 2 | | | 1 | | 11 | 9 | | | | 27 |
| | 10 | 3 | 4 | 5 | 6 | 7 | 8 | 9 | | | | 2 | | | 1 | | 11 | | | | | 28 |
| | 10 | 3 | 4 | 5 | 6 | 7 | 8* | | | | | 2 | | | 1 | | 11 | 9 | 12 | | | 29 |
| | 10 | 3 | 4 | 5 | 6 | 7 | 8 | 9 | | | | 2 | | | 1 | | 11 | | | | | 30 |
| | | 2 | 4 | 5 | 6 | 7 | 8 | 9 | 10 | | | | | 3 | 1 | | 11 | | | | | 31 |
| | | 3 | 4 | 5 | 6 | 7 | | 9 | 10 | | | 2 | | | 1 | | 11 | 8 | | | | 32 |
| | 5 | 3 | 4 | | 6 | 7 | | 9 | 10 | | | 2 | | 12 | 1 | | 11 | 8* | | | | 33 |
| | 10 | 3 | 4 | 5 | 6 | 7 | | 9 | | | | 2 | | 12 | 1 | | 11 | 8* | | | | 34 |
| | 10 | 3 | 4 | 5 | 6* | 7 | 8 | 9 | | | | 2 | | 12 | 1 | | 11 | | | | | 35 |
| | 6 | 3 | 4 | 5 | | 7 | 8 | 9 | 10 | | | 2 | | 12 | 1 | | 11* | | | | | 36 |
| | | 3 | 4 | 5 | 6* | 7 | 8 | 9 | 10 | | | 2 | | 12 | 1 | | 11 | | | | | 37 |
| | | 3 | 4 | 5 | 6 | 7 | | 9 | 10 | | | 2 | | 12 | 1 | | 11 | 8* | | | | 38 |
| | 2 | | | 5 | | 7 | | | 10 | | | | | 3 | 1 | 4 | 11 | 9 | 8 | 6 | | 39 |
| | 6 | 2 | 4 | 5 | | 7 | 8 | 9 | 10 | | | 12 | | 3 | 1 | | 11* | | | | | 40 |
| | 4* | 3 | | 5 | 6 | 7 | | 9 | 10 | | | 2 | | 12 | 1 | | 11 | 8 | | | | 41 |
| | | 2 | 4 | 5 | 6 | 7 | 8 | 9 | 10* | | | 12 | | 3 | 1 | | 11 | | | | | 42 |
| 14 | 32 | 32 | 40 | 36 | 37 | 42 | 33 | 30 | 31 | 14 | | 19 | 5 | 21 | 28 | 3 | 25 | 16 | 1 | 2 | 1 | |
| 1 | 1 | | | | | | | | | 1 | 1 | 2 | 2 | 11 | 1 | | 1 | | 1 | 2 | | |
| 2 | | 5 | 6 | 2 | 11 | 11 | 6 | 6 | | | | | | | | | 1 | 10 | | | | |

# 1979-80

Manager: Dave Sexton

| | | | | | | | |
|---|---|---|---|---|---|---|---|
| 1 | Aug | 18 | (a) | Southampton | D 1-1 | McQueen | 21,768 |
| 2 | | 22 | (h) | West Brom A | W 2-0 | Coppell, McQueen | 53,377 |
| 3 | | 25 | (a) | Arsenal | D 0-0 | | 44,380 |
| 4 | Sep | 1 | (h) | Middlesbrough | W 2-1 | Macari 2 | 51,015 |
| 5 | | 8 | (a) | Aston Villa | W 3-0 | Coppell, Grimes, Thomas | 34,859 |
| 6 | | 15 | (h) | Derby C | W 1-0 | Grimes | 54,308 |
| 7 | | 22 | (a) | Wolves | L 1-3 | Macari | 35,503 |
| 8 | | 29 | (h) | Stoke C | W 4-0 | McQueen 2, McIlroy, Wilkins | 52,596 |
| 9 | Oct | 6 | (h) | Brighton & HA | W 2-0 | Coppell, Macari | 52,641 |
| 10 | | 10 | (a) | West Brom A | L 0-2 | | 27,713 |
| 11 | | 13 | (a) | Bristol C | D 1-1 | Macari | 28,305 |
| 12 | | 20 | (h) | Ipswich T | W 1-0 | Grimes | 50,826 |
| 13 | | 27 | (a) | Everton | D 0-0 | | 37,708 |
| 14 | Nov | 3 | (h) | Southampton | W 1-0 | Macari | 50,215 |
| 15 | | 10 | (a) | Manchester C | L 0-2 | | 50,067 |
| 16 | | 17 | (h) | Crystal P | D 1-1 | Jordan | 52,800 |
| 17 | | 24 | (h) | Norwich C | W 5-0 | Jordan 2, Coppell, Macari, Moran | 46,540 |
| 18 | Dec | 1 | (a) | Tottenham H | W 2-1 | Coppell, Macari | 51,389 |
| 19 | | 8 | (h) | Leeds U | D 1-1 | Thomas | 58,348 |
| 20 | | 15 | (a) | Coventry C | W 2-1 | Macari, McQueen | 25,541 |
| 21 | | 22 | (h) | Nottingham F | W 3-0 | Jordan 2, McQueen | 54,607 |
| 22 | | 26 | (a) | Liverpool | L 0-2 | | 51,073 |
| 23 | | 29 | (h) | Arsenal | W 3-0 | Jordan, McIlroy, McQueen | 54,295 |
| 24 | Jan | 12 | (a) | Middlesbrough | D 1-1 | Thomas | 30,587 |
| 25 | Feb | 2 | (a) | Derby C | W 3-1 | McIlroy, Thomas, B.Powell (og) | 27,783 |
| 26 | | 9 | (h) | Wolves | L 0-1 | | 51,568 |
| 27 | | 16 | (a) | Stoke C | D 1-1 | Coppell | 28,389 |
| 28 | | 23 | (h) | Bristol C | W 4-0 | Jordan 2, McIlroy, Merrick (og) | 43,329 |
| 29 | | 27 | (h) | Bolton W | W 2-0 | Coppell, McQueen | 47,546 |
| 30 | Mar | 1 | (a) | Ipswich T | L 0-6 | | 30,229 |
| 31 | | 12 | (h) | Everton | D 0-0 | | 45,515 |
| 32 | | 15 | (a) | Brighton & HA | D 0-0 | | 29,621 |
| 33 | | 22 | (h) | Manchester C | W 1-0 | Thomas | 56,387 |
| 34 | | 29 | (a) | Crystal P | W 2-0 | Jordan, Thomas | 33,056 |
| 35 | Apr | 2 | (a) | Nottingham F | L 0-2 | | 31,417 |
| 36 | | 5 | (h) | Liverpool | W 2-1 | Greenhoff, Thomas | 57,342 |
| 37 | | 7 | (a) | Bolton W | W 3-1 | Coppell, McQueen, Thomas | 31,902 |
| 38 | | 12 | (h) | Tottenham H | W 4-1 | Ritchie 3, Wilkins | 53,151 |
| 39 | | 19 | (a) | Norwich C | W 2-0 | Jordan 2 | 23,274 |
| 40 | | 23 | (h) | Aston Villa | W 2-1 | Jordan 2 | 45,201 |
| 41 | | 26 | (h) | Coventry C | W 2-1 | McIlroy 2 | 52,154 |
| 42 | May | 3 | (a) | Leeds U | L 0-2 | | 39,625 |

FINAL LEAGUE POSITION: 2nd in Division One

Appearances
Sub Appearances
Goals

FA Cup

| | | | | | | | |
|---|---|---|---|---|---|---|---|
| 3 | Jan | 5 | (a) | Tottenham H | D 1-1 | | |
| R | | 9 | (h) | Tottenham H | L 0-1 | (After extra-time) | |

League Cup

| | | | | | | |
|---|---|---|---|---|---|---|
| 2 | Aug | 29 | (a) | Tottenham H | L 1-2 | |
| | Sep | 5 | (h) | Tottenham H | W 3-1 | |
| 3 | | 26 | (a) | Norwich C | L 1-4 | |

| Bailey | Nicholl | Albiston | McIlroy | McQueen | Buchan | Coppell | Wilkins | Jordan | Macari | Thomas | Ritchie | Paterson | Grimes | Sloan | Houston | Moran | McGrath | Jovanovic | Greenhoff J | |
|---|---|---|---|---|---|---|---|---|---|---|---|---|---|---|---|---|---|---|---|---|
| 1 | 2 | 3 | 4 | 5 | 6 | 7 | 8 | 9 | 10 | 11 | | | | | | | | | | 1 |
| 1 | 2 | 3 | 4* | 5 | 6 | 7 | 8 | 9 | 10 | 11 | 12 | | | | | | | | | 2 |
| 1 | 2 | 3 | 4 | 5 | 6 | 7* | 8 | 9 | 10 | 11 | | 12 | | | | | | | | 3 |
| 1 | 2 | 3 | 4 | 5 | 6 | 7 | 8 | 9 | 10 | 11 | | | | | | | | | | 4 |
| 1 | 2 | 3 | 4 | 5 | 6 | 7 | 8 | 9* | 10 | 11 | | | 12 | | | | | | | 5 |
| 1 | 2 | 3 | 4 | 5 | 6 | 9 | 8 | | 10 | 11 | | | 7 | | | | | | | 6 |
| 1 | 2 | 3 | 4 | 5 | 6 | 9 | 8 | | 10 | 11 | | | 7 | | | | | | | 7 |
| 1 | 2 | 3 | 4 | 5 | 6 | 9 | 8 | | 10* | 11 | | | 7 | 12 | | | | | | 8 |
| 1 | 2 | 3 | 4 | 5 | 6 | 9 | 8 | | 10 | 11 | | | 7 | | | | | | | 9 |
| 1 | 2 | 3 | 4 | 5 | 6 | 9 | 8 | | 10 | 11 | | | 7 | | | | | | | 10 |
| 1 | 2 | 3 | 4 | 5 | 6 | 9 | 8 | | 10 | 11 | | | 7 | | | | | | | 11 |
| 1 | 2 | 3 | 4 | 5 | 6 | 9 | 8 | | 10 | 11 | | | 7 | | | | | | | 12 |
| 1 | 2 | 3* | 4 | 5 | 6 | 9 | 8 | | 10 | 11 | | | 7 | 12 | | | | | | 13 |
| 1 | 2 | | 4 | | 6 | 9 | 8 | | 10 | 11 | | | 7 | | 3 | 5 | | | | 14 |
| 1 | 2 | | 4 | | 6 | 9 | 8 | | 10 | 11 | | | 7 | | 3 | 5 | | | | 15 |
| 1 | 2 | | 4 | | 6 | 7 | 8 | 9 | 10 | 11* | | | 3 | | 12 | 5 | | | | 16 |
| 1 | 2 | | 4 | | 6 | 7 | 8 | 9 | 10 | 11 | | | 3 | | | 5 | | | | 17 |
| 1 | 2 | | 4 | | 6 | 7 | 8 | 9 | 10 | 11 | | | 3 | | | 5 | | | | 18 |
| 1 | 2 | | 4 | | 6 | 7 | 8 | 9 | 10 | 11 | | | 3 | | | 5 | | | | 19 |
| 1 | 2 | | 4 | 5 | 6 | 7 | 8 | 9 | 10 | 11 | | | 3 | | | | | | | 20 |
| 1 | 2 | | 4 | 5 | 6 | 7 | 8 | 9 | 10 | 11 | | | 3 | | | | | | | 21 |
| 1 | 2 | | 4 | 5 | 6 | 7 | 8 | 9 | 10 | 11* | | | 3 | | 12 | | | | | 22 |
| 1 | 2 | | 4 | 5 | 6 | 7 | 8 | 9 | 10 | 11 | | | 3 | | | | | | | 23 |
| 1 | 2 | | 4 | 5 | 6 | 7 | 8 | 9 | 10 | 11* | | | 3 | | 12 | | | | | 24 |
| 1 | 2 | | 4 | 5 | 6 | 7 | | 9 | 10 | 11 | | 12 | 3 | | 8* | | | | | 25 |
| 1 | 2 | | 4 | 5 | 6 | 7 | 8* | 9 | 10 | 11 | | 12 | 3 | | | | | | | 26 |
| 1 | 2 | | 4 | 5 | 6 | 7 | 8 | 9 | 10* | 11 | | | 3 | | 12 | | | | | 27 |
| 1 | 2 | | 4 | 5* | 6 | 7 | 8 | 9 | 10 | 11 | | | 3 | | 12 | | | | | 28 |
| 1 | 2 | | 4 | 5 | 6 | 7 | 8* | 9 | 10 | 11 | | | 3 | | 12 | | | | | 29 |
| 1 | 2* | | 4 | 5 | 6 | 7 | | 9 | 10 | 11 | | | 3 | | 8 | 12 | | | | 30 |
| 1 | 2 | 3 | 4 | 5 | 6 | 7 | 8 | 9 | 10* | 11 | | | | | | | 12 | | | 31 |
| 1 | 2 | 3 | 4 | 5 | 6 | 7 | 8 | 9 | 10 | 11 | | | | | | | | | | 32 |
| 1 | 2 | 3 | 4 | 5 | 6 | 7 | 8 | 9 | 10 | 11* | | | 12 | | | | | | | 33 |
| 1 | 2 | 3 | 4 | 5 | 6 | 7 | 8 | 9 | 10 | 11 | | | | | | | | | | 34 |
| 1 | 2 | 3 | 4 | 5 | 6 | 7 | 8 | 9 | 10 | 11 | | | | | | | | | | 35 |
| 1 | 2 | 3 | | 5 | 6 | 7 | 8 | 9 | 10 | 11 | | | | | | | | | 4 | 36 |
| 1 | 2 | 3 | 4 | 5 | 6 | 7 | 8* | 9 | | 11 | | | 12 | | 10 | | | | | 37 |
| 1 | 2 | 3 | 4 | | 6 | 7 | 8 | 9 | | 11 | | | | | 10 | | | | | 38 |
| 1 | 2 | 3 | 4 | | 6 | 7 | 8 | 9 | | 11 | | | | | 10 | 5 | | | | 39 |
| 1 | 2 | 3 | 4 | | 6 | 7 | | 9 | 10 | 11 | | | | | 8 | 5 | | | | 40 |
| 1 | 2 | 3 | 4 | | 6 | 7 | | 9 | 10 | 11 | | | 12 | | 8* | 5 | | | | 41 |
| 1 | 2 | 3 | 4 | 5 | 6* | 7 | | 9 | 10 | 11 | | | 12 | | 8 | | | | | 42 |
| 42 | 42 | 25 | 41 | 33 | 42 | 42 | 37 | 32 | 39 | 35 | 3 | | 20 | 1 | 14 | 9 | | 1 | 4 | |
| | | | | | | | | | | | | 5 | 1 | 6 | 4 | | 1 | 1 | 1 | |
| | | 6 | 9 | | 8 | 2 | 13 | 9 | 8 | 3 | | | 3 | | | 1 | | | 1 | |

2 own-goals

# 1980-81

Manager: Dave Sexton

| | | | | | | | |
|---|---|---|---|---|---|---|---|
| 1 | Aug | 16 | (h) | Middlesbrough | W 3-0 | Grimes, Macari, Thomas | 54,394 |
| 2 | | 19 | (a) | Wolves | L 0-1 | | 31,955 |
| 3 | | 23 | (a) | Birmingham C | D 0-0 | | 28,661 |
| 4 | | 30 | (h) | Sunderland | D 1-1 | Jovanovic | 51,498 |
| 5 | Sep | 6 | (a) | Tottenham H | D 0-0 | | 40,995 |
| 6 | | 13 | (h) | Leicester C | W 5-0 | Jovanovic 2, Coppell, Grimes, Macari | 43,229 |
| 7 | | 20 | (a) | Leeds U | D 0-0 | | 32,539 |
| 8 | | 27 | (h) | Manchester C | D 2-2 | Albiston, Coppell | 55,918 |
| 9 | Oct | 4 | (a) | Nottingham F | W 2-1 | Coppell, Macari | 29,801 |
| 10 | | 8 | (h) | Aston Villa | D 3-3 | McIlroy 2, Coppell | 38,831 |
| 11 | | 11 | (h) | Arsenal | D 0-0 | | 49,036 |
| 12 | | 18 | (a) | Ipswich T | D 1-1 | McIlroy | 28,572 |
| 13 | | 22 | (a) | Stoke C | W 2-1 | Jordan, Macari | 24,534 |
| 14 | | 25 | (h) | Everton | W 2-0 | Coppell, Jordan | 54,260 |
| 15 | Nov | 1 | (a) | Crystal P | L 0-1 | | 31,449 |
| 16 | | 8 | (h) | Coventry C | D 0-0 | | 42,794 |
| 17 | | 12 | (h) | Wolves | D 0-0 | | 37,959 |
| 18 | | 15 | (a) | Middlesbrough | D 1-1 | Jordan | 20,606 |
| 19 | | 22 | (a) | Brighton & HA | W 4-1 | Jordan 2, Duxbury, McIlroy | 23,293 |
| 20 | | 29 | (h) | Southampton | D 1-1 | Jordan | 46,840 |
| 21 | Dec | 6 | (a) | Norwich C | D 2-2 | Coppell, Bond (og) | 18,780 |
| 22 | | 13 | (h) | Stoke C | D 2-2 | Jordan, Macari | 39,568 |
| 23 | | 20 | (a) | Arsenal | L 1-2 | Macari | 33,730 |
| 24 | | 26 | (h) | Liverpool | D 0-0 | | 57,049 |
| 25 | | 27 | (a) | West Brom A | L 1-3 | Jovanovic | 30,326 |
| 26 | Jan | 10 | (h) | Brighton & HA | W 2-1 | Macari, McQueen | 42,208 |
| 27 | | 28 | (a) | Sunderland | L 0-2 | | 31,910 |
| 28 | | 31 | (h) | Birmingham C | W 2-0 | Jordan, Macari | 39,081 |
| 29 | Feb | 7 | (a) | Leicester C | L 0-1 | | 26,085 |
| 30 | | 17 | (h) | Tottenham H | D 0-0 | | 40,642 |
| 31 | | 21 | (a) | Manchester C | L 0-1 | | 50,114 |
| 32 | | 28 | (h) | Leeds U | L 0-1 | | 45,733 |
| 33 | Mar | 7 | (a) | Southampton | L 0-1 | | 22,698 |
| 34 | | 14 | (a) | Aston Villa | D 3-3 | Jordan 2, McIlroy | 42,182 |
| 35 | | 18 | (h) | Nottingham F | D 1-1 | Burns (og) | 38,205 |
| 36 | | 21 | (h) | Ipswich T | W 2-1 | Nicholl, Thomas | 46,685 |
| 37 | | 28 | (a) | Everton | W 1-0 | Jordan | 25,856 |
| 38 | Apr | 4 | (h) | Crystal P | W 1-0 | Duxbury | 37,954 |
| 39 | | 11 | (a) | Coventry C | W 2-0 | Jordan 2 | 20,201 |
| 40 | | 14 | (a) | Liverpool | W 1-0 | McQueen | 31,276 |
| 41 | | 18 | (h) | West Brom A | W 2-1 | Jordan, Macari | 44,442 |
| 42 | | 25 | (h) | Norwich C | W 1-0 | Jordan | 40,165 |

FINAL LEAGUE POSITION: 8th in Division One

Appearances

Sub Appearances

Goals

FA Cup

| 3 | Jan | 3 | (h) | Brighton & HA | D 2-2 | |
| R | | 7 | (a) | Brighton & HA | W 2-0 | |
| 4 | | 24 | (a) | Nottingham F | L 0-1 | |

League Cup

| 2 | Aug | 27 | (h) | Coventry C | L 0-1 | |
| | Sep | 2 | (a) | Coventry C | L 0-1 | |

Manchester United also played in the first round of the UEFA Cup (see *United in Europe*).

338

| Bailey | Nicholl | Albiston | McIlroy | Moran | Buchan | Coppell | Greenhoff J | Jordan | Macari | Thomas | Grimes | Roche | Ritchie | McGrath | Duxbury | Jovanovic | McGarvey | McQueen | Sloan | Birtles | Whelan | Wilkins | |
|---|---|---|---|---|---|---|---|---|---|---|---|---|---|---|---|---|---|---|---|---|---|---|---|
| 1 | 2 | 3 | 4 | 5 | 6 | 7 | 8 | 9* | 10 | 11 | 12 | | | | | | | | | | | | 1 |
| | 2 | 3 | 4 | 5 | 6 | 9 | 8 | | 10 | 11 | 7* | 1 | 12 | | | | | | | | | | 2 |
| | 2 | 3 | 4 | 5* | 6 | | 8 | | 10 | 11 | | 1 | 9 | | 7 | 12 | | | | | | | 3 |
| 1 | 2 | 3 | 4 | | 6 | 7 | 8 | | 10 | 11 | | | 9 | | | 5 | | | | | | | 4 |
| 1 | 2 | 3 | 4 | | 6 | 7 | 8 | | 10 | 11 | | | 9* | | 12 | 5 | | | | | | | 5 |
| 1 | 2 | 3 | 4 | | 6 | 9 | 8 | | 10* | 11 | 7 | | | | 12 | 5 | | 12 | | | | | 6 |
| 1 | 2 | 3 | 4 | | 6 | 9 | 8 | | 10* | 11 | 7 | | | | 12 | 5 | | | | | | | 7 |
| 1 | 2 | 3 | 4 | | 6 | 9 | 8 | | | 11 | 7 | | | | 10* | 5 | | 12 | | | | | 8 |
| 1 | 2 | 3 | 4 | | 6 | | 8 | 9 | 10 | 11 | 7 | | | | | 5 | | | | | | | 9 |
| 1 | 2 | 3 | 4 | | 6 | | 8 | 9 | 10* | 11 | 7 | | | | 12 | 5 | | | | | | | 10 |
| 1 | 2 | 3 | 4 | | 6 | | 8 | 9 | | 11 | 7 | | | | 10 | 5 | | | | | | | 11 |
| 1 | 2 | 3 | 4 | | 6 | 7 | | 9 | 10 | 11 | | | | | 8 | 5 | | | | | | | 12 |
| 1 | 2 | 3 | 4 | | 6 | 7 | | 9 | 10 | 11 | | | | | 12 | 5* | | | | 8 | | | 13 |
| 1 | 2 | 3 | 4 | 5 | | 7 | | 9 | 10 | 11 | | | | | 6 | | | | | 8 | | | 14 |
| 1 | 2 | 3 | 4 | | 6 | 7 | | 9 | 10 | 11 | | | | | 5 | | | | | 8 | | | 15 |
| 1 | 2 | 3 | 4 | | 6 | 7 | | 9 | 10 | 11 | | | | | 5* | | | 12 | | 8 | | | 16 |
| 1 | 2 | 3 | 4 | 5 | | 7 | | 9 | 10 | 11 | | | | | 6 | | | | | 8 | | | 17 |
| 1 | 2 | 3 | 4 | 5 | | 7 | | 9 | 10 | 11 | | | | | 6 | | | | | 8 | | | 18 |
| 1 | 2 | 3 | 4 | | 6 | 7 | | 9 | | 11 | 12 | | | | 10 | 5 | | | | 8* | | | 19 |
| 1 | | 3 | 4 | 5* | | 7 | | 9 | 10 | | 11 | | | | 6 | 2 | | | | 8 | | 12 | 20 |
| 1 | 2 | 3 | 4 | | 6 | 7 | 8 | 9 | 10 | 11 | | | | | | 5 | | | | | | | 21 |
| 1 | 2 | 3 | 4 | | 6 | 7 | | 9 | 10 | 11 | | | | | 8 | 5 | | | | | | | 22 |
| 1 | 2 | 3 | 4 | | 6 | 7 | | 9 | 10 | 11 | | | | | 8 | 5 | | | | | | | 23 |
| 1 | 2 | 3 | 4 | | 6 | 7 | | 9 | 10 | 11 | | | | | 8 | 5 | | | | | | | 24 |
| 1 | 2 | 3 | 4 | | 6 | 7 | | 9 | 10 | 11 | | | | | 8 | 5 | | | | | | | 25 |
| 1 | 2 | 3 | | | 6 | 7 | | 9 | 10 | 11 | | | | | 12 | | | 5 | | 8 | | 4* | 26 |
| 1 | 2 | 3 | | | 6 | 7 | | 9 | 10 | 11 | | | | | 4 | | | 5 | | 8 | | | 27 |
| 1 | 2 | 3 | 12 | | 6 | 7 | | 9 | 10 | 11* | | | | | 4 | | | 5 | | 8 | | | 28 |
| 1 | 2 | 3 | | | 6 | 7 | | 9 | 10 | 11 | | | | | 4 | | | 5* | | 8 | | 12 | 29 |
| 1 | 2 | 3 | 11 | 5 | 6 | 7 | | | 10 | | | | | | 4 | | | | 9 | 8 | | | 30 |
| 1 | 2 | 3 | 11 | 5 | 6 | 7 | | | 10 | | | | | | 4* | 12 | | | 9 | 8 | | | 31 |
| 1 | 2 | 3 | 11 | 5 | 6 | 7 | | 9 | 10 | | | | | | | | | | | 8 | | 4 | 32 |
| 1 | 2 | 3 | 11 | 5 | 6 | 7 | | 9 | 10 | | | | | | | | | | | 8 | | 4 | 33 |
| 1 | 2 | 3 | 11 | 5 | 6 | 7 | | 9 | 10 | | | | | | | | | | | 8 | | 4 | 34 |
| 1 | 2 | 3 | 11* | 5 | 6 | 7 | | 9 | 10 | | | | | | 12 | | | | | 8 | | 4 | 35 |
| 1 | 2 | 3 | 4 | | 6 | 7 | | 9 | 10 | 11 | | | | | | | | 5 | | 8 | | | 36 |
| 1 | 2* | 3 | 4 | | 6 | 7 | | 9 | 10 | 11 | 12 | | | | | | | 5 | | 8 | | | 37 |
| 1 | | 3 | 4 | | 6 | 7 | | 9 | 10 | 11* | | | | | 2 | | | 5 | | 8 | | 12 | 38 |
| 1 | | 3 | 4 | | 6 | 7 | | 9 | 10 | | | | | | 2 | | | 5 | | 8 | | 11 | 39 |
| 1 | | 3 | 4 | | 6 | 7 | | 9 | 10 | | | | | | 2 | | | 5 | | 8 | | 11 | 40 |
| 1 | | 3 | 4 | | 6 | 7 | | 9 | 10 | | | | | | 2 | | | 5 | | 8 | | 11 | 41 |
| 1 | | 3 | 4 | | 6 | 7 | | 9 | 10 | | | | | | 2 | | | 5 | | 8 | | 11 | 42 |
| 40 | 36 | 42 | 31 | 32 | 26 | 42 | 8 | 33 | 37 | 30 | 6 | 2 | 3 | 1 | 27 | 19 | | | | 25 | | 11 | |
| | | | 1 | | | | | 1 | 1 | 2 | | | 1 | | 6 | 2 | | 2 | | 1 | | 2 | |
| | 1 | 1 | 5 | | | 6 | | 15 | 9 | 2 | 2 | | | | 2 | 4 | | | | 2 | | | |

2 own-goals

# 1981-82

Manager: Ron Atkinson

| | | | | | | | | |
|---|---|---|---|---|---|---|---|---|
| 1 | Aug | 29 | (a) | Coventry C | L | 1-2 | Macari | 19,329 |
| 2 | | 31 | (h) | Nottingham F | D | 0-0 | | 51,496 |
| 3 | Sep | 5 | (h) | Ipswich T | L | 1-2 | Stapleton | 45,555 |
| 4 | | 12 | (a) | Aston Villa | D | 1-1 | Stapleton | 37,661 |
| 5 | | 19 | (h) | Swansea C | W | 1-0 | Birtles | 47,309 |
| 6 | | 22 | (a) | Middlesbrough | W | 2-0 | Birtles, Stapleton | 19,895 |
| 7 | | 26 | (a) | Arsenal | D | 0-0 | | 39,795 |
| 8 | | 30 | (h) | Leeds U | W | 1-0 | Stapleton | 47,019 |
| 9 | Oct | 3 | (h) | Wolves | W | 5-0 | McIlroy 3, Birtles, Stapleton | 46,837 |
| 10 | | 10 | (a) | Manchester C | D | 0-0 | | 52,037 |
| 11 | | 17 | (h) | Birmingham C | D | 1-1 | Coppell | 48,800 |
| 12 | | 21 | (h) | Middlesbrough | W | 1-0 | Moses | 38,342 |
| 13 | | 24 | (a) | Liverpool | W | 2-1 | Albiston, Moran | 41,438 |
| 14 | | 31 | (h) | Notts C | W | 2-1 | Birtles, Moses | 45,928 |
| 15 | Nov | 7 | (a) | Sunderland | W | 5-1 | Stapleton 2, Birtles, Moran, Robson | 27,070 |
| 16 | | 21 | (h) | Tottenham H | L | 1-3 | Birtles | 35,534 |
| 17 | | 28 | (h) | Brighton & HA | W | 2-0 | Birtles, Stapleton | 41,911 |
| 18 | Dec | 5 | (a) | Southampton | L | 2-3 | Robson, Stapleton | 24,404 |
| 19 | Jan | 6 | (h) | Everton | D | 1-1 | Stapleton | 40,451 |
| 20 | | 23 | (a) | Stoke C | W | 3-0 | Birtles, Coppell, Stapleton | 19,793 |
| 21 | | 27 | (h) | West Ham U | W | 1-0 | Macari | 41,291 |
| 22 | | 30 | (a) | Swansea C | L | 0-2 | | 24,115 |
| 23 | Feb | 6 | (h) | Aston Villa | W | 4-1 | Moran 2, Coppell, Robson | 43,184 |
| 24 | | 13 | (a) | Wolves | W | 1-0 | Birtles | 22,481 |
| 25 | | 20 | (h) | Arsenal | D | 0-0 | | 43,833 |
| 26 | | 27 | (h) | Manchester C | D | 1-1 | Moran | 57,830 |
| 27 | Mar | 6 | (a) | Birmingham C | W | 1-0 | Birtles | 19,637 |
| 28 | | 17 | (h) | Coventry C | L | 0-1 | | 34,499 |
| 29 | | 20 | (a) | Notts C | W | 3-1 | Coppell 2, Stapleton | 17,048 |
| 30 | | 27 | (h) | Sunderland | D | 0-0 | | 40,776 |
| 31 | Apr | 3 | (a) | Leeds U | D | 0-0 | | 30,953 |
| 32 | | 7 | (h) | Liverpool | L | 0-1 | | 48,371 |
| 33 | | 10 | (a) | Everton | D | 3-3 | Coppell 2, Grimes | 29,306 |
| 34 | | 12 | (h) | West Brom A | W | 1-0 | Moran | 38,717 |
| 35 | | 17 | (h) | Tottenham H | W | 2-0 | Coppell, McGarvey | 50,724 |
| 36 | | 20 | (a) | Ipswich T | L | 1-2 | Gidman | 25,744 |
| 37 | | 24 | (a) | Brighton & HA | W | 1-0 | Wilkins | 20,750 |
| 38 | May | 1 | (h) | Southampton | W | 1-0 | McGarvey | 40,038 |
| 39 | | 5 | (a) | Nottingham F | W | 1-0 | Stapleton | 18,449 |
| 40 | | 8 | (a) | West Ham U | D | 1-1 | Moran | 26,337 |
| 41 | | 12 | (a) | West Brom A | W | 3-0 | Birtles, Coppell, Robson | 19,707 |
| 42 | | 15 | (h) | Stoke C | W | 2-0 | Robson, Whiteside | 43,072 |

FINAL LEAGUE POSITION: 3rd in Division One

Appearances
Sub Appearances
Goals

FA Cup

| | | | | | | |
|---|---|---|---|---|---|---|
| 3 | Jan | 2 | (a) | Watford | L | 0-1 |

League Cup

| | | | | | | |
|---|---|---|---|---|---|---|
| 2 | Oct | 7 | (a) | Tottenham H | L | 0-1 |
| | | 28 | (h) | Tottenham H | L | 0-1 |

340

| Bailey | Gidman | Albiston | Wilkins | McQueen | Buchan | Coppell | Birtles | Stapleton | Macari | McIlroy | Duxbury | Moses | Moran | Robson | Roche | Nicholl | McGarvey | Grimes | Whiteside | Davies | |
|---|---|---|---|---|---|---|---|---|---|---|---|---|---|---|---|---|---|---|---|---|---|
| 1 | 2 | 3 | 4 | 5 | 6 | 7 | 8 | 9 | 10 | 11 |  |  |  |  |  |  |  |  |  |  | 1 |
| 1 | 2 | 3 | 4 | 5 | 6 | 7 | 8 | 9 | 10 | 11 |  |  |  |  |  |  |  |  |  |  | 2 |
| 1 | 2 | 3 | 4 | 5 | 6 | 7 | 8 | 9 | 10 | 11* | 12 |  |  |  |  |  |  |  |  |  | 3 |
| 1 | 2 | 3 | 4 | 5 | 6 | 7 | 8 | 9 | 10 | 11 |  |  |  |  |  |  |  |  |  |  | 4 |
| 1 | 2 | 3 | 4 | 5 | 6 | 7 | 8 | 9 | 10 | 11* |  | 12 |  |  |  |  |  |  |  |  | 5 |
| 1 | 2 | 3 | 4 | 5 | 6* | 7 | 8 | 9 | 10 |  |  | 12 | 11 |  |  |  |  |  |  |  | 6 |
| 1 | 2 | 3 | 4 | 5 | 6 | 7 | 8 | 9 | 10 |  |  |  | 11 |  |  |  |  |  |  |  | 7 |
| 1 | 2 | 3 | 4 | 5* | 6 | 7 | 8 | 9 | 10 |  |  | 12 | 11 |  |  |  |  |  |  |  | 8 |
| 1 | 2 | 3 | 4 |  | 6 | 7 | 8 | 9 | 10 | 11 |  |  | 5 |  |  |  |  |  |  |  | 9 |
| 1 | 2 | 3 | 4 |  | 6 | 12 | 8* | 9 | 10 | 11 |  |  | 5 | 7 |  |  |  |  |  |  | 10 |
| 1 | 2 | 3 | 4 |  | 6 | 11 | 8 | 9 |  |  |  | 10 | 5 | 7 |  |  |  |  |  |  | 11 |
| 1 | 2 | 3 | 4 |  | 6 | 11 | 8 | 9 |  |  |  | 5 | 10 | 7 |  |  |  |  |  |  | 12 |
| 1 | 2 | 3 | 4 |  | 6 | 11 | 8 | 9 |  |  |  | 10 | 5 | 7 |  |  |  |  |  |  | 13 |
| 1 | 2 | 3 | 4 |  | 6 | 11 | 8 | 9 |  |  | 12 | 5 | 10 | 7* |  |  |  |  |  |  | 14 |
| 1 | 2* | 3 | 4 |  | 6 | 11 | 8 | 9 |  |  | 12 | 10 | 5 | 7 |  |  |  |  |  |  | 15 |
|  |  | 3 | 4 |  | 6* |  | 8 | 9 |  | 11 | 2 | 10 | 5 | 7 | 1 | 12 |  |  |  |  | 16 |
|  | 2 | 3 | 4 |  | 6 |  | 8 | 9 |  | 11 |  | 10 | 5 | 7 | 1 |  |  |  |  |  | 17 |
|  | 2 | 3 | 4 |  | 6 |  | 8 | 9 |  | 11 |  | 10 | 5 | 7 | 1 |  |  |  |  |  | 18 |
| 1 | 2 | 3 | 4 |  | 6 | 11 |  | 9 |  |  |  | 10 | 5 | 7 |  | 8 |  |  |  |  | 19 |
| 1 |  | 3 | 4 | 5 |  | 11 | 8 | 9 |  |  | 10 | 2 | 6 | 7 |  |  |  |  |  |  | 20 |
| 1 |  | 3 | 4 |  | 6 | 11 | 8 | 9 |  |  | 10 | 2 | 5 | 7 |  |  |  |  |  |  | 21 |
| 1 | 12 | 3 | 4 |  | 6* | 11 | 8 | 9 |  |  | 10 | 2 | 5 | 7 |  |  |  |  |  |  | 22 |
| 1 | 2 | 3 | 4 |  | 6 | 11 | 8* | 9 |  |  |  | 10 | 5 | 7 |  |  | 12 |  |  |  | 23 |
| 1 | 2 | 3 | 4 |  | 6 | 11 | 8 | 9 |  |  |  | 10 | 5 | 7 |  |  |  |  |  |  | 24 |
| 1 | 2 | 3 | 4 |  | 6 | 11 | 8 | 9 |  |  |  | 10 | 5 | 7 |  |  |  |  |  |  | 25 |
| 1 | 2 | 3 | 4 |  | 6 | 11 | 8 | 9 |  |  |  | 10 | 5 | 7 |  |  |  |  |  |  | 26 |
| 1 | 2 | 3 | 4 |  | 6 | 11 | 8 | 9 |  |  |  | 10 | 5* | 7 |  |  | 12 |  |  |  | 27 |
| 1 | 2 | 3 | 4 |  | 6 | 11 | 8 | 9 |  |  | 12 | 10 | 5 | 7* |  |  |  |  |  |  | 28 |
| 1 | 2 | 3 | 4 |  | 6 | 11 | 8 | 9 |  |  |  | 10 | 5* | 7 |  |  | 12 |  |  |  | 29 |
| 1 | 2 | 3 | 4 | 5 | 6 | 11 | 8* | 9 |  |  |  | 10 |  | 7 |  |  | 12 |  |  |  | 30 |
| 1 |  | 3 | 4 |  | 6 | 11 |  | 9 |  |  | 2 | 10 | 5 | 7 |  | 8 |  |  |  |  | 31 |
| 1 |  | 3 | 4 |  | 6* | 11 |  | 9 |  |  | 2 | 10 | 5 | 7 |  | 8 | 12 |  |  |  | 32 |
| 1 | 2 | 3 | 4 |  |  | 11 |  | 9 |  |  | 6 | 10* | 5 | 7 |  | 8 | 12 |  |  |  | 33 |
| 1 | 2 | 3 | 4 |  | 6 | 11 |  | 9 |  |  |  |  | 5 | 7 |  | 8 | 10 |  |  |  | 34 |
| 1 | 2 | 3 | 4 |  | 6 | 11 |  | 9 |  |  |  |  | 5 | 7 |  | 8 | 10 |  |  |  | 35 |
| 1 | 2 | 3 | 4 |  | 6* | 12 |  | 9 |  | 11 |  |  | 5 | 7 |  | 8 | 10 |  |  |  | 36 |
| 1 | 2 | 3 | 4 |  | 6 |  |  | 9 |  | 11* |  |  | 5 | 7 |  | 8 | 10 | 12 |  |  | 37 |
| 1 | 2 | 3 | 4 |  | 6 |  |  | 9 |  |  |  |  | 5 | 7 |  | 8 | 10 | 11 |  |  | 38 |
| 1 | 2 | 3 | 4 |  |  | 11 |  | 9 |  |  |  | 6 | 5 | 7 |  | 8 | 10 |  |  |  | 39 |
| 1 | 2 | 3 | 4 |  |  | 11 | 8* | 9 |  |  |  | 6 | 5 | 7 |  | 12 | 10 |  |  |  | 40 |
| 1 | 2 | 3 | 4 |  | 6 | 11 | 8 | 9 |  |  |  |  | 5 | 7 |  |  | 10 |  |  |  | 41 |
| 1 | 2 | 3 | 4 |  | 6 | 11 | 8* |  |  |  |  |  | 5 | 7 |  | 12 | 10 |  | 9 |  | 42 |
| 39 | 36 | 42 | 42 | 21 | 27 | 35 | 32 | 41 | 10 | 12 | 19 | 20 | 30 | 32 | 3 | 10 | 9 | 1 | 1 |  |  |
| 1 |  |  |  |  |  |  | 1 | 1 | 1 |  |  | 5 | 1 |  | 1 | 6 | 2 | 1 |  |  |  |
|  | 1 | 1 | 1 |  |  | 9 | 11 | 13 | 2 | 3 |  | 2 | 7 | 5 |  | 2 | 1 | 1 |  |  |  |

# 1982-83

Manager: Ron Atkinson

| 1 | Aug | 28 | (h) | Birmingham C | W | 3-0 | Coppell, Moran, Stapleton | 48,673 |
|---|---|---|---|---|---|---|---|---|
| 2 | Sep | 1 | (a) | Nottingham F | W | 3-0 | Robson, Whiteside, Wilkins | 23,956 |
| 3 | | 4 | (a) | West Brom A | L | 1-3 | Robson | 24,928 |
| 4 | | 8 | (h) | Everton | W | 2-1 | Robson, Whiteside | 43,186 |
| 5 | | 11 | (h) | Ipswich T | W | 3-1 | Whiteside 2, Coppell | 43,140 |
| 6 | | 18 | (a) | Southampton | W | 1-0 | Macari | 21,700 |
| 7 | | 25 | (h) | Arsenal | D | 0-0 | | 43,198 |
| 8 | Oct | 2 | (a) | Luton T | D | 1-1 | Grimes | 17,009 |
| 9 | | 9 | (h) | Stoke C | W | 1-0 | Robson | 43,132 |
| 10 | | 16 | (a) | Liverpool | D | 0-0 | | 40,853 |
| 11 | | 23 | (h) | Manchester C | D | 2-2 | Stapleton 2 | 57,334 |
| 12 | | 30 | (a) | West Ham U | L | 1-3 | Moran | 31,684 |
| 13 | Nov | 6 | (a) | Brighton & HA | L | 0-1 | | 18,379 |
| 14 | | 13 | (h) | Tottenham H | W | 1-0 | Muhren | 47,869 |
| 15 | | 20 | (a) | Aston Villa | L | 1-2 | Stapleton | 35,487 |
| 16 | | 27 | (h) | Norwich C | W | 3-0 | Robson 2, Muhren | 34,579 |
| 17 | Dec | 4 | (a) | Watford | W | 1-0 | Whiteside | 25,669 |
| 18 | | 11 | (h) | Notts C | W | 4-0 | Duxbury, Robson, Stapleton, Whiteside | 33,618 |
| 19 | | 18 | (a) | Swansea C | D | 0-0 | | 15,748 |
| 20 | | 27 | (h) | Sunderland | D | 0-0 | | 47,783 |
| 21 | | 28 | (a) | Coventry C | L | 0-3 | | 18,945 |
| 22 | Jan | 1 | (h) | Aston Villa | W | 3-1 | Stapleton 2, Coppell | 41,545 |
| 23 | | 3 | (h) | West Brom A | D | 0-0 | | 39,123 |
| 24 | | 15 | (a) | Birmingham C | W | 2-1 | Robson, Whiteside | 19,333 |
| 25 | | 22 | (h) | Nottingham F | W | 2-0 | Coppell, Muhren | 38,615 |
| 26 | Feb | 5 | (a) | Ipswich T | D | 1-1 | Stapleton | 23,804 |
| 27 | | 26 | (h) | Liverpool | D | 1-1 | Muhren | 57,397 |
| 28 | Mar | 2 | (a) | Stoke C | L | 0-1 | | 21,266 |
| 29 | | 5 | (a) | Manchester C | W | 2-1 | Stapleton 2 | 45,400 |
| 30 | | 19 | (h) | Brighton & HA | D | 1-1 | Albiston | 36,264 |
| 31 | | 22 | (h) | West Ham U | W | 2-1 | McGarvey, Stapleton | 30,227 |
| 32 | Apr | 2 | (h) | Coventry C | W | 3-0 | Macari, Stapleton, Gillespie (og) | 36,814 |
| 33 | | 4 | (a) | Sunderland | D | 0-0 | | 31,486 |
| 34 | | 9 | (h) | Southampton | D | 1-1 | Robson | 37,120 |
| 35 | | 19 | (a) | Everton | L | 0-2 | | 21,715 |
| 36 | | 23 | (h) | Watford | W | 2-0 | Cunningham, Grimes | 43,048 |
| 37 | | 30 | (a) | Norwich C | D | 1-1 | Whiteside | 22,233 |
| 38 | May | 2 | (a) | Arsenal | L | 0-3 | | 23,602 |
| 39 | | 7 | (h) | Swansea C | W | 2-1 | Robson, Stapleton | 35,724 |
| 40 | | 9 | (h) | Luton T | W | 3-0 | McGrath 2, Stapleton | 34,213 |
| 41 | | 11 | (a) | Tottenham H | L | 0-2 | | 32,803 |
| 42 | | 14 | (a) | Notts C | L | 2-3 | McGrath, Muhren | 14,395 |

FINAL LEAGUE POSITION: 3rd in Division One

Appearances
Sub Appearances
Goals

FA Cup

| 3 | Jan | 8 | (h) | West Ham U | W | 2-0 | |
|---|---|---|---|---|---|---|---|
| 4 | | 29 | (a) | Luton T | W | 2-0 | |
| 5 | Feb | 19 | (a) | Derby C | W | 1-0 | |
| 6 | Mar | 12 | (h) | Everton | W | 1-0 | |
| SF | Apr | 16 | (n*) | Arsenal | W | 2-1 | (*Palyed at Villa Park, Birmingham.) |
| F | May | 21 | (n†) | Brighton & HA | D | 2-2 | (After extra-time. †Played at Wembley Stadium) |
| R | | 26 | (n†) | Brighton & HA | W | 4-0 | |

Manchester United also played in the first round of the UEFA Cup (see *United in Europe*).

| Bailey | Duxbury | Albiston | Wilkins | Moran | McQueen | Robson | Muhren | Stapleton | Whiteside | Coppell | Grimes | Macari | Buchan | Moses | McGrath P | McGarvey | Gidman | Wealands | Cunningham | Davies | No. |
|---|---|---|---|---|---|---|---|---|---|---|---|---|---|---|---|---|---|---|---|---|---|
| 1 | 2 | 3 | 4 | 5 | 6 | 7 | 8 | 9 | 10 | 11 |  |  |  |  |  |  |  |  |  |  | 1 |
| 1 | 2 | 3 | 4 | 5 | 6 | 7 | 8 | 9 | 10 | 11 |  |  |  |  |  |  |  |  |  |  | 2 |
| 1 | 2 | 3 | 4 | 5 | 6 | 7 | 8 | 9 | 10 | 11 |  |  |  |  |  |  |  |  |  |  | 3 |
| 1 | 2 | 3 | 4 | 5 | 6 | 7 | 8 | 9 | 10 | 11 |  |  |  |  |  |  |  |  |  |  | 4 |
| 1 | 2 | 3 | 4 | 5 | 6 | 7 | 8 | 9 | 10 | 11 |  |  |  |  |  |  |  |  |  |  | 5 |
| 1 | 2 | 3 | 4 |  | 6 | 7 |  | 9 | 10 | 11* | 8 | 12 | 5 |  |  |  |  |  |  |  | 6 |
| 1 | 2 | 3 | 4 | 5 | 6 | 7 |  | 9 | 10 |  | 8 | 11 |  |  |  |  |  |  |  |  | 7 |
| 1 | 2 | 3 | 4 | 5 | 6 | 7 |  | 9 | 10 |  | 8 |  |  | 11 |  |  |  |  |  |  | 8 |
| 1 | 2 | 3 | 4 | 5 | 6 | 7 |  | 9 | 10 |  | 8 |  |  | 11 |  |  |  |  |  |  | 9 |
| 1 | 2 | 3 | 4 | 5 | 6 | 7 |  | 9 | 10 | 11 | 8 |  |  |  |  |  |  |  |  |  | 10 |
| 1 | 2 | 3 | 4 | 5 | 6 | 7 | 8* | 9 | 10 | 11 |  | 12 |  |  |  |  |  |  |  |  | 11 |
| 1 | 2 | 3 |  | 5 |  | 7 | 8 | 9 | 10 | 11 | 4 |  | 6 |  |  |  |  |  |  |  | 12 |
| 1 | 2 | 3 | 5* |  | 6 | 7 | 8 | 9 | 10 | 11 |  | 12 |  | 4 |  |  |  |  |  |  | 13 |
| 1 | 2 | 3 |  |  | 6 | 7 | 8 | 9 | 10 | 11 |  |  |  | 4 | 5 |  |  |  |  |  | 14 |
| 1 | 2 | 3 |  | 5 | 6 | 7 | 8 | 9 | 10* | 11 |  |  |  | 4 |  | 12 |  |  |  |  | 15 |
| 1 | 2 | 3 |  | 5 | 6 | 7 | 8 | 9 | 10 | 11 |  |  |  | 4 |  |  |  |  |  |  | 16 |
| 1 | 2 | 3 |  |  | 6 | 7 | 8 | 9 | 10 | 11 |  |  |  | 5 | 4 |  |  |  |  |  | 17 |
| 1 | 2 | 3 |  | 5 | 6 | 7* | 8 | 9 | 10 | 11 | 12 |  |  | 4 |  |  |  |  |  |  | 18 |
| 1 | 2 | 3 |  | 5 | 6 | 7 | 8 | 9 | 10 | 11 |  |  |  | 4 |  |  |  |  |  |  | 19 |
| 1 | 2 | 3 |  | 5 | 6 | 7 | 8 | 9 | 10 | 11 |  |  |  | 4 |  |  |  |  |  |  | 20 |
| 1 | 2 | 3 | 8 | 5 | 6 | 7 |  | 9 |  |  |  | 11 |  | 4 |  | 10 |  |  |  |  | 21 |
| 1 | 2 | 3 |  | 5 | 6 | 7 | 8 | 9 | 10 | 11 |  |  |  | 4 |  |  |  |  |  |  | 22 |
| 1 | 2 | 3 |  | 5 | 6 | 7 | 8 | 9 | 10 | 11 |  |  |  | 4 |  |  |  |  |  |  | 23 |
| 1 | 2 | 3 |  | 5 | 6 | 7 | 8 | 9 | 10 | 11 |  |  |  | 4 |  |  |  |  |  |  | 24 |
| 1 | 2 | 3 |  | 5 | 6 | 7 | 8 | 9 | 10 | 11 |  |  |  | 4 |  |  |  |  |  |  | 25 |
| 1 | 2 | 3 |  | 5 | 6 | 7 | 8 | 9 | 10 | 11 |  |  |  | 4 |  |  |  |  |  |  | 26 |
| 1 | 2 | 3 | 7 | 5* | 6 |  | 8 | 9 | 10 | 11 |  | 12 |  | 4 |  |  |  |  |  |  | 27 |
| 1 | 2 | 3 | 7 |  | 6 |  | 8 | 9 | 10 | 11 |  |  |  | 4 | 5 |  |  |  |  |  | 28 |
| 1 | 2 | 3 | 7 |  | 6 |  | 8 | 9 | 10 | 11 |  |  |  | 4 | 5 |  |  |  |  |  | 29 |
| 1 | 6 | 3 | 7* |  |  |  | 8 | 9 | 10 | 11 | 4 | 12 |  |  | 5 |  | 2 |  |  |  | 30 |
| 1 | 6 | 3 | 7 |  |  |  | 8 | 9* |  | 11 |  | 12 |  | 4 | 5 | 10 | 2 |  |  |  | 31 |
|  | 2 | 3 | 7 |  | 6 |  | 8 | 9 | 10* | 11 |  | 12 |  | 4 | 5 |  |  | 1 |  |  | 32 |
|  | 2 | 3 | 7 |  | 6 |  | 8 | 9 |  | 11 |  |  | 10* | 4 | 5 |  |  | 1 |  |  | 33 |
| 1 | 2 | 3 | 11 |  | 6 | 7 | 8 | 9 | 10 |  |  |  |  | 4 | 5 |  |  |  |  |  | 34 |
|  | 2 | 3 | 8 |  | 6 | 7 |  | 9 | 10* | 11 |  |  |  | 4 | 5 |  |  | 1 | 12 |  | 35 |
|  | 2 | 3* | 8 |  | 6 | 7 |  | 9 | 10 | 11 |  |  |  | 4 | 5 |  |  | 1 | 12 |  | 36 |
| 1 | 2 |  | 8 | 5 | 6 | 7 |  | 9 | 10 |  |  |  | 3 | 4 |  |  |  |  | 11 |  | 37 |
| 1 | 2 |  | 8 | 5 | 6 |  |  |  | 10 |  |  |  | 3 | 4 | 7 | 9 |  |  | 11 |  | 38 |
| 1 | 2 |  | 4* | 5 | 6 | 7 | 8 | 9 |  |  |  |  | 3 |  |  |  |  |  | 11 | 12 | 39 |
| 1 | 2 |  |  | 5 | 6 | 7 | 8 | 9 | 10* |  |  |  | 3 | 4 | 12 |  |  |  | 11 |  | 40 |
| 1 | 2 | 3 |  | 5 |  | 7* | 8 | 9 | 10 |  |  |  |  | 4 | 6 | 12 |  |  |  | 11 | 41 |
|  | 6 | 3 | 7 |  |  |  | 8 | 9 | 10 |  |  |  |  | 4 | 5 |  | 2 | 1 |  | 11 | 42 |
| 37 | 42 | 38 | 26 | 29 | 37 | 33 | 32 | 41 | 39 | 29 | 15 | 2 | 3 | 29 | 14 | 3 | 3 | 5 | 3 | 2 |  |
|  |  |  |  |  |  |  |  |  |  |  | 1 | 7 |  |  | 4 |  |  |  | 2 | 1 |  |
|  | 1 | 1 | 1 | 2 |  | 10 | 5 | 14 | 8 | 4 | 2 | 2 |  | 3 | 1 |  |  |  |  | 1 |  |

1 own-goal

League Cup

| | | | | | | |
|---|---|---|---|---|---|---|
| 2 | Oct | 6 | (h) | Bournemouth | W | 2-0 |
|  |  | 26 | (a) | Bournemouth | D | 2-2 |
| 3 | Nov | 10 | (a) | Bradford C | D | 0-0 |
| R |  | 24 | (h) | Bradford C | W | 4-1 |
| 4 | Dec | 1 | (h) | Southampton | W | 2-0 |
| 5 | Jan | 19 | (h) | Nottingham F | W | 4-0 |
| SF | Feb | 15 | (a) | Arsenal | W | 4-2 |
|  |  | 23 | (h) | Arsenal | W | 2-1 |
| F | Mar | 26 | (n†) | Liverpool | L | 1-2 (After extra-time. †Played at Wembley Stadium) |

# 1983-84

Manager: Ron Atkinson

| 1 | Aug | 27 | (h) | Queen's Park R | W | 3-1 | Muhren 2, Stapleton | 48,742 |
|---|---|---|---|---|---|---|---|---|
| 2 | | 29 | (h) | Nottingham F | L | 1-2 | Moran | 43,005 |
| 3 | Sep | 3 | (a) | Stoke C | W | 1-0 | Muhren | 23,704 |
| 4 | | 6 | (a) | Arsenal | W | 3-2 | Moran, Robson, Stapleton | 42,703 |
| 5 | | 10 | (h) | Luton T | W | 2-0 | Muhren, Albiston | 41,013 |
| 6 | | 17 | (a) | Southampton | L | 0-3 | | 20,674 |
| 7 | | 24 | (h) | Liverpool | W | 1-0 | Stapleton | 56,121 |
| 8 | Oct | 1 | (a) | Norwich C | D | 3-3 | Whiteside 2, Stapleton | 19,290 |
| 9 | | 15 | (h) | West Brom A | W | 3-0 | Albiston, Graham, Whiteside | 42,221 |
| 10 | | 22 | (a) | Sunderland | W | 1-0 | Wilkins | 26,826 |
| 11 | | 29 | (h) | Wolves | W | 3-0 | Stapleton 2, Robson | 41,880 |
| 12 | Nov | 5 | (h) | Aston Villa | L | 1-2 | Robson | 45,077 |
| 13 | | 12 | (a) | Leicester C | D | 1-1 | Robson | 24,409 |
| 14 | | 19 | (h) | Watford | W | 4-1 | Stapleton 3, Robson | 43,111 |
| 15 | | 27 | (a) | West Ham U | D | 1-1 | Wilkins | 23,355 |
| 16 | Dec | 3 | (h) | Everton | L | 0-1 | | 43,664 |
| 17 | | 10 | (a) | Ipswich T | W | 2-0 | Crooks, Graham | 19,779 |
| 18 | | 16 | (h) | Tottenham H | W | 4-2 | Graham 2, Moran 2 | 33,616 |
| 19 | | 26 | (a) | Coventry C | D | 1-1 | Muhren | 21,553 |
| 20 | | 27 | (h) | Notts C | D | 3-3 | Crooks, McQueen, Moran | 41,544 |
| 21 | | 31 | (h) | Stoke C | W | 1-0 | Graham | 40,164 |
| 22 | Jan | 2 | (a) | Liverpool | D | 1-1 | Whiteside | 44,622 |
| 23 | | 13 | (a) | Queen's Park R | D | 1-1 | Robson | 16,308 |
| 24 | | 21 | (h) | Southampton | W | 3-2 | Muhren, Robson, Stapleton | 40,371 |
| 25 | Feb | 4 | (h) | Norwich C | D | 0-0 | | 36,851 |
| 26 | | 7 | (a) | Birmingham C | D | 2-2 | Hogg, Whiteside | 19,957 |
| 27 | | 12 | (a) | Luton T | W | 5-0 | Robson 2, Whiteside 2, Stapleton | 11,265 |
| 28 | | 18 | (a) | Wolves | D | 1-1 | Whiteside | 20,676 |
| 29 | | 25 | (h) | Sunderland | W | 2-1 | Moran 2 | 40,615 |
| 30 | Mar | 3 | (a) | Aston Villa | W | 3-0 | Moses, Robson, Whiteside | 32,874 |
| 31 | | 10 | (h) | Leicester C | W | 2-0 | Hughes, Moses | 39,473 |
| 32 | | 17 | (h) | Arsenal | W | 4-0 | Muhren 2, Robson, Stapleton | 48,942 |
| 33 | | 31 | (a) | West Brom A | L | 0-2 | | 28,104 |
| 34 | Apr | 7 | (h) | Birmingham C | W | 1-0 | Robson | 39,896 |
| 35 | | 14 | (a) | Notts C | L | 0-1 | | 13,911 |
| 36 | | 17 | (a) | Watford | D | 0-0 | | 20,764 |
| 37 | | 21 | (h) | Coventry C | W | 4-1 | Hughes 2, McGrath, Wilkins | 38,524 |
| 38 | | 28 | (h) | West Ham U | D | 0-0 | | 44,124 |
| 39 | May | 5 | (a) | Everton | D | 1-1 | Stapleton | 28,802 |
| 40 | | 7 | (h) | Ipswich T | L | 1-2 | Hughes | 44,257 |
| 41 | | 12 | (a) | Tottenham H | D | 1-1 | Whiteside | 39,790 |
| 42 | | 16 | (a) | Nottingham F | L | 0-2 | | 23,651 |

FINAL LEAGUE POSITION: 4th in Division One

Appearances
Sub Appearances
Goals

FA Cup

| 3 | Jan | 7 | (a) | Bournemouth | L | 0-2 |
|---|---|---|---|---|---|---|

League Cup

| 2 | Oct | 3 | (a) | Port Vale | W | 1-0 | |
|---|---|---|---|---|---|---|---|
| | | 26 | (h) | Port Vale | W | 2-0 | |
| 3 | Nov | 8 | (a) | Colchester U | W | 2-0 | |
| 4 | | 30 | (a) | Oxford U | D | 1-1 | |
| R | Dec | 7 | (h) | Oxford U | D | 1-1 | (After extra-time) |
| 2R | | 19 | (a) | Oxford U | D | 1-2 | (After extra-time) |

Manchester United also reached the semi-final of the European Cup-winners' Cup (see *United in Europe*).

| Bailey | Duxbury | Albiston | Wilkins | Moran | McQueen | Robson | Muhren | Stapleton | Whiteside | Graham | Macari | Gidman | Moses | McGrath | Crooks | Wealands | Hogg | Hughes | Davies | Blackmore | |
|---|---|---|---|---|---|---|---|---|---|---|---|---|---|---|---|---|---|---|---|---|---|
| 1 | 2 | 3 | 4 | 5 | 6 | 7 | 8 | 9 | 10* | 11 | 12 | | | | | | | | | | 1 |
| 1 | 2* | 3 | 4 | 5 | 6 | 7 | 8 | 9 | 10 | 11 | 12 | | | | | | | | | | 2 |
| 1 | | 3 | 4 | 5 | 6 | 7 | 8 | 9 | 10 | 11 | | | 2 | | | | | | | | 3 |
| 1 | | 3 | 4 | 5 | 6 | 7 | 8 | 9 | 10 | 11* | 12 | | 2 | | | | | | | | 4 |
| 1 | | 3 | 4 | 5 | 6 | 7* | 8 | 9 | 10 | 11 | 12 | | 2 | | | | | | | | 5 |
| 1 | 2 | 3 | 4 | 5 | 6 | | 8 | 9 | 10 | 11 | | | 7 | | | | | | | | 6 |
| 1 | 2 | 3 | 4 | 5 | 6 | 7 | 8 | 9 | 10 | 11 | | | | | | | | | | | 7 |
| 1 | 2 | 3 | 4 | 5 | | 7 | 8* | 9 | 10 | 11 | 12 | | 6 | | | | | | | | 8 |
| 1 | 2 | 3 | 4 | 5 | 6 | 7 | 8 | 9 | 10 | 11 | | | | | | | | | | | 9 |
| 1 | 2 | 3 | 4 | 5* | 6 | 7 | | 9 | 10 | 11 | 12 | | 8 | | | | | | | | 10 |
| 1 | 5 | 3 | 4 | | 6 | 7 | 8 | 9 | 10 | 11 | | 2* | 12 | | | | | | | | 11 |
| 1 | 2 | 3 | 4 | 5 | 6 | 7 | | 9 | 10* | 11 | 12 | | 8 | | | | | | | | 12 |
| 1 | 2 | 3 | 4 | 5 | 6 | 7 | | 9 | 10 | 11 | | | 8 | | | | | | | | 13 |
| 1 | 5 | 3 | 4 | | 6 | 7 | 8 | 9 | | 11 | | | 2 | | 10 | | | | | | 14 |
| 1 | 5 | 3 | 4 | | 6 | 7 | 8* | 9 | 12 | 11 | | | 2 | | 10 | | | | | | 15 |
| 1 | 2 | 3 | 4 | 5 | 6 | 7 | | 9 | 11 | | | | 8 | | 10 | | | | | | 16 |
| 1 | 2 | 3 | 4 | 5 | 6 | 7 | | 9 | | 11 | | | 8 | | 10 | | | | | | 17 |
| 1 | 6 | 3 | 4 | 5 | | 7 | 8 | 9* | 10 | 11 | 12 | 2 | | | | | | | | | 18 |
| | 2 | 3 | 4 | 5 | 6 | | 8 | 9 | | 11 | | | 7 | | 10 | 1 | | | | | 19 |
| | 2 | 3 | 4 | 5 | 6 | | 8 | 9 | 12 | 11 | | | 7 | | 10* | 1 | | | | | 20 |
| 1 | 2 | 3 | 4 | 5 | 6 | | 8 | 9 | 10 | 11 | | | 7 | | | | | | | | 21 |
| 1 | 2 | 3 | 4 | 5* | 6 | | 8 | 9 | 10 | 11 | | | 7 | | 12 | | | | | | 22 |
| 1 | 2 | | 4 | 5 | | 7 | 8 | 9 | 10 | 11 | | 3 | | | | | 6 | | | | 23 |
| 1 | 2 | | 4 | 5 | | 7 | 8 | 9 | 10* | 11 | | 3 | | | | | 6 | 12 | | | 24 |
| 1 | 6 | 3 | 4 | 5 | | 7 | 8 | 9 | 10 | 11 | | 2 | | | | | | | | | 25 |
| 1 | 2 | 3 | 4 | 5 | | 7 | | 9 | 10 | 11 | | | 8 | | | | 6 | | | | 26 |
| 1 | 2 | 3 | 4 | 5 | | 7* | 8 | 9 | 10 | 12 | | | 11 | | | | 6 | | | | 27 |
| 1 | 2 | 3 | 4* | 5 | | 7 | 8 | 9 | 10 | 12 | | | 11 | | | | 6 | | | | 28 |
| 1 | 2 | 3 | 4 | 5* | | 7 | 8 | 9 | 10 | 12 | | | 11 | | | | 6 | | | | 29 |
| 1 | 2 | 3 | 4 | | | 7 | 8 | 9 | 10* | 12 | | | 11 | 5 | | | 6 | | | | 30 |
| 1 | 2 | 3 | 4 | 5 | | 7 | 8 | 9 | | | | | 11 | | | | 6 | 10 | | | 31 |
| 1 | 2 | 3 | 4 | 5 | | 7 | 8 | 9 | 10* | | | | 11 | | | | 6 | 12 | | | 32 |
| 1 | 2 | 3 | 4 | 5 | | 7 | | 9 | 10 | 8 | | | 11 | | | | 6 | | | | 33 |
| 1 | 2 | 3 | 4 | 5 | | 7 | | 9 | 10* | 8 | | | 11 | | | | 6 | 12 | | | 34 |
| 1 | 2 | 3 | 4 | 5 | | | | 9 | 10 | | | | 8 | 7 | | | 6 | 12 | 11* | | 35 |
| 1 | 2 | 3 | 4 | 5 | | | | 9 | 10 | 8 | | | 7 | | | | 6 | 11 | | | 36 |
| 1 | 2 | 3 | 4* | 5 | | | | 9 | 12 | 11 | | 8 | 7 | | | | 6 | 10 | | | 37 |
| 1 | 2 | 3 | 4 | 5 | | | | 9 | 12 | 11 | | 8 | 7* | | | | 6 | 10 | | | 38 |
| 1 | 2 | 3 | 4 | 5 | | 7 | | 9 | 12 | | | | 8 | | 6 | | 10 | 11* | | | 39 |
| 1 | 2 | 3 | 4 | 5 | | 7 | | 9 | | 11 | | 8 | 6 | | | | 10 | | | | 40 |
| 1 | 2 | 3 | 4 | 5 | | 7 | | 9* | 12 | 11 | | 8 | 6 | | | | 10 | | | | 41 |
| 1 | 2 | 3 | 4 | 5 | | 7 | | 9 | 12 | 11* | | | 6 | | | | 10 | | | 8 | 42 |
| 40 | 39 | 40 | 42 | 38 | 20 | 33 | 26 | 42 | 30 | 33 | | 4 | 31 | 9 | 6 | 2 | 16 | 7 | 3 | 1 | |
| | | | | | | | | 7 | 4 | 5 | | 4 | | 1 | | | 4 | | | | |
| | | 2 | 3 | 7 | 1 | 12 | 8 | 13 | 10 | 5 | | 2 | 1 | 2 | | | 1 | 4 | | | |

# 1984-85

Manager: Ron Atkinson

| | | | | | | | |
|---|---|---|---|---|---|---|---|
| 1 | Aug | 25 | (h) | Watford | D | 1-1 | Strachan | 53,668 |
| 2 | | 28 | (a) | Southampton | D | 0-0 | | 22,183 |
| 3 | Sep | 1 | (a) | Ipswich T | D | 1-1 | Hughes | 20,876 |
| 4 | | 5 | (h) | Chelsea | D | 1-1 | Olsen | 48,398 |
| 5 | | 8 | (h) | Newcastle U | W | 5-0 | Strachan 2, Hughes, Moses, Olsen | 54,915 |
| 6 | | 15 | (a) | Coventry C | W | 3-0 | Whiteside 2, Robson | 18,312 |
| 7 | | 22 | (h) | Liverpool | D | 1-1 | Strachan | 56,638 |
| 8 | | 29 | (a) | West Brom A | W | 2-1 | Robson, Strachan | 26,292 |
| 9 | Oct | 6 | (a) | Aston Villa | L | 0-3 | | 37,131 |
| 10 | | 13 | (h) | West Ham U | W | 5-1 | Brazil, Hughes, McQueen, Moses, Strachan | 47,559 |
| 11 | | 20 | (h) | Tottenham H | W | 1-0 | Hughes | 54,516 |
| 12 | | 27 | (a) | Everton | L | 0-5 | | 40,742 |
| 13 | Nov | 2 | (h) | Arsenal | W | 4-2 | Strachan 2, Hughes, Robson | 32,279 |
| 14 | | 10 | (a) | Leicester C | W | 3-2 | Brazil, Hughes, Strachan | 23,840 |
| 15 | | 17 | (h) | Luton T | W | 2-0 | Whiteside 2 | 41,630 |
| 16 | | 24 | (a) | Sunderland | L | 2-3 | Hughes, Robson | 25,405 |
| 17 | Dec | 1 | (h) | Norwich C | W | 2-0 | Hughes, Robson | 36,635 |
| 18 | | 8 | (a) | Nottingham F | L | 2-3 | Strachan 2 | 25,902 |
| 19 | | 15 | (h) | Queen's Park R | W | 3-0 | Brazil, Duxbury, Gidman | 36,134 |
| 20 | | 22 | (h) | Ipswich T | W | 3-0 | Gidman, Robson, Strachan | 35,168 |
| 21 | | 26 | (a) | Stoke C | L | 1-2 | Stapleton | 20,985 |
| 22 | | 29 | (a) | Chelsea | W | 3-1 | Hughes, Moses, Stapleton | 42,197 |
| 23 | Jan | 1 | (h) | Sheffield W | L | 1-2 | Hughes | 47,625 |
| 24 | | 12 | (h) | Coventry C | L | 0-1 | | 35,992 |
| 25 | Feb | 2 | (h) | West Brom A | W | 2-0 | Strachan 2 | 36,681 |
| 26 | | 9 | (a) | Newcastle U | D | 1-1 | Moran | 32,555 |
| 27 | | 23 | (a) | Arsenal | W | 1-0 | Whiteside | 48,612 |
| 28 | Mar | 2 | (h) | Everton | D | 1-1 | Olsen | 51,150 |
| 29 | | 12 | (a) | Tottenham H | W | 2-1 | Hughes, Whiteside | 42,908 |
| 30 | | 15 | (a) | West Ham U | D | 2-2 | Robson, Stapleton | 16,674 |
| 31 | | 23 | (h) | Aston Villa | W | 4-0 | Hughes 3, Whiteside | 40,941 |
| 32 | | 31 | (a) | Liverpool | W | 1-0 | Stapleton | 34,886 |
| 33 | Apr | 3 | (h) | Leicester C | W | 2-1 | Robson, Stapleton | 35,590 |
| 34 | | 6 | (h) | Stoke C | W | 5-0 | Hughes 2, Olsen 2, Whiteside | 42,940 |
| 35 | | 9 | (a) | Sheffield W | L | 0-1 | | 39,380 |
| 36 | | 21 | (a) | Luton T | L | 1-2 | Whiteside | 10,320 |
| 37 | | 24 | (h) | Southampton | D | 0-0 | | 31,291 |
| 38 | | 27 | (h) | Sunderland | D | 2-2 | Moran, Robson | 38,979 |
| 39 | May | 4 | (a) | Norwich C | W | 1-0 | Moran | 15,502 |
| 40 | | 6 | (h) | Nottingham F | W | 2-0 | Gidman, Stapleton | 41,775 |
| 41 | | 11 | (a) | Queen's Park R | W | 3-1 | Brazil 2, Strachan | 20,483 |
| 42 | | 13 | (a) | Watford | L | 1-5 | Moran | 20,500 |

FINAL LEAGUE POSITION: 4th in Division One

Appearances
Sub Appearances
Goals

FA Cup

| | | | | | | | |
|---|---|---|---|---|---|---|---|
| 3 | Jan | 5 | (h) | Bournemouth | W | 3-0 | |
| 4 | | 26 | (h) | Coventry C | W | 2-1 | |
| 5 | Feb | 15 | (a) | Blackburn R | W | 2-0 | |
| 6 | Mar | 9 | (h) | West Ham U | W | 4-2 | |
| SF | Apr | 13 | (n*) | Liverpool | D | 2-2 | (After extra-time. *Played at Goodison Park, Liverpool.) |
| R | | 17 | (n†) | Liverpool | W | 2-1 | (†Played at Maine Road, Manchester.) |
| F | May | 18 | (n‡) | Everton | W | 1-0 | (After extra-time. ‡Played at Wembley Stadium) |

League Cup

| | | | | | | |
|---|---|---|---|---|---|---|
| 2 | Sep | 26 | (h) | Burnley | W | 4-0 |
| | Oct | 9 | (a) | Burnley | W | 3-0 |
| 3 | | 30 | (h) | Everton | L | 1-2 |

Appearances grid (shirt numbers; * denotes player substituted, numbers 12 denote substitute used):

| Bailey | Duxbury | Albiston | Moses | Moran | Hogg | Robson | Strachan | Hughes | Brazil | Olsen | Whiteside | Muhren | McQueen | Gidman | Stapleton | Garton | McGrath | Blackmore | Pears | No. |
|---|---|---|---|---|---|---|---|---|---|---|---|---|---|---|---|---|---|---|---|---|
| 1 | 2 | 3 | 4 | 5 | 6 | 7 | 8 | 9 | 10* | 11 | 12 |  |  |  |  |  |  |  |  | 1 |
| 1 | 2 | 3 | 4 | 5 | 6 | 7 | 8 | 9 | 10 | 11 |  |  |  |  |  |  |  |  |  | 2 |
| 1 | 2 | 3 | 4 | 5 | 6 | 7 | 8 | 9 | 10* | 11 | 12 |  |  |  |  |  |  |  |  | 3 |
| 1 | 2 | 3 | 4 | 5 | 6 | 7 | 8 | 9 |  | 11 | 10 |  |  |  |  |  |  |  |  | 4 |
| 1 | 2 | 3 | 4 | 5 | 6 | 7 | 8 | 9 |  | 11 | 10 |  |  |  |  |  |  |  |  | 5 |
| 1 | 2 | 3 | 4 | 5 | 6 | 7 | 8 | 9 |  | 11 | 10 |  |  |  |  |  |  |  |  | 6 |
| 1 | 2 | 3 | 4 | 5* | 6 | 7 | 8 | 9 |  | 11 | 10 | 12 |  |  |  |  |  |  |  | 7 |
| 1 | 2 | 3 | 4 | 5 | 6 | 7 | 8 | 9 | 10 | 11 |  |  |  |  |  |  |  |  |  | 8 |
| 1 | 2 | 3 | 4 | 5 | 6 | 7 |  | 9 | 10 | 11 |  | 8 |  |  |  |  |  |  |  | 9 |
| 1 | 2 | 3 | 4 |  | 6 | 7 | 8 | 9 | 10 | 11 |  |  | 5 |  |  |  |  |  |  | 10 |
| 1 |  | 3 | 4 | 5 | 6 | 7 | 8 | 9 | 10 | 11 |  |  |  | 2 |  |  |  |  |  | 11 |
| 1 |  | 3 | 4 | 5* | 6 | 7 | 8 | 9 | 10 | 11 |  |  |  | 2 | 12 |  |  |  |  | 12 |
| 1 |  | 3 | 4 | 5 | 6 | 7 | 8 | 9 |  | 11 |  |  |  | 2 | 10 |  |  |  |  | 13 |
| 1 |  | 3 | 4 |  | 6 | 7 | 8 | 9 | 10 | 11* | 12 |  | 5 | 2 |  |  |  |  |  | 14 |
| 1 | 6 | 3 | 4 |  |  | 7* | 8 | 9 |  | 11 | 10 |  | 5 | 2 | 12 |  |  |  |  | 15 |
| 1 |  | 3 | 4 |  |  | 7 | 8 | 9 |  | 11* | 10 | 12 | 5 | 2 | 6 |  |  |  |  | 16 |
| 1 |  | 3 | 4 |  |  | 7 | 8 | 9 |  | 11 | 10 |  | 5 | 2 | 6 |  |  |  |  | 17 |
| 1 | 2 |  | 4 |  |  | 7 | 8 |  | 10 | 11 |  |  | 5 |  | 9 | 6 | 3 |  |  | 18 |
| 1 | 6 | 3 | 4 |  |  | 7 | 8 |  | 10 | 11 |  |  | 5 | 2 | 9 |  |  |  |  | 19 |
| 1 | 6 | 3 | 4 |  |  | 7 | 8 | 9 |  | 11 |  |  | 5 | 2 | 10 |  |  |  |  | 20 |
| 1 | 6 | 3 | 4 |  |  | 7 | 8* | 9 | 12 | 11 |  |  | 5 | 2 | 10 |  |  |  |  | 21 |
| 1 | 2 | 3 | 4 |  |  | 7 | 8 |  | 10 | 11 |  |  | 5 |  | 9 |  | 6 |  |  | 22 |
| 1 | 2 | 3 | 4 |  |  | 7 | 8 | 9 | 10 | 11 |  |  | 5 |  |  |  | 6 |  |  | 23 |
|  | 2 | 3 | 4 |  |  | 7* | 8 |  | 10 | 12 | 11 |  | 5 |  | 9 |  | 6 |  | 1 | 24 |
|  |  | 3 | 4 | 5 | 6 |  | 8 | 9 |  | 11 | 10 |  |  | 2 | 7 |  |  |  | 1 | 25 |
|  |  | 3 | 4 | 5 | 6 |  | 8 |  | 10 | 11* | 9 |  |  | 2 | 12 | 7 |  |  | 1 | 26 |
| 1 | 4 | 3 | 5* |  | 6 |  | 8 | 9 |  | 11 | 12 |  |  | 2 | 10 | 7 |  |  |  | 27 |
| 1 | 4 | 3 |  |  | 6 | 7 |  | 9 |  | 11 | 8 |  |  | 2 | 10 | 5 |  |  |  | 28 |
| 1 | 4 | 3 |  |  | 6 | 7 |  | 9 |  | 11 | 8 |  |  | 2 | 10 | 5 |  |  |  | 29 |
| 1 | 4 | 3 |  |  | 6 | 12 | 7 | 9 |  | 11 | 8* |  |  | 2 | 10 | 5 |  |  |  | 30 |
| 1 |  | 3 |  |  | 6 | 7 | 8 | 9 |  | 11 | 4 |  |  | 2 | 10 | 5 |  |  |  | 31 |
| 1 |  | 3 |  |  | 6 | 7 | 8 | 9 |  | 11 | 4 |  |  | 2 | 10 | 5 |  |  |  | 32 |
| 1 |  | 3 |  |  | 6 | 7 | 8 | 9 |  | 11 | 4 |  |  | 2 | 10 | 5 |  |  |  | 33 |
| 1 | 12 | 3 |  |  | 6 | 7* | 8 | 9 |  | 11 | 4 |  |  | 2 | 10 | 5 |  |  |  | 34 |
|  | 4* | 3 |  |  | 6 | 7 | 8 | 9 | 12 | 11 | 4 |  |  | 2 | 10 | 5 |  | 1 |  | 35 |
| 1 |  | 3 |  |  | 6 | 7 |  | 9 |  | 11 | 4 | 8 |  | 2 | 10 | 5 |  |  |  | 36 |
| 1 | 12 | 3 |  |  | 6 | 7 | 8 | 9 |  | 11 | 4 |  |  | 2 | 10* | 5 |  |  |  | 37 |
| 1 | 12 | 3 |  |  | 6 | 7 | 8 | 9 | 10 | 11 | 4 |  | 2* |  |  | 5 |  |  |  | 38 |
| 1 |  | 3 |  |  | 6 | 7 | 8 | 9 |  | 11 | 4 |  |  | 2 | 10 | 5 |  |  |  | 39 |
| 1 |  | 3 | 5* |  | 6 |  | 8 |  | 10 | 11 | 4 | 12 |  | 2 | 9 | 7 |  |  |  | 40 |
| 1 | 7 | 3 | 6* |  |  |  | 8 |  | 10 | 11 | 4 | 12 |  | 2 | 9 | 5 |  |  |  | 41 |
| 1 | 7 | 3 | 6 |  |  |  | 8 | 9 | 10 | 4* | 11 | 12 |  | 2 |  | 5 |  |  |  | 42 |
| 38 | 27 | 39 | 26 | 19 | 29 | 32 | 41 | 38 | 17 | 36 | 23 | 7 | 12 | 27 | 21 | 2 | 23 | 1 | 4 |  |
| 3 |  |  |  |  |  | 1 |  | 3 |  | 4 | 5 |  |  | 3 |  |  |  |  |  |  |
| 1 |  | 3 | 4 |  |  | 9 | 15 | 16 | 5 | 5 | 9 |  | 1 | 3 | 6 |  |  |  |  |  |

Manchester United reached the quarter-finals of the UEFA Cup (see *United in Europe* section).

# 1985-86

Manager: Ron Atkinson

| | | | | | | | |
|---|---|---|---|---|---|---|---|
| 1 | Aug | 17 | (h) | Aston Villa | W | 4-0 | Hughes 2, Olsen, Whiteside | 49,743 |
| 2 | | 20 | (a) | Ipswich T | W | 1-0 | Robson | 18,777 |
| 3 | | 24 | (a) | Arsenal | W | 2-1 | Hughes, McGrath | 37,145 |
| 4 | | 26 | (h) | West Ham U | W | 2-0 | Hughes, Strachan | 50,773 |
| 5 | | 31 | (a) | Nottingham F | W | 3-1 | Barnes, Hughes, Stapleton | 26,274 |
| 6 | Sep | 4 | (h) | Newcastle U | W | 3-0 | Stapleton 2, Hughes | 51,102 |
| 7 | | 7 | (h) | Oxford U | W | 3-0 | Barnes, Robson, Whiteside | 51,820 |
| 8 | | 14 | (a) | Manchester C | W | 3-0 | Albiston, Duxbury, Robson | 48,773 |
| 9 | | 21 | (a) | West Brom A | W | 5-1 | Brazil 2, Blackmore, Stapleton, Strachan | 25,068 |
| 10 | | 28 | (h) | Southampton | W | 1-0 | Hughes | 52,449 |
| 11 | Oct | 5 | (a) | Luton T | D | 1-1 | Hughes | 17,454 |
| 12 | | 12 | (h) | Queen's Park R | W | 2-0 | Hughes, Olsen | 48,845 |
| 13 | | 19 | (h) | Liverpool | D | 1-1 | McGrath | 54,492 |
| 14 | | 26 | (a) | Chelsea | W | 2-1 | Hughes, Olsen | 42,485 |
| 15 | Nov | 2 | (h) | Coventry C | W | 2-0 | Olsen 2 | 46,748 |
| 16 | | 9 | (a) | Sheffield W | L | 0-1 | | 48,105 |
| 17 | | 16 | (h) | Tottenham H | D | 0-0 | | 54,575 |
| 18 | | 23 | (a) | Leicester C | L | 0-3 | | 22,008 |
| 19 | | 30 | (h) | Watford | D | 1-1 | Brazil | 42,181 |
| 20 | Dec | 7 | (h) | Ipswich T | W | 1-0 | Stapleton | 37,981 |
| 21 | | 14 | (a) | Aston Villa | W | 3-1 | Blackmore, Hughes, Strachan | 27,626 |
| 22 | | 21 | (h) | Arsenal | L | 0-1 | | 44,386 |
| 23 | | 26 | (a) | Everton | L | 1-3 | Stapleton | 42,551 |
| 24 | Jan | 1 | (h) | Birmingham C | W | 1-0 | C.Gibson | 43,095 |
| 25 | | 11 | (a) | Oxford U | W | 3-1 | C.Gibson, Hughes, Whiteside | 13,280 |
| 26 | | 18 | (h) | Nottingham F | L | 2-3 | Olsen 2 | 46,717 |
| 27 | Feb | 2 | (a) | West Ham U | L | 1-2 | Robson | 22,642 |
| 28 | | 9 | (a) | Liverpool | D | 1-1 | C.Gibson | 35,064 |
| 29 | | 22 | (h) | West Brom A | W | 3-0 | Olsen 3 | 45,193 |
| 30 | Mar | 1 | (a) | Southampton | L | 0-1 | | 19,012 |
| 31 | | 15 | (a) | Queen's Park R | L | 0-1 | | 23,407 |
| 32 | | 19 | (h) | Luton T | W | 2-0 | Hughes, McGrath | 33,668 |
| 33 | | 22 | (h) | Manchester C | D | 2-2 | C.Gibson, Strachan | 51,274 |
| 34 | | 29 | (a) | Birmingham C | D | 1-1 | Robson | 22,551 |
| 35 | | 31 | (h) | Everton | D | 0-0 | | 51,189 |
| 36 | Apr | 5 | (a) | Coventry C | W | 3-1 | C.Gibson, Robson, Strachan | 17,160 |
| 37 | | 9 | (h) | Chelsea | L | 1-2 | Olsen | 45,355 |
| 38 | | 13 | (h) | Sheffield W | L | 0-2 | | 32,331 |
| 39 | | 16 | (a) | Newcastle U | W | 4-2 | Hughes 2, Robson, Whiteside | 31,840 |
| 40 | | 19 | (a) | Tottenham H | D | 0-0 | | 32,357 |
| 41 | | 26 | (h) | Leicester C | W | 4-0 | Blackmore, Davenport, Hughes, Stapleton | 38,840 |
| 42 | May | 3 | (a) | Watford | D | 1-1 | Hughes | 18,414 |

FINAL LEAGUE POSITION: 4th in Division One

Appearances
Sub Appearances
Goals

FA Cup

| 3 | Jan | 9 | (h) | Rochdale | W | 2-0 |
|---|---|---|---|---|---|---|
| 4 | | 25 | (a) | Sunderland | D | 0-0 |
| R | | 29 | (h) | Sunderland | W | 3-0 |
| 5 | Mar | 5 | (a) | West Ham U | D | 1-1 |
| R | | 9 | (h) | West Ham U | L | 0-2 |

League Cup

| 2 | Sep | 24 | (a) | Crystal P | W | 1-0 |
|---|---|---|---|---|---|---|
| | Oct | 9 | (h) | Crystal P | W | 1-0 |
| 3 | | 29 | (h) | West Ham U | W | 1-0 |
| 4 | Nov | 26 | (a) | Liverpool | L | 1-2 |

348

| Bailey | Gidman | Albiston | Whiteside | McGrath | Hogg | Robson | Moses | Hughes | Stapleton | Olsen | Duxbury | Strachan | Barnes | Brazil | Blackmore | Moran | Garton | Gibson C | Dempsey | Turner | Wood | Gibson T | Sivebaek | Davenport | Higgins | |
|---|---|---|---|---|---|---|---|---|---|---|---|---|---|---|---|---|---|---|---|---|---|---|---|---|---|---|
| 1 | 2 | 3 | 4 | 5 | 6 | 7 | 8* | 9 | 10 | 11 | 12 | | | | | | | | | | | | | | | 1 |
| 1 | 2* | 3 | 4 | 5 | 6 | 7 | | 9 | 10 | 11 | 12 | 8 | | | | | | | | | | | | | | 2 |
| 1 | | 3 | 4 | 5 | 6 | 7 | | 9 | 10 | 11 | 2 | 8 | | | | | | | | | | | | | | 3 |
| 1 | | 3 | 4 | 5 | 6 | 7 | | 9 | 10 | 11 | 2 | 8 | | | | | | | | | | | | | | 4 |
| 1 | | 3 | 4 | 5 | 6 | 7 | | 9 | 10 | | 2 | 8* | 11 | 12 | | | | | | | | | | | | 5 |
| 1 | | 3 | 4 | 5 | 6 | 7 | | 9 | 10* | | 2 | 8 | 11 | 12 | | | | | | | | | | | | 6 |
| 1 | | 3 | 4 | 5 | 6 | 7 | | 9 | 10* | | 2 | 8 | 11 | 12 | | | | | | | | | | | | 7 |
| 1 | | 3 | 4 | 5 | 6 | 7 | | 9 | 10* | | 2 | 8 | 11 | 12 | | | | | | | | | | | | 8 |
| 1 | | 3 | 4 | 5 | 6 | 7 | | 9 | | | 2 | 8* | 10 | 11 | 12 | | | | | | | | | | | 9 |
| 1 | | 3 | 4* | 5 | | 7 | 8 | 9 | 10 | | 2 | | 11 | | 12 | 6 | | | | | | | | | | 10 |
| 1 | | 3 | 4 | 5 | | 7 | 8 | 9 | 10 | | 2 | | 11 | | | 6 | | | | | | | | | | 11 |
| 1 | | 3 | 4 | 5 | | 7 | | 9 | 10 | | 2 | 8 | 11 | | | 6 | | | | | | | | | | 12 |
| 1 | | 3 | 4 | 7 | 6 | | 8* | 9 | 10 | 11 | 2 | | | | 12 | 5 | | | | | | | | | | 13 |
| 1 | | 3 | 4 | 7 | 6 | | | 9 | 10 | | 2 | 8 | 11 | | | 5 | | | | | | | | | | 14 |
| 1 | | 3 | 4 | 7 | 6 | | | 9 | 10 | | | 8 | 11 | | | 5 | 2 | | | | | | | | | 15 |
| 1 | 2 | 3 | 4 | 5 | | 7* | | 9 | 10 | | | 8 | 12 | 11 | | 6 | | | | | | | | | | 16 |
| 1 | 2 | 3 | 4 | 5 | | | | 9 | 10 | | | 8 | 7 | 11 | | 6 | | | | | | | | | | 17 |
| 1 | 2 | 3* | 4 | 7 | 6 | | | 9 | 10 | 11 | | 8 | | | 12 | 5 | | | | | | | | | | 18 |
| 1 | 2 | | 4 | 7 | 6 | | | 9 | 10 | 11 | | 8 | | | 12 | 5* | | 3 | | | | | | | | 19 |
| 1 | 2 | | 4 | 5 | 6 | | | 9* | 10 | 11 | | 8 | | | 12 | | | 3 | 7 | | | | | | | 20 |
| | 2 | | 4 | 5 | | | | 9 | 10* | 11 | | 8 | | | 12 | 7 | 6 | 3 | | 1 | | | | | | 21 |
| 1 | 2 | | 4 | 5 | | | | 9 | 10 | 11 | | 8 | | | | 7 | 6 | 3 | | 1 | | | | | | 22 |
| 1 | 2 | | 4 | 5 | 6 | | | 9 | 11* | | | 8 | | | | 7 | | 3 | | 1 | 12 | | | | | 23 |
| | 2 | 3 | 4 | 5* | | | | 9 | 10 | | | 8 | | | 12 | 7 | 6 | 11 | | 1 | | | | | | 24 |
| 1 | 2 | 3 | 4 | | | | | 9 | 10 | | | 8 | 7 | | | 5 | 6 | 11 | | 1 | | | | | | 25 |
| 1 | 2 | 3 | 4 | | | | | 9 | 10 | 7 | | 8 | | | | 5 | 6 | 11 | | 1 | | | | | | 26 |
| 1 | 2 | 3 | 4 | 5 | | 7* | | 9 | 10 | 8 | | | | | | 6 | | 11 | | 12 | | | | | | 27 |
| | 2 | 3 | 4 | 5 | | | | 9 | 12 | 11* | | 8 | | | | 6 | 10 | | 1 | 8 | 7 | | | | | 28 |
| 2* | 3 | | 5 | | | | | 9 | 10 | 11 | | 7 | | | 4 | 6 | 8 | | 1 | 12 | | | | | | 29 |
| | 3 | | 5 | | | 7 | | 9 | 10 | 11* | 2 | 8 | | | | 6 | 4 | | 1 | 12 | | | | | | 30 |
| | 3 | | 5 | | | | | 9 | 7 | 2 | 8 | | 4* | 6 | | 11 | | 1 | | 12 | 10 | | | | | 31 |
| | 3 | 4 | 5 | | | | | 9 | 12 | 11 | 2 | 8 | | 6* | | 7 | | 1 | | 10 | | | | | | 32 |
| | 3 | 4 | 5 | | | | | 9 | 12 | | 2 | 8 | 11* | | | 7 | | 1 | | 10 | 6 | | | | | 33 |
| | 2 | 3 | 4 | 5 | | 7 | | 9 | 12 | | | 8 | | | | 11* | | 1 | | 10 | 6 | | | | | 34 |
| | 2 | 3 | 4 | 5 | | 7 | | 9 | 12 | | | 8 | | | | 11 | | 1 | | 10* | 6 | | | | | 35 |
| | 2 | 3 | 4 | 5 | | 7 | | 9 | 12 | | | 8 | | | | 11* | | 1 | | 10 | 6 | | | | | 36 |
| | 2 | 3 | | 5 | | 7 | | 9 | 12 | 11 | 4 | 8* | | | | | | 1 | | 10 | 6 | | | | | 37 |
| | 2 | 3 | | 5 | | 7 | | 9 | | 11 | 4 | | | | | | | 1 | 12 | 8 | 10* | 6 | | | | 38 |
| | 2 | 3 | 4 | 5 | | 7 | | 9 | 10 | | | | 11 | | 6 | | | 1 | 8* | 12 | | | | | | 39 |
| | 2 | 3 | 4 | 5 | | | | 9 | 10 | 12 | 7 | | 11 | | 6 | | | 1 | | | 8* | | | | | 40 |
| | 2 | 3 | 4* | 5 | | | | 9 | 10 | 12 | 7 | | 11 | | 6 | | | 1 | | | 8 | | | | | 41 |
| | | 3 | 4 | 5 | 6 | | | 9 | 10 | 12 | 7 | | 11 | | 2 | | | 1 | | | 8* | | | | | 42 |
| 25 | 24 | 37 | 37 | 40 | 17 | 21 | 4 | 40 | 34 | 25 | 21 | 27 | 12 | 1 | 12 | 18 | 10 | 18 | 1 | 17 | 2 | 2 | 11 | 6 | | |
| | | | | | | | | 7 | 3 | 2 | 1 | 1 | | | 10 | | 1 | | | | 1 | 5 | 1 | | | |
| | | 1 | 4 | 3 | | 7 | | 17 | 7 | 11 | 1 | 5 | 2 | 3 | 3 | | | 5 | | | | | 1 | | | |

# 1986-87

Manager: Ron Atkinson until November 1986, then Alex Ferguson OBE.

| 1 | Aug | 23 | (a) | Arsenal | L 0-1 | | 41,382 |
|---|---|---|---|---|---|---|---|
| 2 | | 25 | (h) | West Ham U | L 2-3 | Stapleton, Davenport | 43,306 |
| 3 | | 30 | (h) | Charlton A | L 0-1 | | 37,544 |
| 4 | Sep | 6 | (a) | Leicester C | D 1-1 | Whiteside | 16,785 |
| 5 | | 13 | (h) | Southampton | W 5-1 | Stapleton 2, Olsen, Davenport, Whiteside | 40,135 |
| 6 | | 16 | (a) | Watford | L 0-1 | | 21,650 |
| 7 | | 21 | (a) | Everton | L 1-3 | Robson | 25,843 |
| 8 | | 28 | (h) | Chelsea | L 0-1 | | 33,340 |
| 9 | Oct | 4 | (a) | Nottingham F | D 1-1 | Robson | 34,828 |
| 10 | | 11 | (h) | Sheffield W | W 3-1 | Davenport 2, Whiteside | 45,890 |
| 11 | | 18 | (h) | Luton T | W 1-0 | Stapleton | 39,927 |
| 12 | | 26 | (a) | Manchester C | D 1-1 | Stapleton | 32,440 |
| 13 | Nov | 1 | (h) | Coventry C | D 1-1 | Davenport | 36,946 |
| 14 | | 8 | (a) | Oxford U | L 0-2 | | 13,545 |
| 15 | | 15 | (a) | Norwich C | D 0-0 | | 22,684 |
| 16 | | 22 | (h) | Queen's Park R | W 1-0 | Sivebaek | 42,235 |
| 17 | | 29 | (a) | Wimbledon | L 0-1 | | 12,112 |
| 18 | Dec | 7 | (h) | Tottenham H | D 3-3 | Davenport 2, Whiteside | 35,957 |
| 19 | | 13 | (a) | Aston Villa | D 3-3 | Davenport 2, Whiteside | 29,205 |
| 20 | | 20 | (h) | Leicester C | W 2-0 | C.Gibson, Stapleton | 34,180 |
| 21 | | 26 | (a) | Liverpool | W 1-0 | Whiteside | 40,663 |
| 22 | | 27 | (h) | Norwich C | L 0-1 | | 44,610 |
| 23 | Jan | 1 | (h) | Newcastle U | W 4-1 | Whiteside, Stapleton, Olsen, P.Jackson (og) | 43,334 |
| 24 | | 3 | (a) | Southampton | D 1-1 | Olsen | 20,409 |
| 25 | | 24 | (h) | Arsenal | W 2-0 | Strachan, T.Gibson | 51,367 |
| 26 | Feb | 7 | (a) | Charlton A | D 0-0 | | 15,482 |
| 27 | | 14 | (h) | Watford | W 3-1 | McGrath, Davenport, Strachan | 35,763 |
| 28 | | 21 | (a) | Chelsea | D 1-1 | Davenport | 26,516 |
| 29 | | 28 | (h) | Everton | D 0-0 | | 47,421 |
| 30 | Mar | 7 | (h) | Manchester C | W 2-0 | Robson, Reid (og) | 48,619 |
| 31 | | 14 | (a) | Luton T | L 1-2 | Robson | 12,509 |
| 32 | | 21 | (a) | Sheffield W | L 0-1 | | 29,888 |
| 33 | | 28 | (h) | Nottingham F | W 2-0 | McGrath, Robson | 39,182 |
| 34 | Apr | 4 | (h) | Oxford U | W 3-2 | Davenport 2, Robson | 32,443 |
| 35 | | 14 | (a) | West Ham U | D 0-0 | | 23,486 |
| 36 | | 18 | (a) | Newcastle U | L 1-2 | Strachan | 32,706 |
| 37 | | 20 | (h) | Liverpool | W 1-0 | Davenport | 54,103 |
| 38 | | 25 | (a) | Queen's Park R | D 1-1 | Strachan | 17,414 |
| 39 | May | 2 | (h) | Wimbledon | L 0-1 | | 31,686 |
| 40 | | 4 | (a) | Tottenham H | L 0-4 | | 36,692 |
| 41 | | 6 | (a) | Coventry C | D 1-1 | Whiteside | 23,407 |
| 42 | | 9 | (h) | Aston Villa | W 3-1 | Blackmore, Duxbury, Robson | 35,179 |

FINAL LEAGUE POSITION: 11th in Division One

Appearances

Sub Appearances

Goals

FA Cup

| 3 | Jan | 10 | (h) | Manchester C | W 1-0 |
|---|---|---|---|---|---|
| 4 | | 31 | (h) | Coventry C | L 0-1 |

League Cup

| 2 | Sep | 24 | (h) | Port Vale | W 2-0 |
|---|---|---|---|---|---|
| | Oct | 7 | (a) | Port Vale | W 5-2 |
| 3 | | 29 | (h) | Southampton | D 0-0 |
| R | Nov | 4 | (a) | Southampton | L 1-4 |

350

Player appearances and goals grid (shirt numbers worn; * = substituted)

| Turner | Duxbury | Albiston | Whiteside | McGrath | Moran | Strachan | Blackmore | Stapleton | Davenport | Gibson C | Olsen | Gibson T | Siveback | Hogg | Robson | Moses | Barnes | Walsh | O'Brien | Garton | Gill | Bailey | Wood | |
|---|---|---|---|---|---|---|---|---|---|---|---|---|---|---|---|---|---|---|---|---|---|---|---|---|
| 1 | 2 | 3 | 4 | 5 | 6 | 7 | 8 | 9 | 10 | 11* | 12 | | | | | | | | | | | | | 1 |
| 1 | 2 | 3 | 4 | 5 | 6 | 7 | 8 | 9 | 10 | 11* | 12 | | | | | | | | | | | | | 2 |
| 1 | 2 | 3 | 4* | 5 | 6 | 7 | 8 | 9 | 10 | | 11 | 12 | | | | | | | | | | | | 3 |
| 1 | 8 | 3 | 4 | 5 | | 7 | | 9 | 12 | 11 | 10* | | 2 | 6 | | | | | | | | | | 4 |
| 1 | | 3 | 4 | 5 | 6 | 8* | | 9 | 10 | 11 | 12 | | 2 | | 7 | | | | | | | | | 5 |
| 1 | | 3 | | 5 | 6 | | 8 | 9 | 10 | 11 | | | 2 | | 7 | 4 | | | | | | | | 6 |
| 1 | | 3 | 4* | 5 | 6 | | 8 | 9 | 10 | | 12 | | 2 | | 7 | 11 | | | | | | | | 7 |
| 1 | | 3 | 4* | 5 | 6 | | 8 | 9 | 10 | | 12 | | 2 | | 7 | 11 | | | | | | | | 8 |
| 1 | | 3 | 4 | 5 | 6 | | 8 | 9 | 10 | 11 | | | 2 | | 7 | | | | | | | | | 9 |
| 1 | | 3 | 4 | 5 | | | 8 | 9 | 10 | | | | 2 | 6 | 7 | 11 | | | | | | | | 10 |
| 1 | | 3 | 4 | 5 | | 8* | | 9 | 10 | | 12 | | 2 | 6 | 7 | 11 | | | | | | | | 11 |
| 1 | | 3 | 4 | 5 | | | | 9 | 10 | | | | 2 | 6 | 7 | 8 | 11 | | | | | | | 12 |
| 1 | | 3 | 4 | 5 | | | 8 | 9 | 10 | | 11 | | 2 | 6 | 7* | 12 | | | | | | | | 13 |
| 1 | 2 | 3 | | 5* | 4 | | 7 | 9 | 10 | | 12 | | 6 | | | 8 | 11 | | | | | | | 14 |
| 1 | | 3 | | 5 | 12 | | 8 | 9 | 10 | | 7 | | 2* | 6 | 4 | 11 | | | | | | | | 15 |
| 1 | | 3 | | 5 | | 12 | 8 | 9 | 10 | | 7 | | 2 | 6 | 4 | 11* | | | | | | | | 16 |
| 1 | | 3 | | 5 | 6 | | 8 | 9 | 10 | | 7 | | 2 | | 12 | 4 | 11* | | | | | | | 17 |
| 1 | | 3 | 9 | 5* | 6 | 8 | | 12 | 10 | | 11 | | 2 | | 7 | 4 | | | | | | | | 18 |
| | 3 | | 9 | | 5 | 8 | | 12 | 10* | | 11 | | 2 | 6 | 7 | 4 | | 1 | | | | | | 19 |
| | | 9 | | 5 | 8 | | 12 | 10 | 3 | 11 | | | 2 | 6 | 7 | | | 1 | 4* | | | | | 20 |
| | 6 | | 4 | 5 | 8 | | | 9 | 10 | 3 | 11 | | 2 | | 7 | | | 1 | | | | | | 21 |
| | 6 | | 4 | | 8 | | | 9 | 10 | 3 | 11 | | 2 | | 7* | | | 1 | 12 | 5 | | | | 22 |
| 1 | 7 | | 9* | | 6 | 8 | | 12 | 10 | 3 | 11 | | 2 | | | 4 | 5 | | | | | | | 23 |
| 1 | 2 | | | | 6 | 8 | | 9 | 12 | 3 | 11 | 10 | | | | 4 | 5 | 7* | | | | | | 24 |
| 1 | 3* | | 4 | 12 | 6 | 8 | 7 | 9 | | 11 | 10 | 2 | | | | | 5 | | | | | | | 25 |
| 1 | 4 | | | | 6 | 8 | 12 | 9 | 3 | 11 | 10* | 2 | | | 7 | | 5 | | | | | | | 26 |
| 1 | 4 | | 5 | | 6 | 8 | 12 | 9 | 3 | 11 | 10 | | | | 7 | | 2* | | | | | | | 27 |
| | 2 | | 4 | 5 | 6 | 8 | 12 | 9 | 3 | 11* | 10 | | | | 7 | | | 1 | | | | | | 28 |
| | 2 | | 4 | 5 | 6 | 11 | | 9* | 3 | | 10 | 8 | | | 7 | | 12 | 1 | | | | | | 29 |
| | 4 | 9 | 5 | 6 | 8* | | 12 | 3 | 10 | | | | 2 | | 7 | | 11 | 1 | | | | | | 30 |
| | 4 | 9 | 5 | 6 | 8 | | 12 | 3* | 10 | | | | 2 | | 7 | | 11 | 1 | | | | | | 31 |
| | 3 | 9 | 5 | 6 | 8 | | | 10 | 11 | | 12 | | | | 7 | 4 | 2* | 1 | | | | | | 32 |
| | 6 | 12 | 10 | 5 | | | | 9 | 3 | | | | 2 | | 7 | 8 | | 1 | 4 | 11* | | | | 33 |
| | 6 | 12 | | 5 | | | | 9 | 11 | 3 | | | 2 | | 7 | 8 | | 1 | 4 | 10* | | | | 34 |
| | 2 | 12 | | 5 | 6 | 8 | | 9 | 11 | 3 | 10 | | | | 7* | 4 | | 1 | | | | | | 35 |
| | 2 | 10 | | 5 | 6 | 8 | 12 | 11 | 3 | | 9* | | | | | 4 | | 1 | 7 | | | | | 36 |
| | 7 | 3* | 10 | 5 | 6 | 8 | 12 | 9 | 11 | | | | 2 | | | 4 | | 1 | | | | | | 37 |
| | 2 | 3 | 9 | 5 | 6 | 8 | | 10 | 11 | | | 12 | | | 7 | 4* | | 1 | | | | | | 38 |
| | 2 | 3 | | 5 | 6 | 8 | 12 | 9 | 11 | | 10 | | | | 7 | 4* | | 1 | | | | | | 39 |
| | 4 | 10 | | 5 | 6 | 8 | 12 | | 3 | 11 | | 9 | 2* | | 7 | | | 1 | | | | | | 40 |
| | 4 | 3 | 9 | 5 | 6 | 8* | 12 | | 10 | 11 | | | | | 7 | | | 1 | 2 | | | | | 41 |
| | 4 | 3 | 9* | 5 | 6 | 8 | | 10 | | 11 | 12 | | | | 7 | | | 1 | 2 | | | | | 42 |
| 23 | 32 | 19 | 31 | 34 | 32 | 33 | 10 | 25 | 34 | 24 | 22 | 12 | 27 | 11 | 29 | 17 | 7 | 14 | 9 | 9 | 1 | 5 | 2 | |
| 3 | | | 1 | 1 | 1 | 2 | 9 | 5 | | 6 | 4 | 1 | | 1 | 1 | | | 2 | | | | | | |
| 1 | | 8 | 2 | | 4 | 1 | 7 | 14 | 1 | 3 | 1 | 1 | | | 7 | | | | | | | | | |

2 own-goals

# 1987-88

Manager: Alex Ferguson OBE

| 1 | Aug | 15 | (a) | Southampton | D | 2-2 | Whiteside 2 | 21,214 |
|---|-----|----|-----|-------------|---|-----|-------------|--------|
| 2 | | 19 | (h) | Arsenal | D | 0-0 | | 42,890 |
| 3 | | 22 | (h) | Watford | W | 2-0 | McGrath, McClair | 38,582 |
| 4 | | 29 | (a) | Charlton A | W | 3-1 | McClair, Robson, McGrath | 14,046 |
| 5 | | 31 | (h) | Chelsea | W | 3-1 | McClair, Strachan, Whiteside | 46,478 |
| 6 | Sep | 5 | (a) | Coventry C | D | 0-0 | | 27,125 |
| 7 | | 12 | (h) | Newcastle U | D | 2-2 | Olsen, McClair | 45,137 |
| 8 | | 19 | (a) | Everton | L | 1-2 | Whiteside | 38,439 |
| 9 | | 26 | (h) | Tottenham H | W | 1-0 | McClair | 47,601 |
| 10 | Oct | 3 | (a) | Luton T | D | 1-1 | McClair | 9,137 |
| 11 | | 10 | (a) | Sheffield W | W | 4-2 | McClair 2, Robson, Blackmore | 32,779 |
| 12 | | 17 | (h) | Norwich C | W | 2-1 | Davenport, Robson | 39,345 |
| 13 | | 25 | (a) | West Ham U | D | 1-1 | Gibson | 19,863 |
| 14 | | 31 | (h) | Nottingham F | D | 2-2 | Robson, Whiteside | 44,669 |
| 15 | Nov | 15 | (h) | Liverpool | D | 1-1 | Whiteside | 47,106 |
| 16 | | 21 | (a) | Wimbledon | L | 1-2 | Blackmore | 11,532 |
| 17 | Dec | 5 | (a) | Queen's Park R | W | 2-0 | Davenport, Robson | 20,632 |
| 18 | | 12 | (h) | Oxford U | W | 3-1 | Strachan 2, Olsen | 34,709 |
| 19 | | 19 | (a) | Portsmouth | W | 2-1 | Robson, McClair | 22,207 |
| 20 | | 26 | (a) | Newcastle U | L | 0-1 | | 26,461 |
| 21 | | 28 | (h) | Everton | W | 2-1 | McClair 2 | 47,024 |
| 22 | Jan | 1 | (h) | Charlton A | D | 0-0 | | 37,257 |
| 23 | | 2 | (a) | Watford | W | 1-0 | McClair | 18,038 |
| 24 | | 16 | (h) | Southampton | L | 0-2 | | 35,716 |
| 25 | | 24 | (a) | Arsenal | W | 2-1 | Strachan, McClair | 29,392 |
| 26 | Feb | 6 | (h) | Coventry C | W | 1-0 | O'Brien | 37,144 |
| 27 | | 10 | (a) | Derby C | W | 2-1 | Whiteside, Strachan | 20,016 |
| 28 | | 13 | (a) | Chelsea | W | 2-1 | Bruce, O'Brien | 25,014 |
| 29 | | 23 | (a) | Tottenham H | D | 1-1 | McClair | 25,731 |
| 30 | Mar | 5 | (a) | Norwich C | L | 0-1 | | 19,129 |
| 31 | | 12 | (h) | Sheffield W | W | 4-1 | McClair 2, Blackmore, Davenport | 33,318 |
| 32 | | 19 | (a) | Nottingham F | D | 0-0 | | 27,598 |
| 33 | | 26 | (h) | West Ham U | W | 3-1 | Strachan, Anderson, Robson | 37,269 |
| 34 | Apr | 2 | (h) | Derby C | W | 4-1 | McClair 3, Gibson | 40,146 |
| 35 | | 4 | (a) | Liverpool | D | 3-3 | Robson 2, Strachan | 43,497 |
| 36 | | 12 | (h) | Luton T | W | 3-0 | McClair, Robson, Davenport | 28,830 |
| 37 | | 30 | (h) | Queen's Park R | W | 2-1 | Bruce, Parker (og) | 35,733 |
| 38 | May | 2 | (a) | Oxford U | W | 2-0 | Anderson, Strachan | 8,966 |
| 39 | | 7 | (h) | Portsmouth | W | 4-1 | McClair 2, Davenport, Robson | 35,105 |
| 40 | | 9 | (h) | Wimbledon | W | 2-1 | McClair 2 | 28,040 |

FINAL LEAGUE POSITION: 2nd in Division One

Appearances
Sub Appearances
Goals

FA Cup

| 3 | Jan | 10 | (a) | Ipswich T | W | 2-1 | |
|---|-----|----|-----|-----------|---|-----|--|
| 4 | | 30 | (h) | Chelsea | W | 2-0 | |
| 5 | Feb | 20 | (a) | Arsenal | L | 1-2 | |

League Cup

| 2 | Sep | 23 | (h) | Hull C | W | 5-0 | |
|---|-----|----|-----|--------|---|-----|--|
| | Oct | 7 | (a) | Hull C | W | 1-0 | |
| 3 | | 28 | (h) | Crystal P | W | 2-1 | |
| 4 | Nov | 18 | (a*) | Bury | W | 2-1 | (*Played at Old Trafford, Manchester.) |
| 5 | Jan | 20 | (a) | Oxford U | L | 0-2 | |

| Walsh | Anderson | Duxbury | Moses | McGrath | Moran | Robson | Strachan | McClair | Whiteside | Olsen | Albiston | Davenport | Gibson | Hogg | Garton | Blackmore | O'Brien | Graham | Turner | Bruce | Martin | |
|---|---|---|---|---|---|---|---|---|---|---|---|---|---|---|---|---|---|---|---|---|---|---|
| 1 | 2 | 3 | 4* | 5 | 6 | 7 | 8 | 9 | 10 | 11† | 12 | 14 | | | | | | | | | | 1 |
| 1 | 2 | 3 | 4 | 5 | 6 | 7 | 8 | 9 | 10 | 11 | | | | | | | | | | | | 2 |
| 1 | 2 | 3 | 4 | 5 | 6 | 7 | 8† | 9 | 10 | 11* | 12 | 14 | | | | | | | | | | 3 |
| 1 | 2 | 3 | 4 | 5 | 6 | 7 | 8† | 9 | 10 | 11* | | 12 | 14 | | | | | | | | | 4 |
| 1 | 2 | 7 | 4 | 5 | 6 | | 8 | 9 | 10 | 11 | 3* | | 12 | | | | | | | | | 5 |
| 1 | 2 | 7 | 4 | 5 | 6 | | 8 | 9 | 10 | 11* | 3† | 12 | 14 | | | | | | | | | 6 |
| 1 | 2 | 3 | 4 | 5 | 6 | 7 | 8 | 9 | 10 | 11* | 12 | | | | | | | | | | | 7 |
| 1 | 2 | 3 | 4 | 5 | | 7 | 8* | 9 | 10 | 11 | | 12 | | 6† | 14 | | | | | | | 8 |
| 1 | 2† | 6 | | 5 | | 7 | 8* | 9 | 10 | 11 | | 12 | 3 | 4 | 14 | | | | | | | 9 |
| 1 | | 6 | | 5 | | 7 | 8 | 9 | 10 | 11 | | | 3 | 4 | 2* | 12 | | | | | | 10 |
| 1 | | | 4 | 5 | 6† | 7 | 8* | 9 | 10 | 11 | 12 | | 3 | | | 2 | 14 | | | | | 11 |
| 1 | | | 4 | 5 | 12 | 7 | | 9 | 10 | 11 | 6 | | 3 | | 2* | 8† | 14 | | | | | 12 |
| 1 | 2 | | 4 | 5 | 6 | 7 | 8* | 9 | 11 | 10 | | | 3 | 12 | | | | | | | | 13 |
| 1 | 2 | | 4 | | 6 | 7 | 12 | 9 | 10* | 11 | 8 | 3 | 5 | | | | | | | | | 14 |
| 1 | 2 | | 4 | | 6* | 7 | 8 | 9 | 10 | 11 | 12 | 3 | 5 | | | | | | | | | 15 |
| 1 | 2 | 3* | 4 | | 6 | 7 | | 9 | 10 | 11 | | 12 | 5 | 14 | 8† | | | | | | | 16 |
| | 2 | | 4 | 5 | | 7 | 8 | 9 | | 11 | | 3 | 10 | | | 6 | | | 1 | | | 17 |
| | 2 | | 4 | 5 | | 7* | 8 | 9 | 10 | 11 | | 12 | 6 | | | 3 | | | 1 | | | 18 |
| | 2 | 6 | | 5 | | 7 | 8 | 9 | 10 | 11* | | 12 | 3 | | | | | | 1 | 4 | | 19 |
| 12 | 2 | 6† | | 5 | | 7 | 8 | 9 | 10 | 11 | | 14 | 3* | | | | | | 1 | 4 | | 20 |
| | 2 | 6 | 12 | 5 | | 7 | 8* | 9 | 10† | 11 | | 14 | 3 | | | | | | 1 | 4 | | 21 |
| | 2 | 5 | | | 6† | 7 | 8 | 9 | 10 | 11* | | 12 | 3 | 14 | | | | | 1 | 4 | | 22 |
| | 2 | 6 | | 5† | | 7 | 8 | 9 | 10 | 11 | 12 | 3* | | 14 | | | | | 1 | 4 | | 23 |
| | 2 | 8 | 6 | 5† | | 7 | 12 | 9 | 10 | 11 | | 3* | | 14 | | | | | 1 | 4 | | 24 |
| | 2 | 3 | | | | 7 | 8 | 9 | 10 | 11 | | 12 | 6 | | | 5* | | | 1 | 4 | | 25 |
| | 2 | 3 | | | | 7 | 8 | 9 | 10 | 11 | | 12 | 6 | | | 5* | | | 1 | 4 | | 26 |
| | 2 | 3* | | | | 7 | 8 | 9 | 10 | 11† | 12 | 14 | 6 | | | 5 | | | 1 | 4 | | 27 |
| | 2 | | | | | 7 | 8 | 9 | 10 | 11* | | 12 | 3 | 6 | | 5 | | | 1 | 4 | | 28 |
| | 2† | 3 | 12 | | | 7 | 8 | 9 | 10 | 11 | | 14 | | 6* | | 5 | | | 1 | 4 | | 29 |
| | | 3* | | | 6 | 7 | 8 | 9 | 10 | 11 | | 12 | | | 2 | 5 | | | 1 | 4 | | 30 |
| | | 5 | | | | 7 | 8 | 9 | 10 | 11* | | | 3 | 6 | 2 | 12 | | | 1 | 4 | | 31 |
| | 2 | 5 | | | 12 | 7 | 8 | 9 | 10 | 11† | | | 3 | 6* | | 14 | | | 1 | 4 | | 32 |
| | 2 | 6 | | 5 | | 7 | 8* | 9 | 10 | 11 | | 12 | 3 | | | | | | 1 | 4 | | 33 |
| | 2 | | 4 | 5† | | 7 | 8 | 9 | 10* | 11 | | 12 | 3 | 6 | | 14 | | | 1 | | | 34 |
| | 2 | 6† | | 5 | | 7 | 8 | 9 | 10 | 11 | 12 | 14 | 3* | | | | | | 1 | 4 | | 35 |
| | 2 | 6 | | 5 | | 7 | 8 | 9 | 10 | 11* | | 12 | 3 | | | | | | 1 | 4 | | 36 |
| | 2 | 6 | | 5 | | 7 | 8 | 9 | 10 | 11 | | 12 | 3* | | | | | | 1 | 4 | | 37 |
| | 2* | 6 | | 5 | | 7 | 8 | 9 | 10 | 11 | | 12 | 3 | | | | | | 1 | 4 | | 38 |
| | 2† | 6 | | 5* | | 7 | 8 | 9 | 10 | 11 | | 12 | 3 | 14 | | | | | 1 | 4 | | 39 |
| | 2 | 6* | | 5 | | 7 | 8 | 9 | 10 | 11 | | | 3 | | | | | | 1 | 4 | 12 | 40 |
| 16 | 30 | 39 | 16 | 21 | 20 | 36 | 33 | 40 | 26 | 30 | 5 | 21 | 26 | 9 | 5 | 15 | 6 | 1 | 24 | 21 | | |
| 1 | | 1 | 1 | 1 | | 3 | | 1 | 7 | 6 | 13 | 3 | 1 | 1 | 7 | 11 | | | 1 | | | |
| | 2 | | | 2 | | 11 | 8 | 24 | 7 | 2 | | 5 | 2 | | 3 | 2 | | | | 2 | | |

1 own-goal

# 1988-89

Manager: Alex Ferguson OBE

| 1 | Aug | 27 | (h) | Queen's Park R | D | 0-0 | | 46,377 |
|---|---|---|---|---|---|---|---|---|
| 2 | Sep | 3 | (a) | Liverpool | L | 0-1 | | 42,026 |
| 3 | | 10 | (h) | Middlesbrough | W | 1-0 | Robson | 40,422 |
| 4 | | 17 | (a) | Luton T | W | 2-0 | Davenport, Robson | 11,010 |
| 5 | | 24 | (h) | West Ham U | W | 2-0 | Davenport, Hughes | 39,941 |
| 6 | Oct | 1 | (a) | Tottenham H | D | 2-2 | Hughes, McClair | 29,318 |
| 7 | | 22 | (a) | Wimbledon | D | 1-1 | Hughes | 12,143 |
| 8 | | 26 | (h) | Norwich C | L | 1-2 | Hughes | 36,998 |
| 9 | | 30 | (a) | Everton | D | 1-1 | Hughes | 27,005 |
| 10 | Nov | 5 | (h) | Aston Villa | D | 1-1 | Bruce | 44,804 |
| 11 | | 12 | (a) | Derby C | D | 2-2 | Hughes, McClair | 24,080 |
| 12 | | 19 | (h) | Southampton | D | 2-2 | Robson, Hughes | 37,277 |
| 13 | | 23 | (h) | Sheffield W | D | 1-1 | Hughes | 30,867 |
| 14 | | 27 | (a) | Newcastle U | D | 0-0 | | 20,350 |
| 15 | Dec | 3 | (h) | Charlton A | W | 3-0 | Milne, McClair, Hughes | 31,173 |
| 16 | | 10 | (a) | Coventry C | L | 0-1 | | 19,936 |
| 17 | | 17 | (a) | Arsenal | L | 1-2 | Hughes | 37,422 |
| 18 | | 26 | (h) | Nottingham F | W | 2-0 | Milne, Hughes | 39,582 |
| 19 | Jan | 1 | (h) | Liverpool | W | 3-1 | McClair, Hughes, Beardsmore | 44,745 |
| 20 | | 2 | (a) | Middlesbrough | L | 0-1 | | 24,411 |
| 21 | | 14 | (h) | Millwall | W | 3-0 | Blackmore, Gill, Hughes | 40,931 |
| 22 | | 21 | (a) | West Ham U | W | 3-1 | Strachan, Martin, McClair | 29,822 |
| 23 | Feb | 5 | (h) | Tottenham H | W | 1-0 | McClair | 41,423 |
| 24 | | 11 | (a) | Sheffield W | W | 2-0 | McClair 2 | 34,820 |
| 25 | | 25 | (a) | Norwich C | L | 1-2 | McGrath | 23,155 |
| 26 | Mar | 12 | (a) | Aston Villa | D | 0-0 | | 28,332 |
| 27 | | 25 | (h) | Luton T | W | 2-0 | Milne, Blackmore | 36,335 |
| 28 | | 27 | (a) | Nottingham F | L | 0-2 | | 30,092 |
| 29 | Apr | 2 | (h) | Arsenal | D | 1-1 | Adams (og) | 37,977 |
| 30 | | 8 | (a) | Millwall | D | 0-0 | | 17,523 |
| 31 | | 15 | (h) | Derby C | L | 0-2 | | 34,145 |
| 32 | | 22 | (a) | Charlton A | L | 0-1 | | 12,055 |
| 33 | | 29 | (h) | Coventry C | L | 0-1 | | 29,799 |
| 34 | May | 2 | (h) | Wimbledon | W | 1-0 | McClair | 23,368 |
| 35 | | 6 | (a) | Southampton | L | 1-2 | Beardsmore | 17,021 |
| 36 | | 8 | (a) | Queen's Park R | L | 2-3 | Bruce, Blackmore | 10,017 |
| 37 | | 10 | (h) | Everton | L | 1-2 | Hughes | 26,722 |
| 38 | | 13 | (h) | Newcastle U | W | 2-0 | McClair, Robson | 30,379 |

FINAL LEAGUE POSITION: 11th in Division One

Appearances
Sub Appearances
Goals

FA Cup

| 3 | Jan | 7 | (h) | Queen's Park R | D | 0-0 | |
|---|---|---|---|---|---|---|---|
| R | | 11 | (a) | Queen's Park R | D | 2-2 | (After extra-time) |
| 2R | | 23 | (h) | Queen's Park R | W | 3-0 | |
| 4 | | 28 | (h) | Oxford U | W | 4-0 | |
| 5 | Feb | 18 | (a) | Bournemouth | D | 1-1 | |
| R | | 22 | (h) | Bournemouth | W | 1-0 | |
| 6 | Mar | 18 | (h) | Nottingham F | L | 0-1 | |

League Cup

| 2 | Sep | 28 | (a) | Rotherham U | W | 1-0 |
|---|---|---|---|---|---|---|
| | Oct | 12 | (h) | Rotherham U | W | 5-0 |
| 3 | Nov | 2 | (a) | Wimbledon | L | 1-2 |

| Leighton | Blackmore | Martin | Bruce | McGrath | McClair | Robson | Strachan | Davenport | Hughes | Olsen | O'Brien | Anderson | Duxbury | Garton | Sharpe | Beardsmore | Robins | Donaghy | Gibson | Milne | Gill | Wilson | Maiorana | Whiteside | Brazil | |
|---|---|---|---|---|---|---|---|---|---|---|---|---|---|---|---|---|---|---|---|---|---|---|---|---|---|---|
| 1 | 2 | 3 | 4 | 5 | 6 | 7 | 8 | 9* | 10 | 11 | 12 | | | | | | | | | | | | | | | 1 |
| 1 | 3 | 4 | 5* | 9 | 7 | 8† | 14 | | 10 | 11 | | 2 | 6 | 12 | | | | | | | | | | | | 2 |
| 1 | 3 | 4 | 5 | 9 | 7 | | 8 | | 10 | 11 | | 6 | 2 | | | | | | | | | | | | | 3 |
| 1 | 3 | 4 | 5 | 9 | 7 | | 8 | | 10 | 11 | | 6 | 2 | | | | | | | | | | | | | 4 |
| 1 | 2 | | 4 | 9 | 7 | 8 | 11 | | 10 | 12 | | 6 | 5† | 3* | 14 | | | | | | | | | | | 5 |
| 1 | | | 4 | 5 | 9 | 7 | 8 | 11* | 10 | 12 | | 14 | 6 | 2† | 3 | | | | | | | | | | | 6 |
| 1 | 2 | | 4 | 9 | 7 | 8* | 11† | | 10 | | | 6 | 5 | 3 | 12 | 14 | | | | | | | | | | 7 |
| 1 | 2 | | 4 | 9 | 7 | 8 | 11* | | 10 | 12 | | 6 | 5 | 3 | | | | | | | | | | | | 8 |
| 1 | 3 | | 4 | 9 | 7 | 8* | | | 10 | 11 | | 14 | 5† | 2 | 12 | | | 6 | | | | | | | | 9 |
| 1 | 2 | | 4 | 9 | 7 | 8 | | | 10 | 11 | | 5 | 12 | | | | | 6 | 3* | | | | | | | 10 |
| 1 | 3 | | 4 | 9 | 7 | 8 | | | 10 | 12 | | 5* | 2 | 11 | | | | 6 | | | | | | | | 11 |
| 1 | 3 | | 4 | 9 | 7 | 8 | | | 10 | | | 2 | 11* | | | | | 6 | | 5 | 12 | | | | | 12 |
| 1 | 3† | | 4 | 9 | 7 | 8* | | | 10 | | | 2 | 11 | | | | | 6 | | 5 | 12 | 14 | | | | 13 |
| 1 | 3 | 12 | 4 | 9 | 7 | | | | 10 | | | 2 | 11† | 14 | | | | 6 | | 8* | 5 | | | | | 14 |
| 1 | 5 | 3 | 4 | 9 | 7 | 8 | | | 10 | | | 2 | | | | | | 6 | | 11 | | | | | | 15 |
| 1 | 5 | 3 | 4 | 9 | 7 | 8 | | | 10 | | | 2* | 11 | | | | | 6 | | 14 | 12† | | | | | 16 |
| 1 | 5* | 2† | 4 | 9 | 7 | 8 | | | 10 | | | 3 | 14 | | | | | 6 | | 11 | 12 | | | | | 17 |
| 1 | | 2 | 4 | 9 | 7 | 8 | | | 10 | | | 3 | 5 | | | | | 6 | | 11 | | | | | | 18 |
| 1 | | 2* | 4 | 12 | 9 | 7 | 8† | | 10 | | | 3 | 5 | 14 | | | | 6 | | 11 | | | | | | 19 |
| 1 | | | 4 | 5 | 9 | 7 | | | 10 | | | 3 | 8* | 14 | | | | 6 | | 11 | 2† | 12 | | | | 20 |
| 1 | 8 | 2 | 4 | 9 | | | | | 10 | | | 3 | 5* | | | | | 6 | | 11† | 7 | 12 | 14 | | | 21 |
| 1 | 5 | 3 | 4 | 9 | 7 | 8* | | | 10 | | | 12 | | | | | | 6 | | 11 | 2 | | | | | 22 |
| 1 | 5 | 2 | 4 | 12 | 9 | 7 | 8† | | 10 | | | 3* | 14 | | | | | 6 | | 11 | | | | | | 23 |
| 1 | 5 | 3 | 4 | 2 | 9 | 7 | 8 | | 10* | | | 12 | | | | | | 6 | | 11* | | | | | | 24 |
| 1 | 2† | 12 | 4 | 5 | 9 | 7 | 8 | | 10 | | | 3 | 14 | | | | | 6 | | 11* | | | | | | 25 |
| 1 | 12 | 3† | 4 | 5 | 9 | 7 | 8 | | 10 | 11 | | 2* | | | | | | 6 | | 14 | | | | | | 26 |
| 1 | 3 | 2 | 4 | 5 | 9 | 7 | | | 10 | | | 8* | | | | | | 6 | | 11 | 12 | | | | | 27 |
| 1 | 3 | 12 | 4 | 5* | 9 | 7 | | | 10 | | | 2 | | | 8 | | | 6 | | 11† | 14 | | | | | 28 |
| 1 | 14 | 12 | 4 | 5 | 9 | 7 | | | 10 | | | 2 | | | 8† | | | 3 | | | | 11* | 6 | | | 29 |
| 1 | | 11 | 4 | 5* | 9 | 7 | | | 10 | | | 2 | | | 8 | | | 3 | | | | 12 | 6 | | | 30 |
| 1 | | 3 | 4 | 5 | 9 | | | | 10 | | | 2† | 12 | | 8* | 7 | | 6 | | 14 | 11 | | | | | 31 |
| 1 | | | 4 | 5 | 9 | 7 | | | 10 | | | 2 | | | 8 | 12 | | 3 | | 11* | | | 6 | | | 32 |
| 1 | 11* | | 4 | 5 | 9 | 7 | | | 10 | | | 2 | | | 8 | 12 | | 3 | | | | | 6 | | | 33 |
| 1 | | 11 | 4 | 5 | 9 | 7 | | | 10 | | | 2 | | | 8 | | | 3 | | | | 12 | 6* | | | 34 |
| 1 | 11* | | 4 | 5 | 9 | 7† | | | 10 | | | 2 | | 12 | 8 | | | 3 | | 14 | | | 6 | | | 35 |
| 1 | 5 | 11 | 4 | | 9 | | | | 10 | | | 2 | | 3* | 8 | 12 | | 6 | | 7 | | | | | | 36 |
| 1 | 5* | 11 | 4 | | 9 | | | | 10 | | | 2† | | 3 | 8 | 12 | | 6 | | 7 | | 14 | | | | 37 |
| 1 | 5† | 3 | 4 | | 9 | 7 | | | 10 | | | 2 | | 14 | 8 | 12 | | 6 | | 11* | | | | | | 38 |
| 38 | 26 | 20 | 38 | 18 | 38 | 34 | 21 | 7 | 38 | 6 | 1 | 5 | 16 | 13 | 19 | 17 | 1 | 30 | 1 | 19 | 4 | | 2 | 6 | | |
| | 2 | 4 | | 2 | | | | 1 | | | | 4 | 2 | 1 | 2 | 1 | 3 | 6 | 9 | 1 | 3 | 5 | 4 | 4 | 1 | |
| | 3 | 1 | 2 | 1 | 10 | 4 | 1 | 2 | 14 | 2 | | | | | 3 | | | 1 | | | | | | | | |

1 own-goal

# 1989-90

Manager: Alex Ferguson OBE

| # | Month | Date | | Opponent | Result | Scorers | Attendance |
|---|---|---|---|---|---|---|---|
| 1 | Aug | 19 | (h) | Arsenal | W 4-1 | Bruce, Hughes, Webb, McClair | 47,245 |
| 2 | | 22 | (a) | Crystal P | D 1-1 | Robson | 22,423 |
| 3 | | 26 | (a) | Derby C | L 0-2 | | 22,175 |
| 4 | | 30 | (h) | Norwich C | L 0-2 | | 39,610 |
| 5 | Sep | 9 | (a) | Everton | L 2-3 | McClair, Beardsmore | 37,916 |
| 6 | | 16 | (h) | Millwall | W 5-1 | Hughes 3, Robson, Sharpe | 42,746 |
| 7 | | 23 | (a) | Manchester C | L 1-5 | Hughes | 43,246 |
| 8 | Oct | 14 | (h) | Sheffield W | D 0-0 | | 41,492 |
| 9 | | 21 | (a) | Coventry C | W 4-1 | Hughes 2, Bruce, Phelan | 19,605 |
| 10 | | 28 | (h) | Southampton | W 2-1 | McClair 2 | 37,122 |
| 11 | Nov | 4 | (a) | Charlton A | L 0-2 | | 16,065 |
| 12 | | 12 | (h) | Nottingham F | W 1-0 | Pallister | 34,182 |
| 13 | | 18 | (a) | Luton T | W 3-1 | Wallace, Blackmore, Hughes | 11,141 |
| 14 | | 25 | (h) | Chelsea | D 0-0 | | 46,975 |
| 15 | Dec | 3 | (a) | Arsenal | L 0-1 | | 34,484 |
| 16 | | 9 | (h) | Crystal P | L 1-2 | Beardsmore | 33,514 |
| 17 | | 16 | (h) | Tottenham H | L 0-1 | | 36,230 |
| 18 | | 23 | (a) | Liverpool | D 0-0 | | 37,426 |
| 19 | | 26 | (a) | Aston Villa | L 0-3 | | 41,247 |
| 20 | | 30 | (a) | Wimbledon | D 2-2 | Hughes, Robins | 9,622 |
| 21 | Jan | 1 | (h) | Queen's Park R | D 0-0 | | 34,824 |
| 22 | | 13 | (h) | Derby C | L 1-2 | Pallister | 38,985 |
| 23 | | 21 | (a) | Norwich C | L 0-2 | | 17,370 |
| 24 | Feb | 3 | (h) | Manchester C | D 1-1 | Blackmore | 40,274 |
| 25 | | 10 | (a) | Millwall | W 2-1 | Wallace, Hughes | 15,491 |
| 26 | | 24 | (a) | Chelsea | L 0-1 | | 29,979 |
| 27 | Mar | 3 | (h) | Luton T | W 4-1 | McClair, Hughes, Wallace, Robins | 35,327 |
| 28 | | 14 | (h) | Everton | D 0-0 | | 37,398 |
| 29 | | 18 | (h) | Liverpool | L 1-2 | Whelan (og) | 46,629 |
| 30 | | 21 | (a) | Sheffield W | L 0-1 | | 33,260 |
| 31 | | 24 | (a) | Southampton | W 2-0 | Gibson, Robins | 20,510 |
| 32 | | 31 | (h) | Coventry C | W 3-0 | Hughes 2, Robins | 39,172 |
| 33 | Apr | 14 | (a) | Queen's Park R | W 2-1 | Robins, Webb | 18,997 |
| 34 | | 17 | (h) | Aston Villa | W 2-0 | Robins 2 | 44,880 |
| 35 | | 21 | (h) | Tottenham H | L 1-2 | Bruce | 33,317 |
| 36 | | 30 | (h) | Wimbledon | D 0-0 | | 29,281 |
| 37 | May | 2 | (a) | Nottingham F | L 0-4 | | 21,186 |
| 38 | | 5 | (h) | Charlton A | W 1-0 | Pallister | 35,389 |

FINAL LEAGUE POSITION: 13th in Division One

Appearances

Sub Appearances

Goals

FA Cup

| | | | | | | |
|---|---|---|---|---|---|---|
| 3 | Jan | 7 | (a) | Nottingham F | W 1-0 | |
| 4 | | 28 | (a) | Hereford U | W 1-0 | |
| 5 | Feb | 18 | (a) | Newcastle U | W 3-2 | |
| 6 | Mar | 11 | (a) | Sheffield U | W 1-0 | |
| SF | Apr | 8 | (n*) | Oldham A | D 3-3 | (After extra-time. *Played at Maine Road, Manchester.) |
| R | | 11 | (n*) | Oldham A | W 2-1 | (After extra-time. *Played at Maine Road, Manchester.) |
| F | May | 12 | (n†) | Crystal P | D 3-3 | (After extra-time. †Played at Wembley Stadium.) |
| R | | 17 | (n†) | Crystal P | W 1-0 | (†Played at Wembley Stadium) |

League Cup

| | | | | | | |
|---|---|---|---|---|---|---|
| 2 | Sep | 20 | (a) | Portsmouth | W 3-2 | |
| | Oct | 3 | (h) | Portsmouth | D 0-0 | |
| 3 | | 25 | (h) | Tottenham H | L 0-3 | |

| Leighton | Duxbury | Blackmore | Bruce | Phelan | Donaghy | Robson | Webb | McClair | Hughes | Sharpe | Martin | Graham | Pallister | Robins | Anderson | Beardsmore | Ince | Wallace | Maiorana | Milne | Brazil | Gibson | Sealey | Bosnich | |
|---|---|---|---|---|---|---|---|---|---|---|---|---|---|---|---|---|---|---|---|---|---|---|---|---|---|
| 1 | 2 | 3 | 4 | 5 | 6 | 7 | 8 | 9 | 10 | 11* | 12 | | | | | | | | | | | | | | 1 |
| 1 | 2 | 3 | 4 | 5 | 6 | 7 | 8 | 9 | 10 | 11 | | | | | | | | | | | | | | | 2 |
| 1 | 2 | 6 | 4 | 5 | | 7 | 8 | 9 | 10 | 11 | 3* | 12 | | | | | | | | | | | | | 3 |
| 1 | 2 | 3† | 4 | 5 | | 7* | 8 | 9 | 10 | 11 | 12 | | 6 | 14 | | | | | | | | | | | 4 |
| 1 | 2* | 8 | 4 | 5 | | 7 | | 9 | 10 | 11 | 3† | | 6 | 12 | 14 | | | | | | | | | | 5 |
| 1 | 14 | | 4* | 5 | 3 | 7 | | 9 | 10 | 11 | | | 6 | | 2 | 12 | 8† | | | | | | | | 6 |
| 1 | | | 4 | 5 | 3 | | | 9 | 10 | 12 | | | 6 | | 2 | 7* | 8 | 11 | | | | | | | 7 |
| 1 | 2† | | 4 | 5 | 3 | 7 | | 9 | 10 | 12 | | 14 | 6 | | | | 8 | 11* | | | | | | | 8 |
| 1 | 14 | | 4 | 5 | 2 | 7 | | 9 | 10 | 11* | 3 | | 6 | | | | 8† | 12 | | | | | | | 9 |
| 1 | 12 | | 4 | 5 | 2 | 7 | | 9 | 10 | 11 | 3 | | 6 | | | | 8* | | | | | | | | 10 |
| 1 | 14 | | 4 | 5 | 2* | 7 | | 9 | 10 | 11† | 3 | | 6 | | | | 8 | 12 | | | | | | | 11 |
| 1 | 2 | | 4 | 5 | | 7 | | 9 | 10 | 12 | 3 | | 6 | | | | 8 | 11* | | | | | | | 12 |
| 1 | 2 | | 4 | 5 | | 7 | | 9 | 10 | | 3 | | 6 | | | | 8 | 11 | | | | | | | 13 |
| 1 | 14 | 2 | 4 | 5 | | 7 | | 9 | 10 | | 3† | | 6 | | | 12 | 8 | 11* | | | | | | | 14 |
| 1 | 2* | | 4 | 5 | | 7 | | 9 | 10 | | 3 | | 6 | | | 12 | 8 | 11 | | | | | | | 15 |
| 1 | 14 | | 4 | 5† | | 7 | | 9 | 10* | 12 | 3 | | 6 | | 2 | | 8 | 11 | | | | | | | 16 |
| 1 | 14 | | 4* | 5 | | 7 | | 9 | 10 | | 3 | | 6 | 12 | 2† | | 8 | 11 | | | | | | | 17 |
| 1 | 2 | | 4 | 5 | | 7 | | 9 | 10 | 12 | 3 | | 6 | | | | 8 | 11* | | | | | | | 18 |
| 1 | 14 | 7† | 4 | 5 | | | | 9 | 10 | 11 | 3* | | 6 | 12 | 2 | | 8 | | | | | | | | 19 |
| 1 | 7 | | 4 | 5 | | | | 9 | 10 | 12 | 3 | | 6 | 11 | 2 | | 8* | | | | | | | | 20 |
| 1 | 14 | 8* | 4 | 5 | | | | 9 | 10 | 7† | 3 | | 6 | 11 | 2 | | | 12 | | | | | | | 21 |
| 1 | 14 | 8† | 4 | 5 | | | | 9 | 10 | | 3 | | 6 | 11 | 2 | 7* | | | 12 | | | | | | 22 |
| 1 | 12 | | 4 | 5* | | | | 9 | 10 | | 3 | | 6 | | 2 | 7 | 8† | 11 | 14 | | | | | | 23 |
| 1 | 8 | 7 | 5 | 4* | | | | 9 | 10 | | 3 | | 6 | | 2 | | 12 | 11† | 14 | | | | | | 24 |
| 1 | 8 | 7* | 5 | | | | | 9 | 10 | | 3 | | 6 | 12 | 2† | | 4 | 11 | 14 | | | | | | 25 |
| 1 | 7* | | 4 | 5 | | | 14 | 9 | 10 | | 3 | | 6 | | 2† | 12 | 8 | 11 | | | | | | | 26 |
| 1 | | | 4 | 5 | | | | 9 | 10 | | 3 | | 6 | | 2 | 7 | 8 | 11* | 12 | | | | | | 27 |
| 1 | 2 | 14 | 4 | 5 | | | | 9 | 10* | | 3 | | 6 | | | 7† | 8 | 11 | 12 | | | | | | 28 |
| 1 | 12 | 7 | 4 | 5 | | | | 9 | 10 | | 3 | | 6 | | 2* | 14 | 8 | 11† | | | | | | | 29 |
| 1 | 11* | | 4 | 5 | 2 | | | 9 | 10 | | 3 | | 6 | 12 | | 7† | | | 14 | | | 8 | | | 30 |
| 1 | | | 4 | 5 | 2 | | | 9 | 10† | 12 | 3 | | 6 | | 14 | | 8 | 11 | | | | 7* | | | 31 |
| 1 | | | 4 | 5 | 2* | 7 | | 9 | 10 | 12 | | | 6 | | 14 | | 8 | 11† | | | | 3 | | | 32 |
| | | | 4* | 5 | | 7 | 8 | 9 | 10† | | 3 | | 6 | | 2 | 14 | | 11 | | | | 12 | 1 | | 33 |
| | 12 | | 4 | 5 | | 7 | 8 | 9 | 10 | | 3* | | 6 | | 2† | | | 11 | 14 | | | | 1 | | 34 |
| 1 | 12 | | 4 | 5 | | 7 | 8* | 9 | 10 | | 3 | | 6 | | 2 | | | 11† | 14 | | | | | | 35 |
| | 14 | | 4 | 5 | | | | 9* | 10 | | 3 | | 6 | | 2 | 7 | 8 | 11† | | | | 12 | | 1 | 36 |
| 1 | 2 | 3 | 4 | 5 | 6 | 7 | 8 | 9 | 10 | 11 | | | | | | | | | | | | | | | 37 |
| 1 | | | 4 | 5 | | 7 | 8 | 9 | 10 | | 3 | | 6 | | 2 | | | 11 | | | | | | | 38 |
| 35 | 12 | 19 | 34 | 38 | 13 | 20 | 10 | 37 | 36 | 13 | 28 | | 35 | 10 | 14 | 8 | 25 | 23 | | | | 5 | 2 | 1 | |
| | 7 | 9 | | | 1 | | 1 | 1 | | 5 | 4 | 1 | | 7 | 2 | 13 | 1 | 3 | 1 | 1 | | 1 | 1 | 1 | |
| | | 2 | 3 | | 1 | 2 | 2 | 5 | 13 | 1 | | | 3 | 7 | 2 | | | 3 | | | | 1 | | | |

1 own-goal

357

# 1990-91

Manager: Alex Ferguson OBE

| 1 | Aug | 25 | (h) | Coventry C | W | 2-0 | Bruce, Webb | 46,715 |
|---|-----|----|-----|------------|---|-----|-------------|--------|
| 2 | | 28 | (a) | Leeds U | D | 0-0 | | 29,172 |
| 3 | Sep | 1 | (a) | Sunderland | L | 1-2 | McClair | 26,105 |
| 4 | | 4 | (a) | Luton T | W | 1-0 | Robins | 12,576 |
| 5 | | 8 | (h) | Queen's Park R | W | 3-1 | McClair, Robins 2 | 43,427 |
| 6 | | 16 | (a) | Liverpool | L | 0-4 | | 35,726 |
| 7 | | 22 | (h) | Southampton | W | 3-2 | McClair, Blackmore, Hughes | 41,228 |
| 8 | | 29 | (h) | Nottingham F | L | 0-1 | | 46,766 |
| 9 | Oct | 20 | (h) | Arsenal | L | 0-1 | | 47,232 |
| 10 | | 27 | (a) | Manchester C | D | 3-3 | Hughes, McClair 2 | 36,427 |
| 11 | Nov | 3 | (h) | Crystal P | W | 2-0 | Webb, Wallace | 45,724 |
| 12 | | 10 | (a) | Derby C | D | 0-0 | | 21,115 |
| 13 | | 17 | (h) | Sheffield U | W | 2-0 | Bruce, Hughes | 45,903 |
| 14 | | 25 | (h) | Chelsea | L | 2-3 | Wallace, Hughes | 37,836 |
| 15 | Dec | 1 | (a) | Everton | W | 1-0 | Sharpe | 32,400 |
| 16 | | 8 | (h) | Leeds U | D | 1-1 | Webb | 40,927 |
| 17 | | 15 | (a) | Coventry C | D | 2-2 | Hughes, Wallace | 17,106 |
| 18 | | 22 | (a) | Wimbledon | W | 3-1 | Bruce 2 (2 pens), Hughes | 9,744 |
| 19 | | 26 | (h) | Norwich C | W | 3-0 | Hughes, McClair 2 | 39,801 |
| 20 | | 29 | (h) | Aston Villa | D | 1-1 | Bruce (pen) | 47,485 |
| 21 | Jan | 1 | (a) | Tottenham H | W | 2-1 | Bruce (pen), McClair | 29,399 |
| 22 | | 12 | (h) | Sunderland | W | 3-0 | Hughes 2, McClair | 45,934 |
| 23 | | 19 | (a) | Queen's Park R | D | 1-1 | Phelan | 18,544 |
| 24 | Feb | 3 | (h) | Liverpool | D | 1-1 | Bruce (pen) | 43,690 |
| 25 | | 26 | (a) | Sheffield U | L | 1-2 | Blackmore (pen) | 27,570 |
| 26 | Mar | 2 | (h) | Everton | L | 0-2 | | 45,656 |
| 27 | | 9 | (a) | Chelsea | L | 2-3 | Hughes, McClair | 22,818 |
| 28 | | 13 | (a) | Southampton | D | 1-1 | Ince | 15,701 |
| 29 | | 16 | (a) | Nottingham F | D | 1-1 | Blackmore | 23,859 |
| 30 | | 23 | (h) | Luton T | W | 4-1 | Bruce 2, Robins, McClair | 41,752 |
| 31 | | 30 | (a) | Norwich C | W | 3-0 | Bruce 2 (1 pen), Ince | 18,282 |
| 32 | Apr | 2 | (h) | Wimbledon | W | 2-1 | Bruce, McClair | 36,660 |
| 33 | | 6 | (a) | Aston Villa | D | 1-1 | Sharpe | 33,307 |
| 34 | | 16 | (h) | Derby C | W | 3-1 | Blackmore, McClair, Robson | 32,776 |
| 35 | May | 4 | (h) | Manchester C | W | 1-0 | Giggs | 45,286 |
| 36 | | 6 | (a) | Arsenal | L | 1-3 | Bruce (pen) | 40,229 |
| 37 | | 11 | (a) | Crystal Palace | L | 0-3 | | 25,301 |
| 38 | | 20 | (h) | Tottenham H | D | 1-1 | Ince | 46,791 |

FINAL LEAGUE POSITION: 6th in Division One

Appearances
Sub Appearances
Goals

FA Cup

| 3 | Jan | 7 | (h) | Queen's Park R | W | 2-1 |
|---|-----|---|-----|----------------|---|-----|
| 4 | | 26 | (h) | Bolton W | W | 1-0 |
| 5 | Feb | 18 | (a) | Norwich C | L | 1-2 |

League Cup

| 2 | Sep | 26 | (a) | Halifax T | W | 3-1 |
|---|-----|----|-----|-----------|---|-----|
| | Oct | 10 | (h) | Halifax T | W | 2-1 |
| 3 | | 31 | (h) | Liverpool | W | 3-1 |
| 4 | Nov | 28 | (a) | Arsenal | W | 6-2 |
| 5 | Jan | 16 | (a) | Southampton | D | 1-1 |
| R | | 23 | (h) | Southampton | W | 3-2 |
| SF | Feb | 10 | (h) | Leeds U | W | 2-1 |
| | | 24 | (a) | Leeds U | W | 1-0 |
| F | Apr | 21 | (n*) | Sheffield W | L | 0-1 | (*Played at Wembley Stadium) |

Manchester United also won the European Cup-winners' Cup (see *United in Europe*).

Appearance grid (shirt number worn; * and † denote substitutions).

| Sealey | Irwin | Donaghy | Bruce | Phelan | Pallister | Webb | Ince | McClair | Hughes | Blackmore | Beardsmore | Robins | Anderson | Sharpe | Martin | Wallace | Robson | Walsh | Ferguson | Giggs | Whitworth | Wratten | Bosnich | Kanchelskis | |
|---|---|---|---|---|---|---|---|---|---|---|---|---|---|---|---|---|---|---|---|---|---|---|---|---|---|
| 1 | 2 | 3 | 4 | 5 | 6 | 7 | 8 | 9 | 10 | 11 |  |  |  |  |  |  |  |  |  |  |  |  |  |  | 1 |
| 1 | 2 | 3 | 4 | 5 | 6 | 7 | 8* | 9 | 10 | 11 | 12 |  |  |  |  |  |  |  |  |  |  |  |  |  | 2 |
| 1 | 2 | 3* | 4 | 5 | 6 | 7 | 8 | 9 | 10† | 11 | 12 | 14 |  |  |  |  |  |  |  |  |  |  |  |  | 3 |
| 1 | 2 | 14 | 4 | 5 | 6 | 7 | 8 | 9 | 12 | 3 | 11† | 10* |  |  |  |  |  |  |  |  |  |  |  |  | 4 |
| 1 | 2 |  | 4 | 5 | 6 | 7 | 8 | 9 |  | 3 | 11 | 10 |  |  |  |  |  |  |  |  |  |  |  |  | 5 |
| 1 | 2 | 14 | 4 | 5 | 6† | 7 | 8* | 9 | 10 | 3 | 12 | 11 |  |  |  |  |  |  |  |  |  |  |  |  | 6 |
| 1 | 2† | 3 |  | 5 | 6 | 7 |  | 9 | 10 | 11 | 12 | 8* | 4 | 14 |  |  |  |  |  |  |  |  |  |  | 7 |
| 1 | 2 | 4 |  | 5 | 6 | 7 | 8 | 9 | 12 | 3 | 11† | 10* |  | 14 |  |  |  |  |  |  |  |  |  |  | 8 |
| 1 | 2† |  | 4 | 5 | 6 | 7 | 8 | 9 | 10 | 3 |  | 12 |  | 11* | 14 |  |  |  |  |  |  |  |  |  | 9 |
| 1 | 2 |  | 4 |  | 6 | 7 | 8 | 9 | 10 | 5 |  |  |  | 11* | 3 | 12 |  |  |  |  |  |  |  |  | 10 |
| 1 | 2 |  | 4 | 5 | 6 | 7 | 8 | 9 |  | 3 |  |  |  | 11 | 12 | 10* |  |  |  |  |  |  |  |  | 11 |
| 1 | 2† | 14 | 4 | 5 | 6 | 7 | 8 | 9 | 10 | 3 |  |  |  | 11* |  | 12 |  |  |  |  |  |  |  |  | 12 |
| 1 | 2* |  | 4 | 5 | 6 | 7 | 8 | 9 | 10 | 3 |  |  |  | 11 |  | 12 |  |  |  |  |  |  |  |  | 13 |
| 1 | 2 |  | 4 | 5† | 6 | 7 | 8 | 9 | 10 | 3* |  |  |  | 14 | 12 | 11 |  |  |  |  |  |  |  |  | 14 |
| 1 | 2 | 4 |  | 5 | 6 | 14 | 8† | 9 | 10 | 3 |  |  |  | 7* | 12 | 11 |  |  |  |  |  |  |  |  | 15 |
| 1 | 2* | 14 | 4 | 5† | 6 |  | 8 | 9 | 10 | 3 |  |  |  | 7 |  | 11 | 12 |  |  |  |  |  |  |  | 16 |
| 1 | 14 |  | 4 | 5 | 6 | 7 | 8† | 9 | 10 | 2 |  |  |  | 3* |  | 11 | 12 |  |  |  |  |  |  |  | 17 |
| 1 |  | 3 | 4 | 5 | 6 | 11 | 8 | 9 | 10 | 2* |  |  |  |  |  | 12 | 7 |  |  |  |  |  |  |  | 18 |
| 1 | 2 | 14 | 4 | 12 | 6 | 5 | 8 | 9 | 10 | 3 |  |  |  | 11† |  |  | 7* |  |  |  |  |  |  |  | 19 |
| 1 | 2 |  | 4 | 12 | 6 | 5 | 8 | 9 | 10 | 3 |  |  |  | 11 |  |  | 7* |  |  |  |  |  |  |  | 20 |
| 1 | 2† |  | 4 | 5* | 6 | 7 | 8 | 9 | 10 | 3 | 12 |  |  | 11 | 14 |  |  |  |  |  |  |  |  |  | 21 |
| 1 | 2 |  | 4 | 12 | 6 | 5* | 8† | 9 | 10 | 3 |  |  | 14 | 11 |  |  | 7 |  |  |  |  |  |  |  | 22 |
| 1 | 2 | 6 | 4 | 5 |  |  | 8 | 9 | 10 | 11 | 7* | 12 |  | 14 | 3† |  |  |  |  |  |  |  |  |  | 23 |
| 1 | 2 |  | 4 | 5† | 6 |  | 8* | 9 | 10 | 3 |  |  |  | 11 | 14 | 12 | 7 |  |  |  |  |  |  |  | 24 |
|  | 2 |  |  | 5 | 6 | 4† | 8 | 9 | 10 |  | 12 |  |  |  | 3 | 11 | 7* | 1 | 14 |  |  |  |  |  | 25 |
| 1 | 2† |  |  | 5 | 6 |  | 8 | 9 | 10 |  | 12 |  |  | 7 | 3* | 11 |  |  | 4 | 14 |  |  |  |  | 26 |
| 1 |  |  | 4 | 5 | 6 |  | 8 | 9 | 10 | 2* |  |  |  | 11 | 3 | 12 | 7 |  |  |  |  |  |  |  | 27 |
| 1 |  |  | 4 | 5 | 6 |  | 8 | 9 |  |  | 7* | 12 |  | 11 | 3 | 10 |  |  | 14 | 2† |  |  |  |  | 28 |
| 1 | 2 | 12 | 4 | 5 | 6 |  | 8 | 9 | 10 |  |  |  |  |  | 3* | 11 | 7 |  |  |  |  |  |  |  | 29 |
| 1 | 2 |  | 4 | 5 | 6 |  |  | 9 | 10 | 3 |  |  |  |  | 11 | 8* | 7 |  |  |  |  |  |  |  | 30 |
| 1 | 2* |  | 4 | 5 | 6 | 9 | 8 | 12 | 10 | 3 |  |  |  | 11† |  |  | 7 |  |  |  |  |  |  |  | 31 |
|  | 2 | 3 | 4† | 5 | 6 | 7 | 8 | 9 |  | 10 |  |  |  | 11* |  |  | 1 |  |  | 14 |  |  |  |  | 32 |
| 1 | 2 | 3 | 4 | 5* | 6 |  | 8 | 9 | 10 |  |  |  |  | 11 |  |  | 7 |  |  |  |  |  |  |  | 33 |
|  | 2 | 3 | 4 |  | 6 | 5* | 8 | 12 | 10 | 9 |  |  |  |  | 11 | 7 |  | 1 |  |  |  |  |  |  | 34 |
|  | 2 | 12 | 4 | 5 | 6 | 8 |  | 9 | 10 | 3 |  |  |  |  | 7 |  |  | 1 |  | 11* |  |  |  |  | 35 |
|  | 6 | 4 | 2 |  | 5 | 8 | 9 | 10* | 3 | 12 | 11 |  |  |  | 7† |  |  | 1 | 14 |  |  |  |  |  | 36 |
|  | 2 | 3 | 4 |  | 6* | 5 | 8 |  | 12 | 9† |  |  |  | 11 |  | 10 | 7 |  | 14 |  |  |  | 1 |  | 37 |
|  | 2† | 14 | 4 | 5 | 6 |  | 8 | 9 | 10 | 3 |  |  |  | 11* | 7 |  |  |  |  |  |  |  | 1 |  | 38 |
| 31 | 33 | 17 | 31 | 30 | 36 | 31 | 31 | 34 | 29 | 35 | 5 | 7 | 1 | 20 | 7 | 13 | 15 | 5 | 2 | 1 | 1 |  | 2 | 1 | |
|  | 1 | 8 |  | 3 |  | 1 |  | 2 | 2 |  | 7 | 12 |  | 3 | 7 | 6 | 2 |  | 3 | 1 |  | 2 |  |  | |
|  |  | 13 | 1 |  | 3 | 3 | 13 | 10 | 4 |  | 4 |  |  | 2 |  | 3 | 1 |  |  | 1 |  |  |  |  | |

# 1991-92

Manager: Alex Ferguson OBE

| | | | | | | | |
|---|---|---|---|---|---|---|---|
| 1 | Aug | 17 | (h) | Notts C | W | 2-0 | Hughes, Robson | 46,278 |
| 2 | | 21 | (a) | Aston Villa | W | 1-0 | Bruce(pen) | 39,995 |
| 3 | | 24 | (a) | Everton | D | 0-0 | | 36,085 |
| 4 | | 28 | (h) | Oldham A | W | 1-0 | McClair | 42,078 |
| 5 | | 31 | (h) | Leeds U | D | 1-1 | Robson | 43,778 |
| 6 | Sep | 3 | (a) | Wimbledon | W | 2-1 | Blackmore, Pallister | 13,824 |
| 7 | | 7 | (h) | Norwich C | W | 3-0 | Irwin, McClair, Giggs | 44,946 |
| 8 | | 14 | (a) | Southampton | W | 1-0 | Hughes | 19,264 |
| 9 | | 21 | (h) | Luton T | W | 5-0 | McClair 2, Ince, Hughes, Bruce | 46,491 |
| 10 | | 28 | (a) | Tottenham H | W | 2-1 | Hughes, Robson | 35,087 |
| 11 | Oct | 6 | (h) | Liverpool | D | 0-0 | | 44,997 |
| 12 | | 19 | (h) | Arsenal | D | 1-1 | Bruce | 46,594 |
| 13 | | 26 | (a) | Sheffield W | L | 2-3 | McClair 2 | 38,260 |
| 14 | Nov | 2 | (h) | Sheffield U | W | 2-0 | Hoyland (og), Kanchelskis | 42,942 |
| 15 | | 16 | (a) | Manchester C | D | 0-0 | | 38,180 |
| 16 | | 23 | (h) | West Ham U | W | 2-1 | Giggs, Robson | 47,185 |
| 17 | | 30 | (a) | Crystal P | W | 3-1 | Webb, McClair, Kanchelskis | 29,017 |
| 18 | Dec | 7 | (h) | Coventry C | W | 4-0 | Bruce, Webb, McClair, Hughes | 42,549 |
| 19 | | 15 | (a) | Chelsea | W | 3-1 | Irwin, McClair, Bruce | 23,120 |
| 20 | | 26 | (a) | Oldham A | W | 6-3 | Irwin 2, McClair 2, Kanchelskis, Giggs | 18,947 |
| 21 | | 29 | (a) | Leeds U | D | 1-1 | Webb | 32,638 |
| 22 | Jan | 1 | (h) | Queen's Park R | L | 1-4 | McClair | 38,554 |
| 23 | | 11 | (h) | Everton | W | 1-0 | Kanchelskis | 46,619 |
| 24 | | 18 | (a) | Notts C | D | 1-1 | Blackmore (pen) | 21,055 |
| 25 | | 22 | (h) | Aston Villa | W | 1-0 | Hughes | 45,022 |
| 26 | Feb | 1 | (a) | Arsenal | D | 1-1 | McClair | 41,703 |
| 27 | | 8 | (h) | Sheffield W | D | 1-1 | McClair | 47,074 |
| 28 | | 22 | (h) | Crystal P | W | 2-0 | Hughes 2 | 46,347 |
| 29 | | 26 | (h) | Chelsea | D | 1-1 | Hughes | 44,872 |
| 30 | | 29 | (a) | Coventry C | D | 0-0 | | 23,967 |
| 31 | Mar | 14 | (a) | Sheffield U | W | 2-1 | McClair, Blackmore | 30,183 |
| 32 | | 18 | (a) | Nottingham F | L | 0-1 | | 28,062 |
| 33 | | 21 | (h) | Wimbledon | D | 0-0 | | 45,428 |
| 34 | | 28 | (a) | Queen's Park R | D | 0-0 | | 22,603 |
| 35 | | 31 | (a) | Norwich C | W | 3-1 | Ince 2, McClair | 17,489 |
| 36 | Apr | 7 | (h) | Manchester C | D | 1-1 | Giggs | 46,781 |
| 37 | | 16 | (h) | Southampton | W | 1-0 | Kanchelskis | 43,972 |
| 38 | | 18 | (a) | Luton T | D | 1-1 | Sharpe | 13,410 |
| 39 | | 20 | (h) | Nottingham F | L | 1-2 | McClair | 47,576 |
| 40 | | 22 | (a) | West Ham U | L | 0-1 | | 24,197 |
| 41 | | 26 | (a) | Liverpool | L | 0-2 | | 38,669 |
| 42 | May | 2 | (h) | Tottenham H | W | 3-1 | Hughes 2, McClair | 44,595 |

FINAL LEAGUE POSITION: 2nd in Division One.

Appearances
Sub Appearances
Goals

FA Cup
| | | | | | | | |
|---|---|---|---|---|---|---|---|
| 3 | Jan | 15 | (a) | Leeds U | W | 1-0 | |
| 4 | | 27 | (a) | Southampton | D | 0-0 | |
| R | Feb | 5 | (h) | Southampton | L | 2-2 | (lost 4-2 on pens) |

League Cup
| | | | | | | | |
|---|---|---|---|---|---|---|---|
| 2 | Sep | 25 | (h) | Cambridge U | W | 3-0 | |
| | Oct | 9 | (a) | Cambridge U | D | 1-1 | |
| 3 | | 30 | (h) | Portsmouth | W | 3-1 | |
| 4 | Dec | 4 | (h) | Oldham A | W | 2-0 | |
| 5 | Jan | 8 | (a) | Leeds U | W | 3-1 | |
| SF | Mar | 4 | (a) | Middlesbrough | D | 0-0 | |
| | | 11 | (h) | Middlesbrough | W | 2-1 | (After extra-time) |
| F | Apr | 12 | (n*) | Nottingham F | W | 1-0 | (*Played at Wembley Stadium) |

Manchester United also reached the second round of the European Cup-winners' Cup (see *United in Europe*).

| Schmeichel | Irwin | Blackmore | Bruce | Ferguson | Parker | Robson | Ince | McClair | Hughes | Kanchelskis | Giggs | Pallister | Donaghy | Webb | Phelan | Martin | Robins | Sharpe | Walsh | |
|---|---|---|---|---|---|---|---|---|---|---|---|---|---|---|---|---|---|---|---|---|
| 1 | 2 | 3 | 4 | 5* | 6 | 7 | 8† | 9 | 10 | 11 | 12 | 14 | | | | | | | | 1 |
| 1 | 2 | 3 | 4 | | 6 | 7 | 8 | 9 | 10 | 11 | | | | 5 | | | | | | 2 |
| 1 | 2* | 3† | 4 | | 6 | 7 | 8 | 9 | 10 | 11 | 12 | | | 5 | 14 | | | | | 3 |
| 1 | 3 | 12 | 4 | 14 | 2 | 7 | 8* | 9 | 10 | 11 | | 6 | | 5† | | | | | | 4 |
| 1 | 3 | 11 | 4† | | 2 | 7 | 8* | 9 | 10 | 12 | | 6 | | 5 | 14 | | | | | 5 |
| 1 | 12 | 11 | 4 | | 2 | 7 | | 9 | 10 | 6 | 3 | 8 | | 5* | | | | | | 6 |
| 1 | 3 | 12 | 4 | | 2 | 7 | | 9 | 10 | 8* | 11 | 6 | | 5† | 14 | | | | | 7 |
| 1 | 3 | | 4 | | | 7 | 12 | 9 | 10 | 8* | 11 | 6 | | 5 | 2 | | | | | 8 |
| 1 | 3 | 9* | 4 | | | 7 | 8 | 12 | 10 | | 11 | 6 | | 5 | 2 | | | | | 9 |
| 1 | 3 | 12 | 4 | | | 7 | 8 | 9 | 10 | 5* | 11 | 6 | | | 2 | | | | | 10 |
| 1 | 3 | 5 | 4 | | | 7 | 8† | 9 | 10 | 12 | 11 | 6 | 14 | | 2* | | | | | 11 |
| 1 | 3 | 2 | 4 | | | 7 | 8 | 9 | 10 | 12 | 11 | 6 | | 5* | | | | | | 12 |
| 1 | 3 | 10 | 4* | | 2 | 7 | | 9 | 8 | 11 | | 6 | | 5 | 12 | | | | | 13 |
| 1 | 3 | | 4 | | 2 | 12 | 8* | 9 | 7 | 11† | 14 | 6 | | 5 | | | 10 | | | 14 |
| 1 | 3 | 8 | 4 | | 2 | 7 | 12 | 9 | 10 | | 11 | 6 | | 5* | | | | | | 15 |
| 1 | 3 | 12 | 4 | | 2* | 7 | | 9 | 10 | 8 | 11 | 6 | | 5 | | | | | | 16 |
| 1 | 3* | 12 | 4 | | 2 | 7 | | 9 | 10 | 8 | 11 | 6 | | 5 | | | | | | 17 |
| 1 | 3 | 12 | 4 | | 2* | | 8 | 9 | 10 | 7 | 11 | 6 | | 5 | | | | | | 18 |
| 1 | 3 | 12 | 4 | | 2 | | 8 | 9 | 10 | 7 | 11* | 6 | | 5 | | | | | | 19 |
| 1 | 3* | 12 | 4 | | 2 | 7† | 8 | 9 | 10 | 11 | 14 | 6 | | 5 | | | | | | 20 |
| 1 | 3* | | 4 | | 2 | | 8 | 9 | 10 | 7† | 11 | 6 | 14 | 5 | 12 | | | | | 21 |
| 1 | 3 | | 4 | | 2 | | 8 | 9 | 10 | 12 | | 6 | | 5 | 7* | | 11 | | | 22 |
| 1 | 3* | | 4 | | 2 | | 8 | 9 | 10 | 7 | 11 | 6 | 12 | 5 | | | | | | 23 |
| 1 | 3 | 12 | 4* | | 2 | | 8 | 9 | 10 | 7 | 11† | 6 | | 5 | 14 | | | | | 24 |
| 1 | 3 | | 4 | | | 7 | 8 | 9 | 10 | | 11 | 6 | 2 | 5 | | | | | | 25 |
| 1 | 3 | | 4 | | | 7 | 8* | 9 | 10 | 11 | 12 | 6 | 2 | 5 | | | | | | 26 |
| 1 | 3 | | | | | 7 | 8 | 9 | 10 | 11 | 2* | 6 | 4 | 5† | 14 | | 12 | | | 27 |
| 1 | 3 | 12 | | | | 7 | 8 | 9 | 10 | 11† | 4 | 6 | 2 | 5* | 14 | | | | | 28 |
| | 3 | 14 | 12 | | | 7* | 8 | 9 | 10 | 11† | 4 | 6 | 2 | 5 | | | | | 1 | 29 |
| | 3 | 12 | | | 2 | | 8 | 9 | 10 | 7* | 11 | 6 | 4 | 5 | | | | | 1 | 30 |
| 1 | 3 | 12 | 4* | | 2 | 7 | 8 | 9 | | | 11 | 6 | | 5 | | | 10 | | | 31 |
| 1 | 3 | 2 | 4 | | | | 8 | 9 | 10† | 14 | 12 | 6 | | 5* | 7 | | 11 | | | 32 |
| 1 | 3 | 2 | 4 | | | | 8 | 9 | 10 | 7 | 11 | 6 | | 5* | | | 12 | | | 33 |
| 1 | 3 | | 4 | | | 7 | | 9 | 10 | 8* | 11 | 6 | 2 | 5 | | | 12 | | | 34 |
| 1 | 3 | 12 | 4 | | | 7* | 8 | 9 | 10 | | | 6 | 2 | 5 | | | 11 | | | 35 |
| 1 | 3 | 5* | 4 | | | | 8 | 9 | 10 | 12 | 7 | 6 | 2 | | | | 11 | | | 36 |
| 1 | 3 | | 4 | | 2 | | 8* | 9 | 10 | 7 | 11 | 6 | 12 | 5 | | | | | | 37 |
| 1 | 3 | 12 | 4 | | 2* | | | 9 | 10† | 14 | 7 | 6 | 8 | 5 | | | 11 | | | 38 |
| 1 | 3 | 2 | 4 | | | | | 9 | 12 | 7 | 10 | 6 | 14 | 8* | 5 | | 11 | | | 39 |
| 1 | 3 | 7* | 4 | 14 | | | | 9 | 10 | 12 | 8 | 6 | 2† | 5 | | | 11 | | | 40 |
| 1 | 3 | | 4 | | | 7 | 8 | 9 | 10 | | 11 | 6* | 2 | 5 | | | 12 | | | 41 |
| 1 | 3 | | 4 | | 2 | | 8* | 9 | 10 | 7 | 11 | 6 | | 5 | | | 12 | | | 42 |
| 40 | 37 | 19 | 37 | 2 | 24 | 26 | 31 | 41 | 38 | 28 | 32 | 37 | 16 | 29 | 14 | 1 | 8 | | 2 | |
| | 1 | 14 | 2 | 2 | 1 | 1 | 1 | 1 | 6 | 6 | 3 | 4 | 2 | 4 | 1 | 1 | 6 | | | |
| | | | 4 | 3 | 5 | 4 | 3 | 18 | 11 | 4 | 4 | 1 | 3 | 1 | | | | | | |

# United Against Other
## _____League Clubs_____

Manchester United have met 78 clubs in the Football League since 1892-3. Below is the Reds' home and away record against each club. Some clubs changed their name (e.g. Small Heath became Birmingham City) and some clubs modified their titles (e.g. Leicester Fosse became Leicester City). In all cases the last name used by each club covers all games under previous names. *Signifies that the total includes a game played in the abandoned 1939-40 season.

| | | | HOME | | | | | | AWAY | | |
|---|---|---|---|---|---|---|---|---|---|---|---|
| | P | W | D | L | F | A | W | D | L | F | A |
| ACCRINGTON | 2 | 0 | 1 | 0 | 3 | 3 | 0 | 1 | 0 | 2 | 2 |
| ARSENAL | 146 | 41 | 20 | 12 | 143 | 70 | 18 | 11 | 44 | 84 | 151 |
| ASTON VILLA | 118 | 37 | 12 | 10 | 127 | 59 | 14 | 15 | 30 | 88 | 128 |
| BARNSLEY | 30 | 12 | 2 | 1 | 35 | 7 | 5 | 7 | 3 | 20 | 14 |
| BIRMINGHAM C | 80 | 23 | 8 | 9 | 60 | 34 | 10 | 15 | 15 | 53 | 62 |
| BLACKBURN R | 62 | 15 | 8 | 8 | 61 | 38 | 10 | 7 | 14 | 55 | 66 |
| BLACKPOOL | 80 | 26 | 8 | 6 | 83 | 34 | 17 | 9 | 14 | 66 | 60 |
| BOLTON W | 92 | 23 | 9 | 14 | 78 | 53 | 11 | 11 | 24 | 52 | 88 |
| BRADFORD | 18 | 5 | 0 | 4 | 17 | 12 | 3 | 1 | 5 | 13 | 24 |
| BRADFORD C | 42 | 13 | 6 | 2 | 35 | 9 | 5 | 7 | 9 | 26 | 28 |
| BRENTFORD | 10 | 2 | 1 | 2 | 9 | 7 | 2 | 1 | 2 | 10 | 12 |
| BRIGHTON & HA | 8 | 3 | 1 | 0 | 7 | 2 | 2 | 1 | 1 | 5 | 2 |
| BRISTOL C | 34 | 9 | 3 | 5 | 30 | 18 | 5 | 7 | 5 | 17 | 21 |
| BRISTOL R | 2 | 1 | 0 | 0 | 2 | 0 | 0 | 1 | 0 | 1 | 1 |
| BURNLEY | 102 | 30 | 8 | 13 | 116 | 66 | 17 | 8 | 26 | 64 | 91 |
| BURTON U | 24 | 9 | 3 | 0 | 39 | 6 | 5 | 3 | 4 | 22 | 23 |
| BURTON W | 6 | 1 | 1 | 1 | 5 | 3 | 1 | 0 | 2 | 3 | 7 |
| BURY | 38 | 9 | 2 | 8 | 24 | 23 | 10 | 5 | 4 | 34 | 23 |
| CARDIFF C | 26 | 5 | 6 | 2 | 28 | 19 | 8 | 1 | 4 | 22 | 18 |
| CHARLTON A* | 41 | 13 | 4 | 3 | 45 | 20 | 8 | 5 | 8 | 27 | 33 |
| CHELSEA* | 101 | 21 | 16 | 13 | 81 | 47 | 25 | 12 | 14 | 97 | 75 |
| CHESTERFIELD | 20 | 10 | 0 | 0 | 26 | 7 | 3 | 1 | 6 | 15 | 15 |
| COVENTRY C | 56 | 15 | 7 | 6 | 49 | 21 | 8 | 8 | 12 | 34 | 37 |
| CREWE A | 4 | 2 | 0 | 0 | 11 | 1 | 2 | 0 | 0 | 4 | 0 |
| CRYSTAL P | 24 | 8 | 2 | 2 | 22 | 7 | 5 | 3 | 4 | 21 | 22 |
| DARWEN | 12 | 4 | 1 | 1 | 20 | 5 | 2 | 2 | 2 | 7 | 8 |
| DERBY C | 76 | 19 | 10 | 9 | 70 | 39 | 9 | 13 | 16 | 58 | 84 |
| DONCASTER R | 8 | 3 | 1 | 0 | 16 | 0 | 1 | 2 | 1 | 3 | 6 |
| EVERTON | 126 | 32 | 17 | 14 | 107 | 64 | 12 | 16 | 35 | 71 | 140 |
| FULHAM | 42 | 17 | 3 | 1 | 44 | 15 | 6 | 7 | 8 | 34 | 32 |
| GAINSBOROUGH T | 20 | 8 | 2 | 0 | 26 | 7 | 5 | 3 | 2 | 10 | 7 |
| GLOSSOP | 14 | 6 | 1 | 0 | 20 | 5 | 5 | 1 | 1 | 14 | 5 |
| GRIMSBY T* | 37 | 13 | 2 | 4 | 42 | 26 | 4 | 4 | 10 | 26 | 37 |
| HUDDERSFIELD T | 42 | 11 | 9 | 1 | 46 | 21 | 7 | 6 | 8 | 32 | 39 |
| HULL C | 16 | 7 | 1 | 0 | 22 | 4 | 2 | 2 | 4 | 8 | 13 |
| IPSWICH T | 40 | 13 | 2 | 5 | 31 | 13 | 6 | 4 | 10 | 26 | 40 |
| LEEDS C | 2 | 0 | 0 | 1 | 0 | 3 | 1 | 0 | 0 | 3 | 1 |
| LEEDS U | 68 | 13 | 13 | 8 | 51 | 32 | 11 | 12 | 11 | 41 | 40 |
| LEICESTER C | 96 | 32 | 11 | 5 | 115 | 51 | 12 | 11 | 25 | 72 | 90 |
| LEYTON ORIENT | 12 | 3 | 3 | 0 | 13 | 5 | 3 | 1 | 2 | 5 | 3 |
| LINCOLN C | 28 | 10 | 3 | 1 | 34 | 12 | 3 | 1 | 10 | 12 | 28 |
| LIVERPOOL | 118 | 27 | 21 | 11 | 100 | 55 | 13 | 16 | 30 | 62 | 103 |
| LOUGHBOROUGH T | 10 | 5 | 0 | 0 | 23 | 2 | 2 | 2 | 1 | 6 | 5 |

|  | | HOME | | | | | AWAY | | | |
| --- | --- | --- | --- | --- | --- | --- | --- | --- | --- | --- |
|  | P | W | D | L | F | A | W | D | L | F | A |
| LUTON T | 38 | 18 | 0 | 1 | 58 | 10 | 9 | 7 | 3 | 30 | 16 |
| MANCHESTER C | 116 | 23 | 21 | 14 | 87 | 74 | 18 | 22 | 18 | 75 | 86 |
| MIDDLESBROUGH | 74 | 23 | 6 | 8 | 77 | 47 | 12 | 9 | 16 | 56 | 73 |
| MILLWALL | 12 | 5 | 1 | 0 | 22 | 3 | 3 | 2 | 1 | 6 | 4 |
| NELSON | 2 | 0 | 0 | 1 | 0 | 1 | 1 | 0 | 0 | 2 | 0 |
| NEW BRIGHTON T | 6 | 2 | 0 | 1 | 4 | 3 | 2 | 0 | 1 | 7 | 3 |
| NEWCASTLE U | 110 | 33 | 13 | 9 | 125 | 67 | 17 | 12 | 26 | 78 | 111 |
| NORTHAMPTON T | 2 | 1 | 0 | 0 | 6 | 2 | 0 | 1 | 0 | 1 | 1 |
| NORWICH C | 42 | 13 | 5 | 3 | 34 | 10 | 9 | 6 | 6 | 37 | 28 |
| NOTTINGHAM F | 86 | 24 | 11 | 8 | 90 | 54 | 13 | 10 | 20 | 55 | 68 |
| NOTTS C | 48 | 11 | 9 | 4 | 41 | 27 | 9 | 5 | 10 | 33 | 33 |
| OLDHAM A | 32 | 9 | 3 | 4 | 32 | 17 | 5 | 6 | 5 | 31 | 23 |
| OXFORD U | 8 | 4 | 0 | 0 | 13 | 3 | 2 | 0 | 2 | 5 | 4 |
| PLYMOUTH A | 12 | 4 | 1 | 1 | 12 | 7 | 2 | 1 | 3 | 8 | 13 |
| PORT VALE | 36 | 16 | 1 | 1 | 52 | 10 | 5 | 4 | 9 | 24 | 27 |
| PORTSMOUTH | 44 | 13 | 3 | 6 | 38 | 21 | 5 | 9 | 8 | 23 | 30 |
| PRESTON NE | 66 | 15 | 11 | 7 | 51 | 35 | 11 | 9 | 13 | 56 | 55 |
| QUEEN'S PARK R | 30 | 12 | 2 | 1 | 33 | 11 | 4 | 6 | 5 | 18 | 22 |
| ROTHERHAM U | 6 | 3 | 0 | 0 | 9 | 2 | 1 | 1 | 1 | 5 | 5 |
| SHEFFIELD U | 82 | 26 | 4 | 11 | 83 | 47 | 11 | 9 | 21 | 49 | 74 |
| SHEFFIELD W | 96 | 30 | 12 | 6 | 91 | 46 | 11 | 9 | 28 | 62 | 89 |
| SOUTH SHIELDS | 6 | 2 | 1 | 0 | 5 | 1 | 2 | 0 | 1 | 5 | 2 |
| SOUTHAMPTON | 64 | 18 | 7 | 7 | 56 | 35 | 9 | 12 | 11 | 38 | 37 |
| STOCKPORT C | 18 | 7 | 2 | 0 | 21 | 7 | 2 | 0 | 7 | 8 | 11 |
| STOKE C | 70 | 17 | 13 | 5 | 63 | 29 | 9 | 11 | 15 | 40 | 60 |
| SUNDERLAND | 96 | 25 | 12 | 11 | 96 | 60 | 12 | 11 | 25 | 61 | 104 |
| SWANSEA C | 16 | 6 | 2 | 0 | 18 | 6 | 0 | 2 | 6 | 6 | 14 |
| TOTTENHAM H | 110 | 34 | 11 | 10 | 104 | 58 | 13 | 20 | 22 | 67 | 99 |
| WALSALL | 12 | 5 | 1 | 0 | 24 | 1 | 2 | 3 | 1 | 7 | 7 |
| WATFORD | 12 | 4 | 2 | 0 | 13 | 4 | 2 | 2 | 2 | 4 | 7 |
| WEST BROMWICH A | 100 | 26 | 13 | 11 | 102 | 65 | 13 | 11 | 26 | 72 | 98 |
| WEST HAM U | 80 | 24 | 6 | 10 | 91 | 48 | 7 | 10 | 23 | 49 | 70 |
| WIMBLEDON | 12 | 3 | 2 | 1 | 5 | 3 | 2 | 2 | 2 | 9 | 8 |
| WOLVERH'TON W | 80 | 26 | 5 | 9 | 80 | 44 | 10 | 9 | 21 | 55 | 81 |
| YORK C | 2 | 1 | 0 | 0 | 2 | 1 | 1 | 0 | 0 | 1 | 0 |

# United in Wartime

W HEN war was declared in August 1914, the FA and Football League decided to carry on the League and Cup competitions, although many people in Britain felt that the decision was, to say the least, unpatriotic. From 1915-16, however, until the end of the war, first-class soccer was arranged in regional competitions and Manchester United had moderate success in the Lancashire Section.

When Germany invaded Poland in September 1939 and Britain declared war two days later, football's ruling bodies immediately called a halt to proceedings and the League was abandoned after only three matches. United had just started their second season back in Division One and there had just been enough time for a win over Grimsby, a draw with Chelsea and defeat at Charlton. Militiamen Ben Carpenter, Reg Gibson, Stan Pearson, Jack Rowley and Harry Worrall had all been available for the start of the season, despite their military duties.

Two days after the declaration of war, parts of Old Trafford, together with the Lower Broughton training facilities, were requisitioned for military use. And two weeks after the declaration, United played a friendly with Bolton and drew 2-2.

Regional soccer became the order of the day and United were placed in the Western Division where four successive defeats in the last weeks of the 1939-40 season cost them the First Championship played up to Christmas, and a Second Championship from Christmas until the season's end. The Second Championship also included those games played in the League War Cup qualifying and knockout stages, and also matches in the Lancashire Cup.

With so many players on military service, guest players were essential to the continuance of the League. Two of the first to help United were Len Butt of Blackburn Rovers and Tommy Woodward of Bolton, whilst United players to appear with other clubs included Tommy Breen who assisted Belfast Celtic, the club from which he had joined United three years earlier. All but seven of United's pre-war playing staff were in the forces — Stan Pearson was one of the first to join — and the others were on war work.

Wartime football threw up some strange games. Heavy bombing raids in December 1940, forced United to switch their game against Blackburn to Stockport. Rovers had to enlist four spectators to complete their team and United duly won 9-0.

Severe bomb damage on the night of 11 March 1941 meant that United had to move away from Old Trafford altogether. Their last game there was on 8 March when Jack Rowley and Johnny Carey scored hat-tricks in their 7-3 win over Bury. Blackpool were the first team to play United at the adopted home of Maine Road. The Seasiders won 3-2 there on 5 April.

United's first wartime honour came in May that year when they beat Burnley 1-0 to win the Lancashire Cup. Carey scored the goal and John Breedon saved a Brocklebank penalty. The following season, 1941-2, United finished top of the Second Championship. In the first half of the season they had finished fourth and, on 29 November, they gave a first-team debut to Arthur Rowley, 15-year-old brother of Jack. It was Jack Rowley who scored twice in the 2-2 draw with Liverpool that day.

United's other wartime success came in 1944-5 when they reached the League North Cup Final. At Burnden Park, Bolton won 1-0 in the first leg; in the second-leg at Maine Road, Malcolm Barrass scored his second goal of the game with a last-minute header to level the scores and give Bolton the Cup.

United lost players in the war, including Ben Carpenter who had joined them from Burton Town in the 1939 close season. Carpenter was killed on active service. Several others were wounded including Johnny Hanlon who was captured in Crete and held in an Italian PoW camp and later, Stalag IVB in Germany. Allenby Chilton who, like Hanlon, served in the Durham Light Infantry, was wounded during the Normandy landings.

Many of the players who were to become household names made their first appearance for United in wartime football including John Aston, Charlie Mitten, Jimmy Delaney, Henry Cockburn, Johnny Morris and Jack Crompton, although Morris was engaged in more serious matters for some of the time, crossing the Rhine in a Royal Armoured Corps tank.

In 1945-6, the Football League reverted to a more familiar 42-match programme split into Northern and Southern sections. United finished fourth and were knocked out of the FA Cup, which had resumed on a two-legged basis, in the fourth round. On 20 March 1946, United lost 2-1 to a BAOR side in Germany before a crowd of 25,000 British servicemen — and a few Germans, who defied orders not to attend by shinning up some nearby trees.

On 27 October 1945, United had beaten Bolton 2-1 at Maine Road with a new manager in charge. Matt Busby had taken the first steps on a road which was to lead to glories hitherto undreamed of by generations of Manchester United supporters.

*Billy Wrigglesworth (left) and Billy Porter (right) were pre-war players whose careers with United continued into wartime football. Wrigglesworth also managed four League games when peacetime football resumed for 1946-7.*

# 1915-16

Manager: John Robson

| 1 | Sep | 4 | (a) | Oldham A | L 2-3 | Halligan, Wilson | 6,000 |
|---|---|---|---|---|---|---|---|
| 2 | | 11 | (h) | Everton | L 2-4 | Wilson 2 | 10,000 |
| 3 | | 18 | (a) | Bolton W | W 5-3 | West 2, Woodcock 2, A.Davies | 2,000 |
| 4 | | 25 | (h) | Manchester C | D 1-1 | Halligan | 20,000 |
| 5 | Oct | 2 | (a) | Stoke | D 0-0 | | 6,000 |
| 6 | | 9 | (h) | Burnley | L 3-7 | D.Davies, Wilson, Woodcock | 12,000 |
| 7 | | 16 | (a) | Preston NE | D 0-0 | | 2,500 |
| 8 | | 23 | (h) | Stockport C | W 3-0 | Halligan, Hughes, Woodcock | 7,000 |
| 9 | | 30 | (a) | Liverpool | W 2-0 | West, Wilson | 15,000 |
| 10 | Nov | 6 | (h) | Bury | D 1-1 | Woodcock | 7,000 |
| 11 | | 13 | (h) | Rochdale | W 2-0 | A.Davies, Gipps | 4,000 |
| 12 | | 20 | (a) | Blackpool | L 1-5 | Woodcock | 4,000 |
| 13 | | 27 | (h) | Southport Cen | D 0-0 | | 5,000 |
| 14 | Dec | 4 | (h) | Oldham A | W 2-0 | Anderson, Halligan | 2,000 |
| 15 | | 11 | (a) | Everton | L 0-2 | | 7,000 |
| 16 | | 18 | (h) | Bolton W | W 1-0 | Bracegirdle | 6,000 |
| 17 | | 25 | (a) | Manchester C | L 1-2 | Halligan | 20,000 |
| 18 | Jan | 1 | (h) | Stoke | L 1-2 | Woodcock | 8,000 |
| 19 | | 8 | (a) | Burnley | L 4-7 | Travis 4 | 7,000 |
| 20 | | 15 | (h) | Preston NE | W 4-0 | Woodcock 2, Hughes, Halligan | 7,000 |
| 21 | | 22 | (a) | Stockport C | L 1-3 | Woodcock | 5,000 |
| 22 | | 29 | (h) | Liverpool | D 1-1 | Cookson | 10,000 |
| 23 | Feb | 5 | (a) | Bury | L 1-2 | Travis | 3,000 |
| 24 | | 12 | (a) | Rochdale | D 2-2 | Halligan, Woodcock | 2,000 |
| 25 | | 19 | (h) | Blackpool | D 1-1 | Woodcock | 10,000 |
| 26 | | 26 | (a) | Southport Cen | L 0-5 | | 2,000 |

FINAL LEAGUE POSITION: 11th in Lancashire Section (Principal Tournament)

Appearances
Goals

| 27 | Mar | 4 | (h) | Everton | L 0-2 | | 5,000 |
|---|---|---|---|---|---|---|---|
| 28 | | 11 | (a) | Oldham A | L 0-1 | | 650 |
| 29 | | 18 | (h) | Liverpool | D 0-0 | | 13,000 |
| 30 | | 25 | (h) | Manchester C | L 0-2 | | 15,000 |
| 31 | Apr | 1 | (a) | Stockport C | L 3-5 | Campey 2, Winterburn | 5,000 |
| 32 | | 8 | (a) | Everton | L 1-3 | Forster | 14,000 |
| 33 | | 15 | (a) | Oldham A | W 3-0 | Crossley, Halligan, Knowles | 6,000 |
| 34 | | 21 | (h) | Stockport C | W 3-2 | Crossley, Halligan, Woodcock | 9,000 |
| 35 | | 22 | (a) | Liverpool | L 1-7 | Woodcock | 20,000 |
| 36 | | 29 | (a) | Manchester C | L 1-2 | Crossley | 15,000 |

FINAL LEAGUE POSITION: 6th in Lancashire Section Subsidiary (Southern) Tournament

Appearances
Goals

| Mew | Allman | Hudson | Broster | O'Connell | Haywood | Holt | Wilson | Woodcock | Halligan | Lofthouse | Knowles | Knighton | Spratt | Barlow | Davies A | Gipps | Davies D | West | Pennington | Ireland | Anderson | Cubberley W | Travis | Hughes | Wall | Bracegirdle | Cubberley S | Chorley | Hayes | Hilditch | Armstrong | Forster | Winterburn | Walker | Campey | Swann | Lucas | Crossley | # |
|---|---|---|---|---|---|---|---|---|---|---|---|---|---|---|---|---|---|---|---|---|---|---|---|---|---|---|---|---|---|---|---|---|---|---|---|---|---|---|---|
| 1 | 2 | 3 | 4 | 5 | 6 | 7 | 8 | 9 | 10 | 11 | | | | | | | | | | | | | | | | | | | | | | | | | | | | | 1 |
| 1 | 2 | 3 | 4 | 5 | | | 11 | 8 | 10 | 9 | 6 | 7 | | | | | | | | | | | | | | | | | | | | | | | | | | | 2 |
| 1 | | | | 4 | | | 11 | 8 | 10 | | | | 3 | 2 | 5 | 6 | 7 | 9 | | | | | | | | | | | | | | | | | | | | | 3 |
| 1 | | | | 4 | | | 11 | 8 | 10 | | | | | | 5 | 6 | 7 | 9 | 3 | 2 | | | | | | | | | | | | | | | | | | | 4 |
| 1 | 2 | | | 4 | | | 11 | 7 | 8 | | | | | 3 | 5 | 6 | | 10 | | | 9 | | | | | | | | | | | | | | | | | | 5 |
| 1 | | | | | | | 8 | 10 | 11 | | | | | 2 | 5 | 6 | 9 | 7 | 3 | | 4 | | | | | | | | | | | | | | | | | | 6 |
| 1 | 2 | | | 4 | | | 11 | 8 | | | | | | 3 | 5 | 6 | 7 | 10 | | | 9 | | | | | | | | | | | | | | | | | | 7 |
| 1 | 2 | | | 4 | | | | 10 | 9 | | | | | 3 | 5 | 6 | | | | | 8 | | | | 7 | 11 | | | | | | | | | | | | | 8 |
| 1 | | 3 | | 4 | | | 10 | 8 | 11 | | | | | 2 | 5 | 6 | | 9 | | | | | 7 | | | | | | | | | | | | | | | | 9 |
| 1 | | 3 | | 4 | | | 9 | 10 | 8 | | | | | 2 | 5 | 6 | | | | | | | | | 7 | 11 | | | | | | | | | | | | | 10 |
| 1 | | 3 | | 4 | | | 11 | 8 | 10 | | | | | 2 | 5 | 6 | | 9 | | | | | 7 | | | | | | | | | | | | | | | | 11 |
| 1 | | 3 | | 5 | | | | 8 | 10 | | | | | 2 | | 6 | | | | | | | | | 7 | 11 | | 4 | | 9 | | | | | | | | | 12 |
| 1 | | 3 | | 4 | | | | 8 | 10 | | | | | 2 | 5 | 6 | | | | | 9 | | 7 | | | 11 | | | | | | | | | | | | | 13 |
| 1 | | 3 | | 4 | | | | 7 | 10 | | | | | 2 | 5 | 6 | | 9 | | | | | 8 | | | 11 | | | | | | | | | | | | | 14 |
| 1 | | 3 | | 4 | | | | 7 | 9 | | | | | 2 | 5 | 6 | | 8 | | | | | 10 | | | 11 | | | | | | | | | | | | | 15 |
| 1 | | 3 | | 4 | | | | 8 | 10 | | | | | 2 | 5 | 6 | | 9 | | | | | 7 | | | 11 | | | | | | | | | | | | | 16 |
| 1 | | 3 | | 4 | | | | 8 | 10 | | | | | 2 | 5 | 6 | | 9 | | | | | | | 7 | 11 | | | | | | | | | | | | | 17 |
| 1 | | 3 | | 4 | | | | 10 | 9 | | | | | 2 | 5 | 6 | | | | | | | 8 | | | 11 | | | | | | | | | | | | | 18 |
| 1 | | 3 | | 4 | 7 | | | 8 | 10 | | | | | 2 | 5 | 6 | | 9 | | | | | | | | 11 | | | | | | | | | | | | | 19 |
| 1 | | | | 4 | | | | 10 | 9 | | | | | 2 | 5 | 6 | | | | | | | 8 | | 7 | | | | | | | | 11 | | | | | | 20 |
| 1 | | 3 | | 4 | 7 | | | 10 | | | | | | 2 | 5 | 6 | | | | | | | | | 8 | 11 | | | | | | | 9 | | | | | | 21 |
| 1 | | 3 | | 4 | | | | 8 | 7 | | 5 | | | 2 | 10 | 6 | | | | | | | | | | | | | | | | | | | | | | | 22 |
| 1 | | 3 | | | 7 | | | 8 | 9 | | | | | 2 | 5 | 6 | | | | | | 4 | 10 | | | | | | | | | 11 | | | | | | | 23 |
| 1 | 2 | 3 | | 4 | | | | 8 | 9 | | 5 | | | | | 6 | | | | | | | | | | | | | | | | 11 | 7 | | | | | | 24 |
| 1 | | 3 | | 4 | | | | 10 | 9 | | 5 | | | 2 | | 6 | | | | | | | 8 | | 7 | 11 | | | | | | | | | | | | | 25 |
| 1 | | 3 | | | | | | 8 | 10 | | 5 | | | 2 | 4 | 6 | | | | | | | | | 7 | 11 | | | | | | | | | | | | | 26 |
| **26** | **5** | **20** | **2** | **18** | **9** | **1** | **11** | **26** | **23** | **2** | **5** | **1** | **1** | **21** | **22** | **24** | **4** | **11** | **2** | **1** | **5** | **2** | **9** | **2** | **7** | **7** | **1** | **1** | **1** | **3** | **2** | **3** | **2** | | | | | | |
| | | | | | | | | 5 | 12 | 7 | | | | 2 | 1 | 1 | 3 | | | | 1 | | 5 | 2 | | 1 | | | | | | | | | | | | | |
| 1 | | | | 4 | | | | 8 | 10 | | | | | 3 | | 6 | | | | | | | | | | | | | | | | 7 | 11 | 5 | 9 | | | | 27 |
| | | | | 4 | | | | 8 | 10 | | | | | 3 | | 6 | | | | | | | | | | | | | | | | 7 | 11 | 5 | 9 | 1 | 2 | | 28 |
| | | | | | | | | 8 | 10 | | | | | 3 | 5 | 6 | | | | | | | | | | | | | | | | 4 | 11 | | 9 | 1 | 2 | | 29 |
| 1 | | | | | | | | 8 | 10 | | 5 | | | 3 | 4 | 6 | | | | | | | | | | | | | | | | 7 | 11 | 2 | 9 | | | | 30 |
| | | 3 | | 4 | | | | 8 | 11 | | | | | | 5 | 6 | | | | | | | | | | | | | | | | 7 | 10 | | 9 | | | 1 | 31 |
| | | 3 | | | | | | 8 | 9 | | 5 | | | 2 | | 6 | | | | | | | | | | | | | | | | 4 | 11 | | | | | | 32 |
| | | 3 | | | | | | 8 | 9 | | 5 | | | 2 | | 6 | | | | | | | 7 | | | | | | | | | 4 | 11 | | | | 10 | | 33 |
| | | 3 | | | | | | 8 | 9 | | 5 | | | 2 | | 6 | | | | | | | 7 | | | | | | | | | 4 | 11 | | | | 10 | | 34 |
| | | 3 | | | | | | 8 | 10 | | 5 | | | 2 | | 6 | | | | | | | | | | | | | | | | 4 | 11 | | 9 | 7 | | | 35 |
| | | 3 | 7 | | | | | 8 | 10 | | 5 | | | 2 | | 6 | | | | | | | | | | | | | | | | 4 | | | 9 | | | 1 | 36 |
| **2** | | **6** | | **3** | | | | **10** | **10** | | **6** | | | **10** | **3** | **10** | | | | | | | | | | | | | | | | | **10** | **9** | **2** | **4** | **4** | **3** | **4** | |
| | | | | | | | | 2 | 2 | | 1 | | | | | 1 | | | | | | | | | | | | | | | | 4 | 1 | 1 | 2 | | 3 | | |

Match 18: Robinson played number 7; Match 20: Fairhurst played number 3; Match 22: Cookson played number 9, scoring once and Hallworth played number 11; Match 24: James Hodge played number 10; Match 26: Brown played number 9; Match 27: Worrall played number 2; Match 29: Hopkin played number 7; Match 31: Worrall played number 2; Match 32: Wright played number 1, Helme played number 7 and Brooks played number 10; Match 33: Wright played number 1; Match 34: Wright played number 1; Match 35: Wright played number 1; Match 36: Cookson played number 11.

Match 31: Walker listed as playing number 2 by the Football League.

# 1916-17

Manager: John Robson

| | | | | | Result | Scorers | Attendance |
|---|---|---|---|---|---|---|---|
| 1 | Sep | 2 | (h) | Port Vale | D 2-2 | Woodcock 2 | 5,000 |
| 2 | | 9 | (a) | Oldham A | W 2-0 | Armstrong, O'Connell | 5,000 |
| 3 | | 16 | (h) | Preston NE | W 2-1 | Woodcock 2 | 7,000 |
| 4 | | 23 | (a) | Burnley | L 1-7 | Armstrong | 3,000 |
| 5 | | 30 | (a) | Blackpool | D 2-2 | Woodcock 2 | 5,000 |
| 6 | Oct | 7 | (h) | Liverpool | D 0-0 | | 5,000 |
| 7 | | 14 | (a) | Stockport C | L 0-1 | | 4,000 |
| 8 | | 21 | (h) | Bury | W 3-1 | Armstrong 2, Thompson (og) | 5,000 |
| 9 | | 28 | (a) | Stoke | L 0-3 | | 5,000 |
| 10 | Nov | 4 | (h) | Southport Cen | W 1-0 | Woodcock | 6,000 |
| 11 | | 11 | (a) | Blackburn R | W 2-1 | Anderson, Woodcock | 5,000 |
| 12 | | 18 | (h) | Manchester C | W 2-1 | Anderson, Woodcock | 8,000 |
| 13 | | 25 | (a) | Everton | L 2-3 | Anderson, Woodcock | 10,000 |
| 14 | Dec | 2 | (h) | Rochdale | D 1-1 | Anderson | 9,000 |
| 15 | | 9 | (a) | Bolton W | L 1-5 | Anderson | 3,000 |
| 16 | | 23 | (h) | Oldham A | W 3-2 | Anderson 2, Ogden | 5,000 |
| 17 | | 30 | (a) | Preston NE | L 2-3 | Anderson, Woodcock | 6,000 |
| 18 | Jan | 6 | (h) | Burnley | W 3-1 | Anderson 2, Woodcock | 5,000 |
| 19 | | 13 | (h) | Blackpool | W 3-2 | Woodcock 2, Crossley | 5,500 |
| 20 | | 20 | (a) | Liverpool | D 3-3 | Anderson 3 | 12,000 |
| 21 | | 27 | (a) | Stockport C | L 0-1 | | 5,000 |
| 22 | Feb | 3 | (a) | Bury | D 1-1 | Woodcock | 5,000 |
| 23 | | 10 | (h) | Stoke | W 4-2 | Woodcock 2, Ellis, Robinson | 7,000 |
| 24 | | 17 | (a) | Southport Cen | W 1-0 | Ellis | 4,000 |
| 25 | | 24 | (h) | Blackburn R | W 1-0 | Anderson | 5,000 |
| 26 | Mar | 3 | (a) | Manchester C | L 0-1 | | 18,000 |
| 27 | | 10 | (h) | Everton | L 0-2 | | 12,000 |
| 28 | | 17 | (a) | Rochdale | L 0-2 | | 7,000 |
| 29 | | 24 | (h) | Bolton W | W 6-3 | Woodcock 3, Anderson 2, Hilditch | 5,000 |
| 30 | Apr | 6 | (a) | Port Vale | L 0-3 | | 6,000 |

FINAL LEAGUE POSITION: 7th in Lancashire Section (Principal Tournament)

Appearances

Goals

| | | | | | Result | Scorers | Attendance |
|---|---|---|---|---|---|---|---|
| 31 | Mar | 31 | (a) | Stoke | L 1-2 | Ellis | 7,000 |
| 32 | Apr | 7 | (h) | Manchester C | W 5-1 | Anderson 3, Woodcock 2 | 14,000 |
| 33 | | 9 | (h) | Port Vale | W 5-1 | Anderson 3, Travis 2 | 8,000 |
| 34 | | 14 | (h) | Stoke | W 1-0 | Woodcock | 9,000 |
| 35 | | 21 | (a) | Manchester C | W 1-0 | Anderson | 15,000 |
| 36 | | 28 | (a) | Port Vale | L 2-5 | McMenemy, Woodcock | 4,000 |

FINAL LEAGUE POSITION: 4th in Lancashire Section (Subsidiary Tournament)

Appearances

Goals

| Wright | Barlow | Silcock | Molyneux | Buckley | Forster | Hughes E | Wilson | Crossley | Woodcock | Robinson A | Mew | O'Connell | Armstrong G | Brooks C | Winterburn A | Wall | Swann | Hilditch | Bunting | Cookson SP | Cubberley S | Anderson | Siddall | Travis | Davies W | Capper | Connor | Hudson EH | Hamill | Lees | Ogden | Ellis | Leigh | Lomas LV | Barnett | McMenemy | Tremlow | Daniels | Walker | Holt | |
|---|---|---|---|---|---|---|---|---|---|---|---|---|---|---|---|---|---|---|---|---|---|---|---|---|---|---|---|---|---|---|---|---|---|---|---|---|---|---|---|---|---|
|1|2|3|4|5|6|7|8|9|10|11||||||||||||||||||||||||||||||||1|
||2|3|5||4|7|||9||1|6|8|10|11||||||||||||||||||||||||||||2|
||2|3|4|5|6||8||10|11|1||7|||9||||||||||||||||||||||||||3|
||2|3|||6||9||7|11|||8||||1|10|4|5||||||||||||||||||||||4|
||2|3|4||6|||8|10|11||5|7|9|||1|||||||||||||||||||||||||5|
||2|3|4||6|||8||11||5|7|9|||1|10||||||||||||||||||||||||6|
||2|3|||6|||8|9|11|1|5|7|||||10|||4|||||||||||||||||||||7|
||2|3|4||6||||10|11|1|5|8|||||9||||7||||||||||||||||||||8|
||2|3|4||6|||||11|1|5|9|||||10||||7|8|||||||||||||||||||9|
||2|3|4||6||||8|11|1|5||||||10||||9||7|||||||||||||||||||10|
|||3|4||5|||2|10||1||||11|||6||||9|||8|7||||||||||||||||||11|
||2|3|4|5|6||||10|11|1|||||||8||||9|||||7|||||||||||||||12|
||2|3|4|5|6|||7|10|11|||||||1|8||||9|||||||||||||||||||13|
||2||4|5|10||||8|11|1|7|||||||||||9||||||3|6||||||||||||14|
||2|3|4||5||||8||1|||||||6||||9||||||||10|7|11||||||||||15|
||3||2||5|||4|8|11|1|||||||6||||9|||||||||10||7|||||||||16|
||2|3|||5|||4|10||1|||||||8||||9|||||||||||11|7|6||||||||17|
|||3||5|6|||2|10||||||||1|4||||9|||||||||||11|7||8||||||18|
||2|3|||5|||7|10|8||||||||4|||||||||||||||9||6|11||||||19|
|||3|||5||||8|||||||||4||||9|||||||||||11|7|6|10||||||20|
||2|3|||5||||8||1|||||||4||||9|||||||||||11|7|6|10||||||21|
||2|3||5|6||||10|11|1|||||||4||||8||||||||||||7||9||||||22|
||2|3||5|6||||10|8|1|||||||4|||||||||||||||7|9||11||||||23|
||2|3|||6||||9||1|||||||4||||10|||||||||||7|8||11||||||24|
||2|3||5|4|||||||1|||||||8||||9|||||||||||11||6|10||||||25|
||2|3||5|6||||8||1|||||||4||||9|||||||||||11|7||10||||||26|
||2|3||5|6||||8||1|||||||4||||9||||||||||||7||10||||||27|
||2|3||5|6||||8||1|||||||4|||||||7|||||||||11|||10||||||28|
||2|3||4|6||||10||1|||||||5||||9||8||||||||||11||||7|||||29|
||||||||||||1|||||||||||||||||||||||||||9|3||||30|
|1|26|27|14|13|29|2|3|10|26|16|22|8|8|3|2|1|5|24|1|1|1|19|1|2|2|1|1|1|1|1|2|12|10|5|11|2|1|||||
|||||||||1|20|1||1|4|||||1||||16||||||||||1|2||||||||||||

1 own-goal

| | | | | | | | | | | | | | | | | | | | | | | | | | | | | | | | | | | | | | | | | | |
|---|---|---|---|---|---|---|---|---|---|---|---|---|---|---|---|---|---|---|---|---|---|---|---|---|---|---|---|---|---|---|---|---|---|---|---|---|---|---|---|---|---|
|||3|||6||||9||1|||||||4||||8||||||||||||11||||7|2|10|||31|
|||3|||6||||8||1|||||||4||||9|||||7|||||||11|||10||||5||32|
|||3|||6||||8||1|||||||4||||10||9|||7|||||||11|||||||5|2|33|
|||3|||6||||8||1|||||||4||||10||||||||||||11||||9|||5|2|34|
|||3||5|6||||8||1|||||||4||||9||10|||7|||||||11|||||||||35|
|||3||5|6||||8||||||||||4||||10|||||7|||||||11||||9|||||36|
|||6||2|6||||6||5|||||||6||||6||2|||4|||||||6|||1|3|1|1|3|2||
||||||||||4|||||||||||||7||2||||||||||1||||1|||||||

Match 19: Frith played number 1; Match 20: Kite played number 1 and E.K.Hudson played number 2; Match 24: Montgomery played number 5; Match 25: Goddard played number 7; Match 27: Tattum played number 11; Match 28: Pilkington played number 9; Match 30: Preece played number 2, Heath played number 4, Bennett played number 5, Bailey played number 6, Spooner played number 7, Martin played number 8, Wroe played number 10 and Brennan played number 11; Match 31: Bennett played number 5; Match 32: Leah played number 2; Match 34: O.Williams played number 7; Match 35: Allman played number 2; Match 36: Berry played number 1 and Allman played number 2.

Match 31: Barnett listed as playing number 5 by the Football League.

# 1917-18

Manager: John Robson

| 1 | Sep | 1 | (a) | Blackburn R | W | 5-0 | Anderson 3, Meehan, Woodcock | 7,000 |
|---|---|---|---|---|---|---|---|---|
| 2 | | 8 | (h) | Blackburn R | W | 6-1 | Anderson 4, Woodcock 2 | 10,000 |
| 3 | | 15 | (a) | Rochdale | L | 0-3 | | 7,000 |
| 4 | | 22 | (h) | Rochdale | D | 1-1 | Woodcock | 8,000 |
| 5 | | 29 | (a) | Manchester C | L | 1-3 | Anderson | 20,000 |
| 6 | Oct | 6 | (h) | Manchester C | D | 1-1 | Woodcock | 10,000 |
| 7 | | 13 | (a) | Everton | L | 0-3 | | 14,000 |
| 8 | | 20 | (h) | Everton | D | 0-0 | | 8,000 |
| 9 | | 27 | (h) | Port Vale | D | 3-3 | Anderson, Connor, Ellis | 7,000 |
| 10 | Nov | 3 | (a) | Port Vale | D | 2-2 | Anderson, Ellis | 4,000 |
| 11 | | 10 | (h) | Bolton W | L | 1-3 | Ellis | 4,000 |
| 12 | | 17 | (a) | Bolton W | L | 2-4 | Anderson, Ellis | 8,000 |
| 13 | | 24 | (h) | Preston NE | W | 2-1 | Anderson 2 | 9,000 |
| 14 | Dec | 1 | (a) | Preston NE | D | 0-0 | | 8,000 |
| 15 | | 8 | (h) | Blackpool | W | 1-0 | Ellis | 9,000 |
| 16 | | 15 | (a) | Blackpool | W | 3-2 | Woodcock 2, Meehan | 8,000 |
| 17 | | 22 | (a) | Burnley | W | 5-0 | Anderson 3, Connor, Meehan | 5,000 |
| 18 | | 29 | (h) | Burnley | W | 1-0 | Connor | 6,000 |
| 19 | Jan | 5 | (a) | Southport Cen | L | 0-3 | | 4,000 |
| 20 | | 12 | (h) | Southport Cen | D | 0-0 | | 5,000 |
| 21 | | 19 | (a) | Liverpool | L | 1-5 | Woodcock | 20,000 |
| 22 | | 26 | (h) | Liverpool | L | 0-2 | | 10,000 |
| 23 | Feb | 2 | (a) | Stoke | L | 1-5 | Woodcock | 6,000 |
| 24 | | 9 | (h) | Stoke | W | 2-1 | Ellis, Woodcock | 10,000 |
| 25 | | 16 | (h) | Bury | D | 0-0 | | 7,000 |
| 26 | | 23 | (a) | Bury | W | 2-1 | Massey, Woodcock | 6,000 |
| 27 | Mar | 2 | (h) | Oldham A | W | 2-1 | Ellis, Woodcock | 9,000 |
| 28 | | 9 | (a) | Oldham A | L | 0-2 | | 4,000 |
| 29 | | 16 | (h) | Stockport C | W | 2-0 | Buckley 2 | 9,000 |
| 30 | | 23 | (a) | Stockport C | L | 1-2 | Buckley | 5,000 |

FINAL LEAGUE POSITION: 8th in Lancashire Section (Principal Tournament)     Appearances

Goals

| 31 | Mar | 29 | (a) | Manchester C | L | 0-3 | | 10,000 |
|---|---|---|---|---|---|---|---|---|
| 32 | | 30 | (h) | Stoke | W | 2-1 | Stafford, Woodcock | 11,000 |
| 33 | Apr | 1 | (h) | Manchester C | W | 2-0 | Buckley, Woodcock | 10,000 |
| 34 | | 6 | (a) | Stoke C | D | 0-0 | | 8,000 |
| 35 | | 13 | (h) | Port Vale | W | 2-0 | Bourne 2 | 7,000 |
| 36 | | 20 | (a) | Port Vale | L | 0-3 | | 4,000 |

FINAL LEAGUE POSITION: 8th in Lancashire Section (Subsidiary Tournament)     Appearances

Goals

| Mew | Thomas | Silcock | Bunting | Walker | Hilditch | Connor | Meehan | Woodcock | Anderson | Ellis | Roberts WR | Roberts RH | Buckley | Muskett | Harrison | Holt | Robinson | Hopkin | Leah | Rainford | Cookson | Mann | Montgomery | Daniels | Chamberlain | Birks | Allsopp | Knowles | Best | Kinsella-Bates | Williams | Marsden | Southern | McMenemy | Hodgkinson | Bell | McLachlan | Johnson | Match |
|---|---|---|---|---|---|---|---|---|---|---|---|---|---|---|---|---|---|---|---|---|---|---|---|---|---|---|---|---|---|---|---|---|---|---|---|---|---|---|---|
| 1 | 2 | 3 | 4 | 5 | 6 | 7 | 8 | 9 | 10 | 11 |  |  |  |  |  |  |  |  |  |  |  |  |  |  |  |  |  |  |  |  |  |  |  |  |  |  |  |  | 1 |
| 1 |  | 3 | 4 | 5 | 6 | 7 | 8 | 9 | 10 | 11 | 2 |  |  |  |  |  |  |  |  |  |  |  |  |  |  |  |  |  |  |  |  |  |  |  |  |  |  |  | 2 |
| 1 |  | 3 |  | 5 |  | 7 | 8 | 9 |  | 11 |  |  | 2 | 6 | 10 | 4 |  |  |  |  |  |  |  |  |  |  |  |  |  |  |  |  |  |  |  |  |  |  | 3 |
| 1 |  | 3 | 5 |  | 6 | 7 | 8 | 9 | 10 | 11 |  |  |  | 4 |  | 2 |  |  |  |  |  |  |  |  |  |  |  |  |  |  |  |  |  |  |  |  |  |  | 4 |
| 1 |  | 3 | 4 |  | 6 | 7 | 8 | 10 | 9 | 11 |  |  |  |  | 5 | 2 |  |  |  |  |  |  |  |  |  |  |  |  |  |  |  |  |  |  |  |  |  |  | 5 |
| 1 |  | 3 | 4 |  | 6 | 7 | 8 | 10 | 9 |  |  |  |  |  |  | 2 | 5 | 11 |  |  |  |  |  |  |  |  |  |  |  |  |  |  |  |  |  |  |  |  | 6 |
| 1 |  | 3 | 4 |  | 6 | 7 | 8 | 10 | 9 | 11 |  |  |  |  |  | 5 | 2 |  |  |  |  |  |  |  |  |  |  |  |  |  |  |  |  |  |  |  |  |  | 7 |
| 1 |  | 3 |  |  | 6 | 7 | 8 | 10 | 9 | 11 |  |  |  |  |  | 5 |  |  |  | 4 | 2 |  |  |  |  |  |  |  |  |  |  |  |  |  |  |  |  |  | 8 |
| 1 |  | 3 | 4 |  |  | 7 | 8 | 9 | 10 |  |  |  |  |  |  | 5 |  |  |  |  | 2 | 6 | 11 |  |  |  |  |  |  |  |  |  |  |  |  |  |  |  | 9 |
| 1 |  | 3 | 5 |  | 10 | 7 |  | 9 |  | 11 |  |  |  |  |  |  |  |  |  |  |  |  | 8 | 2 | 4 | 6 |  |  |  |  |  |  |  |  |  |  |  |  | 10 |
| 1 |  | 3 | 5 |  | 7 | 8 | 9 |  |  |  |  |  |  |  |  |  | 2 |  |  |  |  |  | 11 |  | 4 | 6 |  |  |  |  |  |  |  |  |  |  |  |  | 11 |
| 1 |  | 3 |  |  | 6 | 7 | 8 | 9 |  | 11 |  |  |  |  |  | 5 |  |  |  |  |  |  | 2 |  |  | 4 |  |  |  |  |  |  |  |  |  |  |  |  | 12 |
| 1 |  | 3 | 4 |  | 7 | 8 |  |  |  |  |  |  |  |  |  |  | 2 |  |  |  |  |  |  |  |  |  |  |  | 6 | 5 |  |  |  |  |  |  |  |  | 13 |
| 1 |  | 3 | 4 |  | 7 | 8 |  | 10 | 11 |  |  |  |  |  |  |  | 2 |  |  |  |  |  |  |  |  |  |  |  | 5 | 6 |  |  |  |  |  |  |  |  | 14 |
| 1 |  |  | 4 |  | 7 | 8 | 9 | 10 |  |  |  |  |  |  |  | 2 |  |  |  |  |  |  |  |  |  |  |  |  | 5 | 6 | 3 |  |  |  |  |  |  |  | 15 |
| 1 |  | 3 | 4 |  | 7 | 8 | 9 | 10 |  |  |  |  |  |  |  |  |  |  |  |  |  |  |  |  |  |  |  |  | 5 | 6 | 2 | 11 |  |  |  |  |  |  | 16 |
| 1 |  | 3 | 4 |  | 7 | 8 | 9 | 10 | 11 |  |  |  |  |  |  |  |  |  |  |  |  |  |  |  |  |  |  |  | 5 | 6 | 2 |  |  |  |  |  |  |  | 17 |
| 1 |  | 3 | 4 |  | 7 | 8 | 9 |  |  |  |  |  |  |  |  | 10 |  |  |  |  |  |  |  |  |  |  |  |  | 5 | 6 | 2 | 11 |  |  |  |  |  |  | 18 |
| 1 |  | 3 | 5 |  | 7 | 4 | 9 |  |  |  |  |  |  |  |  | 10 |  |  |  |  |  |  |  |  |  |  |  |  | 6 |  |  | 11 | 8 |  |  |  |  |  | 19 |
| 1 |  | 3 | 4 |  |  | 8 | 9 | 10 |  |  |  |  |  |  |  |  |  |  |  |  |  |  |  |  |  |  |  | 6 | 5 |  | 2 |  |  | 7 | 11 |  |  |  | 20 |
| 1 |  | 3 | 4 |  | 7 | 8 | 9 | 10 |  |  |  |  |  |  |  |  |  |  |  |  |  |  |  |  | 11 |  |  |  | 5 | 6 | 2 |  |  |  |  |  |  |  | 21 |
| 1 |  | 3 | 4 |  | 7 | 8 | 9 | 10 |  |  |  |  |  |  |  |  |  |  |  |  |  |  |  |  |  |  |  |  | 5 | 6 | 2 | 11 |  |  |  |  |  |  | 22 |
| 1 |  | 3 | 4 |  |  | 8 |  | 10 |  |  |  |  |  |  |  |  |  |  |  |  |  |  |  |  |  |  |  |  | 5 | 6 | 2 | 7 |  | 11 | 9 |  |  |  | 23 |
| 1 |  | 3 | 4 |  |  | 8 |  | 11 | 6 |  |  |  |  |  |  |  |  |  |  |  |  |  |  |  |  |  |  |  | 5 | 7 |  |  |  | 10 |  | 9 | 2 | 24 |
| 1 |  | 3 | 4 |  |  | 8 |  | 10 | 6 |  |  |  |  |  |  |  |  |  |  |  |  |  |  |  |  |  |  |  | 5 |  |  |  | 11 | 7 | 9 | 2 | 25 |
| 1 |  | 3 | 4 |  |  |  |  | 10 | 6 |  |  |  |  |  |  |  |  |  |  |  |  |  |  |  |  |  |  |  | 5 |  |  |  | 11 | 2 |  |  | 26 |
| 1 |  | 3 | 4 |  | 9 | 8 |  | 11 | 6 |  |  |  |  |  |  |  |  |  |  |  |  |  |  |  |  |  |  |  | 5 |  |  |  | 10 |  | 2 | 27 |
| 1 |  | 3 | 4 | 7 | 6 | 8 |  | 10 |  |  |  |  |  |  |  |  |  |  |  |  |  |  |  |  |  |  |  |  | 5 |  |  |  | 11 |  | 2 | 28 |
| 1 |  | 3 | 4 | 7 | 6 | 8 |  | 10 | 9 |  |  |  |  |  |  |  |  |  |  |  |  |  |  |  |  |  |  |  | 5 |  |  |  | 11 |  | 2 | 29 |
| 1 |  | 3 | 4 | 7 | 6 | 8 |  | 10 | 9 |  |  |  |  |  |  |  |  |  |  |  |  |  |  |  |  |  |  |  | 5 |  |  |  | 11 |  |  | 30 |
| 30 | 1 | 29 | 6 | 2 | 29 | 23 | 26 | 26 | 15 | 27 | 1 | 1 | 7 | 2 | 1 | 4 | 4 | 1 | 2 | 3 | 1 | 1 | 1 | 4 | 4 | 2 | 2 | 1 | 2 | 17 | 10 | 8 | 4 | 2 | 10 | 2 | 2 | 6 |  |
|  |  |  |  |  |  |  | 3 | 3 | 12 | 16 | 7 |  |  |  |  | 3 |  |  |  |  |  |  |  |  |  |  |  |  |  |  |  |  |  |  |  |  |  |  |  |

| Mew | Thomas | Silcock | Bunting | Walker | Hilditch | Connor | Meehan | Woodcock | Anderson | Ellis | Roberts WR | Roberts RH | Buckley | Muskett | Harrison | Holt | Robinson | Hopkin | Leah | Rainford | Cookson | Mann | Montgomery | Daniels | Chamberlain | Birks | Allsopp | Knowles | Best | Kinsella-Bates | Williams | Marsden | Southern | McMenemy | Hodgkinson | Bell | McLachlan | Johnson | Match |
|---|---|---|---|---|---|---|---|---|---|---|---|---|---|---|---|---|---|---|---|---|---|---|---|---|---|---|---|---|---|---|---|---|---|---|---|---|---|---|---|
| 1 |  |  | 4 |  | 6 | 8 |  | 10 |  |  |  |  |  |  |  |  |  |  |  |  |  |  |  |  |  |  |  |  |  | 5 |  |  |  |  | 11 |  | 3 |  | 31 |
| 1 |  | 3 | 4 |  | 6 | 8 |  | 10 |  | 9 |  |  |  |  |  |  |  |  |  |  |  |  |  |  |  |  |  |  |  | 5 |  |  |  |  | 11 |  | 2 |  | 32 |
| 1 |  | 3 | 4 |  | 6 | 8 |  | 10 |  | 9 |  |  |  |  |  |  |  |  |  |  |  |  |  |  |  |  |  |  |  | 5 |  |  |  |  | 11 |  | 2 |  | 33 |
| 1 |  | 3 | 4 | 7 | 8 |  |  | 10 |  | 5 |  |  |  |  |  |  |  |  |  |  |  |  |  |  |  |  |  |  |  |  |  | 6 |  |  | 11 |  | 2 | 9 | 34 |
| 1 |  | 3 | 4 |  | 6 | 8 |  | 10 |  | 5 |  |  |  |  |  |  |  |  |  |  |  |  |  |  |  |  |  |  |  |  |  |  |  |  | 11 |  | 2 |  | 35 |
|  |  | 3 | 10 |  | 6 |  |  |  |  | 11 |  |  |  |  |  | 9 |  |  |  |  |  |  |  |  |  |  |  |  |  |  |  |  |  |  | 7 |  | 2 |  | 36 |
| 5 |  | 5 | 6 | 1 | 6 | 4 |  | 6 |  | 5 |  |  |  |  |  | 1 |  |  |  |  |  |  |  |  |  |  |  |  |  | 3 | 1 |  |  |  | 6 |  | 5 |  |  |
|  |  |  | 2 |  |  |  |  |  |  | 1 |  |  |  |  |  |  |  |  |  |  |  |  |  |  |  |  |  |  |  |  |  |  |  |  |  |  |  |  |  |

Match 12: Davies played number 10; Match 13: Moores played number 11; Match 14: Searby played number 9; Match 15: Peplow played number 11; Match 19: Lloyd played number 2; Match 26: Stafford played number 7, Massey played number 8, scoring once and Johnson played number 9; Match 27: Wallwork played number 7; Match 28: Whitehead played number 9; Match 30: Cooper played number 2; Match 31: Cooper played number 2, Bain played number 7 and Richmond played number 9; Match 32: Stafford played number 7, scoring once; Match 33: Capper played number 7; Match 35: Hudson played number 2, Davies played number 7 and Bourne played number 9, scoring twice; Match 36: Underwood played number 1, Sullivan played number 4, Darlington played number 5 and Bourne played number 8.

Match 30: Coyne listed as playing number 2 by the Football League.

# 1918-19

Manager: John Robson

| 1 | Sep | 7 | (h) | Oldham A | L | 1-4 | Meehan | 10,000 |
|---|---|---|---|---|---|---|---|---|
| 2 | | 14 | (a) | Oldham A | W | 2-0 | Myers 2 | 8,000 |
| 3 | | 21 | (h) | Blackburn R | W | 1-0 | Ellis | 6,000 |
| 4 | | 28 | (a) | Blackburn R | D | 1-1 | Ellis | 6,000 |
| 5 | Oct | 5 | (h) | Manchester C | L | 0-2 | | 12,000 |
| 6 | | 12 | (a) | Manchester C | D | 0-0 | | 25,000 |
| 7 | | 19 | (h) | Everton | D | 1-1 | Woodcock | 20,000 |
| 8 | | 26 | (a) | Everton | L | 2-6 | Howarth, Woodcock | 16,000 |
| 9 | Nov | 2 | (h) | Rochdale | W | 3-1 | Coombes 2, Tickle | 10,000 |
| 10 | | 9 | (a) | Rochdale | L | 0-1 | | 6,000 |
| 11 | | 16 | (a) | Preston NE | L | 2-4 | Green 2 | 9,000 |
| 12 | | 23 | (h) | Preston NE | L | 1-2 | Robinson (og) | 12,000 |
| 13 | | 30 | (a) | Bolton W | L | 1-3 | Woodcock | 6,000 |
| 14 | Dec | 7 | (h) | Bolton W | W | 1-0 | Hilditch | 13,000 |
| 15 | | 14 | (a) | Port Vale | L | 1-3 | Woodcock | 4,000 |
| 16 | | 21 | (h) | Port Vale | W | 5-1 | Woodcock 4, Jones | 5,000 |
| 17 | | 28 | (a) | Blackpool | D | 2-2 | Ellis, Woodcock | 4,000 |
| 18 | Jan | 11 | (a) | Stockport C | L | 1-2 | Cookson | 8,000 |
| 19 | | 18 | (h) | Stockport C | L | 0-2 | | 14,000 |
| 20 | | 25 | (a) | Liverpool | D | 1-1 | Langford | 15,000 |
| 21 | Feb | 1 | (h) | Liverpool | L | 0-1 | | 20,000 |
| 22 | | 8 | (a) | Southport Vulcan | L | 1-2 | Jones | 6,000 |
| 23 | | 15 | (h) | Southport Vulcan | L | 1-3 | Meehan | 8,000 |
| 24 | | 22 | (a) | Burnley | L | 2-4 | Hodge 2 | 10,000 |
| 25 | Mar | 1 | (h) | Burnley | W | 4-0 | Hodge 2, Makin, Woodcock | 8,000 |
| 26 | | 8 | (a) | Stoke | W | 2-1 | Albinson, Jones | 10,000 |
| 27 | | 15 | (h) | Stoke | W | 3-1 | Woodcock 2, Hodge | 30,000 |
| 28 | | 22 | (a) | Bury | W | 2-0 | Lomas, Woodcock | 15,000 |
| 29 | | 29 | (h) | Bury | W | 5-1 | Spence 4, Woodcock | 19,000 |
| 30 | Apr | 30 | (h) | Blackpool | W | 5-1 | Hopkin 2, Jones 2, Potts | 22,000 |

FINAL LEAGUE POSITION: 9th in Lancashire Section (Principal Tournament)

Appearances

Goals

| 31 | Apr | 5 | (a) | Port Vale | W | 3-1 | Hopkin, Jones, Woodcock | 8,000 |
|---|---|---|---|---|---|---|---|---|
| 32 | | 12 | (h) | Port Vale | W | 2-1 | Woodcock 2 | 8,000 |
| 33 | | 18 | (a) | Manchester C | L | 0-3 | | 35,000 |
| 34 | | 19 | (h) | Stoke | L | 0-1 | | 30,000 |
| 35 | | 21 | (h) | Manchester C | L | 2-4 | Potts, Spence | 35,000 |
| 36 | | 26 | (a) | Stoke | L | 2-4 | Smith, Spence | 20,000 |

FINAL LEAGUE POSITION: 3rd in Lancashire Section (Subsidiary Tournament) Section 'C'

The leaders of this section qualified for the Lancashire Senior Cup semi-finals.

Appearances

Goals

| Mew | Lumberg | Silcock | Hilditch | Manuel | Clayton | Worsencroft | Meehan | Myers | Woodcock | Ellis | Murray | Coombes | Hodge, James | Connor | Haywood | Williams O | Baguley | Dunn | Reed | Davies A | Howarth | Williams W | Hall | Molyneux | Forster | Tickle | Jones T | Cookson SP | Langford | Peplow | Makin | Hudson EK | Nightingale | Kinsella-Bates | Wall | Hopkin | Albinson | Lomas | |
|---|---|---|---|---|---|---|---|---|---|---|---|---|---|---|---|---|---|---|---|---|---|---|---|---|---|---|---|---|---|---|---|---|---|---|---|---|---|---|---|
| 1 | 2 | 3 | 4 | 5 | 6 | 7 | 8 | 9 | 10 | 11 | | | | | | | | | | | | | | | | | | | | | | | | | | | | | 1 |
| 1 | 2 | 3 | 5 | 6 | 4 | | 10 | 8 | 11 | 7 | 9 | | | | | | | | | | | | | | | | | | | | | | | | | | | | 2 |
| 1 | | 3 | 5 | 6 | 4 | | 9 | 8 | 11 | 7 | 10 | 2 | | | | | | | | | | | | | | | | | | | | | | | | | | | 3 |
| 1 | 2 | 3 | 5 | 6 | 4 | | 9 | 8 | 11 | 10 | | 7 | | | | | | | | | | | | | | | | | | | | | | | | | | | 4 |
| 1 | | 3 | 5 | | 4 | | 9 | 8 | 11 | | 10 | | 6 | 7 | 2 | | | | | | | | | | | | | | | | | | | | | | | | 5 |
| 1 | | 3 | 5 | | 4 | | 8 | 11 | 10 | | 6 | 7 | 2 | 9 | | | | | | | | | | | | | | | | | | | | | | | | | 6 |
| 1 | | 3 | 5 | | 4 | | 9 | 8 | 11 | | 10 | 7 | 6 | 2 | | | | | | | | | | | | | | | | | | | | | | | | | 7 |
| 1 | | 3 | 5 | | 4 | | 8 | | 7 | | | | 2 | | 10 | 11 | 6 | 9 | | | | | | | | | | | | | | | | | | | | | 8 |
| 1 | | 3 | | 4 | | | 8 | 11 | 9 | | 7 | | 2 | | | | | | | | 6 | 5 | 10 | | | | | | | | | | | | | | | | 9 |
| 1 | | 3 | | 4 | | | 8 | 11 | 9 | | 6 | | 2 | | | | | | | | 5 | 10 | | | | | | | | | | | | | | | | | 10 |
| 1 | | 3 | 5 | 4 | | | | 11 | | 6 | 2 | | 7 | | | | | | | | | | 8 | 10 | | | | | | | | | | | | | | | 11 |
| 1 | | 3 | 5 | | 9 | | 11 | 8 | | 6 | 4 | | 7 | | | | | | | | 2 | 10 | | | | | | | | | | | | | | | | | 12 |
| 1 | | 3 | 5 | 9 | 10 | | | 6 | | | | | | | | | | | | | | 11 | 7 | | | | | | | | | | | | | | | | 13 |
| 1 | 2 | 5 | 4 | 10 | | | 7 | 11 | 9 | 3 | | | | | | | | | | | | | | | | | 8 | 3 | 6 | 8 | | | | | | | | | 14 |
| 1 | 3 | 5 | 4 | 10 | | | | | | | | | | | | | | | | | | 11 | 9 | | 2 | 8 | | | | | | | | | | | | | 15 |
| 1 | 2 | 4 | 6 | 10 | 11 | | | 7 | | | | | | | | | | | | | | 9 | 8 | 3 | | | 5 | | | | | | | | | | | | 16 |
| 1 | 2 | 4 | 6 | 10 | 11 | | | 7 | | | | | | | | | | | | | | 8 | 9 | 3 | | | 5 | | | | | | | | | | | | 17 |
| 1 | 2 | 4 | 6 | 9 | 10 | | | | | | | | | | | | | | | | | 8 | 7 | 3 | | | 5 | 11 | | | | | | | | | | | 18 |
| 1 | 2 | 4 | 6 | 9 | 11 | | | | | | | | | | | | | | | | | 8 | 10 | 3 | | | 5 | | | | | | | | | | | | 19 |
| 1 | 2 | 5 | 6 | 9 | 11 | | | 7 | | | | | | | | | | | | | | 8 | 4 | 10 | 3 | | | | | | | | | | | | | | 20 |
| 1 | 2 | 5 | 4 | 10 | 11 | | | | | | | | | | | | | | | | | | 6 | | 3 | | | | | | | | | | | | | | 21 |
| 1 | 2 | 5 | 4 | 9 | | | 7 | 6 | | | | | | | | | | | | | | 8 | | 10 | 3 | | | 11 | | | | | | | | | | | 22 |
| 1 | 2 | 5 | 4 | 8 | | | 7 | 6 | | | | | | | | | | | | | | 9 | | | | | | | 11 | | | | | | | | | | 23 |
| 1 | 2 | | 4 | 10 | 6 | | | 9 | | | | | | | | | | | | | | 7 | 8 | | 3 | | 5 | | 11 | | | | | | | | | | 24 |
| 1 | 2 | 5 | 4 | 10 | 6 | | | 9 | | | | | | | | | | | | | | 7 | | | 3 | | | | 11 | 8 | | | | | | | | | 25 |
| 1 | 2 | 5 | 4 | 10 | | | | 9 | | | | | | | | | | | | | | 7 | | | 3 | | | | 11 | 8 | 6 | | | | | | | | 26 |
| 1 | 2 | 5 | 4 | 10 | 6 | | | 9 | | | | | | | | | | | | | | 7 | | | 3 | | | | 11 | | 8 | | | | | | | | 27 |
| 1 | 2 | 5 | 4 | 10 | | | | 8 | | | | | | | | | | | | | | 7 | 6 | | 3 | | | | 9 | 11 | | | | | | | | | 28 |
| 1 | 2 | 5 | 4 | 10 | | | | 9 | | | | | | | | | | | | | | 7 | | | 3 | 6 | | | 11 | | | | | | | | | | 29 |
| 1 | 2 | 5 | 4 | 8 | | | | 3 | | | | | | | | | | | | | | 9 | | | | | | | 11 | | | | | | | | | | 30 |
| 30 | 3 | 30 | 27 | 1 | 4 | 1 | 30 | 6 | 28 | 19 | 2 | 9 | 12 | 2 | 10 | 3 | 1 | 6 | 1 | 2 | 5 | 1 | 1 | 1 | 2 | 2 | 16 | 6 | 10 | 3 | 14 | 3 | 2 | 5 | 3 | 7 | 2 | 3 | |
| | 1 | | | | | | 2 | 2 | 14 | 3 | | 2 | 5 | | | | | | | | 1 | | | | | | | 1 | 5 | 1 | 1 | | 1 | | | 2 | 1 | 1 | |

1 own-goal

| Mew | Lumberg | Silcock | Hilditch | Manuel | Clayton | Worsencroft | Meehan | Myers | Woodcock | Ellis | Murray | Coombes | Hodge, James | Connor | Haywood | Williams O | Baguley | Dunn | Reed | Davies A | Howarth | Williams W | Hall | Molyneux | Forster | Tickle | Jones T | Cookson SP | Langford | Peplow | Makin | Hudson EK | Nightingale | Kinsella-Bates | Wall | Hopkin | Albinson | Lomas | |
|---|---|---|---|---|---|---|---|---|---|---|---|---|---|---|---|---|---|---|---|---|---|---|---|---|---|---|---|---|---|---|---|---|---|---|---|---|---|---|---|
| 1 | 2 | 4 | | 7 | | | 10 | 6 | | | | 9 | | | | | | | | | | 8 | | | 3 | | | | 11 | | | | | | | | | | 31 |
| 1 | 2 | 4 | | 7 | | | 10 | 6 | | | | 9 | | | | | | | | | | 8 | | | 3 | | | | 11 | | | | | | | | | | 32 |
| 1 | 2 | 5 | 4 | 10 | 6 | | | | | | | 7 | | | | | | | | | | 8 | | | 3 | | | | 11 | | | | | | | | | | 33 |
| 1 | 2 | 5 | 4 | 10 | | | 9 | | 7 | | 8 | | | | | | | | | | | | | | 3 | | | | 11 | 6 | | | | | | | | | 34 |
| 1 | 2 | 5 | 4 | 10 | 6 | | | 3 | | | | | | | | | | | | | | | | | | | | | 11 | | | | | | | | | | 35 |
| 1 | 2 | 5 | 4 | 10 | | | | 3 | | | | | | | | | | | | | | 7 | | | | | | | 11 | | | | | | | | | | 36 |
| 6 | 6 | 6 | | 6 | | | 6 | 4 | | | | 5 | | 1 | | | | 2 | | | | 4 | | | 4 | | | | 6 | 1 | | | | | | | | | |
| | | | | | | | 3 | | | | | | | | | | | | | | | | | | 1 | | | | | | | | | | | 1 | | | |

Match 10: Cope played number 7; Match 11: Green played number 9, scoring twice; Match 13: J.E.Worrall played number 2, Nuttall played number 4 and Duncan played number 8; Match 15: Hilton played number 6 and Braddick played number 7; Match 19: Carr played number 7; Match 21: Carr played number 7, Bourne played number 8 and Smith played number 9; Match 23: Barlow played number 3 and Barnett played number 10; Match 29: Spence played number 8, scoring four times; Match 30: Catlow played number 6, Hodgkiss played number 7 and Potts played number 10, scoring once; Match 31: Walker played number 5; Match 32: Walker played number 5; Match 33: Spence played number 9; Match 35: Norton played number 7, Potts played number 8, scoring once and Spence played number 9, scoring once; Match 36: Grimwood played number 6, Smith played number 8, scoring once and Spence played number 9, scoring once.

Match 15: Haywood listed as playing number 6 by the football League; Match 35: Makin listed as playing number 4 by the Football League.

373

# 1939-40

Manager: Walter Crickmer

| 1 | Aug | 26 | (h) | Grimsby T | W | 4-0 | Bryant, Carey, Pearson, Wrigglesworth | 22,537 |
|---|-----|----|-----|-----------|---|-----|---------------------------------------|--------|
| 2 |     | 30 | (a) | Chelsea | D | 1-1 | Bryant | 15,157 |
| 3 | Sep | 2 | (a) | Charlton A | L | 0-2 | | 8,608 |

FINAL LEAGUE POSITION: 10th in Division One when competition suspended — Appearances / Goals

| 4 | Oct | 21 | (h) | Manchester C | L | 0-4 | | 7,000 |
|----|-----|----|-----|--------------|---|-----|------------------------------------------------|--------|
| 5 |     | 28 | (a) | Chester | W | 4-0 | Pearson 2, Smith 2 | 5,500 |
| 6 | Nov | 11 | (h) | Crewe A | W | 5-1 | Carey, Hanlon, Pearson, Smith, Vose | 3,000 |
| 7 |     | 18 | (a) | Liverpool | L | 0-1 | | 5,000 |
| 8 |     | 25 | (h) | Port Vale | W | 8-1 | Wrigglesworth 5, Asquith, Pearson, Smith | 2,000 |
| 9 | Dec | 2 | (a) | Tranmere R | W | 4-2 | Smith 2, Hanlon, Warner | 2,500 |
| 10 |    | 9 | (a) | Stockport C | W | 7-4 | Pearson 2, Smith 2, Hanlon, McKay, Opp own-goal | 3,000 |
| 11 |    | 23 | (h) | Wrexham | W | 5-1 | Pearson 2, Roughton, Hanlon, Butt | 2,000 |
| 12 | Jan | 6 | (a) | Everton | L | 2-3 | McKay, Smith | 2,500 |
| 13 |    | 20 | (h) | Stoke C | W | 4-3 | Jones 2, Butt, Pearson | 3,000 |
| 14 | Feb | 10 | (a) | Manchester C | L | 0-1 | | 5,000 |
| 15 |    | 24 | (h) | Chester | W | 5-1 | Carey, Manley, Pearson, Opp own-goals 2 | 6,000 |
| 16 | Mar | 9 | (a) | Crewe A | W | 4-1 | Smith 2, Butt, Pearson | 3,000 |
| 17 |    | 16 | (h) | Liverpool | W | 1-0 | Pearson | 6,000 |
| 18 |    | 23 | (a) | Port Vale | W | 3-1 | McKay 2, Pearson | 5,000 |
| 19 |    | 30 | (h) | Tranmere R | W | 6-1 | Smith 3, McKay, Roberts, Roughton | 6,000 |
| 20 | Apr | 6 | (h) | Stockport C | W | 6-1 | Butt 2, Pearson 2, Roughton, Wrigglesworth | 8,000 |
| 21 | May | 6 | (h) | New Brighton | W | 6-0 | Smith 2, Asquith, Butt, Whalley, Wrigglesworth | 1,000 |
| 22 |    | 13 | (a) | Wrexham | L | 2-3 | Butt 2 | 4,000 |
| 23 |    | 18 | (a) | New Brighton | L | 0-6 | | 2,000 |
| 24 |    | 25 | (a) | Stoke C | L | 2-3 | Burdett 2 | 2,000 |
| 25 | Jun | 1 | (h) | Everton | L | 0-3 | | 6,000 |

FINAL LEAGUE POSITION: 4th in War Regional League (Western Division) — Appearances / Goals

## League War Cup

| 1 | Apr | 20 | (h) | Manchester C | L | 0-1 | | 21,874 |
|---|-----|----|-----|--------------|---|-----|-------------------------|--------|
|   |     | 27 | (a) | Manchester C | W | 2-0 | Pearson, Wrigglesworth | 21,569 |
| 2 | May | 4 | (a) | Blackburn R | W | 2-1 | Carey, Smith | 8,800 |
|   |     | 11 | (h) | Blackburn R | L | 1-3 | Carey | 12,551 |

Appearances / Goals

Players (columns, left→right): Breedon, Redwood, Griffiths, Warner, Vose, McKay, Bryant, Carey, Smith, Pearson, Wrigglesworth, Hanlon, Chilton, Whalley, Wassall, Asquith, Roughton, Mitten, Butt, Nicholson, Kilshaw, Jones, Manley, Fairhurst, Roberts, Porter, Toseland, Goddall, Gemmell, Briggs, Burdett, Anderson, Dougal, Matthews, Herd, Doherty, Carter.

| Bre | Red | Gri | War | Vos | McK | Bry | Car | Smi | Pea | Wri | Han | Chi | Wha | Was | Asq | Rou | Mit | Match |
|---|---|---|---|---|---|---|---|---|---|---|---|---|---|---|---|---|---|---|
| 1 | 2 | 3 | 4 | 5 | 6 | 7 | 8 | 9 | 10 | 11 | | | | | | | | 1 |
| 1 | 2 | 3 | 4 | 5 | 6 | 7 | 8 | | 10 | 11 | 9 | | | | | | | 2 |
| 1 | 2 | 3 | 4 | | | 7 | | | 10 | 11 | | 5 | 6 | 8 | 9 | | | 3 |
| 3 | 3 | 3 | 3 | 2 | 2 | 3 | 2 | 1 | 3 | 3 | 1 | 1 | 1 | 1 | 1 | 1 | | |
| | | | | | | | 2 | 1 | | | | | 1 | 1 | | | | |

| Bre | Red | Gri | War | Vos | McK | Bry | Car | Smi | Pea | Wri | Han | Chi | Wha | Was | Asq | Rou | Mit | … | Match |
|---|---|---|---|---|---|---|---|---|---|---|---|---|---|---|---|---|---|---|---|
| 1 | | 3 | 4 | 5 | 6 | 11 | 8 | | 10 | | | 7 | | | | 9 | 2 | | 4 |
| 1 | | 3 | 4 | 5 | 6 | | 8 | 11 | 10 | | | 7 | | | | 9 | 2 | | 5 |
| 1 | | 3 | 6 | 5 | 7 | | 2 | 10 | 8 | 11 | | | | | 4 | 9 | | | 6 |
| 1 | 2 | | 5 | | 6 | | 4 | 9 | 10 | 11 | | 3 | | | | 7 | 8 | | 7 |
| 1 | 2 | | 4 | | 6 | | 5 | 9 | 8 | 11 | 7 | | | | | 10 | 3 | | 8 |
| 1 | 2 | | 4 | | 6 | | 5 | 9 | 10 | 11 | 7 | | | | | 8 | 3 | | 9 |
| 1 | | | 4 | 5 | 6 | | 2 | 9 | 10 | 11 | 7 | | | | 3 | | 8 | | 10 |
| 1 | | 3 | 4 | | 6 | | 5 | 9 | 10 | 11 | 7 | | | | 2 | | 8 | | 11 |
| 1 | | 3 | 4 | | 6 | | 5 | 10 | 9 | 11 | 7 | | | | 2 | | 8 | | 12 |
| 1 | 2 | | 4 | | 6 | | 3 | | 8 | | 9 | | 11 | 5 | 7 | 10 | | | 13 |
| 1 | 2 | | 4 | | 6 | | 10 | 9 | | 11 | | 3 | | 8 | 5 | 7 | | | 14 |
| 1 | 2 | | 4 | | 7 | | 8 | 9 | 10 | | | 3 | | 5 | 11 | 6 | | | 15 |
| 1 | | 3 | 4 | | 6 | | 9 | 8 | 11 | | 2 | | 10 | 7 | 5 | | | | 16 |
| 1 | 2 | | | | 11 | | 4 | 9 | 8 | | 3 | | 10 | 5 | 7 | 6 | | | 17 |
| 1 | 2 | | 5 | | 4 | | 9 | 10 | 8 | 11 | 3 | | 7 | 6 | | | | | 18 |
| | 3 | | 5 | | 4 | | 8 | 10 | 9 | 11 | 2 | | 6 | 1 | 7 | | | | 19 |
| | 3 | | 4 | | 6 | | 7 | 9 | 8 | 11 | 2 | | 10 | 5 | 1 | | | | 20 |
| 1 | 3 | | | | 6 | 9 | 11 | | 4 | 8 | 2 | | 10 | 7 | 5 | | | | 21 |
| 1 | 3 | | | | 6 | 10 | 9 | 11 | 4 | | 2 | | 8 | 7 | 5 | | | | 22 |
| 1 | 3 | | 4 | | 6 | 8 | 9 | 11 | 10 | 2 | | 5 | 7 | | | | | | 23 |
| | 2 | | | | | 10 | 11 | 6 | 7 | 11 | | 1 | 3 | 5 | 9 | 4 | 8 | | 24 |
| | 2 | | | | 6 | 4 | 1 | 3 | 5 | 9 | 7 | 8 | 10 | 11 | | | | | 25 |

Totals (appearances):
18, 21, –, 16, 5, 19, 1, 19, 18, 17, 13, 9, –, 2, –, –, 6, 19 | 3, 1, –, 11, 4, 6, 3, 9, 2, 3, 2, 1, 2, 2, 2, 2, 1, 1, 1, 1, 1, 1

Totals (goals):
1, 1, 5, 2, 16, 15, 7, 4 (Hanlon), 1, 2, 3, 8, 2, 1, 1, 2

3 own-goals

| Bre | Red | Gri | War | Vos | McK | Bry | Car | Smi | Pea | Wri | Han | … | Rou | Mit | … | Rob | Por | Match |
|---|---|---|---|---|---|---|---|---|---|---|---|---|---|---|---|---|---|---|
| 1 | 2 | 7 | 4 | | 6 | | 8 | 9 | 10 | 11 | | | | 3 | | | 5 | 1 |
| 1 | 2 | | 4 | | 6 | | 8 | 9 | 10 | 11 | 7 | | | 3 | | | 5 | |
| 1 | 2 | | 4 | | 6 | | 8 | 9 | | 11 | | | 10 | 3 | | 7 | 5 | 2 |
| 1 | 2 | | 4 | | 6 | | 8 | 9 | | 11 | | | 10 | 3 | | 7 | 5 | |
| 4 | 4 | 1 | 4 | | 4 | | 4 | 4 | 2 | 4 | 1 | | 2 | 4 | | 2 | 4 | |
| | | | | | | | | 2 | 1 | 1 | 1 | | | | | | | |

375

# 1940-41

Manager: Walter Crickmer

| 1 | Aug | 31 | (a) | Rochdale | W | 3-1 | Aston, J.Carey, Smith | 3,000 |
|---|---|---|---|---|---|---|---|---|
| 2 | Sep | 7 | (h) | Bury | D | 0-0 | | 2,000 |
| 3 | | 14 | (a) | Oldham A | L | 1-2 | Farrow | 5,000 |
| 4 | | 21 | (h) | Oldham A | L | 2-3 | Smith 2 | 3,000 |
| 5 | | 28 | (a) | Manchester C | L | 1-4 | Smith | 10,000 |
| 6 | Oct | 5 | (h) | Manchester C | L | 0-2 | | 10,000 |
| 7 | | 12 | (a) | Burnley | W | 1-0 | Warner | 2,500 |
| 8 | | 19 | (h) | Preston NE | W | 4-1 | Dodds 2, Buchan, J.Carey | 3,500 |
| 9 | | 26 | (a) | Preston NE | L | 1-3 | Bryant | 2,200 |
| 10 | Nov | 2 | (h) | Burnley | W | 4-1 | Butt 2, J.Carey, Smith | 1,000 |
| 11 | | 9 | (a) | Everton | L | 2-5 | Dodds, Smith | 1,000 |
| 12 | | 16 | (h) | Everton | D | 0-0 | | 2,000 |
| 13 | | 23 | (a) | Liverpool | D | 2-2 | Smith, Warner | 4,000 |
| 14 | | 30 | (h) | Liverpool | W | 2-0 | Butt, Smith | 700 |
| 15 | Dec | 7 | (a) | Blackburn R | D | 5-5 | Dodds 2, Aston, Bryant, Mitten | 2,000 |
| 16 | | 14 | (h) | Rochdale | L | 3-4 | Smith 2, J.Carey | 1,000 |
| 17 | | 21 | (a) | Bury | L | 1-4 | McKay | 2,000 |
| 18 | | 25 | (a) | Stockport C | W | 3-1 | Smith 2, Burrows | 1,500 |
| 19 | | 28 | (h) | Blackburn R | W | 9-0 | Smith 5, J.Carey 2, Aston, Mitten | 1,500 |
| 20 | Jan | 4 | (a) | Blackburn R | W | 2-0 | Smith 2 | 1,000 |
| 21 | | 11 | (h) | Blackburn R | D | 0-0 | | 2,000 |
| 22 | | 18 | (a) | Bolton W | L | 2-3 | Mears, Smith | 1,000 |
| 23 | | 25 | (h) | Bolton W | W | 4-1 | Pearson 2, J.Carey, Smith | 2,000 |
| 24 | Mar | 1 | (a) | Chesterfield | D | 1-1 | Smith | 2,000 |
| 25 | | 8 | (h) | Bury | W | 7-3 | J.Carey 3, Rowley 3, Smith | 3,000 |
| 26 | | 22 | (a) | Oldham A | W | 1-0 | Smith | 1,500 |
| 27 | | 29 | (a) | Blackpool | L | 0-2 | | 4,000 |
| 28 | Apr | 5 | (h) | Blackpool | L | 2-3 | Mears, Smith | 2,000 |
| 29 | | 12 | (a) | Everton | W | 2-1 | Rowley 2 | 4,000 |
| 30 | | 14 | (a) | Manchester C | W | 7-1 | Rowley 4, Pearson 2, Smith | 10,000 |
| 31 | | 19 | (a) | Chester | W | 6-4 | Rowley 5, J.Carey | 3,500 |
| 32 | | 26 | (a) | Liverpool | L | 1-2 | Rowley | 2,000 |
| 33 | May | 3 | (h) | Liverpool | D | 1-1 | Rowley | 1,500 |
| 34 | | 10 | (a) | Bury | L | 1-5 | Rowley | 2,000 |
| 35 | | 17 | (h) | Burnley | W | 1-0 | J.Carey | 10,000 |

FINAL LEAGUE POSITION: 7th in North Regional League

Appearances
Goals

League War Cup

| 1 | Feb | 15 | (h) | Everton | D | 2-2 | Rowley, Whalley | 5,000 |
|---|---|---|---|---|---|---|---|---|
| | | 22 | (a) | Everton | L | 1-2 | Rowley | 3,000 |

Appearances
Goals

Matches 1-35 inclusive were in the North Regional League. There were 36 teams involved and the positions were decided on goal-average. No reference was made to games played home and away and no points were awarded.
Matches 20, 21, 22, 23, 31 (after extra-time), and 35 were in the Lancashire Cup as well as counting towards the League.

| Breedon | Redwood | Roughton | Warner | Brown | McKay | Bryant | Carey J | Smith | Bellis | Aston | Ainsley | Jones B | Farrow | Bartholomew | O'Donnell | Burbank | Vose | Buchan | Dodds | Jones S | McPhillips | Butt | Mitten | Asquith | Whalley | Porter | Gemmell | Emptage | Wrigglesworth | Burrows | Pearson | Mears | Rowley J | Couser | Carey W | Johnson | Griffiths | Gorman | |
|---|---|---|---|---|---|---|---|---|---|---|---|---|---|---|---|---|---|---|---|---|---|---|---|---|---|---|---|---|---|---|---|---|---|---|---|---|---|---|---|
| 1 | 2 | 3 | 4 | 5 | 6 | 7 | 8 | 9 | 10 | 11 | | | | | | | | | | | | | | | | | | | | | | | | | | | | | 1 |
| 1 | 2 | 3 | 4 | 5 | 6 | 7 | 8 | | | 10 | 11 | 9 | | | | | | | | | | | | | | | | | | | | | | | | | | | 2 |
| 1 | 2 | 3 | 7 | 5 | 6 | | 10 | 9 | | 8 | | | 11 | 4 | | | | | | | | | | | | | | | | | | | | | | | | | 3 |
| 1 | 2 | 3 | | 5 | 6 | | 8 | 9 | 11 | | | | | | 4 | 7 | 10 | | | | | | | | | | | | | | | | | | | | | | 4 |
| 1 | 2 | | 4 | 5 | 6 | 3 | 9 | 11 | | | | | | | | | 8 | | 10 | 7 | | | | | | | | | | | | | | | | | | | 5 |
| 1 | 2 | | 4 | 3 | 6 | | 10 | 9 | | | | | | | | | 7 | 11 | 5 | 8 | | | | | | | | | | | | | | | | | | | 6 |
| 1 | 2 | | 4 | 5 | 6 | 7 | 10 | | | 8 | | | | | | | | | 11 | | 9 | 3 | | | | | | | | | | | | | | | | | 7 |
| 1 | 2 | 3 | 4 | 5 | 6 | 7 | 8 | | | | | | | | | | | | 11 | | | | 10 | 9 | | | | | | | | | | | | | | | 8 |
| 1 | 2 | 3 | 4 | 5 | 6 | 7 | | 9 | | 8 | | | | | | | | | 11 | | | | 10 | | | | | | | | | | | | | | | | 9 |
| 1 | 2 | 3 | 4 | 5 | 6 | 7 | 8 | 9 | | | | | | | | | | | | | | 10 | 11 | | | | | | | | | | | | | | | | 10 |
| 1 | | 3 | 4 | 2 | 6 | 7 | 8 | 9 | | | | | | | | | 5 | | 10 | | | | 11 | | | | | | | | | | | | | | | | 11 |
| 1 | 2 | 3 | 4 | 5 | 6 | 7 | 10 | 9 | | | | | | | | | | | | | | | 11 | 8 | | | | | | | | | | | | | | | 12 |
| 1 | 2 | 3 | 4 | 5 | 6 | 8 | 10 | 9 | | | | | | | | | | | | | | | 11 | | 7 | | | | | | | | | | | | | | 13 |
| 1 | 2 | 3 | 4 | | 6 | 7 | 5 | 9 | | | | | | | | | | | | | | 8 | 11 | 10 | | | | | | | | | | | | | | | 14 |
| 1 | | | 4 | 6 | 7 | 5 | 9 | | | 8 | | | | | | | | | 10 | | | | 11 | | 3 | 2 | | | | | | | | | | | | | 15 |
| 1 | 2 | 3 | 4 | | 6 | | 8 | 9 | | | | | | | | | | | | | | | 11 | | | 5 | | | | 10 | 7 | | | | | | | | 16 |
| 1 | 2 | 3 | 4 | | 6 | 7 | 10 | 9 | | 8 | | | | | | | | | | | | | 11 | | | 5 | | | | | | | | | | | | | 17 |
| 1 | 2 | | 4 | | | 7 | 8 | 9 | | | | | | | | | | | | | | | | | 6 | 5 | | | | 11 | 10 | | | | | | | | 18 |
| 1 | 2 | 3 | 4 | | | 7 | 9 | | | | | | | | | | | | 10 | | | | 11 | | 6 | 5 | | | | 8 | | | | | | | | | 19 |
| 1 | 2 | 3 | 4 | | | | 8 | 9 | | | | | | | | | | | 7 | | | | 11 | | 6 | 5 | | | | | | 10 | | | | | | | 20 |
| 1 | 2 | 3 | 4 | | | 7 | 8 | 9 | | | | | | | | | | | | | | | 11 | | 6 | 5 | | | | | | 10 | | | | | | | 21 |
| | | 3 | 4 | 2 | | 8 | 7 | 9 | | | | | | | | | | | | | | | 11 | | 6 | 5 | | | | | | 10 | | | | | | | 22 |
| 1 | 2 | 3 | 4 | | | 7 | 8 | 9 | | | | | | | | | | | | | | | 11 | | 6 | 5 | | | | | | 10 | | | | | | | 23 |
| 1 | 2 | 3 | 4 | | | 10 | 7 | 8 | 9 | | | | | | | | | | | | | | | | 6 | 5 | | | | | | | 11 | | | | | | 24 |
| 1 | 2 | 3 | 4 | | | 7 | 8 | 9 | | | | | | | | | | | | | | | | | 6 | 5 | | | | | | | 10 | 11 | | | | | 25 |
| 1 | 2 | 3 | 4 | | | 7 | 8 | 9 | | | | | | | | | | | | | | | | | 6 | 5 | | | | | | | 11 | 10 | | | | | 26 |
| 1 | 2 | 3 | 4 | | | | 8 | 9 | | | | | | | | | | | | | | | 11 | | 6 | 5 | | | | | 7 | | 10 | | | | | | 27 |
| 1 | | 2 | 4 | | | 7 | | 9 | | | | | | | | | | | | | | | 11 | | 6 | 3 | | | | | | 10 | 8 | | | | | | 28 |
| | | 3 | 4 | | | 1 | 8 | | 10 | | | | | | | | | | | | | | 11 | | 6 | 5 | | | | | | | 9 | | 2 | | | | 29 |
| 1 | | | 4 | | | 2 | 9 | 8 | | | | | | | | | | | | | | | | 7 | 6 | 5 | | | | | 10 | | 11 | | | 3 | | | 30 |
| 1 | | | 4 | | | | 8 | 10 | | | | | | | | | | | | | | | 11 | | 6 | 5 | | | | 7 | | | 9 | | | 3 | 2 | | 31 |
| 1 | | | 4 | | | | 8 | 9 | | 5 | | | | | | | | | | | | | | 7 | 6 | 3 | | | | | 11 | | | | | | 2 | | 32 |
| 1 | | | 4 | | | | 8 | | | | | | | | | | | | | | | | | | 6 | 5 | | | | | 11 | | 9 | | | | | 2 | 33 |
| 1 | | 3 | 4 | | | | 5 | 8 | | | | | | | | | | | | | | | 11 | | 6 | | | | | 7 | | | 9 | | | | | 2 | 34 |
| 1 | | 3 | 4 | | | | 8 | 7 | | | | | | | | | | | | | | | 11 | | 6 | 5 | | | | 10 | | | 9 | | | | | | 35 |
| 33 | 24 | 26 | 34 | 13 | 19 | 20 | 32 | 32 | 4 | 11 | 1 | 1 | 3 | 3 | 5 | 1 | 3 | 2 | 4 | 1 | 1 | 2 | 21 | 2 | 20 | 19 | 1 | 1 | 2 | 5 | 5 | 4 | 11 | 2 | 1 | 2 | 2 | 2 | |
| | 2 | | 1 | 2 | 12 | 26 | | | | 3 | | | | | | | 1 | | | | | | 1 | 5 | 3 | 2 | | | | 1 | 4 | 2 | 17 | | | | | | |

| Breedon | Redwood | Roughton | Warner | Brown | McKay | Bryant | Carey J | Smith | Bellis | Aston | Ainsley | Jones B | Farrow | Bartholomew | O'Donnell | Burbank | Vose | Buchan | Dodds | Jones S | McPhillips | Butt | Mitten | Asquith | Whalley | Porter | Gemmell | Emptage | Wrigglesworth | Burrows | Pearson | Mears | Rowley J | Couser | Carey W | Johnson | Griffiths | Gorman | |
|---|---|---|---|---|---|---|---|---|---|---|---|---|---|---|---|---|---|---|---|---|---|---|---|---|---|---|---|---|---|---|---|---|---|---|---|---|---|---|---|
| 1 | 2 | 3 | 4 | | | 7 | 8 | 9 | | | | | | | | | | | | | | | 10 | | 6 | 5 | | | | | | | 11 | | | | | | 1 |
| 1 | 2 | 3 | 4 | | | 7 | 8 | 9 | | | | | | | | | | | | | | | 10 | | 6 | 5 | | | | | | | 11 | | | | | | |
| 2 | 2 | 2 | 2 | | | 2 | 2 | 2 | | | | | | | | | | | | | | | 2 | | 2 | 2 | | | | | | | 2 | | | | | | |
| | | | | | | | | | | | | | | | | | | | | | | | | | | 1 | | | | | | | 2 | | | | | | |

Match 18: Stocks played number 3; Match 22: Clorley played number 1; Match 28: Briggs played number 5; Match 29: Wyles played number 7; Match 32: A.Rowley played number 10; Match 33: Watkins played number 7, Topping played number 3 and Olsen played number 10; Match 34: Bagley played number 10; Match 35: Topping played number 2.

Match 34: W.Carey listed as playing number 5 by the Football League.

377

# 1941-42

Manager: Walter Crickmer

| | | | | | | | |
|---|---|---|---|---|---|---|---|
| 1 | Aug | 30 | (h) | New Brighton | W 13-1 | J.Rowley 7, Smith 3, Bryant 2, Mitten | 2,000 |
| 2 | Sep | 6 | (a) | New Brighton | D 3-3 | Carey, Morris, Whalley | 1,500 |
| 3 | | 13 | (a) | Stockport C | W 5-1 | J.Rowley 4, Mitten | 3,000 |
| 4 | | 20 | (h) | Stockport C | W 7-1 | J.Rowley 4, Carey, Mitten, Warner | 2,000 |
| 5 | | 27 | (h) | Everton | L 2-3 | J.Rowley, Smith | 4,000 |
| 6 | Oct | 4 | (a) | Everton | W 3-1 | Carey, J.Rowley, Smith | 6,000 |
| 7 | | 11 | (a) | Chester | W 7-0 | Mitten 2, Smith 2, Morris, Warner, Whalley | 3,500 |
| 8 | | 18 | (h) | Chester | W 8-1 | J.Rowley 4, Smith 2, Bryant, Carey | 2,000 |
| 9 | | 25 | (a) | Stoke C | D 1-1 | Carey | 5,000 |
| 10 | Nov | 1 | (h) | Stoke C | W 3-0 | Carey, J.Rowley, Whalley | 4,000 |
| 11 | | 8 | (h) | Tranmere R | W 6-1 | J.Rowley 5, Smith | 2,000 |
| 12 | | 15 | (a) | Tranmere R | D 1-1 | J.Rowley | 2,000 |
| 13 | | 22 | (a) | Liverpool | D 1-1 | Smith | 10,000 |
| 14 | | 29 | (h) | Liverpool | D 2-2 | J.Rowley 2 | 3,000 |
| 15 | Dec | 6 | (h) | Wrexham | W 10-3 | Carey 4, J.Rowley 3, Smith 2, Bryant | 2,000 |
| 16 | | 13 | (a) | Wrexham | W 4-3 | Morris 4 | 2,500 |
| 17 | | 20 | (a) | Manchester C | L 1-2 | Morris | 10,000 |
| 18 | | 25 | (h) | Manchester C | D 2-2 | J.Rowley, Smith | 20,000 |

FINAL LEAGUE POSITION: 4th in Football League Northern Section (First Championship)      Appearances
Goals

| | | | | | | | |
|---|---|---|---|---|---|---|---|
| 19 | Dec | 27 | (h) | Bolton W | W 3-1 | J.Rowley 2, Morris | 5,500 |
| 20 | Jan | 3 | (a) | Bolton W | D 2-2 | Pearson, J.Rowley | 2,500 |
| 21 | | 10 | (h) | Oldham A | D 1-1 | Morris | 5,000 |
| 22 | | 17 | (a) | Oldham A | W 3-1 | Carey 2, J.Rowley | 6,000 |
| 23 | | 31 | (a) | Southport | W 3-1 | Carey, J.Rowley, Smith | 2,000 |
| 24 | Feb | 14 | (a) | Sheffield U | W 2-0 | Carey, J.Rowley | 12,000 |
| 25 | | 21 | (h) | Preston NE | L 0-2 | | 4,000 |
| 26 | | 28 | (a) | Preston NE | W 3-1 | J.Rowley 2, Carey | 6,000 |
| 27 | Mar | 21 | (a) | Sheffield U | D 2-2 | Catterick, Smith | 6,000 |
| 28 | | 28 | (h) | Southport | W 4-2 | Catterick 2, Carey 2 | 3,000 |
| 29 | Apr | 4 | (a) | Blackburn R | W 2-1 | Catterick, Warner | 5,000 |
| 30 | | 6 | (h) | Blackburn R | W 3-1 | Carey 2, Bryant | 9,000 |
| 31 | | 11 | (h) | Wolves | W 5-4 | Catterick 2, Carey, Morris, Smith | 9,000 |
| 32 | | 18 | (a) | Wolves | L 0-2* | | 12,000 |
| 33 | | 25 | (h) | Oldham A† | W 5-1 | Carey 2, Morris 2, Catterick | 4,000 |
| 34 | May | 2 | (a) | Oldham A† | W 2-1 | Carey, Smith | 2,000 |
| 35 | | 9 | (a) | Blackburn R† | D 1-1 | Carey | 1,500 |
| 36 | | 16 | (h) | Blackburn R† | L 0-1 | | 4,000 |
| 37 | | 23 | (a) | Manchester C | W 3-1 | Worrall 2, Whalley | 6,000 |

FINAL LEAGUE POSITION: 1st in Football League Northern Section (Second Championship)      Appearances
*After extra-time      Goals

In the Second Championship, points were calculated on 23 games and the results also included games played
in the League Cup Qualifying and Knock-out Competition and regional cups (see below).
Matches 19-28 inclusive were also in the League Cup Qualifying Competition.
Matches 29-32 inclusive were also in the League Cup Knock-out Competition.
Matches marked thus † also counted in the Lancashire Cup.

| Breedon | Redwood | Roughton | Waddington | Warner | Whalley | Bryant | Mitten | Smith J | Carey J | Rowley J | Shore | Porter | Fidler | Morris | Taylor | Pearson S | Rowley A | Lee | Wrigglesworth | Roach | Chilton | Griffiths J | Emptage | Catterick | Dougan | Robinson R | Holdcroft | Robinson JA | Worrall H | Dougal J | Hornby | # |
|---|---|---|---|---|---|---|---|---|---|---|---|---|---|---|---|---|---|---|---|---|---|---|---|---|---|---|---|---|---|---|---|---|
| 1 | 2 | 3 | 4 | 5 | 6 | 7 | 8 | 9 | 10 | 11 | | | | | | | | | | | | | | | | | | | | | | 1 |
| 1 | 2 | 3 | | | 6 | 7 | 11 | | 8 | | 4 | 5 | 9 | 10 | | | | | | | | | | | | | | | | | | 2 |
| 1 | | 3 | | 4 | 6 | 7 | 8 | 9 | 2 | 11 | | 5 | | 10 | | | | | | | | | | | | | | | | | | 3 |
| 1 | 2 | 3 | | 4 | 6 | 7 | 8 | 9 | 10 | 11 | | 5 | | | | | | | | | | | | | | | | | | | | 4 |
| 1 | 2 | 3 | | 4 | 6 | 7 | 8 | 9 | 10 | 11 | | 5 | | | | | | | | | | | | | | | | | | | | 5 |
| 1 | 2 | 3 | | 4 | 6 | 7 | 11 | 9 | 10 | 8 | | 5 | | | | | | | | | | | | | | | | | | | | 6 |
| 1 | 2 | | | 4 | 6 | 11 | 8 | 9 | 3 | | 10 | 5 | | 7 | | | | | | | | | | | | | | | | | | 7 |
| 1 | 2 | 3 | | 4 | 6 | 7 | | 9 | 10 | 11 | | 5 | | 8 | | | | | | | | | | | | | | | | | | 8 |
| 1 | 2 | 3 | | 4 | 6 | 7 | 8 | 9 | 10 | 11 | | 5 | | | | | | | | | | | | | | | | | | | | 9 |
| 1 | 2 | 3 | | 4 | 6 | 7 | | 9 | 10 | 11 | | 5 | | 8 | | | | | | | | | | | | | | | | | | 10 |
| 1 | 2 | | | 4 | 6 | 7 | | 9 | 3 | 11 | | 5 | | 8 | 10 | | | | | | | | | | | | | | | | | 11 |
| 1 | 2 | 3 | | 4 | 6 | | 8 | 9 | 10 | 11 | | 5 | | 7 | | | | | | | | | | | | | | | | | | 12 |
| 1 | | 3 | | | 6 | | 8 | 9 | 2 | 11 | 4 | 5 | | 7 | | 10 | | | | | | | | | | | | | | | | 13 |
| 1 | 2 | 3 | | 4 | 6 | 7 | | 9 | 10 | 11 | | 5 | | | | | 8 | | | | | | | | | | | | | | | 14 |
| 1 | 2 | 3 | | 4 | 6 | 7 | | 9 | 10 | 11 | | 5 | | | | | | 8 | | | | | | | | | | | | | | 15 |
| 1 | | 3 | | 4 | 6 | 7 | | 9 | 2 | | 10 | 5 | | 8 | | | | 11 | | | | | | | | | | | | | | 16 |
| 1 | | 3 | | 4 | 6 | 7 | | 9 | 2 | 10 | | 5 | | 8 | | | | | 11 | | | | | | | | | | | | | 17 |
| 1 | | | | | 6 | 7 | 3 | 9 | 10 | | 4 | 5 | | | | 8 | | | 11 | 2 | | | | | | | | | | | | 18 |
| 18 | 13 | 15 | 1 | 15 | 18 | 16 | 11 | 17 | 17 | 15 | 5 | 17 | 1 | 10 | 1 | 2 | 1 | 2 | 2 | 1 | | | | | | | | | | | | |
| | | | | 2 | 3 | 4 | 5 | 14 | 10 | 34 | | | | 7 | | | | | | | | | | | | | | | | | | |
| 1 | | 7 | | | 6 | 2 | 8 | 3 | 9 | 4 | 5 | | | 10 | | | | 11 | | | | | | | | | | | | | | 19 |
| 1 | | | | | 6 | 7 | 2 | 11 | 4 | 3 | | | | 10 | | | | | 5 | | 8 | | 9 | | | | | | | | | 20 |
| 1 | | 3 | | 4 | 6 | 11 | | 8 | 9 | | 5 | | | 7 | | | | | | | 2 | | 10 | | | | | | | | | 21 |
| 1 | | 3 | | 4 | 6 | | | 9 | 10 | 11 | 5 | | | 7 | | | | | | | 8 | | 2 | | | | | | | | | 22 |
| 1 | | 3 | | 4 | 6 | | | 9 | 10 | 11 | 5 | | | 7 | | | | | | | 8 | | 2 | | | | | | | | | 23 |
| 1 | 2 | 3 | | 4 | 6 | 7 | 8 | 9 | 10 | | 5 | | | | | | | | | | 11 | | | | | | | | | | | 24 |
| 1 | | 3 | | 4 | 6 | 11 | | 8 | 10 | | 5 | | | 7 | | | | | | | 9 | | 2 | | | | | | | | | 25 |
| 1 | 2 | 3 | | 4 | 6 | | | 9 | 10 | 11 | 5 | | | 7 | | | | | | | 8 | | | | | | | | | | | 26 |
| 1 | 2 | 3 | | 4 | 6 | 7 | | 9 | 10 | | 5 | | | | | | | | | | 8 | | | 11 | | | | | | | | 27 |
| 1 | | 3 | | 4 | 6 | | | 9 | 10 | | 5 | | | 7 | | | | | | | 8 | | 2 | | 11 | | | | | | | 28 |
| 1 | | 3 | | 4 | 6 | 11 | | | 10 | | 5 | | | 7 | | | | | | | 9 | | 2 | | | | | | | | | 29 |
| 1 | 2 | 3 | | 4 | 6 | 7 | 11 | | 10 | | 5 | | | | | | | | | | 8 | | 9 | | | | | | | | | 30 |
| 1 | | 3 | | 4 | 6 | 7 | | 9 | 10 | | 5 | | | | | | | | | | 8 | | 2 | | 11 | | | | | | | 31 |
| 1 | 2 | 3 | | 4 | 6 | 7 | 8 | | 10 | | 5 | | | | | | | | | | 11 | | 9 | | | | | | | | | 32 |
| 1 | | | | 4 | 6 | 7 | 8 | | 10 | | 5 | | | | | | | | | | 11 | 3 | 2 | | 9 | | | | | | | 33 |
| 1 | | | 4 | | 6 | 7 | 8 | 9 | 10 | | 5 | | | | | | | | | | 11 | 3 | 2 | | | | | | | | | 34 |
| 1 | | | 4 | | 6 | 11 | 8 | 9 | 10 | | 5 | | | 7 | | | | | | | | 3 | 2 | | | | | | | | | 35 |
| 1 | | | 4 | 7 | 6 | 11 | 8 | 3 | 10 | | 5 | | | | | | | | | | 9 | | 2 | | | | | | | | | 36 |
| | | | 4 | | 6 | | 8 | | 10 | | 5 | | | | | | | | | | 2 | | | | | 1 | 3 | 7 | 9 | 11 | | 37 |
| 18 | 5 | 12 | 2 | 15 | 19 | 18 | 2 | 16 | 18 | 2 | 19 | 13 | | 5 | | | 1 | 2 | 6 | 1 | 9 | 1 | 10 | 1 | 1 | 1 | 1 | 1 | 1 | 1 | 1 | |
| | | | | 1 | 1 | 1 | 4 | 14 | 8 | | 5 | 1 | | | | | | | | | 7 | | 2 | | | | | | | | | |

Match 3: Fidler listed as playing number 4, Shore number 9 and Redwood number 11 by the Football League; Match 24: Morris listed as playing number 11 by the Football League.

# 1942-43

Manager: Walter Crickmer

| | | | | | | | |
|---|---|---|---|---|---|---|---|
| 1 | Aug | 29 | (a) | Everton | D 2-2 | Catterick, Pearson | 8,000 |
| 2 | Sep | 5 | (h) | Everton | W 2-1 | Carey, Mitten | 4,000 |
| 3 | | 12 | (h) | Chester | L 0-2 | | 3,000 |
| 4 | | 19 | (a) | Chester | D 2-2 | Catterick, Roughton | 3,000 |
| 5 | | 26 | (a) | Blackburn R | L 2-4 | Bryant, Catterick | 2,000 |
| 6 | Oct | 3 | (h) | Blackburn R | W 5-2 | J.Smith 3, Mitten, Morris | 4,000 |
| 7 | | 10 | (h) | Liverpool | L 3-4 | J.Smith 2, Mitten | 4,000 |
| 8 | | 17 | (a) | Liverpool | L 1-2 | Carey | 12,786 |
| 9 | | 24 | (a) | Stockport C | W 4-1 | Bellis 2, Carey, Opp own-goal | 2,000 |
| 10 | | 31 | (h) | Stockport C | W 3-1 | J.Smith 2, Bellis | 3,000 |
| 11 | Nov | 11 | (h) | Manchester C | W 2-1 | Pearson, Opp own-goal | 9,301 |
| 12 | | 14 | (a) | Manchester C | W 5-0 | J.Smith 3, Bryant 2 | 7,000 |
| 13 | | 21 | (a) | Tranmere R | W 5-0 | Morris 2, J.Smith 2, Opp own-goal | 4,000 |
| 14 | | 28 | (h) | Tranmere R | W 5-1 | Pearson 2, J.Rowley 2, J.Smith | 3,000 |
| 15 | Dec | 5 | (h) | Wrexham | W 6-1 | J.Smith 3, Bellis 2, Bryant | 2,000 |
| 16 | | 12 | (a) | Wrexham | W 5-2 | J.Smith 3, Bryant, Carey | 3,500 |
| 17 | | 19 | (a) | Bolton W | W 2-0 | Carey, Mitten | 2,000 |
| 18 | | 25 | (h) | Bolton W | W 4-0 | Carey 2, Bryant, Roughton | 2,000 |

FINAL LEAGUE POSITION: 4th in Football League North (First Championship)  Appearances
Goals

| | | | | | | | |
|---|---|---|---|---|---|---|---|
| 19 | Dec | 26 | (h) | Chester | W 3-0 | Bellis 2, Mitten | 10,449 |
| 20 | Jan | 2 | (a) | Chester | L 1-4 | J.Smith | 15,000 |
| 21 | | 9 | (a) | Blackpool | D 1-1 | Pearson | 5,000 |
| 22 | | 16 | (h) | Blackpool | W 5-3 | Buchan 3, Bryant, J.Smith | 17,381 |
| 23 | | 23 | (h) | Everton | L 1-4 | J.Smith | 7,764 |
| 24 | | 30 | (a) | Everton | W 5-0 | J.Smith 3, Buchan, Pearson | 14,000 |
| 25 | Feb | 6 | (a) | Manchester C | D 0-0 | | 17,577 |
| 26 | | 13 | (h) | Manchester C | D 1-1 | J.Smith | 16,326 |
| 27 | | 20 | (h) | Crewe A | W 7-0 | J.Smith 3, Pearson 2, Bryant, Morris | 5,000 |
| 28 | | 27 | (a) | Crewe A | W 3-2 | Bryant 2, Broadis | 4,000 |
| 29 | Mar | 6 | (h) | Manchester C | L 0-1 | | 28,962 |
| 30 | | 13 | (a) | Manchester C | L 0-2 | | 36,453 |
| 31 | | 20 | (h) | Bury† | W 4-1 | J.Rowley 3, Broadis | 2,000 |
| 32 | | 27 | (a) | Bury† | W 5-3 | Bellis, Hyde, McKay, J.Smith, R.Smith (og) | 2,000 |
| 33 | Apr | 3 | (h) | Crewe A† | W 4-1 | J.Smith 2, McKay, Hyde | 4,000 |
| 34 | | 10 | (a) | Crewe A† | W 6-0 | J.Smith 2, Black, Bryant, W.Griffiths, Pearson | 2,300 |
| 35 | | 17 | (h) | Oldham A† | W 3-0 | J.Smith 2, Bellis | 5,660 |
| 36 | | 24 | (a) | Oldham A† | L 1-3 | J.Smith | 6,267 |
| 37 | May | 1 | (h) | Sheffield U | W 2-0 | Carey, J.Smith | 5,000 |
| 38 | | 8 | (a) | Liverpool | W 3-1 | Bellis, Pearson, J.Rowley | 18,000 |
| 39 | | 15 | (h) | Liverpool | D 3-3 | J.Rowley 2, Roughton | 9,196 |

FINAL LEAGUE POSITION: 6th in Football League North (Second Championship)  Appearances
Goals

Matches 19-37 inclusive were in the Football League North (Second Championship).
Matches 19-28 inclusive were in the League Cup Qualifying Competition and also counted towards the League
as did Matches 29 & 30 (League War Cup Knock-out Competition).
Matches marked thus † were in the Lancashire Cup of which Matches 38 & 39 were the two-legged Final.
Only the Final games did not also count towards the League.

| Breedon | Griffiths J | Roughton | Porter | Carey | Whalley | Bryant | Smith J | Catterick | Pearson | Mitten | Warner | Roach | Asquith | Kippax | Lee | Morris | Barkas | Chadwick | Shore | Vose | Bellis | Rowley A | Harrison | Hall | McKay | Dimond | Rowley J | Walton | Anderson | Buchan | Broadis | Dougan | Hyde | Griffiths W | Griffiths G | Byrom | Eastwood | Walsh | |
|---|---|---|---|---|---|---|---|---|---|---|---|---|---|---|---|---|---|---|---|---|---|---|---|---|---|---|---|---|---|---|---|---|---|---|---|---|---|---|---|
| 1 | 2 | 3 | 4 | 5 | 6 | 7 | 8 | 9 | 10 | 11 | | | | | | | | | | | | | | | | | | | | | | | | | | | | | 1 |
| 1 | 2 | 3 | 4 | | 8 | 6 | | | | | 10 | 11 | 7 | 5 | 9 | | | | | | | | | | | | | | | | | | | | | | | | 2 |
| 1 | 2 | 3 | 4 | | 6 | 7 | 8 | 9 | | 5 | | | 10 | 11 | | | | | | | | | | | | | | | | | | | | | | | | | 3 |
| 1 | 3 | 5 | 4 | 8 | 6 | 7 | | 9 | | 11 | 2 | | | | 10 | | | | | | | | | | | | | | | | | | | | | | | | 4 |
| 1 | | 2 | 4 | | 6 | 7 | 8 | 9 | | | | | | 5 | | 10 | 3 | 11 | | | | | | | | | | | | | | | | | | | | | 5 |
| 1 | 3 | | 4 | 11 | 6 | 7 | 10 | | | | 8 | 5 | 2 | | 9 | | | | | | | | | | | | | | | | | | | | | | | | 6 |
| 1 | 2 | 3 | 4 | 9 | 6 | 7 | 10 | | | | 8 | 5 | | | | 11 | | | | | | | | | | | | | | | | | | | | | | | 7 |
| 1 | 2 | | 3 | 10 | 6 | 7 | | 9 | | | | | | | | 8 | | | 4 | 5 | 11 | | | | | | | | | | | | | | | | | | 8 |
| 1 | 2 | | 3 | 10 | 6 | 7 | 8 | | | | | | | | | | | | | 5 | 11 | | 9 | 4 | | | | | | | | | | | | | | | 9 |
| 1 | 2 | | 3 | 8 | 6 | | 10 | | | | | | | | 4 | | | | 9 | 5 | 11 | | | | 7 | | | | | | | | | | | | | | 10 |
| 1 | | 2 | 3 | | 6 | 7 | | 9 | | | 10 | 11 | 4 | | | | | | | 5 | 8 | | | | | | | | | | | | | | | | | | 11 |
| 1 | | 2 | 3 | 8 | 6 | 7 | | 9 | | | | | | | 4 | | | | 10 | 5 | 11 | | | | | | | | | | | | | | | | | | 12 |
| 1 | | 2 | 3 | | | 7 | | 9 | | | | | | | 4 | 10 | | 8 | | 5 | 11 | | | | 6 | | | | | | | | | | | | | | 13 |
| 1 | 2 | 3 | 4 | | | 7 | 10 | 9 | | | | | | | 5 | | | | | | | | | | 6 | 8 | 11 | | | | | | | | | | | | 14 |
| 1 | 2 | 3 | 4 | | 10 | 7 | | 9 | | | | | | | 5 | | | | | | 11 | | | | 6 | 8 | | | | | | | | | | | | | 15 |
| 1 | 3 | | 4 | 10 | | 7 | | 9 | | | | | | | 5 | | | | | | 11 | | | | 6 | | | 2 | 8 | | | | | | | | | | 16 |
| 1 | 2 | 3 | 4 | 10 | | 7 | | 9 | | | 8 | 5 | | | | | | | | | | | | | 6 | | | 11 | | | | | | | | | | | 17 |
| 1 | 2 | 3 | 4 | 9 | | 7 | | | | | 11 | 5 | | | | | | | 8 | | | | | | 6 | | 10 | | | | | | | | | | | | 18 |
| **18** | **14** | **13** | **18** | **12** | **13** | **16** | **15** | **5** | **4** | **7** | **15** | **3** | **1** | **1** | **3** | **5** | **1** | **1** | **2** | **6** | **9** | **1** | **1** | **1** | **6** | **2** | **1** | **1** | **1** | **2** | | | | | | | | | |
| | 2 | | 7 | | | 6 | 19 | 3 | 4 | 4 | | | | | | 3 | | | | 5 | | | | | | 2 | | | | | | | | | | | | | |

3 own-goals

| Breedon | Griffiths J | Roughton | Porter | Carey | Whalley | Bryant | Smith J | Catterick | Pearson | Mitten | Warner | Roach | Asquith | Kippax | Lee | Morris | Barkas | Chadwick | Shore | Vose | Bellis | Rowley A | Harrison | Hall | McKay | Dimond | Rowley J | Walton | Anderson | Buchan | Broadis | Dougan | Hyde | Griffiths W | Griffiths G | Byrom | Eastwood | Walsh | |
|---|---|---|---|---|---|---|---|---|---|---|---|---|---|---|---|---|---|---|---|---|---|---|---|---|---|---|---|---|---|---|---|---|---|---|---|---|---|---|---|
| 1 | 2 | 3 | 5 | 10 | 4 | 8 | | | 7 | | | | | | | | | | | | 11 | | | | 6 | | | | | | | 9 | | | | | | | 19 |
| 1 | 2 | 3 | 5 | 8 | 11 | | 9 | | | | 4 | 7 | | | 10 | | | | | | | | 6 | | | | | | | | | | | | | | | | 20 |
| 1 | | 2 | 3 | 8 | 6 | 7 | | | | 10 | | | 4 | | 9 | | | | | 5 | 11 | | | | | | | | | | | | | | | | | | 21 |
| | 2 | 3 | 5 | 6 | 7 | 9 | | 8 | | | | | | | 4 | | | | 10 | | | | | 11 | | | | | | | | | | | | | | | 22 |
| | 2 | 3 | 5 | 6 | 7 | 9 | | | | | | | | | 4 | 8 | | | 10 | | | | | 11 | | | | | | | | | | | | | | | 23 |
| | 2 | | 5 | 6 | 7 | 9 | | | 10 | | | | | | 4 | | | | | 11 | | | | | | | | | 8 | | | | | | | | | | 24 |
| 1 | 2 | 3 | 5 | | 6 | 7 | | 9 | | | | | | | 4 | | | | | 11 | | | | | | | | | 8 | | | | | | | | | | 25 |
| 1 | 2 | 3 | 5 | 8 | 6 | 7 | 9 | | | 10 | | | 4 | | | | | | | 11 | | | | | | | | | | | | | | | | | | | 26 |
| 1 | 2 | 3 | | | 6 | 7 | 9 | | 10 | | | | 4 | | | | | | 8 | | 11 | | | | | | | | | | | | | | | | | | 27 |
| 1 | 2 | | 3 | | 6 | 7 | | | | | | | 4 | | | 8 | | | | 5 | 9 | | | | 10 | | | 11 | | | | | | | | | | | 28 |
| 1 | 2 | 3 | 5 | 6 | 7 | 8 | | | | 10 | 4 | | | | | | | | | | 11 | | | | | | | | | 11 | | | | | | | | | 29 |
| 1 | 2 | 3 | 5 | 6 | 11 | 8 | | | | 10 | 4 | | | | | | | | | | | | | | | | | 9 | | | | | | | | | | | 30 |
| 1 | 2 | 3 | 5 | 4 | | | 8 | | | | | | | | | | | | | 9 | | | 6 | 11 | | | | | | | | | | 10 | 7 | | | | 31 |
| 1 | 3 | | 5 | | 7 | 9 | | | 10 | 11 | 4 | | | | | | | | | | | | | | | | | | 2 | | | 8 | | | | | | | 32 |
| 1 | 3 | | | 7 | | 10 | | | | | | | | | | 11 | | | | 4 | | | | | | | | | 8 | 9 | | | 2 | 5 | | | | 33 |
| 1 | 3 | | | 11 | 6 | | 10 | | | 8 | | | | | | | | | | 9 | | | | | | | | | | | | | 2 | 5 | | | | 34 |
| 1 | 3 | | | 6 | 7 | | 10 | | | 11 | 4 | | | | | | | | | 9 | 5 | 8 | | | | | | | | | | | 2 | | | | | 35 |
| 1 | 3 | | | 6 | 7 | | 10 | | | | | | | | | 11 | | | | 9 | | | | | | | | | | | | | 2 | | | | | 36 |
| | 2 | | | 9 | 6 | 7 | 10 | | | | | | | | | 4 | | | | 11 | | | | | | | | | | | | | | | | | 5 | | 37 |
| | | 3 | | | 6 | 7 | | 8 | | 10 | | | | | | | | | | 9 | | | | | | | | 11 | | | | | | | 2 | | 5 | 4 | 38 |
| | 2 | | | | 6 | 7 | 8 | | 10 | | | | | | | | | | | 11 | | | | | | | | 9 | | | | | | | 3 | | 5 | 4 | 39 |
| **15** | **9** | **20** | **8** | **11** | **21** | **18** | **16** | | **12** | **1** | **13** | **1** | | **1** | **5** | | **2** | **17** | **2** | **8** | **6** | **1** | | **5** | **2** | **2** | **2** | **4** | **2** | **2** | **3** | **2** | | | | | | | |
| | 1 | | 1 | | 5 | 19 | 6 | 1 | | | 1 | | | | 5 | | | 2 | 6 | | 4 | 2 | | | 2 | 1 | | | | | | | | | | | | | |

1 own-goal

Match 22: Burnett played number 1; Match 23: King played number 1; Match 24: Scales played number 1 and Kirkman played number 3; Match 25: Brocklebank played number 10; Match 27: T.Smith played number 5; Match 29: Dainty played number 9; Match 30: Worrall played number 7; Match 32: Haigh played number 6; Match 33: Chilton played number 6; Match 34: White played number 4 and Black played number 7, scoring once; Match 36: Martindale played number 4, Woodruff played number 5 and Newsome played number 8; Match 37: Robinson played number 1, Westwood played number 3 and Williams played number 8; Matches 38 & 39: Radcliffe played number 1.

Match 28: A.Rowley listed as playing number 10 by the Football League; Match 30: A.Rowley listed as playing number 9 by the Football League; Match 32: J.Rowley listed as playing number 11 by the Football League.

# 1943-44

Manager: Walter Crickmer

| | | | | | | | |
|---|---|---|---|---|---|---|---|
| 1 | Aug | 28 | (h) | Stockport C | W | 6-0 Bellis 2, Smith 2, McDonald, McKay | 3,000 |
| 2 | Sep | 4 | (a) | Stockport C | D | 3-3 McDonald 2, Bryant | 2,000 |
| 3 | | 11 | (h) | Everton | W | 4-1 McDonald 2, Broadis, Smith | 10,000 |
| 4 | | 18 | (a) | Everton | L | 1-6 Bellis | 14,000 |
| 5 | | 25 | (h) | Blackburn R | W | 2-1 Bryant 2 | 5,000 |
| 6 | Oct | 2 | (a) | Blackburn R | L | 1-2 Roughton | 3,000 |
| 7 | | 9 | (h) | Chester | W | 3-1 Bellis 3 | 5,000 |
| 8 | | 16 | (a) | Chester | L | 4-5 Smith 2, McKay, Opp own-goal | 4,000 |
| 9 | | 23 | (a) | Liverpool | W | 4-3 S.Pearson 2, McDonald, Smith | 15,000 |
| 10 | | 30 | (h) | Liverpool | W | 1-0 McKay | 13,647 |
| 11 | Nov | 6 | (a) | Manchester C | D | 2-2 S.Pearson, Smith | 15,157 |
| 12 | | 13 | (h) | Manchester C | W | 3-0 Bryant, Morris, Smith | 8,958 |
| 13 | | 20 | (h) | Tranmere R* | W | 6-3 Mitten 4, Smith 2 | 2,000 |
| 14 | | 27 | (a) | Tranmere R | W | 1-0 Mckay | 2,500 |
| 15 | Dec | 4 | (a) | Wrexham | W | 4-1 Morris 2, Bryant, Smtih | 3,500 |
| 16 | | 11 | (h) | Wrexham | W | 5-0 S.Pearson 3, Smith 2 | 2,500 |
| 17 | | 18 | (h) | Bolton W | W | 3-1 Morris, Smith, Warner | 4,800 |
| 18 | | 25 | (a) | Bolton W | W | 3-1 Smith 2, Bryant | 8,000 |

FINAL LEAGUE POSITION: 2nd in Football League North (First Championship)    Appearances
        *Match abandoned after 85 minutes but the score stood    Goals

| | | | | | | | |
|---|---|---|---|---|---|---|---|
| 19 | Dec | 27 | (h) | Halifax T | W | 6-2 S.Pearson 3, Smith 2, A.Rowley | 13,500 |
| 20 | Jan | 1 | (a) | Halifax T | D | 1-1 Smith | 4,000 |
| 21 | | 8 | (a) | Stockport C | W | 3-2 Brook 2, Bryant | 4,500 |
| 22 | | 15 | (h) | Stockport C | W | 4-2 Smith 3, Brook | 5,000 |
| 23 | | 22 | (h) | Manchester C | L | 1-3 Smith | 12,372 |
| 24 | | 29 | (a) | Manchester C | W | 3-2 J.Rowley 2, Smith | 18,569 |
| 25 | Feb | 5 | (a) | Bury | W | 3-0 S.Pearson 2, Smith | 5,159 |
| 26 | | 12 | (h) | Bury | D | 3-3 Brook, Bryant, McKay | 6,896 |
| 27 | | 19 | (h) | Oldham A | W | 3-2 Smith 3 | 7,028 |
| 28 | | 26 | (a) | Oldham A | D | 1-1 Bryant | 6,768 |
| 29 | Mar | 4 | (a) | Wrexham | W | 4-1 Bryant, Morris, J.Rowley, Smith | 12,000 |
| 30 | | 11 | (h) | Wrexham | D | 2-2 S.Pearson, Smith | 12,248 |
| 31 | | 18 | (a) | Birmingham | L | 1-3 Smith | 16,000 |
| 32 | | 25 | (h) | Birmingham | D | 1-1 J.Rowley | 32,992 |
| 33 | Apr | 1 | (a) | Bolton W | L | 0-3 | 2,500 |
| 34 | | 8 | (h) | Bolton W | W | 3-2 Bryant 2, Morris | 13,044 |
| 35 | | 10 | (a) | Manchester C | L | 1-4 Bryant | 19,000 |
| 36 | | 15 | (h) | Burnley | W | 9-0 Smith 3, Brook 2, Bryant 2, J.Rowley 2 | 4,000 |
| 37 | | 22 | (a) | Burnley | D | 3-3 Brook 2, Smith | 2,500 |
| 38 | | 29 | (h) | Oldham A | D | 0-0 | 2,000 |
| 39 | May | 6 | (a) | Oldham A | W | 3-1 Morris, Sloan, Opp own-goal | 1,658 |

FINAL LEAGUE POSITION: 9th in Football League North (Second Championship)    Appearances
        Goals

Matches 19-28 were also in the League War Cup Qualifying Competition.
Matches 29-32 inclusive were also in the League War Cup Knock-out Competition.

| Breedon | Griffiths J | Roughton | McKay | Porter | Warner | Whalley | Bryant | Smith J | McDonald J | Bellis | Pearson S | Broadis | Vose | Morris | Williams | Walton | Hyde | Cockburn | Mitten | Walmsley | Dimond | Pearson L | Watton | Brook | Black | Wilson | Rowley J | Rowley A | Gibson | Cochrane | Liddell | Brierley | Wood | Norris | Hacking | Gallon | Fenner | Grundy | Match |
|---|---|---|---|---|---|---|---|---|---|---|---|---|---|---|---|---|---|---|---|---|---|---|---|---|---|---|---|---|---|---|---|---|---|---|---|---|---|---|---|
| 1 | 2 | 3 | 4 | 5 | 6 | 7 | 8 | 9 | 10 | 11 | | | | | | | | | | | | | | | | | | | | | | | | | | | | | 1 |
| 1 | 2 | 3 | 8 | 5 | 4 | 6 | 7 | 9 | 11 | 10 | | | | | | | | | | | | | | | | | | | | | | | | | | | | | 2 |
| 1 | 2 | 3 | 6 | | 4 | 5 | | 10 | 11 | 7 | 9 | 8 | | | | | | | | | | | | | | | | | | | | | | | | | | | 3 |
| 1 | 2 | 3 | 6 | | 4 | 7 | 9 | | 11 | 10 | 8 | | 5 | | | | | | | | | | | | | | | | | | | | | | | | | | 4 |
| 1 | 2 | 3 | | 5 | 4 | 6 | 7 | 8 | 11 | 10 | | | | | 9 | | | | | | | | | | | | | | | | | | | | | | | | 5 |
| 1 | 2 | 3 | | 5 | 4 | 6 | 7 | 8 | 11 | 10 | | | | | 9 | | | | | | | | | | | | | | | | | | | | | | | | 6 |
| 1 | 2 | 3 | 8 | 5 | 4 | 6 | 7 | | 11 | 9 | | | | | 10 | | | | | | | | | | | | | | | | | | | | | | | | 7 |
| 1 | 2 | | 4 | 6 | 5 | 7 | 8 | 10 | 11 | 9 | | | | | | | 3 | | | | | | | | | | | | | | | | | | | | | | 8 |
| 1 | 2 | 3 | | 6 | 5 | 7 | 8 | 10 | 11 | 4 | | | | | 9 | | | | | | | | | | | | | | | | | | | | | | | | 9 |
| 1 | 2 | 3 | 4 | 6 | 5 | 7 | | 10 | | 11 | | | | | 9 | | 8 | | | | | | | | | | | | | | | | | | | | | | 10 |
| 1 | 2 | 3 | 8 | 5 | 4 | 6 | | 10 | | 11 | | | | | 9 | 7 | | | | | | | | | | | | | | | | | | | | | | | 11 |
| 1 | 2 | 3 | 9 | 5 | 4 | 6 | 7 | 10 | | 11 | | | 8 | | | | | | | | | | | | | | | | | | | | | | | | | | 12 |
| 1 | | 3 | 6 | 5 | 4 | | 7 | 10 | | | | | | | | | | 2 | 8 | 9 | 11 | | | | | | | | | | | | | | | | | | 13 |
| | 2 | 3 | 4 | 6 | 5 | 7 | 8 | 9 | | 11 | | | | | | | | | 1 | 10 | | | | | | | | | | | | | | | | | | | 14 |
| 1 | | 3 | 9 | 5 | 4 | 6 | 7 | 10 | | 11 | | | | | 8 | | | 2 | | | | | | | | | | | | | | | | | | | | | 15 |
| 1 | | 3 | 6 | 5 | 4 | | 7 | 10 | | | | | | 9 | | | | 2 | | | | 11 | 8 | | | | | | | | | | | | | | | | 16 |
| 1 | | 3 | 4 | 5 | 6 | | 7 | 10 | | | | | 9 | | 8 | | | 2 | | 11 | | | | | | | | | | | | | | | | | | | 17 |
| 1 | | 3 | 6 | 5 | | 7 | | 10 | | | | | | | 11 | | | 8 | 2 | | | | | 4 | 9 | | | | | | | | | | | | | | 18 |
| **17** | **13** | **17** | **15** | **16** | **14** | **15** | **15** | **8** | **14** | **10** | **2** | **1** | **7** | **1** | **7** | **1** | **1** | **2** | **1** | **1** | **1** | **1** | **1** | **1** | **1** | | | | | | | | | | | | | | |
| | | 1 | 4 | 4 | 1 | 6 | 16 | 6 | 6 | 1 | | | 4 | | 4 | | | | | | | | | | | | | | | | | | | | | | | | |

1 own-goal

| Breedon | Griffiths J | Roughton | McKay | Porter | Warner | Whalley | Bryant | Smith J | McDonald J | Bellis | Pearson S | Broadis | Vose | Morris | Williams | Walton | Hyde | Cockburn | Mitten | Walmsley | Dimond | Pearson L | Watton | Brook | Black | Wilson | Rowley J | Rowley A | Gibson | Cochrane | Liddell | Brierley | Wood | Norris | Hacking | Gallon | Fenner | Grundy | Match |
|---|---|---|---|---|---|---|---|---|---|---|---|---|---|---|---|---|---|---|---|---|---|---|---|---|---|---|---|---|---|---|---|---|---|---|---|---|---|---|---|
| | 2 | 6 | 5 | | | 7 | 9 | | | | | | | 10 | | | 3 | | 1 | | | | | | | | 4 | 8 | 11 | | | | | | | | | | 19 |
| 1 | | | 6 | 5 | 4 | | 7 | 9 | | | | | | 10 | | | 2 | | 11 | | | | | | 8 | | 3 | | | | | | | | | | | | 20 |
| 1 | | 3 | 6 | 5 | 4 | | 7 | 9 | | | | | | 10 | | | 2 | | 11 | | | | | | 8 | | | | | 11 | | | | | | | | | 21 |
| 1 | | 3 | 6 | 5 | 4 | | 7 | 9 | | | | | | 10 | | | 2 | | | | | | | | 8 | | | | | | 11 | | | | | | | | 22 |
| | | 3 | 10 | 5 | 4 | | 7 | 9 | | | | | | | | | 2 | | | | | | | | 8 | | | | | | | 1 | 11 | 6 | | | | | 23 |
| 1 | | 3 | | 5 | 4 | | 7 | 9 | | | | | | 10 | | 8 | 2 | | | | | | | 6 | | | 11 | | | | | | | | | | | | 24 |
| | | 3 | 6 | 5 | 4 | | 9 | | | | | | | 11 | 8 | 7 | 2 | | | | | | 10 | | | | | | | | | 1 | | | | | | | 25 |
| | 2 | 3 | 6 | 5 | 4 | 11 | 7 | 9 | | | | | | | 10 | | | | | | | | | | | | | | | | | | | 8 | 1 | | | | 26 |
| | 5 | 3 | 6 | | 4 | | 7 | 9 | | | | | | | 8 | | 2 | | | | | | | | | | 1 | | | | | | | | | 10 | 11 | | 27 |
| | 2 | 3 | 6 | 5 | 4 | 8 | 7 | | | | | | | | 9 | | | | | | | | | | | | | | | | | | | | | 10 | 11 | 1 | 28 |
| 1 | | 3 | | 5 | 4 | | 7 | 9 | | | | | | 10 | 8 | | 2 | | | | | | | 6 | | | 11 | | | | | | | | | | | | 29 |
| 1 | | 3 | | 5 | 4 | | 7 | 9 | | | | | | 10 | 8 | | 2 | | | | | | | 6 | | | | | | | | | | | | | 11 | | 30 |
| 1 | 2 | 3 | 6 | 5 | 4 | | 7 | 9 | | 11 | | | | | 10 | | | | | | | | | 8 | | | | | | | | | | | | | | | 31 |
| 1 | | 3 | | 5 | 4 | | 7 | 9 | | | | | | 8 | | | 2 | | 11 | | | | | 6 | | | 10 | | | | | | | | | | | | 32 |
| 1 | | 3 | 10 | 5 | 4 | 6 | 9 | | | | | | | | 8 | | 2 | | | | | | | | | | | | | | | | | | | | 11 | | 33 |
| 1 | | 3 | 6 | 5 | 4 | | 9 | | | | | | | | 8 | | 2 | | | | | | | 10 | | | | | | | | | | | | | 11 | | 34 |
| 1 | | | 6 | 3 | 4 | 5 | 7 | 9 | | | | | | | | | | | | | | | | | | | | | | | | | | 10 | | | 11 | | 35 |
| | 6 | 5 | 4 | 3 | | | 7 | 9 | | | | | | | | | 2 | | | | | | | 10 | | | 11 | | | | | | | | | | | 1 | 36 |
| | 6 | 5 | 4 | 3 | | | 7 | 9 | | | | | | | | | 2 | | | | | | | | 8 | | | | | | | | | | | 10 | | | 37 |
| 1 | | | 6 | 3 | 4 | | 7 | 9 | | | | | | | | | 2 | | | | | | | | | | | | | | | | | 10 | | | | | 38 |
| 1 | | | 6 | 5 | 4 | | 7 | 9 | | | | | | | | | 2 | | | | | | | | 8 | | | | | | | | | | 10 | | | | 39 |
| **14** | **7** | **12** | **17** | **20** | **20** | **6** | **20** | **18** | | **2** | **6** | | **11** | | **18** | | | **2** | **1** | | | | **15** | **2** | **5** | **1** | **1** | **1** | **3** | **1** | **1** | **5** | **1** | **3** | **6** | **2** | | | |
| | | | 1 | | | 9 | 19 | | | | | | | | 6 | | 2 | | | | | | 8 | | 6 | 1 | | | | | | 8 | | 6 | 1 | | | 1 | |

1 own-goal

Match 33: Tomlinson played number 7; Match 34: Bootle played number 7; Match 35: Barker played number 2 and Tyrell played number 8; Match 37: Bailey played number 10 and Tilling played number 11; Match 38: Woodruff played number 5 and Gardner played number 11; Match 39: Watson played number 3 and Sloan played number 11, scoring once.

Match 1: H.McDonald listed as playing number 10 and A.Porter number 5 by the Football League; Matches 2 & 3: H.McDonald listed as playing number 11 by the Football League; Match 20: Hyde listed as playing number 4 by the Football League; Match 26: Morris listed as playing number 8 by Football League. Match 34: Norris listed as playing number 8 by Football League. Match 38: Rudman listed as playing number 4 by Football League.

# 1944-45

Manager: Walter Crickmer

| 1 | Aug | 26 | (a) | Everton | W | 2-1 | Mycock, Currier | 15,000 |
|---|---|---|---|---|---|---|---|---|
| 2 | Sep | 2 | (h) | Everton | L | 1-3 | Bryant | 10,000 |
| 3 | | 9 | (h) | Stockport C | L | 3-4 | Mycock 2, Bryant | 8,000 |
| 4 | | 16 | (a) | Stockport C | D | 4-4 | Mycock 2, Bryant, Smith | 6,000 |
| 5 | | 23 | (h) | Bury | D | 2-2 | Mycock, Walton | 6,000 |
| 6 | | 30 | (a) | Bury | L | 2-4 | Mycock, Woodcock | 4,636 |
| 7 | Oct | 7 | (a) | Chester | L | 0-2 | | 5,000 |
| 8 | | 14 | (h) | Chester | W | 1-0 | Freer | 3,000 |
| 9 | | 21 | (h) | Tranmere R | W | 6-1 | Mycock 2, Bryant, Chadwick, Dougan, Mitten | 8,000 |
| 10 | | 28 | (a) | Tranmere R | W | 4-2 | Bryant 2, Mycock, Opp own-goal | 1,500 |
| 11 | Nov | 4 | (a) | Liverpool | L | 2-3 | Mycock, Woodcock | 17,610 |
| 12 | | 11 | (h) | Liverpool | L | 2-5 | Mitten, Mycock | 5,000 |
| 13 | | 18 | (h) | Manchester C | W | 3-2 | Morris 2, Mycock | 20,764 |
| 14 | | 25 | (a) | Manchester C | L | 0-4 | | 18,657 |
| 15 | Dec | 2 | (a) | Crewe A | W | 4-1 | Bryant 2, Chadwick, Mycock | 7,000 |
| 16 | | 9 | (h) | Crewe A | W | 2-0 | Bowden, Morris | 5,000 |
| 17 | | 16 | (h) | Wrexham | W | 1-0 | Ireland | 6,000 |
| 18 | | 23 | (a) | Wrexham | L | 1-2 | Morris | 7,200 |

FINAL LEAGUE POSITION: 30th in Football League North (First Championship)   Appearances
Goals

| 19 | Dec | 26 | (a) | Sheffield U | W | 4-3 | Morris 2, Bainbridge, Chadwick | 12,000 |
|---|---|---|---|---|---|---|---|---|
| 20 | | 30 | (a) | Oldham A | W | 4-3 | Mycock 2, Chadwick, Smith | 6,617 |
| 21 | Jan | 6 | (h) | Huddersfield T | W | 1-0 | Smith | 8,000 |
| 22 | | 13 | (a) | Huddersfield T | D | 2-2 | Cockburn, Smith | 6,146 |
| 23 | Feb | 3 | (h) | Manchester C | L | 1-3 | Mitten | 30,000 |
| 24 | | 10 | (a) | Manchester C | L | 0-2 | | 22,923 |
| 25 | | 17 | (h) | Bury | W | 2-0 | Mitten, Whalley | 5,000 |
| 26 | | 24 | (a) | Bury | L | 1-3 | Bainbridge | 6,000 |
| 27 | Mar | 3 | (h) | Oldham A | W | 3-2 | Chadwick, Rowley, Whalley | 10,000 |
| 28 | | 10 | (a) | Halifax T | L | 0-1 | | 6,000 |
| 29 | | 17 | (h) | Halifax T | W | 2-0 | Chadwick, Roach | 8,000 |
| 30 | | 24 | (a) | Burnley | W | 3-2 | Rowley 2, Chadwick | 15,000 |
| 31 | | 31 | (h) | Burnley | W | 4-0 | Smith 3, Bryant | 25,523 |
| 32 | Apr | 2 | (a) | Blackpool | L | 1-4 | Wrigglesworth | 14,000 |
| 33 | | 7 | (h) | Stoke C | W | 6-1 | Rowley 2, Wrigglesworth 2, Bryant, Smith | 45,616 |
| 34 | | 14 | (a) | Stoke C | W | 4-1 | Bryant 2, McCulloch, Opp own-goal | 5,000 |
| 35 | | 21 | (a) | Doncaster R | W | 2-1 | Bellis, Smith | 29,177 |
| 36 | | 28 | (h) | Doncaster R | W | 3-1 | Wrigglesworth 3 | 31,728 |
| 37 | May | 5 | (h) | Chesterfield | D | 1-1 | Bellis | 32,013 |
| 38 | | 12 | (a) | Chesterfield | W | 1-0 | McDowell | 32,000 |
| 39 | | 19 | (a) | Bolton W | L | 0-1 | | 40,000 |
| 40 | | 26 | (h) | Bolton W | D | 2-2 | Bryant, Wrigglesworth | 57,395 |

FINAL LEAGUE POSITION: 9th in Football League North (Second Championship)   Appearances
Goals

Matches 20-29 inclusive were also played in the League War Cup Qualifying Competition.
Matches 30 & 31 and 33-40 inclusive were also played in the League War Cup Knock-out Competition.
Matches 37 & 38 were in the two-legged semi-final; Matches 39 & 40 were in the two-legged Final and Manchester United finished runners-up.

384

| Breedon | Walton | Roughton | Warner | Porter | Whalley | Bryant | Currier | Mycock | McInnes | Bartholemew | Morris | Crompton | Roach | McKay | Smith J | Chadwick | Makin | Johnson A | Woodcock | Capper | Cockburn | Briggs | Dougan | Freer | Mitten | Jones A | Bowden | Hession | Ireland | Bainbridge | McDonald J | Rowley J | Bellis | Keeley | McCulloch | Wrigglesworth | Chilton | White | Match |
|---|---|---|---|---|---|---|---|---|---|---|---|---|---|---|---|---|---|---|---|---|---|---|---|---|---|---|---|---|---|---|---|---|---|---|---|---|---|---|---|
| 1 | 2 | 3 | 4 | 5 | 6 | 7 | 8 | 9 | 10 | 11 |  |  |  |  |  |  |  |  |  |  |  |  |  |  |  |  |  |  |  |  |  |  |  |  |  |  |  |  | 1 |
| 1 | 2 | 3 | 4 | 5 | 6 | 7 | 10 | 9 | 11 | 8 |  |  |  |  |  |  |  |  |  |  |  |  |  |  |  |  |  |  |  |  |  |  |  |  |  |  |  |  | 2 |
| 1 | 2 | 3 | 4 | 5 | 6 | 7 | 10 | 9 |  |  | 11 | 8 |  |  |  |  |  |  |  |  |  |  |  |  |  |  |  |  |  |  |  |  |  |  |  |  |  |  | 3 |
|  | 2 |  |  | 5 | 6 | 7 | 10 | 9 |  |  |  |  | 1 | 3 | 4 | 8 | 11 |  |  |  |  |  |  |  |  |  |  |  |  |  |  |  |  |  |  |  |  |  | 4 |
|  | 2 | 3 | 4 | 5 |  | 7 |  | 9 |  |  |  |  | 1 |  | 6 | 10 |  | 11 | 8 |  |  |  |  |  |  |  |  |  |  |  |  |  |  |  |  |  |  |  | 5 |
| 1 | 2 | 3 | 4 | 5 |  | 7 |  | 9 |  |  |  |  |  |  | 6 | 10 |  |  |  | 8 | 11 |  |  |  |  |  |  |  |  |  |  |  |  |  |  |  |  |  | 6 |
| 1 | 2 |  |  |  |  |  |  | 9 |  | 11 |  |  | 3 |  | 6 | 8 |  |  |  | 10 | 4 | 5 | 7 |  |  |  |  |  |  |  |  |  |  |  |  |  |  |  | 7 |
| 1 | 2 | 3 | 4 |  |  | 7 |  | 9 |  |  |  |  |  |  | 6 | 10 |  |  |  | 8 | 5 | 11 |  |  |  |  |  |  |  |  |  |  |  |  |  |  |  |  | 8 |
| 1 | 2 | 3 | 4 |  | 6 | 7 |  | 9 |  |  |  |  |  |  |  | 10 |  |  |  |  | 5 | 11 | 8 |  |  |  |  |  |  |  |  |  |  |  |  |  |  |  | 9 |
| 1 | 2 | 3 | 4 |  | 6 | 7 |  | 9 |  |  |  |  |  |  |  | 8 |  |  |  | 11 | 10 | 5 |  |  |  |  |  |  |  |  |  |  |  |  |  |  |  |  | 10 |
|  | 2 | 3 | 4 |  |  | 7 | 8 | 9 |  |  |  |  | 1 |  | 10 | 11 |  |  |  | 6 |  | 5 |  |  |  |  |  |  |  |  |  |  |  |  |  |  |  |  | 11 |
| 1 | 2 | 3 | 4 |  | 6 | 7 |  | 9 |  |  | 10 |  |  |  |  | 11 |  |  |  |  | 5 |  | 8 |  |  |  |  |  |  |  |  |  |  |  |  |  |  |  | 12 |
| 1 | 2 |  | 4 |  | 5 | 7 |  | 9 |  |  | 8 |  | 3 | 6 | 10 | 11 |  |  |  |  |  |  |  |  |  |  |  |  |  |  |  |  |  |  |  |  |  |  | 13 |
| 1 | 2 |  | 4 |  | 5 |  |  | 9 |  |  | 8 |  | 3 | 6 | 10 |  |  |  |  | 11 |  |  |  |  | 7 |  |  |  |  |  |  |  |  |  |  |  |  |  | 14 |
| 1 | 2 | 3 | 4 |  | 5 | 7 |  | 9 |  |  | 8 |  | 11 | 6 |  | 10 |  |  |  |  |  |  |  |  |  |  |  |  |  |  |  |  |  |  |  |  |  |  | 15 |
| 1 | 11 | 3 | 4 |  | 5 | 7 |  | 9 |  |  | 8 |  | 2 | 6 |  |  |  |  |  |  |  |  |  |  | 10 |  |  |  |  |  |  |  |  |  |  |  |  |  | 16 |
|  |  | 3 | 4 |  | 5 | 7 |  | 9 |  |  | 8 |  | 1 | 2 | 6 |  | 10 |  |  |  |  |  |  |  |  | 8 | 11 |  |  |  |  |  |  |  |  |  |  |  | 17 |
|  |  | 3 |  |  | 5 |  |  | 9 |  |  | 8 | 1 | 2 |  |  | 7 |  |  |  | 6 |  | 4 |  |  |  | 11 | 10 |  |  |  |  |  |  |  |  |  |  |  | 18 |
| 13 | 16 | 14 | 15 | 6 | 14 | 16 | 3 | 18 | 2 | 3 | 8 | 5 | 8 | 10 | 8 | 9 | 1 | 1 | 4 | 3 | 4 | 6 | 2 | 1 | 3 | 1 | 2 | 1 | 1 |  |  |  |  |  |  |  |  |  |  |
| 1 |  |  |  |  |  |  |  |  |  |  |  | 8 | 1 | 14 |  | 4 |  |  | 1 | 2 |  | 2 |  |  | 1 | 1 | 2 |  | 1 |  | 1 |  |  |  |  |  |  |  |  |  |

1 own-goal

| Breedon | Walton | Roughton | Warner | Porter | Whalley | Bryant | Currier | Mycock | McInnes | Bartholemew | Morris | Crompton | Roach | McKay | Smith J | Chadwick | Makin | Johnson A | Woodcock | Capper | Cockburn | Briggs | Dougan | Freer | Mitten | Jones A | Bowden | Hession | Ireland | Bainbridge | McDonald J | Rowley J | Bellis | Keeley | McCulloch | Wrigglesworth | Chilton | White | Match |
|---|---|---|---|---|---|---|---|---|---|---|---|---|---|---|---|---|---|---|---|---|---|---|---|---|---|---|---|---|---|---|---|---|---|---|---|---|---|---|---|
| 1 |  |  |  | 5 | 9 |  |  |  |  |  | 10 |  | 2 | 4 | 8 | 7 |  |  |  | 6 |  |  |  |  |  |  |  |  |  |  |  | 11 | 3 |  |  |  |  |  |  | 19 |
|  | 3 |  | 4 | 7 |  | 10 |  |  |  |  | 1 | 2 | 6 | 9 | 11 |  |  |  | 8 |  |  | 5 |  |  |  |  |  |  |  |  |  |  |  |  |  |  |  |  | 20 |
| 3 |  | 4 |  | 5 | 7 |  | 10 |  |  |  | 8 | 1 | 2 | 6 | 9 |  |  |  |  | 11 |  |  |  |  |  |  |  |  |  |  |  |  |  |  |  |  |  |  | 21 |
| 3 |  | 4 |  | 5 |  | 10 |  |  |  |  | 1 | 2 | 6 | 9 |  |  |  |  |  | 11 | 7 |  |  |  |  |  | 8 |  |  |  |  |  |  |  |  |  |  |  | 22 |
| 2 | 3 | 4 |  |  | 7 | 10 |  |  |  |  | 8 | 1 |  | 6 | 9 |  |  |  |  | 5 |  | 11 |  |  |  |  |  |  |  |  |  |  |  |  |  |  |  |  | 23 |
| 5 |  | 3 |  | 4 | 7 | 10 |  |  |  |  | 1 | 2 | 6 | 9 | 8 |  |  |  |  | 11 |  |  |  |  |  |  |  |  |  |  |  |  |  |  |  |  |  |  | 24 |
| 3 |  | 4 |  | 5 | 9 |  |  |  |  |  | 1 | 2 | 6 | 7 |  |  |  |  | 8 |  | 11 |  |  |  |  | 10 |  |  |  |  |  |  |  |  |  |  |  |  | 25 |
| 3 |  | 4 |  | 5 | 7 |  |  |  |  |  | 1 | 2 | 6 | 9 | 8 |  |  |  |  |  |  |  |  |  |  | 10 |  |  |  |  |  |  |  |  |  |  |  |  | 26 |
| 3 |  | 4 |  | 5 |  | 9 |  |  |  |  | 1 | 2 | 6 |  | 11 | 8 |  |  |  |  |  |  |  |  | 7 | 10 |  |  |  |  |  |  |  |  |  |  |  |  | 27 |
| 3 | 2 | 4 |  | 5 | 7 | 8 |  |  |  |  | 1 |  | 6 | 9 |  |  |  |  |  |  |  |  |  |  | 11 | 10 |  |  |  |  |  |  |  |  |  |  |  |  | 28 |
| 2 | 3 | 4 |  | 5 |  |  |  |  |  |  | 1 | 10 | 8 | 7 |  |  |  |  |  |  |  |  |  |  |  | 11 |  |  |  |  |  |  |  |  |  |  |  |  | 29 |
| 2 | 3 | 4 |  | 5 | 9 |  |  |  |  |  | 1 |  | 8 | 11 |  |  |  |  |  |  |  |  |  |  | 7 |  |  | 6 | 10 |  |  |  |  |  |  |  |  |  | 30 |
| 2 | 3 | 4 |  | 5 | 7 |  |  |  |  |  | 1 |  | 8 | 11 |  |  |  |  |  |  |  |  |  |  | 9 | 10 | 6 |  |  |  |  |  |  |  |  |  |  |  | 31 |
| 3 | 2 |  |  | 5 | 9 |  |  |  |  |  | 1 | 6 | 8 | 7 |  | 4 |  |  |  |  |  |  |  |  | 11 |  |  |  |  |  |  |  |  |  |  |  |  |  | 32 |
| 2 | 3 | 4 |  | 5 | 9 |  |  |  |  |  | 1 |  | 8 | 7 |  |  |  |  |  |  |  |  |  |  | 10 |  |  | 11 | 6 |  |  |  |  |  |  |  |  |  | 33 |
| 2 | 3 |  |  | 5 | 9 |  |  |  |  |  | 1 | 10 | 8 | 7 |  |  |  |  |  |  |  |  |  |  | 4 | 11 | 6 |  |  |  |  |  |  |  |  |  |  |  | 34 |
| 2 | 3 | 4 |  | 5 | 9 |  |  |  |  |  | 1 |  | 8 | 7 |  |  |  |  |  |  |  |  |  |  | 10 |  | 11 |  |  |  |  |  |  |  |  |  |  |  | 35 |
| 2 | 3 | 4 |  | 5 | 9 |  |  |  |  |  | 1 |  | 8 | 7 |  |  |  |  |  |  |  |  |  |  | 10 |  | 11 | 6 |  |  |  |  |  |  |  |  |  | 36 |
| 2 | 3 | 4 |  | 5 | 9 |  |  |  |  |  | 1 |  | 8 | 7 |  |  |  |  |  |  |  |  |  |  | 10 |  | 11 | 6 |  |  |  |  |  |  |  |  |  | 37 |
| 2 | 3 |  |  | 5 | 9 |  |  |  |  |  | 1 |  | 8 |  |  |  |  |  |  |  |  |  |  |  | 11 |  | 7 | 6 | 4 |  |  |  |  |  |  |  |  |  | 38 |
| 2 | 3 | 4 |  | 5 | 9 |  |  |  |  |  | 1 |  | 7 |  |  |  |  |  |  |  |  |  |  |  | 11 | 6 | 8 |  |  |  |  |  |  |  |  |  |  | 39 |
| 2 | 3 | 4 |  | 5 | 7 |  |  |  |  |  | 1 |  |  |  |  |  |  |  |  |  |  |  |  |  | 11 |  | 6 |  |  |  |  |  |  |  |  |  |  | 40 |
| 1 | 20 | 15 | 17 | 21 | 19 | 7 | 3 | 21 | 10 | 11 | 18 | 16 | 3 | 4 | 2 | 1 | 3 | 4 | 1 | 3 | 6 | 2 | 3 | 11 | 7 | 3 |  |  |  |  |  |  |  |  |  |  |  |  |  |
|  | 2 | 5 |  | 2 |  |  | 2 |  | 1 |  | 8 | 5 |  |  | 1 |  |  | 2 |  |  | 2 | 5 | 2 |  | 1 | 7 |  |  |  |  |  |  |  |  |  |  |  |  |  |

1 own-goal

Match 26: Boyes played number 11; Match 29: P.Robinson played number 6 and Mercer played number 9; Match 32: Gallon played number 10; Match 35: Glaister played number 6; Match 38: McDowell played number 10 and scored once; Match 39: Sloan played number 10; Match 40: Astbury played number 8, Sloan played number 9 and Glidden played number 10.

Match 13: Roughton listed as played number 3 by the Football League.

# 1945-46

Manager: Matt Busby

| 1 | Aug | 25 | (a) | Huddersfield T | L | 2-3 | Smith 2 | 7,672 |
|---|---|---|---|---|---|---|---|---|
| 2 | Sep | 1 | (h) | Huddersfield T | L | 2-3 | Koffman, Rowley | 28,000 |
| 3 | | 8 | (h) | Chesterfield | L | 0-2 | | 15,000 |
| 4 | | 12 | (a) | Middlesbrough | L | 1-2 | Davie | 10,000 |
| 5 | | 15 | (a) | Chesterfield | D | 1-1 | Bryant | 10,000 |
| 6 | | 20 | (a) | Stoke C | W | 2-1 | Hullett, Reid | 18,000 |
| 7 | | 22 | (a) | Barnsley | D | 2-2 | Cockburn, Hullett | 11,000 |
| 8 | | 29 | (h) | Barnsley | D | 1-1 | Smith | 20,000 |
| 9 | Oct | 6 | (h) | Everton | D | 0-0 | | 30,697 |
| 10 | | 13 | (a) | Everton | L | 0-3 | | 35,000 |
| 11 | | 20 | (a) | Bolton W | D | 1-1 | Wrigglesworth | 20,000 |
| 12 | | 27 | (h) | Bolton W | W | 2-1 | Carey, Worrall | 27,272 |
| 13 | Nov | 3 | (h) | Preston NE | W | 6-1 | Rowley 2, Smith 2, Warner, Worrall | 22,072 |
| 14 | | 10 | (a) | Preston NE | D | 2-2 | Bainbridge, Smith | 13,000 |
| 15 | | 17 | (a) | Leeds U | D | 3-3 | Hanlon 2, Buckle | 10,000 |
| 16 | | 24 | (h) | Leeds U | W | 6-1 | Buckle 2, Wrigglesworth 2, Hanlon, Rowley | 21,312 |
| 17 | Dec | 1 | (h) | Burnley | D | 3-3 | Hullett 3 | 17,429 |
| 18 | | 8 | (a) | Burnley | D | 2-2 | Hanlon, Smith | 8,000 |
| 19 | | 15 | (h) | Sunderland | W | 2-1 | Smith 2 | 19,500 |
| 20 | | 22 | (a) | Sunderland | L | 2-4 | Smith, Wrigglesworth | 18,000 |
| 21 | | 25 | (a) | Sheffield U | L | 0-1 | | 13,000 |
| 22 | | 26 | (h) | Sheffield U | L | 2-3 | Carey, Hullett | 35,000 |
| 23 | | 29 | (h) | Middlesbrough | W | 4-1 | Rowley 2, Smith 2 | 18,937 |
| 24 | Jan | 12 | (h) | Grimsby T | W | 5-0 | Rowley 3, Bainbridge, Smith | 20,789 |
| 25 | | 19 | (a) | Grimsby T | L | 0-1 | | 9,000 |
| 26 | Feb | 2 | (h) | Blackpool | W | 4-2 | Rowley 2, Bainbridge, Wrigglesworth | 18,033 |
| 27 | | 9 | (h) | Liverpool | W | 2-1 | Smith 2 | 33,000 |
| 28 | | 16 | (a) | Liverpool | W | 5-0 | Hanlon 2, Rowley 2, Wrigglesworth | 37,197 |
| 29 | | 23 | (a) | Bury | D | 1-1 | Hanlon | 16,391 |
| 30 | Mar | 2 | (h) | Bury | D | 1-1 | Hanlon | 30,921 |
| 31 | | 9 | (h) | Blackburn R | W | 6-2 | Rowley 3, Hanlon 2, Delaney | 31,422 |
| 32 | | 16 | (a) | Blackburn R | W | 3-1 | Smith 2, Pearson | 8,000 |
| 33 | | 23 | (a) | Bradford | L | 1-2 | Carey | 13,498 |
| 34 | | 27 | (a) | Blackpool | W | 5-1 | Pearson 3, Carey, Wrigglesworth | 10,000 |
| 35 | | 30 | (h) | Bradford | W | 4-0 | Aston, Delaney, Rowley, Wrigglesworth | 36,791 |
| 36 | Apr | 6 | (h) | Manchester C | L | 1-4 | Aston | 62,144 |
| 37 | | 13 | (a) | Manchester C | W | 3-1 | Hanlon, Pearson, Rowley | 50,440 |
| 38 | | 19 | (a) | Newcastle U | W | 1-0 | Pearson | 50,000 |
| 39 | | 20 | (h) | Sheffield W | W | 4-0 | Pearson 2, Delaney, Rowley | 34,000 |
| 40 | | 22 | (h) | Newcastle U | W | 4-1 | Delaney, Mitten, Rowley, Wrigglesworth | 39,173 |
| 41 | | 27 | (a) | Sheffield W | L | 0-1 | | 12,000 |
| 42 | May | 4 | (h) | Stoke C | W | 2-1 | Buckle, Pearson | 37,773 |

FINAL LEAGUE POSITION: 4th in Football League North

Appearances
Goals

## FA Cup

| 3 | Jan | 5 | (a) | Accrington S | D | 2-2 | |
|---|---|---|---|---|---|---|---|
| | | 9 | (h) | Accrington S | W | 5-1 | (Aggregate 7-3) |
| 4 | | 26 | (h) | Preston NE | W | 1-0 | |
| | | 30 | (a) | Preston NE | L | 1-3 | (Aggregate 2-3) |

Appearances and shirt-number grid (numbers = shirt number worn by each player in each match; bottom two rows = total appearances and goals).

| Crompton | Walton | Wilson | Warner | Whalley | McKay | Bryant | Smith J | Hanlon | Koffman | Wrigglesworth | Roach | Chilton | Worrall F | Rowley J | Roughton | Comer | Mycock | Cockburn | Davie | Bainbridge | Dimond | Landers | Reid | Hullett | Keeley | Rhodes | Carey J | Buckle | Tapken | Langford | Vose | Gallacher | Delaney | Pearson S | Aston | Mitten | Hamlett | Match |
|---|---|---|---|---|---|---|---|---|---|---|---|---|---|---|---|---|---|---|---|---|---|---|---|---|---|---|---|---|---|---|---|---|---|---|---|---|---|---|
| 1 | 2 | 3 | 4 | 5 | 6 | 7 | 8 | 9 | 10 | 11 |  |  |  |  |  |  |  |  |  |  |  |  |  |  |  |  |  |  |  |  |  |  |  |  |  |  |  | 1 |
| 1 | 2 |  | 4 | 5 |  |  | 8 | 9 | 10 |  |  | 3 | 6 | 7 | 11 |  |  |  |  |  |  |  |  |  |  |  |  |  |  |  |  |  |  |  |  |  |  | 2 |
| 1 |  |  | 4 | 5 | 9 |  | 7 |  |  |  | 11 | 2 | 6 |  |  | 3 | 8 | 10 |  |  |  |  |  |  |  |  |  |  |  |  |  |  |  |  |  |  |  | 3 |
| 1 | 2 |  | 4 | 5 |  |  |  | 9 |  |  | 11 | 3 |  |  |  |  |  | 6 | 7 | 10 | 8 |  |  |  |  |  |  |  |  |  |  |  |  |  |  |  |  | 4 |
| 1 | 2 |  | 8 | 5 |  |  | 7 |  |  |  | 11 |  | 6 |  |  | 3 |  | 10 | 4 |  |  |  |  | 9 |  |  |  |  |  |  |  |  |  |  |  |  |  | 5 |
| 1 | 2 |  | 4 | 5 |  |  | 7 |  |  |  | 11 | 3 |  |  |  |  |  | 6 |  |  |  |  |  | 8 |  | 9 | 10 |  |  |  |  |  |  |  |  |  |  | 6 |
| 1 |  |  | 5 | 6 |  |  | 7 |  |  |  | 11 | 2 | 8 |  | 10 |  | 3 | 4 |  |  |  |  |  |  | 9 |  |  |  |  |  |  |  |  |  |  |  |  | 7 |
| 1 | 2 |  | 4 | 5 |  |  | 8 |  |  |  | 11 | 3 | 6 | 7 |  |  |  | 9 |  |  |  |  |  |  |  |  |  |  |  |  |  |  |  |  |  |  |  | 8 |
| 1 | 2 |  | 4 | 5 |  |  | 8 |  |  |  | 11 | 3 | 6 | 7 | 9 |  |  | 10 |  |  |  |  |  |  |  |  |  |  |  |  |  |  |  |  |  |  |  | 9 |
| 1 | 2 |  | 4 | 5 |  |  | 8 |  |  |  | 11 | 3 |  | 7 |  |  |  | 6 |  |  |  |  |  |  |  | 9 | 10 |  |  |  |  |  |  |  |  |  |  | 10 |
| 1 | 2 |  | 4 | 5 |  | 7 | 8 |  |  |  | 11 | 3 |  |  |  |  |  | 6 |  |  |  |  |  |  |  |  | 10 |  |  |  |  |  |  |  |  |  |  | 11 |
| 1 | 2 |  | 4 | 5 |  |  |  | 9 |  |  | 11 | 3 |  | 7 | 10 |  |  | 6 |  |  |  |  |  |  |  |  | 8 |  |  |  |  |  |  |  |  |  |  | 12 |
| 1 |  |  | 4 | 2 |  |  |  | 9 |  |  | 11 | 3 | 5 | 7 | 10 |  |  | 6 |  |  |  |  |  |  |  |  | 8 |  |  |  |  |  |  |  |  |  |  | 13 |
| 1 | 2 |  | 4 | 5 |  |  |  | 9 |  |  | 11 | 3 |  | 7 | 10 |  |  | 6 |  | 8 |  |  |  |  |  |  |  |  |  |  |  |  |  |  |  |  |  | 14 |
| 1 | 2 |  | 4 | 5 |  |  |  | 9 | 7 |  | 11 | 3 |  |  |  |  |  | 6 |  |  |  |  |  |  |  |  | 8 | 10 |  |  |  |  |  |  |  |  |  | 15 |
| 1 | 2 |  | 4 | 5 |  |  |  | 9 | 7 |  | 11 | 3 |  | 10 |  |  |  | 6 |  |  |  |  |  |  |  |  | 8 |  |  |  |  |  |  |  |  |  |  | 16 |
| 1 | 2 |  | 4 | 3 |  | 8 | 7 |  |  |  |  | 5 | 11 |  |  |  |  | 6 |  |  |  |  |  |  |  | 9 | 10 |  |  |  |  |  |  |  |  |  |  | 17 |
| 1 | 2 |  | 4 | 3 |  |  |  | 9 | 7 |  | 11 |  | 5 |  |  |  |  | 6 |  |  |  |  |  |  |  |  | 10 | 8 |  |  |  |  |  |  |  |  |  | 18 |
| 1 | 2 |  | 4 | 3 |  |  |  | 9 | 7 |  | 11 |  | 5 |  |  |  |  | 6 |  |  |  |  |  |  |  |  | 8 | 10 |  |  |  |  |  |  |  |  |  | 19 |
| 1 | 2 |  | 4 | 3 |  |  |  | 9 | 7 |  | 11 |  | 5 |  |  |  |  | 6 |  | 10 |  |  |  |  |  |  | 8 |  |  |  |  |  |  |  |  |  |  | 20 |
| 1 | 2 |  | 4 | 3 |  |  |  | 9 | 7 |  | 11 |  | 5 |  |  |  |  | 6 |  | 10 |  |  |  |  |  |  | 8 |  |  |  |  |  |  |  |  |  |  | 21 |
|  | 2 |  | 4 | 3 |  |  |  |  | 7 |  |  |  | 5 | 11 |  |  |  | 6 |  |  |  |  |  |  |  | 9 | 8 | 10 |  | 1 |  |  |  |  |  |  |  | 22 |
| 1 | 3 |  | 4 | 2 |  |  |  | 9 | 7 |  | 11 |  | 5 |  |  |  | 8 | 6 |  |  |  |  |  |  |  |  | 10 |  |  |  |  |  |  |  |  |  |  | 23 |
| 1 | 3 |  | 4 | 5 |  |  |  | 9 | 7 |  | 8 | 2 |  | 11 |  |  |  | 6 |  |  |  |  |  |  |  |  | 10 |  |  |  |  |  |  |  |  |  |  | 24 |
| 1 | 3 |  |  | 2 |  |  |  | 9 | 7 |  | 11 | 4 |  |  |  |  |  | 6 |  |  |  |  |  | 5 |  |  | 10 |  | 5 |  |  |  |  |  |  |  |  | 25 |
|  | 3 |  | 4 | 2 |  |  |  |  | 7 |  | 10 |  | 6 | 11 |  |  |  | 9 |  |  |  |  |  |  |  |  |  |  | 1 |  | 5 | 8 |  |  |  |  |  | 26 |
|  | 3 |  | 4 | 2 |  |  | 8 | 9 |  |  | 11 |  | 5 |  |  |  |  | 6 |  |  |  |  |  |  |  |  | 10 |  | 1 |  |  |  |  | 7 |  |  |  | 27 |
|  | 3 |  | 4 | 2 |  |  |  | 9 |  |  | 11 |  | 5 | 10 |  |  |  | 6 |  |  |  |  |  |  |  |  | 8 |  | 1 |  |  |  |  | 7 |  |  |  | 28 |
|  | 3 |  | 4 | 2 |  |  |  | 9 |  |  | 11 | 10 | 5 |  |  |  |  | 6 |  |  |  |  |  |  |  |  | 8 |  | 1 |  |  |  |  | 7 |  |  |  | 29 |
|  | 3 |  | 4 | 2 |  |  |  | 9 |  |  | 11 |  | 5 |  |  |  |  | 6 |  |  |  |  |  |  |  |  | 8 |  | 1 |  |  |  |  | 7 |  |  |  | 30 |
|  | 3 |  |  | 2 |  |  | 8 | 9 |  |  |  | 5 | 11 |  |  |  |  | 6 |  |  |  |  |  |  |  |  | 4 |  | 1 |  |  |  |  | 7 | 10 |  |  | 31 |
|  | 3 |  |  | 2 |  |  | 8 | 9 |  |  |  | 5 | 11 |  |  |  |  | 6 |  |  |  |  |  |  |  |  | 4 |  | 1 |  |  |  |  | 7 | 10 |  |  | 32 |
|  | 3 |  |  | 2 |  |  |  | 9 |  |  | 11 | 5 |  |  |  |  |  | 6 |  |  |  |  |  |  |  |  | 4 |  | 1 |  |  |  |  | 7 | 10 |  |  | 33 |
|  | 3 |  |  | 2 |  |  |  |  |  |  | 11 | 5 |  |  |  |  |  | 6 |  |  |  |  |  |  |  |  | 4 |  | 1 |  |  |  |  | 7 | 10 | 9 |  | 34 |
|  | 3 |  |  | 2 |  |  |  |  |  |  | 11 | 5 |  |  |  |  |  | 6 |  |  |  |  |  |  |  |  | 4 |  | 1 |  |  |  |  | 7 | 10 | 9 |  | 35 |
|  | 3 |  |  | 2 |  |  |  | 9 |  |  |  | 5 |  |  |  |  |  | 6 |  |  |  |  |  |  |  |  | 4 |  | 1 |  |  |  |  | 7 | 10 | 8 |  | 36 |
| 1 | 3 |  | 4 |  |  |  |  | 9 |  |  | 7 | 5 |  | 10 |  |  |  | 6 |  |  |  |  |  |  |  |  | 2 |  |  |  |  |  |  | 8 |  |  | 11 | 37 |
| 1 | 3 |  | 4 |  |  |  |  |  |  |  | 7 | 5 |  | 10 |  |  |  | 6 |  |  |  |  |  |  |  |  | 2 |  |  |  |  |  | 9 | 8 |  |  | 11 | 38 |
| 1 | 3 |  |  | 6 |  |  |  |  |  |  | 7 | 5 |  | 10 |  |  |  | 4 |  |  |  |  |  |  |  |  | 2 |  |  |  |  |  | 9 | 8 |  |  | 11 | 39 |
| 1 | 3 |  | 4 |  |  |  |  | 9 |  |  | 7 | 5 |  | 10 |  |  |  | 6 |  |  |  |  |  |  |  |  | 2 |  |  |  |  |  |  | 8 |  |  | 11 | 40 |
| 1 | 3 |  | 4 |  |  |  |  |  |  |  | 11 | 5 |  | 10 |  |  |  | 6 |  |  |  |  |  |  |  |  | 2 |  |  |  |  |  |  | 7 | 8 | 9 |  | 41 |
| 1 |  |  |  | 5 |  |  |  |  |  |  | 11 | 3 | 9 |  |  |  |  | 6 |  |  |  |  |  |  |  |  | 10 |  |  |  |  |  |  | 7 | 8 | 4 | 2 | 42 |
| 30 | 36 | 3 | 33 | 38 | 1 | 8 | 22 | 24 | 2 | 36 | 14 | 31 | 7 | 28 | 4 | 1 | 3 | 38 | 1 | 7 | 1 | 1 | 1 | 5 | 1 | 1 | 27 | 6 | 12 | 1 | 1 | 1 | 1 | 15 | 12 | 5 | 4 | |
|  |  |  | 1 |  |  | 1 | 17 | 11 | 1 | 9 |  |  | 2 | 20 |  |  | 1 | 1 |  | 3 |  |  |  | 1 |  |  | 6 | 4 |  |  |  | 4 |  | 4 | 9 | 2 | 1 | |

Match 23: Walton listed as playing number 3 by the Football League.

# United in the FA Cup

**1886-7**
**Round 1**
**Oct 30 v Fleetwood Rangers (a) 2-2** Referee Norris
awarded tie to Fleetwood because Newton Heath
refused to play extra-time
*Doughty 2*
Beckett; Powell, Mitchell, Burke, J.Davies, Howells,
Earp, Longton, J.Doughty, Gotheridge, L.Davies.
*Att: 2,000*

**1889-90**
**Round 1**
**Jan 18 v Preston NE (a) 1-6**
*Craig*
Hay; Harrison, Powell, R.Doughty, J.Davies, J.Owen,
Farman, Craig, J.Doughty, G.Owen, Wilson.
*Att: 7,900*

**1890-91**
**1st Qualifying Round**
**Oct 4 v Higher Walton (h*) 2-0**
*Farman, Evans*
Slater; Mitchell, Powell, R.Doughty, Ramsey, J.Owen,
Farman, Stewart, Evans, Milarvie, Sharpe.
*Att: 3,000*
*Higher Walton drawn at home but agreed to play
at North Road in order to collect greater receipts.
**2nd Qualifying Round**
**Oct 25 v Bootle Reserves (a) 0-1**
Gyves; Powell, J.Owen, Mitchell, Felton, Rattigan,
O'Shaugnessey, Dale, Turner, Craig, Donnelly.
*Att: 500*
Newton Heath fielded their reserve side.

**1891-2**
**1st Qualifying Round**
**Oct 3 v Ardwick (h) 5-1**
*Farman 2, Doughty, Sneddon, Edge*
Slater; McFarlane, Clements, R.Doughty, Stewart,
J.Owen, Farman, Edge, Sneddon, Sharpe, Henrys.
*Att: 11,000*
**2nd Qualifying Round**
**Oct 24 v Heywood (scratched). Won outright**
Match played as a friendly which Newton Heath won
3-2.
**3rd Qualifying Round**
**Nov 14 v South Shore (a) 2-0**
*Farman, J.Doughty*
Slater; McFarlane, Clements, J.Owen, Stewart,
Henrys, Farman, J.Doughty, R.Doughty, Sneddon,
Edge.
*Att: 2,000*
**4th Qualifying Round**
**Dec 5 v Blackpool (h) 3-4**
*Edge 2, Farman*
Slater; McFarlane, Clements, R.Doughty, Stewart,
J.Owen, Farman, Denman, Sneddon, Henrys, Edge.
*Att: 4,000*

**1892-3**
**Round 1**
**Jan 21 v Blackburn R (a) 0-4**
Davies; Mitchell, Clements, Perrins, Stewart,
F.C.Erentz, Farman, Hood, Donaldson, T.Fitzsim-
mons, Colville.
*Att: 7,000*

**1893-4**
**Round 1**
**Jan 27 v Middlesbrough (h) 4-0**
*Donaldson 2, Farman, Peden*
Fall; Mitchell, F.C.Erentz, Perrins, Stewart, Davidson,
Farman, Hood, Donaldson, McNaught, Peden.
*Att 5,000*
**Round 2**
**Feb 10 v Blackburn R (h) 0-0 a.e.t.**
Fall; Mitchell, F.C.Erentz, Perrins, Stewart, Davidson,
Clarkin, Parker, Donaldson, McNaught, Peden.
*Att: 18,000*
**Replay**
**Feb 17 v Blackburn R (a) 1-5**
*Donaldson*
Fall; Mitchell, F.C.Erentz, Perrins, Stewart, Davidson,
Clarkin, Hood, Donaldson, McNaught, Peden.
*Att 5,000*

**1894-5**
**Round 1**
**Feb 2 v Stoke (h) 2-3**
*Smith, Peters*
Douglas; J.McCartney, F.C.Erentz, Perrins,
McNaught, Stewart, Clarkin, Donaldson, Millar,
Smith, Peters.
*Att: 7,000*

**1895-6**
**Round 1**
**Feb 1 v Kettering T (h) 2-1**
*Donaldson, Smith*
Ridgway; Dow, Collinson, D.Fitzsimmons, Perrins,
Cartwright, Kennedy, Donaldson, Cassidy, Smith,
Peters.
*Att 6,000*
**Round 2**
**Feb 15 v Derby C (h) 1-1**
*Kennedy*
Ridgway; Collinson, F.C.Erentz, D.Fitzsimmons,
McNaught, Cartwright, Clarkin, Donaldson, Kennedy,
Smith, Peters.
*Att: 20,000*
**Replay**
**Feb 19 v Derby C (a) 1-5**
*Donaldson*
Ridgway; Collinson, F.C.Erentz, D.Fitzsimmons,
McNaught, Cartwright, Clarkin, Donaldson, Kennedy,
Smith, Peters.
*Att: 6,000*

**1896-7**
**3rd Qualifying Round**
**Dec 12 v West Manchester (h) 7-0**
*Cassidy 2, Gillespie 2, Rothwell 2, Bryant*
Barrett; Stafford, F.C.Erentz, McNaught, Jenkyns, Smith, Bryant, Rothwell, Cassidy, Gillespie, Donaldson.
*Att: 6,000*
**4th Qualifying Round**
**Jan 2 v Nelson (h) 3-0**
*Cassidy, Donaldson, Gillespie*
Barrett; Stafford, F.C.Erentz, Draycott, Jenkyns, McNaught, Bryant, Cassidy, Donaldson, Gillespie, Smith.
*Att: 5,000*
**5th Qualifying Round**
**Jan 16 v Blackpool (h) 2-2**
*Gillespie, Donaldson*
Barrett; Stafford, F.C.Erentz, McNaught, Jenkyns, Cartwright, Bryant, Smith, Donaldson, Cassidy, Gillespie.
*Att: 1,500*
**Replay**
**Jan 20 v Blackpool (a) 2-1**
*Boyd, Cassidy*
Barrett; Stafford, F.C.Erentz, Draycott, Jenkyns, McNaught, Bryant, Donaldson, Boyd, Gillespie, Cassidy.
*Att: 1,500*
**Round 1**
**Jan 30 v Kettering T (h) 5-1**
*Cassidy 3, Donaldson 2*
Barrett; Stafford, F.C.Erentz, Draycott, Jenkyns, Cartwright, Bryant, McNaught, Donaldson, Gillespie, Cassidy.
*Att: 5,000*
**Round 2**
**Feb 13 v Southampton (a) 1-1**
*Donaldson*
Barrett; Stafford, F.C.Erentz, McNaught, Jenkyns, Cartwright, Bryant, Donaldson, Boyd, Gillespie, Cassidy.
*Att: 8,000*
**Replay**
**Feb 17 v Southampton (h) 3-1**
*Bryant 2, Cassidy*
Barrett; Stafford, Cartwright, McNaught, Jenkyns, Smith, Bryant, Donaldson, Boyd, Gillespie, Cassidy.
*Att: 7,000*
**Round 3**
**Feb 27 v Derby C (a) 0-2**
Barrett; Stafford, Cartwright, Draycott, Jenkyns, McNaught, Bryant, Donaldson, Boyd, Gillespie, Cassidy.
*Att: 12,000*

**1897-8**
**Round 1**
**Jan 29 v Walsall (h) 1-0**
*Opponent own-goal*
Barrett; F.C.Erentz, H.Erentz, Draycott, McNaught, Cartwright, Bryant, Collinson, Boyd, Cassidy, Dunn.
*Att: 6,000*
**Round 2**
**Feb 12 v Liverpool (h) 0-0**
Barrett; F.C.Erentz, H.Erentz, Draycott, McNaught, Cartwright, Bryant, Collinson, Boyd, Cassidy, Dunn.
*Att: 12,000*

**Replay**
**Feb 16 v Liverpool (a) 1-2**
*Collinson*
Barrett; F.C.Erentz, H.Erentz, Draycott, McNaught, Cartwright, Bryant, Collinson, Boyd, Cassidy, Gillespie.
*Att: 6,000*

**1898-9**
**Round 1**
**Jan 28 v Tottenham H (a) 1-1**
*Cassidy*
Barrett; Stafford, F.C.Erentz, Draycott, Pepper, W.Morgan, Bryant, Collinson, Cassidy, Cunningham, Gillespie.
*Att: 15,000*
**Replay**
**Feb 1 v Tottenham H (h) 3-5**
*Bryant 3*
Barrett; Stafford, F.C.Erentz, Draycott, W.Morgan, Cartwright, Bryant, Collinson, Cassidy, Cunningham, Gillespie.
*Att: 6,000*

**1899-1900**
**3rd Qualifying Round**
**Oct 28 v South Shore (a) 1-3**
*Jackson*
Barrett; Stafford, F.C.Erentz, W.Morgan, Griffiths, Cartwright, Bryant, Jackson, Blackmore, Cassidy, Roberts.
*Att: 3,000*

**1900-01**
**Supplementary Round**
**Jan 5 v Portsmouth (h) 3-0**
*Griffiths, Jackson, Stafford*
Whitehouse; Stafford, F.C.Erentz, W.Morgan, Griffiths, Cartwright, Schofield, H.Morgan, Leigh, Jackson, Fisher.
*Att: 5,000*
**Round 1**
**Feb 9 v Burnley (h) 0-0**
Whitehouse; Stafford, F.C.Erentz, W.Morgan, Griffiths, Cartwright, Schofield, H.Morgan, Leigh, Jackson, Fisher.
*Att: 8,000*
**Replay**
**Feb 13 v Burnley (a) 1-7**
*Schofield*
Whitehouse; Stafford, F.C.Erentz, W.Morgan, Collinson, Cartwright, Schofield, H.Morgan, Leigh, Heathcote, Fisher.
*Att: 4,000*

**1901-02**
**Intermediate Round**
**Dec 14 v Lincoln C (h) 1-2**
*Fisher*
Whitehouse; Stafford, F.C.Erentz, Cartwright, Griffiths, Banks, Schofield, W.Morgan, Smith, Preston, Fisher.
*Att: 4,000*

**1902-03**
**3rd Qualifying Round**
**Nov 1 v Accrington S (h) 7-0**
*Williams 3, Peddie, Richards, Pegg, Morgan*
Whitehouse; Stafford, Read, W.Morgan, Griffiths,

Banks, Pegg, Richards, Peddie, Williams, Hurst.
*Att: 6,000*
**4th Qualifying Round**
**Nov 13 v Oswaldtwistle Rovers (h) 3-2**
*Pegg, Beadsworth, Williams*
Saunders; Rothwell, Read, Morgan, Griffiths, Banks,
Schofield, Pegg, Turner, Beadsworth, Williams.
*Att: 5,000*
**5th Qualifying Round**
**Nov 29 v Southport Central (h) 4-1**
*Pegg 3, Banks*
Birchenough; Rothwell, Read, Downie, Griffiths,
Banks, Schofield, Richards, Pegg, Beadsworth, Peddie.
*Att: 6,000*
**Intermediate Round**
**Dec 13 v Burton U (h) 1-1**
*Griffiths*
Birchenough; Rothwell, Read, Downie, Griffiths,
Cartwright, Schofield, Richards, Pegg, Peddie, Hurst.
*Att: 6,000*
**Replay**
**Dec 17 v Burton U (h*) 3-1**
*Schofield, Pegg, Peddie*
Birchenough; Rothwell, Read, Downie, Griffiths,
Cartwright, Schofield, Beadsworth, Pegg, Peddie,
Hurst.
*Att: 7,000*
*Both games played at home.
**Round 1**
**Feb 7 v Liverpool (h) 2-1**
*Peddie 2*
Birchenough; Stafford, Rothwell, Downie, Griffiths,
Cartwright, Street, Pegg, Peddie, Smith, Hurst.
*Att: 15,000*
**Round 2**
**Feb 21 v Everton (a) 1-3**
*Griffiths*
Birchenough; Rothwell, Read, Downie, Griffiths,
Cartwright, Street, Pegg, Peddie, Smith, Hurst.
*Att: 15,000*

**1903-04**
**Intermediate Round**
**Dec 12 v Small Heath (h) 1-1**
*Schofield*
Sutcliffe; Bonthron, Blackstock, Downie, Griffiths,
Cartwright, Schofield, Morrison, Grassam, Pegg,
S.Robertson.
*Att: 10,000*
**Replay**
**Dec 16 v Small Heath (a) 1-1 a.e.t.**
*Arkesden*
Sutcliffe; Bonthron, Blackstock, Downie, Griffiths,
Cartwright, Schofield, Morrison, Grassam, Arkesden,
S.Robertson.
*Att: 5,000*
**Second Replay**
**Dec 21 v Small Heath (at Bramall Lane) 1-1 a.e.t.**
*Schofield*
Sutcliffe; Bonthron, Blackstock, Cartwright, Griffiths,
Gaudie, S.Robertson, Arkesden, Grassam, Morrison,
Schofield.
*Att: 3,000*
**Third Replay**
**Jan 11 v Small Heath (at Hyde Road) 3-1**
*Arkesden 2, Grassam*
Sutcliffe; Bonthron, Read, Downie, Griffiths,

Cartwright, Schofield, Morrison, Grassam, Arkesden,
Wilkinson.
*Att: 9,372*
**Round 1**
**Feb 6 v Notts C (a) 3-3**
*Downie, Schofield, Arkesden*
Sutcliffe; Bonthron, Hayes, Downie, Griffiths,
A.Robertson, Schofield, Morrison, Grassam,
Arkesden, S.Robertson.
*Att: 12,000*
**Replay**
**Feb 10 v Notts C (h) 2-1**
*Morrison, Pegg*
Sutcliffe; Bonthron, Hayes, Downie, Griffiths,
Cartwright, Schofield, Morrison, Pegg, Arkesden,
S.Robertson.
*Att: 18,000*
**Round 2**
**Feb 20 v Sheffield W (a) 0-6**
Sutcliffe; Bonthron, Hayes, Downie, Griffiths,
Cartwright, Schofield, Morrison, Pegg, Arkesden,
S.Robertson.
*Att: 22,051*

**1904-05**
**Intermediate Round**
**Jan 14 v Fulham (h) 2-2**
*Mackie, Arkesden*
Moger; Bonthron, Hayes, Downie, Bell, A.Robertson,
A.Schofield, Grassam, Mackie, Arkesden, Williams.
*Att: 17,000*
**Replay**
**Jan 18 v Fulham (a) 0-0 a.e.t.**
Moger; Bonthron, Hayes, Downie, Fitchett, Bell,
A.Schofield, Lyons, Grassam, Arkesden, Williams.
*Att: 15,000*
**Second Replay**
**Jan 23 v Fulham (at Villa Park) 0-1**
Moger; Bonthron, Hayes, Downie, Fitchett, Bell,
A.Schofield, Grassam, Mackie, Arkesden, Hartwell.
*Att: 6,000*

**1905-06**
**Round 1**
**Jan 13 v Staple Hill (h) 7-2**
*Beddow 3, Picken 2, Allen, Williams*
Moger; Bonthron, Holden, Downie, Roberts, Bell,
A.Schofield, Allen, Beddow, Picken, Williams.
*Att: 7,560*
**Round 2**
**Feb 3 v Norwich C (h) 3-0**
*Downie, Peddie, Sagar*
Moger; Bonthron, Holden, Downie, Roberts, Bell,
A.Schofield, Peddie, Sagar, Picken, Williams.
*Att: 10,000*
**Round 3**
**Feb 24 v Aston Villa (h) 5-1**
*Picken 3, Sagar 2*
Moger; Bonthron, Holden, Downie, Roberts, Bell,
A.Schofield, Peddie, Sagar, Picken, Wombwell.
*Att: 35,500*
**Round 4**
**Mar 10 v Woolwich Arsenal (h) 2-3**
*Peddie, Sagar*
Moger; Bonthron, Holden, Downie, Roberts, Bell,
A.Schofield, Peddie, Sagar, Picken, Wombwell.
*Att: 26,500*

**1906-07**
**Round 1**
**Jan 12 v Portsmouth (a) 2-2**
*Picken, Wall*
Moger; Holden, Blackstock, Duckworth, Roberts, Bell, Meredith, Wombwell, Menzies, Picken, Wall.
*Att: 24,329*
**Replay**
**Jan 16 v Portsmouth (h) 1-2**
*Wall*
Moger; Bonthron, Holden, Downie, Duckworth, Bell, Meredith, Wombwell, Menzies, Picken, Wall.
*Att: 8,000*

**1907-08**
**Round 1**
**Jan 11 v Blackpool (h) 3-1**
*Wall 2, Bannister*
Moger; Holden, Stacey, Duckworth, McGillivray, Bell, Meredith, Bannister, J.Turnbull, A.Turnbull, Wall.
*Att: 11,747*
**Round 2**
**Feb 1 v Chelsea (h) 1-0**
*A.Turnbull*
Moger; Holden, Burgess, Duckworth, Roberts, Bell, Meredith, Bannister, J.Turnbull, A.Turnbull, Wall.
*Att: 25,184*
**Round 3**
**Feb 22 v Aston Villa (a) 2-0**
*A.Turnbull, Wall*
Moger; Stacey, Holden, Burgess, Roberts, Bell, Meredith, Bannister, Berry, A.Turnbull, Wall.
*Att: 12,777*
**Round 4**
**Mar 7 v Fulham (a) 1-2**
*J.Turnbull*
Moger; Stacey, Burgess, Duckworth, Roberts, Bell, Meredith, Bannister, J.Turnbull, A.Turnbull, Wall.
*Att: 41,000*

**1908-09**
**Round 1**
**Jan 16 v Brighton & HA (h) 1-0**
*Halse*
Moger; Stacey, Hayes, Duckworth, Roberts, Bell, Halse, A.Turnbull, J.Turnbull, Wall, Meredith.
*Att: 8,300*
**Round 2**
**Feb 6 v Everton (h) 1-0**
*Halse*
Moger; Stacey, Hayes, Duckworth, Roberts, Bell, Halse, Livingstone, J.Turnbull, A.Turnbull, Wall.
*Att: 35,217*
**Round 3**
**Feb 20 v Blackburn R (h) 6-1**
*A.Turnbull 3, J.Turnbull 3*
Moger; Stacey, Hayes, Duckworth, Roberts, Bell, Halse, Livingstone, J.Turnbull, A.Turnbull, Wall.
*Att: 38,500*
**Round 4**
**Mar 6 v Burnley (a) 0-1 (abandoned after 72 mins)**
Moger; Stacey, Hayes, Duckworth, Roberts, Bell, Meredith, Halse, J.Turnbull, A.Turnbull, Wall.
*Att: 15,471*
**Round 4**
**Mar 10 v Burnley (a) 3-2**
*J.Turnbull 2, Halse*

Moger; Stacey, Hayes, Duckworth, Roberts, Bell, Meredith, Halse, J.Turnbull, A.Turnbull, Wall.
*Att: 16,850*
**Semi-final**
**Mar 27 v Newcastle U (at Bramall Lane) 1-0**
*Halse*
Moger; Stacey, Hayes, Duckworth, Roberts, Bell, Meredith, Halse, J.Turnbull, A.Turnbull, Wall.
*Att: 40,118*
**Final**
**Apr 24 v Bristol C (at the Crystal Palace) 1-0**
*A.Turnbull*
Moger; Stacey, Hayes, Duckworth, Roberts, Bell, Meredith, Halse, J.Turnbull, A.Turnbull, Wall.
*Att: 71,401*

**1909-10**
**Round 1**
**Jan 15 v Burnley (a) 0-2**
Moger; Stacey, Hayes, Duckworth, Roberts, Curry, Meredith, Picken, Halse, A.Turnbull, Wall.
*Att: 16,628*

**1910-11**
**Round 1**
**Jan 14 v Blackpool (a) 2-1**
*Picken, West*
Moger; Donnelly, Stacey, Duckworth, Roberts, Bell, Meredith, Picken, West, A.Turnbull, Wall.
*Att: 12,000*
**Round 2**
**Feb 4 v Aston Villa (h) 2-1**
*Halse, Wall*
Moger; Donnelly, Stacey, Duckworth, Roberts, Bell, Meredith, Halse, West, A.Turnbull, Wall.
*Att: 65,101*
**Round 3**
**Feb 25 v West Ham U (a) 1-2**
*A.Turnbull*
Edmonds; Donnelly, Stacey, Duckworth, Roberts, Bell, Meredith, Halse, West, A.Turnbull, Wall.
*Att: 26,000*

**1911-12**
**Round 1**
**Jan 13 v Huddersfield T (h) 3-1**
*West 2, Halse*
Edmonds; Holden, Stacey, Duckworth, Roberts, Bell, Meredith, Halse, West, A.Turnbull, Wall.
*Att: 19,579*
**Round 2**
**Feb 3 v Coventry C (a) 5-1**
*Halse 2, West, Turnbull, Wall*
Edmonds; Holden, Stacey, Duckworth, Whalley, Bell, Meredith, Halse, West, A.Turnbull, Wall.
*Att: 17,130*
**Round 3**
**Feb 24 v Reading (a) 1-1**
*West*
Edmonds; Linkson, Stacey, Duckworth, Roberts, Bell, Meredith, Halse, West, A.Turnbull, Wall.
*Att: 24,069*
**Replay**
**Feb 29 v Reading (h) 3-0**
*A. Turnbull 2, Halse*
Edmonds; Linkson, Stacey, Duckworth, Roberts, Bell, Meredith, Halse, West, A.Turnbull, Wall.
*Att: 29,511*

**Round 4**
**Mar 9 v Blackburn R (h) 1-1**
*Opponent own-goal*
Edmonds; Linkson, Stacey, Duckworth, Roberts, Bell,
Meredith, Halse, West, A.Turnbull, Wall.
*Att: 59,300*
**Replay**
**Mar 14 v Blackburn R (a) 2-4 a.e.t.**
*West 2*
Edmonds; Linkson, Stacey, Duckworth, Roberts, Bell,
Meredith, Halse, West, A.Turnbull, Wall.
*Att: 39,296*

**1912-13**
**Round 1**
**Jan 11 v Coventry C (h) 1-1**
*Wall*
Beale; Hodge, Stacey, Duckworth, Roberts, Whalley,
Meredith, A.Turnbull, Anderson, West, Wall.
*Att: 11,500*
**Replay**
**Jan 16 v Coventry C (a) 2-1**
*Anderson, Roberts*
Beale; Hodge, Stacey, Duckworth, Roberts, Whalley,
Meredith, A.Turnbull, Anderson, West, Wall.
*Att: 20,042*
**Round 2**
**Feb 1 v Plymouth A (a) 2-0**
*Anderson, Wall*
Beale; Hodge, Stacey, Duckworth, Roberts, Whalley,
Meredith, A.Turnbull, Anderson, Hamill, Wall.
*Att: 21,700*
**Round 3**
**Feb 22 v Oldham A (a) 0-0**
Beale; Hodge, Stacey, Duckworth, Roberts, Whalley,
Meredith, Hamill, Anderson, West, Wall.
*Att: 26,932*
**Replay**
**Feb 26 v Oldham A (h) 1-2**
*West*
Beale; Hodge, Stacey, Duckworth, Roberts, Whalley,
Meredith, A.Turnbull, Anderson, West, Wall.
*Att: 31,180*

**1913-14**
**Round 1**
**Jan 10 v Swindon T (a) 0-1**
Beale; Hodge, Stacey, Knowles, Livingstone, Whalley,
Meredith, A.Turnbull, Woodcock, West, Wall.
*Att: 18,187*

**1914-15**
**Round 1**
**Jan 9 v Sheffield W (a) 0-1**
Beale; Hodge, Stacey, Hunter, O'Connell, Cookson,
Meredith, Fox, Anderson, West, Wall.
*Att: 23,248*

**1919-20**
**Round 1**
**Jan 10 v Port Vale (a) 1-0**
*Toms*
Mew; Moore, Silcock, Grimwood, Hilditch, Whalley,
Meredith, Meehan, Toms, Woodcock, Hopkin.
*Att: 14,549*
**Round 2**
**Jan 31 v Aston Villa (h) 1-2**
*Woodcock*

Mew; Moore, Spence, Grimwood, Hilditch, Whalley,
Meredith, Potts, Woodcock, Meehan, Hopkin.
*Att: 48,600*

**1920-21**
**Round 1**
**Jan 8 v Liverpool (a) 1-1**
*Miller*
Mew; Barlow, Silcock, Harris, Grimwood, Forster,
Harrison, Bisset, Miller, Partridge, Hopkin.
*Att: 40,000*
**Replay**
**Jan 12 v Liverpool (h) 1-2**
*Partridge*
Mew; Hofton, Silcock, Harris, Grimwood, Albinson,
Harrison, Bisset, Miller, Partridge, Hopkin.
*Att: 30,000*

**1921-2**
**Round 1**
**Jan 7 v Cardiff C (h) 1-4**
*Sapsford*
Mew; Radford, Scott, Hilditch, McBain, Harris,
Gibson, Lochhead, Spence, Sapsford, Partridge.
*Att: 25,726*

**1922-3**
**Round 1**
**Jan 13 v Bradford C (a) 1-1**
*Partridge*
Mew; Radford, Silcock, Hilditch, Barson, Grimwood,
Wood, Lochhead, Spence, Goldthorpe, Partridge.
*Att: 27,000*
**Replay**
**Jan 17 v Bradford C (h) 2-0**
*Barber, Goldthorpe*
Mew; Radford, Silcock, Hilditch, Barson, Grimwood,
Barber, Lochhead, Spence, Goldthorpe, Partridge.
*Att: 27,791*
**Round 2**
**Feb 3 v Tottenham H (a) 0-4**
Mew; Radford, Silcock, Hilditch, Barson, Grimwood,
Myerscough, Lochhead, Lievesley, Goldthorpe,
Partridge.
*Att: 38,333*

**1923-4**
**Round 1**
**Jan 12 v Plymouth A (h) 1-0**
*McPherson*
Steward; Radford, Moore, Bennion, Barson, Hilditch,
Mann, Bain, Spence, Lochhead, McPherson.
*Att: 35,700*
**Round 2**
**Feb 2 v Huddersfield T (h) 0-3**
Steward; Silcock, Moore, Bennion, Barson, Hilditch,
Mann, Henderson, Spence, Lochhead, McPherson.
*Att: 66,673*

**1924-5**
**Round 1**
**Jan 10 v Sheffield W (a) 0-2**
Steward; Moore, Jones, Mann, Grimwood, Hilditch,
Spence, Smith, Henderson, Kennedy, McPherson.
*Att: 35,079*

**1925-6**
**Round 3**
**Jan 9 v Port Vale (a) 3-2**
*Spence 2, McPherson*
Steward; Moore, Silcock, Mann, Hilditch, Grimwood, Spence, Smith, McPherson, Rennox, Thomas.
*Att: 14,841*
**Round 4**
**Jan 30 v Tottenham H (a) 2-2**
*Spence, Thomas*
Mew; Moore, Silcock, Hilditch, Haslam, Mann, Spence, Hanson, McPherson, Rennox, Thomas.
*Att: 40,000*
**Replay**
**Feb 3 v Tottenham H (h) 2-0**
*Spence, Rennox*
Mew; Moore, Silcock, Hilditch, Haslam, Mann, Spence, Hanson, McPherson, Rennox, Thomas.
*Att: 45,000*
**Round 5**
**Feb 20 v Sunderland (a) 3-3**
*Smith 2, McPherson*
Mew; Moore, Silcock, McCrae, Barson, Mann, Spence, Smith, McPherson, Rennox, Thomas.
*Att: 50,500*
**Replay**
**Feb 24 v Sunderland (h) 2-1**
*Smith, McPherson*
Mew; Moore, Silcock, McCrae, Barson, Mann, Spence, Smith, McPherson, Rennox, Thomas.
*Att: 58,661*
**Round 6**
**Mar 6 v Fulham (a) 2-1**
*Smith, McPherson*
Mew; Moore, Silcock, McCrae, Barson, Mann, Spence, Smith, McPherson, Rennox, Hannaford.
*Att: 28,699*
**Semi-final**
**Mar 27 v Manchester C (at Bramall Lane) 0-3**
Steward; Moore, Silcock, McCrae, Barson, Mann, Spence, Smith, McPherson, Rennox, Thomas.
*Att: 46,450*

**1926-7**
**Round 3**
**Jan 8 v Reading (a) 1-1**
*Bennion*
Steward; Moore, Silcock, Bennion, Hilditch, Barson, Spence, Smith, McPherson, Sweeney, Partridge.
*Att: 28,918*
**Replay**
**Jan 12 v Reading (h) 2-2 a.e.t.**
*Spence, Sweeney*
Steward; Moore, Silcock, Bennion, Hilditch, Barson, Spence, Hanson, McPherson, Sweeney, Partridge.
*Att: 29,122*
**Second Replay**
**Jan 17 v Reading (at Villa Park) 1-2**
*McPherson*
Steward; Moore, Silcock, Bennion, Hilditch, Barson, Spence, Rennox, McPherson, Sweeney, Partridge.
*Att: 16,500*

**1927-8**
**Round 3**
**Jan 14 v Brentford (h) 7-1**
*Hanson 4, Spence, McPherson, Johnston*

Richardson; Jones, Silcock, Bennion, Mann, Wilson, Spence, Hanson, McPherson, Johnston, Partridge.
*Att: 18,538*
**Round 4**
**Jan 28 v Bury (a) 1-1**
*Johnston*
Richardson; Jones, Silcock, Bennion, Mann, Wilson, Spence, Hanson, McPherson, Johnston, Williams.
*Att: 25,000*
**Replay**
**Feb 1 v Bury (h) 1-0**
*Spence*
Richardson; Jones, Silcock, Bennion, Mann, Wilson, Spence, Hanson, McPherson, Johnston, Williams.
*Att: 48,001*
**Round 5**
**Feb 18 v Birmingham (h) 1-0**
*Johnston*
Steward; Jones, Silcock, Bennion, Mann, Wilson, Spence, Hanson, Nicol, Johnston, Partridge.
*Att: 52,568*
**Round 6**
**Mar 3 v Blackburn R (a) 0-2**
Richardson; Moore, Jones, Bennion, Mann, Wilson, Spence, Hanson, Williams, Johnston, Partridge.
*Att: 42,312*

**1928-9**
**Round 3**
**Jan 12 v Port Vale (a) 3-0**
*Spence, Hanson, Taylor*
Steward; Moore, Silcock, Spencer, Mann, Wilson, Spence, Hanson, Williams, Sweeney, Taylor.
*Att: 17,519*
**Round 4**
**Jan 26 v Bury (h) 0-1**
Steward; Moore, Silcock, Spencer, Mann, Wilson, Spence, Rawlings, Thomas, Sweeney, Thomson.
*Att: 40,558*

**1929-30**
**Round 3**
**Jan 11 v Swindon T (h) 0-2**
Steward; Moore, Jones, Taylor, Hilditch, Wilson, Spence, Ball, McLachlan, Rowley, Boyle.
*Att: 33,226*

**1930-31**
**Round 3**
**Jan 10 v Stoke C (a) 3-3**
*Reid 3*
Steward; Mellor, Dale, Bennion, Hilditch, Wilson, Ramsden, Warburton, Reid, Gallimore, McLachlan.
*Att: 23,415*
**Replay**
**Jan 14 v Stoke C (h) 0-0 a.e.t.**
Steward; Mellor, Dale, Bennion, Hilditch, Wilson, Ramsden, Warburton, Reid, Gallimore, McLachlan.
*Att: 22,013*
**Second Replay**
**Jan 19 v Stoke C (at Anfield) 4-2**
*Hopkinson 2, Spence, Gallimore*
Steward; Mellor, Dale, Bennion, Hilditch, McLachlan, Spence, Warburton, Thomson, Gallimore, Hopkinson.
*Att: 11,788*

393

**Round 4**
**Jan 24 v Grimsby T (a) 0-1**
Steward; Mellor, Dale, Bennion, Hilditch, McLachlan,
Spence, Warburton, Reid, Gallimore, Hopkinson.
*Att: 15,000*

**1931-2**
**Round 3**
**Jan 9 v Plymouth A (a) 1-4**
*Reid*
Steward; Mellor, Silcock, Bennion, McLenahan,
Hilditch, Spence, Johnston, Ridding, Reid,
MacLachlan.
*Att: 28,000*

**1932-3**
**Round 3**
**Jan 14 v Middlesbrough (h) 1-4**
*Spence*
Moody; Mellor, Silcock, Vincent, Frame, McLenahan,
Spence, Chalmers, Ridding, Reid, Stewart.
*Att: 36,991*

**1933-4**
**Round 3**
**Jan 13 v Portsmouth (h) 1-1**
*McLenahan*
Hall; Jones, Silcock, Vose, McMillen, Manley, Hine,
McGillivray, Ball, McLenahan, Stewart.
*Att: 23,283*
**Replay**
**Jan 17 v Portsmouth (a) 1-4**
*Ball*
Hall; Jones, Nevin, Vose, McMillen, Manley, Brown,
Hine, Ball, McLenahan, Stewart.
*Att: 18,748*

**1934-5**
**Round 3**
**Jan 12 v Bristol R (a) 3-1**
*Bamford 2, Mutch*
Hall; Griffiths, T.Jones, Robertson, Vose, McKay,
Bryant, Mutch, Bamford, Rowley, Manley.
*Att: 20,400*
**Round 4**
**Jan 26 v Nottingham F (a) 0-0**
Hacking; Griffiths, Porter, Robertson, Vose, McKay,
Cape, Mutch, Bamford, Rowley, T.J.Jones.
*Att: 32,862*
**Replay**
**Jan 30 v Nottingham F (h) 0-3**
Hacking; Griffiths, T.Jones, Robertson, Vose, McKay,
Bryant, Mutch, Bamford, Rowley, T.J.Jones.
*Att: 33,851*

**1935-6**
**Round 3**
**Jan 11 v Reading (a) 3-1**
*Mutch 2, Manley*
Hall; Griffiths, Porter, Brown, Vose, McKay, Bamford,
Gardner, Mutch, Rowley, Manley.
*Att: 25,844*
**Round 4**
**Jan 25 v Stoke C (a) 0-0**
Hall; Griffiths, Porter, Brown, Vose, McKay, Bamford,
Gardner, Mutch, Rowley, Manley.
*Att: 32,286*

**Replay**
**Jan 29 v Stoke C (h) 0-2**
Hall; Griffiths, Porter, Brown, Vose, McKay, Bryant,
Rowley, Mutch, Ferrier, Manley.
*Att: 34,440*

**1936-7**
**Round 3**
**Jan 16 v Reading (h) 1-0**
*Bamford*
Breen; Vose, Roughton, Brown, Winterbottom,
Whalley, Bryant, Mutch, Bamford, McKay, Lang.
*Att: 36,668*
**Round 4**
**Jan 30 v Arsenal (a) 0-5**
Breen; Redwood, Roughton, Brown, Winterbottom,
Whalley, Bryant, Mutch, Bamford, McKay,
Wrigglesworth.
*Att: 45,637*

**1937-8**
**Round 3**
**Jan 8 v Yeovil T (h) 3-0**
*Baird, Bamford, Pearson*
Breen; Redwood, Roughton, Brown, Vose, McKay,
Bryant, Baird, Bamford, Pearson, Rowley.
*Att: 49,004*
**Round 4**
**Jan 22 v Barnsley (a) 2-2**
*Baird, Carey*
Breen; Redwood, Roughton, Brown, Vose, McKay,
Bryant, Baird, Bamford, Carey, Rowley.
*Att: 35,549*
**Replay**
**Jan 26 v Barnsley (h) 1-0**
*Baird*
Breen; Redwood, Roughton, Savage, Vose, McKay,
Bryant, Baird, Bamford, Carey, Rowley.
*Att: 33,601*
**Round 5**
**Feb 12 v Brentford (a) 0-2**
Breen; Redwood, Roughton, Brown, Vose, Manley,
Bryant, Baird, Bamford, Carey, Rowley.
*Att: 24,147*

**1938-9**
**Round 3**
**Jan 7 v West Brom A (a) 0-0**
Tapken; Redwood, Griffiths, Warner, Vose, McKay,
Wrigglesworth, Wassall, Hanlon, Carey, Rowley.
*Att: 23,900*
**Replay**
**Jan 11 v West Brom A (h) 1-5**
*Redwood*
Tapken; Redwood, Griffiths, Warner, Gladwin,
McKay, Wrigglesworth, Wassall, Hanlon, Carey,
Smith.
*Att: 17,641*

**1945-6**
**Round 3 (1st leg)**
**Jan 5 v Accrington S (a) 2-2**
*Smith, Wrigglesworth*
Crompton; Whalley, Roach, Warner, Chilton,
Cockburn, Hanlon, Carey, Smith, Rowley,
Wrigglesworth.
*Att: 9,968*

**Round 3 (2nd leg)**
**Jan 9 v Accrington S (h) 5-1 (agg 7-3)**
*Rowley 2, Bainbridge, Wrigglesworth, opp og*
Crompton; Whalley, Roach, Warner, Carey, Cockburn, Hanlon, Rowley, Smith, Bainbridge, Wrigglesworth.
*Att: 15,339*
**Round 4 (1st leg)**
**Jan 26 v Preston NE (h) 1-0**
*Hanlon*
Crompton; Whalley, Walton, Warner, Chilton, Cockburn, Hanlon, Smith, Rowley, Carey, Wrigglesworth.
*Att: 36,237*
**Round 4 (2nd leg)**
**Jan 30 v Preston NE (a) 1-3 (agg 2-3)**
*Hanlon*
Crompton; Whalley, Walton, Warner, Chilton, Cockburn, Hanlon, Smith, Rowley, Carey, Wrigglesworth.
*Att: 21,000*

**1946-7**
**Round 3**
**Jan 11 v Bradford (a) 3-0**
*Rowley 2, Buckle*
Crompton; Aston, McGlen, Warner, Chilton, Carey, Delaney, Morris, Rowley, Pearson, Buckle.
*Att: 26,990*
**Round 4**
**Jan 25 v Nottingham F (h) 0-2**
Fielding; Aston, McGlen, Warner, Chilton, Carey, Delaney, Morris, Rowley, Pearson, Buckle.
*Att: 58,641*

**1947-8**
**Round 3**
**Jan 10 v Aston Villa (a) 6-4**
*Pearson 2, Morris 2, Delaney, Rowley*
Crompton; Carey, Aston, Anderson, Chilton, Cockburn, Delaney, Morris, Rowley, Pearson, Mitten.
*Att: 58,683*
**Round 4**
**Jan 24 v Liverpool (h*) 3-0**
*Morris, Rowley, Mitten*
Crompton; Carey, Aston, Anderson, Chilton, Cockburn, Delaney, Morris, Rowley, Pearson, Mitten.
*Att: 74,000*
*Played at Goodison Park.
**Round 5**
**Feb 7 v Charlton A (h*) 2-0**
*Warner, Mitten*
Crompton; Carey, Aston, Warner, Chilton, Cockburn, Delaney, Morris, Rowley, Pearson, Mitten.
*Att: 33,312*
*Played at Leeds Road, Huddersfield.
**Round 6**
**Feb 28 v Preston NE (h*) 4-1**
*Pearson 2, Rowley, Mitten*
Crompton; Carey, Aston, Anderson, Chilton, Cockburn, Delaney, Morris, Rowley, Pearson, Mitten.
*Att: 74,213*
*Played at Maine Road.
**Semi-final**
**Mar 13 v Derby C (at Hillsborough) 3-1**
*Pearson 3*
Crompton; Carey, Aston, Anderson, Chilton,

Cockburn, Delaney, Morris, Rowley, Pearson, Mitten.
*Att: 60,000*
**Final**
**Apr 24 v Blackpool (at Wembley) 4-2**
*Rowley 2, Pearson, Anderson*
Crompton; Carey, Aston, Anderson, Chilton, Cockburn, Delaney, Morris, Rowley, Pearson, Mitten.
*Att: 99,000*

**1948-9**
**Round 3**
**Jan 8 v Bournemouth & Boscombe A (h) 6-0**
*Burke 2, Rowley 2, Pearson, Mitten*
Crompton; Carey, Aston, Cockburn, Chilton, McGlen, Delaney, Pearson, Burke, Rowley, Mitten.
*Att: 55,012*
**Round 4**
**Jan 29 v Bradford (h) 1-1**
*Mitten*
Crompton; Carey, Aston, Cockburn, Chilton, McGlen, Delaney, Morris, Rowley, Pearson, Mitten.
*Att: 82,771*
**Replay**
**Feb 5 v Bradford (a) 1-1 a.e.t.**
*Mitten*
Crompton; Carey, Aston, Cockburn, Chilton, McGlen, Buckle, Pearson, Burke, Rowley, Mitten.
*Att: 30,000*
**Second Replay**
**Feb 7 v Bradford (h) 5-0**
*Burke 2, Rowley 2, Pearson*
Crompton; Carey, Aston, Cockburn, Chilton, McGlen, Buckle, Pearson, Burke, Rowley, Mitten.
*Att: 70,434*
**Round 5**
**Feb 12 v Yeovil T (h) 8-0**
*Rowley 5, Burke 2, Mitten*
Crompton; Carey, Aston, Cockburn, Chilton, McGlen, Delaney, Pearson, Burke, Rowley, Mitten.
*Att: 81,565*
**Round 6**
**Feb 26 v Hull C (a) 1-0**
*Pearson*
Crompton; Ball, Aston, Cockburn, Chilton, McGlen, Delaney, Pearson, Burke, Rowley, Mitten.
*Att: 55,000*
**Semi-final**
**Mar 26 v Wolves (at Hillsborough) 1-1 a.e.t.**
*Mitten*
Crompton; Carey, Aston, Cockburn, Chilton, McGlen, Delaney, Anderson, Rowley, Person, Mitten.
*Att: 62,250*
**Replay**
**Apr 2 v Wolves (at Goodison Park) 0-1**
Crompton; Carey, Aston, Cockburn, Chilton, McGlen, Delaney, Pearson, Burke, Rowley, Mitten.
*Att: 73,000*

**1949-50**
**Round 3**
**Jan 7 v Weymouth (h) 4-0**
*Rowley 2, Pearson, Delaney*
Feehan; Carey, Aston, Cockburn, Chilton, McGlen, Delaney, Bogan, Rowley, Pearson, Mitten.
*Att: 38,284*
**Round 4**
**Jan 28 v Watford (a) 1-0**
*Rowley*

Lancaster; Carey, Aston, Warner, Chilton, Cockburn, Delaney, Bogan, Rowley, Pearson, Mitten.
*Att: 32,800*

**Round 5**
**Feb 11 v Portsmouth (h) 3-3**
*Mitten 2, Pearson*
Lancaster; Carey, Aston, Warner, Chilton, Cockburn, Delaney, Bogan, Rowley, Pearson, Mitten.
*Att: 53,688*

**Replay**
**Feb 15 v Portsmouth (a) 3-1**
*Delaney, Downie, Mitten*
Feehan; Carey, Aston, Warner, Chilton, Cockburn, Delaney, Bogan, Rowley, Downie, Mitten.
*Att: 49,962*

**Round 6**
**Mar 4 v Chelsea (a) 0-2**
Crompton; Carey, Aston, Warner, Chilton, Cockburn, Delaney, Downie, Rowley, Pearson, Mitten.
*Att: 70,362*

**1950-51**
**Round 3**
**Jan 6 v Oldham A (h) 4-1**
*Pearson, Aston, Birch, Whyte (og)*
Allen; Carey, McGlen, Lowrie, Chilton, Cockburn, Birkett, Pearson, Aston, Birch, McShane.
*Att: 37,161*

**Round 4**
**Jan 27 v Leeds U (h) 4-0**
*Pearson 3, Rowley*
Allen; Carey, Redman, Gibson, Chilton, Cockburn, Birkett, Pearson, Aston, Birch, Rowley.
*Att: 55,434*

**Round 5**
**Feb 10 v Arsenal (h) 1-0**
*Pearson*
Allen; Carey, Redman, Gibson, Chilton, Cockburn, Birkett, Pearson, Aston, Birch, Rowley.
*Att: 55,058*

**Round 6**
**Feb 24 v Birmingham C (a) 0-1**
Allen; McNulty, Carey, Gibson, Chilton, Cockburn, Birkett, Pearson, Aston, Birch, Rowley.
*Att: 50,000*

**1951-2**
**Round 3**
**Jan 12 v Hull C (h) 0-2**
Allen; McNulty, Byrne, Carey, Chilton, Cockburn, Berry, Pearson, Rowley, Downie, Bond.
*Att: 43,517*

**1952-3**
**Round 3**
**Jan 10 v Millwall (a) 1-0**
*Pearson*
Wood; Aston, Byrne, Carey, Chilton, Cockburn, Berry, Downie, Lewis, Pearson, Rowley.
*Att: 35,652*

**Round 4**
**Jan 31 v Walthamstow Avenue (h) 1-1**
*Lewis*
Wood; Aston, Byrne, Carey, Chilton, Cockburn, Berry, Downie, Lewis, Pearson, Rowley.
*Att: 34,748*

**Replay**
**Feb 5 v Walthamstow Avenue (a*) 5-2**
*Rowley 2, Byrne, Lewis, Pearson*
Wood; Aston, Byrne, Carey, Chilton, Cockburn, Berry, Lewis, Rowley, Pearson, Pegg.
*Att: 49,119*
*Played at Highbury

**Round 5**
**Feb 14 v Everton (a) 1-2**
*Rowley*
Wood; Aston, Byrne, Carey, Chilton, Cockburn, Berry, Lewis, Rowley, Pearson, Pegg.
*Att: 77,920*

**1953-4**
**Round 3**
**Jan 9 v Burnley (a) 3-5**
*Blanchflower, Taylor, Viollet*
Wood; Foulkes, Byrne, Whitefoot, Chilton, Edwards, Berry, Blanchflower, Taylor, Viollet, Rowley.
*Att: 54,000*

**1954-5**
**Round 3**
**Jan 8 v Reading (a) 1-1**
*Webster*
Wood; Foulkes, Byrne, Gibson, Chilton, Edwards, Berry, Blanchflower, Webster, Viollet, Rowley.
*Att: 26,000*

**Replay**
**Jan 12 v Reading (h) 4-1**
*Webster 2, Viollet, Rowley*
Wood; Foulkes, Byrne, Gibson, Chilton, Edwards, Berry, Blanchflower, Webster, Viollet, Rowley.
*Att: 24,578*

**Round 4**
**Jan 29 v Manchester C (a) 0-2**
Wood; Foulkes, Byrne, Gibson, Chilton, Edwards, Berry, Blanchflower, Taylor, Viollet, Rowley.
*Att: 75,000*

**1955-6**
**Round 3**
**Jan 7 v Bristol R (a) 0-4**
Wood; Foulkes, Byrne, Colman, Jones, Whitefoot, Berry, Doherty, Taylor, Viollet, Pegg.
*Att: 35,872*

**1956-7**
**Round 3**
**Jan 5 v Hartlepools U (a) 4-3**
*Whelan 2, Berry, Taylor*
Wood; Foulkes, Byrne, Colman, Jones, Edwards, Berry, Whelan, Taylor, Viollet, Pegg.
*Att: 17,264*

**Round 4**
**Jan 26 v Wrexham (a) 5-0**
*Whelan 2, Taylor 2, Byrne*
Wood; Foulkes, Byrne, Colman, Jones, Edwards, Webster, Whelan, Taylor, Viollet, Pegg.
*Att: 34,445*

**Round 5**
**Feb 16 v Everton (h) 1-0**
*Edwards*
Wood; Foulkes, Byrne, Colman, Jones, Edwards, Berry, Whelan, Taylor, Viollet, Pegg.
*Att: 61,803*

**Round 6**
**Mar 2 v Bournemouth & Boscombe A (a) 2-1**
*Berry 2*
Wood; Foulkes, Byrne, Colman, Jones, McGuinness,
Berry, Whelan, Edwards, Viollet, Pegg.
*Att: 28,799*
**Semi-final**
**Mar 23 v Birmingham C (at Hillsborough) 2-0**
*Berry, Charlton*
Wood; Foulkes, Byrne, Colman, Blanchflower,
Edwards, Berry, Whelan, Charlton, Viollet, Pegg.
*Att: 65,107*
**Final**
**May 4 v Aston Villa (at Wembley) 1-2**
*Taylor*
Wood; Foulkes, Byrne, Colman, Blanchflower,
Edwards, Berry, Whelan, Taylor, Charlton, Pegg.
*Att: 100,000*

**1957-8**
**Round 3**
**Jan 4 v Workington (a) 3-1**
*Viollet 3*
Gregg; Foulkes, Byrne, Colman, M.Jones, Edwards,
Morgans, Charlton, T.Taylor, Viollet, Scanlon.
*Att: 21,000*
**Round 4**
**Jan 25 v Ipswich T (h) 2-0**
*Charlton 2*
Gregg; Foulkes, Byrne, Colman, M.Jones, Edwards,
Morgans, Charlton, T.Taylor, Viollet, Scanlon.
*Att: 53,550*
**Round 5**
**Feb 19 v Sheffield W (h) 3-0**
*Brennan 2, Dawson*
Gregg; Foulkes, Greaves, Goodwin, Cope, Crowther,
Webster, E.Taylor, Dawson, Pearson, Brennan.
*Att: 59,848*
**Round 6**
**Mar 1 v West Brom A (a) 2-2**
*E.Taylor, Dawson*
Gregg; Foulkes, Greaves, Goodwin, Cope, Crowther,
Webster, E.Taylor, Dawson, Pearson, Charlton.
*Att: 58,250*
**Replay**
**Mar 5 v West Brom A (h) 1-0**
*Webster*
Gregg; Foulkes, Greaves, Goodwin, Cope, Harrop,
Webster, E.Taylor, Dawson, Pearson, Charlton.
*Att: 60,000*
**Semi-final**
**Mar 22 v Fulham (at Villa Park) 2-2**
*Charton 2*
Gregg; Foulkes, Greaves, Goodwin, Cope, Crowther,
Webster, E.Taylor, Dawson, Pearson, Charlton.
*Att: 69,745*
**Replay**
**Mar 26 v Fulham (at Highbury) 5-3**
*Dawson 3, Charlton, Brennan*
Gregg; Foulkes, Greaves, Goodwin, Cope, Crowther,
Webster, E.Taylor, Dawson, Charlton, Brennan.
*Att: 38,000*
**Final**
**May 3 v Bolton W (at Wembley) 0-2**
Gregg; Foulkes, Greaves, Goodwin, Cope, Crowther,
Dawson, E.Taylor, Charlton, Viollet, Webster.
*Att: 100,000*

**1958-9**
**Round 3**
**Jan 10 v Norwich C (a) 0-3**
Gregg; Foulkes, Carolan, Goodwin, Cope, McGuinness,
Bradley, Quixall, Viollet, Charlton, Scanlon.
*Att: 38,000*

**1959-60**
**Round 3**
**Jan 9 v Derby C (a) 4-2**
*Goodwin, Charlton, Scanlon, Barrowcliffe (og)*
Gregg; Foulkes, Carolan, Goodwin, Cope, Brennan,
Dawson, Quixall, Viollet, Charlton, Scanlon.
*Att: 33,297*
**Round 4**
**Jan 30 v Liverpool (a) 3-1**
*Charlton 2, Bradley*
Gregg; Foulkes, Carolan, Setters, Cope, Brennan,
Bradley, Quixall, Viollet, Charlton, Scanlon.
*Att: 56,736*
**Round 5**
**Feb 20 v Sheffield W (h) 0-1**
Gregg; Foulkes, Carolan, Setters, Cope, Brennan,
Bradley, Quixall, Viollet, Charlton, Scanlon.
*Att: 66,350*

**1960-61**
**Round 3**
**Jan 7 v Middlesbrough (h) 3-0**
*Dawson 2, Cantwell*
Gregg; Brennan, Cantwell, Setters, Foulkes, Nicholson,
Quixall, Stiles, Dawson, Pearson, Charlton.
*Att: 49,184*
**Round 4**
**Jan 28 v Sheffield W (a) 1-1**
*Cantwell*
Briggs; Brennan, Cantwell, Setters, Foulkes, Nicholson,
Viollet, Stiles, Dawson, Pearson, Charlton.
*Att: 58,000*
**Replay**
**Feb 1 v Sheffield W (h) 2-7**
*Dawson, Pearson*
Briggs; Brennan, Cantwell, Setters, Foulkes, Nicholson,
Quixall, Stiles, Dawson, Pearson, Charlton.
*Att: 65,243*

**1961-2**
**Round 3**
**Jan 6 v Bolton W (h) 2-1**
*Nicholson, Herd*
Gaskell; Brennan, Dunne, Nicholson, Foulkes, Setters,
Chisnall, Giles, Herd, Lawton, Charlton.
*Att: 42,202*
**Round 4**
**Jan 31 v Arsenal (h) 1-0**
*Setters*
Gaskell; Brennan, Dunne, Nicholson, Foulkes, Setters,
Chisnall, Stiles, Lawton, Giles, Charlton.
*Att: 54,082*
**Round 5**
**Feb 17 v Sheffield W (h) 0-0**
Gaskell; Brennan, Dunne, Setters, Foulkes, Nicholson,
Chisnall, Giles, Herd, Lawton, Charlton.
*Att: 59,553*
**Replay**
**Feb 21 v Sheffield W (a) 2-0**
*Charlton, Giles*

Gaskell; Brennan, Dunne, Stiles, Foulkes, Setters, Quixall, Giles, Herd, Lawton, Charlton.
*Att: 62,969*
**Round 6**
**Mar 10 v Preston NE (a) 0-0**
Gaskell; Brennan, Dunne, Nicholson, Foulkes, Setters, Chisnall, Giles, Cantwell, Lawton, Charlton.
*Att: 37,521*
**Replay**
**Mar 14 v Preston NE (h) 2-1**
*Herd, Charlton*
Gaskell; Brennan, Dunne, Stiles, Foulkes, Setters, Quixall, Giles, Herd, Lawton, Charlton.
*Att: 63,468*
**Semi-final**
**Mar 31 v Tottenham H (at Hillsborough) 1-3**
*Herd*
Gaskell; Dunne, Cantwell, Stiles, Foulkes, Setters, Quixall, Giles, Herd, Lawton, Charlton.
*Att: 65,000*

**1962-3**
**Round 3**
**Mar 4 v Huddersfield T (h) 5-0**
*Law 3, Giles, Quixall*
Gregg; Brennan, Cantwell, Stiles, Foulkes, Setters, Giles, Quixall, Herd, Law, Charlton.
*Att: 47,703*
**Round 4**
**Mar 11 v Aston Villa (h) 1-0**
*Quixall*
Gregg; Brennan, Cantwell, Stiles, Foulkes, .Setters, Giles, Quixall, Herd, Law, Charlton.
*Att: 52,265*
**Round 5**
**Mar 16 v Chelsea (h) 2-1**
*Quixall, Law*
Gregg; Brennan, Cantwell, Stiles, Foulkes, Setters, Giles, Quixall, Herd, Law, Charlton.
*Att: 48,298*
**Round 6**
**Mar 30 v Coventry C (a) 3-1**
*Charlton 2, Quixall*
Gregg; Brennan, Dunne, Crerand, Foulkes, Setters, Giles, Quixall, Herd, Law, Charlton.
*Att: 44,000*
**Semi-final**
**Apr 27 v Southampton (at Villa Park) 1-0**
*Law*
Gaskell; Dunne, Cantwell, Crerand, Foulkes, Setters, Giles, Stiles, Herd, Law, Charlton.
*Att: 65,000*
**Final**
**May 25 v Leicester C (at Wembley) 3-1**
*Herd 2, Law*
Gaskell; Dunne, Cantwell, Crerand, Foulkes, Setters, Giles, Quixall, Herd, Law, Charlton.
*Att: 100,000*

**1963-4**
**Round 3**
**Jan 4 v Southampton (a) 3-2**
*Crerand, Moore, Herd*
Gaskell; Dunne, Cantwell, Crerand, Foulkes, Setters, Anderson, Moore, Charlton, Moore, Herd, Best.
*Att: 29,164*

**Round 4**
**Jan 25 v Bristol R (h) 4-1**
*Law 3, Herd*
Gaskell; Dunne, Cantwell, Crerand, Foulkes, Setters, Herd, Chisnall, Charlton, Law, Best.
*Att: 55,772*
**Round 5**
**Feb 15 v Barnsley (a) 4-0**
*Law 2, Best, Herd*
Gaskell; Brennan, Dunne, Crerand, Foulkes, Setters, Herd, Stiles, Charlton, Law, Best.
*Att: 38,076*
**Round 6**
**Feb 29 v Sunderland (h) 3-3**
*Charlton, Best, Hurley (og)*
Gaskell; Brennan, Dunne, Crerand, Foulkes, Setters, Herd, Stiles, Charlton, Law, Best.
*Att: 63,700*
**Replay**
**Mar 4 v Sunderland (a) 2-2 a.e.t.**
*Charlton, Law*
Gaskell; Brennan, Dunne, Crerand, Foulkes, Setters, Herd, Chisnall, Charlton, Law, Best.
*Att: 68,000*
**Second Replay**
**Mar 9 v Sunderland (at Leeds Road, Huddersf'ld) 5-1**
*Law 3, Chisnall, Herd*
Gaskell; Brennan, Dunne, Crerand, Foulkes, Setters, Herd, Chisnall, Charlton, Law, Best.
*Att: 54,952*
**Semi-final**
**Mar 14 v West Ham U (at Hillsborough) 1-3**
*Law*
Gaskell; Brennan, Dunne, Crerand, Foulkes, Setters, Herd, Chisnall, Charlton, Law, Best.
*Att: 65,000*

**1964-5**
**Round 3**
**Jan 9 v Chester (h) 2-1**
*Kinsey, Best*
P.Dunne; Brennan, A.Dunne, Crerand, Foulkes, Stiles, Connelly, Charlton, Herd, Kinsey, Best.
*Att: 40,000*
**Round 4**
**Jan 30 v Stoke C (a) 0-0**
P.Dunne; Brennan, A.Dunne, Crerand, Foulkes, Stiles, Connelly, Charlton, Herd, Law, Best.
*Att: 53,009*
**Replay**
**Feb 3 v Stoke C (h) 1-0**
*Herd*
P.Dunne; Brennan, A.Dunne, Crerand, Foulkes, Stiles, Connelly, Charlton, Herd, Law, Best.
*Att: 50,814*
**Round 5**
**Feb 20 v Burnley (h) 2-1**
*Crerand, Law*
P.Dunne; Brennan, A.Dunne, Crerand, Foulkes, Stiles, Connelly, Charlton, Herd, Law, Best.
*Att: 54,000*
**Round 6**
**Mar 10 v Wolves (a) 5-3**
*Law 2, Crerand, Herd, Best*
P.Dunne; Brennan, A.Dunne, Crerand, Foulkes, Stiles, Connelly, Charlton, Herd, Law, Best.
*Att: 53,581*

**Semi-final**
**Mar 27 v Leeds U (at Hillsborough) 0-0**
P.Dunne; Brennan, A.Dunne, Crerand, Foulkes,
Stiles, Connelly, Charlton, Herd, Law, Best.
*Att: 65,000*
**Replay**
**Mar 31 v Leeds U (at City Ground, Nottingham) 0-1**
P.Dunne; Brennan, A.Dunne, Crerand, Foulkes,
Stiles, Connelly, Charlton, Herd, Law, Best.
*Att: 46,300*

**1965-6**
**Round 3**
**Jan 22 v Derby C (a) 5-2**
*Best 2, Law 2, Herd*
Gregg; Dunne, Cantwell, Crerand, Foulkes, Stiles,
Best, Law, Charlton, Herd, Aston.
*Att: 33,827*
**Round 4**
**Feb 12 v Rotherham U (h) 0-0**
Gregg; Dunne, Cantwell, Crerand, Foulkes, Stiles,
Best, Law, Charlton, Herd, Connelly.
*54,263*
**Replay**
**Feb 15 v Rotherham U (a) 1-0 a.e.t.**
*Connelly*
Gregg; Brennan, Dunne, Crerand, Foulkes, Stiles, Best,
Law, Charlton, Herd, Connelly.
*Att: 23,500*
**Round 5**
**Mar 5 v Wolves (a) 4-2**
*Law 2, Herd, Best*
Gregg; Brennan, Dunne, Crerand, Foulkes, Stiles, Best,
Law, Charlton, Herd, Connelly.
*Att: 53,500*
**Round 6**
**Mar 26 v Preston NE (a) 1-1**
*Herd*
Gregg; Brennan, Dunne, Crerand, Foulkes, Stiles, Best,
Law, Charlton, Herd, Connelly.
*Att: 37,876*
**Replay**
**Mar 30 v Preston NE (h) 3-1**
*Law 2, Connelly*
Gregg; Brennan, Dunne, Crerand, Foulkes, Stiles,
Connelly, Law, Charlton, Herd, Aston.
*Att: 60,433*
**Semi-final**
**Apr 23 v Everton (at Burnden Park) 0-1**
Gregg; Brennan, Dunne, Crerand, Foulkes, Stiles,
Anderson, Law, Charlton, Herd, Connelly.
*Att: 60,000*

**1966-7**
**Round 3**
**Jan 28 v Stoke C (h) 2-0**
*Law, Herd*
Stepney; Dunne, Noble, Crerand, Foulkes, Stiles, Best,
Law, Sadler, Herd, Charlton.
*Att: 63,500*
**Round 4**
**Feb 18 v Norwich C (h) 1-2**
*Law*
Stepney; Dunne, Noble, Crerand, Sadler, Stiles, Ryan,
Law, Charlton, Herd, Best.
*Att: 63,409*

**1967-8**
**Round 3**
**Jan 27 v Tottenham H (h) 2-2**
*Best, Charlton*
Stepney; Dunne, Burns, Crerand, Sadler, Fitzpatrick,
Best, Kidd, Charlton, Law, Aston.
*Att: 63,500*
**Replay**
**Jan 31 v Tottenham H (a) 0-1 a.e.t.**
Stepney; Dunne, Burns, Crerand, Sadler, Fitzpatrick,
Best, Kidd, Charlton, Herd, Aston.
*Att: 57,200*
**1968-9**
**Round 3**
**Jan 4 v Exeter C (a) 3-1**
*Fitzpatrick, Kidd, Newman (og)*
Stepney; Dunne, Burns, Fitzpatrick, James, Stiles,
Best(Sadler), Kidd, Charlton, Law, Sartori.
*Att: 18,500*
**Round 4**
**Jan 25 v Watford (h) 1-1**
*Law*
Rimmer; Kopel, Dunne, Fitzpatrick, James, Stiles,
Morgan, Best, Charlton, Law, Sartori.
*Att: 63,498*
**Replay**
**Feb 3 v Watford (a) 2-0**
*Law 2*
Stepney; Fitzpatrick, Dunne, Crerand, James, Stiles,
Morgan, Kidd, Charlton, Law, Best.
*Att: 34,000*
**Round 5**
**Feb 8 v Birmingham C (a) 2-2**
*Law, Best*
Stepney; Fitzpatrick, Dunne, Crerand, James, Stiles,
Morgan, Kidd, Charlton, Law, Best.
*Att: 52,500*
**Replay**
**Feb 24 v Birmingham C (h) 6-2**
*Law 3, Kidd, Morgan, Crerand*
Stepney; Fitzpatrick, Dunne, Crerand, James, Stiles,
Morgan, Kidd, Charlton, Law, Best.
*Att: 61,932*
**Round 6**
**Mar 1 v Everton (h) 0-1**
Stepney; Fitzpatrick, Dunne, Crerand, James, Stiles,
Morgan, Kidd, Charlton, Law, Best.
*Att: 63,464*
**1969-70**
**Round 3**
**Jan 3 v Ipswich T (a) 1-0**
*McNeil (og)*
Stepney; Edwards, Brennan, Burns, Ure, Sadler,
Morgan(Aston), Crerand, Charlton, Kidd, Best.
*Att: 29,552*
**Round 4**
**Jan 24 v Manchester C (h) 3-0**
*Kidd 2, Morgan*
Stepney; Edwards, Burns, Crerand, Ure, Sadler,
Morgan, Sartori, Charlton, Kidd, Aston.
*Att: 63,417*
**Round 5**
**Feb 7 v Northampton T (a) 8-2**
*Best 6, Kidd 2*
Stepney; Edwards, Dunne, Crerand, Ure, Sadler,
Morgan, Sartori, Charlton(Burns), Kidd, Best.
*Att: 21,771*

**Round 6**
**Feb 21 v Middlesbrough (a) 1-1**
*Sartori*
Stepney; Edwards, Dunne, Crerand, Ure, Sadler, Morgan, Sartori, Charlton, Kidd, Best.
*Att: 40,000*
**Replay**
**Feb 25 v Middlesbrough (h) 2-1**
*Charlton, Morgan*
Stepney; Dunne, Burns, Crerand, Ure, Sadler, Morgan, Sartori, Charlton, Kidd, Best.
*Att: 63,418*
**Semi-final**
**Mar 14 v Leeds U (at Hillsborough) 0-0**
Stepney; Edwards, Dunne, Crerand, Ure, Sadler, Morgan, Sartori, Charlton, Kidd, Best.
*Att: 55,000*
**Replay**
**Mar 23 v Leeds U (at Villa Park) 0-0 a.e.t.**
Stepney; Edwards, Dunne, Crerand, Sadler, Stiles, Morgan, Sartori(Law), Charlton, Kidd, Best.
*Att: 62,500*
**Second Replay**
**Mar 26 v Leeds U (at Burnden Park) 0-1**
Stepney; Edwards, Dunne, Crerand, Sadler, Stiles Morgan, Sartori(Law), Charlton, Kidd, Best.
*Att: 56,000*
**Third-place Play-off**
**Apr 10 v Watford (at Highbury) 2-0**
*Kidd 2*
Stepney; Stiles, Dunne, Crerand, Ure, Sadler, Morgan, Fitzpatrick, Charlton, Kidd, Best.
*Att: 15,105*

**1970-71**
**Round 3**
**Jan 2 v Middlesbrough (h) 0-0**
Rimmer; Fitzpatrick, Dunne, Crerand, Ure, Sadler, Morgan, Best, Charlton, Kidd, Law.
*Att: 47,824*
**Replay**
**Jan 5 v Middlesbrough (a) 1-2**
*Best*
Rimmer; Fitzpatrick, Dunne, Crerand, Edwards, Sadler, Morgan, Best, Charlton, Kidd(Gowling), Law.
*Att: 41,000*

**1971-2**
**Round 3**
**Jan 15 v Southampton (a) 1-1**
*Charlton*
Stepney; O'Neil, Burns, Gowling, Edwards, Sadler, Morgan, Kidd(McIlroy), Charlton, Law, Best.
*Att: 30,190*
**Replay**
**Jan 19 v Southampton (h) 4-1 a.e.t.**
*Best 2, Sadler, Aston*
Stepney; O'Neil, Burns, Gowling, Edwards, Sadler, Morgan, McIlroy(Aston), Charlton, Law, Best.
*Att: 50,960*
**Round 4**
**Feb 5 v Preston NE (a) 2-0**
*Gowling 2*
Stepney; O'Neil, Burns, Gowling, James, Sadler, Morgan, Kidd, Charlton, Law, Best.
*Att: 27,025*

**Round 5**
**Feb 26 v Middlesbrough (h) 0-0**
Stepney; O'Neil, Dunne, Burns, James, Sadler, Morgan, Gowling, Charlton, Law, Best.
*Att: 53,850*
**Replay**
**Feb 29 v Middlesbrough (a) 3-0**
*Morgan, Charlton, Best*
Stepney; O'Neil, Dunne, Burns, James, Sadler, Morgan, Gowling, Charlton, Law, Best.
*Att: 39,683*
**Round 6**
**Mar 18 v Stoke C (h) 1-1**
*Best*
Stepney; O'Neil, Dunne, Buchan, James, Sadler (Gowling), Morgan, Kidd, Charlton, Law, Best.
*Att: 54,226*
**Replay**
**Mar 22 v Stoke C (a) 1-2 a.e.t.**
*Best*
Stepney; O'Neil, Dunne, Gowling, James, Buchan, Morgan(McIlroy), Kidd, Charlton, Law, Best.
*Att: 49,192*

**1972-3**
**Round 3**
**Jan 13 Wolves (a) 0-1**
Stepney; Young, Forsyth, Law, Sadler, Buchan, Morgan, W.Davies, Charlton, Kidd(Dunne), Graham.
*Att: 40,005*

**1973-4**
**Round 3**
**Jan 5 v Plymouth A (h) 1-0**
*Macari*
Stepney; Young, Forsyth, B.Greenhoff, Holton, Buchan, Morgan, Macari, Kidd, Graham, Martin (McIlroy).
*Att: 31,810*
**Round 4**
**Jan 26 v Ipswich T (h) 0-1**
Stepney; Buchan, Forsyth, B.Greenhoff, Holton, James, Morgan, Macari(Kidd), McIlroy, Young, Martin.
*Att: 37,177*

**1974-5**
**Round 3**
**Jan 4 v Walsall (h) 0-0**
Stepney; Young, Houston, B.Greenhoff, Sidebottom, Buchan, Morgan(R.Davies), McIlroy, Pearson, Macari, Daly.
*Att: 43,353*
**Replay**
**Jan 7 v Walsall (a) 2-3 a.e.t.**
*McIlroy, Daly*
Stepney; Young, Houston, B.Greenhoff, Sidebottom, Buchan, McCalliog, McIlroy, Pearson, Macari, Daly(R.Davies).
*Att: 18,105*

**1975-6**
**Round 3**
**Jan 3 v Oxford U (h) 2-1**
*Daly 2*
Stepney; Forsyth(Nicholl), Houston, Daly, B.Greenhoff, Buchan, Coppell, McIlroy, Pearson, Macari, Hill.
*Att: 41,082*

400

**Round 4**
**Jan 24 v Peterborough U (h) 3-1**
*Forsyth, McIlroy, Hill*
Stepney; Forsyth, Houston, Daly, B.Greenhoff,
Buchan, Coppell, McIlroy, Pearson, Macari, Hill.
*Att: 56,352*
**Round 5**
**Feb 14 v Leicester C (a) 2-1**
*Daly, Macari*
Stepney; Forsyth, Houston, Daly, B.Greenhoff,
Buchan, Coppell, McIlroy, Pearson, Macari,
Hill(McCreery).
*Att: 34,000*
**Round 6**
**Mar 6 v Wolves (h) 1-1**
*Daly*
Stepney; Forsyth, Houston, Daly, B.Greenhoff,
Buchan, Coppell, McIlroy, Pearson, Macari, Hill.
*Att: 59,433*
**Replay**
**Mar 9 v Wolves (a) 3-2 a.e.t.**
*B.Greenhoff, McIlroy, Pearson*
Stepney; Forsyth, Houston, Daly, B.Greenhoff,
Buchan, Coppell, McIlroy, Pearson, Macari (Nicholl),
Hill.
*Att: 44,373*
**Semi-final**
**Apr 3 v Derby C (at Hillsborough) 2-0**
*Hill 2*
Stepney; Forsyth, Houston, Daly, B.Greenhoff, Buchan,
Coppell, McIlroy, Pearson, McCreery, Hill.
*Att: 55,000*
**Final**
**May 1 v Southampton (at Wembley) 0-1**
Stepney; Forsyth, Houston, Daly, B.Greenhoff,
Buchan, Coppell, McIlroy, Pearson, Macari,
Hill(McCreery).
*Att: 100,000*


**1976-7**
**Round 3**
**Jan 8 v Walsall (h) 1-0**
*Hill*
Stepney; Nicholl, Houston, McIlroy, B.Greenhoff,
Buchan, Coppell(Daly), J.Greenhoff, Pearson, Macari,
Hill.
*Att: 48,870*
**Round 4**
**Jan 29 v Queen's Park R (h) 1-0**
*Macari*
Stepney; Nicholl, Houston, McIlroy, B.Greenhoff,
Buchan, Coppell, J.Greenhoff, Pearson, Macari, Hill.
*Att: 57,422*
**Round 5**
**Feb 26 v Southampton (a) 2-2**
*Macari, Hill*
Stepney; Nicholl, Houston, McIlroy, B.Greenhoff,
Buchan, Coppell, J.Greenhoff(McCreery), Pearson,
Macari, Hill.
*Att: 29,137*
**Replay**
**Mar 8 v Southampton (h) 2-1**
*J.Greenhoff 2*
Stepney; Nicholl, Houston, McIlroy, B.Greenhoff,
Buchan, Coppell, J.Greenhoff, Pearson, Macari, Hill.
*Att: 58,103*

**Round 6**
**Mar 19 v Aston Villa (h) 2-1**
*Houston, Macari*
Stepney; Nicholl, Houston, McIlroy, B.Greenhoff
(McCreery), Buchan, Coppell, J.Greenhoff, Pearson,
Macari, Hill.
*Att: 57,089*
**Semi-final**
**Apr 23 v Leeds U (at Hillsborough) 2-1**
*Coppell, J.Greenhoff*
Stepney; Nicholl, Houston, McIlroy, B.Greenhoff,
Buchan, Coppell, J.Greenhoff, Pearson, Macari, Hill.
*Att: 55,000*
**Final**
**May 21 v Liverpool (at Wembley) 2-1**
*Pearson, J.Greenhoff*
Stepney; Nicholl, Albiston, McIlroy, B.Greenhoff,
Buchan, Coppell, J.Greenhoff, Pearson, Macari,
Hill(McCreery).
*Att: 100,000*


**1977-8**
**Round 3**
**Jan 7 v Carlisle U (a) 1-1**
*Macari*
Roche; Nicholl, Albiston, McIlroy, B.Greenhoff,
Buchan, Coppell, J.Greenhoff, Pearson, Macari,
Grimes(McCreery).
*Att: 21,710*
**Replay**
**Jan 11 v Carlisle U (h) 4-2**
*Pearson 2, Macari 2*
Roche; Nicholl, Albiston, McIlroy, Houston, Buchan,
Coppell, J.Greenhoff, Pearson, Macari, Hill.
*Att: 54,156*
**Round 4**
**Jan 28 v West Brom A (h) 1-1**
*Coppell*
Roche; Nicholl, Albiston, McIlroy, Houston, Buchan,
Coppell, Jordan, Pearson, Macari, Hill.
*Att: 57,056*
**Replay**
**Feb 1 v West Brom A (a) 2-3 a.e.t.**
*Pearson, Hill*
Roche; Nicholl, Albiston(J.Greenhoff), McIlroy,
Houston, Buchan, Coppell, Jordan, Pearson, Macari,
Hill.
*Att: 37,086*


**1978-9**
**Round 3**
**Jan 15 v Chelsea (h) 3-0**
*Coppell, J.Greenhoff, Grimes*
Bailey; B.Greenhoff, Houston, McIlroy, McQueen,
Buchan, Coppell, J.Greenhoff, Pearson, Nicholl,
Grimes.
*Att: 38,743*
**Round 4**
**Jan 31 v Fulham (a) 1-1**
*J.Greenhoff*
Bailey; B.Greenhoff, Houston, McIlroy, McQueen,
Buchan, Coppell, J.Greenhoff, Pearson(Nicholl),
Macari, Thomas.
*Att: 25,229*

**Replay**
**Feb 12 v Fulham (h) 1-0**
*J.Greenhoff*
Bailey; B.Greenhoff, Albiston, McIlroy, McQueen, Buchan, Coppell, J.Greenhoff, Ritchie, Macari, Thomas.
*Att: 41,200*
**Round 5**
**Feb 20 v Colchester U (a) 1-0**
*J.Greenhoff*
Bailey; B.Greenhoff(Nicholl), Albiston, McIlroy, McQueen, Buchan, Coppell, J.Greenhoff, Ritchie, Macari, Thomas.
*Att: 13,171*
**Round 6**
**Mar 10 v Tottenham H (a) 1-1**
*Thomas*
Bailey; Nicholl, Albiston, McIlroy, McQueen, Buchan, Coppell, J.Greenhoff, Ritchie(Jordan), Grimes, Thomas.
*Att: 51,800*
**Replay**
**Mar 14 v Tottenham H (h) 2-0**
*McIlroy, Jordan*
Bailey; Nicholl, Albiston, McIlroy, McQueen, Buchan, Coppell, J.Greenhoff, Jordan, Grimes, Thomas.
*Att: 55,584*
**Semi-final**
**Mar 31 v Liverpool (at Maine Road) 2-2**
*Jordan, B.Greenhoff*
Bailey; Nicholl, Albiston, McIlroy, McQueen, Buchan, Coppell, J.Greenhoff, Jordan, B.Greenhoff, Thomas.
*Att: 52,524*
**Replay**
**Apr 4 v Liverpool (at Goodison Park) 1-0**
*J.Greenhoff*
Bailey; Nicholl, Albiston, McIlroy, McQueen, Buchan, Coppell, J.Greenhoff, Jordan, Macari (Ritchie), Thomas.
*Att: 53,069*
**Final**
**May 12 v Arsenal (at Wembley) 2-3**
*McQueen, McIlroy*
Bailey; Nicholl, Albiston, McIlroy, McQueen, Buchan, Coppell, J.Greenhoff, Jordan, Macari, Thomas.
*Att: 100,000*

**1979-80**
**Round 3**
**Jan 5 v Tottenham H (a) 1-1**
*McIlroy*
Bailey; Nicholl, Houston, McIlroy, McQueen, Buchan, Coppell, Wilkins, Jordan, Macari, Thomas.
*Att: 45,207*
**Replay**
**Jan 9 v Tottenham H (h) 0-1 a.e.t.**
Bailey; Nicholl, Houston, McIlroy, McQueen, Buchan, Coppell, Wilkins, Jordan, Macari, Thomas.
*Att: 53,762*

**1980-81**
**Round 3**
**Jan 3 v Brighton & HA (h) 2-2**
*Duxbury, Thomas*

Bailey; Nicholl, Albiston, McIlroy(Duxbury), Jovanovic, Moran, Coppell, Birtles, Jordan, Macari, Thomas.
*Att: 42,199*
**Replay**
**Jan 7 v Brighton & HA (a) 2-0**
*Nicholl, Birtles*
Bailey; Nicholl, Albiston, Wilkins(Duxbury), McQueen, Buchan, Coppell, Birtles, Jordan, Macari, Thomas.
*Att: 26,915*
**Round 4**
**Jan 24 v Nottingham F (a) 0-1**
Bailey; Nicholl, Albiston, Wilkins, McQueen, Buchan, Coppell, Birtles, Jordan, Macari, Thomas.
*Att: 34,110*

**1981-2**
**Round 3**
**Jan 2 v Watford (a) 0-1**
Bailey; Gidman, Albiston, Wilkins, Moran, Buchan, Robson, Birtles, Stapleton, Moses(Macari), McIlroy.
*Att: 26,104*

**1982-3**
**Round 3**
**Jan 8 v West Ham U (h) 2-0**
*Stapleton, Coppell*
Bailey; Duxbury, Albiston, Moses, Moran, McQueen, Robson, Muhren, Stapleton, Whiteside, Coppell.
*Att: 44,143*
**Round 4**
**Jan 29 v Luton T (a) 2-0**
*Moses, Moran*
Bailey; Duxbury, Albiston, Moses, Moran, McQueen, Robson, Muhren, Stapleton, Whiteside, Coppell.
*Att: 20,516*
**Round 5**
**Feb 19v Derby C (a) 1-0**
*Whiteside*
Bailey; Duxbury, Albiston, Moses, Moran, McQueen, Robson, Muhren, Stapleton, Whiteside, Coppell.
*Att: 33,022*
**Round 6**
**Mar 12 v Everton (h) 1-0**
*Stapleton*
Bailey; Duxbury(Macari), Albiston, Moses, Moran, McQueen, Wilkins, Muhren, Stapleton, Whiteside, Coppell.
*Att: 58,198*
**Semi-final**
**Apr 16 v Arsenal (at Villa Park) 2-1**
*Robson, Whiteside*
Bailey; Duxbury, Albiston, Moses, Moran(McGrath), McQueen, Robson, Wilkins, Stapleton, Whiteside, Grimes.
*Att: 46,535*
**Final**
**May 21 v Brighton & HA (at Wembley) 2-2 a.e.t.**
*Stapleton, Wilkins*
Bailey; Duxbury, Albiston, Wilkins, Moran, McQueen, Robson, Muhren, Stapleton, Whiteside, Davies.
*Att: 100,000*
**Replay**
**May 26 v Brighton & HA (at Wembley) 4-0**
*Robson 2, Muhren, Whiteside*

Bailey; Duxbury, Albiston, Wilkins, Moran, McQueen, Robson, Muhren, Stapleton, Whiteside, Davies.
*Att: 92,000*

**1983-4**
**Round 3**
**Jan 2 v AFC Bournemouth (a) 0-2**
Bailey; Moses, Albiston(Macari), Wilkins, Hogg, Duxbury, Robson, Muhren, Stapleton, Whiteside, Graham.
*Att: 14,782*

**1984-5**
**Round 3**
**Jan 5 v AFC Bournemouth (h) 3-0**
*Strachan, McQueen, Stapleton*
Bailey; Duxbury, Albiston, Moses, McQueen, McGrath, Robson, Strachan, Stapleton, Hughes, Muhren.
*Att: 32,080*

**Round 4**
**Jan 26 v Coventry C (h) 2-1**
*Hughes, McGrath*
Pears; Gidman, Albiston, Moses, Moran, Hogg, McGrath, Strachan, Whiteside, Hughes(Brazil), Olsen.
*Att: 38,039*
**Round 5**
**Feb 15 v Blackburn R (a) 2-0**
*Strachan, McGrath*
Bailey; Gidman, Albiston, Moses, Moran, Hogg, McGrath, Strachan, Hughes, Whiteside, Olsen.
*Att: 22,692*
**Round 6**
**Mar 9 v West Ham U (h) 4-2**
*Whiteside 3, Hughes*
Bailey; Gidman, Albiston, Duxbury, McGrath, Hogg, Strachan, Whiteside, Hughes, Stapleton, Olsen.
*Att: 46,769*
**Semi-final**
**Apr 13 v Liverpool (at Goodison Park) 2-2 a.e.t.**
*Robson, Stapleton*
Bailey; Gidman, Albiston, Whiteside, McGrath, Hogg, Robson, Strachan, Hughes, Stapleton, Olsen.
*Att: 51,690*
**Replay**
**Apr 17 v Liverpool (at Maine Road) 2-1**
*Robson, Hughes*
Bailey; Gidman, Albiston, Whiteside, McGrath, Hogg,

Robson, Strachan, Hughes, Stapleton, Olsen.
*Att: 45,775*
**Final**
**May 18 v Everton (at Wembley) 1-0 a.e.t.**
*Whiteside*
Bailey; Gidman, Albiston(Duxbury), Whiteside, McGrath, Moran, Robson, Strachan, Hughes, Stapleton, Olsen.
*Att: 100,000*

**1985-6**
**Round 3**
**Jan 9 v Rochdale (h) 2-0**
*Stapleton, Hughes*
Turner; Duxbury, Albiston, Whiteside, Higgins, Garton, Blackmore, Strachan, Hughes(Olsen), Stapleton, C.Gibson.
*Att: 40,223*
**Round 4**
**Jan 25 v Sunderland (a) 0-0**
Bailey; Gidman, Albiston, Whiteside, McGrath, Moran, Robson, Strachan, Stapleton, Blackmore, Olsen.
*Att: 35,284*
**Replay**
**Jan 29 v Sunderland (h) 3-0**
*Olsen 2, Whiteside*
Bailey; Gidman, Albiston, Whiteside, McGrath, Moran, Robson, Strachan(Blackmore), Stapleton, Olsen, C.Gibson.
*Att: 43,402*
**Round 5**
**Mar 5 v West Ham U (a) 1-1**
*Stapleton*
Turner; Duxbury, Albiston, Whiteside, McGrath, Moran, Robson(Olsen), Strachan, Hughes, Stapleton, C.Gibson.
*Att: 26,441*
**Replay**
**Mar 9 v West Ham U (h) 0-2**
Turner; Duxbury, Albiston, Whiteside, McGrath, Higgins(Blackmore), Olsen, Strachan, Hughes, Stapleton, C.Gibson.
*Att: 30,441*

**1986-7**
**Round 3**
**Jan 10 v Manchester C (h) 1-0**
*Whiteside*
Turner; Sivebaek, C.Gibson, Whiteside, Garton,

*Gary Bailey looks thoughtful as his United colleagues show off the FA Cup which they have just won with ten men against Everton in 1985.*

Moran, Duxbury, Strachan, Stapleton, Davenport (T.Gibson), Olsen.
*Att: 54,294*
**Round 4**
**Jan 31 v Coventry C (h) 0-1**
Turner; Sivebaek, Duxbury, Whiteside, Garton, Moran, Blackmore(McGrath), Strachan, Stapleton (Davenport), T.Gibson, Olsen.
*Att: 49,082*


**1987-8**
**Round 3**
**Jan 10 v Ipswich T (a) 2-1**
*D'Avray (og), Anderson*
Turner; Anderson, Duxbury, Bruce, Moran, Moses (Olsen), Robson, Strachan, McClair, Whiteside, Gibson(Davenport).
*Att: 23,012*
**Round 4**
**Jan 30 v Chelsea (h) 2-0**
*Whiteside, McClair*
Turner; Anderson, Duxbury, Bruce, Blackmore (O'Brien), Hogg, Robson, Strachan, McClair, Whiteside, Olsen.
*Att: 50,716*
**Round 5**
**Feb 20 v Arsenal (a) 1-2**
*McClair*
Turner; Anderson, Gibson, Bruce, Duxbury, Hogg(O'Brien), Davenport, Strachan, McClair, Whiteside, Olsen(Blackmore).
*Att: 54,161*


**1988-9**
**Round 3**
**Jan 7 v Queen's Park R (h) 0-0**
Leighton; Gill, Martin, Bruce, Beardsmore, Donaghy, Robson(Wilson), Robins, McClair, Hughes, Milne.
*Att: 36,222*
**Replay**
**Jan 11 v Queen's Park R (a) 2-2 a.e.t.**
*Gill, Graham*
Leighton; Martin, Sharpe(Graham), Bruce, Beardsmore, Donaghy, Gill, Blackmore(Wilson), McClair, Hughes, Milne.
*Att: 22,236*
**Second replay**
**Jan 23 v Queen's Park R (h) 3-0**
*McClair 2 (1 pen), Robson*
Leighton; Martin, Sharpe, Bruce, Blackmore (Beardsmore), Donaghy, Robson, Strachan, McClair, Hughes, Milne(McGrath).
*Att: 46,257*
**Round 4**
**Jan 28 v Oxford U (h) 4-0**
*Hughes, Bruce, J.Phillips (og), Robson*
Leighton; Blackmore, Sharpe(Beardsmore), Bruce, McGrath(Gill), Donaghy, Robson, Strachan, McClair, Hughes, Milne.
*Att: 47,754*
**Round 5**
**Feb 18 v AFC Bournemouth (a) 1-1**
*Hughes*
Leighton; Blackmore, Martin(Sharpe), Bruce, McGrath, Donaghy, Robson, Strachan, McClair, Hughes, Milne.
*Att: 12,500*

**Replay**
**Feb 22 v AFC Bournemouth (h) 1-0**
*McClair*
Leighton; Blackmore, Sharpe, Bruce, McGrath, Donaghy, Robson, Strachan, McClair, Hughes, Milne(Gill).
*Att: 52,422*
**Round 6**
**Mar 18 v Nottingham F (h) 0-1**
Leighton; Beardsmore, Sharpe(Martin), Bruce, McGrath, Donaghy, Robson, Strachan, McClair, Hughes, Milne(Blackmore).
*Att: 55,052*

**1989-90**
**Round 3**
**Jan 7 v Nottingham F (a) 1-0**
*Robins*
Leighton; Anderson, Martin, Bruce, Phelan, Pallister, Beardsmore, Blackmore(Duxbury), McClair, Hughes, Robins
*Att: 23,072*
**Round 4**
**Jan 28 v Hereford U (a) 1-0**
*Blackmore*
Leighton; Anderson, Martin, Donaghy, Duxbury, Pallister, Blackmore, Ince(Beardsmore), McClair, Hughes, Wallace.
*Att: 13,777*
**Round 5**
**Feb 18 v Newcastle U (a) 3-2**
*Robins, Wallace, McClair*
Leighton; Anderson, Martin, Bruce, Phelan, Pallister, Robins(Beardsmore), Duxbury(Ince), McClair, Hughes, Wallace
*Att: 31,748*
**Round 6**
**Mar 11 v Sheffield U (a) 1-0**
*McClair*
Leighton; Anderson(Duxbury), Martin, Bruce, Phelan, Pallister, Robins, Ince, McClair, Hughes, Wallace
*Att: 34,344*
**Semi-final**
**Apr 8 v Oldham A (at Maine Road) 3-3 a.e.t.**
*Robson, Webb, Wallace*
Leighton; Martin(Robins), Gibson, Bruce, Phelan, Pallister, Robson(Wallace), Ince, McClair, Hughes, Webb
*Att: 44,026*
**Replay**
**Apr 11 v Oldham A (at Maine Road) 2-1 a.e.t.**
*McClair, Robins*
Leighton; Ince, Martin(Robins), Bruce, Phelan, Pallister, Robson, Webb(Gibson), McClair, Hughes, Wallace
*Att: 35,005*
**Final**
**May 12 v Crystal P (at Wembley) 3-3 a.e.t.**
*Hughes 2, Robson*
Leighton; Ince, Martin(Blackmore), Bruce, Phelan, Pallister(Robins), Robson, Webb, McClair, Hughes, Wallace
*Att: 80,000*
**Replay**
**May 17 v Crystal P (at Wembley) 1-0**
*Martin*
Sealey; Ince, Martin, Bruce, Phelan, Pallister, Robson, Webb, McClair, Hughes, Wallace
*Att: 80,000*

**1990-91**
**Round 3**
**Jan 7 v Queen's Park Rangers (h) 2-1**
*Hughes, McClair*
Sealey; Irwin, Blackmore, Bruce, Webb, Pallister, Robson, Ince, McClair, Hughes, Sharpe.
*Att: 35,065*
**Round 4**
**Jan 26 v Bolton W (h) 1-0**
*Hughes*
Sealey; Irwin, Blackmore, Bruce, Phelan (Robins), Pallister, Robson, Webb, McClair, Hughes, Sharpe.
*Att: 43,293*
**Round 5**
**Feb 18 v Norwich C (a) 1-2**
*McClair*
Sealey; Irwin, Martin(Wallace), Bruce, Blackmore, Pallister, Robson, Ince, McClair, Hughes, Sharpe.
*Att: 23,058*

**1991-92**
**Round 3**
**Jan 15 v Leeds U (a) 1-0**
*Hughes*
Schmeichel; Parker, Irwin, Bruce, Webb, Pallister, Kanchelskis, Ince, McClair, Hughes, Giggs.
*Att: 31,819*
**Round 4**
**Jan 27 v Southampton (a) 0-0**
Schmeichel; Parker, Irwin, Donaghy, Webb, Pallister, Robson, Ince, McClair, Hughes, Blackmore(Giggs).
*Att: 19,506*
**Round 4 (Replay)**
**Feb 5 v Southampton (h) 2 2 a.e.t. Southampton won 4-2 on penalties**
*Kanchelskis, McClair*
Schmeichel; Parker, Irwin, Donaghy(Sharpe), Webb, Pallister, Robson, Ince, McClair, Giggs, Kanchelskis (Hughes).
*Att: 33,414*

405

# UNITED IN THE
# Football League Cup
## (SUBSEQUENTLY CALLED THE MILK CUP THEN THE LITTLEWOODS CUP)

**1960-61**
**Round 1**
**Oct 19 v Exeter C (a) 1-1**
*Dawson*
Gregg; Setters, Brennan, Stiles, Foulkes, Nicholson, Dawson, Lawton, Viollet, Pearson, Scanlon.
*Att: 14,494*
**Replay**
**Oct 26 v Exeter C (h) 4-1**
*Quixall 2 (1 pen), Giles, Pearson*
Gaskell; Dunne, Carolan, Stiles, Cope, Nicholson, Dawson, Giles, Quixall, Pearson, Scanlon.
*Att: 15,662*
**Round 2**
**Nov 2 v Bradford C (a) 1-2**
*Viollet*
Gregg; Setters, Brennan, Bratt, Foulkes, Nicholson, Dawson, Giles, Viollet, Pearson, Scanlon.
*Att: 4,670*


**1966-7**
**Round 2**
**Sep 14 v Blackpool (a) 1-5**
*Herd*
P.Dunne; Brennan, A.Dunne, Crerand, Foulkes, Stiles, Connelly, Best, Sadler, Herd, Aston.
*Att: 15,570*


**1969-70**
**Round 2**
**Sep 3 v Middlesbrough (h) 1-0**
*Sadler*
Stepney; Fitzpatrick, Dunne, Crerand, James, Sadler, Morgan, Kidd(Gowling), Charlton, Givens, Best.
*Att: 38,939*
**Round 3**
**Sep 23 v Wrexham (h) 2-0**
*Kidd, Best*
Stepney; Fitzpatrick, Dunne, Burns, Ure, Sadler, Morgan, Kidd, Charlton, Aston, Best.
*Att: 48,347*
**Round 4**
**Oct 14 v Burnley (a) 0-0**
Stepney; Fitzpatrick, Dunne, Burns, Ure, Sadler, Morgan, Kidd, Charlton, Aston, Best.
*Att: 27,959*
**Replay**
**Oct 20 v Burnley (h) 1-0**
*Best*
Stepney; Fitzpatrick(Sartori), Dunne, Burns, Ure, Sadler, Morgan, Kidd, Charlton, Aston, Best.
*Att: 50,275*

**Round 5**
**Nov 12 v Derby C (a) 0-0**
Stepney; Brennan, Dunne, Burns, Ure, Sadler, Sartori, Best, Charlton, Law, Aston.
*Att: 38,895*
**Replay**
**Nov 19 v Derby C (h) 1-0**
*Kidd*
Stepney; Fitzpatrick, Dunne, Burns, Ure, Sadler, Best, Kidd, Charlton, Law(Sartori), Aston.
*Att: 57,393*
**Semi-final (1st leg)**
**Dec 3 v Manchester C (a) 1-2**
*Charlton*
Stepney; Edwards, Dunne, Burns, Ure, Sadler, Best, Kidd, Charlton, Stiles, Aston.
*Att: 55,799*
**Semi-final (2nd leg)**
**Dec 17 v Manchester C (h) 2-2 (agg 3-4)**
*Edwards, Law*
Stepney; Edwards, Dunne, Stiles, Ure, Sadler, Morgan, Crerand, Charlton, Law, Best.
*Att: 63,418*


**1970-71**
**Round 2**
**Sep 9 v Aldershot (a) 3-1**
*Law, Kidd, Best*
Rimmer; Edwards, Dunne(James), Fitzpatrick, Ure, Sadler, Stiles, Law, Charlton, Kidd, Best.
*Att: 18,509*
**Round 3**
**Oct 7 v Portsmouth (h) 1-0**
*Charlton*
Rimmer; Donald, Burns, Fitzpatrick, Ure, Sadler (Aston), Morgan, Gowling, Charlton, Kidd, Best.
*Att: 32,068*
**Round 4**
**Oct 28 v Chelsea (h) 2-1**
*Best, Charlton*
Rimmer; Edwards, Dunne, Fitzpatrick, James, Sadler, Aston, Best, Charlton, Kidd, Law(Burns).
*Att: 47,565*
**Round 5**
**Nov 18 v Crystal P (h) 4-2**
*Kidd 2, Charlton, Fitzpatrick*
Rimmer; Watson, Dunne, Fitzpatrick, James, Sadler, Law, Best, Charlton, Kidd, Aston.
*Att: 48,961*
**Semi-final (1st leg)**
**Dec 16 v Aston Villa (h) 1-1**
*Kidd*
Rimmer; Watson, Dunne, Fitzpatrick, James, Stiles, Sartori, Best, Charlton, Kidd, Aston.
*Att: 48,889*

**Semi-final (2nd leg)**
**Dec 23 v Aston Villa (a) 1-2 (agg 2-3)**
*Kidd*
Rimmer; Fitzpatrick, Dunne, Crerand, Ure, Sadler,
Morgan, Best, Charlton, Kidd, Law.
*Att: 58,667*

**1971-2**
**Round 2**
**Sep 7 v Ipswich T (a) 3-1**
*Best 2, Morgan*
Stepney; O'Neil, Dunne, Gowling, James, Sadler,
Morgan, Kidd, Charlton, Best Aston.
*Att: 28,143*
**Round 3**
**Oct 6 v Burnley (h) 1-1**
*Charlton*
Stepney; O'Neil, Dunne, Gowling, James, Sadler,
Morgan, Kidd, Charlton, Best, Aston.
*Att: 44,600*
**Replay**
**Oct 18 v Burnley (a) 1-0**
*Charlton*
Stepney; O'Neil, Dunne, Gowling, James, Sadler,
Morgan, Kidd, Charlton, Law, Best.
*Att: 27,511*
**Round 4**
**Oct 27 v Stoke C (h) 1-1**
*Gowling*
Stepney; O'Neil, Burns, Gowling, James, Sadler,
Morgan, Kidd(Aston), Charlton, Law, Best.
*Att: 47,062*
**Replay**
**Nov 8 v Stoke C (a) 0-0 a.e.t.**
Stepney; O'Neil, Burns, Gowling, James, Sadler,
Morgan, Kidd(Aston), Charlton, McIlroy, Best.
*Att: 40,805*
**Second replay**
**Nov 15 v Stoke C (a) 1-2**
*Best*
Stepney; O'Neil, Burns, Gowling James, Sadler,
Morgan, McIlroy, Charlton, Sartori, Best.
*Att: 42,249*

**1972-3**
**Round 2**
**Sep 6 v Oxford U (a) 2-2**
*Charlton, Law*
Stepney; O'Neil, Dunne(McIlroy), M.Buchan, James,
Sadler, Morgan, Charlton, Law, Best, Storey-Moore.
*Att: 16,560*
**Replay**
**Sep 12 v Oxford U (h) 3-1**
*Best 2, Storey-Moore*
Stepney; Fitzpatrick, M.Buchan, Young, James,
Sadler, Morgan, Law(McIlroy), Charlton, Best,
Storey-Moore.
*Att: 21,486*
**Round 3**
**Oct 3 v Bristol R (a) 1-1**
*Morgan*
Stepney; Donald, Dunne, Young, James, M.Buchan,
Morgan, Kidd, Charlton, Best, Storey-Moore.
*Att: 33,957*

**Replay**
**Oct 11 v Bristol R (h) 1-2**
*McIlroy*
Stepney; Watson, Dunne, Young, James, M.Buchan,
Morgan, Kidd(McIlroy), Charlton, Best, Storey-
Moore.
*Att: 29,349*

**1973-4**
**Round 2**
**Oct 8 v Middlesbrough (h) 0-1**
Stepney; M.Buchan, Young, B.Greenhoff, Holton,
James, Morgan, Daly, Macari(G.Buchan), Kidd,
Graham.
*Att: 23,906*

**1974-5**
**Round 2**
**Sep 11 v Charlton A (h) 5-1**
*Macari 2, Houston, McIlroy, Warman (og)*
Stepney; Forsyth(Young), Houston, Martin, Holton,
M.Buchan, Morgan, McIlroy, Macari, McCalliog,
Daly.
*Att: 21,616*
**Round 3**
**Oct 9 v Manchester C h) 1-0**
*Daly*
Stepney; Forsyth, Albiston, B.Greenhoff, Holton,
M.Buchan, Morgan, McIlroy, Pearson(Macari),
McCalliog, Daly.
*Att: 55,159*
**Round 4**
**Nov 13 v Burnley (h) 3-2**
*Macari 2, Morgan*
Stepney; Forsyth, Houston, B.Greenhoff(Morgan),
Sidebottom, M.Buchan, Macari, McIlroy, Pearson,
McCalliog, Daly.
*Att: 46,275*
**Round 5**
**Dec 4 v Middlesbrough (a) 0-0**
Stepney; Forsyth, Houston, B.Greenhoff, Holton,
M.Buchan, Morgan(Young), McIlroy, Pearson,
Macari, Daly.
*Att: 36,005*
**Replay**
**Dec 18 v Middlesbrough (h) 3-0**
*McIlroy, Pearson, Macari*
Stepney; Young, Houston, B.Greenhoff, Sidebottom,
M.Buchan, Morgan, McIlroy, Pearson, Macari,
Daly(McCalliog).
*Att: 49,501*
**Semi-final (1st leg)**
**Jan 15 v Norwich C (h) 2-2**
*Macari 2*
Stepney; Forsyth, Houston, B.Greenhoff, James,
M.Buchan, Morgan, McIlroy, Daly(Young), Macari,
McCalliog.
*Att: 58,010*
**Semi-final (2nd leg)**
**Jan 22 v Norwich C (a) 0-1 (agg 2-3)**
Stepney; Forsyth, Houston, B.Greenhoff,
James(Young), M.Buchan, Morgan, McIlroy, Daly,
Macari, McCalliog.
*Att: 31,621*

**1975-6**
**Round 2**
**Sep 10 v Brentford (h) 2-1**
*McIlroy, Macari*
Stepney; Nicholl, Houston, Jackson(Grimshaw),
B.Greenhoff, M.Buchan, Coppell, McIlroy, Pearson,
Macari, Daly.
*Att: 25,286*
**Round 3**
**Oct 8 v Aston Villa (a) 2-1**
*Coppell, Macari*
Stepney; Nicholl, Houston, Jackson, B.Greenhoff,
M.Buchan, Coppell, McIlroy, Pearson, Macari, Daly.
*Att: 41,447*
**Round 4**
**Nov 12 v Manchester C (a) 0-4**
Roche; Nicholl, Houston, Jackson(McCreery),
B.Greenhoff, M.Buchan, Coppell, McIlroy, Pearson,
Macari, Daly.
*Att: 50,182*

**1976-7**
**Round 2**
**Sep 1 v Tranmere R (h) 5-0**
*Daly 2, Pearson, Macari, Hill*
Stepney; Nicholl, Houston, Daly, B.Greenhoff,
M.Buchan, Coppell, McIlroy(McCreery), Pearson,
Macari, Hill.
*Att: 37,586*
**Round 3**
**Sep 22 v Sunderland (h) 2-2**
*Pearson, Clarke (og)*
Stepney; Nicholl, Houston, Daly, B.Greenhoff,
M.Buchan, McCreery, McIlroy, Pearson, Macari, Hill.
*Att: 46,170*
**Replay**
**Oct 4 v Sunderland (a) 2-2 a.e.t.**
*Daly, B.Greenhoff*
Stepney; Nicholl, Houston, Daly, Waldron,
M.Buchan, Coppell, McIlroy, McCreery, B.Greenhoff
(Albiston), Hill.
*Att: 46,170*
**Second replay**
**Oct 6 v Sunderland (h) 1-0**
*B.Greenhoff*
Stepney; Nicholl, Houston, Daly, B.Greenhoff,
M.Buchan, Coppell, McIlroy, McCreery, Macari, Hill
(Albiston).
*Att: 47,689*
**Round 4**
**Oct 27 v Newcastle U (h) 7-2**
*Hill 3, Nicholl, Houston, Coppell, Pearson*
Stepney; Nicholl, Albiston, Daly, B.Greenhoff,
Houston, Coppell, McIlroy, Pearson(McGrath),
Macari, Hill.
*Att: 52,002*
**Round 5**
**Dec 1 v Everton (h) 0-3**
Stepney; Forsyth, Albiston, Daly(McCreery),
Paterson, B.Greenhoff, Coppell, McIlroy, Pearson,
Jackson, Hill.
*Att: 57,738*

**1977-8**
**Round 2**
**Aug 30 v Arsenal (a) 2-3**
*McCreery, Pearson*

Stepney; Nicholl, Albiston, Grimes, B.Greenhoff
(McGrath), M.Buchan, Coppell, McCreery, Pearson,
Macari, Hill.
*Att: 36,171*

**1978-9**
**Round 2**
**Aug 30 v Stockport C (a*) 3-2**
*McIlroy, J.Greenhoff, Jordan*
Roche; B.Greenhoff, Albiston, McIlroy, McQueen,
M.Buchan, Coppell, J.Greenhoff, Jordan, Macari,
Grimes.
*Att: 41,761*
*Played at Old Trafford
**Round 3**
**Oct 4 v Watford (h) 1-2**
*Jordan*
Roche; Albiston, Houston, B.Greenhoff(McCreery),
McQueen, M.Buchan, Coppell, J.Greenhoff, Jordan,
McIlroy, Grimes.
*Att: 40,534*

**1979-80**
**Round 2 (1st leg)**
**Aug 29 v Tottenham H (a) 1-2**
*Thomas*
Bailey; Nicholl, Albiston, Paterson, McQueen,
M.Buchan, Ritchie, Wilkins, Jordan, Macari, Thomas.
*Att: 29,163*
**Round 2 (2nd leg)**
**Sep 5 v Tottenham H (h) 3-1 (agg 4-3)**
*Coppell, Thomas, Miller (og)*
Bailey; Nicholl, Albiston, McIlroy, Houston(Ritchie),
M.Buchan, Coppell, Wilkins, Jordan, Macari,
Thomas.
*Att: 48,292*
**Round 3**
**Sep 26 v Norwich C (a) 1-4**
*McIlroy*
Bailey; Nicholl, Albiston, McIlroy(Ritchie), McQueen,
M.Buchan, Grimes, Wilkins, Coppell, Macari,
Thomas.
*Att: 18,312*

**1980-81**
**Round 2 (1st leg)**
**Aug 27 v Coventry C (h) 0-1**
Bailey; Nicholl, Albiston, McIlroy, Jovanovic,
M.Buchan, Coppell, J.Greenhoff(Sloan), Ritchie,
Macari, Thomas.
*Att: 31,656*
**Round 2 (2nd leg)**
**Sep 2 v Coventry C (a) 0-1 (agg 0-2)**
Bailey; Nicholl, Albiston, McIlroy, Jovanovic,
M.Buchan, Coppell, J.Greenhoff, Ritchie, Macari,
Thomas.
*Att: 18,946*

**1981-2**
**Round 2 (1st leg)**
**Oct 7 v Tottenham H (a) 0-1**
Bailey; Gidman, Albiston, Wilkins, Moran, M.Buchan,
Coppell, Birtles(Duxbury), Stapleton, McIlroy,
Robson.
*Att: 39,333*
**Round 2 (2nd leg)**
**Oct 28 v Tottenham H (h) 0-1 (agg 0-2)**

Bailey; Gidman, Albiston, Wilkins, Moran, M.Buchan, Robson, Birtles, Stapleton, Moses, Coppell.
*Att: 55,890*

## 1982-3
**Round 2 (1st leg)**
**Oct 6 v AFC Bournemouth (h) 2-0**
*Redknapp (og), Stapleton*
Bailey; Duxbury, Albiston, Wilkins, Moran, McQueen, Robson, Grimes, Stapleton, Beardsley (Whiteside), Moses.
*Att: 22,091*
**Round 2 (2nd leg)**
**Oct 26 v AFC Bournemouth (a) 2-2 (agg 4-2)**
*Muhren, Coppell*
Bailey; Duxbury, Albiston, Wilkins(Macari), Grimes, M.Buchan, Robson, Muhren, Stapleton, Whiteside, Coppell.
*Att: 13,226*
**Round 3**
**Nov 10 v Bradford C (a) 0-0**
Bailey; Duxbury, Albiston, Moses, McGrath, McQueen, Robson, Muhren, Stapleton, Whiteside, Coppell.
*Att: 15,568*
**Replay**
**Nov 24 v Bradford C (h) 4-1**
*Moses, Albiston, Moran, Coppell*
Bailey; Duxbury, Albiston, Moses, Moran, McQueen, Robson, Muhren, Stapleton, Macari, Coppell (Whiteside).
*Att: 24,507*
**Round 4**
**Dec 1 v Southampton (h) 2-0**
*McQueen, Whiteside*
Bailey; Duxbury, Albiston, Moses, Moran, McQueen, Robson, Muhren, Stapleton, Whiteside, Coppell.
*Att: 28,378*
**Round 5**
**Jan 19 v Nottingham F (h) 4-0**
*McQueen 2, Coppell, Robson*
Bailey; Duxbury, Albiston, Moses, Moran, McQueen, Robson, Muhren, Stapleton, Whiteside, Coppell.
*Att: 44,413*
**Semi-final (1st leg)**
**Feb 15 v Arsenal (a) 4-2**
*Coppell 2, Whiteside, Stapleton*
Bailey; Duxbury, Albiston, Moses, Moran, McQueen, Robson, Muhren, Stapleton, Whiteside, Coppell.
*Att: 43,136*
**Semi-final (2nd leg)**
**Feb 23 v Arsenal (h) 2-1 (agg 6-3)**
*Coppell, Moran*
Bailey; Duxbury, Albiston, Moses, Moran, McQueen, Robson(Wilkins), Muhren, Stapleton, Whiteside, Coppell.
*Att: 56,635*

**Final**
**Mar 26 v Liverpool (at Wembley) 1-2 a.e.t.**
*Whiteside*
Bailey; Duxbury, Albiston, Moses, Moran(Macari), McQueen, Wilkins, Muhren, Stapleton, Whiteside, Coppell.
*Att: 100,000*

## 1983-4
**Round 2 1st lg**
**Oct 3 v Port Vale (a) 1-0**
*Stapleton*
Bailey; Duxbury(Moses), Albiston, Wilkins, Moran, McGrath, Robson, Muhren, Stapleton, Whiteside, Graham.
*Att: 19,885*
**Round 2 (2nd leg)**
**Oct 26 v Port Vale (h) 2-0 (agg 3-0)**
*Whiteside, Wilkins*
Bailey; Gidman, Albiston, Wilkins, Duxbury, McQueen, Robson, Moses, Stapleton, Whiteside (Hughes), Graham.
*Att: 23,589*
**Round 3**
**Nov 8 v Colchester U (a) 2-0**
*McQueen, Moses*
Bailey; Duxbury, Albiston, Wilkins, Moran, McQueen, Robson, Moses, Stapleton, Whiteside (Macari), Graham.
*Att: 13,031*
**Round 4**
**Nov 30 v Oxford U (a) 1-1**
*Hughes*
Bailey; Duxbury, Albiston, Wilkins, Moran, McQueen, Robson, Moses, Stapleton, Whiteside, Hughes.
*Att: 13,739*
**Replay**
**Dec 7 v Oxford U (h) 1-1 a.e.t.**
*Stapleton*
Bailey; Duxbury, Albiston, Wilkins, Moran, McQueen, Robson, Moses, Stapleton, Whiteside, Graham.
*Att: 27,459*
**Second replay**
**Dec 19 v Oxford U (a) 1-2 a.e.t.**
*Graham*
Wealands; Moses, Albiston, Wilkins, Moran, Duxbury, Robson(Macari), Muhren, Stapleton, Whiteside, Graham.
*Att: 13,912*

## 1984-5
**Round 2 (1st leg)**
**Sep 26 v Burnley (h) 4-0**
*Hughes 3, Olsen*
Bailey; Duxbury, Albiston, Moses, Garton, Hogg, Robson, Muhren, Hughes, Whiteside(Brazil), Graham.
*Att: 28,383*
**Round 2 (2nd leg)**
**Oct 9 v Burnley (a) 3-0 (agg 7-0)**
*Brazil 2, Olsen*
Bailey; Duxbury, Albiston, Moses, Moran, Hogg, Strachan, Blackmore, Stapleton, Brazil, Olsen.
*Att: 12,690*
**Round 3**
**Oct 30 v Everton (h) 1-2**
*Brazil*
Bailey; Gidman, Albiston, Moses, Moran, Hogg, Robson, Strachan, Hughes, Brazil, Olsen(Stapleton).
*Att: 50,918*

**1985-6**
**Round 2 (1st leg)**
**Sep 24 v Crystal P (a) 1-0**
*Barnes*
Bailey; Duxbury, Albiston, Whiteside, McGrath, Moran, Robson, Blackmore, Stapleton, Brazil, Barnes.
*Att: 21,507*
**Round 2 (2nd leg)**
**Oct 9 v Crystal P (h) 1-0 (agg 2-0)**
*Whiteside*
Bailey; Duxbury, Albiston, Whiteside, McGrath, Moran, Robson, Olsen, Hughes(Brazil), Stapleton, Barnes.
*Att: 26,118*
**Round 3**
**Oct 29 v West Ham U (h) 1-0**
*Whiteside*
Bailey; Duxbury(Brazil), Albiston, Whiteside, Moran, Hogg, McGrath, Olsen, Hughes, Stapleton, Barnes.
*Att: 32,056*
**Round 4**
**Nov 26 v Liverpool (a) 1-2**
*McGrath*
Bailey; Gidman, Blackmore, Whiteside, Moran, Hogg, McGrath, Strachan, Stapleton, Brazil, Olsen.
*Att: 41,291*

**1986-7**
**Round 2 (1st leg)**
**Sep 24 v Port Vale (h) 2-0**
*Stapleton, Whiteside*
Turner; Duxbury, Albiston, Whiteside, McGrath, Moran, Robson, Strachan, Stapleton, Davenport, Moses.
*Att: 18,906*
**Round 2 (2nd leg)**
**Oct 7 v Port Vale (a) 5-2 (agg 7-2)**
*Moses 2, Stapleton, Barnes, Davenport*
Turner; Sivebaek, Albiston, Moses, McGrath, Moran (Whiteside), Robson, Strachan, Stapleton(T.Gibson), Davenport, Barnes.
*Att: 10,486*
**Round 3**
**Oct 29 v Southampton (h) 0-0**
Turner; Duxbury, Albiston, Whiteside, McGrath, Hogg, Robson, Moses(Olsen), Stapleton, Davenport (T.Gibson), Barnes.
*Att: 23,639*
**Replay**
**Nov 4 v Southampton (a) 1-4**
*Davenport*
Turner; Duxbury, Albiston, Whiteside(Wood), McGrath, Hogg, Moses, Olsen, Stapleton, Davenport, C.Gibson(Moran).
*Att: 17,915*

**1987-8**
**Round 2 (1st leg)**
**Sep 23 v Hull C (h) 5-0**
*McGrath, Davenport, Whiteside, Strachan, McClair*
Walsh; Anderson, Gibson, Moses(Garton), McGrath, Duxbury, Robson, Strachan, McClair, Whiteside, Davenport.
*Att: 25,041*
**Round 2 (2nd leg)**
**Oct 7 v Hull C (a) 1-0 (agg 6-0)**
*McClair*

Turner; Blackmore, Gibson(O'Brien), Garton, McGrath, Duxbury(Graham), Robson, Strachan, McClair, Whiteside, Olsen.
*Att: 13,586*
**Round 3**
**Oct 28 v Crystal P (h) 2-1**
*McClair 2*
Turner; Anderson, Gibson, Duxbury, Garton, Moran, Robson(Blackmore), Strachan, McClair, Whiteside, Davenport(Olsen).
*Att: 27,283*
**Round 4**
**Nov 18 v Bury (a*) 2-1**
*Whiteside, McClair*
Walsh; Anderson, Gibson(O'Brien), Duxbury, Blackmore, Davenport(Moses), Robson, Strachan, McClair, Whiteside, Olsen.
*Att: 33,519*                    *Played at Old Trafford
**Round 5**
**Jan 20 v Oxford U (a) 0-2**
Turner; Anderson, Gibson, Blackmore, Moran(Hogg), Duxbury, Robson, Strachan(Davenport), McClair, Whiteside, Olsen.
*Att: 12,658*

**1988-9**
**Round 2 (1st leg)**
**Sep 28 v Rotherham U (a) 1-0**
*Davenport*
Leighton; Blackmore, Sharpe(Beardsmore), Bruce, McGrath, Duxbury, Robson, Strachan(Olsen), McClair, Hughes, Davenport.
*Att: 12,592*
**Round 2 (2nd leg)**
**Oct 12 v Rotherham U (h) 5-0**
*McClair 3, Robson, Bruce*
Leighton; Beardsmore, Blackmore, Bruce, Garton, Duxbury(Robins), Robson(Davenport), Strachan, McClair, Hughes, Sharpe.
*Att: 20,597*
**Round 3**
**Nov 2 v Wimbledon (a) 1-2**
*Robson*
Leighton; Blackmore, Gibson, Bruce, Garton, Duxbury(Strachan), Robson, O'Brien, McClair, Hughes, Olsen(Anderson).
*Att: 10,864*

**1989-90**
**Round 2 (1st leg)**
**Sep 20 v Portsmouth (a) 3-2**
*Ince 2, Wallace*
Leighton; Anderson, Donaghy, Beardsmore, Phelan, Pallister, Robson(Duxbury), Ince, McClair(Sharpe), Hughes, Wallace.
*Att: 18,072*
**Round 2 (2nd leg)**
**Oct 3 v Portsmouth (h) 0-0**
Leighton; Duxbury, Donaghy, Bruce, Phelan, Pallister, Robson, Ince, McClair, Hughes, Wallace
*Att: 26,698*
**Round 3**
**Oct 25 v Tottenham H (h) 0-3**
Leighton; Donaghy, Martin(Maiorana), Bruce, Phelan, Pallister, Robson, Ince, McClair, Hughes, Sharpe
*Att: 45,759*

410

**1990-91**
**Round 2 (1st leg)**
**Sep 26 v Halifax T (a) 3-1**
*Blackmore, McClair, Webb*
Leighton; Irwin, Blackmore, Donaghy, Phelan, Pallister, Webb, Ince(Martin), McClair, Hughes (Robins), Beardsmore.
*Att: 7,500*
**Round 2 (2nd leg)**
**Oct 10 v Halifax T (h) 2-1**
*Bruce, Anderson*
Sealey; Anderson, Blackmore(Wallace), Bruce, Phelan, Pallister, Webb, Irwin(Robins), McClair, Hughes, Martin.
*Att: 22,295*
**Round 3**
**Oct 31 v Liverpool (h) 3-1**
*Bruce, Hughes, Sharpe*
Sealey; Irwin, Blackmore, Bruce, Phelan(Donaghy), Pallister, Webb, Ince, McClair, Hughes(Wallace), Sharpe.
*Att: 42,033*
**Round 4**
**Nov 28 v Arsenal (a) 6-2**
*Sharpe 3, Blackmore, Hughes, Wallace*
Sealey; Irwin, Blackmore, Bruce(Donaghy), Phelan, Pallister, Sharpe, Ince, McClair, Hughes, Wallace.
*Att: 40,884*
**Round 5**
**Jan 16 v Southampton (a) 1-1**
*Hughes*
Sealey; Donaghy, Blackmore, Bruce, Phelan, Pallister, Robson, Webb(Irwin), McClair, Hughes, Sharpe.
*Att: 21,011*
**Replay**
**Jan 23 v Southampton (h) 3-2**
*Hughes 3*
Sealey; Irwin(Donaghy), Blackmore, Bruce, Phelan, Pallister, Robson, Webb, McClair, Hughes, Sharpe (Robins)
*Att: 41,093*
**Semi-final (1st leg)**
**Feb 10 v Leeds U (h) 2-1**
*Sharpe, McClair*
Sealey; Irwin(Donaghy), Martin(Wallace), Bruce, Blackmore, Pallister, Robson, Ince, McClair, Hughes, Sharpe.
*Att: 34,050*
**Semi-final (2nd leg)**
**Feb 24 v Leeds U (a) 1-0**
*Sharpe*
Sealey; Donaghy, Blackmore, Webb(Martin), Phelan, Pallister, Robson, Ince, McClair, Hughes, Sharpe.
*Att: 32,014*
**Final**
**Apr 21 v Sheffield W (at Wembley) 0-1**
Sealey; Irwin, Blackmore, Bruce, Webb(Phelan), Pallister, Robson, Ince, McClair, Hughes, Sharpe.
*Att: 80,000*

**1991-92**
**Round 2 (1st leg)**
**Sep 25 v Cambridge U (h) 3-0**
*Giggs, McClair, Bruce*
Walsh; Phelan, Irwin, Bruce, Webb(Giggs), Pallister, Robson, Ince, McClair, Hughes, Blackmore.
*Att: 30,934*

**Round 2 (2nd leg)**
**Oct 9 v Cambridge U (a) 1-1**
*McClair*
Wilkinson; Donaghy, Irwin, Bruce, Blackmore, Pallister(Robins), Robson, Ince, McClair, Hughes, Martin(Giggs).
*Att: 9,248*
**Round 3**
**Oct 31 v Portsmouth (h) 3-1**
*Robins 2, Robins*
Schmeichel; Parker, Irwin(Robins), Bruce, Webb, Pallister(Robson), Donaghy, Kanchelskis, McClair, Blackmore, Giggs.
*Att: 29,543*
**Round 4**
**Dec 4 v Oldham A (h) 2-0**
*McClair, Kanchelskis*
Schmeichel; Parker, Irwin, Bruce, Webb, Pallister, Robson(Ince), Kancheslskis, McClair, Hughes, Giggs (Blackmore)
*Att: 38,550*
**Round 5**
**Jan 8 v Leeds U (a) 3-1**
*Blackmore, Kanchelskis, Giggs*
Schmeichel; Parker, Blackmore, Bruce, Webb, Pallister, Kanchelskis(Sharpe), Ince, McClair, Hughes (Giggs), Donaghy.
*Att: 28,886*
**Semi-final (1st leg)**
**Mar 4 v Middlesbrough (a) 0-0**
Schmeichel; Parker, Irwin, Donaghy(Phelan), Webb, Pallister, Robson, Ince(Sharpe), McClair, Hughes, Giggs.
*Att: 25,572*
**Semi-final (2nd leg)**
**Mar 11 v Middlesbrough (h) 2-1 a.e.t.**
*Sharpe, Giggs*
Schmeichel; Parker, Irwin, Bruce, Webb, Pallister, Robson, Ince, McClair, Sharpe(Robins), Giggs.
*Att: 45,875*
**Final**
**Apr 12 v Nottingham F (at Wembley) 1-0**
*McClair*
Schmeichel; Parker, Irwin, Bruce, Phelan, Pallister, Kanchelskis(Sharpe), Ince, McClair, Hughes, Giggs.
*Att: 76,810*

*Celebrations after the 1992 Rumeblows Cup Final victory over Nottingham Forest at Wembley.*

*One of United's emerging young stars, Ryan Giggs, chases Forest's Darren Wassell.*

# Watney Cup

**1970**
**Round 1**
**Aug 1 v Reading (a) 3-2**
*Charlton 2, Edwards*
Stepney; Edwards, Dunne, Crerand, Ure, Sadler, Morgan, Law(Fitzpatrick), Charlton, Kidd, Best.
*Att: 18,348*

**Semi-final**
**Aug 5 v Hull City (a) 1-1 aet**
*Law*
Stepney; Edwards, Dunne(Stiles), Crerand, Ure, Sadler, Morgan, Law, Charlton, Kidd, Best.
*Att: 34,007*
United won 4-3 on penalties.

**Final**
**Aug 8 v Derby County (a) 1-4**
*Best*
Stepney; Edwards, Dunne, Crerand, Ure, Sadler, Morgan(Stiles), Law(Fitzpatrick), Charlton, Kidd, Best.
*Att: 32,049*

**1971**
**Round 1**
**Jul 31 v Halifax Town (a) 1-2**
*Best*
Stepney; Fitzpatrick, Dunne, Crerand(Burns), James, Sadler, Morgan, Gowling(Kidd), Charlton, Law, Best.
*Att: 19,765*

# Anglo-Italian Tournament

**1972-73**
**Group One**
**Feb 21 v Fiorentina (h) 1-1**
*Holton*
Stepney; Young, Forsyth, Graham, Holton(Jones), Buchan, Morgan, Kidd(Fletcher), Charlton, Macari, Martin.
*Att: 23,951*

**Group One**
**Mar 21 v Lazio (a) 0-0**
Rimmer; Young, Buchan, Graham, Holton, James, Morgan, Kidd(Fletcher), Charlton, Macari(Anderson), Martin.
*Att: 52,834*

**Group One**
**Apr 4 v Bari (h) 3-1**
*Law, Storey-Moore, Martin*
Stepney; Young, Forsyth, Martin, James, Sadler, Morgan, Daly, Anderson, Law, Storey-Moore (McGivern).
*Att: 14,303*
**Group One**
**May 2 v Verona (a) 4-1**
*Charlton 2, Olney, Fletcher*
Rimmer; Young, Sidebottom, Graham, Holton, Buchan, Morgan(Olney), Anderson, Charlton, Macari (Fletcher), Daly.
*Att: 8,168*
United failed to qualify for the semi-finals.

# FA Charity Shield

**1908**
**Apr 27 v Queen's Park R (at Stamford Bridge) 1-1**
*Meredith*
Moger; Stacey, Burgess, Duckworth, Roberts, Bell, Meredith, Bannister, J.Turnbull, A.Turnbull, Wall.
*Att: 6,000*
**Replay**
**Aug 29 v Queen's Park R (at Stamford Bridge) 4-0**
*Turnbull 3, Wall*
Moger; Stacey, Burgess, Duckworth, Roberts, Bell, Meredith, Bannister, J.Turnbull, Picken, Wall.
*Att: 60,000*

**1911**
**Sep 25 v Swindon T (at Stamford Bridge) 8-4**
*Halse 6, Turnbull, Wall.*
Edmonds; Hofton, Stacey, Duckworth, Roberts, Bell, Meredith, Hamill, Halse, Turnbull, Wall.
*Att: 10,000*

**1948**
**Oct 6 v Arsenal (a) 3-4**
*Burke, Rowley, Smith (og)*
Crompton; Carey, Aston, Anderson, Chilton, Warner, Delaney, Morris, Burke, Rowley, Mitten.
*Att: 31,000*

**1952**
**Sep 24 v Newcastle U (h) 4-2**
*Rowley 2, Downie, Byrne*
Wood; McNulty, Aston, Carey, Chilton, Gibson, Berry, Downie, Rowley, Pearson, Byrne.
*Att: 11,381*

**1956**
**Oct 24 v Manchester C (a) 1-0**
*Viollet*
Wood(Gaskell); Foulkes, Byrne, Colman, Jones, Edwards, Berry, Whelan, Taylor, Viollet, Pegg.
*Att: 30,495*

**1957**
**Oct 22 v Aston Villa (h) 4-0**
*Taylor 3, Berry*
Wood; Foulkes, Byrne, Goodwin, Blanchflower, Edwards, Berry, Whelan, Taylor, Viollet, Pegg.
*Att: 27,923*

**1963**
**Aug 17 v Everton (a) 0-4**
Gaskell; A.Dunne, Cantwell, Crerand, Foulkes, Setters, Giles, Quixall, Herd, Law, Charlton.
*Att: 54,840*

**1965**
**Aug 14 v Liverpool (h) 2-2**
*Best, Herd*
P.Dunne; Brennan, A.Dunne, Crerand, Cantwell, Stiles, Best(Anderson), Charlton, Herd, Law, Aston.
*Att: 48,502*

**1967**
**Aug 12 v Tottenham H (h) 3-3**
*Charlton 2, Law*
Stepney; Brennan, A.Dunne, Crerand, Foulkes, Stiles, Best, Kidd, Charlton, Law, Aston.
*Att: 54,106*

**1977**
**Aug 13 v Liverpool (at Wembley) 0-0**
Stepney; Nicholl, Albiston, McIlroy, B.Greenhoff, M.Buchan, Coppell, J.Greenhoff(McCreery), Pearson, Macari, Hill.
*Att: 82,000*

**1983**
**Aug 20 v Liverpool (at Wembley) 2-0**
*Robson 2*
Bailey; Duxbury, Albiston, Wilkins, Moran, McQueen, Robson, Muhren(Gidman), Stapleton, Whiteside, Graham.
*Att: 92,000*

**1985**
**Aug 10 v Everton (at Wembley) 0-2**
Bailey; Gidman, Albiston, Whiteside, McGrath, Hogg, Robson, Duxbury(Moses), Hughes, Stapleton, Olsen.
*Att: 82,000*

**1990**
**Aug 19 v Liverpool (at Wembley) 1-1**
*Blackmore*
Sealey; Irwin, Donaghy, Bruce, Phelan, Pallister, Blackmore, Ince, McClair, Hughes, Wallace(Robins).
*Att: 66,558*

*Robson and Stapleton parade the 1983 Charity Shield.*

# United in Europe

## European Cup

**1956-7**
**Preliminary Round (1st leg)**
**Sep 12 v RSC Anderlecht (a) 2-0**
*Viollet, Taylor*
Wood; Foulkes, Byrne, Colman, Jones, Blanchflower,
Berry, Whelan, Taylor, Viollet, Pegg.
*Att: 35,000*
**Preliminary Round (2nd leg)**
**Sep 26 v RSC Anderlecht (h*) 10-0 (agg 12-0)**
*Viollet 4, Taylor 3, Whelan 2, Berry*
Wood; Foulkes, Byrne, Colman, Jones, Edwards,
Berry, Whelan, Taylor, Viollet, Pegg.
*Att: 40,000*
*Played at Maine Road
**Round 1 (1st leg)**
**Oct 17 v Borussia Dortmund (h*) 3-2**
*Viollet 2, Pegg*
Wood; Foulkes, Byrne, Colman, Jones, Edwards,
Berry, Whelan, Taylor, Viollet, Pegg.
*Att: 75,598*
*Played at Maine Road
**Round 1 (2nd leg)**
**Nov 21 v Borussia Dortmund (a) 0-0 (agg 3-2)**
Wood; Foulkes, Byrne, Colman, Jones, McGuinness,
Berry, Whelan, Taylor, Edwards, Pegg.
*Att: 44,570*

**Quarter-final (1st leg)**
**Jan 16 v Athletic Bilbao (a) 3-5**
*Taylor, Viollet, Whelan*
Wood; Foulkes, Byrne, Colman, Jones, Edwards,
Berry, Whelan, Taylor, Viollet, Pegg.
*Att: 60,000*
**Quarter-final (2nd leg)**
**Feb 6 v Athletic Bilbao (h*) 3-0 (agg 6-5)**
*Viollet, Taylor, Berry*
Wood; Foulkes, Byrne, Colman, Jones, Edwards,
Berry, Whelan, Taylor, Viollet, Pegg.
*Att: 70,000*
*Played at Maine Road
**Semi-final (1st leg)**
**Apr 11 v Real Madrid (a) 1-3**
*Taylor*
Wood; Foulkes, Byrne, Colman, Blanchflower,
Edwards, Berry, Whelan, Taylor, Viollet, Pegg.
*Att: 135,000*
**Semi-final (2nd leg)**
**Apr 25 v Real Madrid (h) 2-2 (agg 3-5)**
*Taylor, Charlton*
Wood; Foulkes, Byrne, Colman, Blanchflower,
Edwards, Berry, Whelan, Taylor, Charlton, Pegg.
*Att: 65,000*

*Bilbao goalkeeper Carmelo punches clear from Viollet and Taylor as United surge forward during their 3-0
European Cup win over the Spaniards in February 1957.*

415

**1957-8**
**Preliminary Round (1st leg)**
**Sep 25 v Shamrock Rovers (a) 6-0**
*Taylor 2, Whelan 2, Pegg, Berry*
Wood; Foulkes, Byrne, Goodwin, Blanchflower,
Edwards, Berry, Whelan, T.Taylor, Viollet, Pegg.
*Att: 45,000*
**Preliminary Round (2nd leg)**
**Oct 2 v Shamrock Rovers (h) 3-2 (agg 9-2)**
*Viollet 2, Pegg*
Wood; Foulkes, Byrne, Colman, Jones, McGuinness,
Berry, Webster, T.Taylor, Viollet, Pegg.
*Att: 33,754*
**Round 1 (1st leg)**
**Nov 20 v Dukla Prague (h) 3-0**
*Webster, Taylor, Pegg*
Wood; Foulkes, Byrne, Colman, Blanchflower,
Edwards, Berry, Whelan, T.Taylor, Webster, Pegg.
*Att: 60,000*
**Round 1 (2nd leg)**
**Dec 4 v Dukla Prague (a) 0-1 (agg 3-1)**
Wood; Foulkes, Byrne, Colman, Jones, Edwards,
Scanlon, Whelan, T.Taylor, Webster, Pegg.
*Att: 35,000*
**Quarter-final (1st leg)**
**Jan 14 v Red Star Belgrade (h) 2-1**
*Colman, Charlton*
Gregg; Foulkes, Byrne, Colman, Jones, Edwards,
Morgans, Charlton, T.Taylor, Viollet, Scanlon.
*Att: 60,000*
**Quarter-final (2nd leg)**
**Feb 5 v Red Star Belgrade (a) 3-3 (agg 5-4)**
*Charlton 2, Viollet*
Gregg; Foulkes, Byrne, Colman, Jones, Edwards,
Morgans, Charlton, T.Taylor, Viollet, Scanlon.
*Att: 55,000*
**Semi-final (1st leg)**
**May 8 v AC Milan (h) 2-1**
*Taylor (pen), Viollet*
Gregg; Foulkes, Greaves, Goodwin, Cope, Crowther,
Morgans, E.Taylor, Webster, Viollet, Pearson.
*Att: 44,880*
**Semi-final (2nd leg)**
**May 14 v AC Milan (a) 0-4 (agg 2-5)**
Gregg; Foulkes, Greaves, Goodwin, Cope, Crowther,
Morgans, E.Taylor, Webster, Viollet, Pearson.
*Att: 80,000*

**1965-6**
**Preliminary Round (1st leg)**
**Sep 22 v HJK Helsinki (a) 3-2**
*Connelly, Herd, Law*
Gaskell; Brennan, A.Dunne, Fitzpatrick, Foulkes,
Stiles, Connelly, Charlton, Herd, Law, Aston.
*Att: 25,000*
**Preliminary Round (2nd leg)**
**Oct 6 v HJK Helsinki (h) 6-0 (agg 9-2)**
*Connelly 3, Best 2, Charlton*
P.Dunne; Brennan, A.Dunne, Crerand, Foulkes,
Stiles, Connelly, Best, Charlton, Law, Aston.
*Att: 30,388*
**Round 1 (1st leg)**
**Nov 17 v ASK Vorwärts (a) 2-0**
*Law, Connelly*
Gregg; A.Dunne, Cantwell, Crerand, Foulkes, Stiles,
Best, Law, Charlton, Herd, Connelly.
*Att: 40,000*

**Round 1 (2nd leg)**
**Dec 1 v ASK Vorwärts (h) 3-1 (agg 5-1)**
*Herd 3*
P.Dunne; A.Dunne, Cantwell, Crerand, Foulkes,
Stiles, Best, Law, Charlton, Herd, Connelly.
*Att: 30,082*
**Quarter-final (1st leg)**
**Feb 2 v Benfica (h) 3-2**
*Herd, Law, Foulkes*
Gregg; A.Dunne, Cantwell, Crerand, Foulkes, Stiles,
Best, Law, Charlton, Herd, Connelly.
*Att: 64,035*
**Quarter-final (2nd leg)**
**Mar 9 v Benfica (a) 5-1 (agg 8-3)**
*Best 2, Charlton, Connelly, Crerand*
Gregg; Brennan, A.Dunne, Crerand, Foulkes, Stiles,
Best, Law, Charlton, Herd, Connelly.
*Att: 75,000*
**Semi-final (1st leg)**
**Apr 13 v FK Partizan Belgrade (a) 0-2**
Gregg; Brennan, A.Dunne, Crerand, Foulkes, Stiles,
Best, Law, Charlton, Herd, Connelly.
*Att: 60,000*
**Semi-final (2nd leg)**
**Apr 20 v FK Partizan Belgrade (h) 1-0 (agg 1-2)**
*Stiles*
Gregg; Brennan, A.Dunne, Crerand, Foulkes, Stiles,
Anderson, Law, Charlton, Herd, Connelly.
*Att: 62,500*

**1967-8**
**Round 1 (1st leg)**
**Sep 20 v Hibernians (Malta) (h) 4-0**
*Sadler 2, Law 2*
Stepney; Dunne, Burns, Crerand, Foulkes, Stiles, Best,
Sadler, Charlton, Law, Kidd.
*Att: 43,912*
**Round 1 (2nd leg)**
**Sep 27 v Hibernians (Malta) (a) 0-0 (agg 4-0)**
Stepney; Dunne, Burns, Crerand, Foulkes, Stiles, Best,
Sadler, Charlton, Law, Kidd.
*Att: 25,000*
**Round 2 (1st leg)**
**Nov 15 v FK Sarajevo (a) 0-0**
Stepney; Dunne, Burns, Crerand, Foulkes, Sadler,
Fitzpatrick, Kidd, Charlton, Best, Aston.
*Att: 45,000*
**Round 2 (2nd leg)**
**Nov 29 v FK Sarajevo (h) 2-1 (agg 2-1)**
*Best, Aston*
Stepney; Brennan, Dunne, Crerand, Foulkes, Sadler,
Burns, Kidd, Charlton, Best, Aston.
*Att: 62,801*
**Quarter-final (1st leg)**
**Feb 28 v Górnik Zabrze (h) 2-0**
*Kidd, Florenski (og)*
Stepney; Dunne, Burns, Crerand, Sadler, Stiles, Best,
Kidd, Charlton, Ryan, Aston.
*Att: 63,456*
**Quarter-final (2nd leg)**
**Mar 13 v Górnik Zabrze (a) 0-1 (agg 2-1)**
Stepney; Dunne, Burns, Crerand, Sadler, Stiles,
Fitzpatrick, Charlton, Herd, Kidd, Best.
*Att: 105,000*

416

**Semi-final (1st leg)**
**Apr 24 v Real Madrid (h) 1-0**
*Best*
Stepney; Dunne, Burns, Crerand, Sadler, Stiles, Best, Kidd, Charlton, Law, Aston.
*Att: 63,500*
**Semi-final (2nd leg)**
**May 15 v Real Madrid (a) 3-3 (agg 4-3)**
*Foulkes, Sadler, Zocco (og)*
Stepney; Brennan, Dunne, Crerand, Foulkes, Stiles, Best, Kidd, Charlton, Sadler, Aston.
*Att 125,000*
**Final**
**May 29 v Benfica (at Wembley) 4-1 a.e.t**
*Charlton 2, Best, Kidd*
Stepney; Brennan, Dunne, Crerand, Foulkes, Stiles, Best, Kidd, Charlton, Sadler, Aston.
*Att: 100,000*


**1968-9**
**Round 1 (1st leg)**
**Sep 18 v Waterford (a) 3-1**
*Law 3*
Stepney(Rimmer); Dunne, Burns, Crerand, Foulkes, Stiles, Best, Law, Charlton, Sadler, Kidd.
*Att: 48,000*
**Round 1 (2nd leg)**
**Oct 2 v Waterford (h) 7-1 (agg 10-2)**
*Law 4, Stiles, Burns, Charlton*
Stepney; Dunne, Burns, Crerand, Foulkes, Stiles, Best, Law, Charlton, Sadler, Kidd.
*Att: 41,750*

**Round 2 (1st leg)**
**Nov 13 v RSC Anderlecht (h) 3-0**
*Law 2, Kidd*
Stepney; Brennan, Dunne, Crerand, Sadler, Stiles, Ryan, Kidd, Charlton, Law, Sartori.
*Att: 51,000*
**Round 2 (2nd leg)**
**Nov 27 v RSC Anderlecht (a) 1-3 (agg 4-3)**
*Sartori*
Stepney; Kopel, Dunne, Crerand, Foulkes, Stiles, Fitzpatrick, Law, Charlton, Sadler, Sartori.
*Att: 40,000*
**Quarter-final (1st leg)**
**Feb 26 v Rapid Vienna (h) 3-0**
*Best 2, Morgan*
Stepney; Fitzpatrick, Dunne, Crerand, James, Stiles, Morgan, Kidd, Charlton, Law, Best.
*Att: 61,932*
**Quarter-final (2nd leg)**
**Mar 5 v Rapid Vienna (a) 0-0 (agg 3-0)**
Stepney; Fitzpatrick, Dunne, Crerand, James, Stiles, Morgan, Kidd, Charlton, Sadler, Best.
*Att: 52,000*
**Semi-final (1st leg)**
**Apr 23 v AC Milan (a) 0-2**
Rimmer; Brennan, Fitzpatrick, Crerand, Foulkes, Stiles(Burns), Morgan, Kidd, Charlton, Law, Best.
*Att: 80,000*
**Semi-final (2nd leg)**
**May 15 v AC Milan (h) 1-0 (agg 1-2)**
*Charlton*
Rimmer; Brennan, Burns, Crerand, Foulkes, Stiles, Morgan, Kidd, Charlton, Law, Best.
*Att: 63,103*

*Matt Busby is congratulated by his players after United's 1968 European Cup success. Busby was soon to be knighted for his services to football.*

# European Cup-Winners' Cup

**1963-4**
**Round 1 (1st leg)**
**Sep 25 v Willem II (a) 1-1**
*Herd*
Gregg; A.Dunne, Cantwell, Crerand, Foulkes, Setters,
Herd, Chisnall, Sadler, Law, Charlton.
*Att: 20,000*
**Round 1 (2nd leg)**
**Oct 15 v Willem II (h) 6-1 (agg 7-2)**
*Law 3, Charlton, Chisnall, Setters*
Gregg; A.Dunne, Cantwell, Crerand, Foulkes, Setters,
Quixall, Chisnall, Herd, Law, Charlton.
*Att: 46,272*
**Round 2 (1st leg)**
**Dec 3 v Tottenham H (a) 0-2**
Gaskell; A.Dunne, Cantwell, Crerand, Foulkes,
Setters, Quixall, Stiles, Herd, Law, Charlton.
*Att: 57,447*
**Round 2 (2nd leg)**
**Dec 10 v Tottenham H (h) 4-1 (agg 4-3)**
*Charlton 2, Herd 2*
Gaskell; A.Dunne, Cantwell, Crerand, Foulkes,
Setters, Quixall, Chisnall, Sadler, Herd, Charlton.
*Att: 50,000*
**Quarter-final (1st leg)**
**Feb 26 v Sporting Club Lisbon (h) 4-1**
*Law 3, Charlton*
Gaskell; Brennan, A.Dunne, Crerand, Foulkes, Setters,
Herd, Stiles, Charlton, Law, Best.
*Att: 60,000*
**Quarter-final (2nd leg)**
**Mar 18 v Sporting Club Lisbon (a) 0-5 (agg 4-6)**
Gaskell; Brennan, A.Dunne, Crerand, Foulkes, Setters,
Herd, Chisnall, Charlton, Law, Best.
*Att: 40,000*

**1977-8**
**Round 1 (1st leg)**
**Sep 14 v AS Saint-Etienne (a) 1-1**
*Hill*
Stepney; Nicholl, Albiston, McIlroy(Grimes),
B.Greenhoff(Houston), Buchan, McGrath, McCreery,
Pearson, Coppell, Hill.
*Att: 33,678*
**Round 1 (2nd leg)**
**Oct 5 v AS Saint-Etienne (h\*) 2-0 (agg 3-1)**
*Coppell, Pearson*
Stepney; Nicholl, Albiston, McIlroy, B.Greenhoff,
Buchan, Coppell, J.Greenhoff, Pearson(McGrath),
Macari, Hill.
*Att: 31,634*
*\*Played at Home Park, Plymouth.*
**Round 2 (2nd leg)**
**Oct 19 v FC Porto (a) 0-4**
Stepney; Nicholl, Albiston, McIlroy, Houston
(Forsyth), Buchan, McGrath(Grimes), McCreery,
Coppell, Macari, Hill.
*Att: 70,000*
**Round 2 (2nd leg)**
**Nov 2 v FC Porto (h) 5-2 (agg 5-6)**
*Coppell 2, Nicholl, Murca 2 (2 og's)*
Stepney; Nicholl, Albiston, McIlroy, Houston,
Buchan, McGrath, Coppell, Pearson, McCreery, Hill.
*Att: 51,831*

**1983-4**
**Round 1 (1st leg)**
**Sep 14 v Dukla Prague (h) 1-1**
*Wilkins*
Bailey; Duxbury, Albiston, Wilkins, Moran,
McQueen, Robson(Gidman), Muhren(Moses),
Stapleton, Macari, Graham.
*Att: 39,745*
**Round 1 (2nd leg)**
**Sep 27 v Dukla Prague (a) 2-2 (agg 3-3)\***
*Robson, Stapleton*
Bailey; Duxbury, Albiston, Wilkins, Moran,
McQueen, Robson, Muhren, Stapleton, Whiteside,
Graham.
*Att: 28,850*
*\*Won on away goals rule.*
**Round 2 (1st leg)**
**Oct 19 v Spartak Varna (a) 2-1**
*Robson, Graham*
Bailey; Duxbury, Albiston, Wilkins, Moran, McQueen,
Robson, Muhren, Stapleton, Whiteside, Graham.
*Att: 40,000*
**Round 2 (2nd leg)**
**Nov 2 v Spartak Varna (h) 2-0 (agg 4-1)**
*Stapleton 2*
Bailey; Duxbury, Albiston, Moses, Moran(Dempsey),
McQueen, Robson, Macari, Stapleton, Whiteside
(Hughes), Graham.
*Att: 39,079*
**Round 3 (1st leg)**
**Mar 7 v FC Barcelona (a) 0-2**
Bailey; Duxbury, Albiston, Wilkins, Moran, Hogg,
Robson, Muhren, Stapleton, Hughes(Graham), Moses.
*Att: 70,000*
**Round 3 (2nd leg)**
**Mar 21 v FC Barcelona (h) 3-0 (agg 3-2)**
*Robson 2, Stapleton*
Bailey; Duxbury, Albiston, Wilkins, Moran, Hogg,
Robson, Muhren, Stapleton, Whiteside(Hughes),
Moses.
*Att: 58,547*
**Semi-final (1st leg)**
**Apr 11 v Juventus (h) 1-1**
*Davies*
Bailey; Duxbury, Albiston, McGrath, Moran, Hogg,
Graham, Moses, Stapleton, Whiteside, Gidman
(Davies).
*Att: 58,171*
**Semi-final (2nd leg)**
**Apr 25 v Juventus (a) 1-2 (agg 2-3)**
*Whiteside*
Bailey; Duxbury, Albiston, Wilkins, Moran, Hogg,
McGrath, Moses, Stapleton(Whiteside), Hughes,
Graham.
*Att: 64,655*

**1990-91**
**Round 1 (1st leg)**
**Sep 19 v Pécsi Munkás (h) 2-0**
*Blackmore, Webb*
Sealey; Irwin, Blackmore, Bruce, Phelan, Pallister,
Webb, Ince(Sharpe), McClair, Robins(Hughes),
Beardsmore.
*Att: 26,411*

**Round 1 (2nd leg)**
**Oct 3 v Pécsi Munkás (a) 1-0**
*McClair*
Sealey; Anderson, Donaghy, Bruce, Pallister, Phelan, Webb, Blackmore, McClair, Hughes, Martin(Sharpe).
*Att: 15,000*
**Round 2 (1st leg)**
**Oct 23 v Wrexham (h) 3-0**
*McClair, Bruce, Pallister*
Sealey; Blackmore, Martin, Bruce, Sharpe, Pallister, Webb, Ince(Beardsmore), McClair, Hughes, Wallace(Robins).
*Att: 29,405*
**Round 2 (2nd leg)**
**Nov 7 v Wrexham (a) 2-0**
*Robins, Bruce*
Sealey; Iwin, Blackmore, Bruce, Phelan, Pallister, Webb, Ince(Donaghy), McClair(Martin), Robins, Wallace.
*Att: 13,327*
**Quarter-final (1st leg)**
**Mar 6 v Montpellier (h) 1-1**
*McClair*
Sealey; Blackmore, Martin(Wallace), Donaghy, Phelan, Pallister, Robson, Ince, McClair, Hughes, Sharpe.
*Att: 41,942*
**Quarter-final (2nd leg)**
**Mar 19 v Montpellier (a) 2-0**
*Blackmore, Bruce*
Sealey; Irwin, Blackmore, Bruce, Phelan, Pallister, Robson, Ince(Martin), McClair, Hughes, Sharpe.
*Att: 20,500*
**Semi-final (1st leg)**
**Apr 10 v Legia Warsaw (a) 3-1**
*McClair, Hughes, Bruce*
Sealey; Irwin, Blackmore, Bruce, Phelan(Donaghy), Pallister, Webb, Ince, McClair, Hughes, Sharpe.
*Att: 17,500*

**Semi-final (2nd leg)**
**Apr 24 v Legia Warsaw (h) 1-1**
*Sharpe*
Walsh; Irwin, Blackmore(Donaghy), Bruce, Phelan, Pallister, Robson, Webb, McClair, Hughes, Sharpe.
*Att: 44,269*
**Final**
**May 15 v Barcelona (at Rotterdam) 2-1**
*Hughes 2*
Sealey; Irwin, Blackmore, Bruce, Phelan, Pallister, Robson, Ince, McClair, Hughes, Sharpe.
*Att: 45,000*

**1991-92**
**Round 1 (1st leg)**
**Sep 18 v Athinaikos (a) 0-0**
Schmeichel; Phelan, Irwin, Bruce, Webb, Pallister, Robins, Ince, McClair, Hughes, Beardsmore(Wallace)
*Att: 11,000*
**Round 1 (2nd leg)**
**Oct 2 v Athinaikos (h) 2-0**
*Hughes, McClair*
Schmeichel; Phelan, Martin(Beardsmore), Bruce, Kanchelskis, Pallister, Robson, Ince, McClair, Hughes, Wallace(Robins).
*Att: 35,023*
**Round 2 (1st leg)**
**Oct 23 v Atlético Madrid (a) 0-3**
Schmeichel; Parker, Irwin, Pallister, Bruce, Webb, Ince(Martin), Robson, McClair, Hughes, Phelan.
*Att: 50,000*
**Round 2 (2nd leg)**
**Nov 6 v Atlético Madrid (h) 1-1**
*Hughes*
Walsh; Parker, Blackmore, Bruce, Webb, Phelan(Martin), Robson, Robins(Pallister), McClair, Hughes, Giggs.
*Att: 39,654*

# Inter-Cities Fairs Cup

**1964-5**
**Round 1 (1st leg)**
**Sep 23 v Djurgårdens IF (a) 1-1**
*Herd*
P.Dunne; Brennan, A.Dunne, Crerand, Foulkes, Stiles, Connelly, Charlton, Herd, Setters, Best.
*Att: 6,537*
**Round 1 (2nd leg)**
**Oct 27 v Djurgårdens IF (h) 6-1 (agg 7-2)**
*Law 3, Charlton 2, Best*
P.Dunne; Brennan, A.Dunne, Crerand, Foulkes, Stiles, Connelly, Charlton, Herd, Law, Best.
*Att: 38,437*
**Round 2 (1st leg)**
**Nov 11 v Borussia Dortmund (a) 6-1**
*Charlton 3, Herd, Law, Best*
P.Dunne; Brennan, A.Dunne, Crerand, Foulkes, Stiles, Connelly, Charlton, Herd, Law, Best.
*Att: 25,000*

**Round 2 (2nd leg)**
**Dec 2 v Borussia Dortmund (h) 4-0 (agg 10-1)**
*Charlton 2, Connelly, Law*
P.Dunne; Brennan, A.Dunne, Crerand, Foulkes, Stiles, Connelly, Charlton, Herd, Law, Best.
*Att: 31,896*
**Round 3 (1st leg)**
**Jan 20 v Everton 1-1**
*Connelly*
P.Dunne; Brennan, A.Dunne, Crerand, Foulkes, Stiles, Connelly, Charlton, Herd, Law, Best.
*Att: 50,000*
**Round 3 (2nd leg)**
**Feb 9 v Everton (a) 2-1 (agg 3-2)**
*Connelly, Herd*
P.Dunne; Brennan, A.Dunne, Crerand, Foulkes, Stiles, Connelly, Charlton, Herd, Law, Best.
*Att: 54,397*

**Quarter-final (1st leg)**
**May 12 v RC Strasbourg (a) 5-0**
*Law 2, Connelly, Charlton, Herd*
P.Dunne; Brennan, A.Dunne, Crerand, Foulkes,
Stiles, Connelly, Charlton, Herd, Law, Best.
*Att: 30,000*
**Quarter-final (2nd leg)**
**May 19 v RC Strasbourg (h) 0-0 (agg 5-0)**
P.Dunne; Brennan, A.Dunne, Crerand, Foulkes,
Stiles, Connelly, Charlton, Herd, Law, Best.
**Att: 34,188**
**Semi-final (1st leg)**
**May 31 v Ferencváros (h) 3-2**
*Herd 2, Law*
P.Dunne; Brennan, A.Dunne, Crerand, Foulkes,
Stiles, Connelly, Charlton, Herd, Law, Best.
*Att: 39,902*

**Semi-final (2nd leg)**
**Jun 6 v Ferencváros (a) 0-1 (agg 3-3)**
P.Dunne; Brennan, A.Dunne, Crerand, Foulkes,
Stiles, Connelly, Charlton, Herd, Law, Best.
*Att: 50,000*
**Play-off**
**Jun 16 v Ferencváros (a) 1-2**
*Connelly*
P.Dunne; Brennan, A.Dunne, Crerand, Foulkes,
Stiles, Connelly, Charlton, Herd, Law, Best.
*Att: 60,000*

# UEFA Cup

**1976-7**
**Round 1 (1st leg)**
**Sep 15 v Ajax Amsterdam (a) 0-1**
Stepney; Nicholl, Houston, Daly(McCreery),
B.Greenhoff, Buchan, Coppell, McIlroy, Pearson,
Macari, Hill.
*Att: 30,000*
**Round 1 (2nd leg)**
**Sep 29 v Ajax Amsterdam (h) 2-0 (agg 2-1)**
*McIlroy, Macari*
Stepney; Nicholl, Houston, Daly(Albiston),
B.Greenhoff, Buchan, Coppell, McIlroy, McCreery,
Macari, Hill(Paterson).
*Att: 58,918*
**Round 2 (1st leg)**
**Oct 20 v Juventus (h) 1-0**
*Hill*
Stepney; Nicholl, Albiston, Daly(McCreery),
B.Greenhoff, Houston, Coppell, McIlroy, Pearson,
Macari, Hill.
*Att: 59,000*
**Round 2 (2nd leg)**
**Nov 3 v Juventus (a) 0-3 (agg 1-3)**
Stepney; Nicholl, Albiston, Daly, B.Greenhoff,
Houston, Coppell, McIlroy(McCreery), Pearson,
Macari(Paterson), Hill.
*Att: 66,632*

**1980-81**
**Round 1 (1st leg)**
**Sep 17 v Widzew Lódź (h) 1-1**
*McIlroy*
Bailey; Nicholl(Duxbury), Albiston, McIlroy,
Jovanovic, Buchan, Grimes, J.Greenhoff, Coppell,
Macari, Thomas.
*Att: 38,037*
**Round 1 (2nd leg)**
**Oct 1 v Widzew Lódź (a) 0-0 (agg 1-1)\***
Bailey; Nicholl, Albiston, McIlroy, Jovanovic,
M.Buchan(Moran), Grimes, Coppell, Jordan,
Duxbury, Thomas.
*Att: 40,000*
*Lost on away goals rule.

**1982-3**
**Round 1 (1st leg)**
**Sep 15 v Valencia CF (h) 0-0**
Bailey; Duxbury, Albiston, Wilkins, Buchan, McQueen,
Robson, Grimes, Stapleton, Whiteside, Coppell.
*Att: 46,588*
**Round 1 (2nd leg)**
**Sep 29 v Valencia CF (a) 1-2 (agg 1-2)**
*Robson*
Bailey; Duxbury, Albiston, Wilkins, Moran, Buchan
(Macari), Robson, Grimes, Stapleton, Whiteside,
Moses(Coppell).
*Att: 35,000*

**1984-5**
**Round 1 (1st leg)**
**Sep 19 v Raba Vasas ETO (h) 3-0**
*Robson, Muhren, Hughes*
Bailey; Duxbury, Albiston, Moses, Moran, Hogg,
Robson, Muhren, Hughes, Whiteside, Olsen.
*Att: 33,119*
**Round 1 (2nd leg)**
**Oct 3 v Raba Vasas ETO (a) 2-2 (agg 5-2)**
*Brazil, Muhren*
Bailey; Duxbury, Albiston, Moses, Moran, Hogg,
Robson(Gidman), Muhren, Hughes, Brazil, Olsen.
*Att: 26,000*
**Round 2 (1st leg)**
**Oct 24 v PSV Eindhoven (a) 0-0**
Bailey; Gidman, Albiston, Moses, Moran, Hogg,
Robson, Strachan, Hughes, Brazil, Olsen.
*Att: 27,500*
**Round 2 (2nd leg)**
**Nov 7 v PSV Eindhoven (h) 1-0 a.e.t. (agg 1-0)**
*Strachan*
Bailey; Gidman, Albiston, Moses, Moran(Garton),
Hogg, Robson, Strachan, Hughes, Stapleton
(Whiteside), Olsen.
*Att: 39,281*
**Round 3 (1st leg)**
**Nov 28 v Dundee U (h) 2-2**
*Strachan, Robson*
Bailey; Gidman, Albiston, Moses, McQueen, Duxbury,
Robson, Strachan, Hughes, Whiteside(Stapleton), Olsen.
*Att: 48,278*

**Round 3 (2nd leg)**
**Dec 12 v Dundee U (a) 3-2 (agg 5-4)**
*Hughes, Muhren, McGinnis (og)*
Bailey; Gidman, Albiston, Moses, McQueen, Duxbury,
Robson, Strachan, Hughes, Stapleton, Muhren.
*Att: 21,821*
**Quarter-final (1st leg)**
**Mar 6 v Videoton (h) 1-0**
*Stapleton*

Bailey; Gidman, Albiston, Duxbury, McGrath, Hogg,
Strachan, Whiteside, Hughes, Stapleton, Olsen.
*Att: 35,432*
**Quarter-final (2nd leg)**
**Mar 20 v Videoton (a) 0-1 a.e.t. Lost 5-4 on penalties**
Bailey; Gidman, Albiston, Duxbury, McGrath, Hogg,
Robson(Olsen), Strachan, Hughes, Stapleton,
Whiteside.
*Att: 25,000*

# European Super Cup

**1991**
**Nov 19 v Red Star Belgrade (h) 1-0**
*McClair*
Schmeichel; Irwin, Martin(Giggs), Bruce, Webb,
Pallister, Kanchelskis, Ince, McClair, Hughes,
Blackmore.
*Att: 22,110*

*Steve Bruce with the European Super Cup after United's 1-0 win over Red Star Belgrade.*

# World Club Championship

**1968**
**First leg**
**Sep 25 v Estudiantes de la Plata (a) 0-1**
Stepney; Dunne, Burns, Crerand, Foulkes, Stiles,
Morgan, Sadler, Charlton, Law, Best.
*Att: 55,000*

**Second leg**
**Oct 16 v Estudiantes de la Plata (h) 1-1 (agg 1-2)**
*Morgan*
Stepney; Brennan, Dunne, Crerand, Foulkes, Sadler,
Morgan, Kidd, Charlton, Law(Sartori), Best.
*Att: 63,500*

# FA Youth Cup Finals

**1952-53**
**1st leg**
**May 4 v Wolves (h) 7-1**
*McFarlane 2, Lewis 2, Pegg, Scanlon, Whelan*
Clayton; Fulton, Kennedy, Colman, Cope, Edwards,
McFarlane, Whelan, Lewis, Pegg, Scanlon.
*Att: 20,934*
**2nd leg**
**May 9 v Wolves (a) 2-2 (agg 9-3)**
*Lewis, Whelan*
Clayton; Fulton, Kennedy, Colman, Cope, Edwards,
McFarlane, Whelan, Lewis, Pegg, Scanlon.
*Att: 14,290*

**1953-54**
**1st leg**
**Apr 23 v Wolves (h) 4-4**
*Edwards 2, Pegg 2 (1 pen)*
Hawksworth; Beswick, Rhodes, Colman, Harrop,
McGuinness, Littler, Edwards, Charlton, Pegg,
Scanlon.
*Att: 18,246*
**2nd leg**
**Apr 26 v Wolves (a) 1-0 (agg 5-4)**
*Pegg (pen)*
Hawksworth; Beswick, Rhodes, Colman, Harrop,
McGuinness, Littler, Edwards, Charlton, Pegg,
Scanlon.
*Att: 28,651*

**1954-55**
**1st leg**
**Apr 27 v West Bromwich A (h) 4-1**
*Colman 2, Charlton, Beckett*
Hawksworth; Queenan, Rhodes, Colman, Jones,
McGuinness, Beckett, Brennan, Edwards, Charlton,
Fidler.
*Att: 16,696*
**2nd leg**
**Apr 30 v West Bromwich A (a) 3-0 (agg 7-1)**
*Charlton, Edwards, Cooke (og)*
Hawksworth; Queenan, Rhodes, Colman, Jones,
McGuinness, Beckett, Brennan, Edwards, Charlton,
Fidler.
*Att: 8,335*

**1955-56**
**1st leg**
**Apr 30 v Chesterfield (h) 3-2**
*Carolan, Charlton, Pearson*
Hawksworth; Queenan, Jones, Carolan, Holland,
McGuinness, Morgans, Pearson, Dawson, Charlton,
Fidler.
*Att: 25,544*
**2nd leg**
**May 7 v Chesterfield (a) 1-1 (agg 4-3)**
*Fidler*
Hawksworth; Queenan, Jones, Carolan, Holland,
McGuinness, Morgans, Pearson, Dawson, Charlton,
Fidler.
*Att: 15,838*

**1956-57**
**1st leg**
**May 2 v West Ham U (a) 3-2**
*Dawson, Lawton, Hunter*
Gaskell; Smith, Madison, English, Holland, Bratt,
Morgans, Lawton, Dawson, Pearson, Hunter.
*Att: 14,000*
**2nd leg**
**May 7 v West Ham U (h) 5-0 (agg 8-2)**
*Morgans, Hunter, Pearson 3*
Gaskell; Smith, Madison, English, Holland, Bratt,
Morgans, Lawton, Dawson, Pearson, Hunter.
*Att: 23,349*

**1963-64**
**1st leg**
**Apr 27 v Swindon T (a) 1-1**
*Best*
Rimmer; Duff, Noble, McBride, Farrar, Fitzpatrick,
Anderson, Best, Sadler, Kinsey, Aston.
*Att: 17,000*
**2nd leg**
**Apr 30 v Swindon T (h) 4-1 (agg 5-2)**
*Sadler 3, Aston*
Rimmer; Duff, Noble, McBride, Farrar, Fitzpatrick,
Anderson, Best, Sadler, Kinsey, Aston.
*Att 25,563*

**1981-82**
**1st leg**
**Apr 26 v Watford (h) 2-3**
*Blackmore, Dempsey*
P.Hughes; Hill, Scott, Hogg, Garton, Blackmore,
Pearson, Dempsey, Whiteside, M.Hughes, Docherty
(Wood).
*Att: 7,280*
**2nd leg**
**May 6 v Watford (a) 4-4 a.e.t. (agg 6-7)**
*M.Hughes 2, Dempsey, Whiteside*
P.Hughes; Hill, Scott, Hogg, Garton, Williams
(Wood), Blackmore, Dempsey, Whiteside, M.Hughes,
Docherty.
*Att: 8,000*

**1985-86**
**1st leg**
**24 Apr v Manchester C (h) 1-1**
*Harvey*
Walsh; Gill, Martin, Scott, Gardner, Bottomley,
Murphy, Todd, Cronin, Wilson(Hopley), Harvey.
*Att: 7,602*
**2nd leg**
**29 Apr v Manchester C (a) 0-2 (agg 1-3)**
Walsh; Gill, Martin, Scott, Gardner, Harvey, Murphy,
Todd, Cronin, Bottomley(Hopley), Goddard.
*Att: 18,158*

# United Internationals

Many players won additional caps with other clubs but the totals given here are solely for appearances made while Manchester United players. Before 1924 there was only one 'Ireland' team. In that year the Republic of Ireland began separate matches. That position is reflected here. For some time, Northern Ireland could, for Home International matches, select players born in the Republic. Johnny Carey was one such player who won caps with both countries. The date given for each match is the actual year in which that match was played.

## England

**Anderson V.A.** 1987 v West Germany; 1988 v Hungary, Colombia (3).

**Aston J.** 1948 v Denmark, Wales, Switzerland; 1949 v Scotland, Sweden, Norway, France, Republic of Ireland, Wales, Northern Ireland, Italy; 1950 v Scotland, Portugal, Belgium, Chile, USA, Northern Ireland (17).

**Bailey G.R.** 1985 v Republic of Ireland, Mexico (2).

**Berry J.J.** 1953 v Argentina, Chile, Uruguay; 1956 v Sweden (4).

**Bradley W.** 1959 v Italy, Mexico (sub), USA (3).

**Byrne R.W.** 1954 v Scotland, Yugoslavia, Hungary, Belgium, Switzerland, Uruguay, Northern Ireland, Wales, West Germany; 1955 v Scotland, France, Spain, Portugal, Denmark, Wales, Northern Ireland, Spain; 1956 v Scotland, Brazil, Sweden, Finland, West Germany, Northern Ireland, Wales, Yugoslavia, Denmark; 1957 v Scotland, Republic of Ireland, Denmark, Republic of Ireland, Wales, Northern Ireland, France. (33).

**Charlton R.** 1958 v Scotland, Portugal, Yugoslavia, Northern Ireland, USSR, Wales; 1959 v Scotland, Italy, Brazil, Peru, Mexico, USA, Wales, Sweden; 1960 v Scotland, Yugoslavia, Spain, Hungary, Northern Ireland, Luxembourg, Spain, Wales; 1961 v Scotland, Mexico, Portugal, Italy, Austria, Luxembourg, Wales, Portugal, Northern Ireland; 1962 v Austria, Scotland, Switzerland, Peru, Hungary, Argentina, Bulgaria, Brazil; 1963 v France, Scotland, Brazil, Czechoslovakia, East Germany, Switzerland, Wales, Rest of World, Northern Ireland; 1964 v Scotland, Uruguay, Portugal, Republic of Ireland, USA (sub), Brazil, Argentina, Northern Ireland, Holland; 1965 v Scotland, Wales, Austria, Northern Ireland, Spain; 1966 v West Germany, Scotland, Yugoslavia, Finland, Norway, Poland, Uruguay, Mexico, France, Argentina, Portugal, West Germany, Northern Ireland, Czechoslovakia, Wales; 1967 v Scotland, Wales, Northern Ireland, USSR; 1968 v Scotland, Spain (twice), Sweden, Yugoslavia, USSR, Romania, Bulgaria; 1969 v Romania, Northern Ireland, Wales, Scotland, Mexico, Brazil, Holland, Portugal; 1970 v Holland, Wales, Northern Ireland, Colombia, Ecuador, Romania, Brazil, Czechoslovakia, West Germany (106).

**Chilton A.C.** 1950 v Northern Ireland; 1951 v France (2).

**Cockburn H.** 1946 v Northern Ireland, Republic of Ireland, Wales; 1948 v Scotland, Italy, Denmark, Northern Ireland, Switzerland; 1949 v Scotland, Sweden; 1951 v Argentina, Portugal, France (13).

**Connelly J.M.** 1965 v Hungary, Yugoslavia, Sweden. Wales, Austria, Northern Ireland; 1966 v Scotland, Norway, Denmark, Uruguay (10).

**Coppell S.J.** 1977 v Italy; 1978 v West Germany, Brazil, Wales, Northern Ireland, Scotland, Hungary, Denmark, Republic of Ireland, Czechoslovakia; 1979 v Northern Ireland (twice), Wales (sub), Scotland, Bulgaria, Austria, Denmark, Northern Ireland; 1980 v Republic of Ireland (sub), Spain, Argentina, Wales, Scotland, Belgium, Italy, Romania (sub), Switzerland; 1981 v Romania, Brazil, Wales, Scotland, Switzerland, Hungary (twice); 1982 v Scotland, Finland, France, Czechoslovakia, Kuwait, West Germany, Luxembourg; 1983 Greece (42).

**Duxbury M.** 1983 v Luxembourg; 1984 v France, Wales, Scotland, USSR, Brazil, Uruguay, Chile, East Germany, Finland (10).

**Edwards D.** 1955 v Scotland, France, Spain, Portugal; 1956 v Scotland, Brazil, Sweden, Finland, West Germany, Northern Ireland, Denmark; 1957 v Scotland, Republic of Ireland, Denmark, Republic of Ireland, Wales, Northern Ireland, France (18).

*Bobby Charlton, holder of 106 England caps and, at the time of writing, scorer of the record number of goals for England with 49, although Gary Lineker is pushing for the record.*

**Foulkes W.A.** 1954 v Northern Ireland (1).
**Greenhoff B.** 1976 v Wales, Northern Ireland, Republic of Ireland, Finland, Italy; 1977 v Holland, Northern Ireland, Wales, Scotland, Brazil, Argentina, Uruguay; 1978 v Brazil, Wales, Northern Ireland, Scotland (sub), Hungary (sub) (17).
**Halse H.J.** 1909 v Austria (1).
**Hill G.A.** 1976 v Italy, Republic of Ireland (sub), Finland (sub); 1977 v Luxembourg, Switzerland (sub), Luxembourg (6).
**Kidd B.** 1970 v Northern Ireland, Ecuador (sub) (2).
**McGuinness W.** 1958 v Northern Ireland; 1959 v Mexico (2).
**Mew J.W.** 1920 v Ireland (1).
**Pallister, G.A.** 1991 v Cameroon (sub), Turkey, Germany (3).
**Parker, P.A.** 1991 v Germany (1).
**Pearson J.S.** 1976 v Wales, Northern Ireland, Scotland, Brazil, Finland, Republic of Ireland; 1977 v Holland (sub), Wales, Scotland, Brazil, Argentina, Uruguay, Italy (sub); 1978 v West Germany, Northern Ireland (15).
**Pearson S.C.** 1948 v Scotland, Northern Ireland; 1949 v Scotland, Northern Ireland, Italy; 1951 v Portugal; 1952 v Scotland, Italy (8).
**Pegg D.** 1957 v Republic of Ireland (1).
**Phelan M.C.** 1989 v Italy (sub) (1).
**Roberts C.** 1905 v Ireland, Wales, Scotland (3).
**Robson B.** 1981 v Hungary; 1982 v Northern Ireland, Wales, Holland, Scotland, Finland, France, Czechoslovakia, West Germany, Spain, Denmark, Greece, Luxembourg; 1983 v Scotland, Hungary, Luxembourg; 1984 v France, Northern Ireland, Scotland, USSR, Brazil, Uruguay, Chile, East Germany, Finland, Turkey; 1985 v Republic of Ireland, Romania, Finland, Scotland, Italy, Mexico, West Germany, USA, Romania, Turkey; 1986 v Israel, Mexico, Portugal, Morocco, Northern Ireland; 1987 v Spain, Northern Ireland, Turkey, Brazil, Scotland, Turkey, Yugoslavia; 1988 v Holland, Hungary, Scotland, Colombia, Switzerland, Republic of Ireland, Holland, USSR, Denmark, Sweden, Saudi Arabia; 1989 v Greece, Albania (twice), Chile, Scotland, Poland, Denmark, Poland, Italy, Yugoslavia; 1990 v Czechoslovakia, Uruguay, Tunisia, Republic of Ireland, Holland; 1991 v Cameroon, Republic of Ireland, Turkey (77).
**Rowley J.F.** 1948 v Switzerland; 1949 v Sweden, France, Northern Ireland, Italy; 1952 v Scotland (6).
**Sadler D.** 1967 v Northern Ireland, USSR; 1970 v Ecuador (sub); East Germany (4).
**Sharpe L.S.** 1991 v Republic of Ireland (sub) (1).
**Silcock J.** 1921 v Wales, Scotland; 1923 v Sweden (3).
**Spence J.W.** 1926 v Belgium, Northern Ireland (2).
**Stepney A.C.** 1968 v Sweden (1).
**Stiles N.P.** 1965 v Scotland, Hungary, Yugoslavia, Sweden, Wales, Austria, Northern Ireland, Spain; 1966 v Poland, West Germany, Scotland, Norway, Denmark, Poland, Uruguay, Mexico, France, Argentina, Portugal, West Germany, Northern Ireland, Czechoslovakia, Wales; 1967 v Scotland; 1968 v USSR; 1969 v Romania; 1970 v Northern Ireland, Scotland (28).
**Taylor T.** 1953 v Argentina, Chile, Uruguay; 1954 v Belgium, Switzerland; 1956 v Scotland, Brazil, Sweden, Finland, West Germany, Northern Ireland, Yugoslavia (sub), Denmark; 1957 v Republic of Ireland, Denmark, Republic of Ireland, Wales, Northern Ireland, France (19).
**Viollet D.S.** 1960 v Hungary; 1961 v Luxembourg (2).
**Wall G.** 1907 v Wales; 1908 v Ireland; 1909 v Scotland; 1910 v Wales, Scotland; 1912 v Scotland; 1913 v Ireland (7).
**Webb N.J.** 1989 v Sweden; 1990 v Italy (sub); 1992 v France, Hungary, Brazil (sub) (5).
**Wilkins R.G.** 1979 v Denmark, Northern Ireland, Bulgaria; 1980 v Spain, Argentina, Wales (sub), Northern Ireland, Scotland, Belgium, Italy, Spain; 1981 v Spain (sub), Romania, Brazil, Wales, Scotland, Switzerland, Hungary (sub); 1982 v Northern

*Bryan Robson, who won over 70 caps whilst with United and proved an inspirational skipper of England.*

Ireland, Wales, Holland, Scotland, Finland, France, Czechoslovakia, Kuwait, West Germany, Spain, Denmark, West Germany; 1983 v Denmark; 1984 v Northern Ireland, Wales, Scotland, USSR, Brazil, Uruguay, Chile (38).
**Wood R.E.** 1954 v Northern Ireland, Wales; 1956 v Finland (3).

# Scotland

**Albiston A.R.** 1982 v Northern Ireland; 1983 v Uruguay, Belgium, East Germany; 1984 v Wales, England, Yugoslavia, Iceland, Spain; 1985 v Spain, Wales, East Germany; 1986 v Holland, Uruguay (14).
**Bell A.** 1912 v Ireland (1).
**Buchan M.M.** 1972 v Wales, Yugoslavia, Czechoslovakia, Brazil, Denmark (twice); 1973 v England; 1974 v West Germany, Northern Ireland, Wales, Norway, Brazil, Yugoslavia, East Germany; 1975 v Spain, Portugal, Denmark, Romania; 1976 v Finland, Czechoslovakia; 1977 v Chile, Argentina, Brazil, East Germany, Wales (sub); 1978 v Northern Ireland, Peru, Iran, Holland, Austria, Norway, Portugal (32).
**Burns F.S.** 1969 v Austria (1).
**Crerand P.T.** 1963 v Northern Ireland; 1965 v England, Poland, Finland, Poland (5).
**Delaney J.** 1947 v England, Northern Ireland, Wales; 1948 v England (4).
**Forsyth A.** 1973 v England; 1974 v East Germany, Spain; 1975 v Northern Ireland (sub), Romania, Denmark (6).
**Graham G.** 1973 v England, Wales, Northern Ireland, Switzerland (sub), Brazil (sub) (5).
**Holton J.A.** 1973 v Wales, Northern Ireland, England, Switzerland, Brazil, Czechoslovakia, West Germany; 1974 v Northern Ireland, Wales, England, Norway, Zaire, Brazil, Yugoslavia, East Germany (15).
**Houston S.M.** 1975 v Denmark (1).
**Jordan J.** 1978 v Bulgaria, Northern Ireland, England, Peru, Iran, Holland, Austria, Portugal; 1979 v Wales (sub), Northern Ireland, England, Norway, Belgium; 1980 v Northern Ireland (sub), Wales, England, Poland; 1981 v Israel, Wales, England (20).
**Law D.** 1962 v Wales, Northern Ireland; 1963 v England, Austria, Norway, Republic of Ireland, Spain, Norway, Wales; 1964 v England, West Germany, Wales, Finland, Northern Ireland; 1965 v England, Spain, Poland, Finland, Northern Ireland, Poland; 1966 v England, Wales; 1967 v England, USSR, Northern Ireland; 1968 v Austria; 1969 v West Germany, Northern Ireland; 1972 v Peru, Northern Ireland, Wales, England, Yugoslavia, Czechoslovakia, Brazil (35).
**Leighton J.** 1988 v Colombia, England, Norway; 1989 v Cyprus, France, Cyprus, England, Chile, Yugoslavia, France, Norway; 1990 v Argentina, Malta (sub), Costa Rica, Sweden, Brazil (16).
**McBain N.** 1922 v England (1).
**McClair B.J.** 1987 v Bulgaria; 1988 v Malta (sub), Spain (sub), Norway, Yugoslavia, Italy (sub); 1989 v Cyprus, France (sub), Norway (sub); 1990 v Argentina (sub), Bulgaria; 1991 v Bulgaria, San Marino, Switzerland (sub), Romania; 1992 v Northern Ireland, USA, Canada (sub) (18).
**McQueen G.** 1978 v Bulgaria, Northern Ireland, Wales, Austria, Norway, Portugal; 1979 v Northern Ireland, England, Norway, Peru, Austria, Belgium; 1981 v Wales (13).
**Macari L.** 1973 v England, Wales (sub), Northern Ireland (sub), England; 1975 v Sweden, Portugal (sub), Wales, England (sub), Romania; 1977 v Northern Ireland (sub), England (sub), Chile, Argentina, East Germany, Wales; 1978 v Bulgaria, Peru (sub), Iran (18).
**Miller T.** 1921 v Ireland, England (2).
**Morgan W.** 1972 v Peru, Yugoslavia, Czechoslovakia, Brazil; Denmark (twice); 1973 v England, Wales, Northern Ireland, England, Switzerland, Brazil, Czechoslovakia (twice), West Germany; 1974 v West Germany, Northern Ireland, Belgium (sub), Brazil, Yugoslavia (20).
**Strachan G.D.** 1985 v Spain (sub), England, Iceland, Wales, Australia; 1986 v Romania, Denmark, West Germany, Uruguay, Bulgaria, Republic of Ireland; 1987 v Republic of Ireland, Hungary; 1989 v France (sub) (14).

# Wales

**Bennion S.R.** 1925 v Scotland; 1926 v Scotland; 1927 v Scotland, England; 1928 v Northern Ireland, Scotland, England; 1929 v Northern Ireland, Scotland; 1931 v Northern Ireland (10).

**Blackmore C.G.** 1985 v Norway (sub), Scotland (sub), Hungary (sub); 1986 v Saudi Arabia, Republic of Ireland, Uruguay, Finland; 1987 v USSR, Finland, Czechoslovakia, Denmark (twice), Czechoslovakia; 1988 v Yugoslavia, Sweden, Malta, Italy, Holland, Finland; 1989 v Israel, West Germany, Finland, Holland, West Germany; 1990 v Costa Rica, Belgium, Luxembourg; 1992 v Republic of Ireland (sub), Austria, Romania (sub), Holland. (31).

**Burke T.** 1887 v England, Scotland; 1888 v Scotland (3).

**Davies A.** 1983 v Northern Ireland, Brazil; 1984 v England, Northern Ireland, Iceland (twice); 1985 v Norway (7).

**Davies Jos.** 1888 v England, Ireland, Scotland; 1889 v Scotland; 1890 v England (5).

**Davies R.W.** 1972 v England; 1973 v Scotland (sub), Northern Ireland (3).

**Doughty J.** 1887 v Ireland, Scotland; 1888 v England, Ireland, Scotland; 1889 v Scotland; 1890 v England (7).

**Doughty R.** 1888 v Ireland, Scotland (2).

**Giggs R.J.** 1991 v Germany (sub), Luxembourg (sub); 1992 v Romania (sub) (3).

**Hughes L.M.** 1984 v England, Northern Ireland, Iceland, Spain, Iceland; 1985 v Norway, Scotland, Spain, Norway, Scotland, Hungary; 1986 v Uruguay; 1988 v Holland, Finland; 1989 v Israel, Sweden, West Germany, Finland, West Germany; 1990 v Costa Rica, Denmark, Belgium, Luxembourg; 1991 v Belgium, Iceland, Poland, Germany, Brazil, Germany, Luxembourg; 1992 v Republic of Ireland, Romania, Holland (33).

**Jenkyns C.A.L.** 1897 v Ireland (1).

**Jones T.** 1926 v Northern Ireland; 1927 v England, Northern Ireland; 1930 v Northern Ireland (4).

**Meredith W.H.** 1907 v Ireland, Scotland, England; 1908 v England, Ireland; 1909 v Scotland, England, Ireland; 1910 v Scotland, England, Ireland; 1911 v Ireland, Scotland, England; 1912 v Scotland, England, Ireland; 1913 v Ireland, Scotland, England; 1914 v Ireland, Scotland, England; 1920 v Ireland, Scotland, England (26).

**Moore G.** 1963 v Scotland; 1964 v Northern Ireland (2).

**Owen G.** 1889 v Scotland, Ireland (2).

**Owen J.** 1892 v England (1).

**Owen W.** 1888 v England; 1889 v England, Scotland, Ireland (4).

**Powell J.** 1887 v England, Scotland; 1888 v England, Ireland, Scotland (5).

**Thomas H.** 1927 v England (1).

**Thomas M.R.** 1978 v Turkey; 1979 v West Germany, Malta (sub), Republic of Ireland, West Germany (sub), Turkey; 1980 v England, Scotland, Northern Ireland, Czechoslovakia; 1981 v Scotland, England, USSR (13).

**Warner J.** 1939 v France (1).

**Webster C.** 1957 v Czechoslovakia; 1958 v Hungary, Mexico, Brazil (4).

**Williams D.R.** 1928 v Scotland, England (2).

# Northern Ireland (and Ireland before 1924)

**Anderson T.** 1973 v Cyprus, England, Scotland, Wales, Bulgaria, Portugal (6).

**Best G.** 1964 v Wales, Uruguay, England, Switzerland (twice), Scotland; 1965 v Holland (twice), Albania, Scotland, England, Albania; 1966 v England; 1967 v Scotland; 1968 v Turkey; 1969 v England, Scotland, Wales, USSR; 1970 v Scotland, England, Wales, Spain; 1971 v Cyprus (twice), England, Scotland, Wales, USSR; 1972 v Spain, Bulgaria; 1973 v Portugal (32).

**Blanchflower J.** 1954 v Wales, England, Scotland; 1955 v Scotland; 1956 v Wales, England, Scotland; 1957 v Portugal, Scotland, England, Italy; 1958 v Italy (12).

**Breen T.** 1937 v Wales, England, Scotland; 1938 v Scotland; 1939 v Wales (5).

**Briggs W.R.** 1962 v Wales (1).

**Carey J.J.** 1946 v England, Scotland; 1947 v Wales, England; 1948 v England, Scotland; 1949 v Wales (7).
**Crooks W.** 1922 v Wales (1).
**Donaghy M.M.** 1988 v Spain; 1989 v Spain, Malta, Chile, Republic of Ireland; 1990 v Norway, Yugoslavia, Denmark, Austria; 1991 v Poland, Yugoslavia, Faroe Islands (twice), Austria, Denmark; 1992 v Scotland, Lithuania (17).
**Gregg H.** 1958 v Wales, Czechoslovakia, Argentina, West Germany, France, England; 1959 v Wales, Scotland, England; 1960 v Wales, England, Scotland; 1961 v Scotland, Greece; 1963 v Scotland, England (16).
**Hamill M.** 1912 v England; 1914 v England, Scotland (3).
**Jackson T.A.** 1975 v Sweden, Norway, Yugoslavia; 1976 v Holland, Belgium; 1977 v West Germany, England, Scotland, Wales, Iceland (10).
**Lyner D.** 1922 v England (1).
**McCreery D.** 1976 v Scotland (sub), England, Wales, Holland, Belgium; 1977 v West Germany, England, Scotland, Wales, Iceland (twice), Holland, Belgium; 1978 v Scotland, England, Wales, Republic of Ireland, Denmark, Bulgaria; 1979 v England, Bulgaria, Wales, Denmark (23).
**McGrath R.C.** 1976 v Belgium; 1977 v West Germany, England, Scotland, Wales, Iceland (twice), Holland, Belgium; 1978 v Scotland, England, Wales, Bulgaria (sub); 1979 v England (twice; both sub) (15).
**McIlroy S.B.** 1972 v Spain, Scotland (sub); 1974 v Scotland, England, Wales, Norway, Sweden; 1975 v Yugoslavia, England, Scotland, Wales, Sweden, Norway, Yugoslavia; 1976 v Scotland, England, Wales, Holland, Belgium; 1977 v England, Scotland, Wales, Iceland (twice), Holland, Belgium; 1978 v Scotland, England, Wales, Republic of Ireland, Denmark, Bulgaria; 1979 v England, Bulgaria, England, Scotland, Wales, Denmark, England, Republic of Ireland; 1980 v Israel, Scotland, England, Wales, Sweden, Portugal; 1981 v Scotland, Portugal, Scotland, Sweden, Scotland, Israel (52).
**McMillan S.T.** 1962 v England, Scotland (2).
**McMillen W.S.** 1933 v England; 1934 v Scotland; 1936 v Scotland (3).
**Nicholl J.M.** 1976 v Israel, Wales (sub), Holland, Belgium; 1977 v England, Scotland, Wales, Iceland (twice), Holland, Belgium; 1978 v Scotland, England, Wales, Republic of Ireland, Denmark, Bulgaria 1979 v England, Bulgaria, England, Scotland, Wales, Denmark, England, Republic of Ireland; 1980 v Israel, Scotland, England, Wales, Australia (thrice), Sweden, Portugal; 1981 v Scotland, Portugal, Scotland, Sweden, Scotland, Israel; 1982 v England (41).
**Nicholson J.J.** 1960 v Scotland; 1961 v Wales, Greece, England; 1962 v Wales, Holland, Poland, England, Scotland, Poland (10).
**Sloan T.** 1979 v Scotland, Wales (sub), Denmark (sub) (3).
**Whiteside N.** 1982 v Yugoslavia, Honduras, Spain, Austria, France, West Germany, Albania; 1983 v Turkey, Austria, Turkey, West Germany, Scotland; 1984 v England, Wales, Finland, Romania, Israel, Finland; 1985 v England, Spain, Turkey, Romania, England; 1986 v France, Denmark, Morocco, Algeria, Spain, Brazil, England; 1987 v Israel, England, Yugoslavia, Turkey; 1988 v Poland, France (36).

# Republic of Ireland
**Breen T.** 1937 v Switzerland, France (2).
**Brennan S.A.** 1965 v Spain (twice); 1966 v Austria, Belgium, Spain, Turkey, Spain; 1969 v Czechoslovakia, Denmark, Hungary, Scotland, Czechoslovakia, Denmark, Hungary; 1970 v Poland (sub), West Germany (16).
**Cantwell N.** 1961 v Scotland (twice), Czechoslovakia (twice); 1962 v Austria, Iceland (twice); 1963 v Scotland, Austria; 1964 v Spain, England, Poland; 1965 v Spain (thrice); 1966 v Austria, Belgium, Spain; 1967 v Turkey (19).
**Carey B.** 1992 v USA (sub) (1).
**Carey J.J.** 1937 v Norway; 1938 v Czechoslovakia, Poland, Switzerland, Poland; 1939 v Hungary (twice), Germany; 1946 v Portugal, Spain, England; 1947 v Spain, Portugal; 1948 v Portugal, Spain, Switzerland; 1949 v Belgium, Portugal, Sweden,

Spain, Finland, England, Finland, Sweden; 1950 v Norway; 1951 v Argentina, Norway; 1952 v France; 1953 v Austria (29).
**Carolan J.E.** 1959 v Sweden; 1960 v Chile (2).
**Daly G.A.** 1973 v Poland (sub), Norway; 1974 v Brazil (sub), Uruguay (sub); 1975 v West Germany B, Switzerland (sub); 1976 v England, Turkey, France (9).
**Dunne A.P.** 1962 v Austria, Iceland; 1963 v Scotland, Austria; 1964 v Spain, Poland, Norway, England, Poland; 1965 v Spain (thrice); 1966 v Austria, Belgium, Spain, Turkey, Spain; 1968 v Poland, Denmark; 1969 v Hungary (twice); 1970 v Sweden; 1971 v Italy, Austria (24).
**Dunne P.A.J.** 1965 v Spain (thrice); 1966 v West Germany, Turkey (5).
**Giles M.J.** 1959 v Sweden; 1960 v Chile, Wales, Norway; 1961 v Scotland (twice), Czechoslovakia (twice); 1962 v Austria, Iceland; 1963 v Scotland (11).
**Givens D.J.** 1969 v Denmark, Hungary, Scotland, Czechoslovakia, Denmark, Hungary (6).
**Grimes A.A.** 1978 v Turkey, Poland, Norway (sub), England (sub); 1979 v Bulgaria, USA, Northern Ireland; 1980 v England, Cyprus; 1981 v Czechoslovakia, West Germany B (sub), Poland; 1982 v Algeria, Spain; 1983 v Spain (15).
**Irwin D.J.** 1990 v Morocco, Turkey; 1991 v Wales, England, Poland, USA, Hungary, Poland; 1992 v Wales, USA, Albania, USA (sub) (12).
**McGrath P.** 1985 v Italy (sub), Israel, England, Norway (sub), Switzerland (twice, both sub), Denmark; 1986 v Wales, Iceland, Czechoslovakia, Belgium, Scotland, Poland; 1987 v Scotland, Bulgaria, Belgium, Brazil, Luxembourg (twice), Bulgaria; 1988 v Yugoslavia, Poland, Norway, England, Holland, Northern Ireland; 1989 v France, Hungary, Spain, Malta, Hungary (31).
**Martin M.P.** 1973 v USSR, Poland, France, Norway, Poland; 1974 v Brazil, Uruguay, Chile, USSR, Turkey; 1975 v West Germany B, Switzerland, USSR, Switzerland (14).
**Moran K.R.** 1980 v Switzerland, Argentina, Belgium, France, Cyprus; 1981 v Wales (sub), Belgium, Czechoslovakia, West Germany B, Poland, France; 1982 v Algeria, Iceland, Holland, Malta; 1984 v Israel, Mexico; 1985 v Denmark, Iceland, Czechoslovakia, Belgium, Scotland, Poland; 1987 v Scotland, Bulgaria, Belgium, Brazil, Luxembourg (twice), Bulgaria, Israel; 1988 v Romania, Yugoslavia, Poland, Norway, England, USSR, Holland (38).
**O'Brien L.F.** 1987 v Brazil, Israel (sub); 1988 v Romania (sub), Yugoslavia (sub), Poland (sub), Tunisia (6).
**Roche P.J.** 1974 v USSR, Turkey; 1975 v West Germany B, Switzerland, USSR, Switzerland, Turkey (7).
**Stapleton F.A.** 1981 v Holland, France; 1982 v Algeria, Holland, Iceland, Spain; 1983 v Malta, Spain, Iceland, Holland, Malta; 1984 v Israel, Poland, China, Norway, Denmark; 1985 v Italy, Israel, England, Norway, Switzerland (twice), USSR, Denmark; 1986 v Uruguay, Iceland, Czechoslovakia (sub), Belgium, Scotland, Poland; 1987 v Scotland, Bulgaria, Belgium, Luxembourg (34).
**Whelan L.A.** 1956 v Holland, Denmark; 1957 v England (twice) (4).

# Denmark

**Olsen J.** 1984 v Austria, Norway, Switzerland; 1985 v East Germany (sub), USSR, Republic of Ireland; 1986 v Northern Ireland, Bulgaria, Poland (sub), Paraguay, Scotland, Uruguay (sub), West Germany, Spain, East Germany, West Germany, Czechoslovakia (sub); 1987 v Czechoslavkia (sub), Sweden, West Germany, Wales; 1988 v Austria, Hungary, Czechoslovakia, Belgium (sub) (25).
**Schmeichal, P.** 1991 v Italy, Sweden, Faroe Islands, Austria, Northern Ireland (5)
**Sivebaek J.** 1986 v Northern Ireland, Bulgaria, Norway, Poland Scotland (sub), West Germany, East Germany, Finland, West Germany; 1987 v Finland (sub), Czechoslovakia (11).

# USSR

**Kanchelskis A.** 1991 v Hungary, England, Argentina, Cyprus, Sweden, Italy, Norway, Hungary, Italy, Cyprus; 1992 v Spain, England (12).

### Yugoslavia
**Jovanović N.** 1980 v Luxembourg, Denmark; 1982 v Northern Ireland, Spain, Honduras (5).

### Rest of the World
**Law D.** 1963 v England (1).

### Rest of Europe
**Carey J.J.** 1947 v Great Britain (1).
**Charlton R.** 1964 v Scandinavia (1).
**Law D.** 1964 v Scandinavia (1).

# 'B' Internationals

## England
**Bailey G.R.** 1980 v USA, Australia (2).
**Berry J.J.** 1952 v Holland (1).
**Byrne R.W.** 1953 v Scotland; 1954 v Scotland, West Germany (3).
**Cockburn H.** 1949 v Holland (1).
**Edwards D.** 1954 v West Germany, Switzerland; 1955 v West Germany; 1956 v Switzerland (4).
**Greenhoff B.** 1978 v Czechoslovakia (1).
**Hill G.A.** 1978 v West Germany (1).
**Ince P.E.C.** 1992 v France (1)
**Pallister G.A.** 1989 v Italy, Yugoslavia (sub); 1990 v Czechoslovakia, Algeria; 1991 v Iceland; 1992 v France (6).
**Pegg D.** 1956 v Switzerland (1).
**Robson B.** 1990 v Algeria (1)
**Rowley J.F.** 1949 v Holland (1).
**Sharpe L.S.** 1992 v CIS (1).
**Taylor T.** 1956 v Scotland, Switzerland (2).
**Wallace D.L.** 1990 v Algeria (sub) (1).
**Webb N.J.** 1990 v Czechoslovakia, Algeria; 1991 v Spanish Olympic XI; 1992 v CIS (4).
**Wood R.E.** 1954 v Scotland (1).

## Scotland
**McClair B.J.** 1990 v East Germany (1).

## Wales
**Lawton C.T.** 1992 v Canada (sub) (1)

## Northern Ireland
**Nicholson J.J.** 1959 v France; 1960 v France (2).
**Shiels J.** 1960 v France (1).

## Republic of Ireland
**Brazil D.M.** 1990 v England

# Unofficial Internationals

## England
**Greenhoff B.** 1976 v Team America (1).

**Kidd B.** 1970 v Colombia (1).
**Pearson J.S.** 1976 v Team America (1).
**Stiles N.P.** 1970 v Colombia, Ecuador XI (2).

## All-Ireland
**Martin M.P.** 1973 v Brazil (1).

### The Three v The Six (Common Market Celebration)
Charlton R. 1973

### United Kingdom v Wales (Welsh FA Celebration)
**Best G.** 1969 (1).
**Charlton R.** 1969 (1).

# Wartime Internationals

## England
**Rowley J.F.** 1944 v Wales (1).

# Victory Internationals

## England
**Hilditch C.G.** 1919 v Wales (1).
**Mitten C.** 1946 v Scotland* (1).
**Walton J.W.** 1946 v Scotland * (1). *Bolton Disaster Fund Match.*

## Scotland
**Delaney J.** 1946 v England, Switzerland (2).

## Wales
**Meredith W.H.** 1919 v England (twice) (2).
**Warner J.** 1946 v Northern Ireland (1).

### Northern Ireland (and Ireland before 1924)
**Breen T.** 1946 v England, Scotland, Wales (3).
**Carey J.J.** 1946 v Scotland, Wales (2).
**O'Connell P.** 1919 v Scotland (1).

## Wartime Inter-League Match
**Rowley J.F.** 1944 v Scottish League

# Amateur Internationals

## England
**Bradley W.** 1958 v Finland, Northern Ireland, South Africa, Wales (4).
**Hardman H.P.** 1908 v Belgium, Germany, Sweden, Ireland (4).
**Pinner M.J.** 1961 v Republic of Ireland, Scotland, France (3).
**Walton J.A.** 1952 v Northern Ireland, Wales Scotland (3).

## United Kingdom
**Hardman H.P.** 1908 Olympic Games v Sweden, Holland, Denmark (3).

# Commonwealth Internationals' (FA Tours)

**Duckworth R** 1910 v South Africa (1).
**Hilditch C.G.** 1920 v South Africa (thrice) (3).
**Mew J.W.** 1920 v South Africa (1).
**Wall G.** 1910 v South Africa (thrice) (3).
**Woodcock W.** 1920 v South Africa (twice) (2).

# Under-23 Internationals

## England

**Aston J.** 1969 v Wales (1).
**Charlton R.** 1958 v Poland, Czechoslovakia; 1959 v France, Hungary; 1960 v Scotland, Italy (6).
**Chisnall J.P.** 1963 v Wales, West Germany; 1964 v Scotland, France (4).
**Coppell S.J.** 1976 v Hungary (1).
**Edwards D.** 1954 v Italy; 1955 v Italy, Scotland; 1956 v Scotland; 1957 v Romania, Czechoslovakia (6).
**Edwards P.F.** 1970 v Bulgaria (sub), West Germany, Sweden (3).
**Foulkes W.A.** 1955v Italy, Scotland (2).
**Gowling A.E.** 1971 v Switzerland (1).
**Greenhoff B.** 1974 v Yugoslavia, France (sub), Czechoslovakia; 1976 v Hungary (4).
**Hill G.A.** 1976 v Hungary (1).
**Kidd B.** 1967 v Wales, Italy; 1968 v Scotland; 1969 v Holland, Belgium (sub), Wales, USSR; 1970 v Scotland, West Germany, Sweden (10).
**McGuinness W.** 1958 v Poland, Czechoslovakia; 1959 v France, Hungary (4).
**Pearson J.S.** 1976 v Hungary (1).
**Pegg D.** 1956 v Scotland; 1957 v Scotland, Romania (3).
**Sadler D.** 1967 v Scotland, Wales; 1969 v Portugal (3).
**Scanlon A.J.** 1958 v Poland, Czechoslovakia; 1959 v France, Italy, West Germany (5).
**Setters M.E.** 1960 v Scotland, Holland, East Germany, Poland, Israel (5).
**Stiles N.P.** 1965 v Scotland, West Germany, Czechoslovakia (3).
**Whitefoot J.** 1954 v Italy (1).
**Wood R.E.** 1954 v Italy (1).

## Scotland

**Burns F.S.** 1968 v England (1).
**Forsyth A.** 1974 v Wales (1).
**Holton J.A.** 1973 v Wales (1).
**Houston S.M.** 1975 v Sweden, Romania (2).

## Wales

**Griffiths C.L.** 1974 v England, Scotland (2).
**Moore G.** 1963 v England, Scotland; 1964 v Northern Ireland (3).
**Morgans K.G.** 1958 v Scotland; 1959 v Scotland (2).

## Northern Ireland

**Briggs W.R.** 1962 v Wales (1).
**Nicholson J.J.** 1962 v Wales; 1963 v Wales; 1964 v Wales (3).
**Whiteside N.** 1989 v Republic of Ireland (1).

## Republic of Ireland

**Brazil D.M.** 1989 v Northern Ireland; 1990 v Northern Ireland (2).
**Dunne P.A.J.** 1966 v France (1).
**Brazil D.M.** 1990 v Northern Ireland.
**McEwan F.** 1966 v France (1).
**O'Brien R.** 1973 v France (1).

# Under-21 Internationals

## England

**Bailey G.R.** 1979 v Wales, Bulgaria, Denmark; 1980 v Scotland (twice), East Germany; 1981 v Norway; 1982 v Denmark, Greece; 1983 v Hungary; 1984 v France (twice), Italy, Spain (14).

**Beardsmore R.P.** 1989 v Greece, Albania (sub), Poland, Bulgaria, USA (5).

**Duxbury M.** 1980 v Switzerland (sub); 1981 v Republic of Ireland (sub), Romania (sub), Switzerland, Norway; 1982 v West Germany (twice) (7).

**Martin L.A.** 1989 v Greece (sub), Albania (sub) (2).

**Moses R.M.** 1981 v Hungary (1).

**Robins M.G.** 1990 v Portugal, France, USSR, Czechoslovakia, Hungary (sub), Poland (6).

**Sharpe L.S.** 1989 v Greece; 1990 v Portugal (sub), France, USSR, Czechoslovakia, Hungary, Poland (sub), Republic of Ireland (8).

**Walsh G.** 1987 v West Germany, Yugoslavia (2).

## Scotland

**Albiston A.R.** 1976 v Czechoslovakia; 1977 v Wales, Switzerland (twice), Czechoslovakia (5).

**Hogg G.J.** 1984 v Yugoslavia, West Germany, Iceland; 1985 v Spain (4).

**McGarvey S.T.** 1982 v England (sub), Belgium; 1983 v Switzerland, Belgium (4).

## Wales

**Blackmore C.G.** 1983 v Norway, Bulgaria, Yugoslavia (3).

**Clark J.** 1978 v Scotland (1).

**Davies A.** 1981 v France (twice); 1982 v Holland, Norway, Yugoslavia; 1983 v Bulgaria (6).

**Giggs R.J.** 1991 v Poland (1).

**Graham D.W.T.** 1990 v England (sub) (1).

**Hughes L.M.** 1982 v Norway, Yugoslavia; 1983 v Norway, Bulgaria, Yugoslavia (5).

## Northern Ireland

**McCreery D.** 1978 v Republic of Ireland (1).

**Nicholl J.M.** 1978 v Republic of Ireland (1).

**Sloan T.** 1978 v Republic of Ireland (1).

## Republic of Ireland

**Brazil D.M.** 1986 v Scotland; 1987 v Scotland, Belgium; 1989 v Senegal, Bulgaria, England, French School of Excellence (7).

**Carey B.** 1992 v Switzerland (1)

**Grimes A.A.** 1978 v Northern Ireland; 1979 v Poland (2).

**Russell M.C.** 1986 v Belgium, Scotland; 1987 v Scotland (3).

**Toal K.M.** 1991 v Poland (sub), Turkey; 1992 v Switzerland (3).

**Whelan A.G.** 1981 v England (1).

## Football League

**Allen R.A.** 1950 v Irish League; 1951 v League of Ireland (2).

**Aston J.** 1950 v Scottish League (twice) (2).

**Beale R.H.** 1913 v Scottish League (1).

**Berry J.J.** 1954 v League of Ireland (1).

**Bryant W.** 1897 v Irish League (1).

**Burgess H.** 1907 v Irish League; 1908 v Scottish League (2).

**Byrne R.W.** 1954 v League of Ireland, Irish League; 1955 v Scottish League, League of Ireland; 1956 v Irish League, League of Ireland (6).

**Charlton R.** 1961 v Scottish League, League of Ireland, Italian League; 1962 v Scottish League; 1964 v Italian League; 1965 v Scottish League; 1966 v Scottish League; 1968 v Scottish League (8).

**Cockburn H.** 1950 v Scottish League (1).
**Connelly J.M.** 1966 v Irish League (1).
**Duckworth R.** 1910 v Irish League, Southern League; 1911 v Southern League, Irish League; 1912 v Scottish League (5).
**Edwards D.** 1954 v Irish League; 1955 v Scottish League; 1956 v League of Ireland; 1957 v Scottish League (4).
**Edwards P.F.** 1970 v Irish League (1).
**Foulkes W.A.** 1954 v League of Ireland; 1955 v Scottish League (2).
**Gibson C.J.** 1987 v Irish League (1).
**Halse H.J.** 1908 v Irish League; 1911 v Southern League, Irish League (3).
**Hayes J.V.** 1910 v Scottish League (1).
**Hofton L.** 1911 v Southern League, Irish League (2).
**Kidd B.** 1970 v Scottish League (1).
**McGrath P.** 1987 v Rest of the World (1).
**McGuinness W.** 1958 v Irish League (1).
**Mew J.W.** 1921 v Scottish League (1).
**Morris J.** 1948 v Scottish League, Irish League (2).
**Pallister G.A.** 1990 v Irish League (1).
**Pearson S.C.** 1952 v Irish League (1).
**Quixall A.** 1958 v Scottish League (1).
**Roberts C.** 1905 v Scottish League; 1906 v Irish League; 1907 v Scottish League; 1909 v Scottish League; 1911 v Scottish League; Southern League, Irish League; 1912 v Irish League (8).
**Robson B.** 1987 v Rest of the World (1).
**Rowley J.F.** 1948 v League of Ireland; 1952 v Irish League (2).
**Sadler D.** 1970 v Irish League; 1971 v League of Ireland (2).
**Scanlon A.J.** 1959 v Irish League (1).
**Silcock J.** 1921 v Scottish League, Irish League; 1926 v Scottish League (3).
**Spence J.W.** 1926 v Irish League (1).
**Stepney A.C.** 1968 v Scottish League; 1970 v Scottish League (2).
**Stiles N.P.** 1965 v Scottish League; 1966 v Scottish League; 1968 v Scottish League (3).
**Sutcliffe J.W.** 1903 v Irish League (1).
**Taylor T.** 1956 v Irish League, League of Ireland (2).
**Viollet D.S.** 1956 v League of Ireland; 1959 v League of Ireland (twice) (3).
**Wall G.** 1909 v Irish League; 1910 v Scottish League, Southern League; 1912 v Southern League, Irish League (5).
**West E.J.** 1912 v Southern League (1).
**Whalley A.** 1913 v Irish League (1).
**Whiteside N.** 1987 v Rest of the World (sub) (1).
**Wood R.E.** 1954 v League of Ireland, Irish League; 1956 v Irish League (3).

# England Trial Matches

**Beale R.H.** 1914 North v England (1).
**Duckworth R.** 1912 Stripes v Whites (1).
**Griffiths J.** 1936 Possibles v Probables (1).
**Holden R.H.** 1908 North v South (1).
**Mew J.W.** 1921 North v England (1).
**Roberts C.** 1905 North v South; 1909 North v South; 1912 Stripes v Whites; 1913 England v North (4).
**Silcock J.** 1921 North v England; 1928 The Rest v England (2).
**Spence J.W.** 1927 England v The Rest (1).
**Stacey G.** 1912 Stripes v Whites (1).
**Vose G.** 1936 Possibles v Probables (1).
**Wall G.** 1907 North v South; 1908 North v South; 1911 Stripes v Whites (3).
**Whalley A.** 1914 North v England (1).
*In Stripes v Whites, the Whites were the senior side.*

# Manchester United Career Records

Below are the career records for all United players in major competitions since 1886. They include the three matches of the 1939-40 season, but exclude abandoned matches etc. Football League Test Matches are under 'Europe' column and indicated thus*.

| Player | Played | League App | League Gls | FA Cup App | FA Cup Gls | FL Cup App | FL Cup Gls | Europe App | Europe Gls | Total App | Total Gls |
|---|---|---|---|---|---|---|---|---|---|---|---|
| AINSWORTH A | 1933 | 2 | 0 | 0 | 0 | 0 | 0 | 0 | 0 | 2 | 0 |
| AITKEN J | 1895 | 2 | 1 | 0 | 0 | 0 | 0 | 0 | 0 | 2 | 1 |
| ALBINSON G | 1920 | 0 | 0 | 1 | 0 | 0 | 0 | 0 | 0 | 1 | 0 |
| ALBISTON AR | 1974-88 | 364/15 | 6 | 36 | 0 | 38/2 | 1 | 26/1 | 0 | 464/18 | 7 |
| ALLAN JT | 1904-06 | 35 | 21 | 1 | 1 | 0 | 0 | 0 | 0 | 36 | 22 |
| ALLEN RA | 1950-52 | 75 | 0 | 5 | 0 | 0 | 0 | 0 | 0 | 80 | 0 |
| ALLMAN A | 1914 | 12 | 0 | 0 | 0 | 0 | 0 | 0 | 0 | 12 | 0 |
| AMBLER A | 1899-1900 | 10 | 1 | 0 | 0 | 0 | 0 | 0 | 0 | 10 | 1 |
| ANDERSON G | 1911-14 | 80 | 37 | 6 | 2 | 0 | 0 | 0 | 0 | 86 | 39 |
| ANDERSON J | 1947-48 | 33 | 1 | 6 | 1 | 0 | 0 | 0 | 0 | 39 | 2 |
| ANDERSON T | 1972-73 | 13/6 | 2 | 0 | 0 | 0 | 0 | 0 | 0 | 13/6 | 2 |
| ANDERSON VA | 1987-91 | 50/4 | 2 | 7 | 1 | 6/1 | 0 | 1 | 0 | 64/5 | 4 |
| ANDERSON WJ | 1963-66 | 7/2 | 0 | 2 | 0 | 0 | 0 | 1 | 0 | 10/2 | 0 |
| ARKESDEN TA | 1902-05 | 70 | 28 | 9 | 5 | 0 | 0 | 0 | 0 | 79 | 33 |
| ASQUITH B | 1939 | 1 | 0 | 0 | 0 | 0 | 0 | 0 | 0 | 1 | 0 |
| ASTLEY JE | 1925-26 | 2 | 0 | 0 | 0 | 0 | 0 | 0 | 0 | 2 | 0 |
| ASTON J snr | 1946-53 | 253 | 29 | 29 | 1 | 0 | 0 | 0 | 0 | 282 | 30 |
| ASTON J jnr | 1964-71 | 139/16 | 25 | 5/2 | 1 | 12/3 | 0 | 8 | 1 | 164/21 | 27 |
| BAILEY GR | 1978-87 | 294 | 0 | 31 | 0 | 28 | 0 | 20 | 0 | 373 | 0 |
| BAIN D | 1922-23 | 22 | 9 | 1 | 0 | 0 | 0 | 0 | 0 | 23 | 9 |
| BAIN J | 1899 | 2 | 1 | 0 | 0 | 0 | 0 | 0 | 0 | 2 | 1 |
| BAIN J | 1924-27 | 4 | 0 | 0 | 0 | 0 | 0 | 0 | 0 | 4 | 0 |
| BAINBRIDGE W | 1945 | 0 | 0 | 1 | 1 | 0 | 0 | 0 | 0 | 1 | 1 |
| BAIRD HC | 1936-37 | 49 | 15 | 4 | 3 | 0 | 0 | 0 | 0 | 53 | 18 |
| BALDWIN T | 1974 | 2 | 0 | 0 | 0 | 0 | 0 | 0 | 0 | 2 | 0 |
| BALL J | 1947-49 | 22 | 0 | 1 | 0 | 0 | 0 | 0 | 0 | 23 | 0 |
| BALL JT | 1929-34 | 47 | 17 | 3 | 1 | 0 | 0 | 0 | 0 | 50 | 18 |
| BALL WH | 1902 | 4 | 0 | 0 | 0 | 0 | 0 | 0 | 0 | 4 | 0 |
| BAMFORD T | 1934-37 | 98 | 53 | 11 | 4 | 0 | 0 | 0 | 0 | 109 | 57 |
| BANKS J | 1901-02 | 40 | 0 | 4 | 1 | 0 | 0 | 0 | 0 | 44 | 1 |
| BANNISTER J | 1906-09 | 57 | 7 | 4 | 1 | 0 | 0 | 0 | 0 | 61 | 8 |
| BARBER J | 1922-23 | 3 | 1 | 1 | 1 | 0 | 0 | 0 | 0 | 4 | 2 |
| BARLOW C | 1919-21 | 29 | 0 | 1 | 0 | 0 | 0 | 0 | 0 | 30 | 0 |
| BARNES PS | 1985-87 | 19/1 | 2 | 0 | 0 | 5 | 2 | 0 | 0 | 24/1 | 4 |
| BARRETT F | 1896-97 | 118 | 0 | 14 | 0 | 0 | 0 | *4 | 0 | 136 | 0 |
| BARSON F | 1922-27 | 140 | 4 | 12 | 0 | 0 | 0 | 0 | 0 | 152 | 4 |
| BEADSWORTH A | 1902 | 9 | 1 | 3 | 1 | 0 | 0 | 0 | 0 | 12 | 2 |
| BEALE RH | 1912-14 | 105 | 0 | 7 | 0 | 0 | 0 | 0 | 0 | 112 | 0 |
| BEARDSLEY PA | 1982 | 0 | 0 | 0 | 0 | 1 | 0 | 0 | 0 | 1 | 0 |
| BEARDSMORE RP | 1988- | 30/26 | 4 | 4/4 | 0 | 3/1 | 0 | 1/2 | 0 | 38/33 | 4 |
| BECKETT T | 1886 | 0 | 0 | 1 | 0 | 0 | 0 | 0 | 0 | 1 | 0 |
| BEDDOW JH | 1904-06 | 33 | 12 | 1 | 3 | 0 | 0 | 0 | 0 | 34 | 15 |
| BEHAN W | 1933 | 1 | 0 | 0 | 0 | 0 | 0 | 0 | 0 | 1 | 0 |
| BELL A | 1902-12 | 278 | 10 | 28 | 0 | 0 | 0 | 0 | 0 | 306 | 10 |
| BENNION SR | 1921-32 | 286 | 2 | 15 | 1 | 0 | 0 | 0 | 0 | 301 | 3 |
| BENT G | 1954-56 | 12 | 0 | 0 | 0 | 0 | 0 | 0 | 0 | 12 | 0 |
| BERRY JJ | 1951-57 | 247 | 37 | 15 | 4 | 0 | 0 | 11 | 3 | 273 | 44 |
| BERRY W | 1906-08 | 13 | 1 | 1 | 0 | 0 | 0 | 0 | 0 | 14 | 1 |
| BEST G | 1963-73 | 361 | 137 | 46 | 21 | 25 | 9 | 34 | 11 | 466 | 178 |

| Player | Played | League App | Gls | FA Cup App | Gls | FL Cup App | Gls | Europe App | Gls | Total App | Gls |
|---|---|---|---|---|---|---|---|---|---|---|---|
| BIELBY PA | 1973 | 2/2 | 0 | 0 | 0 | 0 | 0 | 0 | 0 | 2/2 | 0 |
| BIRCH B | 1949-51 | 11 | 4 | 4 | 1 | 0 | 0 | 0 | 0 | 15 | 5 |
| BIRCHENOUGH H | 1902 | 25 | 0 | 5 | 0 | 0 | 0 | 0 | 0 | 30 | 0 |
| BIRKETT C | 1950 | 9 | 2 | 4 | 0 | 0 | 0 | 0 | 0 | 13 | 2 |
| BIRTLES G | 1980-82 | 57/1 | 11 | 4 | 1 | 2 | 0 | 0 | 0 | 63/1 | 12 |
| BISSETT G | 1919-21 | 40 | 10 | 2 | 0 | 0 | 0 | 0 | 0 | 42 | 10 |
| BLACK R | 1931-33 | 8 | 3 | 0 | 0 | 0 | 0 | 0 | 0 | 8 | 3 |
| BLACKMORE CG | 1983- | 138/34 | 19 | 15/5 | 1 | 22/2 | 3 | 11 | 2 | 186/41 | 25 |
| BLACKMORE P | 1899 | 1 | 0 | 1 | 0 | 0 | 0 | 0 | 0 | 2 | 0 |
| BLACKSTOCK T | 1903-06 | 34 | 0 | 4 | 0 | 0 | 0 | 0 | 0 | 38 | 0 |
| BLANCHFLOWER J | 1951-57 | 105 | 26 | 6 | 1 | 0 | 0 | 5 | 0 | 116 | 27 |
| BLEW WH | 1905 | 1 | 0 | 0 | 0 | 0 | 0 | 0 | 0 | 1 | 0 |
| BLOTT SP | 1909-12 | 19 | 2 | 0 | 0 | 0 | 0 | 0 | 0 | 19 | 2 |
| BOGAN T | 1949-50 | 29 | 7 | 4 | 0 | 0 | 0 | 0 | 0 | 33 | 7 |
| BOND JE | 1951-52 | 20 | 4 | 1 | 0 | 0 | 0 | 0 | 0 | 21 | 4 |
| BONTHRON RP | 1903-06 | 119 | 3 | 15 | 0 | 0 | 0 | 0 | 0 | 134 | 3 |
| BOOTH W | 1900 | 2 | 0 | 0 | 0 | 0 | 0 | 0 | 0 | 2 | 0 |
| BOSNICH M | 1989-91 | 3 | 0 | 0 | 0 | 0 | 0 | 0 | 0 | 3 | 0 |
| BOYD H | 1896-98 | 52 | 32 | 7 | 1 | 0 | 0 | *3 | 2 | 62 | 35 |
| BOYD WG | 1934 | 6 | 4 | 0 | 0 | 0 | 0 | 0 | 0 | 6 | 4 |
| BOYLE TW | 1928-29 | 16 | 6 | 1 | 0 | 0 | 0 | 0 | 0 | 17 | 6 |
| BRADBURY L | 1938 | 2 | 1 | 0 | 0 | 0 | 0 | 0 | 0 | 2 | 1 |
| BRADLEY W | 1958-61 | 63 | 20 | 3 | 1 | 0 | 0 | 0 | 0 | 66 | 21 |
| BRATT H | 1960 | 0 | 0 | 0 | 0 | 1 | 0 | 0 | 0 | 1 | 0 |
| BRAZIL AB | 1984-85 | 18/13 | 8 | 0/1 | 0 | 4/3 | 3 | 2 | 1 | 24/17 | 12 |
| BRAZIL DM | 1988- | 0/2 | 0 | 0 | 0 | 0 | 0 | 0 | 0 | 0/2 | 0 |
| BREEDON J | 1935-39 | 38 | 0 | 0 | 0 | 0 | 0 | 0 | 0 | 38 | 0 |
| BREEN T | 1936-38 | 65 | 0 | 6 | 0 | 0 | 0 | 0 | 0 | 71 | 0 |
| BRENNAN SA | 1957-69 | 291/1 | 3 | 36 | 3 | 4 | 0 | 24 | 0 | 355/1 | 6 |
| BRETT FB | 1921 | 10 | 0 | 0 | 0 | 0 | 0 | 0 | 0 | 10 | 0 |
| BRIGGS WR | 1960-61 | 9 | 0 | 2 | 0 | 0 | 0 | 0 | 0 | 11 | 0 |
| BROOKS WH | 1898 | 3 | 3 | 0 | 0 | 0 | 0 | 0 | 0 | 3 | 3 |
| BROOME AH | 1922 | 1 | 0 | 0 | 0 | 0 | 0 | 0 | 0 | 1 | 0 |
| BROOMFIELD H | 1907 | 9 | 0 | 0 | 0 | 0 | 0 | 0 | 0 | 9 | 0 |
| BROWN J | 1932-33 | 40 | 17 | 1 | 0 | 0 | 0 | 0 | 0 | 41 | 17 |
| BROWN J | 1935-38 | 102 | 1 | 8 | 0 | 0 | 0 | 0 | 0 | 110 | 1 |
| BROWN RB | 1947-48 | 4 | 0 | 0 | 0 | 0 | 0 | 0 | 0 | 4 | 0 |
| BROWN W | 1892 | 7 | 0 | 0 | 0 | 0 | 0 | 0 | 0 | 7 | 0 |
| BROWN W | 1896 | 7 | 2 | 0 | 0 | 0 | 0 | 0 | 0 | 7 | 2 |
| BRUCE SR | 1987- | 162 | 25 | 21 | 1 | 19 | 4 | 12 | 4 | 214 | 34 |
| BRYANT W | 1896-99 | 109 | 27 | 14 | 6 | 0 | 0 | *4 | 0 | 127 | 33 |
| BRYANT W | 1934-39 | 151 | 44 | 9 | 0 | 0 | 0 | 0 | 0 | 160 | 44 |
| BUCHAN G | 1973 | 0/3 | 0 | 0 | 0 | 0/1 | 0 | 0 | 0 | 0/4 | 0 |
| BUCHAN MM | 1971-82 | 376 | 4 | 39 | 0 | 30 | 0 | 10 | 0 | 455 | 4 |
| BUCKLE EW | 1946-49 | 20 | 6 | 4 | 1 | 0 | 0 | 0 | 0 | 24 | 7 |
| BUCKLEY FC | 1906 | 3 | 0 | 0 | 0 | 0 | 0 | 0 | 0 | 3 | 0 |
| BULLOCK KJ | 1930 | 10 | 3 | 0 | 0 | 0 | 0 | 0 | 0 | 10 | 3 |
| BUNCE W | 1902 | 2 | 0 | 0 | 0 | 0 | 0 | 0 | 0 | 2 | 0 |
| BURGESS H | 1906-09 | 49 | 0 | 3 | 0 | 0 | 0 | 0 | 0 | 52 | 0 |
| BURKE RS | 1946-48 | 28 | 16 | 6 | 6 | 0 | 0 | 0 | 0 | 34 | 22 |
| BURKE T | 1886 | 0 | 0 | 1 | 0 | 0 | 0 | 0 | 0 | 1 | 0 |
| BURNS FS | 1967-71 | 111/10 | 6 | 11/1 | 0 | 10/1 | 0 | 10/1 | 1 | 142/13 | 7 |
| BYRNE D | 1933 | 4 | 3 | 0 | 0 | 0 | 0 | 0 | 0 | 4 | 3 |
| BYRNE RW | 1951-57 | 245 | 17 | 18 | 2 | 0 | 0 | 14 | 0 | 277 | 19 |
| CAIRNS J | 1894-98 | 2 | 0 | 0 | 0 | 0 | 0 | 0 | 0 | 2 | 0 |
| CAMPBELL WC | 1893 | 5 | 1 | 0 | 0 | 0 | 0 | 0 | 0 | 5 | 1 |
| CANTWELL N | 1960-66 | 123 | 6 | 14 | 2 | 0 | 0 | 7 | 0 | 144 | 8 |
| CAPE JP | 1933-36 | 59 | 18 | 1 | 0 | 0 | 0 | 0 | 0 | 60 | 18 |
| CAPPER A | 1911 | 1 | 0 | 0 | 0 | 0 | 0 | 0 | 0 | 1 | 0 |
| CAREY JJ | 1937-52 | 306 | 17 | 38 | 1 | 0 | 0 | 0 | 0 | 344 | 18 |

| Player | Played | League App | Gls | FA Cup App | Gls | FL Cup App | Gls | Europe App | Gls | Total App | Gls |
|---|---|---|---|---|---|---|---|---|---|---|---|
| CARMAN J | 1897 | 3 | 1 | 0 | 0 | 0 | 0 | 0 | 0 | 3 | 1 |
| CAROLAN JF | 1958-60 | 66 | 0 | 4 | 0 | 1 | 0 | 0 | 0 | 71 | 0 |
| CARSON A | 1892 | 13 | 3 | 0 | 0 | 0 | 0 | 0 | 0 | 13 | 3 |
| CARTMAN HR | 1922 | 3 | 0 | 0 | 0 | 0 | 0 | 0 | 0 | 3 | 0 |
| CARTWRIGHT WG | 1895-1903 | 228 | 8 | 27 | 0 | 0 | 0 | *2 | 0 | 257 | 8 |
| CASHMORE AA | 1913 | 3 | 0 | 0 | 0 | 0 | 0 | 0 | 0 | 3 | 0 |
| CASSIDY J | 1892-99 | 152 | 90 | 15 | 9 | 0 | 0 | *7 | 1 | 174 | 100 |
| CASSIDY L | 1947-51 | 4 | 0 | 0 | 0 | 0 | 0 | 0 | 0 | 4 | 0 |
| CHALMERS WS | 1932-33 | 34 | 1 | 1 | 0 | 0 | 0 | 0 | 0 | 35 | 1 |
| CHAPMAN W | 1926-27 | 26 | 0 | 0 | 0 | 0 | 0 | 0 | 0 | 26 | 0 |
| CHARLTON R | 1956-72 | 604/2 | 199 | 79 | 19 | 24 | 7 | 45 | 22 | 752/2 | 247 |
| CHESTER RA | 1935 | 13 | 1 | 0 | 0 | 0 | 0 | 0 | 0 | 13 | 1 |
| CHESTERS A | 1929-31 | 9 | 0 | 0 | 0 | 0 | 0 | 0 | 0 | 9 | 0 |
| CHILTON AC | 1939-54 | 353 | 3 | 37 | 0 | 0 | 0 | 0 | 0 | 390 | 3 |
| CHISNALL JP | 1961-63 | 35 | 8 | 8 | 1 | 0 | 0 | 4 | 1 | 47 | 10 |
| CHORLTON T | 1913 | 4 | 0 | 0 | 0 | 0 | 0 | 0 | 0 | 4 | 0 |
| CHRISTIE D | 1908 | 2 | 0 | 0 | 0 | 0 | 0 | 0 | 0 | 2 | 0 |
| CHRISTIE J | 1902 | 1 | 0 | 0 | 0 | 0 | 0 | 0 | 0 | 1 | 0 |
| CLARK J | 1899 | 9 | 0 | 0 | 0 | 0 | 0 | 0 | 0 | 9 | 0 |
| CLARK J | 1976-77 | 0/1 | 0 | 0 | 0 | 0 | 0 | 0 | 0 | 0/1 | 0 |
| CLARKIN J | 1893-95 | 67 | 23 | 5 | 0 | 0 | 0 | *2 | 0 | 74 | 23 |
| CLAYTON G | 1956 | 2 | 0 | 0 | 0 | 0 | 0 | 0 | 0 | 2 | 0 |
| CLEAVER H | 1902 | 1 | 0 | 0 | 0 | 0 | 0 | 0 | 0 | 1 | 0 |
| CLEMENTS JE | 1891-93 | 36 | 0 | 4 | 0 | 0 | 0 | *2 | 0 | 42 | 0 |
| CLEMPSON F | 1949-52 | 15 | 2 | 0 | 0 | 0 | 0 | 0 | 0 | 15 | 2 |
| COCKBURN H | 1946-54 | 243 | 4 | 32 | 0 | 0 | 0 | 0 | 0 | 275 | 4 |
| COLLINSON C | 1946 | 7 | 0 | 0 | 0 | 0 | 0 | 0 | 0 | 7 | 0 |
| COLLINSON J | 1895-1900 | 62 | 16 | 9 | 1 | 0 | 0 | 0 | 0 | 71 | 17 |
| COLMAN E | 1955-57 | 85 | 1 | 9 | 0 | 0 | 0 | 13 | 1 | 107 | 2 |
| COLVILLE J | 1892 | 9 | 1 | 1 | 0 | 0 | 0 | 0 | 0 | 10 | 1 |
| CONNACHAN J | 1898 | 4 | 0 | 0 | 0 | 0 | 0 | 0 | 0 | 4 | 0 |
| CONNAUGHTON JP | 1971 | 3 | 0 | 0 | 0 | 0 | 0 | 0 | 0 | 3 | 0 |
| CONNELL TE | 1978 | 2 | 0 | 0 | 0 | 0 | 0 | 0 | 0 | 2 | 0 |
| CONNELLY JM | 1964-66 | 79/1 | 22 | 13 | 2 | 1 | 0 | 19 | 11 | 112/1 | 35 |
| CONNOR E | 1909-10 | 15 | 2 | 0 | 0 | 0 | 0 | 0 | 0 | 15 | 2 |
| COOKSON SP | 1914 | 12 | 0 | 1 | 0 | 0 | 0 | 0 | 0 | 13 | 0 |
| COPE R | 1956-60 | 93 | 2 | 10 | 0 | 1 | 0 | 2 | 0 | 106 | 2 |
| COPPELL SJ | 1974-82 | 320/2 | 54 | 36 | 4 | 25 | 9 | 11/1 | 3 | 392/3 | 70 |
| COUPAR J | 1892-1901 | 32 | 9 | 0 | 0 | 0 | 0 | *2 | 1 | 34 | 10 |
| COYNE PD | 1975 | 1/1 | 1 | 0 | 0 | 0 | 0 | 0 | 0 | 1/1 | 1 |
| CRAIG T | 1889-90 | 0 | 0 | 2 | 1 | 0 | 0 | 0 | 0 | 2 | 1 |
| CRAVEN C | 1938 | 11 | 2 | 0 | 0 | 0 | 0 | 0 | 0 | 11 | 2 |
| CRERAND PT | 1962-70 | 304 | 10 | 43 | 4 | 4 | 0 | 41 | 1 | 392 | 15 |
| CROMPTON J | 1945-56 | 191 | 0 | 20 | 0 | 0 | 0 | 0 | 0 | 211 | 0 |
| CROOKS GA | 1983 | 6/1 | 2 | 0 | 0 | 0 | 0 | 0 | 0 | 6/1 | 2 |
| CROWTHER S | 1957-58 | 13 | 0 | 5 | 0 | 0 | 0 | 2 | 0 | 20 | 0 |
| CUNNINGHAM J | 1898 | 15 | 2 | 2 | 0 | 0 | 0 | 0 | 0 | 17 | 2 |
| CUNNINGHAM LP | 1982 | 3/2 | 1 | 0 | 0 | 0 | 0 | 0 | 0 | 3/2 | 1 |
| CURRY JJ | 1908-10 | 13 | 0 | 1 | 0 | 0 | 0 | 0 | 0 | 14 | 0 |
| DALE | 1890 | 0 | 0 | 1 | 0 | 0 | 0 | 0 | 0 | 1 | 0 |
| DALE J | 1947 | 2 | 0 | 0 | 0 | 0 | 0 | 0 | 0 | 2 | 0 |
| DALE W | 1928-31 | 64 | 0 | 4 | 0 | 0 | 0 | 0 | 0 | 68 | 0 |
| DALTON E | 1907 | 1 | 0 | 0 | 0 | 0 | 0 | 0 | 0 | 1 | 0 |
| DALY GA | 1973-76 | 107/4 | 23 | 9/1 | 5 | 17 | 4 | 4 | 0 | 137/5 | 32 |
| DAVENPORT P | 1985-89 | 72/19 | 22 | 2/2 | 0 | 8/2 | 4 | 0 | 0 | 83/23 | 26 |
| DAVIDSON WR | 1893-94 | 40 | 2 | 3 | 0 | 0 | 0 | *1 | 0 | 44 | 2 |
| DAVIES A | 1981-83 | 6/1 | 0 | 2 | 0 | 0 | 0 | 0/1 | 1 | 8/2 | 1 |
| DAVIES JE | 1886-89 | 0 | 0 | 2 | 0 | 0 | 0 | 0 | 0 | 2 | 0 |
| DAVIES J | 1892 | 7 | 0 | 1 | 0 | 0 | 0 | *2 | 0 | 10 | 0 |
| DAVIES L | 1886 | 0 | 0 | 1 | 0 | 0 | 0 | 0 | 0 | 1 | 0 |

438

| Player | Played | League | | FA Cup | | FL Cup | | Europe | | Total | |
|---|---|---|---|---|---|---|---|---|---|---|---|
| | | App | Gls | App | Gls | App | Gls | App | Gls | App | Gls |
| DAVIES RT | 1974 | 0/8 | 0 | 0/2 | 0 | 0 | 0 | 0 | 0 | 0/10 | 0 |
| DAVIES WR | 1972 | 15/1 | 4 | 1 | 0 | 0 | 0 | 0 | 0 | 16/1 | 4 |
| DAWSON AD | 1956-71 | 80 | 45 | 10 | 8 | 3 | 1 | 0 | 0 | 93 | 54 |
| DEAN H | 1931 | 2 | 0 | 0 | 0 | 0 | 0 | 0 | 0 | 2 | 0 |
| DELANEY J | 1946-50 | 164 | 25 | 19 | 3 | 0 | 0 | 0 | 0 | 183 | 28 |
| DEMPSEY MJ | 1983-86 | 1 | 0 | 0 | 0 | 0 | 0 | 0/1 | 0 | 1/1 | 0 |
| DENMAN J | 1891 | 0 | 0 | 1 | 0 | 0 | 0 | 0 | 0 | 1 | 0 |
| DENNIS W | 1923 | 3 | 0 | 0 | 0 | 0 | 0 | 0 | 0 | 3 | 0 |
| DEWAR N | 1932-33 | 36 | 14 | 0 | 0 | 0 | 0 | 0 | 0 | 36 | 14 |
| DOHERTY J | 1952-57 | 25 | 7 | 1 | 0 | 0 | 0 | 0 | 0 | 26 | 7 |
| DONAGHY B | 1905 | 3 | 0 | 0 | 0 | 0 | 0 | 0 | 0 | 3 | 0 |
| DONAGHY MM | 1988- | 76/13 | 0 | 10 | 0 | 10/4 | 0 | 2/3 | 0 | 98/20 | 0 |
| DONALD IR | 1972 | 4 | 0 | 0 | 0 | 2 | 0 | 0 | 0 | 6 | 0 |
| DONALDSON R | 1892-97 | 131 | 56 | 16 | 10 | 0 | 0 | *8 | 0 | 155 | 66 |
| DONNELLY | 1890 | 0 | 0 | 1 | 0 | 0 | 0 | 0 | 0 | 1 | 0 |
| DONNELLY A | 1908-12 | 34 | 0 | 3 | 0 | 0 | 0 | 0 | 0 | 37 | 0 |
| DOUGAN T | 1938 | 4 | 0 | 0 | 0 | 0 | 0 | 0 | 0 | 4 | 0 |
| DOUGHTY J | 1886-91 | 0 | 0 | 3 | 3 | 0 | 0 | 0 | 0 | 3 | 3 |
| DOUGHTY R | 1891-96 | 0 | 0 | 5 | 1 | 0 | 0 | *3 | 0 | 8 | 1 |
| DOUGLAS W | 1893-95 | 55 | 0 | 1 | 0 | 0 | 0 | *1 | 0 | 57 | 0 |
| DOW JM | 1893-95 | 48 | 6 | 1 | 0 | 0 | 0 | *1 | 0 | 50 | 6 |
| DOWNIE ALB | 1902-09 | 172 | 12 | 19 | 2 | 0 | 0 | 0 | 0 | 191 | 14 |
| DOWNIE JD | 1948-52 | 110 | 35 | 5 | 1 | 0 | 0 | 0 | 0 | 115 | 36 |
| DRAYCOTT WL | 1896-98 | 81 | 6 | 10 | 0 | 0 | 0 | *4 | 0 | 95 | 6 |
| DUCKWORTH R | 1903-12 | 225 | 11 | 26 | 0 | 0 | 0 | 0 | 0 | 251 | 11 |
| DUNN W | 1897 | 10 | 0 | 2 | 0 | 0 | 0 | 0 | 0 | 12 | 0 |
| DUNNE AP | 1960-72 | 414 | 2 | 54/1 | 0 | 21 | 0 | 40 | 0 | 529/1 | 2 |
| DUNNE PAJ | 1964-65 | 45 | 0 | 7 | 0 | 1 | 0 | 13 | 0 | 66 | 0 |
| DUXBURY M | 1980-90 | 274/25 | 6 | 20/5 | 1 | 32/2 | 0 | 17/1 | 0 | 343/33 | 7 |
| DYER JA | 1905 | 1 | 0 | 0 | 0 | 0 | 0 | 0 | 0 | 1 | 0 |
| EARP J | 1886 | 0 | 0 | 1 | 0 | 0 | 0 | 0 | 0 | 1 | 0 |
| EDGE A | 1891 | 0 | 0 | 3 | 3 | 0 | 0 | 0 | 0 | 3 | 3 |
| EDMONDS H | 1910-11 | 43 | 0 | 7 | 0 | 0 | 0 | 0 | 0 | 50 | 0 |
| EDWARDS D | 1952-57 | 151 | 20 | 12 | 1 | 0 | 0 | 12 | 0 | 175 | 21 |
| EDWARDS PF | 1969-72 | 52/2 | 0 | 10 | 0 | 4 | 1 | 0 | 0 | 66/2 | 1 |
| ELLIS D | 1923 | 11 | 0 | 0 | 0 | 0 | 0 | 0 | 0 | 11 | 0 |
| ERENTZ FC | 1892-1901 | 280 | 9 | 23 | 0 | 0 | 0 | *7 | 0 | 310 | 9 |
| ERENTZ H | 1897 | 6 | 0 | 3 | 0 | 0 | 0 | 0 | 0 | 9 | 0 |
| EVANS G | 1890 | 0 | 0 | 1 | 1 | 0 | 0 | 0 | 0 | 1 | 1 |
| EVANS S | 1923 | 6 | 2 | 0 | 0 | 0 | 0 | 0 | 0 | 6 | 2 |
| FALL JW | 1893 | 23 | 0 | 3 | 0 | 0 | 0 | *1 | 0 | 27 | 0 |
| FARMAN AH | 1889-94 | 51 | 18 | 7 | 6 | 0 | 0 | *3 | 4 | 61 | 28 |
| FEEHAN I | 1949 | 12 | 0 | 2 | 0 | 0 | 0 | 0 | 0 | 14 | 0 |
| FELTON G | 1890 | 0 | 0 | 1 | 0 | 0 | 0 | 0 | 0 | 1 | 0 |
| FERGUSON D | 1927 | 4 | 0 | 0 | 0 | 0 | 0 | 0 | 0 | 4 | 0 |
| FERGUSON D | 1990- | 4/5 | 0 | 0 | 0 | 0 | 0 | 0 | 0 | 4/5 | 0 |
| FERGUSON J | 1931 | 8 | 1 | 0 | 0 | 0 | 0 | 0 | 0 | 8 | 1 |
| FERRIER RJ | 1935-37 | 18 | 4 | 1 | 0 | 0 | 0 | 0 | 0 | 19 | 4 |
| FIELDING WJ | 1946 | 6 | 0 | 1 | 0 | 0 | 0 | 0 | 0 | 7 | 0 |
| FISHER J | 1900-01 | 42 | 2 | 4 | 1 | 0 | 0 | 0 | 0 | 46 | 3 |
| FITCHETT J | 1902-04 | 16 | 1 | 2 | 0 | 0 | 0 | 0 | 0 | 18 | 1 |
| FITTON GA | 1931-32 | 12 | 2 | 0 | 0 | 0 | 0 | 0 | 0 | 12 | 2 |
| FITZPATRICK JHN | 1964-72 | 111/6 | 8 | 11 | 1 | 12 | 1 | 7 | 0 | 141/6 | 10 |
| FITZSIMMONS D | 1895-99 | 28 | 0 | 3 | 0 | 0 | 0 | 0 | 0 | 31 | 0 |
| FITZSIMMONS T | 1892-93 | 27 | 6 | 1 | 0 | 0 | 0 | *2 | 0 | 30 | 6 |
| FLETCHER P | 1972-73 | 2/5 | 0 | 0 | 0 | 0 | 0 | 0 | 0 | 2/5 | 0 |
| FOGGON A | 1976 | 0/3 | 0 | 0 | 0 | 0 | 0 | 0 | 0 | 0/3 | 0 |
| FOLEY G | 1899 | 7 | 1 | 0 | 0 | 0 | 0 | 0 | 0 | 7 | 1 |
| FORD JB | 1908-09 | 5 | 0 | 0 | 0 | 0 | 0 | 0 | 0 | 5 | 0 |
| FORSTER T | 1919-21 | 35 | 0 | 1 | 0 | 0 | 0 | 0 | 0 | 36 | 0 |

439

| Player | Played | League App | Gls | FA Cup App | Gls | FL Cup App | Gls | Europe App | Gls | Total App | Gls |
|---|---|---|---|---|---|---|---|---|---|---|---|
| FORSYTH A | 1972-77 | 99/2 | 4 | 10 | 1 | 7 | 0 | 0/1 | 0 | 116/3 | 5 |
| FOULKES WA | 1952-69 | 563/3 | 7 | 61 | 0 | 3 | 0 | 52 | 2 | 679/3 | 9 |
| FOX | 1914 | 0 | 0 | 1 | 0 | 0 | 0 | 0 | 0 | 1 | 0 |
| FRAME T | 1932-33 | 51 | 4 | 1 | 0 | 0 | 0 | 0 | 0 | 52 | 4 |
| GALLIMORE SH | 1930-33 | 72 | 19 | 4 | 1 | 0 | 0 | 0 | 0 | 76 | 20 |
| GARDNER CR | 1935-36 | 16 | 1 | 2 | 0 | 0 | 0 | 0 | 0 | 18 | 1 |
| GARTON WF | 1984-88 | 39/2 | 0 | 3 | 0 | 5/1 | 0 | 0/1 | 0 | 47/4 | 0 |
| GARVEY J | 1900 | 6 | 0 | 0 | 0 | 0 | 0 | 0 | 0 | 6 | 0 |
| GASKELL JD | 1957-66 | 96 | 0 | 16 | 0 | 1 | 0 | 5 | 0 | 118 | 0 |
| GAUDIE R | 1903 | 7 | 0 | 1 | 0 | 0 | 0 | 0 | 0 | 8 | 0 |
| GIBSON CJ | 1985- | 74/5 | 9 | 8/1 | 0 | 7 | 0 | 0 | 0 | 89/6 | 9 |
| GIBSON R | 1921 | 11 | 0 | 1 | 0 | 0 | 0 | 0 | 0 | 12 | 0 |
| GIBSON TB | 1985-87 | 14/9 | 1 | 1/1 | 0 | 0/2 | 0 | 0 | 0 | 15/12 | 1 |
| GIBSON TRD | 1950-54 | 108 | 0 | 6 | 0 | 0 | 0 | 0 | 0 | 114 | 0 |
| GIDMAN J | 1981-86 | 94/1 | 4 | 9 | 0 | 5 | 0 | 7/2 | 0 | 115/3 | 4 |
| GIGGS R | 1990- | 33/7 | 5 | 2/1 | 0 | 5/3 | 3 | 1 | 0 | 41/11 | 8 |
| GILES MJ | 1959-62 | 99 | 10 | 13 | 2 | 2 | 1 | 0 | 0 | 114 | 13 |
| GILL AGD | 1986-88 | 5/5 | 1 | 2/2 | 1 | 0 | 0 | 0 | 0 | 7/7 | 2 |
| GILLESPIE M | 1896-90 | 74 | 17 | 11 | 4 | 0 | 0 | *4 | 0 | 89 | 21 |
| GIPPS T | 1912-14 | 23 | 0 | 0 | 0 | 0 | 0 | 0 | 0 | 23 | 0 |
| GIVENS DJ | 1969 | 4/4 | 1 | 0 | 0 | 1 | 0 | 0 | 0 | 5/4 | 1 |
| GLADWIN GWE | 1936-38 | 27 | 1 | 1 | 0 | 0 | 0 | 0 | 0 | 28 | 1 |
| GODSMARK G | 1899 | 9 | 4 | 0 | 0 | 0 | 0 | 0 | 0 | 9 | 4 |
| GOLDTHORPE EH | 1922-24 | 27 | 15 | 3 | 1 | 0 | 0 | 0 | 0 | 30 | 16 |
| GOODWIN FJ | 1954-59 | 95 | 7 | 8 | 1 | 0 | 0 | 3 | 0 | 106 | 8 |
| GOODWIN W | 1920-21 | 7 | 1 | 0 | 0 | 0 | 0 | 0 | 0 | 7 | 1 |
| GOTHERIDGE J | 1886 | 0 | 0 | 1 | 0 | 0 | 0 | 0 | 0 | 1 | 0 |
| GOURLAY J | 1898 | 1 | 0 | 0 | 0 | 0 | 0 | 0 | 0 | 1 | 0 |
| GOWLING AE | 1967-71 | 64/7 | 18 | 6/2 | 2 | 7/1 | 1 | 0 | 0 | 77/10 | 21 |
| GRAHAM A | 1983-84 | 33/4 | 5 | 1 | 0 | 6 | 1 | 6/1 | 1 | 46/5 | 7 |
| GRAHAM DWT | 1987- | 1/1 | 0 | 0/1 | 1 | 0/1 | 0 | 0 | 0 | 1/3 | 1 |
| GRAHAM G | 1972-74 | 41/2 | 2 | 2 | 0 | 1 | 0 | 0 | 0 | 44/2 | 2 |
| GRAHAM J | 1893 | 4 | 0 | 0 | 0 | 0 | 0 | 0 | 0 | 4 | 0 |
| GRASSAM W | 1903-04 | 29 | 13 | 8 | 1 | 0 | 0 | 0 | 0 | 37 | 14 |
| GREAVES ID | 1954-59 | 67 | 0 | 6 | 0 | 0 | 0 | 2 | 0 | 75 | 0 |
| GREEN RE | 1933 | 9 | 4 | 0 | 0 | 0 | 0 | 0 | 0 | 9 | 4 |
| GREENHOFF B | 1973-78 | 218/3 | 13 | 24 | 2 | 19 | 2 | 6 | 0 | 267/3 | 17 |
| GREENHOFF J | 1976-80 | 94/3 | 26 | 18/1 | 9 | 4 | 1 | 2 | 0 | 118/4 | 36 |
| GREENWOOD W | 1900 | 3 | 0 | 0 | 0 | 0 | 0 | 0 | 0 | 3 | 0 |
| GREGG H | 1957-66 | 210 | 0 | 24 | 0 | 2 | 0 | 11 | 0 | 247 | 0 |
| GRIFFITHS CL | 1973 | 7 | 0 | 0 | 0 | 0 | 0 | 0 | 0 | 7 | 0 |
| GRIFFITHS J | 1933-39 | 168 | 1 | 8 | 0 | 0 | 0 | 0 | 0 | 176 | 1 |
| GRIFFITHS W | 1898-1904 | 157 | 27 | 18 | 3 | 0 | 0 | 0 | 0 | 175 | 30 |
| GRIMES AA | 1977-82 | 62/28 | 10 | 5 | 1 | 6 | 0 | 4/2 | 0 | 77/30 | 11 |
| GRIMSHAW A | 1975 | 0/1 | 0 | 0 | 0 | 0/1 | 0 | 0 | 0 | 0/2 | 0 |
| GRIMWOOD JB | 1919-26 | 196 | 8 | 9 | 0 | 0 | 0 | 0 | 0 | 205 | 8 |
| GRUNDY J | 1899-1900 | 11 | 3 | 0 | 0 | 0 | 0 | 0 | 0 | 11 | 3 |
| GYVES | 1890 | 0 | 0 | 1 | 0 | 0 | 0 | 0 | 0 | 1 | 0 |
| HACKING J | 1933-34 | 32 | 0 | 2 | 0 | 0 | 0 | 0 | 0 | 34 | 0 |
| HALL J | 1933-35 | 67 | 0 | 6 | 0 | 0 | 0 | 0 | 0 | 73 | 0 |
| HALL J | 1925 | 3 | 0 | 0 | 0 | 0 | 0 | 0 | 0 | 3 | 0 |
| HALL P | 1903 | 8 | 2 | 0 | 0 | 0 | 0 | 0 | 0 | 8 | 2 |
| HALSE HJ | 1907-11 | 109 | 41 | 15 | 9 | 0 | 0 | 0 | 0 | 124 | 50 |
| HALTON RL | 1936 | 4 | 1 | 0 | 0 | 0 | 0 | 0 | 0 | 4 | 1 |
| HAMILL M | 1911-13 | 57 | 2 | 2 | 0 | 0 | 0 | 0 | 0 | 59 | 2 |
| HANLON JJ | 1938-48 | 64 | 20 | 6 | 2 | 0 | 0 | 0 | 0 | 70 | 22 |
| HANNAFORD C | 1925-26 | 11 | 0 | 1 | 0 | 0 | 0 | 0 | 0 | 12 | 0 |
| HANSON J | 1924-29 | 138 | 47 | 9 | 5 | 0 | 0 | 0 | 0 | 147 | 52 |
| HARDMAN HP | 1908 | 4 | 0 | 0 | 0 | 0 | 0 | 0 | 0 | 4 | 0 |
| HARRIS FE | 1919-21 | 46 | 2 | 3 | 0 | 0 | 0 | 0 | 0 | 49 | 2 |
| HARRIS T | 1926 | 4 | 1 | 0 | 0 | 0 | 0 | 0 | 0 | 4 | 1 |

| Player | Played | League App | Gls | FA Cup App | Gls | FL Cup App | Gls | Europe App | Gls | Total App | Gls |
|---|---|---|---|---|---|---|---|---|---|---|---|
| HARRISON C | 1889 | 0 | 0 | 1 | 0 | 0 | 0 | 0 | 0 | 1 | 0 |
| HARRISON WE | 1920-21 | 44 | 5 | 2 | 0 | 0 | 0 | 0 | 0 | 46 | 5 |
| HARROP RW | 1957-58 | 10 | 0 | 1 | 0 | 0 | 0 | 0 | 0 | 11 | 0 |
| HARTWELL W | 1903-04 | 3 | 0 | 1 | 0 | 0 | 0 | 0 | 0 | 4 | 0 |
| HASLAM G | 1921-27 | 25 | 0 | 2 | 0 | 0 | 0 | 0 | 0 | 27 | 0 |
| HAWORTH R | 1926 | 2 | 0 | 0 | 0 | 0 | 0 | 0 | 0 | 2 | 0 |
| HAWKSWORTH A | 1956 | 1 | 0 | 0 | 0 | 0 | 0 | 0 | 0 | 1 | 0 |
| HAY T | 1889 | 0 | 0 | 1 | 0 | 0 | 0 | 0 | 0 | 1 | 0 |
| HAYDOCK F | 1960-62 | 6 | 0 | 0 | 0 | 0 | 0 | 0 | 0 | 6 | 0 |
| HAYES JV | 1900-10 | 115 | 2 | 13 | 0 | 0 | 0 | 0 | 0 | 128 | 2 |
| HAYWOOD H | 1932-33 | 4 | 2 | 0 | 0 | 0 | 0 | 0 | 0 | 4 | 2 |
| HAYWOOD JF | 1913-14 | 26 | 0 | 0 | 0 | 0 | 0 | 0 | 0 | 26 | 0 |
| HEATHCOTE J | 1899-1901 | 7 | 0 | 1 | 0 | 0 | 0 | 0 | 0 | 8 | 0 |
| HENDERSON W | 1921-24 | 34 | 17 | 2 | 0 | 0 | 0 | 0 | 0 | 36 | 17 |
| HENDRY J | 1892 | 2 | 1 | 0 | 0 | 0 | 0 | 0 | 0 | 2 | 1 |
| HENRYS A | 1891-92 | 3 | 0 | 3 | 0 | 0 | 0 | 0 | 0 | 6 | 0 |
| HERD DG | 1961-67 | 201/1 | 114 | 35 | 15 | 1 | 1 | 25 | 14 | 262/1 | 144 |
| HERON FTR | 1957-60 | 3 | 0 | 0 | 0 | 0 | 0 | 0 | 0 | 3 | 0 |
| HIGGINS W | 1901 | 10 | 0 | 0 | 0 | 0 | 0 | 0 | 0 | 10 | 0 |
| HIGGINS MN | 1985-87 | 6 | 0 | 2 | 0 | 0 | 0 | 0 | 0 | 8 | 0 |
| HIGSON J | 1901 | 5 | 1 | 0 | 0 | 0 | 0 | 0 | 0 | 5 | 1 |
| HILDITCH CG | 1919-31 | 301 | 7 | 21 | 0 | 0 | 0 | 0 | 0 | 322 | 7 |
| HILL GA | 1975-77 | 100/1 | 39 | 17 | 6 | 7 | 4 | 8 | 2 | 132/1 | 51 |
| HILLAM CE | 1933 | 8 | 0 | 0 | 0 | 0 | 0 | 0 | 0 | 8 | 0 |
| HINE EW | 1932-34 | 51 | 12 | 2 | 0 | 0 | 0 | 0 | 0 | 53 | 12 |
| HODGE James | 1910-19 | 79 | 2 | 7 | 0 | 0 | 0 | 0 | 0 | 86 | 2 |
| HODGE John | 1913-14 | 30 | 0 | 0 | 0 | 0 | 0 | 0 | 0 | 30 | 0 |
| HODGES FC | 1919-20 | 20 | 4 | 0 | 0 | 0 | 0 | 0 | 0 | 20 | 4 |
| HOFTON L | 1910-20 | 17 | 0 | 1 | 0 | 0 | 0 | 0 | 0 | 18 | 0 |
| HOGG GJ | 1983-87 | 82/1 | 1 | 8 | 0 | 7/1 | 0 | 10 | 0 | 107/2 | 1 |
| HOLDEN RH | 1904-12 | 106 | 0 | 11 | 0 | 0 | 0 | 0 | 0 | 117 | 0 |
| HOLT J | 1899 | 1 | 1 | 0 | 0 | 0 | 0 | 0 | 0 | 1 | 1 |
| HOLTON JA | 1972-74 | 63 | 5 | 2 | 0 | 4 | 0 | 0 | 0 | 69 | 5 |
| HOMER TP | 1909-11 | 25 | 14 | 0 | 0 | 0 | 0 | 0 | 0 | 25 | 14 |
| HOOD W | 1892-93 | 33 | 6 | 3 | 0 | 0 | 0 | *2 | 0 | 38 | 6 |
| HOOPER AH | 1909-13 | 7 | 1 | 0 | 0 | 0 | 0 | 0 | 0 | 7 | 1 |
| HOPKIN F | 1919-20 | 70 | 8 | 4 | 0 | 0 | 0 | 0 | 0 | 74 | 8 |
| HOPKINS J | 1898 | 1 | 0 | 0 | 0 | 0 | 0 | 0 | 0 | 1 | 0 |
| HOPKINSON S | 1930-33 | 51 | 10 | 2 | 2 | 0 | 0 | 0 | 0 | 53 | 12 |
| HOUSTON SM | 1973-79 | 204/1 | 13 | 22 | 1 | 16 | 2 | 6/1 | 0 | 248/2 | 16 |
| HOWARTH JT | 1921 | 4 | 0 | 0 | 0 | 0 | 0 | 0 | 0 | 4 | 0 |
| HOWELLS E | 1886 | 0 | 0 | 1 | 0 | 0 | 0 | 0 | 0 | 1 | 0 |
| HUDSON EK | 1913-14 | 11 | 0 | 0 | 0 | 0 | 0 | 0 | 0 | 11 | 0 |
| HUGHES LM | 1983- | 227/8 | 85 | 30/1 | 11 | 26/1 | 10 | 21/3 | 7 | 304/13 | 113 |
| HULME A | 1907-08 | 4 | 0 | 0 | 0 | 0 | 0 | 0 | 0 | 4 | 0 |
| HUNTER GH | 1913-14 | 22 | 2 | 1 | 0 | 0 | 0 | 0 | 0 | 23 | 2 |
| HUNTER RJ | 1958 | 1 | 0 | 0 | 0 | 0 | 0 | 0 | 0 | 1 | 0 |
| HUNTER W | 1912 | 3 | 2 | 0 | 0 | 0 | 0 | 0 | 0 | 3 | 2 |
| HURST DJ | 1902 | 16 | 4 | 5 | 0 | 0 | 0 | 0 | 0 | 21 | 4 |
| IDDON R | 1925-26 | 2 | 0 | 0 | 0 | 0 | 0 | 0 | 0 | 2 | 0 |
| INCE PEC | 1989- | 87/2 | 6 | 11/1 | 0 | 15/1 | 2 | 10 | 0 | 123/4 | 8 |
| INGLIS WW | 1925-28 | 14 | 1 | 0 | 0 | 0 | 0 | 0 | 0 | 14 | 1 |
| IRWIN D | 1990- | 70/2 | 4 | 6 | 0 | 14/1 | 0 | 8 | 0 | 98/3 | 4 |
| JACKSON TA | 1975-76 | 18/1 | 0 | 0 | 0 | 4 | 0 | 0 | 0 | 22/1 | 0 |
| JACKSON W | 1899-1900 | 61 | 12 | 3 | 2 | 0 | 0 | 0 | 0 | 64 | 14 |
| JAMES SR | 1968-74 | 129 | 4 | 12 | 0 | 17/1 | 0 | 2 | 0 | 160/1 | 4 |
| JENKYNS CAL | 1896-97 | 35 | 5 | 8 | 0 | 0 | 0 | *4 | 1 | 47 | 6 |
| JOHN WR | 1936 | 15 | 0 | 0 | 0 | 0 | 0 | 0 | 0 | 15 | 0 |
| JOHNSON SC | 1900 | 1 | 0 | 0 | 0 | 0 | 0 | 0 | 0 | 1 | 0 |
| JOHNSTON WG | 1927-31 | 71 | 24 | 6 | 3 | 0 | 0 | 0 | 0 | 77 | 27 |
| JONES D | 1937 | 1 | 0 | 0 | 0 | 0 | 0 | 0 | 0 | 1 | 0 |

| Player | Played | League App | League Gls | FA Cup App | FA Cup Gls | FL Cup App | FL Cup Gls | Europe App | Europe Gls | Total App | Total Gls |
|---|---|---|---|---|---|---|---|---|---|---|---|
| JONES EP | 1957 | 1 | 0 | 0 | 0 | 0 | 0 | 0 | 0 | 1 | 0 |
| JONES M | 1950-57 | 103 | 1 | 7 | 0 | 0 | 0 | 10 | 0 | 120 | 1 |
| JONES OJ | 1898 | 2 | 0 | 0 | 0 | 0 | 0 | 0 | 0 | 2 | 0 |
| JONES T | 1924-36 | 189 | 0 | 11 | 0 | 0 | 0 | 0 | 0 | 200 | 0 |
| JONES TJ | 1934 | 20 | 4 | 2 | 0 | 0 | 0 | 0 | ✔ 0 | 22 | 4 |
| JORDAN J | 1977-80 | 109 | 37 | 11/1 | 2 | 4 | 2 | 1 | 0 | 125/1 | 41 |
| JOVANOVIC N | 1979-80 | 20/1 | 4 | 1 | 0 | 2 | 0 | 2 | 0 | 25/1 | 4 |
| KANCHELSKIS A | 1990- | 29/6 | 5 | 2 | 1 | 4 | 2 | 1 | 0 | 36/6 | 8 |
| KELLY JW | 1975 | 0/1 | 0 | 0 | 0 | 0 | 0 | 0 | 0 | 0/1 | 0 |
| KENNEDY F | 1923-24 | 17 | 4 | 1 | 0 | 0 | 0 | 0 | 0 | 18 | 4 |
| KENNEDY PA | 1954 | 1 | 0 | 0 | 0 | 0 | 0 | 0 | 0 | 1 | 0 |
| KENNEDY WJ | 1895-96 | 30 | 11 | 3 | 1 | 0 | 0 | 0 | 0 | 33 | 12 |
| KERR H | 1903 | 2 | 0 | 0 | 0 | 0 | 0 | 0 | 0 | 2 | 0 |
| KIDD B | 1967-73 | 195/8 | 52 | 24/1 | 8 | 20 | 7 | 16 | 3 | 255/9 | 70 |
| KINLOCH J | 1892 | 1 | 0 | 0 | 0 | 0 | 0 | 0 | 0 | 1 | 0 |
| KINSEY AJ | 1964 | 0 | 0 | 1 | 1 | 0 | 0 | 0 | 0 | 1 | 1 |
| KNOWLES F | 1911-14 | 46 | 1 | 1 | 0 | 0 | 0 | 0 | 0 | 47 | 1 |
| KOPEL F | 1967-68 | 8/2 | 0 | 1 | 0 | 0 | 0 | 1 | 0 | 10/2 | 0 |
| LANCASTER JG | 1949 | 2 | 0 | 2 | 0 | 0 | 0 | 0 | 0 | 4 | 0 |
| LANG T | 1935-36 | 12 | 1 | 1 | 0 | 0 | 0 | 0 | 0 | 13 | 1 |
| LANGFORD L | 1934-35 | 15 | 0 | 0 | 0 | 0 | 0 | 0 | 0 | 15 | 0 |
| LAPPIN HH | 1900-02 | 27 | 4 | 0 | 0 | 0 | 0 | 0 | 0 | 27 | 4 |
| LAW D | 1961-72 | 305/4 | 171 | 44/2 | 34 | 11 | 3 | 33 | 28 | 393/6 | 236 |
| LAWSON RR | 1900 | 3 | 0 | 0 | 0 | 0 | 0 | 0 | 0 | 3 | 0 |
| LAWTON N | 1959-62 | 36 | 6 | 7 | 0 | 1 | 0 | 0 | 0 | 44 | 6 |
| LEE E | 1898-99 | 11 | 5 | 0 | 0 | 0 | 0 | 0 | 0 | 11 | 5 |
| LEIGH T | 1899-1900 | 43 | 15 | 3 | 0 | 0 | 0 | 0 | 0 | 46 | 15 |
| LEIGHTON J | 1988-91 | 73 | 0 | 14 | 0 | 7 | 0 | 0 | 0 | 94 | 0 |
| LEONARD HD | 1920 | 10 | 5 | 0 | 0 | 0 | 0 | 0 | 0 | 10 | 5 |
| LEWIS E | 1952-55 | 20 | 9 | 4 | 2 | 0 | 0 | 0 | 0 | 24 | 11 |
| LIEVESLEY L | 1931 | 2 | 0 | 0 | 0 | 0 | 0 | 0 | 0 | 2 | 0 |
| LIEVESLEY W | 1922 | 2 | 0 | 1 | 0 | 0 | 0 | 0 | 0 | 3 | 0 |
| LINKSON OHS | 1908-12 | 55 | 0 | 4 | 0 | 0 | 0 | 0 | 0 | 59 | 0 |
| LIVINGSTONE GT | 1908-13 | 43 | 4 | 3 | 0 | 0 | 0 | 0 | 0 | 46 | 4 |
| LOCHHEAD AW | 1921-25 | 147 | 50 | 6 | 0 | 0 | 0 | 0 | 0 | 153 | 50 |
| LONGAIR W | 1894 | 1 | 0 | 0 | 0 | 0 | 0 | 0 | 0 | 1 | 0 |
| LONGTON | 1886 | 0 | 0 | 1 | 0 | 0 | 0 | 0 | 0 | 1 | 0 |
| LOWRIE T | 1947-49 | 13 | 0 | 1 | 0 | 0 | 0 | 0 | 0 | 14 | 0 |
| LYDON G | 1930-31 | 3 | 0 | 0 | 0 | 0 | 0 | 0 | 0 | 3 | 0 |
| LYNER D | 1922 | 3 | 0 | 0 | 0 | 0 | 0 | 0 | 0 | 3 | 0 |
| LYNN S | 1947-49 | 13 | 0 | 0 | 0 | 0 | 0 | 0 | 0 | 13 | 0 |
| LYONS G | 1903-05 | 4 | 0 | 1 | 0 | 0 | 0 | 0 | 0 | 5 | 0 |
| MACARI L | 1972-83 | 311/18 | 78 | 31/3 | 8 | 22/5 | 10 | 9/1 | 1 | 373/27 | 97 |
| McBAIN N | 1921-22 | 42 | 2 | 1 | 0 | 0 | 0 | 0 | 0 | 43 | 2 |
| McCALLIOG J | 1973-74 | 31 | 7 | 1 | 0 | 5/1 | 0 | 0 | 0 | 37/1 | 7 |
| McCARTHY P | 1911 | 1 | 0 | 0 | 0 | 0 | 0 | 0 | 0 | 1 | 0 |
| McCARTNEY W | 1903 | 13 | 1 | 0 | 0 | 0 | 0 | 0 | 0 | 13 | 1 |
| McCARTNEY WJ | 1894 | 18 | 1 | 1 | 0 | 0 | 0 | *1 | 0 | 20 | 1 |
| McCLAIR BJ | 1987- | 190/3 | 70 | 24 | 11 | 28 | 14 | 13 | 5 | 255/3 | 100 |
| McCLELLAND J | 1936 | 5 | 1 | 0 | 0 | 0 | 0 | 0 | 0 | 5 | 1 |
| McCRAE JJ | 1925 | 9 | 0 | 4 | 0 | 0 | 0 | 0 | 0 | 13 | 0 |
| McCREERY D | 1974-78 | 48/39 | 7 | 1/6 | 0 | 4/4 | 1 | 4/3 | 0 | 57/52 | 8 |
| MacDONALD K | 1922-23 | 9 | 2 | 0 | 0 | 0 | 0 | 0 | 0 | 9 | 2 |
| McDONALD W | 1931-33 | 27 | 4 | 0 | 0 | 0 | 0 | 0 | 0 | 27 | 4 |
| MacDOUGALL EJ | 1972 | 18 | 5 | 0 | 0 | 0 | 0 | 0 | 0 | 18 | 5 |
| McFARLANE NW | 1953 | 1 | 0 | 0 | 0 | 0 | 0 | 0 | 0 | 1 | 0 |
| McFARLANE R | 1891 | 0 | 0 | 3 | 0 | 0 | 0 | 0 | 0 | 3 | 0 |
| McFETTERIDGE D | 1894 | 1 | 0 | 0 | 0 | 0 | 0 | 0 | 0 | 1 | 0 |
| McGARVEY ST | 1890-82 | 13/12 | 3 | 0 | 0 | 0 | 0 | 0 | 0 | 13/12 | 3 |
| McGILLIVRAY C | 1933 | 8 | 0 | 1 | 0 | 0 | 0 | 0 | 0 | 9 | 0 |

442

| Player | Played | League | | FA Cup | | FL Cup | | Europe | | Total | |
|---|---|---|---|---|---|---|---|---|---|---|---|
| | | App | Gls | App | Gls | App | Gls | App | Gls | App | Gls |
| McGILLIVRAY J | 1907-08 | 3 | 0 | 1 | 0 | 0 | 0 | 0 | 0 | 4 | 0 |
| McGLEN W | 1946-51 | 110 | 2 | 12 | 0 | 0 | 0 | 0 | 0 | 122 | 2 |
| McGRATH P | 1982-89 | 159/4 | 12 | 15/3 | 2 | 13 | 2 | 4 | 0 | 191/7 | 16 |
| McGRATH RC | 1976-80 | 12/16 | 1 | 0 | 0 | 0/2 | 0 | 3/1 | 0 | 15/19 | 1 |
| McGUINNESS W | 1955-59 | 81 | 2 | 2 | 0 | 0 | 0 | 2 | 0 | 85 | 2 |
| McILROY SB | 1971-81 | 320/22 | 57 | 35/3 | 6 | 25/3 | 6 | 10 | 2 | 390/28 | 71 |
| McILVENNY E | 1950 | 2 | 0 | 0 | 0 | 0 | 0 | 0 | 0 | 2 | 0 |
| McKAY W | 1933-39 | 171 | 15 | 13 | 0 | 0 | 0 | 0 | 0 | 184 | 15 |
| MACKIE C | 1904 | 5 | 3 | 2 | 1 | 0 | 0 | 0 | 0 | 7 | 4 |
| McLACHLAN GH | 1929-32 | 110 | 4 | 6 | 0 | 0 | 0 | 0 | 0 | 116 | 4 |
| McLENAHAN H | 1929-32 | 112 | 11 | 4 | 1 | 0 | 0 | 0 | 0 | 116 | 12 |
| McMILLAN ST | 1961-62 | 15 | 6 | 0 | 0 | 0 | 0 | 0 | 0 | 15 | 6 |
| McMILLEN WS | 1933-34 | 27 | 2 | 2 | 0 | 0 | 0 | 0 | 0 | 29 | 2 |
| McNAUGHT JR | 1893-97 | 140 | 12 | 17 | 0 | 0 | 0 | *5 | 0 | 162 | 12 |
| McNULTY T | 1949-53 | 57 | 0 | 2 | 0 | 0 | 0 | 0 | 0 | 59 | 0 |
| McPHERSON FC | 1923-27 | 159 | 45 | 16 | 7 | 0 | 0 | 0 | 0 | 175 | 52 |
| McQUEEN G | 1977-84 | 184 | 20 | 21 | 2 | 16 | 4 | 7 | 0 | 228 | 26 |
| McSHANE H | 1950-53 | 56 | 8 | 1 | 0 | 0 | 0 | 0 | 0 | 57 | 8 |
| MAIORANA G | 1988- | 2/5 | 0 | 0 | 0 | 0/1 | 0 | 0 | 0 | 2/6 | 0 |
| MANLEY T | 1931-38 | 188 | 40 | 7 | 1 | 0 | 0 | 0 | 0 | 195 | 41 |
| MANN FD | 1922-29 | 180 | 5 | 17 | 0 | 0 | 0 | 0 | 0 | 197 | 5 |
| MANN H | 1931 | 13 | 2 | 0 | 0 | 0 | 0 | 0 | 0 | 13 | 2 |
| MANNS T | 1933 | 2 | 0 | 0 | 0 | 0 | 0 | 0 | 0 | 2 | 0 |
| MARSHALL AE | 1902 | 6 | 0 | 0 | 0 | 0 | 0 | 0 | 0 | 6 | 0 |
| MARTIN LA | 1987- | 55/17 | 1 | 13/1 | 1 | 4/2 | 0 | 4/4 | 0 | 76/24 | 2 |
| MARTIN MP | 1972-74 | 33/7 | 2 | 2 | 0 | 1 | 0 | 0 | 0 | 36/7 | 2 |
| MATHIESON W | 1892-93 | 10 | 2 | 0 | 0 | 0 | 0 | 0 | 0 | 10 | 2 |
| MEEHAN T | 1919-20 | 51 | 6 | 2 | 0 | 0 | 0 | 0 | 0 | 53 | 6 |
| MELLOR J | 1930-36 | 116 | 0 | 6 | 0 | 0 | 0 | 0 | 0 | 122 | 0 |
| MENZIES AW | 1906-07 | 23 | 4 | 2 | 0 | 0 | 0 | 0 | 0 | 25 | 4 |
| MEREDITH WH | 1906-20 | 303 | 35 | 29 | 0 | 0 | 0 | 0 | 0 | 332 | 35 |
| MEW JW | 1912-25 | 186 | 0 | 13 | 0 | 0 | 0 | 0 | 0 | 199 | 0 |
| MILARVIE R | 1890 | 0 | 0 | 1 | 0 | 0 | 0 | 0 | 0 | 1 | 0 |
| MILLAR G | 1894 | 6 | 5 | 1 | 0 | 0 | 0 | 0 | 0 | 7 | 5 |
| MILLER J | 1923 | 4 | 1 | 0 | 0 | 0 | 0 | 0 | 0 | 4 | 1 |
| MILLER T | 1920 | 25 | 7 | 2 | 1 | 0 | 0 | 0 | 0 | 27 | 8 |
| MILNE R | 1988- | 19/4 | 3 | 7 | 0 | 0 | 0 | 0 | 0 | 26/4 | 3 |
| MITCHELL A | 1886-93 | 54 | 0 | 7 | 0 | 0 | 0 | *3 | 0 | 64 | 0 |
| MITCHELL A | 1932 | 1 | 0 | 0 | 0 | 0 | 0 | 0 | 0 | 1 | 0 |
| MITTEN C | 1946-49 | 142 | 50 | 19 | 11 | 0 | 0 | 0 | 0 | 161 | 61 |
| MOGER HH | 1903-11 | 242 | 0 | 22 | 0 | 0 | 0 | 0 | 0 | 264 | 0 |
| MOIR I | 1960-64 | 45 | 5 | 0 | 0 | 0 | 0 | 0 | 0 | 45 | 5 |
| MONTGOMERY A | 1905 | 3 | 0 | 0 | 0 | 0 | 0 | 0 | 0 | 3 | 0 |
| MONTGOMERY J | 1914-20 | 27 | 1 | 0 | 0 | 0 | 0 | 0 | 0 | 27 | 1 |
| MOODY J | 1931-32 | 50 | 0 | 1 | 0 | 0 | 0 | 0 | 0 | 51 | 0 |
| MOORE CW | 1919-29 | 309 | 0 | 19 | 0 | 0 | 0 | 0 | 0 | 328 | 0 |
| MOORE G | 1963 | 18 | 4 | 1 | 1 | 0 | 0 | 0 | 0 | 19 | 5 |
| MORAN KR | 1978-88 | 228/3 | 21 | 18 | 1 | 24/1 | 2 | 13/1 | 0 | 283/5 | 24 |
| MORGAN H | 1900 | 20 | 4 | 3 | 0 | 0 | 0 | 0 | 0 | 23 | 4 |
| MORGAN W | 1896-1902 | 143 | 6 | 9 | 1 | 0 | 0 | 0 | 0 | 152 | 7 |
| MORGAN W | 1968-75 | 236/2 | 25 | 27 | 4 | 24/1 | 3 | 4 | 1 | 291/3 | 33 |
| MORGANS KG | 1957-60 | 17 | 0 | 2 | 0 | 0 | 0 | 4 | 0 | 23 | 0 |
| MORRIS J | 1946-48 | 83 | 32 | 9 | 3 | 0 | 0 | 0 | 0 | 92 | 35 |
| MORRISON T | 1902-03 | 29 | 7 | 7 | 1 | 0 | 0 | 0 | 0 | 36 | 8 |
| MORTON BW | 1935 | 1 | 0 | 0 | 0 | 0 | 0 | 0 | 0 | 1 | 0 |
| MOSES RM | 1981-88 | 143/7 | 7 | 11 | 1 | 22/2 | 4 | 12/1 | 0 | 188/10 | 12 |
| MUHREN AJH | 1982-84 | 65/5 | 13 | 8 | 1 | 11 | 1 | 8 | 3 | 92/5 | 18 |
| MURRAY RD | 1937 | 4 | 0 | 0 | 0 | 0 | 0 | 0 | 0 | 4 | 0 |
| MUTCH G | 1934-37 | 112 | 46 | 8 | 3 | 0 | 0 | 0 | 0 | 120 | 49 |
| MYERSCOUGH J | 1920-22 | 33 | 8 | 1 | 0 | 0 | 0 | 0 | 0 | 34 | 8 |

443

| Player | Played | League | | FA Cup | | FL Cup | | Europe | | Total | |
|---|---|---|---|---|---|---|---|---|---|---|---|
| | | App | Gls | App | Gls | App | Gls | App | Gls | App | Gls |
| NEVIN GW | 1933 | 4 | 0 | 1 | 0 | 0 | 0 | 0 | 0 | 5 | 0 |
| NEWTON P | 1933 | 2 | 0 | 0 | 0 | 0 | 0 | 0 | 0 | 2 | 0 |
| NICHOLL JM | 1974-81 | 188/9 | 3 | 22/4 | 1 | 14 | 1 | 10 | 1 | 234/13 | 6 |
| NICHOLSON JJ | 1960-65 | 58 | 5 | 7 | 1 | 3 | 0 | 0 | 0 | 68 | 6 |
| NICOL G | 1927-28 | 6 | 2 | 1 | 0 | 0 | 0 | 0 | 0 | 7 | 2 |
| NOBLE R | 1965-66 | 31 | 0 | 2 | 0 | 0 | 0 | 0 | 0 | 33 | 0 |
| NORTON JP | 1913-14 | 37 | 3 | 0 | 0 | 0 | 0 | 0 | 0 | 37 | 3 |
| NUTTALL TA | 1911-12 | 16 | 4 | 0 | 0 | 0 | 0 | 0 | 0 | 16 | 4 |
| O'BRIEN LF | 1986-88 | 16/15 | 2 | 0/2 | 0 | 1/2 | 0 | 0 | 0 | 17/19 | 2 |
| O'BRIEN W | 1901 | 1 | 0 | 0 | 0 | 0 | 0 | 0 | 0 | 1 | 0 |
| O'CONNELL P | 1914 | 34 | 2 | 1 | 0 | 0 | 0 | 0 | 0 | 35 | 2 |
| OLIVE RL | 1952 | 2 | 0 | 0 | 0 | 0 | 0 | 0 | 0 | 2 | 0 |
| OLSEN J | 1984-89 | 119/20 | 21 | 13/3 | 2 | 10/3 | 1 | 6/1 | 0 | 148/27 | 24 |
| O'NEIL TP | 1970-72 | 54 | 0 | 7 | 0 | 7 | 0 | 0 | 0 | 68 | 0 |
| O'SHAUGNESSEY | 1890 | 0 | 0 | 1 | 0 | 0 | 0 | 0 | 0 | 1 | 0 |
| OWEN | 1898 | 1 | 0 | 0 | 0 | 0 | 0 | 0 | 0 | 1 | 0 |
| OWEN G | 1889 | 0 | 0 | 1 | 0 | 0 | 0 | 0 | 0 | 1 | 0 |
| OWEN J | 1889-91 | 0 | 0 | 6 | 0 | 0 | 0 | 0 | 0 | 6 | 0 |
| OWEN W | 1934-35 | 17 | 1 | 0 | 0 | 0 | 0 | 0 | 0 | 17 | 1 |
| PAGE LA | 1931-32 | 12 | 0 | 0 | 0 | 0 | 0 | 0 | 0 | 12 | 0 |
| PALLISTER GA | 1989- | 108/3 | 4 | 14 | 0 | 20 | 0 | 12/1 | 1 | 154/4 | 5 |
| PAPE AA | 1924-25 | 18 | 5 | 0 | 0 | 0 | 0 | 0 | 0 | 18 | 5 |
| PARKER B | 1893 | 11 | 0 | 1 | 0 | 0 | 0 | 0 | 0 | 12 | 0 |
| PARKER P | 1991- | 24/2 | 0 | 3 | 0 | 6 | 0 | 2 | 0 | 35/2 | 0 |
| PARKER TA | 1930-31 | 17 | 0 | 0 | 0 | 0 | 0 | 0 | 0 | 17 | 0 |
| PARKINSON R | 1899 | 15 | 7 | 0 | 0 | 0 | 0 | 0 | 0 | 15 | 7 |
| PARTRIDGE AE | 1920-28 | 148 | 16 | 12 | 2 | 0 | 0 | 0 | 0 | 160 | 18 |
| PATERSON SW | 1976-79 | 3/3 | 0 | 0 | 0 | 2 | 0 | 0/2 | 0 | 5/5 | 0 |
| PAYNE E | 1908 | 2 | 1 | 0 | 0 | 0 | 0 | 0 | 0 | 2 | 1 |
| PEARS S | 1984 | 4 | 0 | 1 | 0 | 0 | 0 | 0 | 0 | 5 | 0 |
| PEARSON M | 1957-62 | 68 | 12 | 7 | 1 | 3 | 1 | 2 | 0 | 80 | 14 |
| PEARSON SC | 1937-53 | 315 | 128 | 30 | 21 | 0 | 0 | 0 | 0 | 345 | 149 |
| PEARSON JS | 1974-77 | 138/1 | 55 | 22 | 5 | 12 | 5 | 6 | 1 | 178/1 | 66 |
| PEDDIE JH | 1902-06 | 112 | 52 | 9 | 6 | 0 | 0 | 0 | 0 | 121 | 58 |
| PEDEN J | 1893 | 28 | 7 | 3 | 1 | 0 | 0 | *1 | 0 | 32 | 8 |
| PEGG D | 1952-57 | 127 | 24 | 9 | 0 | 0 | 0 | 12 | 4 | 148 | 28 |
| PEGG E | 1902-03 | 41 | 13 | 10 | 7 | 0 | 0 | 0 | 0 | 51 | 20 |
| PEGG JK | 1947 | 2 | 0 | 0 | 0 | 0 | 0 | 0 | 0 | 2 | 0 |
| PEPPER F | 1898 | 7 | 0 | 1 | 0 | 0 | 0 | 0 | 0 | 8 | 0 |
| PERRINS G | 1892-95 | 92 | 0 | 6 | 0 | 0 | 0 | *4 | 0 | 102 | 0 |
| PETERS J | 1894-95 | 46 | 13 | 4 | 1 | 0 | 0 | *1 | 0 | 51 | 14 |
| PHELAN MC | 1989- | 82/7 | 2 | 8 | 0 | 12/2 | 0 | 12 | 0 | 114/9 | 2 |
| PICKEN JB | 1905-10 | 113 | 39 | 8 | 7 | 0 | 0 | 0 | 0 | 121 | 46 |
| PINNER MJ | 1960 | 4 | 0 | 0 | 0 | 0 | 0 | 0 | 0 | 4 | 0 |
| PORTER W | 1934-37 | 61 | 0 | 4 | 0 | 0 | 0 | 0 | 0 | 65 | 0 |
| POTTS AA | 1913-19 | 27 | 5 | 1 | 0 | 0 | 0 | 0 | 0 | 28 | 5 |
| POWELL J | 1886-90 | 0 | 0 | 4 | 0 | 0 | 0 | 0 | 0 | 4 | 0 |
| PRENTICE JH | 1919 | 1 | 0 | 0 | 0 | 0 | 0 | 0 | 0 | 1 | 0 |
| PRESTON S | 1901-02 | 33 | 14 | 1 | 0 | 0 | 0 | 0 | 0 | 34 | 14 |
| PRINCE AJ | 1914 | 1 | 0 | 0 | 0 | 0 | 0 | 0 | 0 | 1 | 0 |
| PRINCE D | 1893 | 2 | 0 | 0 | 0 | 0 | 0 | 0 | 0 | 2 | 0 |
| PUGH J | 1921-22 | 2 | 0 | 0 | 0 | 0 | 0 | 0 | 0 | 2 | 0 |
| QUINN JJ | 1908-09 | 2 | 0 | 0 | 0 | 0 | 0 | 0 | 0 | 2 | 0 |
| QUIXALL A | 1958-63 | 165 | 50 | 14 | 4 | 1 | 2 | 3 | 0 | 183 | 56 |
| RADCLIFFE G | 1898 | 1 | 0 | 0 | 0 | 0 | 0 | 0 | 0 | 1 | 0 |
| RADFORD C | 1920-23 | 91 | 1 | 5 | 0 | 0 | 0 | 0 | 0 | 96 | 1 |
| RAMSDEN CW | 1927-30 | 14 | 3 | 2 | 0 | 0 | 0 | 0 | 0 | 16 | 3 |
| RAMSEY R | 1890 | 0 | 0 | 1 | 0 | 0 | 0 | 0 | 0 | 1 | 0 |
| RATTIGAN | 1890 | 0 | 0 | 1 | 0 | 0 | 0 | 0 | 0 | 1 | 0 |
| RAWLINGS WE | 1927-29 | 35 | 19 | 1 | 0 | 0 | 0 | 0 | 0 | 36 | 19 |
| READ TH | 1902-03 | 35 | 0 | 7 | 0 | 0 | 0 | 0 | 0 | 42 | 0 |

| Player | Played | League App | League Gls | FA Cup App | FA Cup Gls | FL Cup App | FL Cup Gls | Europe App | Europe Gls | Total App | Total Gls |
|--------|--------|-----|-----|-----|-----|-----|-----|-----|-----|-----|-----|
| REDMAN W | 1950-53 | 36 | 0 | 2 | 0 | 0 | 0 | 0 | 0 | 38 | 0 |
| REDWOOD H | 1935-39 | 89 | 3 | 7 | 1 | 0 | 0 | 0 | 0 | 96 | 4 |
| REID T | 1928-32 | 96 | 63 | 5 | 4 | 0 | 0 | 0 | 0 | 101 | 67 |
| RENNOX C | 1924-26 | 60 | 24 | 8 | 1 | 0 | 0 | 0 | 0 | 68 | 25 |
| RICHARDS CH | 1902 | 8 | 1 | 3 | 1 | 0 | 0 | 0 | 0 | 11 | 2 |
| RICHARDS W | 1901 | 9 | 1 | 0 | 0 | 0 | 0 | 0 | 0 | 9 | 1 |
| RICHARDSON LH | 1925-28 | 38 | 0 | 4 | 0 | 0 | 0 | 0 | 0 | 42 | 0 |
| RIDDING W | 1931-33 | 42 | 14 | 2 | 0 | 0 | 0 | 0 | 0 | 44 | 14 |
| RIDGWAY JA | 1895-97 | 14 | 0 | 3 | 0 | 0 | 0 | 0 | 0 | 17 | 0 |
| RIMMER JJ | 1967-72 | 34 | 0 | 3 | 0 | 6 | 0 | 2/1 | 0 | 45/1 | 0 |
| RITCHIE AT | 1977-80 | 26/7 | 13 | 3/1 | 0 | 3/2 | 0 | 0 | 0 | 32/10 | 13 |
| ROACH J | 1945 | 0 | 0 | 2 | 0 | 0 | 0 | 0 | 0 | 2 | 0 |
| ROBBIE DM | 1935 | 1 | 0 | 0 | 0 | 0 | 0 | 0 | 0 | 1 | 0 |
| ROBERTS 'Bogie' | 1898-99 | 9 | 2 | 1 | 0 | 0 | 0 | 0 | 0 | 10 | 2 |
| ROBERTS C | 1903-12 | 271 | 22 | 28 | 1 | 0 | 0 | 0 | 0 | 299 | 23 |
| ROBERTS RHA | 1913 | 2 | 0 | 0 | 0 | 0 | 0 | 0 | 0 | 2 | 0 |
| ROBERTSON A(*) | 1903-05 | 33 | 1 | 2 | 0 | 0 | 0 | 0 | 0 | 35 | 1 |
| ROBERTSON A | 1903-04 | 28 | 10 | 6 | 0 | 0 | 0 | 0 | 0 | 34 | 10 |
| ROBERTSON T | 1903 | 3 | 0 | 0 | 0 | 0 | 0 | 0 | 0 | 3 | 0 |
| ROBERTSON WS | 1933-35 | 47 | 1 | 3 | 0 | 0 | 0 | 0 | 0 | 50 | 1 |
| ROBINS MG | 1988- | 19/29 | 11 | 4/4 | 3 | 0/7 | 2 | 4/2 | 1 | 27/42 | 17 |
| ROBINSON JW | 1919-21 | 21 | 3 | 0 | 0 | 0 | 0 | 0 | 0 | 21 | 3 |
| ROBINSON M | 1931 | 10 | 0 | 0 | 0 | 0 | 0 | 0 | 0 | 10 | 0 |
| ROBSON B | 1981- | 310/5 | 72 | 32 | 9 | 44/1 | 5 | 22 | 7 | 408/6 | 93 |
| ROCHE PJ | 1974-81 | 46 | 0 | 4 | 0 | 3 | 0 | 0 | 0 | 53 | 0 |
| ROGERS M | 1977 | 1 | 0 | 0 | 0 | 0 | 0 | 0 | 0 | 1 | 0 |
| ROTHWELL C | 1893-96 | 2 | 1 | 1 | 2 | 0 | 0 | 0 | 0 | 3 | 3 |
| ROTHWELL H | 1902 | 22 | 0 | 6 | 0 | 0 | 0 | 0 | 0 | 28 | 0 |
| ROUGHTON WG | 1936-38 | 86 | 0 | 6 | 0 | 0 | 0 | 0 | 0 | 92 | 0 |
| ROUND E | 1909 | 2 | 0 | 0 | 0 | 0 | 0 | 0 | 0 | 2 | 0 |
| ROWE J | 1913 | 1 | 0 | 0 | 0 | 0 | 0 | 0 | 0 | 1 | 0 |
| ROWLEY HB | 1928-36 | 173 | 55 | 7 | 0 | 0 | 0 | 0 | 0 | 180 | 55 |
| ROWLEY JF | 1937-54 | 380 | 182 | 42 | 26 | 0 | 0 | 0 | 0 | 422 | 208 |
| ROYALS EJ | 1911-13 | 7 | 0 | 0 | 0 | 0 | 0 | 0 | 0 | 7 | 0 |
| RYAN J | 1965-69 | 21/3 | 4 | 1 | 0 | 0 | 0 | 2 | 0 | 24/3 | 4 |
| SADLER D | 1963-73 | 266/6 | 22 | 22/1 | 1 | 22 | 1 | 16 | 3 | 326/7 | 27 |
| SAGAR C | 1905-06 | 30 | 20 | 3 | 4 | 0 | 0 | 0 | 0 | 33 | 24 |
| SAPSFORD GD | 1919-21 | 52 | 16 | 1 | 1 | 0 | 0 | 0 | 0 | 53 | 17 |
| SARTORI C | 1968-71 | 26/13 | 4 | 9 | 1 | 3/2 | 0 | 2 | 1 | 40/15 | 6 |
| SARVIS W | 1922 | 1 | 0 | 0 | 0 | 0 | 0 | 0 | 0 | 1 | 0 |
| SAUNDERS J | 1901-02 | 12 | 0 | 1 | 0 | 0 | 0 | 0 | 0 | 13 | 0 |
| SAVAGE RE | 1937 | 4 | 0 | 1 | 0 | 0 | 0 | 0 | 0 | 5 | 0 |
| SAWYER F | 1899-1900 | 6 | 0 | 0 | 0 | 0 | 0 | 0 | 0 | 6 | 0 |
| SCANLON AJ | 1954-60 | 115 | 34 | 6 | 1 | 3 | 0 | 3 | 0 | 127 | 35 |
| SCHMEICHEL P | 1991- | 40 | 0 | 3 | 0 | 6 | 0 | 3 | 0 | 52 | 0 |
| SCHOFIELD AJ | 1900-06 | 157 | 30 | 22 | 5 | 0 | 0 | 0 | 0 | 179 | 35 |
| SCHOFIELD GW | 1920 | 1 | 0 | 0 | 0 | 0 | 0 | 0 | 0 | 1 | 0 |
| SCHOFIELD J | 1903 | 2 | 0 | 0 | 0 | 0 | 0 | 0 | 0 | 2 | 0 |
| SCHOFIELD P | 1921 | 1 | 0 | 0 | 0 | 0 | 0 | 0 | 0 | 1 | 0 |
| SCOTT J | 1921 | 23 | 0 | 1 | 0 | 0 | 0 | 0 | 0 | 24 | 0 |
| SCOTT J | 1952-56 | 3 | 0 | 0 | 0 | 0 | 0 | 0 | 0 | 3 | 0 |
| SEALEY LJ | 1989-91 | 33 | 0 | 4 | 0 | 8 | 0 | 8 | 0 | 53 | 0 |
| SETTERS ME | 1959-64 | 159 | 12 | 25 | 1 | 2 | 0 | 7 | 1 | 193 | 14 |
| SHARPE LS | 1988- | 59/17 | 4 | 8/2 | 0 | 11/4 | 7 | 6/2 | 1 | 84/25 | 12 |
| SHARPE WH | 1890-91 | 0 | 0 | 2 | 0 | 0 | 0 | 0 | 0 | 2 | 0 |
| SHELDON J | 1910-12 | 26 | 1 | 0 | 0 | 0 | 0 | 0 | 0 | 26 | 1 |
| SIDEBOTTOM A | 1972-73 | 16 | 0 | 2 | 0 | 2 | 0 | 0 | 0 | 20 | 0 |
| SILCOCK J | 1919-33 | 423 | 2 | 26 | 0 | 0 | 0 | 0 | 0 | 449 | 2 |
| SIVEBAEK J | 1985-87 | 29/2 | 1 | 2 | 0 | 1 | 0 | 0 | 0 | 32/2 | 1 |
| SLATER JF | 1890-91 | 0 | 0 | 4 | 0 | 0 | 0 | 0 | 0 | 4 | 0 |

| Player | Played | League | | FA Cup | | FL Cup | | Europe | | Total | |
|---|---|---|---|---|---|---|---|---|---|---|---|
| | | App | Gls | App | Gls | App | Gls | App | Gls | App | Gls |
| SLOAN T | 1978-80 | 4/7 | 0 | 0 | 0 | 0/1 | 0 | 0 | 0 | 4/8 | 0 |
| SMITH AC | 1926 | 5 | 1 | 0 | 0 | 0 | 0 | 0 | 0 | 5 | 1 |
| SMITH J | 1937-45 | 37 | 14 | 5 | 1 | 0 | 0 | 0 | 0 | 42 | 15 |
| SMITH L | 1902 | 8 | 1 | 2 | 0 | 0 | 0 | 0 | 0 | 10 | 1 |
| SMITH R | 1894-1900 | 93 | 35 | 7 | 2 | 0 | 0 | *1 | 0 | 101 | 37 |
| SMITH TG | 1923-26 | 83 | 12 | 7 | 4 | 0 | 0 | 0 | 0 | 90 | 16 |
| SMITH W | 1901 | 16 | 0 | 1 | 0 | 0 | 0 | 0 | 0 | 17 | 0 |
| SNEDDON J | 1891 | 0 | 0 | 3 | 1 | 0 | 0 | 0 | 0 | 3 | 1 |
| SPENCE JW | 1919-32 | 481 | 158 | 29 | 10 | 0 | 0 | 0 | 0 | 510 | 168 |
| SPENCER CW | 1928-29 | 46 | 0 | 2 | 0 | 0 | 0 | 0 | 0 | 48 | 0 |
| SPRATT W | 1914-19 | 13 | 0 | 0 | 0 | 0 | 0 | 0 | 0 | 13 | 0 |
| STACEY G | 1907-14 | 241 | 9 | 26 | 0 | 0 | 0 | 0 | 0 | 267 | 9 |
| STAFFORD H | 1895-1902 | 183 | 0 | 17 | 1 | 0 | 0 | 0 | 0 | 200 | 1 |
| STAPLETON FA | 1981-87 | 204/19 | 60 | 21 | 7 | 26/1 | 6 | 14/1 | 5 | 265/21 | 78 |
| STEPHENSON R | 1895 | 1 | 1 | 0 | 0 | 0 | 0 | 0 | 0 | 1 | 1 |
| STEPNEY AC | 1966-77 | 433 | 2 | 44 | 0 | 35 | 0 | 23 | 0 | 535 | 2 |
| STEWARD A | 1920-31 | 309 | 0 | 17 | 0 | 0 | 0 | 0 | 0 | 326 | 0 |
| STEWART W | 1932-33 | 46 | 7 | 3 | 0 | 0 | 0 | 0 | 0 | 49 | 7 |
| STEWART WS | 1890-94 | 76 | 5 | 9 | 0 | 0 | 0 | *2 | 0 | 87 | 5 |
| STILES NP | 1960-70 | 311 | 17 | 38 | 0 | 7 | 0 | 36 | 2 | 392 | 19 |
| STONE H | 1893-94 | 6 | 0 | 0 | 0 | 0 | 0 | *1 | 0 | 7 | 0 |
| STOREY-MOORE I | 1971-73 | 39 | 11 | 0 | 0 | 4 | 1 | 0 | 0 | 43 | 12 |
| STRACHAN GD | 1984-89 | 155/5 | 33 | 22 | 2 | 12/1 | 1 | 6 | 2 | 195/6 | 38 |
| STREET E | 1902 | 1 | 0 | 2 | 0 | 0 | 0 | 0 | 0 | 3 | 0 |
| SUTCLIFFE JW | 1903 | 21 | 0 | 7 | 0 | 0 | 0 | 0 | 0 | 28 | 0 |
| SWEENEY EE | 1925-29 | 27 | 6 | 5 | 1 | 0 | 0 | 0 | 0 | 32 | 7 |
| TAPKEN NH | 1938 | 14 | 0 | 2 | 0 | 0 | 0 | 0 | 0 | 16 | 0 |
| TAYLOR C | 1924-29 | 28 | 6 | 2 | 1 | 0 | 0 | 0 | 0 | 30 | 7 |
| TAYLOR E | 1957-58 | 22 | 2 | 6 | 1 | 0 | 0 | 2 | 1 | 30 | 4 |
| TAYLOR T | 1952-57 | 166 | 112 | 9 | 5 | 0 | 0 | 14 | 11 | 189 | 128 |
| TAYLOR W | 1921 | 1 | 0 | 0 | 0 | 0 | 0 | 0 | 0 | 1 | 0 |
| THOMAS H | 1921-29 | 128 | 12 | 7 | 1 | 0 | 0 | 0 | 0 | 135 | 13 |
| THOMAS MR | 1978-80 | 90 | 11 | 13 | 2 | 5 | 2 | 2 | 0 | 110 | 15 |
| THOMSON A | 1929-30 | 3 | 1 | 2 | 0 | 0 | 0 | 0 | 0 | 5 | 1 |
| THOMSON E | 1907-08 | 4 | 0 | 0 | 0 | 0 | 0 | 0 | 0 | 4 | 0 |
| THOMPSON J | 1913 | 6 | 1 | 0 | 0 | 0 | 0 | 0 | 0 | 6 | 1 |
| THOMPSON JE | 1936-37 | 3 | 1 | 0 | 0 | 0 | 0 | 0 | 0 | 3 | 1 |
| THOMPSON W | 1893 | 3 | 0 | 0 | 0 | 0 | 0 | 0 | 0 | 3 | 0 |
| TOMS WE | 1919-20 | 13 | 3 | 1 | 1 | 0 | 0 | 0 | 0 | 14 | 4 |
| TOPPING HW | 1932-34 | 12 | 1 | 0 | 0 | 0 | 0 | 0 | 0 | 12 | 1 |
| TRANTER WJ | 1963 | 1 | 0 | 0 | 0 | 0 | 0 | 0 | 0 | 1 | 0 |
| TRAVERS GE | 1913-14 | 21 | 4 | 0 | 0 | 0 | 0 | 0 | 0 | 21 | 4 |
| TURNBULL A | 1906-14 | 220 | 90 | 25 | 10 | 0 | 0 | 0 | 0 | 245 | 100 |
| TURNBULL JM | 1907-09 | 67 | 36 | 9 | 6 | 0 | 0 | 0 | 0 | 76 | 42 |
| TURNER | 1890 | 0 | 0 | 1 | 0 | 0 | 0 | 0 | 0 | 1 | 0 |
| TURNER CR | 1985-88 | 64 | 0 | 8 | 0 | 7 | 0 | 0 | 0 | 79 | 0 |
| TURNER J | 1898-1902 | 3 | 0 | 1 | 0 | 0 | 0 | 0 | 0 | 4 | 0 |
| TURNER R | 1898 | 2 | 0 | 0 | 0 | 0 | 0 | 0 | 0 | 2 | 0 |
| TYLER S | 1923 | 1 | 0 | 0 | 0 | 0 | 0 | 0 | 0 | 1 | 0 |
| URE JF | 1969-70 | 47 | 1 | 8 | 0 | 10 | 0 | 0 | 0 | 65 | 1 |
| VALENTINE R | 1904-05 | 10 | 0 | 0 | 0 | 0 | 0 | 0 | 0 | 10 | 0 |
| VANCE J | 1895-96 | 11 | 1 | 0 | 0 | 0 | 0 | 0 | 0 | 11 | 1 |
| VINCENT E | 1931-33 | 64 | 1 | 1 | 0 | 0 | 0 | 0 | 0 | 65 | 1 |
| VIOLLET DS | 1952-61 | 259 | 159 | 18 | 5 | 2 | 1 | 12 | 13 | 291 | 178 |
| VOSE G | 1933-39 | 197 | 1 | 14 | 0 | 0 | 0 | 0 | 0 | 211 | 1 |
| WALDRON C | 1976 | 3 | 0 | 0 | 0 | 1 | 0 | 0 | 0 | 4 | 0 |
| WALKER DA | 1962 | 1 | 0 | 0 | 0 | 0 | 0 | 0 | 0 | 1 | 0 |
| WALKER R | 1898 | 2 | 0 | 0 | 0 | 0 | 0 | 0 | 0 | 2 | 0 |
| WALL G | 1905-14 | 287 | 89 | 29 | 9 | 0 | 0 | 0 | 0 | 316 | 98 |
| WALLACE DL | 1989- | 36/9 | 6 | 6/2 | 2 | 3/3 | 2 | 3/2 | 0 | 48/16 | 10 |

| Player | Played | League App | Gls | FA Cup App | Gls | FL Cup App | Gls | Europe App | Gls | Total App | Gls |
|---|---|---|---|---|---|---|---|---|---|---|---|
| WALSH G | 1986- | 37 | 0 | 0 | 0 | 3 | 0 | 2 | 0 | 42 | 0 |
| WALTON JA | 1951 | 2 | 0 | 0 | 0 | 0 | 0 | 0 | 0 | 2 | 0 |
| WALTON JW | 1945-47 | 21 | 0 | 2 | 0 | 0 | 0 | 0 | 0 | 23 | 0 |
| WARBURTON A | 1929-33 | 35 | 10 | 4 | 0 | 0 | 0 | 0 | 0 | 39 | 10 |
| WARNER J | 1892 | 22 | 0 | 0 | 0 | 0 | 0 | 0 | 0 | 22 | 0 |
| WARNER J | 1938-47 | 105 | 1 | 13 | 1 | 0 | 0 | 0 | 0 | 118 | 2 |
| WASSALL JV | 1935-39 | 46 | 6 | 2 | 0 | 0 | 0 | 0 | 0 | 48 | 6 |
| WATSON W | 1970-72 | 11 | 0 | 0 | 0 | 3 | 0 | 0 | 0 | 14 | 0 |
| WEALANDS JA | 1982-83 | 7 | 0 | 0 | 0 | 1 | 0 | 0 | 0 | 8 | 0 |
| WEBB NJ | 1989- | 70/4 | 8 | 9 | 1 | 13 | 1 | 9 | 1 | 101/4 | 11 |
| WEBSTER C | 1953-58 | 65 | 26 | 9 | 4 | 0 | 0 | 5 | 1 | 79 | 31 |
| WEDGE FE | 1897 | 2 | 2 | 0 | 0 | 0 | 0 | 0 | 0 | 2 | 2 |
| WEST EJ | 1910-14 | 166 | 72 | 15 | 8 | 0 | 0 | 0 | 0 | 181 | 80 |
| WETHERELL J | 1896 | 2 | 0 | 0 | 0 | 0 | 0 | 0 | 0 | 2 | 0 |
| WHALLEY A | 1909-19 | 97 | 6 | 9 | 0 | 0 | 0 | 0 | 0 | 106 | 6 |
| WHALLEY H | 1935-46 | 33 | 0 | 6 | 0 | 0 | 0 | 0 | 0 | 39 | 0 |
| WHELAN AG | 1980 | 0/1 | 0 | 0 | 0 | 0 | 0 | 0 | 0 | 0/1 | 0 |
| WHELAN LA | 1954-57 | 79 | 43 | 6 | 4 | 0 | 0 | 11 | 5 | 96 | 52 |
| WHITEFOOT J | 1949-55 | 93 | 0 | 2 | 0 | 0 | 0 | 0 | 0 | 95 | 0 |
| WHITEHOUSE J | 1900-02 | 59 | 0 | 5 | 0 | 0 | 0 | 0 | 0 | 64 | 0 |
| WHITEHURST W | 1955 | 1 | 0 | 0 | 0 | 0 | 0 | 0 | 0 | 1 | 0 |
| WHITESIDE KD | 1907 | 1 | 0 | 0 | 0 | 0 | 0 | 0 | 0 | 1 | 0 |
| WHITESIDE N | 1981-89 | 193/13 | 47 | 24 | 10 | 26/3 | 9 | 11/2 | 1 | 254/18 | 67 |
| WHITNEY J | 1895-1900 | 3 | 0 | 0 | 0 | 0 | 0 | 0 | 0 | 3 | 0 |
| WHITTAKER W | 1895 | 3 | 0 | 0 | 0 | 0 | 0 | 0 | 0 | 3 | 0 |
| WHITTLE J | 1931 | 1 | 0 | 0 | 0 | 0 | 0 | 0 | 0 | 1 | 0 |
| WHITWORTH N | 1990-91 | 1 | 0 | 0 | 0 | 0 | 0 | 0 | 0 | 1 | 0 |
| WILCOX TWJ | 1908 | 2 | 0 | 0 | 0 | 0 | 0 | 0 | 0 | 2 | 0 |
| WILKINS RC | 1979-83 | 158/2 | 7 | 10 | 1 | 14/1 | 1 | 8 | 1 | 190/3 | 10 |
| WILKINSON H | 1903 | 8 | 0 | 1 | 0 | 0 | 0 | 0 | 0 | 9 | 0 |
| WILKINSON IM | 1991- | 0 | 0 | 0 | 0 | 1 | 0 | 0 | 0 | 1 | 0 |
| WILLIAMS DR | 1927-28 | 31 | 2 | 4 | 0 | 0 | 0 | 0 | 0 | 35 | 2 |
| WILLIAMS F | 1902 | 8 | 0 | 2 | 4 | 0 | 0 | 0 | 0 | 10 | 4 |
| WILLIAMS F | 1930 | 3 | 0 | 0 | 0 | 0 | 0 | 0 | 0 | 3 | 0 |
| WILLIAMS H | 1922 | 5 | 2 | 0 | 0 | 0 | 0 | 0 | 0 | 5 | 2 |
| WILLIAMS H | 1904-05 | 33 | 7 | 4 | 1 | 0 | 0 | 0 | 0 | 37 | 8 |
| WILLIAMS J | 1906 | 3 | 1 | 0 | 0 | 0 | 0 | 0 | 0 | 3 | 1 |
| WILLIAMS W | 1901 | 4 | 0 | 0 | 0 | 0 | 0 | 0 | 0 | 4 | 0 |
| WILLIAMSON J | 1919 | 2 | 0 | 0 | 0 | 0 | 0 | 0 | 0 | 2 | 0 |
| WILSON DG | 1988 | 0/4 | 0 | 0/2 | 0 | 0 | 0 | 0 | 0 | 0/6 | 0 |
| WILSON E | 1889 | 0 | 0 | 1 | 0 | 0 | 0 | 0 | 0 | 1 | 0 |
| WILSON JT | 1926-31 | 130 | 3 | 10 | 0 | 0 | 0 | 0 | 0 | 140 | 3 |
| WILSON T | 1907 | 1 | 0 | 0 | 0 | 0 | 0 | 0 | 0 | 1 | 0 |
| WINTERBOTTOM W | 1936-37 | 25 | 0 | 2 | 0 | 0 | 0 | 0 | 0 | 27 | 0 |
| WOMBWELL R | 1904-06 | 47 | 3 | 4 | 0 | 0 | 0 | 0 | 0 | 51 | 3 |
| WOOD J | 1922 | 15 | 1 | 1 | 0 | 0 | 0 | 0 | 0 | 16 | 1 |
| WOOD NA | 1985-86 | 2/1 | 0 | 0 | 0 | 0/1 | 0 | 0 | 0 | 2/2 | 0 |
| WOOD RE | 1949-58 | 178 | 0 | 15 | 0 | 0 | 0 | 12 | 0 | 205 | 0 |
| WOODCOCK W | 1913-19 | 58 | 20 | 3 | 1 | 0 | 0 | 0 | 0 | 61 | 21 |
| WORRALL H | 1946-47 | 6 | 0 | 0 | 0 | 0 | 0 | 0 | 0 | 6 | 0 |
| WRATTEN P | 1990-91 | 0/2 | 0 | 0 | 0 | 0 | 0 | 0 | 0 | 0/2 | 0 |
| WRIGGLESWORTH W | 1936-46 | 30 | 8 | 7 | 2 | 0 | 0 | 0 | 0 | 37 | 10 |
| YATES W | 1906 | 3 | 0 | 0 | 0 | 0 | 0 | 0 | 0 | 3 | 0 |
| YOUNG J | 1906 | 2 | 0 | 0 | 0 | 0 | 0 | 0 | 0 | 2 | 0 |
| YOUNG TA | 1970-75 | 69/14 | 1 | 5 | 0 | 5/4 | 0 | 0 | 0 | 79/18 | 1 |

*United stars of '92. Top (left to right): Paul Parker, Mike Phelan, Dennis Irwin. Bottom (left to right): Andrei Kanchelskis, Peter Schmeichel and Lee Sharpe.*